UNEQUAL
SISTERS

UNEQUAL SISTERS

A MULTI-CULTURAL READER IN U.S. WOMEN'S HISTORY

Edited by
Vicki L. Ruiz and
Ellen Carol DuBois

SECOND EDITION

ROUTLEDGE
New York • London

Published in 1994 by

Routledge
29 West 35th Street
New York, NY 10001

Published in Great Britain by

Routledge
11 New Fetter Lane
London EC4P 4EE

Library of Congress Cataloging-in-Publication Data
Unequal sisters : a multicultural reader in U.S. women's history /
    edited by Vicki L. Ruiz and Ellen Carol DuBois.—2nd ed.
        p.   cm.
    Includes bibliographical references nd index.
    ISBN 0-415-90891-4 (HB)   ISBN 0-415-90892-2 (PB)
    1. Women—United States—History—Cross-cultural studies.   2. Sex
role—United States—History—Cross-cultural studies.   3. Afro
-American women—History.   I. Ruiz, Vicki. II. DuBois, Ellen
Carol, 1947–   .
HQ1410.U54   1994
305.4′0973—dc20   94-2430
                                                                                      CIP

British Library Cataloging-in-Publication Data is available.

Table of Contents

Acknowledgments

The "daughter" of *Unequal Sisters* was crafted with good humor, patience, and friendship. The generous comments by Lois Banner, Robert Dawidoff, and Lynn Dumenil considerably strengthened our introduction to the second edition. We thank Valerie Matsumoto and Peggy Pascoe, who labored through successive drafts and whose comments helped us clarify our shared vision of multicultural women's histories. We especially appreciate the meticulous line-by-line editing of Peggy Pascoe and Lois Banner. Brian Niiya, the bibliographer at the Asian American Studies Library, UCLA, deserves the credit for the enhanced format of the bibliographies. Kira Hilden-Minton, Matthew Lasar, and Alicia Rodríquez contributed diligent and efficient research assistance, and Sandra Campbell provided indispensable secretarial support. A special note of thanks is reserved for Cecelia Cancellaro and her editorial assistant Maura Burnett. A superlative editor in every way, Cecelia Cancellaro has our deepest admiration and respect. Almost four years has passed since the appearance of the first edition of *Unequal Sisters*, and much has changed—for the better—in U.S. women's history and in our own lives. We gratefully acknowledge the support and encouragement of our students, of our readers, and of each other. For his love and laughter, Vicki L. Ruiz adds a personal note of appreciation to her compañero, Victor Becerra.

Introduction to the Second Edition
Vicki L. Ruiz and Ellen Carol DuBois

In the introduction to the first edition of *Unequal Sisters*, we wrote:

Well into its second decade, the field of women's history stands at a crossroads. Growing demands for the recognition of "difference"—the diversity of women's experiences—can no longer be satisfied by token excursions into the histories of minority women, lesbians, and the working class. The journey into women's history itself has to be remapped. From many quarters comes the call for a more complex approach to women's experiences, one that explores not only the conflicts between women and men but also the conflicts among women; not only the bonds among women but also the bonds between women and men. Only such a multifaceted perspective will be sufficient "to illuminate the interconnections among the various systems of power that shape women's lives."[1]

In *Unequal Sisters* we seek to address such issues in the context of American women's history. In particular, this anthology highlights scholarship on women of color, from which we draw more than half of our articles. In addition, other selections explore "difference" with respect to class and sexual orientation. The dynamics of race and gender, however, are the pivotal point of this collection.

Most of the early work in U.S. women's history paid little attention to race, and assumed instead a universal women's experience, defined in contrast to "man's" history. While a stark focus on the difference between the male and female past helped to legitimize women's history, the past it explored was usually only that of middle-class white women. In this uniracial model, the universal man of American history was replaced with the universal woman.

For instance, much of nineteenth-century women's history scholarship rests on the assumption that women's lives were lived in a separate domestic "sphere," on which basis they were able to claim a kind of social power distinct from that of men. This concept grew out of the historical experience of white, leisured women. And despite historians' earnest efforts to include less privileged women—notably female slaves and immigrant wives—the narrative line of women's history could not help but marginalize them. These other histories came across either as exotic or deviant, providing no clue to the larger history of American womanhood. In this uniracial model, race and gender cannot be brought into the same theoretical field. White women appear "raceless," their historical experiences determined solely by gender. By contrast, the distinct historical experiences of women of color, to the degree that they are acknowledged, are credited solely to race. The uniracial framework leads women's historians, eager to expand their range, right into the trap of "women-and-minorities," a formula that accentuates rather than remedies the invisibility of women of color.

While the notion of a universal female past focuses on power relations between men and women, scholarship has begun to appear that explores power relations *between women*— of different races, classes, and cultures. Slaveowner and slave, mistress and maid, reformer and immigrant, social worker and client are some of the many relationships of inequality that run through American women's history. When focused on questions of race, we term this sort of approach "biracial." Scholarship in this biracial mode benefits from a paradigm for examining power, not only between men and women but also within women's history itself. This biracial approach shatters the notion of a universal sisterhood. Simply stated, it permits feminist historians to discard celebration for confrontation, and allows them to explore the dynamics through which women have oppressed other women.

While the biracial approach has effectively broken through the notion of a universal female experience, it has its limits. The framework itself leads the historian to focus her examination on the relation between a powerful group, almost always white women, and minority women, the varieties of whose experiences are too often obscured. In other words, the historical emphasis is on white power, and women of color have to compete for the role of "other." The historical testimonies of women of color thus tend to be compacted into a single voice. The biracial framework has helped create a situation in which the demand for a greater understanding of race can be reduced to a black-and-white analysis— literally and figuratively.

Much as the uniracial framework in women's history is closely associated with the Northeast, the biracial model has its own regional bias, and seems best to describe the Southeast. For the possibilities of a richer palette for painting women's history, we turn to "the West." Western women's historians are taking the lead in moving beyond biracialism, if only because the historical experiences of the region require a multifaceted approach. Given the confluence of many cultures and races in this region—Native American, Mexican, Asian, Black and Anglo—grappling with race at all requires a framework that has more than two positions. Nor is white history always center stage. Even the term "the West" only reflects one of several historical perspectives; the Anglo "West" is also the Mexican "North," the Native American "homeland," and the Asian "East." Nor are the possibilities for such an approach limited to one region. Even in areas that seem racially homogenous or in which the struggle between two races understandably preoccupies historians, there are other peoples and positions to consider.

To describe this third framework, the one we seek to elaborate in *Unequal Sisters*, we use the term "multicultural." We chose the term "multicultural" over "multiracial" because we seek to focus on the interplay of many races and cultures, because we acknowledge that not all white women's histories can be categorized under one label, and because we seek to suggest that the term "race" needs to be theorized rather than assumed. As a framework for women's history, a multicultural approach poses a variety of challenges to scholarship. Many groups of women, rarely explored or incorporated into women's history, await further study. There are distinctions to note, comparisons to be made, among different groups of women, with respect to family life, forms of work, definitions of womanhood, sources of power, bonds among women. The various forms of white domination must be examined for their impact on women's history: the dispossession of Mexican land after 1848; the genocide and relocation of Native Americans; the legal exclusion of Asian Americans. Even slavery takes on multiple meanings for women's history through a multicultural lens. Finally, a multicultural approach to women's history invites the study of cultural contact and transformation, so important in understanding the development of family patterns, child-rearing practices, sexuality, and other cultural arenas crucial to women's history concerns.

In U.S. history, race has coincided closely with class. The segmentation of people of color in lower-echelon industrial, service, and agricultural jobs has served to blunt their opportunities for economic mobility. The multicultural framework allows for an analysis that takes class into account, not as a separate variable, but as an intertwined component of both race and gender. The history of women cannot be studied without considering both race and class. Similarly, working-class culture cannot really be understood without reference to gender and race. Many of the essays in this volume provide insight into the structural and ideological components of class, as it interplays with race and gender in the formation of women's consciousness.

At the risk of overreaching, it does seem that a multicultural approach, one in which many pasts can be explored simultaneously, may be the only way to organize a genuinely national, a truly inclusive, history of women. As Jacquelyn Dowd Hall has written, women's history must develop "a historical practice that turns on partiality, that is self-conscious about perspective, that releases multiple voices rather than competing orthodoxies, and that, above all, nurtures an 'internally differing but united political community'."[2] To allow for overlapping narratives and to recognize multiple forms of power, this is both an old populist dream and a postmodern challenge.

Such a kaleidoscopic approach undoubtedly runs the risk of fragmentation. But in moving beyond the notion of women's history as a monolith, coherence need not be abandoned. "We should not have to choose between a common legacy and cultural diversity, especially in a nation where diversity is a legacy," writes James Quay, director of the California Council of the Humanities.[3] We hope, in this volume and in the future scholarship it may encourage, to contribute to a reconceptualization of American women's history, as a series of dialectical relations among and across races and classes of women, representing diverse cultures and unequal power.

During the past three years, we have witnessed a dramatic flowering of multicultural women's history. This growth in scholarship has made possible the revision and expansion of *Unequal Sisters*. A timely and substantial second edition seems entirely in the spirit of the first collection: inasmuch as we originally saw in multicultural scholarship a way to challenge confining paradigms and premature orthodoxies, we want to keep this anthology a venue for changes in U.S. women's history. This revised edition also reflects our continuing conviction that, despite obligatory lip service in many women's history collections and much feminist theory, work linking race and gender remains underrepresented.

Multicultural women's history has developed despite (or perhaps because) of an intense debate over its legitimacy. This debate ranges all the way from the most rarefied circles of academia through the most easily accessible forms of popular culture. The critiques of multiculturalism also range along the political spectrum. To conservatives, multiculturalism so fragments the narrative as to make a coherent account of American history impossible. Ultraconservative radio jockey Rush Limbaugh insists that multiculturalism teaches children "how horrible America is."[4] From the center, Arthur Schlesinger Jr. worries that multicultural history will erode a general sense of national identity and public education. "The cult of ethnicity," he writes, "exaggerates differences, intensifies resentments and antagonisms, drives ever deeper the awful wedges between races and nationalities."[5]

Those on the left also have concerns. Postcolonialists decry the homogenizing or sanitizing tendencies of multiculturalism, seeing "diversity" as a glossy cover for race, gender, class, and heterosexual domination. Micaela Di Leonardo worries that such scholarship "runs away from admitting class stratification as fast as its little Disneyland-doll, Benettonad legs can carry it."[6] Similarly, Russell Leong's poem "Beware of the M Word" suggests that multiculturalism obscures conflict behind the screen of diversity:

> and color without clashes
> color without classes
> is blind
> is no color at all . . .
> ....
> We cannot be reduced
> to a single definition
> to one word
> one vision
> one spirit[7]

As the debates rage on, however, multicultural women's history continues to flourish. There is no single political agenda, goal, or pattern to this research, which can express an expanded appreciation of American democracy or provide withering critiques of white privilege and power. Readers can find both celebrations of minority cultures and heart-breaking accounts of painful legacies of oppression, slavery, dispossession, and humiliation. Multicultural history can concentrate on the discrete nature of various historical experiences, or it can build on the multiplicity of separate histories to create comparative frameworks.

We have our own idea of what multicultural women's history can and should do. We see multicultural women's history contributing substantially to a new, complex and more satisfying synthesis of the American past. At its best, multicultural history not only opens up social categories, including gender, race, class, culture, region, generation, and sexual orientation; it brings them together through comparative analyses, studies of unequal power dynamics, and explorations of intercultural borders.

Feminist scholars are now at the stage of exploring a variety of synthetic frames to make harmony of this apparent cacophony. As editors, we continue to rely, at least partially, on a linear, national, political, and economic framework of the sort American historians have long cherished. For instance, the triptych of articles on suffrage explores the relations of different groups of women to a single, national, political development, the Nineteenth Amendment. Similarly, the transformation of the American economy from family-based subsistence production to a segmented, wage-based labor force provides a framework for integrating women's diverse experiences across race and region.

By itself, however, we do not believe that a single narrative framework can be flexible enough to incorporate the many different historical experiences and identities of American women. Shading U.S. history with overlapping narratives, such as those rooted in region, helps us to bring out the range of women's experience without unduly sacrificing coherence. We also think that room must be made in our historical accounts for the stages of the female life cycle, as they both unify and differentiate women's everyday experiences. For instance, attending to generational differences among women reveals distinct and sometimes antagonistic expectations with respect to work, family, and sexuality.

The success of the continuing search for synthesis in multicultural history depends on how well its practitioners meet two sets of analytical challenges. The first of these is the building of bridges across the conceptual territories of race, class, and gender. It seems quite clear to us at this point that research on gender and race has permanently altered concepts of class in American history. What we mean by "working class" now has to feature domestic, service, and agricultural labor along with industrial work, and to explore family economies rather than simply subsume women and children under male workers. What we mean by "middle class" has similarly been expanded, notably by reconceptualizing "female domesticity" as a crusading middle-class culture advanced by female moral authority. Americanization, directed in different ways to mothers and daughters in immigrant families, can be seen not simply as an assault on ethnic cultures but as the continuing expansion of these middle-class norms. Also, in our opinion, theoretical linkages between race and gender, especially as they illuminate sexuality, have become much stronger in the last few years. As Tessie Liu argues in the concluding article of this edition, "By understanding how race is a *gendered* social category," we can better understand the why and how of historical differences among women. "In a male-dominated system, regulating *social* relationships through racial metaphors necessitates control over women."

The second set of issues facing multicultural history comes from the new scholarship in literary criticism and cultural analysis. We think of multicultural history as a way to establish the context within which voices long ignored can be heard. And yet, what constitutes historical "voice" and how we, from our own positions in the present, can hear all the women of the past, is a very complex matter. "Experience" is the fundamental category of all social history; yet these other disciplines have alerted us to the importance of systems of expression—of discourse and representation—for structuring experience. As a result, historical "experience" no longer seems simple and unmediated. In addition, inasmuch as these representational systems reflect power inequalities in any given society, how do we acknowledge them and yet continue to hear what has been so invigorating in multicultural women's history, the independent voices of those farthest from the centers of power? We do not want to become so engulfed in theoretical abstractions that we lose touch with human action; and yet we can no longer avoid analyzing the languages, attending to the silences, and decoding the symbols by which people place themselves in history. In the end, situating historical experience and understanding how it has been constructed may help us to arrive at a new, more inclusive synthesis.

Let us turn now to the bases on which we have selected articles for the second edition. We have enlarged the collection to include thirty-six articles, twenty-four of which directly address the experiences of women of color. We particularly recognize the need to offer our readers an expanded view into scholarship in indigenous women's history and to diversify the historical coverage of Asian American women.

Comparative studies in U.S. women's history constitute a significant direction in the field, and we have chosen to include several examples of such work. Not only does such scholarship help us move towards a more unified narrative, but comparative women's history allows us to revisit and recast the cornerstones of women's history—for instance, sexuality, wage work, domesticity, and reform—in light of the new literature on women of color, lesbians, and working-class women. Comparisons must also cross political borders, as well as cultural ones. For example, Sylvia Van Kirk's essay on "Sarah Ballenden and the Foss-Pelly Scandal" and Vicki Ruiz's study of the Houchen Settlement House in El Paso add nuanced dimensions to the shifting interplay of class, colonialism, race and gender on both the Canadian frontier and the Mexico-Texas border.

The second edition also highlights, more than the first, the methods by which we expand our historical repertory and reclaim voices long silenced, closeted, and overlooked. In terms of archival research, the essays in this edition demonstrate that a panoply of historical evidence exists, tucked away in libraries and museums, and that the greater challenge is not just to unearth it, but to interpret and contextualize its many meanings. Similarly, the work of oral history, so crucial to expanding both the gender and ethnic boundaries of history, does not end with the interview. The words on tape do not represent unvarnished history, but an interpretation of the past through the filter of memory and the mediation of the interviewer.

We maintain our conviction, as we wrote in the first edition, that "history is unavoidably political." Peggy Pascoe reflects in this volume on history "as a kind of conversation between the past and present in which we travel through time to examine the cultural assumptions— and the possibilities—of our own society as well as the societies before us." We hope that the second edition of *Unequal Sisters* not only expands our historical knowledge across race, ethnicity, sexual orientation, class, and gender, but helps foster for all of us a stronger civic culture of mutual regard and recognition. We continue to learn from each other's history.

Notes

1. We want to thank Joanne Meyerowitz, for this phrasing of our project in personal correspondence with the editors.
2. Hall, "Partial Truths," *Signs: Journal of Women in Culture and Society* (Summer 1989), 14, 4, p. 908.
3. Quay, "The Learning Society and the New American Legacy," *Humanities News* (Spring 1989), vol. 11, p. 4.
4. Rush Limbaugh, III, *The Way Things Ought To Be* (New York: Pocket Books, 1992), p. 211.
5. Schlesinger Jr., *The Disuniting of America: Reflections on a Multicultural Society*, (New York: W. W. Norton, 1992), p. 102.
6. Di Leonardo, "White Fright," *Village Voice* (May 18, 1993), p. 40.
7. Leong, *California Sociologist*, (Winter-Summer 1991), vol. 14, no. 1–2, pp. 7–10.

UNEQUAL
SISTERS

1

Beyond the Search for Sisterhood: American Women's History in the 1980s

Nancy A. Hewitt

I

One of the principal projects of the contemporary feminist movement in the United States has been the development of a sense of community among women, rooted in their common oppression and expressed through a distinctive women's culture. This project is premised on the patriarchal assumptions accepted by the majority of North America's early feminist leaders: the gender is the primary source of oppression in society and is the model for all other forms of oppression.[1] American women's historians of the 1960s and 1970s not only accepted the premises and projects of the women's movement but also helped to establish them. The bonds that encircled past generations of women were initially perceived as restrictive, arising from female victimization at the hands of patriarchs in such institutions as medicine, education, the church, the state, and the family. Historians soon concluded, however, that oppression was a double-edged sword; the counterpart of subordination in or exclusion from male-dominated domains was inclusion in an all-female enclave. The concept of womanhood, it soon appeared, bound women together even as it bound them down.[2] The formative works in American women's history have focused on the formation of these separate sexual spheres, particularly among the emerging urban bourgeoisie in the first half of the nineteenth century. Reified in prescriptive literature, realized in daily life, and ritualized in female collectivities, this "woman's sphere" came to be seen as the foundation of women's culture and community in antebellum America.[3]

Though feminists, including scholars, have perceived community as a source of support and solidarity for women, both history and politics affirm that a strong sense of community can also be a source of exclusion, prejudices, and prohibitions. For the past decade, the women's movement itself has been accused of forming its own exclusive community, characterized by elitism, ethnocentrism, and a disregard for diversity. At the same time, students of black and working-class women's lives have argued that the notion of a single women's community rooted in common oppression denies the social and material realities of caste and class in America.[4] Yet as the concept of community has become increasingly problematic for women's historians, it has also become increasingly paradigmatic. This article will evaluate the current paradigm in American women's history—premised on patriarchy and constructed around community—by comparing the creation, conditions and practices of communal life among black and white working-class women with that among the white bourgeoisie in the nineteenth and early twentieth centuries.

Reprinted with permission from *Social History*, vol. 10, October, 1985.

The community that has become the cornerstone of North American women's history was discovered within the Victorian middle class. There a "rich female subculture" flourished "in which women, relegated to domesticity, constructed powerful emotional and practical bonds with each other."[5] Three distinct but related investigations converged to illuminate this enclave of sisterhood. Barbara Welter first identified the construction of a new ideology of gender in the years 1820 to 1860 that defined the "true woman" as pious, pure, domestic, and submissive. Nancy Cott correlated this ideology with a separation of women and men into distinct spheres of activity, at least among New England's middling classes. For this group, commercial and industrial developments in the late eighteenth and early nineteenth centuries simultaneously consigned married women to domesticity and launched men on public careers. Carroll Smith-Rosenberg then discovered within the private domain a dynamic "world of love and ritual" in which a distinct set of values was elaborated into a richly textured women's culture.[6]

Though each of these authors regarded her work as speculative and carefully noted parameters of time, region, and class, the true woman/separate spheres/woman's culture triad became the most widely used framework for interpreting women's past in the United States. The articles and arguments presented by the architects of the paradigm are widely quoted, reprinted frequently, summarized in textbooks and popular histories, reproduced in curriculum packets, and elaborated upon in an array of scholarly studies. By gendering the Victorian landscape and evaluating historical patterns and processes in women's own terms, the historians of bourgeois womanhood have established concepts and categories that now shape the analysis of all groups of American women.[7]

Historians soon traced the bonds of womanhood into public arenas and across race and class barriers. According to Cott, the "doctrine of woman's sphere opened to women (reserved for them) the avenues of domestic influence, religious morality, and child nurture. It articulated a social power based on their special female qualities."[8] That social power was first revealed in church and charitable societies and in educational missions, then was gradually expanded into campaigns for moral reform, temperance, the abolition of slavery, and even women's rights.[9] By the late nineteenth century, domestic skills and social power would converge in "social housekeeping," embracing and justifying women's participation in urban development, social welfare programs, social work, the settlement house movement, immigrant education, labor reform, and electoral politics.[10]

At the same time that middle-class wives reached across the domestic threshold, they also apparently, though more haltingly, stepped across the moat dividing them from women of other classes and races. Some plantation mistresses, for instance, decried, at least in their private diaries, the sexual double standard reflected in white men's abuse of slave women. In at least one southern town, free black and white women seemed to adopt a common set of values grounded in personalism: both races were "more attuned to the needs and interests of other women, more concerned with economic security, more supportive of organized charity, and more serious about the spiritual life than men."[11] White working-class women were also soon caught in the web of womanhood. One historian noted that this web could be paralyzing for an individual working woman, but added that "when a strong enough wind is blowing, the whole web and all the women in it can be seen to move and this is a new kind of movement, a new source of power and connectedness."[12] Those connections, moreover, stretched across economic strata as industrialization created "an oppressive leisure life" for affluent women and "an oppressive work life" for their laboring sisters, forging a "bond of sisterhood" across classes.[13]

Elaborations on and extensions of female community multiplied rapidly. Women on wagon trains heading west, worshippers in evangelical revivals and in Quaker meeting houses, prostitutes on the Comstock Lode, mill workers in Lowell boarding houses, and immigrants on the streets of Lawrence and the stoops of Providence loved and nurtured one another, exchanged recipes, gossip, and herbal remedies, swapped food and clothing, shared childrearing and domestic chores, covered for each other at work, protected one another from abusive fathers, husbands, lovers, and bosses, and supported each other in birth and death.[14] For each group, these "friendship and support networks" could also become "crucibles in which collective acts of rebellion were formed."[15] Middle-class "re-bels" formed single-sex public associations to ameliorate social ills and eradicate social evils. Quaker farm wives, in Seneca Falls, Waterloo, and Rochester, New York, attacked the "repeated injuries and usurpations on the part of man toward woman."[16] Lowell mill operatives on strike for higher wages vowed that "none will go back, unless they receive us all as one."[17] In Lawrence, New York's Lower East Side, Cripple Creek, Colorado, and Tampa, Florida, immigrant women—as wives and wage-earners—united shop-floor struggle with neighborhood discontent and employed the resources of their everyday life as weapons in the class struggle.

How could the bonds of womanhood, first forged in the domestic enclaves of the Victorian bourgeoisie, have filtered through the walls dividing private and public domains, affluent and poor, native-born and immigrant, black and white? The answer provided by the authors of the woman's community construct was a combination of patriarchy and modernization. Patriarchy explained what women held in common—sexual vulnerability, domestic isolation, economic and educational deprivation, and political exclusion. Modern-ization served as the causal mechanism by which the ideology of separate spheres and the values of "true womanhood" were dispersed throughout the society.[18] Employing modern-ization as the mechanism of change allowed North American scholars to recognize broad forces—industrialization, urbanization and class stratification—and collective psychological developments—the growth of individualism and the search for autonomy—while main-taining the primacy of gender.[19] In addition, the "trickle down" method by which societies supposedly become modern suggested that the analysis of elite women could provide an appropriate framework for understanding and predicting the experiences of all women. Finally, the teleological bent of modernization obscures conflict and thereby reinforced the notion that bonds among women based on gender are stronger than barriers between women based on class or race.

The adoption of modernization by leading social, including women's, historians has carried us a great distance from Jesse Lemisch's early plea for a history written "from the bottom up."[20] As more feminist scholars pursued studies of black and white working-class life, however, they demanded renewed attention to the complexity of women's experience and recognition of the conflict that it engenders. At the same time, students of bourgeois women began debating woman's specific role in modernization: was she the repository of traditional values, the happy humanizer of modernity, a victim of male-dominated forces, or an eager agent of Progress? Those who compared the experiences of privileged and poor women in the Victorian era concluded that, if modernization occurred, it led not to the inclusion of women in a universal sisterhood but rather to the dichotomization of women along class lines into the pious and pure "modern" woman and the prurient and parasitical "pre-modern" woman.[21] Students of the Third World were even more adamant that women, rather than gaining by the development of a new domesticated ideal, lost "traditional forms of power and authority on the road to 'emancipation' from premodern lifeways."[22]

In addition, some women's historians attacked the concept of modernization itself as vague, untested, "nebulous," "both one-dimensional and elastic," or as "a piece of post-capitalist ideology."[23] This last criticism focused on the cornerstone of the current paradigm—the separation of spheres—suggesting that it may have been culturally prescribed by dominant sectors of society to divide classes against themselves. It is not clear, however, that either the working classes or the bourgeoisie itself actually patterned their lives according to such prescriptions. Certainly bourgeois women were not so separated from same-class men as to disengage them from the prejudices and power inherent in their class position. Evidence of this appears in white suffragists' use of racist rhetoric, Protestant charitable ladies' denial of aid to Catholics, affluent women's refusal to support working women's strikes, moral reformers' abhorrence of working-class sexual mores, and settlement house educators' denigration of immigrant culture.[24] Finally, students of black women's history reject the teleological design of modernization. Like contemporary black feminists, they argue that the concept of a woman's community derived from white women's experience distorts the reality of black lives and ignores the ways that white solidarity, including sisterhood, has served to deny rights to blacks, including women.[25]

II

We can most fully illuminate the value and limits of women's community by examining the bonds of womanhood among that group furthest removed from the Victorian parlor, Southern slaves. Slave women functioned within two communities in the antebellum era: one structured by white masters; the other by slaves themselves. The key to women's roles in both was work. In the former, labor was imposed upon blacks as their principal obligation; in the latter, labor was a primary concern by necessity. In both arenas, women's work embraced the production of goods and services and the production of human beings.[26] In both worlds and in both forms of work, the sexual division of labor encouraged women to band together for sustenance, security, and sociability.

In the fields, the master's house, and the slave quarters, black women often performed sex-specific tasks and worked in sex-segregated groups. Plantation owners generally differentiated field work by gender—"women hoed while men plowed"—though such lines were frequently ignored when the need arose.[27] Then, women carted manure, shovelled, cut trees, hauled lumber, drove teams and cleared land. Even when performing tasks similar to those of men, women did not always work side-by-side with slaves. The "trash gang" was one form of an all-female work group. It was composed of pregnant and nursing mothers, young girls and old women who were assigned the lighter work of raking stubble or pulling weeds while other female teams hoed and picked the cotton.[28] On rice plantations, the division of labor by gender was probably even more regularized and rigid.

Within the master's house, on all plantations, work was highly sex-segregated.[29] Female slaves cooked and sewed, nursed and reared children, and performed a wide array of domestic chores. Here, even more than in the fields, women worked in all-female circles in which the older trained the younger in work-related skills and survival techniques. The latter had a specific meaning for house slaves who were trapped by the division of sexual labor and by their proximity to white men in a highly charged and potentially abusive situation. The "passionlessness" of "true women" was counterposed, by white males, to the sexual insatiability of blacks, justifying the rape of female slaves and enhancing white profits if coercion led to conception. The testimony of ex-slaves suggests that they rarely found refuge in the sympathies of white mistresses, who were as likely to take out their frustrations on the victim as the victimizer, and thus slave women learned early the importance of self-reliance and of black sisterhood.[30]

Once slaves were safely ensconced in their own quarters, they joined in the collective performance of essential labors, such as food preparation, household maintenance, and child care. Here as in the fields, women and men performed some overlapping tasks, but they often did so in sex-segregated circles. Other chores they specifically divided along gender lines: fishing and hunting were for men, gardening and cooking were for women. However, the value placed on men's and women's work was more equal among blacks than whites. Certain female skill, such as cooking, sewing, quilting, or healing, were highly regarded since knowledge in these areas was essential to the survival of the slave community. Midwives were of particular importance. Though male physicians were reshaping the birth process among affluent whites, childbirth remained an all-female ritual among blacks and one that occurred with much greater frequency and hazard.[31] Childrearing was probably also more clearly defined as black rather than white women's work, especially since slave women often nursed and cared for the children of their owners as well as their own family. The emphasis on the slave mother's role was reinforced by both white masters and slaves themselves. As masters imposed a matrifocal structure on slave families, black women drew on their own self-identification with maternity to cement their central position in the slave family and community.[32]

Slave women, like their bourgeois counterparts, functioned in a sex-segregated world; but without access to land, cash, or the fruits of one's labor, slave women and men were denied the measures that defined status in bourgeois society. In general, the absence of such measures equalized men's and women's status and allowed women in particular to develop criteria for determining self-worth that were relatively independent of men, white or black.[33] Yet despite this development of a woman's sphere and a set of women's values, slave women did not define themselves in opposition to their male counterparts. Rather, black women forged bonds of sisterhood and then wielded them as weapons in the fight for black community survival. Moreover, though defined in part by women's roles in reproduction and domesticity, black womanhood was not an extension of white womanhood nor did sisterly feelings among slaves extend, except on rare occasions, to white mistresses.[34]

From the perspective of the slave experience, then, strong communal ties among women were rooted not in the culture-bound concept of the separation of spheres but in the material realities of the sexual division of labor. That division assigned men and women to distinct but complementary roles. In this context, strong bonds among women strengthened the community as a whole, providing support for the interests of slave men and a defense against domination by white women and men. This same dynamic—of a sexual division of labor resulting in complementary roles, the development of bonds among women and the use of those bonds in defense of community interests, and the formation of a strong sense of identity among same-class women that served as a barrier to universal sisterhood—can be traced for other groups on nineteenth-century working women. In western mining and eastern mill towns at mid-century and in northern immigrant and southern industrial centers at the turn of the century, women banded together to perform essential labor and then wielded their collective power in defense of same-class men and in defiance of other-class women.[35]

In towns where the primary form of work was rigidly sex-typed, such as deep shaft mining or textile manufacturing, women and men formed distinct circles of association in the workplace as well as in the household and community. Yet even in industrial centers of the late nineteenth century, where both men and women worked for wages, sex-segregation within factories and the continued assignment of domestic chores to females assured the development of a sense of community based on gender. A variety of work-related experiences shaped the bonds of womanhood among wage earners. In Lowell, Massachusetts, for instance, young mill operatives taught each other skills, substituted for each other at work, warned each other of a foreman's approach, and shared meals, leisure hours, and even beds at company-owned boarding-houses. A half-century later in nearby Lawrence, immigrant daughters gathered at an appointed corner in the pre-dawn hours to "walk each other to the mills"—talking all the way and sharing information on wages and working conditions in the different factories. On returning home in the evening, the bonds were tightened further. As one worker recounted: "Back then you see this is how you lived—you slept in shifts, we all lived like one then. One kitchen we all used and we all knew each other."[36]

Working-class housewives shared similar burdens across communities and across time. Combining their efforts and expertise in cooking, childcare, sewing, nursing, and laundry, housewives provided each other with advice, missing items for recipes, hand-me-down clothes, soap flakes, a moment's respite from child minding, and an extra pair of hands.[37] Communal spaces, such as stoops, streets, churches, groceries, and bath houses became forums for the exchange of "gossip," including the latest information on wages, prices, and rents. These women were also in charge of providing emotional support, food, and general assistance during life crises, organizing social functions for children and adults, supplying welfare services to widows and orphans, and socializing young girls into proper family, work, and courtship patterns.

The importance of these bonds of womanhood was strikingly visible when workers walked off their jobs; the ability of a community to survive without wages was often related to women wage earners' militancy and to the resources hoarded and distributed by non-wage earning housewives. Triumphs on the shop floor were directly tied to the tenaciousness of working-class women in keeping their families and neighborhoods fed and functioning. Evidence now abounds that striking women "often outdid men in militancy." It was "harder to induce women to compromise"; they were "more likely to hold out to the bitter end . . . to obtain exactly what they want."[38] This militancy was strengthened when men joined women in unions and on picket lines.

It is true that skilled craftsmen and male union leaders sought to exclude women from their benefits and that women in the garment industry and elsewhere called strikes over the objections of male advisors. The most virulent sexism of union men, however, surfaced when the sexual division of labor appeared to be breaking down and in doing so threatened wage scales set by skilled men. In this situation it was often women of different racial or ethnic backgrounds who challenged existing male jobs; and skilled workers were hostile to any intrusions from these groups whether by women or men. When the sexual division of labor placed men and women in different industries or in different jobs in the same industry, thus eliminating the threat of job loss and wage cuts, men and women joined forces to protect their common economic interests.[39] In Massachusetts, for instance, the Lowell Female Labor Reform Association and the New England Workingman's Association combined efforts to gain a ten-hour law for industry. In Troy and Cohoes, New York, iron molders and laundresses supported each other in alternating strikes. In western Pennsylvania, miners and textile operatives, often contributing to the same family income, received benefits from better contracts in either industry. In North Carolina, women finally overcame opposition of union leaders, joined the Textile Workers Union of America and the Tobacco Workers International Union, and played significant and militant roles in numerous strikes and labor actions.[40]

Moreover, both male and female workers benefited from the community networks woven by non-wage earning women that served as a safety net in times of economic crisis. In Cripple Creek, Colorado, for instance, where there were few wage-earning possibilities for women, miners' wives ran soup kitchens, boycotted anti-union merchants, walked picket lines, defended union offices against soldiers, printed union papers in lieu of jailed editors, raised bail bonds, and provided food for incarcerated members of the Western Federation of Miners. In 1912, the housewives of Lawrence extended their customary communal cooking efforts to provide meals for strikers' families, and older women shouldered more than their normal burden of childcare so younger women could join picket lines. Housewives also went door-to-door, and store-to-store, collecting food, clothing, and funds, using their power as consumers to pressure merchants into supporting strike activities. Standard household items became weapons against union foes with scalding water, red pepper, and household shears always at the ready. The "gossip" networks of more peaceful periods and the communal spaces where women daily congregated became the communication centers for strike organization. The strategies developed there were often put into effect by the women themselves. They paraded through the neighborhoods jeering, hooting, and hissing at potential scabs; cornered strikebreakers and stripped them on the streets; and brandished sewing scissors to cut the backs of soldier's uniforms, thus "exposing their yellow insides."[41] In addition, in all striking communities, it was women, in individual families and neighborhood circles, who stretched the available food, nursed the sick and wounded, exchanged essential items, and sustained the emotional as well as physical resources of strikers and their families.

The sisterly bonds that bolstered working-class communities, like those among slaves, extended from the domestic enclave into the public domain, were forged from material necessity, and were employed in the interests of men as well as women. The very tightness of the web thus formed often served as a wall against women of other social, economic, ethnic, or racial groups. In western mining camps, for instance, prostitutes and dance hall girls formed their own sisterly circles through the exchange of "small favors, the sharing of meals, fashion advice, and sewing," yet miners' wives recognized no common bonds. Here the division of sexual labor between "good" girls and "bad" girls served to divide working-class women against themselves. Yet at the same time, miners' wives refused to support women of the merchant and professional families in the "civic housekeeping" crusades against gambling houses and brothels since crusade leaders sided with employers and against workers whenever strikes occurred.[42]

Lowell mill operatives were less hostile to the town's "ladies" who they believed would be "compassionate" to any who were "in want"; but they claimed nonetheless that "we prefer to have the disposing of our charities in our own hands."[43] While willing to dispense that charity to Yankee sisters and brothers, native-born mill operatives refused to extend it to the Irish and French-Canadian women who began flooding the mills at mid-century. An even more direct confrontation between communities of working women occurred in Atlanta in 1896. There it was the attempt to introduce black women into textile jobs that led to a strike and the formation of a union by previously unorganized white women. The union's first victory was the ouster of the newly recruited black employees. In the tobacco towns of North Carolina, the lines between black and white communities were subtler but no less definitively drawn; and they were clearly rooted in the racial and sexual divisions of labor. Black women, who suffered from lower wages and more frequent layoffs than whites, were hired by white women co-workers as domestic servants during slack seasons.[44] This practice eased the tension between white working-class husbands and wives as the latter suffered under the double burden of wage work and house work while also reinforcing, both symbolically and pragmatically, the racial specificity of Southern sisterhood.

III

If we take these experiences of community among women and project them back upon the Victorian bourgeoisie, we find important parallels. The separation of spheres which supposedly arose from an ideological barrier between men's and women's worlds may be more usefully analyzed as a transformation in the sexual division of labor. Occurring in the midst of commercial and industrial development, the new division provided for more specialized roles for each sex and thereby assured their mutual dependency in the production of goods and services and the reproduction of human beings. Bourgeois women, rather than retreating into an isolated domestic enclave that was a haven from class concerns and conflicts, became central actors in the family and the community: in both arenas their labor was essential to class formation.[45] Still, they performed their tasks in sex-segregated groups; and a particular set of female rituals and values did emerge from these groups as it did among women in other economic, ethnic, and racial enclaves.

The sexual division of labor rigidified among the emerging bourgeoisie by the mid-nineteenth century as middle-class, and especially married, women retreated from the cash nexus and from the fecundity of their foremothers. Home-bound wives were not idle, however. They continued to produce children's and women's clothing and a variety of other goods, and they provided a wide range of services for their families—laundry, cleaning, food preparation, shopping, and childcare. The assistance of domestic servants relieved privileged women of some of the most arduous physical labor, but the majority of middle-class women were confronted with ever-expanding duties as furniture became more elaborate, home entertainments more prevalent, and consumerism more pervasive.[46] Overall, the "felicity of families" was increasingly dependent on wives who were "properly methodical and economical in their distributions and expenditures of time."[47]

The greatest transformation for these women in the use of time was the shift in emphasis from the production of goods to the production of human beings. The declining birth rate affected bourgeois women in two ways. First, the assumed a greater role in policing sexual activity, their own and others, accepting in the process a new sexual identity of "passionlessness." Second, the nurturing and socialization of bourgeois children became more complex in this period and mothers shouldered most of the added burden.[48] From the first months of an infant's life, mothers were admonished to begin "instructing their sons in the principles of liberty and government," preparing them for service in a new array of white-collar and professional careers, and protecting sons and daughters from the "contamination of the streets" and the corruption of their souls.[49] To educate mothers for their new role, advice books, magazines, and mothers' associations flourished: the price of successful progeny was eternal maternal vigilance.

The concern for the maintenance and upward mobility of the family was shared by husbands and wives even as their roles in that achievement were rendered more distinct. This was true in the public as well as the private sphere. It proved impossible to protect children from contaminants and corruption without active community involvement; and bourgeois mothers, with the approval of their husbands, banded together to fight delinquency, destitution, prostitution, profligacy, intemperance, and impiety. Such endeavors extended the sexual division of labor into the public arena where men preferred cash donations and financial and legal advice and women raised and distributed funds and supplied the voluntary labor to establish the first urban welfare systems.[50]

As in the working class, middle-class women were not a unified body in the mid-nineteenth century and, like them, the critical divisions were not along lines of gender but of economic and social interest. And again, these divisions were most visible in the public domain where conflicts among three distinct segments of the emerging bourgeoisie revealed that sibling rivalry was as characteristic as sisterhood. The conflicts, moreover, embraced both the goals and the styles of social activism. In Rochester, New York, for instance, the wives of the city's wealthiest and most powerful men labored "economically, noiselessly, and consistently" to ameliorate the worst effects of rapid urban growth. At the other end of the middle-class spectrum, the wives of farmers and small traders, outside the circles of local political influence, asserted that "commotion shows signs of vitality" and organized demonstrations, wore bloomers instead of long skirts, and socialized in mixed racial company in their attempt to foment a "thorough Re-organization of Society." In between these extremes, the wives of upwardly mobile entrepreneurs insisted that there was a proper role for women "between the doll and the Amazon," apparently located in orphan asylums, homes for delinquent boys and "friendless" women, temperance crusades, and female auxiliaries to men's political associations.[51] In each case, the women had the support of male kin and neighbors; and together, the men and women of each class segment sought to channel social change in the direction of their own material and social interests.[52]

It was those in between the Amazons and the dolls who most fully embraced the tenets of true womanhood, yet it was precisely these upwardly mobile, public-minded women who most often substituted class hegemony for sisterly harmony. The "contradiction in the exercise of bourgeois women's historical agency" was most evident for this group: "that women both wielded power and that their power was not always progressive."[53] Indeed, the adherence of privileged women to a narrow and class-bound definition of women's proper sphere while a boon to their own sense of community was a barrier to their inclusion of women from other social and economic circumstances. Bourgeois women's new roles in production and reproduction were rooted in a "decentralized home system" in which each married woman was wholly responsible for the care and nurture of her own individual family, "passionlessness" combined with vigilant maternity, moral and spiritual superiority that justified women's power in the family and entry into the public domain, voluntary labor, and the belief in the natural and universal differentiation of the sexes in biological, intellectual, emotional, and economic terms.[54] When "true women" attempted to extend these "benefits" and beliefs to all women, they failed to recognize the value that white and black working-class women placed on their own carefully constructed communities and therefore created antipathy in their search for unity.

"True women," as educators, writers, dispensers of charity and missionaries to the heathen touted their own lifestyle, expressed and covered its contradictions in their public espousals of privatized domesticity, and took little cognizance of the values and mores of those being aided.[55] Even those female reformers who demonstrated genuine concern for the problems faced by women across classes did not necessarily offer solutions that were more attentive to cultural and social differences among women. In the desire to eliminate the sexual double standard, for instance, middle-class moral reformers offered prostitutes the wages of domestic servants as a substitute for the wages of sin and sought to replace sexual pleasure with passionlessness in order to curb what they saw as the dangers of unbridled lust. Their marginal concern for fertility control became the primary focus of female activists by the late nineteenth century. In family planning campaigns, the economic burden of large numbers of children and the technical control of conception led women to advocate the small nuclear family as the model for all groups, without attention to different cultural and social meanings of motherhood. Similarly, affluent wives claimed solidarity with working-class sisters in the fight against alcohol, yet few temperance leaders helped working-class women organize on their own behalf or supported divorce as an option for abused wives. All three groups of bourgeois reformers advocated state regulation of the vices they abhorred, the use to charity to aid deserving victims, and the intervention of male physicians to apply scientific solutions to moral dilemmas. In each case, these solutions lessened working-class women's control over their own lives and instead increased the powers of the dominant class in shaping the most intimate aspects of working-class women's lives.[56]

In the attempt to free working women from the hazards of long hours and poor working conditions, middle-class women again rejected the strategy of supporting grassroots organizational efforts. Instead, they aligned themselves, sometimes inadvertently, with concerned politicians and chauvinistic union leaders in demanding protective legislation to reduce the hours and workload of female wage earners. Even those privileged women with more progressive views, who established working alliances with laboring sisters through such associations as the Women's Trade Union League, often supported an activist agenda that placed the priorities of the women's movement—suffrage—above the bread-and-butter issues crucial to the workers.[57] Also, most middle-class women genuinely believed that the "family wage," by which the male head of household received a sufficient salary to support his wife and children, was the best hope for society and for working women. Yet, as upwardly mobile black and immigrant women discovered, when women's wages and their domestic labor became or were perceived as less essential to the family, the household became more clearly a den of inequity.[58]

This domesticated den, however, was the centerpiece of most bourgeois reform efforts. Aid was offered to individual families who most closely resembled the privatized ideal. Thus, alms were distributed to "respectable" families in impoverished neighborhoods. Birth control was dispensed to married women in stable relationships to remove the taint of promiscuity from family planning clinics. Poor women in urban and rural areas were forced to hide, limit, or relinquish their communal modes of child care and healing to gain access to public health programs, nursing services, and well-baby clinics. Americanization courses taught immigrant daughters to emulate bourgeois lifestyles and to evacuate the crowded stoops and communal kitchens for the privatized home.[59]

Finally, middle-class women, believing that they were essentially different from men, advocated the establishment of single-sex associations and thereby created divisions within those working-class communities which they had supposedly entered to assist.[60] They were aided, no doubt, by working-class men who alternately excluded women from their class-based organizations, attempted to gain control of potentially successful working-class women's campaigns, or ignored women's issues in pursuit of their own agenda. Thus, in the garment workers' strike of 1908, union leaders only offered support once the women had walked off the job. In the tenant's rights movement and the kosher meat boycotts in New York City, women "pioneered as the organizers of protests," but men took over "when the higher levels of the structure first emerged."[61] In anti-lynching campaigns in the South, it was black women who fought to safeguard their male kin against false rape accusations and vigilante justice, while black men concentrated on gaining property and political rights.[62] Yet even the difficulties of organizing with same-class men did not necessarily assure the success of women's cross-class alliances. Some working-class women remained in organizations dominated by men; some forged temporary alliances with more affluent women to achieve limited goals; and some struggled with the advantages and ambiguities of dual affiliations with same-class men and middle-class women. For instance, despite male takeover of the leadership positions in the tenant's rights movement and the kosher meat boycotts, women remained active in large numbers in both movements. Many black and white working-class women who joined forces with more affluent women in the anti-lynching crusade or the Women's Trade Union League only remained active until their immediate goal was achieved. Those working-class women who attempted to maintain dual affiliations with same-class men and other-class women did so at great personal cost.[63]

Whichever path working-class women chose, they demonstrated the limits of any universal notion of sisterhood. That women attempted cross-class alliances more frequently than men cannot be doubted and does indicate certain commonalities in the experience of womanhood in North America in the nineteenth and early twentieth centuries. Yet evidence from the lives of slaves, mill operatives, miners' wives, immigrants, and southern industrial workers as well as from "true women" indicates that there was no single woman's culture or sphere. There was a culturally dominant definition of sexual spheres promulgated by an economically, politically, and socially dominant group. That definition was firmly grounded in the sexual division of labor appropriate to that class, just as other definitions developed based on the sexual division of labor in other class and racial groups. All of these divisions were characterized by sufficient sex-stereotyping to assure the formation of distinct female circles of labor and distinct rituals and values rooted in that laboring experience. To date historians have focused on the parallels in the establishment of women's spheres across classes, races, and ethnic groups and have asserted certain commonalities among them, assuming their common origin in the modernization of society during the nineteenth century. A closer examination now reveals that no such universal sisterhood existed, and in fact that the development of a sense of community among various classes of women served as a barrier to an all-embracing bond of womanhood. Finally, it is now clear that privileged women were willing to wield their sex-specific influence in ways that, intentionally or unintentionally, exploited other women in the name of "true womanhood."

The quest to integrate women into historical analysis has already moved beyond the search for sisterhood. Yet like charitable ladies, plantation mistresses, settlement house residents, and Women's Trade Union League founders of the nineteenth and early twentieth centuries, women's historians continue to employ the rhetoric of community despite the reality of conflict. In highlighting the importance of collective action for women and the centrality of woman-constructed networks for community-wide campaigns, feminist scholars have demonstrated women's historical agency. Now we must recognize that that agency is not only our legacy but also our labrys, and like any double-edged weapon it cuts both ways: women influenced and advocated change, but they did so within the context of their particular social and material circumstances.

Sisterhood—the sharing of essential emotional and economic resources among females—was central to the lives of nearly all groups of American women from the antebellum era to the early twentieth century and was rooted in the sexual division of labor in the family, the work-place, the community, and the political arena. It was during this same period that cultural elites sought to impose a universal definition of the female character on society-at-large through the "cult of true womanhood." If women's historians now accept that ideology as the basis for cross-class and inter-racial sisterhood, we only extend the hegemony of the antebellum bourgeoisie. To recognize and illuminate the realities of all women's historical experience, we must instead acknowledge that for most nineteenth- and early twentieth-century women, and their modern counterparts, community was more a product of material conditions and constraints than of ideological dictates. And that therefore diversity, discontinuity, and conflict were as much a part of the historical agency of women as of men.

Notes

I would like to thank Ron Atkinson, Ardis Cameron, Wendy Goldman, Steven Lawson, and Marcus Rediker for their thoughtful readings of many drafts of this article and for their faith in its completion. Geoff Eley and the participants in the "Communities of Women" session at the Sixth Berkshire Conference on the History of Women were also essential sources of encouragement and ideas.

1. The classic statements include Millett, *Sexual Politics* (1970); Firestone, *The Dialectic of Sex* (1970); Brownmiller, *Against Our Will* (1975); Morgan (ed.), *Sisterhood is Powerful* (1970), and Firestone and Koedt (eds.), *Notes from the Second Year* (1970). Only in the late 1970s did significant numbers of feminist scholars

in the United States begin seriously to consider socialist perspectives in their discussions of women's oppression; an integrated socialist-feminist analysis is distant and, moreover, is not a goal of a major portion of American feminist scholars. See, for example, Sargent (ed.), *Women and Revolution* (1981); and Eisenstein (ed.), *Capitalist Patriarchy and the Case for Socialist Feminism* (1979).

2. The quote and the clearest statement of its implications can be found in Cott, *The Bonds of Womanhood* (1977), 1. For examples of early historical studies of patriarchy and patriarchal institutions, see Banner and Hartman (eds.), *Clio's Consciousness Raised* (1974); Carroll (ed.), *Liberating Women's History* (1976); and the entire issue of *Feminist Studies*, III, 1/2 (Fall 1975).

3. The antebellum period, roughly 1820 to 1860, has received the most attention from women's historians; specific concepts and frameworks derived from antebellum studies will be discussed on pp. 2–3 in this book.

4. This position has been articulated most clearly with reference to race. See, for example, Dill, "Race, Class, and Gender" (1983); Palmer, "White Women Black Women" (1983); Fisher, "Guilt and Shame in the Women's Movement" (1983). For a debate on the concept of women's culture by leading women's historians, see DuBois, Buhle, Kaplan, Lerner, and Smith-Rosenberg, "Politics and Culture in Women's History" (1980). While most black women are also working women or working-class women, the studies of black women in the United States have generally focused specifically on slavery or on cultural aspects of black life. Studies of working-class women, on the other hand, have almost always focused on white women. A recent exception is Janiewski, *Sisterhood Denied* (1985).

5. The quote is from Sara Evans, "Rethinking Women's Lives" (1983), who was summarizing the current state of women's history for readers of *In These Times*, a popular socialist weekly.

6. Welter, "The Cult of True Womanhood" (1966); Cott, *Bonds of Womanhood*; and Smith-Rosenberg, "The Female World of Love and Ritual" (1975).

7. These concepts, though supposedly linked to the economic and social developments of the early 1800s, have been projected back into analyses of colonial women and forward to twentieth-century studies. See, for example, Norton, *Liberty's Daughters* (1980); Kerber, "Daughters of Columbia" (1974); Tentler, *Wage-Earning Women* (1979). Feminist anthropologists initially suggested that the division of men and women into public and private spheres might be even more timeless. See, Rosaldo, "Woman, Culture, and Society" (1974).

8. Cott, *Bonds of Womanhood*, 200.

9. The earliest suggestions of this position appear in Flexner, *A Century of Struggle* (1959); and Sinclair, *The Emancipation of the American Woman* (1965). More detailed studies based on the doctrine of woman's sphere can be found in Epstein, *The Politics of Domesticity* (1981); Hersh, *The Slavery of Sex* (1978); Melder, *The Beginnings of Sisterhood* (1977); and Smith-Rosenberg, *Religion and the Rise of the City* (1971).

10. See, for example, Flexner, *Century of Struggle* (1959); Davis, *Spearheads for Reform* (1967); Seller, "The Education of the Immigrant Woman" (1982); Borden, *Women and Temperance* (1980); Buhle, *Women and American Socialism* (1981); and Scott, *Making the Invisible Woman Visible* (1984).

11. Quote from Lebsock, *The Free Women of Petersburg* (1984), xix. See also Scott, "Women's Perspective on the Patriarchy" (1982); and, for an overstated example, see Clinton, *The Plantation Mistress* (1983).

12. Tax, *The Rising of the Women* (1980), 7.

13. Quote from the middle-class leaders of the Women's Trade Union League in Jacoby, "The Women's Trade Union League and American Feminism" (1971), 205, 206.

14. Faragher and Stansell, "Women and Their Families on the Overland Trail" (1979); Jeffrey, Review in *Signs* (1982); Cott, "Young Women in the Second Great Awakening" (1975); Boylan, "Evangelical Womanhood in the Nineteenth Century" (1978), and "Women in Groups" (1984); Goldman, *Gold Diggers and Silver Miners* (1981); Dublin, "Women, Work and Protest" (1971); Cameron, "Women's Culture and Working-Class Activism" (1983); and Smith, "Our Own Kind" (1978). Similar patterns for England and France are traced in Ross, "Survival Networks" (1983); Hufton, "Women and the Family Economy" (1975); and Smith, *Ladies of the Leisure Class* (1981).

15. Quote from Rapp, Ross, and Bridenthal, "Examining Family History" (1983), 244.

16. Quote from *Report of the Woman's Rights Convention, Held at Seneca Falls, N.Y.* (1848). See also, Smith-Rosenberg, "Beauty, the Beast and the Militant Woman" (1971); Melder, *Beginnings of Sisterhood* (1977); and Hewitt, *Women's Activism and Social Change* (1984).

17. Quoted in Dublin, "Women, Work and Protest," 52. See also, Cameron, "Women's Culture"; Tax, *Rising of the Women*, chs. 8 and 9; and Jameson, "Imperfect Unions" (1971).

18. Among the most influential works using a modernization framework are Cott, *Bonds of Womanhood*; Smith-Rosenberg, "Beauty, the Beast"; Degler, *At Odds* (1980); Kraditor (ed.), *Up From the Pedestal* (1968); and Smith, "Family Limitation" (1973). Cott is the most explicit in acknowledging her debt to historical modernization literature (*Bonds of Womanhood*, 3–5).

19. For examples of historical modernization literature, See Brown, "Modernization and the Modern Personality" (1972); and Weinstein and Platt, *The Wish to be Free* (1969). For a statement of the general theory, see Black, *The Dynamics of Modernization* (1966); and Inkeles, "Making Men Modern" (1969).

20. Lemisch, "The American Revolution Seen from the Bottom Up" (1967).

21. This dichotomization has affected both European and American women. See, for example, Ehrenreich and English, *For Her Own Good* (1979), ch. 2; and Davidoff, "Class and Gender in Victorian England" (1983).

22. Quote from Jackson, Review in *Signs* (1983), 304. See also, Sacks, *Sisters and Wives* (1979); and Bénéria and Sens, "Class and Gender Inequalities and Women's Role in Economic Development" (1982).

23. See, for example, Kessler-Harris, *Out to Work* (1982), preface; Rapp, Ross, and Bridenthal, "Examining Family History", 233; Freidman, "Women's History and the Revision of Southern History" (1983) and Pleck, "Women's History" (1983).

24. Among those questioning the degree of separation between men's and women's spheres in the middle class are Hewitt, *Women's Activism* (1984); Ryan *Cradle of the Middle Class* (1981); May, "Expanding the Past" (1982); and Rothman "Sex and Self-control" (1982). On evidence of class prejudice among women, see Kraditor, *The Ideas of the Woman Suffrage Movement* (1965), chs. 6 and 7; Hewitt, *Women's Activism*, ch. 5; Jacoby, "Women's Trade Union League" (1971), 218–21; and Gordon and DuBois, "Seeking Ecstasy on the Battlefield" (1983).

25. See, for example, Davis, *Women, Race, and Class* (1981); Dill, "Race, Class and Gender" (1983); Edwards, *Rape, Racism, and the White Women's Movement* (n. d.); Freidman, "Women's History and the Revision of Southern History"; Harley and Terborg-Penn (eds.), *The Afro-American Woman* (1978); Hooks, *Ain't I A Woman* (1981); Hull, Scott, and Smith (eds.), *But Some of Us Are Brave* (1982); Lerner, *The Majority Finds Its Past* (1979), chs. 5, 6, and 7; Palmer, "White Woman/Black Women" (1983); and Simson, "The Afro-American Woman" (1983).

26. Throughout this article I will be employing Frederick Engels' definition of production which has a dual character; "on the one side, the production of the means of existence, of food, clothing, and shelter and the tools necessary for that production; on the other side, the production of human beings themselves, the propagation of the species." Under this latter, I also include social reproduction which embraces childrearing and domestic labor as well as childbearing. Quoted in Engles, *The Origin of the Family, Private Property and the State* (1972).

27. Quote from White, "Female Slaves" (1983). I am indebted to White's analysis throughout the section on slave women. See also, Davis, *Women, Race and Class*; Blassingame, *The Slave Community* (1972); Gutman, *The Black Family in Slavery and Freedom* (1976); Genovese, *Roll, Jordan, Roll* (1972); and Lerner (ed.), *Black Women in White America* (1972), 7–72.

28. White, "Female Slaves", 251–3.

29. While black women were assigned to men's work in the fields, especially during busy seasons, black men were apparently never assigned to "women's" work in the household even under dire circumstances.

30. For slave testimony, see Brent, *Incidents in the Life of a Slave Girl* (1861); and Keckley, *Behind the Scenes* (1868). Both are analyzed in Simson, "Afro-American Woman." See also Lerner (ed.), *Black Women*, 47–51, 150–63; and Lebsock, *Free Women of Petersburg* (1984), Introduction.

31. On the transition to male physicians among affluent whites and the resulting effects on female rituals, see Scholten " 'On the Importance of the Obstetrick Art' " (1977).

32. On black motherhood, see White, "Female Slaves," 256- 8; Cody, "Naming, Kinship, and Estate Dispersal" (1982); Genovese, *Roll, Jordan, Roll*; and Gutman, *The Black Family*. For a comparison of Southern white men's and women's roles in childrearing, see Smith, "Autonomy and Affection" (1983). On contemporary black women's views of mothering, see Stack, *All Our Kin* (1974); and Black Woman's Liberation Group, "Statement on Birth Control" (1970).

33. See, White, "Female Slaves," 256–8. On similar patterns in African cultures, See Sacks, *Sisters and Wives*.

34. See, Simson, "Afro-American Woman," and Lebsock, *Free Women of Petersburg* (1984), 139–40.

35. Throughout the rest of this article, same-class will be used to identify women and men of the same ethnicity and race as well as the same economic status.

36. Quote from Cameron, "Women's Culture," 6. See also, Dublin, "Women, Work, and Protest."

37. See, for example, Cameron, "Women's Culture"; Jameson, "Imperfect Unions" (1971); Ross, "Survival Networks" (1983); and Smith, "Our Own Kind" (1978).

38. Kessler-Harris, *Out to Work*, 160. For other examples see 247–8.

39. For a brilliant analysis of the conflicts between male unionists and women workers, see Kessler-Harris, "Where Are the Organized Women Workers?" (1975). See also, Cooper, "From Hand Craft to Mass Production" (1981). For a discussion of male-female co-operation, see, Brenner and Ramas, "Rethinking Women's Oppression" (1984), 44–9.

40. See, for example, Dublin, "Women, Work and Protest," 58–61; Walkowitz, *Worker City, Company Town*

(1978), chs. 3–5; Kessler-Harris, "Where Are the Organized Women Workers?" 100 and n. 34; and Janiewski, "Sisters under Their Skins" (1983).

41. Quote from Cameron, "Women's Culture," 10–11. See also, Jameson, "Imperfect Unions," especially 191–3.

42. On prostitutes, quote is from Jeffrey, Review in *Signs* (1982), 146. On miners' wives' responses, see Jameson, "Imperfect Unions," 180, 184–6, and 188–9.

43. Quoted in Dublin, "Women, Work and Protest" (1971), 53.

44. Janiewski, "Sisters under Their Skins," 26, 29–30.

45. See, Ryan, *Cradle of the Middle Class* (1981), chs. 4 and 5; and Hewitt, *Women's Activism*, ch. 7.

46. On changes in domestic work and domestic servitude, see Strasser, *Never Done* (1982); and Dudden, *Serving Women* (1983). In addition, women had less help from children with the expansion of public education. For an analysis of the variation in (or lack of) hours spent on housework as a result of technological changes, see Hartmann, "The Family as a Locus of Gender, Class, and Political Struggle" (1981); and Vanek, "Time Spent in Housework" (1974).

47. Judith Sargent Murray, a late eighteenth century educator, quoted in Kerber, "Daughters of Liberty" (1974), 91.

48. On the first effect, see Cott, "Passionlessness" (1978); and Smith, "Family Limitation" (1973). On the second, see Kuhn, *The Mother's Role in Childhood Education* (1974); Folbre, "Of Patriarchy Born" (1983); Minge-Kalman, "The Industrial Revolution and the European Family" (1978); and Ryan, *Cradle of the Middle Class* (1981), ch. 5.

49. Quote from Dr. Benjamin Rush in Kerber, "Daughters of Columbia" (1974), 91; and Ryan, *Cradle of the Middle Class*, 148.

50. Numerous community studies, both published and in progress, make this point clearly. See particularly, Hewitt, *Women's Activism*; Scott, *Making the Invisible Woman Visible* (1984); and Ryan, *Cradle of the Middle Class*. Current research on Cincinnati by Caroline Blum and on St. Louis by Marion Hunt provide further evidence.

51. Quoted in Hewitt, *Women's Activism*, 17, 189–90, and 209; see also 243–52 generally.

52. See Hewitt, *Women's Activism*, ch. 7; and Ryan, *Cradle of the Middle Class*, ch. 3.

53. Newton, Ryan, and Walkowitz (eds.), *Sex and Class* (1983), editors' introduction, 9.

54. On the development of the "decentralized home system," see Hartmann, "The Family as the Locus of Gender, Class and Political Struggle" (1981).

55. See, for example, Kathryn Kish Sklar, *Catharine Beecher* (1973); Kelley, *Private Woman, Public Stage* (1984); and Young, "Women, Civilization, and the Indian Question" (1982).

56. See Gordon and DuBois, "Seeking Ecstasy on the Battlefield" (1983); Ryan, "The Power of Women's Networks" (1979); Gordon, *Woman's Body, Woman's Right*, (1976); and Borden, *Women and Temperance* (1980). The outstanding example of moral reform studies, focused on England, is Walkowitz, *Prostitution and Victorian Society* (1980). Early investigations into working-class and minority groups suggest that they construct their sexuality and morality differently from the bourgeoisie. See, for instance, Dannenbaum, "The Origins of Temperance Activism and Militancy Among American Women" (1981); Duberman, Eggan and Clemmer, "Documents in Hopi Sexuality" (1979); Peiss, " 'Charity Girls' and City Pleasures" (1983); and Simson, "Afro-American Woman."

57. See Kessler-Harris, "Where Are the Organized Women Workers?" (1975); Jacoby, "Women's Trade Union League"; and Dye, "Creating a Feminist Alliance" (1971).

58. Cameron has found evidence of immigrant women's opposition to the "family wage" in Lawrence, Massachusetts, in the 1880s based on women's fear of losing power in the family. (Personal correspondence with the author.) On changes in status with upward mobility, see especially, Terborg-Penn, "Black Male Perspectives on the Nineteenth-Century Woman" (1978); and Lerner (ed.), *Black Women* (1972), 290–4. For the importance of women's control of economic resources to their status in society, see Sacks, *Sisters and Wives* (1979); and Brown, "Iroquois Women" (1975).

59. See, Hewitt, *Women's Activism*, ch. 7; Gordon, *Woman's Body* (1976), chs. 9 and 10; Zeidenstein (ed.), *Learning About Rural Women* (1979), introduction; and Seller, "Education of the Immigrant Woman" (1982).

60. The vast majority of charitable, missionary, moral reform, temperance, and antislavery societies were single-sex associations in the antebellum era as were the largest women's organizations at the turn of the century—the women's clubs, temperance societies and suffrage associations. For this same pattern in these and other movements, see Freedman, "Separation as Strategy" (1979).

61. Quote from Lawson and Barton, "Sex Roles in Social Movements" (1980), 231. See also Tax, *Rising of the Women*, ch. 6; and Hyman, "Immigrant Women and Consumer Protest" (1980).

62. See, Davis, *Women, Race, and Class* (1981), ch. 11. On black women's struggles to work with black men and/or white women, see Neverdon-Morton, "The Black Women's Struggle" (1978); Barnett, *On Lynching* (1969); and Hall, *Revolt Against Chivalry* (1979). An excellent summary of differences in black men's and

women's approach to public activism was presented by Darlene Clark Hines at the Southern Historical Association meetings in Charleston, South Carolina, in November 1983.

63. See, for example, Kessler-Harris, "Organizing the Unorganizable" (1971).

References

Banner, Lois and Mary Hartman, eds. *Clio's Consciousness Raised.* New York: Harper and Row, 1974.

Barnett, Ida B. Wells. *On Lynching* (New York: Arno Press, 1969).

Beneria, Lourdes and Gita Sens. "Class and Gender Inequalities and Women's Role in Economic Development: Theoretical and Practical Implications." *Feminist Studies* 8 (Spring 1982): 152–76.

Black, Cyril E. *The Dynamics of Modernization.* New York: Free Press, 1966.

Black Women's Liberation Group, Mount Vernon, New York. "Statement on birth control," in Robin Morgan, ed., *Sisterhood is Powerful: An Anthology.* New York: Vintage, 1970.

Blassingame, John W. *The Slave Community: Plantation Life in the Antebellum South.* New York: Oxford University Press, 1972.

Borden, Ruth. *Women and Temperance: The Quest for Power and Liberty, 1873–1900.* Philadelphia: Temple University Press, 1980.

Boylan, Anne M. "Evangelical Womanhood in the Nineteenth Century: The Role of Women in Sunday Schools." *Feminist Studies* 4 (October 1978): 62–80.

Boylan, Anne M. "Women in Groups: An Analysis of Women's Benevolent Organizations in New York and Boston, 1797–1840." *Journal of American History* 71 (December 1984): 497–523.

Brenner, Johanna and Maria Ramas. "Rethinking Women's Oppression." *New Left Review* 144 (March–April 1984): 44–49.

Brent, Linda (alias of Harriet Brent Jacobs). *Incidents in the Life of a Slave Girl,* ed. with an introduction by Lydia Maria Child. Boston: 1861.

Brown, Judith K. "Iroquois Women. An Ethnohistoric Note," in Rayna R. Reiter, ed. *Toward an Anthropology of Women.* New York: Monthly Review Press, 1975.

Brown, Richard D. "Modernization and the Modern Personality in Early America, 1600–1865." *Journal of Interdisciplinary History* 11 (1972): 201–28.

Brownmiller, Susan. *Against Our Will: Men, Women, and Rape.* New York: Simon and Schuster, 1975.

Buhle, Mary Jo. *Women and American Socialism, 1870–1920.* Champagne-Urbana: University of Illinois Press, 1981.

Cameron, Ardis. "Women's Culture and Working-Class Activism." Paper presented at the Social Science History Association meeting, Washington, D.C., November 1983.

Cantor, Milton and Bruce Laurie, eds. *Class, Sex, and the Woman Worker.* Contributions in Labor History. Westport, CT: Greenwood Press, 1971.

Carroll, Berenice A., ed. *Liberating Women's History: Theoretical and Critical Essays.* Chicago: University of Illinois Press, 1976.

Clinton, Catherine. *The Plantation Mistress: Woman's World in the Old South.* New York: Pantheon Books, 1983.

Cody, Cheryll Ann. "Naming, Kinship, and Estate Dispersal: Notes on Slave Family Life on a South Carolina Plantation, 1786 to 1833." *William and Mary Quarterly* 31 (January 1982): 192–211.

Cooper, Patricia. "From Hand Craft to Mass Production: Men, Women, and Work Culture in American Cigar Factories, 1900–1919." Ph.D. dissertation, University of Maryland, 1981.

Cott, Nancy. "Passionlessness: An Interpretation of Victorian Sexual Ideology, 1790 to 1850." *Signs* 55 (1978): 219–36.

Cott, Nancy. "Young Women in the Second Great Awakening in New England." *Feminist Studies* 3 (Fall 1975): 15–29.

Cott, Nancy. *The Bonds of Womanhood: 'Woman's Sphere' in New England, 1780–1835.* New Haven: Yale University Press, 1977.

Dannenbaum, Jed. "The Origins of Temperance Activism and Militancy among American Women." *Journal of Social History* 14 (Winter 1981): 235–52.

Davidoff, Leonore. "Class and gender in Victorian England," in Judith Newton, Mary Ryan, and Judith Walkowitz, eds. *Sex and Class in Women's History.* Boston & London: Routledge and Kegan Paul, 1983.

Davis, Allen F. *Spearheads for Reform: The Social Settlements and the Progressive Movement, 1890–1914.* New York: Oxford University Press, 1967.

Davis, Angela Y. *Women, Race, and Class.* New York: Random House, 1981.

degler, Carl. *At Odds: Women and the Family in America from the Revolution to the Present.* New York: Oxford University Press, 1980.

DiCaprio, Lisa. "Women's Liberation: Yesterday and Today." *The Guardian,* 7 November 1984.

Dill, Bonnie Thornton. "Race, Class, and Gender: Prospects for an all-inclusive Sisterhood." *Feminist Studies,* 9 (Spring 1983): 131–50.

Duberman, Martin B., Fred Eggan, and Richard Clemmer. "Documents in Hopi Sexuality: Imperialism, Culture, and Resistance." *Radical History Review* 20 (Spring–Summer 1979): 99–130.

Dublin, Thomas. "Women, Work and Protest in the Early Lowell Mills: 'The Oppressing Hand of Avarice Would Enslave Us'," in Milton Cantor and Bruce Laurie, eds. *Class, Sex, and the Woman Worker.* Westport, CT: Greenwood Press, 1971.

DuBois, Ellen, Mari Jo Buhle, Temma Kaplan, Gerda Lerner, and Carroll Smith-Rosenberg. "Politics and Culture in Women's History: A Symposium." *Feminist Studies* 6 (Spring 1980): 26–84.

Dudden, Faye E. *Serving Women: Household Service in Nineteenth-Century America.* Middletown, Ct: Wesleyan University Press, 1983.

Dye, Nancy Schrom. "Creating a Feminist Alliance: Sisterhood and Class Conflict in the New York Women's Trade Union League, 1903–1914," in Milton Cantor and Bruce Laurie, eds. *Class, Sex, and the Woman Worker.* Westport, CT: Greenwood Press, 1971.

Edwards, Alison. *Rape, Racism, and the White Women's Movement: An Answer to Susan Brownmiller.* Chicago: Sojourner Truth Organization, n.d.

Ehrenreich, Barbara and Deirdre English. *For Her Own Good: 150 Years of Advice to Women.* Garden City, NY: Doubleday, 1979.

Eisenstein, Zillah R., ed. *Capitalist Patriarchy and the Case for Socialist Feminism.* New York: Monthly Review Press, 1979.

Engels, Frederick. *The Origin of the Family, Private Property and the State,* ed. with an introduction by Eleanor Leacock. New York: International Publishers, 1972.

Epstein, Barbara. *The Politics of Domesticity: Women, Evangelicalism, and Temperance in Nineteenth-Century America.* Middletown, Ct: Wesleyan University, 1981.

Evans, Sara. "Rethinking Women's Lives." *In These Times* (January 1983): 19–25.

Faragher, Johnny Mack and Christine Stansell. "Women and Their Families on the Overland Trail to California and Oregon, 1842–1867," in Nancy Cott and Elizabeth Pleck, eds. *A Heritage of Her Own: Towards a New Social History of American Women.* New York: Simon and Schuster, 1979.

Firestone, Shulamith. *The Dialectic of Sex: The Case for Feminist Revolution.* New York: William Morrow, 1970.

Firestone, Shulamith and Anne Koedt, eds. *Notes from the Second Year: Major Writings of Radical Feminists.* New York: Radical Feminist Publications, 1979.

Fisher, Berenice. "Guilt and Shame in the Women's Movement: The Radical Ideal of Action and Its Meaning for Feminist Intellectuals." *Feminist Studies* 10 (Summer 1984): 185–212.

Flexner, Eleanor. *A Century of Struggle: The Women's Rights Movement in the United States.* Cambridge, MA: Harvard University Press, 1959.

Folbre, Nancy. "Of Patriarchy Born: The Political Economy of Fertility Decisions." *Feminist Studies* 9 (Summer 1983): 261–84.

Freedman, Estelle. "Separation as Strategy: Female Institution Building and American Feminism, 1870–1930." *Feminist Studies* 5 (Fall 1979): 512–29.

Freidman, Jean E. "Women's History and the Revision of Southern History," in Joanne Hawks and Shelia Skemp, eds. *Sex, Race, and the Role of Women in the South.* Jackson: University of Mississippi Press, 1983.

Genovese, Eugene. *Roll, Jordan, Roll: The World the Slaves Made.* New York: Vintage Press, 1972.

Goldman, Marion B. *Gold Diggers and Silver Miners: Prostitution and Social Life on the Comstock Lode.* Ann Arbor: University of Michigan Press, 1981.

Gordon, Linda. *Woman's Body, Woman's Right: A Social History of Birth Control in America.* New York: Grossman Publishers, 1976.

Gordon, Linda and Ellen DuBois. "Seeking Ecstasy on the Battlefield: Danger and Pleasure in Nineteenth-Century Feminist Sexual Thought." *Feminist Studies* 9 (Spring 1983): 7–25.

Gutman, Herbert. *The Black Family in Slavery and Freedom, 1750–1925.* New York: Pantheon Books, 1976.

Hall, Jacquelyn Dowd. *Revolt Against Chivalry: Jessie Daniel Ames and the Women's Campaign Against Lynching.* New York: Columbia University Press, 1979.

Harley, Sharon and Rosalyn Terborg-Penn, eds. *The Afro-American Women: Struggles and Images.* Port Washington, NY: Kennikat Press, 1978.

Hartmann, Heidi. "The Family as a Locus of Gender, Class, and Political Struggle: The Example of Housework." *Signs* 6 (Spring 1981): 366–94.

Hawks, Joanne V. and Sheila L. Skemp, eds. *Sex, Race, and the Role of Women in the South.* Jackson: University of Mississippi Press, 1983.

Hersh, Blanche Glassman. *The Slavery of Sex: Feminist-Abolitionists in America.* Chicago: University of Illinois Press, 1978.

Hewitt, Nancy A. *Women's Activism and Social Change: Rochester, New York, 1822–1872.* Ithaca, NY: Cornell University Press, 1984.

Hooks, Bell. *Ain't I A Woman: Black Women and Feminism.* Boston: South End Press, 1981.

Hufton, Olwen. "Women and the Family Economy." *French Historical Studies* 9 (Spring 1975): 1–22.

Hull, Gloria T., Patricia Bell Scott, and Barbara Smith, eds. *But Some of Us are Brave: All the Women are White, All the Blacks are Men.* Old Westbury, NY: The Feminist Press, 1982.

Hyman, Paula. "Immigrant Women and Consumer Protest: The New York City Kosher Meat Boycott of 1902." *American Jewish History* 70 (September 1980): 91–105.

Inkeles, Alex. "Making Men Modern: On the Causes and Consequences of Individual Change in Six Developing Countries." *American Journal of Sociology* 75 (1969): 208–25.

Jackson, Jean E. Review. *Signs* 9 (Winter 1983): 304.

Jacoby, Robin Miller. "The Women's Trade Union League and American Feminism," in Milton Cantor and Bruce Laurie, eds. *Class, Sex, and the Woman Worker.* Westport, CT: Greenwood Press, 1971.

Jameson, Elizabeth. "Imperfect Unions: Class and Gender in Cripple Creek, 1894–1904," in Milton Cantor and Bruce Laurie, eds. *Class, Sex, and the Woman Worker.* Westport, CT: Greenwood Press, 1971.

Janiewski, Dolores. *Sisterhood Denied: Race, Class, and Gender in a New South Community.* Philadelphia: Temple University Press, 1985.

Janiewski, Dolores. "Sisters Under Their Skins: Southern Working Women, 1880–1950," in Joanne Hawks and Shelia Skemp, eds. *Sex, Race, and the Role of Women in the South.* Jackson: University of Mississippi Press, 1981.

Jeffrey, Julie Roy. Review. *Signs* 8 (Autumn 1982): 143–6.

Keckley, Elizabeth. *Behind the Scenes.* New York: G. W. Carleton and Co., 1868.

Kelley, Mary. *Private Woman, Public Stage: Literary Domesticity in Nineteenth-Century America.* New York: Oxford University Press, 1984.

Kerber, Linda K. "Daughters of Columbia: Educating Women for the Republic, 1787–1805," in Stanley Elkins and Eric McKitrick, eds. *The Hofstadter Aegis: A Memorial.* New York: Alfred A. Knopf, 1974.

Kerber, Linda K. and Jane DeHart Mathews, eds. *Women's America: Refocusing the Past.* New York: Oxford University Press, 1982.

Kessler-Harris, Alice. *Out to Work: A History of Wage-Earning Women in America.* New York: Oxford University Press, 1982.

Kessler-Harris, Alice. "Where are the Organized Women Workers?" *Feminist Studies* 3 (Fall 1975): 92–110.

Kraditor, Aileen S. *The Ideas of the Woman Suffrage Movement, 1890–1920.* New York: Columbia University Press, 1965.

Kraditor, Aileen S., ed. *Up From the Pedestal.* New York: Quadrangle, 1968.

Kuhn, Anne L. *The Mother's Role in Childhood Education: New England Concepts, 1830–1860.* New Haven: Yale University Press, 1974.

Lawson, Ronald and Stephen E. Barton. "Sex Roles in Social Movements: A Case Study of the Tenant Movement in New York City." *Signs* 6 (Winter 1980): 230–47.

Lebsock, Suzanne. "Free Black Women and the Question of Matriarchy," in Joanne Hawks and Shelia Skemp, eds. *Sex, Race, and the Role of Women in the South.* Jackson: University of Mississippi Press, 1983.

Lebsock, Suzanne. *The Free Women of Petersburg: Status and Culture in a Southern Town, 1784–1860.* New York: W. W. Norton, 1984.

Lemisch, Jesse. "The American Revolution Seen from the Bottom Up," in Barton J. Bernstein, ed. *Towards a New Past: Dissenting Essays in American History.* New York: Vintage Books, 1967.

Lerner, Gerda, ed. *Black Women in White America.* New York: Vintage Books, 1972.

Lerner, Gerda. *The Majority Finds Its Past.* New York: Oxford University Press, 1979.

May, Elaine Tyler. "Expanding the Past: Recent Scholarship on Women in Politics and Work." *Reviews in American History* (December 1982): 216–33.

Melder, Keith. *The Beginnings of Sisterhood: The Woman's Rights Movement in the United States, 1800–1849.* New York: Schocken Books, 1977.

Millett, Kate. *Sexual Politics.* New York: Doubleday, 1970.

Minge-Kalman, Wanda. "The Industrial Revolution and the European Family: The Institutionalization of

'Childhood' as a Market for Family Labor." *Comparative Studies in Society and History* 20 (July 1978): 454–67.

Morgan, Robin, ed. *Sisterhood is Powerful: An Anthology.* New York: Vintage Books, 1970.

Neverdon-Morton, Cynthia. "The Black Women's Struggle for Equality in the South, 1895–1925," in Sharon Harley and Rosalyn Terborg-Penn, eds. *Afro-American Woman: Struggles and Images.* Port Washington, NY: Kennikat Press, 1978.

Newton, Judith L., Mary P. Ryan, and Judith R. Walkowitz, eds. *Sex and Class in Women's History.* History Workshop Series. New York and London: Routledge and Kegan Paul, 1983.

Norton, Mary Beth. *Liberty's Daughters: The Revolutionary Experience of American Women, 1750–1800.* Boston: Little, Brown, 1980.

Palmer, Phyllis Marynick. "White Women/Black Women: The Dualism of Female Identity and Experience in the United States." *Feminist Studies* 9 (Spring 1983): 151–70.

Peiss, Kathy. " 'Charity Girls' and City Pleasures: Historical Notes on Working-class Women's Sexuality, 1880–1920," in Ann Snitow, Christine Stansell, and Sharon Thompson, eds. *Powers of Desire.* New York: Monthly Review Press, 1983.

Pleck, Elizabeth H. "Women's History: Gender as a Category of Historical Analysis," in James B. Gardner and George Rollie Adams, eds. *Ordinary People and Everyday Life: Perspectives on the New Social History.* Nashville, TN: American Association of State and Local History, 1983.

Rapp, Rayna, Ellen Ross, and Renata Bridenthal. "Examining Family History," in Judith Newton, Mary Ryan and Judith Walkowitz, eds. *Sex and Class in Women's History.* New York and London: Routledge and Kegan Paul, 1983.

Report of the Woman's Rights Convention, Held at Seneca Falls, N.Y., 19 and 20 July 1848. Rochester: John Dick, 1848.

Rosaldo, Michelle Zimbalist. "Woman, Culture, and Society: A Theoretical Overview," in Rosaldo and Louise Lamphere, eds. *Woman, Culture, and Society.* Stanford, CA: Stanford University Press, 1974.

Ross, Ellen. "Survival Networks: Women's Neighborhood Sharing in London before World War I." *History Workshop* 15 (Spring 1983): 4–27.

Rothman, Ellen K. "Sex and Self-control: Middle-class Courtship in America, 1770–1870." *Journal of Social History* 15 (Spring 1982): 409–25.

Ryan, Mary P. *Cradle of the Middle Class: Family and Community in Oneida County, New York, 1780–1865.* Cambridge: Cambridge University Press, 1981.

Ryan, Mary P. "The Power of Women's Networks: A Case Study of Female Moral Reform in America." *Feminist Studies* 4 (Spring 1979): 66–86.

Sacks, Karen. *Sisters and Wives: The Past and Future of Sexual Equality.* Westport, CT: Greenwood Press, 1979.

Sargent, Lydia, ed. *Women and Revolution: A Discussion of the Unhappy Marriage of Marxism and Feminism.* Political Controversies Series, 2. Boston: South End Press: 1981.

Scholten, Catharine M. " 'On the Importance of the Obstetrick art': Changing Customs of Childbirth in America, 1760–1825." *William and Mary Quarterly* 34 (1977): 426–45.

Scott, Anne Firor. "Women's Perspective on the Patriarchy in the 1850s," in Jean E. Freidman and William G. Shade, eds. *Our American Sisters: Women in American Life and Thought.* 3rd edition. Lexington, MA: D.C. Heath and Co., 1982.

Scott, Anne Firor. *Making the Invisible Woman Visible.* Chicago: University of Illinois Press, 1984.

Seller, Maxine. "The Education of the Immigrant Woman, 1900–1935," in Linda Kerber and Jane Mathews, eds. *Women's America: Refocusing the Past.* New York: Oxford University Press, 1982.

Simson, Rennie. "The Afro-American Woman: The Historical Context of the Construction of Sexual Identity," in Ann Snitow, Christine Stansell, and Sharon Thompson, eds. *Powers of Desire.* New York: Monthly Review Press, 1983.

Sinclair, Andrew. *The Emancipation of the American Woman.* New York: Harper and Row, 1965.

Sklar, Kathryn Kish. *Catharine Beecher: A Study in American Domesticity.* New Haven: Yale University Press, 1973.

Smith-Rosenberg, Carroll. "Beauty, the Beast and the Militant Woman: A Case Study in Sex Roles and Social Stress in Jacksonian America." *American Quarterly,* 23 (October 1971): 562–84.

Smith-Rosenberg, Carroll. "The Female World of Love and Ritual: Relations between Women in Nineteenth-century America." *Signs* 1 (Autumn 1975): 1–29.

Smith-Rosenberg, Carroll. *Religion and the Rise of the City: The New York City Mission Movement, 1812–1870.* Ithaca, NY: Cornell University Press, 1971.

Smith, Bonnie G. *Ladies of the Leisure Class: The Bourgeoises in Northern France in the Nineteenth Century.* Princeton, NJ: Princeton University Press, 1981.

Smith, Daniel Blake. "Autonomy and Affection: Parents and Children in Chesapeake Families," in Michael

Gordon, ed. *The American Family in Social-Historical Perspective.* 3rd edition. New York: St. Martin's Press, 1983.

Smith, Daniel Scott. "Family Limitation, Sexual Control, and Domestic Feminism in Victorian America." *Feminist Studies* 1 (Winter–Spring 1973): 40–57.

Smith, Judith. "Our Own Kind: Family and Community Networks in Providence." *Radical History Review,* 17 (Spring 1978): 99–120.

Snitow, Ann, Christine Stansell, and Sharon Thompson, eds. *Powers of Desire.* New York: Monthly Review Press, 1983.

Stack, Carol. *All Our Kin: Strategies for Survival in a Black Community.* New York: Harper Books, 1974.

Strasser, Susan. *Never Done: A History of American Housework.* New York: Pantheon Books, 1982.

Tax, Meredith. *The Rising of the Women: Feminist Solidarity and Class Conflict, 1880–1917.* New York: Monthly Review Press, 1980.

Tentler, Leslie Woodcock. *Wage-Earning Women: Industrial Work and Family Life in the United States, 1900–1930.* New York: Oxford University Press, 1979.

Terborg-Penn, Rosalyn. "Black Male Perspectives on the Nineteenth-century Woman," in Sharon Harley and Rosalyn Terborg-Penn, eds. *Afro-American Woman: Struggles and Images.* Port Washington, NY: Kennikat Press, 1978.

Vanck, Joann. "Time Spent in Housework." *Scientific American* (November 1974): 116–21.

Walkowitz, Daniel J. *Worker City, Company Town: Iron and Cotton Worker Protest in Troy and Cohoes, New York, 1855–1884.* Chicago: University of Illinois Press, 1978.

Walkowitz, Judith R., *Prostitution and Victorian Society: Women, Class and the State.* New York: Cambridge University Press, 1980.

Weinstein, Fred and Gerald Platt. *The Wish to be Free: Society, Psyche, and Value Change.* Berkeley: University of California Press, 1969.

Welter, Barbara. "The Cult of True Womanhood, 1820–1860." *American Quarterly* 18 (Summer 1966): 151–74.

White, Deborah G. "Female Slaves: Sex Roles and Status in the Antebellum Plantation South." *Journal of Family History* (Fall 1983): 248–61.

Young, Mary E. "Women, Civilization, and the Indian Question," in Linda Kerber and Jane Mathews, eds. *Women's America: Refocusing the Past.* New York: Oxford University Press, 1982.

Zeidenstein, Sondra, eds. *Learning About Rural Women.* New York: Population Council, 1979.

2

Female Slaves:
Sex Roles and Status in the
Antebellum Plantation South

Deborah Gray White

In his study of the black family in America, sociologist E. Franklin Frazier theorized that in slave family and marriage relations, women played the dominant role. Specifically, Frazier wrote that "the Negro woman as wife or mother was the mistress of her cabin, and, save for the interference of master and overseer, her wishes in regard to mating and family matters were paramount." He also insisted that slavery had schooled the black woman in self-reliance and self-sufficiency and that "neither economic necessity nor tradition had instilled in her the spirit of subordination to masculine authority" (1939:125). The Frazier thesis received support from other social scientists, including historians Kenneth Stampp (1956:344) and Stanley Elkins (1959:130), both of whom held that slave men had been emasculated and stripped of their paternity rights by slave masters who left control of slave households to slave women. In his infamous 1965 national report, Daniel Patrick Moynihan (1965:31) lent further confirmation to the Frazier thesis when he alleged that the fundamental problem with the modern black family was the "often reversed roles of husband and wife," and then traced the origin of the "problem" back to slavery.

Partly in response to the criticism spawned by the Moynihan Report, historians reanalyzed antebellum source material, and the matriarchy thesis was debunked. For better or worse, said historians Robert Fogel and Stanley Engerman (1974:141), the "dominant" role in slave society was played by men. Men were dominant, they said, because men occupied all managerial and artisan slots, and because masters recognized the male head of the family group. From historian John Blassingame we learned that by building furnishings and providing extra food for their families, men found indirect ways of gaining status. If a garden plot was to be cultivated, the husband "led" his wife in the family undertaking (1972:92). After a very thoughtful appraisal of male slave activities, historian Eugene Genovese concluded that "slaves from their own experience had come to value a two-parent, male-centered household, no matter how much difficulty they had in realizing the ideal" (1974:491–492). Further tipping the scales toward patriarchal slave households, historian Herbert Gutman argued that the belief that matrifocal households prevailed among slaves was a misconception. He demonstrated that children were more likely to be named after their fathers than mothers, and that during the Civil War slave men acted like fathers and husbands by fighting for their freedom and by protecting their wives and children when they were threatened by Union troops or angry slaveholders (1976:188–191, 369–386).

Reprinted with permission from the *Journal of Family History*, vol. 8, Fall, 1983 (JAI Press, Inc., Greenwich, CT).

With the reinterpretation of male roles came a revision of female roles. Once considered dominant, slave women were now characterized as subordinated and sometimes submissive. Fogel and Engerman found proof of their subordinated status in the fact that they were excluded from working in plow gangs and did all of the household chores (1974:141–142). Genovese maintained that slave women's "attitude toward housework, especially cooking, and toward their own femininity," belied the conventional wisdom "according to which women unwittingly helped ruin their men by asserting themselves in the home, protecting their children, and assuming other normally masculine responsibilities (1974:500). Gutman found one Sea Island slave community where the black church imposed a submissive role upon married slave women (1976:72).

In current interpretations of the contemporary black family the woman's role has not been "feminized" as much as it has been "deemphasized." The stress in studies like those done by Carol Stack (1974) and Theodore Kennedy (1980), is not on roles per se but on the black family's ability to survive in flexible kinship networks that are viable bulwarks against discrimination and racism. These interpretations also make the point that black kinship patterns are not based exclusively on consanguineous relationships but are also determined by social contacts that sometimes have their basis in economic support.

Clearly then, the pendulum has swung away from the idea that women ruled slave households, and that their dominance during the slave era formed the foundation of the modern day matriarchal black family. But how far should that pendulum swing? This paper suggests that we should tread the road that leads to the patriarchal slave household and the contemporary amorphous black family with great caution. It suggests that, at least in relation to the slave family, too much emphasis has been placed on what men could not do rather than on what women could do and did. What follows is not a comprehensive study of female slavery, but an attempt to reassess Frazier's claim that slave women were self-reliant and self-sufficient through an examination of some of their activities, specifically their work, their control of particular resources, their contribution to their households and their ability to cooperate with each other on a daily basis. Further, this paper will examine some of the implications of these activities, and their probable impact on the slave woman's status in slave society, and the black family.

At the outset a few points must be made about the subject matter and the source material used to research it. Obviously, a study that concentrates solely on females runs the risk of overstating woman's roles and their importance in society. One must therefore keep in mind that this is only one aspect, although a very critical one, of slave family and community life. In addition, what follows is a synthesis of the probable sex role of the average slave woman on plantations with at least twenty slaves.[1] In the process of constructing this synthesis I have taken into account such variables as plantation size, crop, region of the South, and the personal idiosyncrasies of slave masters. Finally, in drawing conclusions about the sex role and status of slave women, I have detailed their activities and analyzed them in terms of what anthropologists know about women who do similar things in analogous settings. I took this approach for two reasons. First, information about female slaves cannot be garnered from sources left by slave women because they left few narratives, diaries or letters. The dearth of source material makes it impossible to draw conclusions about the slave woman's feelings. Second, even given the ex-slave interviews, a rich source material for this subject, it is almost impossible to draw conclusions about female slave status from an analysis of their individual personalities. Comments such as that made by the slave woman. Fannie, to her husband Bob, "I don't want no sorry nigger around me," perhaps says something about Fannie, but not about all slave women (Egypt et al., 1945:184). Similarly, for every mother who grieved over the sale of her children there was probably a father whose heart was also broken. Here, only the activities of the slave woman will be examined in an effort to discern her status in black society.

Turning first to the work done by slave women, it appears that they did a variety of heavy and dirty labor, work which was also done by men. In 1853, Frederick Olmsted saw South Carolina slaves of both sexes carting manure on their heads to the cotton fields where they spread it with their hands between the ridges in which cotton was planted. In Fayetteville, North Carolina, he noticed that women not only hoed and shovelled but they also cut down trees and drew wood (Olmsted, 1971:67, 81). The use of women as lumberjacks occurred quite frequently, especially in the lower South and Southwest, areas which retained a frontier quality during the antebellum era. Solomon Northrup, a kidnapped slave, knew women who wielded the ax so perfectly that the largest oak or sycamore fell before their well-directed blows. An Arkansas ex-slave remembered that her mother used to carry logs (Osofsky, 1969:308–309; Rawick, 1972, vol. 10, pt. 5:54). On Southwestern plantations women did all kinds of work. In the region of the Bayou Boeuf women were expected to "plough, drag, drive team, clear wild lands, work on the highway," and do any other type of work required of them (Osofsky, 1969:313). In short, full female hands frequently did the same kind of work as male hands.

It is difficult, however, to say how often they did the same kind of field work, and it would be mistake to say that there was no differentiation of field labor on Southern farms and plantations. The most common form of differentiation was that women hoed while men plowed. Yet, the exceptions to the rule were so numerous as to make a mockery of it. Many men hoed on a regular basis. Similarly, if a field had to be plowed and there were not enough male hands to do it, then it was not unusual for an overseer to command a strong woman to plow. This could happen on a plantation of twenty slaves or a farm of five.[2]

It is likely, however, that women were more often called to do the heavy labor usually assigned to men after their childbearing years. Pregnant women, and sometimes women breastfeeding infants, were usually given less physically demanding work.[3] If, as recent studies indicate (see Dunn, 1977:58; Gutman, 1976:50, 74, 124, 171; Trussell, 1978:504), slave women began childbearing when about twenty years of age and had children at approximately two and a half year intervals, at least until age thirty-five, slave women probably spent a considerable amount of time doing tasks which men did not do.[4] Pregnant and nursing women were classified as half-hands or three-quarters hands and such workers did only some of the work that was also done by full hands. For instance, it was not unusual for them to pick cotton or even hoe, work done on a regular basis by both sexes. But frequently, they were assigned to "light work" like raking stubble or pulling weeds, which was often given to children and the elderly.[5]

Slave women might have preferred to be exempt from such labor, but they might also have gained some intangibles from doing the same work as men. Anthropologists (Mullings, 1976:243–244; Sacks, 1974:213–222) have demonstrated that in societies where men and women are engaged in the production of the same kinds of goods and where widespread private property is not a factor, participation in production gives women freedom and independence. Since neither slave men nor women had access to, or control over, the products of their labor, parity in the field may have encouraged egalitarianism in the slave quarters. In Southern Togo, for instance, where women work alongside their husbands in the field because men do not alone produce goods which are highly valued, democracy prevails in relationships between men and women (Rocher et al., 1962:151–152).

But bondswomen did do a lot of traditional "female work" and one has to wonder whether this work, as well as the work done as a "half-hand," tallied on the side of female subordination. In the case of the female slave, domestic work was not always confined to the home, and often "woman's work" required skills that were highly valued and even coveted because of the place it could purchase in the higher social echelons of the slave world. For example, cooking was definitely "female work" but it was also a skilled occupation. Good cooks were highly respected by both blacks and whites, and their occupation was raised in status because the masses of slave women did not cook on a regular basis. Since field work occupied the time of most women, meals were often served communally. Female slaves therefore, were, for the most part, relieved of this traditional chore, and the occupation of "cook" became specialized.[6]

Sewing too was often raised above the level of inferior "woman's work." All females at one time or another had to spin and weave. Occasionally each woman was given cloth and told to make her family's clothes, but this was unusual and more likely to happen on small farms than on plantations. During slack seasons women probably did more sewing than during planting and harvesting seasons, and pregnant women were often put to work spinning, weaving and sewing. Nevertheless, sewing could be raised to the level of a skilled art, especially if a woman sewed well enough to make the white family's clothes. Such women were sometimes hired out and allowed to keep a portion of the profit they brought their master and mistress (Rawick, 1972, vol. 17, 158; SHC, White Hill Plantation Books:13; Rawick, 1972, vol. 2, pt. 2:114).

Other occupations which were solidly anchored in the female domain, and which increased a woman's prestige, were midwifery and doctoring. The length of time and extent of training it took to become a midwife is indicated by the testimony of Clara Walker, a former slave interviewed in Arkansas, who remembered that she trained for five years under a doctor who became so lazy after she had mastered the job that he would sit down and let her do all the work. After her "apprenticeship" ended she delivered babies for both slave and free, black and white (Rawick, 1972, vol. 10, pt. 5:21). Other midwives learned the trade from a female relative, often their mother, and they in turn passed the skill on to another female relative.

A midwife's duty often extended beyond delivering babies, and they sometimes became known as "doctor women." In this capacity they cared for men, women, and children. Old women, some with a history of midwifery and some without, also gained respect as "doctor women." They "knowed a heap about yarbs [herbs]," recalled a Georgia ex-slave (Rawick, 1972, vol. 2, pt. 2:112).[8] Old women had innumerable cures, especially for children's diseases, and since plantation "nurseries" were usually under their supervision, they had ample opportunity to practice their art. In sum, a good portion of the slave's medical care, particularly that of women and children, was supervised by slave women.

Of course, not all women were hired-out seamstresses, cooks, or midwives; a good deal of "female work" was laborious and mundane. An important aspect of this work, as well as of the field work done by women, was that it was frequently done in female groups. As previously noted, women often hoed while men plowed. In addition, when women sewed they usually did so with other women. Quilts were made by women at gatherings called, naturally enough, "quiltins." Such gatherings were attended only by women and many former slaves had vivid recollections of them. The "quiltin's and spinnin' frolics dat de women folks had" were the most outstanding remembrances of Hattie Anne Nettles, an Alabama ex-slave (Rawick, 1972, vol. 6:297, 360). Women also gathered, independent of male slaves, on Saturday afternoons to do washing. Said one ex-slave, "they all had a regular picnic of it as they would work and spread the clothes on the bushes and low branches of the tree to dry. They would get to spend the day together" (Rawick, 1972, vol. 7:315).

In addition, when pregnant women did field work they sometimes did it together. On large plantations the group they worked in was sometimes known as the "trash gang." This gang, made up of pregnant women, women with nursing infants, children and old slaves,was primarily a female work gang.[9] Since it was the group that young girls worked with when just being initiated into the work world of the plantation, one must assume that it served some kind of socialization function. Most likely, many lessons about life were learned by twelve-year-old girls from this group of women who were either pregnant or breastfeeding, or who were grandmothers many times over.

It has been noted that women frequently depended on slave midwives to bring children into the world; their dependence on other slave women did not end with childbirth but continued through the early life of their children. Sometimes women with infants took their children to the fields with them. Some worked with their children wrapped to their backs, others laid them under a tree. Frequently, however, an elderly woman watched slave children during the day while their mothers worked in the field. Sometimes the cook supervised young children at the master's house.[10] Mothers who were absent from their children most of the day, indeed most of the week, depended on these surrogate mothers to assist them in child socialization. Many ex-slaves remember these women affectionately. Said one South Carolinian: "De old lady, she looked after every blessed thing for us all day long en cooked for us right along wid de mindin' " (Rawick, 1972, vol. 2, pt. 1:99).

Looking at the work done by female slaves in the antebellum South, therefore, we find that sex role differentiation in field labor was not absolute but that there was differentiation in other kinds of work. Domestic chores were usually done exclusively by women, and certain "professional" occupations were reserved for females. It would be a mistake to infer from this differentiation that it was the basis of male dominance. A less culturally biased conclusion would be that women's roles were different or complementary. For example, in her overview of African societies, Denise Paulme notes that in almost all African societies, women do most of the domestic chores, yet they lead lives that are quite independent of men. Indeed, according to Paulme, in Africa, "a wife's contribution to the needs of the household is direct and indispensable, and her husband is just as much in need of her as she of him" (1963:4). Other anthropologists have suggested that we should not evaluate women's roles in terms of men's roles because in a given society, women may not perceive the world in the same way that men do (Rogers, 1978:152–162). In other words, men and women may share a common culture but on different terms, and when this is the case, questions of dominance and subservience are irrelevant. The degree to which male and female ideologies are different is often suggested by the degree to which men and women are independently able to rank and order themselves and cooperate with members of their sex in the performance of their duties. In societies where women are not isolated from one another and placed under a man's authority, where women cooperate in the performance of household tasks, where women form groups or associations, women's roles are usually complementary to those of men, and the female world exists independently of the male world. Because women control what goes on in their world, they rank and order themselves vis à vis other women, not men, and they are able to influence decisions made by their society because they exert pressure as a group. Ethnographic studies of the Igbo women of Eastern Nigeria (Tanner, 1974:146–150), the Ga women of Central Accra in Ghana (Robertson, 1976:115–132), and the Patani of Southern Nigeria (Leis, 1974, 221–242) confirm these generalizations. Elements of female slave society—the chores done in and by groups, the intrasex cooperation and dependency in the areas of child care and medical care, the existence of high echelon female slave occupations—may be an indication, not that slave women were inferior to slave men, but that the roles were complementary and that the female slave world allowed women the opportunity to rank and order themselves and obtain a sense of self which was quite apart from the men of their race and even the men of the master class.

That bondswomen were able to rank and order themselves is further suggested by evidence indicating that in the community of the slave quarters certain women were looked to for leadership. Leadership was based on either one or a combination of factors, including occupation, association with the master class, age, or number of children. It was manifested in all aspects of female slave life. For instance, Louis Hughes, an escaped slave, noted that each plantation had a "forewoman who . . . had charge of the female slaves and also the boys and girls from twelve to sixteen years of age, and all the old people that were feeble" (Hughes, 1897:22).Bennett H. Barrow repeatedly lamented the fact that Big Lucy, one of his oldest slaves, had more control over his female slaves than he did: "Anica, Center, Cook Jane, the better you treat them the worse they are. Big Lucy, the Leader, corrupts every young negro in her power" (Davis, 1943:191).[11] When Elizabeth Botume went to the Sea Islands after the Civil War, she had a house servant, a young woman named Amy who performed her tasks slowly and sullenly until Aunt Mary arrived from Beaufort. In Aunt Mary's presence the obstreperous Amy was "quiet, orderly, helpful and painstaking" (Botume, 1893:132).[12]

Another important feature of female life, bearing on the ability of women to rank and order themselves independently of men, was the control women exercised over each other by quarreling. In all kinds of sources there are indications that women were given to fighting and irritating each other. From Jesse Belflowers, the overseer of the Allston rice plantation in South Carolina, Adele Petigru Allston learned that "mostly mongst the Woman," there was "goodeal of quarling and disputing and telling lies" (Easterby, 1945:291). Harriet Ware, a northern missionary, writing from the Sea Islands in 1863 blamed the turmoil she found in black community life on the "tongues of the women" (Pearson, 1906:210).[13] The evidence of excessive quarreling among women hints at the existence of a gossip network among female slaves. Anthropologists (Rosaldo, 1974:10–11, 38; Stack, 1974:109–115; Wolfe, 1974:162) have found gossip to be a principal strategy used by women to control other women as well as men. Significantly, the female gossip network, the means by which community members are praised, shamed, and coerced, is usually found in societies where women are highly dependent on each other and where women work in groups or form female associations.[14]

In summary, when the activities of female slaves are compared to those of women in other societies a clearer picture of the female slave sex role emerges. It seems that slave women were schooled in self-reliance and self-sufficiency but the "self" was more likely the female slave collective than the individual slave woman. On the other hand, if the female world was highly stratified and if women cooperated with each other to a great extent, odds are that the same can be said of men, in which case neither sex can be said to have been dominant or subordinate.

There are other aspects of the female slave's life that suggest that her world was independent of the male slave's and that slave women were rather self-reliant. It has long been recognized (Blassingame, 1972: 77–103) that slave women did not derive traditional benefits from the marriage relationship, that there was no property to share and essential needs like food, clothing, and shelter were not provided by slave men. Since in almost all societies where men consistently control women, that control is based on male ownership and distribution of property and/or control of certain culturally valued subsistence goods, these realities of slave life had to contribute to female slave self-sufficiency and independence from slave men. The practice of "marrying abroad," having a spouse on a different plantation, could only have reinforced this tendency, for as ethnographers(Noon, 1949:30–31; Rosaldo, 1974:36, 39) have found, when men live apart from women, they cannot control them.[15] We have yet to learn what kind of obligations brothers, uncles, and male cousins fulfilled for their female kin, but it is improbable that wives were controlled by husbands whom they saw only once or twice a week. Indeed, "abroad marriages" may have intensified female intradependency.

The fact that marriage did not yield traditional benefits for women, and that "abroad marriages" existed, does not mean that women did not depend on slave men for foodstuffs beyond the weekly rations, but since additional food was not guaranteed, it probably meant that women along with men had to take initiatives in supplementing slave diets. So much has been made of the activities of slave men in this sphere (Blassingame, 1972:92; Genovese, 1974:486) that the role of slave women has been overlooked.[16] Female house slaves, in particular, were especially able to supplement their family's diet. Mary Chesnut's maid, Molly, made no secret of the fact that she fed her offspring and other slave children in the Confederate politician's house. "Dey gets a little of all dat's going," she once told Chesnut (Chesnut, 1905:348). Frederick Douglass remembered that his grandmother was not only a good nurse but a "capital hand at catching fish and making the nets she caught them in" (1855:27). Eliza Overton, an ex-slave, remembered how her mother stole, slaughtered, and cooked one of her master's hogs. Another ex-slave was not too bashful to admit that her mother "could hunt good ez any man." (Rawick, 1972, vol. 11:53, 267.)[17] Women, as well as men, were sometimes given the opportunity to earn money. Women often sold baskets they had woven, but they also earned money by burning charcoal for blacksmiths and cutting cordwood (Olmsted, 1971:26; Rawick, 1972, vol. 7; 23). Thus, procuring extra provisions for the family was sometimes a male and sometimes a female responsibility, one that probably fostered a self-reliant and independent spirit.

The high degree of female cooperation, the ability of slave women to rank and order themselves, the independence women derived from the absence of property considerations in the conjugal relationship, "abroad marriages," and the female slave's ability to provide supplementary foodstuffs are factors which should not be ignored in considerations of the character of the slave family. In fact, they conform to the criteria most anthropologists (Gonzalez, 1970:231–243; Smith, 1956; 257–260, 1973:125; Tanner, 1974:129–156) list for that most misunderstood concept—matrifocality. Matrifocality is a term used to convey the fact that women *in their role as mothers* are the focus of familial relationships. It does not mean that fathers are absent; indeed two-parent households can be matrifocal. Nor does it stress a power relationship where women rule men. When *mothers* become the focal point of family activity, they are just more central than are fathers to a family's continuity and survival as a unit. While there is not set model for matrifocality, Smith (1973:125) has noted that in societies as diverse as Java, Jamaica, and the Igbo of eastern Nigeria, societies recognized as matrifocal, certain elements are constant.[18] Among these elements are female solidarity, particularly in regard to their cooperation within the domestic sphere. Another factor is the economic activity of women which enables them to support their children independent of fathers *if they desire to do so or are forced to do so.* The most important factor is the supremacy of the mother-child bond over all other relationships (Smith, 1973:139–142).

Female solidarity and the "economic" contribution of bondswomen in the form of medical care, foodstuffs, and money has already been discussed; what can be said of the mother-child bond? We know from previous works on slavery (Bassett, 1925:31, 139, 141; Kemble, 1961:95, 127, 179; Phillips, 1909:I, 109, 312) that certain slaveholder practices encouraged the primacy of the mother-child relationship. These included the tendency to sell mothers and small children as family units, and to accord special treatment to pregnant and nursing women and women who were exceptionally prolific. We also know (Gutman, 1976:76) that a husband and wife secured themselves somewhat from sale and separation when they had children. Perhaps what has not been emphasized enough is the fact that it was the wife's childbearing and her ability to keep a child alive that were the crucial factors in the security achieved in this way. As such, the insurance against sale which husbands and wives received once women had borne and nurtured children heads the list of female contributions to slave households.

In addition to slaveowner encouragement of close mother-child bonds there are indications that slave women themselves considered this their most important relationship.[19] Much has been made of the fact that slave women were not ostracized by slave society when they had children out of "wedlock" (Genovese, 1974:465–466; Gutman, 1976:74, 117–118). Historians have usually explained this aspect of slave life in the context of slave sexual norms which allowed a good deal of freedom to young unmarried slave women. However, the slave attitude concerning "illegitimacy" might also reveal the importance that women, and slave society as a whole, placed on the mother role and the mother-child dyad. For instance, in the Alabama community studied by Charles S. Johnson (1934:29, 66–70) in the 1930s, most black women felt no guilt and suffered no loss of status when they bore children out of wedlock. This was also a community in which, according to Johnson, the role of the mother was "of much greater importance than in the more familiar American family group." Similarly, in his 1956 study of the black family in British Guyana, Smith (1956:109, 158, 250–251) found the mother-child bond to be the strongest in the whole matrix of social relationships, and it was manifested in a lack of condemnation of women who bore children out of legal marriage. If slave women were not ostracized for having children without husbands, it could mean that the mother-child relationship took precedence over the husband-wife relationships.

The mystique which shrouded conception and childbirth is perhaps another indication of the high value slave women placed on motherhood and childbirth. Many female slaves claimed that they were kept ignorant of the details of conception and childbirth. For instance, a female slave interviewed in Nashville, noted that at age twelve or thirteen, she and an older girl went around to parsley beds and hollow logs looking for newborn babies. "They didn't tell you a thing," she said (Egypt et al., 1945:10; Rawick, 1972, vol. 16:15). Another ex-slave testified that her mother told her that doctors brought babies, and another Virginia ex-slave remembered that "people was very particular in them days. They wouldn't let children know anything:" (Egypt et al., 1945:8; Rawick, 1972, vol. 16:25. See also Rawick, 1972, vol. 7:3–24 and vol. 2:51–52). This alleged naiveté can perhaps be understood if examined in the context of motherhood as a *rite de passage*. Sociologist Joyce Ladner (1971:177–263) found that many black girls growing up in a ghetto area of St. Louis in the late 1960s were equally ignorant of the facts concerning conception and childbirth. Their mothers had related only "old wives tales" about sex and childbirth even though the community as one where the mother-child bond took precedence over both the husband-wife bond and the father-child bond. In this St. Louis area, having a child was considered the most important turning point in a black girl's life, a more important *rite de passage* than marriage. Once a female had a child all sorts of privileges were bestowed upon her. That conception and childbirth were cloaked in mystery in antebellum slave society is perhaps an indication of the sacredness of motherhood. When considered in tandem with the slave attitude toward "illegitimacy," the mother-child relationship emerges as the most important familial relationship in the slave family.

Finally, any consideration of the slave's attitude about motherhood and the expectations which the slave community had of childbearing women must consider the slave's African heritage. In many West African tribes the mother-child relationship is and has always been the most important of all human relationships.[20] To cite one of many possible examples, while studying the role of women in Ibo society, Sylvia Leith-Ross (1939:127) asked an Ibo woman how many of ten husbands would love their wives and how many of ten sons would love their mothers. The answer she received demonstrated the precedence which the mother-child tie took: "Three husbands would love their wives but seven sons would love their mothers."

When E. Franklin Frazier (1939:125) wrote that slave women were self-reliant and that they were strangers to male slave authority he evoked an image of an overbearing, even brawny woman. In all probability visions of Sapphire danced in our heads as we learned from Frazier that the female slave played the dominant role in courtship, marriage and family relationships, and later from Elkins (1959:130) that male slaves were reduced to childlike dependency on the slave master. Both the Frazier and Elkins theses have been overturned by historians who have found that male slaves were more than just visitors to their wives' cabins, and women something other than unwitting allies in the degradation of their men. Sambo and Sapphire may continue to find refuge in American folklore but they will never again be legitimized by social scientists.

However, beyond the image evoked by Frazier is the stark reality that slave women did not play the traditional female role as it was defined in nineteenth-century America, and regardless of how hard we try to cast her in a subordinate or submissive role in relation to slave men, we will have difficulty reconciling that role with the plantation realities. When we consider the work done by women in groups, the existence of upper echelon female slave jobs, the intradependence of women in childcare and medical care; if we presume that the quarreling or "fighting and disputing" among slave women is evidence of a gossip network and that certain women were elevated by their peers to positions of respect, then what we are confronted with are slave women who are able, within the limits set by slave-owners, to rank and order their female world, women who identified and cooperated more with other slave women than with slave men. There is nothing abnormal about this. It is a feature of many societies around the world, especially where strict sex role differentiation is the rule.

Added to these elements of female interdependence and cooperation were the realities of chattel slavery that decreased the bondsman's leverage over the bondswoman, made female self-reliance a necessity, and encouraged the retention of the African tradition which made the mother-child bond more sacred than the husband-wife bond. To say that this amounted to a matrifocal family is not to say a bad word. It is not to say that it precluded male-female cooperation, or mutual respect, or traditional romance and courtship. It does, however, help to explain how African-American men and women survived chattel slavery.

Notes

1. The majority of the available source material seems to be from plantations or farms with more than one or two slave families. Relatively few ex-slave interviewees admit to being one of only three or four slaves. If Genovese is right and at least half of the slaves in the South lived on units of twenty slaves or more, this synthesis probably describes the life of a majority of slave women (Genovese, 1974:7).
2. For other examples of work done by female slaves and indications that they did the same work required of men, see Nairne. 1732:60; Kemble. 1961:65; Olmsted. 1971:67–81; Olsmsted. 1907:81; Drew,1969:92; Rawick, 1972, vol. 13, pt. 4:357; vol 6:46, 151, 158, 270, 338.
3. See Rawick, 1972, vol. 4, pt. 3:160; Hughes, 1897:22, 41; Rawick, 1972, vol. 10, pt. 7:255; Olmsted, 1856:430; SHC, Plantation Instructions; Olmsted, 1971:78. 175; Kemble, 1961:87. 179; Drew, 1969:128; Davis, 1943:127.

4. Although Fogel and Engerman cite the slave woman's age at first birth as 22.5, other historians, including Gutman and Dunn, found that age to be substantially lower—Gutman a range from 17 to 19, and Dunn (average age at first birth on the Mount Airy, Virginia Plantation) 19.22 years. More recently, economists Trussell and Steckel have found the age to be 20.6 years (Fogel and Engerman, 1974:137–138; Dunn, 1977;58; Gutman, 1976:50, 75, 124, 171; Trussell and Steckel, 1978:504.

5. For examples, see n. 3.

6. For an example of the privileges this occupation *could* involve, see Chesnut, 1905:24.

7. For other examples of midwives see Rawick, vol. 6:256, 318; vol. 16:90–91; vol. 10, pt. 5:125. The job status of the midwife needs to be examined more closely than is possible here. Midwives were curers whose duty usually extended beyond delivering babies. Occasionally their cures spilled over into witchcraft or voodoo, and slaves who practiced these arts were often feared.

8. See also Rawick, 1972, vol. 2, pt. 2:55; vol. 17:174; Olmsted, 1907:76.

9. Sometimes pregnant women were made to weave, spin, or sew, in which case they usually did it with other women. The term "trash gang" was probably used only on very large plantations, but units of pregnant women, girls, elderly females, as well as boys and elderly men, probably worked together on a farm with twenty slaves. See n. 2.

10. See, for instance, Olmsted, 1856:423 and Phillips, 1909:I.127.

11. Big Lucy thwarted all of the Barrow's instructions and her influence extended to the men also; see Davis, 1943:168.173.

12. On a given plantation there could be a number of slave women recognized by other slave women as leaders. For instance, when Frances Kemble first toured Butler Island she found that the cook's position went to the oldest wife in the settlement.

13. Additional evidence that women quarreled can be found in a pamphlet stating the terms of an overseer's contract: "Fighting, particularly amongst the women . . . is to be always rigorously punished." Similarly, an ex-slave interviewed in Georgia noted that "sometimes de women uster git whuppins for fightin." See Bassett, 1925:32 and Rawick, 1972, vol. 12, pt. 2:57.

14. Gossip is one of many means by which women influence political decisions and interpersonal relationships. In Taiwan, for instance, women gather in the village square and whisper to each other. In other places, such as among the Marina of Madagascar, women gather and shout loud insults at men or other women. In still other societies, such as the black ghetto area studied by Carol Stack, the gossip network takes the form of a grapevine. See Rosaldo 1974:10–11; Wolf, 1974:162; and Stack, 1974:109–115.

15. For instance, it is thought that Iroquois women obtained a high degree of political and economic power partly because of the prolonged absences of males due to trading and warfare (Noon, 1949:30–31).

16. Of male slaves who provided extra food, John Blassingame wrote: "The slave who did such things for his family gained not only the approbation of his wife, but he also gained status in the quarters." According to Genovese, "the slaves would have suffered much more than many in fact did from malnutrition and the hidden hungers of nutritional deficiencies if men had not taken the initiative to hunt and trap animals."

17. For other examples of women who managed to provide extra food for their families see Rawick, 1972, vol. 16:16; Brent, 1861:9.

18. See also Smith, 1956:257–260; Tanner, 1974:129–156.

19. Gutman suggests that the husband-wife and father-child dyad were as strong as the mother-child bond. I think not. It has been demonstrated that in most Western Hemisphere black societies as well as in Africa, the mother-child bond is the strongest and most enduring bond. This does not mean that fathers have no relationship with their children or that they are absent. The father-child relationship is of a more formal nature than the mother-child relationship. Moreover, the conjugal relationship appears on the surface, to be similar to the Western norm in that two-parent households prevail, but, when competing with consanguineous relationships, conjugal affiliations usually lose. See Gutman, 1976:79; Smith, 1970:62–70; Smith, 1973:129; Stack, 1974:102–105.

20. See Paulme, 1963:14; Tanner, 1974:1147; Fortes, 1939:127.

References

Bassett, John Spencer (1925). The Southern Plantation Overseer. As Revealed in his Letters, Northhampton, Massachusetts: Southworth Press.

Bibb, Henry (1969). Narrative of the Life and Adventures of Henry Bibb. In Gilbert Osofsky, ed., Puttin on Ole Massa. 51-171. New York: Harper and Row Publishers.

Blassingame, John W. (1972). The Slave Community: Plantation Life in the Antebellum South. New York: Oxford University Press.

Botume, Elizabeth Hyde (1893). First Days Amongst the Contrabands. Boston: Lee and Shepard Publishers.

Brent, Linda (1861). Incidents in the Life of a Slave Girl. Ed. Lydia Maria Child. Boston: by the author.

Brown, William Wells (1969). Narrative of William Wells Brown. In Osofsky, 1969: 173–223.

Chesnut, Mary Boykin (1905). A Diary From Dixie. Ed. Ben Ames Williams. New York: D. Appleton and Company.

Davis, Adwon Adams (1943). Plantation Life in the Florida Parishes of Louisiana 1836–1846 as Reflected in the Diary of Bennett H. Barrow. New York: Columbia University Press.

Drew, Benjamin (1969). The Refugee: A North Side View of Slavery. Boston: Addison Wesley.

Dunn, Richard (1977). "The Tale of Two Plantations: Slave Life at Mesopotamia in Jamaica and Mount Airy in Virginia, 1799–1828." William and Mary Quarterly 34:32–65.

Easterby, J. E., ed. (1945). The South Carolina Rice Plantations as Revealed in the Papers of Robert W. Allston. Chicago: University of Chicago Press.

Egypt, Ophelia S., J. Masuoka and Charles S. Johnson, eds. (1945). Unwritten History of Slavery: Autobiographical Accounts of Negro Ex-slaves. Nashville: Fisk University Press.

Elkins, Stanley M. (1959). Slavery: A Problem in American Institutional and Intellectual Life. 2nd ed. Chicago: University of Chicago Press.

Fogel, Robert William and Stanley Engerman (1974). Time on the Cross: The Economics of American Negro Slavery. Boston: Little, Brown.

Fortes, Mayer (1939). "Kinship and Marriage among the Ashanti." In A. R. Radcliffe-Brown and Daryll Forde, eds. African Systems of Kinship and Marriage. 252–284. London: Routledge and Kegan Paul.

Frazier, E. Franklin (1939). The Negro Family in the United States. Chicago: University of Chicago Press.

Genovese, Eugene (1974). Roll, Jordan, Roll: The World the Slaves Made. New York: Vintage Books.

Gutman, Herbert (1976). The Black Family in Slavery and Freedom, 1750–1925. New York: Pantheon Books.

Gonzalez, Nancie (1970). "Toward a Definition of Matrifocality." In Norman E. Whitten, Jr. and John F. Szwed, eds. Afro-American Anthropology: Contemporary Perspectives, 231–243. New York: The Free Press.

Hafkin, Nancy J. and Edna G. Bay (1976). Women in Africa: Studies in Social and Economic Change. Stanford: Stanford University Press.

Hughes, Louis (1897). Thirty Years a Slave. Milwaukee: South Side Printing.

Johnson, Charles S. (1934). Shadow of the Plantation. Chicago: University of Chicago Press.

Kemble, Frances Anne (1961). Journal of a Residence on a Georgian Plantation. Ed. John A. Scott. New York: Alfred Knopf.

Kennedy, Theodore R. (1980). You Gotta Deal With It: Black Family Relations in a Southern Community, New York: Oxford University Press.

Ladner, Joyce (1971). Tomorrow's Tomorrow: The Black Woman. New York: Doubleday.

Leis, Nancy B. (1974). "Women in Groups: Ijaw Women's Associations." In Rosaldo and Lamphere, 1974:223–242.

Leith-Ross, Sylvia (1939). African Women: A Study of the Ibo of Nigeria. London: Routledge and Kegan Paul.

Moynihan, Daniel Patrick (1965). The Negro Family: The Case for National Action. Washington, D.C.: Government Printing Office.

Mullings, Leith (1976). "Women and Economic Change in Africa." In Hafkin, 1976:239–264.

Nairne, Thomas (1732). A Letter from South Carolina. London: J. Clark.

Noon, John A. (1949). Law and Government of the Grand River Iroquois. New York: Viking.

Northup, Solomon (1969). Twelve Years a Slave: Narrative of Solomon Northup. In Osofsky, 1969:225–406.

Olmsted, Frederick L. (1856). A Journey in the Seaboard Slave States. New York: Dix and Edwards.

———. (1907). A Journey in the Back Country, New York: G. P. Putnam's Sons.

———. (1971). The Cotton Kingdom. Ed. David Freeman Hawke. New York: Bobbs-Merrill.

Osofsky, Gilbert, ed. (1969). Puttin' on Ole Massa. New York: Harper and Row.

Paulme, Denise, ed. (1963). Women of Tropical Africa. Berkeley: University of California Press.

Pearson, Elizabeth Ware, ed. (1906). Letters from Port Royal Written at the Time of the Civil War. Boston: W. B. Clarke.

Phillips, Ulrich B. (1909). Plantation and Frontier Documents 1649–1863. 2 vols. Cleveland: Arthur H. Clarke.

Rawick, George, ed. (1972). The American Slave: A Composite Autobiography, 19 vols. Westport, Connecticut. Greenwood Press.

Robertson, Claire (1976). "Ga Women and Socioeconomic Change in Accra. Ghana." In Hafkin, 1976:111–134.

Rocher, Guy, R. Clignet, and F. N. N'sougan Agblemagon (1962). "Three Preliminary Studies: Canada. Ivory Coast, Togo." International Social Science Journal 14:130–156.

Rogers, Susan Carol (1978). "Woman's Place: A Critical Review of Anthropological Theory." Comparative Studies in Society and History, 20:123–162.

Rosaldo, Michelle (1974). "Woman. Culture and Society: A Theoretical Overview." In Rosaldo and Lamphere, 1974:17–42.

Rosaldo, Michelle and Louise Lamphere, eds. (1974). Woman, Culture and Society. Stanford: Stanford University Press.

Sacks, Karen (1974). "Engels Revisited: Women, the Organization of Production, and Private Property." In Rosaldo and Lamphere, 1974:207–222.

Smith, Raymond T. (1956). The Negro Family in British Guiana: Family Structure and Social Status in the Villages. London: Routledge and Kegan Paul.

———. (1970). "The Nuclear Family in Afro-American Kinship." Journal of Comparative Family Studies 1:55–70.

———. (1973). "The Matrifocal Family." In Jack Goody, ed., The Character of Kinship, 121–144. London: Cambridge University Press.

Southern Historical Collection [SHC] Bayside Plantation Records (1846–1852) Plantation Instructions (undated) White Hill Plantation Books (1817–1860).

Stack, Carol (1974). All Our Kin: Strategies for Survival in a Black Community. New York: Harper and Row.

Stampp, Kenneth (1956). The Peculiar Institution: Slavery in the Ante-Bellum South. New York: Vintage Books.

Tanner, Nancy (1974). "Matrifocality in Indonesia and Africa and Among Black Americans." In Rosaldo and Lamphere, 1974: 129–156.

Trussell, James and Richard Steckel (1978). "Age of Slaves at Menarche and Their First Birth." Journal of Interdisciplinary History 8:477–505.

Wolf, Margery (1974). "Chinese Women: Old Skill in a New Context." In Rosaldo and Lamphere, 1974: 157–172.

3

Cherokee Women and the Trail of Tears

Theda Perdue

One hundred and fifty years ago, in 1839, the United States forced the Cherokee Nation west of the Mississippi River to what later would become the state of Oklahoma. The Cherokees primarily occupied territory in the Southeast that included north Georgia, northeastern Alabama, southeastern Tennessee, and southwestern North Carolina. In the three decades preceding removal, they experienced a cultural transformation. Relinquishing ancient beliefs and customs, the leaders of the nation sought to make their people culturally indistinguishable from their white neighbors, in the hope that through assimilation they could retain their ancestral homeland. White land hunger and racism proved too powerful, however, and the states in which the Cherokees lived, particularly Georgia, demanded that the federal government extinguish the Indians' title and eject them from the chartered boundaries of the states. The election of Andrew Jackson in 1828 strengthened the states' cause.

While President Jackson promoted the policy of removing eastern Indians to the west, he did not originate the idea. Thomas Jefferson first suggested that removal beyond the evils of "civilization" would benefit the Indians and provide a justification for his purchase of Louisiana. In 1808 to 1810 and again in 1817 to 1819, members of the Cherokee Nation migrated to the west as the Cherokee land base shrank. But the major impetus for total removal came in 1830 when Congress, at the urging of President Jackson, passed the Indian Removal Act which authorized the President to negotiate cessions of Indian land in the east and transportation of native peoples west of the Mississippi. Although other Indian Nations, such as the Choctaws, signed removal treaties right away, the Cherokees refused. The Nations' leaders retained legal counsel and took its case against repressive state legislation to the United States Supreme Court (*Cherokee Nation v. Georgia*, 5 Peters 1). The Cherokee Nation won, however, on the grounds that the Cherokees constituted a "domestic dependent" nation—not a foreign state under the U.S. Constitution. The state's failure to respond to the decision and the federal government's refusal to enforce it prompted an unauthorized Cherokee faction to negotiate removal. In December 1835, these disaffected men signed the Treaty of New Echota by which they exchanged the Cherokee Nation's territory in the southeast for land in the west. The United States Senate ratified the treaty, and in the summer of 1838, soldiers began to round up Cherokees for deportation. Ultimately, the Cherokees were permitted to delay until fall and to manage their own removal, but this leniency did little to ameliorate the experience the Cherokees called the "trail of tears." The weather was unusually harsh that winter; cold, disease, hunger, and exhaustion claimed the lives of at least four thousand of the fifteen thousand people who travelled the thousand miles to the west.[1]

The details of Cherokee removal have been recounted many times by scholars and

Reprinted with permission from the *Journal of Women's History*, Vol. I, No. 1 (Spring 1989).

popular writers. The focus of these accounts has tended to be political: they have dealt primarily with the United States' removal policy, the negotiation of removal treaties, and the political factionalism which the removal issue created within Cherokee society. In other words, the role of men in this event has dominated historical analysis. Yet women also were involved, and it seems appropriate to reexamine the "trail of tears" using gender as a category of analysis. In particular, what role did women play in removal? How did they regard the policy? Did their views differ from those of men? How did the removal affect women? What were their experiences along the "trail of tears"? How did they go about reestablishing their lives in their new homes in the West? How does this kind of analysis amplify or alter our understanding of the event?

The Treaty of New Echota by which the Cherokee Nation relinquished its territory in the Southeast was signed by men.[2] Women were present at the rump council that negotiated the treaty, but they did not participate in the proceedings. They may have met in their own council—precedents for women's councils exist—but if they did, no record remains. Instead, they probably cooked meals and cared for children while their husbands discussed treaty terms with the United States commissioner. The failure of women to join in the negotiation and signing of the Treaty of New Echota does not necessarily mean that women were not interested in the disposition of tribal land, but it does indicate that the role of women had changed dramatically in the preceding century.

Traditionally, women had a voice in Cherokee government.[3] They spoke freely in council, and the War Woman (or Beloved Woman) decided the fate of captives. As late as 1787, a Cherokee woman wrote Benjamin Franklin that she had delivered an address to her people urging them to maintain peace with the new American nation. She had filled the peace pipe for the warriors, and she enclosed some of the same tobacco for the United States Congress in order to unite symbolically her people and his in peace. She continued:

> I am in hopes that if you Rightly consider that woman is the mother of All—and the Woman does not pull Children out of Trees or Stumps nor out of old Logs, but out of their Bodies, so that they ought to mind what a woman says.[4]

The political influence of women, therefore, rested at least in part on their maternal biological role in procreation and their maternal role in Cherokee society, which assumed particular importance in the Cherokee's matrilineal kinship system. In this way of reckoning kin, children belonged to the clan of their mother, and their only relatives were those who could be traced through her.[5]

The Cherokees were not only matrilineal, they also were matrilocal. That is, a man lived with his wife in a house which belonged to her, or perhaps more accurately, to her family. According to the naturalist William Bartram, "Marriage gives no right to the husband over the property of his wife; and when they part she keeps the children and property belonging to them."[6] The "property" that women kept included agricultural produce— corn, squash, beans, sunflowers, and pumpkins—stored in the household's crib. Produce belonged to women because they were the principal farmers. This economic role was ritualized at the Green Corn Ceremony every summer, when an old woman presented the new corn crop. Furthermore, eighteenth-century travelers and traders normally purchased corn from women instead of men, and in the 1750s the garrison at Fort Loudoun, in present-day eastern Tennessee, actually employed a female purchasing agent to procure corn.[7] Similarly, the fields belonged to the women who tended them, or rather to the women's lineages. Bartram observed that "their fields are divided by proper marks and their harvest is gathered separately."[8] While the Cherokees technically held land in common and anyone could use unoccupied land, improved fields belonged to specific matrilineal households.

Perhaps this explains why women signed early deeds conveying land titles to the Proprietors of Carolina. Agents who made these transactions offered little explanation for the signatures of women on these documents. In the early twentieth century, a historian speculated that they represented a "renunciation of dower," but it may have been that the women were simply parting with what was recognized as theirs, or they may have been representing their lineages in the negotiations.[9]

As late as 1785, women still played some role in the negotiation of land transactions. Nancy Ward, the Beloved Woman of Chota, spoke to the treaty conference held at Hopewell, South Carolina to clarify and extend land cessions stemming from Cherokee support of the British in the American Revolution. She addressed the assembly as the "mother of warriors" and promoted a peaceful resolution to land disputes between the Cherokees and the United States. Under the terms of the Treaty of Hopewell, the Cherokees ceded large tracts of land south of the Cumberland River in Tennessee and Kentucky and west of the Blue Ridge Mountains in North Carolina. Nancy Ward and the other Cherokee delegates to the conference agreed to the cession not because they believed it to be just but because the United States dictated the terms of the treaty.[10]

The conference at Hopewell was the last treaty negotiation in which women played an official role, and Nancy Ward's participation in that conference was somewhat anachronistic. In the eighteenth century, the English as well as other Europeans had dealt politically and commercially with men, since men were the hunters and warriors in Cherokee society and Europeans were interested primarily in military alliances and deerskins. As relations with the English grew increasingly important to tribal welfare, women became less significant in the Cherokee economy and government. Conditions in the Cherokee Nation following the American Revolution accelerated the trend. In their defeat, the Cherokees had to cope with the destruction of villages, fields, corn cribs, and orchards which had occurred during the war, and the cession of hunting grounds which accompanied the peace. In desperation, they turned to the United States government, which proposed to convert the Cherokees into replicas of white pioneer farmers in the anticipation that they would then cede additional territory (presumably hunting grounds they no longer needed).[11] While the government's so-called "civilization" program brought some economic relief, it also helped produce a transformation of gender roles and social organization. The society envisioned for the Cherokees, one which government agents and Protestant missionaries zealously tried to implement, was one in which a man farmed and headed a household composed only of his wife and children. The men who gained power in eighteenth-century Cherokee society—hunters, warriors, and descendants of traders—took immediate advantage of this program in order to maintain their status in the face of a declining deerskin trade and pacification, and then diverted their energy, ambition, and aggression into economic channels. As agriculture became more commercially viable, these men began to farm or to acquire African slaves to cultivate their fields for them. They also began to dominate Cherokee society, and by example and legislation, they altered fundamental relationships.[12]

In 1808, a Council of headmen (there is no evidence of women participating) from Cherokee towns established a national police force to safeguard a person's holdings during life and "to give protection to children as heirs to their father's property, and to the widow's share," thereby changing inheritance patterns and officially recognizing the patriarchal family as the norm. Two years later, a council representing all seven matrilineal clans, but once again apparently including no women, abolished the practice of blood vengeance. This action ended one of the major functions of clans and shifted the responsibility for punishing wrongdoers to the national police force and tribal courts. Matrilineal kinship clearly did not have a place in the new Cherokee order.[13]

We have no record of women objecting to such legislation. In fact, we know very little about most Cherokee women because written documents reflect the attitudes and concerns of a male Indian elite or of government agents and missionaries. The only women about whom we know very much are those who conformed to expectations. Nancy Ward, the Beloved Woman who favored peace with the United States, appears in the historical records, while other less cooperative Beloved Women are merely unnamed, shadowy figures. Women such as Catherine Brown, a model of Christian virtue, gained the admiration of missionaries, and we have a memoir of Brown's life; other women who removed their children from mission schools incurred the missionaries' wrath, and they merit only brief mention in mission diaries. The comments of government agents usually focused on those native women who demonstrated considerable industry by raising cotton and producing cloth (in this case, Indian men suffered by comparison), not those who grew corn in the matrilineage's fields.[14] In addition to being biased and reflecting only one segment of the female population, the information from these sources is secondhand; rarely did Indian women, particularly traditionalists, speak for themselves.

The one subject on which women did speak on two occasions was land. In 1817 the United States sought a large cession of Cherokee territory and removal of those who lived on the land in question. A group of Indian women met in their own council, and thirteen of them signed a message which was delivered to the National Council. They advised the council:

> The Cherokee ladys now being present at the meeting of the Chiefs and warriors in council have thought it their duties as mothers to address their beloved Chiefs and warriors now assembled.
> Our beloved children and head men of the Cherokee nation we address you warriors in council[. W]e have raised all of you on the land which we now have, which God gave us to inhabit and raise provisions[. W]e know that our country has once been extensive but by repeated sales has become circumscribed to a small tract and never have thought it our duty to interfere in the disposition of it till now, if a father or mother was to sell all their lands which they had to depend on[,] which their children had to raise their living on[,] which would be bad indeed and to be removed to another country[. W]e do not wish to go to an unknown country which we have understood some of our children wish to go over the Mississippi but this act of our children would be like destroying your mothers. Your mother and sisters ask and beg of you not to part with any more of our lands.[15]

The next year, the National Council met again to discuss the possibility of allotting Cherokee land to individuals, an action the United States government encouraged as a preliminary step to removal. Once again, Cherokee women reacted:

> We have heard with painful feelings that the bounds of the land we now possess are to be drawn into very narrow limits. The land was given to us by the Great Spirit above as our common right, to raise our children upon, & to make support for our rising generations. We therefore humbly petition our beloved children, the head men and warriors, to hold out to the last in support of our common rights, as the Cherokee nation have been the first settlers of this land; we therefore claim the right of the soil. . . . We therefore unanimously join in our meeting to hold our country in common as hitherto.[16]

Common ownership of land meant in theory that the United States government had to obtain cessions from recognized, elected Cherokee officials who represented the wishes of the people. Many whites favored allotment because private citizens then could obtain individually owned tracts of land through purchase, fraud, or seizure. Most Cherokees recognized this danger and objected to allotment for that reason. The women, however, had an additional incentive for opposing allotment. Under the laws of the states in which the Cherokees lived and of which they would become citizens if land were allotted, married women had few property rights. A married woman's property, even property she held prior to her marriage, belonged legally to her husband.[17] Cherokee women and matrilineal households would have ceased to be property owners.

The implications for women became apparent in the 1830s, when Georgia claimed its law was in effect in the Cherokee country. Conflicts over property arose because of uncertainty over which legal system prevailed. For example, a white man, James Vaught, married the Cherokee, Catherine Gunter. She inherited several slaves from her father, and Vaught sold two of them to General Isaac Wellborn. His wife had not consented to the sale and so she reclaimed her property and took them with her when the family moved west. General Wellborn tried to seize the slaves just as they were about to embark, but a soldier, apparently recognizing her claim under Cherokee law, prevented him from doing so. After removal, the General appealed to Principal Chief John Ross for aid in recovering the slaves, but Ross refused. He informed Wellborn: "By the laws of the Cherokee Nation, the property of husband and wife remain separate and apart and neither of these can sell or dispose of the property of the other." Had the Cherokees accepted allotment and come under Georgia law, Wellborn would have won.[18]

The effects of the women's protests in 1817 and 1818 are difficult to determine. In 1817 the Cherokees ceded tracts of land in Georgia, Alabama, and Tennessee, and in 1819 they made an even larger cession. Nevertheless, they rejected individual allotments and strengthened restrictions on alienation of improvements. Furthermore, the Cherokee Nation gave notice that they would negotiate no additional cessions—a resolution so strongly supported that the United States ultimately had to turn to a small unauthorized faction in order to obtain the minority treaty of 1835.[19]

The political organization which existed in the Cherokee Nation in 1817 to 1818 had made it possible for women to voice their opinion. Traditionally, Cherokee towns were politically independent of one another, and each town governed itself through a council in which all adults could speak. In the eighteenth century, however, the Cherokees began centralizing their government in order to restrain bellicose warriors whose raids jeopardized the entire nation, and to negotiate as a single unit with whites. Nevertheless, town councils remained important, and representatives of traditional towns formed the early National Council. This National Council resembled the town councils in that anyone could address the body. Although legislation passed in 1817 created an Executive Committee, power still rested with the council, which reviewed all committee acts.[20]

The protests of the women to the National Council in 1817 and 1818 were, however, the last time women presented a collective position to the Cherokee governing body. Structural changes in Cherokee government more narrowly defined participation in the National Council. In 1820 the council provided that representatives be chosen from eight districts rather than from traditional towns, and in 1823 the committee acquired a right of review over acts of the council. The more formalized political organization made it less likely that a group could make its views known to the national government.[21]

As the Cherokee government became more centralized, political and economic power rested increasingly in the hands of a few elite men who adopted the planter lifestyle of the white, antebellum South. A significant part of the ideological basis for this lifestyle was the cult of domesticity, in which the ideal woman confined herself to home and hearth while men contended with the corrupt world of government and business.[22] The elite adopted the tenets of the cult of domesticity, particularly after 1817, when the number of Protestant missionaries, major proponents of this feminine ideal, increased significantly, and their influence on Cherokee society broadened.

The extent to which a man's wife and daughters conformed to the idea quickly came to be one measure of his status. In 1818 Charles Hicks, who later served as Principal Chief, described the most prominent men in the Nation as "those who have for the last 10 or 20 years been pursuing agriculture & kept their women & children at home & in comfortable circumstances." Eight years later, John Ridge, one of the first generation of Cherokees to have been educated from childhood in mission schools, discussed a Cherokee law which protected the property rights of a married woman and observed that "in many respects she has exclusive & distinct control over her own, particularly among the less civilized." The more "civilized" presumably left such matters to men. Then Ridge described suitable activities for women: "They sew, they weave, they spin, they cook our meals and act well the duties assigned them by Nature as mothers." Proper women did not enter business or politics.[23]

Despite the attitudes of men such as Hicks and Ridge, women did in fact continue as heads of households and as businesswomen. In 1828 the *Cherokee Phoenix* published the obituary of Oo-dah-less who had accumulated a sizeable estate through agriculture and commerce. She was "the support of a large family," and she bequeathed her property "to an only daughter and three grandchildren." Oo-dah-less was not unique. At least one-third of the heads of household listed on the removal roll of 1835 were women. Most of these were not as prosperous as Oo-dah-less, but some were even more successful economically. Nineteen owned slaves (190 men were slaveholders), and two held over twenty slaves and operated substantial farms.[24]

Nevertheless, these women had ceased to have a direct voice in Cherokee government. In 1826 the council called a constitutional convention to draw up a governing document for the nation. According to legislation which provided for election of delegates to the convention, "No person but a free male citizen who is full grown shall be entitled to vote." The convention met and drafted a constitution patterned after that of the United States. Not surprisingly, the constitution which male Cherokees ratified in 1827 restricted the franchise to "free male citizens" and stipulated that "no person shall be eligible to a seat in the General Council, but a free Cherokee male, who shall have attained the age of twenty-five." Unlike the United States Constitution, the Cherokee document clearly excluded women, perhaps as a precaution against women who might assert their traditional right to participate in politics instead of remaining in the domestic sphere.[25]

The exclusion of women from politics certainly did not produce the removal crisis, but it did mean that a group traditionally opposed to land cession could no longer be heard on the issue. How women would have voted is also unclear. Certainly by 1835, many Cherokee women, particularly those educated in mission schools, believed that men were better suited to deal with political issues than women, and a number of women voluntarily enrolled their households to go west before the forcible removal of 1838 to 1839. Even if women had united in active opposition to removal, it is unlikely that the United States and aggressive state governments would have paid any more attention to them than they did to the elected officials of the nation who opposed removal or the fifteen thousand Cherokees, including women (and perhaps children), who petitioned the United States Senate to reject the Treaty of New Echota. While Cherokee legislation may have made women powerless, federal authority rendered the whole Nation impotent.

In 1828 Georgia had extended state law over the Cherokee Nation, and white intruders who invaded its territory. Georgia law prohibited Indians, both men and women, from testifying in court against white assailants, and so they simply had to endure attacks on person and property. Delegates from the Nation complained to Secretary of War John H. Eaton about the lawless behavior of white intruders:

> Too many there are who think it an act of trifling consequence to oust an Indian family from the quiet enjoyment of all the comforts of their own firesides, and to drive off before their faces the stock that gave nourishment to the children and support to the aged, and appropriate it to the satisfaction of avarice.[26]

Elias Boudinot, editor of the bilingual *Cherokee Phoenix*, even accused the government of encouraging the intruders in order to force the Indians off their lands, and he published the following account:

> A few days since two of these white men came to a Cherokee house, for the purpose, they pretended, of buying provisions. There was no person about the house but one old woman of whom they inquired for some corn, beans etc. The woman told them she had nothing to sell. They then went off in the direction of the field belonging to this Cherokee family. They had not gone but a few minutes when the woman of the house saw a heavy smoke rising from that direction. She immediately hastened to the field and found the villains had set the woods on fire but a few rods from the fences, which she found already in a full blaze. There being a very heavy wind that day, the fire spread so fast, that her efforts to extinguish it proved utterly useless. The entire fence was therefore consumed in a short time. It is said that during her efforts to save the fence the men who had done the mischief were within sight, and were laughing heartily at her.

The Georgia Guard, established by the state to enforce its law in the Cherokee country, offered no protection and, in fact, contributed to the lawlessness. The *Phoenix* printed the following notice under the title "Cherokee Women, Beware.":

> It is said that the Georgia Guard have received orders, from the Governor we suppose, to inflict corporeal punishment on such females as shall hereafter be guilty of insulting them. We presume they are to be the judges of what constitutes *insult*.[27]

Despite harassment from intruders and the Guard, most Cherokees had no intention of going west, and in the spring of 1838 they began to plant their crops as usual. Then United States soldiers arrived, began to round up the Cherokees, and imprisoned them in stockades in preparation for deportation. In 1932 Rebecca Neugin, who was nearly one hundred years old, shared her childhood memory and family tradition about removal with historian Grant Foreman:

> When the soldier came to our house my father wanted to fight, but my mother told him that the soldiers would kill him if he did and we surrendered without a fight. They drove us out of our house to join other prisoners in a stockade. After they took us away, my mother begged them to let her go back and get some bedding. So they let her go back and she brought what bedding and a few cooking utensils she could carry and had to leave behind all of our other household possessions.[28]

Rebecca Neugin's family was relatively fortunate. In the process of capture, families were sometimes separated and sufficient food and clothing were often left behind. Over fifty years after removal, John G. Burnett, a soldier who served as an interpreter, reminisced:

Men working in the fields were arrested and driven to stockades. Women were dragged from their homes by soldiers whose language they could not understand. Children were often separated from their parents and driven into the stockades with the sky for a blanket and the earth for a pillow.

Burnett recalled how one family was forced to leave the body of a child who had just died and how a distraught mother collapsed of heart failure as soldiers evicted her and her three children from their homes.[29] After their capture, many Cherokees had to march miles over rugged mountain terrain to the stockades. Captain L. B. Webster wrote his wife about moving eight hundred Cherokees from North Carolina to the central depot in Tennessee: "We were eight days in making the journey (80 miles), and it was pitiful to behold the women & children, who suffered exceedingly—as they were all obliged to walk, with the exception of the sick."[30]

Originally the government planned to deport all the Cherokees in the summer of 1838, but the mortality rate of the three parties that departed that summer led the commanding officer, General Winfield Scott, to agree to delay the major removal until fall. In the interval, the Cherokees remained in the stockades, where conditions were abysmal. Women in particular often became individual victims of their captors. The missionary Daniel Butrick recorded the following episode in his journal:

> The poor Cherokees are not only exposed to temporal evils, but also to every species of moral desolation. The other day a gentleman informed me that he saw six soldiers about two Cherokee women. The women stood by a tree, and the soldiers with a bottle of liquor were endeavoring to entice them to drink, though the women, as yet were resisting them. He made this known to the commanding officer but we presume no notice was taken of it, as it was reported that those soldiers had those women with them the whole night afterwards. A young married woman, a member of the Methodist society was at the camp with her friends, though her husband was not there at the time. The soldiers, it is said, caught her, dragged her about, and at length, either through fear, or otherwise, induced her to drink; and then seduced her away, so that she is now an outcast even among her own relatives. How many of the poor captive women are thus debauched, through terror and seduction, that eye which never sleeps, alone can determine.[31]

When removal finally got underway in October, the Cherokees were in a debilitated and demoralized state. A white minister who saw them as they prepared to embark noted: "The women did not appear to as good advantage as did the men. All, young and old, wore blankets which almost hid them from view."[32] The Cherokees had received permission to manage their own removal, and they divided the people into thirteen detachments of approximately one thousand each. While some had wagons, most walked. Neugin rode in a wagon with other children and some elderly women, but her older brother, mother, and father "walked all the way."[33] One observer reported that "even aged females, apparently nearly ready to drop in the grave, were traveling with heavy burdens attached to the back." Proper conveyance did not spare well-to-do Cherokees the agony of removal, the same observer noted:

> One lady passed on in her hack in company with her husband, apparently with as much refinement and equipage as any of the mothers of New England; and she was a mother too and her youngest child, about three years old, was sick in her arms, and all she could do was to make it comfortable as circumstances would permit. . . . She could only carry her dying child in her arms a few miles farther, and then she must stop in a stranger-

land and consign her much loved babe to the cold ground, and that without pomp and ceremony, and pass on with the multitude.[34]

This woman was not alone. Journals of the removal are largely a litany of the burial of children, some born "untimely."[35]

Many women gave birth alongside the trail: at least sixty-nine newborns arrived in the West.[36] The Cherokees' military escort was often less than sympathetic. Daniel Butrick wrote in his journal that troops frequently forced women in labor to continue until they collapsed and delivered "in the midst of the company of soldiers." One man even stabbed an expectant mother with a bayonet.[37] Obviously, many pregnant women did not survive such treatment. The oral tradition of a family from southern Illinois, through which the Cherokees passed, for example, includes an account of an adopted Cherokee infant whose mother died in childbirth near the family's pioneer cabin. While this story may be apocryphal, the circumstances of Cherokee removal make such traditions believable.[38]

The stress and tension produced by the removal crisis probably accounts for a post-removal increase in domestic violence, of which women usually were the victims. Missionaries reported that men, helpless to prevent seizure of their property and assaults on themselves and their families, vented their frustrations by beating wives and children. Some women were treated so badly by their husbands that they left them, and this dislocation contributed to the chaos in the Cherokee Nation in the late 1830s.[39]

Removal divided the Cherokee Nation in a fundamental way, and the Civil War magnified that division. Because most signers of the removal treaty were highly acculturated, many traditionalists resisted more strongly the white man's way of life and distrusted more openly those Cherokees who imitated whites. This split between "conservatives," those who sought to preserve the old ways, and "progressives," those committed to change, extended to women. We know far more, of course, about "progressive" Cherokee women who left letters and diaries which in some ways are quite similar to those of upper-class women in the antebellum South. In letters, they recounted local news such as "they had Elick Cockrel up for steeling horses" and "they have Charles Reese in chains about burning Harnages house" and discussed economic concerns: "I find I cannot get any corn in this neighborhood, and so of course I shall be greatly pressed in providing provision for my family." Nevertheless, family life was the focus of most letters: "Major is well and tryes hard to stand alone he will walk soon. I would write more but the baby is crying."[40]

Occasionally we even catch a glimpse of conservative women who seem to have retained at least some of their original authority over domestic matters. Red Bird Smith, who led a revitalization movement at the end of the nineteenth century, had considerable difficulty with his first mother-in-law. She "influenced" her adopted daughter to marry Smith through witchcraft and, as head of the household, meddled rather seriously in the couple's lives. Interestingly, however, the Kee-Too-Wah society which Red Bird Smith headed had little room for women. Although the society had political objectives, women enjoyed no greater participation in this "conservative" organization than they did in the "progressive" republican government of the Cherokee Nation.[41]

Following removal, the emphasis of legislation involving women was on protection rather than participation. In some ways, this legislation did offer women greater opportunities than the law codes of the states. In 1845 the editor of the *Cherokee Advocate* expressed pride that "in this respect the Cherokees have been considerably in advance of many of their white brethren, the rights of their women having been amply secured almost ever since they had written laws." The Nation also established the Cherokee Female Seminary to provide higher education for women, but like the education women received before removal, students studied only those subjects considered to be appropriate for their sex.[47]

Removal, therefore, changed little in terms of the status of Cherokee women. They had lost political power before the crisis of the 1830s, and events which followed relocation merely confirmed new roles and divisions. Cherokee women originally had been subsistence-level farmers and mothers, and the importance of these roles in traditional society had made it possible for them to exercise political power. Women, however, lacked the economic resources and military might on which political power in the Anglo-American system rested. When the Cherokees adopted the Anglo-American concept of power in the eighteenth and nineteenth centuries, men became dominant. But in the 1830s the chickens came home to roost. Men, who had welcomed the Anglo-American basis for power, now found themselves without power. Nevertheless, they did not question the changes they had fostered. Therefore, the tragedy of the trail of tears lies not only in the suffering and death which the Cherokees experienced but also in the failure of many Cherokees to look critically at the political system which they had adopted—a political system dominated by wealthy, highly acculturated men, and supported by an ideology that made women (as well as others defined as "weak" or "inferior") subordinate. In the removal crisis of the 1830s, men learned an important lesson about power; it was a lesson women had learned well before the "trail of tears."

Notes

1. The standard account of Cherokee removal is Grant Foreman, *Indian Removal. The Emigration of the Five Civilized Tribes of Indians* (Norman, OK, 1932), pp. 229–312. Also see Ronald N. Satz, *American Indian Policy in the Jacksonian Era* (Lincoln, NE., 1975); Dale Van Every, *Disinherited: The Lost Birthright of the American Indian* (New York, 1966); William G. McLoughlin, "Thomas Jefferson and the Beginning of Cherokee Nationalism, 1806 to 1809," *William and Mary Quarterly*, 3d ser., 32 (1975), pp. 547–80; Thurman Wilkins, *Cherokee Tragedy: The Story of the Ridge Family and the Decimation of a People* (New York, 1970); Gary E. Moulton, *John Ross: Cherokee Chief* (Athens, GA, 1978); Russell Thornton, "Cherokee Population Losses during the Trail of Tears: A New Perspective and a New Estimate," *Ethnohistory* 31 (1984); pp. 289–300. Other works on the topic include Gloria Jahoda, *The Trail of Tears* (New York, 1975), Samuel Carter, *Cherokee Sunset: A Nation Betrayed* (Garden City, N.Y., 1976); John Ehle, *The Trail of Tears: The Rise and Fall of the Cherokee Nation* (New York, 1988). A good collection of primary documents can be found in the *Journal of Cherokee Studies* 3 (1978). For the context in which the removal policy developed, see Francis Paul Prucha, *American Indian Policy in the Formative Years: The Indian Trade and Intercourse Acts, 1790–1834* (Cambridge, MA, 1962). Not all Cherokees went west; see John R. Finger, *The Eastern Band of Cherokees, 1819–1900* (Knoxville, TN, 1984).

2. Charles J. Kappler, ed., *Indian Affairs: Laws and Treaties*, 5 vols. (Washington, 1904–1941), 2, pp. 439–49.

3. While some similarities to the role of women among the Iroquois exist, the differences are significant. Both had matrilineal kinship systems and practiced the same fundamentally sexual division of labor, but the Cherokees had no clan mothers who selected headmen, an important position among the Iroquois of the Five Nations. The Cherokees were an Iroquoian people, but linguists believe that they separated from the northern Iroquois thousands of years ago. Certainly, the Cherokees had been in the Southeast long enough to be a part of the southeastern cultural complex described by Charles Hudson in *The Southeastern Indians* (Knoxville, 1976). Yet where women were concerned, the Cherokees differed from other southeastern peoples. James Adair, an eighteenth-century trader, gave the following analysis: "The Cherokees are an exception to all civilized or savage nations in having no laws against adultery; they have been a considerable while under a petticoat-government, and allow their women full liberty to plant their brows with horns as oft as they please, without fear of punishment" (James Adair, *Adair's History of the American Indian*, ed. Samuel Cole Williams [Johnson City, TN, 1930], pp. 152–53). Indeed, Adair was correct that Cherokee women enjoyed considerable sexual autonomy. Furthermore, they seem to have exercised more political power than other eighteenth-century native women in the Southeast. Earlier sources, however, describe "queens" who ruled southeastern peoples other than the Cherokee. See Edward Gaylord Bourne, ed.,

Narratives of the Career of Hernando de Soto (2 vols.) (New York, 1922), 1, pp. 65–72. Consequently, the unusual role of women in Cherokee society cannot be attributed definitively to either Iroquoian or southeastern antecedents.

4. Samuel Hazard, ed., *Pennsylvania Archives, 1787*, 12 vols., (Philadelphia, 1852–56), 11, pp. 181–82. See also Theda Perdue, "The Traditional Status of Cherokee Women," *Furman Studies* (1980), pp. 19–25.

5. The best study of the aboriginal Cherokee kinship system is John Phillip Reid, *A Law of Blood: The Primitive Law of the Cherokee Nation* (New York, 1970). Also see William H. Gilbert, *The Eastern Cherokees* (Washington, 1943) and Alexander Spoehr, *Changing Kinship Systems: A Study in the Acculturation of the Creeks, Cherokee, and Choctaw* (Chicago, 1947).

6. William Bartram, "Observations on the Creek and Cherokee Indians, 1789," *Transactions of the American Ethnological Society* 3, pt. 1 (1954), p. 66.

7. William L. McDowell, ed., *Documents Relating to Indian Affairs, 1754–1765* (Columbia, SC, 1970), p. 303; Henry Timberlake, *Lieut. Henry Timberlake's Memoirs, 1756–1765*, ed. Samuel Cole Williams (Johnson City, TN, 1927), pp. 89–90; Benjamin Hawkins, *Letters of Benjamin Hawkins, 1796–1806*, vol. 9 of *Georgia Historical Society Collections* (Savannah, Geo., 1916), p. 110; Adair, *Adair's History*, pp. 105–17.

8. William Bartram, ed., *The Travels of William Bartram*, ed. Mark Van Doren (New York, 1940), p. 90.

9. Alexander S. Salley, ed., *Narratives of Early Carolina, 1650–1708* (New York, 1911), p. 90.

10. *American State Papers*, Class 2: *Indian Affairs*, 2 vols. (Washington, 1832), 1, p. 41. For Nancy Ward, see Ben Harris McClary, "Nancy Ward: Last Beloved Woman of the Cherokees," *Tennessee Historical Quarterly* 21 (1962), pp. 336–52; Theda Perdue, "Nancy Ward" in *Portraits of American Women*, Catherine Clinton and Ben Barker-Benfield, eds. (New York, St. Martin's Press, 1991).

11. Prucha, *American Indian*, pp. 213–49; Bernard W. Sheehan, *Seeds of Extinction: Jeffersonian Philanthropy and the American Indian* (Chapel Hill, NC, 1973); Robert F. Berkhofer, Jr., *Salvation and the Savage: An Analysis of Protestant Missions and American Indian Response* (Lexington, KY, 1965).

12. William G. McLoughlin, *Cherokee Renascence in the New Republic* (Princeton, 1986); William G. McLoughlin, *Cherokees and Missionaries, 1789–1839* (New Haven, CT, 1984); Henry T. Malone, *Cherokees of the Old South: A People in Transition* (Athens, GA, 1956); Theda Perdue, *Slavery and the Evolution of Cherokee Society, 1540–1866* (Knoxville, TN, 1979).

13. *Laws of the Cherokee Nation: Adopted by the Council at Various Times, Printed for the Benefit of the Nation* (Tahlequah, Cherokee Nation, 1852), pp. 3–4.

14. Rufus Anderson, *Memoir of Catherine Brown, A Christian Indian of the Cherokee Nation* (Philadelphia, 1832); Hawkins, p. 20.

15. Presidential Papers Microfilm: Andrew Jackson (Washington, 1961), Series 1, Reel 22; also mentioned in *Journal of Cyrus Kingsbury*, 13 February, 1817, Papers of the American Board of Commissioners for Foreign Missions, Houghton Library, Harvard University, Cambridge, MA (hereafter cited as American Board Papers).

16. Brainerd Journal, 30 June, 1818 (American Board Papers).

17. For women's property rights in the United States, see Mary Beard, *Woman as a Force in History: A Study in Traditions and Realities* (New York, 1946); Marylynn Salmon, "Women and Property in South Carolina: The Evidence from Marriage Settlements, 1730–1830," *William and Mary Quarterly*, 3d ser., 39 (1982), pp. 655–85; Marylynn Salmon, "Equality or Submersion? *Feme Covert* Status in Early Pennsylvania," in *Women of America*, ed. Carol Berkin and Mary Beth Norton (Boston, 1979); Marylynn Salmon, " 'Life Liberty and Dower': The Legal Status of Women after the Revolution," in *Women, War and Revolution*, ed. Carol Berkin and Clara Lovett, eds. (New York, 1980); Norma Basch, "Invisible Women: The Legal Fiction of Marital Unity in Nineteenth-Century America," *Feminist Studies* 5 (1979), pp. 346–66; Norma Basch, *In the Eyes of the Law: Women, Marriage, and Property in Nineteenth-Century New York* (Ithaca, NY, 1982); Albie Sachs and Joan Hoff-Wilson, *Sexism and the Law: A Study of Male Beliefs and Legal Bias in Britain and the United States* (New York, 1979); Suzanne Lebsock, *The Free Women of Petersburg: Status and Culture in a Southern Town, 1784–1860* (New York, 1984).

18. Louis Wyeth to R. Chapman and C.C. Clay, 16 May 1838, Memorial of Isaac Wellborn to Martin Van Buren, n.d., Writ of the Morgan County (Alabama) Court, 9 June, 1838 (Letters Received by the Office of Indian Affairs, 1824–1881, RG 75, National Archives, Washington); Joel R. Poinsett to Mathew Arbuckle, 17 December, 1838, John Ross to Joel R. Poinsett, 18 July, 1839 (John Ross Papers, Thomas Gilcrease Institute, Tulsa, Okla.).

19. Charles C. Royce, *Indian Land Cessions in the United States* (Washington, 1900), pp. 684–85, 696–97.

20. V. Richard Persico, Jr., "Early Nineteenth-Century Cherokee Political Organization," in *The Cherokee Indian Nation: A Troubled History*, Duane H. King, ed., (Knoxville, TN, 1979), pp. 92–109.

21. *Laws of the Cherokee Nation*, pp. 14–18, 31–32.

22. The classic article is Barbara Welter, "The Cult of True Womanhood, 1820–1860," *American Quarterly* 18

(1966), pp. 151–74. Also see Glenna Matthews, *"Just a Housewife": The Rise and Fall of Domesticity in America* (New York, 1987). In *The Plantation Mistress. Woman's World in the Old South* (New York, 1982), Catherine Clinton points out that southern women, particularly from the planter class, did not exactly fit the model for northern women. Yet Cherokee women may have conformed more closely to that model than many other southern women because of the influence of northern missionaries. See Theda Perdue, "Southern Indians and the Cult of True Womanhood," in *The Web of Southern Social Relations: Essays on Family Life, Education, and Women*, Walter J. Fraser, Jr., R. Frank Saunders, Jr., and Jon L. Wakelyn, Jr., eds. (Athens, Ga., 1985), pp. 35–51. Also see Anne Firor Scott, *The Southern Lady: From Pedestal to Politics, 1830–1930* (Chicago, 1970), pp. 3–21; Mary E. Young, "Women, Civilization, and the Indian Question," in *Clio Was a Woman. Studies in the History of American Women*, Mabel E. Deutrich and Virginia C. Purdy, eds. (Washington, 1980).

23. Ard Hoyt, Moody Hall, William Chamberlain, and D. S. Butrick to Samuel Worcester, 25 July, 1818 (American Board Papers); John Ridge to Albert Gallatin, 27 February, 1826 (John Howard Payne Papers, Newberry Library, Chicago, IL [hereafter cited as Payne papers]).

24. *Cherokee Phoenix*, 2 July, 1828; Census of 1835 (Henderson Roll), RG 75, Office of Indian Affairs, National Archives, Washington; R. Halliburton, Jr., *Red over Black: Black Slavery among the Cherokee Indians* (Westport, CT, 1977), pp. 181–92. Robert Bushyhead, a native Cherokee speaker from Cherokee, North Carolina, identified the gender of names on the Henderson Roll.

25. *Laws of the Cherokee Nation*, pp. 79, 120–21.

26. George Lowrey, Lewis Ross, William Hicks, R. Taylor, Joseph Vann, and W. S. Shorey to John H. Eaton, 11 February, 1830, Letters received, Office of Indian Affairs, 1824–1881, National Archives, Washington.

27. *Cherokee Phoenix*, 26 March, 1831, 16 July, 1831.

28. Foreman, *Indian Removal*, pp. 302–303.

29. John G. Burnett, "The Cherokee Removal through the Eyes of a Private Soldier," *Journal of Cherokee Studies* 3 (1978), p. 183.

30. Capt. L. B. Webster, "Letters from a Lonely Soldier," *Journal of Cherokee Studies* 3 (1978), p. 154.

31. Journal of Daniel S. Butrick, n.d. (Payne Papers). There is another Butrick journal in the American Board Papers. The one in the Payne papers is as much a commentary as a personal narrative.

32. J. D. Anthony, *Life and Times of Rev. J. D. Anthony* (Atlanta, 1896).

33. Foreman, *Indian Removal*, pp. 302–303.

34. "A Native of Maine, Traveling in the Western Country," *New York Observer*, 26 January, 1839.

35. A good example is B. B. Cannon, "An Overland Journey to the West (October–December 1837)," *Journal of Cherokee Studies* 3 (1978), pp. 166–173.

36. "Emigration Detachments," *Journal of Cherokee Studies* 3 (1978), pp. 186–87.

37. Butrick Journal (Payne Papers).

38. Story related by unidentified member of an audience at Warren Wilson College, Black Mountain, NC, January, 1983.

39. Butrick Journal, 30 April, 1839, 2 May, 1839 (American Board Papers).

40. Edward Everett Dale and Gaston Litton, eds., *Cherokee Cavaliers: Forty Years of Cherokee History as Told in the Correspondence of the Ridge-Watie-Boudinot Family* (Norman, OK, 1939), pp. 20–21, 37–38, 45–46. For comparison, see Scott, *Southern Lady*, and Clinton, *Plantation Mistress*.

41. *Indian Pioneer History*, 113 vols. (Oklahoma Historical Society, Oklahoma City), 9; pp. 490–91; Robert K. Thomas, "The Redbird Smith Movement," in *Symposium on Cherokee and Iroquois Culture*, William N. Fenton and John Gulick, eds. (Washington, 1961).

42. *Cherokee Advocate*, 27 February, 1845; Rudi Halliburton, Jr., "Northeastern Seminary Hall," *Chronicles of Oklahoma* 51 (1973–74), pp. 391–98; *Indian Pioneer History* I, p. 394.

4

To Earn Her Daily Bread: Housework and Antebellum Working-Class Subsistence

Jeanne Boydston

In 1845, in a volume entitled *The Sanitary Condition of the Laboring Population of New York*, former city health inspector John H. Griscom published his observations on the health of New York City's working poor. He sketched a bleak scene. Forced into crowded, tinderbox tenements that lacked adequate light or ventilation, and subjected daily to the waste that leached in from streets, outhouses, and animal yards, the laboring classes seemed to Griscom bound for extinction.[1]

Middle-class reformers like Griscom tended to raise these specters as a way of deploring the alleged sloth and intemperance of the poor, rather than as a means of examining the economy that created the poverty.[2] Nevertheless, the conditions they so vividly documented have remained a subject of special interest to American historians. For these were the transitional generations—the households that lived the lurching transformations toward wage dependency. By the late 1870s, the number of people working solely for wages in manufacturing, construction, and transportation alone was almost equivalent to the size of the entire population in 1790.[3] The strategies that enabled working-class households to survive the intervening period tell us much, not only about the making of the American working classes, but equally important, about the making of American industrial capitalism itself.

Historians have generally described the coming of industrialization in terms of changes in paid work. The transformation has been framed as one from a community of comparatively independent producers to a class of wageworkers, forced for their survival to sell labor as a commodity on the capitalist market. This approach defines the problem of antebellum working-class subsistence as a question of pay. Wages are taken to correspond to "means of support" along the lines of Paul Faler's conclusion that by 1830 Lynn shoemakers ". . . were full time wage earners with no important means of support other than . . . their income from shoemaking."[4]

Certainly, this emphasis reflects the way in which paid workers themselves formulated the problem of household survival. When the Philadelphia cordwainers complained in 1805 that the "pittance of subsistence" they received in wages was inadequate to provide "a fair and just support for our families,"[5] they expressed a conflation of "subsistence" and "wages" that was common among antebellum wage earners. The clearest and most consistent statement of that conflation was in the growing insistence upon a "family wage." A demand for a wage for husbands high enough to eliminate the need for daughters and wives to work for pay, the "family wage" was based on an assumption that cash income constituted

Reprinted with permission from the author and © MARHO: The Radical Historians' Organization. Originally appeared in *Radical History Review* 35, April 1986.

the entirety of the family subsistence: a "family wage" to the male head would, workingmen insisted, permit the mechanic to provide ". . . a livelihood for himself and [his family]" from his "earnings" alone.[6]

Nevertheless, recent work in American social history suggests that this strict equation of wages with "means of support" does not accurately describe the range of strategies through which the nineteenth-century working classes pieced together their livelihoods. Christine Stansell has pointed to the importance of casual labor—"peddling, scavenging, and the shadier arts of theft and prostitution"—in "making ends meet" in the households of the laboring poor in mid-nineteenth-century New York City.[7] Judith E. Smith has noted the dense networks of resource-sharing (including the sharing of food) that existed among immigrant families in turn-of-the-century Providence, Rhode Island.[8] Examining the grass-roots politics of socialism in early twentieth-century New York City, Dana Frank has demonstrated the power of housewives, in their work as shoppers, to force down food prices through community-based boycotts.[9] Each of these studies offers a vision of a survival economy based, not solely on the cash income of waged labor, but on a far larger and more intricate fabric of resources.

In this essay, I will argue that the antebellum working classes did indeed rely for their subsistence upon means of support other than their wages. Among the key economic resources of antebellum working-class households was housework itself—the unwaged (although not always unremunerated) labor that wives performed within their own families. Working-class women understood their obligations as mothers and wives to extend from such unpaid labor as child-rearing, cooking, and cleaning to such casualized forms of cash-earning as taking in boarders and vending. In the course of this work, their labor represented a substantial economic benefit—both to their families and to the employers who paid their husbands' wages. Within the household, wives' labor produced as much as half of the family subsistence. Beyond the household, the value of housework accrued to the owners of mills and factories and shops, who were able to pay "subsistence" wages at levels which in fact represented only a fraction of the real price of workers' survival.

The distinctive value of housewives' labor lies largely unrecognized in the traditional Marxist analysis which has informed so much of the study of working-class history. This results from the way in which Marx formulated the concept of "means of subsistence." Marx defined "subsistence" as "the labour-time necessary for the production [and reproduction] of labour-power"—that is, the labor-time required to insure the survival of the wage earner both from day to day and from generation to generation.[10] But Marx assumed that the working class bought its entire subsistence on the market, with cash. In his discussion of the sale of labor-power, for example, he identified "the means of subsistence" as "articles" that "must be bought or paid for," some "every day, others every week, others every quarter and so on."[11] He mentioned food, fuel, clothing, and furniture as examples. Having thus conceptually limited "subsistence" to what had to be purchased with income, Marx made a parallel limitation of the concept of "necessary labour-time" to labor-time that earned money.

Limiting the definition of subsistence to that which had to be purchased with cash was a convenience for Marx, whose focus was on the potential of money to obscure inequalities in the buying and selling of labor. He reasoned that the price of labor, the wage, represented very different values to the worker and to the capitalist. The worker received the cost of subsistence; the capitalist purchased all that labor could produce in a given period of time. As the capitalist was able to increase the value labor produced over the cost of keeping labor alive, he gained for himself a "surplus value" which was the origin of new capital. Formulated in this way, the cash exchange—*money*, with its "inherent" "possibility . . . of a quantitative incongruity between price and magnitude of value"—became key to Marx's analysis.

Marx was not entirely consistent in this formulation, however. One sometimes glimpses in *Capital* his own acknowledgment of the limitations of his analysis. His original definition of the value of labor-power as "the labour-time necessary for the production, and consequently also the reproduction" of labor in no way excludes the labor-time required to search the docks or borrow food in a period of shortage, for example.[13] At one point, moreover, he defined "subsistence" as the variety of resources "physically indispensable" to survival.[14] This definition might well include the labor of processing food into a digestible state, of nursing the sick back to health, and of tending small children—all of this routine in the labor of working-class housework. Finally, in his analysis of surplus value, Marx acknowledged that the wage might not always represent the value of subsistence. The capitalist could increase his margin of surplus value "by pushing the wage of the worker down below the value of his labour-power"—that is, below subsistence level.[15] This was not a mere hypothetical possibility for Marx, who acknowledged "the important part which this method plays in practice. . . ." But he found himself "excluded from considering it here by our assumption that all commodities, including labour-power, are bought and sold at their full value."[16]

Housework, however, was not bought and sold at its full value. Indeed, it was not bought and sold at all, but rather was exchanged directly for subsistence, in the manner of barter, within the family. Nonetheless, the cooking and cleaning, scavenging and borrowing, nursing and mending and child-rearing which made up housework was clearly necessary to produce a husband's labor-power. In other words, it was constituent in the total labor-time represented by the commodity—labor-power—the husband would sell on the market. At one point in his discussion of money, Marx noted that the *quantitative* contradiction expressed by the price could also become a *qualitative* one—that "a thing can, formally speaking, have a price without having a value."[17] The history of housework had left this labor in just the opposite position: it had a value without having a price. This distinguished housework from the forms of labor Marx was examining, but it did not exclude it from the process through which the surplus value of industrial capitalism was realized.

Indeed, for the Northeastern United States at least, evidence suggests that the denial of the economic worth of housework was a historical process integral to the development of industrial capitalism.[18] The Europeans who settled the region in the seventeenth century appear to have recognized the economic contribution of wives' work. A largely subsistence-oriented people, New England Puritans defined the household as the "economical society"[19] and understood that family survival required the wife's work in the garden, the barnyard, and the larder as much as it required the husband's work in the fields and meadows and barn. Court records bear testimony to the perceived importance of wives' labor, in the form of actions to overturn a husband's will when magistrates concluded that the wife's share did not accurately reflect her "diligence and industry" in "the getting of the Estate."[20]

At the same time, colonial society contained the ideological foundations for later denial of the economic worth of wives' labor. As ministers reminded women, husbands—not wives—were the public representatives of the household: "Our Ribs were not ordained to be our Rulers."[21] Wives' subordination was embedded in the English common law that the Puritans brought with them to New England. As *feme covert*, a wife's legal identity was subsumed under that of her husband, who was recognized as the owner of her labor-time, the products of that labor-time, and any cash realized from the sale of either the labor or its products. However much individual males acknowledged individual wives' economic worth, the tradition of law identified that worth with the husband. Thus, Marx's assumption, throughout *Capital*, that the "possessor" of labor-power and "the person whose labour-power it is" were one and the same person was historically inaccurate for housework in America from the beginning of English settlement.[22]

Mediated early on by the local nature of economic activity, wives' coverture became a more critical factor in the history of housework during the eighteenth century. Over the course of that century, the elaboration of cash markets and the growing competition among males for wages and property served to enhance the importance of money as a primary socially recognized index of economic worth. In public discussions of the economy, that is to say, industriousness was increasingly associated with money-making, while work that did not bring cash payment came scarcely to be recognized as work at all. This changing perception applied even to discussions of farming, still a largely subsistence-oriented activity. As Jared Eliot contended, the absence of a cash market ". . . tends to enervate and abate the Vigor and Zeal" of the farmer and "renders him Indolent."[23] Working for the most part without prospect of payment, and unable to lay legal claim to payment even when it was made, the prototype of the free worker who labored outside of the cash marketplace was the wife.

This is not to say that wives never sold their labor, or the products of their labor, directly for cash.[24] But wives' formal relationship to the market remained ambiguous at best—as men's was not. Over the course of the eighteenth century, as the importance of cash markets increased, the absence of a formal relationship with those markets rendered women *as a group* less visible as participants in and contributors to the economy. Remunerated or not, their labor was conceptually subsumed under the labor of the person who owned it, their husbands. Laurel Thatcher Ulrich has suggested that by the mid-eighteenth century, the husband who would acknowledge the individuality of his wife's paid labor (as distinct from his own claim as head of household) was a rare exception.[25]

The growing equation of cash with economic value created for women palpable contradictions between experience and ideology. At a time when even the comparatively prosperous Esther Edwards Burr numbered among her labors cooking, cleaning, baking, seeing to her family's provision of vegetables, fruits, beverages, and dairy produce, whitewashing walls, spinning, raising two children, covering chair bottoms, and making, remaking, and mending clothes,[26] colonial newspapers taunted that wives "want[ed] sense, and every kind of duty" and spent their time "more trifling than a baby."[27] From merely "owning" the family labor pool, husbands had now been ideologically identified as the *whole* of the family labor pool.

But the growing cultural invisibility of the economic value of the wife's labor in the family was not limited to the well-off. Indeed, by the end of the eighteenth century, the material conditions of survival in poor households provided a solid foundation, within the experience of working-class families themselves, for this new conception of the relation of men's paid labor or household support. As Ruth Schwartz Cowan has argued, one of the first effects of the coming of industrialization was the removal of men's labor from the household.[28] As poorer families could no longer provide land to their sons and as the growing power of masters and retailing middlemen undercut the traditional lines of advancement for journeymen in the trades, men experienced a dislocation in their ability to provide their share of the household maintenance. Under economic siege in the provision of their traditional portion of the family's subsistence, working-class men responded by conflating that *part* with the *whole* of the family economy. Certainly, this conflation was made easier by the general and growing invisibility of the economic value of housework among the middle classes. But working-class men appear to have first expressed the conflation in the course of attempting to articulate and protest changes in the nature and status of their own labor. Like the Philadelphia cordwainers, early nineteenth-century journeymen hatters

complained that the erosion of the apprenticeship system was preventing them from "gain-
[ing] an honest livelihood for themselves and families. . . ." and the seamen who gathered
at New York's City Hall to protest the Embargo Act in 1808 sought "wages which may
enable them to support their families. . . ."[29]

Similarly, it was in this context that the demand for the family wage was forged; as
Martha May has observed, workingmen recognized that under existing conditions, "the
working-class family would be unable to maintain a tolerable standard of living or retain
its customs and traditions."[30] But in the context of a society in which men's "ownership"
of the family labor-time had already been transformed into a perception that men were
the only laborers in the family economy, the "family wage" ideal worked to reinforce the
invisibility of the wife's contribution. As workingmen searched for a language through
which to express concretely the brutalization of the paid workplace and the deterioration of
their standard of living, the "family wage" ideal incorporated an ideal of female domesticity,
including a distinction between women's household activities and economic labor. Workingmen's newspapers contrasted the "odious, cruel, unjust and tyrannical system" of the
factory to the rejuvenative powers of the home.[31] *The Northern Star and Freeman's Advocate*
agreed that, "It is in the calm and quiet retreat of domestic life that relaxation from toil is
obtained. . . ."[32] Early trade unionist William Sylvis waxed sentimental about the charm of
women's mission

> to guide the tottering footsteps of tender infancy in the paths of rectitude and virtue, to
> smooth down the wrinkles of our perverse nature, to weep over our shortcomings, and
> make us glad in the days of our adversity, to counsel, and console us in our declining
> years.[33]

In working-class as well as middle-class representations, counsel, comfort, and consolation
had become the products of women's labor in the home.

Behind the rhetoric of female domesticity, however, antebellum working-class wives
continued to engage in a complex array of subsistence-producing labor. They worked
primarily as unpaid laborers in the family, where their work was of two general types. On
the first level, wives (as well as children) were responsible for finding ways to increase the
household provisions without spending cash. The most common form of this labor was
scavenging—for food, for discarded clothing, for household implements, and for fuel. On
the outskirts of cities and in smaller communities, wives and daughters collected bullrushes
(which could be used to make chair bottoms), cattails (which could be used to stuff
mattresses), and broom straw.[34] In the cities, women of the laboring poor haunted docks
and wharves in search of damaged goods, and examined the refuse of the streets and
marketplaces for food, cloth, or furniture which would be useful to their families.

Often carried out as an entirely legal enterprise, in practice the work of scavenging
sometimes shaded into theft, another of the strategies through which families of the laboring
poor added to their larders.[35] Throughout the antebellum period, both Black and white
women appeared in court to face charges of the theft of common and basic household
implements: washtubs, frying pans, kettles, clothing, and other items that seem destined,
not for resale, but for immediate consumption. When Mary Brennan stole a three-dollar
pair of shoes from Percy S. White in 1841, "[s]he assigned her great destitution as the
sole cause of the theft."[36]

Among more prosperous working-class families, shopping, household manufacturing,
and gardening also functioned as means of avoiding cash outlays. Food bought in quantity
was cheaper; grown in a garden, it was virtually free.[37] While the labor of gardening was

often shared among family members, by the antebellum period, marketing (which men had often done in earlier times) was women's work. In addition, some women continued to manufacture their own candles and make their own soap, and most women manufactured mattresses, pillows, linen, curtains, and clothing, and repaired furniture and garments.

Working-class wives worked not only to avoid spending money altogether, but also to reduce the size of necessary expenditures. Important for both of these ends was the maintenance of friendly contacts with neighbors, to whom one might turn for goods or services either as a regular supplement to one's own belongings or in periods of emergency. New to a building, neighborhood, or community, a woman depended upon her peers for information on the cheapest places to shop, the grocers least likely to cheat on weights and prices, and the likely spots for scavenging. Amicable relations with one's neighbors could yield someone to sit with a sick child or a friend from whom to borrow a pot or a few pieces of coal. In the event of fire, women often found that it was neighboring females who "exerted themselves in removing goods and furniture, and also in passing water" through the bucket brigade.[38] A history of friendly relations motivated one woman "to [go] herself to Whitehall after a load [of wood provided as public support], and . . . to see it delivered" when her neighbor's family was in danger of going without heat.[39]

Scarcity created tensions between cooperation and competition that required careful calculation. Boston's Mary Pepper complained that a neighbor had her run in as a drunk for no other reason than to get her evicted: "An its all along of your wanting my little place becaise ye cant pay the rent for your own, . . ." she charged.[40] Pepper was a single mother, responsible for the entirety of the household economy. Perhaps she had not had time to develop the bonds of mutual aid and obligation that might have prompted her neighbors to protect rather than complain of her. On the other hand, perhaps no amount of friendliness could have overridden a neighbor's need for her apartment. Indeed, Pepper herself may have acquired it by similar means.

Working-class wives also provided the bulk of the labor necessary to transform raw materials into items that the family could consume. That is to say, they hauled coal and wood, laid fires, and cooked the raw corn meal, beans, onions, potatoes, and occasional meat that comprised the mainstay of working-class diets. Among working-class households able to afford cloth, wives made many of the family's garments and linens. Where clothing was scavenged and/or handed down, wives did the mending, the lengthening, the letting out and taking in. They lugged water into the dwelling—or else they carried laundry out—so that the family clothing could be washed. They carried the garbage from the building—or, more convenient and less backbreaking, sometimes simply threw it out of a window onto the streets.

Poverty simplified this labor. Since there was seldom enough money to buy food ahead or in large quantities, poorer wives spent relatively less time than middling wives in either food preparation or preservation. A table, a chair, some blankets and rags for mattresses, a cooking pot, and a few utensils might well constitute the sum of the household furnishings, requiring little of the general upkeep that occupied so much of the time of wives in wealthier families or even in more prosperous working-class households. Among the working poor, providing warmth, food, and clothing took precedence over providing a scrubbed and scoured environment. Moreover, exacting standards of cleanliness were to little avail in city tenant houses in which there were no outlets for the soot and fumes of cooking and into which water might run "at every storm."[41]

It was not uncommon for working-class wives also to be responsible for bringing some cash into the household economy. The regularity of this labor varied from household to household, depending not only on the size but also on the reliability of the husband's wage packet. Facing systemic economic hardship, married Black women were more likely to undertake regular outside work—as cooks, nurses, washerwomen, and maids. (Among whites, paid domestic service was commonly limited to single women.) Both Black and white married women became seamstresses. Both sometimes became street vendors. If they lacked the twenty-five-cent-a-day fee to rent a market stall, then from sidewalks and carts they hawked roots and herbs they had dug themselves, or fruits, vegetables, candy, eggs, peanuts, coffee, or chocolate.[42] Some women collected rags to sell to paper manufacturers, "poking into the gutters after rags before the stars go to bed."[43] If their husbands had employment building canals and railroads, wives sometimes took jobs for a season as cooks and laundresses for the entire work camp.[44]

But much of the cash-earning of working-class wives was even less visible than these examples suggest. Virtually every wife whose husband worked in close proximity to the household (be he a tailor or a tavern-keeper) was expected to contribute labor as his assistant. In this capacity, her portion of the labor was seldom distinguished by a separate wage or fees paid directly in her name. Rather, her work was subsumed under her husband's pay, or absorbed into an enterprise identified as exclusively his. For example, it is only in the course of a criminal prosecution in 1841 that it becomes clear on the record that John Cronin's wife "generally tended the junk shop" that bore his name.[45] Equally invisible was the cash-earning that women performed by taking boarders into the household. In this instance, they exchanged their labor as cooks and maids, and sometimes as washerwomen and seamstresses, for a payment to the household. Virtually indistinguishable in nature from the labor they performed for free for their families, and enmeshed in that work in the course of the daily routine, boarding could nonetheless add as much as three or four dollars a week to the household budget.

Through all of this, wives also took primary responsibility for nursing elderly or sick household members and for child-rearing. In the conditions of the nineteenth-century city, the latter was a responsibility that brought special anxieties. The dangers of the city to children were legion—fires, horses running out of control, unmarked wells, unfenced piers, disease, as well as temptations to theft and prostitution as means of making some money. In families where the household economy required that the mother or children go out to work, or that the mother focus her attention on needlework, for example, within the household, close supervision was impossible. This is not to suggest, as did the middle-class reformers of the period, that these parents were negligent. Within the demand for the family wage, and for working-class female domesticity, was a demand for a household in which children could be protected and better cared for. Wage earning men longed for the day when "our wives, no longer doomed to servile labor, will be . . . the instructors of our children."[46]

The distinction between "paid labor" and "housework" implied in working-class men's yearning for the domestic ideal persisted in later nineteenth-century analyses of women's unpaid labor and was eventually replicated in *Capital*. Because wives' work was largely unpaid, and because husbands came to the marketplace as the "possessors" of their wives' labor, Marx did not address the role of housework in the labor exchange that led to surplus value. Neither did he attend to the dynamics which permitted the husband to lay claim, in the price of his own labor, to the value of his wife's work.

The exchange value of housework is elusive, but it is not impossible to calculate. Some of it was directly paid, even when done by a wife in the context of her family duties—vending and needlework, for example. But even that labor for which wives were *not* paid when they worked in the context of their own families *was* paid when performed in the context of someone else's family, that is, as domestic service. The equivalence was direct, for in the antebellum period paid domestic service and unpaid housework were the same labor, often performed by the same woman, only in different locations and in different parts of her workday or workweek. Since paid domestic servants were customarily provided with room and board in addition to their wages, moreover, their earnings represented a price over and above food, shelter, and warmth, or, understood as an equivalent for housework, over and above the wife's basic maintenance.

In northeastern cities in 1860, cooks (who frequently also did the laundry) earned between three and four dollars a week. Seamstresses averaged two-and-a-half dollars a week, and maids made about the same amount. On the market, caring for children was at the lower end of the pay scale, commanding perhaps two dollars a week. Taken at an average, this puts the price of a wife's basic housework at about three dollars a week—or $150 dollars a year—excluding the value of her own maintenance.[47]

To this should be added the value of goods a wife might make available within the family for free or at a reduced cost. Among poorer households, this was the labor of scavenging. A rag rug found among the refuse was worth fifty cents, an old coat several dollars. Flour for a week, scooped from a broken barrel on the docks, could save the household almost a dollar in cash outlay.[48] When Mary Brennan stole the pair of shoes, she avoided a three-dollar expenditure (or would have, had she been successful). In these ways, a wife with a good eye and a quick hand might easily save her family a dollar a week—or fifty dollars or so over the course of the year.

Not all working-class wives scavenged. In households with more cash, wives were likely to spend that labor-time in other forms of purchase-avoidance work. By shopping carefully, buying in bulk, and drying or salting extra food, a wife could save ten to fifty percent on the family food budget, or about a dollar a week on an income of $250 a year.[49] Wives who kept kitchen gardens could, at the very least, produce and preserve potatoes worth a quarter a week, or some ten to fifteen dollars a year.[50]

But there was also the cash that working-class wives brought into the household—in the form of needlework, vending, taking in boarders, running a grocery or a tavern from her kitchen, or working unpaid in her husband's trade. A boarder might pay four dollars a week into the family economy. Subtracting a dollar and a half for food and rent, the wife's labor-time represented $2.50 of that sum, or $130 a year.[51] Needlewomen averaged about two dollars a week, or a hundred dollars a year.[52] Calculated on the basis of a "helper" in a trade, the wife's time working in her husband's occupation (for example, alongside her husband shoemaker, for the equivalent of a day a week) was worth some twenty dollars a year.[53]

The particular labor performed by a given woman depended on the size and resources of her household. In this way, housework remained entirely embedded within the family. Yet we can estimate a general market price of housework by combining the values of the individual activities that made it up: perhaps $150 for cooking, cleaning, laundry, and child-rearing, even in poor households another fifty dollars or so saved through scavenging and wise shopping, another fifty dollars or so in cash brought directly into the household. This would set the price of a wife's labor-time among the laboring poor at roughly $250 a year beyond maintenance, or in the neighborhood of four hundred dollars a year when the price of a single woman's maintenance purchased on the market (about $170 a year) is included. In households with more income, where the wife could focus her labor on money-saving and on taking in a full-time boarder, that price might reach over five hundred dollars annually, or between six hundred and seven hundred dollars including maintenance.

The shift in the nature of and increase in the value of wives' work as a husband's income increased seems not to have been entirely lost on males, who advised young men that if they meant to get ahead, they should "get married."[54] This difference by income may also further explain the intersection of gender and economic interests which informed workingmen's ideal of female domesticity. Women's wages were low—kept that way in part by the rhetoric surrounding the family wage ideal. Given this, a wife working without pay at home may have been more valuable to the family maintenance than a wife working for pay—inside or outside the home. Similarly, the low levels of women's wages meant that few women could hope to earn the $170 a year necessary to purchase their maintenance on the market. This was true even for women in industrial work. While a full-time seamstress who earned $2.50 a week and was employed year-round would earn only $130 a year, an Irishwoman with ten years seniority in the Hamilton mills earned only about $2.90 a week in 1860, or about $150 a year.[55]

Because of her need for access to cash, the wife's dependence on a wage-earner within the family was particularly acute. She was not the only member benefiting from the amalgamation of labors that the household represented, however. A single adult male, living in New York City in 1860, could scarcely hope to get by on less than $250 a year: four dollars a week for room and board ($208 a year) and perhaps fifteen dollars a year for minimal clothing meant an outlay of almost $225 before laundry, medicines, and other occasional expenses.[56] Many working-class men did not earn $225 a year, and for them access to the domestic labor of a wife might be the critical variable in achieving a maintenance. Even men who did earn this amount might find a clear advantage in marrying, for a wife saved money considerably over and above the cost she added for her own maintenance.

Historians have frequently analyzed the working-class family as a collectivity, run according to a communal ethic. But by both law and custom the marital exchange was not an even one. Finally the husband owned not only the value of his own labor-time, but the value of his wife's as well—as expressed, for example, in cash or cooked food, manufactured or mended clothing, scavenged dishes or food, and in children raised to an age at which they, too, could contribute to the household economy. There is no evidence that working-class males were prepared to give up the prerogatives of manhood. To the contrary, as we have seen, the rhetoric of the family wage suggests that they were engaged in a historical process of strengthening those claims.

Perhaps it would seem absurd to quibble over who owned the poverty or near-poverty that so often characterized working-class households. There were things to be owned, however, and ownership could prove the determining factor of subsistence or destitution if the household broke up. First, the husband possessed his own maintenance, and any improvements in it which became possible as a result of the labor of his wife and children. He also owned whatever furnishings the family had accumulated. Although a table, a chair, clothing, bedding, and a few dishes seem (and were) scant enough property, they were the stuff of which life-and-death transactions were made in the laboring classes; pawned overnight, for example, clothes were important "currency" to cover the rent until payday. The husband also owned the children his wife raised, and whose wages (when they reached their mid-teens) might amount to several hundred dollars a year—almost as much as his own. Even while they were quite young, children might be helpful in scavenging fuel and food.

To be sure, wives commonly benefited from some or all of these sources of value, and both personal and community norms tended to restrain husbands from taking full advantage of their positions. Not only the affectional bonds of the family, but the expanding cultural emphasis on the husband as the "protector" and "provider" may have helped mediate emotionally the structural inequities of the household.

At the same time, community norms did not prevent the expression of individual self-interest in marriage, and the stresses of material hardship were as likely to rend as to create mutualities of concern. The frequency of incidents in which a wife had her husband arrested for battery and then "discharged at her request" suggests a complex, and less than romantic, dynamic of dependence in antebellum families. The continuing development of cash exchange networks throughout the antebellum period, and the relegation of barter largely to domestic transactions, had heightened that dynamic. A man could wear dirty clothes or look for cheaper accommodations or eat less to reduce his cash outlay, even if these choices might prove destructive in the long run. But the mariner's wife who stood with her four children on New York's docks, begging her husband for half of his wages, was in a far more extreme position of dependency. Her husband preferred to remain on board ship—with his wages.[57]

Husbands were not the only ones to benefit from the economic value of housework and from its invisibility. Employers were enabled by the presence of this sizeable but uncounted labor in the home to pay both men and women wages which were, in fact, below the level of subsistence. At a time when the level of capital accumulation in the Northeast remained precariously low and when, as a result, most new mills did not survive ten years, the margin of profit available from sub-subsistence wages was crucial.

Occasionally, mill owners acknowledged that the wages they paid did not cover maintenance. One agent admitted:

> . . . I regard my work-people just as I regard my machinery. So long as they can do my work *for what I choose to pay them*, I keep them, getting out of them all I can. . . . [H]ow they fare outside my walls I don't know, nor do I consider it my business to know. They must look out for themselves. . . .[58]

More often, however, both capitalists and the political economists who rose in their defense maintained that they did indeed care about their workers, and that the wages they paid represented the true value of the labor they received, including the value of producing that labor. In 1825, for example, John McVickar caused to be reprinted in the United States the *Encyclopedia Britannica* discussion of political economy, which asserted that "the cost of producing artificers, or labourers, regulates the wages they obtain. . . ."[59] Eleven years later, in *Public and Private Economy*, Theodore Sedgwick carried this optimism about the relationship of wages to subsistence one step further—at the same time revealing the dangerous uses to which the belief that wages represented subsistence could be put. Since "a little, a very little only" was required to maintain labor, Sedgwick argued, even at current levels of payment "in the factories of New England, very large numbers [of workers] may annually lay up half their wages; many much more. . . ."[60] Presumably, wages not only covered, but exceeded the value of maintenance. The other shoe would fall, again and again, as employers used the fact of working-class survival to justify further cuts in wages. The value of unpaid housework in mediating those cuts would remain invisible.

Although there is no evidence that capitalists consciously thought of it in this way, it was clearly in the interests of capital for housework to remain invisible. Following the lines of Marx's analysis, some scholars have concluded that, since it was unwaged, housework could not have created surplus value—that there must be a discrete exchange of money for that process to occur. Marx recognized, though, that the nature of the individual transaction was less important than its part in the general movement of capital. In the case of housework, which Marx did not examine, it was the very unwaged character of the labor that made it so profitable to capital. Traded first to the husband for partial subsistence, it then existed in the husband's labor as an element of subsistence made available to capital for free. Indeed, housework had achieved just the reverse of the qualitative contradiction Marx predicted: it had a value without having a price. Excluding the cash that working-class wives brought into the household, housework added several hundred dollars a year to the value of working-class subsistence—several hundred dollars which the employer did not have to pay as a part of the wage packet. Had the labor of housework been counted, wages would have soared to roughly twice their present levels. And as factory and mill owners knew well, "profits must vary inversely as wages, that is, they must fall as wages rise, and rise as wages fall."[61]

It is important to recognize that employers were able to appropriate the value of house-work in part because the people they were paying *also* appropriated it. Paid workers protested many things during the antebellum period—long hours, pay cuts, production speed-ups—but there is no evidence that they objected to the fiction that wages were meant to cover the full value of household maintenance. Indeed, to have questioned that premise would have been to question the very structure of the gender system and of the family as socially constituted in the history of the northeastern United States. In this way, capital's claim to the surplus value of the wife's labor existed through and was dependent upon the husband's claim to that same value. So long as husbands understood their status as men (and so as heads of households) to depend upon the belief that they were the primary, if not the sole, "providers" of the family, the value of housework would remain unacknowledged by—and profitable to—their employers.

The history of industrialization—in the United States and elsewhere—has been written largely as a history of paid work. Housework, where it has been included at all, has been fitted into the historical scheme merely as an ancillary factor: family life felt the shock waves of industrialization, but the epicenter of the quake was elsewhere—in the realm of "productive" labor. Marx himself drew the distinction between "productive" and "reproductive" work. He realized, however, as historians since have tended to forget, that the lines between these spheres were artificial: " . . . every social process of production is at the same time a process of reproduction."[62] The case of women's unpaid labor in the antebellum northeastern United States suggests that the opposite is also accurate. Only when we make the changing conditions and relations of housework integral parts of the narrative of economic and social transformation will our telling of the story become complete.

Notes

I would like to thank Betsy Blackmar, Carol Karlsen, Lori Ginzberg, Ileen DeVault, Nancy F. Cott and the Columbia Seminar on Working Class History for their helpful criticisms of various drafts of this article. I am also grateful to Rutgers University for its support, through the Henry Rutgers Research Fellowship.

1. John H. Griscom, *The Sanitary Condition of the Laboring Population of New York* (New York: Arno Press, 1970; orig. pub. 1845), *passim.*

2. For discussions of the attitudes of middle-class reformers toward the poor in the antebellum period, see Carroll Smith Rosenberg, *Religion and the Rise of the American City: The New York City Mission Movement, 1812–1870* (Ithaca: Cornell University Press, 1971) and Paul Boyer, *Urban Masses and Moral Order in America, 1820–1920* (Cambridge: Harvard University Press, 1978). For a contemporary example, in addition to Griscom's, see Charles Loring Brace, *The Dangerous Classes of New York, and Twenty Years' Work Among Them* (New York: WynKoop and Hallenbeck, 1872).

3. U.S. Bureau of the Census, *Historical Statistics of the United States, Part 1* (Washington, D.C.: United States Government Printing Office, 1975), Series A 6–8, p. 8 and Series D 167–181, p. 139.

4. Paul G. Faler, *Mechanics and Manufacturers in the Early Industrial Revolution: Lynn, Massachusetts, 1780–1860* (Albany: State University of New York Press, 1981), p. 84.

5. "The Address to the Working Shoemakers of the City of Philadelphia to the Public," as quoted in John Commons et al., *History of Labor in the United States*, vol. I (New York: The Macmillan Company, 1918), pp. 141–42.

6. As quoted in Martha May, "Bread Before Roses: American Workingmen, Labor Unions and the Family Wage" in Ruth Milkman, ed., *Women, Work and Protest: A Century of U.S. Women's Labor History* (Boston: Routledge and Kegan Paul, 1985), p. 3.

7. Christine Stansell, "Women, Children, and the Uses of the Streets: Class and Gender Conflict in New York City, 1850–1869," *Feminist Studies* 8/2 (Summer 1982), pp. 312–13. This essay also appears as chapter 8 in this volume.

8. Judith E. Smith, "Our Own Kind: Family and Community Networks in Providence," *Radical History Review* 17 (Spring 1978), pp. 99–120.

9. Dana Frank, "Housewives, Socialists, and the Politics of Food: The 1917 New York Cost-of-Living Protests," *Feminist Studies* 11/2 (Summer 1985), pp. 255–85.

10. Karl Marx, *Capital*, trans. Ben Fowkes (New York: Vintage Books, 1977), I: 274.

11. Marx, *Capital*, I: 276.

12. Marx, *Capital*, I: 196.

13. Marx, *Capital*, I: 274.

14. Marx, *Capital*, I: 277.

15. Marx, *Capital*, I: 431.

16. Marx, *Capital*, I: 431.

17. Marx, *Capital*, I: 197.

18. For a more detailed discussion of the transformation of housework as an aspect of industrialization, see Jeanne Boydston, "Home and Work: The Industrialization of Housework in the Northeastern United States from the Colonial Period to the Civil War" (Unpublished dissertation, Yale University, 1984).

19. For example, William Perkins gave his 1631 sermon on "oeconomie" the subtitle, "Or, Household-Government: A Short Survey of the Right Manner of Erecting and Ordering a Family. . . ."

20. William Brigham, *The Compact with the Charter and Laws of the Colony of New Plymouth* (Boston: Dutton and Wentworth, 1836), p. 281.

21. William Secker, "*A Wedding Ring for the Finger* . . ." (Boston: Samuel Green, 1690), n.p.

22. See for example Marx's discussion of the sale of labor power in *Capital*, I: 271.

23. Jared Eliot, *Essays Upon Field Husbandry in New England and Other Papers, 1748–1762*, Harry J. Carman and Rexford G. Tugwell, eds. (New York, 1942), as quoted in Richard L. Bushman, *From Puritan to Yankee: Character and the Social Order in Connecticut, 1690–1765* (New York: W. W. Norton and Company, 1967), pp. 26–27.

24. See, for example, Laurel Thatcher Ulrich, " 'A Friendly Neighbor': Social Dimensions of Daily Work in Northern Colonial New England," *Feminist Studies* 6/2 (Summer 1980), pp. 392–405, and Joan M. Jensen, "Cloth, Butter and Boarders: Women's Household Production for the Market," *The Review of Radical Political Economics* 12/2 (Summer 1980), pp. 14–24.

25. Ulrich, " 'A Friendly Neighbor,' " pp. 394–95.

26. Carol F. Karlsen and Laurie Crumpacker, eds., *The Journal of Esther Edwards Burr, 1754–1757* (New Haven: Yale University Press, 1984), *passim*.

27. "A-La-Mode, for the Year 1756," *Boston Evening Post*, Supplement, March 8, 1756; "By the Ranger," *Boston Evening Post*, October 16, 1758.

28. Ruth Schwartz Cowan, *More Work for Mother: The Ironies of Household Technology from the Open Hearth to the Microwave* (New York: Basic Books, Inc., 1983), pp. 63–67.

29. *American State Papers, 1789–1815*, vol. 2: *Finance* (Washington: Gales and Seaton, 1832), p. 257; George Daitman, "Labor and the 'Welfare State' in Early New York," *Labor History* 4 (Fall 1963), p. 252.

30. May, "Bread before Roses," p. 4.

31. *The Man*, May 13, 1835, as quoted in Commons, *History of Labor*, p. 388.

32. *The Northern Star and Freeman's Advocate*, January 2, 1843.

33. James C. Sylvis, ed., *Life, Speeches, Labors, and Essays of William H. Sylvis* (Philadelphia: Claxton, Remsen, and Haffelfinger, 1872), p. 120.

34. Susan May Strasser, *Never Done: A History of American Housework* (New York: Pantheon, 1982), p. 18.

35. For an excellent discussion of the uses of theft as an economic tool among the antebellum laboring poor, see Stansell, "Women, Children, and the Uses of the Streets," *passim*.

36. For examples, see the *New York Tribune*, April 12, 14, 19, and 20, 1841, and May 17, 1841. The quotation is from April 20, 1841.

37. See below, n. 48.

38. *Boston Evening Transcript*, September 20, 1830.

39. Ezra Stiles Ely, *Visits of Mercy*, I (6th ed.; Philadelphia: S. F. Bradford, 1829), p. 88.

40. *Boston Evening Transcript*, July 27, 1830.

41. Griscom, *Sanitary Condition*, p. 9.

42. See, for example, Solon Robinson, *Hot Corn: Life Scenes in New York Illustrated* (New York: Dewitt and Davenport, 1854), p. 31, and Thomas F. DeVoe, *The Market Book, Containing a Historical Account of the Public Markets in the Cities of New York, Boston, Philadelphia and Brooklyn* (New York: Burt Franklin, 1862), p. 370.

43. Robinson, *Hot Corn*, p. 198.

44. DeVoe, *The Market Book*, p. 463; Robert Ernst, *Immigrant Life in New York City, 1825–1863* (New York: King's Crown Press, 1949), p. 66.

45. *New York Tribune*, April 22, 1841.

46. William English, as quoted in Martha May, "Bread Before Roses," p. 5.

47. Wages are from Edgar W. Martin, *The Standard of Living in 1860: American Consumption Levels on the Eve of the Civil War* (Chicago: The University of Chicago Press, 1942), p. 177, and Faye E. Dudden, *Serving Women: Household Service in Nineteenth-Century America* (Middletown, Conn.: Wesleyan University Press, 1983), p. 149.

48. This is calculated on the basis of an average weekly budget for a working-class family of five, as itemized in the *New York Tribune* in 1851. According to that budget, flour could be bought in bulk at five dollars a barrel, a barrel lasting a family of five about eight weeks. Since the *Tribune* budget assumes a family with an annual income over five hundred dollars (and therefore able to benefit from the savings of buying in bulk), I have increased the cost by thirty per cent. See Norman Ware, *The Industrial Worker, 1840–1860: The Reaction of American Industrial Society to the Advance of the Industrial Revolution* (New York: Quadrangle/ The New York Times Book Company, 1974), p. 33. On savings from buying in bulk, see Griscom, *Sanitary Condition*, p. 8. Other cash values are found in Martin, *Standard of Living*, p. 122, and in Richard Osborn Cummings, *The American and His Food: A History of Food Habits in the United States* (Chicago: University of Chicago Press, 1941), p. 75.

49. See above, n. 48.

50. Based on figures provided in Ware, *The Industrial Worker*, p. 33.

51. Martin, *Standard of Living*, p. 168.

52. Martin, *Standard of Living*, p. 177.

53. This calculation is based on wages in Carroll D. Wright, *Comparative Wages, Prices, and Cost of Living* (Boston: Wright and Potter Printing Company, 1889), pp. 47 and 55. It provides a very conservative index for wives' work; wives frequently had skills far beyond the "helper" level.

54. Grant Thorburn, *Sketches from the Note-book of Lurie Todd* (New York: D. Fanshaw, 1847), p. 12. Thorburn recommended marriage as a sensible economic decision for young men earning as little as five hundred dollars a year—more than males of the laboring poor, but within the range of better-paid workingmen.

55. Thomas Dublin, *Women at Work: The Transformation of Work and Community in Lowell, Massachusetts, 1826–1860* (New York: Columbia University Press, 1979), Table 11:12, p. 197.

56. See Martin, *Standard of Living*, p. 168, for the average weekly cost of room and board for a single, adult male living in New York City.

57. Ely, *Visits of Mercy*, p. 194.

58. Quoted in Ware, *The Industrial Worker*, p. 77. Emphasis mine.

59. John McVickar, *Outlines of Political Economy* (New York: Wilder and Campbell, 1825), p. 107.

60. Theodore Sedgwick, *Public and Private Economy* (New York: Harper and Brothers, 1836), pp. 30 and 225.

61. McVickar, *Outlines*, p. 144.

62. Marx, *Capital*, I: 711.

5

La Tules of Image and Reality: Euro-American Attitudes and Legend Formation on a Spanish-Mexican Frontier

Deena J. González

In the summer of 1846, Doña Gertrudis Barceló stood at an important crossroad. Exempted from the hardships and tribulations endured by the women around her, Barceló had profited enormously from the "gringo" merchants and itinerant retailers who had arrived in Santa Fé after the conquest. The town's leading businesswoman, owner of a gambling house and saloon, and its most unusual character, Barceló exemplified an ingenious turnaround in the way she and others in her community began resolving the problem of the Euro-American, now lodged more firmly than ever in their midst. Barceló also epitomized the growing dilemma of dealing with newcomers whose culture and orientation differed from hers.

Since 1821, people like Barceló had seen traders enter their town and change it. But local shopkeepers and vendors had done more than observe the developing marketplace. They had forged ahead, establishing a partnership with the adventurers who brought manufactured items and textiles to Santa Fé while exporting the products of Nuevo México, including gold, silver, and equally valuable goods, such as Navajo blankets and handwoven rugs.[1]

Barceló's life and activities were indisputably anchored in a community shaped by a changing economy, as well as by other political, social, and cultural demands. Orthodox interpretations of her life have overlooked the primacy of the surrounding turmoil. Moreover, by 1846, she would become the female object of the easiest, most exaggerated misunderstandings bred by such complicated frontier situations. The exaggerations have been examined from several perspectives; but standard works have failed to assess the role that sex and gender played in discussions of Barceló's business and personality.[2] The outcome has been the creation of a legend around her, one directly shaped by the disruptions experienced by her generation and focused on her business and her sex.

Gertrudis Barceló was said to have controlled men and to have dabbled in local politics, but these insinuations do not form the core of her legend. Rather, reporters of her time, professional historians today, and novelists have debated her morals, arguing about her influence over political leaders and speculating about whether she was operating a brothel. These concerns are consistently revealed in early accounts of Barceló by writers and soldiers recalling their experiences in the "hinterlands" of northern Mexico. The negative images and anti-Mexican stereotypes in these works not only stigmatized Barceló but also helped legitimize the Euro-Americans' conquest of the region. Absorbed and reiterated by succeeding generations of professional historians and novelists, the legend of Barceló has obscured the complex reality of cultural accommodation and ongoing resistance.

Moreover, the legend evolving around Barceló affected the lives of other Spanish-Mexican women. Her supposed moral laxity and outrageous dress were generalized to include all the women of Santa Fé. Susan Shelby Magoffin, the first Euro-American woman to travel down the Santa Fé Trail, observed in 1846 that "These were dressed in the Mexican style; large sleeves, short waists, ruffled skirts, and no bustles—which latter looks exceedingly odd in this day of grass skirts and pillows. All danced and smoked cigarittos, from the old woman with false hair and teeth [Doña Tula], to the little child."[3]

This was not the first account of La Tules, as Barceló was affectionately called (in reference either to her slimness or to her plumpness, because *tules* means "reed").[4] Josiah Gregg, a trader during the 1830s, said that La Tules was a woman of "loose habits," who "roamed" in Taos before she came to Santa Fé.[5] In his widely read *Commerce of the Prairies*, Gregg linked local customs—smoking, gambling, and dancing—to social and moral disintegration. La Tules embodied, for him and others, the extent of Spanish-Mexican decadence.

La Tules's dilemmas predated 1846 and, at a social and economic level, portended a community's difficulties, which were not long in developing. Governing officers in Chihuahua had already sent word of a crackdown on illegal trafficking,[6] Bishop Zubiría in Durango issued a pastoral limiting church holidays and celebrations, in an effort to economize on expenses but also on priests' time. This pastoral gave added emphasis to the regulations descending on New Mexicans, who now became aware that the Catholic church, too, was reconsidering its obligations. In this period, Barceló and other Spanish-Mexicans experienced the tightening grip of the Mexican state, which was bent on rooting out uncontrolled trading; but they gained a reprieve accidentally. As orders arrived from the church concerning the condition of Christians on the northern frontier, the United States chose to invade, hurling General Stephen Kearny and his troops toward the capital city.[7]

Barceló's activities and business acumen demonstrated, despite these pressures, the *vecinos*' (residents') proven resilience and the town's characteristic adaptability. But in the 1840s Barceló also became the object of intense Euro-American scrutiny and harsh ridicule. She was an expert dealer at monte, a card game named after the *monte* (mountain) of cards that accumulated with each hand. She drew hundreds of dollars out of merchants and soldiers alike; it was the former who embellished her name and reputation, imbuing her facetiously with characteristics of superiority and eccentricity.

Josiah Gregg, the trader, first brought Barceló notoriety because his book described her as a loose woman. But Gregg also argued that money from gambling eventually helped elevate her moral character.[8] A Protestant, and a doctor in failing health, Gregg respected only her gift—the one he understood best—for making money. During her lifetime, she became extraordinarily wealthy, and for that reason as well, Gregg and others would simultaneously admire and disdain her.

In the face of such contradictory attitudes toward her, Barceló ventured down a trail of her own choosing. Not quite as rebellious as Juana Lopes, who had defied husband and judge alike, she nevertheless achieved personal autonomy. Several times, she appeared before magistrates to pay fines, testifying once against an indicted judge who had pocketed her money. She even involved her family in her pursuits, and they were fined along with her.[9] As early as 1825, she was at the mining camp outside of Santa Fé, Real del Oro, doing a brisk business at monte.[10] By the 1830s, the card dealer was back in town, enticing Euro-Americans to gamble under terms she prescribed. At her saloon, she served the men alcohol as she dealt rounds of cards. Controlling consumption as well as the games, Barceló accommodated the newcomers, but on her own terms. "Shrewd," Susan Shelby Magoffin, wife of the trader Samuel Magoffin, called Barceló in 1846.[11]

Barceló had proven her shrewdness long before that. Since the 1820s, Barceló had engaged in an extremely profitable enterprise. Gambling, dubbed by observers the national pastime, was ubiquitous, and by the mid-1830s nearly every traveler and merchant felt compelled to describe Barceló's contributions to the game.[12] Matt Field, an actor and journalist from Missouri, depicted Barceló's saloon as a place where her "calm seriousness was alone discernible, and the cards fell from her fingers as steadily as though she were handling only a knitting needle. . . . Again and again the long fingers of Señora Toulous swept off the pile of gold, and again were they replaced by the unsteady fingers of her opponent."[13] By any account, Euro-Americans could understand what drove Barceló. Because they recognized in her their own hungry search for profit, they embellished their stories and, just as frequently, maligned her.

When Barceló died in 1852, she was worth over ten thousand dollars, a sum twice as high as most wealthy Spanish-Mexican men possessed and larger than the average worth of Euro-Americans in Santa Fé.[14] Her properties were extensive: she owned the saloon, a long building with large rooms, and she had an even larger home not far from the plaza. She made enough money to give generously to the church and to her relatives, supporting families and adopting children.[15] Military officers claimed that she entertained lavishly and frequently.[16]

Dinners, dances, gambling, and assistance to the poverty-stricken elevated Barceló to a special place in New Mexican society, where she remained throughout her life. The community respected her, since it tolerated atypical behavior in others and rarely seemed preoccupied with what Barceló represented. Even her scornful critics were struck by how well received and openly admired the woman with the "red hair and heavy jewelry" was among Santa Fé's "best society."[17]

What was it about Nuevo México in the two decades before the war that allowed a woman like Barceló to step outside the accepted boundaries of normal or typical female behavior, make a huge sum of money, undergo excessive scrutiny, primarily by newcomers to Santa Fé, and yet be eulogized by her own people? Some answers lie within her Spanish-Mexican community, which, although beset by persisting problems, had flexibility and an inclination toward change. Others lie in the general position and treatment of women in that society.

Court records and other documents reveal that Santa Fé's women were expected to defer to men but did not, that they were bound by a code of honor and respectability but often manipulated it to their advantage, and that they were restrained by fathers and brothers from venturing too far out of family and household but frequently disobeyed them. One professional historian has argued that social codes in colonial New Mexican society, with their twin emphasis on honor and virtue, were primarily metaphors for expressing hierarchical relationships, but also served to resolve conflict as much as to restrict women.[18] Women's behavior and the espoused social ideals of restraint, respectability, and deference were at cross-purposes, especially in a community that was supremely concerned about the appearance of honor, if not its reality. Separate requirements based on gender—or what the society would label appropriate masculine and feminine virtues—occupied an equally important place in these social codes, and also concerned power and the resolution of conflict.

Barceló's gambling and drinking violated the rigid codes organizing appropriate female behavior, but such behavior was not the key to her distinctiveness. Rather, her success as a businesswoman and gambler gave her a unique independence ordinarily denied women. Thus, the most hostile comments about her frequently came from Spanish-Mexican women.

In particular, complaints filed against Barceló reveal the extent of other women's animosity, not men's, and were usually thinly disguised as aspersions on her honor. In 1835, Ana María Rendón remonstrated that Barceló and Lucius Thruston, a migrant from Kentucky, were cohabiting.[19] In fact, Barceló's husband lived in the same house, indicating that Thruston was probably a boarder. Honor lay in the proof, and Barceló achieved both by defending herself and her husband as well. Another time, Barceló complained about a slanderous comment made by Josefa Tenório and was also exonerated.[20] Spanish-Mexicans of Santa Fé remained a litigious people, and they waged battles on many fronts. The *alcalde* court (local court) prevailed as the best place to seek resolution. However, Catholic Spanish-Mexican *vecinos* were generally a forgiving people, especially where slander and gossip were involved. Barceló forgave Ana María Rendón's complaint when Rendón retracted it, and the records are filled with similar recantations in other cases.[21]

At issue, then, were not Barceló's violations of gender and social codes—she had in part moved beyond that—but the others' violations of her good name and reputation. On one level, their hostility and outright distrust of Barceló were vendettas directed against a neighbor on the road to wealth and prestige. On another, women upheld the gender code (albeit with some trepidation) because, in complaining about Barceló, they defended themselves and their society. Even when she was fined for gambling, the amounts were so minuscule that they neither halted Barceló's gambling nor conveyed a forceful message about modifying social behavior.[22]

Barceló, a married woman, would not have been able to step outside the boundaries of her society, nor would Manuela Baca or Juana Lopes in the previous decade, if there were no disjunction between the idealized married life and the conditions that stood in the way of its realization—conditions such as taking in boarders or having children out of wedlock. Rallitas Washington, Barceló's grandniece born out of wedlock, as well as hundreds of other women whose mothers were unmarried, formed a decidedly heterodox, yet devoutly Catholic, community.[23] In relationships as in personal behavior, these women's lack of conformity did not shake the conscience of a community as much as needle it.

Beyond cultural mores and behavioral codes, though, what might go unrecognized is that women of the Far West who defied the rules might have been viewed from the outset as marginal. When not ignored completely, women who have existed outside the boundaries of a society of community—or who have been ostracized for various reasons—have frequently been termed outlaws and burdened with characteristics obscuring their social or economic conditions. That may have been standard procedure for marginal women everywhere.[24]

But marginality signifies not only the transgression of social boundaries but also the aftermath of such transgression; it represents the fate of people who press against those boundaries and afterward must live on the edges of society. Barceló cleverly crossed social and sexual barriers to gamble, make money, buy property, and influence politicians, but she avoided marginality. She did not regard herself as a marginal woman, nor was she necessarily marginalized, except by Euro-Americans. She was unusual and she was mocked for it, but not by her own people. In fact, her life and legend are interesting precisely because, in the eyes of observers, she came to represent the worst in Spanish-Mexican culture while, as a Spanish-Mexican, she mastered the strategies and methods of the Americanizers; she achieved what they had professed in speeches and reports originally to want for all New Mexicans.[25]

Barceló's life and her legend contradict orthodox notions of marginality in a situation of conquest. In their writings, conquerors maligned and ostracized her. The opinions they expressed and the images they drew of her sealed her legend in the popular imagination, because their works were distributed throughout the United States. Translated into several languages, Gregg's *Commerce of the Prairies* was reprinted three times between 1844, when it first appeared, and 1857. Thousands of readers learned through him of the "certain female of very loose habits, known as La Tules."[26] What Gregg and the others could not communicate to their audience was that La Tules was adaptable, and that, before their eyes, she had begun disproving their notion that Spanish-Mexicans were "lazy and indolent."[27] She contradicted James Josiah Webb's contention that all Spanish-Mexicans did was "literally dance from the cradle to the grave."[28] Barceló's busy saloon hosted nightly fandangos, or dances, and their organizer easily became the target of Webb's manipulation of stereotype. Dancing, drinking, and gambling—the order was often changed according to how much the writer wanted to emphasize licentious behavior—gave these Protestant travelers pause, and they quickly made use of the observations to fictionalize Barceló's, and all women's, lives.

But the tales about La Tules are important in another respect. Fictitious representations marginalized Barceló because they shrouded her life in mystery and called forth several stereotypes about Mexicans. Yet Barceló was hardly the excessive woman the travelers depicted. Instead, she became pivotal in the achievement of their conquest. Worth thousands of dollars, supportive of the army, friendly to accommodating politicians, Barceló was in the right place to win over Spanish-Mexicans for the intruders. Using business and political skills, she made the saloon the hub of the town's social and economic life, and at the hall she kept abreast of the latest political developments. Politicians and military officers alike went there seeking her opinion, or involved her in their discussions about trade or the army.[29] As adviser and confidante, she took on a role few other women could have filled. If she existed on the fringes of a society, it was because she chose to place herself there—a woman with enormous foresight who pushed against her own community's barriers and risked being labeled by the travelers a madam or a whore.

Such caricatures denied her contributions to the economy and the society. Had she not been a gambler, a keeper of a saloon, or a woman, she might have been praised for her industry and resourcefulness, traits that antebellum Americans valued in their own people.[30] But from the point of view of the writers, the admirable qualities of a woman who lived by gambling and who was her own proprietor would have been lost on Protestant, middle-class readers. Furthermore, they could hardly imagine, let alone tolerate, the diversity Santa Fé exhibited. It became easier to reaffirm their guiding values and walk a literary tightrope by making La Tules a symbol of Spanish-Mexican degeneracy or an outcast altogether. Barceló had exceeded their wildest expectations, and in their eyes she was an outlaw.

Yet the aspersions heaped on Barceló were not designed solely to obscure her personality and life or to make her activities legendary. They created an image that fit the Euro-Americans' preconceptions about Spanish-Mexicans. Thus described to the readers, the image of Barceló in the travel documents merely confirmed older, pernicious stereotypes. Many recalled the *leyenda negra* (black legend) of the sixteenth century, when Spaniards were objectified as a fanatical, brutal people.[31] Historians and others have traced another critical stage in the development of anti-Mexican fervor to the antebellum period, when expansionist dreams and sentiments of such politicians as Senator Thomas Hart Benton gave rise to a continued confusion about Spanish-Mexican culture.[32] Not only travelers from the United States but residents in general harbored deep prejudices toward Spanish-Mexicans.[33] The travelers of the nineteenth century thus represented broader racial attitudes and demonstrated the ethnocentrism of a population back home.

Racial slurs and derogatory comments about Mexicans appeared regularly in the *Congressional Record*, in newspapers, and, not coincidentally, in travel accounts.[34] Speeches and statements consistently equated brown skin with promiscuity, immorality, and decay. Albert Pike, who arrived in New Mexico from New England in 1831, called the area around Santa Fé "bleak, black, and barren;"[35] New Mexicans, he said, were "peculiarly blessed with ugliness."[36] The chronicler of a military expedition to New Mexico in the 1840s, Frank Edwards, said that all Mexicans were "debased in all moral sense"[37] and amounted to little more than "swarthy thieves and liars."[38] The same judgments were made later, long after the war had ended, and reflect the persistence of the same thinking. The historian Francis Parkman argued that people in the West could be "separated into three divisions, arranged in order of their merits: white men, Indians, and Mexicans; to the latter of whom the honorable title of 'whites' is by no means conceded."[39] In the same period, William H. Emory of the boundary commission declared that the "darker colored" races were inevitably "inferior and syphilitic."[40]

These select references—and there are hundreds of other comments like them—describe a set of racist attitudes and ethnocentric beliefs from the Jacksonian period that carried into Santa Fé. Travelers thus mirrored the intrinsic values of a nation encroaching on Mexican territory, and were fueled by the heightened fervor over destiny and superiority.

Scholars have assessed the genre of travel guides and recollections as contributions to literature and have debated its special characteristics of construction, organization, and distortion.[41] But the books had something besides literary appeal; they sold rapidly in a country hungry for information about the West. Many planned visits and escapes to the healthier climates of the Southwest, while others intended to live in warmer areas and to find markets for their goods: such motives had inspired Gregg to leave Missouri for Santa Fé. Although he and his fellow adventurers were genuinely curious about Mexicans and about what the West had to offer, one important consequence of their visits, vacations, and reports, at least for Barceló, was that the migrants also brought capital to Santa Fé.[42] The accounts cannot, therefore, be considered only as travel literature; they do not, as some have argued, simply unveil anti-Mexican, anti-Catholic sentiment.[43] Rather, they describe—from the outside in, from the perspective of the colonizer—the systematic movement of an ethnocentric people to Santa Fé and reveal the interest in the promise of continued prosperity in the Southwest.

Travel writers of the nineteenth century, however, were also conscious of the desires and proclivities of their readers. Hence, these writers described the unsavory material culture (Matt Field gazed upon the adobe buildings and labeled Santa Fé's houses a testament to "the power of mud")[44] and the miserable conditions because they thought the objectionable portraits would suit their audience. Assessed today, the writers and their reflections continue to convey the overwhelmingly persistent attitudes, values, and ideas of a conquering group interpreting others. Except for a government official, Brantz Mayer, whose book indicted United States travelers by citing their prejudices against Mexicans, these writers mainly exhibited condescension and an implied, if not outspoken, sense of superiority.[45]

This uniformity in outlook is not the only characteristic binding these works and suggesting their significance in conquest. Many of the writers patterned their books after previously published accounts, such as Zebulon Pike's narrative of his reconnaissance trips in the early nineteenth century.[46] Imitating his organization and style, such writers as Gregg exaggerated La Tules's appearance, blamed her for the ruin of many "wayward youth," and imitated previous travelogues in other ways to portray and dismiss the wretched condition of the Spanish-Mexicans. Barceló's smoking and gambling were but two of the most widely reported vices. George Brewerton, writing for *Harper's Magazine* in the 1850s, continued the tradition. To the growing list of those at fault, he added the duplicitous New Mexican priests, for stifling individuality and stunting well-being:

> Here were the men, women, and children—the strong man, the mother, and the lisping child—all engaged in the most debasing of vices, gambling, the entire devotion to which is the besetting sin of the whole Mexican people. . . . What better could you have expected from an ignorant, priest-ridden peasantry, when those whom they are taught to reverence and respect, and who should have been their prompters to better things, not only allow, but openly practice this and all other iniquities?[47]

The popularity of gambling and drinking among all people prompted Brewerton and his predecessors to decry the pervasive debauchery—which, it seemed, only they, as Americans, could relieve. They failed to understand that Spanish-Mexicans loved celebration and socializing. The church organized parties, pageants, and social affairs on varied occasions; yet even officially sanctioned church holidays or the days when patron saints were honored did not escape Euro-American comments.[48] Brewerton found "rude engravings" of saints everywhere, among rich and poor, which he said would be "decked out by the females of the family with all sorts of tawdry ornaments."[49] He wondered about people who would use a doll to represent the Virgin Mary. Brewerton failed, in his rigid anti-Catholic viewpoint, to understand the beauty and intricacy of the *bultos* and *retablos* (icons and altarpieces). Catholicism, in Brewerton's opinion, did nothing but give Spanish-Mexicans occasion to revel in superstition, or to drink and dance. A community's way of celebrating—even the pious processions when the Virgin and the saints were paraded through town for all to worship in the annual outpouring of public devotion—was lost on Protestants: "During this whole time the city exhibited a scene of universal carousing and revelry. All classes abandoned themselves to the most reckless dissipation and profligacy. . . . I never saw a people so infatuated with the passion for gaming."[50] Whether commemorating saints or gathering for entertainment and diversion, Spanish-Mexicans appeared lascivious.

To the Protestant mind, nothing short of the complete elimination of gambling would lift New Mexicans out of their servility and make them worthy of United States citizenship. The Jacksonian Americans wanted to replace gambling with industry and enterprise. To them, gambling stemmed from a fundamental lack of faith in the individual, and it was risky besides. Travelers called monte a game of chance; they said that it required no particular skills and brought undeserved wealth.[51] By that logic, La Tules, a dealer par excellence, was not an entrepreneur; her wealth was undeserved because it sprang from "unbridled passions."[52] Her gravest sin against Protestant ethics became not the unskilled nature of her trade or her undeserved success, but her lack of restraint: her wealth was uncontrolled. Yet initial misgivings about Barceló and the games passed after many entertaining evenings at the gambling house. Once soldiers and others began going there, they lingered, and returned often.[53] Deep-seated anti-Mexican feelings and moralistic judgments gave way to the profits that awaited them if they won at monte, or the pleasures to be savored each evening in Santa Fé even if they lost.

At the numerous tables that lined Barceló's establishment, men who could not speak Spanish and people who did not understand English learned a new language. Card games required the deciphering of gestures and facial expressions but did not depend on any verbal communication. Soldiers and travelers new to Santa Fé understood easily enough what was important at the gaming table. Over cards, the men and women exchanged gold or currency in a ritual that emblazoned their meetings with new intentions. Drinking, cursing, and smoking, the soldiers and others unloaded their money at the table; if Barceló profited, they lost. But the game was such a diversion for the lonely soldiers that they hardly seemed to mind. The stakes grew larger at every turn, and many dropped away from the table to stand at the bar. Barceló's saloon took care of those who did not gamble as well as those who lost. Sometimes a group of musicians arrived and began playing. Sometimes women—who, if not gambling, had been observing the scene—cleared a space in the long room, and dancing began.[54]

Barceló did more than accommodate men by inviting them to gamble. She furthered their adjustment to Santa Fé by bringing them into a setting that required their presence and money. At the saloon, the men were introduced to Spanish-Mexican music, habits, and humor. They could judge the locals firsthand, and could observe a community's values and habits through this single activity. After they had a few drinks, their initial fears and prejudices gradually yielded to the relaxed, sociable atmosphere of the gambling hall.

In the spring of 1847, Lieutenant Alexander Dyer first visited the saloon. By June, his journal listed attendance at no fewer than forty fandangos and described numerous visits to La Tules's saloon. Frequently, cryptic citations indicated his rush to abandon the journal for the card games: "at the Me. House tonight" meant a visit to the monte house, and it appeared dozens of times in any given month.[55] Dyer's "Mexican War Journal" leaves the distinct impression that a soldier's life, for those of his stripe, involved a constant round of entertainment; visits and parties at Barceló's hall were part of an officer's busy social life.

Thus, rhetoric about gambling or cavorting lessened with time. If visitors did not entirely accept the sociable atmosphere, they were sufficiently lonely for Euro-American women and companionship to go to Barceló's saloon and attend other events to which they were invited. When Kearny and his officers went to Mass on their first Sunday in town, they endeared themselves to Spanish-Mexicans.[56] Some soldiers at the fort, like Dyer, had little choice but to adapt, because they were assigned to Santa Fé for two years. Other newcomers, however, were shocked into submission.

Finding much to upset them, visitors were nevertheless impressed by the scenic grandeur of Santa Fé and the environs. James Ohio Pattie remained as awed by Taos Mountain, stretching fifteen thousand feet high, as he was intrigued by the native life below it. He puzzled over differences: "I had expected to find no difference between these people and our own, but their language. I was never so mistaken. The men and women were not clothed in our fashion."[57]

Nine days later, Pattie reached Santa Fé, and this time his tone grew prosaic:

> The town contains between four and five thousand inhabitants. It is situated on a large plain. A handsome stream runs through it, adding life and beauty to a scene striking and agreeable from the union of amenity and cultivation around, with the distant view of snow clad mountains. It is pleasant to walk on the flat roofs of the houses in the evening, and look on the town and plain spread below.[58]

In a few weeks, Pattie had reached Chihuahua City, traveling the considerable distance in a short time. He described it as the "largest and handsomest town I had ever seen."[59] The trek across treacherous deserts, the long unbroken plain, and probably the fact that Spanish-Mexicans were much friendlier to him than Indians (whom he feared and loathed) changed Pattie's original reservations.

But travel records contain an underlying difficulty: they tend to freeze their author's thoughts in time, and do not reveal the extent of the adaptations or changes a writer might have experienced. Many travelers evidently did not find anything to admire or enjoy in Santa Fé, but some did. Although locked into a particular time and a special setting, the men, after consistent reflection and observation, relaxed their worst fears. Pattie's descriptions might not have been atypical in that regard.

Court cases offer other impressions of how sojourning Euro-Americans changed their organizing concepts and values. The evidence is especially suggestive for those who began making a transition to becoming settlers. In the 1820s, Julian Green was fined for gambling at monte; on the same day, the judge assessed a fine against Barceló.[60] In 1850, the census lists Green, with a woman named María, in a household containing six children; all have Spanish first names.[61] Another *vecino*, Marcelo Pacheco, sued William Messervy for slander in the 1840s, calling the merchant "a trespasser who thinks he owns everything."[62] He won his case, and Messervy had to pay a fine. Perhaps Green and Messervy were perplexed about Santa Fé's ways, as many migrants had been, but because they paid their fines and stayed in Santa Fé, they changed.

Investigations in these records delineate the onset of the newcomers' accommodation. Barceló was not the only one practicing accommodation; it worked in two directions. Whether obeying the community's laws or breaking them, new men were adjusting to life away from home. Santa Fé modified the settling Euro-Americans, at times even the sojourning ones, and Barceló had begun to socialize them in the traditions of an older settlement. The people of the Dancing Ground continued their practice of accepting newcomers, particularly those who seemed able to tolerate, if not embrace, the community's religious and secular values.

At the same time, the conquering soldiers were armed, as the merchants Gregg and Webb were, with purpose and commitment. Military men brought plans and realized them: a fort above the town was begun the day after Kearny marched into Santa Fé. Soldiers built a two-story-high flagstaff, and the imposing structure on the plaza attracted visitors from the Dancing Ground, who came supposedly to admire it, but probably also were there to assess the military's strength.[63] What better symbol than a new garrison and an obtrusive monument rising high for all the people to notice? Soldiers hailed these crowning achievements as signs of blessings from God to a nation destined to control the hemisphere, but locals were not so pleased.

A new wave of resistance derailed Barceló's efforts to help resettle Euro-Americans in Santa Fé. Nevertheless, even after her death in 1852, Barceló's legend continued to indicate that her role extended beyond the immediate helping hand she had lent Euro-Americans. No documents written by her, except a will, have survived to tell whether she even recognized her accomplishment, or if she read much into the assistance she had given the American cause. Her wealth would suggest that she might have harbored an understanding of her influential status in the process of colonization. One fact remains, whether she realized it or not: beginning with her, the accommodation of Euro-Americans proceeded on several levels. Barceló had inaugurated the first, at the gambling hall, and she set the stage as well for the second, when women began marrying the newcomers.

But as one retraces the original surrounding tensions—deriving from the steady and continuing presence of traders, merchants, and soldiers—and juxtaposes them against Barceló's achievement as an architect of a plan that reconciled the Euro-American to Santa Fé, the realities of displacement and encroachment must not be forgotten. Lieutenant Dyer reported problems as he observed them, and he commented a year after his arrival in Santa Fé: "Still it began to be apparent that the people generally were dissatisfied with the change."[64] In January 1847, resisters in Taos caught and scalped Governor Charles Bent, leaving him to die.[65] In the spring, a lieutenant who had been pursuing horse thieves was murdered, and forty-three Spanish-Mexicans were brought to Santa Fé to stand trial for the crime.[66] In October of the same year, some months after several revolts had been suppressed and their instigators hanged, Dyer reported "a large meeting of citizens at the Palace," where speakers expressed "disaffection at the course of the commissioned officers."[67]

Local dissatisfaction and political troubles had not subsided, in spite of Barceló's work. In the late 1840s, Navajos and Apaches stepped up their raids, and reports filtered in of surrounding mayhem.[68] The garrisoned soldiers grew impatient and acted rashly, and Dyer reported that "a Mexican was unfortunately shot last night by the sentinel at my store house. Tonight we have a rumor that the Mexicans are to rise and attack us."[69] The government in Santa Fé was being forced again to come to terms with each new case of racial and cultural conflict, because it was still charged with trying murders and treason, and it had now become the seat for initiating solutions. Problems no longer brewed outside; they had been brought home by accommodated Euro-Americans.

But Barceló should not be blamed here, as she has been by some, for so many problems. She symbolized the transformations plaguing her people. She symbolized as well how an older community had handled the arrival of men from a new, young nation still seeking to tap markets and find a route to the Pacific. Moreover, she exemplified contact and conflict between independent female Catholics and westering male Protestants. The political and social constraints within which she existed had not disappeared as a community contemplated what to do with the strangers among them.

The people of Santa Fé did not kill any newcomers as residents of Taos had. Surrounding the Dancing Ground, stories and legends of other people resisting Americanization were about to begin, and these no longer emphasized accommodation. Barceló was unusual in that way as well. She was of a particular time and a special place. The famed resister to American encroachment, Padre Antonio José Martínez of Taos, opposed (in his separatist plans and principles) all that Barceló had exemplified. A legend developed around him that stands in interesting contrast to La Tules's.[70]

Yet, in New Mexico and throughout the West, resistance was giving way to Euro-American encroachment. Richard Henry Dana, traveling in California during the 1830s, mourned the seemingly wasted opportunity presented by land still in the possession of Spanish-Mexicans: "In the hands of an enterprising people, what a country this might be!"[71] His fellow sojourners to New Mexico concurred. What Dana and the other Euro-Americans failed to see was that the land and its communities were already in the hands of such enterprising persons as Barceló. But rather than acknowledge the truth, they disparaged her; their conquerors' minds could not comprehend her intellect, enterprise, and success. Barceló, they believed, had erred. Yet in giving herself to the conquest, but not the conquerors, she survived and succeeded. She drew betting clients to her saloon; they played but lost, she gambled and won. In the end, the saloon that attracted conquerors released men who had been conquered.

Notes

1. Josiah Gregg, *The Commerce of the Prairies*, ed. Max Moorhead (Norman: University of Oklahoma Press, 1964), pp. 105–106. (Originally published 1844.)
2. Fray Angélico Chávez, "Doña Tules: Her Fame and Her Funeral," *El Palacio* 62 (August 1950), pp. 227–234; Janet Lecompte, "The Independent Women of Hispanic New Mexico, 1821–1846," *Western Historical Quarterly* 22 (January 1981), pp. 25–26.
3. Stella Drumm, ed., *The Diary of Susan Shelby Magoffin 1846–1847: Down the Santa Fé Trail and into Mexico* (Lincoln: University of Nebraska Press, 1982), p. 145.

4. Tules was the diminutive for Gertrudis. See Marc Simmons, *The Little Lion of the Southwest: A Life of Manuel Antonio Cháves* (Chicago: University of Chicago Press, 1983), p. 55.

5. Gregg, *Commerce of the Prairies*, p. 168.

6. Howard R. Lamar, *Far Southwest* (New York: Norton, 1970), p. 55.

7. On the church, see "Zubiría Pastoral," 1840, Archives of the Archdiocese of Santa Fé, Coronado Collection, University of New Mexico, microfilm, LDD, no. 2; and "Bishop Zubiría's Visitation," 1845, Archives of the Archdiocese of Santa Fé, box 4, book 89.

8. Gregg, *Commerce of the Prairies*, pp. 168–169.

9. See Trinidad Barceló, June 9, 1825, Probate Court Journals, Mexican Archives of New Mexico, New Mexico State Records Center, microfilm, roll 26, frame 187.

10. Janet Lecompte, "La Tules and the Americans," *Arizona and the West* (Autumn 1978), p. 220.

11. Drumm, *Diary of Susan Shelby Magoffin*, p. 120.

12. For Gregg's comments, see *Commerce of the Prairies*, pp. 168–169; for other comments, see William Clark Kennedy, *Persimmon Hill: A Narrative of St. Louis and the Far West* (Norman: University of Oklahoma Press, 1948), p. 191; and John E. Sunder, ed., *Matt Field on the Santa Fé Trail* (Norman: University of Oklahoma Press, 1960), p. 206.

13. Sunder, *Matt Field*, p. 209.

14. For comparison, see Table 6.2 in Angelina F. Veyna, " 'It is My Last Wish That . . .' A Look at Colonial Nuevo Mexicanas through their Testaments," in *Building With Our Hands: Directions in Chicana Scholarship*, eds. Beatríz Pesquera and Adela dé la Torre (Berkeley: University of California Press, 1993), p. 95.

15. Will of Gertrudis Barceló, Santa Fé County Records, Wills and Testaments, 1848–1856, book A–1, p. 154.

16. John Galvin, ed., *Western America in 1846–1847: The Original Travel Diary of Lieutenant J.W. Abert, Who Mapped New Mexico for the United States Army* (San Francisco: J. Howell, 1966), p. 75; see Abert's report in *Senate Executive Document* no. 23, 29th Cong., 1st sess.

17. Gregg, *Commerce of the Prairies*, pp. 168–169.

18. Ramón Arturo Gutiérrez, in a paper presented at the annual meeting of the Western Historical Association, Salt Lake City, October 12, 1984.

19. See Lecompte, "La Tules," p. 222, and the source, Complaint of Ana María Rendón to the alcalde, Probate Court Journals, 1835, roll 20.

20. Complaint of Ana María Rendón.

21. Lecompte, "La Tules," p. 222; for recantations, see Complaint against José Tenório, January 15, 1828, and November 14, 1829, Probate Court Journals, roll 8, frame 310; Petition of Juan Francisco Gonzales, Probate Court Journals, 1829, roll 10, frame 177.

22. Gertrudis Barceló, June 9, 1825, Probate Court Journals, roll 26, frame 186.

23. On the issues of illegitimacy and legitimacy, see Ramón Arturo Gutiérrez, "Marriage, Sex and the Family: Social Change in Colonial New Mexico, 1690–1846," Ph.D. diss., University of Wisconsin-Madison, 1980. For examples of the church's stance on legitimacy and baptism, see Books of Baptisms, 1826–1841, Archives of the Archdiocese of Santa Fé, New Mexico State Records Center, microfilm.

24. On the Far West, see George M. Blackburn and Sherman L. Richards, "The Prostitutes and Gamblers of Virginia City, Nevada: 1870," *Pacific Historical Review* 48, no. 2 (May 1979), pp. 239–258; and Lawrence B. de Graaf, "Race, Sex and Region: Black Women in the American West, 1850–1920," *Pacific Historical Review* 49, no. 2 (May 1980), pp. 285–313. For earlier periods and for women of two different worlds, see Adelaida del Castillo, "Malintzín Tenépal: A Preliminary Look into a New Perspective," in *Essays on La Mujer*, eds. Rosaura Sánchez and Rosa Martínez Cruz (Los Angeles: Chicano Studies Research Center, University of California, 1977), pp. 124–149; and Marina Warner, *Joan of Arc: The Image of Female Heroism* (New York: Knopf, 1981).

25. For speeches, see Kearny's in Ralph Emerson Twitchell, *The Story of the Conquest of Santa Fé: New Mexico and the Building of Old Fort Marcy, A.D. 1846* (Santa Fe: Historical Society of New Mexico, 1923), p. 30; for another, see *Santa Fe Republican*, January 22, 1848; and for an earlier version of the same ideas but espoused in the United States, see *Richmond Enquirer*, May 11, 1847; for a report and discussion on the benefits a railroad would bring, see the *Western Journal*, vol. 1, p. 260, and the *Richmond Daily Union*, May 13, 1847.

26. Gregg, *Commerce of the Prairies*, p. 168.

27. Waddy Thompson, *Recollections of Mexico* (New York: Wiley and Putnam, 1846), p. 23.

28. James Josiah Webb, "Memoirs, 1844–1889," Museum of New Mexico, History Library, Santa Fe, manuscript, p. 46; James Ohio Pattie, *The Personal Narrative of James O. Pattie, of Kentucky* (Ann Arbor: University of Michigan Press, 1966), p. 120 (originally published 1831).

29. Simmons, *Little Lion*, p. 55; for the officers at the game of monte, see Walter Briggs, "The Lady They Called Tules," *New Mexico Magazine* 39 (1971), pp. 9–16.

68 / Deena J. González

30. For an overview, see Edward Pessen, *Jacksonian America: Society, Personality and Politics* (Homewood, Ill,: Row, Peterson, 1969). For criticism of the attendant values, see Herman Melville, *The Confidence-Man: His Masquerade* (New York: New American Library, 1964; originally published 1857); for an interpretation of the novel, see Roy Harvey Pearce, "Melville's Indian Hater: A Note on the Meaning of 'The Confidence-Man,'" *Publications of the Modern Language Association* 67 (1952), pp. 942–948.

31. The legend's origins have been traced to several sources, among them Bartolomé de las Casas, *In Defense of the Indians*, trans. Stafford Poole (De Kalb: Northern Illinois University Press, 1974). For other arguments about the origins, see Stanley T. Williams, *The Spanish Background of American Literature* (New York: Shoe String Press, 1968), and Philip Wayne Powell, *Tree of Hate: Propaganda and Prejudices Affecting United States Social Relations with the Hispanic World* (New York: Basic Books, 1971).

32. Thomas Hart Benton, Speech on the Oregon Question, May 28, 1846, Senate Document, *Congressional Globe*, 29th Cong., 1st sess., pp. 915, 917.

33. For earlier statements, see Joel Roberts Poinsett, *Notes on Mexico Made in the Autumn of 1822* (New York: Praeger, 1969), pp. 40, 120–122 (originally published 1824); for a detailed survey of attitudes toward Mexicans, see Philip Anthony Hernández, "The Other Americans: The American Image of Mexico and Mexicans, 1550–1850," Ph.D. diss., University of California, Berkeley, 1974.

34. Dr. Adolphus Wislizenus, "Memoir of a Tour to Northern Mexico," *Senate Miscellaneous Document*, 30th Cong., 1st sess., pp. 2–3. For an example of an anti-Mexican travel account in Texas, see Mary Austin Holley, *Observations, Historical, Geographical, and Descriptive* (Austin: University of Texas Press, 1935), p. 128 (originally published 1833); in California, see Alfred Robinson, *Life in California* (New York: Da Capo, 1969), p. 73 (originally published 1846).

35. Albert Pike, *Prose Sketches and Poems, Written in the Western Country with Additional Stories*, ed. David Weber (Albuquerque: University of New Mexico Press, 1967), p. 7.

36. *Ibid.*, p. 275. For a Euro-American woman's reactions during visits to Santa Fe, see Jane Austin, Letter to her "Dear Brother," October 23, 1846, Museum of New Mexico, History Library, Santa Fe, box 4, p. 1.

37. Frank S. Edwards, *A Campaign in New Mexico with Colonel Doniphan* (Philadelphia: Carey and Hart, 1847), p. 132.

38. *Ibid.*, p. 50.

39. Francis Parkman, *The California and Oregon Trail: Being Sketches of Prairie and Rocky Mountain Life . . .* (New York: Putnam, 1849), p. 360.

40. W. H. Emory, "Notes of a Military Reconnaissance from Fort Leavenworth, in Missouri, to San Diego, in California . . . Made in 1846–7, with the Advanced Guard of the Army of the West," *House Executive Document* no. 41, 30th Cong., 1st sess., p. 110.

41. Mabel Major, Rebecca Smith, and T. M. Pearce, *Southwest Heritage: A Literary History with Bibliography* (Albuquerque: University of New Mexico Press, 1938). For deciphering distortion, see Robert A. LeVine and Donald Campbell, *Ethnocentrism: Theories of Conflict, Ethnic Attitudes, and Group Behavior* (New York: Wiley, 1972).

42. Richard Onofre Ulibarri, "American Interest in the Spanish-Mexican Southwest, 1803–1848," Ph.D. diss., University of Utah, 1963, p. 80.

43. Ray Allen Billington, *The Protestant Crusade, 1800–1860: A Study of the Origins of American Nativism* (1938; rpt. Gloucester, Mass.: Peter Smith, 1963), pp. 75, 223–230. For a comment by Webb, see Ralph Bieber, ed., *Adventures in the Santa Fe Trade, 1844–1847, by James Josiah Webb* (Glendale, Ca.: Arthur H. Clark, 1931), p. 102.

44. Sunder, *Matt Field*, p. 194.

45. Brantz Mayer, *Mexico, as It Was and as It Is* (Philadelphia: G. B. Zieber, 1847); for an example of an observer who vacillated in his opinions about Mexicans, see Abiel Abbot Livermore, *The War with Mexico Reviewed* (Boston: American Peace Society, 1850).

46. Susan Reyner Kenneson, "Through the Looking-Glass: A History of Anglo-American Attitudes towards the Spanish-Americans and Indians of New Mexico," Ph.D. diss., Yale University, 1978, p. 130.

47. George Brewerton, "Incidents of Travel in New Mexico," *Harper's Magazine* 47 (April 1854), p. 589.

48. Gregg, *Commerce of the Prairies*, pp. 173, 179–180.

49. Brewerton, "Incidents," p. 578.

50. Thomas James, *Three Years among the Indians and Mexicans* (Philadelphia: Lippincott, 1962), pp. 88–89 (originally published 1916).

51. Gregg, *Commerce of the Prairies*, pp. 167–168.

52. Brewerton, "Incidents," p. 588.

53. Alexander B. Dyer, "Mexican War Journal, 1846–1848," Museum of New Mexico, History Library, manuscript, pp. 80–81, 84, 118–119.

54. "Gen. Kearny and the Army of the West: Extracts from the Journal of Lieut. Emory," *Niles National Register* 71 (November 7, 1846), p. 158.

55. Dyer, "Mexican War Journal," p. 96.

56. Drumm, *Diary of Susan Shelby Magoffin*, p. 138; for an example of the continuing partnership between the church and the military, see the inauguration of Governor David Meriwether in Gunther Barth, *Instant Cities: Urbanization and the Rise of San Francisco and Denver* (New York: Oxford University Press, 1975), p. 70.

57. Pattie, *Narrative*, p. 41.

58. *Ibid.*, p. 44.

59. *Ibid.*, p. 110.

60. Testimony of Julian Green, June 9, 1825, Probate Court Journals, roll 20, frame 188.

61. United States Bureau of the Census, Seventh Census of Population, for Santa Fe, 1850 (microfilm, New Mexico State Records Center).

62. Complaint of Marcelo Pacheco, April 11, 1846, Probate Court Journals, roll 32, frame 185. See also the Euro-Americans fined for "making fandangos without licenses," Jury Book, 1848–1856, Probate Court Journal, Santa Fe County Records, pp. 137–140.

63. James Madison Cutts, *The Conquest of California and New Mexico by the Forces of the United States in the Years 1846–1847* (Philadelphia: Carey and Hart, 1947), p. 84.

64. Alexander Dyer to Robert Johnston, February 14, 1847, Museum of New Mexico, History Library, box 4, p. 2.

65. Lamar, *Far Southwest*, p. 68.

66. Dyer to Johnston, February 14, 1847, pp. 2–3.

67. Dyer, "Mexican War Journal," p. 97.

68. *Ibid.*, p. 62; on Navajo and Apache raids, see David J. Weber, *The Mexican Frontier, 1821–1846: The American Southwest under Mexico* (Albuquerque: University of New Mexico Press, 1982), pp. 92–93.

69. Dyer, "Mexican War Journal," p. 82.

70. On Martínez's activities, see Lamar, *Far Southwest*, p. 72; on the legend, see E. K. Francis, "Padre Martínez: A New Mexico Myth," *New Mexico Historical Review* 31 (October 1956), pp. 265–289; for a short biography, see Pedro Sánchez, "Memorias sobre la vida del presbitero don Antonio José Martínez," in *Northern Mexico on the Eve of the United States Invasion*, ed. David Weber (New York: Arno Press, 1976); in the same collection, see "Historia consisa del cura de Taos Antonio José Martínez" (originally published in *El Historiador*, May 4, 1861).

71. Richard Henry Dana, *Two Years Before the Mast* (New York: New American Library, 1864), p. 136. (Originally published 1840.)

6

Native American Women and Agriculture: A Sencca Case Study

Joan M. Jensen

At the time Europeans first arrived in North America, and for centuries after, Native American women dominated agricultural production in the tribes of the eastern half of the United States.[1] In many of these tribes, the work of the women provided over half of the subsistence and secured for them not only high status but also public power. Yet this immense contribution to the economy and to the culture of the Native Americans has never been studied systematically by historians. We have no complete history of Indian agriculture.[2] We have no study of how women functioned in these agricultural societies. We do not know what happened to the women and their agricultural production under the impact of the Europeans' invasion (Carrier, 1923; Holder, 1970; Terrell & Terrell, 1974; Wallace, 1970; Will & Hyde, 1917). Using the Seneca women, I would like to provide a prototype of what we can learn about the history of Native American women and agriculture.

Several theories have recently been presented by anthropologists to describe the status of women. Peggy Sanday (1973, 1974) has suggested that there is a high correlation between female status and a balanced division of labor and that women do not develop public power unless some of their energies are employed in economic production. Judith Brown (1970a, 1970b) has argued that women must not only produce in agricultural societies but must also control the means of production—land, seeds, tools—and the methods of work to achieve public power. The history of the Seneca women seems to confirm both these theories and also to show that this power, once achieved, was difficult to dislodge even by the combined efforts of missionaries, government, and reformers.

Unfortunately, we have no verbatim transcripts from early Native American women about agricultural production. Our only account is by Buffalo Woman, a Hidatsa who provided a lengthy description of the philosophy and techniques of agriculture in 1912. Buffalo Woman spent over a year with an anthropologist in North Dakota demonstrating in minute detail the cultivation, planting, and hoeing process. She described the cooperative work groups of the women and sang their work songs. Her account conveys a feeling of the pride and care with which Native American women performed their work. But to develop a picture of the community power women derived from this agricultural production, and the struggle to maintain that power under the impact of change, we must turn to the records of those who were the agents of change. If used critically, these records provide a starting point for the study of Native American women and agriculture (Wilson, 1917).

When White colonists arrived in the seventeenth century they found many of the best

Reprinted by permission of the author and Plenum Publishing Corporation. Originally published in *Sex Roles: A Journal of Research*, vol. 3, 1977.

bottomlands near creeks and rivers cleared, sometimes abandoned, but often filled with the neat and clean corn fields of the Native American women. An early account by Roger Williams told of the "very loving sociable speedy way" in which men and women joined together to clear fields, and how women planted, weeded, hilled, gathered, and stored the corn. In some areas, tribal women had as many as 2,000 acres under cultivation and in most areas they had accumulated surpluses which were traded to hungry settlers (Carrier, 1923). Colonists were often more interested in commerce than in laborious clearing and planting, and even when engaged in agriculture many were not careful farmers. Records mention that Native American women sometimes ridiculed colonists for neglecting to keep their fields well weeded.

At first colonists occupied abandoned fields or purchased cleared fields from the Native Americans. War soon added a third method by which the colonists obtained fields. "Now," said Edward Waterhouse after the Indian attack of 1622 in Virginia, "their cleared grounds in all their villages (which are situated in the fruitfullest places of the land) shall be inhabited by us, whereas heretofore the grubbing of woods was the greatest labour" (quoted by Washburn, 1971). During the next 300 years the Native American agricultural societies underwent a drastic transformation as trade, warfare, and disease disrupted their subsistence economies. The Seneca, like other tribes, felt the impact of these disruptions on their economy.

The foremothers of the Seneca were among the women of the League of the Iroquois whose well-tended fields surrounded their western New York villages, and whose origin myth began with a female deity falling from the sky to give birth to the first woman. Sky Woman brought earth, seeds, and roots from which wild trees, fruits, and flowers grew. The domestic plants—potatoes, beans, squash, corn, and other crops—sprang from the grave of Sky Woman's daughter. Later, according to several corn legends, the Corn Maiden brought corn to the Seneca, taught the women how to plant, how to prepare the corn, how to dance the corn dances, and which songs to sing at the dances. Seneca women believed that a great power pervaded all nature and endowed every element with intelligence. Each clod of soil, each tree, each stalk of corn, had life and consciousness. At a winter ceremony each year the women gave thanks for every object in nature. At springtime they offered thanks to the sap and sugar from the maple trees, which they made into syrup. Later there were planting feasts, a June strawberry feast, then a corn feast, and finally completing the cycle, a harvest feast. The purpose of these feasts was to show that life was desired and that the people were thankful for it (Hewitt, 1918; Parker, 1923, 1926).

Seneca family life centered on the longhouse, a joint tenement shared by families of kin, the entire clan household being composed of as many as fifty or sixty people. The domestic economy of each household was regulated by an older woman who distributed household stores to families and guests. Households were clustered in compact villages of twenty to thirty houses or in larger towns of 100 to 150 houses. The more densely populated towns usually shifted location every ten years; the smaller towns might occupy the same site for twenty years or more. These compact towns proved particularly vulnerable to seventeenth-century disease and warfare. In 1668, for example, almost 250 people in one town died of disease, and, in one month in 1676, sixty small children in another town died from pneumonia. The French destroyed large Seneca towns in 1687 and 1696 (Hawley, 1884; Morgan, 1965).

Communal living, as practiced by the Seneca, provided stable care for all the children of the village. Children inherited their property and place in the clan through their mothers; and women who were childless or had few children adopted any orphan children. Seneca women showed extraordinary affection for their children, as one of the earliest Jesuit visitors observed in 1668, and children had great respect for their parents. Elders in the longhouse shared the responsibility of teaching children necessary physical and social survival skills. After their mothers had arranged their marriage, a young couple traditionally joined one of the mothers' communal households.[3] In no case did the couple set up a separate nuclear family. According to early Jesuit accounts, most marriages were monogamous, but a few Seneca women had two husbands. If husbands were absent too long or failed to provide their share of subsistence for the household, the woman would take another marriage partner (Hawley, 1884; Lafitau, 1724).

Seneca women had possessory rights to all cultivated land within the tribal area. The women's clans distributed the land to households according to their size, and organized farming communally. Each year, the women of the town elected a chief matron who directed the work. Sick and injured members of these mutual aid societies had a right to assistance in planting and harvesting; and after hoeing the owner of each parcel of land would provide a feast for all the women workers. According to Mary Jemison, the Irish captive who spent the second half of the eighteenth century with Seneca women, their work was less onerous than that of White women (Seaver, 1824). They had no drivers or overseers and worked in the fields as leisurely as they wished with their children beside them. The women formed *Toñwisas*, ritual groups to encourage the good favor of the "three sisters"—corn, beans, and squash. The leaders of these groups performed rites, carrying armfuls of corn and loaves of corn bread around a kettle of corn soup. After harvest, women braided or stored the corn in corncribs or shelled and stored it in bark barrels. Women later ground the corn in large oak mortars with four-foot-long maple wood pestles. The rhythmic sound of the women grinding corn was the first sound heard in the villages each morning (Parker, 1968b; Seaver, 1824).

Seneca women also controlled the distribution of surplus food and—by virtue of the right to demand captives as replacement for murdered kinspeople—often influenced warfare. The matrilineal Seneca women retained a powerful position in the community through control of land and agriculture. Women had their own councils and were represented in the council of the civil rulers by a male speaker, the most famous of whom was Red Jacket. Women also had the power to elect the civilian rulers and to depose those guilty of misconduct, incompetence, or disregard of the public welfare (Parker, 1952; Wallace, 1970).

By the 1780s the Senecas had already experienced the most common disruptions of agricultural village life: warfare, disease, and trade. The Seneca were one of the League of Six Nations who supported the British, in part because the American revolutionaries offered them no guarantee of the peaceful possession of their territory. In August 1779, on General Washington's orders, American troops under John Sullivan laid waste to the Seneca lands. By army estimates, they uprooted, girdled, or chopped down 1,500 orchard trees; destroyed 60,000 bushels of corn, 2,000 to 3,000 bushels of beans, and cucumbers, watermelons, and pumpkins in such quantities, one major recalled, as to be "almost incredible to a civilized people" (Parker, 1968b). An estimated 500 acres of cultivated crops were destroyed, along with forty large towns and villages of communal longhouses. The warriors fled to the protection of the British and the women and children hid in the forests. Although Washington had urged the capture of women as well as men, none were taken, and the refugees crowded into Fort Niagara that winter where the British furnished meat and rations. The next spring the Seneca women returned to plant corn, potatoes, and pumpkins along the bottoms of the south side of Buffalo Creek at the eastern tip of Lake Erie and made maple sugar in their old way. Smallpox ravaged the communities the following year, however, and deaths led to demoralization and loss of confidence. The corn supply again was exhausted and the people applied to Fort Niagara for supplies. The officer at Fort Niagara complained that the Seneca had improvident habits but he sent the supplies (Fenton, 1956; G. H. Harris, 1903; Houghton, 1920).

By 1789, trade had also drastically altered the women's way of life. They now had iron and steel hoes, awls, needles, shears, and cloth. Women has substituted cloth for fur garments and beads for porcupine quills in much of their decorated work. The estimated contact population of 10,000 had been reduced to several thousand survivors. There were about 2,000 in western New York along the Buffalo and Cazenovia creeks clustered in three or four villages.

Women retained their political power, however. When Washington sent Colonel Proctor to obtain the support of the Seneca in negotiating with other tribes in May 1791, the women intervened to urge peaceful negotiation. It was a time of crisis for the Seneca. Warriors had just brought in an Indian scalp with the story that White people were making war. The rulers had met in council and refused to negotiate. Next morning the elder women appeared before Colonel Proctor's lodge, where he was talking with a number of chiefs, and announced that they had considered his proposition:

> you ought to hear and listen to what we, women shall speak, as well as to the sachems; for *we are the owners of this land,*—and it is ours. It is we that plant it for our and their use. Hear us, therefore, for we speak of things that concern us while our men shall say more to you; for we have told them. (quoted by Stone, 1841, p. 56)

Later that day the council reassembled and Red Jacket, the spokesman for the women, announced that the women were "to conclude what ought to be done by both sachems and warriors," and that the women had decided that for the good of them and their children a peace delegation would be sent (Stone, 1841).

Women also spoke during the negotiations of the Treaty of 1794 with the United States government. In 1797 they still had a dominant voice. When Thomas Morris arrived in August of that year to negotiate a land sale for his father, the women again vetoed the decision of the sachems and insisted, "It is we, the women, who own the land" (quoted by Parker, 1952). Morris promised the women that if they agreed to the treaty, they would never again know want. Warriors often went to White settlements to sell furs and buy foods while the women and children might go hungry, he reminded them. He said that the $100,000 offered to them for the land could be put in a bank so that "in times of scarcity, the women and children of your nation can be fed." The warriors supported the treaty, because Morris promised that hunting rights would not be impaired. To the women Morris offered special gifts and a string of wampum to remind them—should they turn down the offer and then become impoverished—of the wealth they had rejected.

Certainly, this was economic pressure of the rankest kind, and yet, given the difficult circumstances, it is easy to see why the women decided to sell the land. Morris's tactics were successful. "This had an excellent effect on the women [who] at once declared themselves for selling, and the business began to wear a better aspect," Morris wrote in his journal (quoted by Parker, 1952).

Government and speculators had reduced the land of the women. The way was now open for teachers and missionaries to end women's domination over agriculture. The Quakers had dispatched their first mission to the Seneca in 1789 to teach the men agriculture and the women "useful arts," but the people exhibited little interest. Two years later a Seneca leader appealed to Washington to teach the men how to plow and the women to spin and weave. Washington sent a teacher; and the Secretary of State, Timothy Pickering, urged the Six Nations to fence their lands, raise livestock, and farm "as white people do" (Howland, 1903). Buffalo Creek and other villages refused to admit teachers or missionaries.

The leader who appealed to Washington for technical assistance was Cornplanter, who was not a traditional chief.[4] He spoke only for his own village on the Allegheny River; there he exercised unusual power because he had received personal title to the land for negotiating the sale of Indian lands to Pennsylvania (Parker, 1927). The Quakers were quick to accept Cornplanter's invitation and soon arrived at the Allegheny village ready to retrain both men and women. At this time women were tending the fields and men were trading furs. The women refused to appear, though the Quakers specifically asked to talk to them. To the men, the Quakers proposed an incentive system, promising to pay cash to men who would raise wheat, rye, corn, potatoes, and hay, and to women who would spin thread from flax and wool. Later the Quakers conducted an experiment to prove that plowed fields produced a greater yield than fields hoed by women. It was "unreasonable" the Quakers argued, to allow mothers, wives, and sisters to work all day in the fields and woods, and men to "play" with bows and arrows. The men warned the Quakers not to expect too much (Deardorff & Snyderman, 1956).

The Reverend Elkanah Holmes (1903) reported that the Tuscarora tribe of the Iroquois told him in 1800 that among the Senecas and the western tribes women did all the field work. Among the Tuscarora, the men had already begun to substitute agricultural work for hunting and Holmes reported them at work in the fields alongside the women planting, hoeing, and harvesting corn. In 1801, however, the Seneca requested oxen to plow with and spinning wheels. By 1804, a Quaker reported a large plow at work in a Seneca village above Buffalo Creek drawn by three yoke of oxen and attended by three Native American men; he reported considerable "progress" in agriculture (Holmes, 1903).

At Allegheny two Quaker women soon began to teach spinning and weaving, and in 1806 Seneca women promised to take up these White women's arts. Gayantgogwus, sister of Cornplanter and one of the most influential persons in the community, brought her granddaughter and another young relative to show visiting Quakers how they could knit and spin. The Quakers urged the men to spread out their farms, arguing that it was better for farming and cattle raising to be separated. The Quakers also introduced wheat and other new crops. Already 100 families had chosen to fence their farms individually and to embrace the nuclear family, while 30 new homes clustered at Cold Springs (Deardorff & Snyderman, 1956; Visit of Gerald T. Hopkins, 1903; Wallace, 1970).

We do not know what prompted women at Allegheny to adopt their new role so quickly. Brazilian women, moving more recently from a women's work group to a shared work situation with men, have explained that they wanted to share the burden of supplying food more equally with men whose ability to hunt had decreased with the decline in game. They also wanted the benefits in consumer goods which a cash income would bring. Among the Seneca women, there was a split. Some of the older women saw the change as a threat to their strong position in the community and reasserted their traditional powers against the divisive new economy and way of life being forced upon them. Old women advised their daughters to use contraceptives and abortion and, if necessary, to leave husbands who took up the new ways. Handsome Lake, who had recently replaced Cornplanter as the new chief of the League of the Iroquois, attacked the older women. "The Creator is sad because of the tendency of old women to breed mischief," he warned. He accused them of witchcraft (Murphy & Murphy, 1974; Parker, 1968a).

Witchcraft accusations occur when social relations are ambiguous and tensions cannot otherwise be resolved. They are often an instrument for breaking off relations or withdrawing community protection from certain individuals (Douglas, 1970). The older Seneca women formed a rival faction to the changes which Cornplanter, Handsome Lake, and the Quakers wished to institute, and a power block which Handsome Lake wished to break. The accusations split the ranks of the women still further and realigned some in support of the new system and its leaders. Handsome Lake made many accusations among the Senecas and, though he opposed them, some executions did occur. In a few cases, accusations were followed with trials by council and swift execution. One old woman was reported cut down while at work in her corn field in 1799. Another was reported executed on the spot after a council decided on her guilt. Four of the "best women in the nation" narrowly escaped execution at Sandusky when the executioners refused to carry out the sentence. Probably not many old women died but the lesson was clear (Houghton, 1920; Smith, 1988; Wallace, 1970).

As Handsome Lake, Cornplanter, and the Quakers asserted their influence more clearly over the village of Allegheny and its agricultural pattern, the witchcraft accusations ceased. Handsome Lake became the prophet of the supremacy of the husband-wife relationship over the mother-daughter relationship. Men were to harvest food for their families, build good houses, keep horses and cattle; women were to be good housewives. By 1813 Seneca women were operating spinning wheels, and two Seneca men, trained by the Quakers as village weavers, turned out 200 yards of linen and wool cloth that year. Well pleased with the transition at Allegheny, the Quakers estimated that the average farm had ten acres, horses or oxen, cows, and pigs. In 1821, a painted box sent from the first school portrayed Seneca girls learning to spin and weave with quotes from the Bible above their busy activity: "She layeth her hands to the spindle, and hands hold the distaff . . . . She looketh well to her household and eateth not the bread of Idleness" (Fenton, 1956; Wallace, 1970).

While Allegheny seemed a model agricultural village and thus—the Quakers hoped— on its way to eventual Christianity, the villages at Buffalo Creek were still in crisis. During 1818 to 1822, there was an outbreak of witchcraft accusations at Buffalo Creek and women were executed there and at Tuscarora. Like the women of Allegheny, the older women of these communities seemed to be opposing the new order. Jabez Backus Hyde, a Presbyterian schoolteacher, reported from Buffalo Creek in 1820 that

> Their ancient manner of subsistence is broken up and when they appear willing and desirous to turn their attention to agriculture, their ignorance, the inveteracy of their old habits, and disadvantage under which they labor, soon discourage them; though they struggle hard little is realized to their benefit, besides the continual dread they live in of losing their possessions. If they build they know not who will inhabit. If they make fields they know not who will cultivate them. They know the anxiety of their white neighbors to get possession of their lands. (Hyde, 1903, 215).

When the New York Missionary Society requested that a mission be established at Buffalo Creek, the Seneca there called a council to debate the matter. Men and women, converts and traditionalists, agreed to allow a mission to be established, and in 1819 the first evangelical minister arrived to preach and teach. Subsidized by the government to teach agriculture to the boys and instructed by the mission society to teach all the children to work and be industrious, the new school attempted to teach girls to knit and sew. But the little girls proved especially troublesome and, when disciplined, complained to their parents. Complaints brought objections by the chiefs and a request that the children be persuaded and coaxed into obedience and, if disobedient, left to the parent to reprove. If all else failed, the child could be considered heathen and expelled. Such a doctrine of education was unacceptable, the Reverend T. S. Harris (1903) confided to his journal, because "the rod is the plan of God's own appointment."

Despite Harris' severity with the young girls, the school supplied a new community focus to replace the old communal activities being destroyed by fences and isolated farming.

A group of older non-Christian women soon appeared before Harris and asked to be taught as well. The minister agreed that the school would do so as soon as a female teacher was procured. Education and new skills learned in a group were attractive alternatives to the isolation of the new farmsteads and compatible with the women's new relationship to the economy. The third wife of Red Jacket—he was now leader of the anti-Christian faction—left him to join the church, and twenty persons, mostly women, asked the minister to instruct them. A number of women adopted Christian names and became members of the mission (T. S. Harris, 1903).

The years between 1837 and 1845 were times of trouble for the Seneca and for other tribes who were all being pressured to move west of the Mississippi. As early as 1818 a delegation of Cherokee women had opposed westward removal and urged missionaries to help them maintain the bounds of the lands they possessed. Cherokee women took up the ways of White women to prove their worthiness to remain on their land. They learned to spin and weave and to wear bonnets and allowed their men to replace them in the fields. Their efforts were ignored by the government. When the army took the Cherokee women out of Georgia in 1839, they left a large number of spinning wheels and looms behind. Other Cherokee women fled to the mountains with a small band who refused to leave. Seminole women, deported that same year from Florida, criticized the men for allowing deportation and for refusing to die on their native soil (Foreman, 1953; Malone, 1956).

The Senecas would have been forcibly removed too, but for the efforts of the Quakers and the missionary Asher Wright, who had moved to Buffalo Creek in 1831. The Quakers mobilized public opinion against a treaty calling for removal of all the Senecas, and Wright helped negotiate a compromise treaty allowing them to keep the Allegheny and Cattaraugus reservations but giving up the valuable Buffalo Creek land (*Case of the Seneca Indians*, 1840; Fenton, 1956).

When the Seneca voted on the compromise treaty, there was still no consensus, which traditionally would have meant rejection. The Quakers charged that bribery and secrecy had been responsible for the majority of the chiefs signing the first treaty and that many opposed the compromise treaty as well. The Buffalo Creek Seneca were especially bitter at the removal, held a meeting, and resolved to have nothing to do with Christian Indians, missionaries, or the gospel. Under protest, they were removed from the Buffalo Creek reservation 35 miles south to the Cattaragus reservation. Their ancestral lands eventually became part of the city of Buffalo (Caswell, 1892; Fenton, 1956).

At the time of the negotiations in 1838, the women were still working the land, making beadwork, brooms, baskets, and other articles for sale, and picking berries to sell at local markets. The women bathed twice a week and dressed neatly in beaded skirts of brightly colored calico, long tunics and leggings, and wore their hair parted in the middle and tied back loose or in a knot with ribbons. They acted and felt, remarked Henry Dearborn (1904), Adjutant General for Massachusetts, "on a perfect equality" with their husbands, advised and influenced them, and were treated well in turn. "She lives with him from love," noted Dearborn a bit wistfully in his journal, "for she can obtain her own means of support better than he can." Senecas still traced descent through the female and were affectionate, careful, kind, and laborious in the care of their little children. They were "equals and quite as independent in all that is general to both, and each separately forming his or her duties as things proper and indispensable for the interest and happiness of themselves in their several domestic private and common relations" (Dearborn, 1904).

Other Whites assured Dearborn that the condition of the Seneca, despite appearances, was deplorable, the men and women intemperate and dissolute and not able to raise sufficient provisions for their support. Once the flats of Buffalo Creek had been one continuous corn field, said one informant; now the fields were overgrown and the Senecas' chief subsistence was begging. Judge Paine of nearby Aurora advised emigration before the Seneca became extinct. All groups were equally wretched, the judge told the visitor, and they were causing great injury to those around by obstructing agriculture. Land values would be enhanced if the White people owned and settled the land, one trader assured Dearborn (Dearborn, 1904).

Dearborn was skeptical about the "pretended mercies of the villainous white man," and romantic about "the noble race of the Senecas." Yet he concluded they must be forced to work and that all efforts at change must begin with the women, who had traditionally tilled the land, manufactured the clothing, and managed the domestic and economic concerns of the family. First, the land must be divided and owned in severalty to be sold, devised, or inherited as with Whites. Representation must be by landowners only. Cattle and plows should be provided to the men to break up the land, and hoes, rakes, and shovels to the women. Children should be taught to read and write and premiums should be given mothers for each twelve-year-old son who regularly worked on the land or at some mechanical trade; and at sixteen, the sons should be allowed half this premium. In one generation, Dearborn (1904) wrote, in words reformers would echo through the century with each new plan to "civilize the Indians," all the Native Americans would be good farmers skilled in the useful mechanical arts, independent, intelligent, industrious, and on the march to "moral excellence and refinement." The "ridiculous" corn feast and other rites, said Dearborn, must be abandoned.

Dearborn had already witnessed the corn feast where a third of the assembled people were women—teenagers of fourteen to old matrons. Five women had distributed the food—corn, beans, squash, vegetables, and deer soup—in baskets and kettles to the other women who then carried the food to their families—husbands and children scattered in groups on the grass—or home. The feast symbolized the fact: women were still in charge of production and distribution of the food (Dearborn, 1904).

Seneca women continued their important economic role in the community. In 1846 they were reported by anxious Quakers as still working in the fields, wearing their traditional tunic and leggings, living in log huts with earth floors, and cooking a pot of venison stew for the family's main meal (Kelsey, 1917). Quakers urged Seneca men to withdraw their women from the fields, for the domestic duties of the household and, at a council meeting with the Seneca that year, a female Quaker appealed to the women to change, arguing that "to mothers, properly belongs the care and management of the education of their children." The Seneca woman Guanaea responded that it was the earnest desire of the Seneca women in council to have their children instructed in the manner desired and to do all in their power to cooperate in and promote that goal (Kelsey, 1917). As a result of this meeting, the Quakers opened a Female Manual Labor School at Cattaraugus where young women under 20 were taught to card and spin wool, knit stockings, cut out and make garments, wash and iron clothes, make bread, do plain cooking, and perform "every other branch of good housewifery, pertaining to a country life" (Kelsey, 1917).

Published records do not indicate what role the women had in the establishment of a republican government with laws and a constitution in 1848. The communities had lost seventy people in a typhoid epidemic, and political dissension again divided the people. Presumably, however, the women performed their traditional role in divesting the old chiefs of their horns, the symbol of life tenure, to allow the new constitution to be legally established. Under the new constitution men and women elected three judges to the judiciary and eighteen legislators to the council. Three-fourths of the voters and three-fourths of all the mothers had to ratify all decisions.[5] While confirming important political power to the women, the new constitution also legitimized the replacement of consensus by majority rule among the women, thereby acknowledging the fragmentation of their power. That same year, 1848, White women were meeting less than a hundred miles away at Seneca Falls to demand the right to vote and be heard in the politics of their nation (Caswell, 1982; *Constitution of the "government by chiefs,"* 1854).

The Seneca women were also able to continue to exert economic control over the annuities paid by the federal government from the interest on a trust fund from the sale of their lands. This was the money that Morris had promised would allow them to live forever without poverty if they gave up their lands. The Seneca annuities were first paid in blankets, calico, and yarn annually at Buffalo Creek. As with other tribes, these annuities were a main source of complaint against government policies. Native Americans often complained because some treaties had set a particular sum in gold to be paid in food and commodities, but financial fluctuations, especially inflation, reduced the quantity of goods received, sometimes by half. In addition, businesses with government contracts were notorious in their willingness to supply poor quality goods, and government officials were known for their willingness to purchase commodities which the Native Americans did not want and could not use. A cash payment was soon substituted for the Senecas, funds allotted to the heads of families, and tribal members encouraged to buy from merchants licensed to sell on the reservation. After 1834, allegedly to end frauds, Congress decided the money would go to the chiefs. Chiefs thereafter represented the tribes and received the money from the government; but among the Seneca the money was then divided by the chiefs among the mothers of the families, usually depending on their need. The women were given credit by the merchants and thus were able to retain some control over the distribution of food and commodities. The annuities were never enough to prevent poverty, however. In 1850, the Seneca received only $18,000. Still the $50 to $80 each woman received annually was an important supplement to her earnings. The women also attempted to make the chiefs accountable not only to the women, but sometimes to White creditors as well (Allen, 1903; Morgan, 1904; Trennert, 1973; U.S. Congress, 1867; E. E. White, 1965).

Nor were Seneca women agreed on the benefits of the White women's culture, which the Christians worked so hard to inculcate. During the 1850s Laura Wright, the missionary wife of Asher Wright, established an orphanage to care for young children and began to instruct the older women in their wifely duties. She believed women should be taught to be Christian housekeepers, needlewomen, and laundresses, and planned to buy material and teach them to make garments for sale. She began by sponsoring dinners at which she gave lessons in making clothing, housekeeping, and child care. But during these dinners, the non-Christians—still at least a third of the women—would gather outside in an opposition meeting to ridicule the converts. They considered sewing a ruse to break down the old religion and insisted on observing the old rites (Caswell, 1892).

Later Ms. Wright borrowed $800 to invest in material and contracted to supply the government with 650 duck coats and red flannel shirts for the western tribes. Several women even purchased sewing machines on credit, hoping to pay for them with the proceeds from the contract. After a long wait, the government finally paid for the garments, but the amount was so small that the women did not consider it worth their time to continue sewing for sale. They did, however, continue to sell their beaded work, baskets, and berries to nearby Whites, and they continued to farm (Caswell, 1892).

By all evidence, the Seneca women still had a strong political, religious, and economic role in the 1850s. It is surprising, therefore, that when the Victorian anthropologist Lewis Henry Morgan began his studies of the Iroquois in 1846, he did not perceive the importance of the economic role of the women.[6] It was not that he believed the Native American women were unproductive. He noted in his journals of 1862 (L. A. White, 1959), while visiting the western tribes: "Among all our Indian nations the industry of the women is proverbial." But he encouraged the women in domestic manufacture, the products of which could be purchased by government agents to reimburse the women for their labor. The women then would support the whole tribe, he suggested, and after a time the men would unite with them in the labor. Such a plan might have been good half a century earlier, but industrialization had already made it unlikely that women would continue domestic manufacturing, as Laura Wright had found out.' Among the Native American women only traditional manufactures, such as pottery and blanket weaving in the Southwest, ever provided much of an income and even then it was very low (Fee, 1974; Morgan, 1965; L. A. White, 1959).

Like other American men, Morgan continued to place his main hope for the progress of all women in the "affections" between the sexes, in the perfection of the monogamous family, the education of women, and private ownership of land. After a visit to the Iroquois in 1846, he claimed that the males considered the women to be inferior, dependent, and their servants—and that the women agreed. Later Morgan wrote of the power the Iroquois women exercised through their clans, but he never mentioned the economic functions of the women as he meticulously traced their kinship systems. He certainly did not agree with Frederick Engels, who drew upon Morgan for *The Origin of the Family, Private Property and the State,* but who concluded that the only way to liberate women was to bring them back into public industry and abolish the monogamous family as an economic unit (Engels, 1972; Fee, 1974; Morgan, 1904; Sacks, 1974).

By the end of the nineteenth century, Morgan's goals had become those of most reformers in America who were concerned about the "Indian problem." In the 1870s the federal government began encouraging the training of a few Native Americans for "higher spheres," that is, to teach common school. Some Seneca women from the Cattaraugus orphanage, which was now named the Thomas Indian School and now financed by the state of New York, went to Oswego Normal School or Genesco State Normal School. Most, however, went to Hampton Normal and Agricultural School; there from 1878 Indians were taught in classes separate from the Black students, though both groups were expected to become agriculturalists, mechanics, or teachers. Hundreds of young Native Americans were educated in the East in "rigidly organized society," anthropologist Alice Fletcher wrote, so that they could resist the restless experimenting and energy of the West when sent there as teachers. The Carlisle Indian School in Pennsylvania was founded on the same principles as Hampton, with the difference that its founder did not believe Native Americans should be exposed to Black students and accepted only Indians (Hampton Institute, 1888).

In 1881, Secretary of the Interior Carl Schurz praised the Carlisle School for keeping the girls busy "in the kitchen, dining-room, sewing-room, and with other domestic work" (quoted by Prucha, 1973). The education of Indian girls was particularly important, he wrote, because he felt that the Indian woman had only been a beast of burden, disposed of like an article of trade at maturity, and treated by her husband alternately with "animal fondness" and "the cruel brutality of the slave driver." Attachment to the home would civilize the Indians, he predicted, and it was the woman's duty to make the home attractive. She must become the center of domestic life and thus gain respect and self-respect. "If we educate the girls of to-day," Schurz predicted with the reformer's usual assurance, "we educate the mothers of to-morrow, and in educating those mothers we prepare for the education of generations to come" (quoted by Prucha, 1973).

Reformers quite commonly ignored the agricultural traditions of the women and insisted that Indians had all depended on game for subsistence. The reformers argued that the Indians had no right to the land because they had simply roamed over it like buffalo. Reformers always saw the key to civilization in the family, a family in which the man held the land. Individualism, private ownership, the nuclear family—all were marshalled to defend the breakup of reservation life. Tribal government meant socialism to many and thus had to be destroyed. Daughters, the reformers were fond of saying, must be educated and married under the laws of the land instead of sold "at a tender age for a stipulated price into concubinage to gratify the brutal lusts of ignorance and barbarism" (quoted by Prucha, 1973). Coeducation would lift the Indian woman out of servility and degradation, said Seth Low, later president of Columbia University, so that their husbands and men generally would "treat them with the same gallantry and respect which is accorded their move favored white sisters" (quoted by Prucha, 1973). The plan for education remained the same: cooking, sewing, laundry work, teaching.

During the years while reformers spoke long and piously of breaking up tribal life, the Seneca women struggled with disease and lack of food. Cholera, smallpox, and typhoid fever swept the reservations in the 1880s. A drought caused the loss of the corn and potato crop, and the orchards produced little fruit. The government further reduced the annuities. When Laura Wright died in 1886, after fifty-three years of missionary work among the Seneca, she was still giving out meat and flour, and trying to devise a plan for a Gospel Industrial Institute where women could learn to cook and sew and clean (Caswell, 1892).

At the Thomas Indian School, the old educational goals of the early nineteenth century were translated into modern terms by the Whites and continued into the twentieth century. In the classes of 1907 the boys were taught agriculture, the girls "household science." The school reported with confidence in 1910 that girls needed instruction in the comfortable, sanitary, and economic arrangement and management of the home. Girls learned to make quilts and buttonholes and nightdresses and to mend socks. They were trained for general laundry work and scientific cooking, for their own homes and for the homes of others. During vacation they might earn as much as $4 per week as domestics in one of the local homes in Silver Creek or Buffalo (Thomas Indian Schools, 1906, 1911, 1914). The most intelligent young women were also channeled into teaching and targeted to teach on other reservations. Many, however, dropped out of Hampton and returned to the reservation. Some were ill, others were needed at home.

White educators expected most Seneca women to marry and settle on the reservation. Many women did marry and continue to live on the reservation. Others taught for a few years or cleaned and washed dishes for Silver Creek families. In 1910, the Census recorded 2,907 Senecas, all but about 200 in the State of New York (U.S. Department of Commerce, 1915). Over 60 percent of the 1,266 males were gainfully employed, mainly as farmers and farm laborers, although a few worked in the railroad, chemistry, and building industries. Less than 12 percent of the 1,219 women were gainfully employed, although girls were more likely than boys to attend school and 75 percent of them could read and speak English. The women's occupations were reflective of their place in the White world: twenty-three were servants, six were dressmakers, and six were teachers. Still thirty-one were listed as farmers and eight as basket makers, reflecting how tenaciously the older women had maintained their traditional occupations (U.S. Department of Commerce, 1937).

According to the Census of 1910 (U.S. Department of Commerce, 1915), 85 percent of all Native American men twenty-five to forty-four years of age were gainfully employed while over 80 percent of the Native American women of the same age were not. Of the 19.6 percent of Native American women who were gainfully employed, almost one-third were employed in traditional White women's work—as servants, laundresses, and teachers. More than two-thirds were employed in home industry—manufacturing baskets, pottery and textiles—or as farm laborers and farmers. These two-thirds, while engaged in occupations considered traditional for the Native American woman, were actually in new occupations geared to the market economy and reserved for working-class women of certain ethnic groups. Black, German-American, and Swedish-American women, along with Mexican-American and Japanese-American women, were still in the fields. Immigrant women still stitched in their tenement houses. A Cherokee woman in the fields of an Oklahoma farmer, a Navajo woman weaving outside her Arizona hogan, a Seneca woman cleaning the home of a White New Yorker—all were accepted in practice as working women but considered exceptions to the ideal that the Native American woman's place was now in the home.

The policy of the federal government, of missionaries, and of reformers to move the Native American woman from her traditional role as farmer into the accepted White woman's role as housewife and mother and to move the man from his traditional role of hunter and warrior into the accepted White man's role of farmer seemed to have been successful. Native American men had developed a functional relationship to the dominant White man's economy and Native American women had retreated to a dysfunctional relationship with the economy, that is, they expressed their productivity indirectly through the home and husband.

What Carl Sauer (1969) has called the "Neolithic agricultural revolution," the domestication of plants by women, was ending in North America approximately 5,000 years after the revolution of the plow began in Mesopotamia. Whether or not plow culture began as the German geographer Eduard Hahn suggested—with sacred oxen drawing the ceremonial cart and pulling the plow, a phallic symbol for the insemination of the receptive earth—the husbandman had taken over agricultural operations in many areas of the world and the women had retired to the house and to garden work. Male hierarchies prevailed where cattle, plowed fields, and wagons became dominant institutions. Wherever the plow was introduced, women lost their old relationship to the agricultural economy. The process in North America was now almost complete (Sauer, 1969).

In spite of the disappearance of their traditional economic function, Native American women continued to be active in tribal organizations and to display independence and strength in arranging their lives. In addition, they kept alive older traditions which conflicted with the new ideology of private property, profit, and subordination of women to men. Many reservation lands were lost and divided, but some tribes clung to their communal lands, refused to divide land into separate plots permanently, refused to give up their annuities, and continued to believe in the Native American culture as a better way of life than that which the White Americans had offered to them. The U.S. Commissioner of Indian Affairs (1910) reported that he was still trying to get rid of the Seneca annuities but the tribe had refused. They still held lands communally and their tribal organizations were strong. The Seneca tribe had maintained its control over the reservation and its internal government. They refused to recognize the White man's marriage laws. Marriage was often cohabitation and divorce separation at pleasure, complained one government official. Such conditions were "abhorrent to the finer sensibilities of civilized mankind," he told the U.S. Commissioner of Indian Affairs (Lurie, 1972; Randle, 1951; U.S. Commissioner of Indian Affairs, 1910, 1915).

Seneca mothers had not lost their reverence for the land. Though agriculture was now male and plow dominated and some Seneca men participated in the industrial, large-scale, technological, and profit-oriented agriculture, the older attitudes from the matrilineal subsistence agriculture survived. Their relation to the land had made the women strong and enabled them to keep alive the belief that the purpose of land is more than just to bring profits to those willing to exploit it.

Notes

1. Criticism by many women helped the development of this article at different stages. Anthropologists Bea Medicine and Peggy Sanday, women historians at Arizona State University, and community women in Phoenix all made valuable contributions to its evolution.
2. I use the term *agriculture* rather than *horticulture* because horticulture, alone with "hoe culture," has so often been used negatively (Kramer, 1967).
3. It is not clear from early accounts whether the Seneca couple always joined the household of the woman. Parker (1952) says the couple lived with her women for the first year, then with his women. Other accounts say the Seneca couples joined the husband's household. The Seneca may have changed from living with the wife's clan to living with the husband's clan because of the increasing military demands on the tribe (Martin & Voorhies, 1975).
4. Cornplanter's mother was a hereditary matron of the Wolf clan who passed over him to nominate her younger full-blooded son as sachem. Cornplanter had no official title but became an elder and was given the right to sign treaties because of his military role. His mother later lived in his village.
5. The Seneca replaced this new government with the older "government by chiefs" in 1854 but people of both sexes over the age of 21 had to consent to the sale or lease of reservation land under this second constitution.
6. The reason for Morgan's reluctance to discuss women's production seems to have been his desire to protect Native Americans from criticism by Whites. Since Morgan believed that male industry replacing female industry was a sign of progress, he seldom commented on the widespread women's work, but praised men's labor when he found it.
7. Many White women sewed at home during the Civil War and into the twentieth century, and later Puerto Rican women stitched nightgowns for wealthy New Yorkers in their island slums, but women resorted to sewing in their homes only when desperate.

References

Allen, O. Personal recollections of Captains Jones and Parrish and the payment of Indian annuities in Buffalo. *Buffalo Historical Society Proceedings*, 1903, *6*, 539–542.

Brown, J. K. Economic organization and the position of women among the Iroquois. *Ethnohistory*, 1970, *17*, 151–67.(a)

Brown, J. K. A note on the division of labor by sex. *American Anthropologist*, 1970, *72*, 1073–1078.(b)

Carrier, L. *The beginnings of agriculture in America.* New York: McGraw-Hill, 1923.

Case of the Seneca Indians in the state of New York. Philadelphia: Merrihew & Thompson, 1840.

Casewell, H. S. *Our life among the Iroquois Indians.* Boston: Congressional Sunday School, 1892.

Constitution of the "government by chiefs" of the Seneca nation of Indians. Buffalo, N.Y.: Thomas & Lathrop, 1854.

Dearborn, H. A. S. Journals. *Buffalo Historical Society Proceedings*, 1904, *7*, 60–137.

Deardorff, M. H., & Snyderman, G. S. A nineteenth-century journal of a visit to the Indians of New York. *American Philosophical Society Proceedings*, 1956, *100*, 583–612.

Douglas, M. (Ed.). *Witchcraft: Confessions and accusations.* London: Tavistock, 1970.

Engels, F. *The origin of the family, private property and the state.* New York: International, 1972.

Fee, E. The sexual policies of Victorian social anthropology. In M. Hartman & L. W. Banner (Eds.), *Clio's consciousness raised: New perspectives on the history of women.* New York: Harper & Row, 1974.

Fenton, W. N. Toward the gradual civilization of the Indian natives: The missionary and linguistic work of Asher Wright (1803–1875) among the Senecas of western New York. *American Philosophical Society Proceedings*, 1965, *100*, 567–581.

Foreman, G. *Indian removal: The emigration of the five civilized tribes of Indians.* Norman, Okla.: University of Oklahoma Pres, 1953.

Hampton Institute. *Ten years' work for Indians at the Hampton Normal and Agricultural Institute, 1879–1888,* 1888.

Harris, G. H. Life of Horatio Jones. *Buffalo Historical Society Publications*, 1903, *6*, 383–514.

Harris, T. S. Journals. *Buffalo Historical Society Proceedings*, 1903, *6*, 313–379.

Hawley, C. *Early chapters of Seneca history: Jesuit missions in Sonnontouan, 1656–1684*, Auburn, N.Y.: Cayuga County Historical Society Collections, 1884

Hewitt, J. N. B. (Ed.). Seneca fiction, legends and myths. In U.S. Bureau of American Ethnology, *Annual Report 1910–1911*. Washington, D.C., 1918.

Holder, P. *The hoe and the horse on the plains: A study of cultural development among North American Indians*. Lincoln, Neb.: University of Nebraska Press, 1970.

Holmes, E. Letters from Fort Niagara in 1800. *Buffalo Historical Society Publications*, 1903, *6*, 187–204.

Houghton, F. The history of the Buffalo Creek reservation. *Buffalo Historical Society Publications*, 1920, *24*, 3–181.

Howland, H. P. The Seneca mission at Buffalo Creek. *Buffalo Historical Society Publications*, 1903, *6*, 125–160.

Hyde, J. B. Teacher among the Senecas. *Buffalo Historical Society Proceedings*, 1903, *6*, 245–270.

Kelsey, R. W. *Friends and the Indians, 1655–1917*. Philadelphia: Friends on Indian Affairs, 1917.

Kramer, F. L. Eduard Hahn and the end of the "three stages of man." *Geographical Review*, 1967, *57*, 73–89.

Lafitau, J. F. *Moeures des sauvages Ameriquains*. 2 vols. Paris: Hochereau, 1724.

Lurie, N. O. Indian women: A legacy of freedom. In R. L. Iacopi (Ed.), *Look to the mountain top*. San Jose, Calif.: Gousha, 1972.

Malone, H. T. *Cherokees of the old south: A people in transition*. Athens, Ga.: University of Georgia Press, 1956.

Martin, M. K. & Voorhies, B. *Female of the species*. New York & London: Columbia University Press, 1975.

Morgan, L. H. *Houses and house-life of the American aborgines*. Chicago & London: University of Chicago Press, 1965.

Morgan, L. H. *League of the Ho-De-No-Sau-Nee or Iroquois*. New York: Dodd Mead, 1904.

Murphy, Y. & Murphy, R. F. *Women of the forest*. New York & London: Columbia University Press, 1974.

Parker, A. C. *Seneca myths and folk tales*. Buffalo, N.Y.: Buffalo Historical Society, 1923.

Parker, A. C. Analytical history of the Seneca Indians. *New York State Archeological Association Researches and Transactions*, 1926, *6*, 1–162.

Parker, A. C. Notes on the ancestry of Cornplanter. *New York State Archeological Association Researches and Transactions*, 1927, *7*, 4–22.

Parker, A. C. *Red Jacket: Last of the Seneca*. New York: McGraw-Hill, 1952.

Parker, A. C. The code of Handsome Lake, the Seneca prophet. In W. N. Fenton (Ed.), *Parker on the Iroquois*. Syracuse, N.Y.: Syracuse University Press, 1968.(a)

Parker, A. C. Iroquois uses of maize and other food plants. In W. N. Fenton (Ed.), *Parker on the Iroquois*. Syracuse, N.Y.: Syracuse University Press, 1968.(b)

Prucha, F. P. (Ed.). *Americanizing the American Indians: Writings by the "Friends of the Indian" 1880–1900*. Cambridge, Mass.: Harvard University Press, 1973.

Randle, M. C. Iroquois women, then and now. In W. N. Fenton (Ed.), *Symposium on local diversity in Iroquois culture* (Bureau of American Ethnology Bulletin No. 149). Washington, D.C. 1951.

Sacks, K. Engels revisited: Women, the organization of production, and private property. In M. Z. Rosaldo & L. Lamphere (Eds.), *Woman, culture and society*. Stanford, Calif.: Stanford University Press, 1974.

Sanday, P. R. Toward a theory of the status of women. *American Anthropologist*, 1973, *75*, 1682–1700.

Sanday, P. R. Female status in the public domain. In M. Z. Rosaldo & L. Lamphere (Eds.), *Woman, culture and society*. Stanford, Calif.: Stanford University Press, 1974.

Sauer, C. O. *Seeds, spades, hearths and herds: The domestication of animals and foodstuffs* (2nd ed.). Cambridge, Mass.: Massachusetts Institute of Technology, 1969.

Seaver, J. E. *Life of Mary Jemison: White woman of the Genesee*. Canandaigua, N.Y.: Beamis, 1824.

Smith, D. Witches and demonism of the modern Iroquois. *Journal of American Folk-Lore*, 1888, *1*, 184–193.

Stone, W. L. *The life and times of Red-Jacket, or Sa-Go-Ye-Wat-Ha*. New York & London: Wiley & Putnam, 1841.

Terrell, J., & Terrell, D. M. *Indian women of the western morning: Their life in early America*. New York: Dial, 1974.

Thomas Indian Schools. *Annual Report for 1906*. Albany, New York State, 1906.

Thomas Indian Schools. *Annual Report for 1910*. Albany, New York State, 1911.

Thomas Indian Schools. *Annual Report for 1913*. Albany, New York State, 1914.

Trennert, R. A. William Medill's war with the Indian traders, 1847. *Ohio History*, 1973, *82*, 46–62.

U.S. Commissioner of Indian Affairs, *Report 1910*. Washington, D.C., 1910.

U.S. Commissioner of Indian Affairs. *Senecas and other Indians.* Washington, D.C., 1915.

U.S. Congress, Joint Special Committee on the Conditions of the Indian Tribes. *Report.* Washington, D.C., 1867.

U.S. Department of Commerce, Bureau of the Census. *Indian population in the United States and Alaska, 1910.* Washington, D.C., 1915.

U.S. Department of Commerce, Bureau of the Census. *Indian population of the United States and Alaska.* Washington, D.C., 1937.

Visit of Gerald T. Hopkins. *Buffalo Historical Society Proceedings,* 1903, *6,* 217–222.

Wallace, A. *The death and rebirth of the Seneca.* New York: Knopf, 1970.

Washburn, W. *Red man's land/white man's law: A Study of the past and present status of the American Indian.* New York: Scribner's, 1971.

White, E. E. *Experiences of a special agent.* Norman, Okla.: University of Oklahoma Press, 1965.

White, L. A. (Ed.). *Lewis Henry Morgan: The Indian journals, 1859–1862.* Ann Arbor, Mich.: University of Michigan Press, 1959.

Will, G. F., & Hyde, G. E. *Corn among the Indians of the upper Missouri.* Lincoln, Neb.: University of Nebraska Press, 1917.

Wilson, G. L. *Agriculture of the Hidatsa Indians: An Indian interpretation* (University of Minnesota Studies in the Social Sciences No. 9). Minneapolis: University of Minnesota Press, 1917.

7

The Domestication of Politics:
Women and American Political Society, 1780–1920

Paula Baker

On one subject all of the nineteenth-century antisuffragists and many suffragists agreed: a woman belonged in the home. From this domain, as wife, as daughter, and especially as mother, she exercised moral influence and insured national virtue and social order. Woman was selfless and sentimental, nurturing and pious. She was the perfect counterpoint to materialistic and competitive man, whose strength and rationality suited him for the rough and violent public world. Despite concurrence on the ideal of womanhood, antisuffragists and suffragists disagreed about how women could best use their power of moral superiority. Suffragists believed that the conduct and content of electoral politics—voting and office holding—would benefit from women's special talents. But for others, woman suffrage was not only inappropriate but dangerous. It represented a radical departure from the familiar world of separate spheres, a departure that would bring, they feared, social disorder, political disaster, and, most important, women's loss of position as society's moral arbiter and enforcer.[1]

The debates over female suffrage occurred while the very functions of government were changing. In the late nineteenth and early twentieth centuries, federal, state, and municipal governments increased their roles in social welfare and economic life. With a commitment to activism not seen since the first decades of the nineteenth century, Progressive-era policy makers sought ways to regulate and rationalize business and industry. They labored to improve schools, hospitals, and other public services. These efforts, halting and incomplete as they were, brought a tradition of women's involvement in government to public attention.[2] Indeed, from the time of the Revolution, women used, and sometimes pioneered, methods for influencing government from outside electoral channels. They participated in crowd actions in colonial America and filled quasi-governmental positions in the nineteenth century; they circulated and presented petitions, founded reform organizations, and lobbied legislatures. Aiming their efforts at matters connected with the well-being of women, children, the home, and the community, women fashioned significant public roles by working from the private sphere.[3]

The themes of the debates—the ideology of domesticity, the suffrage fight, the re-emergence of governmental activism, and the public involvement of nineteenth-century women—are familiar. But what are the connections among them? Historians have told us much about the lives of nineteenth-century women. They have explained how women gained political skills, a sense of consciousness as women, and feelings of competence and

Reprinted by permission of the author. Originally published in the *American Historical Review*, vol. 89, June 1984.

self-worth through their involvement in women's organizations. But as important as these activities were, women were also shaped by—and in turn affected—American government and politics. Attention to the interaction between women's political activities and the political system itself can tell us much about the position of women in the nineteenth century. In addition, it can provide a new understanding of the political society in which women worked—and which they helped change.[4]

In order to bring together the histories of women and politics, we need a more inclusive definition of politics than is usually offered. "Politics" is used here in a relatively broad sense to include any action, formal or informal, taken to affect the course or behavior of government or the community.[5] Throughout the nineteenth century, gender was an important division in American politics. Men and women operated, for the most part, in distinct political subcultures, each with its own bases of power, modes of participation, and goals. In providing an intellectual and cultural interpretation of women and politics, this essay focuses on the experiences of middle-class women. There is much more we need to learn about the political involvement of women of all classes in the years prior to suffrage; this essay must, therefore, be speculative. Its purpose is to suggest a framework for analyzing women and politics and to outline the shape that a narrative history of the subject could take.

The basis and rationale for women's political involvement already existed by the time of the Revolution.[6] For both men and women in colonial America, geographically bounded communities provided the fundamental structures of social organization. The most important social ties, economic relationships, and political concerns of individuals were contained within spatially limited areas. Distinctions between the family and community were often vague; in many ways, the home and the community were one.[7] There were, to be sure, marked variations from place to place; community ties were weaker, for example, in colonial cities and in communities and regions with extensive commercial and market connections, such as parts of the South.[8] Still, clear separations existed between men and women in their work and standards of behavior, and most women probably saw their part in the life of the community as the less important. A little-changing round of household tasks dominated women's lives and created a routine that they found stifling. Women had limited opportunities for social contact, and those they had were almost exclusively with other women. They turned work into social occasions, and they passed the milestones of their lives in the supportive company of female friends and relatives. But, however confining, separation provided a basis for a female culture—though not yet for female politics.[9]

Differences between men's and women's political behavior were muted in the colonial period, compared with what they later became. In many places, men who did not own land could not vote because governments placed property restrictions on suffrage. Both men and women petitioned legislatures to gain specific privileges or legal changes. Citizens held deferential attitudes toward authority; elections were often community rituals embodying codes of social deference. A community's "best" men stood for election and were returned to office year after year, and voters expected candidates to "treat" potential supporters by providing food and drink before and on election day. Deferential politics, however, weakened by the middle of the eighteenth century. Economic hardship caused some men to question the reality of a harmony of interests among classes, and the Great Awakening taught others to question traditional authorities. Facing a growing scarcity of land, fathers could no longer promise to provide for their sons, which weakened parental control. This new willingness to question authority of all sorts was a precondition for the Revolution and was, in turn, given expression by republican thought.[10]

Republicanism stressed the dangers posed to liberty by power and extolled the advantages of mixed and balanced constitutions. In a successful republic, an independent, virtuous, watchful, and dispassionate citizenry guarded against the weakness and corruption that threatened liberty. Although interpreted by Americans in different ways, republicanism provided a framework and a rationale for the Revolution. It furnished prescriptions for citizenship and for the relationship between citizens and the state. And it helped unify a collection of local communities racked by internal divisions and pressures.[11]

While the ideology and process of the Revolution forced a rethinking of fundamental political concepts, this re-evaluation did not extend to the role of women. As Linda K. Kerber persuasively argued, writers and thinkers in the republic tradition were concerned more with criticizing a particular political administration than with examining traditional assumptions about the political role of all inhabitants. Given their narrow intentions, they were not obliged to reconsider the position of women in the state. The language of republicanism also tended to make less likely the inclusion of women. Good republicans were, after all, self-reliant, given to simple needs and tastes, decisive, and committed first to the public interest. These were all "masculine" qualities; indeed, "feminine" attributes— attraction to luxury, self-indulgence, timidity, dependence, passion—were linked to corruption and posed a threat to republicanism. Moreover, women did not usually own land— the basis for an independent citizenry and republican government.[12]

Despite their formal prepolitical status, women participated in the Revolution. They were central to the success of boycotts of imported products and, later, to the production of household manufactures. Their work on farms and in businesses in their husbands' absences was a vital and obvious contribution. Women's participation also took less conventional forms. Edward Countryman recounted instances in which groups of women, angered at what they saw as wartime price-gouging, forced storekeepers to charge just prices. During and after the war, women also took part in urban crowd actions, organized petition campaigns, and formed groups to help soldiers and widows. Some even met with legislatures to press for individual demands.[13] Whatever their purposes, all of these activities were congruent with women's identification with the home, family, and community. In boycotts of foreign products and in domestic manufacture during the Revolution, women only expanded traditional activities. In operating farms and businesses, they stepped out of their sphere temporarily for the well-being of their families. Because separations between the home and community were ill defined in early America, women's participation in crowd actions can also be seen as a defense of the home. As Countryman and others pointed out, a communalist philosophy motivated the crowd actions of both men and women. Crowds aimed to redress the grievances of the whole community. Women and men acted not as individuals but as members of a community—and with the community's consent.[14]

Women's political participation took place in the context of the home, but the important point is that the home was a basis for political action. As Kerber and Mary Beth Norton have shown, the political involvement of women through the private sphere took new forms by the beginning of the nineteenth century. Women combined political activity, domesticity, and republican thought through motherhood. Although outside of formal politics, mothering was crucial: by raising civic-minded, virtuous sons, they insured the survival of the republic. On the basis of this important task, women argued for wider access to education and justified interest and involvement in public affairs. As mothers women were republicans; they possessed civic virtue and a concern for the public good. Their exclusion from traditionally defined politics and economics guaranteed their lack of interest in personal gain. Through motherhood, women attempted to compensate for their exclusion from the formal political world by translating moral authority into political influence. Their political demands, couched in these terms, did not violate the canons of domesticity to which many men and women held.[15]

During the nineteenth century, women expanded their ascribed sphere into community service and care of dependents, areas not fully within men's or women's politics. These tasks combined public roles and administration with nurturance and compassion. They were not fully part of either male electoral politics and formal governmental institutions or the female world of the home and family. Women made their most visible public contributions as founders, workers, and volunteers in social service organizations.[16] Together with the social separation of the sexes and women's informal methods of influencing politics, political domesticity provided the basis for a distinct nineteenth-century women's political culture.

Although the tradition, tactics, and ideology for the political involvement of women existed by the first decades of the nineteenth century, a separate political culture had not yet taken shape. Women's style of participation and their relationship to authority were not yet greatly different from those of many men. Until the 1820s—and in some states even later—property restrictions on suffrage disfranchised many men. Even for those granted the ballot, political interest and electoral turnout usually remained low.[17] During the early years of the republic, deferential political behavior was again commonplace. Retreating from the demands of the Revolutionary period, most citizens once again seemed content to accept the political decisions made by the community's most distinguished men. This pattern persisted until new divisions split communities and competing elites vied for voters' support.[18]

Changes in the form of male political participation were part of a larger transformation of social, economic, and political relationships in the early nineteenth century. The rise of parties and the re-emergence of citizen interest in politics had a variety of specific sources. In some places, ethnic and religious tensions contributed to a new interest in politics and shaped partisan loyalties. Recently formed evangelical Protestant groups hoped to use government to impose their convictions about proper moral behavior on the community, a goal opposed by older Protestant groups and Catholics. Other kinds of issues—especially questions about the direction of the American political economy—led to political divisions. Citizens were deeply divided about the direction the economy ought to take and the roles government ought to play. They thought attempts to tie localities to new networks and markets in commerce and agriculture could lead to greater prosperity, but such endeavors also meant that economic decisions were no longer made locally and that both the social order and the values of republicanism could be in danger. Local party leaders linked these debates to national parties and leaders,[19] and the rise of working men's parties in urban areas seemed to spring from a similar set of questions and sense of unease about nineteenth-century capitalism.[20]

Whatever their origin, parties also served other less explicitly "political" purposes. The strength of antebellum parties lay in their ability to fuse communal and national loyalties. The major parties were national organizations, but they were locally based: local people organized rallies, printed ballots, worked to gain the votes of their friends and neighbors. Through political activities in towns and cities, parties gained the support of men and translated their feelings into national allegiances.[21] Political organization provided a set pattern of responses to divisive questions, which raised problems to the national level and served to defuse potential community divisions. Indeed, by linking local concerns to national institutions and leaders, parties took national political questions out of the local context.[22]

The local base of the Democrats and Whigs allowed them to take contradictory positions on issues in different places. Major party leaders searched for issues that enabled them to distinguish their own party from the opposition, while keeping their fragile constituencies intact. At the same time, local politics returned in most places to search for consensual, nonpartisan solutions to community questions.[23]

The rise of a national two-party system in the 1820s and 1830s inaugurated a period of party government and strong partisan loyalties among voters that lasted until after the turn of the twentieth century. Parties, through the national and state governments, distributed resources to individuals and corporations, and patronage to loyal partisans. Throughout most of the nineteenth century, roughly three-quarters of the eligible electorate cast their ballots in presidential elections. The organization and identity of the parties changed, but the pre-eminence of partisanship and government-by-party remained. Party identifications and the idea of partisanship passed from fathers to sons.[24]

Partisan politics characterized male political involvement, and its social elements help explain voters' enthusiastic participation. Parties and electoral politics united all white men, regardless of class or other differences, and provided entertainment, a definition of manhood, and the basis for a male ritual. Universal white manhood suffrage implied that, since all men shared the chance to participate in electoral politics, they possessed political equality. The right to vote was something important that men held in common. And, as class, geography, kinship, and community supplied less reliable sources of identification than they had at an earlier time, men could at least define themselves in reference to women. Parties were fraternal organizations that tied men together with others like themselves in their communities, and they brought men together as participants in the same partisan culture.[25]

Election campaigns celebrated old symbols of the republic and, indeed, manhood. Beginning as early as William Henry Harrison's log cabin campaign in 1840, parties conducted entertaining extravaganzas. Employing symbols that recalled glorious old causes (first, the Jacksonian period and, later, the Civil War), men advertised their partisanship. They took part in rallies, joined local organizations, placed wagers on election results, read partisan newspapers, and wore campaign paraphernalia. In large and small cities military-style marching companies paraded in support of their party's candidates, while in rural areas picnics and pole raisings served to express and foster partisan enthusiasm.[26]

Party leaders commonly used imagery drawn from the experience of war: parties were competing armies, elections were battles, and party workers were soldiers. They commented approvingly on candidates who waged manly campaigns, and they disparaged nonpartisan reformers as effeminate.[27] This language and the campaigns themselves gathered new intensity in the decades following the Civil War. The men who marched in torchlight parades recalled memories of the war and demonstrated loyalty to the nation and to their party. Women participated, too, by illuminating their windows and cheering on the men; sometimes the women marched alongside the men, dressed as patriotic figures like Miss Liberty.[28] The masculine character of electoral politics was reinforced on election day. Campaigns culminated in elections held in saloons, barber shops, and other places largely associated with men. Parties and electoral politics, in short, served private, sociable purposes.

Just as the practice and meaning of electoral politics changed in the early nineteenth century, so did the function of government. State and local governments gradually relinquished to the marketplace the tasks of regulating economic activity, setting fair prices, and determining product standards. State governments limited the practice of granting corporate charters on an individual basis and, instead, wrote uniform procedures that applied to all applicants. These governments also reduced, and finally halted, public control of businesses and private ventures in which state money had been invested. A spate of state constitutional revisions undertaken from the 1820s through the 1840s codified these changes in the role of government in economic life. In state after state, new constitutions limited the power of the legislatures. Some of this power was granted to the courts, but most authority passed to the entrepreneurs. This transformation in governance is just beginning to be re-evaluated by political historians.[29] For our purposes, the important point is that governments largely gave up the tasks of regulating the economic and social behavior of the citizenry.

The rise of mass parties and characteristic forms of male political participation separated male and female politics. When states eliminated property qualifications for suffrage, women saw that their disfranchisement was based solely on sex. The idea of separate spheres had a venerable past, but it emerged in the early nineteenth century with a vengeance. Etiquette manuals written by both men and women prescribed more insistently the proper behavior for middle-class ladies. Woman's attributes—physical weakness, sentimentality, purity, meekness, piousness—were said to disqualify her for traditional public life. Motherhood was now described as woman's special calling— a "vocation," in Nancy Cott's term—that, if performed knowledgeably and faithfully, represented the culmination of a woman's life.[30] While a handicap for traditional politics, her emotional and guileless nature provided strengths in pursuing the important tasks of binding community divisions and upholding moral norms.

At the same time, political activity expanded in scope and form. New organizations for women proliferated in small and large cities and became forums for political action.[31] These organizations took on some of the tasks—the care of dependents and the enforcement of moral norms—that governments had abandoned. If not maintained by church, government, and community, the social order would be preserved by woman and the home. Women's positions outside traditionally defined politics and their elevated moral authority took on new importance and may have allowed men to pursue individual economic and social ends with less conflict. Through selfless activities in the home and community, women could provide stability.[32]

As historians of women have pointed out, one of the ironies of Jacksonian democracy was the simultaneous development of the "cult of true womanhood" and rhetoric celebrating the equality of men.[33] These developments were related and carried ramifications for both male politics and woman's political role. The notion of womanhood served as a sort of negative referent that united all white men. It might, indeed, have allowed partisan politics to function as a ritual, for it made gender, rather than other social or economic distinctions, the most salient political division. Men could see past other differences and find common ground with other men.

"Womanhood" was more than just a negative referent, for it assigned the continued safety of the republic to the hands of disinterested, selfless, moral women. In the vision of the framers of the Constitution, government was a self-regulating mechanism that required good institutions to run properly—not, as in classical republicanism, virtuous citizens. Men's baser instincts were more dependable than their better ones; hence, the framers made self-interest the basis for government. While politics and public life expressed selfish motives, private life—the home—maintained virtue. The republican vocabulary lingered into the nineteenth century, but key words gained new meanings that were related to private behavior. "Liberty," "independence," and "freedom" had economic as much as political connotations, while "virtue" and "selflessness" became attributes of women and the home. Because order was thought to be maintained by virtuous women, men could be partisans and could admit that community divisions existed.[34] At the same time, male electoral participation defined politics. As the idea of parties gained citizens' acceptance and other modes of participation were closed off or discouraged, electoral participation stood as the condoned means of political expression.

Women's political demands and actions that too closely approached male prerogatives met with resistance. Women fought hard—and sometimes successfully—in state legislatures to end legal discrimination. But even their victories had as much to do with male self-interest as with women's calls for justice.[35] Still, they slowly gained legal rights in many states. And since male politics determined what was public and political, most of those demands by women that fell short of suffrage were seen as private and apolitical. The political activities of women in clubs and in public institutions achieved a considerable degree of male support. Women reformers not only drew little visible opposition from men but often received male financial support. Women's moral nature gave them a reason for public action, and, since they did not have the vote, such action was considered "above" politics.

Ideas about womanhood and separate spheres, as well as forces as diverse as urbanization and the resurgence of revival religion, gave women's political activity a new prominence. But that female sphere had now grown. Men and women would probably have agreed that the "home" in a balanced social order was the place for women and children. But this definition became an expansive doctrine: home was anywhere women and children were. Influential women writers such as Catharine Beecher described a "domestic economy" in which women combined nurturance and some of the organizational methods of the new factory system to run loving, yet efficient, homes. Others expanded the profession of motherhood to include all of society, an argument that stressed the beneficial results that an application of feminine qualities had on society as a whole.[36] This perspective on motherhood and the home included not only individual households but all women and children and the forces that affected their lives. And it had a lasting appeal. As late as 1910, feminist and journalist Rheta Childe Dorr asserted: "Woman's place is Home. . . . But Home is not contained within the four walls of an individual house. Home is the community. The city full of people is the Family. The public school is the real Nursery. And badly do the Home and Family need their mother."[37] Many nineteenth-century women found this vision of the home congenial: it encouraged a sense of community and responsibility toward all women, and it furnished a basis for political action.

Throughout the nineteenth century women participated in politics through organizations that worked to correct what they defined as injustices toward women and children. The ideas and institutions through which women acted, however, changed significantly over time. Early organizations, including moral reform societies and local benevolent organizations, based their political action on the notions of the moral superiority of women and an expansive woman's sphere. By the mid-nineteenth century, new groups rejected that vision. Early suffrage organizations insisted on rights for women and the independence to move outside of the woman's sphere. Although they by no means fully dismissed the notion of women's moral superiority, their tactics and ideology flowed from different sources, such as the abolition movement. Still later, a new generation of clubwomen returned to the idea of a woman's sphere but rejected sentimentality in favor of the scientific and historical vision of the Gilded Age. They stressed how scientific motherhood, if translated into efficient, nonpartisan, and tough-minded public action, could bring social progress. Temperance activists and suffragists in the late nineteenth century wanted political equality so that the special qualities of womanhood could be better expressed and exercised: femininity provided a sort of expertise needed in formal politics. Drawing on the growing body of works that recount the public activities of women, we can illustrate how the nineteenth-century female political culture operated.

Some of the earliest examples of women's organizations were benevolent and moral reform societies. These groups, usually located in cities, were staffed and managed by middle-class women.[38] Unable to believe that women voluntarily acted in ways that were in conflict with the strictures of the woman's sphere, they blamed their charges' misfortunes on male immorality. For example, the Female Benevolent Society and the Female Moral Reform Society, both in New York City and both most active in the 1830s, concentrated their efforts on eradicating moral lapses such as prostitution. Since no woman would choose such an unwomanly vocation, they reasoned, they blamed the moral inferiority of men and the scarcity of economic opportunities for women for this degradation of womanhood.

Such an analysis of the causes of unwomanly behavior encouraged women in benevolent groups to broaden their efforts and concerns. Organized women inaugurated employment services, trained women for work as seamstresses and housekeepers, and gathered funds to aid poor women. These reformers were also alarmed at the treatment of women in prisons; they feared these women were brutalized and immodestly mixed with male inmates. Hence they worked for prison reform and persuaded state and municipal governments to appoint female guards and police matrons, as well as to set up halfway houses and prisons for women. Other groups dedicated themselves to helping elderly women, poor women, children, and orphans. They were joined by clubwomen in working for dress reform, health and sex education, and education for women.[39] As their concerns widened, so did the variety of their tactics. One group published the names of prostitutes' clients that were gathered by members who held vigils outside of brothels. When moral suasion and shame seemed ineffective, they turned to law. Reformers lobbied legislators to pass measures that would protect women, children, and the home. They also launched successful petition drives. A New York State group persuaded legislators to introduce a bill that would make adultery and seduction punishable crimes. During the next three years, they put pressure on assemblymen by publishing the names of representatives who voted against the measure. It passed. Members of charitable organizations also worked to see legislation enacted that protected married women's property.[40]

These demands, like all of the political actions of the antebellum groups, were fully congruent with a broad vision of the woman's sphere. We should recognize, too, that the vision of the home as embracing all women and children had an important corollary: "woman" was a universal category in the minds of organized women, as it was for others who held the doctrine of separate spheres. Because all women shared certain qualities, and many the experience of motherhood, what helped one group of women benefited all. "Motherhood" and "womanhood" were powerful integrating forces that allowed women to cross class, and perhaps even racial, lines.[41] They also carried moral and political clout. Hence, women's groups celebrated the special moral nature of women, usually in contrast to men's capacity for immoral behavior. The nature of woman simply suited her to ensure the moral and social order, which sometimes necessitated the assistance of the state.

The culmination of this strain of female political culture was the Woman's Parliament, convened by Sorosis, a professional women's club in New York City, in 1869. Supporters envisioned creating a parallel government with responsibilities complementing woman's nature: education, prisons, reform schools, parks, recreation, political corruption, and social policy in general—tasks that male partisan politics handled poorly, if at all. Participants intended the parliament to be elected by all women at large, and, although it met only once, the Woman's Parliament was the fullest expression of the transfer of woman's sphere to politics.[42] Nonetheless, the members of the Woman's Parliament rejected woman suffrage, even though they were prepared to operate a separate government. Suffrage represented the antithesis of the glorification of separate spheres that lay behind the political activities of the early organizations. For these women and many men, suffrage was indeed a radical demand.[43] By involving women in the male political arena, women's right to vote threatened to end political separation. It implied—and suffragists argued—that men and women should be treated as individuals, equal in abilities and talents, and that neither men nor women were blessed with a special nature. Women's suffrage threatened the fraternal, ritualistic character of male politics, just as it promised to undercut female political culture.

The early suffrage movement developed from women's participation in the abolition movement, particularly the Garrisonian wing, but there was no simple connection between the two. Women, as Ellen DuBois pointed out, did not need involvement in abolitionism to recognize their oppression. Rather, from their experience women gained political skills, an ideology distinct from the doctrine of separate spheres, and a set of tactics. They learned about political organization and public speaking, found humanism an attractive alternative to evangelical Protestantism and woman's special nature, and discovered Garrisonian moral suasion to be a useful way of making political demands. Abolitionism taught women how to turn women's rights into a political movement. Moreover, the rejection of their demands by the Radical Republicans showed them the unreliability of the established political parties and the necessity for an independent movement.[44] Yet the early suffrage movement was notably unsuccessful. The organization itself split over questions of tactics and purpose. A few Western states passed woman suffrage amendments, but apparently for reasons other than women's demands. By the 1880s, many states allowed women to vote in school elections, and even to serve on school boards. But, on the whole, the movement made little headway until the turn of the century.[45]

Neither the equality nor the liberal individualism promised by the early suffragists found a receptive audience in the nineteenth century. Throughout the late nineteenth and early twentieth centuries, women's political activities were characterized by voluntary, locally based moral and social reform efforts. Many women had a stake in maintaining the idea of separate spheres. It carried the force of tradition and was part of a feminine identity, both of which were devalued by the individualism that suffrage implied. Separate spheres allowed women to wield power of a sort. They could feel that their efforts showed some positive result and that public motherhood contributed to the common good. Moreover, men were unwilling to vote for suffrage amendments. The late nineteenth century was the golden age of partisan politics: at no time before or since did parties command the allegiance of a higher percentage of voters or have a greater hand in the operation of government. Indeed, in the extremes of political action of both men and women during the late nineteenth century—torchlight parades and the Woman's Parliament—there were hints of earnest efforts to hold together a social and political system that was slipping from control. At any rate, separate political cultures had nearly reached the end of existence.

Throughout the nineteenth century, the charitable work of women aimed to remedy problems like poverty, disease, and helplessness. But after the Civil War the ideas that informed women's efforts, as well as the scope of their work, markedly changed. New perceptions about the function of the state and a transformed vision of society came out of the experience of the war. It had illustrated the importance of loyalty, duty, centralization, and organization and encouraged a new sense of American nationality. Even as the federal government drew back from its wartime initiatives, many Americans were recognizing the shortcomings of limited government. Amid rapid urbanization and industrialization, the economic system nationalized and reached tighter forms of organization. Social thinkers and political activists discovered limits in the ability of traditional Protestantism, liberalism, or republicanism to explain their world. Some even questioned the idea of moral authority itself and turned to a positivistic interpretation of Spencerian sociology, which stressed the inevitability of historical progress and touted science as the height of human achievement. While the system had its critics, it more commonly was justified by a faith in historical progress.[46]

Women's political culture reflected these changes. The work of Northern women in the Sanitary Commission illustrates some of the directions that their politics took. The commission, a voluntary but quasi-governmental organization founded by male philanthropists, set out to supply Northern troops with supplies and medical care. Volunteers, they argued, were too often distracted by the suffering of individuals, and community-based relief got in the way. Unsentimental and scientific, the members of the commission felt they best understood the larger purpose and the proper way to deal with the magnitude of the casualties. Women served as nurses in the commission, as they did in army hospitals and voluntary community relief operations. They moved women's traditional roles of support, healing, and nurturance into the public sphere. At the same time, their experiences taught them the limits of sentiment and the need for discipline. Women such as Clara Barton, Dorthea Dix, Mary Livermore, and Mother Bickerdyke gained public acclaim for their services. Well-to-do Northern women raised a substantial amount of money for the commission by running "Sanitary Fairs." They collected contributions, sold items donated by men and women, and publicly celebrated the Union's cause.[47]

The commission is an important example of women's participation in politics. The acceptance and expansion of the woman's sphere, professionalization, and the advancement of science over sentiment were repeated in other Gilded Age female organizations. Some middle-class groups saw socialism as the solution to heightened class tensions, and, for a time, such groups formed alliances with working-class and socialist organizations. In Chicago, the Illinois Woman's Alliance cooperated with the Trade and Labor Assembly on efforts to secure legislation of interest to both groups. Yet such alliances grew increasingly rare as socialists were discredited.[48]

Organized women found a more permanent method in social science. Especially in its early reformist stage, social science tied science to traditional concerns of women.[49] The methods and language of social science—data collection, detached observation, and an emphasis on prevention—influenced the political work of women. In the South, women in church and reform groups adopted these methods to address what they perceived as the important social dislocations created by the Civil War. Gilded Age "friendly visitors" spent time with the poor, gathering information and providing a presumably uplifting example. They did little more, since alms giving was bad for the poor because it discouraged work, and, by standing in the way of progress, it was also a detriment to the race. Even more "scientific," Progressive-era settlement workers later mocked the friendly visitors' pretensions. They saw the Gilded Age ladies as lacking in compassion and blind to the broader sources of poverty and, hence, the keys to its prevention. Later still, professional social workers, further removed from sentimentality, replaced the settlement workers and their approaches.[50] Yet in the Gilded Age, social science provided women with quasi-professional positions and an evolutionary argument for women's rights. It also contributed a logic for joining forces with formal governmental institutions, because social science taught the importance of cooperation, prevention, and expertise. This faith in the scientific method and in professionalism eventually led to a devaluation of voluntary work and to the relinquishment of social policy to experts in governmental bureaucracies.[51]

The temperance movement illustrates another way that women fused domesticity and politics. It engaged more women than any other nineteenth-century cause and shows how women could translate a narrow demand into a political movement with wide concerns. Temperance appealed to women because it addressed a real problem—one that victimized women—and because, as a social problem, it fell within the woman's sphere. The temperance movement developed through a number of stages and gained momentum especially during the Second Great Awakening. Its history as a women's movement, however, began with the temperance crusade during the years following the Civil War. In small cities and towns in the East and Midwest, groups of women staged marches and held vigils outside or conducted prayer meetings inside saloons, which sometimes coerced their owners to close. In some places, they successfully enlisted the aid of local governments. In most towns, however, the saloons reopened after a short period of "dry" enthusiasm.[52]

The Women's Christian Temperance Union was a descendant of the temperance crusade. It, too, relied on Protestant teachings, women's sense of moral outrage, and the belief in women's moral superiority. Throughout its history, the WCTU was involved in working for legislation such as high license fees and local option. But under the leadership of Frances Willard, the organization, while still defining temperance as its major goal, moved far beyond its initial concerns and closer to the Knights of Labor, the Populist party, and the Christian Socialists and away from the tactics and ideology of the temperance crusade. Like these Gilded Age protest movements, the WCTU turned a seemingly narrow demand of group interest into a critique of American society.[53] Indeed, the ability of the WCTU to cast the traditional concerns of women in terms of a broad vision and of the public good helps explain its success. But that success was in part the result of its flexible organization. Although centrally directed, the WCTU was locally organized, which allowed the branches to determine their own concerns and projects within the general directives of the leadership. Willard's WCTU inaugurated the "Do Everything" policy, which allowed local organizations to choose projects as they saw fit. The WCTU made temperance the basis of demands for a wide range of reforms. Alcohol abuse, they argued, was a symptom, not a cause, of poverty, crime, and injustices done to women. Therefore, the WCTU organized departments in areas such as labor, health, social purity, peace, education, and, eventually, suffrage. The locals were directly involved in electoral politics: small-town women worked for "dry" candidates, while the Chicago Union supported the Socialist party.[54]

The WCTU's call for the vote for women nearly split the organization. It supported suffrage not for the sake of individual rights but because the ballot could allow women to serve better the causes of temperance, the home, and the public good. American politics and economics in the late nineteenth century contained enough examples of the baneful results of unrestrained self-interest, from political corruption to avaricious corporations. The efforts of women to deal locally with social problems were no longer sufficient in a nation where the sources were extralocal, and created by male, self-interested political and economic behavior. Woman's vote, they argued, would express her higher, selfless nature. The WCTU combined the woman's sphere with suffrage under the rubric of "Home Protection," an argument that implied feminine values belonged within traditionally defined politics. While taking traditional domestic concerns seriously, the WCTU taught women how to expand them into wider social concern and political action. With greater success than any other nineteenth-century women's group, it managed to forge the woman's sphere into a broadly based political movement.

Other groups—notably the second generation of woman suffragists and clubwomen—also attempted to combine the woman's sphere and women's rights. In this effort, woman suffrage remained divisive. As DuBois and Carl Degler have shown, the threat woman suffrage posed to the doctrine of separate spheres helps explain why the struggle was so long and bitterly fought. But an examination of the political context can provide further insights. The antisuffragists' most powerful argument was that suffrage was dangerous because it threatened the existence of separate spheres. If women voted, they would abandon the home and womanly virtues. The differences between the sexes would be obscured: men would lose their manhood and women would begin to act like men. Throughout the nineteenth century, those arguments struck a chord. Participation in electoral politics did define manhood. Women also had a stake in maintaining their sphere and the power it conferred. But by the end of the century profound social, economic, and political changes made that antisuffrage argument—and the separate male and female political cultures—less persuasive to many women—and many men.

The nature of electoral politics changed significantly during the early twentieth century. Gone were not only the torchlight parades but also most of the manifestations of the male political culture that those parades symbolized. Voter turnout began to decline, and men's allegiance to political parties waned. In the broadest sense, these changes can be traced to the effects of rapid urbanization and industrialization.[55] In the nineteenth century, partisan politics was a local experience, resting on certain sorts of community relationships. In the partisan press and campaigns, politics meant economic policy. Locally, such issues were handled in an individualistic, partisan manner; on the national level, abstract discussions of distant economic questions supplied the basis for a partisan faith.

But by the early twentieth century the communities in which voters' loyalties were formed had changed. Men's most important relationships were no longer contained solely within geographically defined localities but were instead scattered over distances. Their political ties were no longer exclusively with neighbors but also with people having similar economic or other interests. Male political participation began to reflect this shift. Men increasingly replaced or supplemented electoral participation with the sorts of single-issue, interest-group tactics that women had long employed. Moreover, political parties that dealt with problems on an individualistic basis now seemed less useful because economic and political problems demanded more than individualistic solutions.[56] The sum of these changes in nineteenth-century patterns of electoral participation was to lessen the importance of partisan politics for men. In hindsight, at least, woman suffrage presented less of a threat to a male political culture and to manhood.

Even more important, the antisuffragists could no longer argue so forcefully that the vote would take women out of the home. Government had assumed some of the substantive functions of the home by the early twentieth century. Politics and government in the nineteenth century had revolved almost entirely around questions of sectional, racial, and economic policies. To be sure, governments, especially at the state level, spent the largest portion of their budgets on supporting institutions like schools, asylums, and prisons.[57] But election campaigns and partisan political discussions largely excluded mention of these institutions. In the Progressive era, social policy—formerly the province of women's voluntary work—became public policy. Women themselves had much to do with this important transition—a transition that in turn changed their political behavior.

Women continued to exercise their older methods of political influence, but now they directed their efforts through new institutions. Women's clubs—united in 1890 as the General Federation of Women's Clubs—were one important means. Beginning as self-improvement organizations, many clubs soon focused on social and cultural change. These women sought to bring the benefits of motherhood to the public sphere. They set up libraries, trade schools for girls, and university extension courses, and they worked to introduce home economics courses, to improve the physical environment of schools, and to elect women to school boards. They also sponsored legislation to eliminate sweatshops and provide tenement-house fire inspection. Clubwomen interested in sanitary reforms helped enact programs for clean water and better sewage disposal. In many cities, they raised money for parks and playgrounds. Clubs were also important in pressing for a juvenile court system and for federal public health legislation, such as the 1906 Pure Food and Drug Act.[58]

But by the Progressive period, these women recognized that their efforts—and even public motherhood—were not enough. The scope of these problems meant that reform had to be concerned with more than the care of women and children. Charity had real limits. Problems were not solvable, or even treatable, at the local level. Despite attempts to uplift them, the poor remained poor, and women began to identify the problem as having broader sources. The municipal housekeepers needed the help of the state: along, they were powerless to remove the source of the problem, only to face the growing number of its victims. As Mary Beard explained in 1915,

> It is the same development which has characterized all other public works—the growth from remedy to prevention, and the growth is stable for the reason that it represents economy in the former waste of money and effort and because popular education is leading to the demand for prevention and justice rather than charity. In this expansion of municipal functions there can be little dispute as to the importance of women. Their hearts touched in the beginning by human misery and their sentiments aroused, they have been led into manifold activities in attempts at amelioration, which have taught them the breeding places of disease, as well as of vice, crime, poverty, and misery. Having learned that effectively to "swat the fly" they must swat its nest, women have also learned that to swat disease they must swat poor housing, evil labor conditions, ignorance, and vicious interests.[59]

What Beard described was the process by which politics became domesticated. Women's charitable work had hardly made a dent in the social dislocations of industrial society. The problems were unsolvable at the local level because they were not local problems. And, since the goal of these women was to prevent abstract, general problems—to prevent poverty rather than to aid poor people—the methods of antebellum organizations would not suffice. Hence, the state—the only institution of sufficient scope—had to intervene. Women therefore turned their efforts toward securing legislation that addressed what they perceived to be the sources of social problems—laws to compensate victims of industrial accidents, to require better education, to provide adequate nutrition, and to establish factory and tenement inspection, for example.[60] Clubwomen pointed proudly to playgrounds that they had founded and later donated to local governments.[61] Thus women passed on to the state the work of social policy that they found increasingly unmanageable.

Historians have not yet explicitly addressed the questions of how and why governments took on these specific tasks. In the broadest sense, the willingness of government to accept these new responsibilities has to do with the transformation of liberalism in the early twentieth century. Liberalism came to be understood not as individualism and laissez faire but as a sense of social responsibility coupled with a more activist, bureaucratic, and "efficient" government. This understanding of government and politics meshed nicely with that of women's groups. Both emphasized social science ideas and methods, organization, and collective responsibility for social conditions. Thus there were grounds for cooperation, and the institutions that women created could easily be given over to government. Yet the character of collective action varied. The business corporation created the model for the new liberalism, while politically active women and some social thinkers took the family and small community as an ideal.[62] But whatever the mechanism, as governments took up social policy—in part because of women's lobbying—they became part of the private domain.

The domestication of politics, then, was in large part women's own handiwork. In turn, it contributed to the end of separate political cultures. First, it helped women gain the vote. Suffrage was no longer either a radical demand or a challenge to separate spheres, because the concerns of politics and of the home were inextricable. At the same time, it did not threaten the existence of a male political culture because that culture's hold had already attenuated. The domestication of politics was connected, too, with the changed ideas of citizens about what government and politics were for. Each of these developments, illustrating ties between transformations in politics and the role of women, merits further attention.

Recovering from a period of apathy and discouragement, the women's suffrage campaign enjoyed renewed energy in the early twentieth century. The second generation of suffragists included home protection in their arguments in favor of votes for women. They noted that the vote would not remove women from the home and that electoral politics involved the home and would benefit from women's talents. Suffragists argued that women's work in World War I proved their claims to good citizenship. They also took pains to point out what the vote would not do. Indeed, the suffragists made every conceivable argument, from equal rights to home protection to the need for an intelligent electorate. Such a wide array of practical claims did not necessarily represent a retreat from the radicalism of Elizabeth Cady Stanton's generation. Suffragists often presented arguments in response to accusations by the opposition. If opponents claimed that woman suffrage would destroy the home, suffragists replied that it would actually enhance family life. The suffragist's arguments, moreover, reflected a transition in political thought generally. Just as Stanton's contemporaries spoke in the language of Garrisonian abolitionism, the later suffragists framed their ideas in the language of science, racism, efficiency, and cooperation. This does not make their nativist or racist rhetoric any less objectionable, but it does mean that second-generation suffragists were working within a different cultural and intellectual environment.[63]

But organization, not argumentation, was the key to winning the vote for the second generation. They discarded a state-by-state strategy and concentrated on winning a national amendment. Under the leadership of Carrie Chapman Catt and others, suffragists patterned their organization after a political machine, mimicking male politics. The suffrage campaign featured a hierarchical organization, with workers on the district level who received guidance, funds, and speakers from the state organizations, which in turn were supported by the national organization. They conducted petition campaigns to illustrate the support that suffrage had from women and men. They held parades and pageants to demonstrate that support and gather publicity. To be sure, suffragists pointed to the positive results votes for women could bring. But most of all, they aimed to show that woman suffrage—whatever it meant—was inevitable.[64]

Suffragists considered the suffrage referenda in New York to be pivotal tests. Victory there would provide crucial publicity for the cause and lend credence to the notion of inevitability. In 1915 the referendum lost by a fairly wide margin in a fiercely fought campaign; only five scattered upstate counties supported the referendum. Two years later, woman suffrage was back on the ballot. This time, the suffragists concentrated their efforts on district work in major cities. Curiously, the election approached with much less fanfare than that of 1915. The suffragists apparently had won their battle of attrition. The amount and tone of the newspaper coverage suggests that woman suffrage was indeed considered inevitable, and the referendum passed, almost entirely because of the support it received in the cities. The election results point to important patterns. The woman suffrage referendum ran poorly in areas where the prohibition vote was high or where high voter turnout and other manifestations of the nineteenth-century culture of politics were still visible. Here, women's suffrage was still a threat. Conversely, it ran well in cities, especially in certain immigrant wards and places where the Socialist vote was high—where nineteenth-century political patterns had never taken hold or had already disappeared. Men who had no stake in maintaining the old culture of politics seemed more likely to support woman suffrage. In the South, where the right to vote was tied to both manhood and white supremacy, woman suffrage also met stiff resistance.[65]

That woman suffrage had little impact on women or politics has been considered almost axiomatic by historians. It failed to help women achieve equality. It did not result in the disaster antisuffragists imagined. Women did not vote as a reform bloc or, indeed, in any pattern different from men. Woman suffrage simply doubled the electorate. Historians have traced the reasons for the negligible impact of woman suffrage to the conservative turn of the second-generation suffragists, including their single-minded pursuit of the vote and home protection arguments. But to dismiss woman suffrage as having no impact is to miss an important point. It represented the endpoint of nineteenth-century womanhood and woman's political culture. In a sense, the antisuffragists were right. Women left the home, in a symbolic sense; they lost their place above politics and their position as the force of moral order. No longer treated as a political class, women ceased to act as one. At the same time, politics was unsexed. Differences between the political involvement of men and women decreased, and government increasingly took on the burden of social and moral responsibility formerly assigned to the woman's sphere.

The victory of woman suffrage reflected women's gradual movement away from a separate political culture. By the early twentieth century, the growing number of women who worked for wages provided palpable examples of the limits of notions about a woman's place. Certainly by the 1920s, the attachment of women to the home could not be taken for granted in the same way it had in the nineteenth century, in part because by the 1920s the home was something of an embarrassment. Many men and women rejected domesticity as an ideal. The "new woman" of the 1920s discarded nineteenth-century womanhood by adopting formerly male values and behavior.[66] To be sure, most women probably did not meet the standard of the "new woman," but that ideal was the cultural norm against which women now measured their behavior. Women thus abandoned the home as a basis for a separate political culture and as a set of values and way of life that all women shared.

Women rejected the form and substance of nineteenth-century womanhood. Municipal housekeepers and charity workers saw that the responsibility for social policy was not properly theirs: only government had the scope and potentially the power to deal with national problems. Society seemed too threatening and dangerous to leave important responsibilities to chance, and women to whom municipal housekeeping was unknown seemed to sense this. They also surrendered to government functions that had belonged to the woman's sphere. Given the seemingly overwhelming complexities and possibilities for grievous errors, women were willing to take the advice of experts and government aid in feeding their families and rearing and educating their children. Tradition offered little guidance; the advice of their mothers, who grew up during the mid- and late nineteenth century, could well have seemed anachronistic in an urban and industrial society. Their own experiences could lead to wrong decisions in a rapidly changing society. Moreover, abandoning the functions of the old-fashioned woman's sphere allowed a new independence. Women made some gains, but they also lost the basis for a separate political culture.[67]

Lacking a sense of common ground, women fragmented politically. Their rejection of the woman's sphere as an organizing principle discouraged women from acting as a separate political bloc. Without political segregation to unite them, differences among groups of women magnified. What benefited professional women might be superfluous, even damaging, to the interests of working-class women. Women did not vote as a bloc on "women's" issues because there were no such issues, just as there were no issues that reflected the common interests of all men. The commonality that women had derived from the home in the nineteenth century disappeared, leaving women to splinter into interest groups and political parties. Organizing a separate women's party held little appeal for women because they could not find issues on which to unite.[68] Women were also no longer "above" politics. Their political behavior benefited from neither the veneration of the home and the moral power it bestowed nor the aura of public concern that their older informal methods of participation communicated.

It almost goes without saying that women gained little real political power upon winning the vote. Men granted women the vote when the importance of the male culture of politics and the meaning of the vote changed. Electoral politics was no longer a male right or a ritual that dealt with questions that only men understood. Instead, it was a privilege exercised by intelligent citizens. Important positions in government and in the parties still went to men. Woman suffrage was adopted just at the time when the influence of parties and electoral politics on public policy was declining. By the early twentieth century, interest groups and the formation of public opinion were more effective ways to influence government, especially the new bureaucracies that were removed from direct voter accountability.[69]

As differences between political participation and men and women lessened in the early twentieth century, the role of government changed. Government now carried moral authority and the obligations it implied. That governments often chose not to use that authority is not the point. What matters is that citizens wanted more from government, in the way of ethical political behavior and of policies that ensured economic and social stability. To exercise moral authority, government needed to behave in moral ways. Citizens expected office holders to separate their public actions from their private interests and wanted a civil service system to limit the distribution of public rewards for party work. Even in the 1920s, citizens held government responsible for encouraging a growing economy and social order. When the methods employed in the 1920s for accomplishing these goals—government orchestration of self-regulating functional groups—proved lacking, government took a larger hand in directing social and economic policy.[70]

Even more fundamentally, Americans' perceptions of the distinctions between the public and private spheres were transformed by the 1920s. Although it has not received sufficient scholarly attention, some of the outlines of this change are discernable. In the nineteenth century, social and cultural separations between what was public and what was private were well-defined, at least in theory. The public world included politics, economics, and work outside of the home, while the private sphere meant the home and family. These sharp delineations provided a sense of stability. The lines were often crossed: women, for example, worked outside of the home. And, while women brought their "private" concerns to the "public" sphere, men's political involvement served private ends. This paradox suggests a rethinking of the meanings of public and private in the nineteenth century, one that has implications for understanding public life in the twentieth. Social definitions of public and private blurred in the twentieth century, re-creating an obfuscation similar to that of colonial America. In a sense, the existence of spheres was denied. The personal was political and the political was evaluated in regard to personal fulfillment. Citizens judged office holders on the basis of personality. Men and women shunned the traditional public world of voting and holding office to concentrate their attention on private life. Although not a descent into confusion (the separations between public and private had also been murky in the nineteenth century), these changes pointed to a complex and vastly different understanding of the meaning of public and private from the one held by people in the nineteenth century.[71]

Women played important, but different, parts in two major turning points in American political history, transformations that coincided with changes in the roles of women. In the Jacksonian period, the cultural assignment of republican virtues and moral authority to womanhood helped men embrace partisanship and understand electoral politics as social drama. The social service work of female organizations filled some of the gaps created as governments reduced the scope of their efforts. Two political cultures operated throughout the remainder of the nineteenth century. The female culture was based on the ideology of domesticity and involved continued expansion of the environs of the "home." Women carried out social policy through voluntary action. They practiced a kind of interest-group politics, by directing their attention to specific issues and exercising influence through informal channels. Male politics consisted of formal structures: the franchise, parties, and holding office. For many men, this participation was as much social as it was political, and it contributed to a definition of manhood.

Women had a more active part in the political changes of the Progressive period. They passed on their voluntary work—social policy—to governments. Men now sought to influence government through nonelectoral means, as women had long done. Electoral politics lost its masculine connotations, although it did not cease to be male dominated. Voting, ideally, had less to do with personal loyalties than with self-interested choices. Women voted. They did so in somewhat smaller numbers than men, and they held few important party or governmental positions. But sharp separations between men's and women's participation abated. In this process, individual women gained opportunities. "Woman," however, lost her ability to serve as a positive moral influence and to implement social policy.

Much work on women's political involvement is necessary before we can fully understand the connections between women's activities and American politics. But if either is to be understood, the two must be considered together. Gaining a broader understanding of "politics" is one way to begin doing so. This interpretation should consider the political system as a whole, and include both formal and informal means of influence. It could thus embrace voluntary activities, protest movements, lobbying, and other kinds of ways in which people attempt to direct governmental decisions, together with electoral politics and policy making. In determining what activities might be termed "political" we might adapt John Dewey's definition of the "public." For Dewey, the "public as a state" included "all modes of associated behavior . . . [that] have exclusive and enduring consequences which involve others beyond those directly engaged in them."[72] This understanding suggests that the voluntary work of nineteenth-century women was part of the political system. Although directed at domestic concerns, the activities of women's organizations were meant to affect the behavior of others, as much as—or more than—were ballots cast for Grover Cleveland. Given such a definition of politics, political historians could come to different understandings of the changes in and connections between political participation and policy making.

Historians of women could find new contexts in which to place their work. Students of both subjects need to go beyond the definition of "political" offered by nineteenth-century men.

Notes

A number of individuals commented on earlier versions of this essay, including Dee Garrison, Kathleen W. Jones, Suzanne Lebsock, Richard L. McCormick, Wilson Carey McWilliams, John F. Reynolds, Thomas Slaughter, and Warren I. Susman. I am grateful for their criticism, advice, and encouragement.

1. Accounts of the suffrage campaign include William H. Chafe, *Women and Equality* (New York, 1977); Carl N. Degler, *At Odds: Women and the Family in America from the Revolution to the Present* (New York, 1980), chap. 14; Ellen Carol DuBois, *Feminism and Suffrage: The Emergence of an Independent Women's Movement in America, 1848–1869* (Ithaca, N.Y., 1978); Eleanor Flexner, *Century of Struggle: The Woman's Rights Movement in the United States* (Cambridge, Mass., 1959); Alan P. Grimes, *The Puritan Ethic and Woman Suffrage* (New York, 1967); Aileen S. Kraditor, *The Ideas of the Woman Suffrage Movement, 1890–1920* (New York, 1965); David Morgan, *Suffragists and Democrats in America* (East Lansing, Mich., 1970); William L. O'Neill, *Everyone Was Brave: A History of American Feminism* (Chicago, 1969); Ross Evan Paulson, *Woman's Suffrage and Prohibition* (Glenview, Ill., 1973); and Anne F. Scott and Andrew M. Scott, *One-Half of the People: The Fight for Woman Suffrage* (Philadelphia, 1975). Important treatments of the ideology of domesticity include Nancy F. Cott, *The Bonds of Womanhood: "Woman's Sphere" in New England, 1790–1835* (New Haven, 1975); Daniel Scott Smith, "Family Limitation, Sexual Control, and Domestic Feminism in Victorian America," in Mary Hartman and Lois W. Banner, eds., *Clio's Consciousness Raised* (New York, 1974), 119–33; Kathryn Kish Sklar, *Catharine Beecher: A Study in American Domesticity* (New Haven, 1973); and Barbara Welter, "The Cult of True Womanhood, 1820–1860," *American Quarterly*, 18 (1966): 151–74.

2. Syntheses of the vast number of works on Progressive reform include John W. Chambers II, *The Tyranny of Change: America in the Progressive Era, 1900–1917* (New York, 1980); Otis L. Graham, *The Great Campaign: Reform and War in America, 1900–1928* (Englewood Cliffs, N.J., 1971); Arthur S. Link and Richard L. McCormick, *Progressivism* (Arlington Heights, Ill., 1983); Samuel P. Hays, *The Response to Industrialism, 1885–1914* (Chicago, 1957); William L. O'Neill, *The Progressive Years: America Comes of Age* (New York, 1975); and Robert Wiebe, *The Search for Order, 1877–1920* (New York, 1967). For a good recent review essay, see Daniel T. Rodgers, "In Search of Progressivism," *Reviews in American History*, 10 (1982): 113–32.

3. Numerous works have appeared over the past decade that deal with the public activities of middle-class women. These works most often examine particular groups and attempt to trace the development of a feminist consciousness in the nineteenth century. See, for example, Barbara Berg, *The Remembered Gate—Origins of American Feminism: Women and the City, 1800–1860* (New York, 1978); Karen Blair, *The Clubwoman as Feminist: True Womanhood Redefined, 1868–1914* (New York, 1980); Ruth Bordin, *Woman and Temperance: The Quest for Power and Liberty, 1873–1900* (Philadelphia, 1981); Mari Jo Buhle, *Women and American Socialism, 1870–1920* (Urbana, Ill., 1981); Cott, *The Bonds of Womanhood;* Barbara Leslie Epstein, *The Politics of Domesticity: Women, Evangelism, and Temperance in Nineteenth-Century America* (Middletown, Conn., 1981); Estelle B. Freedman, "Separatism as Strategy: Female Institution-Building and American Feminism, 1870–1930," *Feminist Studies,* 5 (1979): 512–29; Linda K. Kerber, *Women of the Republic: Intellect and Ideology in Revolutionary America* (Chapel Hill, N.C., 1980); William Leach, *True Love and Perfect Union: The Feminist Reform of Sex and Society* (New York, 1980); Gerda Lerner, "The Lady and the Mill Girl: Changes in the Status of Women in the Age of Jackson," 15–30, "Community Work of Black Club Women," 83–93, "Political Activities of Anti-Slavery Women," 94–111, and "Black and White Women in Confrontation and Interaction," 112–28, in her *The Majority Finds Its Past: Placing Women in History* (New York, 1979); J. Stanley Lemons, *The Woman Citizen: Social Feminism in the 1920s* (Urbana, Ill., 1973); Keith E. Melder, *Beginnings of Sisterhood: The American Woman's Rights Movement, 1800–1850* (New York, 1977); Mary Beth Norton, *Liberty's Daughters: The Revolutionary Experience of American Women, 1750–1800* (Boston, 1980); Mary P. Ryan, *Cradle of the Middle Class: The Family in Oneida County, New York, 1790–1865* (Cambridge, Mass., 1981); and Anne Firor Scott, *The Southern Lady: From Pedestal to Politics, 1830–1930* (Chicago, 1970). A number of contemporary accounts are especially useful. See Mary R. Beard, *Women's Work in Municipalities* (New York, 1915); Jane Cunningham Croly, *The History of the Women's Club Movement in America* (New York, 1898); Mary A. Livermore, *My Story of the War* (Hartford, Conn., 1896), and "Women and the State," in William Meyers, ed., *Women's Work in America* (Hartford, Conn., 1889); and Frances E. Willard, *Woman and Temperance: Or, the Work and Workers of the Women's Christian Temperance Union* (Hartford, Conn., 1883).

4. A number of studies examine the treatment of women in American political thought. These include Zillah Eisenstein, *The Radical Future of Liberal Feminism* (New York, 1981); Jean Bethke Elshtain, *Public Man, Private Woman: Women in Social and Political Thought* (Princeton, N.J., 1981); Kerber, *Women of the Republic*; and Susan Moller Okin, *Women in Western Political Thought* (Princeton, N.J., 1979). Historical treatments of women in politics include William H. Chafe, *The American Woman: Her Changing Social, Economic, and Political Roles, 1920–1970* (New York, 1972), 24–47; Jane Gruenebaum, "Women in Politics" in Richard M. Pious, ed., *The Power to Govern: Assessing Reform in the United States*, Proceedings of the Academy of Political Science, no. 34 (New York, 1981), 104–20; Gerda Lerner, ed., *The Female Experience: An American Documentary* (Indianapolis, 1977), 317–22, and Sheila M. Rothman, *Woman's Proper Place: A History of Changing Ideals and Practices, 1870 to the Present* (New York, 1978), 102–32, 136–53.

5. "Government" refers to the formal institutions of the state and their functions. "Policy" includes efforts by those within these institutions as well as by those outside them to shape social or economic conditions with the support of "government."

6. Cott, *The Bonds of Womanhood*; Kerber, *Women of the Republic*; Norton, *Liberty's Daughters*; and Ryan, *Cradle of the Middle Class*. Also see Linda Grant DePauw, *Founding Mothers: Women in the Revolutionary Era* (New York, 1975); and Joan Hoff-Wilson, "The Illusion of Change: Women and the American Revolution," in Alfred H. Young, ed., *The American Revolution: Explorations in the History of American Radicalism* (DeKalb, Ill., 1976), 383–444. Of these works, only Kerber's and Norton's explicitly set out to answer questions about women and politics, and their analyses differ on important points. On the basis of an examination of women's diaries and other papers, Norton argued that the Revolution and republicanism significantly changed the role of women. Family relationships, for example, grew more egalitarian, and women developed a new appreciation of their competence and skills outside the home. Kerber's analysis of American political thought in relationship to women, however, suggests that neither republicanism nor the Revolution had a positive effect on the role of women. Rather, republican thought assumed women were apolitical. But by the early nineteenth century an ideology of motherhood allowed women to combine domesticity with political action.

7. Thomas Bender, *Community and Social Change in America* (New Brunswick, N.J., 1978), 68; Paul Boyer and Stephen Nissenbaum, *Salem Possessed: The Social Origins of Witchcraft* (Cambridge, Mass., 1971), 151; Richard L. Bushman, *From Puritan to Yankee: Character and the Social Order in Connecticut, 1690–1765* (New York, 1970), chaps. 1, 2; John Demos, *A Little Commonwealth: Family Life in Plymouth Colony* (New York, 1970), 182–85, chap. 4; James Henretta, *The Evolution of American Society, 1700–1815: An Interdisciplinary Analysis* (Lexington, Mass., 1973), 23–31; Ryan, *Cradle of the Middle Class*, chap. 1; and Michael Zuckerman, *Peaceable Kingdoms: New England Towns in the Eighteenth Century* (New York, 1970).

8. Bender, *Community and Social Change*, 62–67; Michael Kammen, *Colonial New York* (New York, 1975), 290; Paul G. E. Clemens, *The Atlantic Economy and Colonial Maryland's Eastern Shore: From Tobacco to Grain* (Ithaca, N.Y., 1980); James T. Lemon, *The Best Poor Man's Country: A Geographical Study of Early Southeastern Pennsylvania* (Baltimore, 1972); Edmund S. Morgan, *American Slavery, American Freedom: The Ordeal of Colonial Virginia* (New York, 1975); 149–79; Darrett B. Rutman, *Winthrop's Boston* (Chapel Hill, N.C., 1965); and Samuel Bass Warner, Jr., *The Private City: Philadelphia in Three Periods of Its Growth* (Philadelphia, 1968), chap. 1.

9. Kerber, *Women of the Republic*, chap. 1; and Norton, *Liberty's Daughters*, chaps. 1–3.

10. Among the many works on colonial political practices, see, for example, Charles S. Sydnor, *Gentlemen Freeholders: Political Practices in Washington's Virginia* (Chapel Hill, N.C., 1952); and Robert Zemsky, *Merchants, Farmers, and River Gods: An Essay on Eighteenth-Century Politics* (Boston, 1971). On changing attitudes toward authority, see Bushman, *Puritan to Yankee*, 138–63, 264–87; Jay Fliegelman, *Prodigals and Pilgrims: The American Revolution against Patriarchal Authority, 1750–1800* (Cambridge, Mass., 1982); Philip J. Greven, Jr., *Four Generations: Population, Land, and Family in Colonial Andover, Massachusetts* (Ithaca, N.Y., 1970), chaps. 7, 8; Robert A. Gross, *The Minutemen and Their World* (New York, 1976); and Gary B. Nash, *The Urban Crucible: Social Change, Political Consciousness, and the Origins of the American Revolution* (Cambridge, Mass., 1979).

11. Reviews of the literature on republicanism include Robert E. Shalhope, "Toward a Republican Synthesis: The Emergence of an Understanding of Republicanism in American Historiography," *William and Mary Quarterly*, 3d ser., 29 (1972); 49–80, and "Republicanism and Early American Historiography," *ibid.*, 39 (1982): 334–56. The articles in Young's *The American Revolution* illustrate divisions in the republican consensus.

12. Kerber, *Women of the Republic*, chap. 2.

13. Edward Countryman, *A People in Revolution: The American Revolution and Political Society in New York, 1760–1790* (Baltimore, 1981), 43–44; Kerber, *Women of the Republic*, chaps. 2–3; Nash, *The Urban Crucible*, chap. 7; Norton, *Liberty's Daughters*, chaps. 6–7; and Julia Cherry Spruill, *Women's Life and Work in the Southern Colonies* (Chapel Hill, N.C., 1938; reprint edn., New York, 1972), 232–45.

14. Countryman, *A People in Revolution*; Eric Foner, *Tom Paine and Revolutionary America* (New York, 1976),

chaps. 2, 5; Pauline Maier, "Popular Uprisings and Civil Authority in Eighteenth-Century America," *William and Mary Quarterly*, 3d ser., 27 (1970): 3–35; E. P. Thompson, "The Moral Economy of the English Crowd in the Eighteenth Century," *Past & Present*, 50 (1971): 76–136; and Warner, *The Private City*, pt. 1.

15. Kerber, *Women of the Republic*, chaps. 7, 9; and Norton, *Liberty's Daughters*, chap. 9. Some works suggest that republicanism was not a cause of more egalitarian family relationships, of new education for women to enhance their roles as better wives and mothers, or of women's use of the home to gain political influence. Jay Fliegelman, for example, persuasively argued that by the middle of the eighteenth century the older notion of the patriarchal family was under attack. It was being replaced by a new ideal—one drawn from Locke and the Scottish common-sense philosophers. Examining these writings and popular novels, he showed that the new model, which called for affectionate and egalitarian relationships with children and humane child rearing designed to prepare children for rational independence and self-sufficiency, was in place well before 1776. In fact, the rhetoric of the Revolution was replete with images portraying the importance of personal autonomy and of parental respect for the individuality of children who had come of age. Thus, a cultural revolution against patriarchal authority preceded the Revolution. (Fliegelman's analysis, however, chiefly concerns sons, not daughters, and it deals with questions not directly related to relationships between men and women.) Furthermore, the "republican mother" was not an ideal limited to America. Traian Stoianovich showed that an ideology of domesticity similar in content to republican motherhood had appeared in a systemized form in France by the late seventeenth century. See Fliegelman, *Prodigals and Pilgrims*; and Stoianovitch, "Gender and Family: Myths, Models, and Ideologies," *History Teacher*, 15 (1981): 70–84.

16. For the idea that women's political activity through organizations filled an undefined space in American government and politics, see Suzanne Lebsock, *The Free Women of Petersburg: Status and Culture in a Southern Town, 1784–1860* (New York, 1984), chap. 7.

17. On electoral participation in the early nineteenth century, see Ronald P. Formisano, "Deferential-Participant Politics: The Early Republic's Political Culture," *American Political Science Review* [hereafter, *APSR*], 68 (1974): 473–87; and Paul Kleppner, *Who Voted? The Dynamics of Electoral Turnout, 1870–1980* (New York, 1982), chap. 3: "The Era of Citizen Mobilization, 1840–1900." For a discussion of the increasing rates of participation, their timing, and their causes, see Richard P. McCormick, "New Perspectives on Jacksonian Politics," *AHR*, 65 (1959–60): 288–301.

18. The rise and decline—indeed, the existence—of deference in male political behavior remains widely debated by political historians. Ronald P. Formisano has provided a good review of this literature in "Deferential-Participation Politics." A number of studies of individual communities illustrate the appearance of competing elites and new community divisions and citizens' demands. See Bender, *Community and Social Change*, 100–08; Michael Frisch, *Town into City: Springfield, Massachusetts, and the Meaning of Community, 1840–1880* (Cambridge, Mass., 1972), 32–53, 179–201; and Harry L. Watson, *Jacksonian Politics and Community Conflict: The Emergence of the Second Party System in Cumberland County, North Carolina* (Baton Rouge, La., 1981), 82–108.

19. I have drawn my discussion of the connections between economic issues and party formation from Watson's *Jacksonian Politics and Community Conflict*, which imaginatively blends many of the themes and approaches historians have most recently advanced to explain nineteenth-century political life. Watson combined a refurbished economic interpretation, the assumption that citizens cared deeply about economic issues, a concern for questions about political culture, attention to republican ideology and quantitative methods, and a social analysis of politics in his account of party formation. Although such assumptions, methods, and concerns will probably continue to influence political historians, a good deal of debate remains about the development of parties and the meaning of partisanship. Richard P. McCormick argued that the legal framework governing elections (as well as the revival of the contest for the presidency) best explains the rising pitch of partisan behavior and that parties were fundamentally electoral machines, unconcerned with issues. See McCormick, *The Second American Party System*. Others, however, have found that ethnic and religious tensions among citizens can account for partisan divisions. See Lee Benson, *The Concept of Jacksonian Democracy: New York as a Test Case* (Princeton, N.J., 1961); Ronald P. Formisano, *The Birth of Mass Political Parties: Michigan, 1827–1861* (Princeton, N.J., 1971); Paul Kleppner, *The Cross of Culture: A Social Analysis of Midwestern Politics, 1850–1900* (New York, 1970); and Michael F. Holt, *Forging a Majority: The Formation of the Republican Party in Pittsburgh, 1848–1860* (New Haven, Conn., 1969). For recent historiographic analyses of Jacksonian politics, see Ronald P. Formisano, "Toward a Reorientation of Jacksonian Politics: A Review of the Literature, 1959–1975," *Journal of American History* [hereafter, *JAH*], 63 (1976–77): 42–65; and Sean Wilentz, "On Class and Politics in Jacksonian America," *Reviews in American History*, 10 (1982): 45–63. Richard L. McCormick evaluated the work of those offering an ethnic and religious interpretation. See McCormick, "Ethno-Cultural Interpretations of Nineteenth-Century American Voting Behavior," *Political Science Quarterly*, 89 (1974): 351–77.

20. Discussions of working men's parties include Bruce Laurie, *Working People of Philadelphia, 1800–1850*

(Philadelphia, 1980); and Edward Pessen, *Most Uncommon Jacksonians: The Political Leaders of the Early Labor Movement* (Albany, N.Y., 1967), 11–33. The Antimasonic party, strongest in rural areas, offered a moral critique of American politics and society; see Benson, *The Concept of Jacksonian Democracy*, 14–38. Ronald P. Formisano provided an analysis of both parties; see *The Transformation of Political Culture: Massachusetts Parties, 1790s–1840s* (New York, 1983), 197–224.

21. See Jean H. Baker, *Affairs of Party: The Political Culture of Northern Democrats in the Mid-Nineteenth Century* (Ithaca, N.Y., 1983), chaps. 1, 2; Benson, *The Concept of Jacksonian Democracy*; Formisano, *The Birth of Mass Political Parties*, chaps. 2, 7; and Watson, *Jacksonian Politics and Community Conflict*, 151–86, 269–77, 297–99, 312–13.

22. For a discussion of the removal of national issues from local politics, see Bender, *Community and Social Change*, 104.

23. On the positions on issues taken by various parties, see McCormick, *Second American Party System*; and Michael F. Holt, *The Political Crisis of the 1850s* (New York, 1978). Richard P. McCormick's view that parties were primarily electoral machines conflicts with that of Holt, who argued that parties needed clear divisions between them to maintain the voters' interest. For consensual politics at the local level, especially in settled towns, see Hal S. Barron, "After the Great Transformation: The Social Processes of Settled Rural Life in the Nineteenth-Century North," in Steven Hahn and Jonathan Prude, eds., *Rural Societies in Nineteenth-Century America: Essays in Social History* (Chapel Hill, N.C., forthcoming); Bender, *Community and Social Change*, 104–05; and Stuart Blumin, *The Urban Threshold: Growth and Change in a Nineteenth-Century Community* (Chicago, 1976), 144, 148.

24. For discussions of nineteenth-century voting patterns, see Walter Dean Burnham, "The Changing Shape of the American Political Universe," *APSR*, 59 (1965): 7–28; Paul Kleppner, *Who Voted*, chap. 3; and Richard L. McCormick, "The Party Period and Public Policy: An Exploratory Hypothesis," *JAH*, 66 (1979–80): 279–98. Although they agree on a description of political behavior in the nineteenth century, these accounts differ on periodization, focus, and explanations for the demise of nineteenth-century patterns. I have adopted McCormick's emphases on the continuities of partisan behavior throughout most of the nineteenth century and the links between distribution and partisanship. For the best account of the connections between partisanship and family, see Baker, *Affairs of Party*, chap. 1.

25. Daniel Calhoun suggested that fears about gender replaced fears about tyranny in the political thought of the nineteenth century; Calhoun, *The Intelligence of a People* (Princeton, N.J., 1973), 188–205. For a discussion of partisan politics as a way of re-creating fraternal relations, see Wilson Carey McWilliams, *The Idea of Fraternity in America* (Berkeley and Los Angeles, 1973), chap. 3, 243–53. For an account from the Progressive era, see Mary Kingsbury Simkhovitch, "Friendship and Politics," *Political Science Quarterly*, 17 (1902): 189–205.

26. Descriptions and analyses of campaign rituals include Robert Gray Gunderson, *The Log Cabin Campaign* (Lexington, Ky., 1957), 1–11, 108–47, 210–18; Richard Jensen, *The Winning of the Midwest: Social and Political Conflict, 1888–1896* (Chicago, 1971), 1–33, and "Armies, Admen, and Crusaders: Types of Presidential Election Campaigns," *History Teacher*, 2 (1969): 33–50; Michael E. McGerr, "Political Spectacle and Partisanship in New Haven, 1860–1900," paper presented at the Seventy-Fifth Annual Meeting of the Organization of American Historians, held in Philadelphia, April 1982; and McCormick, *The Second American Party System*, 15–16, 30–31, 75–76, 88, 145, 157–58, 268–76. Lewis O. Saum, drawing on a vast number of diaries, documented citizens' participation in campaigns and the laconic reactions to antebellum politics; Saum, *The Popular Mood of Pre-Civil War America* (Westport, Conn., 1980), 149–57.

27. Party politicians often spoke of reformers—those men outside of the party—in terms that questioned the reformers' masculinity. Most of all, reformers were seen as politically impotent. Men whose loyalty to a party was questionable were referred to, for example, as the "third sex" of American politics, "man-milliners," and "Miss-Nancys." This suggests that men, like women, were limited in the forms that their political participation could take. Works that note these charges of effeminacy include Lois W. Banner, *Elizabeth Cady Stanton: A Radical for Woman's Rights* (Boston, 1980), 43; Geoffrey Blodgett, "Reform Thought and the Genteel Tradition," in H. Wayne Morgan, ed., *The Gilded Age* (2d edn., Syracuse, N.Y., 1970), 56–57; Richard Hofstadter, *Anti-Intellectualism in American Life* (New York, 1963), 179–91; and Alan Trachtenberg, *The Incorporation of America: Culture and Society in the Gilded Age* (New York, 1982), 163–65. In addition to this language, phallic imagery and symbolism had an important place in nineteenth-century electoral politics. Psychohistorians might find a good deal of underlying meaning in the long ballot (reformers favored the short form) and pole raisings, for example, as well as in partisans' charges of sexual impotence. Political historians, however, have as yet failed to examine the rituals and symbols of partisan contests in regard to their sexual connotations.

28. Formisano, *Transformation of Political Culture*, 266; McGerr, "Political Spectacle and Partisanship,"; and Saum, *The Popular Mood of Pre-Civil War America*, 153.

29. On economic policy and constitutional revision, see Wallace D. Farnham, " 'The Weakened Spring of

106 / Paula Baker

Government': A Study in Nineteenth-Century American History," *AHR*, 68 (1962–63); 662–80; L. Ray Gunn, "Political Implications of General Incorporation Laws in New York to 1860," *Mid-America*, 59 (1977): 171–91; Oscar Handlin and Mary Flug Handlin, *Commonwealth: A Study of the Role of Government in the American Economy—Massachusetts, 1774–1861* (New York, 1947); Louis Hartz, *Economic Policy and Democratic Thought: Pennsylvania, 1776–1850* (Cambridge, Mass., 1948); James Willard Hurst, *Law and the Conditions of Freedom in the Nineteenth-Century United States* (Madison, Wisc., 1956), chaps. 1, 2; and Morton Keller, *Affairs of State: Public Life in Late Nineteenth-Century America* (Cambridge, Mass., 1977), 71–81. On changes in social policy, see Jeremy P. Felt, *Hostages of Fortune: Child Labor Reform in New York State* (Syracuse, N.Y., 1956), 17–37; and Walter I. Trattner, *From Poor Law to Welfare State: A History of Social Welfare in America* (New York, 1974), chaps. 2–4.

30. Cott, *The Bonds of Womanhood*, chap. 2; Berg, *The Remembered Gate*, chaps. 2–4; Degler, *At Odds*, chaps. 3–5; Ann Douglas, *The Feminization of American Culture* (New York, 1977), 65–90, 107–11; Sklar, *Catharine Beecher*, 87, 151–67, 212–13; Mary P. Ryan, *Womanhood in America: From Colonial Times to the Present* (1975; 2d edn., New York, 1979), 142–74; Carroll Smith-Rosenberg, "Beauty, the Beast, and the Militant Woman: A Case Study in Sex Roles and Social Stress in Jacksonian America," *American Quarterly*, 4 (1971): 562–84; Ryan, *Womanhood in America*, 85–92; and Welter, "Cult of True Womanhood."

31. Mary P. Ryan argued that these new organizations prepared women for a domesticity confined to the conjugal family; *Cradle of the Middle Class*, esp. 9–18. Perhaps Berg made the strongest case for the political importance of early nineteenth-century women's organizations, for she contended that these early reform groups provided the groundwork for American feminism; *The Remembered Gate*, esp. 6–7, 174–75, 240–42.

32. Welter, "Cult of True Womanhood"; and Sklar, *Catharine Beecher*, 126–29, 151–67, 172, 212–13.

33. The phrase is Welter's; see "The Cult of True Womanhood." Since the appearance of her work, historians of women have concentrated on questions different from those Welter asked about the concurrent rise of the woman's sphere and male egalitarianism. Welter explored the relationship between the two and found that the new insistence on woman's place compensated for the lack of restraint on male political and economic ambitions. Scholars have since focused on the impact of domesticity on feminism. Some historians, taking a "cultural" approach, have seen the roots of feminism in women's organizations and domesticity. Others, notably Ellen DuBois, have found this inadequate. They have argued that, in order to understand the origins of feminism, historians should pay closest attention to explicitly "political" concerns in the nineteenth century. For an introduction to this debate, see "Politics and Culture in Women's History: A Symposium," *Feminist Studies*, 6 (1980): 26–54. Studies of the woman's sphere in the Jacksonian period include Berg, *The Remembered Gate*; Cott, *The Bonds of Womanhood*; Lerner, "The Lady and the Mill Girl"; Glenda Riley, "The Subtle Subversion: Changes in the Traditionalist Image of the American Woman," *Historian*, 32 (1970): 210–27; Sklar, *Catharine Beecher*, esp. 134–36, 155–67; Smith-Rosenberg, "Beauty, the Beast, and the Militant Woman"; and Ryan, *Womanhood in America*, 85–92.

34. Gordon Wood, *The Creation of the American Republic, 1776–1787* (Chapel Hill, N.C., 1969). For an economic understanding of the republican vocabulary, see Rowland Berthoff, "Independence and Attachment, Virtue and Interest: From Republican Citizen to Free Enterpriser, 1787–1837," in Bushman *et al.*, eds., *Uprooted Americans: Essays to Honor Oscar Handlin* (Boston, 1979), 97–124. In a related vein, Merle Curti discussed economic arguments for national loyalty; see Curti, *The Roots of American Loyalty* (New York, 1946), chap. 4. On connections between domesticity and Jacksonian democracy, see Lawrence J. Friedman, *Inventors of the Promised Land* (New York, 1975), chap. 4; and Sklar, *Catharine Beecher*, 80–89, 155–63.

35. Degler, *At Odds*, 332–33; and Suzanne D. Lebsock, "Radical Reconstruction and the Property Rights of Southern Women," *Journal of Southern History*, 43 (1977): 195–216. Lebsock noted that opposition to women speakers, along with new forms of ritual deference, appeared in the middle of the nineteenth century, and she suggested that men may have reacted to women's increasing power in the private sphere by encroaching on their public roles; *Free Women of Petersburg*, chap. 7.

36. Mary P. Ryan referred to women who wished to apply motherhood to the public sphere as "social housekeepers"; *Womanhood in America*, 142–47, 226–35. For other studies that consider the expansion and articulation of domesticity, see Cott, *The Bonds of Womanhood*; Linda Gordon, *Woman's Body, Woman's Right: A Social History of Birth Control* (New York, 1976), 95–115, 126–36; Ryan, *Cradle of the Middle Class*; and Sklar, *Catharine Beecher*, 80–89, 96, 135–37, 151–67, 193–94, 203, 221–22, 264–65.

37. Dorr, *What Eight Million Women Want* (Boston, 1919; reprint edn., New York, 1971), 327.

38. Berg, *The Remembered Gate*, esp. chap. 7; Degler, *At Odds*, 279–86, 298–316; Cott, *The Bonds of Womanhood*, 149–59; Melder, *Beginnings of Sisterhood*, 40–43, 50–60, 64–76; Ryan, *Cradle of the Middle Class*, chap. 3; and Smith-Rosenberg, "Beauty, the Beast, and the Militant Woman."

39. Both Berg and Melder stressed the anti-male rhetoric of these early organizations; Melder, *Beginnings of Sisterhood*, chap. 4, esp. 55. Also see Riley, "Subtle Subversion"; Mary P. Ryan, "The Power of Women's Networks: A Case Study of Female Moral Reform in Antebellum America," *Feminist Studies*, 5 (1979): 66–

85; Smith-Rosenberg, "Beauty, the Beast, and the Militant Woman"; Blair, *Clubwoman as Feminist*; Estelle B. Freedman, *Their Sisters' Keepers: Women's Prison Reform in America, 1830–1930* (Ann Arbor, Mich., 1981), 22–35; and Leach, *True Love and Perfect Union*, chaps. 6–7.

40. Berg, *The Remembered Gate*, 183–85. For comparable examples, see Melder, *Beginnings of Sisterhood*, chap. 4; and Ryan, "The Power of Women's Networks."

41. On the possibility of racial cooperation, see Blanche Glassman Hersh, *The Slavery of Sex: Feminist Abolitionists in America* (Urbana, Ill., 1978). Gerda Lerner has explicated the difficulty of such cooperation; see "Black and White Women in Interaction and Confrontation."

42. On the Woman's Parliament, see Blair, *Clubwoman as Feminist*, 39–45, 73.

43. DuBois, *Feminism and Suffrage*. Also see Degler, *At Odds*, chap. 7; and Scott and Scott, *One-Half the People*.

44. DuBois, *Feminism and Suffrage*.

45. Fourteen states admitted women to the electorate at least for school elections. Four states—Wyoming, Colorado, Idaho, and Utah—passed full woman suffrage amendments. On the conservative, nonfeminist motives behind the passage of woman suffrage in the Western states, see Grimes, *Puritan Ethic and Woman Suffrage*. For Sarah Churske Stevens's account of her successful race for school superintendent in Markate County, Minnesota, in 1890, see Lerner, *Female Experience*, 361–73.

46. George M. Frederickson, *The Inner Civil War: Northern Intellectuals and the Crisis of the Union* (New York, 1965); James Gilbert, *Designing the Industrial State: The Intellectual Pursuit of Collectivism in America, 1880–1940* (Chicago, 1972); Peter Dobkin Hall, *The Organization of American Culture, 1700–1900: Private Institutions, Elites, and the Origins of American Nationality* (New York, 1982), 218–70; Thomas L. Haskell, *The Emergence of Professional Social Science: The American Social Science Association and the Nineteenth-Century Crisis of Authority* (Urbana, Ill., 1977); Keller, *Affairs of State;* Leach, *True Love and Perfect Union;* and Trachtenberg. *The Incorporation of America.*

47. L. P. Brockett and Mary C. Vaughn, *Women's Work in the Civil War* (Philadelphia, 1967); Ann Douglas, "The War Within: Women Nurses in the Union Army," *Civil War History*, 18 (1972): 197–212; Fredrickson, *The Inner Civil War*, 98–112, 212–16; Livermore, *My Story of the War;* Rothman, *Woman's Proper Place,* 71–74; and Ryan, *Womanhood in America,* 226–28.

48. Buhle, *Women and American Socialism;* Ann D. Gordon and Mari Jo Buhle, "Gender Politics and Class Conflict: Chicago in the Gilded Age," paper presented at the Upstate Women's History Conference, held in Binghamton, New York, October 1981.

49. Social science was for Franklin Sanborn, a leader of the American Social Science Association, "the feminine gender of Political Economy, . . . very receptive of particulars but little capacity of general and aggregate matters." Sanborn, as quoted in Haskell, *Emergence of Professional Social Science,* 137.

50. On women and social science, see Gordon and Buhle, "Gender Politics and Class Conflict"; Leach, *True Love and Perfect Union,* 316–22, 324–46; and Rothman, *Woman's Proper Place,* 108–12. Transitions in reform thought and tactics are traced in Paul Boyer, *Urban Masses and Moral Order, 1820–1920* (Cambridge, Mass., 1978); Robert H. Bremner, *From the Depths. The Discovery of Poverty in the United States* (New York, 1956); Fredrickson, *The Inner Civil War,* 98–112, 119–216; Roy Lubove, *The Professional Altruist: The Emergence of Social Work as a Career, 1880–1930* (Cambridge, Mass., 1965), 2–20, 81–82, 84; and David P. Thelen, *The New Citizenship: The Origins of Progressivism in Wisconsin, 1885–1900* (Columbia, Mo., 1972). On the South, see James L. Leloudis II, "School Reform in the New South: The Women's Association for the Betterment of Public School Houses in North Carolina, 1902–1919," *JAH,* 69 (1982–83): 886–909; and Scott, *Southern Lady,* chap. 6.

51. For an examination of changing attitudes about voluntarism, see Kathleen D. McCarthy, *Noblesse Oblige. Charity and Cultural Philanthropy in Chicago, 1849–1929* (Chicago, 1982), esp. 27–50.

52. On women's activity in early temperance organizations, see Jed Dannenbaum, "The Origins of Temperance Activism and Militancy among American Women," *Journal of Social History,* 15 (1981–82): 235–52; Epstein, *The Politics of Domesticity,* 93–114; and Eliza Daniel ("Mother") Stewart, *Memories of the Crusade: A Thrilling Account of the Great Uprising of the Women of Ohio in 1873 against the Liquor Crime* (Columbus, Ohio, 1889; reprint edn., 1972).

53. Willard attempted to ally the WCTU with the Prohibitionists and later the Populists. For a time, she also considered supporting the Republican party but found it an unreliable partner. On Willard's relationship and that of the WCTU to the parties and reform movements of the Gilded Age, see Jack S. Blocker, Jr., "The Politics of Reform: Populists, Prohibitionists, and Woman Suffrage, 1891–1892," *Historian,* 34 (1975): 614–32; Ruth Bordin, "Frances Willard and the Practice of Political Influence," paper presented at the Seventy-Sixth Annual Meeting of the Organization of American Historians, held in Cincinnati, Ohio, April 1983; Buhle, *Women and American Socialism,* 60–69, 80–89; Epstein, *The Politics of Domesticity,* 137–47; and Joseph R. Gusfield, *Symbolic Crusade: Status Politics and the American Temperance Movement* (Urbana, Ill., 1963), 88–96.

54. Bordin, *Woman and Temperance*; Buhle, *Women and American Socialism*, 54–60, 70–89; Degler, *At Odds*, 338–39; Gordon and Buhle, "Gender Politics and Class Conflict"; and Epstein, *The Politics of Domesticity*, chap. 5.

55. Historians and political scientists have devoted a good deal of attention to changing patterns of electoral politics in the early twentieth century. Still, much controversy remains. For different points of view, see Burnham, "The Changing Shape of the American Political Universe"; Philip E. Converse, "Change in the American Electorate," in Angus Campbell and Converse, eds., *The Human Meaning of Social Change* (New York, 1972), 263–337; J. Morgan Kousser, *The Shaping of Southern Politics: Suffrage Restrictions and the Establishment of the One-Party South, 1880–1910* (New Haven, Conn., 1974); and Jerrold G. Rusk, "The Effect of the Australian Ballot on Split-Ticket Voting," *APSR*, 64 (1970): 1220–38. Other important works tie changes in electoral politics to the transformation of governance in the twentieth century. See Hays, *Response to Industrialism*; Paul Kleppner, *The Third Electoral System, 1853–1892: Parties, Voters, and Political Cultures* (Chapel Hill, N.C., 1979), and *Who Voted*, chap. 4; Richard L. McCormick, "The Discovery That Business Corrupts Politics: A Reappraisal of the Origins of Progressivism," *AHR*, 86 (1981): 247–74; and Wiebe, *The Search for Order*. The interpretation offered here blends elements of these approaches along with the findings of studies of late nineteenth-century community life. It owes the most to Samuel P. Hays, "Political Parties and the Community-Society Continuum," in William Nisbet Chambers and Walter Dean Burnham, eds., *The American Party Systems: Stages of Political Development* (2d edn., New York, 1975), 152–81.

56. On the connection between community change and partisan behavior, see Hays, "Political Parties and the Community-Society Continuum"; Kleppner, *Who Voted*; and Paula Baker, "The Culture of Politics in the Late Nineteenth Century: Community and Political Behavior in Rural New York," *Journal of Social History* (forthcoming). The relationship between partisanship and forms of policy making is analyzed in McCormick, "The Party Period and Public Policy."

57. Gerald N. Grob, "The Political System and Social Policy in the Nineteenth Century: Legacy of the Revolution," *Mid-America*, 58 (1976): 5–19.

58. Blair, *Clubwoman as Feminist*; Marlene Stein Wortman, "Domesticating the Nineteenth-Century American City," *Prospects: An Annual of American Cultural Studies*, 3 (1977): 531–72; Rothman, *Woman's Proper Place*, 102–26, 112–27; and Margaret Gibbons Wilson, *The American Woman in Transition: The Urban Influence, 1870–1920* (Westport, Conn., 1979), 91–99. Women in the South engaged in similar work through women's clubs and church organizations; see Leloudis, "School Reform in the New South"; John Patrick McDowell, *The Social Gospel in the South: The Women's Home Mission Movement in the Methodist Episcopal Church, South, 1886–1939* (Baton Rouge, La., 1982); and Scott, *Southern Lady*, chap. 6. Middle-class black women worked through separate organizations in the nineteenth century. See Lynda F. Dickson, "The Early Club Movement among Black Women in Denver, 1890–1925" (Ph.D. dissertation, University of Colorado, 1982); Tullia Hamilton, "The National Association of Colored Women's Clubs" (Ph.D. dissertation, Emory University, 1978); and Gerda Lerner, "Community Work of Black Women's Clubs," and "Black and White Women in Interaction and Confrontation." For clubwomen's descriptions of their work, see Croly, *History of the Women's Club Movement*; Gerda Lerner, ed., *Black Women in White America: A Documentary History* (New York, 1972), chap. 8; and Mary I. Wood, *The History of the General Federation of Women's Clubs for the First Twenty-Two Years of Its Organization* (New York, 1912).

59. Beard, *Women's Work*, 221.

60. *Ibid.*, chap. 6–7; Wilson, *American Woman in Transition*; Rothman, *Woman's Proper Place*, 119–27; and Wortman, "Domesticating the Nineteenth-Century American City."

61. Wortman, "Domesticating the Nineteenth-Century American City"; and Leloudis, "School Reform in the New South." For contemporary accounts, see Beard, *Women's Work*, chaps. 9–11; Wood, *History of the General Federation*, 120–209; and Dorr, *What Eight Million Women Want*.

62. Among the many works that trace the transition in liberal thought, see Theodore J. Lowi, *The End of Liberalism: The Second Republic of the United States* (2d edn., New York, 1979), chaps. 1–3; R. Jeffrey Lustig, *Corporate Liberalism: The Origins of Modern American Political Theory, 1890–1920* (Berkeley and Los Angeles, 1982); William E. Nelson, *The Roots of American Bureaucracy, 1830–1900* (Cambridge, Mass., 1982); and James Weinstein, *The Corporate Ideal in the Liberal State, 1900–1918* (Boston, 1968). Discussions of the family and the small community as a model are provided in Jean B. Quandt, *From the Small Town to the Great Community: The Social Thought of Progressive Intellectuals* (New Brunswick, N.J., 1970); and Wortman, "Domesticating the Nineteenth-Century American City." Although historians have not yet fully described the mechanism by which government took on work that had been the responsibility of voluntary organizations, a few hypotheses seem safe. Municipal governments were undoubtedly responding to demands for better social services—ones in part created by women's attempts to form public opinion. Turning to existing institutions would have been a logical choice for municipal governments. Office holders may also have seen

new opportunities for patronage—opportunities that gained importance as older sources (service contracts arranged with private businesses, for example) fell under attack.

63. The second generation has been presented as conservative even by those historians who have regarded suffrage as a radical demand. See Degler, *At Odds*, 357–61; and Ellen DuBois, ed., *Elizabeth Cady Stanton and Susan B. Anthony: Correspondence, Writings, Speeches* (New York, 1981), 192–93. The most detailed analysis of the suffrage movement's conservative turn are Kraditor, *Ideas of the Woman Suffrage Movement*; and O'Neill, *Everyone Was Brave*.

64. DuBois pointed out that the second-generation suffragists' insistence on nonpartisanship is an indication that the vote—rather than what women might do with it—was their major goal; *Elizabeth Cady Stanton and Susan B. Anthony*, 182–83. The suffragists' new campaign tactics owed a large debt to the publicity-gathering techniques of the Congressional Union. For a good account of the course of the suffrage campaign, see Carrie Chapman Catt, *Woman Suffrage and Politics: The Inner Story of the Suffrage Movement* (1923; 2d edn., New York, 1926), 189–91, 212, 284–99, 302–15. Also see Flexner, *Century of Struggle*, 262–65, 271, 285; and Sharon Hartman Strom, "Leadership and Tactics in the American Woman Suffrage Movement: A New Perspective from Massachusetts," *JAH*, 62 (1975–76): 296–315.

65. The counties that supported suffrage in 1915 were Chautauqua, Schenectady, Chemung, Broome, and Tompkins. The lowest support for the referenda in both 1915 and 1917—as low as 30 percent—occurred in the counties of Livingston, Yates, Ulster, Lewis, Albany, and Columbia. Preliminary calculations suggest that in places where women's groups had a long history of public action, where men's organizations (such as agricultural societies) had increasing involvement in interest-group politics, and where the Socialist vote was high voters were more likely to support suffrage. The southern-tier counties, for example, illustrate the first two hypotheses. Schenectady County, like certain wards in New York City, supported Socialist candidates. Rough calculations also suggest that comparatively high levels of turnout and low incidence of split-ticket voting occurred in places where suffrage was unpopular. Nearly half of New York's sixty-two counties supported suffrage in 1917, but the greatest gains were made in New York, Bronx, Kings, Richmond, and Westchester counties. For studies of the New York City campaign, see Doris Daniels, "Building a Winning Coalition: The Suffrage Fight in New York State," *New York History*, 60 (1979): 59–88; and Elinor Lerner, "Immigrant and Working-Class Involvement in the New York City Suffrage Movement, 1905–1917: A Study in Progressive Era Politics" (Ph.D. dissertation, University of California, Berkeley, 1981). Both Daniels and Lerner emphasized the support suffrage received from immigrant groups—especially Jewish voters—and Socialist voters. Lerner noted that men who voted for suffrage probably knew many women who were financially independent. Neither, however, put the race in the context of long-term political patterns.

66. Paula S. Fass, *The Damned and the Beautiful: American Youth in the 1920s* (New York, 1977). Ironically, motherhood was ritualized and glorified just as the domestic ideal declined. See Kathleen W. Jones, "Mother's Day: The Creation, Promotion, and Meaning of a New Holiday in the Progressive Era," *Texas Studies in Literature and Language*, 22 (1980): 176–96. For a review of the work on women in the 1920s, see Estelle B. Freedman, "The New Woman: Changing Views of Women in the 1920s," *JAH*, 61 (1974–75): 373–93. Also useful is Freda Kirchwey, *Our Changing Morality: A Symposium* (New York, 1924).

67. On the changed relationship between doctors and mothers, see Kathleen W. Jones, "Sentiment and Science: The Late Nineteenth-Century Pediatrician as Mother's Advisor," *Journal of Social History*, 17 (1983–84): 79–96. Jones stressed the reciprocal relationship between women and professionals, noting that women initially sought experts' advice and helped shape the profession of pediatrics. For accounts of women as more passive recipients of expert intrusion, see Barbara Ehrenreich and Deirdre English, *For Her Own Good: One Hundred Fifty Years of the Experts' Advice to Women* (Garden City, N.J., 1978); Christopher Lasch, *Haven in a Heartless World: The Family Besieged* (New York, 1977); and Rothman, *Woman's Proper Place*.

68. Felice Dosik Gordon, "After Winning: The New Jersey Suffragists, 1910–1947" (Ph.D. dissertation, Rutgers University, 1982). In an important recent article, Estelle B. Freedman has argued that women's separate institutions provided a degree of influence lost when women joined organizations that included both sexes; see "Separatism as Strategy."

69. On the rise of interest groups in politics, see Richard L. McCormick, *From Realignment to Reform: Political Change in New York State, 1893–1910* (Ithaca, N.Y., 1981), 151–155, 173–77, 264–71; Herbert F. Margulies, *The Decline of the Progressive Movement in Wisconsin, 1890–1920* (Madison, Wisc., 1968); and Mansel G. Blackford, *The Politics of Business in California, 1890–1920* (Columbus, Ohio, 1977). The image of the intelligent client—in this case, the voter—was common in the late nineteenth and early twentieth centuries. It applied even to motherhood. See Jones, "Sentiment and Science"; and Rothman, *Woman's Proper Place*, 97–99. A classic study that illustrates men's adoption of women's political tactics is Peter H. Odegard, *Pressure Politics: The Story of the Anti-Saloon League* (New York, 1928).

70. Ellis Hawley, *The Great War and the Search for a Modern Order: A History of the American People and Their*

Institutions, 1917–1933 (New York, 1979), 80–109; and Louis Galambos, *Competition and Cooperation: The Emergence of a National Trade Association* (Baltimore, 1966).

71. Christopher Lasch, *The Culture of Narcissism: American Life in an Age of Diminishing Expectations* (New York, 1979); and Richard Sennett, *The Fall of Public Man: On the Social Psychology of Capitalism* (1974; 2d edn., New York, 1976). On the transition from "character" to "personality" in twentieth-century culture, a transition that has important implications for the study of politics, see Warren I. Susman, " 'Personality' and the making of Twentieth-Century Culture," in John Higham and Paul K. Conkin, eds., *New Directions in American Intellectual History* (Baltimore, 1979), 212–26.

72. John Dewey, *The Public and Its Problems* (New York, 1927), 27. As a refinement, "consequences" might be considered political only if they represent attempts to change prescriptions for behaviors and attitudes that are enshrined in law or custom, whether done through legal or informal means.

8

Women, Children, and the Uses of the Streets: Class and Gender Conflict in New York City, 1850–1860

Christine Stansell

On a winter day in 1856, an agent for the Children's Aid Society (CAS) of New York encountered two children out on the street with market baskets. Like hundreds he might have seen, they were desperately poor—thinly dressed and barefoot in the cold—but their cheerful countenances struck the gentleman, and he stopped to inquire into their circumstances. They explained that they were out gathering bits of wood and coal their mother could burn for fuel and agreed to take him home to meet her. In a bare tenement room, bereft of heat, furniture, or any other comforts, he met a "stout, hearty woman" who, even more than her children, testified to the power of hardihood and motherly love in the most miserable circumstances. A widow, she supported her family as best she could by street peddling; their room was bare because she had been forced to sell her clothes, furniture, and bedding to supplement her earnings. As she spoke, she sat on a pallet on the floor and rubbed the hands of the two younger siblings of the pair from the street. "They were tidy, sweet children," noted the agent, "And it was very sad to see their chilled faces and tearful eyes." Here was a scene that would have touched the heart of Dickens, and seemingly many a chillier mid-Victorian soul. Yet in concluding his report, the agent's perceptions took a curiously harsh turn.

> Though for her pure young children too much could hardly be done, in such a woman there is little confidence to be put . . . it is probably, some cursed vice has thus reduced her, and that, if her children be not separated from her, she will drag them down, too.[1]

Such expeditions of charity agents and reformers into the households of the poor were common in New York between 1850 and 1860. So were such harsh and unsupported judgments of working-class mothers, judgments which either implicitly or explicitly converged in the new category of the "dangerous classes." In this decade, philanthropists, municipal authorities, and a second generation of Christian evangelicals, male and female, came to see the presence of poor children in New York's streets as a central element of the problem of urban poverty. They initiated an ambitious campaign to clear the streets, to change the character of the laboring poor by altering their family lives, and, in the process, to eradicate poverty itself. They focused their efforts on transforming two elements of laboring-class family life, the place of children and the role of women.

There was, in fact, nothing new about the presence of poor children in the streets, nor was it new that women of the urban poor should countenance that presence. For centuries,

This article is reprinted from *Feminist Studies*, volume 8, number 2 (Summer 1982): 309–335, by permission of the publisher, *Feminist Studies, Inc.*, c/o Women's Studies Program, University of Maryland, College Park, MD 20742.

poor people in Europe had freely used urban public areas—streets, squares, courts, and marketplaces—for their leisure and work. For the working poor, street life was bound up not only with economic exigency, but also with childrearing, family morality, sociability, and neighborhood ties. In the nineteenth century, the crowded conditions of the tenements and the poverty of great numbers of metropolitan laboring people made the streets as crucial an arena as ever for their social and economic lives. As one New York social investigator observed, "In the poorer portions of the city, people live much and sell mostly out of doors."[2]

How, then, do we account for this sudden flurry of concern? For reformers like the agent from the CAS, street life was antagonistic to ardently held beliefs about childhood, womanhood and, ultimately, the nature of civilized urban society. The middle class of which the reformers were a part was only emerging, an economically ill-defined group, neither rich nor poor, just beginning in the antebellum years to assert a distinct cultural identity. Central to its self-conception was the ideology of domesticity, a set of sharp ideas and pronounced opinions about the nature of a moral family life. The sources of this ideology were historically complex and involved several decades of struggles by women of this group for social recognition, esteem, and power in the family. Nonetheless, by midcentury, ideas initially developed and promoted by women and their clerical allies had found general acceptance, and an ideology of gender had become firmly embedded in an ideology of class. Both women and men valued the home, an institution which they perceived as sacred, presided over by women, inhabited by children, frequented by men. The home preserved those social virtues endangered by the public world of trade, industry, and politics, a public world which they saw as even more corrupting and dangerous in a great city like New York.[3]

Enclosed, protected, and privatized, the home and the patterns of family life on which it was based thus represented to middle-class women and men a crucial institution of civilization. From this perspective, a particular geography of social life—the engagement of the poor in street life rather than in the enclave of the home—became in itself evidence of parental neglect, family disintegration, and a pervasive urban social pathology. Thus in his condemnation of the impoverished widow, the CAS agent distilled an entire analysis of poverty and a critique of poor families: the presence of her children on the streets was synonymous with a corrupt family life, no matter how disguised it might be. In the crusade of such mid-Victorian reformers to save poor children from their parents and their class lie the roots of a long history of middle-class intervention in working-class families, a history which played a central part in the making of the female American working class.

Many historians have shown the importance of antebellum urban reform to the changing texture of class relations in America, its role in the cultural transformations of urbanization and industrialization.[4] Confronted with overcrowding, unemployment, and poverty on a scale theretofore unknown in America, evangelical reformers forged programs to control and mitigate these pressing urban problems, programs which would shape municipal policies for years to come. Yet their responses were not simply practical solutions, the most intelligent possible reactions to difficult circumstances; as the most sensitive historians of reform have argued, they were shaped by the world view, cultural affinities, conceptions of gender, class prejudices, and imperatives of the reformers themselves. Urban reform was an interaction in which, over time, both philanthropists and their beneficiaries changed. In their experience with the reformers, the laboring poor learned—and were forced—to accommodate themselves to an alien conception of family and city life. Through their work with the poor, the reformers discovered many of the elements from which they would forge their own class and sexual identity, still ill-defined and diffuse in 1850; women, particularly, strengthened their role as dictators of domestic and familial standards for all classes of Americans. The reformers' eventual triumph in New York brought no solutions to the problem of poverty, but it did bring about the evisceration of a way of urban life and the legitimation of their own cultural power as a class.

The conflict over the streets resonated on many levels. Ostensibly the reformers aimed to rescue children from the corruptions and dangers of the city streets; indeed the conscious motives of many, if not all, of these well-meaning altruists went no further. There were many unquestioned assumptions, however, on which their benevolent motives rested, and it is in examining these assumptions that we begin to see the challenge which these middle-class people unwittingly posed to common practices of the poor. In their cultural offensive, reformers sought to impose on the poor conceptions of childhood and motherhood drawn from their own ideas of domesticity. In effect, reformers tried to implement their domestic beliefs through reorganizing social space, through creating a new geography of the city. Women were especially active; while male reformers experimented, through a rural foster home program, with more dramatic means of clearing the streets, middle-class ladies worked to found new working-class homes, modeled on their own, which would establish a viable alternative to the thoroughly nondomesticated streets. Insofar as the women reformers succeeded, their victory contributed to both the dominance of a class and of a specific conception of gender. It was, moreover, a victory which had enduring and contradictory consequences for urban women of all classes. In our contemporary city streets, vacated, for the most part, of domestic life yet dangerous for women and children, we see something of the legacy of their labors.

Children's Uses of the Streets

Unlike today, the teeming milieu of the New York streets in the mid-nineteenth century was in large part a children's world. A complex web of economic imperatives and social mores accounted for their presence there, a presence which reformers so ardently decried. Public life, with its panoply of choices, its rich and varied texture, its motley society, played as central a role in the upbringing of poor children as did private, domestic life in that of their more affluent peers. While middle-class mothers spent a great deal of time with their children (albeit with the help of servants), women of the laboring classes condoned for their offspring an early independence—within bounds—on the streets. Through peddling, scavenging, and the shadier arts of theft and prostitution, the streets offered children a way to earn their keep, crucial to making ends meet in their households. Street life also provided a home for children without families—the orphaned and abandoned—and an alternative to living at home for the especially independent and those in strained family circumstances.

Such uses of the streets were dictated by exigency, but they were also intertwined with patterns of motherhood, parenthood, and childhood. In contrast to their middle- and upper-class contemporaries, the working poor did not think of childhood as a separate stage of life in which girls and boys were free from adult burdens, nor did poor women consider mothering to be a full-time task of supervision. They expected their children to work from an early age, to "earn their keep" or to "get a living," a view much closer to the early modern conceptions which Philippe Ariès describes in *Centuries of Childhood*.[5] Children were little adults, unable as yet to take up all the duties of their elders, but nonetheless bound to do as much as they could. To put it another way, the lives of children, like those of adults, were circumscribed by economic and familial obligations. In this context, the poor expressed their care for children differently than did the propertied classes. Raising one's children properly did not mean protecting them from the world of work; on the contrary, it involved teaching them to shoulder those heavy burdens of labor which were the common lot of their class, to be hardworking and dutiful to kin and neighbors. By the same token, laboring children gained an early autonomy from their parents, an autonomy alien to the experience of more privileged children. But there were certainly generational tensions embedded in these practices: although children learned independence within the bounds of family obligation, their self-sufficiency also led them in directions that parents could not always control. When parents sent children out to the streets, they could only partially set the terms of what the young ones learned there.

Street selling, or huckstering, was one of the most common ways for children to turn the streets to good use. Through the nineteenth century, this ancient form of trade still flourished in New York alongside such new institutions of mass marketing as A.T. Stewart's department store.[5] Hucksters, both adults and children, sold all manner of necessities and delicacies. In the downtown business and shopping district, passers-by could buy treats at every corner: hot sweet potatoes, bake-pears, teacakes, fruit, candy, and hot corn. In residential neighborhoods, hucksters sold household supplies door to door: fruits and vegetables in season, matchsticks, scrub brushes, sponges, strings, and pins. Children assisted adult hucksters, went peddling on their own, and worked in several low-paying trades which were their special province: crossing-sweeping for girls; errand running, bootblacking, horse holding, and newspaper selling for boys.[6] There were also the odd trades in which children were particularly adept, those unfamiliar and seemingly gratuitous forms of economic activity which abounded in nineteenth-century metropolises: one small boy whom a social investigator found in 1859 made his living in warm weather by catching butterflies and peddling them to canary owners.[7]

Younger children, too, could earn part of their keep on the streets. Scavenging, the art of gathering useful and salable trash, was the customary chore for those too small to go out streetselling. Not all scavengers were children; there were also adults who engaged in scavenging full-time, ragpickers who made their entire livelihoods from "all the odds and ends of a great city."[8] More generally, however, scavenging was children's work. Six- or seven-year-olds were not too young to set out with friends and siblings to gather fuel for their mothers. Small platoons of these children scoured neighborhood streets, ship and lumber yards, building lots, demolished houses, and the precincts of artisan shops and factories for chips, ashes, wood, and coal to take home or peddle to neighbors. "I saw some girls gathering cinders," noted Virginia Penny, New York's self-styled Mayhew. "They burn them at home, after washing them."[9]

The economy of rubbish was intricate. As children grew more skilled, they learned how to turn up other serviceable cast-offs. "These gatherers of things lost on earth," a journal had called them in 1831. "These makers of something out of nothing."[10] Besides taking trash home or selling it to neighbors, children could peddle it to junk dealers, who in turn vended it to manufacturers and artisans for use in industrial processes. Rags, old rope, metal, nails, bottles, paper, kitchen grease, bones, spoiled vegetables, and bad meat all had their place in this commercial network. The waterfront was especially fruitful territory: there, children foraged for loot which had washed up on the banks, snagged in piers, or spilled out on the docks. Loose cotton shredded off bales on the wharves where the southern packet ships docked, bits of canvas and rags ended up with paper- and shoddy-manufacturers (shoddy, the cheapest of textiles, made its way back to the poor in "shoddy" ready-made clothing). Old rope was shredded and sold as oakum, a fiber used to caulk ships. Whole pieces of hardware—nails, cogs, and screws—could be resold: broken bits went to iron- and brass-founders and coppersmiths to be melted down; bottles and bits of broken glass, to glassmakers.[11] The medium for these exchanges were the second-hand shops strung along the harbor which carried on a bustling trade with children despite a city ordinance prohibiting their buying from minors.[12] "On going down South Street I met a gang of small Dock Thieves . . . had a bag full of short pieces of old rope and iron," William Bell, police inspector of second-hand shops, reported on a typical day on the beat in 1850. The malefactors were headed for a shop like the one into which he slipped incognito, to witness the mundane but illegal transaction between the proprietor and a six-year-old boy, who sold him a glass bottle for a penny.[13] The waterfront also yielded trash which could be used at home rather than vended: tea, coffee, sugar, and flour spilled from sacks and barrels, and from the wagons which carried cargo to nearby warehouses.[14]

By the 1850s, huckstering and scavenging were the only means by which increasing numbers of children could earn their keep. A decline in boys' positions as artisans' apprentices and girls' positions as domestic servants meant that the streets became the most accessible employer of children. Through the 1840s, many artisan masters entirely rearranged work in their shops to take advantage of a labor market glutted with impoverished adults, and to survive within the increasingly cutthroat exigencies of New York commerce and manufacturing. As a result, apprenticeship in many trades had disappeared by 1850. Where it did survive, the old perquisites, steady work and room and board, were often gone: boys' work, like that of the adults they served, was irregular and intermittent.[15]

There were analogous changes in domestic service. Until the 1840s, girls of the laboring classes had easily found work as servants, but in that decade, older female immigrants, whom employers preferred for their superior strength, crowded them out of those positions. By the early 1850s, domestic service was work for Irish and German teenagers and young women. In other industrial centers, towns like Manchester and Lowell, children moved from older employments into the factories; New York, however, because of high ground rents and the absence of sufficient water power, lacked the large establishments which gave work to the young in other cities.[16] Consequently, children and adolescents, who two generations earlier would have worked in more constrained situations, now flooded the streets.

The growth of the street trades meant that increasing numbers of children worked on their own, away from adult supervision. This situation magnified the opportunities for illicit gain, the centuries-old pilfering and finagling of apprentices and serving-girls. When respectable parents sent their children out to scavenge and peddle, the consequences were not always what they intended: these trades were an avenue to theft and prostitution as well as to an honest living. Child peddlers habituated household entryways, with their hats and umbrellas and odd knickknacks, and roamed by shops where goods were often still, in the old fashion, displayed outside on the sidewalks.[17] And scavenging was only one step removed from petty theft. The distinction between gathering spilled flour and spilling flour oneself was one which small scavengers did not always observe. Indeed, children skilled in detecting value in random objects strewn about the streets, the seemingly inconsequential, could as easily spot value in other people's property. As the superintendent of the juvenile asylum wrote of one malefactor, "He has very little sense of moral rectitude, and thinks it but little harm to take small articles."[18] A visitor to the city in 1857 was struck by the swarms of children milling around the docks, "scuffling about, wherever there were bags of coffee and hogshead of sugar." Armed with sticks, "they 'hooked' what they could."[19] The targets of pilfering were analogous to those of scavenging: odd objects, unattached to persons. The prey of children convicted of theft and sent to the juvenile house of correction in the 1850s included, for instance, a bar of soap, a copy of the *New York Herald*, lead and wood from demolished houses, and a board "valued at 3¢."[20] Police Chief George Matsell reported that pipes, tin roofing, and brass doorknobs were similarly endangered.[21] Thefts against persons, pickpocketing and mugging, belonged to another province, that of the professional child criminal.

Not all parents were concerned about their children's breaches of the law. Reformers were not always wrong whey they charged that by sending children to the streets, laboring-class parents implicitly encouraged them to a life of crime. The unrespectable poor did not care to discriminate between stolen and scavenged goods, and the destitute could not afford to. One small boy picked up by the CAS told his benefactors that his parents had sent him out chip picking with the instructions, "you can take it wherever you can find it"—although like many children brought before the charities, this one was embroidering his own innocence and his parents' guilt.[22] But children also took their own chances, without their parents' knowledge. By midcentury, New York was the capital of American crime, and there was a place for children, small and adept as they were, on its margins. Its full-blown economy of contraband, with the junk shops at the center, allowed children to exchange pilfered and stolen goods quickly and easily: anything, from scavenged bottles to nicked top hats could be sold immediately.

As scavenging shaded into theft, so it also edged into another street trade, prostitution. The same art of creating commodities underlay both. In the intricate economy of the streets, old rope, stray coal, rags, and sex all held the promise of cash, a promise apparent to children who from an early age learned to be "makers of something out of nothing." For girls who knew how to turn things with no value into things with exchange value, the prostitute's act of bartering sex into money would have perhaps seemed daunting, but nonetheless comprehensible. These were not professional child prostitutes; rather, they turned to the lively trade in casual prostitution on occasion or at intervals to supplement other earnings. One encounter with a gentleman, easy to come by in the hotel and business district, could bring the equivalent of a month's wages in domestic service, a week's wages seamstressing, or several weeks' earnings huckstering. Such windfalls went to pay a girl's way at home or, more typically, to purchase covertly some luxury—pastries, a bonnet, cheap jewelry, a fancy gown—otherwise out of her reach.

Prostitution was quite public in antebellum New York. It was not yet a statutory offense, and although the police harassed streetwalkers and arrested them for vagrancy, they had little effect on the trade. Consequently, offers from men and inducements from other girls were common on the streets, and often came a girl's way when she was out working. This is the reason a German father tried to prevent his fourteen-year-old daughter from going out scavenging when she lost her place in domestic service. "He said, 'I don't want you to be a rag-picker. You are not a child now—people will look at you—you will come to harm,' " as the girl recounted the tale.[23] The "harm" he feared was the course taken by a teenage habitué of the waterfront in whom Inspector Bell took a special interest in 1851. After she rejected his offer of a place in service, he learned from a junk shop proprietor that, along with scavenging around the docks, she was "in the habit of going aboard the Coal Boats in that vicinity and prostituting herself."[24] Charles Loring Brace, founder of the CAS, claimed that "the life of a swill-gatherer, or coal-picker, or chiffonier '[ragpicker] in the streets soon wears off a girl's modesty and prepares her for worse occupation," while Police Chief Matsell accused huckster-girls of soliciting the clerks and employees they met on their rounds of counting houses.[25]

While not all girls in the street trades were as open to advances as Brace and Matsell implied, their habituation to male advances must have contributed to the brazenness with which some of them could engage in sexual bartering. Groups of girls roamed about the city, sometimes on chores and errands, sometimes only with an eye for flirtations, or being "impudent and saucy to men," as the parents of one offender put it.[26] In the early 1830s, John R. McDowall, leader of the militant Magdalene Society, had observed on fashionable Broadway "females of thirteen and fourteen walking the streets without a protector, until some pretended gentleman gives them a nod, and takes their arm and escorts them to houses of assignation."[27] McDowall was sure to exaggerate, but later witnesses lent credence to his description. In 1854, a journalist saw nearly fifty girls soliciting one evening as he walked a mile up Broadway, while diarist George Templeton Strong referred to juvenile prostitution as a permanent feature of the promenade in the early 1850s: "no one can walk the length of Broadway without meeting some hideous troop of ragged girls."[28] But despite the entrepreneurial attitude with which young girls ventured into prostitution, theirs was a grim choice, with hazards which, young as they were, they could not always foresee. Nowhere can we see more clearly the complexities of poor children's lives in the public city. The life of the streets taught them self-reliance and the arts of survival, but this education could also be a bitter one.

The autonomy and independence which the streets fostered through petty crime also extended to living arrangements. Abandoned children, orphans, runaways, and particularly independent boys made the streets their home: sleeping out with companions in household areas, wagons, marketplace stalls, and saloons. In the summer of 1850, the *Tribune* noted that the police regularly scared up thirty or forty boys sleeping along Nassau and Ann streets; they included boys with homes as well as genuine vagabonds.[29] Police Chief Matsell reported that in warm weather, crowds of roving boys, many of them sons of respectable parents, absented themselves from their families for weeks.[30] Such was Thomas W., who came to the attention of the CAS; "sleeps in stable," the case record notes, "Goes home for clean clothes; and sometimes for his meals."[31] Thomas's parents evidently tolerated the arrangement, but this was not always the case. Rebellious children, especially boys, evaded parental demands and discipline by living on the streets full-time. Thus John Lynch left home because of some difficulty with his father: he was sent on his parents' complaint to the juvenile house of correction on a vagrancy charge.[32]

Reformers like Matsell and the members of the CAS tended to see such children as either orphaned or abandoned, symbols of the misery and depravity of the poor. Their perception, incarnated by writers like Horatio Alger in the fictional waifs of sentimental novels, gained wide credibility in nineteenth-century social theory and popular thought. Street children were essentially "friendless and homeless," declared Brace. "No one cares for them, and they care for no one."[33] His judgment, if characteristically harsh, was not without truth. If children without parents had no kin or friendly neighbors to whom to turn, they were left to fend for themselves. Such was the story of the two small children of a deceased stonecutter, himself a widower. After he died, "they wandered around, begging cold victuals, and picking up, in any way they were able, their poor living."[34] William S., fifteen years old, had been orphaned when very young. After a stay on a farm as an indentured boy, he ran away to the city, where he slept on the piers and supported himself by carrying luggage off passenger boats: "William thinks he has seen hard times," the record notes.[35] But the testimony garnered by reformers about the "friendless and homeless" young should also be taken with a grain of salt. The CAS, a major source of these tales, was most sympathetic to children who appeared before the agents as victims of orphanage, desertion, or familial cruelty; accordingly, young applicants for aid sometimes presented themselves in ways which would gain them the most favor from philanthropists. The society acknowledged the problem, although it claimed to have solved it: "runaways frequently come to the office with fictitious stories. . . . Sometimes a truant has only one parent, generally the mother, and she is dissipated, or unable to control him. He comes to the office . . . and tells a fictitious story of orphanage and distress."[36] Yet in reality, there were few children so entirely exploited and "friendless" as the CAS believed.

Not surprisingly, orphanage among the poor was a far more complex matter than reformers perceived. As Carol Groneman has shown, poor families did not disintegrate under the most severe difficulties of immigration and urbanization.[37] In the worst New York slums, families managed to keep together and to take in those kin and friends who lacked households of their own. Orphaned children as well as those who were temporarily parentless—whose parents, for instance, had found employment elsewhere—typically found homes with older siblings, grandparents, and aunts. The solidarity of the laboring-class family, however, was not as idyllic as it might seem in retrospect. Interdependence also bred tensions which weighed heavily on children, and in response, the young sometimes chose—or were forced—to strike out on their own. Step-relations, so common in this period, were a particular source of bad feelings. Two brothers whom a charity visitor found sleeping in the streets explained that they had left their mother when she moved in with another man after their father deserted her.[38] If natural parents died, step-parents might be particularly forceful about sending children "on their own hook." "We haven't got no father nor mother," testified a twelve-year-old wanderer of himself and his younger brother. Their father, a shoemaker, had remarried when their mother died; when he died, their stepmother moved away and left them, "and they could not find out anything more about her."[39]

Moreover, the difficulties for all, children and adults, of finding work in these years of endemic underemployment created a kind of half-way orphanage. Parents emigrating from New York could place their boys in apprenticeships which subsequently collapsed and cast the children on their own for a living. The parents of one boy, for example, left him at work in a printing office when they moved to Toronto. Soon after they left, he was thrown out of work; to support himself he lived on the streets and worked as an errand boy, newsboy and bootblack.[40] Similarly, adolescents whose parents had left them in unpleasant or intolerable situations simply struck out on their own. A widow boarded her son with her sister when she went into service; the boy ran away when his aunt "licked him."[41] Thus a variety of circumstances could be concealed in the category of the street "orphan."

All these customs of childhood and work among the laboring poor were reasons for the presence of children, girls and boys, in the public life of the city, a presence which reformers passionately denounced. Children and parents alike had their uses for the streets. For adults, the streets allowed their dependents to contribute to their keep, crucial to making ends meet in the household economy. For girls and boys, street life provided a way to meet deeply ingrained family obligations. This is not to romanticize their lives. If the streets provided a way to meet responsibilities, it was a hard and bitter, even a cruel one. Still, children of the laboring classes lived and labored in a complex geography, which reformers of the poor perceived only as a stark tableau of pathology and vice.

To what degree did their judgments of children redound on women? Although reformers included both sexes in their indictments, women were by implication more involved. First, poverty was especially likely to afflict women.[42] To be the widow, deserted wife, or orphaned daughter of a laboring man, even a prosperous artisan, was to be poor; female self-support was synonymous with indigence. The number of self-supporting women, including those with children, was high in midcentury New York: in the 1855 census report for two neighborhoods, nearly 60 percent of six hundred working women sampled had no adult male in the household. New York's largest charity reported in 1858 that it aided 27 percent more women than men.[43] For women in such straits, children's contributions to the family income were mandatory. As a New York magistrate had written in 1830: "of the children brought before me for pilfering, nine out of ten are those whose fathers are dead, and who live with their mothers."[44] Second, women were more responsible than men for children, both from the perspective of reformers and within the reality of the laboring family. Mothering, as the middle class saw it, was an expression of female identity, rather than a construction derived from present and past social conditions. Thus the supposedly neglectful ways of laboring mothers reflected badly not only on their character as parents, but also on their very identity as women. When not depicted as timid or victimized, poor women appeared as unsavory characters in the annals of reformers: drunken, abusive, or, in one of the most memorable descriptions, "sickly-looking, deformed by over work . . . weak and sad-faced."[45] Like prostitutes, mothers of street children became a kind of half-sex in the eyes of reformers, outside the bounds of humanity by virtue of their inability or unwillingness to replicate the innate abilities of true womanhood.

Reformers and Family Life

In the 1850s, the street activities of the poor, especially those of children, became the focus of a distinct reform politics in New York. The campaign against the streets, one element in a general cultural offensive against the laboring classes which evangelical groups had carried on since the 1830s, was opened in 1849 by Police Chief Matsell's report to the public on juvenile delinquency. In the most hyperbolic rhetoric, he described a "deplorable and growing evil" spreading through the streets. "I allude to the constantly increasing number of vagrants, idle and vicious children of both sexes, who infest our public thorough-fares."[46] Besides alerting New York's already existing charities to the presence of the dangerous classes, Matsell's exposé affected a young Yale seminarian, Charles Loring Brace, just returned from a European tour and immersed in his new vocation of city missionary. Matsell's alarmed observations coalesced with what Brace had learned from his own experiences working with boys in the city mission. Moved to act, Brace in 1853 founded the CAS, a charity which concerned itself with all poor children, but especially with street "orphans." Throughout the 1850s, the CAS carried on the work Matsell had begun, documenting and publicizing the plight of street children.[47] In large measure because of its efforts, the "evil" of the streets became a central element in the reform analysis of poverty and a focus of broad concern in New York.

Matsell, Brace, and the New York philanthropists with whom they associated formed—like their peers in other northeastern cities—a closely connected network of secular and moral reformers. By and large, these women and men were not born into New York's elite, as were those of the generation who founded the city's philanthropic movement in the first decades of the century. Rather, they were part of an emerging middle class, typically outsiders to the ruling class, either by birthplace or social status.[48] Although much of the ideology which influenced reformers' dealings with the poor is well known, scholars have generally not explored the extent to which their interactions with the laboring classes were shaped by developing ideas of gentility: ideas, in turn, based upon conceptions of domestic life. Through their attempts to recast working-class life within these conceptions, this still-inchoate class sharpened its own vision of urban culture and its ideology of class relations. Unlike philanthropists in the early nineteenth century, who partook of an older attitude of tolerance to the poor and of the providential inevitability of poverty, mid-Victorians were optimistic that poverty could be abolished by altering the character of their wards as workers, citizens, and family members. The reformers of the streets were directly concerned with the latter. In their efforts to teach the working poor the virtues of the middle-class home as a means of self-help, they laid the ideological and programmatic groundwork for a sustained intervention in working-class family life.

What explains the sudden alarm about the streets at midcentury? The emergence of street life as a target of organized reform was partly due to the massive immigrations of those years, which created crises of housing, unemployment, and crime. The influx of Irish and German immigrants in the 1840s greatly increased the presence of the poor in public areas. Thousands of those who arrived after 1846 wandered through the streets looking for housing, kin, work, or, at least, a spot to shelter them from the elements. A news item from 1850 reported a common occurrence.

> Six poor women with their children, were discovered Tuesday night by some police officers, sleeping in the alleyway, in Avenue B, between 10th and 11th streets. When interrogated they said they had been compelled to spend their nights wherever they could obtain any shelter. They were in a starving condition, and without the slightest means of support.[49]

Indeed, severe overcrowding in the tenements meant that more of the poor strayed outside, particularly in hot weather. "The sidewalks, cellar doors, gratings, boxes, barrels, etc. in the densely populated streets were last night literally covered with gasping humanity, driven from their noisome, unventilated dens, in search of air," reported the *Tribune* several weeks later.[50]

The existence of the new police force, organized in 1845, also aggravated the reformers' sense of crisis by broadening their notions of criminal behavior. The presence of these new agents of mediation between the poor and the propertied shed light on a milieu which theretofore had been closed to the genteel. Indeed, the popularization of the idea of the dangerous classes after 1850 was partly due to publicized police reports and to accounts written by journalists who accompanied the police on their rounds. The "vicious" activities of the laboring classes were elaborated in such reports as Matsell's, published in pamphlet form for philanthropic consumption, and novelists' and journalists' exposés like those of Ned Buntline and Charles Dickens's description of Five Points in his *American Notes*.

The police also seem to have enforced prohibitions on street life with their own definitions of juvenile crime. Because conceptions of vagrancy depended on whether the police considered the child's presence in the streets to be legitimate, it is possible that some of the high number of juvenile commitments—about two thousand a year[51]—can be attributed to conflicting notions of the proper sphere of children. Brace was struck by the drama of children, police, and mothers in Corlear's Hook (now the Lower East Side). The streets teemed with

> wild ragged little girls who were flitting about . . . some with baskets and poker gathering rags, some apparently seeking chances of stealing. . . . The police were constantly arresting them as "vagrants," when the mothers would beg them off from the good-natured justices, and promise to train them better in the future.[52]

As for petty larceny, that at least some of the arrests were due to an ambiguity about what constituted private property was testified to by one New York journalist. The city jail, he wrote, was filled, along with other malefactors, "with young boys and girls who have been caught asleep on cellar doors or are suspected of the horrible crime of stealing junk bottles and old iron!"[53] As children's presence in the public realm became inherently criminal, so did the gleaning of its resources. The distinction between things belonging to no one and things belonging to someone blurred in the minds of propertied adults as well as propertyless children.

There were, then, greater numbers of children in the New York streets after 1845, and their activities were publicized as never before. Faced with an unprecedented crisis of poverty in the city, reformers fastened on their presence as a cause rather than a symptom of impoverishment. The reformers' idea that the curse of poor children lay in the childrearing methods of their parents moved toward the center of their analysis of the etiology of poverty, replacing older notions of divine will.[54] In the web of images of blight and disease which not only reflected but also shaped the midcentury understanding of poverty, the tenement house was the "parent of constant disorders, and the nursery of increasing vices," but real parents were the actual agents of crime.[55] In opposition to the ever more articulate and pressing claims of New York's organized working men, this first generation of "experts" on urban poverty averred that familial relations rather than industrial capitalism were responsible for the misery which any clear-headed New Yorker could see was no transient state of affairs. One of the principal pieces of evidence of "the ungoverned appetites, bad habits, and vices"[56] of laboring-class parents was the fact that they sent their offspring out to the streets to earn their keep.

The importance of domesticity to the reformers' own class identity fostered this shift of attention from individual moral shortcomings to the family structure of a class. For these middle-class dwellers, the home was not simply a place of residence; it was a focus of social life and a central element of class-consciousness, based on specific conceptions of femininity and childrearing. There, secluded from the stress of public life, women could devote themselves to directing the moral and ethical development of their families. There, protected from the evils of the outside world, the young could live out their childhoods in innocence, freed from the necessity of labor, cultivating their moral and intellectual faculties.[57]

From this vantage point, the laboring classes appeared gravely deficient. When charity visitors, often ladies themselves, entered the households of working people, they saw a domestic sparseness which contradicted their deepest beliefs about what constituted a morally sustaining family life.[58] "[Their] ideas of domestic comfort and standard of morals, are far below our own," wrote the Association for Improving the Condition of the Poor (AICP).[59] The urban poor had intricately interwoven family lives, but they had no *homes*. Middle-class people valued family privacy and intimacy: among the poor, they saw a promiscuous sociability, an "almost fabulous gregariousness."[60] They believed that the moral training of children depended on protecting them within the home; in poor neighborhoods, they saw children encouraged to labor in the streets. The harshness and intolerance with which midcentury reformers viewed the laboring classes can be partly explained by the disparity between these two ways of family life. "Homes—in the better sense—they never know," declared one investigating committee; the children "graduate in every kind of vice known in that curious school which trains them—the public street."[61] The AICP scoffed at even using the word: "Homes . . . if it is not a mockery to give that hallowed name to the dark, filthy hovels where many of them dwell."[62] To these middle-class women and men, the absence of home life was not simply due to the uncongenial physical circumstances of the tenements, nor did it indicate the poor depended upon another way of organizing their family lives. Rather, the homelessness of this "multitude of half-naked, dirty, and leering children"[63] signified an absence of parental love, a neglect of proper childrearing which was entwined in the habits and values of the laboring classes.

The Children's Aid Society

Although Brace shared the alarm and revulsion of reformers like Matsell at the "home-lessness" of the poor, he also brought to the situation an optimistic liberalism, based upon his own curious and ambiguous uses of domesticity. In his memoirs of 1872, looking back on two decades of work with the New York laboring classes, Brace took heart from the observation that the absence of family life so deplored by his contemporaries actually operated to stabilize American society. Immigration and continual mobility disrupted the process by which one generation of laboring people taught the next a cultural identity, "that continuity of influence which bad parents and grandparents exert."[64] Brace wrote this passage with the specter of the Paris Commune before him; shaken, like so many of his peers, by the degree of organization and class consciousness among the Parisian poor, he found consolation on native ground in what others condemned. "The mill of American life, which grinds up so many delicate and fragile things, has its uses, when it is turned on the vicious fragments of the lower strata of society."[65]

It was through the famed placing-out system that the CAS turned the "mill of American life" to the uses of urban reform. The placing-out program sent poor city children to foster homes in rural areas where labor was scarce. With the wages-fund theory, a common Anglo-American liberal reform scheme of midcentury, which proposed to solve the problem of metropolitan unemployment by dispersing the surplus of labor, the society defended itself against critics' charges that "foster parents" were simply farmers in need of cheap help, and placing-out, a cover for the exploitation of child labor.[66] At first, children went to farms in the nearby countryside, as did those the city bound out from the Almshouse, but in 1854 the society conceived the more ambitious scheme of sending parties of children by railroads to the far Midwest: Illinois, Michigan, and Iowa. By 1860, 5,074 children had been placed out.[67]

At its most extreme, the CAS only parenthetically recognized the social and legal claims of working-class parenthood. The organization considered the separation of parents and children a positive good, the liberation of innocent, if tarnished, children from the tyranny of unredeemable adults. Here, as in so many aspects of nineteenth-century reform, the legacy of the Enlightenment was ambiguous: the idea of childhood innocence it had bequeathed, socially liberating in many respects, also provided one element of the ideology of middle-class domination.[68] Since the CAS viewed children as innocents to be rescued and parents as corrupters to be displaced, its methods depended in large measure on convincing children themselves to leave New York, with or without parental knowledge or acquiescence. Street children were malleable innocents in the eyes of the charity, but they were also little consenting adults, capable of breaking all ties to their class milieu and families. To be sure, many parents did bring their children to be placed out, but nonetheless, the society also seems to have worked directly through the children.[69] In 1843, the moral reformer and abolitionist Lydia Maria Child had mused that the greatest misfortune of "the squalid little wretches" she saw in the New York streets was that they were not orphans.[70] The charity visitors of the CAS tackled this problem directly: where orphans were lacking, they manufactured them.

Placing-out was based on the thoroughly middle-class idea of the redeeming influence of the Protestant home in the countryside.[71] There, the morally strengthening effects of labor, mixed with the salutary influences of domesticity and female supervision, could remold the child's character. Thus domestic ideology gave liberals like Brace the theoretical basis for constructing a program to resocialize the poor in which force was unnecessary. Standards of desirable behavior could be internalized by children rather than beaten into them, as had been the eighteenth-century practice. With home influence, not only childrearing but the resocialization of a class could take the form of subliminal persuasion rather than conscious coercion.[72]

Earlier New York reformers had taken a different tack with troublesome children. In

1824, the Society for the Reformation of Juvenile Delinquents had established an asylum, the House of Refuge, to deal with juvenile offenders. As in all the new institutions for deviants, solitary confinement and corporal punishment were used to force the recalcitrant into compliance with the forces of reason.[73] But Brace thought the asylum, so prized by his predecessors, was impractical and ineffectual. Asylums could not possibly hold enough children to remedy the problem of the New York streets in the 1850s; moreover, the crowding together of the children who were incarcerated only reinforced the habits of their class.[74] The foster home, however, with its all-encompassing moral influence, could be a more effective house of refuge. "We have wished to make every kind of religious family, who desired the responsibility, an Asylum or a Reformatory Institution . . . by throwing about the wild, neglected little outcast of the streets, the love and gentleness of home."[75] The home was an asylum, but it was woman's influence rather than an institutional regimen that accomplished its corrections.

This is an overview of the work of the CAS, but on closer examination, there was also a division by sex in the organization, and domesticity played different roles in the girls' and boys' programs. The emigrants to the West seem to have been mostly boys: they seem to have been more allured by emigration than were girls, and parents were less resistant to placing out sons than daughters. "Even as a beggar or pilferer, a little girl is of vastly more use to a wretched mother than her son," the society commented. "The wages of a young girl are much more sure to go to the pockets of the family than those of a boy."[76] Brace's own imagination was more caught up with boys than girls; his most inventive efforts were directed at them. Unlike most of his contemporaries, he appreciated the vitality and tenacity of the street boys; his fascination with the Western scheme came partly from the hope that emigration would redirect their toughness and resourcefulness, "their sturdy independence,"[77] into hearty frontier individualism.[78] Similarly, the agents overseeing the foster home program were men, as were the staff members of the society's much-touted Newsboys' Lodging-House, a boardinghouse where, for a few pennies, newsboys could sleep and eat. The Lodging-House, was, in fact, a kind of early boys' camp, where athletics and physical fitness, lessons in entrepreneurship (one of its salient features was a savings bank), and moral education knit poor boys and gentlemen into a high-spirited but respectable masculine camaraderie.[79]

Women were less visible in the society's literature, their work less well-advertised, since it was separate from Brace's most innovative programs. The women of the CAS were not paid agents like the men, but volunteers who staffed the girls' programs: a Lodging-House and several industrial schools. The work of the women reformers was, moreover, less novel than that of the men. Rather than encouraging girls to break away from their families, the ladies sought the opposite: to create among the urban laboring classes a domestic life of their own. They aimed to mold future wives and mothers of a reformed working class: women who would be imbued with a belief in the importance of domesticity and capable of patterning their homes and family lives on middle-class standards.

Yet it was this strategy of change, rather than Brace's policy of fragmentation, which would eventually dominate attempts to reform working-class children. The ladies envisioned homes which would reorganize the promiscuously sociable lives of the poor under the aegis of a new, "womanly" working-class woman. In the CAS industrial schools and Lodging-House, girls recruited off the streets learned the arts of plain sewing, cooking, and house-cleaning, guided by the precept celebrated by champions of women's domestic mission that "nothing was so honorable as industrious *house-work*."[80] These were skills which both prepared them for waged employment in seamstressing and domestic service and outfitted them for homes of their own; as the ladies proudly attested after several years of work, their students entered respectable married life as well as honest employment. "Living in homes reformed through their influence,"[81] the married women carried on their female mission, reformers by proxy.

Similarly, the women reformers instituted meetings to convert the mothers of their students to a new relationship to household and children. Classes taught the importance of sobriety, neat appearance, and sanitary housekeeping: the material basis for virtuous motherhood and a proper home. Most important, the ladies stressed the importance of keeping children off the streets and sending them to school. Here, they found their pupils particularly recalcitrant. Mothers persisted in keeping children home to work and cited economic reasons when their benefactresses upbraided them. The CAS women, however, considered the economic rationale a pretense for the exploitation of children and the neglect of their moral character. "The larger ones were needed to 'mind' the baby," lady volunteers sardonically reported, "or go out begging for clothes . . . and the little ones, scarcely bigger than the baskets on their arms, must be sent out for food, or chips, or cinders."[82] The Mothers' Meetings tried, however unsuccessfully, to wean away laboring women from such customary practices to what the ladies believed to be a more nurturant and moral mode of family life: men at work, women at home, children inside.

In contrast to the male reformers, the women of the society tried to create an intensified private life within New York itself, to enclose children within tenements and schools rather than to send them away or incarcerate them in asylums. There is a new, optimistic vision of city life implied in their work. With the establishment of the home across class lines, a renewed city could emerge, its streets free for trade and respectable promenades, and emancipated from the inconveniences of pickpockets and thieves, the affronts of prostitutes and hucksters, the myriad offenses of working-class mores and poverty. The "respectable" would control and dominate public space as they had never before. The city would itself become an asylum on a grand scale, an environment which embodied the eighteenth-century virtues of reason and progress, the nineteenth-century virtues of industry and domesticity. And as would befit a city for the middle class, boundaries between public and private life would be clear: the public space of the metropolis would be the precinct of men, the private space of the home, that of women and children.

In the work of the CAS female volunteers lies the roots of the Americanization campaign which, half a century later, reshaped the lives of so many working-class immigrants. The settlement houses of turn-of-the-century New York would expand the mothers' classes and girls' housekeeping lessons into a vast program of nativist assimilation. Female settlement workers would assure immigrant mothers and daughters that the key to decent lives lay in creating American homes within the immigrant ghettoes: homes that were built on a particular middle-class configuration of possessions and housekeeping practices and a particular structure of family relations. And, as in the 1850s, the effort to domesticate the plebeian household would be linked to a campaign to clear the streets of an ubiquitous, aggressive, and assertive working-class culture.

Neither the clearing of the streets nor the making of the working-class home were accomplished at any one point in time. Indeed, these conflicts still break out in Manhattan's poor and working-class neighborhoods. Today, in the Hispanic *barrios* of the Upper West and Lower East sides and in black Harlem, scavenging and street huckstering still flourish. In prosperous quarters as well, where affluent customers are there for the shrewd, the battle continues between police on the one hand, hucksters and prostitutes on the other. Indeed, the struggle over the streets has been so ubiquitous in New York and other cities in the last 150 years that we can see it as a structural element of urban life in industrial capitalist societies. As high unemployment and casualized work have persisted in the great cities, the streets have continued to contain some of the few resources for the poor to make ends meet. At the same time, the social imagination of the poor, intensified by urban life, has worked to increase those resources. All the quick scams—the skills of the con men, street musicians, beggars, prostitutes, peddlers, drug dealers, and pickpockets—are arts of the urban working poor, bred from ethnic and class traditions and the necessities of poverty.

Neither is the conflict today, however, identical to the one which emerged in the 1850s. The struggle over the streets in modern New York takes place in a far different context, one defined by past victories of reformers and municipal authorities. Vagrancy counts against children are now strengthened by compulsory school legislation; child labor laws prohibit most kinds of child huckstering; anti-peddling laws threaten heavy fines for the unwary. Most important, perhaps, the mechanisms for "placing out" wandering children away from "negligent" mothers are all in place (although the wholesale breakdown of social services in New York has made these provisions increasingly ineffectual, creating a new problem in its wake). The street life of the working poor survives in pockets, but immeasurably weakened, continually under duress.

In more and more New York neighborhoods, the rich and the middle-class can walk untroubled by importunate prostitutes, beggars, and hucksters. The women gossiping on front stoops, the mothers shouting orders from upstairs windows, and the housewife habitués of neighborhood taverns have similarly disappeared, shut away behind heavily locked doors with their children and television sets. New York increasingly becomes a city where a variant of the nineteenth-century bourgeois vision of respectable urban life is realized. NO LOITERING/PLAYING BALL/SITTING/PLAYING MUSIC ON SIDEWALKS IN FRONT OF BUILDINGS placards on the great middle-class apartment houses warn potential lingerers. The sidewalks are, indeed, often free of people, except for passers-by and the doormen paid to guard them. But as Jane Jacobs predicted so forcefully two decades ago, streets cleared for the respectable have become free fields for predators. The inhabitants of modern-day New York, particularly women and children, live in a climate of urban violence and fear historically unprecedented save in wartime. In the destruction of the street life of the laboring poor, a critical means of creating urban communities and organizing urban space has disappeared. As the streets are emptied of laboring women and children, as the working-class home has become an ideal, if not a reality, for ever-widening sectors of the population, the city of middle-class hopes becomes ever more bereft of those ways of public life which once mitigated the effects of urban capitalism.

Notes

Many colleagues commented on drafts of this essay. My thanks especially to the participants in the Bard College Faculty Seminar at which the paper was originally presented, and to my friends Ellen Ross, Judith Walkowitz, and Sean Wilentz.

1. Children's Aid Society, (hereafter referred to as CAS), *Third Annual Report* (New York, 1856), 26–27.
2. Virginia Penny, *The Employments of Women* (Boston, 1863), 317.
3. For the class character of the New York reformers, see Carroll Smith-Rosenberg, *Religion and the Rise of the American City: The New York City Mission Movement, 1812–1870* (Ithaca, N.Y.: Cornell University Press, 1971), 6. For a more recent and ambitious analysis of the class base of the evangelical reform movement, see Mary Ryan, *Cradle of the Middle Class* (Cambridge: Cambridge University Press, 1981).
4. The literature on antebellum reform is voluminous. Two of the most helpful books specifically treating New York are Thomas Bender, *Toward an Urban Vision: Ideas and Institutions in Nineteenth-Century America* (Lexington, Ky.: University Press of Kentucky, 1975); and Paul Boyer, *Urban Masses and Moral Order in America, 1820–1920* (Cambridge, Mass.: Harvard University Press, 1978).
5. Philippe Ariès, *Centuries of Childhood: A Social History of Family Life* (New York: Random House, 1965).
6. Penny, *Employments of Women*, 133–34, 143–44, 150–52, 168, 421, 473, 484; William Burns, *Life in New*

York: *In Doors and Out of Doors* (New York, 1851); Phillip Wallys, *About New York: An Account of What a Boy Saw on a Visit to the City* (New York, 1857), 50; CAS, *First Annual Report* (1854), 23–24, *Seventh Annual Report* (1860), 16.

7. Penny, *Employments of Women*, 484.
8. Charles L. Brace, *The Dangerous Classes of New York and Twenty Years' Work Among Them* (New York, 1872), 152–53.
9. Penny, *Employments of Women*, 444.
10. *New York Mirror* 9 (1831): 119, quoted in the I.N.P. Stokes Collection, New York Public Library, New York, 461.
11. Brace, *Dangerous Classes*, 152–53; Penny, *Employments of Women*, 122, 435, 444, 467, 484–85; Solon Robinson, *Hot Corn: Life Scenes in New York Illustrated* (New York, 1854), 207; CAS *Second Annual Report* (1855), 36; see also Sean Wilentz's "Crime, Poverty and the Streets of New York City: The Diary of William H. Bell 1850–51," *History Workshop* 7 (Spring 1979): 126–55.
12. *Laws and Ordinances . . . of the City of New York* (1817), 112.
13. Bell Diary, 25 November 1850.
14. See also *Daily Tribune*, 16 March 1850.
15. Sean Wilentz, *Chants Democratic: New York City and the Rise of the American Working Class* (New York, Oxford University Press, 1983). In this respect as in many others, I am deeply indebted to Sean Wilentz for my understanding of New York history.
16. Victor S. Clark, *History of Manufactures in the United States*, 3 vols. (New York: McGraw-Hill Book Company, 1929), 1:351. For the lack of children's factory employment, see CAS, *Seventh Annual Report* (1860), 7.
17. The aggressive character of juveniles on the streets and the prevalence of juvenile petty theft is discussed in David R. Johnson, "Crime Patterns in Philadelphia, 1840–70," in *The Peoples of Philadelphia: A History of Ethnic Groups and Lower Class Life, 1790–1940*, ed. Allen F. Davis and Mark H. Haller (Philadelphia: Temple University Press, 1973).
18. New York House of Refuge Papers, Case Histories, New York State Library, Albany, 12 June 1852.
19. Wallys, *About New York*, 43.
20. House of Refuge Papers, Case Histories, 3 April 1854, 14 March 1855.
21. "Semi-Annual Report of the Chief of Police," *Documents of the Board of Aldermen*, vol. 17, p. 1 (1850), 59–60.
22. CAS, *Fifth Annual Report* (1858), 38.
23. Brace, *Dangerous Classes*, 120.
24. Bell Diary, 10 June 1851.
25. Brace, *Dangerous Classes*, 154; "Semi-Annual Report," 63.
26. House of Refuge Papers, Case Histories, vol. 1, case no. 61.
27. John R. McDowall, *Magdalen Facts* (New York, 1832), 53.
28. Allan Nevins and Milton Halsey Thomas, eds., *The Diary of George Templeton Strong* , 2 vols. (New York: The MacMillan Company, 1952), 2: 57 (entry for 7 July 1851).
29. *New York Daily Tribune*, 3 June 1850.
30. "Semi-Annual Report," 65.
31. CAS, *Second Annual Report* (1855), 45.
32. House of Refuge Papers, Case Histories, 3 April 1854.
33. Brace, *Dangerous Classes*, 91.
34. CAS, *Fifth Annual Report* (1858), 39–40.
35. CAS, *Second Annual Report* (1855), 45.
36. CAS, *Sixth Annual Report* (1859), 67.
37. Carol Groneman (Pernicone), "The 'Bloody Ould Sixth': A Social Analysis of a New York City Working-Class Community in the Mid-Nineteenth Century" (Ph.D. dissertation, University of Rochester, 1973).
38. CAS, *Sixth Annual Report* (1859), 67–68. Brace also notes the connection of step-parents and child vagrancy in *Dangerous Classes*, 39.
39. CAS, *Fifth Annual Report* (1858), 61.
40. CAS, *Sixth Annual Report* (1859), 58.
41. CAS, *Fourth Annual Report* (1857), 43–44.
42. See my essay "Origins of the Sweatshop," in *Working-Class America: Essays in the New Labor History*, ed. Michael Frish and Daniel Walkowitz (Urbana: University of Illinois Press, 1982), for an extended treatment of this point.
43. New York State Census, 1855, Population Schedules, Ward 4, Electoral District 2, and Ward 17, Electoral District 3, MSS at County Clerk's Office, New York City; Association for Improving the Condition of the Poor, *Fifteenth Annual Report* (New York, 1858), 38.

44. Letter reprinted in Matthew Carey, "Essays on the Public Charities of Philadelphia," *Miscellaneous Essays* (Philadelphia, 1830), 161.

45. CAS, *Third Annual Report* (1856), 27.

46. "Semi-Annual Report," 58.

47. Miriam Z. Langsam, *Children West: A History of the Placing-Out System in the New York Children's Aid Society* (Madison, Wis.: State Historical Society of Wisconsin, 1964).

48. Boyer, *Urban Masses,* stresses the role of charity work in providing status and fellowship for newcomers to the city. Brace was from a family of declining Connecticut gentry; Matsell was born into an artisan family, became a dyer by trade, and rose to prominence and fortune in the city through Tammany Hall politics. See Emma Brace, ed., *The Life of Charles Loring Brace . . . Edited by His Daughter* (New York, 1894); "George W. Matsell," *The Palimpsest* 5 (July 1924): 237–248.

49. *New York Daily Tribune,* 4 July 1850.

50. *Ibid.,* 31 July 1850.

51. From "Reports of Commitments to First District Prison published in Commissioners of the Almshouse," *Annual Reports* (1850–60).

52. Brace, *Dangerous Classes,* 145.

53. George C. Foster, *New York In Slices; By an Experienced Carver* (New York, 1849), 20.

54. Rosenberg, *Religion and the Rise of the American City,* 3, 29.

55. New York Assembly, *Report of the Select Committee Appointed to Examine into the Condition of Tenant Houses in New-York and Brooklyn,* Assembly doc. 205, 80th sess., 1857, 12.

56. CAS, *Third Annual Report* (1856), 29.

57. The best works on nineteenth-century domesticity are Nancy F. Cott, *The Bonds of Womanhood: "Woman's Sphere" in New England, 1780–1835* (New Haven, Yale University Press, 1977); Ann Douglas, *The Feminization of American Culture* (New York: Avon, 1978); Kathryn Kish Sklar, *Catharine Beecher: A Study in American Domesticity* (New Haven: Yale University Press, 1973).

58. Here I strongly disagree with the view of the sisterly relations between women and charity workers and their wards presented in Barbara Berg, *The Remembered Gate: Origins of American Feminism—the Women and the City, 1800–1860* (New York: Oxford University Press, 1975).

59. Association for Improving the Condition of the Poor, *Thirteenth Annual Report* (1856), 23.

60. New York Assembly, *Report of the Select Committee,* 20.

61. *Ibid.,* 51.

62. Association for Improving the Condition of the Poor, *Fourteenth Annual Report* (1857), 21.

63. CAS, *Third Annual Report* (1856), 4.

64. Brace, *Dangerous Classes,* 46–47.

65. *Ibid.*

66. CAS, *Sixth Annual Report* (1859), 9.

67. Figures are from Langsam, *Children West,* 64.

68. Michel Foucault has most forcefully analyzed this ambiguity. See *Madness and Civilization: A History of Insanity in the Age of Reason* (New York: Random House, 1973)

69. See the appendices in CAS, *Annual Reports* (1854–60).

70. Lydia Maria Child, *Letters from New York* (London, 1843), 62.

71. CAS, *Third Annual Report* (1856), 8.

72. This is similar to the shift in criminal law from corporal punishment to the more enlightened environmental techniques of the penitentiary. See Michael Ignatieff, *A Just Measure of Pain: the Penitentiary in the Industrial Revolution, 1750–1850* (New York: Pantheon, 1978).

73. *Ibid.*

74. CAS, *First Annual Report* (1854), 7; *Second Annual Report* (1855), 5. See also Boyer, *Urban Masses,* 94–95.

75. CAS, *Second Annual Report* (1855), 5.

76. CAS, *Fifth Annual Report* (1858), 17.

77. Brace, *Dangerous Classes,* 100.

78. See Boyer, *Urban Masses,* 94–107; and Brace, *Dangerous Classes,* 98–99.

79. Brace, *Dangerous Classes,* 99–105.

80. CAS, *Ninth Annual Report* (1862), 13. See also *First Annual Report* (1854), 7, 9.

81. CAS, *Tenth Annual Report* (1863), 23; *Seventh Annual Report* (1860), 8.

82. CAS, *Eleventh Annual Report* (1864), 28.

9

"The Reputation of a Lady": Sarah Ballenden and the Foss-Pelly Scandal

Sylvia Van Kirk

A visitor to the Big House and Lower Fort Garry today is quickly transported back to the year 1850, when the fort was in its heyday as the administrative headquarters of the Governor of Assiniboia. The life and times of Red River are brought alive not only by guides impersonating the occupants of the fort, but by the reenactment of the trial of *Foss v. Pelly et. al*, which took place in July 1850. This sensational trial, which had serious repercussions for the elite of Red River, also significantly illuminates the position of women in the fur trade society of mid-nineteenth-century Manitoba.

The trial focused on the character of one of the most socially prominent women in the community, Sarah Ballenden, the native wife of the chief factor in charge of the Hudson's Bay Company's (HBC) Red River district. Her fate provides insight into the operation of the sexual double standard of Victorian society—to retain social standing a woman had to be free of any hint of impropriety. That Mrs. Ballenden was guilty of adultery, as her slanderers charged, was never actually proved; yet her reputation, indeed, her life was ruined. Her supposed lover, Captain Foss, in attempting to clear her reputation by suing her accusers for defamatory conspiracy, may unwittingly have sealed her demise, for such "a stain" once publicly attached to a woman's character "could not easily be washed off" and the community was henceforth primed to believe the worst.[1]

Other important themes for women's history also emerge. In examining the circumstances surrounding the trial, it is apparent that certain other women were among Sarah Ballenden's chief accusers. Paradoxically, although patriarchal mores have often victimized women, women themselves can often be seen to have staunchly upheld these norms and to have been most anxious to see any violation punished. The reasons for such "unsisterly" action should be confronted squarely by feminist historians; cases such as the Foss-Pelly scandal reveal that such behavior was rooted in women's social and economic entrapment in marriage. The rivalry among women in nineteenth-century Red River, however, was compounded by the issue of race.

Fur trade society in Rupert's Land had resulted from decades of intermarriage among incoming white fur traders with Indian and, later, mixed-blood women.[2] It is significant that for decades, in Western Canada, both white women and Christian missionaries had been conspicuously absent. The founding of the Red River settlement in 1811 provided a base from which these two "civilizing" elements could intrude into fur trade society. In a broader context, the Foss-Pelly scandal reflected the racial and social tensions which had been developing in Red River in the early nineteenth century. Racist attitudes, particularly

Reprinted by permission of the author and *Manitoba History* (Spring 1986).

with regard to women, can be seen in the attempts of the missionaries to enforce their concepts of morality upon a society that had developed its own indigenous customs. But the scandal also threatened the position of Anglicized mixed-bloods in the social elite of Red River. Sarah Ballenden, as the wife of the HBC's chief officer in the colony, had symbolized the success of this group. Indeed, it was even predicted that this vivacious, young, mixed-blood woman was "destined to raise her whole caste above European ladies in their influence on society here."[3]

In 1848, when John Ballenden was appointed chief factor in charge of the Red River district, he and his wife returned to a society where acculturated mixed-blood women were allowed to feature more prominently than they had a decade or so earlier. In 1830 Governor George Simpson had sent shock waves through fur trade society by abandoning his "country wife," Margaret Taylor, and returning to Rupert's Land with his young cousin Frances as his bride. He had apparently hoped to create an all-white elite in Red River, for his wife's society was restricted to those few other white wives whose husbands had respectable positions in the colony—Mrs. Donald McKenzie, the Swiss-born wife of the Governor of Assiniboia, and Mrs. David Jones and Mrs. William Cockran, the wives of the Anglican clergymen.[4] Prominent settlers and officers who had native wives appear to have left them behind when being entertained by the Simpsons; as one mixed-blood officer in the company's service resentfully observed, "things are not on the same footing as formerly."[5]

Within a few years, however, Simpson's intentions had been undermined, not only because of the inability of white ladies such as his own wife to adjust to the rigors of life in Rupert's Land, but because of the loyalty which other HBC officers evinced for their native mates. In 1833, with the appointment of Chief Factor Alexander Christie as Governor of Assiniboia, his mixed-blood wife was given the opportunity to occupy a most prominent position in Red River society. Although Simpson agreed that Christie was the best man for the job, he had initially discounted him because he had a native family *à la façon du pays*.[6] When a clerk at Moose Factory, Christie had taken as his wife Ann, a daughter of HBC officer John Thomas and his Cree wife Meenish. Ann Christie's acceptability in Red River society was, no doubt, much increased when she was formally married to her husband by the Reverend David Jones on 10 February, 1835.[7] Although many couples such as the Christies had lived faithfully for years as husband and wife, their unions, because they were without benefit of clergy, had been denounced as "living in sin" by the missionaries, who were particularly prone to hypocritically chastizing the native women for this shameful state.[8]

Certainly in Red River, the centre of "civilization" in Rupert's Land, church marriage had replaced the fur trade custom of marriage *à la façon du pays* by the early 1830s. By this time too, the missionaries' establishment of schools in the colony increasingly reflected the fur traders' concern to have their children acculturated to the norms of British society. Company officers emphasized that when they sent *their* daughters to boarding school in Red River, they wanted them to acquire the accomplishments of ladies, such as music, drawing, and dancing, and their virtue was to be closely safeguarded.[9] Such a genteel upbringing, it was hoped, would enable these young women to overcome the taint of their mixed blood and enhance their marriageability in the eyes of young officers coming into the company's service. Both Ann Cockran, and later Mary Jones, whose husband established the Red River Academy in 1832, supervised the education of fur traders' daughters, some of whom were sent from the far corners of Rupert's Land.

One of these was Sarah McLeod, a daughter of Chief Trader Alexander Roderick McLeod and his native wife. Born in 1818, Sarah had spent her early years at posts in the Mackenzie and Columbia districts before being sent to Mrs. Cockran at Red River, probably around 1830.[10] By the time she was eighteen, this young woman's beauty and accomplishments had turned the promising young HBC clerk John Ballenden into an ardent suitor; the couple's marriage, which was celebrated on 10 December, 1836 by the Reverend William Cockran, was one of the highlights of the Red River season.[11] Even James Hargrave, whose opposition to mixed marriages was well known, enthusiastically congratulated Ballenden on his choice. Sarah, he declared, was "a delightful creature," and his friend had "every reason to consider himself a happy man." When going on furlough, Hargrave further promised Ballenden that should he visit his family in Orkney, he would assure them of the merits of Mrs. Ballenden: "Should I find any old country prejudices remaining depend on it I shall pass a sponge over them."[12] As the wife of a rising young officer, Mrs. Ballenden enjoyed life in Red River and she was quite disappointed to have to leave the settlement when her husband was posted to Sault Ste. Marie in 1840.[13] That native wives had regained esteem in the colonial elite was symbolized in the Ballendens choosing to name their first child "Anne Christie" in honour of the wife of the Governor of Assiniboia.[14]

Ironically, the decline in racial exclusiveness that characterized Red River in the late 1830s and forties helped to set the stage for a fierce social rivalry between white and acculturated mixed-blood women which was to reach its climax in the Foss-Pelly scandal. During this time a small group of British women, who had arrived in Red River initially as schoolmistresses, experienced a considerable increase in status by marrying retired company officers who formed part of the colony's elite. After the death of their native wives, such notables as James Bird, Robert Logan, J.P. Pruden and John Charles all married former schoolmistresses.[15] Their new wives, although they had to accommodate themselves to being stepmothers to large mixed-blood families, now possessed the wherewithal to become leaders in Red River society. According to one observer, the not-so-gentle art of social climbing had come to Red River:

> We have now some rich old fellows that have acquired large fortunes in the service, have got married to European females and cut a dash, have introduced a system of extravagance into the place that is followed by all that can afford it.[16]

Evidently quite a pecking order developed, with people becoming so sensitive about their social position that when Duncan Finlayson assumed the governorship of Assiniboia in 1839, he complained that it would have required "Beau Nash" to regulate the movements of fashionable Red River couples. Finlayson's genteel wife, a sister of Frances Simpson, was apparently appalled by the social pretensions of the colony; she retreated behind a veil of ill health which contributed to her husband's desire to give up his post as soon as possible.[17]

Mrs. Christie, on the other hand, was delighted to resume her position as Governor's lady when her husband was reappointed in 1844.[18] Anxious that native women not be outdone, she was instrumental in promoting a match between her daughter Margaret, who had been educated in England, and company officer John Black the following year. While some of Black's contemporaries expressed surprise that he should have been "caught in that quarter," his wife considered that her marriage had sealed her position within the elite and was inclined to think herself "far above the rest of the native Ladies."[19] A woman's social standing was, however, determined not on her own account but by her husband's position. Thus in 1848, when the Ballendens took up residence at Upper Fort Garry, it was Sarah Ballenden, not Margaret Black, who was the highest-ranking native woman in the fort.

Mrs. Ballenden's delight in returning to Red River had been dampened by her husband suffering a stroke on the canoe voyage inland; that he made the recovery he did owed much to his wife's devoted nursing.[20] In spite of her domestic cares, Sarah Ballenden was both eager and able to play an active role in the social life of the colony, as befitted the wife of the HBC's chief officer. She organized dinner parties and balls, and the christening of her new daughter in the fall of 1849 was reported to be a "splendid entertainment with abundance of champagne."[21] The baby was named "Frances Isobel Simpson" after Governor Simpson's genteel British wife and her sister. As part of her social duties, Mrs. Ballenden also presided, with her husband, over the officers' mess at Upper Fort Garry, where she attracted the admiration of several of the other officers. In the light of subsequent events, it is significant that Sarah spurned the advances of one of these, the fort's accountant A. E. Pelly,[22] but was herself much more susceptible to the charms of a gallant Irishman, Captain Christopher Vaughan Foss. A career soldier, Foss had come out to Red River in 1848 as second in command of the Chelsea Pensioners under Major William Caldwell, who now succeeded Christie as Governor of Assiniboia. Having been stationed at the Upper Fort, Captain Foss was allowed to occupy a seat at the mess table at the company's expense and he quickly ingratiated himself with the Ballendens. Ballenden himself declared that Foss was "an agreeable fellow and will, I daresay, become very popular."[23]

It appears that Sarah Ballenden's beauty and her prominent social position made her an object of envious gossip, particularly among certain white women in Red River. As one observer assessed the situation, "the poor woman seems to have had a watch set on her from the moment of her arrival, every act word or deed was marked and commented upon by certain parties."[24] Her popularity with men excited much speculation. Hadn't her virtue, like many native girls, been suspect during her early days in Red River? Could Captain Foss be simply her platonic friend? Mrs. Robert Logan, one of the lesser ex-schoolmistresses, was heard to remark that Ballenden's wife was a woman who "must always have a sweetheart as well as a husband."[25] Indeed, suggestive hints which originated with Mrs. Ballenden's German servant girl, Catherine Winegart, about the relationship between her mistress and the captain were seized upon and magnified until, by the summer of 1849, it was widely rumored that Foss's attentions to Ballenden's wife were "of such a character as to entitle Mr. B. to a divorce."[26]

This gossip was to fall on the receptive ears of two new white women who arrived in Red River in the fall of 1849. The first was Anne Clouston, the daughter of the Company's agent at Stromness, who came out to Rupert's Land to be married to the aforementioned A. E. Pelly, a relative of the London Governor of the company, Sir John H. Pelly.[27] The couple were married at York Factory by The Rt. Revd. David Anderson, the first Anglican bishop of Rupert's Land, who had come by the same ship as Miss Clouston. The Bishop, a widower with three children, was accompanied by his sister Margaret, who was to look after his household and help with the running of the academy. Miss Anderson appears to have been the epitome of the straitlaced, sharp-tongued spinster.[28]

Upon her arrival at the Upper Fort, Mrs. Pelly was much disconcerted to find that in spite of her connections, she was obliged to give precedence to Mrs. Ballenden, a woman whom, due to race and reputation, she did not consider her social equal. The Orkney woman evidently intended to play the great lady, for even Letitia Hargrave, who had come out to York Factory from Scotland in 1840, had been aghast at the extravagance of her trousseau:

> Anne brought an immense quantity of finery 5 perfectly new bonnets besides that she wore on board, & scarves, handkerchiefs & shawls as if she had been going to Calcutta.[29]

Instead of the deference she expected, Anne Pelly found that her fastidious and fainting ways were the object of ridicule at the mess table, especially by Captain Foss, who was evidently in the habit of making telling remarks to Mrs. Ballenden. Pelly's wife was so incensed by the insulting manner in which she considered she was treated that she actually made herself ill; her husband withdrew from the mess in a huff and shunned the Ballendens.[30]

In Mrs. Pelly's view the behavior of Captain Foss and Mrs. Ballenden at the mess table, coupled with what she had heard from Catherine Winegart, was enough for her to importune Major Caldwell that such immorality could not be condoned.[31] Ballenden's popularity made Caldwell hesitate to take any open action, but after the chief factor left in June to meet Governor Simpson at Fort Alexander, a concerted effort was made to exclude his wife from respectable company. The Major forbade his family to associate with Mrs. Ballenden, Miss Anderson and the Bishop refused to countenance her, and the Cockrans advised some of Sarah's close friends that she was no longer fit company. Most humiliating of all, Mrs. Black, who had shown a preference for the society of Mrs. Pelly, now openly cut her fellow countrywoman.[32]

Upon hearing the rumors circulating about them, Mrs. Ballenden and Captain Foss were determined to fight back to prove their innocence. Sarah took refuge with Recorder Adam Thom and his wife, who had acted as godmother to her last child. With Thom's aid, a sworn statement was obtained from Catherine Winegart denying any knowledge of an illicit relationship between her mistress and Captain Foss.[33] The Captain, meanwhile, posted a notice on the shop door at the Upper Fort, denouncing Pelly for circulating "false and calumnious" reports, and announcing his intention to seek legal redress. When John Black, who had been given temporary charge of the post, insisted that the notice be removed, Foss began to suspect that Black was in league with Pelly to disgrace their superior.[34] Upon his return with the Governor at the end of June, Ballenden was much relieved to be assured by Thom that his investigations had convinced him that there was no truth to the reports about Mrs. Ballenden. Ballenden, however, decided that he should postpone his furlough and resume charge of the Upper Fort, but, almost immediately, he was forced to resign because of the actions of Black and Pelly. Mr. Black confronted him with a sworn deposition by the mess cook John Davidson and his English wife implicating Sarah with Captain Foss; it had been sworn in front of Governor Simpson, as was a similar statement by Mr. Pelly.[35]

The upshot of these charges was that Captain Foss brought a suit of defamatory conspiracy against Pelly, Davidson and their wives for having accused him of "criminal intercourse with a married woman"; his sole purpose, he claimed, was "to clear the reputation of a Lady."[36] The three-day trial which began on July 16 threw Red River into a turmoil; such was the excitement occasioned by the case, lamented Simpson, that "all the inhabitants thought it proper to espouse one side or the other and to regard the verdict as a personal triumph or a personal injury."[37] From a judicial point of view, the trial was highly irregular, notably because the judge Adam Thom had previously acted for the prosecution. Furthermore, the question as to whether the defendants had really been the instigators of a defamatory conspiracy was lost sight of as the trial concentrated on proving Mrs. Ballenden's guilt or innocence. Numerous witnesses were called, but their evidence proved extremely vague and circumstantial; most of them had to admit they had just heard and repeated rumors concerning Foss and Mrs. Ballenden. The testimony of some of the women, especially Mrs. Cockran and Miss Anderson, was full of innuendo and undisguised hostility.[38] Finally, after several hours of deliberation, the jury declared that Captain Foss and Mrs. Ballenden had been unjustly slandered, and the defendants were required to pay heavy damages—Pelly, three hundred pounds; Davidson, one hundred pounds.[39]

That nearly all of the jurors were Anglophone mixed-bloods may have influenced the stiff fines, for much racial animosity was engendered by the case. Chief among Sarah

Ballenden's accusers were those who championed the supremacy of white women: the Protestant clergy, particularly Bishop Anderson and Reverend Cockran; Governor Caldwell; and some of the lesser company officers. On the other hand, most of her supporters were either Anglophone mixed-bloods or married to native women. Two of her most ardent defenders were Dr. John Bunn, a prominent mixed-blood, and the colony's sheriff Alexander Ross, who was married to an Indian woman and had numerous daughters. The Anglophone mixed-bloods who desired to be assimilated into white society viewed the attack on Mrs. Ballenden as an attempt to discredit mixed-blood women which would threaten their position in Red River society. In the words of one cogent observer, the affair seemed to be "a strife of Blood."[40] Adam Thom, whose part in the proceedings had temporarily lessened his unpopularity among the mixed-blood community, denounced the intended racial slur. "Altho Mrs. B. might not have so much starch in her face" he declared, "she had as much virtue in her heart as any *exotic*."[41] There can be no doubt that Anne Pelly's air of superiority occasioned much resentment and was a root cause of trouble. Her brother, Chief Trader Robert Clouston, wrote acidly to his father-in-law Donald Ross:

> . . . my sister is *not a native*—therefore must have the ill-will of that class. She has self respect and acts in a manner entitling her to the respect of others therefore she must have the enmity of those who have lost the sense of shame.[42]

Thus the colonial elite was seriously split along predominantly racial lines when the new Associate Governor of the Hudson's Bay Company, Eden Colvile, arrived in the fall of 1850 with his English wife Anne. Despite her declared innocence, Mrs. Ballenden had continued to be shunned by "the nobs of womankind," particularly Mrs. Caldwell, Miss Anderson and Mrs. Cockran. The bad feelings resulting from the scandal created an impossible social situation. Colvile wrote in exasperation to Simpson:

> Altogether the state of things is most unpleasant though somewhat ludicrous, withal. For instance, today, the Bishop & his sister were calling on us, & in the middle of the visit I heard a knock at the door & suspecting who it was rushed out & found Mr. & Mrs. Ballenden. I had to cram them into another room till the Bishop's visit was over, but as he was then going to see the Pelly's he had to pas through this room, so that I had to bolt out & put them into a third room. It was altogether like a scene in a farce.[43]

Colvile, who took over the governorship of the colony from the unpopular Caldwell, would have reinstated Ballenden at Upper Fort Garry, but Black insisted upon retaining the charge for the coming year. The Ballendens removed to Lower Fort Garry where they took up quarters in the Big House, and the Governor delighted Ballenden by admitting Sarah to the company of his wife. Since Ballenden himself believed in his wife's innocence, Colvile, who was anxious to restore harmony, deemed it only fair that she should be allowed back into society. As the summer wore on, Colvile found Mrs. Ballenden's behavior so discreet and proper that he began to think that the "poor woman had been more sinned against than sinning." The parsons and their women were "very strait-laced," he declared, and the colony "a dreadful place for scandal."[44]

For his part, Captain Foss, who had been divested of his company privileges, had been away at York Factory most of the late summer, supervising the arrival of another contingent of pensioners. It was expected that he would soon leave the settlement permanently, but Foss changed his mind and decided to winter in Red River, likely because of a disagreement with the company over some property.[45] He took up residence at the home of Donald

McKenzie, a retired Company officer, and remained popular with the Anglophone mixed-blood community.[46] By the fall, however, Chief Factor Ballenden had made up his mind that he should go to Britain for medical treatment. He felt confident in leaving his wife and family under the protection of Governor Colvile; there was no lively mess table at the Lower Fort, but Mrs. Ballenden was to take her meals with the clerk W. D. Lane.[47]

These winter arrangements began auspiciously enough, but by early December Sarah Ballenden was again hopelessly entangled in scandal's web. An incriminating note, allegedly from Sarah to Captain Foss, was delivered into the hands of Adam Thom, who, forthwith, presented Governor Colvile with a copy. In the note, Mrs. Ballenden, proposing to take advantage of Colvile's absence at the Upper Fort, invited her "darling Christopher" to pay her a visit. The original having been delivered, although it was never revealed by whom, Foss apparently effected the rendezvous, although no one actually reported having seen him at the Lower Fort.[48] When Colvile returned home on December 5, he did not confront Mrs. Ballenden as to her conduct; now convinced of her deceit, he abruptly ceased all association between her and his family. A few days later, Sarah further incriminated herself, in his eyes, by driving from the fort alone and paying an afternoon visit to the McKenzie home where Foss was living.[49]

This turn of events, the news of which spread rapidly through the community, confirmed Mrs. Ballenden's accusers in the belief that she had been guilty of immoral conduct all along. Several of her supporters now also felt obliged to desert her cause: both Dr. Bunn and Adam Thom changed sides.[50] But while Thom deemed it necessary to write to Ballenden, now in Scotland, of his wife's falseness, others, notably Alexander Ross, remained unconvinced of her guilt. An intriguing, if frustratingly cryptic, series of notes also reveals that Mrs. Ballenden received sympathetic support from her nephew, A. G. B. Bannatyne, a clerk at the Upper Fort, and her messmate, W. D. Lane. Realizing that she was now *persona non grata* at the fort, Sarah, accompanied by her nephew, left on January 11 to live at "Green's old place" with members of the Ross family. Bannatyne enlisted Lane's aid to provide his aunt with a stove and other articles for her comfort, and expressed the hope that she might now "pass the remainder of the winter *more pleasantly than the commencement.*"[51]

It is a popular misconception, current both then and today, that Mrs. Ballenden left the fort to live with Captain Foss. This is incorrect and, in spite of an undoubtedly close surveillance, no one could report any further evidence of an affair between her and the Captain.[52] By this time Sarah, who already had several young children in her care, was well along in her eighth pregnancy, and she gave birth to a son on June 15.[53] Shortly after this, the baby's father returned from furlough and Captain Foss left the settlement for good.[54] No record remains of Ballenden's reunion with his wife after his long absence. When far away in Scotland, grief-stricken and angry, he had contemplated divorce, but now refused to pursue this course even though pressured by "respectable" society to do so.[55] It was reported, by Thom and Colvile, that during the summer the unhappy Sarah had "confessed" and thrown herself upon her husband's mercy. But Ballenden himself casts doubt on such an occurrence in a private letter to Simpson in which he asks the governor to cease in his condemnation of his wife:

> No further proceedings, on my part, against her, will ever take place, indeed, did no other reason exist, they would be worse than useless, as there is no proof, notwithstanding Mr Thoms opinion to the contrary. . . . I entreat of you, for my sake, *if not for hers*, to cease, and let her rest in peace—if that is now possible.[56]

In the fall of 1851, Ballenden was posted to Fort Vancouver, and it appears that he would have taken his wife with him had her health been up to the long journey across the Rockies. Instead, he endeavored to settle Sarah comfortably in a rented house near The Rapids in the settlement. But Sarah Ballenden, now vilified as a "fallen woman," was to pass a wretched and lonely winter. Her health seriously deteriorated; according to one of her few friends, "if there is such a thing as dying of a broken heart, she cannot live long."[57] In the summer of 1852, finding the situation in Red River unbearable and hoping to travel with the annual brigade to join her husband, Mrs. Ballenden and her children moved to Norway House, where she was generously received by Chief Factor George Barnston and his mixed-blood wife Ellen. Barnston, who had been a friend of Sarah's father and known her since childhood, declared that she might "always find an asylum where I live. Surely utter helplessness merits aid."[58]

The only letters written by Sarah Ballenden known to have survived date from this period. Charming notes written to thank W. D. Lane for his help in forwarding her belongings and in securing a servant for her, they also indicate that she was far from well. "I feel stronger," she wrote in July, "but *cough* very much still."[59] In 1853, Ballenden's own poor health forced him to retire from the Columbia, and he arranged for his nephew to take his wife and family to Scotland where he planned to retire. There is evidence that a poignant reunion between husband and wife took place in Edinburgh before Sarah died of consumption in December of that year. When writing a short time later to his daughter Eliza, Ballenden referred movingly to the concern which "your own dear mother" had expressed about the welfare of her children as she lay on her deathbed.[60]

The fate of Sarah Ballenden, who was only thirty-five years old when she died, was a tragic one. In terms of assessing her guilt, it is worth considering Alexander Ross's belief that she had been a victim of jealousy and revenge. "After what I had seen at the trial," declared Ross, "and the unfounded malice got up in certain circles, no earthly power will convince me that she is guilty, till that guilt be proved."[61] Indeed, if Captain Foss and Mrs. Ballenden *had* been guilty of an adulterous affair, it seems highly unlikely that they would have actively invited the risk of exposure brought by the trial. Certainly those accused of the conspiracy had motives for wishing to discredit one or both parties. Mrs. Pelly's envy of Sarah Ballenden's social position complemented her husband's desire for revenge: he had not only been spurned by Sarah himself but had lost a large sum through gambling to Captain Foss.[62] The Davidsons, recently arrived from England, appear to have resented their inferior position at the fort; Mrs. Davidson was particularly piqued at being required to perform household duties which she considered beneath her dignity, especially for a mixed-blood mistress.[63] John Black's motivation for making the Davidsons' accusations public were seen as highly suspect. One observer declared that the chief trader hoped to disgrace Ballenden so his superior would be forced to resign and Black would regain charge of the fort as he was to have done during Ballenden's absence on furlough.[64]

It seems significant that when the scandal blew up the second time, none of the defendants sued for redress of damages. Thus it is not beyond the realm of possibility that Sarah Ballenden was framed; the incriminating note was not signed, and found its way most conveniently into the hands of Adam Thom. On the other hand, although there was little opportunity for them to meet after the trial, it is possible that the friendship which existed between Sarah Ballenden and Captain Foss was developing into something deeper. If indeed, Mrs. Ballenden had attempted a surreptitious meeting with the Captain, she was certainly betrayed, although it was never revealed by whom or for what reason. In sum, the historical evidence does not justify supporting Reverend Cockran's observation that "whenever a rumour of this kind is in circulation, I have always found them [sic] to turn out correct."[65]

Whatever the case, Sarah Ballenden paid a heavy price. She became a social outcast, her reputation ruined. According to the double standard of British morality, it was women who must uphold the sexual purity of society and any deviation must be punished. Ironically, the mixed-blood woman's strongest condemnation came not from men but from other women. In this situation the women behaved in a petty and vindictive manner; yet ultimately they were more deserving of pity than censure. Their actions stemmed in large measure from their being reduced to a precarious dependency on male protectors and, unlike the men, they were locked into a marital system which gave them no autonomous way of establishing their status or worth. The racism evinced by white women in Red River, while as inexcusable as that of their male counterparts, was aggravated by what, in their view, was a concrete threat to their own welfare in the competition for eligible husbands.

The fall of Sarah Ballenden had the effect of intensifying racial prejudice in nineteenth-century fur trade society. Implicit in some of the attitudes expressed during the trial was the belief that a certain moral weakness was inherent in women of even part-Indian extraction. In the opinion of Chief Trader Robert Campbell, for example, the Foss-Pelly scandal served as a striking lesson of the folly of marrying a native woman:

It is too well known that few indeed of those joined to the ebony and half ebony damsels of the north are happy or anything like it; . . . few or none of them have pleasure, comfort or satisfaction of their Families.[66]

While not all incoming company officers in the 1850s followed Campbell's example of marrying a British woman, those who continued to marry "daughters of the country" restricted their choice to highly acculturated daughters of wealthy Hudson's Bay families who studiously endeavored to disassociate themselves from their native heritage. Certainly by the post-1870 period, the mixed marriage which had been a central part of the fabric of Red River society had become an increasingly peripheral phenomenon.

Notes

1. Public Archives of Canada, James Hargrave Correspondence, vol. 7, p. 1716, Duncan Finlayson to Hargrave, August 12, 1839.
2. For a detailed discussion of the role played by native women in the development of fur trade society, see Sylvia Van Kirk, *"Many Tender Ties": Women in Fur Trade Society in Western Canada 1670–1870* (Winnipeg: Watson & Dwyer, 1980), chs. 1–6.
3. Hudson's Bay Company Archives, D. 5/31, f. 247, James Bird to Gov. Simpson, Aug. 8, 1851.
4. H.B.C.A., B.135/c/2. f. 64d, G. Simpson to J. G. McTavish, April 10, 1831.
5. H.B.C.A., Ermatinger Correspondence, Copy 23, f. 271, W. Sinclair to E. Ermatinger, Aug. 18, 1831.
6. H.B.C.A., B.135/c/2. f. 106, Simpson to McTavish, June 29, 1833.
7. H.B.C.A., E.4/16, f. 243, Register of Marriages; Copy of Will of John Thomas, Sr. (1822). In several sources, Anne Christie has been incorrectly identified as the daughter of HBC Governor Thomas Thomas.
8. See Van Kirk, *"Many Tender Ties,"* pp. 153–158, 165.
9. *Ibid.*, pp. 147–149.
10. The identity of Alexander Roderick McLeod's wife has not been discovered. In the papers relating to his estate she is described as "an Indian Woman of the half breed Caste", see H.B.C.A., A.36/10, f. 18; Provincial Archives of Manitoba, Records of the General Quarterly Court of Assiniboia, *"Foss v. Pelly et. al.,* 16–18 July 1850," p. 203.
11. G. P. de T. Glazebrook, ed., *The Hargrave Correspondence, 1821–1843* (Toronto: Champlain Society, vol. 24, 1938), pp. 249–250; H.B.C.A., E.4/lb, f. 248d, Register of Marriages; Chief Factor John Stuart, who

acted as Sarah's guardian, gave his consent to the marriage (H.B.C.A., D.5/14, f.275) and the bride received a dowry of £350 from her father (H.B.C.A., D.5/12, fos. 243–244).

12. P.A.C., Hargrave Correspondence. vol. 23, letterbook 14, Hargrave to Mrs. T. Isbister, May 28, 1839 and letterbook 15, Hargrave to J. Ballenden, Sept. 7, 1839.

13. *Ibid.*, vol. 8, p. 1891, Ballenden to Hargrave, Jan. 30, 1841.

14. Public Record Office, England, Prob. 11, 2257, f. 667, Will of John Ballenden (1854).

15. See Van Kirk, *"Many Tender Ties,"* pp. 189–90.

16. Glenbow Foundation Archives, Calgary, James Sutherland papers, Jas. Sutherland to John Sutherland, Aug. 7, 1838.

17. P.A.C., Hargrave Correspondence, vol. 8, p. 2193, Finlayson to Hargrave, Dec. 18, 1841.

18. H.B.C.A., D.5/9, f.373d. D. Finlayson to Simpson, Dec. 18, 1843.

19. *Ibid.*, D.5/13, fos. 395d–96, Finlayson to Simpson, April 8, 1845; Provincial Archives of British Columbia, Donald Ross Papers, John McBeath to Donald Ross, Aug. 6, 1850.

20. H.B.C.A., D.5/29, f. 422, Ballenden to Simpson, Dec. 30, 1850; P.A.M., *Foss v. Pelly*, p. 218.

21. P.A.C., Hargrave Correspondence, vol. 27, Letitia Hargrave to Flora Mactavish, June 1, 1850.

22. P.A.M., *Foss v. Pelly*, pp. 202–203.

23. H.B.C.A., D.5/23, f.383, Ballenden to Simpson, Nov. 29, 1848. For further information on Captain Foss and his relations with the Hudson's Bay Company, see E. E. Rich, ed., *Eden Colvile's Letters, 1849–52* (London: H.B.R.S., vol. 19, 1956).

24. P.A.B.C., D. Ross Papers, Wm. Todd to Donald Ross, July 20, 1850.

25. P.A.M., *Foss v. Pelly*, pp. 185–86, 203.

26. Margaret A. MacLeod, ed., *The Letters of Letitia Hargrave* (Toronto: Champlain Society, vol. 28, 1947), p. 247.

27. P.A.B.C., D. Ross Papers, Robert Clouston to Donald Ross, June 29, 1849.

28. H.B.C.A., D.5/30, f. 206, Adam Thom to Simpson, Feb. 5, 1851.

29. MacLeod, *Letitia's Letters*, p. 247; see also P.A.C., Hargrave Correspondence, vol. 27, Letitia to her mother, Dec. 14, 1851.

30. P.A.B.C., D. Ross Papers, A. E. Pelly to D. Ross, Aug. 1, 1850; P.A.M., *Foss v. Pelly*, pp. 185, 196.

31. *Ibid.*, pp. 183, 193, 213–14.

32. P.A.C., Hargrave Correspondence, vol. 15, p. 4533, Wm. Todd to Hargrave, July 13, 1850 and p. 4581, John Black to Hargrave, Aug. 6, 1850; P.A.M., *Foss v. Pelly*, p. 187; MacLeod, *Letitia's Letters*, p. 255.

33. P.A.M., *"Foss vs. Pelly"*, p. 207.

34. H.B.C.A., A.12/5, fos. 178–179, Memo for Gov. Simpson.

35. P.A.M., *Foss v. Pelly*, pp. 199–202.

36. Charges were also to have been laid against the Blacks but these were dropped (MacLeod, *Letitia's Letters*, p. 255); P.A.M., *Foss v. Pelly*, p. 181.

37. H.B.C.A., D.4/71, fos. 265–266d, Simpson to J. Black, Dec. 18, 1850.

38. P.A.B.C., D. Ross Papers, J. Ballenden to Ross, Aug. 1, 1850; H.B.C.A., D.5/28, f. 437d, Adam Thom to Simpson, Aug. 15, 1850.

39. Foss never actually collected the £100 from Davidson, maintaining that it was the principle not the money he was really interested in (*Foss v. Pelly*, p. 181).

40. P.A.B.C., D. Ross Papers, R. Clouston to Ross, Dec. 17, 1850.

41. MacLeod, *Letitia's Letters*, p. 256.

42. P.A.B.C., D. Ross Papers, R. Clouston to Ross, Sept. 28, 1850.

43. Rich, *Colvile's Letters*, p. 193.

44. *Ibid.*, 195.

45. *Ibid.*, 47–65.

46. This Donald McKenzie had been a lesser officer in the service of the Hudson's Bay Company; he was married to a half-breed woman, Matilda Bruce.

47. Rich, *Colvile's Letters*, 195, 197. The published version mistakenly reads Jane instead of Lane.

48. *Ibid.*, p. 201

49. *Ibid.*

50. H.B.C.A., D.5/30, fos. 47–53, John Black to Simpson, Jan. 8, 1851 and f. 203, Adam Thom to Simpson, Feb. 5, 1851.

51. University of British Columbia Archives, W. D. Lane Papers, Folder 1, letter 12, A. G. B. Bannatyne to Lane, Jan. 9, 1851. Colvile (p. 204) states that Mrs. Ballenden went to live at one Cunninghame's; this was likely the home of one of the married daughters of Alexander Ross by that name.

52. Rich, *Colvile's Letters*, pp. 204, 210.

53. Will of John Ballenden; U.B.C.A., Lane Papers, Bannatyne to Lane, Monday evening, "Poor Aunt has got

a son yesterday morning about 7 o'clock". Like many of the notes between Bannatyne and Lane, this one is not dated, but from other evidence it can be established that it was written on June 16, 1851.

54. Rich, *Colvile's Letters*, p. 65.
55. H.B.C.A., D.5/31, f. 143d, Black to Simpson, July 26, 1851.
56. *Ibid.*, D.5/32, f. 323 Ballenden to Simpson, Dec. 5, 1851.
57. *Ibid.*, D.5/31, f. 206, A. Ross to Simpson, Aug. 1, 1851.
58. P.A.B.C., D. Ross Papers, G. Barnston to Ross, July 22, 1852.
59. U.B.C.A., Lane Papers, Folder 1, letter 15, Sarah Ballenden to W. D. Lane, July 20, 1852.
60. H.B.C.A., D.4/74, f. 212, Simpson to A. McDermot, Feb. 6, 1854; J. J. Healy, *Women of Red River* (Winnipeg, 1923), p. 195.
61. H.B.C.A., D.5/31, f. 206, A. Ross to Simpson, Aug. 1, 1851.
62. MacLeod, *Letitia's Letters*, p. 247.
63. P.A.M., *Foss v. Pelly*, p. 207.
64. P.A.B.C., Ross Papers, Wm. Todd to Ross, July 20, 1850.
65. P.A.M., *Foss v. Pelly*, p. 187.
66. H.B.C.A., D.5/37, fos. 458–59, Robert Campbell to Simpson, Aug. 31, 1853.

10

Gender Systems in Conflict: The Marriages of Mission-Educated Chinese American Women, 1874–1939

Peggy Pascoe

As soon as Wong Ah So entered the United States in 1922, she was sold into prostitution. Her owner, a Chinese woman who moved her from one town to another, took most of her earnings, but Wong Ah So scraped up extra money to send to her impoverished family in Hong Kong. When the man who had helped smuggle her into the country demanded $1000 for his services, Wong Ah So, who was afraid of him, borrowed the money to pay him. Shortly afterwards, she developed an illness, apparently venereal disease, that required daily treatment and interfered with her work as a prostitute.

In February 1924, Protestant missionaries raided the residential hotel in Fresno, California, where Wong Ah So was staying. Wong Ah So was frightened. Her owner had tried to keep her away from missionaries by telling her that their leader, Donaldina Cameron, "was in the habit of draining blood from the arteries of newly 'captured' girls and drinking it to keep up her own vitality."[1] But Wong Ah So was also tired, sick, and afraid that she could not repay her heavy debts. She agreed to enter Cameron's Presbyterian Mission Home in San Francisco. Wong Ah So would live in the Mission Home for only a little more than a year, but the course of the rest of her life would be changed by her contact with missionary women.[2]

From the late nineteenth century to the present, accounts like that of Wong Ah So fed the white American taste for exoticism and formed a unique genre in the popular mythology of American race relations. Missionary women called them "rescue" stories and saw them as skirmishes in a righteous battle against sexual slavery. Newspaper reporters exploited the stories for sensational copy, attracting readers with provocative headlines such as "Slave Girls Taken in Raid on Chinese," or "Woman Tells of Traffic in Slave Girls."[3] Anti-Chinese politicians relied on images of so-called "Chinese slave girls" to bolster their successful 1882 campaign to restrict the immigration of Chinese laborers.

In the rescue genre, sensational images of victimized Chinese women were accompanied by equally sensational portrayals of nefarious Chinese organizations—the tongs—that kidnapped, enslaved, and exploited prostitutes. Because rescue stories suggested that every Chinese organization thrived on organized vice, they left scandalized readers ignorant of the distinction between the tongs that controlled prostitution and the Chinese family and district associations that had little connection to the trade.[4]

In order to counter these racially based stereotypes, scholars of Chinese America writing in the 1960s and 1970s tried to desensationalize the Chinese American past by shifting attention away from organized vice. Trying to convince their readers that Chinese immi-

Reprinted with permission from the *Journal of Social History*, volume 22, June 1989.

grants were model Americans, they depicted tongs as misunderstood benevolent institutions and did their best to ignore prostitution altogether.[5]

Their silence on the subject of prostitution came at the same time that another group of historians was mounting a trenchant critique of American racism. In these writings, Protestant missionaries were, for the first time, given their full share of the blame for American racism and ethnocentrism. Historians of race used rescue stories like that of Wong Ah So to demonstrate the racist attitudes and cultural condescension of Victorian missionaries, with the term "rescue" used skeptically, in quotation marks.[6] From their efforts, we have come to a much fuller understanding of the ways in which missionary adoption of racial stereotypes helped maintain white American dominance over minority groups.

The alternatives available to Chinese immigrant women in American Chinatowns were conditioned by Victorian racial hierarchies, but they were also affected by the conflict between gender systems revealed in the contact between Chinese immigrant women and Protestant women reformers.[7] Because rescue stories illuminate both race relations and gender systems, missionary records are an ideal source for exploring the complexity of race *and* gender relations between dominant groups and minority groups in American society.[8] To explore these issues, I will use the case files of the Presbyterian Mission Home that Wong Ah So entered in 1924 as a window on gender relations in San Francisco's Chinatown at the turn of the century.

Specifically, I want to do three things: first, describe the two different gender systems idealized in China and in nineteenth-century America; second, show how the immigrant context made Chinese women in San Francisco particularly vulnerable to exploitation yet, at the same time, put some of them in a particularly opportune position to challenge traditional male prerogatives; and finally, show how Chinese immigrant women used the conflict between traditional Chinese and Victorian American gender systems to shape one set of possibilities for a distinctive Chinese American culture.

Let's begin with the gender system of traditional China, the set of ideals Wong Ah So and many other immigrant women were raised to emulate.[9] In traditional China, families provided the social glue of society, and families focused their energies on the importance of raising male heirs to carry on the lineage.[10] For this reason, young girls were considered to be less important than young boys from birth. Especially—but not only—in impoverished families, young girls might be sold to pay debts or expected to demonstrate their filial piety by working for wages. Something like this happened to Wong Ah So when her mother bargained with a young man who told them that in San Francisco, Wong Ah So could make money to support her family as an entertainer at Chinese banquets. When the young man offered the mother $450 for her daughter, Wong Ah So went to California.[11]

Although historians should be cautious in equating cultural ideals with individual behavior, there is little doubt that Wong Ah So understood and accepted her subordinate position in this traditional gender system. Even after she awoke from her dreams of fancy entertaining to the harsh reality of prostitution in immigrant California, Wong Ah So's letters to her mother in Hong Kong were framed in traditional terms. "Daughter is not angry with you," she wrote in one letter later found and saved by missionary women, "It seems to be just my fate." Dutifully reciting familiar stories of Chinese children renowned for their filial piety, she promised her mother that "after I have earned money by living this life of prostitution, I will return to China and become a Buddhist nun." "By accomplishing these two things," she ended rather hopefully, "I shall have attained all the requirements of complete filial piety."[12]

The full weight of the gender system of traditional China descended on young women at the time of marriage. Matches were generally arranged by go-betweens, with little personal contact between prospective mates. In and of themselves, new brides held little status until they produced male heirs; until then, they were expected to serve their mothers-in-law. Whether mothers or daughters-in-law, women were expected to display female submission to male authority. Thus Wong Ah So knew by heart what she called "the three great obediences:" "At home, a daughter should be obedient to her parents; after marriage, to her husband; after the death of her husband, to her son."[13]

The subordination of young wives was ensured by a series of social sanctions. Wives who didn't produce male heirs might find their husbands taking concubines; there was a highly stratified system of prostitution from which such concubines could be chosen.[14] Furthermore, wives who didn't behave according to custom might find themselves divorced and sent back to their own families in disgrace.[15] Even young wives' most forceful weapon of complaint—committing suicide to protest against bad treatment—brought social judgment on their in-laws only at the cost of their own lives.[16]

Young women who adapted to the constraints of this traditional patriarchal system, however, could achieve significant social status later in life as mothers and mothers-in-law. As Wong Ah So noted, evidently trying to resign herself to her situation, "Now I may be somebody's daughter, but some day I may be somebody's mother."[17] Wives who gave birth to sons could look forward to becoming mothers-in-law, a position of some authority within the patrilineal lineage.[18]

By the late nineteenth century, when Chinese immigration to the United States was in full swing, the traditional system of patriarchal control was beginning to lose some of its power in China. In Kwangtung, the area from which most immigrants to America came, some young women who were able to find employment in the sericulture industry were mounting a "marriage resistance" movement and entering all-women's houses rather than living with parents or in-laws.[19] Their relative freedom was based on a unique combination of economic circumstances that allowed them to support themselves outside of marriage.

It appears that most Chinese women who immigrated to America were more impoverished and less able to challenge the traditional ideals of marriage head-on than the marriage resisters of their native land. Yet when immigrant women reached the United States, they encountered a Victorian gender system that stood in some contrast to the traditional gender system of late nineteenth-century China. Victorian Americans held up an ideal some historians have called "companionate" marriage. According to these historians, companionate marriage differed from traditional marriage in significant respects. Companionate unions were based on attraction between spouses rather than parental arrangement and in them, at least according to the ideal, women were idealized as nurturant mothers and sexually pure moral guardians.[20]

Yet, as feminist historians have pointed out, Victorian marriages also reflected an unequal arrangement of gender power.[21] Companionate marriage may have differed from traditional marriage, but women who held to the Victorian ideal gained affection and moral influence at the cost of legal and economic powerlessness. Throughout the nineteenth century, middle-class American women had to fight for such basic rights as the chance to be considered legal guardians of their own children. Often deprived of formal control over their property, women were expected by society to be the economic dependents of men, a status that sharply limited their alternatives in and outside of marriage.

The ideal of companionate marriage was the rhetorical panacea put forth by the middle-class women who established the Presbyterian Mission Home Wong Ah So entered in San Francisco. Yet the Mission Home matrons who espoused companionate marriage were themselves single women devoted to professional careers in missionary work, women who had encountered in their own lives few of the daily restraints of Victorian marriage and who occupied a somewhat marginal place within the Victorian gender system.[22] Their single status and their public activism combined, not always smoothly, with their advocacy of companionate marriage to offer a striking example to the Chinese immigrant women with whom they came in contact.

Thus, while both the Victorian American and traditional Chinese gender systems were patriarchal, the two forms of patriarchy were significantly different. In the Victorian gender system, women's status rested not on their position as mothers-in-law but on their ability to parlay their supposedly "natural" nurturing influence into a form of moral authority recognized by white Americans. To Victorians, a display of female moral authority rooted in sexual purity was the only sure measure of women's standing in society. As a result, missionary women believed that women who didn't fit Victorian definitions of female morality were oppressed and subjugated examples of the victimization of women. Thus Donaldina Cameron, the Presbyterian Mission Home matron, was fond of saying that Chinese prostitutes were "the most helpless and oppressed group of women and children who live within the borders of these United States of America."[23]

Clearly, this Victorian analysis of women's position rested in part on an ethnocentric—at times even racist—belief in the superiority of American culture. Victorian assumptions can be seen in the words of Presbyterian Mission Home workers, who had long insisted that "the first step upwards from heathenism to civilization is the organization of a home on Christian principles."[24] In ideological terms, missionary women equated the emancipation of women with the adoption of middle-class Victorian marriages in which husbands' traditional powers could be reduced by wives' moral influence, conveniently ignoring the legal and economic powerlessness Victorian women endured. Further, as long as they held to the assumptions of the Victorian gender system, missionaries could not disentangle their critique of the treatment of women in traditional societies from their assumption of racial and cultural superiority.

The cultural ideas of these two distinct gender systems clashed in American Chinatowns, where a unique pattern of immigration rendered Chinese immigrant women easily exploitable even as it held before them the promise of unprecedented opportunity. At the root of this unique social context was an extreme numerical imbalance between male immigrants (who formed the vast majority of the Chinese population in America) and the much smaller number of female immigrants. The number of Chinese women who traveled to the United States in the nineteenth century was so small that by 1882, when American exclusion legislation cut Chinese immigration drastically, the sex ratio in Chinese immigrant communities was already sharply skewed. In California, there were twenty-two Chinese men for every Chinese woman in 1890; in 1920, there were still five Chinese men for every Chinese woman.[25]

This population imbalance created a demand for sexual services that sustained a thriving network of organized prostitution in Chinese immigrant communities.[26] Only a few married Chinese women traveled to America, since respectable young wives were expected to remain with in-laws in China.[27] Most of the female immigrants were young women who, like Wong Ah So, were placed into prostitution. Young women entered prostitution by a variety of means. Very few Chinese prostitutes were independent entrepreneurs. Many had been enticed into dubious marriages in China only to be sold into the trade on their arrival in America. Others had been purchased from their poverty-stricken parents; still others had been kidnapped by procurers and smuggled into American ports.

Compared to white American prostitutes of the same period, Chinese prostitutes were particularly powerless; in fact, many were kept in conditions that render some truth to the sensational stereotype of the "Chinese slave girl."[28] Some were indentured, with few hopes of paying off their contracts; others were virtually enslaved. Most were under the control of tong leaders and their henchmen, many of whom operated with the collusion of white officials.

Thus, the skewed sex ratio of immigrant Chinatowns increased the vulnerability of Chinese immigrant women to sexual exploitation. At the same time, however, the extreme sexual imbalance also offered unusual opportunities for those immigrant women who could find a way to take advantage of them. As Lucie Cheng has noted, both the skewed sex ratio and the absence of established in-laws created unique opportunities for immigrant prostitutes to marry in order to leave prostitution behind.[29]

And here is where rescue homes founded by Protestant women came in. Rescue homes gave missionary women space and time to impose the Victorian gender system and its ideal of companionate marriage on Chinese immigrant women. Even the very term "rescue home" is a significant clue to their intentions. It conveyed the twin goals of Protestant women: on the one hand, they wanted to "rescue" Chinese women who had been sold or enticed into prostitution; on the other, they wanted to inculcate in all women their particular concept of the "Christian home." Protestant women believed that their institutions would separate women victims from the men who preyed on them, providing space for the supposedly natural virtues of Victorian "true womanhood"—purity and piety—to come to the surface.[30] These Victorian ideals clashed with the more traditional gender system held by Chinese women. Nowhere was this conflict between gender systems more intense than in the Presbyterian Mission Home for Chinese women, founded in San Francisco in 1874 and in operation until 1939.[31]

Support for Victorian female values was built into the institutional routine of the Presbyterian Mission Home. The Victorian conception of female purity, for example, was ensured by drawing strict boundaries between the rescue home and the surrounding community. Such a strategy seemed like mere common sense to missionary women who believed that the Chinese women who entered the institution were the innocent victims of predatory men. Mission Home officials had been threatened by tong members and local white gangs so frequently that they saw every venture outside the Home as potentially dangerous.[32] In their view, structured isolation was a necessary protection. As a result, Mission Home residents were never allowed outside the institution without escorts; in the early years, they were even hidden behind a screen at church services.[33]

Further, the Home had trusted doorkeepers whose job it was to screen visitors—men in particular—and keep them away from the women within.[34] Contact with people outside the Home was limited to those approved by the mission staff—schoolteachers, employers judged suitable for domestic servants, and young men of "good" character who had been scrutinized by staff members. Matrons read all incoming and outgoing mail and confiscated letters they thought would prove detrimental to the residents' journey toward true womanhood.[35]

Victorian female piety was encouraged in the Mission Home by continual attempts to convert residents to Protestant Christianity. Morning and evening prayers, with more extended sessions on weekends, were the rule. Since matrons were determined that "the Bible shall be deeply implanted within [residents'] minds" in case they were "ever again surrounded with heathen influence," Protestantism permeated institutional educational activities.[36] Training in scripture was thought to be such a fundamental part of the Mission Home education that managers once cancelled an arrangement with the Board of Education to provide a teacher for the Home because "the staff felt that she did not give the religious influence necessary," even though the decision meant that they had to finance a replacement themselves.[37]

Along with this emphasis on purity and piety came a routine of constant busyness, which was desired both as a means of training in domesticity and as a way of keeping rescue home residents from looking longingly at their old lives. The day began with 7 A.M. prayers, followed by breakfast, an hour of supervised housework, morning and afternoon school classes, dinner, a 7 P.M. prayer meeting, a study session, and then lights out.[38] Each resident cleaned her own room and did her own laundry in addition to the shared household tasks. Pairs of women were assigned each day to special tasks—cooking the Chinese and American meals, perhaps, or caring for the few babies in residence at any one time, a favorite assignment. The staff depended on the most trusted residents to translate, for most missionaries did not speak Chinese. Older residents also assisted in rescue work, litigation, and the critical initial encounters with new entrants. Younger ones recited lessons or performed skits at the monthly public fund-raising meetings held at the Home.

The capstone to all this training in purity, piety, and domesticity was the marriage of a rescue home resident. Missionary women believed that, by separating "degraded" women from their unsuitable liaisons with male "betrayers" and allowing them to regain their supposedly natural moral purity, Christian homes would be formed in which moral wives and mothers would preside, their womanhood respected and honored by kindly Protestant husbands. Accordingly, matrons kept count of the number of "Christian homes" formed by residents and considered them the surest measure of institutional success. They lavished praise on young married couples, orchestrated elaborate wedding celebrations, and published photographs accompanied by society-page-style descriptions of the ceremonies.[39]

Given the relatively small population of Chinese immigrant women, the numbers of these marriages are impressive. Mission Home workers claimed that by 1888, only fourteen years after the establishment of the institution, fifty-five Home residents had been married; by 1901, they took credit for 160 such marriages.[40] No comparable summary figures are available for the twentieth century, but, extrapolating from the average number of marriages recorded in occasional yearly statistics, I estimate that as many as 266 Chinese women married after residing in the Home in the period between 1874 and 1928.[41] By combining information from Chinese Mission Home publications between 1874 and 1928 with information from the institutional case files between 1907 and 1928 (case files before that date were destroyed in the San Francisco earthquake of 1906), we can locate specific information on 114 marriages.[42] These marriages can be divided into two groups—those of prostitutes marrying suitors chosen well before entering the Mission Home and those arranged directly by Mission Home officials.

For the first two decades of its existence, the Presbyterian Mission Home survived by attracting women of the first group—Chinese prostitutes with suitors who exchanged prostitution for marriage by agreeing to submit to a concentrated mission-administered dose of the Victorian gender system. In the context of immigrant Chinatowns, marriage offered young women social respectability and a chance at financial security without the traditional period of apprenticeship to mothers-in-law, since so many in-laws remained in China.[43] But, for the typical prostitute, the chance to marry was limited by the virtual slavery of the tong-controlled prostitution system. Tong leaders were reluctant to release prostitutes under any conditions, and when they did let women go, they demanded exorbitant fees (ranging from $300 to $3,000) to offset their initial investment and expected loss of earnings.[44] Women who ran away without paying these fees could expect to be tracked down by tong "highbinders" or enforcers.

Under these circumstances, running away from prostitution was no small feat. To achieve it, young women had to find a way to escape from their owners' control long enough to enter the Presbyterian Mission Home; in fact rescue homes sometimes lived up to their names when mission workers accompanied by white policemen with hatchets in hand "rescued" young prostitutes directly from brothels. What prompted most prostitutes to take such a daring step was the hope of marriage—typically, they had made plans to marry young men who were unable or unwilling to buy out their contracts or purchase their persons.

The early pattern can be seen in a letter addressed to Mission Home workers in 1886 by a young man who asked missionaries to collect his fiancé. He wrote:

> I have the case of a prostitute named Ah _____, to bring forward to your notice . . . I wish to succor her, but fear for my life. I also wish to redeem her, and have not sufficient means for that purpose. I find it hard to rescue her from her state of bondage. I thought of running away with her, but dread her keepers and accomplices' violence to me if intercepted. Even if we are furnished with wings, it is difficult to fly. . . . This girl wishes to enter your school. Here I have few friends of my own surname, so I am powerless to rescue her here. For this reason I have instead written to you for aid. I beseech you, with pitying heart and ability, to save her from her present difficulties and sufferings. This accomplished, there will be happiness all around.

The writer went on to give specifics for the proposed rendezvous with missionaries, telling them that "if you get her I will take her home, and give a reward of $50 to your school. I will not change my words."[45] In this case the young man's hopes came to naught—the missionaries arrived at the agreed site some time after the woman in question did—but the letter outlines a chain of events that was commonplace at the Mission Home.

In the years between 1874 and 1900, a steady stream of prostitutes with suitors approached the Home to obtain protection from the tongs so they could marry. Mission Home workers offered assistance only to women who agreed to reside in the institution for six months to a year.[46] Loi Kum, who entered the Home in July 1879, was one of them. According to Mission workers, Loi Kum "ran away to escape a dissolute life" and appeared at their doorstep "accompanied by a friend, who proposes to make her his wife."[47] By agreement with Mission officials, Loi Kum remained in the Home for several months. When her fiancé returned to arrange for their marriage, the missionaries were reluctant to let her go. They put the young man off several times by requiring him to pay $72 for her board and to obtain a legal marriage license. Finally, however, the wedding took place on July 16, 1880, almost a year after Loi Kum had entered the institution.[48] She and her husband left the Mission Home secure in the knowledge that they would have behind them the force of mission workers' access to police power and judicial authority should they be pursued by tong members.

Because missionaries harbored deep reservations about the young men who brought prostitutes to the Home, they did little to publicize these marriages. Only twenty-seven such cases, a figure I suspect underestimates their frequency, are visible in the sources I collected about Home residents, most mentioned only in passing. When they could, missionaries convinced women to break off their engagements with the men who accompanied them to the Home and choose mission-approved husbands instead. These cases they documented more carefully. Mission officials made so much of the case of Chun Ho, a woman who had, they said, "entered the Home . . . promised . . . in marriage to a Chinese Romanist, but as light came into her mind both the Buddhist and the Romanist religion became distasteful to her, and she voluntarily gave him up" that a group of young women in Ohio offered to contribute to the Home on her behalf.[49] Always ambivalent about their role in facilitating the marriages of prostitutes to non-Protestant men, missionaries wanted to abandon the practice from the first, but not until the turn of the century were they able to do so.[50]

In the meantime, however, San Francisco Presbyterian women had expanded their mission and their rescue work to include neglected or abused children as well as betrothed prostitutes. Some children were brought to the Home by child protection authorities; others were left there by struggling immigrant parents who wanted an inexpensive refuge or an English education for their children. As these young girls grew into adulthood, they, too, were married, again with considerable intervention on the part of Mission Home workers.[51] Eighty-seven of these marriages, which form the second type under consideration here, can be followed in resident information sources.

Perhaps the first such marriage was that of Ah Fah, held on Saturday, April 13, 1878. Ah Fah married Ng Noy, a Chinese Christian man employed as a servant. The service was conducted in Chinese by a Presbyterian missionary and attended by Mission Home workers as well as friends of the couple. One of the missionary guests wrote a lengthy account of the event. Displaying typical racial attitudes, she commented approvingly that "this organization of a home on Christian principles" was "the first step upwards from heathenism to civilization." On behalf of Protestant women, she wished the newly-married couple well, trusting, she said, that their "future housekeeping" would "indeed be a *home-keeping.*"[52]

To arrange for the marriages of long-term residents like Ah Fah, missionaries screened applicants chosen from the many Chinese immigrant men who approached the Mission Home looking for wives. Matrons quizzed applicants about their previous marital status, their religious convictions, and their financial prospects in the belief that, as they put it, "he who would win a member of the Mission Home family for his wife must present the very best credentials."[53] Only those Chinese men who fit the white Protestant ideal of the Christian gentleman were allowed to write or call on Mission Home residents.[54]

Chinese men had several motivations for seeking Mission Home brides. First, they were handicapped in finding wives by the skewed sex ratio of the Chinese immigrant community in San Francisco. Second, they had few other alternatives. Intermarriage was not a possibility for them, since Chinese immigrants were prohibited from marrying whites by California miscegenation laws.[55] Bringing a bride from China was at least equally difficult. Few minor merchants had the financial resources to pay for the trip, and those who did found themselves at the mercy of unpredictable immigration officials. For these reasons, there was no shortage of suitors for Mission Home residents. Mission Home employee Tien Fu Wu found that she was approached by potential suitors even on a trip to Boston. "Everybody is after me for girls," she wrote to Donaldina Cameron back in San Francisco, jokingly adding, "I might as well open a Matrimony Bureau here in the east."[56] Mission marriages, then, were sought out by Chinese immigrant men. They also represented a significant advance in social status for Mission Home women, many of whom had originally been destined for lives of prostitution, neglect, abuse, or hardworking poverty.

In fact, mission-arranged marriages placed immigrant women at a particular level of the emerging social structure of San Francisco's Chinatown. In contrast to the social structure in China, which was dominated by scholars and officials, the social structure in immigrant Chinatowns in America was dominated by merchants. The wealthiest of these merchants tended to disdain immigrant women and had the resources to seek brides in China. A step below these wealthy merchants, however, stood a group of less prosperous merchants who were destined to become significant as growing immigrant communities came to depend on them for goods, services, and community leadership.[57] It was these minor merchants, many of whom started with very little, who most actively sought—and accomplished—marriage with Presbyterian Mission Home residents. Although historians have largely ignored the immigrant marriages that were formed in this period (commonly referred to as the "bachelor" years of San Francisco's Chinatown), it is possible to argue that, by pairing promising Chinese merchants with young women inculcated with Victorian family ideology, mission- arranged marriages created a core of middle-class Protestant Chinese American families in many cities.[58]

Some Mission Home husbands achieved considerable prominence. One example was Ng Poon Chew, the husband of Mission Home resident Chun Fa. Chun Fa had been brought to the Home at age six when a Chinese informant told the juvenile authorities that she was suffering regular beatings at the hands of the woman who had purchased her. She married Ng, who had studied under a Taoist priest in China, attended a Christian mission school in the United States, and taken a degree in theology from the San Francisco Theological Seminary. After several years of conducting mission work with Chinese immigrants in southern California, Ng returned to San Francisco to edit the *Chung Sai Yat Po,* an influential daily paper that catered to Chinatown merchants.[59] The Ngs had five children. Of their daughters, one became a piano teacher, one graduated from the University of California, and a third became the first Chinese American woman to be accepted as a (kindergarten) teacher by the Oakland Board of Education. Their son, Edward, achieved notice as the first Chinese American man to be commissioned by the Army in World War I.[60]

It was not only in San Francisco that Mission Home marriages contributed to the development of a Chinese American middle class. Presbyterian Mission Home workers received marriage inquiries from Chinese immigrant men all over the country and used them to establish mission-influenced satellite communities in other areas. As a result, small communities of Mission Home women formed in Los Angeles, Philadelphia, New Orleans, Portland, Minneapolis, Boston, and Chicago. The Philadelphia community, for example, began when Qui Ngun married Wong John in the late 1890s. In 1901, another Mission Home resident, Choi Qui, traveled to Philadelphia and married Wong John's cousin Wong Moy. At the beginning of their married life, Choi Qui and her husband set up housekeeping with the older couple. In 1915, Mission Home resident Jean Leen married Won Fore in the same city. When mission helper Tien Fu Wu brought Jean Leen to Philadelphia for her wedding, she used the occasion to visit all the other ex-Home residents in the area. A few years later, Mission Home officials sent Augusta Chan to live with and assist Qui Ngun. In 1922, Qui Ngun's daughter Eliza sent a wedding invitation to "grandma" Donaldina Cameron, matron of the Presbyterian Mission Home.[61]

Thus, for both groups of women—prostitutes with suitors and children raised in the institution—the Mission Home facilitated marriages. Whether the residents entered the Home specifically for this reason or came there for other reasons, whether they entered the Home voluntarily or involuntarily, mission marriages seem to have offered Chinese immigrant women something of value. Despite the missionaries' preoccupation with Protestantism, the number of marriages far exceeded the number of baptisms among Mission Home residents. By 1901, for example, Mission Home officials claimed 160 marriages but only 100 baptisms.[62]

In fact, the prospect of mission marriages proved so appealing that some already-married women came to the Mission Home in search of new husbands. Some of these women had, like Wong Ah So, been the victims of men who had deceived them into technical marriage ceremonies to smuggle them into the country. Others had been married quite legitimately according to Chinese custom but wanted to leave incompatible mates. One such woman wrote matron Donaldina Cameron in 1923 to ask her to "let me enter your Home and study English [because] I am going to divorce with my husband for the sake of free from repression." "I understand," she explained, "that you as a Superintendent of the Home, always give aid to those who suffer from ill-treatment at home."[63]

Mission workers, who were horrified by the deceptions and conditioned by racial and cultural bias to believe that Chinese marriages weren't really marriages at all, did help many women secure annulments or divorces. In at least a handful of these cases, missionaries arranged for new husbands as well.[64] Occasional facilitation of second marriages persisted despite the fact that it exposed the Mission Home to criticism from observers in the white community. One lawyer who participated in a divorce proceeding initiated by a Mission Home resident could not restrain his sarcasm. When the divorce was declared final, he commented acidly that "the cute little defendant is now at liberty to marry whomsoever the good lord may direct across her path."[65]

The Mission Home offered married women more than the chance to form new marriages—it also offered them a chance to jockey for position vis-à-vis their current husbands. In fact, workers at the Presbyterian Mission Home were repeatedly asked to intervene on behalf of unhappy Chinese immigrant wives. The numbers of these cases were probably considerably larger than the numbers of mission-arranged marriages. In the early years of the Home, matrons were reluctant to acknowledge how many unhappy wives they admitted, but during the twentieth century they faced the issue more squarely. Statistics from the five-year period between 1923 and 1928 show seventy-eight such "domestic cases" admitted (in a period in which fifteen resident marriages were performed).[66] Without more information from the nineteenth-century period, we can only guess at the total number of women who might have entered the Home with domestic complaints between 1874 and 1928, but eighty-four individual cases can be followed closely from resident information sources.

In domestic cases, several complaints loomed large. The most frequent was wife abuse. When unhappy wives complained of mistreatment at the hands of their husbands, they were granted temporary shelter in the Mission Home while missionaries, shocked at the ritualized complaints they heard, made it their business to shape unhappy marriages into the Victorian companionate mode. Because they believed that "the fault usually lies with the husband," missionaries almost always tried to ensure better treatment for the wife.[67] One woman, Mrs. Tom She Been, entered the Home "badly bruised from a beating" at the hands of her husband. Her husband, a well-known Chinese doctor, apologized to the missionaries and asked his wife to return to him, but not until the secretary of the Chinese Legation offered to intercede on her behalf did the woman agree.[68] Missionaries were not, of course, always successful in solving the problem. One young woman who twice sought help from the Mission Home and both times went back to her husband committed suicide in March 1924.[69]

Other Chinese immigrant women approached the Home in order to gain leverage in polygamous marriages. One such woman, Mrs. Yung, requested help from the Mission Home after her husband took a concubine. Although concubinage was a recognized institution in China, Yung's own mother advised her to resist it. "I know," she wrote to her daughter in the Home, "how the second wife has brought all these accusations against you, causing your husband to maltreat you and act savagely. . . . You must make him send the concubine back to China. . . . It isn't right to acquire a concubine and especially this concubine." Mr. Yung, backed up by his father, apparently refused, but when Mrs. Yung complained to the Mission Home, Protestant women speedily arranged for the deportation of the concubine.[70]

Still other Chinese immigrant women came to the Mission Home to flee from marriages arranged by their parents that were distasteful to them. The unsatisfied ex-resident who committed suicide was one of them. As word got around that Mission Home workers were hostile to arranged marriages, a number of young women found their way to the institution soon after their parents proposed unappealing matches. Bow Yoke, a young woman whose father had accepted $600 for agreeing to make her the second wife of a much older man, refused to go along with the plan. She fled to the Police Station, and then to the Mission Home, before it could be carried out.[71]

Still another group of married women sought help from missionaries when the death of their husbands placed them under unprecedented control by relatives. This was the case with one ex-prostitute who had been known to Mission Home officials for several years. The young woman had refused earlier invitations to come to the Mission Home because soon after becoming a prostitute she was successfully ransomed by a man who paid $4,400 for her; she married her redeemer soon afterwards. She later explained to a Mission official that "he [her husband] was good to her and therefore she did not have to come to the Mission."[72] She did, however, come to the Mission Home when, after her husband's death, his nephew demanded that she return to him all the jewelry she had received as wedding presents.[73] Other widows, who feared that relatives would send them back to China or sell them or their children, also approached the Home.[74]

The possibility of Mission Home intervention offered Chinese immigrant women in any of these positions bargaining room to improve the terms of their marriages or their relations with relatives. In one quite typical case, a woman entered the Presbyterian Mission Home in 1925 and did not return to her husband until mission workers convinced him to sign an agreement stipulating that: 1) he would not use opium, 2) he would treat her with "kindness and consideration" and "provide for them as comfortable a home as his income will permit," 3) he would give her money to care for herself and her children, and 4) if she died he would give the children to the Mission Home or to their grandmother (rather than selling them).[75]

Missionaries intervened not only in the marriages of strangers who approached them, but also in the marriages of women who had resided in and married from the Mission Home. A look at these interventions shows how Chinese immigrant women and, later, their American-born daughters, used the conflict between the traditional Chinese gender system and the Victorian gender system in Mission Home marriages to shape their options in Chinese American communities.

Most of the public—and some of the private—accounts of Mission Home marriages stressed how thoroughly Chinese immigrant women adopted the Victorian gender system and its correlate, the ideal of companionate marriage. One of the Mission Home women in Philadelphia, for example, described her marriage to Mission Home superintendent Donaldina Cameron in a letter written during a lengthy illness. "My husband has been nursing me day and night," she reported, "he even gave up his restaurant to another party to look after, so he can nurse me, altho, our restaurant is the largest one in town." She went on to say that "he treats me like a real Christian. I regret very much that Heaven doesn't give me longer time to be with him. Yet, I thank God and you [Cameron] that we have had one another for more than ten years. As husband and wife we are most satisfied."[76]

As this example suggests, some mission marriages did mirror the companionate ideals of Victorianism, but I think it would be more correct to say that, faced with the conflict between two distinct gender systems, Chinese immigrant women sifted through the possibilities and fashioned their own end-product, one that reveals some of the weaknesses of the Victorian gender system for women. The argument must remain speculative here, because most of the sources come not from the women who entered the Mission Home, married, and remained in contact with missionaries, but from those who refused to enter the Home in the first place or who ran away after a short residence. Still, the Mission Home case files suggest just how selectively immigrant women responded to missionary overtures.

The files show, for example, the attitudes held by young prostitutes who refused to enter the Mission Home in the first place. Despite their sexual exploitation, young prostitutes were accustomed to receiving fine clothing and gifts of cash or jewelry from their customers or their owners. Unless they had chosen a particular husband or found themselves especially ill-treated by their owners, they were unlikely to trade these material advantages for the general promise of Victorian moral respectability and economic dependence on husbands. On one occasion in 1897, when the Mission Home accepted sixty prostitutes arrested in a government raid, the matron recorded that the women "shrieked and wailed beating the floor with their shoes" and "denounc[ed] the Home in no unmeasured terms." The matron removed the angriest prostitutes to another room, but even those remaining rejected her offer of "protection" and residence in the Home "with scorn and derision."[77]

The disdain of these prostitutes was echoed by another group of Mission Home residents—young Chinese American women judged by American courts to be the victims of "immoral" men. Such young women were much more likely than abused children or unhappy wives to criticize the most coercive aspect of the Mission Home—the attempt to mold all women to fit the Victorian belief that women were "naturally" morally pure and pious.[78] In 1924, for example, Rose Seen, an unhappy fourteen-year-old girl who longed to be reunited with her lover, Bill, a Chinese man who had been charged with contributing to her delinquency, was sent to the Presbyterian Mission Home. In a note addressed "to my dearest beloved husband," Seen pleaded with Bill "to find some easy job and go to work so just to make them think you are not lazy and go to church on Sunday so pretend that you were a Christian cause Miss Cameron does not allow the girls to marry a boy that doesn't go to work."[79] When this plan failed (Mission Home women confiscated the note and reported Bill to his probation officer), Seen tried another tack. Remaining in the Home for more than a year, she and a fellow resident convinced Mission Home officials of their sincerity to the extent that they were entrusted with the funds of a student group. In December 1925, however, both young women ran away from the Home, taking the money and some jewelry, hoping to reunite with Bill and his friends.[80]

By running away from the Mission Home, Rose Seen escaped the moral supervision of missionaries. Amy Wong, a married ex-resident, was not so lucky. When she came to the Mission Home asking for help in a marital dispute, Protestant women decided that she, not her husband, was in the wrong. They promptly suggested that she sign an agreement that echoed those they ordinarily presented to husbands. According to its terms, her husband would take her back if she gave up smoking, drinking, gambling, and attending the Chinese theater and if she agreed "not to be out later than ten o'clock at night without my husband's knowledge and consent, or in his company." Additionally, she was to attend church and part-time school regularly, and to spend the rest of her time working to earn money for further education.[81] The Wong agreement is the only one of its kind among Mission Home sources, but the Victorian pattern of female purity and piety it sought to enforce was a common assumption on the part of Protestant women.

Yet, even though women like Rose Seen and Amy Wong eschewed the moral restrictiveness of Victorian culture, the clash between traditional and Victorian ideologies in immigrant Chinatowns rendered certain tenets of the traditional Chinese gender system particularly vulnerable. For Chinese women who had decided to marry, the traditional Chinese family ideals upheld by immigrant communities contrasted with important realities, including the relative absence of in-laws and the difficulty young men had in finding wives. In such a situation, Chinese immigrant women used the Home to help tip the balance between vulnerability and opportunity in immigrant Chinatowns—to facilitate forming marriages and to exert some control over relations within marriage itself.

Perhaps we can best understand this process by returning once again to the case of Wong Ah So, whose life so clearly reveals the connection between individual experience and shifts in the gender system of Chinese immigrant communities. After residing in the Mission Home for one year, Wong Ah So married an aspiring merchant who had established a foothold in Boise, Idaho.[82] A few years later, Wong Ah So wrote a letter to missionary Donaldina Cameron at the Presbyterian Mission Home. She started out by displaying the gratitude expected by Mission Home workers. "Thank you," she wrote, "for rescuing me and saving my soul and wishing peace for me and arranging for my marriage."[83] Wong Ah So had more than thank-you's on her mind, though: she had written to ask for help with her marriage. Her husband, she said, was treating her badly. Her complaints were three: first, her husband had joined the Hop Sing tong; second, he refused to educate his daughters (by a previous wife); and third, he was so unhappy that Wong Ah So did not provide him with children that he had threatened to go to China to find a concubine to have a son for him.[84]

In this letter, it is possible to see not only a conflict between two gender systems but also to see how Wong Ah So's ideals had changed over the years since she left China behind. As a former prostitute who had suffered from illness, she may have been unable to have the son whose birth would earn her female authority in traditional culture; in any case, what she wanted now was an education for her step-daughters. As a result, she had come to question the traditional ideals her husband still held. To retain his power, her husband threatened to return to China to find a willing concubine, a step that would have reinforced Won Ah So's vulnerability. To offset his power, Wong Ah So invoked the aid of Mission Home women, who, reading Wong Ah So's carefully worded charges as an all-too-familiar indictment of "heathen" behavior, promptly sent a local Protestant woman to investigate.

Wong Ah So's case is especially revealing, but it was hardly unique. Because the Presbyterian Mission Home offered immigrant women a pathway to marriage in immigrant Chinatowns, its sources show in concentrated form the clash between traditional Chinese and Victorian gender systems. The clash itself, however, was a society-wide process. Many Chinese immigrant women in America, in or outside of Mission Homes, found themselves in a position to use the gap between gender systems to maneuver for specific protections for individual women. Their dreams were played out over and over again as immigrant Chinatowns transformed themselves into Chinese American communities in the early twentieth century. Yet even as Wong Ah So made her plea to missionary women, the context of the clash between gender systems was changing dramatically.

After the turn of the century, the steps toward individual autonomy that Chinese immigrant women had made in negotiating between gender systems in the United States were overshadowed by the steps women were taking in revolutionary China. By 1937, when social scientists Norman S. Hayner and Charles N. Reynolds conducted a series of interviews with Chinese immigrants, they discovered that Chinese women from China were often "shocked by the attitude of American-born Chinese . . . [and believed] that American Chinese, and women in particular, have stood still or lagged while their sisters in China have been progressing."[85] The emergence of Chinese feminism offered Chinese immigrant women in contact with feminist ideas a critique of traditional male power beyond that offered by Victorian missionary women, thus reducing the appeal of the Mission Home.[86]

At the same time, the strength and vitality of the Mission Home was sapped by the decline of the Victorian gender system within American society, the disintegration of a separate women's reform movement, and a general reevaluation of the thrust of Protestant women's missionary work.[87] Although Mission Home matron Donaldina Cameron and many of her San Francisco followers remained devoted to rescue work, the Mission Home became the target of national Presbyterian officials who, in 1939, moved mission operations to new quarters with room for no more than six residents. The reshaped mission, under the direction of Lorna Logan, planned to offer "a program of broad community service" instead of rescue work focused on Chinese women and girls.[88]

In such a changed context, the Mission Home had little to offer either Chinese or white women. At its height, however, rescue work had granted white missionary matrons—and a few selected Chinese protégés—an alternative to marriage that reduced their marginality in the Victorian gender system even while it required them to espouse companionate marriage as the proper goal for all women. For Chinese immigrant women, rescue work offered something else—a pathway to marriage which, while it required them, too, to espouse the rhetoric of companionate marriage and to risk the ethnocentrism of missionaries, gave them some leverage in reducing traditional male power. In this way, the conflict between gender systems seen in the San Francisco Mission Home allowed Chinese immigrant women to shape one set of possibilities for a Chinese American culture.

Notes

An earlier version of this paper was presented at the Seventh Berkshire Conference on the History of Women at Wellesley College in June 1987. I would like to thank the following colleagues for their research suggestions and critiques of earlier drafts of this essay: Sucheng Chan, Estelle Freedman, Dave Gutiérrez, Yukiko Hanawa, Susan Johnson, Valerie Matsumoto, Sucheta Mazumdar, Stacey Oliker, Beverly Purrington, Jack Tchen, Anne Walthall, Ann Waltner, Richard White, Anand Yang and Judy Yung.

1. Carol Green Wilson, *Chinatown Quest: The Life Adventures of Donaldina Cameron* (Stanford, 1931), 209.

2. Information about Wong Ah So has been compiled from inmates files #258 and #260, Cameron House, San Francisco, California (numbers assigned by author during research); Fisk University Social Science Institute, *Orientals and Their Cultural Adjustment* (Nashville, 1946), 31–35; *Women and Missions* 2 (1925–26): 169–172; and "Slave, Rescued in Fresno, Is Brought Here," *San Francisco Chronicle*, February 10, 1924.

3. Donaldina Cameron biographical file, *San Francisco Chronicle* newspaper morgue collection, California Historical Society, San Francisco, California.

4. See, for example, Alexander McLeod, *Pigtails and Gold Dust* (Caldwell, ID, 1947) and, to a somewhat lesser degree, Richard Dillon, *The Hatchetmen* (New York, 1962).

5. See, for example, S. W. Kung, *Chinese in American Life: Some Aspects of Their History, Status, Problems, and Contributions* (Seattle, 1962); Betty Lee Sung, *Mountain of Gold: The Story of the Chinese in America* (New York, 1967); Francis L. K. Hsu, *The Challenge of the American Dream: The Chinese in the United States* (Belmont, CA, 1971); and H. Brett Melendy, *The Oriental Americans* (New York, 1972).

6. See, for example, Stuart Creighton Miller, *The Unwelcome Immigrant: The American Image of the Chinese, 1785–1882* (Berkeley, 1969); Alexander Saxton, *The Indispensable Enemy: Labor and the Anti-Chinese Movement in California* (Berkeley, 1971); Victor G. and Brett de Bary Nee, *Longtime Californ': A Documentary Study of an American Chinatown* (New York, 1972); Stanford M. Lyman, *Chinese Americans* (New York, 1974); and Ronald T. Takaki, *Iron Cages: Race and Culture in Nineteenth-Century America* (New York, 1979).

7. Only in the past decade have there been serious scholarly attempts to analyze the significance of prostitution within the Chinese immigrant community or to explore the experiences of prostitutes themselves. See Lucie Cheng Hirata, "Free, Endentured, Enslaved: Chinese Prostitutes in Nineteenth-Century America," *Signs* 5 (1979): 3–29 and "Chinese Immigrant Women in Nineteenth-Century California," in *Women of America: A History*, ed. Carol Ruth Berkin and Mary Beth Norton (Boston, 1979), 223–41; Judy Yung, *Chinese Women of America: A Pictorial History* (Seattle, 1986), 18–23; and also Ruthanne Lum McCunn's biographical novel, *Thousand Pieces of Gold* (San Francisco, 1981). I would define a gender system as the way in which any

given society creates, maintains, and reproduces its ideas about gender for women and men. My definition is adapted from a landmark article by Gayle Rubin, "The Traffic in Women: Notes on the 'Political Economy' of Sex," in *Toward an Anthropology of Women*, ed. Rayna R. Reiter (New York, 1975), 157–210; 159.

8. To date, most historians of women who focused on missionary sources used them to understand missionary women rather than to understand relations between missionaries and the minority groups they targeted for their work. See, however, Jane Hunter, *The Gospel of Gentility: American Women Missionaries in Turn-of-the-Century China* (New Haven, 1984) and Joan Jacobs Brumberg, "Zenanas and Girlless Villages: The Ethnology of American Evangelical Women, 1870–1910," *Journal of American History* 69 (September 1982): 347–71 and "The Ethnological Mirror: American Evangelical Women and Their Heathen Sisters, 1870–1910," in *Women and the Structure of Society*, ed. Barbara J. Harris and JoAnn K. McNamara (Durham, 1984), 108–128.

9. For information on the traditional Chinese gender system, see Margery Wolf and Roxane Witke, eds., *Women in Chinese Society* (Stanford, 1975). Scholarship on the Chinese family has been flourishing of late, and is too extensive to be reviewed here. For a sense of the issues at stake, see Maurice Freedman, "The Family in China, Past and Present," *Pacific Affairs* 34 (Winter 1961–62): 323–36; Charlotte Ikels, "The Family Past: Contemporary Studies and the Traditional Chinese Family," *Journal of Family History* 6 (Fall 1981): 334–40; and James L. Watson, "Chinese Kinship Reconsidered: Anthropological Perspectives on Historical Research," *China Quarterly* 92 (December 1982): 589–622.

10. This generalization holds true despite the fact that ordinarily only the richest—and luckiest—families were able to reach the cultural ideal of the multigenerational family gathered under one roof. For a twentieth-century example of one of the rare peasant families able to maintain the extended family ideal, see Margery Wolf, *The House of Lim: A Study of a Chinese Farm Family* (New York, 1968); for an example of a nineteenth-century woman unable—but still determined—to reach the ideal, see Ning Lao T'ai-T'ai, *A Daughter of Han: The Autobiography of a Chinese Working Woman*, ed. Ida Pruitt (New Haven, 1945).

11. *Orientals and Their Cultural Adjustment*, 31; *Women and Missions* 2 (1925–26): 169.

12. Wong Ah So to her mother, n.d., inmate file #260, Cameron House, San Francisco. The letter has been reprinted in *Orientals and Their Cultural Adjustment*, 34–35 and in *Women and Missions* 2 (1925–26): 169–172.

13. *Ibid.*

14. Sue Gronewald, "Beautiful Merchandise: Prostitution in China, 1860–1936," *Women and History* 1 (Spring 1982).

15. Olga Lang, *Chinese Family and Society* (New Haven, 1946), ch. 4.

16. Margery Wolf, "Women and Suicide in China," in *Women in Chinese Society*, 111–42.

17. Wong Ah So to her mother, n.d., inmate file #260, Cameron House, San Francisco.

18. Lang, *Chinese Family and Society*, ch. 5; Wolf, "Women and Suicide in China," 111–42.

19. Lang, *Chinese Family and Society*, 53, 108–9; Marjorie Topley, "Marriage Resistance in Rural Kwangtung," in *Women in Chinese Society*, 67–88.

20. Robert Griswold, *Family and Divorce in California, 1840–1890: Victorian Illusions and Everyday Realities* (Albany, 1982), 1–17; Carl Degler, *At Odds: Women and the Family in America from the Revolution to the Present* (New York, 1980), 3–25; Ellen Rothman, *Hands and Hearts: A History of Courtship in America* (New York, 1984), ch. 1.

21. Linda Gordon, for example, points out that what family historians have called the emergence of the companionate family was actually "the reconstruction of patriarchy" and Mary Ryan critiques the development of family history by exploring the gap between family ideology and women's reality. See Linda Gordon, "Child Abuse, Gender, and the Myth of Family Independence: A Historical Critique," *Child Welfare* 64 (May–June 1985): 213–23 and Mary P. Ryan, "The Explosion of Family History," *Reviews in American History* 10 (December 1982): 180–95. Other feminist historians have seen companionate marriage as a development of the twentieth rather than the nineteenth century. See Elaine T. May, *Great Expectations: Marriage and Divorce in Post-Victorian America* (Chicago, 1980) and Christina Simmons, "Companionate Marriage and the Lesbian Threat," *Frontiers* 4 (1979): 54–59.

22. Examinations of the complex relation of women reformers to the Victorian gender system include: Christine Stansell, *City of Women: Sex and Class in New York, 1789–1860* (New York, 1986), pp. 199–16; Linda Gordon, "Family Violence, Feminism, and Social Control," *Feminist Studies* 12 (Fall 1986): 453–78; Elizabeth Pleck, "Challenges to Traditional Authority in Immigrant Families," in *The American Family in Social-Historical Perspective*, 3rd ed., ed. Michael Gordon (New York, 1983), 504–17; Barbara L. Epstein, *The Politics of Domesticity: Women, Evangelism, and Temperance in Nineteenth-Century America* (Middletown, 1981); and Kathryn Kish Sklar, *Catharine Beecher: A Study in American Domesticity* (New Haven, 1973). Examinations that focus directly on Protestant missionary women include Sarah Deutsch, *No Separate Refuge: Culture, Class, and Gender on an Anglo-Hispanic Frontier in the American Southwest, 1880–1940* (New York, 1987), 63–86; Brumberg, "Zenanas and Girlless Villages;" Hunter, *The Gospel of Gentility*; Rosemary Skinner

Keller, "Lay Women in the Protestant Tradition," in *Women and Religion in America*, vol. 1, ed. Rosemary P. Ruether and Rosemary S. Keller (San Francisco, 1983), 242–53; and Patricia R. Hill, *The World Their Household: The American Woman's Foreign Mission Movement and Cultural Transformation, 1870–1920* (Ann Arbor, 1984).

23. Donaldina Cameron, speech outline, inmate file #260, Cameron House, San Francisco.

24. M.H.F., "A Christian Chinese Wedding," *Occident*, May 1, 1978, 6.

25. Figures taken from "The Ratio of Chinese Women to Men Compared to the Ratio of Women to Men in the Total Population of California, 1850–1970," document included with Hirata, "Chinese Immigrant Women in Nineteenth-Century California," 241.

26. The dynamics of this network are best described in Hirata, "Free, Endentured, Enslaved," and I have relied on this article for much of the discussion that follows.

27. Mary Chapman, "Notes on the Chinese in Boston," *Journal of American Folklore* 5 (1892): 321–24; Stanford M. Lyman, "Marriage and the Family Among Chinese Immigrants to America, 1850–1960," *Phylon* 29 (Winter 1968): 321–30.

28. See Jacqueline Baker Barnhart, "Working Women: Prostitution in San Francisco from the Gold Rush to 1900" (Ph.D. Dissertation, University of California, Santa Cruz, 1976), for the comparison.

29. Hirata, "Chinese Immigrant Women in Nineteenth-Century California," 237.

30. The virtues of true womanhood were first identified in Barbara Welter, "The Cult of True Womanhood, 1820–1860," *American Quarterly* 16 (1966): 151–74.

31. Most earlier accounts of the Presbyterian Mission Home are focused on the life of its most famous matron, Donaldina Cameron. See Wilson, *Chinatown Quest;* Mildred Crowl Martin, *Chinatown's Angry Angel: The Story of Donaldina Cameron* (Palo Alto, 1977); and Laurene Wu McClain, "Donaldina Cameron: A Reappraisal," *Pacific Historian* 27 (Fall 1983): 25–35.

32. *Woman's Work*, July 1892, 179; Woman's Occidental Board of Foreign Missions, *Annual Report*, 1896, 66.

33. Occidental Branch, Woman's Foreign Missionary Society, *Annual Report*, 1878, 7.

34. Woman's Occidental Board of Foreign Missions, *Annual Report*, 1903, 54–55.

35. Woman's Occidental Board of Foreign Missions, *Annual Report*, 1895, 57; Ethel Higgins to Mrs. C. S. Brattan, February 19, 1921, inmate file #109; Ethel Higgins to C. W. Mathews, August 28, 1922, inmate file #108, Cameron House, San Francisco.

36. *Occident*, April 13, 1881, 7.

37. Grace M. King, "Presbyterian Chinese Mission Home," 9, ms. Report for the California State Board of Charities and Corrections, November–December 1919, Cadwallader Papers, San Francisco Theological Seminary.

38. California Branch, Woman's Foreign Missionary Society, *Annual Report*, 1876, 20–21; Woman's Occidental Board of Foreign Missions, *Annual Report*, 1895, 58–59; *Occidental Board Bulletin*, November 1, 1901, 15; King, "Presbyterian Chinese Mission Home," 9.

39. For typical examples, see M.H.F., "A Christian Chinese Wedding," *Occident*, May 1, 1878, 6; *Occidental Board Bulletin*, February 1, 1902, 34; and *Women and Missions* 5 (1928–29): 184–85.

40. Occidental Board, Woman's Foreign Missionary Society, *Annual Report*, 1888, 52–61; Woman's Occidental Board of Foreign Missions, *Annual Report*, 1901. Mission marriages reflected a larger phenomenon occurring within the Chinese immigrant community in California. Lucie Cheng's figures indicate that in 1870, there were 3,536 adult Chinese women in California, 2,157 of whom were listed in the census as prostitutes and 753 of whom were listed as "keeping house." By 1880, when exclusionist sentiment was already beginning to take effect, there were 3,171 adult Chinese women in California, 759 of whom were listed in the census as prostitutes and 1,445 as "keeping house." Cheng cautions that "most of this increase [in the number of Chinese housewives] occurred outside of San Francisco County." Hirata, "Chinese Immigrant Women in Nineteenth-Century California," 227–28, 236.

41. Mission Home officials reported a yearly total of marriages in 33 of the 54 annual reports issued between 1874 and 1928. A total of 163 marriages were reported, for an average of 4.9 marriages per year. If we assume that the same average number of marriages were performed in each of the 21 years for which marriage statistics are not available, 102.9 additional marriages would have occurred during these years, thus my estimated total of 266 marriages. This total would be smaller than the summary totals occasionally claimed by Mission Home officials.

42. Besides the annual reports, which contain a great deal of information about individual Home residents, published Mission Home sources include: *Woman's Work for Woman* (Woman's Foreign Missionary Society and Woman's Presbyterian Board of Missions of the Northwest) 1875–1878; *Occident* (a San Francisco Presbyterian newspaper) 1876–1899; *Woman's Work* (Woman's Foreign Missionary Societies of the Presbyterian Church) 1885–1895; *Home Mission Monthly* (Women's Executive Committee of Home Missions of the Presbyterian Church) 1886–1902; *Occidental Board Bulletin* (Woman's Occidental Board of Foreign Missions)

1900–1903; *Far West* (Woman's Home and Foreign Mission Boards of the Presbyterian Church of California) 1907–1920; *Women and Missions* (Board of Missions, Presbyterian Church in the U.S.A.) 1924–1939; *"920" Newsletter* (Woman's Occidental Board of Foreign Missions) 1933–1939; and a series of individually titled pamphlets. I have seen 288 confidential inmate files still in the possession of Cameron House, San Francisco, California. To protect the confidentiality of the women and men mentioned in them, I have referred to the files by numbers I assigned during research. When my information about a particular resident or her husband comes from case files rather than from previously published sources, I have used pseudonyms in the text. All pseudonyms are pointed out in the appropriate footnotes.

43. Hirata, "Chinese Immigrant Women in Nineteenth Century California," 237, Hirata, "Free, Endentured, Enslaved," 19.

44. Woman's Occidental Board of Foreign Missions, *Annual Report*, 1907, 71; *Occident*, January 15, 1879, 6.

45. Occidental Board, Woman's Foreign Missionary Society, *Annual Report*, 1886, 50–51.

46. California Branch, Woman's Foreign Missionary Society, *Annual Report*, 1875, 19.

47. *Occident*, September 17, 1879, 6.

48. *Occident*, August 25, 1880, 7.

49. *Occident*, September 6, 1876, 285.

50. The policy is discussed in California Branch, Woman's Foreign Missionary Society, *Annual Report*, 1875, 19 and "Corrections on Tentative Report of the Presbyterian Chinese Mission Home, San Francisco, California," May 7, 1935, Correspondence file, Cameron House, San Francisco.

51. It should be noted, however, that the Presbyterian Mission Home did single out and support a small number of Home residents through higher education programs ranging from kindergarten training to medical school, and these young women were generally encouraged not to marry in order to make the most of their hard-won professional skills.

52. M.H.F., "A Christian Chinese Wedding," *Occident*, May 1, 1878, 6.

53. Woman's Occidental Board of Foreign Missions, *Annual Report*, 1909, 77.

54. On the role of the Christian gentleman, see Rothman, *Hands and Hearts*, ch. 6; Charles E. Rosenberg, "Sexuality, Class, and Role in Nineteenth-Century America," *American Quarterly* 25 (May 1973): 131–53; Lewis Perry, " 'Progress, Not Pleasure, Is Our Aim': The Sexual Advice of an Antebellum Radical," *Journal of Social History* 12 (Spring 1979): 354–67; and Kathleen D. McCarthy, *Noblesse Oblige: Charity and Cultural Philanthropy in Chicago, 1849–1929* (Chicago, 1982), 53–75.

55. Megumi Dick Osumi, "Asians and California's Anti-Miscegenation Laws," in *Asian and Pacific American Experiences: Women's Perspectives*, ed. Nobuya Tsuchida (Minneapolis, 1982), 1–37.

56. Tien Fu Wu to Donaldina Cameron, June 13, 1915, inmate file #269, Cameron House, San Francisco, California.

57. June Mei, "Socioeconomic Developments among the Chinese in San Francisco, 1848–1906," in *Labor Immigration Under Capitalism: Asian Workers in the U.S. Before World War II*, ed. Lucie Cheng and Edna Bonacich (Berkeley, 1984), 370–401; Shepard Schwartz, "Mate Selection among New York City's Chinese Males, 1931–38," *American Journal of Sociology* 56 (May 1951): 562–68.

58. Victor and Brett de Bary Nee, for example, use the term "bachelor society" to describe the years from the beginning of Chinese immigration through the 1920s. See Nee and Nee, *Longtime Californ,'* 11.

59. For an analysis of *Chung Sai Yat Po's* coverage of women's issues, see Judy Yung, "The China Connection: The Impact of China's Feminist Movement on the Social Awakening of Chinese American Women, 1900–1911," paper presented at the Seventh Berkshire Conference on the History of Women, Wellesley College, June 19–21, 1987.

60. *Occident*, May 18, 1892, 11; Woman's Occidental Board of Foreign Missions, *Annual Report*, 1892, 52 and 1909, 76; *Occidental Board Bulletin*, July 1, 1902; *Far West*, November 1918, 3–4; Mrs. E. V. Robbins, *How Do the Chinese Girls Come to the Mission Home?*, 4th ed. (N.p., n.d.); Corinne K. Hoexter, *From Canton to California: The Epic of Chinese Immigration* (New York, 1976).

61. *Occident*, February 7, 1900, 18–19; *Occidental Board Bulletin*, November 1, 1901, 10, December 1, 1901, January 1, 1902, 12, and February 1, 1902, 3–4; inmate files #53 and #98, Cameron House, San Francisco, California.

62. Woman's Occidental Board of Foreign Missions, *Annual Report*, 1901.

63. Letter to Donaldina Cameron, January 3, 1923, inmate file #62, Cameron House, San Francisco, California.

64. *Occident*, April 4, 1887; Occidental Branch, Woman's Foreign Missionary Society, *Annual Report*, 1878, 9; *Occident*, January 27, 1886, 11; Woman's Occidental Board of Foreign Missions, *Annual Report*, 1915, 87–88; inmate files #12, #119, #189, #237, Cameron House, San Francisco, California.

65. V. L. Hatfield to Donaldina Cameron, October 6, 1923, in inmate file #189, Cameron House, San Francisco, California.

66. "Admissions, 1923–1928" and "Dismissals, 1923–1928," folder 6, box 3, record group 101, Files of the

Department of Educational and Medical Work, 1878–1966, Board of National Missions, Presbyterian Historical Society, Philadelphia, Pennsylvania.

67. Woman's Occidental Board of Foreign Missions, *Annual Report*, 1900, 73.

68. *Occident*, February 28, 1900, 11; Woman's Occidental Board of Foreign Missions, *Annual Report*, 1900, 73.

69. Biographical sketch and newspaper clippings (*San Francisco Call*, March 4,1924; *San Francisco Examiner*, March 4, 1924; and *San Francisco Chronicle*, March 5, 1924), inmate file #56, Cameron House, San Francisco, California.

70. Case of Mrs. Yung (pseudonym), inmate file #167, Cameron House, San Francisco, California.

71. Woman's Occidental Board of Foreign Missions, *Annual Report*, 1907, 68–69.

72. "Statement by Miss Tien Fuh Wu," inmate file #63, Cameron House, San Francisco, California.

73. "Statement [of resident]," inmate file #63, Cameron House, San Francisco, California.

74. See, for example, *Occident*, December 23, 1885, 11; *Occident*, September 6, 1876, 285; *Occident*, January 24, 1877, 5; *Occident*, March 7, 1900, 18; Woman's Occidental Board of Foreign Missions, *Annual Report*, 1910, 64.

75. "Agreement," August 8, 1925, inmate file #30, Cameron House, San Francisco, California.

76. Ex-resident to Donaldina Cameron, June 1, 1928, inmate file #111, Cameron House, San Francisco, California.

77. Woman's Occidental Board of Foreign Missions, *Annual Report*, 1894, 60–61.

78. See, for example, Woman's Occidental Board of Foreign Missions, *Annual Report*, 1899, 74–81.

79. Rose Seen (pseudonym) to Bill Wong (pseudonym), n.d., inmate file #176, Cameron House, San Francisco, California.

80. "Two Slave Girls Flee With $1000," *San Francisco Daily News*, December 22, 1925; "Slave Girls Turn Thieves," *San Francisco Chronicle*, December 23, 1925; both clippings in inmate file #115, Cameron House, San Francisco, California.

81. Case of Amy Wong (pseudonym), "Agreement, September 13, 1927," inmate file #211, Cameron House, San Francisco, California.

82. Wong Ah So to Donaldina Cameron, October 24, 1928, inmate file #258, Cameron House, San Francisco, California.

83. *Ibid.*

84. *Ibid.*

85. Norman S. Hayner and Charles N. Reynolds, "Chinese Family Life in America," *American Sociology Review* 2 (October 1937): 630–37.

86. One of the major conduits for the dissemination of Chinese feminism was the *Chung Sai Yat Po*, the newspaper run by Mission Home resident Chun Fa's husband Ng Poon Chew. See Yung, "The China Connection," for an analysis.

87. May, *Great Expectations*; Rosalind Rosenberg, *Beyond Separate Spheres: Intellectual Roots of Modern Feminism* (New Haven, 1982); Estelle Freedman, "Separatism as Strategy: Female Institution Building and American Feminism, 1870–1930," *Feminist Studies* 5 (Fall 1979): 512–29; Paula Baker, "The Domestication of Politics: Women and American Political Society, 1780–1920," *American Historical Review* 89 (June 1984): 620–47; Hill, *The World Their Household*, ch. 6; and Lois A. Boyd and R. Douglas Brackenridge, *Presbyterian Women in America: Two Centuries of a Quest for Status* (Westport, CT, 1983), ch. 4.

88. Presbyterian Church, *Board Reports*, 1939, 96–98; 1940, 41. See Lorna Logan, *Ventures in Mission: The Cameron House Story* (Wilson Creek, WA, 1976), 47–92 for her account of the changes. The new quarters were abandoned in 1949 and all the Presbyterian social services for Chinese Americans were once again consolidated in the old building at 920 Sacramento Street, where they remain to this day. The building was later renamed Cameron House.

11

Black and White Visions of Welfare: Women's Welfare Activism, 1890–1945

Linda Gordon

One of the pleasures of historical scholarship is that it may lead into unexpected paths, and what begins as a frustration—say, from an apparent shortage of sources—may end as a new opening. This essay began as an attempt to examine gender differences in visions of public welfare among reformers. Having compiled material about women welfare activists who were mainly white, I found I could not distinguish the influence of gender from that of race in their perspectives. (Indeed, to many white historians, the racial characteristics of the white people we studied were invisible until we began to learn from minority historians to ask the right questions.) So I set up a comparison between Black and white women welfare activists, with results that were illuminating about both groups. Three major areas of difference between Black and white women's ideas emerged: first, about the nature of entitlement, between a Black orientation toward universal programs, and a white orientation toward supervised, means-tested ones; second, in attitude toward mothers' employment; third, in strategies for protecting women from sexual exploitation. In what follows I want both to show how those differences were manifest and to suggest their roots in historical experience.[1]

Several historians have recently studied Black women's civic contributions, but Black women's reform campaigns have not usually been seen as part of welfare history. How many discussions of settlement houses include Victoria Earle Matthews's White Rose Mission of New York City, or Margaret Murray Washington's Elizabeth Russell Settlement at Tuskegee, Alabama, or Janie Porter Barrett's Locust Street Social Settlement in Hampton, Virginia, or Lugenia Burns Hope's Neighborhood Union in Atlanta, Georgia, or many others? In examining this activism from a welfare history perspective I came to understand how the standard welfare histories had been by definition white-centered. It was possible to make the widespread welfare reform activity of minority women visible only by changing the definition of the topic and its periodization.[2]

The white experience has defined the very boundaries of what we mean by welfare. Whites were by 1890 campaigning for *government programs* of cash relief and of regulation such as the Pure Food and Drugs Act and anti-child-labor laws. These welfare programs had racial content, not only in the perspectives of the reformers (white) but also in the identification of their objects (largely the immigrant working class, which, although white, was perceived as racially different by turn-of-the-century reformers). The programs also had class content, visible, for example, in their rejection of traditional working-class cooperative

Reprinted with permission from *The Journal of American History* 78, September 1991.

benevolent societies. Moreover, because of these orientations, welfare in the late nineteenth century was increasingly conceived as an *urban* reform activity.[3]

By contrast African Americans, still concentrated in the South and in rural communities, had been largely disfranchised by this time, and even in the North had much less power than whites, certainly less than elite whites, to influence government. Southern states had smaller administrative capacities and were more paltry in their provision of public services, even to whites. African Americans did campaign for governmental programs and had some success; at the federal level, they had won an Office of Negro Health Work in the United States Public Health Service, and they had gotten some resources from the extension programs of the United States Department of Agriculture. Nevertheless, Black welfare activity, especially before the New Deal, consisted to a great extent of *building private institutions*. Black women welfare reformers created schools, old people's homes, medical services, community centers. Attempting to provide for their people what the white state would not, they even raised private money for public institutions. For example, an Atlanta University study of 1901 found that in at least three southern states (Virginia, North Carolina, and Georgia) the private contribution to the Negro public schools was greater than that from tax moneys.[4] For example, a teacher in Lowndes County, Alabama, appealed for funds in 1912.

> Where I am now working there are 27,000 colored people. . . . In my school district there are nearly 400 children. I carry on this work eight months in the year and receive for it $290, out of which I pay three teachers and two extra teachers. The State provides for three months' schooling. . . . I have been trying desperately to put up an adequate school building for the hundreds of children clamoring to get an education. To complete it . . . I need about $800.[5]

Thus a large proportion of their political energy went to raising money, and under the most difficult circumstances—trying to collect from the poor and the limited middle class to help the poor. White women raised money, of course, but they also lobbied aldermen and congressmen, attended White House conferences, and corresponded with Supreme Court justices; Black women had less access to such powerful men and spent proportionally more of their time organizing bake sales, rummage sales, and church dinners. One detailed example may illustrate this: the Gate City Kindergartens, established in Atlanta in 1905.

> Another method of raising funds was through working circles throughout the city. . . . From Bazaars held at Thanksgiving time, lasting as long as a week, when every circle was responsible for a day, one day of which a turkey dinner was served. Money was made by sales in items of fancy work, aprons, etc., canned fruit, cakes and whatever could be begged. The association realized as much as $250.00 at a Bazaar. From track meets sponsored by colleges, and participated in by the children of the public school, $100.00 gate receipts were cleared. Food and cake sales brought at times $50.00. April sales brought $50.00, and one time the women realized as much as $100.00 from the sale of aprons. Sales of papers, magazines and tin foil brought as much as $50.00. A baby contest brought $50.00. Intercollegiate contest brought $100. Post-season baseball games realized as much as $25.00. Sales of soap wrappers, soap powder wrappers, saved and collected from housewives, and baking powder coupons brought $25.00. . . . [the list is twice this long]

It cost twelve hundred dollars in cash to maintain the kindergartens each year. In addition donations in kind were vital: all five kindergartens were housed in donated locations; clothes were constantly solicited for the needy children; for several years Procter & Gamble gave five boxes of Ivory soap annually.[6] Some Black welfare activists were adept at raising white money but had to accept sometimes galling strings, and even the most successful tried to shift their economic dependence to their own people.[7] No doubt some of these money-raising activities were also pleasurable and community-building social occasions, but often they were just drudgery, and those doing the work hated it. Jane Hunter, a Cleveland Black activist, wrote that "this money getting business destroys so much of ones real self, that we cannot do our best."[8]

This essay uses a limited comparison—between Black and white women reformers—to alter somewhat our understanding of what welfare *is* and to bring into better visibility gender and race (and class) influences on welfare thinking. The essay uses two kinds of data: written and oral history records of the thoughts of these activists, and a rudimentary collective biography of 145 Black and white women who were national leaders in campaigns for public welfare between 1890 and 1945.[9] This method emerges from the premise expressed by the feminist slogan, "The personal is political": that political views and activities are related not only to macroeconomic and social conditions but also to personal circumstances—such as family experiences and occupational histories.

My approach uses a broad definition of welfare. I include reformers who sought regulatory laws, such as the Pure Food and Drugs Act, compulsory education, and anti-child-labor regulations. I do not include reformers who worked mainly on labor relations, civil rights, women's rights, or a myriad of other reform issues not centrally related to welfare.[10] In categorizing many different activists, I had to ignore many differences in order to make broad generalization possible. This method inevitably obscures context and some fascinating personalities. Many more monographs are necessary, but I notice that historical thinking develops through a constant interplay between monographs and syntheses; I hope that this essay, because of its very breadth, will stimulate more monographs.

I did not form this sample according to a random or other formal selection principle. Instead I identified members of my sample gradually during several years of research on welfare campaigns and then tracked down biographical information. The process is a historian's form of snowball sampling, because often tracking down one activist produces references to another. Naturally, there are many bits of missing information because biographical facts are difficult to find for many women, especially minority women. I make no claim to having created a representative sample or an exhaustive list. But, on the methodological principle of saturation, I doubt that my generalizations would be much altered by the addition of more individuals.

To bound my sample, I included only those who were national leaders—officers of national organizations campaigning for welfare provision or builders of nationally important institutions, such as hospitals, schools, or asylums. (For more on the sample, see the Appendix.) These leaders were not typical welfare activists; more typical were those who worked exclusively locally, and their personal profiles might be quite different. But the national leaders had a great deal of influence on the thinking of other women. I included only activists prominent chiefly after 1890 because it was in the 1890s that such key national organizations as the National Association of Colored Women (NACW) began and that white women welfare activists began a marked emphasis on *public* provision. I followed welfare activism until 1945 because I wanted to look at broad patterns of ideas across a long period of policy debate; I ended in 1945 because after that date, among white women, there was a marked decline in such agitation, and among Blacks, a shift in emphasis to civil rights.

My approach sacrifices, of course, change over time. Substantial generational as well as individual differences among women had to be put aside. For example, the early Black activists were, on average, more focused on race uplift and the later more on integration; during this period the mass northward migration of Blacks shifted reformers' concerns not only away from the South but also increasingly toward urban problems. The white women welfare activists of the 1890s tended to divide between Charity Organization Society devotees and settlement advocates; by the 1930s, they were more united in promoting professionalism in public assistance. Nevertheless, I am convinced that there are enough continuities to justify this periodization, continuities that will emerge in the discussion below.

The two groups thus formed were in many ways not parallel. For example, the white women were mainly from the Northeast or Midwest, and there were few southern white women—only sixteen percent of the group were either born or active in the South, whereas a majority of the Black women were born in the South. For another example, many of the Black women were educators by occupation, while white women who were educators were few. But these divergences are part of what I am trying to identify, part of the differences in Black and white women's perspectives. Among whites, northerners contributed more to national welfare models than did southerners. And education had particular meanings for African Americans and was integrated into campaigns for the welfare of the race in a distinctive way. Generalizing among a variety of women of several generations, the comparison naturally eclipses some important distinctions, but it does so to illuminate others that are also important.[11]

I identified sixty-nine Black women as national leaders in welfare reform. Separating the white from the Black women was not my decision: the networks were almost completely segregated. First, the national women's organizations were segregated; those that included Blacks, such as the Young Women's Christian Association (YWCA), had separate white and Black locals. Second, since Black women rarely held government positions, they rarely interacted with white women officially. Third, the national network of white women reformers usually excluded Black women even when they could have been included.[12] The exclusion of Black women from the white women's clubs and the ignoring or trivializing of life-and-death Black issues, such as lynching, have been amply documented.[13] To cite but one example, one of the most important women in the New Deal–Mary McLeod Bethune—was not a part of the tight, if informal, caucus that the white New Deal women formed.[14] There were important counterexamples, interracial efforts of significant impact, particularly local ones: in Chicago, for instance, white settlement and charity workers joined Black reformers in campaigning for public services for dependent children, establishing the Chicago Urban League, and responding to the 1919 race riot. In the South interracial efforts arose from evangelical religious activity. Some white members of this sample group worked with the Commission of Interracial Cooperation, forming its Women's Council, which had 805 county-level groups by 1929.[15] The national YWCA became a forum for communication between Black and white women. But these efforts were marked by serious and sometimes crippling white prejudice, and the core networks of women remained segregated.

While the Black group was created in part by white racism, it was also created from the inside, so to speak, by personal friendships. Often these relationships were born in schools and colleges and continued thereafter, strengthened by the development of Black sororities after 1908. The creation of national organizations and networks extended relationships and ideas among these Black women leaders across regional boundaries. For example, the Phillis Wheatley Home for the protection of single Black urban women, established by Jane Hunter in Cleveland in 1911, spurred the opening of similar homes in Denver, Atlanta,

Seattle, Boston, Detroit, Chicago, Greenville, Winston-Salem, Toledo, and Minneapolis by 1934. When Fannie Barrier Williams spoke in Memphis in 1896, she had never been in the South before, having grown up in upstate New York and settled in Chicago.[16] More and more the women began to travel widely, despite the difficult and humiliating conditions of travel for Black women. Friendships could be intense, despite distance; Black women early in the twentieth century, like white women, sometimes spoke openly of their strong emotional bonds. Darlene Clark Hine quotes Jane Hunter writing Nannie Burroughs, "It was so nice to see you and to know your real sweet self. Surely we will . . . cultivate a lasting friendship. I want to be your devoted sister in kindred thought and love." At other times Hunter wrote to Burroughs of her loneliness "for want of a friend."[17] Mutual support was strong. When in the 1930s the president and trustees of Howard University, led by Abraham Flexner, tried to force Howard's dean of women, Lucy D. Slowe, to live on campus with her girls (something the dean of men was not, of course, required to do) and she refused to comply, a whole network of women interceded on her behalf. A group of five asked for a meeting with Flexner, which he refused. Another group of women interviewed trustees in New York and reported to Slowe their perceptions of the situation. Mary McLeod Bethune urged her to be "steadfast" and campaigned for her among sympathetic Howard faculty.[18] The network was divided by cliques and encompassed conflicts and even feuds. Yet it had a "bottom line" of loyalty. Even those who criticized Bethune for insufficient militance understood her to be absolutely committed to the network of Black women.[19]

The Black women's network was made more coherent by its members' common experience as educators and builders of educational institutions. Education was the single most important area of activism for Black women. The majority of women in this sample taught at one time or another, and thirty-eight percent were educators by profession. For many, reform activism centered around establishing schools, from kindergartens through colleges, such as Nannie Burroughs's National Training School for Women and Girls in Washington, D.C., or Lucy Laney's Haines Institute in Augusta, Georgia, or Arenia Mallory's Saints' Industrial and Literary Training School in Mississippi. In his 1907 report on economic cooperation among Negro Americans, for example, W.E.B. Du Bois counted 151 church-connected and 161 nonsectarian private Negro schools. Although he did not discuss the labor of founding and maintaining these institutions, we can guess that women contributed disproportionately.[20]

Another Black welfare priority was the establishment of old people's homes, considered by Du Bois the "most characteristic Negro charity." These too, according to the early findings of Du Bois, were predominantly organized by women.[21] But if we were to take the period 1890 to 1945 as a whole, the cause second to education was health. Black hospitals, while primarily initiated by Black and white men, depended on crucial support from Black women. Between 1890 and 1930, African Americans created approximately two hundred hospitals and nurse-training schools, and women often took charge of the community organizing and fund-raising labor. Over time Black women's health work changed its emphasis, from providing for the sick in the 1890s to preventive health projects after about 1910. Yet even in the first decade of the century, Du Bois found that most locations with considerable Black populations had beneficial and insurance societies that paid sickness as well as burial benefits; these can be traced back a century before Du Bois studied them. In several cities the societies also paid for medicines and actually created their own health maintenance organizations (HMOs). With the dues of their members they hired physicians, annually or on a quarterly basis, to provide health care for the entire group.[22]

Many women's clubs made health work their priority. The Washington, D.C., Colored YWCA built a program around visiting the sick. The Indianapolis Woman's Improvement

Club focused on tuberculosis, attempting to make up for the denial of service to Blacks by the Indianapolis board of health, the city hospital, and the Marion County tuberculosis society. The preventive health emphasis was stimulated in part by educational work. For example, Atlanta's Neighborhood Union did a survey of conditions in the Black schools in 1912 to 1913 that revealed major health problems; in 1916 this led the Neighborhood Union to establish a clinic that offered both health education and free medical treatment. Possibly the most extraordinary individual in Black women's public health work was Modjeska Simkins, who used her position as director of Negro work for the antituberculosis association of South Carolina to inaugurate a program dealing with the entire range of Black health problems, including maternal and infant mortality, venereal disease (VD), and malnutrition as well as tuberculosis. Perhaps the most ingenious women's program was Alpha Kappa Alpha's Mississippi Health Project. These Black sorority women brought health care to sharecroppers in Holmes County, Mississippi, for several weeks every summer from 1935 to 1942. Unable to rent space for a clinic because of plantation owners' opposition, they turned cars into mobile health vans, immunizing over 15,000 children and providing services such as dentistry and treatment for malaria and VD for 2,500 to 4,000 people each summer.[23]

These reformers were united also through their churches, which were centers of networking and of activism, in the North as well as the South. Indeed, more locally active, less elite Black women reformers were probably even more connected to churches; the national leadership was moving toward more secular organization, while remaining more church-centered than white women welfare leaders. Black churches played a large role in raising money, serving in particular as a conduit for appeals for white money, through missionary projects.[24]

The YWCA also drew many of these women together. Victoria Matthews's White Rose Mission influenced the YWCA, through its leader Grace Dodge, to bring Black women onto its staff, which experience groomed many Black women leaders.[25]

And despite the fact that these were national leaders, they shared a regional experience. At least fifty-seven percent were born in the South. More important, perhaps, two-thirds of these migrated to the Northeast, Midwest, and mid-Atlantic regions, thus literally spreading their network as they fled Jim Crow and sought wider opportunity.[26]

Most members of this network were married—eighty-five percent. More than half of the married women had prominent men as spouses, and their marriages sometimes promoted their leadership positions.[27] Lugenia Burns Hope was the wife of John Hope, first Black president of Atlanta University; Irene Gaines was the wife of an Illinois state legislator. Ida Wells-Barnett's husband published Chicago's leading Black newspaper. George Edmund Haynes, husband of Elizabeth, was a Columbia Ph.D., a professor at Fisk, an assistant to the secretary of labor from 1918 to 1921, and a founder of the Urban League. George Ruffin, husband of Josephine, was a Harvard Law graduate, a member of the Boston City Council, and Boston's first Black judge. Most of the women, however, had been activists before marriage, and many led lives quite independent of their husbands. (Of these married women, twenty percent were widowed, divorced, or separated.)

Their fertility pattern was probably related to their independence. Of the whole group, forty-three percent had no children; and of the married women, thirty-four percent had no children (there were no unmarried mothers).[28] (In comparison, thirty-one percent of the white married women in this sample were childless.) It thus seems likely that these women welfare activists used birth control, although long physical separations from their husbands may have contributed to their low fertility.[29] In their contraceptive practices these women may have been as modern as contemporary white women of comparable class position.

For most African American women a major reason for being in the public sphere after marriage was employment, due to economic necessity; but for this group of women, economic need was not a driving pressure. A remarkable number had prosperous parents.[30] Crystal Fauset's father, although born a slave, was principal of a Black academy in Maryland. Elizabeth Ross Haynes's father went from slavery to ownership of a fifteen-hundred-acre plantation. Addie Hunton's father was a substantial businessman and founder of the Negro Elks. Mary Church Terrell's mother *and* father were successful in business. Most Black women in the sample had husbands who could support them; fifty-one percent of the married women had high-professional husbands—lawyers, physicians, ministers, educators.[31] The women of this network were also often very class-conscious, and many of the clubs that built their collective identity were exclusive, such as the sororities, the Chautauqua Circle, and the Twelve in Atlanta. The fact that about forty percent were born outside the South provides further evidence of their high status, since the evidence suggests that the earlier northward migrants were the more upwardly mobile.[32] In all these respects, this group probably differed from typical local activists, who were less privileged. Yet even among this elite group only a tiny minority—twelve percent—were not employed.[33] To be sure, this economic privilege was only relative to the whole Black population; on average, the Black women's network was less wealthy than the white women's. Even those who were born to middle-class status were usually newly middle-class, perhaps a generation away from slavery and without much cushion against economic misfortune. Still, among many whites the first and most important emblem of middle-class status was a woman's domesticity. One can safely conclude that one meaning of these women's combining of public and family lives was the greater acceptance among African Americans, for many historical reasons, of the public life of married women.

The Black women's national network was made more homogeneous by educational attainment, high social status, and a sense of superiority to the masses that brought with it obligations of service. Of the Black women, eighty-three percent had a higher education, comparable to the proportion of white women, and thirty-five percent had attended graduate school. These figures may surprise those unfamiliar with the high professional achievement patterns of Black women between 1890 and 1945. The full meaning of the statistics emerges when one compares them with the average educational opportunities for Blacks in the United States at this time. In the earliest year for which we have figures, 1940, only one percent of Afro-Americans, male and female, had four or more years of college. Moreover, only forty-one percent of the women in this sample attended Black colleges, whereas those colleges conferred eighty-six percent of all Black undergraduate degrees in the period from 1914 to 1936.[34] Several women in this sample who were born into the middle class described learning for the first time in adulthood of the conditions of poverty in which most African Americans lived—an ignorance characteristic of prosperous whites but rarer among Blacks. As Alfreda Duster, Ida Wells-Barnett's daughter, recalled, "It was difficult for me to really emphathize with people who had come from nothing, where they had lived in cottages, huts in the South, with no floor and no windows and had suffered the consequences of the discrimination and the hardships of the South."[35] Many Black women joined Du Bois in emphasizing the importance of building an intellectual and professional elite, calling upon the "leading" or "intelligent" or "better class of" Negroes to take initiatives for their people. Class and status inequalities, measured by such markers as money, occupation, and skin color, created tensions in this network, as comparable inequalities did in the white network.[36] Some thought of their obligations in the eugenic terms that were so fashionable in the first three decades of this study. "I was going to multiply my ability and my husband's by six," Alfreda Duster said in describing her decision to have six children.[37] Such thinking had somewhat different meanings for Blacks than for whites, however, reflecting their awareness that race prejudice made it difficult for educated, prosperous Blacks to escape the discrimination and pejorative stereotyping that held back all African Americans. As Ferdinand Barnett, later to become the husband of Ida B. Wells, put it in 1879, "One vicious, ignorant Negro is readily conceded to be a type of all the rest, but a Negro educated and refined is said to be an exception. We must labor to reverse this rule; education and moral excellence must become general and characteristic, with ignorance and depravity the exception."[38]

Indeed, the high social status and prosperity common in this group should not lead us to forget the discrimination and humiliation that they faced. Their high levels of skills and education were frustrated by lack of career opportunity. Sadie Alexander, from one of the most prominent Black families in the United States, was the first Black woman Ph.D., degree from the University of Pennsylvania. But she could not get an appropriate job because of her color, and was forced to work as an assistant actuary for a Black insurance company. Anna Arnold Hedgeman, one of the youngest women in this sample, from a small Minnesota town where she had attended integrated schools and churches, graduated from Hamline University in St. Paul and then discovered that she could not get a teaching job in any white institution. Instead she went to work in Holly Springs, Mississippi, until she found the Jim Crow intolerable. Despite the relatively large Black middle class in Washington, D.C., African American women there could not generally get clerical jobs in the federal government until the 1940s.[39]

Moreover, this Black activism was born in an era of radically worsening conditions for most Afro-American women, in contrast to the improving conditions for white women. The older women in this network had felt segregation intensify in their adult lifetimes; there was widespread immiseration and denial of what political power they had accumulated after the emancipation. In the 1920s the second Ku Klux Klan attracted as many as six million members. These experiences, so rarely understood by whites, further reinforced the bonds uniting Black women and influenced their welfare visions.[40]

The seventy-six white women, like the Blacks, constituted a coherent network. Most of them knew each other, and their compatibility was cemented by a homogeneous class, religious, and ethnic base. Most had prosperous, many even prominent parents; virtually all were of north European, Protestant backgrounds, from the Northeast or Midwest. The nine Jewish members were hardly representative of Jewish immigrants: five had wealthy German-Jewish parents (Elizabeth Brandeis Raushenbush, Hannah Einstein, Josephine and Pauline Goldmark, and Lillian Wald). There were three Catholics (Josephine Brown, Jane Hoey, and Agnes Regan), but they were hardly typical of Catholics in the United States in the period: they were all native-born of prosperous parents. The shared Protestantism of the others was more a sign of similar ethnic background than of avid religious commitment, for few were churchgoers or intense believers, and churches did not organize their welfare activities.

The great majority (eighty-six percent) were college-educated, and sixty-six percent attended graduate school. By contrast, in 1920 fewer than one percent of all American women held college degrees. It is worth recalling, however, that eighty-three percent of the Black women were college-educated, and their disproportion to the Black population as a whole was even greater. The white women had attended more expensive, elite schools; thirty-seven percent had graduated from one of the New England women's colleges.

The white women had even more occupational commonality than the Blacks. The great majority were social workers.[41] To understand this correctly we must appreciate the changing historical meanings of *social work*. Prior to the Progressive Era, the term did not refer to a profession but to a range of helping and reform activity; the word *social* originally emphasized the reform, rather than the charity, component. Here it is relevant that many had mothers active in social reform.[42] The early twentieth-century professionalization of social work has often been conceptualized as creating a rather sharp break both with amateur friendly visiting and with political activism. The experience of the women I am studying suggests otherwise: well into the 1930s they considered casework, charity, and reform politics as "social work." By contrast to the Afro-American women, very few were educators, a pattern that suggests that creating new educational institutions was no longer a reform priority for white women and that other professional jobs, especially governmental, were open to them.[43]

The whites had at least as much geographical togetherness as the Black women. Sixty-eight percent worked primarily in the New England and mid-Atlantic states—hardly surprising since the national headquarters of the organizations they worked for were usually located there. Moreover, fifty-seven percent had worked in New York City during the Progressive Era or the 1920s. New York City played a vanguard role in the development of public services and regulation in the public interest, and women in the network were influential in that city's welfare programs. New York City settlement houses specialized in demonstration projects, beginning programs on a small, private scale and then getting them publicly funded. The settlements initiated vocational guidance programs, later adopted by the public schools; they initiated use of public schools for after-hours recreation programs and public health nursing. Lillian Wald, head of the Henry Street Settlement, coordinated the city's response to the 1919 influenza epidemic. The settlements lobbied for municipal legislation regulating tenements and landlord-tenant relations, and milk purity and prices. In 1917 the Women's City Club of New York City opened a Maternity Center in Hell's Kitchen, where they provided prenatal nursing care and education and housekeeping services for new mothers. Expanded to ten locations in Manhattan, this effort served as a model for the bill that eventually became the Sheppard-Towner Act. The Women's City Club provided an important meeting place for many of these women, and it can serve as an indicator of their prosperity: members had to pay substantial dues and an initiation fee, and the club purchased a mansion on Thirty-fifth Street and Park Avenue for $160,000 in 1917.[44]

Some of these white women had been active in party politics even before they had the vote. Some had been in the Socialist Party, and many were active in the 1912 Progressive Party campaign. Most, however, preferred nonpartisan public activism. During the late 1920s and 1930s they became more active in political parties, and transferred their allegiances to the Democratic Party. Here too New York was important, because the political figure who most attracted these women to the Democrats was Franklin D. Roosevelt, in his governorship and then his presidency. Several women who had been active in reform in the city, notably Belle Moskowitz, Rose Schneiderman, and Eleanor Roosevelt, took on statewide roles. The Al Smith campaign of 1928 promoted more division than unity, however, because most women social workers were critical of his "wet" positions and his association with machine politics. The reassuring presence of his aide Moskowitz and Franklin Roosevelt's "aide" Eleanor Roosevelt was critical in bringing their network into the Democratic Party.[45]

The Black network also underwent a political realignment from Republican to Democratic, but with different meanings, largely associated with migration northward, because the southern Democratic party was essentially closed to Blacks. Ironically, this transition was also in part effectuated by Eleanor Roosevelt, who became the symbol of those few white political leaders willing to take stands on racial equality.[46] Nevertheless Eleanor Roosevelt did not create an integrated network, nor was she able to swing the white network to support the leading Black demand during the Roosevelt administration: a federal antilynching law.

Women in both networks taught, mentored, even self-consciously trained each other. Among Blacks this occurred in colleges, in white-run organizations such as the YWCAs, and in Black organizations such as sororities, the National Association of Colored Women, and many local groups. A higher proportion of the white than of the Black women worked in settlement houses—probably partly because so many of the white women were single. That experience strongly encouraged intergenerational connections and intimacy, because the younger or newer volunteers actually lived with their elders, seeing them in action. In the civic organizations, leaders groomed, protected, and promoted their protégées: Jane Addams did this with Alice Hamilton, Lillian Wald, and Florence Kelley; Sophonisba Breckinridge launched her student Grace Abbott's career by placing her at the head of the newly formed Immigrants' Protective League; the whole network campaigned for Abbott and then for Frances Perkins to become secretary of labor.[47] Such involvements continued when network members became federal or state officials, with other members as their employees. The chiefs of the Children's and Women's bureaus—the two key federal agencies run by women—exercised extraordinary involvement in the personal lives of their employees. Mary Anderson, for example, head of the Women's Bureau, corresponded frequently with her employees in other parts of the country about their family lives, advising them, for example, about the care of aging parents.[48]

It is quite possible that Black women's personal and professional support networks were just as strong; there is less evidence because, as several historians of African American women have suggested, Black women left fewer private papers than did white.[49] Given this caveat, the white women's network does appear to differ in one measure of mutual dependence. The great majority of the white women were single—only thirty-four percent had ever been married, and only eighteen percent remained married during their peak political activity (forty-two percent of those who ever married were divorced, separated, or widowed). Only twenty-eight percent had children. In this respect they are probably quite different from many local welfare activists, a group that included less elite and more married women. Moreover, twenty-eight percent were in relationships with other women that might have been called "Boston marriages" a few decades before.[50] (My figure is a conservative one since I counted only those women for whom I could identify a specific partner. It does not include such women as Edith Rockwood who lived until her death in 1953 with Marjorie Heseltine of the Children's Bureau and Louise Griffith of the Social Security Agency and who built and owned a summer house jointly with Marion Crane of the Children's Bureau.[51]) At the time these relationships were mainly not named at all, although Mary ("Molly") Dewson referred to her mate as "partner." Contemporaries usually perceived them as celibate.[52] Today some of these women might be called lesbian, but there is much controversy among historians as to whether it is ahistorical to apply the word to that generation, a controversy I wish to avoid here since it is not relevant to my argument. What is relevant is not their sexual activity but their dependence on other women economically, for jobs; for care in grief, illness, and old age; for vacation companionship; for every conceivable kind of help. Despite their singleness, their efforts were very much directed to family and child welfare. It is remarkable to contemplate that so many women who became symbols of matronly respectability and asexual "social motherhood" led such unconventional private lives.

Moreover, they turned this mutual dependency into a political caucus. When lesbian history was first being written, these relationships between women were seen, first, in exclusively private and individual terms, and, second, as a life-style that isolated them from the heterosexual social and cultural mainstream. Recently, Estelle Freedman and Blanche Wiesen Cook have helped change that paradigm.[53] The women's female bonding did not disadvantage them but brought them political power, and they got it without making the sacrifices of personal intimacy that men so often did. Privileged women that they were, several of them had country homes, and groups would often weekend together; we can be sure that their conversation erased distinctions between the personal and the political, between gossip and tactics.

In truth we do not know how different these white women's relationships were from Black women's. Many Black married women, such as Bethune and Charlotte Hawkins Brown, lived apart from their husbands (but so did several white women counted here as married, such as Perkins); and a few Black women, such as Dean Lucy Slowe of Howard, lived in Boston marriages. Many Blacks in this sample spoke critically not only of men but of marriage, and feared its potential to demobilize women. Dorothy Height lamented that the "over-emphasis on marriage has destroyed so many people."[54]

Both white and Black women, if single, experienced a sense of betrayal when a friend married; and both, if about to marry, feared telling their single comrades.[55] In time, particularly from the 1930s on, the white women's sense that marriage and activity in the public sphere were incompatible choices diminished, and more married activists appeared.[56] This change, however, only makes it the more evident that throughout the period, Black women had greater willingness, necessity, or ability to combine marriage and public activism, through coping strategies that may have included informal marital separations.

The white women's friendship network was particularly visible among the most prominent women because they took it with them to their prominent and well-documented jobs. Their friendships transcended boundaries between the public and private sectors, between government and civic organization. In this way they created what several historians have begun calling a "women's political culture"—but again we must remember that this concept has referred primarily to white women. The powerful settlement houses, Hull House and the Henry Street Settlement, for example, became virtually a part of municipal government and were able to command the use of tax money when necessary. When women gained governmental positions, there was as much extra-agency as intra-agency consultation and direction. In its first project, collecting data on infant mortality, the Children's Bureau used hundreds of volunteers from this organizational network to help. In 1920, Florence Kelley of the National Consumers' League (NCL) listed investigations the Women's Bureau should undertake, and these were done. Mary Anderson of the Women's Bureau arranged for the NCL to draft a bill for protection of female employees for the state of Indiana, and Anderson herself wrote comments on the draft. In 1922 Anderson wrote Mary Dewson of the NCL asking her to tone down her critical language about the National Woman's Party, and Dewson complied; in 1923 Dewson asked Anderson to help her draft a response to the National Woman's Party that was to appear in the *Nation* under Dewson's name.

Such cooperation continued throughout the New Deal. A good example was the Women's Charter, an attempt made in 1936, in response to the increased intensity of the campaign for the Equal Rights Amendment (ERA), to negotiate a settlement between the two sides of the women's movement. An initial meeting was attended by representatives of the usual white women's network civic organizations—YWCA, League of Women Voters, Women's Trade Union League, American Association of University Women (AAUW), Federation of Business and Professional Women—as well as several state and federal government women. The first draft of the charter was written by Anderson, still head of the Women's Bureau; Frieda Miller, then head of the women's section of the New York State Department of Labor; Rose Schneiderman, formerly of the National Recovery Administration (until the Supreme Court overruled it) and soon to become head of the New York State Department of Labor; and Mary Van Kleeck. The drafting of the charter exemplifies two of the findings regarding this network: the importance of New York and the predominance of single women.[57]

Singleness did not keep these women from useful connections with men, however. These connections came with kinship and class, if not with marriage. Clara Beyer got her "in" to the network because Felix Frankfurter recommended her to administer the 1918 District of Columbia minimum wage law. She then brought in Elizabeth Brandeis, the daughter of Louis Brandeis, to share the job with her. Brandeis's two sisters-in-law, Josephine and Pauline Goldmark, were also active in this network. Sophonisba Breckinridge, Florence Kelley, Julia Lathrop, and Katherine Lenroot were daughters of senators or congressmen. Loula Dunn's father and two grandfathers had been in the Alabama legislature. Susan Ware computed, about a different but overlapping group of New Deal women, that almost fifty percent (thirteen of twenty-eight) were from political families.[58] These women often learned politics in their households, and knew where to get introductions and referrals to politically influential people when they needed them. When Beyer said, "It was my contacts that made [me] so valuable, that I could go to these people," she was speaking about both her women's network and her male connections.[59]

With these group characteristics in mind, I want to examine the welfare ideas of these two networks.

One major difference in the orientation of the two groups was that the whites, well into the Great Depression, more strongly saw themselves as helping others—people who were "other" not only socially but often also ethnically and religiously. The perspective of the white network had been affected particularly by large-scale immigration, the reconstitution of the urban working class by people of non-WASP origin, and residential segregation, which grouped the immigrants in ghettos not often seen by the white middle class. Much has been written about the arrogance and condescension these privileged social workers showed their immigrant clients. Little has been done to discover the impact of the immigrant population on the reformers' own ideas. The Black/white comparison suggests that ethnic difference between the white poor and white reformers not only discouraged identification but also slowed the reformers' development of a structural understanding of the origins of poverty, as opposed to one that blamed individual character defects, however environmentally caused. Thus into the 1940s, the great majority of the white women in this sample supported welfare programs that were not only means-tested but also "morals-tested," continuing a distinction between the worthy and the unworthy poor. They believed that aid should always be accompanied by expert supervision and rehabilitation so as to inculcate into the poor work habits and morals that they so often (or so the reformers believed) lacked. (And, one might add, they did not mind the fact that this set up a sexual double standard in which women aid recipients would be treated differently and more severely than men recipients.)[60]

In comparison, Black women were more focused on their own kind. Despite the *relative* privilege of most of them, and there was criticism from Blacks of the snobbery of some of these network members, there was less distance between helper and helped than among white reformers. There was less chronological distance, for all their privileges were so recent and so tenuous. There was less geographical distance, for residential segregation did not allow the Black middle class much insulation from the Black poor. Concentrating their efforts more on education and health, and proportionally less on charity or relief, meant that they dealt more often with universal needs than with those of the particularly unfortunate, and sought to provide universal, not means-tested, services.

These were differences of degree and should not be overstated. Most of the white women in this sample favored environmental analyses of the sources of poverty. Many Black women's groups engaged in classic charity activity. In the 1890s Washington, D.C., Black women volunteered to work with the Associated Charities in its "stamp work," a program designed to inculcate thrift and saving among the poor. In the depression of 1893 these relatively prosperous Black "friendly visitors" donated supplies of coal and food staples. The Kansas Federation of Women's Clubs, Marilyn Brady found, clung to all the tenets of the "cult of true womanhood" except, perhaps, for fragility. As Ena Farley wrote of the Boston League of Women for Community Service, "Their patronage roles toward others less fortunate than themselves not only dramatized their relative superiority within the minority structure, but also gave them the claim to leadership and power positions." But these programs must be understood in a context in which the needy were far more numerous, and the prosperous far fewer, than among whites.[61]

This does not mean that there was no condescension among Black women. Black leaders shared with white ones the conviction that the poor needed training, to develop not only skills but also moral and spiritual capacities. Mary Church Terrell could sound remarkably like a white clubwoman.

> To our poor, benighted sisters in the Black Belt of Alabama we have gone and we have been both a comfort and a help to these women, through the darkness of whose ignorance of everything that makes life sweet or worth the living, no ray of light would have penetrated but for us. We have taught them the ABC of living by showing them how to make their huts more habitable and decent with the small means at their command and how to care for themselves and their families.[62]

Like the Progressive Era white female reformers, the Blacks emphasized the need to improve the sexual morals of their people.[63] Fannie Barrier William declared that the colored people's greatest need was a better and purer home life—that slavery had destroyed home ties, the sanctity of marriage, and the instincts of motherhood.[64]

Concern for sexual respectability by no means represented one class or stratum imposing its values on another; for Black as for white women it grew also from a feminist, or womanist, desire to protect women from exploitation, a desire shared across class lines. But this priority had profoundly different meanings for Black women reformers. Not only were Black women more severely sexually victimized, but combatting sexual exploitation was for Blacks inseparable from race uplift in general, as white sexual assaults against Black women had long been a fundamental part of slavery and racial oppression. Indeed, Black activists were far in advance of white feminists in their campaigns against rape and their identification of that crime as part of a system of power relations, and they did not assume that only *white* men were sexual aggressors. The historian Darlene Clark Hine suggests that efforts to build recreational programs for boys also reflected women's strategies for protecting girls from assault. Nevertheless, given the difficulties of affecting change in the aggressors, many Black welfare reformers focused on protecting potential victims. Many of the earliest Black urban institutions were homes designed to protect working women. Black women's considerable contribution to the founding and development of the Urban League had such motives. Just as the efforts by white welfare reformers to protect girls and women contained condescending and victim-blaming aspects, particularly inasmuch as they were directed at different social groups (immigrants, the poor), so victim-blaming was present among Black reformers too. The problem of sex exploitation could not be removed from intrarace class differences that left some Black women much more vulnerable than others, not only to assault but also to having their reputations smeared; Black, like white, women defined their middle-class status in part by their sexual respectability. But their sexual protection efforts were so connected to uplift for the whole race, without which the reformers could not enjoy any class privileges, that the victim-blaming was a smaller part of their message than among whites.[65]

Moreover, despite the sense of superiority among some, the Black women reformers could not easily separate their welfare from their civil rights agitation.[66] As Deborah White puts it, "The race problem . . . inherently included the problems of poverty."[67] Race uplift work was usually welfare work by definition, and it was always conceived as a path to racial equality. And Black poverty could not be ameliorated without challenges to white domination. A nice example: in 1894 Gertrude Mossell, in a tribute to Black women's uplift activity, referred to Ida Wells's antilynching campaign as "philanthropy." Several of these women, notably Terrell and Anna J. Cooper, were among the first rebels against Booker T. Washington's domination because of their attraction both to academic educational goals for their people and to challenges to segregation.[68] Those who considered themselves women's rights activists, such as Burroughs, Terrell, and Cooper, particularly protested the hypocrisy in the white feminists' coupling of the language of sisterhood with the practice of Black exclusion—as in Terrell's principled struggle, as an elderly woman, to gain admission to the District of Columbia chapter of the American Association of University Women.

To be sure, there was a shift in emphasis from race uplift and thus institution-building in the first part of this long period of study to the struggle against segregation in the second. But the shift was only visible in overview, because many women activists had been challenging racism from early in their careers. Williams, for example, as early as 1896, insisted that white women needed to learn from Blacks.[69] YWCA women such as Eva Bowles, Lugenia Burns Hope, and Addie Hunton struggled against discrimination in the YWCA soon after the first colored branch opened in 1911. Charlotte Hawkins Brown, who was noted and sometimes criticized for her snobbery and insistence on "respectability," nevertheless "made it a practice, whenever insulted in a train or forced to leave a pullman coach and enter the Jim Crow car, to bring suit." At least one lawyer, in 1921, tried to get her to accept a small settlement, but she made it clear that her purpose was not financial compensation but justice.[70] Cooper, whose flowery and sentimental prose style might lead one to mistake her for a "soft," accommodating, spirit, rarely let a slur against Negroes go unprotested. She wrote to the Oberlin Committee against Al Smith in 1928 that she could not "warm up very enthusiastically with religious fervor for Bible 'fundamentalists' who have nothing to say about lynching Negroes or reducing whole sections of them to a state of peonage."[71]

The many women who had always challenged racism made a relatively smooth transition to a civil rights emphasis in their welfare work. There were conflicts about separatist versus integrationist strategies from the beginning of this period, not only in women's participation in leading Black discourse but also in women's own projects. For example, Jane Hunter's establishment of a Black YWCA in Cleveland evoked much Black criticism, especially from those who thought her success in raising white money sprang from her decision not to challenge the white YWCA. Yet most Black women in this network used separate institution-building and antisegregation tactics at the same time. Nannie Burroughs, noted for her work as an educator promoting Black Christian and vocational education, urged a boycott of the segregated public transportation system of Washington, D.C., in 1915.[72] (And Burroughs was Hunter's model.) In the 1930s Burroughs denounced the Baptist leadership and resisted its control so strongly that that church almost cut off financial support for the National Training School for Girls that she had worked so hard and long to build. " 'Don't wait for deliverers,' she admonished her listeners. . . . 'There are no deliverers. They're all dead. . . . The Negro must serve notice . . . that he is ready to die for justice.' " The Baptists relented, but Burroughs was still provoking white churchmen a decade later. In 1941 she canceled an engagement to speak for the National Christian Mission because the hierarchy insisted on precensoring her speech.[73] "The Negro is oppressed not because he is a Negro—but because he'll take it."[74] Bethune, who began her career as founder of a Black college, and was criticized by some for her apologias for segregated New Deal programs, was walking a picket line in front of Peoples Drugs in the District of Columbia, demanding jobs for colored youth, in 1939 even while still at the National Youth Administration.[75]

Moreover, the greater emphasis on civil rights never eclipsed uplift strategies. From the New Deal on, Black government leaders were simultaneously trying to get more Black women hired, protesting the passing over of qualified Black applicants, and working to improve the qualifications and performance of Black individuals. In 1943 Corinne Robinson of the Federal Public Housing Authority organized a skit, entitled *Lazy Daisy*, which called upon Black government workers to shed slothful habits.[76] Nannie Burroughs in 1950 complained that the average Negro "gets up on the installment plan—never gets dressed fully until night, and by then he is completely disorganized." But that is because, she explained, "He really has nothing to get up to." To repeat: there was for these women no inherent contradiction between race uplift and antidiscrimination thinking.[77]

These Black welfare activists were also militant in their critique of male supremacy, that militance, too, arising from their work for the welfare of the race. Deborah White has argued that the Black women's clubs, more than the white, claimed leadership of the race for women. Charlotte Hawkins Brown declared her own work and thoughts were just as important as Booker T. Washington's.[78] Moreover, their ambitions were just as great as those of the white women: Afro-Americans spoke of uplifting their race; white women described themselves as promoting the general welfare, but only because their focus on their own race was silent and understood. Whether or not these women should be called feminists (and they certainly did not call themselves that), they shared characteristics of the white group that has been called "social feminists"; their activism arose from efforts to advance the welfare of the whole public, not just women, in a context where, they believed, men did not or could not adequately meet the needs.[79]

Black and white women welfare reformers also differed in their thinking about women's economic role. The white women, with few exceptions, tended to view married women's economic dependence on men as desirable, and their employment as a misfortune; they accepted the family wage system and rarely expressed doubts about its effectiveness, let alone its justice. There was substantial variation within this network and change over time in its members' view of the family wage. There was also substantial contradiction. Beginning in the 1890s, women social investigators repeatedly demonstrated that the family wage did not work, because most men did not earn enough, because some men became disabled, and because others were irresponsible toward their families. Sybil Lipschultz has shown that between two key Supreme Court briefs written by women in the white network—for *Muller v. Oregon* in 1908, and for *Adkins v. Children's Hospital* in 1923—the grounds for protective legislation changed considerably. The brief for *Muller* privileged sacred motherhood and treated women's wage labor as an anomaly that should be prevented; the brief for *Adkins* argued from women's weaker position in the labor market and the need for government to intervene because it was not an anomaly.[80] Yet when the women's welfare network moved away from protective labor legislation toward public assistance or family policy, its recommendations presupposed that the desirable position for women was as domestic wives and mothers dependent on male earnings. The many unmarried women in the network viewed their own singleness as a class privilege and a natural condition for women active in the public sphere, and felt that remaining childless was an acceptable price for it. They were convinced that single motherhood and employment among mothers meant danger. They feared relief to single mothers offered without counseling or employment offered to mothers other than temporarily, because they resisted establishing single-mother families as durable institutions.[81]

This is where the social work legacy is felt. The white reformers were accustomed to, and felt comfortable with, supervising. Long after Jane Addams with her environmentalist, democratic orientation became their hero, they continued to identify with the Charity Organization Society fear of "pauperizing" aid recipients by making it too easy for them and destroying their work incentive—and they feared that too much help to deserted women, for example, would do just this, let men off the hook. They did not share the belief of many contemporary European socialists that aid to single mothers should be a matter of right, of entitlement. Even Florence Kelley, herself a product of a European socialist education, defended the family wage as the appropriate goal of reform legislation. A divorced mother herself, she nevertheless lauded "the American tradition that men support their families, the wives throughout life," and lamented the "retrograde movement" that made the man no longer the breadwinner. The U.S. supporters of mothers' pensions envisioned aid as a gift to the deserving, and felt an unshakable responsibility to supervise single mothers and restore marriages and wives' dependency on husbands whenever possible. This "white" view was clearly a class perspective as well. A troubling question is unavoidable: Did these elite white women believe that independence was a privilege of wealth to which poor women ought not aspire?[82]

The Black women reformers also held up breadwinner husbands and nonemployed wives as an ideal; Black and white women spoke very similarly about the appropriate "spheres" of the two sexes, equally emphasizing motherhood.[83] The difference I am describing here is not diametric. Lucy D. Slowe, dean of women at Howard, believed that working mothers caused urban juvenile delinquency, and she called for campaigns to "build up public sentiment for paying heads of families wages sufficient to reduce the number of Negro women who must be employed away from home to the detriment of their children and of the community in general."[84] Personally, many of the married Black activists had trouble prevailing upon their husbands to accept their activities, and some were persuaded to stay home. Ardie Halyard, recollecting the year 1920, described the process:

> Interviewer: How did your husband feel about your working?
> Halyard: At first, he thought it was very necessary. But afterwards, when he became able to support us, it was day in and day out, "When are you going to quit?"[85]

Dorothy Ferebee's husband could not tolerate her higher professional status. Inabel Lindsay promised her husband not to work for a year and then slid into a lifelong career by taking a job that she promised was only temporary.[86]

Mixed as it was, acceptance of married women's employment as a long-term and widespread necessity was much greater among Blacks than among whites. Fanny Jackson Coppin had argued in the 1860s for women's economic independence from men, and women were active in creating employment bureaus. We see the greater Black acknowledgement of single mothers in the high priority Black women reformers gave to organizing kindergartens, then usually called day nurseries. In Chicago, Cleveland, Atlanta, Washington, and many other locations, daytime child-care facilities were among the earliest projects of women's groups. Terrell called establishing them her first goal, and her first publication was the printed version of a speech she had delivered at a National American Woman Suffrage Association convention, which she sold for twenty-five cents a copy to help fund a kindergarten.[87] In poor urban white neighborhoods the need for child care may have been nearly as great, and some white activists created kindergartens, but proportionally far fewer. Virtually no northern white welfare reformers endorsed such programs as long-term or permanent services until the 1930s and 1940s; until then even the most progressive, such as Kelley, opposed them even as temporary solutions, fearing they would encourage the exploitation of women through low-wage labor.[88]

Black women decried the effects of the "double day" on poor women as much as did white reformers. They were outspoken in their criticism of men who failed to support families. Burroughs wrote, "Black men sing too much 'I Can't Give You Anything But Love, Baby.' "[89] But their solutions were different. From the beginning of her career, Burroughs understood that the great majority of Black women would work all their lives, and she had to struggle against continuing resistance to accepting that fact to get her National Training School funded. And most Black women activists projected a favorable view of working women and women's professional aspirations. Elizabeth Ross Haynes wrote with praise in 1922 of "the hope of an economic independence that will some day enable them [Negro women] to take their places in the ranks with other working women."[90] Sadie Alexander directly attacked the view that a married woman's ideal should be domesticity. She saw that in an industrial society the work of the housewife would be increasingly seen as "valueless consumption" and that women should "place themselves again among the producers of the world."[91]

This high regard for women's economic independence is also reflected in the important and prestigious role played by businesswomen in Black welfare activity. One of the best-known and most revered women of this network was Maggie Lena Walker, the first woman bank president in the United States. Beginning work at the age of fourteen in the Independent Order of St. Luke, a mutual benefit society in Richmond, Virginia, that provided illness and burial insurance as well as social activity for Blacks, in 1903 she established the St. Luke Penny Savings Bank. Walker became a very wealthy woman. She devoted a great deal of her money and her energy to welfare activity, working in the National Association for the Advancement of Colored People (NAACP), the National Association of Wage Earners, and local Richmond groups. In the context of Afro-American experience, Walker's business was itself a civil rights and community welfare activity; many reformers, including prominently Bethune and Du Bois, believed that economic power was a key to Black progress. The St. Luke enterprise stimulated Black ownership and employment. They opened a Black-owned department store in Richmond, thus threatening white economic power, and met intense opposition from white businessmen; indeed, a white Retail Dealers' Association was formed to crush the store. Several noteworthy businesswomen-activists got rich manufacturing cosmetics for Blacks: the mother-daughter team, C. J. Walker and A'Lelia Walker (not related to Maggie Walker) of Pittsburgh and Indianapolis, and Annie Turnbo Malone of St. Louis. Reformer Jane Hunter was respected not only because of her welfare contributions but also because, once penniless, she left an estate of over four hundred thousand dollars at her death; as was Sallie Wyatt Stewart, who left over one hundred thousand dollars in real estate.[92]

These factors suggest considerable differences in orientations (among the numerous similarities) between white and Black women activists, although the preliminary stage of research on this topic requires us to consider the differences more as hypotheses than as conclusions. First, Black women claimed leadership in looking after the welfare of their whole people more than did comparable whites. Because of this assumption of race responsibility, and because for Blacks welfare was so indistinguishable from equal rights, Black women emphasized programs for the unusually needy less, and universal provision more, than did white women. Perhaps in part because education was so important a part of the Black women's program, and because education developed for whites in the United States as a universal public service, Blacks' vision of welfare provision followed that model. Among whites, a relatively large middle class encouraged reformers to focus their helping efforts on others, and kept alive and relatively uncriticized the use of means and morals testing as a way of distributing help, continuing the division of the "deserving" from the "undeserving" poor. Among the Black reformers, despite their relatively elite position, welfare appeared more closely connected with legal entitlements, not so different from the right to vote or to ride the public transportation system.[93] Had their ideas been integrated into the white women's thinking, one might ask, would means testing and humiliating invasions of privacy have been so uniformly accepted in programs such as Aid to Families with Dependent Children (AFDC), over which the white women's network had substantial influence?

Another difference is the Black women's different attitude toward married women's employment. Most of the white women welfare reformers retained, until World War II, a distinctly head-in-the-sand and even somewhat contradictory attitude toward it: it was a misfortune, not good for women, children, or men; helping working mothers too much would tend to encourage it. Thus they were more concerned to help—sometimes to force—single mothers to stay home than to provide services that would help working mothers, such as child care or maternity leave. Black women were much more positive about women's employment. Despite their agreement that a male family wage was the most desirable arrangement, they doubted that married women's employment would soon disappear, or that it could be discouraged by making women and children suffer for it. In relation to this race difference, it is hard to ignore the different marital status of the majority of the women in the two groups: Most of the Black women had themselves had the experience of combining public-sphere activism with marriage, if less often with children.[94] Perhaps the fact that most of the white women had dispensed with marriage and family, probably largely by choice, made them see the choice between family and work as an acceptable one, oblivious to the different conditions of such "choice" among poorer women.

Third, Black and white welfare reformers differed considerably about how to protect women from sexual exploitation. Black welfare reformers were more concerned to combine the development of protective institutions for women with an antirape discourse. Among whites, rape was not an important topic of discussion during this period, and in protective work for women and girls, male sexuality was treated as natural and irrepressible. It is not clear how the Black activists would have translated antirape consciousness into welfare policy, had they had the power to do so, but it seems likely that they would have tried.

There were also substantial areas of shared emphases between white and Black women. Both groups oriented much of their welfarist thinking to children, rarely questioning the unique responsibility of women for children's welfare. Neither group questioned sexual "purity" as an appropriate goal for unmarried women. Both groups used women's organizations as their main political and social channels. Both emphasized the promotion of other women into positions of leadership and jobs, confident that increasing the numbers of women at the "top" would benefit the public welfare. Both believed that improving the status of women was essential to advancing the community as a whole. At the same time, both groups, in the 1920s, were moving away from explicitly feminist discourse and muting their public criticisms of what we would today call sexism. Moreover they shared many personal characteristics: low fertility, relatively high economic and social status, very high educational attainment.

These impressions raise more questions than they answer. I wonder, for example, what the relation was between the national leaders and local rank-and-file activists: Were the leaders "representative" of "constituencies"? One might hypothesize that local activists were more often married and less elite, since singleness and prosperity were probably among the factors that allowed women to travel and to function nationally. To what extent were the Black/white differences functions of chronology? White reformers were, for instance, active in building educational institutions in the nineteenth century; by the early twentieth century the institutions they needed were in place. Further research might also make it possible to identify historical circumstances that contributed to these race differences, circumstances such as migration, changing demand for labor, immigration, and its closure.

I approached this evidence as part of a general inquiry into welfare thinking in the United States in this century. In this project I found, as have several other historians, that the white women's reform network—but not the Black—had some influence on welfare policy, particularly in public assistance programs. I have tried to show here that this influence was as much colored by race as by gender. The white women's influence supported the legacies in our welfare programs of means testing, distinguishing the deserving from the undeserving, moral supervision of female welfare recipients, failing to criticize men's sexual behavior, and discouraging women's employment. Black women's influence on federal welfare programs was negligible in this period; indeed, the leading federal programs—old-age insurance, unemployment compensation, workmen's compensation, and the various forms of public assistance such as AFDC—were expressly constructed to exclude Blacks. It is not too late now, however, to benefit from a review of Black women's welfare thought as we reconsider the kind of welfare state we want.[95]

Appendix

The women in these samples were selected because they were the leaders of national organizations that lobbied for welfare programs (such as the National Consumers' League, the National Child Labor Committee, the National Association of Colored Women, or the National Council of Negro Women), or government officials responsible for welfare programs who were also important advocates of such programs, or builders of private welfare institutions. Women who were simply employees of welfare programs or institutions were not included; for example, educators were only included when they were builders of educational institutions. For the Blacks, this sample of welfare activists overlaps extensively with a sample one might construct of clubwomen and political activists, but not exactly; for example, Ida Wells-Barnett is not here because she must be categorized as primarily a civil rights, not a welfare, campaigner. Among the whites this sample overlaps, somewhat with "social feminists," but those who were primarily labor organizers, for example, are not included.

Some of what appear to be race differences are differences of historical time and circumstance. Thus a study of women between, say, 1840 and 1890 would have included more white women educators (because white women were then working to build educational institutions, as Black women were later) and more white married women (because the dip in the marriage rate among college-educated white women occurred later). Regional differences are also produced by this definition of the samples: a focus on local or state, as opposed to national activity would have led to the inclusion of more western and southern women, for example; women in the Northeast and mid-Atlantic were more likely to be important in national politics because New York and Washington, D.C., were so often the headquarters of national activities

In order to simplify this list, only a single, general, major area of welfare activism is given for each woman. Because many women were active in several areas, the identifications given here do not necessarily conform to some figures in the text, for example, how many women were social workers or educators. The categories for the white and Black women are not the same. Among the whites I gave more specific identifications to indicate the importance of several key arenas, such as the National Consumers' League and the United States Children's Bureau. To use such specific identifications among the Black women would have been uninformative, since virtually all were, for example, active in the NACW. Furthermore, a few Black women participated in such a variety of welfarist activity organized through the NACW, sororities, or other women's organizations that I could define their major sphere as simply club work.

Table 1. Selected Black Women Welfare Activists

Name	Main Reform	Name	Main Reform
Alexander, Sadie Tanner Mossell	Civil rights	Jones, Verina Morton	Social work
Anthony, Lucille	Health	Laney, Lucy Craft	Education
Ayer, G. Elsie	Education	Lawton, Maria Coles Perkins	Education
Barnes, Margaret E.	Education	Lindsay, Inabel Burns	Education
Barrett, Janie Porter	Education	Lyle, Ethel Hedgeman	Club
Bearden, Bessye	Civil rights	Mallory, Arenia Cornella	Education
Bethune, Mary McLeod	Education	Malone, Annie M. Turnbo	Education
Bowles, Eva Del Vakia	Social work	Marsh, Vivian Osborne	Club
Brawley, Ruth Merrill	Social work	Matthews, Victoria Earle	Social work
Brown, Charlotte Hawkins	Education	Mays, Sadie Gray	Social work
Brown, Sue M.	Education	McCrorey, Mary Jackson	Social work
Burroughs, Nannie Helen	Education	McDougald, G. Elsie Johnson	Education
Callis, Myra Colson	Employment	McKane, Alice Woodby	Health
Carter, Ezella	Education	Merritt, Emma Frances Grayson	Education
Cary, Alice Dugged	Child welfare	Nelson, Alice Ruth Dunbar	Social work
Cook, Coralie Franklin	Education	Pickens, Minnie McAlpin	Civil rights
Cooper, Anna Julia Haywood	Education	Randolph, Florence	Club
Davis, Belle	Health	Ridley, Florida Ruffin	Club
Davis, Elizabeth Lindsey	Club	Ruffin, Josephine St. Pierre	Club
Dickerson, Addie W.	Club	Rush, Gertrude E.	Social work
Faulkner, Georgia M. DeBaptiste	Social work	Saddler, Juanita Jane	Civil rights
Fauset, Crystal Bird	Civil rights	Snowden, Joanna Cecilia	Social work
Ferebee, Dorothy Boulding	Health	Stewart, Sallie Wyatt	Social work
Gaines, Irene McCoy	Civil rights	Talbert, Mary Barnett	Civil rights
Harris, Judia C. Jackson	Social work	Taylor, Isabelle Rachel	Social work
Haynes, Elizabeth Ross	Civil rights	Terrell, Mary Eliza Church	Civil rights
Hedgeman, Anna Arnold	Civil rights	Walker, A'Lelia	Social work
Height, Dorothy I.	Civil rights	Walker, Maggie Lena	Social work
Hope, Lugenia Burns	Social work	Warren, Sadie	Social work
Hunter, Jane Edna Harris	Social work	Washington, Margaret Murray	Education
Hunton, Addie D. Waites	Civil rights	Wells, Eva Thornton	Social work
Jackson, Juanita Elizabeth	Civil rights	Wheatley, Laura Frances	Education
Jeffries, Christina Armistead	Civil rights	Williams, Fannie Barrier	Social work
Johnson, Bertha La Branche	Education	Young, Mattie Dover	Social work
Johnson, Kathryn Magnolia	Civil rights		

Table 2. Selected White Women Welfare Activists

Name	Main Reform	Name	Main Reform
Abbott, Edith	Social work	Kelley, Florence Molthrop	Consumers' League
Abbott, Grace	Children's Bureau	Kellor, Frances (Alice)	Immigrant welfare
Addams, Jane	Settlement	Lathrop, Julia Clifford	Childrens' Bureau
Amidon, Beulah Elizabeth	Social work	Lenroot, Katherine Frederica	Children's Bureau
Anderson Mary	Women's Bureau	Loeb, Sophie Irene Simon	Mothers' pension
Armstrong,	Social Security	Lundberg, Emma Octavia	Children's Bureau
Barbara Nachtrieb		Maher, Amy	Social Security
Armstrong, Florence Arzelia	Social Security	Mason, Lucy Randolph	Consumers' League
Beyer, Clara Mortenson	Children's Bureau	McDowell, Mary Eliza	Settlement
Blair, Emily Newell	Democratic party	McMain, Eleanor Laura	Settlement
Bradford, Cornelia Foster	Settlement	Miller, Frieda Segelke	Women's Bureau
Breckinridge,	Social work	Moskowitz, Belle Israels	Democratic party
Sophonisba Preston		Newman, Pauline	Women's Bureau
Brown, Josephine Chapin	Social work	Perkins, Frances	Social Security
Burns, Eveline Mabel	Social Security	Peterson, Agnes L.	Women's Bureau
Cannon, Ida Maud	Medical social work	Pidgeon, Mary Elizabeth	Women's Bureau
Colcord, Joanna	Social work	Rankin, Jeannette Pickering	Congresswoman
Coyle, Grace Longwood	Social work	Raushenbush,	Unemployment
Crane, Caroline Bartlett	Sanitation reform	Elizabeth Brandeis	
Deardorff, Neva Ruth	Social work	Regan, Agnes Gertrude	Social work
Dewson, Mary W. (Molly)	Democratic party	Richmond, Mary Ellen	Social work
Dinwiddie, Emily Wayland	Housing reform	Roche, Josephine Aspinall	Consumers' League
Dudley, Helena Stuart	Settlement	Roosevelt, (Anna) Eleanor	Social work
Dunn, Loula Friend	Social work	Schneiderman, Rose	Labor
Eastman, Crystal (Catherine)	Industrial health	Sherwin, Belle	Club
Einstein, Hannah Bachman	Mothers' pensions	Simkhovitch, Mary Kingsbury	Settlement
Eliot, Martha May	Children's Bureau	Springer, Gertrude Hill	Social work
Ellickson, Katherine Pollak	Social Security	Switzer, Mary Elizabeth	Social work
Elliott, Harriet Wiseman	Democratic party	Taft, (Julia) Jessie	Social work
Engle, Lavinia Margaret	Social Security	Thomas, M. Carey	Education
Evans, Elizabeth Glendower	Consumers' League	Towle, Charlotte Helen	Social work
Fuller, Minnie Ursala	Child welfare		(academic)
Goldmark, Josephine Clara	Consumers' League	Vaile, Gertrude	Social work
Goldmark, Pauline Dorothea	Consumers' League	Van Kleeck, Mary Abby	Women's Bureau
Gordon, Jean Margaret	Consumers' League	Wald, Lillian D.	Settlement
Hall, Helen	Settlement	White, Sue Shelton	Democratic party
Hamilton, (Amy) Gordon	Social work	Wood, Edith Elmer	Housing reform
Hamilton, Alice	Industrial health	Woodbury,	Children's Bureau
Hoey, Jane Margueretta	Social Security	Helen Laura Sumner	
Iams, Lucy Virginia Dorsey	Housing reform	Woodward, Ellen Sullivan	Social work
Keller, Helen	Health reform		

Notes

For critical readings of this article in draft I am indebted to Lisa D. Brush, Nancy Cott, Elizabeth Higginbotham, Evelyn Brooks Higginbotham, Jacquelyn D. Hall, Stanlie James, Judith Walzer Leavitt, Gerda Lerner, Adolph Reed, Jr., Anne Firor Scott, Kathryn Kish Sklar, Susan Smith, David Thelen, Susan Traverso, Bill Van Deburg, Deborah Gray White, and anonymous readers for this journal. I could not meet all the high standards of these scholars, many of whom took a great deal of time and care with this sprawling essay, but several of them not only offered valuable insights but also saved me from some errors resulting from my venture into a new field, and I am extremely grateful.

1. For a critique of gender bias in existing welfare scholarship and an explanation of the need for further research about the influence of gender, see the introduction to Linda Gordon, ed., *Women, the State, and Welfare* (Madison, 1990), pp. 9–35.

2. One of the subjects of this study, Inabel Burns Lindsay, former dean of the Howard University School of Social Work, wrote a dissertation on this topic at the University of Pittsburgh in 1952, and published Inabel Burns Lindsay, "Some Contributions of Negroes to Welfare Services, 1865–1900," *Journal of Negro Education*, 25 (Winter 1956), pp. 15–24. Her publication did not spark others, however. A valuable collection of documents is Edyth L. Ross, ed., *Black Heritage in Social Welfare, 1860–1930* (Metuchen, 1978). Neither publication considers the particular role of women. For suggestions that Black women participated more in organized activity than did white women, see Anne Firor Scott, "Most Invisible of All: Black Women's Voluntary Associations," *Journal of Southern History*, 56 (February, 1990), p. 5; and Ena L. Farley, "Caring and Sharing since World War I: The League of Women for Community Service—A Black Volunteer Organization in Boston," *Umoja*, 1 (Summer 1977), pp. 1–12. Victoria Earle Matthews's surname is sometimes spelled "Mathews." Ralph E. Luker, "Missions, Institutional Churches, and Settlement Houses: The Black Experience, 1885–1910," *Journal of Negro History*, 69 (Summer/Fall 1984), pp. 101–13; Dorothy C. Salem, *To Better Our World: Black Women in Organized Reform, 1890–1920* (Brooklyn, 1990), pp. 44–45; Sharon Harley, "Beyond the Classroom: The Organizational Lives of Black Female Educators in the District of Columbia, 1890–1930," *Journal of Negro Education*, 51 (Summer 1982), p. 262; Jacqueline Anne Rouse, *Lugenia Burns Hope: Black Southern Reformer* (Athens, GA, 1989); Elizabeth Lasch, "Female Vanguard in Race Relations: 'Mother Power' and Blacks in the American Settlement House Movement," paper delivered at the Berkshire Conference on the History of Women, Rutgers University, June 1990 (in Linda Gordon's possession). Since the Black settlements were often called missions and were often more religious than typical white settlements, historians have not clearly recognized the broad range of services they provided and the organizational/agitational centers they became.

3. On public social welfare programs attacking working-class self-help programs in England, see Stephen Yeo, "Working-Class Association, Private Capital, Welfare, and the State in the Late Nineteenth and Twentieth Centuries," in *Social Work, Welfare, and the State*, ed. Noel Parry *et al.* (London, 1979). Self-help associations of the poor were probably as common in the United States as in England.

4. Charles L. Coon, "Public Taxation and Negro Schools," quoted in W.E.B. Du Bois, ed., *Efforts for Social Betterment among Negro Americans* (Atlanta, 1909), p. 29. The tax money spent on Black schools was, of course, proportionally and absolutely far less than that spent on white.

5. Cynthia Neverdon-Morton, *Afro-American Women of the South and the Advancement of the Race, 1895–1925* (Knoxville, 1989), p. 79.

6. Louie D. Shivery, "The History of the Gate City Free Kindergarten Association" (from a 1936 Atlanta University M.A. thesis), in *Black Heritage in Social Welfare*, ed. Ross, pp. 261–62.

7. Tera Hunter, " 'The Correct Thing': Charlotte Hawkins Brown and the Palmer Institute," *Southern Exposure*, 11 (Sept./Oct., 1983), pp. 37–43; Sandra N. Smith and Earle H. West, "Charlotte Hawkins Brown," *Journal of Negro Education*, 51 (Summer 1982), pp. 191–206.

8. Darlene Clark Hine, " 'We Specialize in the Wholly Impossible': The Philanthropic Work of Black Women," in *Lady Bountiful Revisited: Women, Philanthropy, and Power*, ed. Kathleen D. McCarthy (New Brunswick, 1990), p. 84.

9. For help in gathering and analyzing biographical data, I am indebted to Lisa Brush, Bob Buchanan, Nancy Isenberg, Nancy MacLean, and Susan Traverso.

10. For a discussion of the definition of welfare, see Gordon, ed., *Women, the State, and Welfare*, pp. 19–35; and Linda Gordon, "What Does Welfare Regulate?" *Social Research*, 55 (Winter 1988), pp. 609–30. Child labor is both a welfare and a labor reform issue. I have included it here because, for so many women active in this cause, it seemed a logical, even inevitable, continuation of other child welfare activity; opposition to child labor was a much-used argument for mothers' pensions and Aid to Families with Dependent Children.

11. Although my focus is on welfare, a similar predominance of northern whites and southern Blacks occurred

among the national women's organizations. For example, Margaret (Mrs. Booker T.) Washington was the first southerner to be head of any national secular women's group—in her case, the National Association of Colored Women (NACW). See Darlene Rebecca Roth, "Matronage: Patterns in Women's Organizations, Atlanta, Georgia, 1890–1940" (Ph.D. diss., George Washington University, 1978), p. 81. On the integration of education into campaigns for welfare by African Americans, see, for example, Elizabeth Higginbotham, "Too Much to Ask: The Costs of Black Female Success," ch. 3, "Socialized for Survival" (in Elizabeth Higginbotham's possession).

12. Of the 69 black women, 5 held governmental positions: Mary McLeod Bethune was director of the Division of Negro Affairs at the National Youth Administration under Franklin D. Roosevelt; Alice Cary was a traveling advisor to the Department of Labor during World War I; Crystal Fauset was a state legislator from Philadelphia and race relations advisor to the Works Progress Administration during the New Deal; Anna Hedgeman was assistant to the New York City commissioner of welfare in 1934. By contrast, 53 percent of the white women held federal government positions, and 58 percent held state positions.

13. Neverdon-Morton, *Afro-American Women of the South*, pp. 191–236; Rosalyn Terborg-Penn, "Discrimination against Afro-American Women in the Woman's Movement, 1830–1920," in *The Afro-American Woman: Struggles and Images*, ed. Sharon Harley and Rosalyn Terborg-Penn (Port Washington, 1978), pp. 17–27.

14. These white reformers were not more racist than the men engaged in similar activity and often less. Eight white women from this sample were among the founding members of the National Association for the Advancement of Colored People (NAACP): Jane Addams, Florence Kelley, Julia Lathrop, Sophonisba Breckinridge, Mary McDowell, Lillian Wald, and Edith and Grace Abbott.

15. Steven J. Diner, "Chicago Social Workers and Blacks in the Progressive Era." *Social Service Review*, 44 (December, 1970), pp. 393–410; Sandra M. Stehno, "Public Responsibility for Dependent Black Children: The Advocacy of Edith Abbott and Sophonisba Breckinridge," *Social Service Review*, 62 (September, 1988), pp. 485–503; Gerda Lerner, *Black Women in White America: A Documentary History* (New York, 1972), p. 459; Salem, *To Better Our World*, pp. 248–50; Jacquelyn Dowd Hall, *Revolt against Chivalry: Jessie Daniel Ames and the Women's Campaign against Lynching* (New York, 1979), p. 66.

16. Jacqueline Rouse, biographer of Lugenia Burns Hope of Atlanta, lists ten other Black activists who, with Hope, formed a close southern network by about 1910; Bethune in Florida, Nettie Napier and M.L. Crosthwait in Tennessee, Jennie Moton and Margaret Washington in Alabama, Maggie Lena Walker in Virginia, Charlotte Hawkins Brown and Mary Jackson McCrorey in North Carolina, and Lucy Laney and Florence Hunt also in Georgia. Rouse, *Lugenia Burns Hope*, p. 5. Rouse also identifies an overlapping group of Black southern women educators—Hope, Hunt, McCrorey, Washington, Moton, Bethune, with the addition of Marion B. Wilkinson of South Carolina State College; Julia A. Fountain of Morris Brown College in Atlanta; and A. Vera Davage of Clark College in Atlanta, *Ibid*, p. 55. Paula Giddings, *In Search of Sisterhood: Delta Sigma Theta and the Challenge of the Black Sorority Movement* (New York, 1988). Darlene Rebecca Roth found that Black clubwomen retained closer ties with their schools than did white clubwomen. Roth, "Matronage," p. 183. Hine, " 'We Specialize in the Wholly Impossible,' " pp. 70–93; Fannie Barrier Williams, "Opportunities and Responsibilities of Colored Women," in *Afro-American Encyclopaedia; or, the Thoughts, Doings, and Sayings of the Race*, ed. James T. Haley (Nashville, 1896), pp. 146–61.

17. Hine, " 'We Specialize in the Wholly Impossible'," p. 83.

18. On the attempt to force Lucy D. Slowe to live in the women's dormitory, see the letters in folder 59, box 90-3, and folder 100, box 90-4, Lucy D. Slowe Papers (Moorland-Spingarn Research Center, Howard University, Washington, D.C.), esp. Coralie Franklin Cook et al. to Lucy D. Slowe, June 9, 1933, folder 9, box 90-2, *ibid*.; Clayda J. Williams to Slowe, August 23, 1993, *ibid*.; Mary McLeod Bethune to Slowe, November 23, 1933, folder 28, *ibid*. Howard University was notorious for its discriminatory treatment of women, backward even in relation to other colleges at the time. On Howard, see Giddings, *In Search of Sisterhood*, p. 43.

19. For remarks made about Bethune at the 1938 National Conference of Negro Women White House Conference, praising her for not being satisfied to be the token Black but struggling to increase Black representation in the New Deal, see folder 4, box 1, series 4, pp. 27–28, National Council of Negro Women Papers (Mary McLeod Bethune Museum and Archives, Washington, D.C.).

20. Tullia Brown Hamilton also found this focus on education predominant among the Black women reformers she studied. Tullia Brown Hamilton, "The National Association of Colored Women, 1896–1920" (Ph.D. diss. Emory University, 1978), pp. 45–46. Similarly Roth found that even among Atlanta's most elite organization of Black women, the Chautauqua Circle, all had been employed as teachers; Roth, "Matronage," p. 181. Melinda Chateauvert found that women graduates of Washington, D.C.'s elite Black Dunbar High School (who outnumbered males two to one around 1910) were overwhelmingly likely to go on to the district's free Miner Teacher's College to become teachers; Melinda Chateauvert, "The Third Step: Anna Julia Cooper and Black Education in the District of Columbia," *Sage*, 5 (Student Supplement 1988), pp.

7–13. For the same conclusion, see Carol O. Perkins, "The Pragmatic Idealism of Mary McLeod Bethune," *ibid.* (Fall 1988), pp. 30–36. W.E.B. Du Bois, ed., *Economic Cooperation among Negro Americans* (Atlanta, 1907), pp. 80–88.

21. Du Bois, ed., *Efforts for Social Betterment among Negro Americans*, pp. 65–77. For a northern local example, see Russell H. Davis, *Black Americans in Cleveland: From George Peake to Carl B. Stokes, 1796–1969* (Cleveland, 1972), p. 192.

22. Darlene Clark Hine, *Black Women in White: Racial Conflict and Cooperation in the Nursing Profession, 1890–1950* (Bloomington, 1989), p. xvii; Edward H. Beardsley, *A History of Neglect: Health Care for Blacks and Mill Workers in the Twentieth-Century South* (Knoxville, 1987), p. 101; Susan L. Smith, "The Black Women's Club Movement: Self-Improvement and Sisterhood, 1890–1915" (M.A. thesis, University of Wisconsin, Madison, 1986); Susan L. Smith, "Black Activism in Health Care, 1890–1950," paper delivered at the conference "Black Health: Historical Perspectives and Current Issues," University of Wisconsin, Madison, April 1990 (in Gordon's possession); Salem, *To Better Our World*, p. 74; Du Bois, *Economic Cooperation among Negro Americans*, pp. 92–103; Du Bois, *Efforts for Social Betterment among Negro Americans*, pp. 17–22; Scott, "Most Invisible of All," p. 6; Claude F. Jacobs, "Benevolent Societies of New Orleans Blacks during the Late Nineteenth and Early Twentieth Centuries," *Louisiana History*, 29 (Winter 1988), pp. 21–33; Kathleen C. Berkeley, " 'Colored Ladies Also Contributed': Black Women's Activities from Benevolence to Social Welfare, 1866–1896," in *The Web of Southern Social Relations: Women, Family, and Education*, ed. Walter J. Fraser, Jr., R. Frank Saunders, Jr., and Jon L. Wakelyn (Athens, Ga., 1985), pp. 181–203.

23. Colored YWCA, *Fifth and Sixth Years Report, May 1909–May 1911* (Washington, n.d.), pp. 10–11 (Library, State Historical Society of Wisconsin, Madison); I am indebted to Bob Buchanan for this reference. Earline Rae Ferguson, "The Woman's Improvement Club of Indianapolis: Black Women Pioneers in Tuberculosis Work, 1903–1938," *Indiana Magazine of History*, 84 (September 1988), pp. 237–61; Darlene Clark Hine, *When the Truth Is Told: A History of Black Women's Culture and Community in Indiana, 1875–1950* (Indianapolis, 1981). The Atlanta Neighborhood Union also worked against tuberculosis. Cynthia Neverdon-Morton, "Self-Help Programs as Educative Activities of Black Women in the South, 1895–1925: Focus on Four Key Areas," *Journal of Negro Education*, 51 (Summer 1982), pp. 207–21; Walter R. Chivers, "Neighborhood Union: An Effort of Community Organization," *Opportunity*, 3 (June 1925), pp. 178–79. Modjeska Simkins's work is briefly summarized in Beardsley, *History of Neglect*, pp. 108–12. Smith, "Black Women's Club Movement"; Smith, "Black Activism in Health Care."

24. Fannie Barrier Williams, "Social Bonds in the 'Black Belt' of Chicago: Negro Organizations and the New Spirit Pervading Them." *Charities*, (October 7, 1905), pp. 40–44; Scott, "Most Invisible of All," p. 8.

25. The Young Women's Christian Association (YWCA) was segregated, and these activists fought that segregation. Nevertheless, as Dorothy Height points out forcefully in her interview, "It was unmatched by any other major group drawn from the major white population" in the opportunities it offered to Black women; Dorothy Height interview by Polly Cowan, February 11, 1974–November 6, 1976, p. 173, Black Women Oral History Project (Schlesinger Library, Radcliffe College, Cambridge, Mass.). See also descriptions of YWCA opportunities in Frankie V. Adams interview by Gay Francine Banks, April 26, 28, 1977, transcript, p. 9, *ibid.*; Salem, *To Better Our World*, p. 46.

26. I could not identify birthplaces for all the women, and those with missing information include some likely to have been southern-born.

27. Others have reached similar conclusions. See Marilyn Dell Brady, "Kansas Federation of Colored Women's Clubs, 1900–1930," *Kansas History*, 9 (Spring 1986), pp. 19–30; Linda Marie Perkins, *Black Feminism and "Race Uplift," 1890–1900* (Cambridge, Mass., 1981), Bunting Institute Working Paper (ERIC microfiche ED 221445), p. 4; Salem, *To Better Our World*, p. 67.

28. In the Black population in general, 7 percent of all married women born 1840–1859 were childless, and 28 percent of those born 1900–1919 were childless. U.S. Department of Commerce, Bureau of the Census, *Historical Statistics of the United States: Colonial Times to 1970* (2 vols., Washington, 1975), I. p. 53.

29. Black women's overall fertility was declining rapidly in this period, falling by one-third between 1880 and 1910, and southern Black women had fewer children than southern white women. Some of this low fertility was attributable to poor health and nutrition. Moreover, the women in this network were virtually all urban, and the fertility of urban Black woman was only half that of rural Black women. See Jacqueline Jones, *Labor of Love, Labor of Sorrow: Black Women, Work, and the Family from Slavery to the Present* (New York, 1985), pp. 122–23. Supporting my view of Black women's use of birth control, see Jessie M. Rodrique, "The Black Community and the Birth-Control Movement," in *Passion and Power: Sexuality in History*, ed. Kathy Peiss and Christina Simmons (Philadelphia, 1989), pp. 138–54. This article offers a convincing criticism of my own earlier work, which overstated Black hostility to birth control campaigns because of their genocidal implications. I also learned from Elizabeth Lasch's unpublished paper that Margaret Murray Washington's settlement at Tuskegee offered a course of study on sex hygiene that included birth control; this suggests

the need for further research on Black women's advocacy of birth control. Lasch, "Female Vanguard in Race Relations." p. 4.

30. I was able to identify 25 percent (17) with prosperous parents.

31. Marilyn Dell Brady found the same marital patterns for Black women reformers in her study of Kansas. Brady, "Kansas Federation of Colored Women's Clubs, 1900–1930," pp. 19–30. The major figures she studied were married and supported by their husbands.

32. Anna Arnold Hedgeman, *The Trumpet Sounds: A Memoir of Negro Leadership* (New York, 1964), pp. 25, 74; Farley, "Caring and Sharing since World War I," pp. 317–37. Hamilton, "National Association of Colored Women," p. 41; Paula Giddings, *When and Where I Enter: The Impact of Black Women on Race and Sex in America* (New York, 1984), p. 108; Berkeley, " 'Colored Ladies Also Contributed',"pp. 185–86.

33. For corroboration on the employment of well-to-do Black women, see Roth, "Matronage," pp. 180–81. On Black women's socialization toward employment, see Inabel Burns Lindsay interview by Marcia Greenlee, May 20–June 7, 1977, transcript, pp. 4, 40, Black Women Oral History Project.

34. Charles S. Johnson, *The Negro College Graduate* (Chapel Hill, 1938), pp. 18–20; U.S. Department of Commerce, Bureau of the Census, *The Social and Economic Status of the Black Population in the United States: An Historical View, 1790–1978* (Washington, 1979), p. 93.

35. Alfreda Duster interview by Greenlee, March 8–9, 1978, transcript, p. 9, Black Women Oral History Project; Hedgeman, *Trumpet Sounds*, pp. 3–28.

36. In my comments on the class attitudes of Black women welfare reformers, I am mainly indebted to the interpretations of Deborah Gray White, especially in Deborah Gray White, "Fettered Sisterhood: Class and Classism in Early Twentieth Century Black Women's History," paper delivered at the annual meeting of the American Studies Association, Toronto, November 1989 (in Gordon's possession). See also Williams, "Social Bonds in the 'Black Belt' of Chicago." On Black discrimination against relatively dark-skinned women, see, for example, Nannie Burroughs, "Not Color But Character," *Voice of the Negro*, 1 (July 1904), pp. 277–79; Duster interview, p. 52; Giddings, *In Search of Sisterhood*, p. 105; Perkins, *Black Feminism and "Race Uplift"*, p. 4; and Nancy Weiss, *Farewell to the Party of Lincoln: Black Politics in the Age of FDR* (Princeton, 1983), p. 139. Berkeley argues against the importance of class differences in the NACW, but I found them substantial. See Berkeley, " 'Colored Ladies Also Contributed.' " On class development among Blacks, see August Meier and David Lewis, "History of the Negro Upper Class in Atlanta, Georgia, 1890–1958," *Journal of Negro Education*, 28 (Spring 1959), pp. 128–39.

37. Duster interview, p. 37.

38. Philip S. Foner, ed., *The Voice of Black America: Major Speeches by Negroes in the United States, 1797–1971* (New York, 1972), p. 462.

39. Hedgeman, *Trumpet Sounds*, pp. 1–28; Chateauvert, "The Third Step"; Height interview, p. 40; Caroline Ware interview by Susan Ware, January 27–29, 1982, transcript, p. 94, Women in Federal Government Oral Histories (Schlesinger Library).

40. Robert Alan Goldberg, *Hooded Empire: The Ku Klux Klan in Colorado* (Urbana, 1981), p. vii.

41. Of the white women reformers, 78 percent had been social workers at some time; 68 percent had social work as their major reform area. I checked to see if the social work background could have been a characteristic of the less prominent women, but this was not the case. The most prominent two-thirds of the group were even more frequently social workers (84 percent).

42. Stanley Wenocur and Michael Reisch, *From Charity to Enterprise: The Development of American Social Work in a Market Economy* (Urbana, 1989), p. 33.

43. Of the white women, 18 percent had held academic jobs at one time; 9 percent were mainly employed as educators. For only 1 percent was education their major reform area.

44. Lillian Wald, *Windows on Henry Street* (Boston, 1934); Mary Kingsbury Simkhovitch, *Neighborhood: Story of Greenwich House* (New York, 1938); William W. Bremer, *Depression Winters: New York Social Workers and the New Deal* (Philadelphia, 1984); George Martin, *Madame Secretary: Frances Perkins* (Boston, 1976), pp. 134–35; Elisabeth Israels Perry, "Training for Public Life: ER and Women's Political Networks in the 1920s," in *Without Precedent: The Life and Career of Eleanor Roosevelt*, Joan Hoff-Wilson and Marjorie Lightman, eds. (Bloomington, 1984), p. 30.

45. Elisabeth Israels Perry, *Belle Moskowitz: Feminine Politics and the Exercise of Power in the Age of Alfred E. Smith* (New York, 1987), pp. 76–77; Walter Trattner, "Theodore Roosevelt, Social Workers, and the Election of 1912: A Note," *Mid-America*, 50 (January, 1968), pp. 64–69. On pre-woman suffrage women's electoral participation, see, for example, S. Sara Monoson, "The Lady and the Tiger: Women's Electoral Activism in New York City before Suffrage," *Journal of Women's History*, 2 (Fall 1990), pp. 100–135.

46. I thank Anne Firor Scott for pointing out this similarity to me.

47. On settlement house relationships, see Virginia Kemp Fish, "The Hull House Circle: Women's Friendships and Achievements," in *Gender, Ideology, and Action: Historical Perspectives on Women's Public Lives*, ed. Janet

Sharistanian (Westport, 1986); and Kathryn Kish Sklar, "Hull House in the 1890s: A Community of Women Reformers," *Signs*, 10 (Summer 1985), pp. 658–77. Lela B. Costin, *Two Sisters for Social Justice: A Biography of Grace and Edith Abbott* (Urbana, 1983), pp. 38–40; Martin, *Madame Secretary*, p. 233.

48. See, for example, Ethel Erickson to Mary Anderson, July 14, 1938, box 1263, Women's Bureau Papers, RG 86 (National Archives); Anderson to Erickson, August 4, 1938, *ibid.*; Erickson to Anderson, July 29, 1942, *ibid.*; Anderson to Erickson, August 1, 1942, *ibid.*

49. Darlene Clark Hine, "Rape and the Inner Lives of Black Women in the Middle West: Preliminary Thoughts on the Culture of Dissemblance," in this volume; Deborah Gray White, "Mining the Forgotten: Manuscript Sources for Black Women's History," *Journal of American History*, 74 (June 1987), pp. 237–42; Elsa Barkley Brown, comment at Berkshire Conference on the History of Women, 1990.

50. The singleness of the white women reformers was characteristic of other women of their race, class, and education in this period. In 1890, for example, over half of all women doctors were single. Of women earning Ph.D.s between 1877 and 1924, three-fourths remained single. As late as 1920, only 12 percent of all professional women were married. See, for example, Carl N. Degler, *At Odds: Women and the Family in America from the Revolution to the Present* (New York, 1980), p. 385. Roth corroborates the significance of marital breaks in the lives of activists, finding that civically active white women in Atlanta in this period were more likely to be widows. Roth, "Matronage," p. 182. On Boston marriages, see Micaela di Leonardo, "Warrior Virgins and Boston Marriages: Spinsterhood in History and Culture," *Feminist Issues*, 5 (Fall 1985), pp. 47–68.

51. Mrs. Tilden Frank Phillips, memoir, February 22, February 26, 1953, folder 22, Edith Rockwood Papers (Schlesinger Library); will of Edith Rockwood, folder 20, *ibid.*

52. Blanche Wiesen Cook, "The Historical Denial of Lesbianism," *Radical History Review*, 20 (Spring/Summer 1979), pp. 60–65. For quotations from a (hostile) contemporary source, see James Johnson, "The Role of Women in the Founding of the United States Children's Bureau," in *"Remember the Ladies": New Perspectives on Women in American History: Essays in Honor of Nelson Manfred Blake*, ed. Carol V.R. George (Syracuse, 1975), p. 191.

53. Cook, "Historical Denial of Lesbianism"; Blanche Wiesen Cook, "Female Support Networks and Political Activism: Lillian Wald, Crystal Eastman, Emma Goldman," in *A Heritage of Her Own*, Nancy F. Cott and Elizabeth H. Pleck, eds. (New York 1979), pp. 412–44; Estelle B. Freedman, "Separatism as Strategy," *Feminist Studies*, 5 (Fall 1979), pp. 512–29.

54. Slowe lived with Mary Burrill, who is treated as a partner in letters to and from Slowe and in letters of condolence to Burrill after Slowe's death in 1937. See letters in box 90–1, Slowe Papers. Height interview, p. 52.

55. Duster interview, p. 11; Wendy Beth Posner, "Charlotte Towle: A Biography" (Ph.D. diss., University of Chicago School of Social Service Administration, 1986), pp. 47, 77–78.

56. Mary Dewson to Clara Beyer, October 12, 1931, folder 40, box 2, Clara Beyer Papers (Schlesinger Library); Ware interview, pp. 40–42; Janice Andrews, "Role of Female Social Workers in the Second Generation: Leaders or Followers," 1989 (in Gordon's possession). The possibility of combining marriage and career had been debated intensely starting in the 1920s, but it was in the 1930s that the change began to be evident. See Lois Scharf. *To Work and to Wed: Female Employment, Feminism, and the Great Depression* (Westport, 1980)

57. Florence Kelley to Anderson, June 28, 1920, box 843, Women's Bureau Papers; Anderson to Dewson, August 23, 1920, *ibid.*; Anderson to Dewson, October 23, 1922, *ibid.*; Dewson to Anderson, June 1,1 923, *ibid.* Anderson to Mary Van Kleeck, January 8, 1937, folder 22, box 1, Mary Anderson Papers (Schlesinger Library); Judith Sealander, "Feminist against Feminist: The First Phase of the Equal Rights Amendment Debate, 1923–1963," *South Atlantic Quarterly*, 81 (Spring 1982), pp. 154–56. Mary R. Beard participated in the early meeting to draft the charter but did not, ultimately, sign it. I thank Nancy Cott for clarification on this point.

58. Susan Ware, *Beyond Suffrage: Woman in the New Deal* (Cambridge, Ma., 1981), pp. 156–57.

59. Vivien Hart, "Watch What We Do: Women Administrators and the Implementation of Minimum Wage Policy, Washington, D.C., 1918–1923," paper delivered at the Berkshire Conference on the History of Women, 1990, p. 31 (in Gordon's possession).

60. Gordon, "What Does Welfare Regulate?"; Barbara Nelson, "The Origins of the Two-Channel Welfare State: Workmen's Compensation and Mothers' Aid," in *Women, the State, and Welfare*, ed. Gordon, pp. 123–57.

61. Brady, "Kansas Federation of Colored Women's Clubs"; Lindsay, "Some Contributions of Negroes to Welfare Services," pp. 15–24; Constance Greene, *The Secret City: A History of Race Relations in the Nation's Capital* (Princeton, 1967), pp. 144–46; Neverdon-Morton, *Afro-American Women of the South*; Neverdon-Morton, "Self-Help Programs as Educative Activities of Black Women in the South"; Farley, "Caring and Sharing since World War I," esp. 4.

62. Mary Church Terrell, "Club Work among Women," *New York Age*, January 4, 1900, p. 1. Although this speech was given in 1900, another given in 1928 uses virtually the same rhetoric. See Mary Church Terrell, "Progress and Problems of Colored Women," *Boston Evening Transcript*, December 15, 1928, folder 132, box 102–4, Mary Church Terrell Papers (Moorland-Spingarn Research Collection).

63. For just a few examples, see Elise Johnson McDougald, "The Task of Negro Womanhood," in *The New Negro: An Interpretation*, ed. Alain Locke (New York, 1925), pp. 369–84; Mary Church Terrell, "Up-To-Date," *Norfolk Journal and Guide*, November 3, 1927, folder W, box 102–2, Terrell Papers; Williams, "Opportunities and Responsibilities of Colored Women"; and many speeches by Slowe, box 90–6, Slowe Papers. See also Perkins, *Black Feminism and "Race Uplift"*.

64. Williams, "Opportunities and Responsibilities of Colored Women," p. 150.

65. White, "Fettered Sisterhood"; Hine, "Rape and the Inner Lives of Black Women in the Middle West." White reformers rhetoric about protecting women named prostitution, not rape, as the problem. See Ellen DuBois and Linda Gordon, "Seeking Ecstasy on the Battlefield: Nineteenth-Century Feminist Views of Sexuality," *Feminist Studies*, 9 (Spring 1983), pp. 7–25; Lillian Wald, "The Immigrant Young Girl," in *Proceedings of the National Conference of Charities and Correction at the Thirty-sixth Annual Session Held in the City of Buffalo, N.Y., June 9th to 16th, 1909* (Fort Wayne, n.d.), p. 264. Jane Edna Hunter, *A Nickel and a Prayer* (Cleveland, 1940); Marilyn Dell Brady, "Organizing Afro-American Girls' Clubs in Kansas in the 1920s," *Frontiers*, 9 (no. 2, 1987), pp. 69–73; Greene, *Secret City*, pp. 144–46; Salem, *To Better Our World*, pp. 44–46; Scott, "Most Invisible of All," p. 15; Monroe N. Work, "Problems of Negro Urban Welfare" (from *Southern Workman*, January 1924) in *Black Heritage in Social Welfare*, ed. Ross, pp. 383–84; "Foreword" (from *Bulletin of National League on Urban Conditions among Negroes*, Report 1912–13), *ibid.*, p. 241; Guichard Parris and Lester Brooks, *Blacks in the City: A History of the National Urban League* (Boston, 1971), pp. 3–10; Hine, " 'We Specialize in the Wholly Impossible,' " p. 73.

66. Evelyn Brooks, "Religion, Politics, and Gender: The Leadership of Nannie Helen Burroughs," *Journal of Religious Thought*, 44 (Winter/Spring 1988), pp. 7–22; Cheryl Townsend Gilkes, "Building in Many Places: Multiple Commitments and Ideologies in Black Women's Community Work," in *Women and the Politics of Empowerment*, Ann Bookman and Sandra Morgen, eds. (Philadelphia, 1988), pp. 53–76.

67. White, "Fettered Sisterhood," p. 5.

68. Mrs. N. F. Mossell, *The Work of the Afro-American Woman* (1894; reprint, Freeport, 1971), p. 32. Ida Wells-Barnett is the woman most associated with this challenge to Booker T. Washington, but she was not included in this sample because she was primarily a civil rights, rather than a welfare, activist. On Anna J. Cooper, see Sharon Harley, "Anna J. Cooper: A Voice for Black Women," in *Afro-American Woman*, Harley and Terborg-Penn, eds., pp. 87–96; and Louise Daniel Hutchinson, *Anna J. Cooper: A Voice from the South* (Washington, 1981). On Mary Church Terrell, see Dorothy Sterling, *Black Foremothers* (New York, 1979); and Elliott Rudwick, *W.E.B. Du Bois: Voice of the Black Protest Movement* (Urbana, 1982), pp. 129–30.

69. Williams, "Opportunities and Responsibilities of Colored Women," p. 157.

70. Story told in Lerner, *Black Women*, pp. 375–76. On the complexity of Brown's attitudes, see Tera Hunter, " 'The Correct Thing' "; and Smith and West, "Charlotte Hawkins Brown."

71. Anna J. Cooper to A. G. Comings, October 1, 1928, folder 5, box 32–1, Anna J. Cooper Papers (Moorland-Spingarn Research Collection). Cooper was another one of those figures who tirelessly challenged racism even in its apparently small or accidental varieties. For example, she wrote to the *Atlantic Monthly* complaining about an article mentioning a poor Negro with lice. *Atlantic Monthly* editors to Cooper, January 31, 1935, folder 5, box 23–1, *ibid.*

72. Hine, " 'We Specialize in the Wholly Impossible' "; Evelyn Brooks Barnett, "Nannie Burroughs and the Education of Black Women," in *Afro-American Woman*, Harley and Terborg-Penn, eds., pp. 97–108; Brooks, "Religion, Politics, and Gender," p. 12.

73. Burroughs, speech at Bethel AME Church in Baltimore, reported in "Baptists May Oust Nannie H. Burroughs," *Chicago Defender*, (September 9, 1939); "Nannie Burroughs Refuses to Speak on National Christian Mission," *Pittsburgh Courier* (February 1, 1941), Burroughs Vertical File (Moorland-Spingarn Research Collection).

74. Burroughs's 1943 remark is quoted in Lerner. *Black Women*, p. 552.

75. On criticism of Bethune, see B. Joyce Ross, "Mary McLeod Bethune and the National Youth Administration: A Case Study of Power Relationships in the Black Cabinet of Franklin D. Roosevelt," *Journal of Negro History*, 60 (January 1975), pp. 1–28. On her defense of the New Deal, see Mary McLeod Bethune, " 'I'll Never Turn Back No More!' " *Opportunity*, 16 (November 1938), pp. 324–26; "Mrs Bethune Praises NYA Courses as 'Bright Ray of Hope for Rural Negroes,' " *Black Dispatch*, (May 1, 1937), Bethune, Vertical File (Moorland-Spingarn Research Collection); "Mrs Bethune Hails Achievements of the New Deal," *Washington Tribune*, (November 12, 1935), *ibid.*; "55,000 Aided by the NYA Program, Says Dr. Bethune," *Washington Tribune*, (April 23, 1938), *ibid.* On her picketing, see photo and caption, "Give US More Jobs," *Washington Afro-American*, (August 12, 1939), *ibid.*

76. Corinne Robinson to Jeanetta Welch Brown, with script of *Lazy Daisy* enclosed, September 22, 1943, folder 274, box 17, series 5, National Council of Negro Women Papers.

77. Era Bell Thompson, "A Message from a Mahogany Blond," *Negro Digest*, 9 (July 1950), p. 31.

78. White, "Fettered Sisterhood"; Smith and West, "Charlotte Hawkins Brown," p. 199.

79. I am in sympathy with Cott's critique of the use of the concept "social feminism," but it remains descriptive of a widely understood phenomenon, and we have as yet no terms to substitute. Nancy F. Cott, "What's in a Name? The Limits of 'Social Feminism'; or, Expanding the Vocabulary of Women's History," *Journal of American History*, 76 (December 1989), pp. 809–29.

80. Sybil Lipschultz, "Social Feminism and Legal Discourse: 1908–1923," *Yale Journal of Law and Feminism*, 2 (Fall 1989), pp. 131–60.

81. Linda Gordon, *Heroes of Their Own Lives: The Politics and History of Family Violence, Boston, 1880–1960* (New York, 1988), pp. 82–115.

82. Florence Kelley, "Minimum-Wage Laws," *Journal of Political Economy*, 20 (December 1912), p. 1003.

83. See, for examples, Roth, "Matronage," p. 87; Brady, "Kansas Federation of Colored Women's Clubs," pp. 19–31; and Marilyn Dell Brady, "Organizing Afro-American Girls' Clubs in Kansas in the 1920s," *Frontiers*, 9 (no. 2, 1987), pp. 69–73.

84. Lucy D. Slowe, "Some Problems of Colored Women and Girls in the Urban Process" [probably 1930s], folder 143, box 90–6, Slowe Papers.

85. Ardie Clark Halyard interview by Greenlee, August 24, 25, 1978, transcript, p. 15, Black Women Oral History Project.

86. Dorothy Boulding Ferebee interview by Merze Tate, December 28–31, 1979, transcript, p. 9, *ibid.*; Lindsay interview, pp. 4–5.

87. Sharon Harley, "For the Good of Family and Race: Gender, Work, and Domestic Roles in the Black Community, 1880–1930," *Signs*, 15 (Winter 1990), pp. 336–49; Helen A. Cook, "The Work of the Woman's League, Washington, D.C.," in *Some Efforts of American Negroes for Their Own Social Betterment*, ed. W. E. B. Du Bois (Atlanta, 1898), p. 57; Du Bois, ed., *Efforts for Social Betterment among Negro Americans*, pp. 119–20, 126–27; Giddings, *When and Where I Enter*, pp. 100–101; Hine, *When the Truth Is Told*, pp. 52–54; Ross, ed. *Black Heritage in Social Welfare*, pp. 233–34; Perkins, *Black Feminism and "Race Uplift"*, pp. 7–8; Allan Spear, *Black Chicago: The Making of a Ghetto, 1890–1920* (Chicago, 1967), p. 102; Stehno, "Public Responsibility for Dependent Black Children"; Harley, "Beyond the Classroom," pp. 254–65; Rouse, *Lugenia Burns Hope*, p. 28; Davis, *Black Americans in Cleveland*, p. 195; Stetson, "Black Feminism in Indiana"; Greene, *Secret City*, pp. 144–46; Mary Church Terrell, *A Colored Woman in a White World* (Washington, 1940), p. 153.

88. The white reformers in the first decades of the twentieth century were campaigning hard for mothers' pensions and feared that daytime child care would be used as an alternative, forcing mothers into poor jobs. But they continued to see mothers' employment as a misfortune. For example, Florence Kelley in 1909 argued that day nurseries should be acceptable only for temporary emergencies and that the social cost of mothers' employment was always too high. "A friend of mine has conceived the monstrous idea of having a night nursery to which women so employed might send their children. And this idea was seriously described in so modern a publication as Charities and the Commons . . . without a word of editorial denunciation." Florence Kelley, "The Family and the Woman's Wage," *Proceedings of the National Conference of Charities and Correction . . . 1909*, pp. 118–21.

89. Giddings, *When and Where I Enter*, p. 205.

90. Barnett, "Nannie Burroughs and the Education of Black Women." For Elizabeth Ross Haynes's statement of 1922, see Lerner, *Black Women*, p. 260.

91. Giddings, *When and Where I Enter*, p. 196.

92. My discussion of Walker is based on Elsa Barkley Brown, "Womanist Consciousness: Maggie Lena Walker and the Independent Order of Saint Luke," *Signs*, 14 (Spring 1989), pp. 610–33. On the significance of Black banks and other businesses, see also Du Bois, *Economic Cooperation Among Negro Americans*, pp. 103–81. Hedgeman, *Trumpet Sounds*, pp. 47–48; *Who's Who in Colored America* (New York, 1927), p. 209; Hine, " 'We Specialize in the Wholly Impossible,' " p. 86; Hine, *When the Truth is Told*, p. 51.

93. This orientation toward entitlement was evident *despite* the southern state governments' relatively smaller size, and it casts doubt on state capacity explanations for reformers' strategies.

94. Although many of the Afro-American women leaders were legally married, it does not necessarily follow that they lived their daily lives in close partnerships with their husbands or carried much domestic labor responsibility.

95. Gordon, "What Does Welfare Regulate?"

12

Sexual Geography and Gender Economy: The Furnished-Room Districts of Chicago, 1890–1930

Joanne Meyerowitz

The broad outlines of the early twentieth-century sexual revolution in the United States are now well known.[1] From roughly 1890 to 1930, public discussions and displays of sexuality multiplied in popular magazines, newspapers, and entertainments. At the same time, women began to adopt more sexual, or at least less modest, styles; shorter skirts, cosmetics, bobbed hair, and cigarettes, once the styles of prostitutes, all seemed evidence of a larger change in mores when adopted by "respectable" working- and middle-class women. Men and women mingled freely in new commercialized recreation industries and in workplaces. And surveys of the middle class revealed increases in premarital intercourse.

Historians have now written at least three versions of this sexual revolution. In the oldest and now standard account, young, middle-class "flappers" rebelled against the repressive standards of their parents by engaging in shocking behavior, such as petting in automobiles, dancing to jazz music, and using bawdy language.[2] A second version of the sexual revolution developed with the growth of the field of U.S. women's history. In this rendition, young feminist bohemians, or independent "new women," influenced by the writings of Freud and other sexologists, experimented sexually and rejected the homosocial sisterhood of earlier women's rights activists.[3] A third variation points to a working-class component. Urban, working-class "rowdy girls" appear as early as the 1830s, but seem to enter historical center stage in precisely the same years that the middle-class "new women" and "flappers" self-consciously rejected Victorian mores. In the workplace and in dance halls, theaters, and amusement parks, young, working-class women adopted an overtly sexual style that dismayed both their parents and middle-class reformers.[4]

This article is a case study of working-class women's sexuality in the furnished-room districts of turn-of-the-century Chicago. In a particular setting, how did women participate in the sexual revolution, and how was their behavior interpreted and publicized? This approach modifies the various versions of the sexual revolution. For one, it locates neglected geographical centers of urban sexual activity—the furnished-room districts—and early active participants in the sexual revolution—the women lodgers. Second, it highlights economic imperatives that motivated and shaped at least part of the sexual revolution. And, finally, it shows how middle-class observers reshaped the experiences of sexually active working-class women, and broadcast them to a larger national audience.

Recently US feminists have engaged in heated debates over the meaning of twentieth-century sexual expression. The debates are polarized between those who emphasize the sexual dangers, such as rape, that oppress women and those who focus on the sensual

Reprinted with permission from *Gender & History*, Vol. 2 No. 3, Autumn 1990.

pleasures that await women.[5] While this article does not enter these debates directly, it suggests the importance of studying sexuality in context. Sexual behavior, of course, is neither inherently dangerous for women nor inherently pleasurable. Like other socially constructed behaviors, its meanings derive from the specific contexts in which it is enacted. This study examines how and why a particular group of women adopted the freer modes of sexual expression that characterized the early twentieth-century sexual revolution. It finds that neither sexual danger nor sensual pleasure provides adequate explanation.

Most major American cities today have a distinct geography of sexuality. That is, one could locate districts and neighborhoods known as the institutional and social centers of various sexual subcultures. Take San Francisco, for example, a city known for its celebration of sexual variety. Upscale heterosexual singles live in apartments and frequent bars in the Marina district. Downscale heterosexual men go to porn shops and massage parlors in the Tenderloin. Female prostitutes sell their services at the corner of 18th and Mission Streets; male prostitutes sell their services on Polk Street. Gay men congregate in the Castro district, and lesbians meet in the bars and coffeehouses in the vicinity of Valencia Street.

A lesser-known geography of sexuality also existed in early twentieth-century American cities. In 1916, sociologist Robert Park identified what he called "moral regions" of the city, "detached milieus in which vagrant and suppressed impulses, passions, and ideals emancipate themselves from the dominant moral order."[6] Park was not the first to define neighborhoods by sexual behavior. At the end of the nineteenth century, a few urban investigators identified the furnished-room districts, or areas where rooming houses abounded, as "moral regions" of sorts, distinct neighborhoods where unconventional sexual behavior flourished.[7] By the early twentieth century, reformers defined a "furnished-room problem" more precisely. In 1906, for example, in a study of Boston's furnished-room district, Albert Benedict Wolfe lamented the "contamination of young men, the deterioration in the modesty and morality of young women, the existence of actual houses of prostitution in the guise of lodging-houses, the laxity of landladies, the large number of informal unions, the general loosening of moral texture."[8] By the late 1910s and 1920s, more dispassionate sociologists explored "a new code of sex relationships" in the furnished room districts of Chicago.[9] Evidence from newspapers, autobiographies, vice reports, and social surveys also suggests that the furnished-room districts were indeed the centers of sexually unconventional subcultures.[10]

By the end of the nineteenth century, most major American cities had furnished-room districts. These often first appeared in the city center, and, later, as business displaced downtown housing, moved out farther along major transportation lines. The large proportion of adult residents and the small proportion of children distinguished these districts demographically from other neighborhoods of the city. A residential street in a furnished-room district usually resembled others in the city: a typical block would consist of single-family homes, buildings of flats, large tenements, or older mansions. The owners of the buildings, however, converted the interiors into one- or two-room dwellings. They might divide a flat into two or three smaller units or divide a large tenement into an "apartment hotel" with as many as one hundred furnished rooms.

In Chicago, three such districts emerged in the late nineteenth century. On the South Side, the furnished-room district included major portions of the Chicago Black community and also what was, before the 1912 raids, the segregated vice district of the city. On the West Side, the district housed a population of predominantly white service and factory workers. A transient male hobo population congregated on the inner boundaries. On the

North Side, where rents were slightly higher, clerical and sales workers lived in rooming houses alongside white service and manufacturing workers, artists, bohemians, and radicals of all stripes. In the early twentieth century, the North Side district included substantial numbers of Irish and Swedish roomers.[11]

These districts burgeoned in the early 1890s when migrants and visitors streamed to Chicago for the World's Columbian Exposition. They continued to grow in the first decades of the twentieth century. By 1923, the Illinois Lodging House Register reported over eighty-five thousand lodgers in about five thousand rooming houses in the three major furnished-room districts. By 1930, residents of the new small unit apartments (with private bathrooms and kitchenettes) joined lodgers in these neighborhoods.[12]

Several distinctive features of the furnished-room districts fostered the development of extramarital sexual relationships. Most obviously, women and men lived together in houses where most people did not live in families. In these neighborhoods, lodgers found numerous opportunities to create social and sexual ties with their peers. Further, the high geographic mobility in the furnished-room districts made informal, transient relationships the norm. One writer went so far as to claim that the entire population of Chicago's North Side furnished-room district changed every four months.[13] This high turnover rate created an atmosphere of anonymity in which lodgers rarely knew their neighbors well. Community pressures to conform to conventional familial roles were weaker than in more settled neighborhoods. And parental authorities were absent. Many rooming-house keepers, eager to keep their tenants, refrained from criticizing or interfering with roomers' sexual behavior.[14] In addition, the predominance of men in the North and West Side districts may have encouraged women to participate in extramarital heterosexual relationships: it would have been easy to meet men and difficult to avoid them.[15]

In any case, the prevalence of prostitution in the furnished-room districts created a climate where open expressions of sexuality were common. In the first decade of the twentieth century, the most prominent vice district of Chicago lay in the South Side furnished-room district. Brothels were tolerated in sections of the West and North Side districts as well.[16] In addition, on the South, West, and North Sides, some keepers of rooming houses and hotels rented rooms by the hour or night to prostitutes and their customers.[17] After the municipal government closed the brothels in the 1910s, social investigators repeatedly found rooming houses and hotels used for prostitution.[18]

In addition to hotels and rooming houses, the "bright-light" centers of the furnished-room districts provided settings in which men and women could socialize. Investors who hoped to profit from the demand by lodgers opened cafeterias, cheap restaurants, tearooms, soft-drink parlors, saloons, dance halls, cabarets, and movie theaters. Residents of the districts turned these institutions into social centers. As one observer noted: "Considerable companionship grows up around these resorts. One is struck by the fact that the same people visit and re-visit the same cabaret time and again."[19]

On the North Side, Clark Street and, on the West Side, Halsted Street were well known for their night life. In 1918, Clark Street alone housed fifty-seven saloons, thirty-six restaurants, and twenty cabarets.[20] On the South Side, the State Street "Stroll" and 35th Street emerged as the "bright-light" centers of the Black community. Dance halls, restaurants, movies, and saloons for Black customers coexisted with "black and tan" cabarets, which offered racially integrated recreation.[21] When young men and women who lived with their parents were out for a night on the town, and when wealthier people went "slumming," they often went to the furnished-room districts of the city.

These areas, it seems, were geographic settings where behavior considered unacceptable elsewhere was accepted matter-of-factly and even encouraged. In residential communities of Chicago, neighbors often stigmatized sexually active unmarried women. For example, Mamie, a young woman who lived with her parents in a working-class neighborhood of Chicago, first encountered problems in 1918 when a policewoman reported her for "unbecoming conduct with sailors." Later, rumor had it that her neighbors talked of signing a petition to expel her from the neighborhood.[22] Contrast Mamie's brief case history with the comment of a student of Chicago's South Side furnished-room district: "It is said that an attractive woman who does not "cash in" is likely to be considered a fool by her neighbors, instead of any stigma being attached to a woman who "hustles" in this neighborhood."[23]

By the early twentieth century, the furnished-room districts of Chicago and other large cities were known as havens for women and men who chose to defy conventions.[24] In addition to migrants and transients, they attracted women and men seeking adventures and a chance to break taboos in a community without parental supervision.[25] Here interested lodgers could enter peer-oriented subcultures that sanctioned extramarital sexual behavior. A 1918 account of Chicago's North Side shows the complex and casual nature of social and sexual relationships:

> [J. and V.] went to the North Clark Street section where they posed as man and wife. They took a couple of furnished rooms, . . . and remained there for two years. Both of them worked, often bringing in as much as $30.00 a week together. They took their meals out and got along very well.
>
> Then two of the girl's sisters came to Chicago to find work and rented rooms next to them. These girls had good intentions but not securing very lucrative positions, they soon learned how to supplement their wages by allowing young men to stay with them.
>
> These girls struck up an acquaintanceship with another girl who used to remain overnight with them now and again when they had been out to a dance or cabaret. J. liked this new girl and as he put it could not "help monkeying with her" and when V. found it out she became extremely jealous and shortly afterwards left him. Her sisters and the other girl followed her.[26]

Other accounts provide additional glimpses of how women formed social networks in the furnished-room districts. In 1911, two women, seventeen and twenty years old, met at a South Side dance hall. The older woman persuaded the younger to room with her on Chicago's North Side. After they moved in together, they made "pick up acquaintances" with men at dance halls and on the street.[27] Around 1913, Myrtle S., who roomed on the North Side, made friends with a woman at the restaurant where she ate her meals. This woman introduced her to a man, Lew W., with whom she spent several evenings drinking beer. Myrtle testified that she lost her virginity when Lew took advantage of her: "one night she lost consciousness after her drink of beer and awoke next morning in the Superior Hotel." Despite this betrayal, she returned to the hotel with Lew on two other occasions. Later, Myrtle met another man at a "chop suey" restaurant.[28]

Some of the social circles that developed in the furnished-room districts were distinguished by unconventional life-styles, sexual preferences, or political leanings. In the North Side district, for example, a subculture of hoboes congregated in and around Washington, or Bughouse, Square. In her autobiography, hobo "Box-Car Bertha" wrote, "Girls and women . . . seemed to keep Chicago as their hobo center. . . . They are centered about the Near North Side, in Bughouse Square, in the cheap roominghouses and light housekeeping establishments, or begged or accepted sleeping space from men or other women there before them." The women hoboes whom Bertha described engaged casually in sexual relationships. One woman, she wrote, had "a group of sweethearts," others lived and traveled with men "to whom by chance or feeling they had attached themselves," and still others engaged in "careless sex relations."[29]

By the 1920s, lesbian communities were also visible.[30] According to blues singer Ma Rainey, a Black bisexual, lesbians frequented State Street, in the South Side rooming-house area. A song she recorded in 1924 included the following among other more sexually suggestive verses:

> Goin' down to spread the news
> State Street women wearing brogan shoes
> Hey, hey, daddy let me shave 'em dry . . .
> There's one thing I don't understand
> Some women walkin' State Street like a man,
> Eeh, hey, hey, daddy let me shave 'em dry.[31]

According to Box-Car Bertha, "several tea shops and bootleg joints on the near-north side . . . catered to lesbians," including many among the Chicago hobo population.[32] Another observer found lesbians in the somewhat less transient population of the North Side furnished-room district's bohemian circles. He, too, noted that homosexual women and men frequented the tearooms of the area and held parties in their rented rooms.[33]

The best-known subcultures of the furnished-room districts were undoubtedly the bohemian circles of artists, intellectuals, and political radicals. In Chicago, Black bohemians congregated in the South Side furnished-room district, and some white socialists and anarchists lived in the West Side district.[34] But the heart of Chicago's bohemia was on the North Side, where one study found that, "Most of the experimenters are young women."[35] In most respects, Chicago's bohemians resembled those of New York's Greenwich Village. Chicago, though, had its own distinctive institutions. The informal Dill Pickle Club provided a setting for lectures, plays, and jazz performances.[36] And the anarchist tradition of soapbox oratory in Washington Square provided a public forum for unconventional speakers.[37]

As in the other subcultures of the furnished-room districts, women who joined bohemian circles expected and often wanted to participate in extramarital sexual activities. For example, Natalie Feinberg, the daughter of working-class Jewish immigrants from Russia, expressed an interest in "free love" before she moved away from her family in Chicago, changed her name to Jean Farway, and "frequented the various gathering places" of the bohemians. According to the sociologist who described her, "She won the reputation of wishing to become a great courtesan."[38]

Historians remember the furnished-room districts primarily for the articulate, "emanci-pated" middle- and upper-class members of bohemian communities. Such people are often seen as vanguards of modern sexuality, women and men who experimented freely with new sexual possibilities learned from Sigmund Freud, Havelock Ellis, and other sexolo-gists.[39] The geography of sexuality helps place the bohemians in context, as only one subculture among several. The furnished-room districts housed working-class women and men as well as middle- and upper-class bohemians. There is no evidence that the "revolu-tion" of a bohemian and middle-class vanguard trickled down to the working class. In fact, it seems more likely that bohemians learned of new sexual possibilities not only from the "highbrow" writings of the sexologists but also from the "lowbrow" behavior of their less intellectual neighbors.[40]

Furnished-room districts not only provide a setting for observing various participants in the sexual revolution; they also reveal the social and economic context that shaped changing sexual mores. Heterosexual relationships in the furnished-room districts included "dating," "pickups," "occasional prostitution," and "temporary alliances." Like professional prostitution and marriage, these were economic as well as sexual and social relationships. Because employers paid self-supporting women wages intended for dependent daughters and wives, many women lodgers worked in low-paying jobs that barely covered subsistence.[41] In an era of rapidly expanding urban consumerism, these women were forced into scrimping and self-denial. By entering sexual relationships, however, they could supplement their wages with free evenings on the town, free meals in restaurants, and sometimes gifts and money. In many cases, the new sexual expression allowed women to participate in the urban consumer economy.

Even in the most innocent dating, men customarily paid for the evening's entertainment. Women, in return, gave limited sexual favors, ranging from charming companionship to sexual intercourse. A 1910 federal report on self-supporting working women stressed the economic value of dating:

> Even if most of the girls do not spend money for amusements, it is no proof that they go without them. Many of the girls have "gentlemen friends" who take them out. "Sure I go out all the time, but it doesn't cost me anything; my gentleman friend takes me," was the type of remark again and again. . . . [G]irls who have "steadies" are regarded as fortunate indeed.[42]

A woman need not have a "steady," however, to benefit from dating. In "pickups," "women met male strangers casually on street corners or in dance halls, restaurants, and saloons. They then spent the evening and sometimes the night with them. In Chicago women attempted to pick men up in dance halls and on the streets. In 1911, for example, a vice investigator in a North Side dance hall encountered several women who asked him "to take them to shows or dances."[43] Ten years later, in the heart of the South Side furnished-room district, Gladys B., an eighteen-year-old Black woman, "went cabareting" with James P. after she picked him up at the corner of 35th and State Streets. They ended the evening in a hotel room.[44] Presumably James paid for the cabarets, the room, and perhaps for Gladys' sexual services. (In this case, he paid more than he bargained for: this mundane pickup became newsworthy only when Gladys escaped in the night with James' wad of money.)

In the early twentieth century, young, working-class women who lived in their parents' homes also participated avidly in the new urban dating patterns promoted by commercialized recreation facilities.[45] For many women lodgers in the furnished-room districts, though, the necessity of supporting themselves on low wages added a special imperative. Lodgers themselves were highly aware of the economic benefits of dating. A waitress said bluntly, "If I did not have a man, I could not get along on my wages."[46] And a taxi dancer stated, "It's a shame a girl can't go straight and have a good time but I've got to get what I get by 'Sex Appeal'."[47] One male resident of the North Side furnished-room district concluded: "[women] draw on their sex as I would on my bank account to pay for the kind of clothes they want to wear, the kind of shows they want to see."[48]

"Occasional prostitution" resembled dates and pickups, but here the economic benefits were even clearer. Women asked men explicitly to pay for the sexual services provided them. These women worked in stores, offices, factories, and restaurants by day and sold their sexual services on occasional nights for extra money. While many women who dated probably exchanged only companionship, flirtation, and petting for evenings on the town, the smaller group of occasional prostitutes stepped up the barter, exchanging sexual intercourse for gifts or money. These women did not necessarily see themselves as prostitutes; they simply played the "sex game" for somewhat higher stakes.[49]

Without watchful relatives nearby, women lodgers could engage in occasional prostitution more easily than working women who lived in their parents' homes. Accordingly, vice investigators in search of occasional prostitutes went to the furnished-room districts to find them. In a North Clark Street saloon, for example, a vice investigator met two women who lived in the North Side district. They worked in a department store for $5.50 per week. "They can't live on this," he reported, "so they 'hustle' on the side." In another case, the investigator reported on a nineteen-year-old migrant from Indiana who worked in a South Side restaurant: "Is not a regular prostitute, goes with men for presents or money. Is poorly paid at restaurant."[50]

With pickups and occasional prostitution, the relationships usually lasted for one night only. In a "temporary alliance," a woman maintained a sexual relationship with one or more "steady" boyfriends, or lived with a man as if she were married. Amy, a twenty-year-old woman who lived on the South Side, worked as a cashier in a downtown restaurant until she met a streetcar conductor who agreed to "keep" her. He had given her a new fall hat and promised to buy her a new winter coat. Amy occasionally went out with other men "to get a little more spending money."[51] Another account of temporary alliances in furnished rooms stated tersely, "For ten months, Marion lived a hand-to-mouth existence, dependent upon the bounty of several men with whom she became intimate."[52] Such alliances were motivated in some cases by "genuine and lasting regard," but in others, "the motive of the girl is simply to find support, and that of the man gratification."[53]

From the limited evidence available, it seems that economic concerns also shaped sexual relationships in the lesbian subculture. Some lesbians depended on men, earning money as prostitutes. Others found higher-paid or wealthier women to support them. For example, in the North Side district in the late 90s, one lesbian, Beatrice, was supported by her lover Peggy, who earned money as a prostitute. Peggy had "had a dozen sweethearts, all lesbian" and had "always supported them." On at least one occasion, some lesbians also adopted a form of gold digging or, more precisely, veiled blackmail. After a North Side party, some lesbians persuaded the wealthier women attending to pay for their companionship: "The lesbians would get their names and addresses and borrow money by saying, 'I met you at . . . [the] party.' " Some lesbians also prostituted themselves to other women.[54]

This emphasis on the economics of sexual relationships should not obscure the sexual dangers or the sensual pleasures that many women experienced. On the one hand, some women lodgers encountered undeniable sexual violence, including rape, and others found themselves betrayed by false promises of marriage.[55] On the other hand, many women clearly enjoyed real relationships in which they found physical pleasure, excitement, and companionship. As one woman stated bluntly, "Frankly, I like intercourse!"[56] Further, the economic dependency in these relationships was not necessarily more exploitative or more oppressive than wives' traditional dependence on husbands or daughters' traditional dependence on fathers.

The financial imperatives are important, though, for they point to a neglected economics of the early twentieth-century sexual revolution. The exchange of sexual services for monetary support moved beyond the marital bedroom and the brothel and into a variety of intermediate forms including dating, pickups, temporary alliances, and occasional prostitution. The sexual revolution was not simply, as one historian has written, "prosperity's child."[57] In the furnished-room districts, economic need shaped sexual experimentation. "What I get is mine. And what they have is mine, too, if I am smart enough to get it," said one self-avowed gold digger, ". . . I'll show you how to take their socks away."[58] "Modern" sexual expression, then, not only threatened women with danger and promised women pleasure; in a variety of forms, it also offered financial reward.

Contemporary feminists who debate the meanings of sexual expression are not the first to define sexuality in terms of danger and pleasure. In the past century and a half, middle-class American commentators, including feminists, have often invested sexual expression with one of two opposing meanings. On the one side, many observers, especially in the nineteenth century, have described nonmarital sexual expression with various stories of danger, disease, decay, and disorder. On the other side, some observers, primarily in the twentieth century, have represented nonmarital sexuality with stories of pleasure, vitality, adventure, and freedom.[59] In both constructions, sexuality was stripped of its everyday contexts and inflated with symbolic meaning. In the early twentieth century, the bourgeois attack on Victorian "sexual repression" marked a self-conscious shift in the dominant discourse from sex as danger to sex as pleasure.[60] As this conception of sexuality changed, the woman lodger played a central symbolic role. Through local and national media, a variety of commentators constructed conflicting interpretations of her unconventional sexual behavior. Reformers, manufacturers of popular culture, and sociologists dominated these debates.[61]

At the turn of the century, reformers presented the woman lodger as a symbol of endangered womanhood. In the organized boarding-home movement, the antiprostitution crusade, and the campaign to improve women's wages, reformers wrote with genuine concern for poorly paid, self-supporting women. With a sense of female solidarity, they deplored the economic hardships faced by the wage-earning woman, but they reserved their greatest distress for her sexual vulnerability.[62] Like most middle-class Americans of their day, they lamented female sexual expression outside marriage, but, unlike many, they rarely blamed the women involved.[63] Following earlier female moral reformers, they read sexual expression as a symbol of female victimization in an increasingly ruthless urban world.[64] These writers portrayed sexually active women lodgers as passive, pure, and impoverished orphans duped, forced, or unduly tempted by scheming men. While they occasionally criticized women lodgers for their "tendency . . . to drift away from sweet and tender home influences," most often they condemned the "vampires" who trapped "poor, innocent little girls."[65] The reformers acknowledged that a woman lodger might enjoy the companionship she found in the furnished-room districts, but "the glare of cheap entertainments and the dangers of the street," they feared, would overpower her.[66] In short, they adopted a stereotype of female weakness and innocence that absolved the woman lodger of responsibility for her own sexual behavior.

The reformers appointed themselves as maternal protectors. In Chicago and other cities, they opened subsidized boarding homes—"veritable virtue-saving stations"—to lure women from commercial rooming houses.[67] By the 1920s, Chicago had over sixty organized homes managed by Protestant, Catholic, Jewish, African American, German, Swedish, Polish, and Norwegian-Danish middle-class women for working women of their own religious, racial, and ethnic background.[68] They established room registries that placed women lodgers with private families in residential neighborhoods. They campaigned for minimum-wage laws because they saw the low pay of women lodgers as a major cause of "immorality." To "outwit evil agents, who would deceive the innocent," they placed charity workers in train stations and police matrons in public dance halls.[69] While they helped women in need of support, they obscured the actions that women lodgers took on their own behalf, and elaborated instead an image of weak-willed women in sexual danger. In fact, well after most reformers had acknowledged the competence of working women living with parents, the "woman adrift," who lodged on her own, bereft of protectors, remained a symbol of endangered womanhood.

A variant of the reformers' discourse reached into popular culture. In the late nineteenth and early twentieth centuries, popular "working girl" romance novels, printed as cheap books or story-paper serials, adopted the image of orphaned, innocent, and imperiled "women adrift."[70] In these melodramatic stories, young, virtuous, native-born, white women endured countless agonies when alone in the city, and eventually married wealthy men. Here the language of female victimization reached its most sensational. Listen to Charlotte M. Stanley, the author of "Violet, the Beautiful Street Singer; or, an Ill-Starred Betrothal": "Oh, what cruel fate was it that had so suddenly altered the safe, smooth current of her young existence and cast her adrift in this frightful seething whirlpool of vice and crime?"[71] In romance novels, the gravest dangers a woman faced were threats to her sexual purity, generally seduction, abduction, procurement, and forced marriage. The queen of romance was probably Laura Jean Libbey, the author of over sixty novels in the late nineteenth century. Libbey created especially naive heroines who endured unusually frequent and frightening perils. In the opening chapters of one Libbey novel, beautiful Junie, an "artless little country lass" alone in the city, spurns the advances of a cad, follows a seemingly kind male stranger "without the least thought of her danger," and falls in the clutches of the cruel Squire Granger, who abducts her.[72] Like the reformers, Libbey publicized the perils of life in the city and sympathized with the lone woman whom she portrayed as passive, innocent, and endangered.

The reformers and romance novelists, though, were fighting a losing battle, in part because the women they hoped to help belied the image of helpless victim. In fact, some women lodgers themselves directly attacked the reformers who treated them as pathetic orphans. In 1890, several "self-respecting and self-supporting" residents of the Chicago YWCA home wrote a blistering letter to a local newspaper:

> The idea seems to be in circulation that we who are unfortunate enough to be independent, are a collection of ignorant, weak-minded young persons, who have never had any advantages, educational or otherwise, and that we are brought here where we will be philanthropically cared for, and the cold winds tempered for us. A matron is provided, and a committee of women who happen to be blessed with a few thousand dollars worth of aristocracy, has charge of the matron.

The women also complained of the furniture and food, and referred to themselves as the "victims of the home."[73]

By the early twentieth century, some reformers began to reassess their outlook. Managers of organized homes and other astute observers could not help note that many women lodgers were competent, assertive, and sexual by choice. Using the fact-gathering methods of the new social science, social investigators met face to face with women who pursued sexual companionship actively.[74] While reformers' concern for the woman lodger continued, they dropped their earlier emphasis on her passivity. Some also began to recognize that wage-earning women had sexual feelings. In 1910, one Chicago antivice crusader, who described self-supporting women as innocent, naive, and unprotected, admitted that "every normal girl or woman has primal instincts just as strong as her brother's."[75] Jane Addams, Louise DeKoven Bowen, and other Chicago reformers rejected earlier images of female passionlessness, and instead blamed overwork, commercialized recreation, and alcohol for bringing out natural yearnings and instincts that they preferred to see repressed.

As reformers observed women lodgers, their fears about sexual danger diminished. They saw that women in the furnished-room districts lived in a world that attached less stigma to female sexual activity. Reformers interviewed women who had given up their chastity without an inkling that they had chosen "a fate worse than death," and they saw that a wage-earning woman might choose to sell or exchange sexual services without ruining her life. "The fact that she has earned money in this way does not stamp her as 'lost' ... " a 1911 federal report stated. "And the ease with which, in a large city, a woman may conceal a fall of this kind, if she desires to do so, also helps make a return to virtuous ways easy ... occasional prostitution holds its place in their minds as a possible resource, extreme, to be sure, but not in the least unthinkable."[76]

By the mid-1910s the observations of reformers coincided with broader changes in middle-class thought and behavior. In the years before World War I, increasing numbers of middle-class urban women adopted the more open sexual behavior of women in the furnished-room districts. This change in middle-class morals further undermined the older image of female innocence and passionlessness, and challenged reformers' fear that female sexual behavior denoted female victimization. After World War I, in a conservative political climate, reformers suffered further from declining public interest and from government repression and indifference.[77]

Ultimately reformers' views on sexuality could not compete with a newer discourse emerging in popular culture. In the early twentieth century, cabaret reviews and movies attracted audiences by using the woman lodger as an appealing symbol of urban vitality, allure, and adventure. In these newer texts, the woman lodger, headstrong and openly sexual, lived freely in a fast-paced urban environment. In the earlier romance novels, unfortunate circumstance—poverty or death in the family—forced timid young women, soon to be victims, from happy parental homes. Or foolish young women left home and soon regretted it. In the newer scenarios, opportunistic women, like Theodore Dreiser's Sister Carrie, chafed at the restriction of domesticity and the dullness of the small town. As one writer concluded, "[The city] is her frontier and in it she is the pioneer."[78] In the earlier discourse, the woman victim's suffering signified the high cost of urban living; in the newer, the woman pioneer's pleasure pointed to its rewards.[79]

By the first decade of the twentieth century, the new image reached national audiences in stories of chorus girls who achieved stardom and married wealth.[80] These women strutted boldly across the stage, displaying their bodies and commanding attention through their sexual appeal. They won wide publicity in 1908 when the trial of Henry Thaw made sensational headlines and reached larger audiences still in a movie, *The Great Trial.* Thaw had murdered architect Stanford White in a jealous rage over White's affair with Thaw's wife, Evelyn Nesbit. During the trial, Nesbit, a former chorus girl, told how wealthy men entertained, courted, and, in her case, married the sexually attractive dancers in cabarets and theaters. As she recounted her rise from the life of a hardworking chorus girl to a life of luxury and extravagance, she announced the material and romantic pleasures available to the sexual, independent wage-earning woman.[81]

In the following years, as the number of movie theaters expanded rapidly and the size of audiences grew, the woman lodger emerged as a central character in the new feature films. At first, in early "white slavery" films, the heroines faced threats to their virtue and sometimes eventual victimization. At the same time, though, in early serials—*The Perils of Pauline* and *The Hazards of Helen*—the heroines, independent from family, were "healthy, robust, and self-reliant." They met available and often moneyed men whom they attracted with their native allure. While they encountered dangers and difficulties, they also enjoyed a daring nightlife in cabarets and dance halls, as well as the high life in opulent villas.[82] By 1915, Mary Pickford, the first major movie queen, was portraying women lodgers who flirted, danced, wore revealing clothing, and enjoyed energetic activities. Always chaste, she combined the purity of the Victorian orphan with the healthy sexuality of the chorus girl. Her exuberance and spunk attracted male suitors, leading to upwardly mobile marriages.[83]

By the 1920s, the movies drew clear connections between independence from family, on the one side, and female sexuality and material gain, on the other. In some movies, the woman lodger was the stock heroine in rags-to-riches stories. *At the Stage Door* typifies the formula: "Mary leaves home to become a chorus girl in New York, and soon she achieves stardom. Philip Pierce, a young millionaire, is attracted to her."[84] As the heterosexual activities and assertive behavior of the independent working woman became more explicit in movies, so did the threat she posed to men.[85] The woman lodger as "gold digger" appeared at least as early as 1915. In *The Model: Or, Women and Wine*, wealthy young Dick Seymour pursues an independent working woman, Marcelle Rigadont, an artist's model. Marcelle, as one character advises her, wants to "play him for a sucker . . . and bleed him for every cent he's got." She finally confesses, "I never loved you—It was only your money I was after."[86] In the 1920s, at least thirty-four films included the "gold digger" with her "aggressive use of sexual attraction."[87]

Although unrecorded forms of entertainment are harder to document, it seems that similar themes appeared in chorus revues at cabarets and theaters. In the opening number of the Midnight Frolic's "Just Girls," staged in 1915, "girls from 24 cities and one small home town came to New York for adventure, men, and a new life." "Sally," a Ziegfield revue staged in 1920, told the story of a working-class orphan who climbed from "the chorus to theatrical fame, wealthy admirers, and riches."[88] By the 1920s, variations on these plot lines appeared repeatedly in new monthly pulp romance magazines such as *True Story* and *True Romances*.

In the late 1910s and 1920s, the new image of women lodgers achieved academic legitimacy in writings by urban sociologists at the University of Chicago. Inaugurated in the 1890s, the academic discipline of sociology moved quickly from an antiurban moralism to more rarefied theoretical questions. In Chicago, sociologists, predominantly male, undertook intensive investigations of urban life, using census data, interviews, and observation. They showed little interest in women or in sexuality per se; rather, they used sexual behavior in the furnished-room districts to bolster their theories of "urban evolution." Sociologist Robert Park wrote, "Everywhere the old order is passing, but the new has not arrived. . . . This is particularly true of the so-called rooming-house area."[89] In this view, the furnished-room districts became the vanguard of urban change, characterized by "disorganization" and "individuation." As these terms suggest, some sociologists saw the furnished-room districts as disturbed, soulless, and lonely.[90] For the most part, though, sociologists had a stronger faith in progress. As the vanguard of urban evolution, the furnished-room districts were, in a sense, the most advanced development of urban life. With a marked ambivalence, sociologists described the residents of furnished-room districts as "emancipated" as frequently as they called them "disorganized."[91]

For sociologists, the woman of the furnished-room districts represented the freedom of urban life. As in movies, the urban woman was seen as released from the "monotony of settled family life" in the small town.[92] From a barren, restricted existence, she moved to "a section of the old frontier transplanted to the heart of the modern city" where, competent and self-seeking, she could pursue her individual desires and ambitions.[93] One particularly blunt sociology student stated, "The homeless woman of modern cities is the emancipated woman."[94] In areas where earlier reformers had discovered sexual exploitation of unprotected women, sociologists now found willing participation. Of dating for money, Frances Donovan wrote, "She is not . . . exploited nor driven into it, but goes with her eyes wide open."[95] Another sociologist asserted, more dubiously, that prostitutes were no longer exploited by procurers or pimps.[96] And, as in the movies, some sociologists depicted the sexually "emancipated" woman as a potential threat to men: "In the quest after the material equipment of life . . . the girl becomes not only an individualist but also—frankly—an opportunist."[97] In earlier reformers' portrayals, men exploited naive women; in sociologists' constructions, women lodgers, like Hollywood "gold diggers," took advantage of men.

No less than earlier images of the innocent victim, new images of the urban pioneer reduced women in furnished-room districts to stereotypes, exaggerating certain features of their lives and neglecting others. Sociologists used self-supporting women as examples of uniquely urban personalities, emphasizing those traits that supported their theories of urban evolution: individualism, unconventional sexual behavior, transient personal relationships, and freedom from social control. Their commitment to the idea of evolutionary progress encouraged them to view these urban features as at least somewhat positive and liberating. At the same time, sociologists undermined reform efforts to alleviate female poverty. They downplayed the negative constraints of low wages, sexual harassment, and economic dependence, and thus suggested that reformers were superfluous, even meddling.

Reformers and romance novelists portrayed women lodgers as passive, passionless, and imperiled, while sociologists, moviemakers, and pulp magazine writers depicted them as active, pleasure-seeking, and opportunistic. The changing discourse marks the waning influence of moral reformers and the rise to cultural power of manufacturers of mass entertainment and academic social scientists. It also highlights a larger change in the portrayal of women in America, from the Victorian angel to the sexy starlet. In the late nineteenth century, women lodgers, alone in the city, epitomized the purity of endangered womanhood; in the early twentieth century, the same women were among the first "respectable" women broadcast as happy sexual objects.

The sexual behavior of women in turn-of-the-century furnished-room districts is not an isolated episode in women's history. Other U.S. historians also describe sexual expression among women lodgers. From at least the 1830s to at least the 1960s, women who supported themselves in the cities sometimes explored the boundaries of sexual convention.[98] In other societies as well, "modern" sexual behavior has reflected in part the changing social and economic relations wrought by wage work and urbanization. The migration of labor to cities has removed some women workers from traditional forms of community or family control and protection, thus opening possibilities for both sexual experimentation and sexual coercion. At the same time, the worldwide gender gap in wages has sustained women's dependence on others, especially on men. In new urban, industrial settings, the traditional exchange of services for support has taken on extrafamilial, sexual forms, including temporary alliances and occasional prostitution.[99]

In turn-of-the-century Chicago, the volume of migrants led entrepreneurs to invest in restaurants, furnished-rooming houses, theaters, cabarets, and dance halls. Women and men flocked to and shaped these institutions, creating new peer-oriented subcultures in specific urban districts. In these districts, most women could not afford to view sex solely in terms of sexual danger or sensual pleasure, for sexual expression was also tied inextricably to various forms of economic reward. In this context, the sexual revolution was, most likely, sometimes oppressive, sometimes exciting, and often an exchange.

The history of women lodgers in the furnished-room districts is important, for these women helped shape the modern sexual expression that other women later adopted. In the furnished-room districts themselves, middle- and upper-class bohemian "new women" observed the unconventional behavior of working-class women who were their neighbors. Middle-class pleasure-seekers and "flappers" may have copied the blueprints of "sexy" behavior they observed while slumming in the districts' cabarets and dance halls. And moviegoers and magazine readers learned from the portrayals of women lodgers, as films, cabarets, and romance magazines used the sexuality of independent wage-earning women to attract and titillate viewers and readers. In these ways, turn-of-the-century women lodgers helped chart the modern American sexual terrain.

Notes

1. This article is reprinted in slightly revised form from Nancy Hewitt, ed., *Women, Families, and Communities: Readings in American History* (Scott Foresman, New York, 1990). It draws on material in Joanne Meyerowitz, *Women Adrift: Independent Wage-Earners in Chicago, 1880–1930* (University of Chicago Press, Chicago, 1988). Thanks to Estelle Freedman, Zane Miller, Leila Rupp, Christina Simmons, and Bruce Tucker for their helpful comments. And special thanks to Nancy Hewitt who helped sustain this article through its strange publication history.

2. Frederick Lewis Allen, *Only Yesterday* (Harper and Brothers, New York, 1931); William Leuchtenburg, *The Perils of Prosperity, 1914–1932* (University of Chicago Press, Chicago, 1958); James McGovern, "The American Woman's Pre-World War I Freedom in Manners and Morals," *Journal of American History*, (September 1968); Gerald E. Critoph, "The Flapper and Her Critics," in Carol V. R. George, ed., *"Remember the Ladies": New Perspectives on Women in American History* (Syracuse University Press, Syracuse, 1975). See also Paula S. Fass, *The Damned and the Beautiful: American Youth in the 1920s* (Oxford University Press, New York, 1977); John Modell, "Dating Becomes the Way of American Youth," in Leslie Page Moch and Gary Stark, eds., *Essays on the Family and Historical Change* (Texas A & M University Press, College Station, Texas, 1983).

3. June Sochen, *The New Woman: Feminism in Greenwich Village, 1910–1920* (Quadrangle Books, New York, 1972); Elaine Showalter, ed., *These Modern Women: Autobiographical Essays from the Twenties* (The Feminist Press, Old Westbury, New York, 1978); Carroll Smith-Rosenberg, "The New Woman as Androgyne: Social Disorder and Gender Crisis, 1870–1936," in Smith-Rosenberg, ed., *Disorderly Conduct: Visions of Gender in Victorian America* (Alfred A. Knopf, New York, 1985); Esther Newton, "The Mythic Mannish Lesbian: Radclyffe Hall and the New Woman," *Signs: Journal of Women in Culture and Society*, (Summer 1984); Ellen Carol DuBois and Linda Gordon, "Seeking Ecstasy on the Battlefield: Danger and Pleasure in Nineteenth-Century Feminist Sexual Thought," in Carole S. Vance, ed., *Pleasure and Danger: Exploring Female Sexuality* (Routledge and Kegan Paul, Boston, 1984); Leila J. Rupp, "Feminism and the Sexual Revolution in the Early Twentieth Century: The Case of Doris Stevens," *Feminist Studies*, (Summer 1989). For an earlier account, see Henry F. May, *The End of American Innocence: A Study of the First Years of Our Own Time, 1912–1917* (Alfred A. Knopf, New York, 1986).

4. Kathy Peiss, *Cheap Amusements: Working Women and Leisure in Turn-of-the-Century New York* (Temple University Press, Philadelphia, 1986); for the nineteenth century, see Christine Stansell, *City of Women: Sex and Class in New York, 1789–1860* (Alfred A. Knopf, New York, 1986).

5. For a summary of these debates, see "Forum: The Feminist Sexuality Debates," *Signs: Journal of Woman in Culture and Society*, (Autumn 1984); Carole S. Vance, "Pleasure and Danger: Toward a Politics of Sexuality," in Vance, ed., *Pleasure and Danger*.

6. Robert Park, "The City: Suggestions for the Investigation of Human Behavior in Urban Environment," in Richard Sennett, ed., *Classic Essays on the Culture of Cities* (Meredith Corporation, New York, 1969), pp. 128–129.

7. Robert Woods, ed., *The City Wilderness: A Settlement Study* (Houghton Mifflin Boston, 1898); see especially William I. Cole's article, "Criminal Tendencies," pp. 166–169.

8. Albert Benedict Wolfe, *The Lodging House Problem in Boston* (Houghton, Mifflin and Co., Boston, 1906), p. 171. See also Franklin Kline Fretz, *The Furnished Room Problem in Philadelphia* (published Ph.D. thesis, University of Pennsylvania, 1912); S. P. Breckinridge and Edith Abbott, "Chicago's Housing Problems: Families in Furnished Rooms," *American Journal of Sociology*, (November 1910), pp. 289–308.

9. Harvey Warren Zorbaugh, *Gold Coast and Slum: A Sociological Study of Chicago's Near North Side* (University of Chicago Press, Chicago, 1929), p. 153.

10. To avoid being unduly influenced by the sociologists' discourse, I have accepted the sociologists' conclusions only when I could corroborate them with evidence from other sources, such as newspapers accounts, reports of reformers, and memoirs.

11. In the 1910s, the South Side district ran from 16th to 33rd Streets and from Clark Street to Prairie Avenue; the West Side district ran from Washington to Harrison Streets and from Ashland Boulevard to Halsted

Street; the North Side district went from Division Street to the Chicago River and from Wells to Rush Streets. Edith Abbott, *The Tenements of Chicago, 1908–1935* (University of Chicago Press, Chicago, 1936).

Information on the population of the furnished room districts was derived from sociological studies and from the Federal Manuscript Census, (Meyerowitz's) samples of Chicago "women adrift," 1880 and 1910, and the tract-by-tract census data found in Ernest W. Burgess and Charles Newcomb, eds., *Census Data of the City of Chicago, 1920* University of Chicago Press, Chicago, 1931), and Ernest W. Burgess and Charles Newcomb, eds. *Census Data of the City of Chicago, 1930* (University of Chicago Press, Chicago, 1933).

12. On growth of districts, see Abbott, *Tenements of Chicago*, ch. 10; also Kimball Young, "Sociological Study of a Disintegrated Neighborhood" (M.A. thesis, University of Chicago, 1918). On the number of lodgers, see T. W. Allison, "Population Movement in Chicago," *Journal of Social Forces*, (May 1924), pp. 529–533. The lodging houses included in the 1923 register were only those with over 10 roomers.

13. Zorbaugh, *Gold Coast and Slum*, p. 72.

14. See Wolfe, *The Lodging Problem in Boston;* for examples of permissive landladies in Chicago, see Louise DeKoven Bowen, *The Straight Girl on the Crooked Path: A True Story* (Juvenile Protective Association of Chicago, Chicago, 1916).

15. In 1920, the sex ratio in the North Side district was 1.4, and in the West Side district, 1.6. In 1930, the ratio in the North Side district was 1.3 and in the West Side district 2.0. In both years, the South Side district, which was more dispersed over a larger area, had a sex ratio of 1.0. These sex ratios were derived from tract-by-tract census data found Burgess and Newcomb, eds., *Census Data of the City of Chicago, 1920* and *Census Data of the City of Chicago, 1930.*

16. Vice Commission of Chicago, *The Social Evil in Chicago: A Study of Existing Conditions with Recommendations by the Vice Commission of Chicago* (Vice Commission of Chicago, Chicago, 1911), pp 87–91.

17. *The Social Evil in Chicago*, pp. 73, 71, 92–94.

18. "Investigation of Commercialized Prostitution," December 1922, Juvenile Protective Association of Chicago Papers 5:92, University of Illinois at Chicago Manuscript Collections.

19. Young, "Sociological Study of a Disintegrated Neighborhood," p. 52.

20. Young, "Sociological Study of a Disintegrated Neighborhood," p. 42; Abbott, *The Tenements of Chicago*, p. 322.

21. James R. Grossman, *Land of Hope: Chicago, Black Southerners, and the Great Migration* (University of Chicago Press, Chicago, 1989), p. 117; E. Franklin Frazier, *The Negro Family in Chicago* (University of Chicago Press, Chicago, 1932), p. 103. See also Carroll Binder, "Negro Active in Business World," Chicago *Daily News*, (5 August 1927); Junius B. Wood, *The Negro in Chicago*, reprint of articles in Chicago *Daily News*, (11–27 December 1916), p. 25.

22. Reckless, "The Natural History of Vice Areas," p. 381.

23. E. H. Wilson, "Chicago Families in Furnished Rooms" (M.A. thesis, University of Chicago, 1929), p. 100.

24. See Young, "Sociological Study of a Disintegrated Neighborhood," p. 54; also Zorbaugh, *Gold Coast and Slum*. As early as 1898, Frederick Bushee suggested that "The lodging houses themselves [in Boston's South End district] are the homes of the queer and questionable of every shade," in Woods, ed., *The City Wilderness*, p. 50.

25. See, for example, Walter C. Reckless, *Vice in Chicago* (University of Chicago Press, Chicago, 1933), pp. 53–54. I use Claude Fischer's definition of subcultures: "social worlds . . . inhabited by persons who share relatively distinctive traits (like ethnicity or occupation), who tend to interact especially with one another, and who manifest a relatively distinct set of beliefs and behaviors." Claude S. Fischer, *The Urban Experience* (Harcourt, Brace, Jovanovich, New York, 1976), p. 36.

26. Young, "Sociological Study of a Disintegrated Neighborhood," p. 79.

27. Case record from Chicago Vice Study File, cited in Walter C. Reckless, *Vice in Chicago*, pp. 53, 54.

28. *Chicago Examiner* (12 April 1913).

29. Box-Car Bertha as told to Dr. Ben L. Reitman, *Sister of the Road: The Autobiography of Box-Car Bertha* (Macauley, New York, 1937), pp. 68, 70, 62, 29.

30. There is some evidence of a lesbian community among prostitutes in Paris as early as the 1880s, and also evidence suggesting that some lesbians in New York participated in the male homosexual subculture there by the 1890s. In general, though, American lesbian communities were not visible until the 1920s, perhaps because the majority of women had fewer opportunities than men to leave family life. Moreover, romantic attachments between women were not usually labeled deviant in America until the early twentieth century. Middle- and upper-class women who lived together as couples in "Boston marriages," for example, were not segregated as outcasts from heterosexual family and friends. On early male homosexual subcultures in American cities, see Jonathan Katz, ed. *Gay American History: Lesbians and Gay Men in the U.S.A.* (Avon Books, New York, 1976), pp. 61–81; John D'Emilio, "Capitalism and Gay Identity," in Ann Snitow, Christine Stansell, and Sharon Thompson, eds, *Powers of Desire: The Politics of Sexuality* (Monthly Review Press, New

York, 1983) and George Chauncey, Jr., "Christian Brotherhood or Sexual Perversion? Sexual Boundaries in the World War One Era," *Journal of Social History*, (Winter 1985). On lesbian prostitutes in Paris and on turn-of-the-century tolerance for lesbianism, see Lillian Faderman, *Surpassing the Love of Men: Romantic Friendship and Love Between Women from the Renaissance to the Present* (William Morrow and Co., New York, 1981), pp. 282, 298.

31. Paul Oliver, *Screening the Blues: Aspects of the Blues Tradition* (Cassell and Co., London, 1968), pp. 225, 226.

32. Box-Car Bertha, *Sister of the Road*, p. 65.

33. "A nurse told me of being called on night duty in an apartment in the 'village' and of being entertained every night by the girls in the apartment across the well, some of whom would put on men's evening clothes, make love to the others, and eventually carry them off in their arms into the bedrooms." Zorbaugh, *Gold Coast and Slum*, p. 100.

34. Frazier, *The Negro Family in Chicago*, p. 103; interview with Eulalia B., conducted by author, 16 October 1980.

35. Zorbaugh, *Gold Coast and Slum*, p. 91.

36. "Dill Pickle Club," in Vivien Palmer, "Documents of History of the Lower North Side," vol. 3, part 2, document 52, Chicago Historical Society.

37. Zorbaugh, *Gold Coast and Slum*, pp. 114–115.

38. Walter Reckless, "The Natural History of Vice Areas in Chicago" (Ph.D. thesis, University of Chicago, 1925), pp. 374, 375. For a similar rejection of social background, see the story of Christina Stranski (a.k.a. DeLoris Glenn) in Paul G. Cressey, *The Taxi-Dance Hall: A Sociological Study in Commercialized Recreation and City Life* (University of Chicago Press, Chicago, 1932), p. 56.

39. On bohemians as a vanguard of sex radicalism, see May, *The End of American Innocence*.

40. A few other historians have suggested that working-class women were pioneers in changing sexual mores. See, for example, Nathan G. Hale, Jr., *Freud and the Americans: The Beginnings of Psychoanalysis in the United States, 1876–1917* (Oxford University Press, New York, 1971), p. 477; Lewis A. Erenberg, *Steppin' Out: New York Nightlife and the Transformation of American Culture, 1890–1930* (Greenwood Press, Westport, Connecticut, 1981); Daniel Scott Smith, "The Dating of the American Sexual Revolution: Evidence and Interpretation," in Michael Gordon, ed., *The American Family in Social-Historical Perspective* (St. Martin's Press, New York, 1973).

41. On women's wages, see Leslie Woodcock Tentler, *Wage-Earning Women: Industrial Work and Family Life in the United States, 1900–1930* (Oxford University Press, New York, 1979).

42. Charles P. Neill, *Wage-Earning Women in Stores and Factories*, vol. 5, *Report on Condition of Woman and Child Wage-Earners in the United States* (Government Printing Office, Washington, D.C., 1910), p. 75.

43. *The Social Evil in Chicago*, p. 186.

44. Chicago *Defender*, (20 August 1921).

45. See Kathy Peiss, " 'Charity Girls' and City Pleasures: Historical Notes on Working-Class Sexuality, 1880–1920," in Snitow, ed., *Powers of Desire*.

46. Louise DeKoven Bowen, *The Girl Employed in Hotels and Restaurants* (Juvenile Protective Association of Chicago, Chicago, 1912).

47. "Alma N.Z———r, "Paul Cressey notes, c.1926, p. 5, Ernest Burgess Papers 129:6, University of Chicago Manuscript Collections.

48. Zorbaugh, *Gold Coast and Slum*, p. 86.

49. Frances Donovan, *The Woman Who Waits* (Arno Press, New York, 1974, originally 1920), pp. 211–220.

50. *The Social Evil in Chicago*, p. 133, 95.

51. *Ibid.*, p. 188.

52. Ruth Shonle Cavan, *Suicide*, (University of Chicago Press, Chicago, 1928), p. 206.

53. Wolfe, *The Lodging House Problem in Boston*, p. 142. In these accounts of heterosexual relationships, most of the women lodgers seem to be under 30 years of age. Older women lodgers were probably somewhat less attractive to the predominantly young male suitors. They also seemed to tire of the nightlife, preferring the more stable support and companionship sometimes provided in marriage. In fact, most women lodgers in Chicago did eventually marry. For a revealing interview with an older woman, see Anderson, "Life History of a Rooming House Keeper," c.1925, Ernest Burgess Papers 127:2, University of Chicago Manuscript Collections.

54. Box-Car Bertha, *Sister of the Road*, pp. 223, 66, 69, 288. This limited evidence of dependent relationships is corroborated by other evidence that early twentieth-century working-class lesbians often adopted somewhat traditional gender roles, with one partner assuming a masculine role. See Katz, *Gay American History*, pp. 383–390. See also Joan Nestle, "The Fem Question," in Vance, ed., *Pleasure and Danger* and Elizabeth Lapovsky Kennedy and Madeline Davis, "The Reproduction of Butch-Fem Roles: A Social Constructionist Approach," in Kathy Peiss and Christina Simmons, eds., *Passion and Power: Sexuality in History* (Temple University Press, Philadelphia, 1989).

55. See, for example, Louise DeKoven Bowen, *A Study of Bastardy Cases* (Juvenile Protective Association, Chicago, 1914).

56. Lillian S.W———n," p. 18, Paul Cressey Notes, Ernest Burgess Papers 129:6, University of Chicago Manuscript Collections.

57. Kenneth Yellis, "Prosperity's Child: Some Thoughts on the Flapper," *American Quarterly*, (Spring 1969).

58. *Chicago Daily Times*, (31 January 1930).

59. I'm not suggesting that the contemporary feminist sexuality debates replicate the earlier discourse, only that contemporary debates are a new, different, and interesting variant of older associations. On sex as danger, see Caroll Smith-Rosenberg, "Sex as Symbol in Victorian Purity: An Ethnohistorical Analysis of Jacksonian America," in John Demos and Sarane Spence Boocock, eds., *Turning Points: Historical and Sociological Essays on the Family* (University of Chicago Press, Chicago, 1978); Paul Boyer, *Urban Masses and Moral Order in America, 1820–1920* (Harvard University Press, Cambridge, Massachusetts, 1978); on sex as pleasure, see Paul Robinson, *The Modernization of Sex: Havelock Ellis, Alfred Kinsey, William Masters and Virginia Johnson* (Harper and Row, New York, 1976). For a general history of the changing dominant discourses on sexuality, see John D'Emilio and Estelle Freedman, *Intimate Matters: A History of Sexuality in America* (Harper and Row, New York, 1988). On late nineteenth- and early twentieth-century feminist variants of the shift from sex as danger to sex as pleasure, see DuBois and Gordon, "Seeking Ecstasy on the Battlefield," in Vance, ed., *Pleasure and Danger*. For formulations in Britain, see Judith Walkowitz, *Prostitution and Victorian Society: Women, Class, and the State* (Cambridge University Press, Cambridge, 1980); Susan Kingsley Kent, *Sex and Suffrage in Britain, 1860–1914* (Princeton University Press, Princeton, 1987); Frank Mort, *Dangerous Sexualities: Medico-Moral Politics in England Since 1830* (Routledge and Kegan Paul, London, 1987). In general, representations of sex as vitality, pleasure, adventure, and freedom have not been studied as closely by historians as representations of sex as danger, disease, decay, and disorder.

60. On the attack on Victorian "sexual repression," see Christina Simmons, "Modern Sexuality and the Myth of Victorian Repression," in Peiss and Simmons, eds., *Passion and Power*. See also Michel Foucault, *The History of Sexuality*, vol. 1 (Vintage Books, New York, 1980).

61. For psychiatrists' contribution to these public discussions, see Elizabeth Lunbeck, " 'A New Generation of Women': Progressive Psychiatrists and the Hypersexual Woman," *Feminist Studies*, (Fall 1987).

62. On late nineteenth-century reformers' interest in working women, see Mari Jo Buhle, "The Nineteenth-Century Woman's Movement: Perspectives on Women's Labor in Industrializing America," unpublished paper, Bunting Institute of Radcliffe College, 1979.

63. For a more detailed discussion of the reformers' position, see Meyerowitz, *Women Adrift*, ch. 3. For a similar combination of feminist sympathy and middle-class moralism in the early to mid-nineteenth century, see Stansell, *City of Women*, pp. 70–74.

64. On earlier reformers, see especially Mary P. Ryan, "The Power of Women's Networks: A Case Study of Female Moral Reform in Antebellum America," *Feminist Studies*, (Spring 1979); Carroll Smith-Rosenberg, "Beauty, the Beast, and the Militant Woman: A Case Study of Sex Roles and Social Stress in Jacksonian America," in Nancy F. Cott and Elizabeth H. Pleck, eds. *A Heritage of Her Own: Toward a New Social History of American Women* (Simon and Schuster, New York, 1979).

65. Women's Christian Association of Chicago, *Fifth Annual Report* (1881), p. 12; Charles Bryon Chrysler, *White Slavery* (n.p., Chicago, 1909), p. 13.

66. Annie Marion MacLean, "Homes for Working Women in Large Cities," *Charities Review*, (July 1899), p. 228.

67. MacLean, "Homes for Working Women," p. 228.

68. Josephine J. Taylor, "Study of YWCA Room Registry," unpublished paper, 1928, Ernest Burgess Papers 138:9, University of Chicago Manuscript Collections; Essie Mae Davidson, "Organized Boarding Homes for Self-Supporting Women in the City of Chicago" (M.A. thesis, University of Chicago, 1914); Ann Elizabeth Trotter, *Housing Non-Family Women in Chicago: A Survey* (Chicago Community Trust, Chicago, c. 1921).

69. YWCA of Chicago, *18th Annual Report* (1894), p. 33. On the national Travelers' Aid movement, see Lynn Y. Weiner, *From Working Girl to Working Mother: The Female Labor Force in the United States, 1820–1980* (University of North Carolina Press, Chapel Hill, 1985). On reforming the dance halls, see Elisabeth I. Perry, " 'The General Motherhood of the Commonwealth': Dance Hall Reform in the Progressive Era," *American Quarterly*, (Winter 1985).

70. For a brief description of the "working girl" novel, see Cathy N. and Arnold E. Davidson, "Carrie's Sisters: The Popular Prototypes for Dreiser's Heroine," *Modern Fiction Studies*, (Autumn 1977).

71. Charlotte M. Stanley, "Violet, the Beautiful Street Singer; or An Ill-Starred Betrothal," *The New York Family Story Paper*, 5 September 1908. See also T. W. Hanshew, "Alone in New York: A Thrilling Portrayal of the Dangers and Pitfalls of the Metropolis," *The New York Family Story Paper*, 30 April 1887.

72. Laura Jean Libbey, *Junie's Love Test* (George Munro, New York, 1883), p. 66.

73. *Sunday Inter Ocean*, (16 November 1890). The women who lived in this YWCA home tended to be white,

native-born women who held more middle-class jobs in offices and stores. Black women and immigrant women also expressed displeasure with forms of housing that invaded their privacy and reduced their initiative. See Meyerowitz, *Women Adrift*, ch. 4.

74. See, for example, Louise DeKoven Bowen, *Safeguards of City Youth at Work and at Play* (Macmillan, New York, 1914), p. 23; Clara E. Laughlin, *The Work-A-Day Girl* (Arno Press, New York, 1974, originally 1913), p. 51.

75. Leona Prall Groetzinger, *The City's Perils* (n.p., c.1910), p. 110.

76. Mary Conyngton, *Relation Between Occupation and Criminality of Women*, vol. 15, *Report on Condition of Woman and Child Wage-Earners in the United States* (Government Printing Office, Washington, D.C., 1911), pp. 102–103.

77. Other factors undermining the reformers' image of passive, endangered women gers included the WWI venereal disease campaign, the decline in the number of women immigrants arriving from Europe, and a slight rise in women's real wages in the 1920s. As these changes occurred, most reformers lost interest in women lodgers; those who maintained their interest lost the power to shape cultural images.

78. Donovan, *The Woman Who Waits*, p. 9.

79. For a more detailed discussion of this newer image, see Meyerowitz, *Women Adrift*, ch. 6.

80. Lois Banner, *American Beauty* (University of Chicago Press, Chicago, 1983), pp. 180–84.

81. On the Thaw trial, see Lewis Erenberg, *Steppin' Out*, p. 53; Lary May, *Screening Out the Past: The Birth of Mass Culture and the Motion Picture Industry* (Oxford University Press, New York, 1980), pp. 34, 43.

82. May, *Screening Out the Past*, pp. 108.

83. *Ibid.*, pp. 119, 142, 143. For a discussion of "heterosocial culture" in earlier films, see Peiss, *Cheap Amusements*, pp. 153–58.

84. Kenneth Munden, ed., *The American Film Institute Catalog, Feature Films, 1921–1929* (R. R. Bowker Co., New York, 1971), p. 29.

85. The 1920s stories which represented sexual expression as pleasurable and adventurous often had a subtext of potential danger (especially to men), as the "gold digger" movies attest.

86. "The Model; Or, Women and Wine," *Picture-Play Weekly*, (12 June 1915), pp. 12–16.

87. Mary P. Ryan, "The Projection of a New Womanhood: The Movie Moderns in the 1920s," in Jean E. Friedman and William G. Shade, eds., *Our American Sisters: Women in American Life and Thought*, 2nd edn., (Allyn and Bacon, Inc., Boston, 1976), p. 376.

88. Erenberg, *Steppin' Out*, pp. 210, 223.

89. Robert E. Park, "Introduction," in Zorbaugh, *Gold Coast and Slum*, p. viii.

90. Ruth Shonle Cavan, *Suicide* 81. Robert E. L. Faris, *Chicago Sociology, 1920–1932* (University of Chicago Press, Midway Reprint, Chicago, 1979, originally 1967), p. 35.

91. See, for examples, Ernest Mowrer, *Family Disorganization: An Introduction to Sociological Analysis* (University of Chicago Press, Chicago, 1927), p. 111; Faris, *Chicago Sociology*, p. 79.

92. Walter C. Reckless, "The Natural History of Vice Areas in Chicago," p. 211.

93. Zorbaugh, *The Gold Coast and the Slum*, p. 199.

94. Reckless, "The Natural History of Vice Areas," p. 209.

95. Donovan, *The Woman Who Waits*, p. 220.

96. W. I. Thomas, *The Unadjusted Girl, With Cases and Standpoint for Behavioral Analysis* (Little, Brown, and Co., Boston, 1923), p. 150.

97. Paul G. Cressey, *The Taxi-Dance Hall*, p. 47.

98. Stansell, *City of Women*, pp. 83–101, 171–192; Linda Gordon, *Woman's Body, Woman's Right: A Social History of Birth Control in America* (Penguin Books, New York, 1977), pp. 203–204; Barbara Ehrenreich, Elizabeth Hess, and Gloria Jacobs, *Re-Making Love: The Feminization of Sex* (Anchor Press/Doubleday, Garden City, New York, 1986), pp. 39–42, 54–62.

99. There is a recent and growing literature on contemporary women migrants in Third World nations. For a good introduction, see the special issue of *International Migration Review*, (Winter 1984) and Annette Fuentes and Barbara Ehrenreich, *Women in the Global Factory* (South End Press, Boston, 1983). For additional references to sexuality, see also Ilsa Schuster, "Marginal Lives: Conflict and Contradiction in the Position of Female Traders in Lusaka, Zambia," in Edna G. Bay, ed., *Women and Work in Africa* (Westview Press, Boulder, 1982) and Sharon Stichter, *Migrant Laborers* (Cambridge University Press, Cambridge, 1985). On capitalism, urbanization, migration, and sexuality in Europe, see the now-classic accounts of the eighteenth century in Edward Shorter, "Illegitimacy, Sexual Revolution and Social Change in Modern Europe," *Journal of Interdisciplinary History*, (Autumn 1971) and Louise A. Tilly, Joan W. Scott, and Miriam Cohen, "Women's Work and Fertility Patterns," *Journal of Interdisciplinary History*, (Winter 1976). Shorter emphasizes the sexual pleasure pursued by women, while Tilly, Scott, and Cohen underscore women's sexual vulnerability. For a more recent account, see Nicholas Rogers, "Carnal Knowledge: Illegitimacy in Eighteenth-Century Westminster," *Journal of Social History*, (Winter 1989).

13

The Uprising of the Thirty Thousand

Meredith Tax

A lull in the struggle,
A truce in the fight,
The whirr of machines
And the dearly brought right,
Just to labor for bread,
Just to work and be fed.

For this we have marched
Through the snow-covered street,
Have borne our dead comrades
While muffled drums beat.
For this we have fought,
For this boon dearly-bought.

We measure our gain
By the price we have paid.
Call the victory great
As the struggle we made;
For we struggled to grow,
And we won. And we know.

Ah, we know, as we hear
Once again the loud hum
Of machines all in motion,
Commanding we come
In our newly-won powers,
To this labor of ours.

Together we suffered
The weary weeks past,
Together we won and
Together at last
As we learn our own might,
We will win the great fight.
                              Mary O'Reilly
                              "After the Strike"[1]

Reprinted with permission of the author from Meredith Tax, *The Rising of the Women* (New York & London: Monthly Review Press, 1980).

On November 22, 1909, the tiny waistmakers' local of the International Ladies Garment Workers Union called a general strike of all the shirtwaist makers in New York. The strike became known as the Uprising of the Thirty Thousand (or, depending on the source, the Twenty Thousand) because that was the approximate number of strikers who rose spontaneously in answer to the union's call. The strike also came to be thought of as the "woman's movement strike," because under the leadership of the Women's Trade Union League, the whole of the women's movement, from the society matrons of the Colony Club to the socialists of the Lower East Side, joined with the strikers, most of whom were teenage girls.

Local 25 of the ILGWU, the shirtwaist makers' local, had rented Cooper Union for the November 22 meeting. Three shirtwaist shops were already on strike—Leiserson's, Rosen Brothers, and the Triangle Waist Company—but union leaders had no idea how many workers outside those three shops would come to the meeting. The crowd began to pour into the hall hours early. People waited patiently, talking mainly in Yiddish. Most of them were teenage girls, nervous and excited at being at their first union meeting. The *Jewish Daily Forward*, a Yiddish socialist paper, reported some of their conversations: "What if a general strike is decided upon? Who knows how many will join in it? Who can tell how long it may last? And what if a motion for a strike will be voted down? When will there be another chance to improve the conditions? Are we to suffer forever?"[2] Soon there was not even standing room in the hall, and the union officers began to scurry around, renting other halls in the neighborhood for the overflow, until Beethoven Hall, the Manhattan Lyceum, and Astoria Hall were full and people were still lining up in the street.

In Cooper Union, the speakers arranged themselves on the platform. Unlike the audience, they were well dressed, prosperous, respectable looking, and almost all men. Chief among them was Samuel Gompers of the AFL; it was considered a coup to have gotten him to come. Then there were other union officials, socialist lawyers, and Mary Dreier of the Women's Trade Union League—an endless series of speakers, none of whom worked in the shirtwaist shops. The speeches went on for two hours. Finally, as the union has described the events in its *Souvenir History of the Strike*:

> Then came the dramatic climax of the evening. At Cooper Union, down in the body of the hall, arose a working girl, a striker, an unknown, who asked the chairman for the privilege of the floor. Many grumbling dissensions came her way, some excitement was visible on the platform, but the chairman held that as she was a striker she had as good a right there as himself, so Clara Lemlich made her way to the platform. She was a striker from the Leiserson shop; she had been assaulted while picketing; she knew from actual experience what her sisters were up against, and that they were tired of oratory; she knew they had come there for business; she knew they were seething with discontent and hatred of their bondage; that they were pulsing with sympathy for their fellow workers and that each was ready, aye, anxious, for the charge into the camp of the common oppressor, and, as has been well said, after an impromptu phillipic in Yiddish, eloquent even to American ears, she put the motion for a general strike, and was unanimously endorsed.
>
> The chairman then cried, "Do you mean faith? Will you take the old Jewish oath?" and up came two thousand right hands, with the prayer, "If I turn traitor to the cause I now pledge, may this hand wither from the arm I now raise," and thus started this historic general strike, probably the greatest struggle for unionism among women the world has ever seen.[3]

Clara Lemlich may have been an "unknown" to the public, but to the Lower East Side labor movement she was already a heroine: she was a founder of the shirtwaist local, had led the walkout in Leiserson's shop, and had been beaten by hired thugs while picketing. During the two weeks she was laid up, her health was the subject of almost daily comment in the *New York Call.*

Clara Lemlich had had to fight since the day she was born in the Ukraine in 1888, so she had become good at it. Her father was an Orthodox Jewish scholar, and as tradition dictated, he did not permit his daughter to learn to read; in particular the study of Russian (as opposed to Yiddish) was forbidden. Clara Lemlich would sneak down to the village to make buttonholes for the little tailor shops, and use the money she earned to pay students to teach her to read Russian. Although her father burned her Russian books, she had already become literate by the time her family fled Russia in 1903—she had even read revolutionary literature.[4]

Clara Lemlich wanted to go to school in New York, but instead she had to go to work to help support her family. She got work in a shirtwaist shop, making the elaborate blouses that were virtually the uniform of working women in this period. She continued to study, however, and hoped to become a doctor. She would work for eleven hours, then walk to the public library, stopping only for a glass of milk, and study until it closed. She would not get home for supper until late at night. She recalled later: "All week long I wouldn't see the daylight. I remember once, when things were slow, they let us out in the middle of the day. 'What!' I said, 'Are all the people on strike? I had never realized that there were so many out during the daytime."[5]

In 1906 Clara Lemlich joined a group of shirtwaist makers who went to the office of the *Jewish Daily Forward* to find out how to form a union. She was one of seven young women and six young men who formed Local 25, at a time when the ILGWU was small and its members mainly comprised of male cloakmakers. She was by then a skilled draper, still saving money to go to school, but she seemed unable to work in a shop without trying to organize it. Even when she vowed to be a "good girl," she found herself talking union two days later. She began to look for work in the smaller shops where she could have more influence. The oppressive conditions in the trade kept her at the boiling point: the forewoman following a girl to the toilet, nagging her to hurry; the new girls being cheated of their pay; the fines; the charges for electricity and needles and thread; the "mistakes" in the pay envelopes that were so difficult to get fixed; the time clock that was fixed so that lunch was twenty minutes short, or was set back an hour so the workers didn't know that they were working overtime.[6]

In 1907 she took part in her first strike, a ten-week strike against speedup in the small shop where she worked at the time. At one of the union meetings she heard strikers arguing about Gompers and his "pure-and-simple trade unionism." She asked one of them what that meant. He asked her to go for a walk, and they walked forty blocks while he gave her her first lesson in Marxism:

> He started with a bottle of milk—how it was made, who made the money from it at every stage of its production. Not only did the boss take the profits, he said, but not a drop of milk did you drink unless he allowed you to. It was funny, you know, because I'd been saying things like that to the girls before. But now I understood it better and I began to use it more often—only with shirtwaists.[7]

She also began taking classes in Marxist theory at the Socialist Party's school, the Rand School.

In 1908 the young women at the Gotham shop, where Clara Lemlich was then working, struck in sympathy when the boss fired men to make room for women, because he could pay them less. The strike failed and the other girls went back to work, but Clara Lemlich stayed outside the shop, distributing boycott leaflets until the boss finally had her arrested for disorderly conduct. This was the first of many such arrests.

She then went to work at Leiserson's. The male operators, who were in a different ILGWU local than the shirtwaist makers, planned a strike without even informing the other workers, many of whom were women. When Clara Lemlich found out about it, she went to their strike meeting and, asking for the floor, gave them a piece of her mind, telling them that if they went out on strike alone they would surely lose, but if they organized, they could take the whole shop with them. They followed her advice and the whole factory struck. Clara Lemlich's leadership was decisive in keeping the Leiserson strike together—certainly the boss thought so, for during the eleven weeks the picket line was outside the shop she was singled out numerous times by his hired thugs. In one battle six of her ribs were broken. In later years she recalled her fearlessness: "Ah—then I had fire in my mouth. . . . What did I know about trade unionism? Audacity—that was all I had—audacity!"[8]

Her militance was an appropriate response to conditions in the shirtwaist industry, which was notorious for irregularity, inefficiency, and severe exploitation. The industry was divided into hundreds of tiny shops, each employing between five and twenty girls and each competing with the others to drive down labor costs and sell more cheaply, but it was dominated by a group of larger shops, each employing between two hundred and three hundred workers. The work was seasonal; all of the workers toiled long hours during the busy season—fifty-six a week with overtime—but were laid off when things were slow. Wages varied greatly, depending on whether the workers were paid on a time or a piecework basis, and whether they were skilled or not. All workers were charged for the equipment they used, and many firms made a twenty percent profit on electricity for sewing machines, and twenty-five percent on needles and thread. Workers were docked an hour's pay for being five minutes late, and were made to pay for a whole length of cloth if they spoiled a corner.[9]

Within the work force there were further inequities, the greatest of which was between women and men. Most of the men were either skilled workers (cutters and pressers)[10] or subcontractors who were given orders by larger bosses and hired female assistants to do the work. The union believed that the subcontracting system had grown up as a result of the disorganization and lack of management skills that characterized the entire garment industry:

> It must first be understood that an overwhelming majority of the proprietors in this trade were laborers themselves but a few years ago, and not being endowed with a superabundance of executive ability or knowledge of modern business methods, especially those belonging to organization, they soon found the details of their business growing too numerous to be handled by personal attention.
>
> Therefore, instead of dividing their factory into departments and employing a foreman to supervise the same, they called in a workman and made a contract with him for a period of three or four months, agreeing to pay him so much a week for so much work turned out. They rented or loaned him the machines and encouraged him to get as much work out of a young girl for as little money as he could, and actually classified it as the speeding up system. By this means the girls' bosses were doubled, the inspection and criticism of her work was doubled, the incessant supervision of her every move was doubled, and two profits to one were taken out of her labor.[11]

In the shirtwaist industry, subcontracting went on inside large factories, where the subcontractors were responsible to a foreman. A subcontractor could pay his female employees what he pleased and usually paid them as little as possible. He had two categories of employees; women who had two or three years of experience and "learners" or apprentices. The union estimated that thirty-seven percent of the workers in the shirtwaist trade were learners, young girls who made from $2.50 to four dollars a week, while about fifty percent were more experienced young women, who made an average of nine dollars a week. The skilled male workers, on the other hand, who made up the remaining fifteen percent of the workforce, made fifteen dollars to twenty-three dollars a week.[12]

It was the skilled male workers and the subcontractors who led the ILGWU and Local 25, and who negotiated for it during the strike. The women workers, the most exploited section of the work force, had their bosses as their union leaders.[13] It is only in the light of this basic structural fact that developments in the union, which became increasingly clear in the years after the strike, can be understood: the absence of women from leadership or even staff positions; the leadership's tendency to look at the women workers as so many cattle who needed a strong leader to look up to, and their desire to run the union like a business. This view of the world stemmed from the leadership's position as employers of the other workers, privileged, skilled, and upwardly mobile. Needless to say, their attitude also rose from the male supremacy of the society as a whole, for they held their positions because of their sex—women did not become subcontractors, cutters, or paid union officials.[14]

If the sexual contradiction was built into the structure of the industry, ethnic differences also made uniting the work force difficult. Russian Jews, Italians, and native-born Americans formed fifty-five percent, thirty-five percent, and seven percent respectively of the women in the trade. The men in the industry were mainly Russian Jews. Of those who actually went out on strike, however, seventy percent were Russian Jewish women, twenty percent were Russian Jewish men, six percent were Italian women, and three percent native-born women. The strikers were thus ninety percent Russian Jewish.[15] The Italians were particularly underrepresented among the strikers, partly, no doubt, because very few of them spoke English and none of the union leaders spoke their language. In fact, the union leaders mainly spoke Yiddish. Not only were the Italians and Jews separated by language and cultural barriers, but the Italians were also newcomers to the industry, brought in to undercut the wages of the Jews. The employers consciously used national differences to divide the work force; according to the union, "they placed an Italian girl beside a Jewess, so that they might not understand each other, and then started stories to arouse race prejudice."[16] There were also problems with the native-born American women, who considered themselves superior to the others. They usually earned more, they worked in different shops, further uptown, and they were unwilling to accept the leadership of "foreigners."

Local 25 did not attempt to deal with these ethnic differences. Overwhelmingly Russian Jewish in membership, it made few efforts to reach the Italians and the "American girls." It was small and weak, and its organizing techniques were primitive. Its usual strategy was to wait until there was a spontaneous movement such as a walkout in a shop. The union would quickly go there and try to sign the workers up, and then negotiate with the boss for union recognition. As described by B. Witashkin, secretary of the local in its early days, this method seldom worked:

> Our organizing work we generally carried on in a stereotyped way. We would issue a circular reading somewhat as follows: "Murder! The exploiters, the blood-suckers, the manufacturers. . . . Pay your dues. . . . Down with the capitalists! Hurrah!" The employers would be somewhat frightened and concede the demands of the union. After the demands would be granted, the workers would drop out of the organization. We would thus gain "recognition" and lose the workers.[17]

By 1909 the number of spontaneous actions indicated that conditions were changing and that it might be possible to use different methods. More workers started to seek out and join the union, and then a small strike wave began in the East Side shops. The first of these was a walkout at the Triangle Waist Company in the fall of 1908. Just before the Jewish holidays, a protesting subcontractor announced that he was sick of being a slave driver and was going to quit. As the foreman began to drag him out, he appealed to his fellow workers: "Brothers and sisters, are you going to sit by your machines and see a fellow workman used this way?" That was all it took; they laid down their work and walked out. The strike lasted only three days, for without an organization or benefits, the workers were quickly driven back.[18] The Triangle management then organized a company union or benefit society whose officers were all relatives of the owners. After a few months some of the workers began to realize what a travesty this "union" was and went to Local 25 for advice. They began to hold small meetings in secret.

Another strike at about this time, also initiated by male subcontractors, was at Rosen Brothers. Two hundred workers went out when the boss refused to pay the price the subcontractors demanded. This strike lasted five weeks; the union was called in to negotiate, and the subcontractors won.

A third strike began in September 1909 at Leiserson's, where Clara Lemlich worked. Leiserson had begun to lay off his experienced workers on the pretext that he had no work to give them. They learned that he was sending their work to a cheaper shop he had started downtown and even giving it on the sly to the learners in their own shop. Outraged, one hundred workers walked out. After the walkout Leiserson immediately advertised for scabs. He also hired thugs—"sluggers," as they were called, led by the "notorious Dominick"—to beat up the picketers.

At this time mass picketing, involving large numbers of workers, was not yet common. Instead, a handful of strikers would walk up and down in front of their shops, wearing placards or carrying signs and trying to persuade the scabs not to go in. The union bent over backwards not to be offensive. It issued rules for the picketers, which it hoped would save them from arrest—a vain hope:

Rules for Pickets

Don't walk in groups of more than two or three.

Don't stand in front of the shop; walk up and down the block.

Don't stop the person you wish to talk to; walk alongside of him.

Don't get excited and shout when you are talking.

Don't put your hand on the person you are speaking to. Don't touch his sleeve or button. This may be construed as a "technical assault."

Don't call anyone "scab" or use abusive language of any kind.

Plead, persuade, appeal, but do not threaten.

If a policeman arrests you and you are sure that you have committed no offence, take down his number and give it to your union officers.[19]

These ladylike instructions did not prevent strikers from being enthusiastically set upon by hired thugs, beaten, and then arrested by the police. If a picketer spoke to a scab, she was arrested and charged with assault or intimidation; the scab was then bribed to swear in court that the striker had grabbed or threatened her. Such daily dramas in front of the Leiserson shop had an unforeseen effect, however: increasingly distressed by this treatment of their fellow workers, a second group of workers walked out, including some Italians. This was the first sign of the labor solidarity that was to become such a remarkable element in the general strike; it certainly amazed the employers, who had succeeded in pitting Italians against Jews for so long.

Three days later, on September 28, 1909, the workers at the nearby Triangle Waist Company, a number of whom had secretly joined Local 25, also went on strike. Management called a meeting of the company union, and one boss quoted the company union's bylaws, which said "no member of this society shall belong to any other organization." He went on to say that those who had joined Local 25 had broken this rule and unless they immediately left the union they would lose their jobs. After the workers held a union meeting and decided to fight back, the company locked them out and advertised for scabs.[20]

The Triangle management went one better on Louis Leiserson's tactic of hiring local gangsters: they hired Broadway prostitutes and their pimps, guessing that the strikers would feel more intimidated that way. The prostitutes beat up ten women in one day.[21] After a striker was beaten, she was charged with assault and fined. On October 14, for instance, twenty-eight strikers were arrested and fined three dollars each—a week's wage for a learner. The drain on the union treasury began to be insupportable, while the male workers lost heart and stopped picketing, not wanting to be beaten up. The women carried on, suffering assault and arrest day after day.[22] Clara Lemlich was arrested seventeen times.

On October 19, a group of policemen broke into the union hall during a meeting. They stared at those present, so they would be able to recognize them on the picket line, then left. Such open intimidation was the last straw: some of the women strikers went to the Women's Trade Union League and appealed for protection against false arrest. The League "allies" began to come down to the picket line to observe and then act as witnesses in court.

Union officials were meanwhile trying to work out a strategy for dealing with the police repression and the unwillingness of the companies to negotiate. The strikers were getting no publicity, except in the Jewish and radical press, and the manufacturers found it easy to subcontract their work to other shops. The union still had few members, little money for strike benefits, and no influence. Nevertheless, it seemed to the officers of Local 25 that the industry was beginning to move and that it might pay to take a chance, particularly since they had neither a treasury nor prestige to risk. So they decided to call a general strike of the whole shirtwaist industry and hope it would catch on. The ILGWU, their own International, thought the plan had no chance of working. Most trade unionists agreed.

Once the members of the Local 25's executive board had decided to call the strike, they had to convince the rest of the union's one hundred members. They called a general meeting on October 21, and used a "strategic ruse": various executive board members and Leiserson strikers sat scattered around the hall and described the dreadful conditions in the trade as if they were representing different shops. They then called for a general strike.[23] They swung the meeting, and the next day the *New York Call* carried the banner headline "25,000 Waist Makers Declare for Strike!" By the day after, the *Call* had realized this joyful news did not correspond to reality and printed a bewildered retraction: "For reasons which the union leaders refuse to divulge, the time for calling the big strike will be kept secret until the blow is ready to fall upon the bosses who are backing up Louis Leiserson . . . and The Triangle Waist Company."[24]

The executive board waited to see how the workers would respond to their call. In the next four weeks, before the general strike was finally declared, about two thousand workers joined the union. Meanwhile, on November 4 the strike got the necessary publicity boost. Mary Dreier, president of the New York Women's Trade Union League (WTUL), socialite, and resident of Beekman Place, was arrested while observing police brutality on the picket line. As the *New York Call* reported the incident:

Mary Dreier . . . was covered with insults and arrested without cause yesterday while doing picket duty in the strike of the Ladies' Waistmakers against the Triangle Waist Company. . . . A member of the Triangle firm heard her speak to one of the girls as she came from work and in the presence of an officer he turned on Miss Dreier and shouted: "You are a liar. You are a dirty liar." Miss Dreier turned to the officer and said, "You heard the language that man addressed to me. Am I not entitled to your protection?" The officer replied, "How do I know you are not a dirty liar?"[25]

She was arrested, then discharged by the judge, who apologized for having mistaken her for a working girl. But the publicity given the arrest was crucial in arousing the interest of the press and the public in both the strike and police brutality, and the union used the occasion to intensify its shop propaganda. When it called a mass meeting for November 22 at Cooper Union, the response was overwhelming. Fifteen thousand workers, mostly young girls, walked out on their jobs the morning after the Cooper Union meeting. By nightfall there were twenty-five thousand on strike, and more joined in the next few days. Only a handful had been union members before the strike, and no one had expected such a huge response—seventy-five percent of the workers in the trade were out on strike.

Most of the women who had been at the meeting and voted to strike went to work the next morning excited but uncertain what they were supposed to do. What happened in Natalya Urosova's shop is typical of the kind of chain reaction that took place:

"But I did not know how many workers in my shop had taken that oath at the meeting. I could not tell how many would go on strike in our factory the next day," said Natalya afterward. "When we came back the next morning to the factory, though, no one went to the dressing-room. We all sat at the machines with our hats and coats beside us, ready to leave. The foreman had no work for us when we got there. But, just as always, he did not tell when there would be any, or if there would be any at all that day. And there was whispering and talking softly all around the room among the machines: 'Shall we wait like this?' 'There is a general strike.' 'Who will get up first?' 'It would be better to be the last to get up, and then the company might remember it of you afterward, and do well for you.' But I told them," observed Natalya with a little shrug, " 'What difference does it make which one is first and which one is last?' Well, so we stayed whispering, and no one knowing what the other would do, not making up our minds for two hours. Then I started to get up." Her lips trembled. "And just at the same minute all—we all got up together, in one second. No one after the other; no one before. And when I saw it—that time— oh, it excites me so yet. I can hardly talk about it. So we all stood up, and all walked out together. And already out on the sidewalk in front, the policemen stood with the clubs. One of them said, 'If you don't behave, you'll get this on your head.' And he shook his club at me.

"We hardly knew where to go—what to do next. But one of the American girls, who knew how to telephone, called up the Women's Trade Union League, and they told us all to come to a big hall a few blocks away."[26]

All through the day the girls streamed out of their shops toward Clinton Hall, the union headquarters. The situation was chaotic. The officers of Local 25 were virtually prisoners in their tiny office, hemmed in by hordes of young women trying to join the union. Thousands of strikers milled about in the streets, unable to find their shop meetings— about twenty different halls were in use—or unable to get into them because of the crowds. Some people wandered around without help for a day or two and then went back to work, demoralized.

It was the WTUL that brought order out of this chaos, though the women of the Socialist

Party were of notable service as well. WTUL women did secretarial and organizational work and were responsible for most of the publicity. The strike was run out of twenty halls, each of which had a woman in charge, sometimes a League member, usually a rank-and-file striker. The male staff of Local 25 was not large enough to do this and to give interviews and conduct negotiations as well, and it was due to this weakness that the women were able to run their own strike and to gain experience doing so. It was they who arranged picketing schedules, made reports on scab and police brutality, wrote leaflets, spoke at other unions, visited rich women to raise money, went to court to bail out strikers or act as witnesses, kept track of the shops that settled, gave out strike benefits to needy workers, organized new women into the union, kept up spirits, and persuaded people not to go back to work.

Local 25 had called a general strike in order to organize the whole industry at one time. This approach put it somewhere between the traditional AFL unions, with their narrow craft orientation and methods, and the IWW's revolutionary industrial unionism. The ILGWU attempted to combine the spirit of industrial unionism with the tactics of craft organization. Had the union been organized on a purely craft basis, for instance, the cutters and the dressmakers might have struck at different times, thus setting up divisions between the workers in the same shop. It was this approach that Clara Lemlich had had to combat when she organized the strike at Leiserson's. In a normal AFL situation, the cutters would have crossed the dressmakers' picket lines and kept on working, even if the company brought in scabs.

The strikers were thus generally grouped by shop, instead of craft, though there were a few language groupings, and each shop formulated its own particular list of demands. The main issue was "union recognition"—which meant a union shop, where a worker would have to join the union to get a job—but the strikers also demanded the abolition of subcontracting, payment every week instead of every two, a fifty-two hour week, no more than two hours a day overtime, and an end to making the workers pay for materials and electricity.[27]

The workers felt the demand for the union shop was critical. In an industry where most work was paid by the piece, and the piece-rate varied wildly from season to season and shop to shop, the only way to set uniform wages and standards was to have the union do so—the employers would always try to undercut each other by cheating the workers. The union would not have the power to standardize the industry unless it could control the supply of labor through the union shop. Needless to say, this demand was extremely controversial. Despite the fact that an arbitration board was established, made up of two representatives of the manufacturers and two of labor (Morris Hillquit, a socialist lawyer, and John Mitchell of the United Mine Workers, then a vice-president of the AFL), the employers would not even discuss the issue of recognition.

Meanwhile the picketing continued through a bitter winter. As before, the pickets were almost entirely women, because it was assumed that they would be handled less roughly than the men.[28] In many cases the women voluntarily gave up their strike benefits so that the married men could get more. The heroism of these shirtwaist strikers was remarked by all observers:

> In spite of being underfed and often thinly clad, the girls took upon themselves the duty of picketing, believing that the men would be more severely handled. Picketing is a physical and nervous strain under the best conditions, but it is the spirit of martyrdom that sends young girls of their own volition, often insufficiently clad and fed, to patrol the streets in midwinter with the temperature low and with snow on the ground, some days freezing

and some days melting. After two or three hours of such exposure, often ill from the cold, they returned to headquarters, which were held for the majority in rooms dark and unheated, to await further orders.

It takes uncommon courage to endure such physical exposure, but these striking girls underwent as well the nervous strain of imminent arrest, the harsh treatment of the police, insults, threats and even actual assaults from the rough men who stood around the factory doors. During the thirteen weeks over six hundred girls were arrested; thirteen were sentenced to five days in the workhouse and several were detained a week or ten days in the Tombs.[29]

Helen Marot thought it was the spirit of the strikers that distinguished this strike from others. She felt it came from the fact that they were women, turning all the cliches about why women couldn't be organized upside down:

> The same temper displayed in the shirtwaist strike is found in other strikes of women, until we have now a trade-union truism, that "women make the best strikers." Women's economic position furnishes two reasons for their being the best strikers; one is their less permanent attitude toward their trade, and the other their lighter financial burdens. While these economic factors help to make women good strikers, the genius for sacrifice and the ability to sustain, over prolonged periods, response to emotional appeals are also important causes. Working women have been less ready than men to make the initial sacrifice that trade-union membership calls for, but when they reach the point of striking they give themselves as fully and instinctively to the cause as they give themselves in their personal relationships. It is important, therefore, in following the action of the shirtwaist makers, to remember that eighty percent were women.[30]

The judges who sentenced the women showed extreme prejudice against the union, strikers, and women who stepped out of their assigned position in the scheme of things. Judge Cornell sentenced strikers to the workhouse—for the offense of picketing—with the words, "I find the girls guilty. It would be perfectly futile for me to fine them. Some charitable woman would pay their fines or they could get a bond. I am going to commit them to the workhouse under the Cumulative Sentence Act, and there they will have an opportunity of thinking over what they have done."[31] Magistrate Olmstead sentenced another girl with the message: "You are on strike against God and Nature, whose firm law is that man shall earn his bread in the sweat of his brow. You are on strike against God."[32] Those who were sent to the workhouse were often only fifteen or sixteen years old. Two WTUL women went to remonstrate with a judge who had sentenced a sixteen-year-old to thirty days, and "tried to make him understand that she had done nothing wrong. We asked if he realized what it would mean to a girl her age to be locked up with prostitutes, thieves, and narcotics addicts. 'Oh,' he said, 'It will be good for her. It will be a vacation.' "[33]

The police and courts went out of their way to classify the strikers as prostitutes as an attempt to break their spirit. Prostitution was never very far from the lives of working women who tried to live on six dollars a week; they had seen women they had grown up with fall into the life of the streets, and the thin barrier between themselves and that life meant a great deal to them. The memoirs of jailed women strikers and radicals in the early part of the century focus rather obsessively on the prostitutes they met. The police and employers called the strikers whores because they were walking the streets shamelessly; they tried to insult them sexually, as if the way to stop them from rebelling as workers was to put them back in their places as sexual objects. At a meeting protesting police brutality, Yetta Ruth, a seventeen-year-old, described her treatment:

'I acted as spokesman for my shop and when the boss, Beekman, told me that he would not accept the terms of the union, walked out and others followed. He then had me arrested for taking out his workers.

"While I was at the station house, on 20th street, the officers treated me in such a manner that a girl is ashamed to talk about. I am only seventeen and many of the insinuations escaped me. But what I did understand was bad enough. . . .

"The policeman asked me with how many men I was living. One officer told me that I was a dirty Socialist and Anarchist. One man said, 'Here is a nice fellow, Yetta, hook onto him.' One policeman showed me a torn pair of pants and asked me to mend them."

The little girl stopped abruptly and her voice failed her. She was urged again to continue and after some hesitation, said, "One man went to some place and winking to me, said: 'Come along, Yetta!' "[34]

The WTUL and socialist women made police repression one of their main issues. On December 3, the League organized a parade down to the mayor's office, led by three League members and three girls who had been arrested. Ten thousand women strikers marched behind. The mayor received their petition politely and promised to read it, and things went on as before.

Despite the forces arrayed against them, these young strikers fought on in an extraordinary fashion. One sixteen-year-old girl came into the union office covered with bruises from head to foot: her father and brothers had beaten her to try to make her go back to work, but she had refused. She begged Helen Marot to find her another place to stay. Another striker swore she'd go to the workhouse the next time she was arrested rather than have the union use its funds to pay her fine.[35] There were women who were arrested time and time again, who seemed able to do without food or sleep, and who spent all their time at meetings or on the picket line. Several observers noted that the most militant strikers were often the most highly paid and skilled workers, though it would seem that they had least to gain from the strike. These were often the women who, as pacesetters or forewomen, organized the work process in the shop; it was a natural transition for them to become leaders in the strike:

"It's because there are so many girls who can't make decent living wages that we had to strike," said one. "I can work unusually fast, and I make $12 a week during the busy season; but there are many who make only $4." All the strikers take it as a matter of course that they shall feel for each other, and act unselfishly on that feeling, too.[36]

The solidarity the strikers built was their greatest achievement, and it is this that makes their strike memorable. They showed the world that the slow entry of millions of women into the U.S. industrial work force had set new conditions for woman's struggle and had liberated women from the privacy of household drudgery in sufficient numbers for them to be able to act together. A number of observers saw them as a working-class analogue to the suffragists, showing what the women's movement could be like when the issues included survival. With the shirtwaist makers' strike, the U.S. working woman showed what she was made of, and even Samuel Gompers had to acknowledge that here was a force to be reckoned with:

The strike . . . brought to the consciousness of the nation a recognition of certain features looming up in its social development. These are the extent to which women are taking up with industrial life, their consequent tendency to stand together in the struggle to protect their common interests as wage earners, the readiness of people of all classes to approve of trade-union methods in behalf of working women, and the capacity of women as strikers to suffer, to do, and to dare in support of their rights.[37]

Looking back on the strike, Helen Marot of the League thought the general-strike gamble had succeeded only because of the unusual history and temperament of the Russian Jewish workers: "The Russian workers who filled New York factories are ever ready to rebel against the suggestion of oppression and are of all people the most responsive to an idea to which is attached an ideal. The union officers understood this and . . . answered, 'Wait and see,' when their friends urged caution before calling a general strike in an unorganized industry."[38]

The Italian and the native-born American women played a less forceful role in the strike than did their Russian Jewish sisters. Although the Americans came out on strike initially, they went back to work after a few weeks. According to Marot, their working conditions and pay were so much better than the Russians' that they did not strike on their own behalf, but because they felt sorry for the rest:

> They acknowledged no interest in common with the others, but if necessary they were prepared to sacrifice a week or two of work. Unfortunately the sacrifice required of them was greater than they had counted on . . . the Russians failed to be grateful, took for granted a common cause and demanded that all shirtwaist makers, regardless of race or creed, continue the strike until they were recognized by the employers as a part of the union. This difference in attitude and understanding was a heavy strain on the generosity of the American girls. It is believed, however, that the latter would have been equal to what their fellow workers expected, if their meetings had been left to the guidance of American men and women who understood their prejudices. . . . It was the daily, almost hourly, tutelage which the Russian men insisted on the American girls' accepting, rather than the prolongation of the strike beyond the time they had expected, that sent the American girls back as "scabs."[39]

Marot and the other women of the League believed that they could have handled the American-born women better than the union did. Their broadmindedness did not extend to the Italian workers. The patronizing tone of the League's analysis of the Italians is common to reform and even labor descriptions of them during a period when they were the most recent immigrants:

> The Italian girls and women . . . are the oppressed of the race, absolutely under the dominance of the men of their family and heavily shackled by old customs and traditions. They are very much afraid of trade unions and everything that involves danger to their job either through strikers or discharge. In the shirtwaist strike they joined the strike, but failed to hold out, and were used successfully as strike breakers, following the instructions of their priest. This was, however, largely due to the fact that they were mostly Sicilians . . . . They have no collective vision. They follow willingly and devotedly a leader whom they trust and the all-important thing therefore is to get the right kind of leader.[40]

Two years later the Italian women of Lawrence proved that they could be as militant as any other strikers, provided they were organized by people who spoke their language and understood their culture and their special needs as women.

If the American-born and Italian women had an ambiguous relationship to the union during the strike, the Black women in the shirtwaist industry had none at all. They were few in number—the 1900 census put the total number of Black working women in New

York at 16,114, and ninety percent of these were domestic workers.[41] Black women were by and large kept out of the factories, and only 803 were listed as dressmakers in New York. Mary White Ovington, a founder of the National Association for the Advancement of Colored People, described the situation of Black women in the garment industry in 1903:

> Colored women have always been known as good sewers, and recently they have studied at their trade in some of the best schools. From 1904 to 1910, the Manhattan Trade School [where Leonora O'Reilly, a member of the NAACP as well as the League, taught sewing] graduated thirty-four girls in dress-making, hand sewing, and novelty making. The public night school on West Forty-Sixth Street . . . has educated hundreds of women in sewing, dressmaking, millinery, and artificial flower-making. . . . Occasionally an employer objects to colored girls, but the Manhattan Trade School repeatedly, in trying to place its graduates, has found that opposition to the Negro has come largely from working girls. Race prejudice has even gone so far as to prevent a colored woman from receiving home work when it entailed her waiting in the same sitting-room with white women. Of course, this is not a universal attitude. In friendly talks with hundreds of New York's white women workers, I have found the majority ready to accept the colored worker. Jewish girls are especially tolerant. They believe that good character and decent manners should count, not color; but an aggressive, combative minority is quite sure that no matter how well-educated or virtuous she may be, no black woman is as good as a white one.[42]

As in many other strike situations, the garment manufacturers made a special effort to keep their few Black workers on during the strike and to recruit other Black women as scabs. This led to a full-scale debate within the Black community: should Black women take jobs as scabs if this was the only way they could break into the industry? Or should they put pressure on the union to enroll them as members, knowing that in the long run their future as workers lay on the side of the labor movement and not the employers?

On January 10, 1910, the *New York Age*, a Black weekly, editorialized on the subject: "Why should Negro working girls pull white working girls' chestnuts out of the fire? The *Age* had been asked to refuse to print advertisements for strikebreakers and to "help induce these colored girls to join the union"; it had not only refused this request but had recruited Black women as ironers for firms that were on strike. The reason: before the strike "Negro girls were not asked to join the union," and it was safe to assume that the union would discriminate against them after the strike, whether they scabbed or not.[43]

The day after the editorial was published, a crisis meeting was called by the Cosmopolitan Club, an organization of Black and white progressives and radicals which Mary White Ovington had helped pull together during her seven years' sociological investigation of the conditions of Afro-American people in New York. The club met in various homes, usually those of Black society leaders in Brooklyn (the Petersons, Mars, Wilbccans) to discuss "various phases of the race question."[44] The meeting was held at the Black community church in Brooklyn on January 21 and passed a historic if little known resolution, which was reprinted in the *New York Call*:

> *Resolved*, That the citizens of Brooklyn in mass meeting assembled, protest and urge the women of color to refrain from acting in the capacity of strikebreakers in the shirtwaist making concerns of New York, because we regard their action as antagonistic to the best interests of labor.
>
> We further urge that, in the event of the successful termination of the strike, organized labor exercise a proper consideration of the claims and demands of the men and women

of color who desire to enter the various trades in the way of employment and the protection of the various labor unions. . . .

Those familiar with negro opinion will feel the significance of this appeal from the leaders of the race. The colored girl is urged, not to enter the market and underbid, accepting any chance to learn a trade, but to refrain from injuring other working women, and whenever possible, to ally herself with the cause of union labor.[45]

If the shirtwaist strikers won their demand for a closed shop, the future of Black workers in the industry would depend on the union's willingness to recruit them. A Brooklyn reader of the *Survey*, a social work magazine, argued that Black women were already excluded from Local 25: "I happened to read your editorial just after I had been talking with a social worker who is much interested in work among the colored people. . . . She told me that colored shirtwaist makers could not get into the union and were likewise not permitted by the union to work in the shops."[46] The Women's Trade League attempted to rebut these accusations of racism within the union, but the numbers cited in their defense are so small as to case doubt upon the question. Margaret Dreier Robins wrote the *Survey* to say that the union did have Black members—*one* in New York and *two* in Philadelphia.[47] And Elizabeth Dutcher, an officer of the New York League, wrote in W.E.B. Du Bois's magazine, the *Horizon*:

In New York, colored girls are not only members of the union, but they have been prominent in the union. One colored girl has been secretary of her shop organization all through the strike and has been very frequently at union headquarters doing responsible work. The editor should also know that meetings were held during the strike at the Fleet Street Methodist Memorial Church (colored) in Brooklyn and the St. Marks Methodist Church in Manhattan and that in both, members of the Ladies' Waist Makers' Union said definitely and publicly that colored girls were not only eligible but welcome to membership.[48]

The Cosmopolitan Club urged that the union make an effort to organize Black workers after the strike, "both for their own protection against the rapacity of their employers, and that they may not be used to take the place of other strikers,"[49] and at its poststrike executive board meeting, the Women's Trade Union League passed a resolution to "offer its services to the National Association for the Protection of Colored Women stating the very great desire of the League to cooperate with them in their efforts to protect the colored women workers through organization."[50] There is no indication that either the League or the union made any further effort.[51] The League does not seem to have actively organized Black women workers until 1919, when their Southern organizer, Mildred Rankin, organized unions of Black teachers and service workers in Virginia, and their first Black organizer, Irene Goins, worked with some success in the Chicago stockyards.[52]

The weaknesses in the work of the ILGWU and the WTUL with Black and Italian workers were only one of the problems they had to confront as the strike wore on. Equally important was the contradiction between those strikers whose shops settled in the early days of the strike and those whose shops held out until the end or never settled at all. Local 25 allowed its member shops to settle and go back to work one by one, like a craft union, rather than holding out for a single settlement, like an industrial one. The shops that settled then took work on a subcontract basis from companies that were still on strike. By November 27, one-third of the strikers had gone back to work. This drastically weakened the economic base of the strike and undermined its collective strength, even though the union treasury benefitted from the dues of those who had gone back to work.[53]

Early in the strike, the biggest employers joined together in an Association of Waist and

Dress Manufacturers which negotiated with the union at the same time as they pledged never to officially recognize it. On December 27, the arbitrators came out with a proposed compromise. The employers said they would "welcome conferences" about contract violations; they would only reinstate former employees "as far as practicable"; and they would not hire new workers until the strikers were back at work. (This clearly left loopholes for blacklisting union militants.) The agreement also stipulated a fifty-two hour week, no discrimination against union members, equal division of work between workers in the slack season, four paid holidays a year, shop negotiations for wages and prices, and an end to making employees pay for equipment.[54] These were substantial concessions, considering conditions in the trade prior to the strike, but they avoided the key question of union recognition. The Association was obdurate in its refusal to agree to this, and the strikers were furious that the union leadership had offered to compromise on this question. When the proposal was explained, " 'Send it back, we will not consider it!' 'We refuse to vote on it!' 'We want recognition of the union!' 'We will go to jail again and win!' and similar exclamations uttered in the highest pitch by 2,000 men and women made further reading impossible."[55]

At this point the united front of workers, AFL, League, suffragists, and women of the Socialist Party that had come together to support the strike began to disintegrate. As Helen Marot noted, the AFL and many of the suffragists deserted the strike because it was becoming too radical.

> An uncompromising attitude is good trade-union tactics up to a certain point, but the shirtwaist makers were violating all traditions. Their refusal to accept anything short of the closed shop indicated to many a state of mind which was as irresponsible as it was reckless. Their position may have been reckless, but it was not irresponsible. Their sometime sympathizers did not realize the endurance of the women or the force of their enthusiasm, but insisted on the twenty to thirty thousand raw recruits becoming sophisticated unionists in thirteen short weeks.[56]

The League and the Socialist Party stuck by the strikers, despite their intransigence. A closer look at the strike support work of the League, the Socialist Party, and the wealthy suffragist "allies" shows how diverse were the elements in this united front, and how unstable was their unity.

The WTUL's list of their activities during the strike shows what an enormous contribution they made:

> (1) We organized a volunteer picket force of allies of 75 League members. This is the first time in our knowledge in the history of trade unions where a volunteer picket corps was organized.
> (2) Organized volunteer legal services, 9 lawyers.
> (3) Furnished bail amounting to $29,000.
> (4) Protested against illegal action on part of police, and interceded for strikers with the City authorities.
> (5) Organized shops.
> (6) Organized parade of 10,000 strikers over night.
> (7) Took part in Arbitration Conference.
> (8) Arranged large meetings where arbitrators representing the Union explained situation to strikers.
> (9) Took active part in shop meetings and paid benefits to those meeting at League headquarters.

(10) Made publicity for strike through the press, through meetings of all descriptions, edited two special strike editions of the *New York Call* and *New York Evening Journal.*
(11) Appealed for funds.[57]

They also sent organizers to help a related strike in Philadelphia, and to raise funds by touring New York State and New England.

Despite all this work, League members did not attempt either to claim credit for more than their due, or to impose caution on the workers who resisted the arbitrated agreement. Although privately they recognized that Local 25 could never have managed to organize such a vast strike without their help, in their public report on the strike they were unequivocal about the union's role: "It is untrue to state, as has been stated, that the League financed and led the strike. The strike was organized and led by the union. Perhaps it is more correct to say that it was organized by the union and led up to a certain point: the point of compromise. When that point was reached the strikers themselves turned leaders, continuing the strike to one of the most remarkable victories in the history of trade unions."[58]

The League emphasized those aspects of the strike that linked the labor and suffrage movements. One of their aims was to help feminists understand the struggles of working-class women, and they felt the strike was a major advance in that respect, even though some of the forms this female solidarity took were slightly bizarre. Borrowing a tactic from the suffragists, the League organized a car caravan to publicize the strike. The cars, lent by various millionaire women, honked their way through the narrow streets of the Lower East Side, "taking on and leaving off pickets. . . . Within the autos rich, fashionable women and poor frail striking girls . . . were making merry over this exceptional affair. It was amusing to see rich women carrying cards on which was proclaimed the need for organization for labor and which demanded shorter hours and increased pay."[59] The cars were no doubt chauffeured.

No aspect of the strike attracted as much attention in the press as the support given it by certain wealthy women, notably Alva Belmont and Anne Morgan. Alva Belmont was the daughter of an Alabama plantation owner and one of New York's most prominent society matrons. She married William K. Vanderbilt and embarked on a lavish campaign to break into New York society's "Four Hundred." After building a three-million-dollar chateau on Fifth Avenue and a two-million-dollar mansion in Newport, she finally achieved her goal, after which she divorced Vanderbilt and married Oliver Hazard Perry Belmont, heir to the New York subway system. She became an ardent suffragist, active first in NAWSA and then in the National Woman's Party.[60]

During the strike she personally financed a mass meeting that was sponsored by the suffragist Political Equality Association and held at the Hippodrome on December 5. Speakers included Dr. Anna Howard Shaw for NAWSA, Leonora O'Reilly for the Women's Trade Union League, and Rose Pastor Stokes for the Socialist Party. Alva Belmont never lost an opportunity to note that the strike showed the need for woman suffrage. After observing at the trials of some of the strikers, she told the press:

> During the six hours I spent in that police court I saw enough to convince me and all who were with me beyond the smallest doubt of the absolute necessity for woman's suffrage—for the direct influence of women over judges, jury and policemen, over every-thing and everybody connected with the so-called course of justice. . . . Every woman who sits complacently amid the comforts of her home, or who moves with perfect ease and independence in her own protected social circle, and says, "I have all the rights I want," should spend one night at the Jefferson Market Court. She would then know that there are other women who have no rights which man or law or society recognizes.[61]

The press was almost as enthralled by Alva Belmont's strike support work as they were with that of Anne Morgan, daughter of robber baron J.P. Morgan ("Mr. Morgan," said a very intimate friend of the family, "naturally has very different views from Anne, but he is a broad-minded man and respects his daughter for thinking and acting for herself. . . . The story that he had angrily sworn to disinherit her for her avowed sympathy with the strikers is absolutely false.")[62] The Morgan financial interests were not involved in the garment industry.

The support of the "millionaire women" climaxed in a fund-raising meeting at the exclusive Colony Club on December 15, when a group of strikers, including Clara Lemlich, told their life stores to the women of the "Four Hundred." Theresa Malkiel, a socialist activist who wrote a fictionalized first-person account of the strike, drew the moral for her readers:

> They've brought me to their fashionable clubhouse to hear about our misery. To tell the truth, I've no appetite to tell it to them, for I've almost come to the conclusion that the gulf between us girls and these rich ladies is too deep to be smoothed over by a few paltry dollars; the girls would probably be the better off in the long run if they did not take their money. They would the sooner realize the great contrast and division of classes; this would teach them to stick to their own. . . . The women gave us a thousand dollars, but what does this amount to? Not even a quarter apiece for each striker.[63]

And in fact, when the strikers voted down the arbitrated agreement, some of their rich supporters began to change their minds. On January 3, the Socialist Party and the League, together with various other organizations, called a meeting at Carnegie Hall to protest police brutality. The 370 arrested strikers sat on the stage, and speakers included Leonora O'Reilly and Morris Hillquit, the Socialist Party lawyer who was one of the arbitrators. At a special press conference the next morning, Anne Morgan deplored the undue influence of the socialists who, she said, were taking advantage of the strike situation to stir up trouble:

> I attended the meeting at Carnegie Hall last night. There was no doubt that some of the girls have been badly treated, both by some of the manufacturers, some of the police, and some of the magistrates. But I deplore the fanatical statements of Morris Hillquit, Leonora O'Reilly and others at such times as these. . . . In these times of stress such meetings should be an appeal to reason and sound judgement, and it is extremely dangerous to allow these Socialist appeals to emotionalism. It is very reprehensible for Socialists to take advantage of these poor girls in these times, and when the working people are in such dire straits, to teach their fanatical doctrines.[64]

Anne Morgan was joined in her attack by her friend Eva McDonald Valesh, a close associate of Samuel Gompers, who had left her job as managing editor of the *American Federationist* to come to New York. When she became involved in the shirtwaist makers' strike, most people were under the impression that she was acting as Gomper's emissary, and she even referred to herself as "general organizer of the AFL."[65] In fact, she was on her own.

Eva McDonald Valesh was peripherally involved in the arbitration agreement that had been rejected by the strikers on December 27, and, like Anne Morgan, she thought it had been voted down because of excessive Socialist Party influence. In a speech at the Woman's Civic Forum a few weeks later she attacked the Socialist Party and included the Women's Trade Union League in her offensive, on the theory that it was a socialist "front" organization. She tried to use the contradiction between men and women in the union as a basis for undermining the strike, telling the *New York Daily Tribune*:

> "The strikers' committee refused to consider any overture but one agreeing to the closed shop. What is that strikers' committee? Eighteen men and two girls were present the day I saw them—the men all socialists, connected with the trade perhaps, but ignorant of what the girls want. And to show you the feminine viewpoint, those girl strikers are actually grateful to the men who are using them for their own purposes. 'It's so nice of the men, who know so much more than we, to serve on our committees,' they say.
>
> "I propose," Mrs. Valesh went on, "to start a campaign against socialism. This strike may be used to pave the way for forming clean, sensible labor unions, and I want to enroll every woman of leisure, every clubwoman, in the movement. The existing unions aren't doing what they ought to stem the tide of socialism in this country. The Women's Trade Union League is dominated by socialists, though I won't deny that they have helped the shirtwaist strikers some.
>
> "Socialism is a menace, and it is alarming to some one who has been, as I have, away from New York for some years, to come back and see how socialism has grown here. I've been down to Clinton Hall [the union office], and I am terrified at the spirit that fills the people who congregate there. There's nothing constructive about socialism. It just makes those ignorant foreigners discontented, sets them against the government, makes them want to tear down. And the socialists are using the strikers."
>
> "How about the suffragists?" demanded Mrs. William H. McCartney.
>
> "That's different," said Mrs. Valesh. "The suffragists have used the strikers, but they've helped them, given them spiritual vision, and, besides, the suffragists say frankly to the strikers, 'We want votes for women,' while the socialists veil their purposes under all sorts of pretenses."[66]

The papers printed Eva McDonald Valesh's comments with great enthusiasm, announcing that she and Anne Morgan were starting a rival organization to the Women's Trade Union League, of which both happened to be members. The League feared that Gompers was behind the attack, and a controversy erupted over whether to expel Eva McDonald Valesh. The socialists in the New York League wanted a public denunciation. Margaret Dreier Robins, the national president, rushed to New York to try to dampen the fire before it got out of control; she and her husband Raymond felt that Eva McDonald Valesh wanted publicity and that if she were openly expelled she would "herald forth how the 'reds' could not stand her great arguments and her mighty influence and had to expel her."[67] Meanwhile Eva McDonald Valesh kept sending in resignations, and the League had to table each one in order to go on with expulsion proceedings. In the end, the New York League—as usual—yielded to Margaret Dreier Robins' persuasions, and kept the expulsion a confidential matter. Reflecting upon this episode, Raymond Robins wrote to his wife, "What an old Pup the Hon. Samuel Gompers really is. It seems that Gompers is worthy of all the Socialists say about him and that the Socialists are worthy of all that Gompers says about them. We shall let these ill tempered and low natured people scrap among themselves. Each knows the smut of the other and they can wash their dirty linen to their souls delight."[68]

In fact, the women of the Socialist Party had played an important role in the united front that supported the strike but had received no public recognition for it. They had come from all over the New York area and, according to their own reports, had been "clerks, organizers, speakers, pickets, watchers, newsies, human sandwiches, solicitors for relief funds, took an active part in the Hippodrome meeting, for which Mrs. Belmont alone received the credit, and helped arrange the demonstration and parade to City Hall."[69] They had initiated the Carnegie Hall meeting, and, once the strikers rejected the arbitrated agreement and other support began to fall away, they collected most of the strike funds.[70] Bitter and hurt by the attacks on them and by the League's unwillingness to defend them publicly, several of the most active socialist women made their own defense:

> If large advertising in the capitalist dailies, so generously given the "society" ladies during the strike, helped, the well-to-do women certainly did everything for them; for the Socialist women's activity was never mentioned by the newspapers until Mr. Gompers and his assistant, Mrs. Valesh, chose to open war on the Socialists.
>
> There has never been a more humiliating position in the history of the labor movement than that occupied by the Socialist women in the shirtwaist strike. So long as they did the work of the black man "Friday" they were tolerated and permitted to go on; but no sooner did they attempt to do anything that would count officially then they were put in the background.
>
> The result was, however, well worth the price; the Socialist women have become a power with the girls themselves.
>
> No wonder Mr. Gompers raises his hands in alarm. The girls have found out by experience who their friends are. They will not allow themselves to be fooled, as did the workingmen.[71]

The strike dragged on through January with less and less hope of a finale as splendid as its opening chords. After December 27, the employers' association refused to arbitrate further; support fell away; some large shops were allowed to settle without mentioning the issues of union shop and recognition, and the union began to settle on whatever basis it could with the remaining firms. On February 15, 1910, the strike was declared over despite the fact that thirteen shops were still on strike, and between one thousand and three thousand workers went back with no gains and no guarantee against blacklisting.[72]

The Triangle Waist Company was one of those in which there was only a partial settlement. One demand that was not met was for adequate fire escapes and open doors—the foremen used to lock the doors for fear the girls might sneak out for a minute's break or steal a few needles or a little thread.[73] Shortly before closing time a year later, on March 25, 1911, the fire alarms began to shrill. Like most garment factories, Triangle was a firetrap, with piles of material lying about, and so much lint that the air itself could catch fire. The factory went up in minutes. There was no sprinkler system. One exit was blocked by fire, the other door was locked, and the workers could not get out. The fire escape let down onto an iron spike fence, impaling the girls trying to jump to the ground. It was a holocaust. Of the five hundred people who worked there, 146 died in the fire and many more were injured. A League member who was passing by described the scene:

> I was coming down Fifth Avenue on the Saturday afternoon when a great, swirling, billowing cloud of smoke swept like a giant streamer out of Washington Square and down upon the beautiful houses in Lower Fifth Avenue. Just as I was turning into the Square two young girls whom I knew to be working in the vicinity came rushing toward me, tears were running from their eyes and they were white and shaking as they caught me by the arm.
>
> "Oh," shrieked one of them, "they are jumping."
>
> "Jumping from ten stories up! They are going through the air like bundles of clothes, and the firemen can't stop them and the policemen can't stop them and nobody can help them at all."
>
> "Fifty of them's jumped already and just think how many there must be left inside yet"—and the girls started crying afresh and rushed away up Fifth Avenue.

> A little old tailor whom I knew came shrieking across the Square, tossing his arms and crying, "Horrible, horrible." He did not recognize me, nor know where he was; he had gone mad with the sight.[74]

Rose Schneiderman of the WTUL made a bitter speech at the memorial meeting held a week later at the Metropolitan Opera House, rented for the occasion by Anne Morgan. She threw out a challenge to the liberal public:

> I would be a traitor to those poor burned bodies if I came here to talk good fellowship. We have tried you good people of the public and we have found you wanting. The old Inquisition had its rack and its thumbscrews and its instruments of torture with iron teeth. We know what these things are today: the iron teeth are our necessities, the thumbscrews the high-powered and swift machinery close to which we must work, and the rack is here in the "fire-proof" structures that will destroy us the minute they catch on fire.
> This is not the first time girls have been burned alive in this city. Every week I must learn of the untimely death of one of my sister workers. Every year thousands of us are maimed. The life of men and women is so cheap and property is so sacred. There are so many of us for one job it matters little if 143 [sic] of us are burned to death.
> We have tried you, citizens; we are trying you now, and you have a couple of dollars for the sorrowing mothers and daughters and sisters by way of a charity gift. But every time the workers come out in the only way they know to protest against conditions which are unbearable, the strong hand of the law is allowed to press down heavily upon us. . . . I can't talk fellowship to you who are gathered here. Too much blood has been spilled. I know from my experience it is up to the working people to save themselves . . . by a strong working-class movement.[75]

The owners of the Triangle firm were tried for negligence but not convicted. The press blamed the fire on a worker who had been smoking. The League embarked on a crusade for stronger legislation for fire protection and better enforcement of existing laws. They printed leaflets informing the workers of the laws and their rights, and did soapboxing on fire protection; Clara Lemlich, blacklisted after the strike, was one of the speakers. League members also helped organize relief and legal aid for the families of the victims. The IWW, which was beginning to be active in the Lower East Side garment industry, sneered at this palliative approach:

> A stirring commentary upon the policy of the league is to be found in the conduct of the Triangle Company. Compelled to seek new quarters, what did they do in the face of "public opinion" and the "vigorous action" of the unions? Go and seek out, with scrupulous care, a real fire-proof building? Not these butchers for profit. THEY RENTED A CONDEMNED BUILDING AND PROCEEDED TO AGAIN DEFY THE LAW TO WHICH THE WOMEN'S TRADE UNION LEAGUE APPEALS TO REMEDY THESE CONDITIONS. The capitalists know that the law is on their side every time, hence they have no fear of it.[76]

Everyone in the labor movement knew that the best way to protect the Lower East Side workers was to have a union strong enough on the shop level to enforce the law and to agitate around safety issues. But although Local 25 had gained enormously from the strike, enrolling twenty thousand members, it quickly went into a decline, and by the fall of 1911 it had only thirty-eight hundred members and little influence.[77] The women of the New York League became increasingly critical of its general strike approach, unless it could be followed up by "effective leadership which instructs the rank and file in the principles of trade unionism and the best method of getting practical results, so that a permanent advance may be established after such a magnificent struggle."[78] The League felt that its responsibility was to the women in the trade, whose interests were not being served by male leadership of Local 25. Helen Marot became disturbed when the idea began to circulate after the fire that another general strike would be necessary to recoup the union's membership. She recommended that the League oppose this and instead endorse candidates for union office who had "constructive" ideas. The League, however, refused to interfere in the union's internal policies, and Marot then wrote a letter to the *Jewish Daily Forward* about the inadequacies of the union's leadership: "It is becoming clear to the League that it is a betrayal of the faith and fine spirit of the girls to encourage them to organize into trade unions if their union is to be dominated by men without business sense or executive ability and by men competent to talk but not to act."[79]

The lack of democracy inherent in an all-male leadership over a female rank and file was exacerbated by a new movement for "protocols"—pacts signed with the garment manufacturers to set up compulsory arbitration boards that would settle conflicts between labor and management as they arose, without strikes. In other words, the ILGWU leadership was prepared to bargain away the power to strike (the only real power the workers had) in order to consolidate its control over the trade. When the idea met with initial success among the male cloakmakers, the ILGWU wanted to extend it to the female waistmakers. The conservatives in Local 25 were strongly in favor of the experiment, as was the AFL leadership; Gompers himself came to the 1912 negotiations that set up the shirtwaist protocol. Some radicals opposed the idea. The rank and file of the union was divided, as was the Women's Trade Union League, which did not publicly endorse the campaign.[80]

The manipulative attitude of the union leadership toward the women workers became clear in these contract negotiations. The protocol was based on the union's ability to keep its members in line; it ruled out any displays of spontaneous militance such as the rejection of the arbitrated agreement in the shirtwaist strike. The manufacturers' association made it clear that they expected the union to "control" the workers.[81] Since there was widespread unrest in the industry, the union decided to stage a theatrical event in January 1913 to give the workers a sense that there was more of a struggle with management than was in fact the case. The workers would vote for another general strike, only this time everything would have been settled beforehand, the strike would last only a few days, and the industry would not be disrupted. As the union's historian described the events:

> Such a strike would give the workers a chance to express "their protest against the bad conditions in the trade" and also create in them a sense that each and all had helped to "uplift the trade." The plan was to issue a call for a general strike; then at the very inception of the strike call a mass meeting of the workers and inform them of the standards agreed upon between the manufacturers' association and the union, and then direct the workers in the shops of the association to return to work . . . the union promised not to sign individual agreements with individual firms, but to refer all employers to the association, which they would be asked to join. It was also understood that the agreement between the association and the union would become effective only if the union succeeded in bringing into its membership the majority of the workers in the trade. . . . The manufacturers agreed to give the union a list of their workers in order to facilitate the work of organization. . . .
>
> The course of the strike was smooth and peaceful. The "girls" accepted the protocol as a *fait accompli*, with some surprise but without much animation. A few thousand Italian "girls" under the leadership of Nicholas Lauretano and other IWWs expressed some dissatisfaction, but were easily pacified.[82]

Under this happy arrangement the membership of Local 25 quickly rose to about twenty-five thousand.[83] But although in theory union and management would now meet to settle the problems of the trade without any disruption from below, in practice it soon became clear that the protocol's machinery didn't work. It took forever to settle grievances, and although the "impartial" arbitration board was supposed to give the workers wage increases and other awards, its decisions never seemed to lead to improvements in wages or working conditions.[84] The employers soon began to introduce speedup measures to gain an edge on competitors, and they refused to give the arbitrators the information necessary to set wages in advance, because that would have entailed releasing information about the next season's styles, and they were afraid rival firms would steal their ideas. They acted in general like benign dictators, and refused to meet with the union officials on an equal footing.[85]

So the protocol broke down. One of its early casualties was the employers' promise to hire union members first. The membership of Local 25 began to decline as a result, until by November 1913, eight months after the protocol was initiated, it was down to about sixteen thousand; it lost three thousand by the end of 1915.[86]

At this point both the manufacturers and union officials agreed that a new protocol was necessary, and in January 1916 they announced an agreement. But when the union called another "general strike" for February 9, 1916—meant to be merely a "demonstration of unity"—they got more than they had bargained for.[87] Rank-and-file women, dissatisfied both with protocolism and with the undemocratic way the union was run, led an open revolt. The ILGWU had made no progress in integrating women into the leadership since the first criticisms made by the Women's Trade Union League, and as a result relations between them had become strained. Late in 1912, Helen Marot informed an ILGWU official in her usual forthright manner that

> the business of the League was to bring women into places of responsibility in the organization of their trade; that we know and he knew if we should now work even with representatives in a general strike that the union would be carried on and controlled by the men, and the women would have no place and power, and probably mostly no voice.[88]

And she summarized the situation in her book *American Labor Unions*, published in 1914:

> It was the strike of the Shirt Waist Makers which gave the first real impetus to the organization of the workers making women's clothing and which placed at last the International Ladies' Garment Workers' Union in its present position—the third largest union affiliated with the American Federation. This union has jurisdiction over one of the largest fields in which women work. It is officered by men who believe that women make good strikers, but who have no confidence in their ability to handle union affairs. They have gone further than any other union in building up organization by protocol agreements with manufacturers without a conscious sentiment or understanding among the workers. They claim that the workers as a whole have no real conception of organization.[89]

In 1916 some of these women not only found a voice but found fists as well:

> A meeting of shop chairmen at No. 175 East Broadway, ended last night in a general fight. Women became hysterical, and Charles Jacobson, a union official, was injured. The fight began because Jacobson, who had charge of the door, refused admission to a crowd who were without tickets.
>
> It was announced that 5,000 of the strikers would return to work this morning. Miss Ida Grabinski, who has been named chairman of one of the dozen committees of women in the new "equal voice" movement, said today that she intends to lay the whole matter

before Samuel Gompers, President of the Federation. She and her followers are not satisfied with the way mere man had conducted the affairs of the union until now.

"The officers of the union boss us worse than the bosses," she said. "Now they tell us to go to work. The next minute they withdraw that order. The women workers comprise more than 65 percent of the union members throughout the country. The association shops have a woman general manager. Why shouldn't we have something to say about what concerns us most?"[90]

Although a large number of dissident workers refused to go back to work at the union's command, they did not succeed in staying out for long, and the strike was over by the end of February.[91]

The ILGWU leadership in this period initiated policies that were to become its general practice: it put stability in the industry first, followed by good fringe benefits and services to its members, who were expected to show their desire for a job and their appreciation of their union benefits by remaining in their place. The separation of men from women in the trade, and the more privileged position of the men—reinforced by the social inequality of women in general—created a strike situation in which the generals were men and the soldiers were women. Only certain kinds of wars can be won by such an army, and a war for women's liberation is not among them. When women fill all the most exploited categories in an industry, a fight for economic justice is inseparable from a struggle for women's liberation. This struggle has yet to take place in the U.S. garment industry.[92] Yet, despite its limitations, the Uprising of the Thirty Thousand brought great gains to women garment workers, gains in self-respect as well as wages. As Clara Lemlich summed it up: "They used to say that you couldn't even organize women. They wouldn't come to union meetings. They were 'temporary' workers. Well, we showed them!"[93]

Notes

1. *The Voice of Labor*, Women's Trade Union League songbook, Leonora O'Reilly papers, Box 15, File 349, Schlesinger Library, Radcliffe College, Cambridge, Mass.
2. As quoted in the *New York Call*, 28 November 1909.
3. Ladies' Waist Makers' Union, *Souvenir History of the Strike* (New York: Ladies' Waistmakers' Union, 1910), pp. 11–12.
4. Paula Scheier, "Clara Lemlich Shavelson," *Jewish Life* 8, no. 95 (November 1954), p. 8.
5. Ibid., p. 9.
6. M. B. Sumner, "Spirit of the Strikers," *Survey* 23 (22 January 1910), p. 554.
7. Scheier, "Clara Lemlich Shavelson," p. 9.
8. Ibid.
9. Louis Levine, *The Women's Garment Workers, A History of the International Ladies Garment Workers' Union* (New York: B. W. Heubsch, Inc., 1924), pp. 146–147.
10. The cutters were not members of Local 25, the shirtwaist makers' local, but of Local 30. They generally had higher wages and worked shorter hours than the women. Two days after the general strike began, 500 members of Local 30 struck in solidarity.
11. Ladies' Waist Makers' Union, *Souvenir History*, pp. 2–3.
12. Woods Hutchinson, M.D., "The Hygienic Aspects of the Shirtwaist Strike," *Survey* 23 (22 January 1910), p. 545.
13. Ibid.
14. The number of working women who were hired as organizers or union staff in this period could be easily counted on one person's fingers. Among them were Rose Schneiderman, Pauline Newman, Gertrude Barnum, and Josephine Casey.
15. Helen Marot, "A Woman's Strike—An Appreciation of the Shirtwaist Makers of New York," in *Proceedings of the American Academy of Political Science, City of New York* 1 (1910), p. 122. Out of the thirty thousand strikers, Marot estimates that six thousand were Russian men, two thousand Italian women, one thousand American women, and twenty-one thousand Russian women.

16. Ladies' Waist Makers' Union, *Souvenir History*, p. 4.
17. Quoted in Levine, *The Women's Garment Workers*, p. 148.
18. Ladies' Waist Makers' Union, *Souvenir History*, p. 2.
19. Sumner, "Spirit of the Strikers," p. 554.
20. *New York Call*, 28 September 1909.
21. *New York Call*, 5 October 1909.
22. Marot, "A Woman's Strike," p. 120.
23. Levine, *The Women's Garment Workers*, p. 152.
24. *New York Call*, 23 October 1909.
25. *New York Call*, 5 November 1909.
26. Sue Ainslie Clark and Edith Wyatt, "Working Girls' Budgets: The Shirtwaist Makers and Their Strike," *McClure's Magazine* 36 (November 1910), p. 81.
27. Marot, "A Woman's Strike," p. 135.
28. Woods Hutchinson, "The Hygienic Aspects," p. 545.
29. Marot, "A Woman's Strike," p. 126.
30. Ibid., p. 124.
31. Clark and Wyatt, "Working Girls' Budgets," p. 82.
32. Levine, *The Women's Garment Workers*, p. 159.
33. Rose Schneiderman, with Lucy Goldthwaite, *All for One* (New York: Paul S. Ericksson, Inc., 1967), p. 93.
34. *New York Call*, 4 December 1909.
35. William Mailly, "How Girls Can Strike," *Progressive Woman* 3, no. 33 (February 1910), p. 6.
36. Grace Potter, "Women Shirt-Waist Strikers Command Sympathy of Public," *New York Call*, 12 December 1909.
37. Levine, *The Women's Garment Workers*, p. 166.
38. Marot, "A Woman's Strike," pp. 123–124.
39. Ibid., pp. 122–123.
40. National Women's Trade Union League, *Proceedings of the Third Biennial Convention* (1911), p. 19.
41. Mary White Ovington, *Half a Man* (New York: Longmans, Green and Company, 1911), pp. 144, 150.
42. Ibid., pp. 161–163.
43. Philip S. Foner, *Women and the American Labor Movement* (New York: Free Press, 1979), pp. 339–340.
44. Mary White Ovington, *The Walls Come Tumbling Down* (New York: Schocken Books, 1970), p. 43.
45. "Woman's Sphere," *New York Call*, 4 January 1910.
46. Alfred T. White, "Shirtwaist Makers' Union," *Survey* 23 (29 January 1910), p. 588.
47. Margaret Dreier Robins, "Shirtwaist Makers' Union," *Survey* 23 (19 February 1910), p. 788.
48. Foner, *Women and the American Labor Movement*, p. 341.
49. *New York Call*, 22 December 1909.
50. Minutes, Executive Board, 21 May 1910, National Women's Trade Union League papers, Library of Congress.
51. The lingerie manufacturers in the white goods shops tried to use Black workers as strikebreakers as they had used them in the white goods general strike of 1913. This failed partly because the strikers threw "missiles" at them, and partly because they were unskilled at the trade. Hyman Berman, "The Era of the Protocol," Ph.D. dissertation, Columbia University, 1956, p. 189.
52. See the National Women's Trade Union League papers, Library of Congress and Mildred Rankin's letters to Margaret Dreier Robins, Robins papers, University of Florida, Gainesville, Florida.
53. Levine, *The Women's Garment Workers*, p. 165.
54. Ibid., p. 163.
55. *New York Call*, 28 December 1909.
56. Marot, "A Woman's Strike," p. 29.
57. *Proceedings of the . . . Convention* (1911), p. 18.
58. "The League and the Strike of the Thirty Thousand," *Annual Report of the Women's Trade Union League of New York, 1909–1910*, p. 3.
59. *New York Call*, 20 December 1909.
60. Aileen S. Kraditor, *The Ideas of the Woman Suffrage Movement, 1890–1920* (New York: Anchor Books, 1971), p. 225.
61. *New York Call*, 21 December 1909.
62. *New York American*, 29 December 1909.
63. Theresa Serber Malkiel, *Diary of a Shirtwaist Striker* (New York: Cooperative Press, 1910), pp. 40–41.
64. *New York Call*, 4 January 1910.
65. Minutes, National Executive Board Meeting, National Women's Trade Union League, 20 May 1910, National Women's Trade Union League papers, Library of Congress.

66. *New York Daily Tribune*, 22 January 1910.

67. Raymond Robins to Margaret Dreier Robins, 5 February 1910, Raymond Robins papers, Wisconsin Historical Society, Box 1, File 1.

68. Raymond Robins to Margaret Dreier Robins, 3 February 1910, Raymond Robins papers, Wisconsin Historical Society, Box 1, File 1.

69. Theresa Malkiel, Meta Stern, and Antoinette Konikow, "Socialist Women and the Shirtwaist Strike," *New York Call*, 8 February 1910.

70. Ibid.

71. Ibid.

72. Levine, *The Women's Garment Workers*, p. 165; *New York Call*, 15 February 1910.

73. Leon Stein, *The Triangle Fire* (New York: J. B. Lippincott Company, 1962), p. 168.

74. Martha Bensley Bruere, "The Triangle Fire," *Life and Labor* 1, no. 5 (May 1911), p. 137.

75. Schneiderman, *All for One*, p. 100. The 143 figure was wrong; 146 died.

76. *Solidarity*, 15 April 1911.

77. Levine, *The Women's Garment Workers*, p. 218.

78. *Proceedings of the . . . Convention* (1911), p. 18.

79. 13 May 1911; quoted by Nancy Schrom Dye, "The Woman's Trade Union League of New York, 1903–1920," Ph.D. dissertation, University of Wisconsin, 1974, p. 182. As the ILGWU continued to call general strikes to organize various branches of the garment industry, the League lost patience, particularly when the strikers included "American girls." Mary Dreier wrote Margaret Dreier Robins on the occasion of the lingerie workers' strike in 1912:

> This strike seems to be as unorganized as the shirtwaist workers—there are some American girls out, very promising material for organization, but the Union has not yet asked our help, though we tooted up to see if we cd help. . . . I wish we had the authority to go straight into any strike situation and make them obey us—I mean of course in these unorganized strikes. It wd be much better all around. (4 January 1912, Margaret Dreier Robins papers, University of Florida, Gainesville).

80. Dye, "The Women's Trade Union League," p. 205. It appears that Leonora O'Reilly, Mollie Schepps, Helen Marot, Melinda Scott, and Maggie Hinchey were against the protocol. Rose Schneiderman and Pauline Newman were presumably for it.

81. Levine, *The Women's Garment Workers*, p. 224.

82. Ibid., pp. 224–225.

83. Ibid., p. 301.

84. Ibid., p. 313.

85. Ibid., pp. 315–316.

86. Ibid., p. 301.

87. Ibid., p. 303.

88. Quoted in Dye, "The Women's Trade Union League," p. 234.

89. Helen Marot, *American Labor Unions* (New York: Henry Holt & Co., 1914), p. 75.

90. *Solidarity*, 26 February 1916.

91. Berman, "The Era of the Protocol," p. 370.

92. The same discrimination against women exists today in the ILGWU, complicated by racial and ethnic factors. In 1970 one-third at the very least of the union's membership were Black, Latin, or Asian, but there was only one minority member on the executive board. Women made up 80 percent of the union membership and in 1970 they too had only one member on the executive board. The union's president, Louis Stolberg, told the *Wall Street Journal*, "Women are very peculiar. I once tried to promote one. She went off and married a man. What the hell can I do?" *Wall Street Journal*, 30 December 1970.

93. Scheier, "Clara Lemlich Shavelson," p. 8.

14

Working Women, Class Relations, and Suffrage Militance: Harriot Stanton Blatch and the New York Woman Suffrage Movement, 1894–1909

Ellen Carol DuBois

More than any other period in American reform history, the Progressive Era eludes interpretation. It seems marked by widespread concern for social justice and by extraordinary elitism, by democratization and by increasing social control. The challenge posed to historians is to understand how Progressivism could simultaneously represent gains for the masses and more power for the classes. The traditional way to approach the period has been to study the discrete social programs reformers so energetically pushed in those years, from the abolition of child labor to the Americanization of the immigrants. Recently, historians' emphasis has shifted to politics, where it will probably remain for a time. Historians have begun to recognize that the rules of political life, the nature of American "democracy," were fundamentally reformulated beginning in the Progressive Era, and that such political change shaped the ultimate impact of particular social reforms.

Where were women in all this? The new focus on politics requires a reinterpretation of women's role in Progressivism. As the field of women's history has grown, the importance of women in the Progressive Era has gained notice, but there remains a tendency to concentrate on their roles with respect to social reform. Modern scholarship on the Progressive Era thus retains a separate spheres flavor; women are concerned with social and moral issues, but the world of politics is male. Nowhere is this clearer than in the tendency to minimize, even to omit, the woman suffrage movement from the general literature on the Progressive Era.[1]

Scholarship on woman suffrage is beginning to grow in detail and analytic sophistication, but it has yet to be fully integrated into overviews of the period.[2] Histories that include woman suffrage usually do so in passing, listing it with other constitutional alterations in the electoral process such as the popular election of senators, the initiative, and the referendum. But woman suffrage was a mass movement, and that fact is rarely noticed. Precisely because it was a mass political movement—perhaps the first modern one—woman suffrage may well illuminate Progressive-Era politics, especially the class dynamics underlying their reformulation. When the woman suffrage movement is given its due, we may begin to understand the process by which democratic hope turned into mass political alienation, which is the history of modern American politics.

To illuminate the origin and nature of the woman suffrage movement in the Progressive Era I will examine the politics of Harriot Stanton Blatch. Blatch was the daughter of Elizabeth Cady Stanton, the founding mother of political feminism. Beginning in the early twentieth century, she was a leader in her own right, initially in New York, later nationally.

Reprinted with permission from *The Journal of American History*, vol. 74, June 1987.

As early as 1903, when politics was still considered something that disreputable men did, like smoking tobacco, Blatch proclaimed: "There are born politicians just as there are born artists, writers, painters. I confess that I should be a politician, that I am not interested in machine politics, but that the devotion to the public cause . . . rather than the individual, appeals to me."[3]

Just as her zest for politics marked Blatch as a new kind of suffragist, so did her efforts to fuse women of different classes into a revitalized suffrage movement. Blatch's emphasis on class was by no means unique; she shared it with other women reformers of her generation. Many historians have treated the theme of class by labeling the organized women's reform movement in the early twentieth century "middle class." By contrast, I have tried to keep open the question of the class character of women's reform in the Progressive Era by rigorously avoiding the term. Characterizing the early twentieth-century suffrage movement as "middle class" obscures its most striking element, the new interest in the vote among women at both ends of the class structure. Furthermore, it tends to homogenize the movement. The very term "middle class" is contradictory, alternatively characterized as people who are not poor, and people who work for a living. By contrast, I have emphasized distinctions between classes and organized my analysis around the relations between them.

No doubt there is some distortion in this framework, particularly for suffragists who worked in occupations like teaching. But there is far greater distortion in using the term "middle class" to describe women like Blatch or Carrie Chapman Catt or Jane Addams. For example, it makes more sense to characterize an unmarried woman with an independent income who was not under financial compulsion to work for her living as "elite," rather than "middle class." The question is not just one of social stratification, but of the place of women in a whole system of class relations. For these new style suffragettes, as for contemporary feminists who write about them, the complex relationship between paid labor, marital status, and women's place in the class structure was a fundamental puzzle. The concept of "middle class" emerged among early twentieth-century reformers, but may ultimately prove more useful in describing a set of relations *between* classes that was coming into being in those years, than in designating a segment of the social structure.

Blatch, examined as a political strategist and a critic of class relations, is important less as a unique figure than as a representative leader, through whose career the historical forces transforming twentieth-century suffragism can be traced. The scope of her leadership offers clues to the larger movement: She was one of the first to open up suffrage campaigns to working-class women, even as she worked closely with wealthy and influential upper-class women; she pioneered militant street tactics and backroom political lobbying at the same time. Blatch's political evolution reveals close ties between other stirrings among American women in the Progressive Era and the rejuvenated suffrage movement. Many of her ideas paralleled Charlotte Perkins Gilman's influential reformulation of women's emancipation in economic terms. Many of Blatch's innovations as a suffragist drew on her prior experience in the Women's Trade Union League. Overall, Blatch's activities suggest that early twentieth-century changes in the American suffrage movement, often traced to the example of militant British suffragettes, had deep, indigenous roots. Among them were the growth of trade unionism among working-class women and professionalism among the elite, changing relations between these classes, and the growing involvement of women of all sorts in political reform.

The suffrage revival began in New York in 1893–1894, as part of a general political reform movement. In the 1890s New York's political reformers were largely upper-class men concerned about political "corruption," which they blamed partly on city Democratic machines and the bosses who ran them, partly on the masses of voting men, ignorant, immigrant, and ripe for political manipulation. Their concern about political corruption and about the consequences of uncontrolled political democracy became the focus of New York's 1894 constitutional convention, which addressed itself largely to "governmental procedures: the rules for filling offices, locating authority and organizing the different branches."[4]

The New York woman suffrage movement, led by Susan B. Anthony, recognized a great opportunity in the constitutional convention of 1894. Focusing on political corruption, Anthony and her allies argued that women were the political reformers' best allies. For while men were already voters and vulnerable to the ethic of partisan loyalty—indeed a man without a party affiliation in the 1890s was damned closed to unsexed—everyone knew that women were naturally nonpartisan. Enfranchising women was therefore the solution to the power of party bosses. Suffragists began by trying to get women elected to the constitutional convention itself. Failing this, they worked to convince the convention delegates to include woman suffrage among the proposed amendments.[5]

Anthony planned a house-to-house canvass to collect signatures on a mammoth woman suffrage petition. For the $50,000 she wanted to fund this effort, she approached wealthy women in New York City, including physician Mary Putnam Jacobi, society leader Catherine Palmer (Mrs. Robert) Abbe, social reformer Josephine Shaw Lowell, and philanthropist Olivia (Mrs. Russell) Sage. Several of them were already associated with efforts for the amelioration of working-class women, notably in the recently formed Consumers' League, and Anthony had reason to think they might be ready to advocate woman suffrage.[6]

The elite women were interested in woman suffrage, but they had their own ideas about how to work for it. Instead of funding Anthony's campaign, they formed their own organization. At parlor meetings in the homes of wealthy women, they tried to strike a genteel note, emphasizing that enfranchisement would *not* take women out of their proper sphere and would *not* increase the political power of the lower classes. Eighty-year-old Elizabeth Stanton, observing the campaign from her armchair, thought that "men and women of the conservative stamp of the Sages can aid us greatly at this stage of our movement."[7]

Why did wealthy women first take an active and prominent part in the suffrage movement in the 1890s? In part they shared the perspective of men of their class that the influence of the wealthy in government had to be strengthened; they believed that with the vote they could increase the political power of their class. In a representative argument before the constitutional convention, Jacobi proposed woman suffrage as a response to "the shifting of political power from privileged classes to the masses of men." The disfranchisement of women contributed to this shift because it made all women, "no matter how well born, how well educated, how intelligent, how rich, how serviceable to the State," the political inferiors of all men, "no matter how base-born, how poverty stricken, how ignorant, how vicious, how brutal." Olivia Sage presented woman suffrage as an antidote to the growing and dangerous "idleness" of elite women, who had forgotten their responsibility to set the moral tone for society.[8]

Yet, the new elite converts also supported woman suffrage on the grounds of changes taking place in women's status, especially within their own class. Jacobi argued that the educational advancement of elite women "and the new activities into which they have been led by it—in the work of charities, in the professions, and in the direction of public education—naturally and logically tend toward the same result, their political equality." She argued that elite women, who had aided the community through organized charity and benevolent activities, should have the same "opportunity to serve the State nobly."

Sage was willing to advocate woman suffrage because of women's recent "strides . . . in the acquirement of business methods, in the management of their affairs, in the effective interest they have evinced in civic affairs."[9]

Suffragists like Jacobi and Sage characteristically conflated their class perspective with the role they saw for themselves as women, contending for political leadership not so much on the grounds of their wealth, as of their womanliness. Women, they argued, had the characteristics needed in politics—benevolence, morality, selflessness, and industry; conveniently, they believed that elite women most fully embodied these virtues. Indeed, they liked to believe that women like themselves were elite *because* they were virtuous, not because they were wealthy. The confusion of class and gender coincided with a more general elite ideology that identified the fundamental division in American society not between rich and poor, but between industrious and idle, virtuous and vicious, community-minded and selfish. On these grounds Sage found the purposeless leisure of wealthy women dangerous to the body politic. She believed firmly that the elite, women included, should provide moral—and ultimately political—leadership, but it was important to her that they earn the right to lead.[10]

The problem for elite suffragists was that woman suffrage meant the enfranchisement of working-class, as well as elite, women. Jacobi described a prominent woman who "had interested herself nobly and effectively in public affairs, . . . but preferred not to claim the right [of suffrage] for herself, lest its concession entail the enfranchisement of ignorant and irresponsible women." An elite antisuffrage organization committed to such views was active in the 1894 campaign as well, led by women of the same class, with many of the same beliefs, as the prosuffrage movement. As Stanton wrote, "The fashionable women are about equally divided between two camps." The antis included prominent society figures Abby Hamlin (Mrs. Lyman) Abbott and Josephine Jewell (Mrs. Arthur) Dodge, as well as Annie Nathan Meyer, founder of Barnard College and member of the Consumers' League. Like the elite suffragists, upper-class antis wanted to insure greater elite influence in politics; but they argued that woman suffrage would decrease elite influence, rather than enhance it.[11]

Elite suffragists' willingness to support woman suffrage rested on their confidence that their class would provide political leadership for all women once they had the vote. Because they expected working-class women to defer to them, they believed that class relations among women would be more cooperative and less antagonistic than among men. Elite women, Jacobi argued before the 1894 convention, would "so guide ignorant women voters that they could be made to counterbalance, when necessary, the votes of ignorant and interested men." Such suffragists assumed that working-class women were too weak, timid, and disorganized to make their own demands. Since early in the nineteenth century, elite women had claimed social and religious authority on the grounds of their responsibility for the women and children of the poor. They had begun to adapt this tradition to the new conditions of an industrial age, notably in the Consumers' League, formed in response to the pleas of women wage earners for improvement in their working conditions. In fact, elite antis also asserted that they spoke for working-class women, but they contended that working-class women neither needed nor wanted to vote.[12]

From an exclusively elite perspective, the antisuffrage argument was more consistent than the prosuffrage one; woman suffrage undoubtedly meant greater political democracy, which the political reform movement of the 1890s most fundamentally feared. Elite suffragists found themselves organizing their own arguments around weak refutations of the antis' objections.[13] The ideological weakness had political implications. Woman suffrage got no serious hearing in the constitutional convention, and the 1894 constitutional revisions designed to "clean up government" ignored women's plea for political equality.

The episode revealed dilemmas, especially with respect to class relations among women, that a successful suffrage movement would have to address. Elite women had begun to aspire to political roles that led them to support woman suffrage, and the resources they commanded would be crucial to the future success of suffrage efforts. But their attraction to woman suffrage rested on a portrait of working-class women and a system of class relations that had become problematic to a modern industrial society. Could elite women sponsor the entrance of working-class women into politics without risking their influence over them, and perhaps their position of leadership? Might not working-class women assume a newly active, politically autonomous role? The tradition of class relations among women had to be transformed before a thriving and modern woman suffrage movement could be built. Harriot Stanton Blatch had the combination of suffrage convictions and class awareness to lead New York suffragists through that transition.

The 1894 campaign, which confronted suffragists with the issue of class, also drew Blatch actively into the American woman suffrage movement. She had come back from England, where she had lived for many years, to receive a master's degree from Vassar College for her study of the English rural poor. A powerful orator, she was "immediately pressed into service . . . speaking every day," at parlor suffrage meetings, often to replace her aged mother.[14] Like her mother, Blatch was comfortable in upper-class circles; she had married into a wealthy British family. She generally shared the elite perspective of the campaign, assuming that "educated women" would lead their sex. But she disliked the implication that politics could ever become too democratic and, virtually alone among the suffragists, criticized all "those little anti-republican things I hear so often here in America, this talk of the quality of votes." And while other elite suffragists discussed working-class women as domestic servants and shop clerks, Blatch understood the centrality of industrial workers, although her knowledge of them was still primarily academic.[15]

Blatch's disagreements with the elite suffrage framework were highlighted a few months after the constitutional convention in an extraordinary public debate with her mother. In the *Woman's Journal,* Stanton urged that the suffrage movement incorporate an educational restriction into its demand, to respond to "the greatest block in the way of woman's enfranchisement . . . the fear of the 'ignorant vote' being doubled." Her justification for this position, so at odds with the principles of a lifetime, was that the enfranchisement of "educated women" best supplied "the imperative need at the time . . . woman's influence in public life." From England, Blatch wrote a powerful dissent. Challenging the authority of her venerated mother was a dramatic act that—perhaps deliberately—marked the end of her political daughterhood. She defended both the need and the capacity of the working class to engage in democratic politics. On important questions, "for example . . . the housing of the poor," their opinion was more informed than that of the elite. She also argued that since "the conditions of the poor are so much harder . . . every working man needs the suffrage more that I do." And finally, she insisted on the claims of a group her mother had ignored, working women.[16]

The debate between mother and daughter elegantly symbolizes the degree to which class threatened the continued vitality of the republican tradition of suffragism. Blatch was able to adapt the republican faith to modern class relations, while Stanton was not, partly because of her participation in the British Fabian movement. As a Fabian, Blatch had gained an appreciation for the political intelligence and power of the working class very rare among elite reformers in the U. S. When she insisted that the spirit of democracy was more alive in England than in the U. S., she was undoubtedly thinking of the development of a working-class political movement there.[17]

Over the next few years, Blatch explored basic assumptions of the woman suffrage faith she had inherited in the context of modern class relations. In the process, like other women reformers of her era, such as Charlotte Perkins Gilman, Florence Kelley, Jane Addams, and numerous settlement house residents and supporters of organized labor, she focused on the relation of women and work. She emphasized the productive labor that women performed, both as it contributed to the larger social good and as it created the conditions of freedom and equality for women themselves. Women had always worked, she insisted. The new factor was the shift of women's work from the home to the factory and the office, and from the status of unpaid to paid labor. Sometimes she stressed that women's unpaid domestic labor made an important contribution to society; at other times she stressed that such unpaid work was not valued, but always she emphasized the historical development that was taking women's labor out of the home and into the commercial economy. The question for modern society was not whether women should work, but under what conditions, and with what consequences for their own lives.[18]

Although Blatch was troubled by the wages and working conditions of the laboring poor, her emphasis on work as a means to emancipation led her to regard wage-earning women less as victims to be succored, than as exemplars to their sex. She vigorously denied that women ideally hovered somewhere above the world of work. She had no respect for the "handful of rich women who have no employment other than organizing servants, social functions and charities." Upper-class women, she believed, should also "work," should make an individualized contribution to the public good, and where possible should have the value of their labor recognized by being paid for it.[19] As a member of the first generation of college-educated women, she believed that education and professional achievement, rather than wealth and refinement, fitted a woman for social leadership.

Turning away from nineteenth-century definitions of the unity of women that emphasized their place in the home, their motherhood, and their exclusion from the economy, and emphasizing instead the unity that productive work provided for all women, Blatch rewrote feminism in its essentially modern form, around work. She tended to see women's work, including homemaking and child rearing, as a mammoth portion of the world's productive labor, which women collectively accomplished. Thus she retained the concept of "women's work" for the sex as a whole, while vigorously discarding it on the individual level, explicitly challenging the notion that all women had the same tastes and talents.[20]

Her approach to "women's work" led Blatch to believe that the interconnection of women's labor fundamentally shaped relations among them. Here were the most critical aspects of her thought. Much as she admired professional women, she insisted that they recognize the degree to which their success rested on the labor of other women, who cared for their homes and their children. "Whatever merit [their homes] possess," Blatch wrote, "is largely due to the fact that the actress when on the stage, the doctor when by her patient's side, the writer when at her desk, has a Bridget to do the homebuilding for her." The problem was that the professional woman's labor brought her so much more freedom than the housemaid's labor brought her. "Side by side with the marked improvement in the condition of the well-to-do or educated woman," Blatch observed, "our century shows little or no progress in the condition of the woman of the people." Like her friend Gilman, Blatch urged that professional standards of work—good pay, an emphasis on expertise, the assumption of a lifelong career—be extended to the nurserymaid and the dressmaker, as well as to the lawyer and the journalist. Until such time, the "movement for the emancipation of women [would] remain . . . a well-dressed movement."[21]

But professional training and better wages alone would not give labor an emancipatory power in the lives of working-class women. Blatch recognized the core of the problem of women's work, especially for working-class women: "How can the duties of mother and wage earner be reconciled?" She believed that wage-earning women had the same desire as professional women to continue to enjoy careers and independence after marriage. "It may be perverse in lowly wage earners to show individuality as if they were rich," Blatch wrote, "but apparently we shall have to accept the fact that all women do not prefer domestic work to all other kinds." But the problem of balancing a career and a homelife was "insoluble—under present conditions—for the women of the people." "The pivotal question for women," she wrote, "is how to organize their work as home-builders and race-builders, how to get that work paid for not in so called protection, but in the currency of the state."[22]

As the female labor force grew in the late nineteenth century, so did the number of married women workers and demands that they be driven from the labor force. The suffrage movement had traditionally avoided the conflict between work and motherhood by pinning the demand for economic equality on the existence of unmarried women, who had no men to support them.[23] Blatch confronted the problem of work and motherhood more directly. In a 1905 article, she drew from the utopian ideas of William Morris to recommend that married women work in small, worker-owned manufacturing shops where they could have more control over their hours and could bring their children with them. Elsewhere, she argued that the workplace should be reorganized around women's needs, rather than assume the male worker's standards, but she did not specify what that would mean. She never solved the riddle of work and children for women—nor have we—but she knew that the solution could not be to force women to choose between the two nor to banish mothers from the labor force.[24]

Blatch's vision of women in industrial society was democratic—all must work and all must be recognized and rewarded for their work—but it was not an egalitarian approach nor one that recognized most working women's material concerns. According to Blatch, women worked for psychological and ethical reasons, as much as for monetary ones. "As human beings we must have work," she wrote; "we rust out if we have not an opportunity to function on something." She emphasized the common promises and problems work raised in women's lives, not the differences in how they worked, how much individual choice they had, and especially in how much they were paid. She was relatively unconcerned with the way work enabled women to earn their livings. No doubt, her own experience partially explains this. As a young woman fresh out of college in the 1870s, she had dared to imagine that her desire for meaningful work and a role in the world need not deprive her of marriage and motherhood, and it did not. Despite her marriage, the birth of two children, and the death of one, she never interrupted her political and intellectual labors. But she also never earned her own living, depending instead on the income from her husband's family's business. In later years, she joked about the fact that she was the only "parasite" in the organization of self-supporting women she headed.[25]

But the contradictions in her analysis of the problem of work and women reflected more than her personal situation. There were two problems of work and women: the long-standing exploitation of laboring women of the working classes and the newly expanding place of paid labor in the lives of all women in bourgeois society. While the two processes were not the same, they were related, and women thinkers and activists of the Progressive period struggled to understand how. As more women worked for pay and outside of the home, how would the meaning of "womanhood" change? What would be the difference between "woman" and "man" when as many women as men were paid workers? And what would be the class difference between women if all of them worked? Indeed, would there be any difference between the classes at all, once the woman of leisure no longer existed? Virtually all the efforts to link the gender and class problems of work for woman were incomplete. If Blatch's analysis of work, like Gilman's, shorted the role of class, others' analyses, for instance Florence Kelley's, underplayed what work meant for women as a sex.

Blatch rethought the principles of political equality in the light of her emphasis on women's work. At an 1898 congressional hearing, Blatch hailed "the most convincing argument upon which our future claims must rest—the growing recognition of the economic value of the work of women."[26] Whereas her mother had based her suffragism on the nineteenth-century argument for natural rights and on the individual, Blatch based hers on women's economic contribution and their significance as a group.

The contradictions in Blatch's approach to women and work also emerged in her attempts to link work and the vote. On the one hand, she approached women's political rights as she did their economic emancipation, democratically: Just as all sorts of women must work, all needed the vote. Wealthy women needed the vote because they were taxpayers and had the right to see that their money was not squandered; women industrial workers needed it because their jobs and factories were subject to laws, which they had the right to shape. On the other hand, she recognized the strategic centrality of the enormous class of industrial workers, whose economic role was so important and whose political power was potentially so great. "It is the women of the industrial class," she explained, "the wage-earners, reckoned by the hundred of thousands, . . . the women whose work has been submitted to a money test, who have been the means of bringing about the altered attitude of public opinion toward woman's work in every sphere of life."[27]

Blatch returned to New York for several extended visits after 1894, and she moved back for good in 1902. She had two purposes. Elizabeth Stanton was dying, and Blatch had come to be with her. Blatch also intended to take a leading role in the New York City suffrage movement. On her deathbed in 1902, Stanton asked Anthony to aid Blatch. However, hampered by Anthony's determination to keep control of the movement, Blatch was not able to make her bid for suffrage leadership until Anthony died, four years later.[28]

Meanwhile, Blatch was excited by other reform efforts, which were beginning to provide the resources for a new kind of suffrage movement. During the first years of the twentieth century two movements contributed to Blatch's political education—a broadened, less socially exclusive campaign against political corruption and a democratized movement for the welfare of working women. By 1907, her combined experience in these two movements enabled her to put her ideas about women and work into practice within the suffrage movement itself.

Women had become more active in the campaign against political corruption after 1894. In New York City, Josephine Shaw Lowell and Mary Putnam Jacobi formed the Woman's Municipal League, which concentrated on educating the public about corruption, in particular the links between the police and organized prostitution. Women were conspicuous in the reform campaigns of Seth Low, who was elected mayor in 1901.[29]

By the early 1900s, moreover, the spirit of political reform in New York City had spread beyond the elite. A left wing of the political reform movement had developed that charged that "Wall Street" was more responsible for political corruption than "the Bowery." Women were active in this wing, and there were women's political organizations with links to the Democratic party and the labor movement, a Women's Henry George Society, and a female wing of William Randolph Hearst's Independence League. The nonelite women in these groups were as politically enthusiastic as the members of the Woman's Municipal League, and considerably less ambivalent about enlarging the electorate. Many of them strongly supported woman suffrage. Beginning in 1905, a group of them organized an Equal Rights League to sponsor mock polling places for women to register their political opinions on election day.[30]

Through the 1900s Blatch dutifully attended suffrage meetings, and without much excitement advocated the municipal suffrage for propertied women, favored by the New York movement's leaders after their 1894 defeat. Like many other politically minded women, however, she found her enthusiasm caught by the movement for municipal political reform. She supported Low for mayor in 1901 and believed that his victory demonstrated "how strong woman's power really was when it was aroused." By 1903 she suggested to the National American Woman Suffrage Association (NAWSA) that it set aside agitation for the vote, so that "the women of the organization should use it for one year, nationally and locally, to pursue and punish corruption in politics." She supported the increasing attention given to "the laboring man" in reform political coalitions, but she pointedly observed that "the working woman was never considered."[31]

However, working-class women were emerging as active factors in other women's reform organizations. The crucial arena for this development was the Women's Trade Union League (WTUL), formed in 1902 by a coalition of working-class and elite women to draw wage-earning women into trade unions. The New York chapter was formed in 1905, and Blatch was one of the first elite women to join. The WTUL represented a significant move away from the tradition of elite, ameliorative sisterhood at work in the 1894 campaign for woman suffrage. Like the Consumers' League, it had been formed in response to the request of women wage earners for aid from elite women, but it was an organization of both classes working together. Blatch had never been attracted to the strictly ameliorative tradition of women's reform, and the shift toward a partnership of upper-class and working-class women paralleled her own thinking about the relation between the classes and the role of work in women's lives. She and other elite women in the WTUL found themselves laboring not for working-class women, but with them, and toward a goal of forming unions that did not merely "uplift" working-class women, but empowered them. Instead of being working- class women's protectors, they were their "allies." Instead of speaking on behalf of poor women, they began to hear them speak for themselves. Within the organization wage earners were frequently in conflict with allies. Nonetheless, the league provided them an arena to articulate a working-class feminism related to, but distinct from, that of elite women.[32]

Although prominent as a suffragist, Blatch participated in the WTUL on its own terms, rather than as a colonizer for suffrage. She and two other members assigned to the millinery trade conducted investigations into conditions and organized mass meetings to interest women workers in unions. She sat on the Executive Council from 1906 through 1909 and was often called on to stand in for President Mary Dreier. Her academic knowledge of "the industrial woman" was replaced by direct knowledge of wage-earning women and their working conditions. She was impressed with what she saw of trade unionism, especially its unrelenting "militance." Perhaps most important, she developed working relations with politically sophisticated working-class women, notably Leonora O'Reilly and Rose Schneiderman. Increasingly she believed that the organized power of labor and the enfranchisement of women were closely allied.[33]

Working-class feminists in the league were drawn to ideas like Blatch's—to conceptions of dignity and equality for women in the workplace and to the ethic of self-support and lifelong independence; they wanted to upgrade the condition of wage-earning women so that they, too, could enjoy personal independence on the basis of their labor. On the one hand, they understood why most working-class women would want to leave their hateful jobs upon marriage; on the other, they knew that women as a group, if not the individual worker, were a permanent factor in the modern labor force. Mary Kenney O'Sullivan of Boston, one of the league's founders, believed that "self support" was a goal for working-class women, but that only trade unions would give the masses of working women the "courage, independence, and self respect" they needed to improve their conditions. She expected "women of opportunity" to help in organizing women workers, because they "owed much to workers who give them a large part of what they have and enjoy," and because "the time has passed when women of opportunity can be self respecting and work *for* others."[34]

Initially, the demand for the vote was less important to such working-class feminists than to the allies. Still, as they began to participate in the organized women's movement on a more equal basis, wage-earning women began to receive serious attention within the woman suffrage movement as well. Beginning about 1905, advocates of trade unionism and the vote for women linked the demands. At the 1906 suffrage convention WTUL member Gertrude Barnum pointed out that "our hope as suffragists lies with these strong working women." Kelley and Addams wrote about the working woman's need for the vote to improve her own conditions. In New York, Blatch called on the established suffrage societies to recognize the importance of the vote to wage-earning women and the importance of wage-earning women to winning the vote. When she realized that existing groups could not adapt to the new challenges, she moved to form her own society.[35]

In January 1907, Blatch declared the formation of a new suffrage organization, the Equality League of Self-Supporting Women. The *New York Times* reported that the two hundred women present at the first meeting included "doctors, lawyers, milliners and shirtmakers."[36] Blatch's decision to establish a suffrage organization that emphasized female "self-support"—lifelong economic independence—grew out of her ideas about work as the basis of women's claim on the state, the leadership role she envisioned for educated professionals, and her discovery of the power and political capacity of trade-union women. The Equality League provided the medium for introducing a new and aggressive style of activism into the suffrage movement—a version of the "militance" Blatch admired among trade unionists.

Initially, Blatch envisioned the Equality League of Self-Supporting Women as the political wing of the Women's Trade Union League. All the industrial workers she recruited were WTUL activists, including O'Reilly, the Equality League's first vice-president, and Schneiderman, its most popular speaker. To welcome working-class women, the Equality League virtually abolished membership fees; the policy had the added advantage of allowing Blatch to claim every woman who ever attended a league meeting in her estimate of its membership. She also claimed the members of the several trade unions affiliated with the Equality League, such as the bookbinders, overall makers, and cap makers, so that when she went before the New York legislature to demand the vote, she could say that the Equality League represented thousands of wage-earning women.[37]

Blatch wanted the Equality League to connect industrial workers, not with "club women" (her phrase), but with educated, professional workers, who should, she thought, replace benevolent ladies as the leaders of their sex. Such professionals—college educated and often women pioneers in their professions—formed the bulk of the Equality League's active membership. Many were lawyers, for instance, Ida Rauh, Helen Hoy, Madeleine Doty, Jessie Ashley, Adelma Burd, and Bertha Rembaugh. Others were social welfare workers, for instance the Equality League's treasurer, Kate Claghorn, a tenement housing inspector and the highest paid female employee of the New York City government. Blatch's own daughter, Nora, the first woman graduate civil engineer in the United States, worked in the New York City Department of Public Works. Many of these women had inherited incomes and did not work out of economic need, but out of a desire to give serious, public substance to their lives and to make an impact on society. Many of them expressed the determination to maintain economic independence after they married.[38]

Although Blatch brought together trade-union women and college-educated profession-als in the Equality League, there were tensions between the classes. The first correspon-dence between O'Reilly and Barnard graduate Caroline Lexow was full of class suspicion and mutual recrimination. More generally, there were real differences in how and why the two classes of working women demanded the vote. Trade-union feminists wanted the vote so that women industrial workers would have power over the labor laws that directly affected their working lives. Many of the college-educated self-supporters were the designers and administrators of this labor legislation. Several of them were, or aspired to be, government employees, and political power affected their jobs through party patronage. The occupation that might have bridged the differences was teaching. As in other cities, women teachers in New York organized for greater power and equal pay. The Equality League frequently offered aid, but the New York teachers' leaders were relatively conservative and kept their distance from the suffrage movement.[39]

Blatch's special contribution was her understanding of the bonds and common interests uniting industrial and professional women workers. The industrial women admired the professional ethic, if not the striving careerism, of the educated working women, and the professionals admired the matter-of-fact way wage-earning women went out to work. The fate of the professional woman was closely tied to that of the industrial worker; the cultural regard in which all working women were held affected both. Blatch dramatized that tie when she was refused service at a restaurant because she was unescorted by a man (that is, because she was eating with a woman). The management claimed that its policy aimed to protect "respectable" women, like Blatch, from "objectionable" women, like the common woman worker who went about on her own, whose morals were therefore questionable. Blatch rejected the division between respectable women and working women, pointing out that "there are five million women earning their livelihood in this country, and it seems strange that feudal customs should still exist here."[40]

The dilemma of economically dependent married women was crucial to the future of both classes of working women. Blatch believed that if work was to free women, they could not leave it for dependence on men in marriage. The professional and working-class members of the Equality League shared this belief, one of the distinguishing convictions of their new approach to suffragism. In 1908, Blatch and Mary Dreier chaired a debate about the housewife, sponsored by the WTUL and attended by many Equality League members. Charlotte Perkins Gilman took the Equality League position, that the unemployed wife was a "parasite" on her husband, and that all women, married as well as unmarried, should work, "like every other self-respecting being." Anna Howard Shaw argued that women's domestic labor was valuable, even if unpaid, and that the husband was dependent on his wife. A large audience attended, and although they "warmly applauded" Gilman, they preferred Shaw's sentimental construction of the economics of marriage.[41]

A month after the Equality League was formed, Blatch arranged for trade-union women to testify before the New York legislature on behalf of woman suffrage, the first working-class women ever to do so. The New York Woman Suffrage Association was still concentrating on the limited, property-based form of municipal suffrage; in lethargic testimony its leaders admitted that they had "no new arguments to present." Everyone at the hearing agreed that the antis had the better of the argument. The Equality League testimony the next day was in sharp contrast. Clara Silver and Mary Duffy, WTUL activists and organizers in the garment industry, supported full suffrage for all New York women. The very presence of these women before the legislature, and their dignity and intelligence, countered the antis' dire predictions about enfranchising the unfit. Both linked suffrage to their trade-union efforts: While they struggled for equality in unions and in industry, "the state" undermined them, by teaching the lesson of female inferiority to male unionists and bosses. "To be left out by the State just sets up a prejudice against us," Silver explained. "Bosses think and women come to think themselves that they don't count for so much as men."[42]

The formation of the Equality League and its appearance before the New York legislature awakened enthusiasm. Lillie Devereux Blake, whose own suffrage group had tried "one whole Winter . . . to [interest] the working women" but found that they were "so overworked and so poor that they can do little for us," congratulated Blatch on here apparent success. Helen Marot, organizing secretary for the New York WTUL, praised the Equality League for "realizing the increasing necessity of including working women in the suffrage movement." Blatch, O'Reilly, and Schneiderman were the star speakers at the 1907 New York suffrage convention. "We realize that probably it will not be the educated workers, the college women, the men's association for equal suffrage, but the people who are fighting for industrial freedom who will be our vital force at the finish," proclaimed the newsletter of the NAWSA.[43]

The unique class character of the Equality League encouraged the development of a new style of agitation, more radical than anything practiced in the suffrage movement since . . . since Elizabeth Stanton's prime. The immediate source of the change was the Women's Social and Political Union of England (WSPU), led by Blatch's comrade from her Fabian days, Emmeline Pankhurst. Members of the WSPU were just beginning to be arrested for their suffrage protests. At the end of the Equality League's first year, Blatch invited one of the first WSPU prisoners, Anne Cobden-Sanderson, daughter of Richard Cobden, to the U.S. to tell about her experiences, scoring a coup for the Equality League. By emphasizing Cobden-Sanderson's connection with the British Labour party and distributing free platform tickets to trade-union leaders, Blatch was able to get an overflow crowd at Cooper Union, Manhattan's labor temple, two-thirds of them men, many of them trade unionists.[44]

The Equality League's meeting for Cobden-Sanderson offered American audiences their first account of the new radicalism of English suffragists, or as they were beginning to be called, suffragettes. Cobden-Sanderson emphasized the suffragettes' working-class origins. She attributed the revival of the British suffrage movement to Lancashire factory workers; the heroic figure in her account was the working-class suffragette, Annie Kenney, while Christabel Pankhurst, later canonized as the Joan of Arc of British militance, went unnamed. After women factory workers were arrested for trying to see the prime minister, Cobden-Sanderson and other privileged women, who felt they "had not so much to lose as [the workers] had," decided to join them and get arrested. She spent almost two months in jail, living the life of a common prisoner and coming to a new awareness of the poor and suffering women she saw there. Her simple but moving account conveyed the transcendent impact of the experience.[45]

Cobden-Sanderson's visit to New York catalyzed a great outburst of suffrage energy; in its wake, Blatch and a handful of other new leaders introduced the WSPU tactics into the American movement, and the word *suffragette* became as common in New York as in London. The "militants" became an increasingly distinct wing of the movement in New York and other American cities. But it would be too simple to say that the British example caused the new, more militant phase in the American movement. The developments that were broadening the class basis and the outlook of American suffragism had prepared American women to respond to the heroism of the British militants.[46]

The development of militance in the American suffrage movement was marked by new aggressive tactics practiced by the WSPU, especially open-air meetings and outdoor parades. At this stage in the development of British militance, American suffragists generally admired the heroism of the WSPU martyrs. Therefore, although the press emphasized dissent within the suffrage movement—it always organized its coverage of suffrage around female rivalries of some sort—the new militant activities were well received throughout the movement. And, conversely, even the most daring American suffragettes believed in an American exceptionalism that made it unnecessary to contemplate going to prison, to suffer as did the British militants.[47]

Despite Blatch's later claims, she did not actually introduce the new tactics in New York City. The first open-air meetings were organized immediately after the Cobden-Sanderson visit by a group called the American Suffragettes. Initiated by Bettina Borrman Wells, a visiting member of the WSPU, most of the American Suffragettes' membership came from the Equal Rights League, the left-wing municipal reform group that had organized mock polling places in New York since 1905. Feminist egalitarians with radical cultural leanings, its members were actresses, artists, writers, teachers, and social welfare workers—less wealthy versions of the professional self-supporters in the Equality League. Their local leader was a librarian, Maud Malone, whose role in encouraging new suffrage tactics was almost as important as, although less recognized than, Blatch's own.[48]

The American Suffragettes held their first open-air meeting in Madison Square on New Year's Eve, 1907. After that they met in the open at least once a week. Six weeks later, they announced they would hold New York's first all-woman parade. Denied a police permit, they determined to march anyway. The twenty-three women in the "parade" were many times outnumbered by the onlookers, mostly working-class men. In a public school to which they adjourned to make speeches, the American Suffragettes told a sympathetic audience that "the woman who works is the underdog of the world"; thus she needed the vote to defend herself. Socialists and working women rose from the floor to support them. Two years later the Equality League organized a much more successful suffrage parade in New York. Several hundred suffragettes, organized by occupation, marched from Fifty-ninth Street to Union Square. O'Reilly, the featured speaker, made "a tearful plea on behalf of the working girl that drew the first big demonstration of applause from the street crowd."[49]

Perhaps because the American Suffragettes were so active in New York City, Blatch held the Equality League's first open-air meetings in May 1908 upstate. Accompanied by Maud Malone, she organized an inventive "trolley car campaign" between Syracuse and Albany, using the interurban trolleys to go from town to town. The audiences expressed the complex class character of the suffrage movement at that moment. In Syracuse Blatch had her wealthy friend Dora Hazard arrange a meeting among the workers at her husband's factory. She also held a successful outdoor meeting in Troy, home of the Laundry Workers' Union, one of the oldest and most militant independent women's trade unions in the country. Albany was an antisuffrage stronghold, and its mayor tried to prevent the meeting, but Blatch outwitted him. The highlight of the tour was in Poughkeepsie, where Blatch and Inez Milholland, then a student at Vassar College, organized a legendary meeting. Since Vassar's male president forbade any woman suffrage activities on college grounds, Blatch and Milholland defiantly announced they would meet students in a cemetery. Gilman, who was extremely popular among college women, spoke, but it was the passionate trade-union feminist, Schneiderman, who was the star.[50]

Blatch believed that the first function of militant tactics was to gain much-needed publicity for the movement. The mainstream press had long ignored suffrage activities. If an occasional meeting was reported, it was usually buried in a small backpage article, focusing on the absurdity and incompetence of women's efforts to organize a political campaign. Gilded Age suffragists themselves accepted the Victorian convention that respectable women did not court public attention. The Equality League's emphasis on the importance of paid labor for women of all classes struck at the heart of that convention. Blatch understood "the value of publicity or rather the harm of the lack of it." She encouraged open-air meetings and trolley car campaigns because they generated much publicity, which no longer held the conventional horror for her followers.[51]

Militant tactics broke through the "press boycott" by violating standards of respectable femininity, making the cause newsworthy, and embracing the subsequent ridicule and attention. "We . . . believe in standing on street corners and fighting our way to recognition, forcing the men to think about us," an *American Suffragette* manifesto proclaimed. "We glory . . . that we are theatrical." The militant pursuit of publicity was an instant success: Newspaper coverage increased immediately; by 1908 even the sneering *New York Times* reported regularly on suffrage. The more outrageous or controversial the event, the more prominent the coverage. Blatch was often pictured and quoted.[52]

The new methods had a second function; they intensified women's commitment to the movement. Militants expected that overstepping the boundary of respectability would etch suffrage beliefs on women's souls, beyond retraction or modification. Blatch caught the psychology of this process. "Society has taught women self-sacrifice and now this force is to be drawn upon in the arduous campaign for their own emancipation," she wrote. "The new methods of agitation, in that they are difficult and disagreeable, lay hold of the imagination and devotion of women, wherein lies the strength of the new appeal, the certainty of victory." Borrman Wells spoke of the "divine spirit of self-sacrifice," which underlay the suffragette's transgressions against respectability and was the source of the "true inwardness of the movement."[53]

If suffrage militants had a general goal beyond getting the vote, it was to challenge existing standards of femininity. "We must eliminate that abominable word ladylike from our vocabularies," Borrman Wells proclaimed. "We must get out and fight." The new definition of femininity the militants were evolving drew, on the one hand, on traditionally male behaviors, like aggression, fighting, provocation, and rebelliousness. Blatch was particularly drawn to the "virile" world of politics, which she characterized as a male "sport" she was sure she could master. On the other hand, they undertook a spirited defense of female sexuality, denying that it need be forfeited by women who participated vigorously in public life. "Women are no longer to be considered little tootsey wootseys who have nothing to do but look pretty," suffragette Lydia Commander declared. "They are determined to take an active part in the community and look pretty too." A member of a slightly older generation, Blatch never adopted the modern sexual ethic of the new woman, but she constantly emphasized the fact that women had distinct concerns that had to be accommodated in politics and industry. These two notes—the difference of the sexes and the repressed ability of women for manly activities—existed side by side in the thought of all the suffrage insurgents.[54]

The militant methods, taking suffrage out of the parlors and into the streets, indicated the new significance of working-class women in several ways. Blatch pointed out that the new methods—open-air meetings, newspaper publicity—suited a movement whose members had little money and therefore could not afford to rent halls or publish a newspaper. As a style of protest, "militance" was an import from the labor movement; WTUL organizers had been speaking from street corners for several years. And disrespect for the standards of ladylike respectability showed at least an impatience with rigid standards of class distinction, at most the influence of class-conscious wage-earning women.[55]

Working-class feminists were eager to speak from the militants' platform, as were many Socialists. A Socialist cadre, Dr. Anna Mercy, organized a branch of the American Suffragettes on the Lower East Side, which issued the first suffrage leaflets ever published in Yiddish. Militants also prepared propaganda in German and Italian and, in general, pursued working-class audiences. "Our relation to the State will be determined by the vote of the average man," Blatch asserted. "None but the converted . . . will come to us. We must seek on the highways the unconverted."[56]

However, it would be a mistake to confuse the suffragettes' radicalism with the radicalism of a working-class movement. The ultimate goal of the suffragettes was not a single-class movement, but a universal one, "the union of women of all shades of political thought and of all ranks of society on the single issue of their political enfranchisement." While the Equality League's 1907 hearing before the state legislature highlighted trade-union suffragists, at the 1908 hearing the league also featured elite speakers, in effect deemphasizing the working-class perspective.[57] Militants could neither repudiate the Socialist support they were attracting, and alienate working-class women, nor associate too closely with Socialists and lose access to the wealthy. Blatch—who actually became a Socialist after the suffrage was won—would not arrange for the Socialist party leader Morris Hillquit to join other prosuffrage speakers at the 1908 legislative hearing. Similarly, the American Suffragettes allowed individual Socialists on their platform but barred Socialist propaganda. Speaking for Socialist women who found the "idea of a 'radical' suffrage movement . . . very alluring," Josephine Conger Kaneko admitted that the suffragettes left her confused.[58]

Moreover, the militant challenge to femininity and the emphasis on publicity introduced a distinctly elite bias; a society matron on an open-air platform made page one while a working girl did not, because society women were obliged by conventions and could outrage by flouting them. In their very desire to redefine femininity, the militants were anxious to stake their claim to it, and it was upper-class women who determined femininity. In Elizabeth Robin's drama about the rise of militance in the British suffrage movement, *The Convert*, the heroine of the title was a beautiful aristocratic woman who became radical when she realized the emptiness of her ladylike existence and the contempt for women obscured by gentlemen's chivalrous gestures. The Equality League brought *The Convert* to New York in 1908 as its first large fund-raising effort; working-class women, as well as elite women, made up the audience. Malone was one of the few militants to recognize and to protest against excessive solicitousness for the elite convert. She resigned from the American Suffragettes when she concluded that they had become interested in attracting "a well-dressed crowd, not the rabble."[59]

Blatch's perspective and associations had always been fundamentally elite. The most well connected of the new militant leaders, she played a major role in bringing the new suffrage propaganda to the attention of upper-class women. She presided over street meetings in fashionable neighborhoods, where reporters commented on the "smart" crowds and described the speakers' outfits in society-page detail. Blatch's first important ally from the Four Hundred was Katherine Duer Mackay, wife of the founder of the International Telephone and Telegraph Company and a famous society beauty. Mackay's suffragism was very ladylike, but other members of her set who followed her into the movement were more drawn to militance: Alva Belmont, a veritable mistress of flamboyance, began her suffrage career as Mackay's protégé. The elitist subtext of militance was a minor theme in 1908 and 1909. But by 1910 becoming a suffragette was proving "fashionable," and upper-class women began to identify with the new suffrage style in significant numbers. By the time suffragette militance became a national movement, its working-class origins and trade-union associations had been submerged, and it was in the hands of women of wealth.[60]

From the beginning, though, class was the contradiction at the suffrage movement's heart. In the campaign of 1894, elite women began to pursue more power for themselves by advocating the suffrage in the name of all women. When Cobden-Sanderson spoke for the Equality League at Cooper Union in 1907, she criticized "idle women of wealth" as the enemies of woman suffrage, and she was wildly applauded. But what did her charge mean? Were all rich women under indictment, or only those who stayed aloof from social responsibility and political activism? Were the militants calling for working-class leadership of the suffrage movement or for cultural changes in bourgeois definitions of womanhood? This ambiguity paralleled the mixed meanings in Blatch's emphasis on working women; it coincided with an implicit tension between the older, elite women's reform traditions and the newer trade-union politics they had helped to usher in; and it was related to a lurking confusion about whether feminism's object was the superfluity of wealthy women or the exploitation of the poor. It would continue to plague suffragism in its final decade, and feminism afterwards, into our own time.

Notes

The author wishes to thank Nancy Cott, Elizabeth L. Kennedy, Anne F. Scott, David Thelen, and Eli Zaretsky for their thoughtful reading and challenging comments on earlier drafts. In addition, the Papers of Elizabeth Cady Stanton and Susan B. Anthony, University of Massachusetts, Amherst, provided generous research assistance.

1. A good overview of political history in the Progressive Era can be found in Arthur S Link and Richard L. McCormick, *Progressivism* (Arlington Heights, Ill., 1983), 26–66. The "separate spheres" framework of Progressive-Era historiography has been identified and challenged by Paula Baker, "The Domestication of Politics: Women and American Political Society, 1780–1920," *American Historical Review*, 89 (June 1984), esp. 639–47; and by Kathryn Kish Sklar, "Hull House in the 1890s: A Community of Women Reformers," *Signs*, 10 (Summer 1985);, 658–77; and Kathryn Kish Sklar, "Florence Kelley and the Integration of 'Women's Sphere' into American Politics, 1890–1921," paper delivered at the annual meeting of the Organization of American Historians, New York, April 1986 (in Sklar's possession).

2. Steven M. Buechler, *The Transformation of the Woman Suffrage Movement: The Case of Illinois, 1850–1920* (New Brunswick, 1986); Mari Jo Buhle and Paul Buhle, eds., *The Concise History of Woman Suffrage: Selections from the Classic Work of Stanton, Anthony, Gage and Harper* (Urbana, 1978); Carole Nichols, *Votes and More for Women: Suffrage and After in Connecticut* (New York, 1983); Anne F. Scott and Andrew Scott, eds., *One Half the People* (Philadelphia, 1975); and Sharon Strom, "Leadership and Tactics in the American Woman Suffrage Movement: A New Perspective from Massachusetts," *Journal of American History*, 52 (Sept. 1975), 296–315.

3. "Mrs. Blatch's Address," clipping, 1903, Women's Club of Orange, N. J., Scrapbooks, IV (New Jersey Historical Society, Trenton). Thanks to Gail Malmgreen for this citation.

4. Richard L. McCormick, *From Realignment to Reform: Political Change in New York State, 1893–1910* (Ithaca, 1979), 53. An excellent account of the political reform movement in the 1890s in New York City can be found in David C. Hammack, *Power and Society: Greater New York at the Turn of the Century* (New York, 1982).

5. Susan B. Anthony and Ida Husted Harper, eds., *The History of Woman Suffrage*, vol. IV: *1883–1900* (Rochester, 1902), 847–52; New York State Woman Suffrage Party, *Record of the New York Campaign of 1894* (New York, 1895); Ida Husted Harper, *The Life and Work of Susan B. Anthony* (3 vols., Indianapolis, 1898–1908), II, 758–76, esp. 759.

6. Mary Putnam Jacobi, "Report of the 'Volunteer Committee' in New York City," in *Record of the New York Campaign*, 217–20; Maud Nathan, *The Story of an Epoch-making Movement* (Garden City, 1926); William Rhinelander Steward, ed., *The Philanthropic Work of Josephine Shaw Lowell* (New York, 1926), 334–56.

7. *New York Times*, April 14, 1894, 2; *ibid.*, April 15, 1894, 5. Mrs. Robert (Catherine) Abbe's suffrage scrapbooks provide extensive documentation of the New York suffrage movement, beginning with this campaign. Mrs. Robert Abbe Collection (Manuscript Division, New York Public Library). Theodore Stanton and Harriot Stanton Blatch, eds., *Elizabeth Cady Stanton As Revealed in Her Letters, Diary and Reminiscences* (2 vols. New York, 1922). II. 299.

8. Mary Putnam Jacobi, "Address Delivered at the New York City Hearing," in *Record of the New York Campaign*, 17–26; Olivia Slocum Sage, "Opportunities and Responsibilities of Leisured Women," *North American Review*, 181 (Nov. 1905), 712–21.

9. *Ibid.*

10. *Ibid.*

11. Jacobi, "Report of the 'Volunteer Committee,' " 217; Stanton and Blatch, eds., *Elizabeth Cady Stanton*, II, 305; *New York Times*, May 3, 1894, 9 Abby Hamlin Abbott and Josephine Jewell Dodge were both Brooklyn residents; the division between suffragists and antis reflected a conflict between the elites of Manhattan and Brooklyn over the 1894 referendum to consolidate the two cities into Greater New York. See Hammack, *Power and Society*, 209.

12. Jacobi, "Address Delivered at the New York City Hearing," 22; *New York Times*, April 12, 1894, 5. "The woman in charge of the [anti] protest . . . told a reporter . . . that her own dressmaker has secured about forty signatories to the protest among working women," *Ibid.*, May 8, 1894, 1.

13. *Woman's Journal*, May 12, 1894, 147.

14. *Ibid.*, May 1894. The study, patterned after Charles Booth and Mary Booth's investigation of the London poor, on which Blatch worked, was published as Harriot Stanton Blatch, "Another View of Village Life," *Westminster Review*, 140 (Sept. 1893), 318–24.

15. Stanton and Blatch, *Elizabeth Cady Stanton*, II, 304; unidentified clipping, April 25, 1894, Scrapbook XX; Susan B. Anthony Collection (Manuscript Division, Library of Congress); *New York Times*, April 25, 1894, *Ibid.*, May 3, 1894, 9; *New York Sun*, April 15, 1894, n.p.

16. *Woman's Journal*, Nov. 3, 1894, 348–49; *Ibid.*, Dec. 22, 1894, 402; *Ibid.*, Jan. 5, 1895, 1. Blatch wrote that her mother's position "pained" her but there is no evidence of any personal conflict between them at this time. *Ibid.*, Dec. 22, 1894, 402.

17. Harriot Stanton Blatch and Alma Lutz, *Challenging Years: The Memoirs of Harriot Stanton Blatch* (New York 1940), 77. *Woman's Journal*, Jan. 18, 1896, 18.

18. *Woman's Journal*, May 12, 1900, 146–47. Along with Blatch and Charlotte Perkins Gilman, Florence Kelley and Jane Addams were the most important figures to focus on women and class. See Charlotte Perkins Gilman, *Women and Economics: A Study of the Economic Relation between Men and Women as a Factor in Social Evolution* (Boston, 1898); Florence Kelley, *Woman Suffrage: Its Relation to Working Women and Children* (Warren, Ohio, 1906); Florence Kelley, "Women and Social Legislation in the United States," *Annals of the American Academy of Political and Social Science*, 56 (Nov. 1914), 62–71; Jane Addams, *Newer Ideals of Peace* (New York, 1907); and Jane Addams, *Twenty Years at Hull House* (New York, 1910). Some of the other women reformers who wrote on women and work early in the century were: Rheta Childe Dorr, *What Eight Million Women Want* (Boston, 1910); Lillian Wald, "Organization among Working Women," *Annals of the American Academy of Political and Social Science*, 27 (May 1906), 638–45; and Anna Garlin Spencer, *Woman's Share in Social Culture* (New York, 1913).

19. Harriot Stanton Blatch, "Specialization of Function in Women," *Gunton's Magazine*, 10 (May 1896), 349–56, esp. 350.

20. *Ibid.*

21. *Ibid.*, 354–55; see also Blatch's comments at a 1904 suffrage meeting in New York, *Woman's Journal*, Dec. 31, 1904, 423.

22. Blatch, "Specialization of Function in Women," 350, 353.

23. See, for example, the response of the New York City Woman Suffrage League to a proposal before the American Federation of Labor to ban women from all nondomestic employment, *New York Times*, Dec. 23, 1898, 7.

24. Harriot Stanton Blatch, "Weaving in a Westchester Farmhouse," *International Studio*, 26 (Oct. 1905), 102–05; *Woman's Journal*, Jan. 21, 1905; *Ibid.*, Dec. 31, 1904, 423.

25. Blatch, "Weaving in a Westchester Farmhouse," 104; Blatch and Lutz, *Challenging Years*, 70–86; Rhoda Barney Jenkins interview by Ellen Carol DuBois, June 10, 1982 (in Ellen Carol DuBois's possession); Ellen DuBois, " 'Spanning Two Centuries': The Autobiography of Nora Stanton Barney," *History Workshop*, no. 22 (Fall 1986), 131–52. esp. 149.

26. Anthony and Harper, eds., *History of Woman Suffrage*, IV , 311.

27. "Mrs. Blatch's Address," Women's Club of Orange, N. J., Scrapbooks; Anthony and Harper, eds., *History of Woman Suffrage*, IV, 311.

28. Harriot Stanton Blatch to Susan B. Anthony, Sept. 26, 1902, in *Epistolary Autobiography*, Theodore Stanton Collection (Douglass College Library, Rutgers University, New Brunswick, N. J.).

29. Oswald Garrison Villard, "Women in New York Municipal Campaign," *Woman's Journal*, March 8, 1902.

30. *New York Times*, Jan. 14, 1901, 7. The Gertrude Colles Collection (New York State Library, Albany) is particularly rich in evidence of the less elite, more radical side of female political reform in these years. On the mock voting organized by the Equal Rights League, see *Woman's Journal*, Dec. 28, 1905, and *New York Times*, Nov. 7, 1906, 9.

31. Anthony and Harper, eds., *History of Woman Suffrage*, IV, 861; Ida Husted Harper, ed., *History of Woman Suffrage*, vol. VI: *1900–1920* (New York, 1922), 454; *New York Times*, March 2, 1902, 8; *Woman's Tribune*, April 25, 1903, 49. After Blatch had become an acknowledged leader of the New York suffrage movement, the co worker who, she felt, most shared her political perspective was Caroline Lexow, daughter of the man who had conducted the original investigation of police corruption in New York in 1894. See Blatch and Lutz, *Challenging Years*, 120–21; and Isabelle K. Savell, *Ladies' Lib: How Rockland Women Got the Vote* (New York, 1979).

32. Minutes, March 29, 1906, reel 1, New York Women's Trade Union League Papers (New York State Labor Library, New York). On the WTUL, see Nancy Schrom Dye, *As Equals and As Sisters: Feminism, the Labor Movement, and the Women's Trade Union League of New York* (Columbia, 1980); and Meredith Tax, *The Rising of the Women: Feminist Solidarity and Class Conflict, 1880–1917* (New York, 1980), 95–124.

33. Dye, *As Equals and As Sisters*, 63; Minutes, April 26, Aug. 23, 1906, New York Women's Trade Union League Papers; *New York Times*, April 11, 1907, 8.

34. Mary Kenney O'Sullivan, "The Need of Organization among Working Women (1905)," Margaret Dreier Robins Papers (University of Florida Library, Gainesville); Sarah Eisenstein, *Give Us Bread but Give Us Roses: Working Women's Consciousness in the United States, 1890 to the First World War* (London, 1983), 146–50.

35. *Woman's Journal*, March 17, 1906, 43; Kelley, *Woman Suffrage;* Jane Addams, *Utilization of Women in Government*, in *Jane Addams: A Centennial Reader* (New York, 1960), 117–18; *Woman's Journal*, Dec. 31, 1904, 423; "Mrs. Blatch's Address," Women's Club of Orange, N. J., Scrapbooks. There was a lengthy discussion of working women's need for the vote, including a speech by Rose Schneiderman, at the 1907 New York State Woman Suffrage Association convention. See Minute Book, 1907–10, New York State Woman Suffrage Association (Butler Library, Columbia University, New York). The WTUL identified woman suffrage as one of its goals by 1907. Dye, *As Equals and As Sisters*, 123.

36. *New York Times*, Jan. 3, 1907, 6; *Woman's Journal*, Jan. 12, 1907, 8.

37. *Progress*, June 1907, Carrie Chapman Catt to Millicent Garrett Fawcett, Oct. 19, 1909, container 5, Papers of Carrie Chapman Catt (Manuscript Division, Library of Congress).

38. *Woman's Journal*, Aug. 17, 1907, 129. On Nora Blatch (who later called herself Nora Stanton Barney), see DuBois, " 'Spanning Two Centuries,' " 131–52. Those self- supporters who, I believe, had independent incomes include Nora Blatch, Caroline Lexow, Lavinia Dock, Ida Rauh, Gertrude Barnum, Elizabeth Finnegan, and Alice Clark. See, for example, on Nora Blatch, *ibid.*, and on Dock, *Notable American Women: The Modern Period*, s.v. "Dock, Lavinia Lloyd."

39. Caroline Lexow to Leonora O'Reilly, Jan. 3, 1908, reel 4, Leonora O'Reilly Papers (Schlesinger Library, Radcliffe College, Cambridge, Mass.); O'Reilly to Lexow, Jan. 5, 1908, *Ibid.*; Robert Doherty, "Tempest on the Hudson: The Struggle for Equal Pay for Equal Work in the New York City Public Schools, 1907–1911," *Harvard Educational Quarterly*, 19 (Winter 1979), 413–39. The role of teachers in the twentieth-century suffrage movement is a promising area for research. For information on teachers' organizations in the Buffalo, New York, suffrage movement, I am indebted to Eve S. Faber, Swarthmore College, "Suffrage in Buffalo, 1898–1913" (unpublished paper. in DuBois's possession).

40. *New York Times*, June 6, 1907, 1.

41. On self-support for women after marriage, see *New York World*, July 26, 1908, 3; and Lydia Kingsmill Commander, "The Self Supporting Woman and the Family," *American Journal of Sociology*, 14 (March 1909), 752–57. On the debate, see *New York Times*, Jan. 7, 1909, 9.

42. *New York Times*, Feb. 6, 1907, 6. Harriot Stanton Blatch, ed., *Two Speeches by Industrial Women* (New York, 1907), esp. 8. The Equality League's bill authorized a voters' referendum on an amendment to the New York constitution, to remove the word "male" from the state's suffrage provisions, thus enfranchising New York women. Since the U. S. Constitution vests power to determine the electorate with the states, the aim was to win full suffrage in federal, as well as state, elections for New York women. With minor alterations, the measure finally passed, but in 1915 New York voters refused to enfranchise the women of their state; a second referendum in 1917 was successful. See Blatch and Lutz, *Challenging Years*, 156–238.

43. *Woman's Tribune*, Feb. 9, 1907, 12; Minutes, April 27, 1909, New York Women's Trade Union League Papers; *Progress*, Nov. 1907.

44. Blatch and Lutz, *Challenging Years*, 100–101; *Progress*, Jan. 1908.

45. *Woman's Journal*, Dec. 28, 1907, 205, 206–7.

46. By 1908, there was a racehorse named "suffragette." *New York Evening Telegram*, Sept. 16, 1908. Blatch noted that once she left England in the late 1890s, she and Emmeline Pankhurst did not communicate until 1907, after they had both taken their respective countries' suffrage movements in newly militant directions. Blatch to Christabel Pankhurst, in Christabel Pankhurst, *Unshackled: How We Won the Vote* (London, 1959), 30.

47. The first American arrests were not until 1917. For American suffragists' early response to the WSPU, see the *Woman's Journal*, May 30, 1908, 87. Even Carrie Chapman Catt praised the British militants at first. *Woman's Journal*, Dec. 12, 1908, 199. For an example of divisive coverage by the mainstream press, see "Suffragist or Suffragette," *New York Times*, Feb. 29, 1908, 6.

48. On Bettina Borrman Wells, see A. J. R., ed., *Suffrage Annual and Women's Who's Who* (London, 1913), 390. Thanks to David Doughan of the Fawcett Library for this reference. The best sources on the Equal Rights League are the Gertrude Colles Collection and *The American Suffragette*, which the group published from 1909 through 1911. See also Winifred Harper Cooley, "Suffragists and 'Suffragettes.'" *World To Day*, 15 (Oct. 1908), 1066–71; and Elinor Lerner, "Jewish Involvement in the New York City Woman Suffrage Movement," *American Jewish History*, 70 (June 1981), 444–45. The American suffragettes found a predecessor and benefactor in seventy-five-year-old Lady Cook, formerly Tennessee Claflin, in 1909 the wife of a titled Englishman. "Our Cook Day," *American Suffragette*, 1 (Nov. 1909). 1.

49. On the first open-air meeting, see *New York Times*, Jan. 1, 1908, 16. On the parade, see *Ibid.*, Feb. 17, 1908, 7; there is also an account in Dort, *What Eight Million Women Want*, 298–99; *New York Evening Journal*, May 21, 1910.

50. Equality League of Self-Supporting Women, *Report for Year 1908–1909* (New York, 1909), 2; Blatch and Lutz, *Challenging Years*, 107–09. On Vassar, see also *New York American*, June 10, 1908.

51. Harriot Stanton Blatch, "Radical Move in Two Years," clipping, Nov. 8, 1908, suffrage scrapbooks, Abbe Collection. Blatch "starred" in a prosuffrage movie, *What Eight Million Women Want*, produced in 1912. Kay Sloan, "Sexual Warfare in the Silent Cinema: Comedies and Melodramas of Woman Suffragism," *American Quarterly*, 33 (Fall 1981), 412–36. She was also very interested in the propaganda possibilities of commercial radio, according to Lee de Forest, a pioneer of the industry, who was briefly married to her daughter. Lee de Forest, *Father of Radio: The Autobiography of Lee de Forest* (Chicago, 1950), 248–49.

52. Mary Tyng, "Self Denial Week," *American Suffragette*, 1 (Aug. 1909); *New York Herald*, Dec. 19, 1908.

53. Blatch, "Radical Move in Two Years"; Mrs. B. Borrman Wells, "The Militant Movement for Woman Suffrage," *Independent*, April 23, 1908, 901–3.

54. "Suffragettes Bar Word Ladylike," clipping, Jan. 13, 1909, Suffrage scrapbooks, abbe Collection; Blatch and Lutz, *Challenging Years*, 91–242; *New York Herald*, March 8, 1908. On militants' views of femininity and sexuality, see also "National Suffrage Convention," *American Suffragette*, 2 (March 1910), 3.

55. Blatch and Lutz, *Challenging Years*, 107; Dye, *As Equals and As Sisters*, 47.

56. *Woman's Journal*, May 30, 1908, 87; Blatch, "Radical Move in Two Years."

57. Borrman Wells, "Militant Movement for Woman Suffrage," 901; *Woman's Journal*, Feb . 29, 1908, 34.

58. *New York Times*, Feb. 11, 1908, 6; [Josephine C. Kaneko], "To Join, or Not to Join," *Socialist Woman*, 1 (May 1908). 6.

59. On *The Convert*, see Equality League, *Report for 1908–1909*, 4; Jane Marcus, "Introduction," in *The Convert* (London, 1980), v–xvi; *New York Call*, Dec. 9, 1908, 6; and Minutes, Dec. 22, 1908, New York Women's Trade Union League Papers. Maud Malone also charged the American Suffragettes with discrimination against Socialists and Bettina Borrman Wells with personal ambition. For her letter of resignation, see *New York Times*, March 27, 1908, 4.

60. *New York Times*, May 14, 1909, 5. On Mackay and her Equal Franchise Society, see *New York Times*, Feb. 21, 1909, part 5, 2. On Blatch's relation to Mackay, see Blatch and Lutz, *Challenging Years*, 118. "As for the suffrage movement, it is actually fashionable now," wrote militant Inez Haynes, who very much approved of the development. "All kinds of society people are taking it up." Inez Haynes to Maud Wood Park, Dec. 2, 1910, reel 11, National American Woman Suffrage Association Papers (Manuscript Division, Library of Congress). Gertrude Foster Brown, another wealthy woman recruited by Blatch, wrote her own history of the New York suffrage movement in which she virtually ignored the role of working-class women. Gertrude Foster Brown, "On Account of Sex," Gertrude Foster Brown Papers, Sophia Smith Collection (Smith College, Northampton, Mass).

15

The Social Awakening of Chinese American Women as Reported in *Chung Sai Yat Po*, 1900–1911

Judy Yung

The first decade of the twentieth century saw the advancement of women's emancipation in both China and the United States.[1] In China the women's cause was furthered by the 1898 Reform Movement, which advocated that China emulate the West and modernize in order to throw off the yoke of foreign domination. Modernization included elevating the status of women in Chinese society. As a result anti-footbinding societies, schools for girls, women's rights organizations and magazines, and the increased participation of women in public affairs became evident, particularly in the cities. Soon after the 1911 Revolution, in which women played limited but conspicuous roles—conveying messages, smuggling arms and ammunition, and serving as nurses and soldiers at the war front—Chinese women in Guangdong Province were among the first to be granted suffrage.[2] Meanwhile in the United States women were becoming more educated, independent of men, and visible in the public sphere. Some actively participated in social reform, in the temperance, peace, and labor movements. At the same time the women's suffrage movement was gaining momentum, with the final push beginning in the 1910s, when eight states, including California, passed a women's suffrage amendment.[3]

What was the response of Chinese American women to the changes taking place in China and the United States? Before we attempt to answer this question, we need to gauge their response by comparing the role and status of Chinese American women in the nineteenth century with that of the early twentieth century.

The first wave of Chinese immigrants to California during the Gold Rush included very few women. Early Chinese sojourners, who intended to strike it rich and return home, did not bring their wives or families with them. Cultural restrictions at home, the lack of funds for traveling, and anti-Chinese sentiment in the West further discouraged the early emigration of Chinese women. As a result, the Chinese male/female ratio in America was as high as 19 to 1 in 1860; 13 to 1 in 1870; 21 to 1 in 1880; and 27 to 1 in 1890.[4] The sexual imbalance, combined with anti-miscegenation laws that prohibited marriages between Chinese and whites, created a need for Chinese prostitution. Given this situation, the prostitution trade thrived, proving immensely profitable for the tongs, or secret societies, in Chinatowns.

The majority of Chinese women in nineteenth-century California were indentured prostitutes, kidnapped, lured, or purchased from poor parents in China and resold in America for high profits. Approximately 85 percent of Chinese women in San Francisco

Reprinted by permission of the author. Originally published in *Chinese America: History and Perspectives*, 1988.

were prostitutes in 1860 and 71 percent in 1870. Treated as chattel and subjected to constant physical and mental abuse, the average prostitute did not outlive her contract terms of four to five years.[5] Those who survived the trade either ran away with the help of lovers, were redeemed by wealthy clients, or sought protection from the police or the missionary homes. In the 1880s while prostitution began to decline due to anti-prostitution laws and the successful rescue raids by Protestant missionaries, the number of Chinese wives began to increase due to the arrival of the merchant class and the marriages of former prostitutes to Chinese men here. Although some women did emigrate alone or came as *mui tsai* or domestic servants, most other Chinese women then were wives who lived either in urban Chinatowns or in remote rural areas. Following Chinese tradition, Chinatown wives seldom left their homes, where in addition to their own housework, they often worked for low wages—sewing, washing, rolling cigars, and making slippers and brooms while caring for their children. In rural areas Chinese wives tended livestock and vegetable gardens, hauled in the catch and dried seafood for export, or took in boarders. Regardless of their residence or their husbands' social status, immigrant wives led hardworking lives and were excluded from participation in almost all public affairs.

The restrictive lives of Chinese American women began to change in the twentieth century. A growing number of Chinese women began to free themselves of social restrictions—working outside the home, appearing in public places, educating their daughters, starting and joining Chinese women's organizations, and participating in community affairs.[6] How and why did this change occur? Were Chinese American women socially awakened by the emancipation of women occurring in China or in the United States?

Unfortunately there is no known body of writings by Chinese American women that can help answer these questions. But one valuable source that has remained relatively untapped until recently is the Chinese American press.[7] Among the most successful and long-lasting Chinese language newspapers of the early twentieth century is *Chung Sai Yat Po* (*CSYP*). Started by Presbyterian minister Ng Poon Chew in 1900, *CSYP* was heavily influenced by both Chinese nationalism and Western middle-class ideology. It favored reform in China and advocated equal rights for Chinese Americans, including women. As *CSYP* enjoyed wide circulation among Chinese Americans until its decline in the 1930s, it played an important advocatory and informational role in the Chinese American community.[8]

A close reading of *CSYP* from 1900 to 1911 supports the contention that the role and status of Chinese American women were indeed beginning to change and that women, especially among the literate, were being influenced more by women's issues and events in China than by developments in the United States.[9] This orientation was due as much to the newspaper's reform platform as to strong feelings of Chinese nationalism in the Chinatown community. Excluded from meaningful participation in American society[10] and aware of the adverse impact of China's weak international status upon their lives in America, Chinese Americans concentrated their attention and energies more on politics in China than in the United States. But as *CSYP* advocated as well as reported, Chinese American leaders were adept at using the American courts and diplomatic channels to fight discrimination.

The need to elevate the status of Chinese women was evidently a concern of *CSYP*. Between 1900 and 1911 approximately 550 articles and 66 editorials on women (2 percent of the newspaper's pages), 26 of which reflected the voices of Chinese women themselves, appeared in *CSYP*.[11] Almost all addressed the same women's issues that were being raised in China: (1) the elimination of "barbaric" practices harmful to women, such as polygamy, slavery, arranged marriages, and especially footbinding; (2) education for women; (3) women's rights; and (4) women's role in national salvation. What follows is a summary and analysis of these articles and editorials as they relate to the social awakening of Chinese American women.

The Campaign Against Footbinding and Other Sexist Practices

Begun in the tenth century as an innovation of palace dancers, footbinding remained a popular practice in China until it was denounced by reformers and outlawed after the 1911 Revolution.[12] A symbol of gentility, bound feet was considered an asset in the marriage market. In practice footbinding prevented women from "wandering," as women with bound feet generally found it difficult to walk unassisted. At the same time it reinforced women's cloistered existence, as Chinese etiquette dictated that a Chinese lady should not appear in public or be seen in the company of men. Bound feet came to symbolize the oppressed state of Chinese women and the decadence of old China. Thus, the eradication of bound feet became one of the rallying points in the Reform Movement in China as well as of reformers in the United States, where women with bound feet could still be found.[13]

The earliest reference to footbinding in *CSYP* appeared in 1902 when the Chinese ambassador's wife, Mme. Wu Tingfang, was quoted as saying that it was "quite unthinkable that footbinding, long considered an evil practice in China, is still in vogue in the United States" (*CSYP*, February 19, 1902).[14] In 1904 a Chinese entrepreneur was openly condemned for putting a Chinese woman with bound feet on display at the St. Louis World's Fair (*CSYP*, June 6, 1904). Front-page editorials argued for an end to foot binding for the following reasons: It was detrimental to a woman's health, was unnatural, caused unnecessary pain and suffering for women, and was a barbaric custom.[15] One editorial specifically urged Chinese American women to discontinue the practice. "How can men treat their wives with such contempt? How can women treat their bodies with such contempt?" the editorial asked. Three reasons were given as to why women overseas would choose to have bound feet: The parents were obstinant and at fault; husbands prized and encouraged its practice; and women in general were still uneducated and unenlightened. Its eradication, the editorial concluded, depended on family upbringing and formal schooling for all girls (*CSYP*, December 9, 1907).

In another article, "Corsets Can Harm Your Health," Dr. Tielun reportedly gave a public speech comparing the harmful effects of wearing corsets with footbinding. "Deforming a natural foot [whereby] Chinese women lose their freedom of movement and endure a life of pain and suffering . . . is just as abusive as that of binding the waist—a most barbaric practice," he said. In an editorial note at the end of the article, the reporter commented as follows: "Wearing corsets, although a vile practice, still gives one more freedom of movement than bound feet. Once the Natural Feet Society advocates our women be released from suffering, I suspect the practice of wearing corsets will also decline" (*CSYP*, August 13, 1909).

In a satire, "Ten Good Points About Footbinding," that appeared in the literature section[16] of *CSYP* on May 24, 1910, the "positive" effects of footbinding included the following: One could always use bound feet as an excuse to escape work; bound feet were an especially important asset for a good marriage if one had an ugly face; and a woman with bound feet could always appear helpless and frail to escape the wrath of an abusive mother-in-law.

Equally creative was a poem of twenty-four stanzas, "An Exhortation Against Footbinding," that appeared in the September 16, 1909 issue:

A daughter's feet,
A daughter's feet,
By nature flesh and blood.
Whether boy,
Whether girl,
Both are born of mother.

Ten fine toes,
Just like siblings,
Harmonious, from same womb.
They want to grow,
Perfect and whole,
To enjoy their natural due.

Why on earth
Are women folk
Infected by strange ways?
Young or old,
Rich or poor,
All desire the three-inch lotus.

In strict confinement,
Inner apartments,
A virtual living hell.
Beneath hemlines,
Bound like dumplings,
Swathed in restraining layers.

Halting steps,
Walking slow,
Ever fearful toppling over.
Circulation impeded,
Blocked and unmoving,
Painful pecks of birds.

And that is why
Among the girls
Few enjoy long life.
Within their chambers,
For what crime,
Are they so tortured? . . .

Imperial orders against footbinding, printed prominently in *CSYP*, gave the campaign against the practice an aura of official sanction. According to a series of Qing edicts, men whose wives had bound feet could not qualify for civil service; girls with bound feet could not attend government-sponsored schools; women with bound feet would be considered of the "mean" or "common" class; and no court honors could be conferred on women with bound feet.[17]

Similar diatribes were aimed at the "barbaric" practices of polygamy, arranged marriages, and keeping slave girls. In an editorial, "Reflections on the Selection of Courtesans by the Qing Court," the emperor was blamed for promoting polygamy and prostitution by setting a poor example. Whereas polygamy was practiced in most undeveloped countries in Asia, monogamy was the general practice in developed countries, according to the article. In conclusion, "If we wish to correct China's morals in order to have a stronger country, we must establish the law of monogamy. If we wish to develop the character of our women ... we must promote schools for girls" (*CSYP*, March 28, 1906)

Free marriage and divorce as practiced in America were evidently controversial issues among Chinese Americans during this period. On the one hand, *CSYP* warned against the pitfalls of free marriage, stressing the need for women to maintain traditional morals.[18] On the other hand, an editorial that appeared on April 26, 1907 advocated the American custom of free marriage, defining a good marriage as one between two persons with compatible interests and personalities. Although divorce was still not socially acceptable, *CSYP* reported with sympathy three cases of divorce among Chinese Americans—two involving wives who claimed they were being forced into prostitution and one involving a wife who claimed her husband had taken a concubine.[19]

Of the two editorials that attacked the custom of keeping slave girls, one pointed out that compared with other countries, China was most guilty of the oppression of women. "For centuries we have erred in teaching our women to be obedient ... to not even step out into the courtyard but remain in their lonely quarters as captive prisoners. . . . Women with bound feet, weakened bodies, and undeveloped intelligence cannot attain equality with men." Such treatment, the editorial continued, was not only detrimental to the interests of women, but since women made up half of the country's population, detrimental to the interests of China (*CSYP*, April 2, 1907). The second editorial exhorted women to learn from Abraham Lincoln's emancipation of black slavery and organize to liberate the slave girls. "If we want to be free, we must first make everyone else free" (*CSYP*, March 16, 1906). In support of the newspaper's reformist platform, both editorials also stressed that keeping slave girls was a sign of China's decadence in the eyes of Western countries and therefore should be eradicated.

Chinese prostitution in the United States was also discussed in *CSYP* editorials. Once a heated topic of debate in the late nineteenth century, Chinese prostitution was on the decline in the early 1900s. However, cases of prostitution were still reported in the newspaper.[20] One case, well covered in *CSYP* for three consecutive months, involved a prostitute by the name of Jingui, who had sought asylum at the Presbyterian mission. She was later arrested on trumped-up charges of grand larceny, and abducted by two Chinese men from a jail near Stanford University. Angered by Jingui's plight and suspecting corruption on the part of local officials, a group of private citizens and university students raised funds, passed resolutions, and held a protest rally on her behalf. In the process of her trial, Jingui revealed that she was born in China and became a prostitute through abduction. The court finally ordered her deported and a full investigation made of alleged corruption on the part of law-enforcement officers.[21]

In another editorial, those involved in the prostitution trade were asked to search their consciences and to mend their ways. With the establishment of shelters for rescued prostitutes by the Presbyterian and Methodist missions, and with a move by both the American government and the imperial government in China to investigate the matter, "your profits will suffer if not your reputation," admonished the editorial (*CSYP*, August 8, 1907).

Although the campaign against footbinding and other sexist practices began in China as part of the 1898 Reform Movement, it soon spread to American Chinatowns, where the same practices were still being followed, although to a lesser degree. Exposed to Western culture and Christianity, constantly criticized and ridiculed for their "heathen" ways by Anglo-Americans, and moved by nationalism to join their compatriots' efforts to reform China, progressive Chinese Americans such as Ng Poon Chew understood well the need to eradicate Chinese practices such as footbinding, polygamy, arranged marriages, and keeping slave girls. Educated Chinese women also rallied behind the campaign, encouraging women in China as well as in America to oppose and free themselves of these sexist practices.

Education for Women

> Two hundred million women—all are naturally endowed with intelligence, mental vigor, and talent. But because they are not educated, they are discarded as useless. A living dream dies under the oppression of husbands. It is greatly lamented (*CSYP*, August 30, 1909).

These feminist sentiments, as expressed in a three-part editorial, "On the Establishment of Independence for Chinese American Women," show *CSYP's* progressive point of view on women's education. Most editorials on the same subject, however, were more conservative and tended to use the following reformist line of reasoning to argue for women's education: Educated women make better wives and mothers; better wives and mothers make better families and citizens; better families and citizens make a stronger China.[22] Another recurring argument stressed that women made up half of China's population. If educated, they would be better able to contribute to their country's prosperity, as did women in Western countries. According to one editorial written by Pan Xuezhen, a female schoolteacher in China:

> Countries in Europe and America are rich and powerful because fundamentally, their women are educated. As to why they are educated, it is because men and women are equal in Europe and America. . . . In France and America, there are women in high offices. In England and America, there are women in astronomy, clerical work, communications, documentation and record keeping, medicine, law, as professors and educators, no different than men. This is because women in these countries are organized to encourage one another to pursue education (*CSYP*, March 4, 1902).

Numerous articles in *CSYP* reported on the establishment of elementary schools, trade schools, medical schools, and teacher-training schools for girls and women in China, especially in the Guangdong Province, from which most Chinese immigrants in American originated.[23] This news not only indicated that reform in the area of education for women was taking place at home but also encouraged overseas Chinese to continue sending remittances home to support schools for girls. Three editorials specifically asked for such support: "An Appeal to Overseas Chinese for Funds to Establish Schools" (*CSYP*, December 14, 1908), "On the Need for Overseas Chinese to Promote Girl Schools" (*CSYP*, December 20, 1909), and "Strengthening Ourselves Through Educating Women" (*CSYP*, April 4, 1910). The last editorial appealed directly to Chinese American women to support schools for girls in China. A number of articles also beseeched Chinese female students studying abroad and Chinese American women to "return home" to teach.[24]

Like their counterparts in China, who were among the earliest advocates of education for girls and women, Protestant missionaries evidently played a similar role in Chinatowns.[25] According to an article in *CSYP* on March 6, 1904, a school to teach Chinese girls Chinese, English, and the fine arts opened at 2 Clay Street under the auspices of the Baptist mission. On January 25, 1911, *CSYP* ran an advertisement announcing a new school established by the Presbyterian mission at 925 Stockton Street to teach girls and women Chinese in the evenings. The newspaper also reported in detail talks given by Chinese Christians encouraging women's education. In a three-part commentary on two speeches delivered at the Baptist and Presbyterian missions by Liu Fengxian, a woman missionary visiting from China, *CSYP* apparently agreed with Liu that women must become educated if they hoped to achieve equality: "Education leads to self-reliance and independence—the essence of freedom and equality . . . the fortuitous future of women for which this reporter truly anticipates" (*CSYP*, September 3, 1909). Earlier this same writer had encouraged Chinese American parents to "breathe in the Western air and bask in the thoughts and ideas of the enlightened. There is no one who does not want women to become educated and useful people in this world" (*CSYP*, September 1, 1909). The second speech was delivered by Mr. Zhong Yongguang at the Presbyterian church on May 25, 1911. According to the newspaper article that appeared the next day, Zhong attributed the devaluation of women to their lack of education and preached that freedom and equality for women could be won through Christianity and education.

Another indication of *CSYP's* support for women's education can be found in the newspaper's coverage of female scholastic achievements, which ranged from short acknowledgments of women graduating from college or professional schools in the United States to an editorial praising outstanding female students.[26] Graduates who expressed interest in returning to China to work, teach, or advocate women's education received special commendation in the newspaper.[27] One editorial, which noted the many female students who were receiving honors in public schools, denounced the Chinese proverb, "Ignorance in a woman is a virtue," and concluded, "We should be grateful that America offers our women education and congratulate the parents and girls on their scholastic achievements" (*CSYP*, June 6, 1904).

As they had in the campaign against footbinding, Protestant missionaries and nationalist reformers took the lead in advocating women's education in China. While Christians believed that educating Chinese women would help to civilize and convert China to Christianity, reformers believed that educating half of the country's population not only would show the rest of the world that China was not decadent but, more importantly, would strengthen the country by encouraging the contributions of all able-minded citizens. Although the latter message was carried in *CSYP*, the issue of women's education took on an added dimension in American Chinatowns. In addition to the nationalist reasons offered, parents were encouraged to educate their daughters because of the American, particularly Christian, emphasis on education for both boys and girls. Yet their children were excluded from attending integrated public schools until the 1920s.[28] Chinese Americans were also led to believe that education would facilitate assimilation into American society and provide improved job opportunities in the future. Yet most Chinese American college graduates could not find jobs in their chosen fields until after World War II. These discriminatory conditions for Chinese Americans only added fuel to the traditional Chinese belief that girls did not need an education. But nonetheless, *CSYP* continued to argue that educating women would help China's cause and lead to equality for women.

Women's Rights

More than any other issue of concern to Chinese American women, the issue of women's rights as covered by *CSYP* indicates clearly the detachment Chinese women felt toward the women's suffrage movement in America and their identification with women's emancipation in China. Although short articles reporting on the struggle to achieve women's rights and suffrage in America as well as in England, Russia, Finland, and Denmark appeared in the newspaper, no mention was made of the involvement of Chinese American women in this struggle.[29] At times *CSYP* even asked why women should be given the right to vote when Chinese men were denied naturalization rights and thus the right to vote.[30]

The names of American feminist leaders during this period—Alice Paul, Carrie Chapman Catt, Elizabeth Gurley Flynn, Crystal Eastman, and Emma Goldman—did not appear in *CSYP*. Instead the newspaper extolled Chinese feminist leaders such as Zhang Zhujun and Xue Jinqin (Sieh King King in the English-language press). Both women were educated in China, Christians, recognized feminist leaders in China, and acclaimed role models for Chinese American women.

According to *CSYP*, Zhang Zhujun came from a well-to-do family in the Cantonese region of China. Taken ill as a child, she stayed in a Western hospital, where she first heard the gospel, chose to be baptized, unbound her feet, and vowed never to marry. After studying Western medicine for three years, Zhang became a doctor and was instrumental in establishing hospitals and vocational schools for girls. At the same time she preached the gospel and advocated women's education, "touring other countries in order to find ways to liberate two million women still in darkness" (*CSYP*, January 21, 1903).

Although there were indications in the newspaper that Zhang intended to visit the United States to seek support for women's education in China, because of illness, she never made the trip.[31] However, two of her articles on education and footbinding were reprinted and featured in *CSYP*. In "The Announcement of the Women's Association for Security Through Learning," which appeared June 9, 10, 11, and 12, 1904, she lamented the miserable conditions for women in China and appealed to Chinese women overseas to support her newly formed Women's Association. According to its bylaws, printed in their entirety, the organization would maintain four schools for girls in China through membership dues and special fund-raising projects. It would also sponsor monthly meetings for members to exchange information and offer mutual support and make an effort to help widows, orphans, and the handicapped. "We must cultivate our intellect in order to be self-reliant, learn skills in order to make our own living, and unite with our comrades for mutual support," she wrote (*CSYP*, June 9, 1904). A commentary in a later issue called Zhang a heroine: By starting the four schools for girls, Zhang was advancing the future of Chinese women and "shaming all those who believe in the absurd idea that ignorance in a woman is a virtue" (*CSYP*, June 16, 1904).

The second article, which appeared July 27, 1904, was the text of a speech Zhang reportedly delivered at the commencement of her practice in Shanghai. In this piece she condemned both the practice of footbinding and the use of cosmetics, emphasizing their harmful effects on women's health. "I beseech women everywhere to practice hygiene and to pursue careers in order to achieve strength and independence. . . . In the future those who support women's rights will not look to Europe but to China," she said (*CSYP*, July 27, 1904).

Acclaimed as a heroine and as the first of Chinese woman orators, Xue Jinqin reportedly delivered her first speech to 500 people in Shanghai in 1901, protesting the Chinese government's intention to grant Russia special rights in Manchuria after the Boxer Rebellion failed.[32] In 1902, at the age of sixteen, Xue registered as a student at a school in Berkeley, having studied earlier in a missionary school in China. "She is petite but ambitious," commented the newspaper reporter. "Her goal, upon completion of her studies, is to return to China to advocate women's education and to free Chinese women of thousand-year-old traditional bindings" (*CSYP*, October 23, 1902).

Xue reportedly made two speeches in San Francisco Chinatown. On November 3, 1902, at the invitation of the Baohuanghui (Society to Protect the Emperor),[33] she spoke at the Danqui Theatre to an audience of 1,000, arguing against footbinding and for women's education (*CSYP*, November 4, 1902). A year later Xue gave another "eloquent and inspiring speech" which again "expounded her views on the role of Chinese women and the need to abolish outdated Chinese customs and emulate the West," this time to an exclusively female audience of 200. She was filling in for reformist leader Lian Qichao, who was unable to attend (*CSYP*, October 12, 1903). *CSYP*, in its New Year issue of 1903, praised her as "an extraordinary woman who brings honor to China" (*CSYP*, January 21, 1903).

CSYP also provided a platform for other feminists who advocated women's rights. A speech delivered in Canton, China, by feminist leader Du Qingqi blamed both men and women for China's state of decline. Men were guilty of oppressing women by denying them education, independence, and nondomestic work, and women were equally guilty for allowing the abridgement of their rights. In order to break the traditional bonds that restrict women's movement and confine them to domestic duties, "women must develop character that can bear the responsibilities of education, reason, judgment, and saving others. This they must do with the mutual love and assistance of their husbands" (*CSYP*, October 25, 1902).

Similar sentiments were echoed in an open letter by the Women's Rights Organization (of China) and in a poem written by Bai Gui, a female scholar. Both drew on classical sayings to illustrate the oppression of women. The letter ended by crying out, "Those who are with us, who are so angry that their hairs stand on end, must raise an army of women to punish the guilty and strip them of their will" (*CSYP*, May 12, 1904). The last refrain of the poem, "Song of Women's Hell," reads:

> I want to arouse women with a rising roar.
> With rage and martial spirit we must unite to set things right.
> Rescuing our sisters out of hell,
> In this will we women be brilliant.
> Though we may die in battle, yet will we be elated
> (*CSYP*, April 8, 1908).

In support of women's emancipation in China, *CSYP* helped to advertise a new women's journal that was to be published weekly in Canton, China. According to the announcement that appeared April 24, 1910, the goals of the journal were to maintain women's morals, advance women's knowledge, promote women's skills, and recover women's rights. *CSYP* encouraged Chinese women overseas to subscribe to it. "The journal can serve as a compass and warning against abuse, thus proving beneficial to all" (*CSYP*, April 24, 1910).

Reports by visitors and by other newspapers on the status of women in China also appeared in *CSYP*. A Baptist minister, recently returned from a conference in Shanghai, commented on the change in women's roles that he witnessed there. "Men and women now have equal rights. Both boys and girls must attend school. Moreover, women recognize the need to learn a skill by which they can firmly establish their independence. Several hundred businesses and factories now employ women workers" (*CSYP*, July 1, 1907). And according to news articles from London and Hong Kong reprinted in *CSYP*, women in China were becoming educated, working in journalism, the military, and commerce, and leading an active public life in the cities.[34]

Such coverage on the issue of women's rights in China encouraged Chinese American women to support women's emancipation in China as well as to examine and challenge their own subordinate role in America. Although the underlying argument for sex equality in China was national salvation, its advocacy in America was also influenced by Protestant values. In either case there were limits to the extent of equality for women. As Ng Poon Chew himself espoused on his lecture tours, women should have the rights of education, livelihood, and free choice of marriage, but "the status of the woman is the home, and there is no excuse for her not being there and rearing a family."[35]

National Salvation

National salvation served as a further impetus to engage Chinese American women in China's politics and to strengthen their identification with their counterparts in China. According to *CSYP*, women on both sides of the ocean expressed their patriotism or nationalism by raising funds for victims of floods and famines and later by supporting the 1911 Revolution. Indeed, it was national crises, such as war and natural disasters in China, that repeatedly called forth a united front among all Chinese and new activism on the part of women in China as well as in America.

When floods and famine occurred in the lower Yangtze River area in 1907 and 1908, *CSYP* reported that female students and women in Guangdong Province donated money and jewelry and raised funds by holding bazaars, giving performances, and selling embroidery and poems.[36] Chinese American women were also moved to action when floods and famines occurred in Jiangbei and Jianquan provinces in 1907 and 1911. In an editorial, "Chinese American Women's Views on Relief Work," women were urged not only to donate their jewelry and their husband's spending money for famine relief, but to encourage others to do likewise. "Things are slowly changing for those here in America. There are now women who are literate and can spread the word" (*CSYP*, May 4, 1907). In 1911 *CSYP* reported a number of fund-raising efforts on behalf of famine relief by Chinese women in Seattle, Portland, Boston, San Francisco, and Oakland.[37] The benefit performance in Seattle was particularly noteworthy, as it was an event marked by interracial harmony. Many Westerners attended, as well as 175 Chinese women out of a total of 400 persons (*CSYP*, February 20, 1911).

As the 1898 Reform Movement waned, failing in its efforts to modernize China and liberate it from foreign domination, popular support turned to Sun Yat-sen's Tongmenghui or Revolutionary Party, which advocated the overthrow of the Qing dynasty and the establishment of a republic. With the support of overseas Chinese money, underground rebels at home attempted eight armed rebellions between 1907 and 1911 in the southern provinces of Guangdong and Guangxi. Victory was not won until the Wuchang uprising of October 10, 1911.[38]

The participation of women in this revolutionary movement in both China and the United States is well documented in *CSYP*. Revolutionary activities on the part of women in China ranged from organizing benefit performances to enlisting in the army.[39] There was reportedly a revolutionary unit in Shanghai consisting of 500 patriotic women, armed and ready to do battle under the leadership of a female commander (*CSYP*, December 9, 1911). Stories of women engaged in dangerous undercover work also appeared in the newspaper—for example, the assassination of Anhui's provincial governor by a female student and the Revolutionary Party's use of women as ammunition smugglers and spies.[40] In another article the patriotism of a female student who tattooed *ai quo* ("love my country") on her right wrist out of frustration was cause for praise. As she told her classmates, she regretted that, being female, she could not challenge a particular traitor to a duel (*CSYP*, October 16, 1911).

Meanwhile Chinese American women were doing their part in support of the revolutionary cause. According to *CSYP*, female orators of the Young China Society were speaking up for the revolution as well as for women's rights. They had also made a two-sided flag—one side bearing the Chinese flag and the other, the flag of the Revolutionary Army (*CSYP*, May 25, 1911). When Dr. Sun Yat-sen, leader of the revolution, spoke to over 600 people in Chinatown, the newspaper noted that there were at least fifty women in attendance.[41] Chinese American women also donated money and jewelry and helped with Red Cross work—fund-raising, preparing bandages and medicines, and sewing garments for the war effort.[42]

In 1907, when the revolutionary heroine Qiu Jin was executed, she was equally mourned and exalted by both Chinese and Chinese American women. Born into the gentry class, Qiu Jin was an accomplished poet, horseback rider, and swordswoman. In response to the failure of the 1898 Reform Movement and the Allied sacking of Peking following the Boxer Rebellion, she resolved to help save China and to fight for women's rights. In 1903 when her arranged marriage proved a failure, she deserted her conservative husband and went to study in Japan. There she became involved in radical politics, participating in the Humanitarian Society, which promoted women's rights and education, and becoming a member of the Tongmenghui. While organizing for the revolution in Zhejiang, she was arrested and executed at the young age of thirty-one. Newspapers in China raged over her unjust execution. So did *CSYP*, which published her biography, accounts of her arrest and death, and poems eulogizing her.[43] One of her followers, Wu Zhiying, wrote a moving account of how hard Giu Jin struggled to get an education in Japan because she believed that only through education could women hope to attain independence (*CSYP*, September 11, 1907). Here again was a Chinese role model and national heroine by which Chinese American women could reaffirm their nationalist and feminist ties with their compatriots in China.

National disasters and the 1911 Revolution gave Chinese and Chinese American women the opportunity to express their patriotism, develop leadership skills, and participate in the public sphere of life. The leaders of the 1911 Revolution, continuing where the 1898 Reform Movement left off in the cause of national salvation, especially encouraged the participation of women because of its strong democratic tenets, thereby helping to groom women for their new roles in public life in the decades to follow.

By examining *CSYP*'s coverage of women's issues from 1900 to 1911, we can see the attention that was given to women's emancipation in China in preference to the women's suffrage movement in America. The newspaper's support of women's emancipation was in keeping with its interest in promoting two key concerns: strengthening China through modernization and advocating equal rights for Chinese Americans. By contrasting the restrictive lives of Chinese immigrant women in the nineteenth century with the changing role of Chinese American women in the early years of the twentieth century, we can begin to gauge the influence of these ideas upon the lives of Chinese American women. Although most Chinese American women probably did not read *CSYP*, they were most likely affected by the public opinion it espoused through their husbands, neighbors, and missionary workers looking after their interest. After the 1911 Revolution, it was no longer considered "fashionable" to have bound feet, concubines, and slave girls. The "new woman" not only sought education for herself and her daughters, but began to take advantage of resources in America, to work outside the home, and to participate in community affairs. Certainly other influences, such as the changing composition of the Chinese American population, the efforts of Protestant missionaries to help Chinese American women, and the opening of job opportunities outside the home for women, also affected the role and status of

Chinese American women during the period under study. But as a progressive record of the views and activities of Chinese American women as well as an influential molder of public opinion, *CSYP* is an important and helpful source for shedding light on the social awakening of Chinese American women at the turn of the century.

Notes

1. An earlier version of this article was published in *Chinese America: History and Perspectives 1988* (San Francisco: Chinese Historical Society of America), 80–102. "Chinese American women" is used in this paper to include all Chinese women in America, foreign born as well as American born.

2. Suffrage for all women in China was not granted until 1931. For a general history of women in China, including a discussion of women's emancipation, see Elizabeth Croll, *Feminism and Socialism in China* (New York: Schocken Books, 1980); Ono Kazuko, *Chinese Women in a Century of Revolution, 1850–1950* (Stanford: Stanford University Press, 1989); and Esther S. Lee Yao, *Chinese Women: Past and Present* (Mesquite, Texas: Ide House, 1983).

3. Suffrage for all women in the United States was not won until 1920. For a general history of women in America, including a discussion of women's emancipation, see Mary P. Ryan, *Womanhood in America* (New York: Franklin Watts, 1983) and June Sochen, *Her Story: A Record of the American Woman's Past* (Sherman Oaks, CA: Alfred Publishing Co., 1981).

4. U.S. Bureau of Census, *Sixteenth Census of the United States: Population, 1940* (Washington, D. C.: Government Printing Office, 1942), vol. 2, 19.

5. For a fuller examination of the lives of Chinese women and prostitutes in nineteenth-century California, see Lucie Cheng Hirata, "Chinese Immigrant Women in Nineteenth-Century California," in *Women in America*, eds. C. R. Berkin and M. B. Norton (Boston: Houghton-Mifflin Company, 1979), 224–44; and Lucie Cheng Hirata, "Free, Indentured, Enslaved: Chinese Prostitution in Nineteenth-Century California," *Signs: Journal of Women in Culture and Society* 5:1 (Autumn 1979), 3–29.

6. On the changing role of Chinese American women, see Judy Yung, *Chinese Women of America: A Pictorial History* (Seattle: University of Washington Press, 1986).

7. For a fuller discussion and list of Chinese American newspapers, see Him Mark Lai, "The Chinese-American Press," in *The Ethnic Press in the United States: A Historical Analysis and Handbook*, ed. Sally M. Miller (New York: Greenwood Press, 1987), 27–43; and Karl Lo and Him Mark Lai, *Chinese Newspapers Published in North America, 1854–1975* (Washington, D. C.: Center for Chinese Research Materials, 1977).

8. *CSYP* is available on microfilm at the Asian American Studies Library and East Asiatic Library, University of California, Berkeley. For a fuller discussion of Ng Poon Chew and *CSYP* see Corinne K. Hoexter, *From Canton to California: The Epic of Chinese Immigration* (New York: Four Winds Press, 1976).

9. According to my computation from U. S. National Archives, "U. S. Census of Population" (manuscript schedules), for San Francisco, California, 1900 and 1910, 17 percent of Chinese American women were literate in 1900 and 43 percent in 1910.

10. For example, Chinese could not become naturalized citizens, intermarry, join white labor unions, attend integrated public schools, or own land.

11. Because so many of the articles and editorials in *CSYP* were either unsigned or signed with pen names, it is difficult to determine how many of the pieces on women were written by women themselves. But twenty-six articles and editorials either carried the bylines of women or quoted from speeches delivered by female orators.

12. For a history of footbinding, see Howard S. Levy, *Chinese Footbinding: The History of a Curious Erotic Custom* (New York: Walton Rawls, 1966).

13. Although a smaller percentage of women had bound feet in America than in China (thirty-six were reported in the 1887 "Annual Report of the Foreign Mission Board of the Presbyterian Church" of San Francisco, 56), the practice was still continued by the merchant class here until the 1911 Revolution.

14. The translations in this paper are by the author, with the assistance of Anne Tsong, Linette Lee, and Ellen Yeung.

15. *CSYP*, July 27, 1904; February 13, 1906; January 2, December 9, 1907.

16. A literature section, consisting of poetry, essays, historical biographies and legends, short stories, songs, and anecdotes, was added to *CSYP* in 1907.

17. *CSYP*, September 5, 26, 1906; October 2, 1907; January 1, 1908.

18. *CSYP*, February 10, 1907; December 10, 1908; March 4, 1910.

19. *CSYP*, July 26, 1902; March 7, 1909; August 27, 1910.

20. *CSYP*, July 20, 1901; May 27, June 28, September 25, October 7, December 16, 1902; December 1, 1903.

21. *CSYP*, March 24, April 2, 3, 5, 13, 14, 16, 25, 28, 30, May 7, 8, 14, 1900.

22. *CSYP*, March 4, 1902; July 14, 1904; April 21, 1905; January 31, 1906; July 8, 1908; October 15, 1909; July 5, 1910.

23. *CSYP*, April 11, 1906; June 28, July 30, August 4, 1908; August 10, 1910.

24. *CSYP*, March 2, June 3, 1907; June 28, 1910. The exclusion of Chinese from mainstream American life heightened nationalist feelings, among them the assumption that regardless of place of birth there was but one motherland for all Chinese living in America—China.

25. On the promotion of education for women in China by Protestant missionaries, see Margaret Burton, *The Education of Women in China* (New York: Fleming H. Revell Company, 1911); and Mary Raleigh Anderson, *Protestant Mission Schools for Girls in South China* (Mobile, Alabama: Hester-Starke Printing Company, 1943).

26. *CSYP*, January 22, 1904; July 8, July 28, August 28, 1908; December 25, 1909; June 7, December 25, 1911.

27. *CSYP*, May 9, 1909; July 12, 1909; September 2, 1909; March 10, 1910; February 6, 1911.

28. On the history of educational discrimination against Chinese Americans, see Victor Low, *The Unimpressible Race: A Century of Educational Struggle by the Chinese in San Francisco* (San Francisco: East/West Publishing Company, 1982).

29. On women's suffrage in America: *CSYP*, August 5, 1904; January 5, 1909; January 10, 1910; February 16, March 23, March 24, April 5, May 12, August 23, September 26, December 6, 1911. England: *CSYP*, August 5, 1908; April 19, September 22, 1909; July 8, November 20, 1910; May 14, November 23, 1911. Russia: June 19, 1911. Finland: April 9, 1907. Denmark: March 25, 1909.

30. *CSYP*, August 31, 1901; October 23, 1902; January 21, 1903.

31. *CSYP*, October 26, 1902; October 8, 1904.

32. *CSYP*, August 31, 1901; October 23, 1902; January 21, 1903.

33. The Baohuanghui supported the creation of a constitutional monarchy in China, in contrast to the Zhigong-tang, which wanted to overthrow the Qing dynasty and restore the Ming, and the Tongmenghui, which wanted to establish a republican government.

34. *CSYP*, October 22, 1907; February 5, 1909.

35. See "Dr. Ng Poon Chew's Views on Love and Marriage" in the Ng Poon Chew manuscript collection, Asian American Studies Library, University of California, Berkeley.

36. *CSYP*, May 1, 1907; August 21, September 30, December 21, 1908.

37. *CSYP*, February 20, March 21, April 19, 21, 23, June 2, 1911.

38. On the history of the reform and revolutionary movements in China, see Jean Chesneaux, Marianne Bastid, and Marie-Claire Bergere, *China: From the Opium Wars to the 1911 Revolution* (New York: Pantheon Books, 1976).

39. *CSYP*, June 11, 1908; November 22, 1911.

40. *CSYP*, July 18, 1907; July 20, 1911. See also Croll, 60–79; and Kazuko, chap. 4.

41. *CSYP*, July 14, 1911. At least a dozen Chinese women were known to have been active members of the San Francisco Branch of the Tongmenghui. See Zeng Bugui, "Sun Zhongshan Yu Jiujinshan Nu Tongmen-ghui Tuan" (Sun Yat-sen and the women members of San Francisco's Tongmenghui), *Zhongshan Xiansheng Yishi* (Anecdotes of Sun Yat-sen), (Beijing: Zhongguo Wen-shi Chubanshe, 1986), 141–42.

42. *CSYP*, February 21, November 13, 19, 21, 27, December 25, 1911.

43. Her biography is given in *CSYP*, September 9, 11, 13, 1907. The accounts of her arrest and death are recorded in *CSYP*, August 22, 31, September 13, 16, 17, 1907. The poems appear in *CSYP*, August 31, September 12, 1907.

16

The Emergence of Feminism in Puerto Rico, 1870–1930

Yamila Azize–Vargas

Without a doubt, the twentieth century can be named the Century of Feminism. Economic, political, and social transformations interacted to significantly change women's status. Puerto Rico was no exception. Here I discuss the principal factors and events that were fundamental to improving women's situation during the first three decades of the twentieth century.

First I give a brief summary of women's education in Puerto Rico during the nineteenth century and then contrast it with the historical changes brought about by the U.S. invasion of Puerto Rico in 1898. U.S. military intervention had a major impact on women's work, particularly with the establishment of the tobacco and needlework industries, which employed thousands of women between 1900 and 1930 in Puerto Rico.

Women's work outside the home and their access to more education contributed to creating the conditions for the emergence of feminism in Puerto Rico. Two major groups emerged: one consisting of working class women, and the second of formally educated and more affluent women. Here I discuss their conflicts and struggles to achieve recognition for women in Puerto Rican society.

Spanish Colonialism and Education

Education stands out as one of the most important forces that molded women's lives. There is little to be said about formal education during the first half of the nineteenth century. The Spanish government was not interested in providing any education to women. What efforts were undertaken were made possible by private institutions and individuals. A very small number of privileged girls were taught exclusively by women professors. Men were prohibited from teaching at or visiting girls' schools. There were very few women professors or girls' schools. In 1860, for example, there were 122 schools for boys and twenty-five for girls. Ten years later, in 1870, the unequal proportion of schools still persisted: 246 schools for boys, sixty-seven for girls.[1]

The quality of women's education was very poor. As Cuesta Mendoza, a historian of this period, has said; "Education for Puerto Rican women in the nineteenth century condemned them to living between saucepans and sewing cases for the rest of their lives."[2] Several prominent Puerto Rican intellectuals spoke out on this issue, among them intellectuals like Eugenio María de Hostos, Salvador Brau, Manuel Fernández Juncos, and Alejandro Tapia y Rivera. Eugenio María de Hostos was one of the very first to endorse educational

Reprinted with permission of the author and *Radical America*, Vol. 23, No. 1, 1989. The present essay is a summary of the author's book *La mujer en la lucha* (Cultural, P.R. 1985)—*Women in Struggle*—which discusses the history of feminism in Puerto Rico from the 1870s to the 1930s.

equity, not only in Puerto Rico, but also in Latin America. In a speech entitled "Scientific Education for Women," Hostos argued that women's inferiority was caused by "social, intellectual and moral restraints" together with "men's monopoly of social power." He proposed that society give women a "scientific" education; that is the only way women "will be emancipated from error and slavery." Exiled from Puerto Rico for political reasons, he worked in Chile and the Dominican Republic to establish educational institutions for women.[3]

After the United States Invasion

The end of the century brought significant changes to Puerto Rico and to women's education and status. After the United States Army invasion in 1898, education became one of the priorities of the metropolitan power. Education was envisioned as an instrument to Americanize the population.[4] More schools were opened, and the number of students and teachers in public education increased dramatically. Coeducation was established and more girls attended school, but their education remained quite different from the boys'. Women's educational inequality was imposed and planned by the United States government, based on U.S. economic interests and needs. World War I was also a determinant factor in implementing educational policy for women.

During the first two decades of the twentieth century, a significant transformation of the Puerto Rican economy took place. The devaluation of the Spanish "peso" immediately after the U.S. invasion created a serious economic crisis on the island. Poor women were forced into jobs based on their traditional education and skills; female employment increased significantly in the needlework and tobacco industries, and in professions such as nursing and teaching. By 1910, women made up more than half the labor force in the field of education and the tobacco industry. In 1919, more then thirty-five thousand women did needlework at home.[5]

World War I severely interrupted commercial relations between the U.S. and the Philippines, the garment industry's main supplier. Puerto Rico, the new colony, provided a new source of cheap labor to the garment industry. There was a desperate need for jobs on the island and, given the critical economic situation, workers' wages were extremely low. Garment firms started to train people, mainly women who traditionally had learned this kind of sewing at home. The training then became institutionalized, as home economics became part of the public school's curriculum for all girls. They were enrolled in home economics programs taught by North Americans. Several commercial needlework corporations, interested in establishing their developing businesses in Puerto Rico, financed these programs or opened their own schools. By 1918, according to the Commissioner of Education, home economics was "so popular" that courses in embroidery and drawn work became part of the curriculum in all Puerto Rican schools.[6]

Along with needlework, U.S. investment was concentrated in tobacco. In contrast to needlework, tobacco production revolved around the factory.[7] Thus, while women's work in the tobacco industry, like needlework, capitalized on their supposed manual abilities, women in the tobacco industry faced quite a different work experience. They had to leave their homes, work with other women and men in a common space, and deal with terrible working conditions.

Women experienced various kinds of discrimination in the needlework and tobacco industries, as well as in education and the other occupations in which they were concentrated. They were paid less than men even when they did the same kind of work. Historical testimonies document women complaining about sexual harassment from their male bosses.

The Puerto Rico Employment Bureau reported and denounced the inhumane working conditions in the garment industry. In the teaching profession, where they constituted a majority, women were forbidden to be members of, or even vote for, the School Board.

Women's oppression in the needlework and tobacco industries contributed to the conditions for the emergence of class and feminist consciousness. Women faced double exploitation: as workers and as women. They were paid less than men, while they continued to be responsible for their households.

Women's Struggles and the *Federación Libre de Trabajadores* (Free Workers' Union)

The first clear signs of protest came from women who worked in the tobacco industry. From the beginning of the twentieth century, newspapers published women's testimonies demanding help from the leaders of the *Federación Libre de Trabajadores* (FLT), then the main labor organization in Puerto Rico. Women demanded the right to organize, to be educated and to be protected from discrimination and harassment. The FLT's first response was rejection. But despite opposition from several male leaders, the women began their organizing drive. By 1904, there were eight women's unions with more than five hundred members.[8] In 1906 and 1907, newspapers reported several strikes by women in the tobacco industry.[9]

The presence of the "lector" (reader) in the tobacco factories played a significant role in the process of women's growing awareness and organization. The reader, paid by the workers, read daily newspapers and major literary works to workers in the factory. Oral testimonies and research document that this "lector" was an agitator who promoted unionization among the tobacco workers.

The high point of these struggles came in 1908, when two women delegates to the Fifth Annual Congress of the FLT presented a resolution demanding an official campaign to promote the unionization of working women in Puerto Rico. Other resolutions approved in that meeting dealt with the right to education, to better working conditions and *the first formal demand for women's suffrage.*[10] The leaders of the tobacco unions, who years before had complained about women's participation in the industry, finally recognized that "they couldn't do anything to stop women in the industry . . . we must then, help them to get organized in unions, to get education; they can't be our enemies, they have to be our allies."[11] Soon after, women also became part of the Board of Directors of the *Federación Libre de Trabajadores.*[12]

Luisa Capetillo

One of the most outstanding women leaders in this movement was Luisa Capetillo. Born in Arecibo, of a Spanish father and French mother, she received a liberal education. Her involvement in the labor movement began in 1907 when she became a "lectora" in one of the tobacco factories. She became actively involved in meetings and strikes, and then worked as a reporter for *Unión Obrera*, the main labor newspaper in Puerto Rico at the time. As a writer she published several books: *Ensayos libertarios* (*Libertarian Essays*, 1907), *La humanidad del futuro* (*The Humanity of the Future*, 1910), *Mi opinión sobre las libertades, derechos y deberes de la mujer* (*My Opinion about Women's Freedom, Rights and Duties*, 1911) and her last, *Influencia de las ideas modernas* (*The Influence of Modern Ideas*, 1916). She wrote on education and the importance of women working outside the home, on the benefits of a communist society free from oppression and religion, on love, and on the future of society. In all her writings she insisted on her affiliation with socialism, on her support for women's liberation, and particularly her defense of "free love." She never married, and had three children in open relationships. Ms. Capetillo traveled to New York, Cuba, the Dominican Republic and Florida, and published the feminist magazine, *La Mujer*. She was arrested in Cuba for wearing slacks. In Puerto Rico she is remembered in a popular song that says: "Doña Luisa Capetillo, intentionally or not, has created a tremendous uproar because of her culottes."[13]

The Suffragist Movement

Several years after the working women's feminist campaigns, another group of women organized the *Liga Femínea de Puerto Rico* (Puerto Rican Feminine League). Founded in 1917 by Ana Roqué de Duprey, its main objective was to fight for women's right to vote. Ana Roqué's commitment to women's rights had begun at the end of the nineteenth century. As the founder and editor of several feminist newspapers, she consistently demanded the right to vote, to education and to the active participation of women in society.[14]

In contrast to the feminist working women, the suffragists from *Liga Femínea* demanded the *restricted* vote. This meant that only those women twenty-one years old and over who knew how to read and write could participate in general elections. In Puerto Rico only one sixth of the female population met those requirements. The suffragist organization, though contemporary with the working women's organization, had a different ideology and different strategies. Working women in labor unions were active in strikes, demanded universal suffrage, and discussed issues affecting the working class as a whole. In contrast, the majority of the suffragists who favored the restricted vote did not share working women's problems or situation, and avoided involvement in militant demonstrations like strikes or other kinds of protests.[15]

The Nineteenth Amendment: Colonialism, Feminism, and the Fight for Universal Suffrage

As early as 1908, the impact of feminist polemics was evident in the political arena. Nemesio Canales, writer and legislator, expressed his solidarity with the resolutions approved at the *Federación Libre de Trabajadores* assembly, and presented a bill demanding "legal emancipation for Puerto Rican women," including universal suffrage. The bill was not approved.[16] This was the first of a series of twelve different bills presented over a twenty-year period.

Besides male opposition, an additional obstacle to women's suffrage involved Puerto Rico's colonial status. Given Puerto Rico's subordination to the United States, several suffragists expected that the Nineteenth Amendment to the U.S. Constitution (passed in 1919, granting *universal* suffrage to all U.S. women citizens twenty-one years or over) would extend to Puerto Rico. Since Puerto Ricans were granted U.S. citizenship in 1917, there was a legal basis for this expectation.

Events were, however, more complicated. Once Congress approved the law, the Puerto Rican Legislature was uncertain about its validity in Puerto Rico. The confusion over the amendment's applicability was clarified by a solitary but militant action by one woman: Genera Pagán.

Born in San Juan at the end of the nineteenth century, Genera Pagán became a tobacco stripper in one of the largest tobacco factories. As a working woman, she faced miserable wages and terrible working conditions. Like other women, Genera realized the importance of syndicalism and militancy to achieve social change. She emerged as a leader during a working women's strike in 1914. Years later, after losing her husband in World War I, she emigrated to New York, where she worked in the garment industry. The feminist movement in the United States was at its height, particularly around the issue of universal suffrage. Shortly after the approval of the Nineteenth Amendment, Genera became involved in the fight for the extension of the new law to Puerto Rico. When she learned about the confusion over the new law, she decided to go back to Puerto Rico and fight for women's rights.[17]

Genera Pagán believed that as a U.S. citizen, the 1919 law applied to her and all Puerto Rican women. Thus, she attempted to register to vote. The Puerto Rican government did not know what to do, so it requested an opinion from the Bureau of Insular Affairs in Washington, D.C. Several months later, the Bureau of Insular Affairs decided that the Nineteenth Amendment was not applicable to Puerto Rico.[18]

Several considerations shaped this outcome. As Ana Roqué pointed out in 1920, in one of the last issues of her feminist newspaper, Puerto Rican legislators feared approving universal suffrage in Puerto Rico for three hundred thousand women. The majority of women were poor, and potential supporters of the Socialist Party, the first political party to support both suffrage for women and working women's labor struggles. Several legislators were quoted in a few newspapers saying that they were afraid of a possible victory by the Socialist Party due to women's electoral support. This explains why Ana Roqué wrote in her newspaper: " . . . if you (the legislators) are afraid of the political power the illiterate class could gain with the vote, *you should restrict the right to vote to literate women.*" Several years later her statement became a prophecy.[19]

The challenge raised by Genara Pagán showed that suffragists were overconfident about the extension of the Nineteenth Amendment to Puerto Rico. Disillusioned with the negotiations, their militancy decreased significantly. *Liga Femínea* disappeared and its leader, Ana Roqué, announced in 1920 that she was temporarily quitting, proclaiming that the "only hope in the universal suffrage struggle lay with working women's organizations." Mercedes Solá, another distinguished suffragist writer and leader, also recognized the importance of solid organizations "like the one built by working women in the struggle for women's rights."[20]

Working Women's Struggle for Universal Suffrage

Working women were, again, the first to raise the banner of feminism at the beginning of the new decade. By 1920, the Socialist Party organized the *Asociación Feminista Popular* (AFP Popular Feminist Association). One of its first activities was a mass rally with special guest speaker, Betty Hall, a very well known North American suffragist.[21] This liaison between Puerto Rican and North American feminists was an important precedent, which influenced future feminist strategies.

Several months after the foundation of the AFP, the suffragists decided to reorganize. A new organization, *Liga Social Sufragista* (Suffragist Social League), was founded. Milagros Benet Newton, an active suffragist who held more conservative views than prior leaders, was elected president. She disapproved of Genera Pagán's defiant acts, and stood in favor of the restricted vote.[22] Her presidency, however, did not last long. She was followed by Ricarda López, one of the founders of the Teachers Federation, who brought significant changes to the League, particularly the defense of universal suffrage.

Subsequently, women's struggles for universal suffrage gained momentum. Two other suffragist groups were organized: *Asociación Puertorriqueña de Mujeres Sufragistas* (Puerto Rican Association of Suffragist Women) and *Liga Panamericana de Mujeres Votantes* (Pan-American Women's League), which followed the conservative direction promoted by Benet Newton. These new organizations took a firm stand in favor of *restricted* suffrage. The majority of the legislators shared this conservative position. Thus, of the eleven proposals presented for legislation, none was as liberal and comprehensive as the one that had been presented by the legislator, Nemesio Canales, in 1908. The majority asked for *restricted* suffrage, fearing the party preference of poor women—the Socialist Party. The Liberal Party, the party in power, of course opposed universal suffrage for women.

The political battle was on, and the debate reached other institutions: civic and religious associations, magazines, and newspapers. For example, cartoons appeared in popular magazines like *El Carnaval* and *El Diluvio*, mocking women's demand for suffrage.[23] The Catholic Church leaders opposed women's vote because it "could interrupt women's destiny, according to God and Nature, to be mothers and housewives."[24] *El Mundo*, one of the leading newspapers at that time, conducted a survey in which the majority of people who responded favored universal suffrage for women.[25] The Teachers Federation approved a resolution demanding women's suffrage.

Building Solidarity with North American Feminists and the Pressure from Washington, D.C.

Over the following years, suffrage was one of the most widely discussed issues in the political arena. By 1927, there was a general consensus among several important civic, professional, and political organizations favoring women's right to vote, but the debate over universal versus restricted suffrage constituted a major obstacle to passing legislation. This debate initially divided the politicians and the feminists. A temporary coalition was formed between the conservative suffragist groups, which supported restricted suffrage, and feminist working women from both the Socialist Party and labor unions, which defended and insisted on universal suffrage. But the issue of restricted versus universal suffrage dissolved this united front. However, liberal suffragists in the *Liga Social Sufragista*, who supported universal suffrage, created a different strategy: lobbying in Washington, D.C.[26]

These liberal suffragists developed an ongoing relationship with the National Woman's Party. (It should be pointed out, however, that before the *Liga* began to seek help from North American suffragists, working women from the Socialist Party had contacted them.) Through their North American contacts, the Puerto Rican suffragists were able to lobby several congressmen. Their efforts paid off; they were able to convince two congressmen to present legislation. In January 1929, the bill moved up to the Committee for Insular Possessions and Territories of the United States Congress, which gave it a favorable recommendation.[27] This legislation then put pressure on the Puerto Rican Legislature to approve women's suffrage. Several months later a new bill, Number 12, was presented in Puerto Rico. If this bill was not approved soon, the U.S. legislation would be enacted. The bill was approved—granting *restricted* suffrage for women. Protests arose immediately. Leaders of the Suffragist Social League,[28] the Socialist Party, and other groups vigorously attacked the discriminatory law.

In 1932, approximately fifty thousand women participated in general elections, the first elections in which a group of women exercised their right to vote. Ironically, María Luisa Arcelay, who was not a feminist and was not involved in feminist struggles, was the first woman elected to the legislature. She had economic power as an owner of several needlework factories, and thus her record as a legislator who lacked interest in feminist issues, and in some instances opposed women's interests. For example, she did not support a bill to raise wages for women in the needlework industry, and did not initiate the bill to grant universal suffrage to women. It was clear that when she had to take sides, she defended her personal economic interests.

Feminist struggles waned during the period following the passage of the suffrage bill. This was also the trend in other countries. Thirty years passed before we witnessed a new wave of feminist activism.

Conclusion

One of the major achievements of contemporary feminist movements has been the rediscovery of their forgotten history. Women can learn many lessons from their predecessors' fights. The history of women's struggles, as this essay on Puerto Rican feminism shows, widens the discussions and perspectives on the current situation for women. Three major issues should be underlined: first, the inexorable relationship between feminism and social class, evident for example in the restricted versus universal suffrage polemic and the selection of María Luisa Arcelay as the first "token woman" in the Puerto Rican Legislature; second, the tremendous importance of international solidarity among women, as was demonstrated by the support and collaboration between Puerto Rican and U.S. feminists; third, women's obtaining of rights and equality when they unite and organize, when they develop a collective commitment to struggle for their rights.[29]

Notes

1. For more information on the history of women's education in Puerto Rico, see Cayetano Coll y Toste, *Historia de la instrucción pública en Puerto Rico hasta el año 1898* (*History of Puerto Rican Public Education up to 1898*) (Editorial Vasco Americana, Spain 1970). Statistics quoted were taken from Juan José Osuna, *A History of Education in Puerto Rico* (Editorial U.P.R. 1949), p. 56.

2. Cuesta Mendoza, A. *Historia de la educación en el Puerto Rico colonial de 1821–1898* (*History of Education in Colonial Puerto Rico from 1821–1898*), vols. I and II, (Imprenta Arte y Cine, República Dominicana, 1948).

3. For more information on Hostos see *Hostos en Santo Domingo, Homenaje de la República Dominicana con motivo del Centenario de Eugenio María de Hostos* (*Hostos in Santo Domingo, Dominican Republic's Homage to Eugenio María de Hostos*) ed. E. Rodíguez Demoncci, 1939, pp. 214–215; Eugenio María de Hostos "La educación científica de la mujer," *Páginas Escogidas* ("Scientific Education for Women," *Selected Pages*) (Colección Estrada, Argentina, 1952), p. 81.

4. Negrón de Montilla, Aida. *Americanization in Puerto Rico and the Public School System 1900–1930.* (Editorial Edil, P.R. 1971).

5. "Major Female Occupations in Puerto Rico, 1899–1930." United States Department of Labor, *The Employment of Women in Puerto Rico* (Washington, D.C. Government Printing Office, 1934).

6. Report of the Governor of Puerto Rico, *Informe del Comisionado de Instrucción* (*Report of the Education Commissioner*). Años 1911, p. 175; 1917 p. 467; Reyes de Martínez Ana. L. *El Desarrollo del programa de economía doméstica en Puerto Rico 1903–1964* (*The Development of the Home Economics Program in Puerto Rico from 1903 to 1964*) (Departamento de Instrucción Pública, Junta Estatal de Instrucción Vocacional, P.R. 1964).

7. Quintero Rivera Angel. "Socialista y tabaquero: La proletización de los artesanos." ("The Socialist and Tobacco Worker: The Proletarization of the Artisans") *Sin Nombre* (January–March, 1978), p. 13, P.R.

8. Iglesias, Igualdad. *El obrerismo en Puerto Rico* (*Workmanship in Puerto Rico*). "La mujer en la organización obrera" ("Women in the Workers' Organizations") (Ed. Juan Ponce de León, España, 1973), pp. 323–327.

9. Unión obrera (periódico) (Workers Union, Newspaper) (September 1, 1910; September 26, 1910; August 26, 1911; July 14, 1911).

10. Federación Libre de Trabajadores, editor (Free Workers Union). *Procedimientos de Sexto Congreso de la Federación Libre de Trabajadores de Puerto Rico* (*Procedures of the 6th Conference of the Free Workers Union of Puerto Rico*) (San Juan, P.R. 1910).

11. Torres, A. *Espíritu de clase* (*Class Spirit*) (Imprenta F.L.T., San Juan, P.R. 1917), pp. 43–44.

12. *Unión Obrera* (*Workers' Union*), (September 1, 1906).

13. Valle, N. *Luisa Capetillo* (San Juan, P.R. 1975).

14. For more information on Ana Roqué see Negrón Muñoz A. *Mujeres de Puerto Rico* (*Women in Puerto Rico*)

(Imprenta Venezuela, San Juan, Puerto Rico 1935); Meléndez, C. "Ana Roqué de Duprey: Biografía en cuatro tiempos," *Figuraciones de Puerto Rico* (Instituto de Cultura Puertorriqueña, San Juan, 1958).

15. For more information on the suffragist organizations, see several of their newspapers: *Pluma de mujer* (1915); *Album puertorriqueño* (1918).
16. Canales, N., *Paliques* (Edit Coquí, San Juan, P.R. 1968).
17. *El Mundo*, (September 3, 1920).
18. *El Mundo*, (September 17, 1920; January 6, 1921).
19. *Heraldo de la mujer*, (October 1919) Author's Emphasis.
20. Solá, M. *Feminismo* (Imprenta Cantero, P.R. 1922).
21. *Unión Obrera*, (December 14, 1920).
22. *El Mundo*, (September 3, 1920).
23. *El Carnaval*, (September 12, 1920), cartoon entitled "Cuando las mujeres voten"; (September 19, 1920), "Cosas del sufragio femenino"; (September 26, 1920), "Y quieren que uno las apoye."
24. *El Mundo*, (September 4, 1920).
25. *El Mundo*, (March, April and May 1923).
26. *El Mundo*, (November 28, 1927).
27. "Confer the right to vote to women of Porto Rico," House of Representatives, Report #1895, 70th Congress, May 1928; "Conferring the Right to Vote upon Porto Rican Women," Senate, Report #1454, 70th Congress, January 18, 1929.
28. *El Mundo*, (May 29, 1929).
29. For more information on the history of feminism in Puerto Rico see Azize, Y. *La mujer en la lucha. Historia del feminismo en Puerto Rico 1898–1930* (*Women's Struggles. History of Feminism in Puerto Rico 1898–1930*). (Editorial Cultural, San Juan, Puerto Rico, 1985); Azize, Y. ed. *La mujer en Puerto Rico. Ensayos de investigación* (*Woman in Puerto Rico, Research Essays*) (Editorial Huracán, P.R. 1987).

17

Womanist Consciousness:
Maggie Lena Walker and the
Independent Order of Saint Luke

Elsa Barkley Brown

In the first decades of the twentieth century Maggie Lena Walker repeatedly challenged her contemporaries to "make history as Negro women." Yet she and her colleagues in the Independent Order of Saint Luke, like most black and other women of color, have been virtually invisible in women's history and women's studies. Although recent books and articles have begun to redress this,[1] the years of exclusion have had an impact more significant than just the invisibility of black women, for the exclusion of black women has meant that the concepts, perspectives, methods, and pedagogies of women's history and women's studies have been developed without consideration of the experiences of black women. As a result many of the recent explorations in black women's history have attempted to place black women inside feminist perspectives which, by design, have omitted their experiences. Nowhere is this exclusion more apparent than in the process of defining women's issues and women's struggle. Because they have been created outside the experiences of black women, the definitions used in women's history and women's studies assume the separability of women's struggle and race struggle. Such arguments recognize the possibility that black women may have both women's concerns and race concerns, but they insist upon delimiting each. They allow, belatedly, black women to make history as women or as Negroes but not as "Negro women." What they fail to consider is that women's issues may be race issues, and race issues may be women's issues.[2]

Rosalyn Terborg-Penn, in "Discontented Black Feminists: Prelude and Postscript to the Passage of the Nineteenth Amendment," an essay on the 1920s black women's movement, of which Walker was a part, persuasively discusses the continuing discrimination in the U. S. women's movement and the focus of black women on "uplifting the downtrodden of the race or . . . representing people of color throughout the world." Subsequently she argues for the "unique nature of feminism among Afro-American women." The editors of *Decades of Discontent: The Women's Movement, 1920–1940*, the 1983 collection on post-Nineteenth Amendment feminism, however, introduce Terborg-Penn's article by mistakenly concluding that these black women, disillusioned and frustrated by racism in the women's movement, turned from women's issues to race issues. Using a framework that does not conceive of "racial uplift, fighting segregation and mob violence" and "contending with poverty" as women's issues, Lois Scharf and Joan Jensen succumb to the tendency to assume that black women's lives can be neatly subdivided, that while we are both black and female, we occupy those roles sequentially, as if one cannot have the two simultaneously in one's

Reprinted with permission of the University of Chicago Press. Originally published in *Signs* 14, Spring 1989.

consciousness of being.[3] Such a framework assumes a fragmentation of black women's existence that defies reality.

Scharf and Jensen's conclusion is certainly one that the white feminists of the 1920s and 1930s, who occupy most of the book, would have endorsed. When southern black women, denied the right to register to vote, sought help from the National Woman's Party, these white feminists rejected their petitions, arguing that this was a race concern and not a women's concern. Were they not, after all, being denied the vote not because of their sex but because of their race?[4]

Black women like Walker who devoted their energies to securing universal suffrage, including that of black men, are not widely recognized as female suffragists because they did not separate their struggle for the women's vote from their struggle for the black vote. This tendency to establish false dichotomies, precluding the possibility that for many racism and sexism are experienced simultaneously, leads to discussions of liberation movements and women's movements as separate entities.

Quite clearly, what many women of color at the United Nations Decade for Women conference held in Nairobi, Kenya, in 1985, along with many other activists and scholars, have argued in recent years is the impossibility of separating the two and the necessity of understanding the convergence of women's issues, race/nationalist issues, and class issues in women's consciousnesses.[5] That understanding is in part hampered by the prevailing terminology: feminism places a priority on women; nationalism or race consciousness, a priority on race. It is the need to overcome the limitations of terminology that has led many black women to adopt the term "womanist." Both Alice Walker and Chikwenye Okonjo Ogunyemi have defined womanism as a consciousness that incorporates racial, cultural, sexual, national, economic, and political considerations.[6] As Ogunyemi explains, "black womanism is a philosophy" that concerns itself both with sexual equality in the black community and "with the world power structure that subjugates" both blacks and women. "Its ideal is for black unity where every black person has a modicum of power and so can be a 'brother' or a 'sister' or a 'father' or a 'mother' to the other. . . . [I]ts aim is the dynamism of wholeness and self-healing."[7]

Walker's and Ogunyemi's terminology may be new, but their ideas are not. In fact, many black women at various points in history had a clear understanding that race issues and women's issues were inextricably linked, that one could not separate women's struggle from race struggle. It was because of this understanding that they refused to disconnect themselves from either movement. They instead insisted on inclusion in both movements in a manner that recognized the interconnection between race and sex, and they did so even if they had to battle their white sisters and their black brothers to achieve it. Certainly the lives and work of women such as Anna Julia Cooper, Mary Church Terrell, and Fannie Barrier Williams inform us of this. Cooper, an early Africanamerican womanist, addressed the holistic nature of the struggle in her address to the World's Congress of Representative Women:

> Let woman's claim be as broad in the concrete as in the abstract. *We take our stand on the solidarity of humanity, the oneness of life,* and the unnaturalness and injustice of all special favoritisms, whether of sex, race, country, or condition. If one link of the chain be broken, the chain is broken. . . . We want, then, as toilers for the universal triumph of justice and human rights, to go to our homes from this Congress, demanding an entrance not through a gateway for ourselves, our race, our sex, or our sect, but a grand highway for humanity. The colored woman feels that woman's cause is one and universal; and that not till . . . race, color, sex, and condition are seen as the accidents, and not the substance of life;

... not till then is woman's lesson taught and woman's cause won–not the white woman's, nor the black woman's, nor the red woman's, but the cause of every man and of every woman who has writhed silently under a mighty wrong. *Woman's wrongs are thus indissolubly linked with all undefended woe, and the acquirement of her "rights" will mean the final triumph of all right over might,* the supremacy of the moral forces of reason, and justice, and love in the government of the nations of earth.[8]

One of those who most clearly articulated womanist consciousness was Maggie Lena Walker. Walker (1867–1934) was born and educated in Richmond, Virginia, graduating from Colored Normal School in 1883. During her school years she assisted her widowed mother in her work as a washerwoman and cared for her younger brother. Following graduation she taught in the city's public school and took courses in accounting and sales. Required to stop teaching when she married Armstead Walker, a contractor, her coursework had well prepared her to join several other black women in founding an insurance company, the Woman's Union. Meanwhile, Walker, who had joined the Independent Order of Saint Luke at the age of fourteen, rose through the ranks to hold several important positions in the order and, in 1895, to organize the juvenile branch of the order. In addition to her Saint Luke activities, Walker was a founder or leading supporter of the Richmond Council of Colored Women, the Virginia State Federation of Colored Women, the National Association of Wage Earners, the International Council of Women of the Darker Races, the National Training School for Girls, and the Virginia Industrial School for Colored Girls. She also helped direct the National Association for the Advancement of Colored People, the Richmond Urban League, and the Negro Organization Society of Virginia.[9]

Walker is probably best known today as the first woman bank president in the United States. She founded the Saint Luke Penny Savings Bank in Richmond, Virginia, in 1903. Before her death in 1934 she oversaw the reorganization of this financial institution as the present-day Consolidated Bank and Trust Company, the oldest continuously existing black-owned and black-run bank in the country. The bank, like most of Walker's activities, was the outgrowth of the Independent Order of Saint Luke, which she served as Right Worthy Grand Secretary for thirty-five years.

The Independent Order of Saint Luke was one of the larger and more successful of the many thousands of mutual benefit societies that have developed throughout Africanamerican communities since the eighteenth century. These societies combined insurance functions with economic development and social and political activities. As such they were important loci of community self-help and racial solidarity. Unlike the Knights of Pythias and its female auxiliary, the Courts of Calanthe, societies like the Independent Order of Saint Luke had a nonexclusionary membership policy; any man, woman, or child could join. Thus men and women from all occupational segments, professional/managerial, entrepreneurial, and working-class, came together in the order. The Independent Order of Saint Luke was a mass-based organization that played a key role in the political, economic, and social development of its members and of the community as a whole.[10]

Founded in Maryland in 1867 by Mary Prout, the Independent Order of Saint Luke began as a women's sickness and death mutual benefit association. By the 1880s it had admitted men and had expanded to New York and Virginia. At the 1899 annual meeting William M. T. Forrester, who had served as Grand Secretary since 1869, refused to accept reappointment, stating that the order was in decline, having only 1,080 members in fifty-seven councils, $31.61 in the treasury, and $400.00 in outstanding debts. Maggie Lena Walker took over the duties of Grand Worthy Secretary at one-third of the position's previous salary.[11]

According to Walker, her "first work was to draw around me *women*."[12] In fact, after the executive board elections in 1901, six of the nine members were women: Walker, Patsie K. Anderson, Frances Cox, Abigail Dawley, Lillian H. Payne, and Ella O. Waller.[13] Under their leadership the order and its affiliates flourished. The order's ventures included a juvenile department, an educational loan fund for young people, a department store, and a weekly newspaper. Growing to include over 100,000 members in 2,010 councils and circles in twenty-eight states, the order demonstrated a special commitment to expanding the economic opportunities within the black community, especially those for women.

It is important to take into account Walker's acknowledgment of her female colleagues. Most of what we know about the order of Saint Luke highlights Walker because she was the leader and spokeswoman and therefore the most visible figure. She was able, however, to function in that role and to accomplish all that she did not merely because of her own strengths and skills, considerable though they were, but also because she operated from the strength of the Saint Luke collective as a whole and from the special strengths and talents of the inner core of the Saint Luke women in particular. Deborah Gray White, in her work on women during slavery, underscores the importance of black women's networks in an earlier time period: "Strength had to be cultivated. It came no more naturally to them than to anyone. . . . If they seemed exceptionally strong it was partly because they often functioned in groups and derived strength from numbers. . . . [T]hey inevitably developed some appreciation of one another's skills and talents. This intimacy enabled them to establish the criteria with which to rank and order themselves." It was this same kind of sisterhood that was Walker's base, her support, her strength, and her source of wisdom and direction.[14]

The women of Saint Luke expanded the role of women in the community to the political sphere through their leadership in the 1904 streetcar boycott and through the *St. Luke Herald's* pronouncements against segregation, lynching, and lack of equal educational opportunities for black children. Walker spearheaded the local struggle for women's suffrage and the voter registration campaigns after the passage of the Nineteenth Amendment. In the 1920 elections in Richmond, fully 80 percent of the eligible black voters were women. The increased black political strength represented by the female voters gave incentive to the growing movement for independent black political action and led to the formation of the Virginia Lily-Black Republican Party. Walker ran on this ticket for state superintendent of public instruction in 1921.[15] Thus Walker and many other of the Saint Luke women were role models for other black women in their community activities as well as their occupations.

Undergirding all of their work was a belief in the possibilities inherent in the collective struggle of black women in particular and of the black community in general. Walker argued that the only way in which black women would be able "to avoid the traps and snares of life" would be to "band themselves together, organize, . . . put their mites together, put their hands and their brains together and make work and business for themselves."[16]

The idea of collective economic development was not a new idea for these women, many of whom were instrumental in establishing the Woman's Union, a female insurance company founded in 1898. Its motto was The Hand That Rocks the Cradle Rules the World.[17] But unlike nineteenth-century white women's rendering of that expression to signify the limitation of woman's influence to that which she had by virtue of rearing her sons, the idea as these women conceived it transcended the separation of private and public spheres and spoke to the idea that women, while not abandoning their roles as wives and mothers, could also move into economic and political activities in ways that would support rather than conflict with family and community. Women did not have to choose between the two spheres; in fact, they necessarily had to occupy both. Indeed, these women's use of this phrase speaks to their understanding of the totality of the task that lay ahead of them as black women. It negates, for black women at least, the public/private dichotomy.

Saint Luke women built on tradition. A well-organized set of institutions maintained community in Richmond: mutual benefit societies, interwoven with extended families and churches, built a network of supportive relations.[18] The families, churches, and societies were all based on similar ideas of collective consciousness and collective responsibility. Thus, they served to extend and reaffirm notions of family throughout the black community. Not only in their houses but also in their meeting halls and places of worship, they were brothers and sisters caring for each other. The institutionalization of this notion of family cemented the community. Community/family members recognized that this had to be maintained from generation to generation; this was in part the function of the juvenile branches of the mutual benefit associations. The statement of purpose of the Children's Rosebud Fountains, Grand Fountain United Order of True Reformers, clearly articulated this:

> Teaching them . . . to assist each other in sickness, sorrow and afflictions and in the struggles of life; teaching them that one's happiness greatly depends upon the others. . . . Teach them to live united. . . . The children of different families will know how to . . . talk, plot and plan for one another's peace and happiness in the journey of life.
>
> Teach them to . . . bear each other's burdens . . . to so bind and tie their love and affections together that one's sorrow may be the other's sorrow, one's distress be the other's distress, one's penny the other's penny.[19]

Through the Penny Savings Bank the Saint Luke women were able to affirm and cement the existing mutual assistance network among black women and within the black community by providing an institutionalized structure for these activities. The bank recognized the meager resources of the black community, particularly black women. In fact, its establishment as a *penny* savings bank is an indication of that. Many of its earliest and strongest supporters were washerwomen, one of whom was Maggie Walker's mother. And the bank continued throughout Walker's leadership to exercise a special commitment to "the small depositor."[20]

In her efforts Walker, like the other Saint Luke women, was guided by a clearly understood and shared perspective concerning the relationship of black women to black men, to the black community, and to the larger society. This was a perspective that acknowledged individual powerlessness in the face of racism and sexism and that argued that black women, because of their condition and status, had a right—indeed, according to Walker, a special duty and incentive—to organize. She argued, "Who is so helpless as the Negro woman? Who is so circumscribed and hemmed in, in the race of life, in the struggle for bread, meat and clothing as the Negro woman?"[21]

In addition, her perspective contended that organizational activity and the resultant expanded opportunities for black women were not detrimental to the home, the community, black men, or the race. Furthermore, she insisted that organization and expansion of women's roles economically and politically were essential ingredients without which the community, the race, and even black men could not achieve their full potential. The way in which Walker described black women's relationship to society, combined with the collective activities in which she engaged, give us some insight into her understanding of the relationship between women's struggle and race struggle.

Walker was determined to expand opportunities for black women. In fulfilling this aim she challenged not only the larger society's notions of the proper place of blacks but also those in her community who held a limited notion of women's proper role. Particularly in light of the increasing necessity to defend the integrity and morality of the race, a "great number of men" and women in Virginia and elsewhere believed that women's clubs, movements "looking to the final exercise of suffrage by women," and organizations of black professional and business women would lead to "the decadence of home life."[22] Women involved in these activities were often regarded as "pullbacks, rather than home builders."[23] Maggie Walker countered these arguments, stressing the need for women's organizations, saying, "Men should not be so pessimistic and down on women's clubs. They don't seek to destroy the home or disgrace the race."[24] In fact, the Richmond Council of Colored Women, of which she was founder and president, and many other women's organizations worked to elevate the entire black community, and this, she believed, was the proper province of women.

In 1908 two Richmond men, Daniel Webster Davis and Giles Jackson, published *The Industrial History of the Negro Race of the United States*, which became a textbook for black children throughout the state. The chapter on women acknowledged the economic and social achievements of black women but concluded that "the Negro Race Needs Housekeepers . . . wives who stay at home, being supported by their husbands, and then they can spend time in the training of their children."[25] Maggie Walker responded practically to those who held such ideas: "The bold fact remains that there are more women in the world than men; . . . if each and every woman in the land was allotted a man to marry her, work for her, support her, and keep her at home, there would still be an army of women left uncared for, unprovided for, and who would be compelled to fight life's battles alone, and without the companionship of man."[26] Even regarding those women who did marry, she contended, "The old doctrine that a man marries a woman to support her is pretty nearly thread-bare to-day." Only a few black men were able to fully support their families on their earnings alone. Thus many married women worked, "not for name, not for glory and honor—but for bread, and for [their] babies."[27]

The reality was that black women who did go to work outside the home found themselves in a helpless position. "How many occupations have Negro Women?" asked Walker. "Let us count them: Negro women are domestic menials, teachers and church builders." And even the first two of these, she feared, were in danger. As Walker perceived it, the expansion of opportunities for white women did not mean a corresponding expansion for black women; instead, this trend might actually lead to an even greater limitation on the economic possibilities for black women. She pointed to the fact that white women's entry into the tobacco factories of the city had "driven the Negro woman out," and she, like many of her sisters throughout the country, feared that a similar trend was beginning even in domestic work.[28]

In fact, these economic realities led members of the Order of Saint Luke to discuss the development of manufacturing operations as a means of giving employment and therefore "a chance in the race of life" to "the young Negro woman."[29] In 1902 Walker described herself as "consumed with the desire to hear the whistle on our factory and see our women by the hundreds coming to work."[30] It was this same concern for the economic status of black women that led Walker and other Saint Luke women to affiliate with the National Association of Wage Earners (NAWE), a women's organization that sought to pool the energies and resources of housewives, professionals, and managerial, domestic, and industrial workers to protect and expand the economic position of black women. The NAWE argued that it was vital that all black women be able to support themselves.[31] Drawing on traditional stereotypes in the same breath with which she defied them, Walker contended that it was in the self-interest of black men to unite themselves with these efforts to secure decent employment for black women: "Every dollar a woman makes, some man gets the direct benefit of same. Every woman was by Divine Providence created for some man; not for some man to marry, take home and support, but for the purpose of using her powers, ability, health and strength to forward the financial . . . success of the partnership into which she may go, if she will. . . . [W]hat stronger combination could ever God make— than the partnership of a business man and a business woman."[32]

By implication, whatever black women as a whole were able to achieve would directly benefit black men. In Walker's analysis family is a reciprocal metaphor for community: family is community and community is family. But this is more than rhetorical style. Her discussions of relationship networks suggest that the entire community was one's family. Thus Walker's references to husbands and wives reflected equally her understandings of male/female relationships in the community as a whole and of those relationships within the household. Just as all family members' resources were needed for the family to be well and strong, so they were needed for a healthy community/family.

In the process of developing means of expanding economic opportunities in the community, however, Walker and the Saint Luke women also confronted white Richmond's notions of the proper place of blacks. While whites found a ban headed by a "Negress" an interesting curiosity,[33] they were less receptive to other business enterprises. In 1905 twenty-two black women from the Independent Order of Saint Luke collectively formed a department store aimed at providing quality goods at more affordable prices than those available in stores outside the black community, as well as a place where black women could earn a living and get a business education. The Saint Luke Emporium employed fifteen women as sales clerks. While this may seem an insignificant number in comparison to the thousands of black women working outside the home, in the context of the occupational structure of Richmond these women constituted a significant percentage of the white-collar and skilled working-class women in the community. In 1900 less than 1 percent of the employed black women in the city were either clerical or skilled workers. That number had quadrupled by 1910, when 222 of the more than 13,000 employed black women listed their occupations as typists, stenographers, bookkeepers, salesclerks, and the like. However, by 1930 there had been a reduction in the numbers of black women employed in clerical and sales positions. This underscores the fact that black secretaries and clerks were entirely dependent on the financial stability of black businesses and in this regard the Independent Order of Saint Luke was especially important. With its fifty-five clerks in the home office, over one-third of the black female clerical workers in Richmond in the 1920s worked for this order. The quality of the work experience was significantly better for these women as compared to those employed as laborers in the tobacco factories or as servants in private homes. They worked in healthier, less stressful environments and, being employed by blacks, they also escaped the racism prevalent in most black women's workplaces. Additionally, the salaries of these clerical workers were often better than those paid even to black professional women, that is, teachers. While one teacher, Ethel Thompson Overby, was receiving eighteen dollars a month as a teacher and working her way up to the top of the scale at forty dollars, a number of black women were finding good working conditions and a fifty-dollar-per-month paycheck as clerks in the office of the Independent Order of Saint Luke. Nevertheless, black women in Richmond, as elsewhere, overwhelmingly remained employed in domestic service in the years 1890–1930.[34]

Located on East Broad Street, Richmond's main business thoroughfare, the Saint Luke Emporium met stiff opposition from white merchants. When the intention to establish the department store was first announced, attempts were made to buy the property at a price several thousand dollars higher than that which the Order of Saint Luke had originally paid. When that did not succeed, an offer of ten thousand dollars cash was made to the order if it would not start the emporium. Once it opened, efforts were made to hinder the store's operations. A white Retail Dealers' Association was formed for the purpose of crushing this business as well as other "Negro merchants who are objectionable . . . because they compete with and get a few dollars which would otherwise go to the white merchant." Notices were sent to wholesale merchants in the city warning them not to sell to the emporium at the risk of losing all business from any of the white merchants. Letters were also sent to wholesale houses in New York City with the same warning. These letters charged that the emporium was underselling the white merchants of Richmond. Clearly, then, the white businessmen of Richmond found the emporium and these black women a threat; if it was successful, the store could lead to a surge of black merchants competing with white merchants and thus decrease the black patronage at white stores. The white merchants' efforts were ultimately successful: the obstacles they put in the way of the emporium, in addition to the lack of full support from the black community itself, resulted in the department store's going out of business seven years after its founding.[35] Though its existence was short-lived and its demise mirrors many of the problems that black businesses faced from both within and without their community, the effort demonstrated the commitment of the Order of Saint Luke to provide needed services for the community and needed opportunities for black women.

Maggie Walker's appeals for support of the emporium show quite clearly the way in which her notions of race, of womanhood, and of community fused. Approximately one year after the opening of the emporium, Walker called for a mass gathering of men in the community to talk, in part, about support for the business. Her speech, "Beniah's Valour; An Address for Men Only," opened with an assessment of white businessmen's and officials' continuing oppression of the black community. In her fine rhetorical style she queried her audience. "Hasn't it crept into your minds that we are being more and more oppressed each day that we live? Hasn't it yet come to you, that we are being oppressed by the passage of laws which not only have for their object the degradation of Negro manhood and Negro womanhood, but also the destruction of all kinds of Negro enterprises?" Then, drawing upon the biblical allegory of Beniah and the lion, she warned, "There is a lion terrorizing us, preying upon us, and upon every business effort which we put forth. The name of this insatiable lion is PREJUDICE. . . . The white press, the white pulpit, the white business associations, the legislature—all . . . the lion with whom we contend daily . . . in Broad Street, Main Street and in every business street of Richmond. Even now . . . that lion is seeking some new plan of attack."[36]

Thus, she contended, the vital question facing their community was how to kill the lion. And in her analysis, "the only way to kill the Lion is to stop feeding it." The irony was that the black community drained itself of resources, money, influence, and patronage to feed its predator.[37] As she had many times previously, Walker questioned the fact that while the white community oppressed the black, "the Negro . . . carries to their bank every dollar he can get his hands upon and then goes back the next day, borrows and then pays the white man to lend him his own money."[38] So, too, black people patronized stores and other businesses in which white women were, in increasing numbers, being hired as salesclerks and secretaries while black women were increasingly without employment and the black community as a whole was losing resources, skills, and finances.[39] Walker considered such behavior racially destructive and believed it necessary to break those ties that kept "the Negro . . . so wedded to those who oppress him."[40] The drain on the resources of the black community could be halted by a concentration on the development of a self-sufficient black community. But to achieve this would require the talents of the entire community/family. It was therefore essential that black women's work in the community be "something more tangible than elegant papers, beautifully framed resolutions and pretty speeches." Rather, "the exercising of every talent that God had given them" was required in the effort to "raise . . . the race to higher planes of living."[41]

The Saint Luke women were part of the Negro Independence Movement that captured a large segment of Richmond society at the turn of the century. Disillusioned by the increasing prejudice and discrimination in this period, which one historian has described as the nadir in U.S. race relations, black residents of Richmond nevertheless held on to their belief in a community that they could collectively sustain.[42] As they witnessed a steady erosion of their civil and political rights, however, they were aware that there was much operating against them. In Richmond, as elsewhere, a system of race and class oppression including segregation, disfranchisement, relegation to the lowest rungs of the occupational strata, and enforcement of racial subordination through intimidation was fully in place by the early twentieth century. In Richmond between 1885 and 1915 all blacks were removed from the city council; the only predominantly black political district, Jackson Ward, was gerrymandered out of existence; the state constitutional convention disfranchised the majority of black Virginians; first the railroads and streetcars, and later the jails, juries, and neighborhoods were segregated; black principals were removed from the public schools and the right of blacks to teach was questioned; the state legislature decided to substitute white for black control of Virginia Normal and College and to strike "and College" from both name and function; and numerous other restrictions were imposed. As attorney J. Thomas Hewin noted, he and his fellow black Richmonders occupied "a peculiar position in the body politics":

> He [the Negro] is not wanted in politics, because his presence in official positions renders him obnoxious to his former masters and their descendants. He is not wanted in the industrial world as a trained handicraftsman, because he would be brought into competition with his white brother. He is not wanted in city positions, because positions of that kind are always saved for the wardheeling politicians. He is not wanted in State and Federal offices, because there is an unwritten law that a Negro shall not hold an office. He is not wanted on the Bench as a judge, because he would have to pass upon the white man's case also. Nor is he wanted on public conveyances, because here his presence is obnoxious to white people.[43]

Assessing the climate of the surrounding society in 1904, John Mitchell, Jr., editor of the *Richmond Planet*, concluded, "This is the beginning of the age of conservatism."[44] The growing movement within the community for racial self-determination urged blacks to depend upon themselves and their community rather than upon whites: to depend upon their own inner strengths, to build their own institutions, and thereby to mitigate the ways in which their lives were determined by the white forces arrayed against them. Race pride, self-help, racial cooperation, and economic development were central to their thinking about their community and to the ways in which they went about building their own internal support system in order to be better able to struggle within the majority system.

The Saint Luke women argued that the development of the community could not be achieved by men alone, or by men on behalf of women. Only a strong and unified community made up of both women and men could wield the power necessary to allow black people to shape their own lives. Therefore, only when women were able to exercise their full strength would the community be at its full strength, they argued. Only when the community was at its full strength would they be able to create their own conditions, conditions that would allow men as well as women to move out of their structural isolation at the bottom of the labor market and to overcome their political impotence in the larger society. The Saint Luke women argued that it was therefore in the self-interest of black men and of the community as a whole to support expanded opportunities for women.

Their arguments redefined not only the roles of women but also the roles and notions of manhood. A strong "race man" traditionally meant one who stood up fearlessly in defense of the race. In her "Address for Men" Walker argued that one could not defend the race unless one defended black women. Appealing to black men's notions of themselves as the protectors of black womanhood, she asked on behalf of all her sisters for their "FRIEND-SHIP, ... LOVE, ... SYMPATHY, ... PROTECTION, and ... ADVICE": "I am asking you, men of Richmond, ... to record [yourselves] as ... the strong race men of our city. . . . I am asking each man in this audience to go forth from this building, determined to do valiant deeds for the Negro Women of Richmond."[45] And how might they offer their friendship, love, and protection; how might they do valiant deeds for Negro womanhood? By supporting the efforts of black women to exercise every talent;[46] by "let[ting] woman choose her own vocation, just as man does his";[47] by supporting the efforts then underway to provide increased opportunities—economic, political, and social—for black women.[48] Once again she drew upon traditional notions of the relationship between men and women at the same time that she countered those very notions. Black men could play the role of protector and defender of womanhood by protecting and defending and aiding women's assault on the barriers generally imposed on women.[49] Only in this way could they really defend the race. Strong race consciousness and strong support of equality for black women were inseparable. Maggie Walker and the other Saint Luke women therefore came to argue that an expanded role for black women within the black community itself was an essential step in the community's fight to overcome the limitations imposed upon the community by the larger society. Race men were therefore defined not just by their actions on behalf of black rights but by their actions on behalf of women's rights. The two were inseparable.

This was a collective effort in which Walker believed black men and black women should be equally engaged. Therefore, even in creating a woman's organization, she and her Saint Luke associates found it essential to create space within the structure for men as well. Unlike many of the fraternal orders that were male or female only, the Order of Saint Luke welcomed both genders as members and as employees. Although the office force was all female, men were employed in the printing department, in field work, and in the bank. Principal offices within the order were open to men and women. Ten of the thirty directors of the emporium were male; eight of the nineteen trustees of the order were male. The Saint Luke women thus strove to create an equalitarian organization, with men neither dominant nor auxiliary. Their vision of the order was a reflection of their vision for their community. In the 1913 Saint Luke Thanksgiving Day celebration of the order, Maggie Walker "thank[ed] God that this is a *woman's* organization, broad enough, liberal enough, and unselfish enough to accord equal rights and equal opportunity to men."[50]

Only such a community could become self-sustaining, self-sufficient, and independent, could enable its members to live lives unhampered by the machinations of the larger society, and could raise children who could envision a different world in which to live and then could go about creating it. The women in the Order of Saint Luke sought to carve a sphere for themselves where they could practically apply their belief in their community and in the potential that black men and women working together could achieve, and they sought to infuse that belief into all of black Richmond and to transmit it to the next generation.

The Saint Luke women challenged notions in the black community about the proper role of women; they challenged notions in the white community about the proper place of blacks. They expanded their roles in ways that enabled them to maintain traditional values of family/community and at the same time move into new spheres and relationships with each other and with the men in their lives. To the larger white society they demonstrated what black men and women in community could achieve. This testified to the idea that women's struggle and race struggle were not two separate phenomena but one indivisible whole. "First by practice and then by precept"[51] Maggie Lena Walker and the Saint Luke women demonstrated in their own day the power of black women discovering their own strengths and sharing them with the whole community.[52] They provide for us today a model of womanist praxis.

Womanism challenges the distinction between theory and action. Too often we have assumed that theory is to be found only in carefully articulated position statements. Courses on feminist theory are woefully lacking in anything other than white, Western, middle-class perspectives; feminist scholars would argue that this is due to the difficulty in locating any but contemporary black feminist thought. Though I have discussed Maggie Lena Walker's public statements, the clearest articulation of her theoretical perspective lies in the organization she helped to create and in her own activities. Her theory and her action are not distinct and separable parts of some whole; they are often synonymous, and it is only through her actions that we clearly hear her theory. The same is true for the lives of many other black women who had limited time and resources and maintained a holistic view of life and struggle.

More important, Maggie Lena Walker's womanism challenges the dichotomous thinking that underlies much feminist theory and writing. Most feminist theory poses opposites in exclusionary and hostile ways: one is black and female, and these are contradictory/problematical statuses. This either/or approach classifies phenomena in such a way that "everything falls into one category or another, but cannot belong to more than one category at the same time."[53] It is precisely this kind of thinking that makes it difficult to see race, sex, and class as forming one consciousness and the resistance of race, sex and class oppression as forming one struggle. Womanism flows from a both/and worldview, a consciousness that allows for the resolution of seeming contradictions "not through an either/or negation but through the interaction" and wholeness. Thus, while black and female may, at one level, be radically different orientations, they are at the same time united, with each "confirming the existence of the other." Rather than standing as "contradictory opposites," they become "complementary, unsynthesized, unified wholes."[54] This is what Ogunyemi refers to as "the dynamism of wholeness." This holistic consciousness undergirds the thinking and action of Maggie Lena Walker and the other Saint Luke women. There are no necessary contradictions between the public and domestic spheres; the community and the family; male and female; race and sex struggle—there is intersection and interdependence.

Dichotomous thinking does not just inhibit our abilities to see the lives of black women and other women of color in their wholeness, but, I would argue, it also limits our ability to see the wholeness of the lives and consciousnesses of even white middle-class women. The thinking and actions of white women, too, are shaped by their race and their class, and their consciousnesses are also formed by the totality of these factors. The failure, however, to explore the total consciousness of white women has made class, and especially race, nonexistent categories in much of white feminist theory. And this has allowed the development of frameworks which render black women's lives invisible. Explorations into the consciousnesses of black women and other women of color should, therefore, be a model for all women, including those who are not often confronted with the necessity of understanding themselves in these total terms. As we begin to confront the holistic nature of all women's lives, we will begin to create a truly womanist studies. In our efforts Maggie Lena Walker and black women like her will be our guide.

Notes

My appreciation is expressed to Mary Kelley, Deborah K. King, Lillian Jones, and the participants in the Community and Social Movements research group of the 1986 Summer Research Institute on Race and Gender, Center for Research on Women, Memphis State University, for their comments on an earlier draft of this article.

1. The recent proliferation of works in black women's history and black women's studies makes a complete bibliographical reference prohibitive. For a sample of some of the growing literature on black women's consciousness, see Evelyn Brooks, "The Feminist Theology of the Black Baptist Church, 1880–1900," in *Class, Race, and Sex: The Dynamics of Control,* ed. Amy Swerdlow and Hanna Lessinger (Boston: G. K. Hall, 1983), 31–59; Hazel V. Carby, *Reconstructing Womanhood: The Emergence of the Afro-American Woman Novelist* (New York: Oxford University Press, 1987); Elizabeth Clark-Lewis, "'This Work Had a' End': The Transition from Live-In to Day Work," Southern Women: The Intersection of Race, Class, and Gender Working Paper no. 2 (Memphis, Tenn.: Memphis State University, Center for Research on Women, 1985); Patricia Hill Collins, "The Social Construction of Black Feminist Thought," *Signs: Journal of Women in Culture and Society* 14, no. 4 (Summer 1989): 745–73; Cheryl Townsend Gilkes, " 'Together and in Harness': Women's Traditions in the Sanctified Church," *Signs* 10, no. 4 (Summer 1985): 678–99; Deborah Gray White, *Ar'n't I a Woman? Female Slaves in the Plantation South* (New York: Norton, 1985). Also note: *Sage: A Scholarly Journal on Black Women,* now in its fifth year, has published issues that focus on education, health, work, mother-daughter relationships, and creative artists.

2. On a contemporary political level, this disassociation of gender concerns from race concerns was dramatically expressed in the 1985 United Nations Decade for Women conference held in Nairobi, Kenya, where the official U. S. delegation, including representatives of major white women's organizations but not one representative of a black women's organization, insisted upon not having the proceedings become bogged down with race and national issues such as apartheid so that it could concentrate on birth control and other "women's" issues. Delegates operating from such a perspective were unable to see African, Asian, and Latin American women who argued for discussion of national political issues as anything other than the tools of men, unfortunate victims unable to discern true women's and feminist struggles. For a discussion of the ways in which these issues were reflected in the Kenya conference, see Ros Young, "Report from Nairobi: The UN Decade for Women Forum," *Race and Class* 27, no. 2 (Autumn 1985): 67–71; and the entire issue of *African Women Rising,* vol. 2, no. 1 (Winter—Spring 1986).

3. See Rosalyn Terborg-Penn, "Discontented Black Feminists: Prelude and Postscript to the Passage of the Nineteenth Amendment," 261–78; Lois Scharf and Joan M. Jensen, "Introduction," 9–10, both in *Decades of Discontent: The Women's Movement, 1920–1940,* ed. Lois Scharf and Joan M. Jensen (Westport, Conn.: Greenwood, 1983).

4. Terborg-Penn, 267. A contemporary example of this type of dichotomous analysis is seen in much of the discussion of the feminization of poverty. Drawing commonalities between the experiences of black and white women, such discussions generally leave the impression that poverty was not a "feminine" problem before white women in increasing numbers were recognized as impoverished. Presumably, before that black women's poverty was considered a result of race; now it is more often considered a result of gender. Linda Burnham has effectively addressed the incompleteness of such analyses, suggesting that they ignore "class, race, and sex as *simultaneously* operative social factors" in black women's lives ("Has Poverty Been Feminized in Black America?" *Black Scholar* 16, no. 2 [March/April 1985]: 14–24 [emphasis mine]).

5. See, e.g., Parita Trivedi, "A Study of 'Sheroes,' " *Third World Book Review* 1, no. 2 (1984): 71–72; Angela Davis, *Women, Race and Class* (New York: Random House, 1981); Nawal el Saadawi, *The Hidden Face of Eve: Women in the Arab World,* trans. Sherif Hetata (Boston: Beacon, 1982); Jenny Bourne, "Towards an Anti-Racist Feminism," *Race and Class* 25, no. 1 (Summer 1983): 1–22; Bonnie Thornton Dill, "Race, Class, and Gender: Prospects for an All-Inclusive Sisterhood," *Feminist Studies* 9, no. 1 (Spring 1983): 131–50; Evelyn Nakano Glenn, *Issei, Nisei, War Bride: Three Generations of Japanese American Women in Domestic Service* (Philadelphia: Temple University Press, 1986); Audre Lorde, *Sister/Outsider: Essays and Speeches* (Trumansburg, N. Y.: Crossing Press, 1984); Barbara Smith, "Some Home Truths on the Contemporary Black Feminist Movement," *Black Scholar* 16, no. 2 (March/April 1985): 4–13; Asoka Bandarage, *Toward International Feminism: The Dialectics of Sex, Race and Class* (London: Zed Press, forthcoming). For

a typology of black women's multiple consciousness, see Deborah K. King, "Race, Class, and Gender Salience in Black Women's Feminist Consciousness" (paper presented at American Sociological Association annual meeting, Section on Racial and Ethnic Minorities, New York, August 1986).

6. Alice Walker's oft-quoted definition is in *In Search of Our Mothers' Gardens: Womanist Prose* (New York: Harcourt, Brace, Jovanovich, 1983), xi–xii: "Womanist. 1 . . . . Responsible. In Charge. *Serious*. 2. . . . Appreciates . . . women's strength. . . . Committed to survival and wholeness of entire people, male *and* female. Not a separatist, except periodically, for health. Traditionally universalist. . . . Traditionally capable. . . . 3. . . . Loves struggle. *Loves* the Folk. Loves herself. *Regardless*, 4. Womanist is to feminist as purple is to lavender." Cheryl Townsend Gilkes's annotation of Alice Walker's definition ("Women, Religion, and Tradition: A Womanist Perspective" [paper presented in workshop at Summer Research Institute on Race and Gender, Center for Research on Women, Memphis State University, June 1986]) has been particularly important to my understanding of this term.

7. Chikwenye Okonjo Ogunyemi, "Womanism: The Dynamics of the Contemporary Black Female Novel in English," *Signs* 11, no. 1 (Autumn 1985): 63–80.

8. May Wright Sewall, ed., *World's Congress of Representative Women* (Chicago, 1893), 715, quoted in Bert James Loewenberg and Ruth Bogin, eds., *Black Women in Nineteenth-Century American Life: Their Words, Their Thoughts, Their Feelings* (University Park: Pennsylvania State University Press, 1976), 330–31 (emphasis mine). See also Anna Julia Cooper, *A Voice from the South: By a Black Woman of the South* (Xenia, Ohio: Aldine, 1892), esp. "Part First."

9. Although there exists no scholarly biography of Walker, information is available in several sources. See Wendell P. Dabney, *Maggie L. Walker and The I. O. of Saint Luke: The Woman and Her Work* (Cincinnati: Dabney, 1927); Sadie Iola Daniel, *Women Builders* (Washington, D. C.: Associated Publishers, 1931), 28–52; Sadie Daniel St. Clair, "Maggie Lena Walker," in *Notable American Women, 1607–1960* (Cambridge, Mass.: Harvard University Press, Belknap, 1971), 530–31; Elsa Barkley Brown, "Maggie Lena Walker and the Saint Luke Women" (paper presented at the Association for the Study of Afro-American Life and History 69th annual conference, Washington, D. C., October 1984), and " 'Not Alone to Build This Pile of Brick': The Role of Women in the Richmond, Virginia, Black Community, 1890–1930" (paper presented at the Midcontinental and North Central American Studies Association joint conference, University of Iowa, April 1983); Lily Hammond, *In the Vanguard of a Race* (New York: Council of Women for Home Missions and Missionary Education Movement of the United States and Canada, 1922), 108–18; A. B. Caldwell, ed., *Virginia Edition*, vol. 5 of *History of the American Negro* (Atlanta: A. B. Caldwell, 1921), 9–11; Rayford Logan, "Maggie Lena Walker," in *Dictionary of American Negro Biography*, ed. Rayford W. Logan and Michael R. Winston (New York: Norton, 1982), 626–27; Gertrude W. Marlowe, "Maggie Lena Walker: African-American Women, Business, and Community Development" (paper presented at Berkshire Conference on the History of Women, Wellesley, Mass., June 21, 1987); Kim Q. Boyd, " 'An Actress Born, a Diplomat Bred'; Maggie L. Walker, Race Woman" (M.A. thesis, Howard University, 1987); Sallie Chandler, "Maggie Lena Walker (1867–1934): An Abstract of Her Life and Activities," 1975 Oral History Files, Virginia Union University Library, Richmond, Va., 1975; Maggie Lena Walker Papers, Maggie L. Walker National Historic Site, Richmond, Va. (hereafter cited as MLW Papers). Fortunately, much of Walker's history will soon be available; the Maggie L. Walker Biography Project, funded by the National Park Service under the direction of Gertrude W. Marlowe, anthropology department, Howard University, is completing a full-scale biography of Walker.

10. Noting the mass base of mutual benefit societies such as the Independent Order of Saint Luke, August Meier has suggested that the activities of these organizations "reflect the thinking of the inarticulate majority better than any other organizations or the statement of editors and other publicists" (*Negro Thought in America, 1880–1915: Racial Ideologies in the Age of Booker T. Washington* [Ann Arbor: University of Michigan Press, 1963], 130).

11. *50th Anniversary—Golden Jubilee Historical Report of the R. W. G. Council I. O. St. Luke, 1867–1917* (Richmond, Va.: Everett Waddey, 1917), 5–6, 20 (hereafter cited as *50th Anniversary*).

12. Maggie L. Walker, "Diary," March 6, 1928, MLW Papers. My thanks to Sylvester Putman, superintendent, Richmond National Battlefield Park, and Celia Jackson Suggs, site historian, Maggie L. Walker National Historic Site, for facilitating my access to these unprocessed papers.

13. *50th Anniversary*, 26.

14. White (n. 1 above), 119–41. Although I use the term "sisterhood" here to refer to this female network, sisterhood for black women, including M. L. Walker, meant (and means) not only this special bond among black women but also the ties amongst all kin/community.

15. Of 260,000 black Virginians over the age of twenty-one in 1920, less than 20,000 were eligible to vote in that year's elections. Poll taxes and literacy tests disfranchised many; white Democratic election officials turned many others away from the polls; still others had given up their efforts to vote, realizing that even

if they successfully cast their ballots, they were playing in "a political game which they stood no chance of winning" (Andrew Buni, *The Negro in Virginia Politics, 1902–1965* [Charlottesville: University of Virginia Press, 1967], 77–88). The high proportion of female voters resulted from whites' successful efforts to disfranchise the majority of black male voters, as well as the enthusiasm of women to exercise this new right; see, e.g., *Richmond News-Leader* (August–October 1920); *Richmond Times-Dispatch* (September–October, 1920). Rosalyn Terborg-Penn (n. 3 above, 275) reports a similarly high percentage of black female voters in 1920s Baltimore. In Richmond, however, black women soon found themselves faced with the same obstacles to political rights as confronted black men. Independent black political parties developed in several southern states where the lily-white Republican faction had successfully purged blacks from leadership positions in that party; see, e.g., George C. Wright, "Black Political Insurgency in Louisville, Kentucky: The Lincoln Independent Party of 1921," *Journal of Negro History* 68 (Winter 1983): 8–23.

16. M. L. Walker, "Addresses," 1909, MLW Papers, cited in Celia Jackson Suggs, "Maggie Lena Walker," TRUTH; *Newsletter of the Association of Black Women Historians* 7 (Fall 1985): 6.

17. Four of the women elected to the 1901 Saint Luke executive board were board members of the Woman's Union, which had officers in Saint Luke's Hall; see advertisements in *Richmond Planet* (August 1898–January 3, 1903).

18. Some of the societies had only women members, including some that were exclusively for the mutual assistance of single mother. For an excellent discussion of the ties among the societies, families, and churches in Richmond, see Peter J. Rachleff, *Black Labor in the South: Richmond, Virginia, 1865–1890* (Philadelphia: Temple University Press, 1984).

19. W. P. Burrell and D. E. Johnson, Sr., *Twenty-Five Years History of the Grand Fountain of the United Order of True Reformers, 1881–1905* (Richmond, Va.: Grand Fountain, United Order of True Reformers, 1909), 76–77.

20. Saint Luke Penny Savings Bank records: Receipts and Disbursements, 1903–1909; Minutes, Executive Committee, 1913; Cashier's Correspondence Book, 1913; Minutes, Board of Trustees, 1913–1915, Consolidated Bank and Trust Company, Richmond, Va.; *Cleveland Plain Dealer* (June 28, 1914), in Peabody Clipping File, Collis P. Huntington Library, Hampton Institute, Hampton, Va. (hereafter cited as Peabody Clipping File), no. 88, vol. 1. See also Works Progress Administration, *The Negro in Virginia* (New York: Hastings House, 1940), 299.

21. This analysis owes much to Cheryl Townsend Gilkes's work on black women, particularly her "Black Women's Work as Deviance: Social Sources of Racial Antagonism within Contemporary Feminism," working paper no. 66 (Wellesley, Mass.: Wellesley College Center for Research on Women, 1979), and " 'Holding Back the Ocean with a Broom': Black Women and Community Work." in *The Black Woman*, ed. LaFrances Rodgers-Rose (Beverly Hills, Calif.: Sage, 1980). Excerpt from speech given by M. L. Walker at 1901 annual Saint Luke convention, *50th Anniversary* (n. 11 above), 23.

22. The prevailing turn-of-the-century stereotype of black women emphasized promiscuity and immorality; these ideas were given prominence in a number of publications, including newspapers, periodicals, philanthropic foundation reports, and popular literature. The attacks by various segments of the white community on the morality of black women and the race at the turn of the century are discussed in Beverly Guy-Sheftall, " 'Daughters of Sorrow': Attitudes toward Black Women, 1880–1920" (Ph.D. diss., Emory University, 1984), 62–86; Darlene Clark Hine, "Lifting the Veil, Shattering the Silence: Black Women's History in Slavery and Freedom," in *The State of Afro-American History: Past, Present, and Future*, ed. Darlene Clark Hine (Baton Rouge: Louisiana State University Press, 1986), 223–49, esp. 234–38; Willi Coleman, "Black Women and Segregated Public Transportation: Ninety Years of Resistance," TRUTH; *Newsletter of the Association of Black Women Historians* 8, no. 2 (1986): 3–10, esp. 7–8; and Paula Giddings, *When and Where I Enter: The Impact of Black Women on Race and Sex in America* (New York: William Morrow, 1984), 82–86. Maggie Walker called attention to these verbal attacks on Negro womanhood in her speech, "Beniah's Valour: An Address for Men only," Saint Luke Hall, March 1, 1906, MLW Papers (n. 9 above). It was in part the desire to defend black women and uplift the race that initiated the formation of the National Federation of Black Women's Clubs.

23. Charles F. McLaurin, "State Federation of Colored Women" (n.p., November 10, 1908), Peabody Clipping File, no. 231, vol. 1.

24. Chandler (n. 9 above), 10–11.

25. Daniel Webster Davis and Giles Jackson, *The Industrial History of the Negro Race of the United States* (Richmond: Virginia Press, 1908), 133. Similar attitudes expressed in the *Virginia Baptist* in 1894 had aroused the ire of the leading figures in the national women's club movement. The *Baptist* had been particularly concerned that women, in exceeding their proper place in the church, were losing their "womanliness" and that "the exercise of the right of suffrage would be a deplorable climax to these transgressions"; see discussion of the *Baptist* in *Women's Era* 1, no. 6 (September 1894): 8.

282 / Elsa Barkley Brown

26. M. L. Walker, "Speech to Federation of Colored Women's Clubs," Hampton, Va., July 14, 1912, MLW Papers (n. 9 above).

27. M. L. Walker, "Speech to the Negro Young People's Christian and Educational Congress," Convention Hall, Washington, D. C., August 5, 1906, MLW Papers.

28. Quotations are from M. L. Walker, "Speech to the Federation of Colored Women's Clubs." These ideas, however, were a central theme in Walker's speeches and were repeated throughout the years. See, e.g., "Speech to the Negro Young People's Christian and Educational Congress" and "Beniah's Valour: An Address for Men Only" (n. 22 above). See also the *St. Luke Herald's* first editorial, "Our Mission" (March 29, 1902), reprinted in *50th Anniversary* (n. 11 above), 26.

29. Excerpt from speech given by M. L. Walker at 1901 annual Saint Luke convention, *50th Anniversary*, 23.

30. See "Our Mission" (n. 28 above).

31. The NAWE, having as its motto "Support Thyself—Work," aimed at making "the colored woman a factor in the labor world." Much of its work was premised upon the belief that white women were developing an interest in domestic science and other "Negro occupations" to such an extent that the prospects for work for young black women were becoming seriously endangered. They believed also that when white women entered the fields of housework, cooking, and the like, these jobs would be classified as professions. It therefore was necessary for black women to become professionally trained in even domestic work in order to compete. Container 308, Nannie Helen Burroughs Papers, Manuscript Division, Library of Congress.

32. M. L. Walker, "Speech to Federation of Colored Women's Clubs" (n. 26 above).

33. See, e.g., "Negress Banker Says If Men Can, Women Can," *Columbus Journal* (September 16, 1909), Peabody Clipping File (n. 20 above), no. 231, vol. 7; see also Chandler (n. 9 above). 32.

34. In 1900, 83.8 percent of employed black women worked in domestic and personal service; in 1930, 76.5 percent. U. S. Bureau of the Census, *Twelfth Census of the United States Taken in the Year 1900, Population Part 1* (Washington, D. C.: Census Office, 1901), *Thirteenth Census of the United States Taken in the Year 1910*, vol 4: *Population 1910—Occupation Statistics* (Washington, D. C.: Government Printing Office, 1914), 595, and *Fifteenth Census of the United States: Population*, vol. 4: *Occupations by States* (Washington, D. C.: Government Printing Office, 1933); Benjamin Brawley, *Negro Builders and Heroes* (Chapel Hill: University of North Carolina Press, 1937), 267–72; U. S. Bureau of the Census, *Fourteenth Census of the United States Taken in the Year 1920*, vol. 4: *Population 1920—Occupations* (Washington, D. C.: Government Printing Office, 1923); Ethel Thompson Overby, *"It's Better to Light a Candle than to Curse the Darkness": The Autobiographical Notes of Ethel Thompson Overby* (1975), copy in Virginia Historical Society, Richmond.

35. The business, which opened the Monday before Easter, 1905, officially closed in January 1912. Information on the emporium is found in *50th Anniversary* (n. 11 above), 55, 76–77; *New York Age*, March 16, 1905, Peabody Clipping File, no. 88, vol. 1, "Maggie Lena Walker Scrapbook," MLW Papers (n. 9 above), 41. The most detailed description of the opposition to the emporium is in M. L. Walker, "Beniah's Valour: An Address for Men Only" (n. 22 above), quote is from this speech.

36. M. L. Walker, "Beniah's Valour: An Address for Men Only."

37. *Ibid.*

38. Chandler (n. 9 above), 30.

39. M. L. Walker, "Beniah's Valour: An Address for Men Only."

40. Chandler, 30.

41. *New York Age* (June 22, 1909), Peabody Clipping File, no. 231, vol. 1.

42. Rayford W. Logan, *The Betrayal of the Negro from Rutherford B. Hayes to Woodrow Wilson* (New York: Collier, 1965; originally published in 1954 as *The Negro in American Life and Thought: The Nadir*).

43. J. Thomas Hewin, "Is the Criminal Negro Justly Dealt with in the Courts of the South?" in *Twentieth Century Negro Literature, or a Cyclopedia of Thought on the Vital Topics Relating to the American Negro*, ed. D. W. Culp (Toronto: J. L. Nichols, 1902), 110–11.

44. *Richmond Planet* (April 30, 1904).

45. M. L. Walker, "Beniah's Valour: An Address for Men Only" (n. 22 above).

46. *New York Age* (June 22, 1909), Peabody Clipping File, no. 231, vol. 1.

47. M. L. Walker, "Speech to the Federation of Colored Women's Clubs" (n. 26 above).

48. M. L. Walker, "Beniah's Valour: An Address for Men Only." This appeal for support of increased opportunities for black women permeated all of Walker's speeches. In her last speeches in 1934 she continued her appeal for support of race enterprises (newspaper clipping [n.p., n.d.], "Maggie Laura Walker Scrapbook," MLW Papers [n. 9 above]). Maggie Laura Walker is Walker's granddaughter.

49. W. E. B. Du Bois, who explored extensively the connection between race struggle and women's struggle in "The Damnation of Women," also challenged men's traditional roles: "The present mincing horror of a free womanhood must pass if we are ever to be rid of the bestiality of a free manhood; *not by guarding the*

weak in weakness do we gain strength, but by making weakness free and strong" (emphasis mine; *Darkwater, Voices from within the Veil* [New York: Harcourt, Brace, & Howe, 1920], 165).

50. M. L. Walker, "Saint Luke Thanksgiving Day Speech," City Auditorium, March 23, 1913, MLW Papers (n. 9 above).

51. M. L. Walker, "Address—Virginia Day Third Street Bethel AME Church," January 29, 1933, MLW Papers.

52. Ogunyemi (n. 7 above; 72–73) takes this idea from Stephen Henderson's analysis of the role of the blues and blues women in the Africanamerican community.

53. The essays in Vernon J. Dixon and Badi G. Foster, eds., *Beyond Black or White: An Alternate America* (Boston: Little, Brown, 1971) explore the either/or and the both/and worldview in relation to Africanamerican systems of analysis; the quote can be found in Dixon, "Two Approaches to Black-White Relations," 23–66, esp. 25–26.

54. Johnella E. Butler explores the theoretical, methodological, and pedagogical implications of these systems of analysis in *Black Studies: Pedagogy and Revolution: A Study of Afro-American Studies and the Liberal Arts Tradition through the Discipline of Afro-American Literature* (Washington D. C.: University Press of America 1981), esp. 96–102.

18

"Go After the Women": Americanization and the Mexican Immigrant Woman, 1915–1929

George J. Sánchez

> The Americanization of the [Mexican] women is as important a part as that of the men. They are harder to reach but are more easily educated. They can realize in a moment that they are getting the best end of the bargain by the change in relationships between men and women which takes place under the new American order ... "Go after the women" should become a slogan among Americanization workers, for after all the greatest good is to be obtained by starting the home off right. The children of these foreigners are the advantages to America, not the naturalized foreigners. These are never 100% Americans, but the second generation may be. "Go after the women" and you may save the second generation for America.
> —Alfred White, Americanization teacher of Mexican girls, 1923[1]

One reaction to Mexican immigration to the United States in the early twentieth century was the establishment of programs aimed at Mexican women explicitly for the purpose of changing their cultural values. Americanization programs, directed toward Mexican immigrants during one of the periods of massive movement across the border, are an important contrast to the debates in Congress and among the American public on the utility of unrestricted Mexican immigration. These programs attempted to transform the values of the Mexican immigrant after arrival, and encouraged them to conform to the American industrial order in a prescribed manner. Older Mexican women were seen as primary targets because of their important role in homemaking and child rearing, but when they proved difficult to Americanize these programs refocused their efforts upon the adolescent American-born Chicana.

The Mexican immigrant woman, therefore, was confronted with the reality of integrating two conflicting cultures. She would be attributed with both the positive and negative sides of *"La Malinche"*—both mother of the Mexican people and traitor to the Mexican race—by members of her own community. Anglo-Americans also classified her as the individual with the most potential to either advance her family into the modern, industrial order of the United States or inhibit them from becoming productive American citizens. Solutions to the "Mexican problem" were placed squarely in her lap.

Paradoxically, the Chicano family has traditionally been viewed as the one institution in Mexican American life that has consistently resisted the forces of assimilation in the United States. According to the argument advanced by Chicano scholars, the stability and insularity

Reprinted by permission of the author. Originally published in the Stanford University Center for Chicano Research Working Paper Series, vol. 6, 1984.

of the Chicano family has acted as a fortress against alien cultural values. Chicanas, in particular, have been seen as the "glue" that keeps the Chicano family together, and they have been designated as the individuals responsible for maintenance of Mexican tradition. The tenacious insistence of social reformers that Mexican women could cast off vestiges of traditional culture calls this assumption into question.

This study will examine the nature of the "problem" of Mexican immigrant women as defined by Americanization programs in California during the period 1915–1929. It will also examine the "solutions" offered by these programs, and the relative success or failure of reformers to carry out their mission of Americanizing Mexican immigrant women in the 1920s. The study is based on the writings of Americanization instructors who worked with Mexican immigrant women in the period and the literature produced by the California Commission on Immigration and Housing, the primary governmental body involved with the state's immigrant population. I have analyzed this literature in order to assess the assumptions these reformers made about the role of women, the family, and work in Mexican culture and American society in the years before the Great Depression. Prior to that, however, Americanization programs must be placed in the context of Mexican immigration to the United States and the variety of responses to it.

The Nature of Mexican Immigration

The movement of Mexicans across the border into the United States increased substantially in the early twentieth century, although immigration from Mexico had been growing since the late 1880s. At its peak from 1910 to 1930, Mexican immigration increased by at least 300 percent.[2] The industrial expansion of the economy in the Southwest created an escalating demand for low-wage labor, and Mexicans took advantage of the economic opportunities available. The development of a transportation system in northern Mexico in the early part of the century facilitated the movement by connecting the populous central plateau of Mexico with the American Southwest. This railroad connection provided the means by which many migrants could escape the political, economic, and social disruption of the Mexican Revolution of 1910. World War I drew workers into war industries and the military, and the subsequent labor vacuum created an additional incentive for American employers to encourage immigration from Mexico. In fact, employers were able to pressure the federal government to establish a temporary admissions program for Mexican workers which served as a catalyst for increased immigration from 1917 to 1920. Although this enlarged flow was temporarily slowed during the recession of 1921, it grew to unprecedented levels during the rest of the decade as restrictions placed upon European and Asian immigration forced more employers to turn to workers from south of the border.[3]

The volume of this migration was nothing less than staggering. Approximately 100,000 persons of Mexican descent or birth lived in the United States in 1900; by 1930, this figure had climbed to 1.5 million. More than one million Mexicans—about 10 percent of Mexico's population—had entered the United States from 1910 to 1930. In 1930, 94 percent of the foreign-born Mexicans living in the U.S. had immigrated since 1900 and 64 percent had entered since 1915.[4]

Movement into the urban centers of the Southwest and Midwest from the countryside characterized this population shift. The Mexican population in Los Angeles more than tripled during the 1920s, making the Los Angeles barrio the largest Mexican community in the world outside of Mexico City. The Mexican populations of San Antonio and El Paso (and Texas in general) experienced between 50 and 100 percent growth in this decade. Even more dramatic was the establishment of completely new centers of Mexican population in the Midwest. The combined Mexican population of Ohio, Illinois, Indiana, and Michigan experienced a 669.2 percent growth in the 1920s, almost all of it concentrated in urban areas, particularly Chicago and Detroit. By 1930, one of every two Mexicans in the United States lived in an urban setting.[5]

The rapid increase in the numbers of Mexican urban dwellers completely transformed the Mexican communities that had existed before the turn of the century. Pressures on available housing in the barrios led to overcrowded, unsanitary living conditions, and eventually forced many residents to move away from traditional centers of Mexican settlement. Barrios expanded rapidly during the World War I years, and newcomers from Mexico no longer entered a well-defined, tight-knit community.[6] The fact that most Mexican migrants to the cities came from the ranks of Mexico's rural poor added burdens on community resources. In addition, the economic position of these migrants in the cities was tenuous at best. At the conclusion of World War I many Mexicans lost their new-found industrial jobs to returning servicemen, and the 1921 depression encouraged rural workers to seek refuge in urban areas already burdened with unemployment.[7]

The nature of Mexican immigration also recast the dynamics between men and women in the barrios. Throughout the first three decades of the twentieth century, men outnumbered women among Mexicans traveling northward at an average ratio of five to four. The greater the distance from the Mexican border and the more rural the community, the lesser the presence of Chicanas and the fewer the number of Chicano families. Chicago by 1930, for example, had 170 Mexican males for every 100 Mexican females, while El Paso had a Mexican male-to-female ratio of 86/100 in the same year. Urban communities as a whole by 1930 had a Mexican male-to-female ratio of 116/100, compared to a 148/100 ratio in rural communities. Los Angeles in this period maintained a fairly even sex ratio, attracting many Mexican immigrant families and balancing single-male immigration from Mexico with male out-migration into California's rural areas.[8]

Cities in the American Southwest also served as focal points for the reconstituting of Mexican familial constellations and the construction of new families north of the border. Los Angeles was often the end point for a reunification of extended families through a chain migration which often saw a male head of household venture out for work alone in the United States and, once settled, send for his wife and children, and often other kin such as brothers, sisters, cousins, and parents. These extended family networks were crucial in both dealing with the disorienting aspects of migration—finding jobs, temporary homes, and possible sickness or death—and in reinforcing native customs, values, and institutions from Mexico.[9] Although few single women emigrated to Los Angeles alone, single Mexican males—otherwise known as "solos"—often established themselves in the city, married American-born Chicanas, and began families of their own. One study of 769 Mexican households in Los Angeles during the 1920s revealed a high birthrate in Mexican families compared to Anglo-American families, and an average number of children per family of 4.3.[10] Clearly, the lives of most Mexican immigrant women and men centered on their families in the early twentieth century.

"The Mexican Problem"

The response of Anglo Americans to this influx of Mexican migrants ranged widely. Restrictionists, consisting primarily of organized labor and nativists, sought to limit the migration; employers fought to keep Mexican immigration unrestricted; and a third group, whom I shall call "Americanists," viewed the restrictionist debate as a secondary concern to the Americanization of the migrants to ensure their cultural allegiance to the United States after arrival.[11]

The most vocal respondents were the restrictionists who wanted to see Mexican immigration contained, stopped, even reversed. Organized labor, under the auspices of the American Federation of Labor (AFL), viewed Mexican immigrants as cheap labor who would compete with "American" workers. Samuel Gompers urged Congress to include Mexico in the quota restrictions, arguing that Mexicans would not be content with farm labor and would soon attempt to enter the trades in the cities. Only months before his death in 1924, Gompers expressed concern that in Los Angeles, "it appeared to me that every other person met on the streets was a Mexican."[12]

In addition to economic interests, racial attitudes influenced restrictionist sentiments. Nativists, including Anglo-American politicians, academics, reporters, and others who believed in Anglo-Saxon racial superiority, waged the longest and most virulent campaign against unrestricted Mexican immigration. After successfully pushing Congress to severely limit immigration from Asia and southern and eastern Europe in 1920, nativists were dismayed to discover that immigration law still allowed for the widespread introduction of "foreigners" who they considered just as, if not more, unassimilable and undesirable. These nativists called for restriction on racial grounds centered on the "Indian" or "Negro" make-up of the Mexican, the social threat to "American standards of living," and arguments based on a view of the Mexican as an unstable citizen in a democracy.[13] Kenneth L. Roberts, writing in *The Saturday Evening Post*, expressed the nativist sentiments clearly when he stated that in Los Angeles, one can:

> ... see the endless streets crowded with the shacks of illiterate, diseased, pauperized Mexicans, taking no interest whatever in the community, living constantly on the ragged edge of starvation, bringing countless numbers of American citizens into the world with the reckless prodigality of rabbits ...[14]

In contrast to these restrictionists, southwestern employers, particularly railroad, agricultural, and mining companies, defended unrestricted Mexican immigration on economic grounds. They were no less racist in their attitudes but stressed the economic advantage of Mexican labor, stressing that "white" laborers would not and should not perform this work. According to these employers, Mexican labor provided the most desirable option for filling their labor shortages and was vital for the survival of their industries. To counteract the racial and political arguments that restrictionists were making, employers stressed that the undesirable traits outlined by nativists actually benefited American society; the Mexican worker, they argued, provided the perfect, docile employee, had no interest in intermixing with Americans, and in fact, returned to Mexico once their labor was no longer needed. W. H. Knox of the Arizona Cotton Growers' Association belittled nativist fears by asking, "Have you ever heard, in the history of the United States, or in the history of the human race, of the white race being overrun by a class of people of the mentality of the Mexicans? I never have. We took this country from Mexico. Mexico did not take it from us. To assume that there is any danger of any likelihood of the Mexican coming in here and colonizing this country and taking it away from us, to my mind, is absurd."[15]

While the battle between restrictionists and employers raged in legislatures and newspaper editorial pages, a third group took a different approach in dealing with the "Mexican problem." Initially, the base of support for the "Americanist" position came from Progressive social reformers, many of whom were middle-class Anglo American women dedicated to the social settlement movement and the "Social Gospel" tradition. These individuals felt that society had an obligation to assimilate the Mexican immigrant and hoped to improve societal treatment of immigrants in general. However, as World War I heightened anxieties concerning immigrants, nativist sentiment began to affect Americanization efforts through the "100 Per Cent American" movement, which wanted to ensure the loyalty of the immigrant to the United States. Additionally, big business took an interest in the Americanization movement as it sought a method to combat radicalism among foreign-born workers. Employers supported efforts to produce loyal, obedient employees, with at least one ultraconservative business group in Los Angeles encouraging a "superpatriotism" which included upholding the "open shop."[16] Americanization activities spread throughout the country in the late 1910s and 1920s with this uneasy alliance of support, and those programs situated in the Southwest had as a primary target the Mexican immigrant.

In California, these "Americanists" first wielded power with the election of a Progressive governor, Hiram Johnson, in 1910. Johnson secured passage of legislation in 1913 establishing a permanent Commission of Immigration and Housing, which investigated the working and living conditions of all immigrants in the state and spearheaded efforts to teach English to foreigners and involve them in Americanization programs.[17] Though governmental bodies and private organizations in other states also sought to Americanize Mexicans, California's program was the most complete attempt to bring together government, business, and private citizens to deal with the "problem of the immigrant" in a scientific and rational fashion. The Commission successfully recruited university academics, religious social workers, government bureaucrats, and middle-class volunteers.

Unlike the debate involving restrictionists and employers, these reformers considered the Mexican immigrant as similar to European immigrants in California at the time. In the eyes of these reformers, Mexicans might have presented a greater challenge than did Italians or Jews, nevertheless they found nothing endemic in the Mexican character that would prevent their eventual assimilation into the "American way of life." What distinguished the Americanization efforts from the social-settlement response to European immigrants before World War I, however, was the cessation of a focus on "immigrant gifts" to American society.[18] In the 1920s, little value was given to Mexican culture in Americanization programs; rather, "Americanists" saw immigrant traditions and customs as impediments to a rapid, thorough integration into American life.

Americanizing the Mexican Woman

As the commission expanded its Americanization programs, commissioners began to center their attention on the Mexican immigrant woman and her potential role in the cultural transformation of her family. In 1915, the state legislature had passed the Home Teacher Act which allowed school districts to employ teachers "to work in the homes of the pupils, instructing children and adults in matters relating to school attendance, . . . in sanitation, in the English language, in household duties, . . . and in the fundamental principles of the American system of government and the rights and duties of citizenship."[19] In the war years, the home teacher became the centerpiece around which Americanization efforts aimed at the Mexican family were concentrated.

Why did the Mexican immigrant woman become the target of Americanization programs? First, Mexican women were seen as the individuals primarily responsible for the transmission of values in the home. According to the strategy advocated by the Americanists, if the Mexican female adopted American values, the rest of her family would certainly follow suit. Pearl Ellis, who worked with Mexican girls in southern California throughout the 1920s, stressed the important "influence of the home" in

creating an employee who is "more dependable and less revolutionary in his tendencies
.... The homekeeper creates the atmosphere, whether it be one of harmony and
cooperation or of dissatisfaction and revolt."[20]

Motherhood, in fact, became the juncture at which the Mexican immigrant woman's
potential role in Americanization was most highly valued. By focusing on the strategic
position of the mother in the Mexican family, Americanization programs hoped to have an
impact on the second generation of Mexicans in the United States, even if the immigrant
generation itself turned out less malleable than expected. Since the father's role in parenting
was assumed to be minimal, cooperation of the Mexican mother was crucial. Americanization
ideology was infused undeniably with the traditional American belief in an exalted role of
motherhood in shaping the future political citizenry of the republic.[21] In the most grandeous
visions of Americanists, the role of the mother loomed incredibly large:

> As the mother furnishes the stream of life to the babe at her breast, so will she shower
> dewdrops of knowledge on the plastic mind of her young child. Her ideals and aspirations
> will be breathed into its spirit, molding its character for all time. The child, in turn, will
> pass these rarer characteristics on to its descendants, thus developing the intellectual,
> physical, and spiritual qualities of the individual, which in mass, are contributions to
> civilization.[15]

Besides creating a home environment that fit in an industrial order, the Americanization
of Mexican women was valued for the direct benefits American society might gain from
labor-force participation of female immigrants. Mexican women were seen as prime targets
for meeting the labor need for domestic servants, seamstresses, laundresses, and service
workers in the Southwest. Black and European immigrant women had not migrated to the
American Southwest in large enough numbers to fill the growing demand in these areas.
Ironically in 1908, a Bureau of Labor inspector had regretfully noted that Mexican "immigrant women have so little conception of domestic arrangements in the United States that
the task of training them would be too heavy for American housewives."[23] A decade later,
Americanization programs were busy training Mexican women to fulfill these tasks.

Importantly, the conflict between the private responsibilities of American women to their
homes and families and the public roles women began to play as workers and citizens in
the 1920s were not addressed in Americanization programs.[24] Americanists were too interested in the contribution Mexican women could make in the transformation of their families
from a rural, preindustrial people to an urban, modern American unit to worry about
"women's proper place." Herbert Gutman, in his important essay, "Work, Culture, and
Society in Industrializing America," has examined the "recurrent tension" produced when
immigrant men and women new to the American industrial order came in contact with the
rigorous discipline of the factory system.[25] Because the Southwest lagged behind the rest
of the nation in industrialization, local reformers were anxious to introduce Mexican women
and men as rapidly as possible into a growing industrial society and inculcate Mexican
families with a "Protestant work ethic." To achieve these ends, the public and private
responsibilities of female were blurred, and in fact Americanists discovered a peculiar
way in which to economize their energy by taking care of both issues at once. By
encouraging Mexican immigrant women to wash, sew, cook, budget, and mother happily
and efficiently, Americans would be assured that Mexican women would be ready to
enter the labor market, while simultaneously presiding over a home that nurtured
American values of economy.

Americanists viewed the ability to speak English as the most fundamental skill necessary for the assimilation of the immigrant, both female and male. English instruction was intended to provide the immigrant with much more than facility with the common language of the United States; it also sought to imbue the foreigner with the values of American society. The commission recommended in 1917 "that employers of immigrants be shown the relation between a unified working force, speaking a common language, and industrial prosperity."[26] In 1918, Mrs. Amanda Matthews Chase, a home teacher in southern California working for the commission, developed a primer for foreign-speaking to teach English by covering "the most essential elements in the home teaching curriculum" and by associating these "with the pupils' own lives and affairs."[27] For example, home teachers were instructed to teach the following song to immigrant women (to the tune, "Tramp, Tramp, Tramp, the Boys are Marching"). The song was intended to instruct them about women's work while they learned twenty-seven new English words:

> We are working every day,
> So our boys and girls can play.
>> We are working for our homes and country, too;
> We like to wash, to sew, to cook,
> We like to write, or read a book,
>> We are working, working, working every day.
> Work, work, work,
> We're always working,
>> Working for our boys and girls,
> Working for our boys and girls,
> For our homes and country, too—
>> We are working, working, working every day.[28]

Despite the concerns of reformers, Mexican women continued to lag behind men in learning the English language. A study of 1,081 Mexican families in Los Angeles conducted in 1921 found that while 55 percent of the men were unable to speak English, an overwhelming 74 percent of the women could not speak the language. Similar gaps existed in English reading and writing.[29] Americanists blamed the patriarchal, outmoded nature of the Mexican family for this discrepancy. "The married Mexican laborer does not allow his wife, as a rule, to attend evening classes," reported Emory Bogardus, a sociologist at the University of Southern California.[30]

Getting the Mexican woman out of her home became a priority for Americanization programs because Americanists saw this as the only avenue available for her intellectual progress and, of course, the only method by which Americanists could succeed in altering her values. Americanists consistently criticized the alleged limitations placed upon the Mexican wife by her husband as traditional and unprogressive. Home teachers visited each Mexican home in their districts individually in order to gain the trust of family members and gradually encourage the husband to allow his wife to attend English-language classes. The scheduling of alternative classes in the afternoons for wives and mothers facilitated this process.[31] According to one Americanization instructor, if left in the home, the Mexican woman's "intellectual ability is stimulated only by her husband and if he be of the average peon type, the stimulation is not very great." The Mexican home, according to the same teacher, "being a sacred institution, is guarded by all the stolid tradition of centuries."[32] If the Mexican home remained such a fortress, Americanists would not be able to accomplish their mission among the Mexican immigrant population.

Americanization programs, however, did not intend to undermine the traditional Mexican family structure; rather these programs depended on the cohesiveness of the Mexican family to achieve their goal of assimilation. Home teachers, even when they did get Mexican women out of the house to attend class, encouraged the acquisition of traditionally feminine skills which could then be utilized within the confines of the household. The conscious strategy of these reformers was to use the Mexican woman as a conduit for creating a home environment well suited to the demands of an industrial economy. In the ditty "The Day's Work," for example, home teachers utilized the following sequence of English phrases to emphasize a woman's contribution to this new order:

> In the morning the women get breakfast.
> Their husbands go to work.
> Their children go to school.
> Then the women get their houses in good order.
> They give the baby its bath.
> They wash, or iron, or cook.
> They get the dinner.
> After dinner they wash the dishes.
> Then they sew, or rest, or visit their friends, or go to school.
> The children must help to cook the supper and wash the
>   dishes.[33]

Changing Family Habits

Two particular areas in which the Mexican female was regarded as crucial in transforming outdated practices in the home were diet and health. Americanization programs encouraged Mexican women to give up their penchant for fried foods, their too-frequent consumption of rice and beans, and their custom of serving all members of the family—from infants to grandparents—the same meal. According to Americanists, the modern Mexican woman should replace tortillas with bread, serve lettuce instead of beans, and broil instead of fry. Malnourishment in Mexican families was not blamed on lack of food or resources, but rather "from not having the right varieties of foods containing constituents favorable to growth and development."[34]

Food and diet management adroitly became tools in a system of social control intended to construct a well-behaved citizenry. A healthy diet was not only seen as essential for proper health; it also was viewed as fundamental for creating productive members of society. In the eyes of reformers, the typical noon lunch of the Mexican child, thought to consist of "a folded tortilla with no filling," became the first step in a life of crime. With "no milk or fruit to whet the appetite" the child would become lazy and subsequently "take food from the lunch boxes of more fortunate children" in order to appease his/her hunger. "Thus," reformers alleged, "the initial step in a life of thieving is taken."[35] Teaching immigrant women proper food values would keep the head of the family out of jail, the rest of the family off the charity lists, and save taxpayers a great amount of money.

Along with diet, health and cleanliness became catchwords for Americanization programs aimed at Mexican women. One of the primary functions of home teachers was to impress upon the minds of Mexican mothers and mothers-to-be "that a clean body and clean mind are the attributes of a good citizen."[36] Reformers working with Mexican women were warned, however, that their task would be a difficult one. "Sanitary, hygienic, and dietic measures are not easily learned by the Mexican. His [sic] philosophy of life flows along the lines of least resistance and it requires far less exertion to remain dirty than to clean up."[37] The lack of cleanliness among Mexicans was blamed for their poor state of health, and this condition was the main reason why the stereotype of the "dirty Mexican" brought concern to the Anglo urban dweller. According to an eminent sociologist working with Americanization programs, Anglo Americans "object to the presence of Mexican children in the schools that their children attend, for fear that the latter will catch a contagious disease. A relatively permanent form of racial antipathy is the result."[38]

The ability of Americanization teachers to inculcate "American" standards of diet, health, and cleanliness upon Mexican women was not viewed as the only essential component in creating a healthy home environment, however. All of the gains made by these programs would be considered lost if the Mexican female bore too many of these nascent citizens. Americanists worried that without limiting family size, the Mexican mother would be unable to train adequately each individual member of her household.

Control of immigrant population growth was a long-standing concern of both those who defined themselves as Progressives and of nativists. Fears of "race suicide" had existed in the Anglo-American mind since the late nineteenth century, when Americans first encountered immigrant groups who exhibited a greater propensity to repopulate themselves than native-born Americans. When this fear was applied to the Mexican immigrant, both nativists and Americanists shared a common concern: the nativist wanted to control Mexican population growth for fear of a "greaser invasion," while Americanists viewed unrestricted population growth as a vestige of Old World ways that would have to be abandoned in a modern industrial world.

Mexican women, according to Americanization strategy, should bear the brunt of the responsibility for family planning. Americanists gave a variety of reasons for the presumed inability of Mexican women to control reproduction: (1) lack of training in sex matters and a primitive sexuality; (2) early marriage of girls due to tradition and the "inherent sentimentality" of the Mexican female; and (3) religiously based opposition to birth control.[39] Despite these barriers, Americanization teachers reported that Mexican mothers were beginning to exhibit discomfort with large families, occasionally inquiring about birth-control measures, and warning other women to delay marriage on the grounds of "much work, too much children."[40]

The Mexican Woman as Worker

Americanists viewed such evidence of changing attitudes as a hopeful sign because limited reproduction opened up new opportunities for Mexican women in and outside the home. Inside the home, Mexican women could devote more time to the "proper" raising of fewer children and creation of an "American" home environment. Outside the home, it created new possibilities for female employment by freeing Mexican women from the heavy burden of constant childrearing. Traditionally, Mexican women had not engaged in wage labor outside the home because of the duties to reproduce and maintain the family unit. If a Mexican immigrant woman worked it was usually before marriage in her late-adolescent or early-adult years.[41]

The new demands of the industrial American Southwest, however, created a need for low-paid, low-status labor in tasks that had traditionally been performed by women inside the home. The labeling of clothing manufacture, laundry, domestic service, and food service as "women's work" presented a problem to employers in these industries in the Southwest. Employers were forced to search for an alternative female labor supply because of restrictions placed upon Asian and European immigration, the paucity of black migration to the Southwest, and the growing demands of Anglo middle-class families for these services. Despite all the traditional objections to Mexican women working outside the home, Americanization programs actively sought to prepare Mexican immigrant women for entrance into these sex- segregated occupations.[42]

The fact that these employment opportunities were in occupations that utilized traditionally female forms of labor made it easier for Americanists to advocate instruction in these tasks without upsetting the traditional social order within the Mexican family. For example, skill at needlework was viewed in Americanization programs as an inherited trait among Mexican women, passed down through generations. Americanization teachers were directed to "strive to foster it in them [so] that we may not lose this valuable contribution to our civilization with the passing of time." This form of encouragement, according to these reformers, should be started as early as possible—by the third year in school at least— since Mexican girls were apt to drop out of school at an early age and would "miss out" on this opportunity to gain "greater respect for the school and for our civilization."[43]

Whatever success Americanization programs had in promoting greater standards of cleanliness and efficiency in home management were seen as having a double benefit for American society. Americanists, for example, stressed the abilities to set a table and to serve food properly. Table etiquette not only encouraged Mexican women to aspire to arrange their meals at home by American standards, but it also discouraged "sloppy appearance and uncleanliness of person [that] would not be tolerated in a waitress and would be the cause of no position or losing one already obtained."[44] Americanists also reasoned that the burden on a private citizen employing a Mexican woman as a domestic servant would be lightened if that woman had already been adequately trained through their programs. As one social worker stated in the late 1920s: "Americans want household help for two or three days a week, and they can, if they will, take Mexican women and teach them. It requires patience to be sure, but there are large numbers of Mexicans who can fill the household gap if the proper conditions are made."[45]

Additionally, encouraging Mexican women to engage in hard work was viewed as an important facet in "curing" the habits of the stereotypical "lazy Mexican." According to one Americanization teacher, *"Quien sabe?"* (who knows) was the philosophy of all of Mexico, and the inability of Mexicans to connect the things that are valued as worthwhile to the effort necessary to obtain them made Mexican laborers inefficient.[46] Another felt that "the laziness of Mexicans" was due to "climate conditions and inherited tendencies" which only hard work could root out.[47] Consequently, putting Mexican women to work would have the effect of promoting discipline in them, which in turn would encourage them to pass on a similar level of self-control to their children.

The Failure of Americanization

Did these programs, in fact, change Mexican family practices and produce "citizens of the republic" who adopted American values and customs? Certainly Americanization programs did produce Mexican converts to the American way of life. Many immigrant women flocked to programs that promised greater social freedom for them, and healthier, more contented lives for family members. By and large, however, Americanization programs failed to change the fundamental cultural practices of Mexican immigrant families for two principal reasons: (1) Mexican immigrants in the 1920s never fully committed themselves to integration into American life. Even when changes in cultural practices did occur, Americanization programs had little role in directing this evolution; (2) The various forces behind Americanization programs never assembled an optimistic ideological approach that might have attracted Mexican immigrant women. Instead, they presented a limited, inconsistent scheme which could not handle the demographic realities of the Mexican immigrant community.

Indeed, most Mexican immigrant families remained unaffected by Americanization efforts throughout the 1920s. A government study in 1930 found that the Mexican immigrant population in California, who had the lowest rate of naturalization of any immigrant group in the state in 1920, actually experienced a decline in the ratio of naturalized Mexicans among the total alien Mexican population from 1920 to 1930.[48] Mexican women remained very unlikely to pursue American citizenship or encourage family members to do so. In fact, in a study conducted in 1923, 55 percent of the Mexican immigrants surveyed considered it their duty to remain politically loyal to Mexico, while almost all of the rest refused to answer the question.[49]

Within the home, little cultural change among the Mexican population was evident. A Mexican sociologist, Manuel Gamio, found that although material possessions often did change among some Mexican immigrants, Mexicans retained their ethics, culture, and loyalty to Mexico to a very large extent.[50] In fact, as the Mexican barrios grew extensively during the 1920s, the need for Mexicans to interact with Anglos lessened. Mexicans were more likely than ever to retain their own cultural values because they experienced minimal contact with Anglo institutions.[51]

The one area in which change is apparent lies in the area of female employment. Textile factories, laundries, hotels, wholesale and retail stores, and bakeries all seem to have been successful in recruiting Mexican women as employees during the 1920s in Los Angeles.[52] Few of these women, however, entered these industries as a result of Americanization efforts; rather, most had little choice in the matter. A study of Mexican women working in Los Angeles industries conducted in 1928 concluded that 62 percent of the women interviewed entered their occupations because of poverty or economic necessity. Moreover, nine-tenths of these women were unmarried, most were under the age of twenty-three, and two-thirds had been born in the United States.[53] It appears as if unmarried older daughters would be the first women to seek employment, rather than older, married Mexican women, because this pattern was more familiar in Mexico and more acceptable in the family and community.[54]

Americanization programs did seem to encourage acculturation among the second generation, although not always in exactly the manner intended. The change in cultural values among children born and/or raised in the United States often led to conflict with Mexican immigrant parents. Sociologist Emory Bogardus noted that during the late 1920s and early 1930s Mexican girls often ran away from home in order to seek pleasure or avoid parental discipline and control.[55] One Mexican immigrant mother explained: "The freedom and independence in this country bring the children into conflict with their parents. They learn nicer ways, learn about the outside world, learn how to speak English, and then they become ashamed of their parents who brought them up here that they might have better advantages." Another Mexican mother placed the blame squarely on American values: "It is because they can run around so much and be so free, that our Mexican girls do not know how to act. So many girls run away and get married. This terrible freedom in this United States. The Mexican girls seeing American girls with freedom, they want it too, so they go where they like. They do not mind their parents; this terrible freedom. But what can the Mexican mothers do? It is the custom, and we cannot change it, but it is bad."[56]

Rather than providing Mexican immigrant women with an attainable picture of assimilation, Americanization programs could only offer these immigrants idealized versions of American values. In reality, what was achieved turned out to be little more than second-class citizenship. The most progressive assumptions behind Americanization programs were never fully shared by the government or business interests involved, and thus they could never be fully implemented. One Americanization teacher who spent the decade working with Mexican immigrants noted with disappointment in 1923 that the newly elected governor of California had eliminated financial provisions for the Americanization program in the public schools from his budget.[57] At least one historian has concluded that the "love affair between the progressive and the businessman" in California inevitably led, in the 1920s, to a blunting of "the cutting edge of progressive social reform."[58] By 1927, the ambivalence of the reformers became apparent when the Commission of Immigration and Housing itself sided with restrictionists, called for an end to unlimited immigration from Mexico, and blamed immigrants for "causing an immense social problem in our charities, schools and health departments."[59] Caught in the middle of a growing debate surrounding Mexican immigration, social reformers were never able to argue forcefully for their own particular program for dealing with the "Mexican problem."

The halfhearted effort of administrators of Americanization programs limited available personnel and resources and ensured that the programs would never be able to cope with the volume of the Mexican migration. The barrios expanded so quickly in the 1920s that any single Americanization teacher found it impossible to keep abreast of the number of new Mexican families in her district who needed a resumption of her program from scratch. Newer areas of Mexican settlement were usually beyond the reach of established Americanization programs entirely. Furthermore, Mexicans experienced a high degree of geographic mobility in this period that easily wiped out whatever progress had been made by these programs in a given community. According to historian Richard Romo, fewer than one-third of Mexicans present in Los Angeles in 1917–1918 were present in the city one decade later.[60] Americanization teacher Amanda Chase acknowledged the extent of this problem when dealing with Mexican women: "I have had in my class record book this year the names of about half as many Mexican women as there are Mexican families in the district. But a third of them moved to other districts."[61] Mexican women could not hope to develop allegiances to the United States when the economic condition of their families forced them to migrate consistently in search of an economic livelihood.

In the end, Americanization programs never had the time to develop sufficiently even to approach a solution to the problems of Mexican immigrants in the United States. With the stock market crash of 1929 and the subsequent Great Depression of the 1930s, all attempts to Americanize Mexican immigrant women came to an abrupt end. Rather than searching for ways to assimilate Mexican immigrants, American society looked for methods to be rid of them altogether. About 500,000 Mexicans left the United States during the 1930s under strong pressure from the government, and up to one-tenth of these individuals had resided in Los Angeles.[62] Americanists joined in these efforts to repatriate Mexican residents; their commitment to improving the conditions of the Mexican female had no place in an economically depressed America.

However short-lived, Americanization programs offer us a unique opportunity to examine the assumptions made about both Mexican and American culture and scrutinize the values of the Progressive era in its waning moments. For a time, a certain group of American citizens felt that the Mexican immigrant woman could be fit into American society, but only in a particular fashion. Her role in the creation of a new industrial order would be to transform her own home into an efficient, productive family unit, while producing law-abiding, loyal American citizens eager to do their duty for capitalist expansion in the American Southwest. Furthermore, once she had learned proper American home care, she would help solve "the servant problem" in Anglo American homes by providing a cheap but efficient form of domestic labor. Americanists felt that they were offering Mexican women an opportunity that they could ill afford to turn down. Apparently most Mexican women in the United States did just that.

Notes

1. Alfred White, "The Apperceptive Mass of Foreigners as Applied to Americanization, the Mexican Group" (University of California, master's thesis, 1923), 34–35.

2. Jose Hernandez Alvarez, "A Demographic Profile of the Mexican Immigration to the United States, 1910–1950," *Journal of Inter-American Studies*, vol. 25 (1983), 472.

3. Mark Reisler, *By the Sweat of Their Brow: Mexican Immigrant Labor in the United States, 1900–1940* (Westport, Conn.: Greenwood Press, 1976), 14–17, 41–42, 55–58.

4. Richard Romo, "Responses to Mexican Immigration, 1910–1930," *Aztlan*, vol. 6, no. 2 (1975), 173; Richard Romo, "The Urbanization of Southwestern Chicanos in the Early Twentieth Century," *New Scholar*, vol. 6 (1977), 194.

5. Romo, "Urbanization," 194–95; Reisler, *Sweat*, 267.

6. For Los Angeles, see Richard Romo, *East Los Angeles: History of a Barrio* (Austin: University of Texas Press, 1983), 77–79; For El Paso, see Mario T. Garcia, *Desert Immigrants: The Mexicans of El Paso, 1880–1920* (New Haven: Yale University Press, 1981), 141–43.

7. Romo, "Responses," 182; Reisler, *Sweat*, 50.

8. Alvarez, "Demographic," 481–82; Romo, "Urbanization," 195–96.

9. Mario T. Garcia, "La Familia: The Mexican Immigrant Family, 1900–1930," in *Work, Family, Sex Roles, Language: The National Association of Chicano Studies, Selected Papers 1979*, Mario Barrera, Alberto Camarillo, Francisco Hernandez, eds. (Berkeley: Tonatiuh-Quinto Sol International, 1980), 120–24.

10. Romo, *East*, 52, 83; Alvarez, "Demographic," 482.

11. My categories largely correspond with those described by John Higham in the restrictionist debate surrounding European immigration, with one notable exception—unlike the Mexican community, European immigrant groups themselves often produced political leaders and organizations who joined employers in fighting against restriction; John Higham, *Strangers in the Land, 1860–1925*, 2nd ed. (New York: Antheneum, 1963), 301–7.

12. Reisler, *Sweat*, 169; Romo, "Responses," 187.

13. Reisler, *Sweat*, 151–69.

14. Kenneth L. Roberts, "The Docile Mexican," *The Saturday Evening Post*, March 10, 1928, 43.

15. U.S. Congress, House, Committee on Immigration and Naturalization, *Hearings on Temporary Admission of Illiterate Mexican Laborers*, 69th Congress, 1st session, 1926, 191, and *Hearings on Seasonal Agricultural Laborers from Mexico*, 46.

16. Higham, *Strangers*, 234–63; Edwin Layton, "The Better America Federation: A Case Study of Superpatriotism," *Pacific Historical Review*, v. 30 (1961), 137–47.

17. Spencer Olin, *California's Prodigal Sons: Hiram Johnson and Progressives, 1911–1917* (Berkeley: University of California Press, 1968), 76–80.

18. See Higham, *Strangers*, 116–23 and Allen F. Davis, *Spearheads for Reform: The Social Settlements and the Progressive Movement, 1890–1914* (New York: Oxford University Press, 1967), 84–102 for a fuller discussion of the treatment of immigrants by social settlements.

19. California, Commission of Immigration and Housing, "The Home Teacher, Immigrant Education Leaflet No. 5" (San Francisco, 1916), 8.

20. Pearl Idelia Ellis, *Americanization through Homemaking* (Los Angeles: Wetzel Publishing Co., 1929), 31.

21. See Linda Kerber, *Women of the Republic: Intellect & Ideology in Revolutionary America* (Chapel Hill: University of North Carolina Press, 1980) for the origins of this ideology.

22. Ellis, *Homemaking*, 65.

23. See Mario T. Garcia, "The Chicana in American History: The Mexican Women of El Paso, 1880–1920—A Case Study," *Pacific Historical Review* 49 (May 1980), 326.

24. Interestingly, the clash between domestic duties and work outside the home became a much-addressed, yet unresolved, issue in the 1920s among middle-class, college-educated Anglo-American women—the very group recruited to become Americanization teachers. See Carl Degler, *At Odds: Women and the Family in American from the Revolution to the Present* (Oxford: Oxford University Press, 1980), 411–13 and Lois Scharf, *To Work and to Wed: Female Employment, Feminism, and the Great Depression* (Westport, CT: Greenwood Press, 1980), 21–43.

25. Herbert G. Gutman, *Work, Culture, and Society in Industrializing America* (New York: Vintage Books, 1977), 13.

26. California, Commission of Immigration and Housing, "A discussion of methods of teaching English to adult foreigners, with a report on Los Angeles County" (Sacramento, 1917), 21.

27. California, Commission of Immigration and Housing, "Primer for Foreign-speaking Women, Part II." Compiled under Mrs. Amanda Matthews Chase (Sacramento, 1918), 3.

28. Ibid., 5.
29. Jay S. Stowell, *The Near Side of the Mexican Question* (New York: George H. Doran Co., 1921), 102.
30. Emory S. Bogardus, *The Mexican in the United States* (Los Angeles: University of Southern California Press, 1934), 81.
31. CIH, "A discussion of methods," 12–14.
32. White, *Apperceptive*, 30.
33. CIH, "Primer," 9.
34. Ellis, *Homemaking*, 19, 21, 29.
35. Ibid., 26.
36. Ibid., 47.
37. Ibid., 64.
38. Bogardus, *Mexican*, 33.
39. Bogardus, *Mexican*, 25; Ellis, *Homemaking*, 61–62.
40. Bogardus, *Mexican*, 26.
41. Garcia, "La Familia," 124–27.
42. For an excellent discussion of occupational sex segregation in this period, see Ruth Milkman, "Women's Work and the Economic Crisis: Some Lessons from the Great Depression," *The Review of Radical Political Economics* 8 (Spring 1976), 75–78.
43. Ellis, *Homemaking*, 15, 13.
44. Ibid., 35.
45. Bogardus, *Mexican*, 43.
46. White, *Apperceptive*, 20.
47. Ellis, *Homemaking*, 43.
48. California, "Mexicans in California: Report of Governor C.C. Young's Mexican Fact-Finding Committee" (Sacramento, 1930), 61–74.
49. Evangeline Hymer, "A Study of the Social Attitudes of Adult Mexican Immigrants in Los Angeles and Vicinity" (University of Southern California, master's thesis, 1923), 51.
50. Manuel Gamio, *Mexican Immigration to the United States: A Study of Human Migration and Adjustment* (New York: Dover Publications, 1971, [1930]), 172–73.
51. Romo, *East*, 162.
52. Ibid., 118.
53. Paul S. Taylor, "Mexican Women in Los Angeles Industry in 1928," *Aztlan*, vol. 11, no. 1 (1980), 103.
54. Garcia, "La Familia," 127; This pattern is similar to that found among Italian immigrant families. See Virginia Yans-McLaughlin, *Family and Community: Italian Immigrants in Buffalo, 1880–1930* (Ithaca: Cornell University Press, 1977), 180–217.
55. Bogardus, *Mexican*, 56–57.
56. Ibid., 29, 28.
57. White, *Apperceptive*, 3.
58. Jackson K. Putnam, "The Persistence of Progressivism in the 1920's: The Case of California," *Pacific Historical Review*, vol. 35 (1966), 398.
59. California, Commission of Immigration and Housing, "Annual Report" (Sacramento, 1927), 8.
60. Romo, *East*, 124–28.
61. CIH, "The Home Teacher," 3.
62. Abraham Hoffman, "Mexican Repatriation Statistics: Some Suggested Alternatives to Carey McWilliams," *Western Historical Quarterly* 3 (October 1972), 391–404; Abraham Hoffman, *Unwanted Mexican Americans in the Great Depression: Repatriation Pressures, 1929–1939* (Tucson: University of Arizona Press, 1974).

19

Dead Ends or Gold Mines? Using Missionary Records in Mexican American Women's History

Vicki L. Ruiz

This essay addresses what is often ill-perceived as the flip side of feminist theory—that is, methodology.[1] How do we use institutional records (for example, missionary reports, pamphlets, and newsletters) to illuminate the experiences and attitudes of women of color? How do we sift through the bias, the self-congratulation, and the hyperbole to gain insight into women's lives? What can these records tell us of women's historical agencies?

I am intrigued (actually, obsessed is a better verb) with questions involving decision-making, specifically with regard to acculturation. What have Mexican women chosen to accept or reject? How have the economic, social, and political environments influenced the acceptance or rejection of cultural messages that emanate from the Mexican community, from U.S. popular culture, from Americanization programs, and from a dynamic coalescence of differing and at times oppositional cultural forms? What were women's real choices? And, to borrow from Jürgen Habermas, how did they move "within the horizon of their lifeworld"?[2] Obviously, no set of institutional records can provide substantive answers, but by exploring these documents in the framework of these larger questions, we place Mexican women at the center of our study, not as victims of poverty and superstition (as they were so often depicted by missionaries) but as women who made choices for themselves and for their families.

Pushed by the economic and political chaos generated by the Mexican Revolution and lured by jobs in U.S. agribusiness and industry, over one million Mexicanos migrated northward between 1910 and 1930. When one thinks of Mexican immigration, one typically visualizes a single male or family group. However, as depicted in figure 1, women also traveled as *solas* ("single women"). Mexicanos settled into the existing barrios and forged new communities in the Southwest and Midwest.[3] El Paso, Texas, was their Ellis Island, and many decided to stay in this bustling border city. In 1900, the Mexican community of El Paso numbered only 8,748 residents, but by 1930, its population had swelled to 68,476. Over the course of the twentieth century, Mexicans have comprised over one-half of El Paso's total population.[4] Inheriting a legacy of colonialism wrought by Manifest Destiny, Mexicans, regardless of nativity, have been segmented into low-paying, low-status jobs. Perceived as cheap labor by Anglo businessmen, they have provided the human resources necessary for the city's industrial and commercial growth. Education and economic advancement proved illusory, as segregation in housing, employment, and schools served as constant reminders of their second-class citizenship. To cite an example of stratification, from

Reprinted with permission from *Frontiers: A Journal of Women's Studies*, vol. XII, no. 1, © Frontiers Editorial Collective.

Figure 1. Las solas: Mexican women arriving in El Paso, 1911. (Courtesy of Rio Grande Historical Collections, University Archives, New Mexico State University, Las Cruces, New Mexico.)

1930 to 1960, only 1.8 percent of El Paso's Mexican work force held high white-collar occupations.[5]

Segundo Barrio or South El Paso has served as the center of Mexican community life. Today, as in the past, wooden tenements and crumbling adobe structures house thousands of Mexicanos and Mexican Americans alike. For several decades, the only consistent source of social services in Segundo Barrio was the Rose Gregory Houchen Settlement House and its adjacent health clinic and hospital. The records of Houchen Settlement form the core of this study.

Founded in 1912 on the corner of Tays and Fifth in the heart of the barrio, this Methodist settlement had two initial goals: (1) to provide a Christian rooming house for single Mexicana wage earners, and (2) to open a kindergarten for area children. By 1918, Houchen offered a full schedule of Americanization programs—citizenship, cooking, carpentry, English instruction, Bible study, and Boy Scouts. The first Houchen staff included three female Methodist missionaries and one "student helper," Ofilia Chávez.[6] Living in the barrio made these women sensitive to the need for low-cost, accessible health care. Infant mortality in Segundo Barrio was alarmingly high. Historian Mario García related the following example: "Of 121 deaths during July [1914], 52 were children under 5 years of age."[7]

In 1920, the Methodist Home Missionary Society responded (at last) to Houchen appeals by assigning Effie Stoltz, a registered nurse, to the settlement. Stoltz's work began in Houchen's bathroom, where she operated a first aid station. More importantly, she persuaded a local physician to visit the residence on a regular basis, and he, in turn, enlisted the services of his colleagues. Within seven months of Stoltz's arrival, a small adobe flat was converted into the Freeman Clinic. Run by volunteers, this clinic provided prenatal exams, well-baby care, and pediatric services; in 1930, it opened a six-bed maternity ward. Seven years later, it would be demolished to make way for the construction of a more modern clinic and a new twenty-two-bed maternity facility—the Newark Methodist Maternity Hospital. Health care at Newark was a bargain. Prenatal classes, pregnancy exams, and infant immunizations were free. Patients paid for medicines at cost, and during the 1940s, thirty dollars covered the hospital bill (see figure 2). Staff members would boast that for less than fifty dollars, payable in installments, neighborhood women could give birth at "one of the best-equipped maternity hospitals in the city."[8]

Houchen Settlement did not linger in the shadows of its adjacent hospital; from 1920 to 1960, it coordinated an array of Americanization activities. These included age- and gender-graded Bible studies, music lessons, Camp Fire Girls, scouting, working girls' clubs, hygiene, cooking, and citizenship classes. Staff members also opened a day nursery to complement the kindergarten program.

In terms of numbers, how successful was Houchen? The records to which I had access gave little indication of the extent of the settlement's client base. Fragmentary evidence for the period 1930 to 1950 suggests that perhaps as many as fifteen thousand to twenty thousand people per year (or approximately one-fourth to one-third of El Paso's Mexican population) utilized its medical and/or educational services. Indeed, one Methodist cited in the 1930s pamphlet boasted that the settlement "reaches nearly fifteen thousand people."[9]

As a functioning Progressive-era settlement, Houchen had amazing longevity from 1912 to 1962. Several Methodist missionaries came to Segundo Barrio as young women and stayed until their retirement. Arriving in 1930, Millie Rickford would live at the settlement for thirty-one years. Two years after her departure, the Rose Gregory Houchen Settlement House (named after a Michigan schoolteacher) would receive a new name, Houchen Community Center. As a community center, it would become more of a secular agency

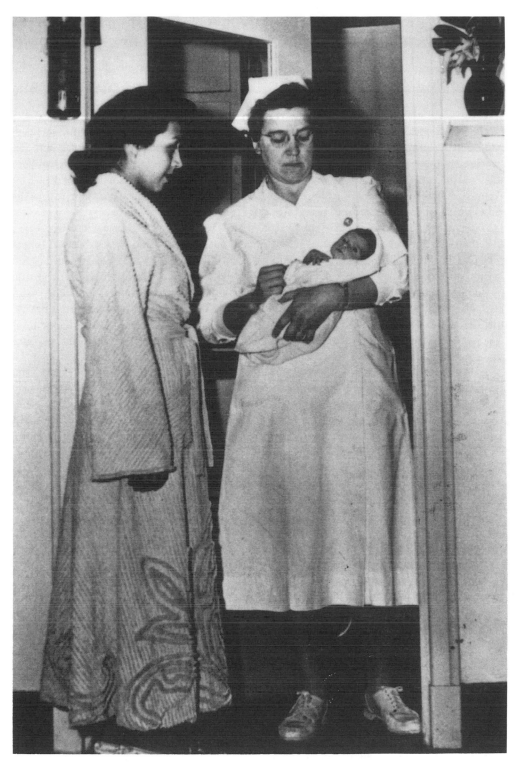

Figure 2. From 1937 to 1976, over 12,000 babies were born at Newark hospital. Although mother and child are unidentified, the nurse is Dorothea Muñoz. (Courtesy of Houchen Community Center.)

staffed by social workers and, at times, Chicano activists.[10] In 1991, the buildings that cover a city block in South El Paso still furnish day care and recreational activities. Along with Bible study, there are classes in ballet folklorico, karate, English, and aerobics. Citing climbing insurance costs (among other reasons), the Methodist church closed the hospital and clinic in December 1986 over the protests of local supporters and community members.[11]

From 1912 until the 1950s, Houchen workers placed Americanization and proselytization at the center of their efforts. Embracing the imagery and ideology of the melting pot, Methodist missionary Dorothy Little explained: "Houchen settlement stands as a sentinel of friendship . . . between the people of America and the people of Mexico. We assimilate the best of their culture, their art, their ideals and they in turn gladly accept the best America has to offer as they . . . become one with us. For right here within our four walls is begun much of the 'Melting' process of our 'Melting Pot'."[12]

To "become one with us" no doubt included a conversion to Methodism. It is important to remember that these missionaries were, indeed, missionaries, and they perceived themselves as harbingers of salvation. In "Our Work at Houchen," it was expressed this way: "Our Church is called El Buen Pastor . . . and that is what our church really is to the people—it is a Good Shepherd guiding our folks out of darkness and Catholocism [sic] into the good Christian life." Along similar lines, one Methodist pamphlet printed during the 1930s equated Catholicism (as practiced by Mexicans) with paganism and superstition. The settlement's programs were couched in terms of "Christian Americanization," and these programs began early.[13]

Like the Franciscan missionaries who trod the same ground three centuries before, the women of Houchen sought to win the hearts and minds of children. Although preschool and kindergarten students spoke Spanish and sang Mexican songs, they also learned English, U.S. history, biblical verses—even etiquette à la Emily Post[14] (see figure 3). The settlement also offered a number of afterschool activities for older children. These included "Little Homemakers," scouting, teen clubs, piano lessons, dance, Bible classes, and story hour. For many years, the most elaborate playground in South El Paso could be found within the outer courtyard of the settlement (see figure 4). A lifelong resident of Segundo Barrio, Elsa Chávez remarked that her mother let her play there on the condition that she not accept any "cookies or Kool-Aid," the refreshments provided by Houchen staff. Other people remembered making similar bargains with their mothers. They could play on the swings and slide, but they could not go indoors.[15] How big of a step was it to venture from the playground to story hour?

Settlement proselytizing did not escape the notice of barrio priests. Clearly troubled by Houchen, a few predicted dire consequences for those who participated in any Protestant-tinged activities. One priest went so far as to tell neighborhood children that it was a sin even to play on the playground equipment. Others, however, took a more realistic stance, and did not chastise their parishioners for utilizing Methodist child-care and medical services. Perhaps as a response to both the Great Depression and suspected Protestant inroads, several area Catholic churches began distributing food baskets and establishing soup kitchens.[16]

Children were not the only people targeted by Houchen. Women, particularly expectant mothers, received special attention. Like the proponents of Americanization programs in California, settlement workers believed that women held a special guardianship over their families' welfare. As head nurse Millie Rickford explained, " 'If we can teach her [the mother-to-be] the modern methods of cooking and preparing foods and simple hygiene habits for herself and her family, we have gained a stride' "[17] (see figure 5).

Figure 3. The task of "Christian Americanization" began early. Here, kindergarten students are taught to say grace during snack time. (Courtesy of Houchen Community Center.)

Figure 4. For many years, the big attraction for neighborhood children was the settlement's elaborate playground. (Courtesy of Houchen Community Center.)

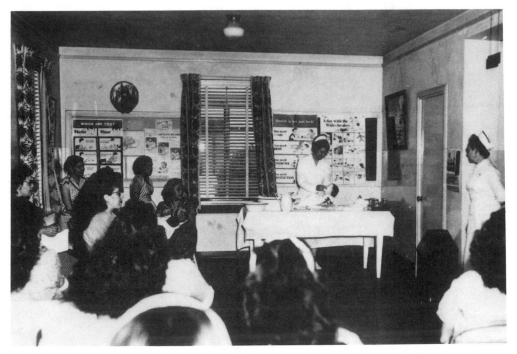

Figure 5. As part of a prenatal class, a Houchen nurse demonstrates the "proper" way to bathe an infant. (Courtesy of Houchen Community Center.)

Houchen's "Christian Americanization" programs were not unique. Between 1910 and 1930, religious and state-organized Americanization projects aimed at the Mexican population proliferated throughout the Southwest. These efforts varied in scale from settlement houses to night classes, and the curriculum generally revolved around cooking, hygiene, English, and civics. Music seemed a universal tool of instruction. One rural Arizona schoolteacher excitedly informed readers of the *Arizona Teacher and Home Journal* that, for the "cause of Americanization," her district had purchased a Victrola and several records, including two Spanish melodies, the " 'Star Spangled Banner', 'The Red, White, and Blue', 'Silent Night', [and] 'Old Kentucky Home'."[18] Houchen, of course, offered a variety of musical activities, beginning with the kindergarten rhythm band of 1927. During the 1940s and 1950s, missionaries offered flute, guitar, ballet, and tap lessons. For fifty cents per week, a youngster could take dance or music classes and perform in settlement recitals[19] (see figure 6). The last figure is not atypical; there apparently were several instances when youngsters were clothed in European peasant styles. For instance, Alice Ruiz, Priscilla Molina, Edna Parra, Mira Gomez, and Aida Rivera, representing Houchen in a local Girl Scout festival held at the Shrine temple, modeled costumes from Sweden, England, France, Scotland, and Lithuania.[20] Some immigrant traditions were valorized more than others. Celebrating Mexican heritage did not figure into the Euro-American orientation pushed by Houchen residents.

Settlement workers held out unrealistic notions of the American dream, romantic constructions of American life. It is as if they endeavored to create a white, middle-class environment for Mexican youngsters, complete with tutus and toe shoes. Cooking classes also became avenues for developing particular tastes. As Minerva Franco recalled, "I'll never forget the look on my mother's face when I first cooked 'Eggs Benedict' which I

Figure 6. The dance recital captures the Eurocentric orientation advocated by Houchen residents. Settlement workers believed that their students could "melt" within the "melting pot." (Courtesy of Houchen Community Center.)

learned to prepare at Houchen."[21] The following passage taken from a report dated February 1942 outlines, in part, the perceived accomplishments of the settlement: "Sanitary conditions have been improving—more children go to school—more parents are becoming citizens, more are leaving Catholicism—more are entering business and public life—and more and more they are taking on the customs and standards of the Anglo people."[22]

There are numerous passages and photographs in the Houchen collection that provide fodder for sarcasm among contemporary scholars. As a Chicana historian, I am of two minds. I respect the settlement workers for their health and child-care services, but I cringe at their ethnocentrism and their romantic idealization of "American" life. Yet, before judging the maternal missionaries too harshly, it is important to keep in mind the social services they rendered over an extended period of time, as well as the environment in which they lived. For example, Houchen probably launched the first bilingual kindergarten program in El Paso, a program that eased the children's transition into an English-only first grade. Nor did Houchen residents denigrate the use of Spanish, and many became fluent Spanish speakers themselves. The hospital and clinic, moreover, were important community institutions for over half a century.[23]

Furthermore, settlement workers could not always count on the encouragement or patronage of Anglo El Paso. In a virulently nativist tract, a local physician, C. S. Babbitt, condemned missionaries like the women of Houchen for working among Mexican and African Americans. In fact, Babbitt argued that religious workers were "seemingly conspiring with Satan to destroy the handiwork of God" because their energies were "wasted on beings . . . who are not in reality the objects of Christ's sacrifice."[24] Perhaps more damaging than this extremist view was the apparent lack of financial support on the part of area Methodist churches. The records I examined revealed little in terms of local donations. The former Michigan schoolteacher whom the settlement was named after bequeathed one thousand dollars for the establishment of an El Paso settlement. The Women's Home Missionary Society of the Newark, New Jersey Conference proved instrumental in raising funds for the construction of both the Freeman Clinic and the Newark Methodist Maternity Hospital. When the clinic first opened its doors in June 1921, all of the medical equipment—everything from sterilizers to baby scales—were gifts from Methodist groups across the nation. The Houchen Day Nursery, however, received consistent financial support from the El Paso Community Chest and, later, the United Way. In 1975, Houchen's board of directors conducted the first community-wide fund-raising drive. Volunteers sought to raise $375,000 to renovate existing structures and to build a modern day-care center. But the Houchen fund-raising slogan—"When people pay their own way, it's your affair . . . not welfare"—makes painfully clear the conservative attitudes toward social welfare harbored by affluent El Pasoans.[25]

The women of Houchen appeared undaunted by the lack of local support. For over fifty years, these missionaries coordinated a multifaceted Americanization campaign among the residents of Segundo Barrio. But how did Mexican women perceive the settlement? What services did they utilize? And to what extent did they internalize the romantic notions of "Christian Americanization"?

Examining Mexican women's agency through institutional records is difficult; it involves getting beneath the text. Furthermore, one must take into account the selectivity of voices. In drafting settlement reports and publications, missionaries chose those voices that would publicize their "victories" among the Spanish-speaking. As a result, quotations abound that heap praise upon praise on Houchen and its staff. For example, in 1939, Soledad Burciaga emphatically declared, "There is not a person, no matter to which denomination they belong, who hasn't a kind word and a heart full of gratitude towards the Settlement House."[26] Obviously, these documents have their limits. Oral interviews and informal discussions with people who grew up in Segundo Barrio give a more balanced, less effusive perspective. Most viewed Houchen as a Protestant-run health-care and afterschool activities center, rather than as the "light-house" [sic] in South El Paso.[27]

In 1949, the term *Friendship Square* was coined as a description for the settlement house, hospital, day nursery, and church. Missionaries hoped that children born at Newark would participate in preschool and afternoon programs, and that eventually they and their families would join the church, El Buen Pastor. And a few did follow this pattern. One of the ministers assigned to El Buen Pastor, Fernando García, had himself been a Houchen kindergarten graduate. Emulating the settlement staff, some young women enrolled in Methodist missionary colleges or served as lay volunteers. Elizabeth Soto, for example, had attended Houchen programs throughout her childhood and adolescence. Upon graduation from Bowie High School, she entered Asbury College to train as a missionary and then returned to El Paso as a Houchen resident. After several years of service, she left settlement work to become the wife of a Mexican Methodist minister. The more common goal among Houchen teens was to graduate from high school and perhaps attend Texas Western, the local college. The first child born at Newark Hospital, Margaret Holguin, took part in settlement activities as a child and later became a registered nurse. According to her *comadre*, Lucy Lucero, Holguin's decision to pursue nursing was "perhaps due to the influence" of head nurse Millie Rickford. Lucero noted, "The only contact I had had with Anglos was with Anglo teachers. Then I met Miss Rickford and I felt, 'Hey, she's human. She's great'." At a time when many (though certainly not all) elementary school-teachers cared little about their Mexican students, Houchen residents offered warmth and encouragement.[28] Based on the selectivity of available data, one cannot make wholesale generalizations about Friendship Square's role in fostering mobility or even aspirations for mobility among the youth of Segundo Barrio. Yet, it is clear that the women of Houchen strove to build self-esteem and encouraged young people to pursue higher education.

Missionaries also envisioned a Protestant enclave in South El Paso, but, to their frustration, very few people responded. The settlement church, El Buen Pastor, had a peak membership of one hundred fifty families. The church itself had an intermittent history. Shortly after its founding in 1897, El Buen Pastor disappeared; it was officially rededicated as part of Houchen in 1932. However, the construction of an actual church on settlement grounds did not begin until 1945. In 1968, the small rock chapel would be converted into a recreation room and thrift shop, as the members of El Buen Pastor and El Mesias (another Mexican-American church) were merged together to form the congregation of the Emmanuel United Methodist Church in downtown El Paso. In 1991, a modern gymnasium occupies the ground where the chapel once stood.[29]

Based on the selective case histories of converts, I suggest that many of those who joined El Buen Pastor were already Protestant. The Dominguez family offers an example. In the words of settlement worker Ruth Kern: "Reyna and Gabriel Dominguez are Latin Americans, even though both were born in the United States. Some members of the family do not even speak English. Reyna was born . . . in a Catholic home, but at the age of eleven years, she began attending The Methodist Church. Gabriel was born in Arizona. His mother was a Catholic, but she became a Protestant when . . . Gabriel was five years old."[30]

The youth programs at Houchen brought Reyna and Gabriel together. After their marriage, the couple had six children, all born at Newark Hospital. The Dominguez family represented Friendship Square's typical success story. Many of the converts were children, and many had already embraced a Protestant faith. In the records I examined, I found only one instance of the conversion of a Catholic adult and one instance of the conversion of an entire Catholic family.[31] It seems that those most receptive to Houchen's religious messages were already predisposed to that direction.

The failure of proselytization cannot be examined solely within the confines of Friendship Square. It is not as if these Methodist women were good social workers but incompetent missionaries. Houchen staff member Clara Sarmiento wrote of the difficulty in building trust among the adults of Segundo Barrio: "Though it is easy for children to open up their hearts to us we do not find it so with the parents." She continued, "It is hard especially because we are Protestant, and most of the people we serve . . . come from Catholic heritage."[32] I would argue that the Mexican community played an instrumental role in thwarting conversion. In a land where the barrio could serve as a refuge from prejudice and discrimination, the threat of social isolation could certainly inhibit many residents from turning Protestant. During an oral interview, a woman who participated in Houchen activities for over fifty years, Estella Ibarra, described growing up Protestant in South El Paso: "We went through a lot of prejudice . . . sometimes my friends' mothers wouldn't let them play with us. . . . When the priest would go through the neighborhood, all the children would run to say hello and kiss his hand. My brothers and I would just stand by and look. The priest would usually come . . . and tell us how we were living in sin. Also, there were times when my brother and I were stoned by other students . . . and called bad names."[33]

When contacted by a Houchen resident, Mrs. Espinosa admitted to being a closet Protestant. As she explained, "I am afraid of the Catholic sisters and [I] don't want my neighbors to know that I am not Catholic-minded." The fear of ostracism, though recorded by Houchen staff, did not figure into their understanding of Mexicano resistance to conversion. Instead, they blamed time and culture. As Dorothy Little succinctly related, "We can not eradicate in a few years what has been built up during ages."[34]

Although a Protestant enclave never materialized, settlement women remained steadfast in their goals of conversion and Americanization, goals that did not change until the mid-to late fifties. Historians Sarah Deutsch and George Sanchez have noted that sporadic, poorly financed Americanization programs made little headway in Mexican communities. Ruth Crocker also described the Protestant settlements in Gary, Indiana, as having only a "superficial and temporary" influence.[35] Yet, even long-term sustained efforts, as in the case of Houchen, had limited appeal. This inability to mold consciousness or identity demonstrates not only the strength of community sanctions but, more significantly, the resiliency of Mexican culture and the astuteness of Mexicanos. Mexican women derived substantive services from Friendship Square in the form of health care and education; however, they refused to embrace the romantic idealizations of American life. Wage-earning mothers who placed their children in the day nursery no doubt encountered an Anglo world quite different from the one depicted by Methodist missionaries, and, thus, they were skeptical of the settlement's cultural ideations (see figure 7). Clara Sarmiento knew from experience that it was much easier to reach the children than their parents.[36]

How did children respond to the ideological undercurrents of Houchen programs? Did Mexican women feel empowered by their interaction with the settlement, or were Methodist missionaries invidious underminers of Mexican identity? In getting beneath the text, the following remarks of Minerva Franco, which appeared in a 1975 issue of *Newark-Houchen News*, raise a series of provocative questions. "Houchen provided . . . opportunities for learning and experiencing. . . . At Houchen I was shown that I had worth and that I was an individual."[37] What did she mean by that statement? Did the settlement house heighten her self-esteem? Did she feel that she was not an individual within the context of her family and neighborhood? Some young women imbibed Americanization so heavily that they rejected their identity. In *No Separate Refuge*, Sarah Deutsch picked up on this theme as she quoted missionary Polita Padilla, "I am Mexican, born and brought up in New Mexico, but much of my life was spent in the Allison School where we had a different training so that the Mexican way of living now seems strange to me." Others, like Estella Ibarra and Rose Escheverría Mulligan, saw little incompatibility between Mexican traditions and Protestantism. Growing up in Los Angeles, Mulligan remembered her religion as reaffirming Mexican values. In her words, "I was beginning to think that the Baptist Church was a little too Mexican. Too much restriction."[38]

Houchen documents reveal glimpses into the formation of identity, consciousness, and values. The Friendship Square calendar of 1949 explicitly stated that the medical care provided at Houchen "is a tool to develop sound minds in sound bodies; for thus it is easier to find peace with God and man. We want to help people develop a sense of values in life." In an era of bleaching creams, the privileging of color—with white as the pinnacle—was an early lesson. Relating the excitement of kindergarten graduation, day nursery head Beatrice Fernandez included in her report a question asked by Margarita, one of the young graduates. "We are all wearing white, white dress, slip, socks and Miss Fernandez, is it alright if our hair is black?"[39] Houchen activities were synonymous with Americanization. A member of the settlement Brownie troop encouraged her friends "to become 'an American or a Girl Scout' at Houchen." Scouting certainly served as a vehicle for Americanization. The all-Mexican Girl and Boy Scout troops of Alpine, Texas, enjoyed visiting El Paso and Ciudad Juárez in the company of Houchen scouts. In a thank-you note, the Alpine Girl Scouts wrote, "Now we can all say we have been to a foreign country."[40]

It is important to remember that Houchen provided a bilingual environment, not a bicultural one. Spanish was the means to communicate the message of Methodism and Christian Americanization. Whether dressing up children as Pilgrims or European peasants, missionaries stressed "American" citizenship and values; yet, outside of conversion, defini-

Figure 7. A wage-earning mother on her way to work escorts her children to the Houchen Day Nursery. (Courtesy of Houchen Community Center.)

tions of those values or of "our American way" remained elusive. Indeed, some of the settlement lessons were not incongruous with Mexican mores. In December 1952, an Anglo settlement worker recorded in her journal the success of a Girl Scout dinner: "The girls learned a lot from it too. They were taught how to set the table, and how to serve the men. They learned also that they had to share, to cooperate, and to wait their turn."[41] The most striking theme is that of individualism. Missionaries emphasized the importance of individual decision-making and individual accomplishment. In recounting her own conversion, Clara Sarmiento explained to a young client, "I chose my own religion because it was my own personal experience and . . . I was glad my religion was not chosen for me."[42]

The Latina missionaries of Houchen served as cultural brokers as they diligently strove to integrate themselves into the community. Until 1950, the Houchen staff usually included one Latina. During the 1950s, the number of Latina (predominately Mexican-American) settlement workers rose to six. Mary Lou López, María Rico, Elizabeth Soto, Febe Bonilla, Clara Sarmiento, María Payan, and Beatrice Fernandez had participated in Methodist outreach activities as children (Soto at Houchen) and had decided to follow in the footsteps of their teachers. In addition, these women had the assistance of five full-time Mexican lay persons.[43] It is no coincidence that the decade of greatest change in Houchen policies occurred at a time when Latinas held a growing number of staff positions. Friendship Square's greater sensitivity to neighborhood needs arose, in part, out of the influence exerted by Mexican clients in shaping the attitudes and actions of Mexican missionaries.

I will further suggest that although Mexican women utilized Houchen's social services, they did not, by and large, adopt its tenets of "Christian Americanization." Children who attended settlement programs enjoyed the activities, but Friendship Square did not always leave a lasting imprint. "My Mom had an open mind, so I participated in a lot of clubs. But I didn't become Protestant," remarked Lucy Lucero. "I had fun and I learned a lot, too." Because of the warm, supportive environment, Houchen settlement is remembered with fondness. However, one cannot equate pleasant memories with the acceptance of the settlement's cultural ideations.[44]

Settlement records bear out the Mexican women's selective use of Houchen's resources. The most complete set of figures I viewed was for the year 1944. During this period, 7,614 people visited the clinic and hospital. The settlement afternoon programs had an average monthly enrollment of 362, and forty children attended kindergarten. Taken together, approximately eight thousand residents of Segundo Barrio utilized Friendship Square's medical and educational offerings. In contrast, the congregation of El Buen Pastor in 1944 included 160 people.[45] Although representing only a single year, these figures indicate the importance of Houchen's medical facilities and of Mexican women's selective utilization of resources.

Implemented by a growing Latina staff, client-initiated changes in Houchen policies brought a realistic recognition of the settlement as a social service agency, rather than as a religious mission. During the 1950s, brochures describing the day nursery emphasized that, although children said grace at meals and sang Christian songs, they would not receive "in any way indoctrination" regarding Methodism. In fact, at the parents' request, Newark nurses summoned Catholic priests to the hospital to baptize premature infants. Client desire became the justification for allowing the presence of Catholic clergy, a policy that would have been unthinkable in the not-too-distant past.[46] Finally, in the new Houchen constitution of 1959, all mention of conversion was dropped. Instead, it conveyed a more ecumenical, nondenominational spirit. For instance, the goal of Houchen Settlement was henceforth "to establish a Christian democratic framework for—individual development, family solidarity, and neighborhood welfare."[47]

Settlement activities also became more closely linked with the Mexican community. During the 1950s, Houchen was the home of two chapters—one for teenagers and one for adults—of the League of United Latin American Citizens (LULAC), the most visible and politically powerful civil rights organization in Texas.[48] Carpentry classes—once the preserve of males—opened their doors to young women, although on a gender-segregated basis. Houchen workers, moreover, made veiled references to the "very dangerous business" of Juárez abortion clinics; however, it appears unclear whether or not the residents themselves offered any contraceptive counseling. But during the early 1960s, the settlement, in cooperation with Planned Parenthood, opened a birth control clinic for "married women." Indeed, a Houchen contraception success story was featured on the front page of a spring newsletter: "Mrs. G——, after having her thirteenth and fourteenth children (twins), enrolled in our birth control clinic; now for one and one half years she has been a happy and non-pregnant mother."[49]

Certainly, Houchen had changed with the times. What factors accounted for the new directions in settlement work? The evidence on the baptism of premature babies seems fairly clear in terms of client pressure, but to what extent did other policies change as the result of Mexican women's input? The residents of Segundo Barrio may have felt more comfortable expressing their ideas, and Latina settlement workers may have exhibited a greater willingness to listen. Though it is a matter of pure speculation at this point, a working coalition of Mexican women that spanned the missionary-client boundary may have accounted for Houchen's more ecumenical tone and greater community involvement. In reviewing Houchen's history, I would argue that Mexican clients, not the missionaries, set the boundaries for interaction. For most women, Houchen was not a beacon of salvation but a medical and social service center run by Methodists. They consciously decided what resources they would utilize, and consciously ignored or sidestepped the settlement's ideological premises. Like women of color in academia, they sought to take advantage of the system without buying into it.

Houchen provides a case study of what I term *cultural coalescence*. Immigrants and their children pick, borrow, retain, and create distinctive cultural forms. There is not a single hermetic Mexican or Mexican-American culture but rather permeable *cultures* rooted in generation, gender, region, class, and personal experience. Chicano scholars have divided Mexican experiences into three generational categories: Mexicano (first generation), Mexican American (second generation), and Chicano (third and beyond).[50] But this general typology tends to obscure the ways in which people navigate across cultural boundaries, as well as their conscious decision-making in the production of culture. However, bear in mind that people of color have not had unlimited choice. Racism, sexism, imperialism, persecution, and social, political, and economic segmentation have all constrained the individual's aspiration, expectations, and decision-making. As an example, young women coming of age during the 1920s may have wanted to be like the flappers they saw on the silver screen or read about in magazines, but few would do more than adopt prevailing fashions. Strict parental supervision, including chaperonage, and the reality of poverty and prejudice served to blunt their ability to emulate the icons of a new consumer society. Young women encountered both the lure of Hollywood and the threat of deportation and walked between the familiarity of tradition and the excitement of experimentation.[51]

The ideations of Americanization were a mixed lot. Religious and secular Americanization programs, the elementary schools, movies, magazines, and radio bombarded the Mexican community with a myriad of models, most of which were idealized, stylized, unrealistic, and unattainable. Even the Spanish-language press promoted acculturation, especially in the realm of consumer culture. Aimed at women, advertisements promised status and affection if the proper bleaching cream, hair coloring, and cosmetics were purchased. "Siga Las Estrellas" [Follow the Stars] beckoned one Max Factor advertisement.[52]

By looking through the lens of cultural coalescence, we can begin to discern the ways in which people select and create cultural forms. The fluidity of cultures offers exciting possibilities for research and discussion. Institutional records, like those of Houchen, are neither dead ends nor gold mines, but points of departure. Creating the public space of the settlement, Methodist missionaries sought to alter the "lifeworld" of Mexican immigrants to reflect their own idealized versions of life in the United States. Settlement workers can be viewed as the narrators of lived experience. And Houchen records reflect the cognitive construction of missionary aspirations and expectations. In other words, the documents revealed more about the women who wrote them than those they served. At another level, one could interpret the cultural ideations of Americanization as indications of an attempt at what Jürgen Habermas has termed "inner colonization."[53] Yet the failure of such projects illustrates the ways in which Mexican women appropriated desired resources, both material (infant immunizations) and psychological (self-esteem), while, in the main, rejecting the ideological messages behind them. The shift in Houchen policies during the 1950s meant more than a recognition of community needs; it represented a claiming of public space by Mexican women clients. Cultural coalescence encompasses both accommodation and resistance, and Mexican women acted, not reacted, to the settlement impulse. When standing at the cultural crossroads, Mexican women blended their options and created their own paths.

Notes

1. I thank Valerie Matsumoto for her unflagging encouragement and insightful comments. I gratefully acknowledge Tom Houghteling, Houchen Community Center executive director, and members of the Houchen board for their permission to use settlement materials. This essay was completed with the support of a University of California, Davis, Humanities Institute Fellowship.

2. Steven Seidman, ed., *Jürgen Habermas on Society and Politics: A Reader* (Boston: Beacon Press, 1989), p. 171.

3. Mario T. García, *Desert Immigrants: The Mexicans of El Paso, 1880–1920* (New Haven: Yale University Press, 1981), pp. 144–145. On a national level, Mexicans formed the "third largest 'racial' group" by 1930, outnumbered only by Anglos and African Americans, according to T. Wilson Longmore and Homer L. Hitt, "A Demographic Analysis of First and Second Generation Mexican Population of the United States: 1930," *Southwestern Social Science Quarterly*, 24 (September 1943), p. 140.

4. Oscar J. Martínez, *The Chicanos of El Paso: An Assessment of Progress* (El Paso: Texas Western Press, 1980), pp. 17, 6.

5. Martínez, *Chicanos*, pp. 29–33, 10. Mario García meticulously documents the economic and social stratification of Mexicans in El Paso; see García, *Desert Immigrants*. In 1960, the proportion of Mexican workers with high white-collar jobs jumped to 3.4 percent, according to Martínez, *Chicanos*, p. 10.

6. "South El Paso's Oasis of Care," *paso del norte*, 1 (September 1982), pp. 42–43; Thelma Hammond, "Friendship Square," (Houchen report, 1969), part of an uncatalogued collection of documents housed at Houchen Community Center, El Paso, Texas, and hereafter referred to as [HF] (for Houchen Files); "Growing With the Century" (Houchen report, 1947) [HF].

7. García, *Desert Immigrants*, p. 145; Effie Stoltz, "Freemen Clinic: A Resumé of Four Years Work" (Houchen pamphlet, 1924) [HF]. It should be noted that Houchen Settlement sprang from the work of Methodist missionary Mary Tripp, who arrived in South El Paso in 1893. However, it was not until 1912 that an actual settlement was established, according to "South El Paso's Oasis of Care," p. 42.

8. Stoltz, "Freeman Clinic"; Hammond, "Friendship Square"; M. Dorothy Woodruff and Dorothy Little, "Friendship Square" (Houchen pamphlet, March 1949) [HF]; "Friendship Square" (Houchen report, circa 1940s) [HF]; "Health Center" (Houchen newsletter, 1943) [HF]; "Christian Health Service" (Houchen report, 1941) [HF]; *El Paso Times* (October 20, 1945).

9. "Settlement Worker's Report" (Houchen report, 1927) [HF]; letter from Dorothy Little to E. Mae Young, dated May 10, 1945 [HF]; letter from Bessie Brinson to Treva Ely, dated September 14, 1958 [HF];

Hammond, "Friendship Square"; Elmer T. Clark and Dorothy McConnell, "The Methodist Church and Latin Americans in the United States" (Board of Home Missions pamphlet, circa 1930s) [HF] My very rough estimate is based on the documents and records to which I had access. I was not permitted to examine any materials then housed at Newark Hospital. The most complete statistics on utilization of services are for the year 1944 and are given in the letter from Little to Young. Because of the deportation and repatriation drives of the 1930s, in which one-third of the Mexican population in the United States was either deported or repatriated, the number of Mexicans in El Paso dropped from 68,476 in 1930 to 55,000 in 1940; by 1960, it had risen to 63,796, according to Martínez, *Chicanos*, p. 6.

10. *El Paso Herald Post* (March 7, 1961); *El Paso Herald Post* (March 12, 1961); "Community Centers" (Women's Division of Christian Service pamphlet, May 1963); "Funding Proposal for Youth Outreach and Referral Report Project" (April 30, 1974), from the private files of Kenton J. Clymer, Ph.D.; *El Paso Herald Post* (January 3, 1983); *El Paso Times* (August 8, 1983).

11. Letter from Tom Houghteling, executive director, Houchen Community Center, to the author, dated December 24, 1990; Tom Houghteling, interview with the author, January 9, 1991.

12. Dorothy Little, "Rose Gregory Houchen Settlement" (Houchen report, February 1942) [HF].

13. *Ibid.*; "Our Work at Houchen" (Houchen report, circa 1940s) [HF]; Woodruff and Little, "Friendship Square"; Jennie C. Gilbert, "Settlements Under the Women's Home Missionary Society," (pamphlet, circa 1920s) [HF]; Clark and McConnell, "The Methodist Church."

14. Anita Hernandez, "The Kindergarten" (Houchen report, circa 1940s) [HF]; "A Right Glad New Year" (Houchen newsletter, circa 1940s) [HF]; Little, "Rose Gregory Houchen Settlement"; "Our Work at Houchen"; Woodruff and Little, "Friendship Square." For more information on the Franciscans, see Ramón Gutiérrez, *When Jesus Came, the Corn Mothers Went Away: Marriage, Sexuality, and Power in New Mexico, 1500–1846* (Stanford, CA: Stanford University Press, 1991).

15. "Settlement Worker's Report"; letter from Little to Young; letter from Brinson to Ely; Friendship Square calendar for 1949 [HF]; Lucy Lucero, interview with the author, October 8, 1983; Elsa Chávez, interview with the author, April 19, 1983; discussion following presentation on "Settlement Houses in El Paso," given by the author at the El Paso Conference on History and the Social Sciences, August 24, 1983, El Paso, Texas. (Tape of presentation and discussion is on file at the Institute of Oral History, University of Texas, El Paso.) Elsa Chávez is a pseudonym used at the person's request.

16. Discussion following "Settlement Houses in El Paso" presentation. The Catholic church never established a competing settlement house. However, during the 1920s in Gary, Indiana, the Catholic diocese opened up the Gary-Alerding Settlement with the primary goal of Americanizing Mexican immigrants. The bishop took such action to counteract suspected inroads made by two local Protestant settlement houses. See Ruth Hutchinson Crocker, "Gary Mexicans and 'Christian Americanization': A Study in Cultural Conflict," in *Forging Community: The Latino Experience in Northwest Indiana, 1919–1975*, James B. Lane and Edward J. Escobar, eds. (Chicago: Cattails Press, 1987), pp. 115–134.

17. "Christian Health Service"; "The Freeman Clinic and the Newark Conference Maternity Hospital" (Houchen report, 1940) [HF]; *El Paso Times* (August 2, 1961); *El Paso Herald Post* (May 12, 1961). For more information on Americanization programs in California, see George J. Sanchez, "'Go After the Women': Americanization and the Mexican Immigrant Woman, 1915–1929," in this volume. The documents reveal a striking absence of adult Mexican male clients. The Mexican men who do appear are either Methodist ministers or lay volunteers.

18. Sanchez, "'Go After the Women',"; Sarah Deutsch, *No Separate Refuge: Culture, Class, and Gender on the Anglo-Hispanic Frontier in the American Southwest, 1880–1940* (New York: Oxford University Press, 1987); "Americanization Notes," *Arizona Teacher and Home Journal*, 11 (January 1923), p. 26. The Methodist and Presbyterian settlements in Gary, Indiana, also couched their programs in terms of "Christian Americanization," according to Hutchinson Crocker, "Gary Mexicans," pp. 118–120.

19. "Settlement Worker's Report"; Friendship Square calendar for 1949; letter from Brinson to Ely; Chávez interview.

20. News clipping from the *El Paso Times* (circa 1950s) [HF].

21. Sanchez, "'Go After the Women',"; *Newark-Houchen News* (September 1975). I agree with George Sanchez that Americanization programs created an overly rosy picture of U.S. life. In his words: "Rather than providing Mexican immigrant women with an attainable picture of assimilation, Americanization programs could only offer these immigrants idealized versions of American life."

22. Little, "Rose Gregory Houchen Settlement."

23. "Settlement Worker's Report"; Hernandez, "The Kindergarten"; "A Right Glad New Year"; Little, "Rose Gregory Houchen Settlement"; "Our Work at Houchen"; Woodruff and Little, "Friendship Square"; "South El Paso's Oasis of Care"; *El Paso Herald Post* (March 7, 1961); *El Paso Herald Post* (March 12, 1961); *El Paso Herald Post* (May 12, 1961).

24. C. S. Babbitt, *The Remedy for the Decadence of the Latin Race* (El Paso, TX: El Paso Printing Company), p. 55 (presented to the Pioneers Association of El Paso, Texas, July 11, 1909, by Mrs. Babbitt, widow of the author; pamphlet courtesy of Jack Redman).

25. "Account Book for Rose Gregory Houchen Settlement (1903–1913)" [HF]; Hammond, "Friendship Square"; "Growing With the Century"; *El Paso Times* (September 5, 1975); Stoltz, "Freeman Clinic"; Woodruff and Little, "Friendship Square"; *El Paso Times* (October 3, 1947); "Four Institutions. One Goal. The Christian Community" (Houchen pamphlet, circa early 1950s) [HF]; Houghteling interview; "A City Block of Service" (script of Houchen slide presentation, 1976) [HF]; *El Paso Times* (January 19, 1977); speech given by Kenton J. Clymer, Ph.D., June 1975 (Clymer Files); *El Paso Times* (May 23, 1975); *Newark-Houchen News* (September 1975). It should be noted that in 1904 local Methodist congregations did contribute much of the money needed to purchase the property upon which the settlement was built. Local civic groups occasionally donated money or equipment and threw Christmas parties for Houchen children, according to "Account Book"; *El Paso Herald Post* (December 14, 1951); *El Paso Times* (December 16, 1951).

26. Vernon McCombs, "Victories in the Latin American Mission" (Board of Home Missions pamphlet, 1935) [HF]; "Brillante Historia de la Iglesia 'El Buen Pastor' El Paso" (Young Adult Fellowship newsletter, December 1946) [HF]; Soledad Burciaga, "Yesterday in 1923" (Houchen report, 1939) [HF].

27. This study is based on a limited number of oral interviews (five to be exact), but they represent a range of interaction with the settlement, from playing on the playground to serving as the minister for El Buen Pastor. It is also informed by a public discussion of my work on Houchen held during an El Paso teachers' conference in 1983. Most of the educators who attended the talk had participated, to some extent, in Houchen activities and were eager to share their recollections (cf. note 15). I am also indebted to students in my Mexican-American history classes when I taught at the University of Texas, El Paso, especially the reentry women, for their insight and knowledge.

28. Woodruff and Little, "Friendship Square"; Hammond, "Friendship Square"; "Greetings for 1946" (Houchen Christmas newsletter, 1946) [HF]; Little, "Rose Gregory Houchen Settlement"; Soledad Burciaga, "Today in 1939" (Houchen report, 1939) [HF]; "Our Work at Houchen"; "Christian Social Service" (Houchen report, circa 1940s) [HF]; Fernando García, interview with the author, September 21, 1983; *El Paso Times* (June 14, 1951); Lucero interview; Vicki L. Ruiz, "Oral History and La Mujer: The Rose Guerrero Story," in *Women on the U.S.-Mexico Border: Responses to Change* (Boston: Allen and Unwin, 1987), pp. 226–227; *Newark-Houchen News* (September 1975).

29. Spanish-American Methodist News Bulletin (April 1946) [HF]; Hammond, "Friendship Square"; McCombs, "Victories"; "El Metodismo en la Ciudad de El Paso," *Christian Herald* (July 1945) [HF]; "Brillante Historia"; "The Door: An Informal Pamphlet on the Work of the Methodist Church Among the Spanish-speaking of El Paso, Texas" (Methodist pamphlet, 1940) [HF]; "A City Block of Service"; García interview; Houghteling interview. From 1932 to 1939, services for El Buen Pastor were held in a church located two blocks from the settlement.

30. A. Ruth Kern, "There Is No Segregation Here," Methodist Youth Fund Bulletin (January–March 1953), p. 12 [HF].

31. *Ibid.*; "The Torres Family" (Houchen report, circa 1940s) [HF]; Estella Ibarra, interview with Jesusita Ponce, November 11, 1982; Hazel Bulifant, "One Woman's Story" (Houchen report, 1950) [HF]; "Our Work at Houchen."

32. Clara Sarmiento, "Lupe" (Houchen report, circa 1950s) [HF].

33. Ibarra interview.

34. Bulifant, "One Woman's Story"; letter from Little to Young.

35. Deutsch, *No Separate Refuge*, pp. 64–66, 85–86; Sanchez, " 'Go After the Women',"; Hutchinson Crocker, "Gary Mexicans," p. 121.

36. Sarmiento, "Lupe." In her study, Ruth Hutchinson Crocker also notes the propensity of Protestant missionaries to focus their energies on children and the selective uses of services by Mexican clients. As she explained, "Inevitably, many immigrants came to the settlement, took what they wanted of its services, and remained untouched by its message" (Hutchinson Crocker, "Gary Mexicans," p. 122).

37. *Newark-Houchen News* (September 1975).

38. Deutsch, *No Separate Refuge*, pp. 78–79; Ibarra interview; interview with Rose Escheverría Mulligan, vol. 27 of *Rosie the Riveter Revisited: Women and the World War II Work Experience*, ed. Sherna Berger Gluck (Long Beach, CA: CSULB Foundation, 1983), p. 24.

39. Friendship Square calendar for 1949; Beatrice Fernandez, "Day Nursery" (Houchen report, circa late 1950s) [HF].

40. "Friendship Square" (Houchen pamphlet, circa 1950s) [HF]; letter to Houchen Girl Scouts from Troop 4, Latin American Community Center, Alpine, Texas, May 18, 1951 [HF].

41. "A Right Glad New Year"; news clipping from the *El Paso Times* (circa 1950s); "Our Work at Houchen";

Little, "Rose Gregory Houchen Settlement"; Anglo settlement worker's journal, entry for December 1952 [HF].

42. *Newark-Houchen News* (September 1975); Sarmiento, "Lupe."

43. Datebook for 1926, settlement worker's private journal, entry for Friday, September 9, 1929 [HF]; "Brillante Historia"; "Report and Directory of Association of Church Social Workers, 1940" [HF]; "May I Come In?" (Houchen brochure, circa 1950s) [HF]; "Friendship Square" (Houchen pamphlet, 1958) [HF]; Mary Lou López, "Kindergarten Report" (Houchen report, circa 1950s) [HF]; Sarmiento, "Lupe"; "Freeman Clinic and Newark Hospital" (Houchen pamphlet, 1954) [HF]; *El Paso Times* (June 14, 1951); "Houchen Day Nursery" (Houchen pamphlet, circa 1950s) [HF]; *El Paso Times* (September 12, 1952). Methodist missionaries seem to have experienced some mobility within the settlement hierarchy. In 1912, Ofilia Chávez served as a "student helper"; forty years later, Beatrice Fernandez would direct the preschool.

44. Chávez interview; Martha González, interview with the author, October 8, 1983; Lucero interview; *Newark-Houchen News* (September 1974).

45. Letter from Little to Young; "The Door"; Woodruff and Little, "Friendship Square."

46. "Houchen Day Nursery"; "Life in a Glass House" (Houchen report, circa 1950s) [HF].

47. Program for first annual meeting, Houchen Settlement and Day Nursery, Freeman Clinic and Newark Conference Maternity Hospital (January 8, 1960) [HF]. It should be noted that thirty years later, there seems to be a shift back to original settlement ideas. Today, in 1991, Houchen Community has regularly scheduled Bible studies, according to letter from Houghteling to the author.

48. Program for Houchen production of "Cinderella" [HF]; letter from Brinson to Ely. For more information on LULAC, see Mario T. García, *Mexican Americans: Leadership, Ideology, and Identity, 1930–1960* (New Haven: Yale University Press, 1989).

49. Bulifant, "One Woman's Story"; "News From Friendship Square" (spring newsletter, circa early 1960s) [HF].

50. As an example of this typology, see García, *Mexican Americans*, pp. 13–22, 295–302. Richard Griswold del Castillo touches on the dynamic nature of Mexican culture in *La Familia: Chicano Families in the Urban Southwest, 1848 to the Present* (Notre Dame, IN: University of Notre Dame Press, 1984).

51. A more developed elaboration of these themes may be found in my essay, " 'Star Struck'. Acculturation, Adolescence, and the Mexican American Woman, 1920–1940," in *Building With Our Hands: New Directions in Chicana Scholarship*, eds. Adela de la Torre and Beatríz Pesquera (Berkeley: University of California Press, 1993).

52. *Ibid.*; *La Opinion* (June 5, 1927); *La Opinion* (January 8, 1938).

53. My understanding and application of the ideas of Jürgen Habermas have been informed by the following works: Jürgen Habermas, *Moral Consciousness and Communicative Action*, trans. Christian Lenhardt and Sherry Weber Nicholsen, intro. Thomas McCarthy (Cambridge, MA.: MIT Press, 1990); Steven Seidman, ed., *Jürgen Habermas on Society and Politics*; Nancy Fraser, *Unruly Practices: Power, Discourse, and Gender in Contemporary Social Theory* (Minneapolis: University of Minnesota Press, 1989); and Seyla Benhabib and Drucilla Cornell, "Introduction: Beyond the Politics of Gender," in *Feminism As Critique*, eds. Benhabib and Cornell (Minneapolis: University of Minnesota Press, 1987).

20

Crossed Boundaries in Interracial Chicago: Pilipino American Families Since 1925

Barbara M. Posadas

On an often snowy, blustery, cold, winter night each December 30, for almost seventy years, the Pilipino community of Chicago has gathered to commemorate the execution of Philippine patriot, Jose Rizal. In recent years, attendance at the dance has been dominated by Pilipino couples newly arrived in the country—the doctors, nurses, accountants, engineers, and other professionals whose emigration from the Islands has boosted the group's population in the city from 1,740 in 1940 to 9,428 in 1970—a pattern resembling that of the United States as a whole where the number rose from 45,563 to 336,731 in the same period. Today, men in tuxedos, their wives in elaborate gowns brought with them from their homeland, and a sprinkling of small children never left with a babysitter dominate at the community festival in which the sounds of many different dialects color the pauses between sets.[1]

In years long past, much was different. The young men who arrived from the Philippines in the 1920s, when the Charleston was the rage, and danced more sedately in the 1930s and 1940s to the big band sounds of Tommy and Jimmy Dorsey, Benny Goodman, and Glenn Miller rarely held professional employment. Though many had come to the United States as self-supporting students to finish high school and obtain an American college degree, few had persisted long enough to accomplish the goals of their youth. They commonly found work in clubs, restaurants, hotels and private homes—the lucky few won enhanced prestige with higher pay and more regularized employment as post office clerks or as attendants on Pullman railway cars, where more than four hundred were hired between 1925 and 1940. At Rizal Day dances throughout these years, these men, now known in Chicago as the "old-timers," were typically accompanied by white, American-born sweethearts and wives, dressed in chiffon, satin, and silk, whose knowledge of the dialects spoken by their partners rarely extended beyond one or two words. Their community has always been interracial.[2]

Though the body of writing on Asian immigrants and their descendants has grown considerably in recent years, historical scholarship continues to slight the Pilipinos in the United States. Over two decades ago, Roger Daniels remarked:

> The history of the Filipino-American should be written soon while the memories of the pioneers can still be tapped. The young men of the 1920s are just a little younger than the century, and the table of mortality is reaping a larger harvest every year.[3]

More recently, in surveying works published in the late 1970s, he noted: "An overwhelming majority of the essays deal with . . . either Chinese or Japanese: other Asian immigrant groups are still largely neglected by scholarship."[4] Only H. Brett Melendy's cross-national study, *Asians in America: Filipinos, Koreans, and East Indians*, offers a useful survey.[5] For additional detail on the pre-1934, first wave of Pilipino immigration, those interested in their history must turn either to brief, early portraits which emphasize or react against viewing Pilipinos as a social problem[6] or to more modern treatments oriented toward an assessment of service needs or toward group consciousness-raising.[7]

Moreover, scholars focusing on the Pilipino experience have concentrated on California and Hawaii, the areas to which most migrated, and have thereby stressed the immigrants' agricultural employment in farm fields and sugar plantations.[8] Given this emphasis on West Coast and Hawaiian Pilipinos, many of whom either never married or failed to form durable family ties, conventional wisdom portrays the old-timer Pilipino, in his later years, as "lonely and alone."[9] Victimization emerges as the common denominator of this generation's life in the United States:

> [M]ost old-timers will sit and talk to a sympathetic ear about their life in America. Their story is pierced not only with humor, but also with bitterness, for many of them have only poverty-line incomes, callous and weather-beaten faces to show for their toil in American farm fields and existence in urban hotels, restaurants and apartments. By material standards, so highly held by American society, the first generation of Philippine Americans has achieved little or left little.[10]

Virtually nothing has yet appeared on Pilipinos who moved permanently from West Coast ports of arrival to major cities in the Midwest and on the East Coast.[11] These Pilipinos, while numerically smaller as a group than the Pacific Coast residents, constitute nonetheless an important element in the generation's history, for they experienced the problems of accommodation and acculturation to American life in an economic and social setting somewhat different from that of the West Coast, and, in addition, confronted these challenges with a significantly higher level of education.[12]

Similarly, the interracial marriages contracted by the old-timers have received scant attention since the 1930s, when these unions were used by advocates of Pilipino exclusion to justify immigration restrictions on moral grounds. The Asian newcomers posed a danger to American society because of their "preference" for white women. Ignoring the demographic reality of an immigrant population overwhelmingly young, single, and male, critics stereotyped Pilipinos as aggressive, uneducated, irresponsible, and prone to fighting and gambling; the women they married were "near-moron white girls."[13] More careful analyses of the social bases of intermarriage, such as those appearing in *Sociology and Social Research* during these years, discussed the topic in legal and statistical terms, or from the perspective of male needs and susceptibilities. The women remained anonymous creatures of ignorance, acquisitiveness, and passion.[14] Their thoughts, actions, and feelings have rarely emerged.[15]

This essay seeks to examine the interracial community formed in Chicago during the late 1920s and early 1930s through a composite utilizing interviews with husbands and wives now in their seventies, for it is through the memories of these couples that the processes of cultural adaptation and racial interaction over an almost fifty-year period can best be analyzed. Through their words, the familial values which they brought to and modified during their marriages can be identified. Through their stories, the support and survival mechanisms which they utilized in combating both familial and social disapproval of their marriages can be assessed.[16]

The Pilipino population in Illinois grew steadily, albeit on a small scale, between 1920, when 164 Island migrants were located by the federal census, and 1930, when their total reached 2,011. By 1940, after a decade of national economic hardship and the virtual stoppage of further mass immigration from the Philippines in 1934 under the terms of the Tydings-McDuffie Act, the state population had declined slightly to 1,930. Thus, the first wave of immigration from the Philippines had produced in Illinois a population less than one-tenth the size of California's 22,636. Other differences were more striking than sheer size, however. More than ninety percent of the Illinois residents lived in Chicago, whereas only 21.4 percent of the California Pilipinos were recorded as living in Los Angeles or San Francisco. This urban-rural dichotomy, clearly reflected in dissimilar occupational distributions, fixed a different group identity in each area. In Chicago, sixty-four percent of the Pilipinos labored as service workers. In California, over sixty percent of the state's much larger Pilipino population worked as agricultural hands, though in Los Angeles and San Francisco, the numbers concentrated in the service sector—seventy-five and eighty-two percent respectively—actually exceeded the Chicago figure (Table 1).[17]

Drastically different levels of schooling for Pilipinos living in Illinois and California further enhanced the contrast. Among Chicagoans, median years of schooling stood at 12.2; for Californians, 6.8. Even in Los Angeles and San Francisco, the figures hovered at nine years. In contrast with the typical West Coast Pilipino, the average Chicago migrant was a high school graduate with some college experience.[18] It is difficult to determine precisely why Chicago drew a more highly educated population, though several factors were undoubtedly important. Many came to continue their schooling. By the mid-1920s, Pilipinos were arriving in Chicago to attend specific colleges and universities in the area. In 1924, 103 students were enrolled at the University of Chicago, Northwestern University, DePaul University and Crane Junior College. Downstate in Urbana, twenty-five Pilipinos studied at the University of Illinois.[19] These immigrants probably came with a high school diploma from the Philippines in hand.[20] Like other Pilipinos seeking an American education, most in Chicago expected to be self-supporting. But they quickly found that the low pay and the long hours of most available service jobs—and the temptations of life in Chicago—limited their successful continuation in school. Caught in the United States by their deeply felt shame at having failed to attain an American degree, many remained in the city, thereby fixing the educational level of the group at a high level.[21] On the other hand, many Pilipinos migrated to Hawaii and the West Coast specifically to find work in agriculture. Like the students, they too hoped to return to their homeland—with money rather than a degree—but found their dreams also limited by American conditions. California's lower educational level is a measure of their entrapment.[22]

These basic patterns also produced a chain migration phenomenon in both areas. In Hawaii and on the West Coast, literate farm laborers wrote home with news of opportunities in agriculture; company recruiters, cognizant of varying economic conditions in different Philippine provinces, sought additional workers in areas where poor prospects and a labor surplus continued. Hence, a steady stream of less-educated Pilipinos, often from the economically depressed Ilocos provinces, flowed into California and Hawaii. Chicagoans, on the other hand, set in motion far smaller chains among relatives and friends who were probably of the same educational level. Because the original Pilipino population came from

Table 1. Pilipinos in Chicago and California: 1940 Education and Occupation

	Chicago	Los Angeles	San Francisco	California
Population	1,097	2,912	1,936	22,636
Median Years Schooling	12.2	9.0	8.9	6.8
Professional & Semiprofessional	3.8	2.2	.8	.7
Farmer & Farm Manager	—	.4	—	1.5
Proprietor, Manager & Official	1.0	1.4	1.1	1.1
Clerical/Sales	11.5	2.0	3.1	1.0
Craftsman/Foreman	3.2	1.8	2.4	.7
Operative	10.5	7.1	6.2	3.1
Domestic Service	4.6	10.3	12.8	4.8
Service	59.1	65.0	69.5	23.4
Farm Laborer	—	2.5	.3	60.8
Nonfarm Laborer	6.2	7.0	3.0	2.7
No Occupation Reported	.2	.3	.7	.3
Total	100.0	100.0	100.0	100.0

Source: U.S. Bureau of the Census, *1940 Census of Population: Characteristics of the Nonwhite Population by Race*, 112; ibid., *Population*, vol. 3, "The Labor Force: Occupation, Industry, Employment, and Income," 874–75.

a variety of provinces, these chains ultimately produced a community of diverse provincial loyalties in Chicago.[23]

The Chicago to which almost 1,800 Pilipinos had migrated by 1930 was an overwhelmingly "ethnic" city of 3.4 million inhabitants, almost ninety percent of whom were either foreign-born whites or their children. Over half a million claimed Polish ancestry; slightly fewer were of German heritage. Russian Jews, Italians, Swedes, Irish, and Czechs all boasted populations of over one hundred thousand. Distinctive neighborhoods, identified by national background, created a patchwork urban landscape of tongues and customs. Minorities comprised a scant 7.1 percent of the city's residents. Most of Chicago's 234,000 Blacks were concentrated in the South Side Black Belt. Among Asians, almost 2,800 Chinese, identified with a bustling Chinatown at Twenty-Second and Wentworth, outnumbered both Pilipinos and the fewer than five hundred Japanese. During the Depression decade, these figures changed little. In 1940, total population remained at 3.4 million; 44,000 additional Black residents expanded ghetto borders; Pilipinos declined by fifty-six.[24]

Among Chicago's white males, unlike Pilipinos, a high school education had not yet become the norm in 1940. The median length of schooling for native-born white males, 9.4 years, indicated completion of at least a grammar school course by more than half; for foreign-born white males, a lower figure, 7.5 years, pertained.[25] These figures reflected an age bias: older men had left school earlier in their lives than their sons. Because few Pilipinos were older than forty-five, they were more likely statistically to have gone farther in school than other Chicagoans. Yet, a correction removing the post-forty-five generation from the calculation would probably not raise the white median to that of the Pilipinos. In 1920, only thirty-two percent of America's high-school-aged youth were enrolled in school; in 1930, the figure had just passed fifty percent for the nation as a whole.[26]

But their additional years of schooling gave Pilipinos little competitive advantage in Chicago. The young men soon found that their skin color defined the occupations which they might enter, the income which they might earn, and the mobility which they might experience. Those in Chicago's service sector, where three-fifths of the Pilipinos worked, had a median yearly income of $824 in 1940; those classified as "operatives" in the city's numerous industries, the twenty-two percent of the population most likely to contain a heavy concentration of white ethnics, took home a median income of $1,092 in that year.[27] While it is true that Pilipinos employed by the Pullman Company—the only Chicago occupational group as yet studied in detail—earned over $1,200 per year, not including tips, after the Brotherhood of Sleeping Car Porters signed its first contract with the company in 1937, even the Pullman attendants experienced racial barriers on the job. Like Black porters, Pilipino attendants found themselves barred from more responsible, more highly paid conductor positions because Pullman restricted these jobs to whites.[28] Thus, if Chicago provided Pilipinos with the best opportunities available in the United States, it is only in comparison with the West Coast situation. By 1940, Pilipinos in Chicago had moved into "clerical" and "craftsmen" categories more rapidly than Los Angeles and San Francisco residents (Table 1). But the disadvantages experienced by Chicago Pilipinos are obvious when the comparison is made with the city's whites (Table 2).

Pilipinos experienced similar problems in housing and recreation. Newcomers in the 1920s found most neighborhoods closed to brown men with low incomes. By this decade, inventive Chicagoans had begun covering the city with restrictive covenants specifically designed to foreclose Black penetration of white areas; other minorities were also excluded. Declared constitutional in 1926, these covenants gave legal teeth to pervasive prejudice. During the 1920s, white Chicago still smarted from the aftermath of the Black-white race riot of 1919. Many white Chicagoans supported the *Chicago Tribune's* policy: "Black Man, Stay South."[29]

Unlike Blacks, Pilipinos were never ghettoized. Many first found housing on the near West Side, in an Italian-dominated, polyglot, ethnic area near the factories and warehouses bordering the central business district. Here, the "Pinoys" frequently clashed with young Italians who viewed brown-skinned men as a challenge to white "turf."[30] Seventy-six-year-old Philip A. Lontoc recalled the dangers of walking alone. Conrado Ocampo remembered that groups of Pilipinos would send one of their number down the street alone while the rest hid. After that brave soul drew an attack, the others would rush to do battle.[31] When Domingo C. Manzon arrived in the city in the mid-1920s, young Pilipinos on the West Side had already formed the Filipino Association of Chicago, an umbrella organization under which the various provincial clubs functioned.

During the next decade, the focus on Chicago's Pilipino community shifted from the near West Side to the near North Side, into an area less linked with a particular ethnic group, an area closer to the "Gold Coast" mansions where many were employed. As on the West Side, Pilipinos found housing in declining apartment buildings, often living in groups to save on expenses. Here too, by 1930, a club house with pool hall, barbershop, and frequent dances appeared. In return for permitting Protestant church services on its premises, the overwhelmingly Catholic Pilipino population secured an annual contribution of approximately two hundred dollars from the board of directors of the Chicago Theological Seminary, which extended its appropriation into the 1940s.[32] Despite this support, however, most Pilipinos remained nominally Catholic. Some travelled to the southern end of the Chicago Loop where, as members of the CYO (Catholic Youth Organization), they attended meetings and movies at the Paulist mission, Old St. Mary's Church. But for most, church attendance was irregular.

On the near North Side, Pilipinos found Chinese restaurants, pool halls, and dance halls which welcomed the money they spent. No specific ethnic group consistently challenged their presence. But around the city and even in the neighborhood where most Pilipinos lived, no one could guarantee Pilipinos freedom from insult or physical violence

Table 2. Chicago: 1940. Male Education and Occupation

	Pilipino	White	Black	Other
Median Years Schooling		7.5FB[a]		
	12.2	9.4NB	7.7	NA
Professional & Semiprofessional	3.8	7.0	3.3	6.1
Farmer & Farm Manager	—	.1	.1	—
Proprietor, Manager & Official	1.0	10.7	2.7	20.9
Clerical/Sales	11.5	22.3	10.1	8.9
Craftsman/Foreman	3.2	20.3	9.2	2.6
Operative	10.5	22.2	20.1	27.3
Domestic Service	4.6	.1	1.4	2.0
Service	59.1	8.8	32.8	29.9
Farm Laborer	—	.1	.1	—
Nonfarm Laborer	6.2	8.1	20.1	2.6
No Occupation Reported	.2	.5	.4	.1
Total	100.0	100.0	100.0	100.0

[a]FB = Foreign-born; NB = Native-born.

Source: U.S. Bureau of the Census, *1950 Census of Population: Characteristics of the Nonwhite Population by Race*, 111–112; *ibid., Population*, vol. 2, "Characteristics of the Population," 642; *ibid., Population*, vol. 3, "The Labor Force," 874–75, 898.

on the streets. This situation, one may speculate, flowed from Chicago's own racial climate, rather than from knowledge of the confrontations occurring between Pilipinos and whites on the West Coast. A city which had succeeded in confining a once-scattered Black population to specific enclaves in the years since 1910 found little need to base its treatment of brown men on the attitudes of white Californians.[33] This basic racial tension was heightened whenever a Pilipino appeared in public with a white woman, and in the 1920s and 1930s, virtually all Chicago Pilipinos found their female contact limited to women who were white.

In 1940, six years after unrestricted immigration by Pilipinos to the United States had been halted by law, Chicago's Pilipino community held 1,298 residents over the age of twenty, of whom only sixty-one were female. This striking sexual imbalance, a ratio of 21:1, had already forced a significant number of men in the community to find wives outside their own group. By 1940, 532 men had married, only fifty-four to Pilipinas; 478, or ninety percent of the marriages within the community, were "mixed."[34]

From the perspective of the men, the choice of an "American" wife is readily understandable, given the likely alternative—remaining single. In addition, in the racially charged atmosphere of Chicago, Pilipinos took pride in their individual ability to date and marry white women despite their persistent dream of returning to the Philippines. But the motivation underlying the women's choice of nonwhite spouses requires more careful consideration. From interviews, a general portrait emerges. The women, in their early twenties when they married, were most frequently the daughters of immigrant parents of the working class. Their educations generally ended after eighth grade, when family custom and financial circumstances dictated their entry into the labor force. As with working-class daughters in general, the earnings of these young women from light factory work, waitressing and, less frequently, office work were turned over to their parents, who returned to the girls a small allowance for clothing, recreation, and other necessities. One elderly woman recalled her own situation in the Polish household in which she grew up:

> I got fifteen dollars a week [filling bottles at a flavoring extract company]. You had to turn your pay over to your mother. Mom gave me five dollars back. It was so hard. If you wanted a pair of silk stockings, the cheapest was a dollar ninety-nine. . . . And if you lost your job, there was hell to pay from Pa until you found another.

While she and her sisters had been sent to work at age fourteen or fifteen, her brothers had attended high school; the youngest, college. Yet, if the work was dull, the pay poor, and the conditions hard both on the job and at home, these young women did win a measure of independence remarkable within the authoritarian confines of the ethnic household. Once the day's work was finished, and their household chores were completed, they ranged far throughout the city in search of recreation; movies and dancing were favored pastimes.[35]

In time, through word passed by sisters, friends, and co-workers, many heard of what seemed a remarkable opportunity. At the Plaza "Dancing School" on North Clark Street, they might earn money while dancing. Another Polish woman reminisced:

> We used to go to the Riverview Ballroom. We loved dancing. All of us girls loved dancing. So we used to go and pay to dance at the Riverview Ballroom and the Trianon. So when we could go to the Plaza School and dance for nothing and make money that was a great thing for us. We thought, "Oh, how wonderful. We can make money and enjoy ourselves," because we just loved dancing. . . . What we earned at the school, that was for our clothes.

Taxi-dance halls such as the Plaza on Chicago's near North Side enabled a young woman to triple her weekly spending money in several evenings; each ten-cent dance ticket collected was split between the proprietor and the dancers.[36]

The dance halls were frequented by men of many nationalities, but among the most regular in attendance were Chicago's Pilipinos, who found that money might buy the feminine companionship their skin color prevented elsewhere. Plaza rules forbade after-hours contact between dancers and patrons, but "you always found a way." In the absence of an outright legal ban against cross-racial unions, even the stringent social taboos then in force failed to prevent relationships from forming. Dating began, and interracial marriage followed.

Immaculately dressed and frequently well-spoken, the Pilipinos presented a level of culture and refinement which the women had not generally experienced. With their courtly ways, the Pilipinos were lavish with attention, good times, and gifts. Those who were still in school or who held regular employment seemed to promise secure futures—at least in the immediate months ahead. Most importantly, first contacts with the Pilipinos came as a stark contrast with the Americans they had dated. One woman recalled:

> I was going out with a Polish fellow . . . but him and his buddy . . . tried to rough me up a little bit, and I lost all faith in him, almost in all men, but when we met the Pilipinos they were so gentle. They were such gentlemen.

Another remembered the trauma of an engagement to an Irish lad, broken only three weeks before the wedding after a mysterious conference between the young man and a priest. Marriage to a Pilipino appeared an escape from the world of their mothers—a world of authoritarian husbands, multiple childbirths, and daughters consigned to a recapitulation of the experience. Like the women's fashionable clothing, their Pilipino husbands were a "modern" choice. Potential problems never crossed their minds. "What did we know! We were green!" And, they were in love.

Not all found their future husbands while working as taxi dancers, but most involvements came through situations in which contact with Pilipinos, if not encouraged, was at least tolerated. Forty-nine years ago, a Czech girl from an Iowa farm community, working as a waitress in the city and sharing an apartment with her sister and brother-in-law, began dating a fellow building resident, a Pilipino, and married him a year later. While Protestant reformers debated "bring[ing] in high-type American girls from outside communities" to counteract "exploitation by women of bad character, 'gold-diggers,' " the Pilipinos' typical pattern of residence, employment, and recreation made likely their choice of working-class, ethnic wives.[37]

The actual decision to marry was often made with speed and on impulse. Though both parties were frequently Catholic, none of the interviewees considered a church wedding necessary or possible at that point.[38] After a five-month courtship, during which they "didn't see each other that often," one couple joined another in eloping to Crown Point, Indiana, the site favored by most interracial couples for the ease with which a license and a ceremony could be obtained. On a wintry, Sunday evening in November 1931, the four hired a taxi for the nearly hundred-mile round-trip, found a Justice of the Peace, and returned that same night to dinner at a Chinese restaurant and a shared apartment. Purchase of rings and thoughts of problems came later.

Confrontations with ethnic families they had seemingly abandoned became a chronic difficulty for the women. Though several marriages met acquiescence—"*You* have to live with him!"—parents more frequently reacted with anger and a tenacious refusal to accept the interracial union for years to come. In one instance, a Polish couple discovered that two daughters, a seventeen-year-old and a twenty-year-old, had both married Pilipinos. Both girls had gone their own way for some time, living at home and working daytime factory jobs to keep a regular sum flowing to the family each week, but also dancing for pay in secret. The parents adamantly refused to meet their new sons-in-law, yet encouraged the girls to visit frequently, hoping that their regard for their mother would eventually draw them back into the family—and away from their unacceptable husbands. The youngest succumbed within a year, and chose a Polish lad for her second matrimonial venture. The eldest continued torn, making weekly visits for five years, before her family relented and, symbolically, gave the couple a blanket for their fifth anniversary. But for three more decades, the couple could never be certain that invitations to family gatherings would arrive addressed to both husband and wife.

Another continuing problem facing the couples was the search for a place of residence. The ease with which the couples had been accepted as they socialized at the taxi-dance hall, at Pilipino clubhouse activities, at cafés on the near North Side and in Chinatown, and at nightclubs in Chicago's Black Belt evaporated all too quickly with the reality of life as husband and wife. Rejection after rejection greeted their answering of "apartment for rent" advertisements and signs. Once a landlord willing to accept a Pilipino and his white wife was found, his building quickly became a haven for other interracial couples, thereby reinforcing the ties among them. In one instance, a large, courtyard apartment building in the nine hundred block of Cornelia Avenue in Chicago's Lake View neighborhood sheltered at least fifteen Pilipino-American families during a twenty-five-year period extending into the 1950s.[39] While not all these residents occupied apartments simultaneously, the effect of even successive occupancy was considerable. Similarly, on the city's near Northwest

Side, in the aging Wicker Park district, at least seven families found apartments within a two-block radius, most in another courtyard building whose owner, a sympathetic Polish widow, had come to value the Pilipino American renters as good tenants. Yet, one white wife recalls "begging" for an apartment for friends—another interracial couple—in the 1950s; the landlady's figurative mental quota had already been reached. Although she relented in this case, she vowed that it would be the last.

Like these buildings, most locations where Pilipino American couples found apartments in Chicago were in white neighborhoods characterized by ethnic mixture rather than identification with a single group. By conscious choice, partners scrupulously avoided Black areas in the belief that residence in the ghetto would further diminish their tenuous status in white society.[40] In their white, multiethnic neighborhoods, couples generally found neighbors to be sociable in the halls and on the sidewalks. Residents of whatever race shared an implicitly understood inability to secure more expensive quarters, though topics of conversation remained explicitly impersonal, and close friendships between white and interracial couples rarely formed. As they came to be known and recognized on their blocks, Pilipino husbands and white wives could more comfortably appear together in this limited sphere.

Such security was not abandoned lightly, and families often remained in their apartments for over a decade, seeking to avoid the anxiety that the search for a new home might bring. During the mid-1950s, one couple attempted to purchase a home near the wife's sister on the far Northwest Side of Chicago, only to be informed after having cashed their savings bonds for the down payment, that the willing seller had come under severe pressure from neighbors unwilling to see the block integrated. For years after the incident, the husband remained so traumatized by the event that neither the pressure of wife nor family could induce him to leave an increasingly dangerous locale. When he did consent to a change, he moved his family to a flat above his widowed father-in-law, knowing that in this way, he might avoid the rejection of strangers. Few Pilipino American couples of the "old-timer" generation secured the American dream—the new home in the suburbs—which captured so many in the years after World War II. Home ownership, when attained, generally meant the purchase of an older home in a city neighborhood, or in a less-developed, often unincorporated, suburban area.

Years after their marriages, other ventures into the wider community remained cautious, as in California, where the daughter of an interracial couple recalled: "Father never walked beside us. He was always either ahead of us or behind us."[41] Chicagoans sometimes sat apart on buses in the early years, and refrained from dining in "American" restaurants for most of their lives.

As they confronted familial and social rejection, the women understandably turned to each other for companionship and understanding. Dinners and parties at each other's apartments, group ventures to Pilipino-sponsored dances at clubs and hotels, outings to Chinese restaurants where prejudice was never a problem—such activities sustained a sense of community. Though "community" never comprised the entire interracial population in any effective sense, smaller cliques formed on the basis of provincial loyalties carried with the men from the Islands; because of work-related contact among husbands at the Pullman Company or in specific hotels; and from residential proximity.

Additionally, the women felt most comfortable with wives originally met just before or immediately after their own marriages—women whose circumstances while single were similar to their own. These women came to be closest friends, capable of discussing openly the frequent "wounds" delivered by outsiders to participants in interracial marriages. And, more importantly, their conversations with female friends helped them to adjust, individually and collectively, to the new culture they encountered in marriage to men from the Philippines. The individual traits exhibited by their husbands, when ascribed to the group, seemed more comprehensible, if not less irritating. Seemingly excessive hospitality, demanding hours in the kitchen from both husband and wife and a virtual open-door policy with regard to the frequency of "company," became the accepted norm as "something we all did." And, while their husbands' tendency to lapse into native dialect when together forced gatherings into a sex-segregated pattern, the women found some relief in collective criticism. These avenues of support were particularly important to women whose husbands worked for the Pullman Company and were customarily away from home for three to six day periods at least half the time. With their husbands gone, visiting among the women took on added importance; in emergencies, friends were nearby, and in ordinary times, lonely hours were filled.[42]

The ability to define and continue more fundamental values was ultimately of greater importance to the endurance of their interracial marriages. Faithfulness to one's spouse and devotion to one's children—traditional moral and familial values—constituted basic norms for those whose marriages survived. For example, couples with children exhibited near uniform agreement that wives should not work outside the home since husbands working for Pullman were out of the city for days at a time. As one wife commented:

> I worked twelve weeks . . . when my kids were small . . . in a plastic place. . . . I liked that better than housework. . . . The youngest ones were going to grammar school. But it never worked out with the kids. It's hard. He's out on the road. . . . If you have kids, you should stay around home.

Tacit agreement was also achieved in other areas. In keeping with the customs of both Pilipino and ethnic cultures, wives exercised considerable control over their husbands' wages, knowing the exact amount of earnings, savings, and expenditures. Decisions regarding purchases were made jointly, and wives never "asked" for money. In contrast with the perpetuation of this tradition, spouses generally abandoned explicit cultural identification in the raising of their children, preferring instead to define a new "American" emphasis. Both Pilipino husbands and ethnic wives believed that becoming "American" would assist their offspring in achieving success. Wives raised in non-English speaking homes and educated in ethnic parochial schools vowed that their children would not be handicapped by a second language and accented English; most sent their children to public schools. Thus, *mestizo* children knew few words in either their mothers' or their fathers' native tongue. Similarly, husbands and wives never learned the original language of the other, a fact which severely limited the Pilipino husbands' communication with their wives' elderly ethnic relatives; conversations between white wives and visitors from the Philippines were conducted in English. In the era during which most of their children grew to maturity, an era before ethnic consciousness came to be emphasized, cultural identity was most visible in the food served at the family table. At parties, husbands' and wives' ethnic specialties appeared side by side; potatoes and rice competed at daily dinners.[43]

These broad spheres of agreement coexisted with areas of subtle tension as well, areas in which agreement or compromise emerged only over time. Trust between marriage partners was sometimes clouded not only by personal incidents, but also by group reputation. For one wife, the dismay and the anger involved in finding that her husband had not made her the beneficiary of his insurance policy after several years of marriage loomed as a grievance even after over forty years. His explanation—that many Pilipinos had been "taken" by American women met at "dancing schools"—had been rejected as irrelevant. Yet, at the same time, she remembered wondering in those early years if he could really "settle down"; "the boys were pretty wild when they were single." And she recalled stalking out of a dance one evening when his attentions to another woman became too obvious. But, as might be expected in marriages which persisted over decades, trust and acceptance grew. Husbands who "strayed" and wives who "ran around" were judged immoral—foolish at best.

Concerns over the planning of a family and the disciplining of children needed resolution as well. While ethnicity and race divided the spouses, many couples "practiced" a common Catholicism. Yet the large-family norm, rarely questioned in the Philippines, found direct challenge from the American wives. Though her husband wanted six children, and maintains his wish to this day, one forceful wife countered effectively:

> I wanted three. I put a stop to it. . . . I could have had a dozen, like my grandma had fifteen. I said forget it. No way. . . . If I had had my way, I would have had one.

In another instance, a wife in her late forties sought support from her gynecologist against a husband who maintained that the religious ceremony performed twenty-five years after their court elopement now precluded the use of birth control; they and their only child, an eleven-year-old born fourteen years after their marriage, then occupied a two and a half room apartment and had few prospects for a quick move to more commodious quarters. In this case, as in the first, the wife's more realistic assessment of economic conditions outweighed her husband's preference for tradition. Similarly, most Pilipino American families were small; American women bore an average of 1.38 children during their marriages to the Pilipinos of this study. Only the rare family unit contained four or five offspring.

Just as the topic of family limitation sometimes caused tension between husbands and wives, so too could differing standards of acceptable behavior for growing children provoke disagreement. In one family, while their daughter was small, the mother accused the father of excessive permissiveness—showering the child with toys, buying the girl high heels before her eighth-grade graduation, and allowing her to "talk back" without severe reprimand. In contrast, once the child reached adolescence, he attempted to enforce a strict code of conduct derived from his own youthful experience with sisters and sweethearts back in the Islands—a code which his wife believed would only encourage their daughter to rebel. Long discussions, late into many nights, debated recurring conflicts over dating and curfew which continued until their daughter accepted a job offer in another city and left the family home. In most families, the mothers took responsibility for setting disciplinary norms, partly because they remained at home while their Pullman husbands traveled. In addition, given the families' emphasis on Americanization, mothers born in the United States seemed more able to guide the adolescents than fathers born abroad, and fathers generally acquiesced in accepting the contention, "that's the way things are done here."

As they aged and as their families grew to maturity, the sources of support for these interracial couples began to change. With the passage of time, both societal and familial antagonisms began to diminish. In the climate of the emerging civil rights movement of the 1960s, and with the migration of a professional population from the Philippines in the years after 1965, the Pilipino old-timers rediscovered their racial heritage and took pride in their survival in a hostile environment for so many years. As their children formed families of their own, without exception marrying men and women of ethnic origins other than Pilipino, and as they frequently found a "success," defined by education and income, which had eluded the Pilipino immigrants and their white wives, the older couples took comfort in a vicarious, ultimate integration into American life. Though many of their children were easily identifiable as Asian in heritage, their culture had become an amalgam of old and new. In the 1960s and 1970s, as they gathered at the Dr. Jose Rizal Community Center in Chicago with the newer, younger, and often more prosperous professionals who had immigrated since 1965, the old-timers sometimes discovered that their attitudes toward politics, family life, and nationality had become more "American" than those of their countrymen.

During the lengthy marriages of the couples surveyed for this study, the social and economic pressures which they faced consistently linked husbands and wives together against the society around them; for this reason, the determination to succeed in their marriages became, for several wives, an explicit and vital goal. Of course, not all interracial marriages formed in these years endured. Many women, once married to Pilipinos, have disappeared completely from view, and without their experiences this picture of interracial life must necessarily remain tentative and incomplete. Yet, in a sense, in seeking the basis of Chicago's Pilipino American community, theirs is not the critical story, for the community derives its heritage from those who formed lasting bonds across racial lines.

Notes

This article, an earlier version of which was presented at The Fifth Berkshire Conference on the History of Women, Vassar College, June 1981, has benefited from the comments and criticism generously offered by Professors Roger Daniels of the University of Cincinnati and Roland L. Guyotte of the University of Minnesota, Morris.

1. U.S. Bureau of the Census, *1940 Census of Population: Characteristics of the Nonwhite Population by Race* (Washington, D.C., 1943), 5–6; U.S. Bureau of the Census, *1970 Census of Population, Subject Reports: Japanese, Chinese, and Filipinos in the United States* (Washington, D.C., 1973), 119, 169; *Associated Filipino Press* (30 December 1934), in Bessie Louise Pierce Notes, Chicago Historical Society.

2. U.S., *1940 Census*, 112. See also, Barbara M. Posadas, "The Hierarchy of Color and Psychological Adjustment in an Industrial Environment: Filipino Immigrants, the Pullman Company and the Brotherhood of Sleeping Car Porters," (Paper delivered at the Eighth Annual Conference on Ethnic and Minority Studies, University of Wisconsin-LaCrosse, 25 April 1980).

3. Roger Daniels, "Comments by Roger Daniels: Filipino Immigration in Historical Perspective," in Josefa M. Saniel, ed., *The Filipino Exclusion Movement: 1927–1935* (Quezon City, Philippines, 1967), 49.

4. Roger Daniels, "North American Scholarship and Asian Immigrants, 1974–1979," *Immigration History Newsletter* eleven (May 1979). Important contributions since the publication of Daniels' article include: Sucheng Chan, *Asian Americans: An Interpretive History* (Boston, 1991); Fred Cordova, *Filipinos: Forgotten Asian Americans* (Dubuque, Iowa, 1983); and Ronald T. Takaki, *Strangers From a Different Shore: A History of Asian Americans* (Boston, 1989).

5. H. Brett Melendy, *Asians in America: Filipinos, Koreans, and East Asians* (Boston, 1977).

6. See for example: Emory S. Bogardus, "The Filipino Immigrant Problem," *Sociology and Social Research* 13 (May–June 1929), 472–479; and "American Attitudes toward Filipinos," *ibid.* 14 (September–October 1929), 59–69; Bruno Lasker, *Filipino Immigration to the Continental United States and Hawaii* (Chicago, 1931); Honorante Mariano, *The Filipino Immigrant in the United States* (1933; San Francisco, 1972); Trinidad A. Rojo, "Social Maladjustment among Filipinos in the United States," *Sociology and Social Research* 21 (1937), 447–457; Benicio T. Catapusan, "The Social Adjustment of Filipinos in the United States," (Ph.D. dissertation, University of Southern California, 1940); Carey McWilliams, "The Little Brown Brother," in *Brothers Under the Skin* (1943; Boston, 1951), 229–249; John H. Burma, "The Background of the Current Situation of Filipino-Americans," *Social Forces* 30 (October 1951), 42–48.

7. Bok Lim C. Kim and Margaret E. Andon, *A Study of Asian Americans in Chicago: Their Socio-Economic Characteristics, Problems and Service Needs* (Washington, D.C., 1975); Wayne S. Wooden and J. H. Monane, "Cultural Community, Cohesion and Constraint: Dynamics of Life Satisfaction among Aged Filipino Men of Hawaii," *Explorations in Ethnic Studies* 3 (July 1980), 25–39; Royal F. Morales, *Makibaka: The Pilipino American Struggle* (Los Angeles, 1973); Jovina Navarro, ed., *Diwang Pilipino: Pilipino Consciousness* (Davis,

1974); Jesse Quinsaat, ed., *Letters in Exile: An Introductory Reader on the History of Pilipinos in America* (Los Angeles, 1976); Jovina Navarro, ed., *Lahing Pilipino: A Pilipino American Anthology* (Davis, 1977).

8. Sonia E. Wallovits, "The Filipinos in California," (M.A. Thesis, University of Southern California, 1966); H. Brett Melendy, "California's Discrimination against Filipinos, 1927–1935," in Saniel, *The Filipino Exclusion Movement,* 3–10; Ruben R. Alcantara, "The Filipino Community in Waialua," (Ph.D. dissertation, University of Hawaii, 1973); Adelaida Castillo, "Filipino Migrants in San Diego, 1900–1946," *Journal of San Diego History* 22 (1976), 26–35; Edwin B. Almirol, "Ethnic Identity and Social Negotiation: A Study of a Filipino Community in California," (Ph.D. dissertation, University of Illinois at Urbana-Champaign, 1977); *ibid.*, "Filipino Voluntary Associations: Balancing Social Pressures and Ethnic Images," *Ethnic Groups* 2 (1978), 65–92; Miriam Sharma, "Pinoy in Paradise: Environment and Adaptation of Pilipinos in Hawaii, 1906–1946," *Amerasia* 7:2 (Fall/Winter 1980), 91–117.

9. Morales, *Makibaka,* 118.

10. Juanita Tamayo Lott, "An Attempt," in Navarro, *Diwang Pilipino,* 9.

11. Exceptions are Albert W. Palmer, *Orientals in American Life* (New York, 1934), which contains an eight-page section on the Chicago community and Benny F. Feria's memoirs, *Filipino Son* (Boston, 1954). See also, Roberto V. Valangca, *Pinoy: The First Wave (1898–1941)* (San Francisco, 1977), which includes the brief reminiscences of several Pilipinos who lived in Chicago; and Precioso M. Nicanor, *Profiles of Notable Filipinos in the U.S.A.* (New York, 1963), which contains biographical sketches of New York Pilipinos.

12. U.S. *1940 Census,* 5, 111–12; U.S. *1960 Census of Population: Characteristics of the Population* 1:15, *Illinois* (Washington, 1963), 58.

13. C. M. Goethe quoted in Melendy, *Asians in America,* 61.

14. On intermarriage, see Alida C. Bowler, "Social Hygiene in Racial Problems—The Filipino," *Journal of Social Hygiene* 18 (1932), 452–457; Nellie Foster, "Legal Status of Filipino Intermarriages in California," *Sociology and Social Research* 16 (May–June 1932), 441–454; Romanzo Adams, *Interracial Marriage in Hawaii: A Study of the Mutually Conditioned Processes of Acculturation and Amalgamation* (1937; Montclair, NJ, 1969); Benicio T. Catapusan, "Filipino Intermarriage Problems in the United States," *Sociology and Social Research* 22 (January–February 1938), 265–272; Severino F. Corpus, "Second Generation Filipinos in Los Angeles," *ibid.* 22 (May–June 1938), 446–451; Constantine Panunzio, "Intermarriage in Los Angeles, 1924–1933," *American Journal of Sociology* 47 (March 1942), 690–701; Randall Risdon, "A Study of Interracial Marriages Based on Data for Los Angeles County," *Sociology and Social Research* 39 (1954), 92–95; and John H. Burma, "Interethnic Marriage in Los Angeles, 1948–1959," *Social Forces* 42 (December 1963), 156–65. See also the discussion of cultural adaptation and conflict in Catapusan, "The Social Adjustment of Filipinos in the United States," 76–88. On U.S. laws governing interracial marriage, see Milton L. Barron, ed., *The Blending American: Patterns of Intermarriage* (Chicago, 1972), 77–84.

15. Iris Brown Buaken, "My Brave New World," *Asia and the Americas* 43 (May 1943), 268–70; Iris Brown Buaken, "You Can't Marry a Filipino: Not If You Live in California," *Commonweal* 41 (16 March 1945), 534–537; Manuel Buaken, *I Have Lived with the American People* (Caldwell, Idaho, 1948), 127–129. On contact between Pilipino men and white women from the male perspective, see Carlos Bulosan, *America Is in the Heart: A Personal History* (New York, 1946).

16. Unless otherwise specified, the material for this paper has been derived from a series of thirteen interviews with American wives and Pilipino husbands conducted during 1979 and 1981. Because of the sensitive nature of the material presented, the respondents remain anonymous. The men and women interviewed consider themselves typical of Chicago's "old-timer" Pilipino community. The Pilipinos' lives reveal varied marital patterns. Some left wives behind in the Islands. Some saw early unions with American women fail. All tried again, and sometimes found greater success—if duration is the measure. Others married once; since they are now in their late seventies and eighties, it would seem, for life. So too, while some women married their Pilipino husbands after an earlier divorce, others entered first marriages which endured. The representativeness of these couples lies, therefore, in the diversity of their experiences. Yet, it is likely that the West Coast pattern differs sharply. California's legal prohibition against Pilipino-white intermarriage, enacted in 1933, effectively foreclosed the option enjoyed by Chicago couples, (see, for example, Iris Brown Buaken, "You Can't Marry a Filipino," and Henry Empeno, *et al.*, "Anti-Miscegenation Laws and the Pilipino," in Quinsaat, ed., *Letters in Exile,* 63–71). The extent, nature and persistence of interracial unions formed on the West Coast without formal ceremony or legalized in other states have yet to be examined; for a brief memoir of a California interracial marriage, see "Frank Coloma," in Vallangca, *Pinoy: The First Wave,* 86–89.

17. U.S. *1940 Census,* 112; *ibid.*, vol. 3, "The Labor Force: Occupation, Industry, Employment, and Income," (Washington, D.C., 1943), 874–875.

18. U.S. *1940 Census,* 111.

19. Leopoldo T. Ruiz, "Filipino Students in the United States," (M.A. thesis, Columbia University, 1924), 40–47.

20. On the extend and impact of American education in the Philippines, see Encarnacion Alzona, *A History of Education in the Philippines, 1565–1930* (Manila, Philippines, 1932) and Glenn Anthony May, *Social Engineering in the Philippines: The Aims, Execution, and Impact of American Colonial Policy, 1900–1913* (Westport, CT, 1980), chs. 5–7.

21. Posadas, "The Hierarchy of Color."

22. Buaken, *I Have Lived with the American People*, 33–38.

23. *Ibid.*, 38; Mariano, *The Filipino Immigrant in the United States*, pp. 10–12.

24. City of Chicago, Department of Development and Planning, *The People of Chicago: Who We Are and Who We Have Been, Census Data on Foreign Born, Foreign Stock and Race, 1837–1970* (Chicago, 1976), 33–39. On ethnic and Black settlement, see, for example: Humbert S. Nelli, *Italians in Chicago, 1880–1930* (New York, 1970) and Allan Spear, *Black Chicago: The Making of a Negro Ghetto, 1890–1920* (Chicago, 1967).

25. U.S. *1940 Census*, vol. 2, "Characteristics of the Population," (Washington, D.C., 1943), 642.

26. David Nasaw, *Schooled to Order: A Social History of Public Schooling in the United States* (New York, 1979), 163.

27. U.S. *1940 Census*, volume 3, "The Labor Force," 874–875, 898.

28. Posadas, "The Hierarchy of Color."

29. Thomas Lee Philpott, *The Slum and the Ghetto: Neighborhood Deterioration and Middle-Class Reform, Chicago, 1880–1930* (New York, 1978), 189; Spear, *Black Chicago*, 202.

30. Palmer, *Orientals in American Life*, 97; Vallangca, *Pinoy: The First Wave*, 84.

31. *Ibid.*, 134.

32. "Minutes of the Board of Directors of Chicago Theological Seminary," (September 1926–November 25, 1942), Chicago Theological Seminary.

33. Spear, *Black Chicago*.

34. U.S. *1940 Census*, 109–110.

35. On the working-class daughters of immigrant families, see Louise Montgomery, *The American Girl in the Stockyards District* (Chicago, 1913), and Leslie Woodcock Tentler, *Wage-Earning Women: Industrial Work and Family Life in the United States, 1900–1930* (New York, 1979), 85–135.

36. *Polk's Chicago (Illinois) City Directory 1928–1929* (Chicago, 1928), 3389. On the "dancing school" milieu in Chicago, see Paul G. Cressey, *The Taxi-Dance Hall: A Sociological Study in Commercialized Recreation and City Life* (Chicago, 1932), especially ch. 7, "The Filipino and the Taxi-Dance Hall," 145–174; and "Anacleto Gorospe," in Vallangca, *Pinoy: The First Wave*, 84–85. Dance halls were also a common form of recreation for the California Pilipinos; see, for example, Benicio Catapusan, "The Filipino Occupational and Recreational Activities in Los Angeles," (M.A. thesis, University of Southern California, 1934), 65–84; Vallangca, *Pinoy: The First Wave*, 50–53; and the fictionalized account set in San Francisco in Precioso M. Nicanor, *Martyrs Never Die* (New York, 1968), 114–123.

37. Palmer, *Orientals in American Life*, 99, 102.

38. The interviewees also recall several marriages between Pilipinos and women of Jewish heritage. In Hawaii, Pilipinos tended to intermarry with Christian women of varied ethnic backgrounds, rather than non-Christian Asian women, (see Adams, *Interracial Marriage in Hawaii*, 180).

39. *City of Chicago Directory* 1 (Chicago, 1950), 206.

40. Similarly, Pilipino members of the predominantly Black Brotherhood of Sleeping Car Porters rarely attended union "soirees," in part because their white wives would not have felt comfortable at the Black social gatherings. See Posadas, "The Hierarchy of Color."

41. Alfredo N. Munoz, *The Filipinos in America* (Los Angeles, 1971), 118.

42. On the preservation of a hospitality "tradition" by Pilipino men in the United States, see Burt W. Aginsky and Ethel G. Aginsky, "The Process of Change in Family Types: A Case Study," *American Anthropologist* 51 (1949), 611–614; and Ruben R. Alcantara, "The Filipino Wedding in Waialua, Hawaii," *Amerasia* 1 (February 1972), 1–12.

43. This tendency toward the Americanization of "hybridized offspring" was noted as early as 1940 in Catapusan, "The Filipino Social Adjustment in the United States," 86.

21

"It Jus Be's Dat Way Sometime":
The Sexual Politics of Women's Blues

Hazel V. Carby

This essay considers the sexual politics of women's blues in the 1920s. Their story is part of a larger history of the production of Afro-American culture within the North American culture industry. My research has concentrated almost exclusively on those black women intellectuals who were part of the development of an Afro-American literature culture and reflects the privileged place that we accord to writers in Afro-American Studies (Carby, 1987). Within feminist theory, the cultural production of black women writers has been analyzed in isolation from other forms of women's culture and cultural presence and has neglected to relate particular texts and issues to a larger discourse of culture and cultural politics. I want to show how the representation of black female sexuality in black women's fiction and in women's blues is clearly different. I argue that different cultural forms negotiate and resolve very different sets of social contradictions. However, before considering the particularities of black women's sexual representation, we should consider its marginality within a white-dominated feminist discourse.

In 1982, at the Barnard conference on the politics of sexuality, Hortense Spillers condemned the serious absence of consideration of black female sexuality from various public discourses including white feminist theory. She described black women as "the beached whales of the sexual universe, unvoiced, misseen, not doing, awaiting *their* verb." The sexual experiences of black women, she argued, were rarely depicted by themselves in what she referred to as "empowered texts": discursive feminist texts. Spillers complained of the relative absence of African-American women from the academy and thus from the visionary company of Anglo-American women feminists and their privileged mode of feminist expression.

The collection of the papers from the Barnard conference, the *Pleasure and Danger* (1984) anthology, has become one of these empowered feminist theoretical texts and Spillers' essay continues to stand within it as an important black feminist survey of the ways in which the sexuality of black American women has been unacknowledged in the public/critical discourse of feminist thought (Spillers, 1984). Following Spillers' lead black feminists continued to critique the neglect of issues of black female sexuality within feminist theory and, indeed, I as well as others directed many of our criticisms toward the *Pleasure and Danger* anthology itself (Carby, 1986).

As black women we have provided articulate and politically incisive criticism which is there for the feminist community at large to heed or to ignore—upon that decision lies the future possibility of forging a feminist movement that is not parochial. As the black

Reprinted by permission of the author and *Radical America*, vol. 20, no. 4, 1986.

feminist and educator Anna Julia Cooper stated in 1892, a woman's movement should not be based on the narrow concerns of white middle class women under the name of "women"; neither, she argued, should a woman's movement be formed around the exclusive concerns of either the white woman or the black woman or the red woman but should be able to address the concerns of all the poor and oppressed (Cooper, 1892).

But instead of concentrating upon the domination of a white feminist theoretical discourse which marginalizes non-white women, I focus on the production of a discourse of sexuality by black women. By analyzing the sexual and cultural politics of black women who constructed themselves as sexual subjects through song, in particular the blues, I want to assert an empowered presence. First, I must situate the historical moment of the emergence of women-dominated blues and establish a theoretical framework of interpretation and then I will consider some aspects of the representation of feminism, sexuality, and power in women's blues.

Movin' On

Before World War I the overwhelming majority of black people lived in the South, although the majority of black intellectuals who purported to represent the interests of "the race" lived in the North. At the turn of the century black intellectuals felt they understood and could give voice to the concerns of the black community as a whole. They were able to position themselves as spokespeople for the "race" because they were at a vast physical and metaphorical distance from the majority of those they represented. The mass migration of blacks to urban areas, especially to the cities of the North, forced these traditional intellectuals to question and revise their imaginary vision of "the people" and directly confront the actual displaced rural workers who were, in large numbers, becoming a black working class in front of their eyes. In turn the mass of black workers became aware of the range of possibilities for their representation. No longer were the "Talented Tenth," the practioners of policies of racial uplift, the undisputed "leaders of the race." Intellectuals and their constituencies fragmented, black union organizers, Marcus Garvey and the Universal Negro Improvement Association, radical black activists, the Sanctified Churches, the National Association of Colored Women, the Harlem creative artists, all offered alternative forms of representation and each strove to establish that the experience of their constituency was representative of the experience of the race.

Within the movement of the Harlem cultural renaissance, black women writers established a variety of alternative possibilities for the fictional representation of black female experience. Zora Neale Hurston chose to represent black people as the rural folk; the folk were represented as being both the source of Afro-American cultural and linguistic forms and the means for its continued existence. Hurston's exploration of sexual and power relations was embedded in this "folk" experience and avoided the cultural transitions and confrontations of the urban displacement. As Hurston is frequently situated as the foremother of contemporary black women writers, the tendency of feminist literary criticism has been to valorize black women as "folk" heroines at the expense of those texts which explored black female sexuality within the context of urban social relations. Put simply, a line of descent is drawn from *Their Eyes Were Watching God* to *The Color Purple*. But to establish the black "folk" as representative of the black community at large was and still is a convenient method for ignoring the specific contradictions of an urban existence in which most of us live. The culture industry, through its valorization in print and in film of *The Color Purple*, for example, can *appear* to comfortably address issues of black female sexuality within a past history and rural context while completely avoiding the crucial issues of black sexual and cultural politics that stem from an urban crisis.

"There's No Earthly Use In Bein Too-Ga-Tha If It Don't Put Some Joy In Yo Life." (Williams, 1981.)

However, two other women writers of the Harlem Renaissance, Jessie Fauset and Nella Larsen, did figure an urban class confrontation in their fiction, though in distinctly different ways. Jessie Fauset became an ideologue for a new black bourgeoisie; her novels represented the manners and morals that distinguished the emergent middle class from the working class. She wanted public recognition for the existence of a black elite that was urbane, sophisticated, and civilized but her representation of this elite implicitly defined its manners against the behavior of the new black proletariat. While it must be acknowledged that Fauset did explore the limitations of a middle-class existence for women, ultimately each of her novels depict independent women who surrender their independence to become suitable wives for the new black professional men.

Nella Larsen, on the other hand, offers us a more sophisticated dissection of the rural/urban confrontation. Larsen was extremely critical of the Harlem intellectuals who glorified the values of a black folk culture while being ashamed of and ridiculing the behavior of the new black migrant to the city. Her novel, *Quicksand* (1928), contains the first explicitly sexual black heroine in black women's fiction. Larsen explores questions of sexuality and power within both a rural and an urban landscape; in both contexts she condemns the ways in which female sexuality is confined and compromised as the object of male desire. In the city Larsen's heroine, Helga, has to recognize the ways in which her sexuality has an exchange value within capitalist social relations while in the country Helga is trapped by the consequences of woman's reproductive capacity. In the final pages of *Quicksand* Helga echoes the plight of the slave woman who could not escape to freedom and the cities of the North because she could not abandon her children and, at the same time, represents how a woman's life is drained through constant childbirth.

But Larsen also reproduces in her novel the dilemma of a black woman who tries to counter the dominant white cultural definitions of her sexuality: ideologies that define black female sexuality as a primitive and exotic. However the response of Larsen's heroine to such objectification is also the response of many black women writers: the denial of desire and the repression of sexuality. Indeed, *Quicksand* is symbolic of the tension in nineteenth and early twentieth-century black women's fiction in which black female sexuality was frequently displaced onto the terrain of the political responsibility of the black woman. The duty of the black heroine toward the black community was made coterminous with her desire as a woman, a desire which was expressed as a dedication to uplift the race. This displacement from female desire to female duty enabled the negotiation of racist constructions of black female sexuality but denied sensuality and in this denial lies the class character of its cultural politics.

It has been a mistake of much black feminist theory to concentrate almost exclusively on the visions of black women as represented by black women writers without indicating the limitations of their middle-class response to black women's sexuality. These writers faced a very real contradiction for they felt that they would publicly compromise themselves if they acknowledged their sexuality and sensuality within a racist sexual discourse thus providing evidence that indeed they were primitive and exotic creatures. But because black feminist theory has concentrated upon the literate forms of black women's intellectual activity the dilemma of the place of sexuality within a literary discourse has appeared as if it were the dilemma of most black women. On the other hand, what a consideration of women's blues allows us to see is an alternative form of representation, an oral and musical women's culture that explicitly addresses the contradictions of feminism, sexuality, and power. What has been called the "Classic Blues" the women's blues of the twenties and early thirties is a discourse that articulates a cultural and political struggle over sexual relations: a struggle that is directed against the objectification of female sexuality within a patriarchal order but which also tries to reclaim women's bodies as the sexual and sensuous subjects of women's song.

Testifyin'

Within black culture the figure of the female blues singer has been reconstructed in poetry, drama, fiction, and art and used to meditate upon conventional and unconventional sexuality. A variety of narratives, both fictional and biographical, have mythologized the woman blues singer and these mythologies become texts about sexuality. Women blues singers frequently appear as liminal figures that play out and explore the various possibilities of a sexual existence; they are representations of women who attempt to manipulate and control their construction as sexual subjects. In Afro-American fiction and poetry, the blues singer has a strong physical and sensuous presence. Shirley Anne Williams wrote about Bessie Smith:

> the thick triangular
> nose wedged
> in the deep brown
> face nostrils
> flared on a last hummmmmmmmm
>
> Bessie singing
> just behind the beat
> that sweet sweet
> voice throwing
> its light on me
>
> I looked in her face
> and seed the woman
> I'd become. A big
> boned face already
> lined and the first line
> in her fo'head was
> black and the next line
> was sex cept I didn't
> know to call it that
> then and the brackets
> round her mouth stood fo
> the chi'ren she teared
> from out her womb. . . . (Williams, 1982)

Williams has argued that the early blues singers and their songs "helped to solidify community values and heighten community morale in the late nineteenth and early twentieth centuries." The blues singer, she says, uses song to create reflection and creates an atmosphere for analysis to take place. The blues were certainly a communal expression of black experience which had developed out of the call and response patterns of work songs from the nineteenth century and have been described as a "complex interweaving of the general and the specific" and of individual and group experience. John Coltrane has described how the audience heard "we" even if the singer said "I." Of course the singers were entertainers but the blues was not an entertainment of escape or fantasy and sometimes directly represented historical events (Williams, 1979).

Sterling Brown has testified to the physical presence and power of Ma Rainey who would draw crowds from remote rural areas to see her "smilin' gold-toofed smiles" and to feel like participants in her performance which articulated the conditions of their social existence. Brown in his poem "Ma Rainey" remembers the emotion of her performance of "Back Water Blues" which described the devastation of the Mississippi flood of 1927. Rainey's original performance becomes in Brown's text a vocalization of the popular memory of the flood and Brown's text constructs itself as a part of the popular memory of the "Mother of the Blues" (Brown, 1981).

Ma Rainey never recorded "Backwater Blues" although Bessie Smith did but local songsters would hear the blues performed in the tent shows or on record and transmit them throughout the community. Ma Rainey and Bessie Smith were among the first women blues singers to be recorded and with Clara Smith, Ethel Waters, Alberta Hunter, Ida Cox, Rosa Henderson, Victoria Spivey, and Lucille Hegamin they dominated the blues-recording industry throughout the twenties. It has often been asserted that this recording of the blues compromised and adulterated a pure folk form of the blues but the combination of the vaudeville, carnival, and minstrel shows and the phonograph meant that the "folk-blues" and the culture industry product were inextricably mixed in the twenties. By 1928 the blues sung by blacks were only secondarily of folk origin and the primary source for the group transmission of the blues was by phonograph which was then joined by the radio.

Bessie Smith, Ma Rainey, Ethel Waters, and the other women blues singers travelled in carnivals and vaudevilles which included acts with animals, acrobats and other circus performers. Often the main carnival played principally for white audiences but would have black sideshows with black entertainers for black audiences. In this way black entertainers reached black audiences in even the remotest rural areas. The records of the women blues singers were likewise directed at a black audience through the establishment of "race records," a section of the recording industry which recorded both religious and secular black singers and black musicians and distributed these recordings through stores in black areas: they were rarely available in white neighborhoods.

When A Woman Gets The Blues . . .

This then is the framework within which I interpret the women blues singers of the twenties. To fully understand the ways in which their performance and their songs were part of a discourse of sexual relations within the black community, it is necessary to consider how the social conditions of black women were dramatically affected by migration, for migration had distinctively different meanings for black men and women. The music and song of the women blues singers embodied the social relations and contradictions of black displacement: of rural migration and the urban flux. In this sense, as singers these women were organic intellectuals; not only were they a part of the community that was the subject of their song but they were also a product of the rural-to-urban movement.

Migration for women often meant being left behind: "Bye Bye Baby" and "Sorry I can't take you" were the common refrains of male blues. In women's blues the response is complex: regret and pain expressed as "My sweet man done gone and left me dead," or

"My daddy left me standing in the door," or "The sound of the train fills my heart with misery." There was also an explicit recognition that if the journey were to be made by women it held particular dangers for them. It was not as easy for women as it was for men to hop freight trains and if money was saved for tickets it was men who were usually sent. And yet the women who were singing the songs had made it North and recorded from the "promised land" of Chicago and New York. So, what the women blues singers were able to articulate were the possibilities of movement for the women who "have ramblin on their minds" and who intended to "ease on down the line" for they had made it—the power of movement was theirs. The train, which had symbolized freedom and mobility for men in male blues songs, became a contested symbol. The sound of the train whistle, a mournful signal of imminent desertion and future loneliness was reclaimed as a sign that women too were on the move. In 1924, both Trixie Smith and Clara Smith recorded "Freight Train Blues." These are the words Clara Smith sang:

> I hate to hear that engine blow, boo hoo.
> I hate to hear that engine blow, boo hoo.
> Everytime I hear it blowin, I feel like ridin too.
>
> That's the freight train blues, I got box cars on my mind.
> I got the freight train blues, I got box cars on my mind.
> Gonna leave this town, cause my man is so unkind.
>
> I'm goin away just to wear you off my mind.
> I'm goin away just to wear you off my mind.
> And I may be gone for a doggone long long time.
>
> I'll ask the brakeman to let me ride the blind.
> I'll ask the brakeman to please let me ride the blind.
> The brakeman say, "Clara, you know this train ain't mine."
>
> When a woman gets the blues she goes to her room and hides.
> When a woman gets the blues she goes to her room and hides.
> When a man gets the blues he catch the freight train and rides.

The music moves from echoing the moaning, mournful sound of the train whistle to the syncopated activity of the sound of the wheels in movement as Clara Smith determines to ride. The final opposition between women hiding and men riding is counterpointed by this musical activity hiding and the determination in Clara Smith's voice. "Freight Train Blues" and then "Chicago Bound Blues," which was recorded by Bessie Smith and Ida Cox, were very popular so Paramount and Victor encouraged more "railroad blues." In 1925 Trixie Smith recorded "Railroad Blues" which directly responded to the line "had the blues for Chicago and I just can't be satisfied" from "Chicago Bound Blues" with "If you ride that train it'll satisfy your mind." "Railroad Blues" encapsulated the ambivalent position of the blues singer caught between the contradictory impulses of needing to migrate North and the need to be able to return for the "Railroad Blues" were headed not for the North but for Alabama. Being able to move both North and South the woman blues singer occupied a privileged space: she could speak the desires of rural women to migrate and voice the nostalgic desires of urban women for home which was both a recognition and a warning that the city was not, in fact, the "promised land."

Men's and women's blues shared the language and experience of the railroad and migration but what that meant was different for each sex. The language of the blues carries this conflict of interests and is the cultural terrain in which these differences were fought over and redefined. Women's blues were the popular cultural embodiment of the way in which the differing interests of black men and women were a struggle of power relations. The sign of the train is one example of the way in which the blues were a struggle within language itself to define the differing material conditions of black women and black men.

Baaad Sista

The differing interests of women and men in the domestic sphere was clearly articulated by Bessie Smith in "In House Blues," a popular song from the mid-twenties which she wrote herself but didn't record until 1931. Although the man gets up and leaves, the woman remains, trapped in the house like a caged animal pacing up and down. But at the same time Bessie's voice vibrates with tremendous power which implies the eruption that is to come. The woman in the house is only barely restrained from creating havoc; her capacity for violence has been exercised before and resulted in her arrest. The music, which provides an oppositional counterpoint to Bessie's voice, is a parody of the supposed weakness of women. A vibrating cornet contrasts with the words that ultimately cannot be contained and roll out the front door.

> Sitting in the house with everything on my mind.
> Sitting in the house with everything on my mind.
> Looking at the clock and can't even tell the time.
>
> Walking to my window and looking outa my door.
> Walking to my window and looking outa my door.
> Wishin that my man would come home once more.
>
> Can't eat, can't sleep, so weak I can't walk my floor.
> Can't eat, can't sleep, so weak I can't walk my floor.
> Feel like calling "murder" let the police squad get me once more.
>
> They woke me up before day with trouble on my mind.
> They woke me up before day with trouble on my mind.
> Wringing my hands and screamin, walking the floor hollerin an crying.
>
> Hey, don't let them blues in here.
> Hey, don't let them blues in here.
> They shakes me in my bed and sits down in my chair.
>
> Oh, the blues has got me on the go.
> They've got me on the go.
> They roll around my house, in and out of my front door.

The way in which Bessie growls "so weak" contradicts the supposed weakness and help-lessness of the woman in the song and grants authority to her thoughts of "murder."

The rage of women against male infidelity and desertion is evident in many of the blues. Ma Rainey threatened violence when she sang that she was "gonna catch" her man "with his britches down," in the act of infidelity, in "Black Eye Blues." Exacting revenge against mistreatment also appears as taking another lover as in "Oh Papa Blues" or taunting a lover who has been thrown out with "I won't worry when you're gone, another brown has got your water on" in "Titanic Man Blues." But Ma Rainey is perhaps best known for the rejection of a lover in "Don't Fish in My Sea" which is also a resolution to give up men altogether. She sang:

> If you don't like my ocean, don't fish in my sea,
> If you don't like my ocean, don't fish in my sea,
> Stay out of my valley, and let my mountain be.
>
> Ain't had no lovin' since God knows when,
> Ain't had no lovin' since God knows when,
> That's the reason I'm through with these no good triflin' men.

The total rejection of men as in this blues and in other songs such as "Trust No Man" stand in direct contrast to the blues that concentrate upon the bewildered, often half-crazed and even paralyzed response of women to male violence.

Sandra Leib (1981) has described the masochism of "Sweet Rough Man," in which a man abuses a helpless and passive woman, and she argues that a distinction must be made between reactions to male violence against women in male and female authored blues. "Sweet Rough Man," though recorded by Ma Rainey, was composed by a man and is the most explicit description of sexual brutality in her repertoire. The articulation of the possibility that women could leave a condition of sexual and financial dependency, reject male violence, and end sexual exploitation was embodied in Ma Rainey's recording of "Hustlin Blues," composed jointly by a man and a woman, which narrates the story of a prostitute who ends her brutal treatment by turning in her pimp to a judge. Ma Rainey sang:

> I ain't made no money, and he dared me to go home.
> Judge, I told him he better leave me alone.
>
> He followed me up and he grabbed me for a fight.
> He followed me up and he grabbed me for a fight.
> He said, "Girl, do you know you ain't made no money tonight."
>
> Oh Judge, tell him I'm through.
> Oh Judge, tell him I'm through.
> I'm tired of this life, that's why I brought him to you.

However, Ma Rainey's strongest assertion of female sexual autonomy is a song she composed herself, "Prove it on Me Blues," which isn't technically a blues song which she sang accompanied by a Tub Jug Washboard Band. "Prove it on Me Blues" was an assertion and an affirmation of lesbianism. Though condemned by society for her sexual preference the singer wants the whole world to know that she chooses women rather than men. The language of "Prove it on Me Blues" engages directly in defining issues of sexual preference as a contradictory struggle of social relations. Both Ma Rainey and Bessie Smith had lesbian relationships and "Prove it on Me Blues" vacillates between the subversive hidden activity of women loving women with a public declaration of lesbianism. The words express a contempt for a society that rejected lesbians. "They say I do it, ain't nobody caught me, They sure got to prove it on me." But at the same time the song is a reclamation of lesbianism as long as the woman publicly names her sexual preference for herself in the repetition of lines about the friends who "must've been women, cause I don't like no men" (Leib, 1981).

But most of the songs that asserted a woman's sexual independence did so in relation to men, not women. One of the most joyous is a recording by Ethel Waters in 1925 called "No Man's Mamma Now." It is the celebration of a divorce that ended a marriage defined as a five year "war." Unlike Bessie Smith, Ethel Waters didn't usually growl, although she could; rather her voice, which is called "sweet-toned," gained authority from its stylistic enunciation and the way in which she almost recited the words. As Waters (1951) said, she tried to be "refined" even when she was being her most outrageous.

> You may wonder what's the reason for this crazy smile,
> Say I haven't been so happy in a long while
> Got a big load off my mind, here's the paper sealed and signed,
> And the judge was nice and kind all through the trial.
> This ends a five year war, I'm sweet Miss Was once more.
>
> I can come when I please, I can go when I please.
> I can flit, fly and flutter like the birds in the trees.
> Because, I'm no man's mamma now. Hey, hey.
>
> I can say what I like, I can do what I like.
> I'm a girl who is on a matrimonial strike;
> Which means, I'm no man's mamma now.
>
> I'm screaming bail
> I know how a fella feels getting out of jail
> I got twin beds, I take pleasure in announcing one for sale.
>
> Am I making it plain, I will never again,
> Drag around another ball and chain.
> I'm through, because I'm no man's mamma now.
>
> I can smile, I can wink, I can go take a drink,
> And I don't have to worry what my hubby will think.
> Because, I'm no man's mamma now.
>
> I can spend if I choose, I can play and sing the blues.
> There's nobody messin with my one's and my twos.
> Because, I'm no man's mamma now.
>
> You know there was a time,
> I used to think that men were grand.
> But no more for mine,
> I'm gonna label my apartment "No Man's Land."
>
> I got rid of my cat cause the cat's name was Pat,
> Won't even have a male fox in my flat,
> Because, I'm no man's mamma now.

Waters' sheer exuberance is infectious. The vitality and energy of the performance celebrates the unfettered sexuality of the singer. The self-conscious and self-referential lines "I can play and sing the blues" situates the singer at the center of a subversive and liberatory activity. Many of the men who were married to blues singers disapproved of their careers, some felt threatened, others, like Edith Johnson's husband, eventually applied enough pressure to force her to stop singing. Most, like Bessie Smith, Ethel Waters, Ma Rainey, and Ida Cox did not stop singing the blues but their public presence, their stardom, their overwhelming popularity, and their insistence on doing what they wanted caused frequent conflict with the men in their personal lives.

Funky And Sinful Stuff

The figure of the woman blues singer has become a cultural embodiment of social and sexual conflict from Gayl Jones' novel *Corregidora* to Alice Walker's *The Color Purple*. The women blues singers occupied a privileged space; they had broken out of the boundaries of the home and taken their sensuality and sexuality out of the private into the public sphere. For these singers were gorgeous and their physical presence elevated them to being referred to as Goddesses, as the high priestesses of the blues, or like Bessie Smith, as the Empress of the blues. Their physical presence was a crucial aspect of their power; the visual display of spangled dresses, of furs, of gold teeth, of diamonds, of all the sumptuous and desirable aspects of their body reclaimed female sexuality from being an objectification of male desire to a representation of female desire.

Bessie Smith wrote about the social criticism that women faced if they broke social convention. "Young Woman's Blues" threads together many of the issues of power and sexuality that have been addressed so far. "Young Woman's Blues" sought possibilities, possibilities that arose from women being on the move and confidently asserting their own sexual desirability.

> Woke up this morning when chickens were crowing for day.
> Felt on the right side of my pillow, my man had gone away.
> On his pillow he left a note, reading I'm sorry you've got my goat.
> No time to marry, no time to settle down.
>
> I'm a young woman and ain't done running around.
> I'm a young woman and ain't done running around.
> Some people call me a hobo, some call me a bum,
> Nobody know my name, nobody knows what I've done.
> I'm as good as any woman in your town,
> I ain't no high yella, I'm a deep killa brown.
>
> I ain't gonna marry, ain't gonna settle down.
> I'm gonna drink good moonshine and run these browns down.
> See that long lonesome road, cause you know its got a end.
> And I'm a good woman and I can get plenty men.

The women blues singers have become our cultural icons of sexual power but what is often forgotten is that they could be great comic entertainers. In "One Hour Mama" Ida Cox used comedy to intensify an irreverent attack on male sexual prowess. The comic does not mellow the assertive voice but on the contrary undermines mythologies of phallic power and establishes a series of woman-centered heterosexual demands.

> I've always heard that haste makes waste,
> So, I believe in taking my time
> The highest mountain can't be raced
> Its something you must slowly climb.
>
> I want a slow and easy man,
> He needn't ever take the lead,
> Cause I work on that long time plan
> And I ain't a looking for no speed.
>
> I'm a one hour mama, so no one minute papa
> Ain't the kind of man for me.

Set your alarm clock papa, one hour that's proper
Then love me like I like to be.

I don't want no lame excuses bout my lovin being so good,
That you couldn't wait no longer, now I hope I'm understood.
I'm a one hour mama, so no one minute papa
Ain't the kind of man for me.

I can't stand no green horn lover, like a rookie goin to war,
With a load of big artillery, but don't know what its for.
He's got to bring me reference with a great long pedigree
And must prove he's got endurance, or he don't mean snap to me.

I can't stand no crowin rooster, what just likes a hit or two,
Action is the only booster of just what my man can do.
I don't want no imitation, my requirements ain't no joke,
Cause I got pure indignation for a guy whats lost his stroke,

I'm a one hour mama, so no one minute papa
Ain't the kind of man for me.
Set your alarm clock papa, one hour that's proper,
Then love me like I like to be.

I may want love for one hour, then decide to make it two.
Takes an hour 'fore I get started, maybe three before I'm through.
I'm a one hour mama, so no one minute papa,
Ain't the kind of man for me.

But this moment of optimism, of the blues as the exercise of power and control over sexuality, was short lived. The space occupied by these blues singers was opened up by race records but race records did not survive the depression. Some of these blues women, like Ethel Waters and Hattie McDaniels, broke through the racial boundaries of Hollywood film and were inserted into a different aspect of the culture industry where they occupied not a privileged but a subordinate space and articulated not the possibilities of black female sexual power but the "Yes, Ma'ams" of the black maid. The power of the blues singer was resurrected in a different moment of black power; re-emerging in Gayl Jones' *Corregidora;* and the woman blues singer remains an important part of our 20th century black cultural reconstruction. The blues singers had assertive and demanding voices; they had no respect for sexual taboos or for breaking through the boundaries of respectability and convention, and we hear the "we" when they say "I."

Notes

This paper was originally a presentation to the conference on "Sexuality, Politics and Power" held at Mount Holyoke College, September 1986. It was reprinted in *Radical America* 20,4 (1986): 9–24. The power of the music can only be fully understood by listening to the songs which should be played as the essay is read.

References

Brown, S. (1980). Ma Rainey. *The Collected Poems of Sterling A. Brown.* New York: Harper and Row.
Carby, H. V. (1986). On the threshold of woman's era: Lynching, empire and sexuality in black feminist theory. In H. L. Gates, Jr. (Ed.), *'Race,' Writing and Difference* (301–16). Chicago: University of Chicago Press.

Carby, H. V. (1987). *Reconstructing Womanhood: The Emergence of the Afro-American Woman Novelist.* New York: Oxford University Press.

Cooper, A. J. (1892). *A Voice from the South.* Xenia, OH: Aldine Publishing House.

Cox, I. (1980). One hour mama. *Mean Mothers.* Rosetta Records, RR 1300.

Leib, S. (1981). *Mother of the Blues: A Study of Ma Rainey.* Amherst: University of Massachusetts Press.

Rainey, G. (1974). *Ma Rainey.* Milestone Records, M47021.

Smith, B. (n.d.). In house blues. *The World's Greatest Blues Singer.* Columbia Records, CG33.

Smith, B. (1972). Young woman's blues. *Nobody's Blues But Mine.* Columbia Records, CG 31093.

Smith, C. (1980). Freight train blues. *Women's Railroad Blues.* Rosetta Records, RR 1301.

Spillers, H. (1984). Interstices: A small drama of words. In C. Vance (Ed.), *Pleasure and Danger: Exploring Female Sexuality* (73–100). London: Routledge and Kegan Paul

Waters, E. (1951). *His Eye is on the Sparrow.* New York: Doubleday & Co., Inc.

Waters, E. (1982). No man's mama. *Big Mamas.* Rosetta Records, RR 1306.

Williams, S. A. (1979). The blues roots of contemporary Afro-American poetry. In M. S. Harper & R. B. Stepto (Eds.), *Chant of Saints* (123–135). Chicago: University of Illinois Press.

Williams, S. A. (1981). The house of desire. In E. Stetson (Ed.), *Black Sister: Poetry by Black American Women, 1746–1980.* Bloomington: Indiana University Press.

Williams, S. A. (1982). Fifteen. *One Sweet Angel Chile.* New York: William Morrow and Co., Inc.

22

Rape and the Inner Lives of Black Women in the Middle West: Preliminary Thoughts on the Culture of Dissemblance

Darlene Clark Hine

One of the most remarked upon but least analyzed themes in Black women's history deals with Black women's sexual vulnerability and powerlessness as victims of rape and domestic violence. Author Hazel Carby put it baldly when she declared "The institutionalized rape of black women has never been as powerful a symbol of black oppression as the spectacle of lynching. Rape has always involved patriarchal notions of women being, at best, not entirely unwilling accomplices, if not outwardly inviting a sexual attack. The links between black women and illicit sexuality consolidated during the antebellum years had powerful ideological consequences for the next hundred and fifty years."[1] I suggest that rape and the threat of rape influenced the development of a culture of dissemblance among Black women. By dissemblance I mean the behavior and attitudes of Black women that created the appearance of openness and disclosure but actually shielded the truth of their inner lives and selves from their oppressors.

To be sure, themes of rape and sexual vulnerability have received considerable attention in the recent literary outpourings of Black women novelists. Of the last six novels I have read and reread, for example, five contained a rape scene or a graphic description of domestic violence.[2] Moreover, this is not a recent phenomenon in Black women's writing.

Virtually every known nineteenth-century female slave narrative contains a reference to, at some juncture, the ever present threat and reality of rape. Two works come immediately to mind: Harriet Jacobs' *Incidents in the Life of a Slave Girl* (1861) and Elizabeth Keckley's *Behind the Scenes, or Thirty Years a Slave, and Four Years in the White House* (1868). Yet there is another thread running throughout these slave narratives—one that concerns these captive women's efforts to resist the misappropriation and to maintain the integrity of their own sexuality.[3] The combined influence of rape (or the threat of rape), domestic violence, and economic oppression is key to understanding the hidden motivations informing major social protest and migratory movements in Afro-American history.

Second only to Black women's concern for sexual preservation is the pervasive theme of the frustration attendant to finding suitable employment. Oral histories and autobiographical accounts of twentieth-century migrating Black women are replete with themes about work. Scholars of Black urban history and Black labor history agree that Black women faced greater economic discrimination and had fewer employment opportunities than did Black men. Black women's work was the most undesirable and least remunerative of all work available to migrants.

As late as 1930 a little over three thousand Black women, or 15 percent, of the Black

Reprinted by permission of the author. Originally published in *Signs* 14, Summer 1989.

female labor force in Chicago were unskilled and semiskilled factory operatives. Thus, over 80 percent of all employed Black women continued to work as personal servants and domestics. Historian Alan H. Spear pointed out that "Negro women were particularly limited in their search for desirable positions. Clerical work was practically closed to them and only a few could qualify as school teachers. Negro domestics often received less than white women for the same work and they could rarely rise to the position of head servant in large households."[4]

Given that many Black women migrants were doomed to work in the same kinds of domestic service jobs they held in the South, one wonders why they bothered to move in the first place. There were some significant differences that help explain this phenomenon. A maid earning seven dollars a week in Cleveland perceived herself to be, and probably was, much better off than a counterpart receiving two dollars and fifty cents a week in Mobile, Alabama. A factory worker, even one whose work was dirty and low status, could and did imagine herself better off than domestic servants who endured the unrelenting scrutiny, interference, and complaints of household mistresses and the untoward advances of male family members.

I believe that in order to understand this historical migratory trend we need to understand the noneconomic motives propelling Black female migration. I believe that many Black women quit the South out of a desire to achieve personal autonomy and to escape both from sexual exploitation from inside and outside of their families and from the rape and threat of rape by white as well as Black males. To focus on the sexual and the personal impetus for Black women's migration in the first several decades of the twentieth century neither dismisses nor diminishes the significance of economic motives. Rather, as historian Lawrence Levine cautioned, "As indisputably important as the economic motive was, it is possible to overstress it so that the black migration is converted into an inexorable force and Negroes are seen once again not as actors capable of affecting at least some part of their destinies, but primarily as beings who are acted upon—southern leaves blown North by the winds of destitution."[5] It is reasonable to assume that some Black women were indeed "southern leaves blown North" and that there were many others who were self-propelled actresses seeking respect, control over their own sexuality, and access to well-paying jobs.

My own research on the history of Black women in the Middle West had led me to questions about how, when, and under what circumstances the majority of them settled in the region. These questions have led to others concerning the process of Black women's migration across time, from the flights of runaway slaves in the antebellum period to the great migrations of the first half of the twentieth century. The most common, and certainly the most compelling, motive for running, fleeing, migrating was a desire to retain or claim some control over ownership of their own sexual beings and the children they bore. In the antebellum period hundreds of slave women risked their lives and those of their loved ones to run away to the ostensibly free states of the Northwest Territory, in quest of an elusive sexual freedom for themselves and freedom from slavery for their children.

Two things became immediately apparent as I proceeded with researching the history and reading the autobiographies of late nineteenth- and early twentieth-century migrating, or fleeing, Black women. First, that these women were sexual hostages and domestic violence victims in the South (or in other regions of the country) did not reduce their determination to acquire power to protect themselves and to become agents of social change once they settled in midwestern communities. Second, the fundamental tension between Black women and the rest of the society—referring specifically to white men, white women, and to a lesser extent, Black men—involved a multifaceted struggle to determine who would control their productive and reproductive capacities and their sexuality. At stake for Black women caught up in this ever evolving, constantly shifting, but relentless war was the acquisition of personal autonomy and economic liberation. Their quest for autonomy, dignity, and access to opportunity to earn an adequate living was (and still is) complicated and frustrated by the antagonisms of race, class, and gender conflict and by differences in regional economies. At heart though, the relationship between Black women and the larger society has always been, and continues to be, adversarial.

Because of the interplay of racial animosity, class tensions, gender role differentiation, and regional economic variations, Black women, as a rule, developed and adhered to a cult of secrecy, a culture of dissemblance, to protect the sanctity of inner aspects of their lives. The dynamics of dissemblance involved creating the appearance of disclosure, or openness about themselves and their feelings, while actually remaining an enigma. Only with secrecy, thus achieving a self-imposed invisibility, could ordinary Black women accrue the psychic space and harness the resources needed to hold their own in the often one-sided and mismatched resistance struggle.

The inclination of the larger society to ignore those considered "marginal" actually enabled subordinate Black women to craft the veil of secrecy and to perfect the art of dissemblance. Yet it could also be argued that their secrecy or "invisibility" contributed to the development of an atmosphere inimical to realizing equal opportunity or a place of respect in the larger society. There would be no room on the pedestal for the southern Black lady. Nor could she join her white sisters in the prison of "true womanhood." In other words, stereotypes, negative images, and debilitating assumptions filled the space left empty due to inadequate and erroneous information about the true contributions, capabilities, and identities of Black women.

This line of analysis is not without problems. To suggest that Black women deliberately developed a culture of dissemblance implies that they endeavored to create, and were not simply reacting to, widespread misrepresentations and negative images of themselves in white minds. Clearly, Black women did not possess the power to eradicate negative social and sexual images of their womanhood. Rather, what I propose is that in the face of the pervasive stereotypes and negative estimations of the sexuality of Black women, it was imperative that they collectively create alternative self-images and shield from scrutiny these private, empowering definitions of self. A secret, undisclosed persona allowed the individual Black woman to function, to work effectively as a domestic in white households, to bear and rear children, to endure the frustration-born violence of frequently under-or unemployed mates, to support churches, to found institutions, and to engage in social service activities, all while living within a clearly hostile white, patriarchal, middle-class America.

The problem this penchant for secrecy presents to the historian is readily apparent. Deborah Gray White has commented about the difficulty of finding primary source material for personal aspects of Black female life: "Black women have also been reluctant to donate their papers to manuscript repositories. That is in part a manifestation of the black woman's perennial concern with image, a justifiable concern born of centuries of vilification. Black women's reluctance to donate personal papers also stems from the adversarial nature of the relationship that countless black women have had with many public institutions, and the resultant suspicion of anyone seeking private information."[6]

White's allusion to "resultant suspicion" speaks implicitly to one important reason why so much of the inner life of Black women remains hidden. Indeed, the concepts of "secrets" and "dissemblance," as I employ them, hint at those issues that Black women believed better left unknown, unwritten, unspoken except in whispered tones. Their alarm, their fear, or their Victorian sense of modesty implies that those who broke the silence provided grist for detractors' mills and, even more ominously, tore the protective cloaks from their inner selves. Undoubtedly, these fears and suspicions contribute to the absence of sophisticated historical discussion of the impact of rape (or threat of rape) and incidences of domestic violence on the shape of Black women's experiences.

However, the self-imposed secrecy and the culture of dissemblance, coupled with the larger society's unwillingness to discard tired and worn stereotypes, has also led to ironic incidences of misplaced emphases. Until quite recently, for example, when historians talked of rape in the slavery experience they often bemoaned the damage this act did to the Black male's sense of esteem and respect. He was powerless to protect his woman from white rapists. Few scholars probed the effect that rape, the threat of rape, and domestic violence had on the psychic development of the female victims. In the late nineteenth and early twentieth centuries, as Carby has indicated, lynching, not rape, became the most powerful and compelling symbol of Black oppression. Lynching, it came to be understood, was one of the major noneconomic reasons why southern Black men migrated North.

The culture of dissemblance assumed its most institutionalized form in the founding, in 1896, of the National Association of Colored Women's Clubs (NACW). This association of Black women quickly became the largest and most enduring protest organization in the history of Afro-Americans. Its size alone should have warranted the same degree of scholarly attention paid to Marcus Garvey's Universal Negro Improvement Association. Not surprisingly, the primary objects of NACW attack were the derogatory images and negative stereotypes of Black women's sexuality. By 1914 it had a membership of fifty thousand, far surpassing the membership of every other protest organization of the time, including the National Association for the Advancement of Colored People and the National Urban League. In 1945, in Detroit, for example, the Detroit Association of Colored Women's Clubs, federated in 1921, boasted seventy-three member clubs with nearly three thousand individual members.[7]

Mary Church Terrell, the first president of the NACW, declared in her initial presidential address that there were objectives of the Black women's struggle that could be accomplished only by the "mothers, wives, daughters, and sisters of this race." She proclaimed, "We wish to set in motion influences that shall stop the ravages made by practices that sap our strength, and preclude the possibility of advancement." She boldly announced, "We proclaim to the world that the women of our race have become partners in the great firm of progress and reform. . . . We refer to the fact that this is an association of colored women, because our peculiar status in this country . . . seems to demand that we stand by ourselves."[8]

At the core of essentially every activity of NACW's individual members was a concern with creating positive images of Black women's sexuality. To counter negative stereotypes many Black women felt compelled to downplay, even deny, sexual expression. The twin obsessions with naming and combatting sexual exploitation tinted and shaped Black women's support even of the woman's suffrage movement. Nannie H. Burroughs, famed religious leader and founder of the National Training School for Women and Girls at Washington, D.C., cajoled her sisters to fight for the ballot. She asserted that with the ballot Black women could ensure the passage of legislation to win legal protection against rapists. Calling the ballot a "weapon of moral defense" she exploded, "when she [a Black woman] appears in court in defense of her virtue, she is looked upon with amused contempt. She needs the ballot to reckon with men who place no value upon her virtue."[9]

Likewise, determination to save young unskilled and unemployed Black women from having to bargain sex in exchange for food and shelter motivated some NACW members to establish boarding houses and domestic service training centers, such as the Phillis

Wheatley Homes, and Burroughs's National Training School. This obsession with providing Black women with protection from sexual exploitation and with dignified work inspired other club members in local communities around the country to support or to found hospitals and nursing training schools.

At least one plausible consequence of this heightened mobilization of Black women was a decline in Black urban birth rates. As Black women became more economically self-sufficient, better educated, and more involved in self-improvement efforts, including participation in the flourishing Black women's club movement in midwestern communities, they had greater access to birth control information. As the institutional infrastructure of Black women's clubs, sororities, church-based women's groups, and charity organizations sunk roots into Black communities it encouraged its members to embrace those values, behaviors, and attitudes traditionally associated with the middle classes. To urban Black middle-class aspirants, the social stigma of having many children did, perhaps, inhibit reproduction. To be sure, over time the gradually evolving male-female demographic imbalance meant that increasingly significant numbers of Black women, especially those employed in the professions, in urban midwestern communities would never marry. The point stressed here, however, is that not having children was, perhaps for the very first time, a choice enjoyed by large numbers of Black women.

There were additional burdens placed upon and awards granted to the small cadre of single, educated, professional Black women who chose not to marry or to bear children. The more educated they were, the greater the sense of being responsible, somehow, for the advance of the race and for the elevation of Black womanhood. They held these expectations of themselves and found a sense of racial obligation reinforced by the demands of the Black community and its institutions. In return for their sacrifice of sexual expression, the community gave them respect and recognition. Moreover, this freedom and autonomy represented a socially sanctioned, meaningful alternative to the uncertainties of marriage and the demands of child rearing. The increased employment opportunities, whether real or imagined, and the culture of dissemblance enabled many migrating Black women to become financially independent and simultaneously to fashion socially useful and autonomous lives, while reclaiming control over their own sexuality and reproductive capacities.

This is not to say that Black women, once settled into midwestern communities, never engaged in sex for pay or occasional prostitution. Sara Brooks, a Black domestic servant from Alabama who migrated to Cleveland, Ohio, in the 1930s, ill-disguised her contempt for women who bartered their bodies. She declared, while commenting on her own struggle to pay the mortgage on her house, "Some women woulda had a man to live in the house and had an outside boyfriend, too, in order to get the house paid for and the bills." She scornfully added, "They meet a man and if he promises en four or five dollars to go to bed, they's grab it. That's called sellin' your own body, and I wasn't raised like that."[10] What escapes Brooks, in this moralizing moment, is that her poor and powerless Black female neighbors were extracting value from the only thing the society now allowed them to sell. As long as they occupied an enforced subordinate position within American society this "sellin' your own body" as Brooks put it, was, I submit, Rape.

In sum, at some fundamental level all Black women historians are engaged in the process of historical reclamation. But it is not enough simply to reclaim those hidden and obscure facts and names of Black foremothers. Merely to reclaim and to narrate past deeds and contributions risks rendering a skewed history focused primarily on the articulate, relatively well-positioned members of the aspiring Black middle class. In synchrony with the reclaiming and narrating must be the development of an array of analytical frameworks which allow us to understand why Black women behave in certain ways and how they acquired agency.

The migration of hundreds of thousands of Black women out of the South between 1915 and 1945, and the formation of thousands of Black women's clubs and the NACW are actions that enabled them to put into place, to situate, a protest infrastructure and to create a self-conscious Black women's culture of resistance. Most significant, the NACW fostered the development of an image of Black women as being super-moral women. In particular, the institutionalization of women's clubs embodied the shaping and honing of the culture of dissemblance. This culture, grounded as it was on the twin prongs of protest and resistance, enabled the creation of positive alternative images of their sexual selves and facilitated Black women's mental and physical survival in a hostile world.

Notes

I benefited greatly from conversations with D. Barry Gaspar and Deborah Gray White. I am grateful to Tiffany Patterson and to Elsa Barkley Brown for their comments. An earlier version of this talk was presented as the endnote address at the First Southern Conference on Women's History, Converse College, Spartanburg, South Carolina, June 10–11, 1988.

1. Hazel V. Carby, *Reconstructing Womanhood: The Emergence of the Afro-American Woman Novelist* (New York: Oxford University Press, 1987), 39.
2. See Terry McMillan, *Mama* (Boston: Houghton Mifflin, 1987); Grace Edwards-Yearwood, *In the Shadow of the Peacock* (New York: McGraw Hill, 1988); Alice Walker, *The Color Purple* (New York: Harcourt Brace Jovanovich, 1982); Toni Morrison, *The Bluest Eye* (New York: Washington Square Press, 1972); Gloria Naylor, *The Women of Brewster Place* (New York: Penguin, 1983).
3. Harriet A. Jacobs, *Incidents in the Life of a Slave Girl Written by Herself,* ed. Jean Fagan Yellin (Cambridge, Mass.: Harvard University Press, 1987). Elizabeth Keckley, *Behind the Scenes, or Thirty Years a Slave, and Four Years in the White House,* introduction by James Olney (New York: Oxford University Press, 1988). See also Rennie Simpson, "The Afro-American Female: The Historical Construction of Sexual Identity," in *The Powers of Desire: The Politics of Sexuality,* ed. Ann Snitow, Sharon Thompson, and Christine Stansell (New York: Monthly Review Press, 1983), 229–35.
4. Alan H. Spear, *Black Chicago: The Making of a Negro Ghetto, 1890–1920* (Chicago: University of Chicago Press, 1967), 34.
5. Lawrence W. Levine, *Black Culture and Black Consciousness: Afro-American Folk Thought from Slavery to Freedom* (New York: Oxford University Press, 1977), 274.
6. Deborah Gray White, "Mining the Forgotten: Manuscript Sources for Black Women's History," *Journal of American History* 74 (June 1987): 237–42, esp. 237–38.
7. Robin S. Peebles, "Detroit's Black Women's Clubs," *Michigan History* 70 (January/February 1986): 48.
8. Darlene Clark Hine, "Lifting the Veil, Shattering the Silence: Black Women's History in Slavery and Freedom," in *The State of Afro-American History: Past, Present, and Future,* ed. Darlene Clark Hine (Baton Rouge: Louisiana State University Press, 1986), 223–49, esp. 236–37.
9. Roslyn Terborg-Penn, "Woman Suffrage: 'First because We Are Women and Second because We Are Colored Women,'" *Truth: Newsletter of the Association of Black Women Historians* (April 1985), 9; Evelyn Brooks Barnett, "Nannie Burroughs and the Education of Black Women," in *The Afro-American Woman,* ed. Roslyn Terborg-Penn and Sharon Harley (Port Washington, N.Y.: Kennikat, 1978), 97–108.
10. Thordis Simonsen, ed., *You May Plow Here: The Narrative of Sara Brooks* (New York: Simon & Schuster, 1987), 219.

23

Disorderly Women: Gender and Labor Militancy in the Appalachian South

Jacquelyn Dowd Hall

The rising sun "made a sort of halo around the crown of Cross Mountain" as Flossie Cole climbed into a neighbor's Model T and headed west down the gravel road to Elizabethton, bound for work in a rayon plant. Emerging from Stoney Creek hollow, the car joined a caravan of buses and self-styled "taxis" brimming with young people from dozens of tiny communities strung along the creek branches and nestled in the coves of the Blue Ridge Mountains of East Tennessee. The caravan picked up speed as it hit paved roads and crossed the Watauga River bridge, passing beneath a sign advertising Elizabethton's new-found identity as a "City of Power." By the time Cole reached the factory gate, it was 7:00 A.M., time to begin another ten-hour day as a reeler at the American Glanzstoff plant.[1]

The machines whirred, and work began as usual. But the reeling room stirred with anticipation. The day before, March 12, 1929, all but seventeen of the 360 women in the inspection room next door walked out in protest against low wages, petty rules, and high-handed attitudes. Now they were gathered at the factory gate, refusing to work but ready to negotiate. When 9:00 A.M. approached and the plant manager failed to appear, they broke past the guards and rushed through the plant, urging their co-workers out on strike. By 1:40 P.M. the machines were idle and the plant was closed.[2]

The Elizabethton conflict rocked Carter County and made national headlines. Before March ended, the spirit of protest had jumped the Blue Ridge and spread through the Piedmont. Gastonia, Marion, and Danville saw the most bitter conflicts, but dozens of towns were shocked by an unexpected workers' revolt.[3]

The textile industry has always been a stronghold of women's labor, and women were central to these events. The most well-known protagonist in the 1929 strikes was, and remains, Gastonia's Ella May Wiggins, who migrated from the mountains, composed ballads for the union, and became a martyr to the workers' cause. But even Ella May Wiggins has been more revered than explained. Memorialized in proletarian novels but slighted by historians, she has joined a long line of working-class heroines who served with devotion and died young. Elizabethton too had it heroines, cast from a more human mold. They were noted by contemporaries sometimes as leaders, more often as pathetic mill girls or as "Amazons" providing comic relief. In historical renditions they have dropped out of sight. The result has been thin description: a one-dimensional view of labor conflict that fails to take culture and community into account.[4]

Elizabethton, of course, is not unusual in this regard. Until recently, historians of trade unionism, like trade unionists themselves, neglected women, while historians of women

Reprinted with permission from the *Journal of American History*, vol. 73, September 1986.

concentrated on the Northeast and the middle class. There were few scholarly challenges to the assumption that women workers in general and southern women in particular were "hard to organize" and that women as family members exercised a conservative pull against class cohesion. Instances of female militancy were seen and not seen.[5] Because they contradicted conventional wisdom, they were easily dismissed.

Recent scholarship has revised that formulation by unearthing an impressive record of female activism.[6] But our task is not only to describe and celebrate but also to contextualize, and thus to understand. In Elizabethton the preindustrial background, the structure of the work force and the industry, the global forces that impinged on local events—these particularities of time and place conditioned women's choices and shaped their identities. Equally important was a private world traditionally pushed to the margins of labor history. Female friendships and sexuality, cross-generational and cross-class alliances, the incorporation of new consumer desires into a dynamic regional culture—these, too, energized women's participation. Women in turn were historical subjects, helping to create the circumstances from which the strike arose and guided by their actions the course the conflict took.

With gender at the center of analysis, unexpected dimensions come into view. Chief among them is the strike's erotic undercurrent, its sexual theme. The activists of Elizabethton belonged to a venerable tradition of "disorderly women," women who, in times of political upheaval, embody tensions that are half-conscious or only dimly understood.[7] Beneath the surface of a conflict that pitted workers and farmers against a new middle class in the town lay an inner world of fantasy, gender ideology, and sexual style.

The melding of narrative and analysis that follows has two major goals. The first is a fresh reading of an important episode in southern labor history, employing a female angle of vision to reveal aspects of the conflict that have been overlooked or misunderstood. The second is a close look at women's distinctive forms of collective action, using language and gesture as points of entry to a culture.

The Elizabethton story may also help to make a more general point. Based as it is on what Michel Foucault has termed "local" or "subjugated" knowledge, that is, perceptions that seem idiosyncratic, naive, and irrelevant to historical explanation, this study highlights the limitations of conventional categories.[8] The women of Elizabethton were neither traditionalists acting on family values nor market-oriented individualists, neither peculiar mountaineers nor familiar modern women. Their irreverence and inventiveness shatter stereotypes and illuminate the intricacies of working-class women's lives.

In 1925 the J. P. Bemberg Company of Barmen, Germany, manufacturer of high-quality rayon yarn by an exclusive stretch spinning process, began pouring the thick concrete floors of its first United States subsidiary. Three years later Germany's leading producer of viscose yarn, the Vereinigte Glanzstoff Fabriken, A.G., of Elberfeld opened a jointly managed branch nearby. A post-World War I fashion revolution, combined with protective tariffs, had spurred the American rayon industry's spectacular growth. As one industry publicist put it, "With long skirts, cotton stockings were quite in order; but with short skirts, nothing would do except sheer, smooth stockings. . . . It was on the trim legs of post-war flappers, it has been said, that rayon first stepped out into big business." Dominated by a handful of European giants, the rayon industry clustered along the Appalachian mountain chain. By World War II over 70 percent of American rayon production took place in the southern states, with 50 percent of the national total in Virginia and Tennessee alone.[9]

When the Bemberg and Glanzstoff companies chose East Tennessee as a site for overseas expansion, they came to a region that has occupied a peculiar place in the American economy and imagination. Since its "discovery" by local-color writers in the 1870s, southern Appalachia has been seen as a land "where time stood still." Mountain people have been romanticized as "our contemporary ancestors" or maligned as "latter-day white barbarians." Central to both images is the notion of a people untouched by modernity. In fact, as a generation of regional scholars has now made clear, the key to modern Appalachian history lies not in the region's isolation but in its role as a source of raw materials and as an outlet for investment in a capitalist world economy.[10]

Frontier families had settled the fertile Watauga River Valley around Elizabethton before the Revolution. Later arrivals pushed farther up the mountains into the hollows carved by fast-falling creeks. Stoney Creek is the oldest and largest of those creek-bed communities. Two miles wide at its base near Elizabethton, Stoney Creek hollow points fourteen miles into the hills, narrowing almost to a close at its upper end, with only a little trail twisting toward the Tennessee-North Carolina line. Here descendants of the original settlers cultivated their own small plots, grazed livestock in woods that custom held open to all, hunted and fished in an ancient hardwood forest, mined iron ore, made whiskey, spun cloth, and bartered with local merchants for what they could not produce at home.[11]

In the 1880s East Tennessee's timber and mineral resources attracted the attention of capitalists in the United States and abroad, and an era of land speculation and railroad building began. The railroads opened the way to timber barons, who stripped away the forests, leaving hillsides stark and vulnerable to erosion. Farmers abandoned their fields to follow the march of the logging camps. Left behind, women and children did their best to pick up the slack. But by the time Carter County was "timbered out" in the 1920s, farm families had crept upward to the barren ridge lands or grown dependent on "steady work and cash wages." Meanwhile, in Elizabethton, the county seat, an aggressive new class of bankers, lawyers, and businessmen served as brokers for outside developers, speculated in land, invested in homegrown factories, and looked beyond the hills for their standards of "push, progress and prosperity."[12]

Carter County, however, lacked Appalachia's grand prize: The rush for coal that devastated other parts of the mountains had bypassed that part of East Tennessee. Nor had county farmers been absorbed into the cotton kingdom, with its exploitative credit system and spreading tenancy. To be sure, they were increasingly hard pressed. As arable land disappeared, farms were divided and redivided. In 1880 the average rural family had supported itself on 140 acres of land; by 1920 it was making do on slightly more than 52 acres. Yet however diminished their circumstances, 84.5 percent still owned their own land. The economic base that sustained traditional expectations of independence, production for use, and neighborly reciprocity tottered but did not give way.[13]

The coming of the rayon plants represented a coup for Elizabethton's aspiring businessmen, who wooed investors with promises of free land, tax exemptions, and cheap labor.[14] But at first the whole county seemed to share the boomtown spirit. Men from Stoney Creek, Gap Creek, and other mountain hamlets built the cavernous mills, then stayed on to learn the chemical processes that transformed the cellulose from wood pulp and cotton linters (the short fibers that remain on cotton seeds after longer, spinnable fibers are removed) into "artificial silk." Women vied for jobs in the textile division where they wound, reeled, twisted, and inspected the rayon yarn. Real-estate prices soared as the city embarked on a frenzied improvement campaign and private developers threw up houses in subdivisions of outlying fields. Yet for all the excitement it engendered, industrialization in Carter County retained a distinctly rural cast. Although Elizabethton's population tripled (from

2,749 in 1920 to 8,093 in 1930), the rayon workers confounded predictions of spectacular urban growth, for most remained in the countryside, riding to work on chartered buses and trains or in taxis driven by neighbors and friends.[15]

Women made up a large proportion of the 3,213 workers in the mills. According to company sources, they held 30 percent of the jobs at the Bemberg plant and a full 44 percent at the larger Glanzstoff mill—where the strike started and the union gained its firmest hold. Between 75 and 80 percent of those female employees were single and aged sixteen to twenty-one. But these figures underestimate the workers' youth, for the company ignored state child-labor laws and hired girls as young as twelve or, more commonly, fourteen. By contrast, a significant proportion of male workers were older, married men. Since no company records have survived, it is impossible to describe the work force in detail, but its general character is clear: The work force was white, drawn predominantly from Elizabethton and Carter County but also from contiguous areas of North Carolina and Virginia. Adult married men, together with a smaller number of teenage boys, dominated the chemical division, while young women, the vast majority of whom commuted from farm homes, processed the finished yarn.[16]

Whether married or single, town- or country-bred, the men who labored in the rayon plants followed in the footsteps of fathers, and sometimes grandfathers, who had combined farming with a variety of wage-earning occupations. To a greater extent than we might expect, young women who had grown up in Elizabethton could also look to earlier models of gainful labor. A search of the 1910 manuscript census found 20 percent (97/507) of women aged fourteen and over in paid occupations. The largest proportion (29.6 percent) were cooks and servants. But close behind were women in what mountain people called "public work": wage-earning labor performed outside a household setting. Most of these (25.1 percent) worked in the town's small cotton and garment mills. Clerks, teachers, and boardinghouse keepers rounded out this employment profile. But a few women pursued more exotic careers. A widowed "authoress—historical" headed a comfortable ten-member household. Living in a boardinghouse with her husband was a thirty-two-year-old woman and her twelve-year-old daughter, apparently members of a traveling theater troupe, their place of business listed as "on the road."[17]

For rayon workers from the countryside, it was a different story. Only 5.2 percent of adult women on Stoney Creek were gainfully employed (33/638). Nineteen of these were farmers. The rest—except for one music teacher—were servants or washerwomen.[18] Such statistics, of course, are notorious for their underestimation of women's moneymaking activities. Nor do they reflect the enormous amount of unpaid labor performed by women on Carter County farms. Still, the contrast is telling, and from it we can surmise two things. The first is that industrialization did not burst upon a static conflict-free "traditional" world. The women who beat a path to the rayon plants came from families that had already been drawn into an economy where money was a key to survival. The second is that the timber industry, which attracted Carter County's men, undermined its agricultural base, and destroyed its natural resources, created few opportunities for rural women. No wonder that farm daughters in the mills counted their blessings and looked on themselves as pioneers. For some the rayon plants offered another way of meeting a farm daughter's obligations to the family economy. But others had more complex motivations, and their route to the factory reflected the changing configuration of mountain women's lives.

Flossie Cole's father owned a tiny farm on Stoney Creek, with a gristmill built from stones he had hauled over the mountain in an ox-drawn sled. When Flossie was "two months and twelve days old," he died in a coal-mining accident in Virginia, leaving his wife with seven children to support. The family kept body and soul together by grinding corn for their neighbors and tending the farm. Cole may have been new to factory labor, but she was no stranger to women's work. While her brothers followed their father's lead to the coal mines, she pursued the two most common occupations of the poorest mountain girls: agricultural labor and domestic service in other people's homes. "We would hire out and stay with people until they got through with us and then go back home. And when we got back home, it was workin' in the corn or wash for people." When Cole lost her job after the strike, she went back to domestic service, "back to the drudge house," as she put it.[19]

Bessie Edens was the oldest of ten children in a family that had been to Illinois and back before the rayon mills arrived. Her father had found a job in a brickyard, but her mother missed the mountains and insisted on coming home. Edens dreamed of an education and begged to go to nursing school. But her parents opposed her plan. At fifteen she too went to work as a servant. "Then I'd come back when Momma had a baby and wait on her, and help if she needed me in any way." When asked fifty years later about a daughter's place on a hardscrabble farm, Edens replied: "The girls were supposed to do housework and work in the fields. They were supposed to be slaves." By the time the rayon plants opened, Edens was married and the mother of two. She left the children with her mother and seized the chance to earn her own money and to contribute to her family's support.[20]

Nettie Reece's father worked for Elizabethton's Empire Chair Company while her mother kept up a seven-acre farm on the outskirts of town. Mrs. Reece also kept four or five cows, ten to fifteen hogs, and one hundred chickens—all that while giving birth to ten children, eight of whom survived. Nettie Reece earned her first fifty cents pulling weeds in a wealthy family's yard. When the Germany factory managers arrived, she waited on tables at their boardinghouse (although her father was indignant when she brought home "tips" and almost made her quit). At fourteen she got a reeling job at the Bemberg plant. To her, work seemed an extension of school, for she was surrounded by girls she had known all her life. "We grew up together," she remembered. "We used to be called the dirty dozen. [When we went to work] it looked like the classroom was walking down the street." Movies, Chautauqua events, and above all the opportunities for courting presented by the sudden gathering of so many young people in the town—these were Nettie Reece's main memories of the eight months she spent at Bemberg before the strike began.[21]

Whether they sought employment out of family need, adventurousness, or thwarted aspiration—or a combination of the three—most saw factory labor as a hopeful gamble rather than a desperate last resort. Every woman interviewed remembered two things: how she got her first job and the size of her first paycheck. "I'll never forget the day they hired me at Bemberg," said Flossie Cole. "We went down right in front of it. They'd come out and they'd say, 'You and you and you,' and they'd hire so many. And that day I was standing there and he picked out two or three more and he looked at me and he said, 'You.' It thrilled me to death." She worked fifty-six hours that week and took home $8.16.[22]

Such pay scales were low even for the southern textile industry, and workers quickly found their income eaten away by the cost of commuting or of boarding in town. When the strike came it focused on the issue of Glanzstoff women's wages, which lagged behind those at the older Bemberg plant. But workers had other grievances as well. Caustic chemicals were used to turn cellulose into a viscous fluid that was then forced through spinnerets, thimble-shaped nozzles pierced with tiny holes. The fine, individual streams coagulated into rayon filaments in an acid bath. In the chemical division men waded through water and acid, exposed all day to a lethal spray. Women labored under less dangerous conditions, but for longer hours and less pay. Paid by the piece, they complained of rising production quotas and what everyone referred to as "hard rules."[23]

Women in particular were singled out for petty regulations, aimed not just at extracting labor but at shaping deportment as well. They were forbidden to wear makeup; in some departments they were required to purchase uniforms. Most galling of all was company surveillance of the washroom. According to Bessie Edens, who was promoted to "forelady" in the twisting room, "men could do what they wanted to in their own department," but women had to get a pass to leave the shop floor. "If we went to the bathroom, they'd follow us," Flossie Cole confirmed, "'fraid we'd stay a minute too long." If they did, their pay was docked; one too many trips and they lost their jobs.[24]

Complaints about the washroom may have had other meanings as well. When asked how she heard that a strike was brewing, Nettie Reece cited "bathroom gossip."[25] As the company well knew, the women's washroom where only a forelady, not a male supervisor could go, might serve as a communications center, a hub of gossip where complaints were aired and plans were formulated.

The German origins of the plant managers contributed to the tension. Once the strike began, union organizers were quick to play on images of an "imported Prussian autocracy." The frontier republicanism of the mountains shaded easily into post-World War I Americanism as strikers demanded their rights as "natural born American citizens" oppressed by a "latter day industrialism." In that they had much in common with other twentieth-century workers, for whom the democratic values articulated during the war became a rallying cry for social justice at home. The nationality of the managers helped throw those values into sharp relief.[26]

Above all, the fact that the plant managers were newcomers to the region made them unusually dependent on second- and third-line supervisors, few of whom could be drawn from established hierarchies of age and skill. The power that shop-floor supervisors thus acquired could cut two ways. If used arbitrarily to hire and fire, it could provoke resentment. At the same time, men and women whose primary concern was the welfare of family and friends might act more as shop stewards than as enforcers of the company will. Reduced to promoting the likes of Bessie Edens to authority over seventy-five young women from her own mountain coves, the managers strengthened their opposition.[27]

Efforts to organize the plants by local American Federation of Labor (AFL) craft unionists had begun at least as early as 1927.[28] But the strike was initiated on March 12, 1929, by women in the Glanzstoff inspection department, by what one observer called "girls in their teens [who] decided not to put up with the present conditions any longer." For weeks Margaret Bowen had been asking for a raise for herself and the section she supervised. That morning she had asked again and once more had been turned away. Christine Galliher remembered the moment well: "We all decided in that department if they didn't give us a raise we wasn't going to work." One by one the other sections sent word: "We are more important than any other department of the plant . . . . Why don't you walk out and we will walk out with you?" At 12:30 the inspectors left their jobs.[29]

On March 13 the women returned to the plant and led the rest of the work force out on strike. Five days later Bemberg workers came out as well. By then the Carter County Chancery Court had handed down two draconian injunctions forbidding all demonstrations against the company. When strikers ignored the injunctions, plant managers joined town officials in convincing the governor to send in the National Guard. The strikers secured a charter from the AFL's United Textile Workers (UTW). Meeting in a place called the Tabernacle, built for religious revivals, they listened to a Baptist preacher from Stoney Creek warn: "The hand of oppression is growing on our people. . . . You women work for practically nothing. You must come together and say that such things must cease to be." Each night more workers "came forward" to take the union oath.[30]

Meanwhile, UTW and Federal Conciliation Service officials arrived on the scene. On

March 22 they reached a "gentlemen's agreement" by which the company promised a new wage scale for "good girl help" and agreed not to discriminate against union members.[31] The strikers returned to work, but the conflict was far from over. Higher paychecks never materialized; union members began losing their jobs. On April 4 local businessmen kidnapped two union organizers and ran them out of town. Eleven days later a second strike began, this time among the women in the Glanzstoff reeling room. "When they blew that whistle everybody knew to quit work," Flossie Cole recalled. "We all just quit our work and rushed out. Some of 'em went to Bemberg and climbed the fence. [They] went into Bemberg and got 'em out of there." With both plants closed by what workers called a "spontaneous and complete walkout," the national union reluctantly promised its support.[32]

This time the conflict quickly escalated. More troops arrived, and the plants became fortresses, with machine guns on the rooftops and armed guardsmen on the ground. The company sent buses manned by soldiers farther up the hollows to recruit new workers and to escort them back to town. Pickets blocked narrow mountain roads. Houses were blown up; the town water main was dynamited. An estimated 1,250 individuals were arrested in confrontations with the National Guard.[33]

As far as can be determined, no women were involved in barn burnings and dynamitings— what Bessie Edens referred to as the "rough . . . stuff" that accompanied the second strike. Men "went places that we didn't go," explained Christine Galliher. "They had big dark secrets . . . the men did." But when it came to public demonstrations, women held center stage. At the outset "hundreds of girls" had ridden down main street "in buses and taxis, shouting and laughing at people who watched them from windows and doorsteps." Now they blocked the road at Gap Creek and refused soldiers' orders that they walk twelve miles to jail in town. "And there was one girl that was awful tough in the bunch. . . . She said, 'No, by God. We didn't walk out here, and we're not walking back!' And she sat her hind end down in the middle of the road, and we all sat down with her. And the law used tear gas on us! . . . And it nearly put our eyes out, but we still wouldn't walk back to town." At Valley Forge women teased the guardsmen and shamed the strikebreakers. In Elizabethton after picket duty, women marched down the "Bemberg Highway . . . draped in the American flag and carrying the colors"—thereby forcing the guardsmen to present arms each time they passed. Inventive, playful, and shrewd, the women's tactics encouraged a holiday spirit. They may also have deflected violence and garnered community support.[34]

Laughter was among the women's most effective weapons. But they also made more prosaic contributions, chief among which was taking responsibility for the everyday tasks of the union. In this they were aided by the arrival of middle-class allies, a series of extraordinary women reformers who provided new models of organizational skill and glimpses of a wider life.

After World War I national women's organizations long interested in working women had looked with increasing concern on the relocation of the female-intensive textile industry to a region where protective legislation was weak and unions were weaker. The National Women's Trade Union League (NWTUL) launched a southern educational campaign. The Young Women's Christian Association (YWCA) strengthened its industrial department and employed a series of talented southern industrial secretaries. In 1927 Louise Leonard left her YWCA post to found the Southern School for Women Workers in Industry. The convergence of interest in the South's women workers intensified with the 1929 strikes. The strikes, in turn, raised reformers' expectations and lent substance to their strategies. Leonard, for instance, visited Elizabethton, recruiting students for the Southern Summer School. Some of those who went returned again and again, and for them the school offered an exciting political education. But the benefit ran both ways. For Leonard the strike confirmed in microcosm the school's larger hopes: The nature of southern industrialization made women the key to unionization; women had led the way at Elizabethton; once reached by the Southern Summer School (and a trade-union movement more sensitive to their needs), women would lead the way throughout the South.[35]

Unlike the YWCA-based reformers, the NWTUL was a newcomer to the region, and to most of its executive committee the South was literally "another nation." Dependent on the writings of journalists and sociologists, NWTUL leaders concluded that southern workers were crippled by poverty and paternalism and that only a roundabout approach through southern liberals would do. The Elizabethton strike persuaded them to take a fresh approach. The NWTUL's twenty-fifth anniversary convention, held in 1929, featured a "dramatic and moving" speech by Margaret Bowen and a historical tableau linking the revolt of the Lowell, Massachusetts, mill girls with "the revolt of the farmers' daughters of the new industrial South today." Matilda Lindsay, director of the NWTUL's southern campaign, became a major presence at Elizabethton and at subsequent conflicts as well.[36]

Within a week after the inspectors' walkout, Matilda Lindsay set up shop in Elizabethton and began coordinating women's union support activities. Women gave out union food vouchers at L. G. Bowles's boardinghouse, where Margaret Bowen lived. They helped to run the union office. Teams of "pretty young girls" distributed handbills and took up contributions at union "tag days" in Knoxville and Asheville. A similar contingent tried to see Gov. Henry H. Horton in Nashville. Failing, they picketed his home. When the strike dragged on, the union leased a boardinghouse for young women and put Lindsay in charge. At the Tennessee Federation of Labor's 1929 convention, UTW officials acknowledged Lindsay's contributions: "She was speaker, adviser, mother, sister, bookkeeper, secretary and stenographer ... [A]nd we are happy to say she did them all without protest and without credit." But the tribute said less about Lindsay than about the distance between the vision of women reformers and the assumptions of trade-union leaders. Whether workers or reformers, women were seen as supporting players, not the best hope for cracking the nonunion South.[37]

In any event, it was workers, not organizers or reformers, who bore the brunt of the struggle and would have to live with its results. And beneath high spirits the terms of battle had begun to change. The militancy of Alfred Hoffmann, the UTW's chief organizer at Elizabethton, matched the strikers' own. But he was hobbled by a national union that lacked the resources and commitment to sustain the strike. Instead of translating workers' grievances into a compelling challenge, the UTW pared their demands down to the bone. On May 26, six weeks after the strike began, the union agreed to a settlement that made no mention of wages, hours, working conditions, or union recognition. The company's only concession was a promise not to discriminate against union members. The workers were less than enthusiastic. According to the strike's most thorough chronicler, "It took nine speeches and a lot of question answering lasting two and a half hours to get the strikers to accept the terms."[38]

The press, for the most part, greeted the settlement as a workers' victory, or at least a satisfactory resolution of the conflict. Anna Weinstock, the first woman to serve as a federal conciliator, was credited with bringing the company to the bargaining table and was pictured as the heroine of the event. "SETTLED BY A WOMAN!" headlined one journal. "This is the fact that astounds American newspaper editors." "Five feet five inches and 120 pounds of femininity; clean cut, even features"—and so on, in great detail. Little was made of Weinstock's own working-class origins. She was simply a "new woman," come to the rescue of a backward mountain folk. The strikers themselves dropped quickly from view.[39]

Louise Leonard had visited Elizabethton only weeks before the UTW capitulated. With her was the left-wing journalist Mary Heaton Vorse. Both were heartened by what they found. In her years of labor reporting, Vorse "had never seen anything to compare with the quality of courage and determination of the Elizabethton strikers." Leonard was impressed not only by the women's leadership but also by the strike's community support.[40] As it turned out, neither "courage and determination" nor community support was sufficient to the strikers' needs. The contest at Elizabethton was an unequal one, with a powerful multinational corporation backed by the armed force of the state pitted against workers who looked to an irresolute national union for support. But it was not so unequal in contemporary eyes as hindsight would have it. To the strikers, as to Vorse and Leonard, the future seemed up for grabs.

Observers at the time and historians since saw the Elizabethton strike as a straightforward case of labor-management strife. But the conflict appeared quite different from within. Everyone interviewed put the blame for low wages on an alliance between the German managers and the "leading citizens" of the town. Preserved in the oral tradition is the story of how the "town fathers" promised the company a supply of cheap and unorganized labor. Bessie Edens put it this way: They told the company that "women wasn't used to working, and they'd work for almost nothing, and the men would work for low wages. That's the way they got the plant here." In this version of events the strike was part of an ongoing tug-of-war. On one side stood workers, farmers, and small merchants linked by traditional networks of trade and kin. On the other, development-minded townspeople cast their lot with a "latter day industrialism" embodied by the rayon plants.[41]

Workers' roots in the countryside encouraged resistance and helped them to mobilize support once the strike began. "These workers have come so recently from the farms and mountains . . . and are of such independent spirit," Alfred Hoffmann observed, "that they 'Don't care if they lose their jobs' and cannot be scared." Asked by reporters what would happen if strike activity cost them their jobs, one woman remarked, "I haven't forgotten to use a hoe," while another said, "We'll go back to the farm."[42] Such threats were not just bravado. High levels of farm ownership sustained cultural independence. Within the internal economy of families, individual fortunes were cushioned by reciprocity; an orientation toward subsistence survived side by side with the desire for cash and store-bought goods.

Stoney Creek farmers were solidly behind the sons and daughters they sent to the factories. In county politics Stoney Creekers had historically marshaled a block vote against the town. In 1929 Stoney Creek's own J. M. Moreland was county sheriff, and he openly took the strikers' side, "I will protect your plant, but not scabs," he warned the company. "I am with you and I want you to win," he cheered the Tabernacle crowd.[43]

Solidarity flowed not only from the farm families of striking workers but also from small merchants who relied on those families for their trade. A grocer named J. D. White turned his store into a union commissary and became a mainstay on the picket line. A strike leader in the twisting room ran a country store and drove his working neighbors into town. "That's why he was pretty well accepted as their leader," said a fellow worker. "Some of them were cousins and other relations. Some of them traded at his store. Some of them rode in his taxi. All intertwined."[44]

The National Guard had divided loyalties. Parading past the plants, the strikers "waved to and called the first names of the guardsmen, for most of the young men in uniforms [were friends of] the men and girls on strike." Even when the local unit was fortified by outside recruits, fraternizing continued. Nettie Reece, like a number of her girlfriends, met her future husband that way; she saw him on the street and "knew that was mine right there." Some guardsmen went further and simply refused to serve. "The use of the National Guard here was the dirtiest deal ever pulled," one protested. "I turned in my equipment when I was ordered to go out and patrol the road. I was dropped from the payroll two weeks later."[45]

In this context of family- and community-based resistance, women had important roles to play. Farm mothers nurtured the strikers' independence simply by cleaving to the land, passing on to their children a heritage at odds with the values of the new order and maintaining family production as a hedge against the uncertainties of a market economy. But the situation of farm mothers had other effects as well, and it would be a mistake to push the argument for continuity too far. As their husbands ranged widely in search of wage labor, women's work intensified while their status—now tied to earning power— declined. The female strikers of Elizabethton saw their mothers as resourceful and strong but also as increasingly isolated and hard pressed. Most important, they no longer looked to their mothers' lives as patterns for their own.[46]

The summer after the strike, Bessie Edens attended the Southern Summer School, where she set the group on its ear with an impassioned defense of women's rights:

> It is nothing new for married women to work. They have always worked. . . . Women have always worked harder than men and always had to look up to the man and feel that they were weaker and inferior. . . . If we women would not be so submissive and take every thing for granted, if we would awake and stand up for our rights, this world would be a better place to live in, at least it would be better for the women.
>
> Some girls think that as long as mother takes in washings, keeps ten or twelve boarders or perhaps takes in sewing, she isn't working. But I say that either one of the three is as hard work as women could do. So if they do that at home and don't get any wages for it, why would it not be all right for them to go to a factory and receive pay for what they do?[47]

Bessie Edens was remarkable in her talent for translating Southern Summer School teachings into the idiom of her own experiences and observations. But scattered through the life histories written by other students are echoes of her general themes.[48] Read in the context of farm daughters' lives—their first-hand exposure to rural poverty, their yearnings for a more expansive world—these stories reflect the "structure of feeling" women brought to the rayon plants and then to the picket line and union hall. Women such as Edens, it seems, sensed the devaluation of women's handicraft labor in the face of cheap consumer goods. They feared the long arm of their mother's fate, resented their father's distant authority, and envied their brother's exploits away from home. By opting for work in the rayon plants, they struck out for their own place in a changing world. When low wages, high costs, and autocratic managers affronted their dignity and dashed their hopes, they were the first to revolt.

The Elizabethton story thus presents another pattern in the female protest tradition. In coal-mining communities a rigid division of labor and women's hardships in company towns have resulted, paradoxically, in the notable militancy of miners' wives. By contrast, tobacco factories have tended to employ married women, whose job commitments and associational lives enable them to assume leadership roles in sustained organizing drives. In yet other circumstances, such as the early New England textile mills or the union insurgency of the 1920s and 1930s, single women initiated independent strikes or provided strong support for male-led, mixed-sex campaigns. Where, as in Elizabethton, people were mobilized as family and community members rather than as individual workers, non-wage-earning women could provide essential support. Once in motion, their daughters might outdo men in militancy, perhaps because they had fewer dependents than their male co-workers and could fall back more easily on parental resources, perhaps because the peer culture and increased independence encouraged by factory labor stirred boldness and inspired experimentation.[49]

The fact of women's initiative and participation in collective action is instructive. Even more intriguing is the gender-based symbolism of their protest style. Through dress, language, and gesture, female strikers expressed a complex cultural identity and turned it to their own rebellious purposes.[50]

Consider, for instance, Trixie Perry and a woman who called herself "Texas Bill." Twenty-eight-year-old Trixie Perry was a reeler in the Glanzstoff plant. She had apparently become pregnant ten years before, had married briefly and then divorced, giving her son her maiden name. Her father was a butcher and a farmer, and she lived near her family on the edge of town. Perry later moved into Elizabethton. She never remarried but went on to have several more children by other men. Texas Bill's background is more elusive. All we know is that she came from out of state, lived in a boardinghouse, and claimed to have been married twice before she arrived in town. These two friends were ringleaders on the picket line. Both were charged with violating the injunction, and both were brought to trial.[51]

Trixie Perry took the stand in a dress sewn from red, white, and blue bunting and a cap made of a small American flag. The prosecuting attorney began his cross-examination:

"You have a United States flag as a cap on your head?"

"Yes."

"Wear it all the time?"

"Whenever I take a notion."

"You are dressed in a United States flag, and the colors?"

"I guess so, I was born under it, guess I have a right to."[52]

The main charge was that Perry and her friend had drawn a line across the road at Gap Creek and dared the soldiers to cross it. Above all they were accused of taunting the National Guard. The defense attorney, a fiery local lawyer playing to a sympathetic crowd, did not deny the charges. Instead, he used the women to mock the government's case. Had Trixie Perry threatened a lieutenant? "He rammed a gun in my face and I told him to take it out or I would knock it out." Had she blocked the road? "A little thing like me block a big road?" What had she said to the threat of a tear gas bomb? "That little old fire cracker of a thing, it won't go off."[53]

Texas Bill was an even bigger hit with the crowd. The defense attorney called her the "Wild Man from Borneo." A guard said she was "the wildest human being I've ever seen." Texas Bill both affirmed and subverted her reputation. Her nickname came from her habit of wearing "cowboy" clothes. But when it was her turn to testify, she "strutted on the stand" in a fashionable black picture hat and a black coat. Besides her other transgressions, she was accused of grabbing a soldier's gun and aiming it at him. What was she doing on the road so early in the morning? "I take a walk every morning before breakfast for my health," Texas Bill replied with what a reporter described as "an assumed ladylike dignity."[54]

Witnesses for the prosecution took pains to contradict Texas Bill's "assumed ladylike dignity." A guardsman complained that she called him a " 'God damned yellow son-of-a-bitch' and then branched out from that." Texas Bill offered no defense: "When that soldier stuck his gun in my face, that did make me mad and I did cuss a little bit and don't deny it." Far from discrediting the strikers, the soldiers' testimony added to their own embarrassment and the audience's delight. In tune with the crowd, the defense attorney "enjoyed making the guards admit they had been 'assaulted' . . . by 16 and 18-year-old girls."[55]

Mock gentility, transgressive laughter, male egos on the line—the mix made for wonderful theater and proved effective in court as well. The judge reserved maximum sentences for three especially aggressive men; all the women and most of the men were found not guilty or were lightly fined. In the end even those convictions were overturned by the state court of appeals.[56]

Trixie Perry and Texas Bill certainly donned the role of "disorderly woman." Since, presumably, only extraordinary circumstances call forth feminine aggression, women's assaults against persons and property constitute a powerful witness against injustice. At the same time, since women are considered less rational and taken less seriously than men, they may meet less resistance and be punished less severely for their crimes.[57]

But Trixie Perry and Texas Bill were not just out of line in their public acts; they also led unconventional private lives. It was that erotic subtext that most horrified officialdom and amused the courtroom crowd. The only extended discussion of the strike that appears in the city council minutes resulted in a resolution that read in part:

> WHEREAS, it has come to [our] attention . . . that the moral tone of this community has been lowered by reason of men and women congregating in various houses and meeting-places in Elizabethton and there practicing lewdness all hours of the night, in defiance of morality, law and order. . . .
>
> NOW, THEREFORE, BE IT RESOLVED, that the police force of the City arrest and place in the City Jail those who are violating the laws by practicing lewdness within the City of Elizabethton. . . .[58]

Union representatives apparently shared, indeed anticipated, the councilmen's concern. Worried by rumors that unemployed women were resorting to prostitution, they had already announced to the press that 25 percent of the strikers had been sent back to their hillside homes, "chiefly young single girls whom we want to keep off the streets." The townsmen and the trade unionists were thus united in drawing a line between good women and bad, with respectability being measured not only by chastity but by nuances of style and language as well.[59] In the heat of the trial, the question of whether or not women—as workers—had violated the injunction took second place to questions about their status *as women*, as members of their sex. Had they cursed? Had they been on the road at odd hours of the day or night? Was Texas Bill a lady or a "wild man from Borneo"? Fearing that "lewd women" might discredit the organizing drive, the organizers tried to send them home. To protect the community's "moral tone," the city council threatened to lock them up.

There is nothing extraordinary about this association between sexual misbehavior and women's labor militancy. Since strikers are often young single women who violate gender conventions by invading public space customarily reserved for men (and sometimes frequented by prostitutes)—and since female aggressiveness stirs up fears of women's sexual power—opponents have often undercut union organizing drives by insinuations of prostitution or promiscuity. Fearing guilt by association, "respectable" women stay away.[60]

What is impressive here is how Trixie Perry and Texas Bill handled the dichotomy between ladyhood and lewdness, good girls and bad. Using words that, for women in particular, were ordinarily taboo, they refused deference and signaled disrespect. Making no secret of their sexual experience, they combined flirtation with fierceness on the picket line and adopted a provocative courtroom style. And yet, with the language of dress—a cap made of an American flag, an elegant wide-brimmed hat—they claimed their rights as citizens and their place in the female community.

Moreover, that community upheld their claims. The defense attorney chose "disorderly women" as his star witnesses, and the courtroom spectators enthusiastically cheered them on. The prosecuting attorney recommended dismissal of the charges against all the women on trial except Trixie Perry, Texas Bill, and a "hoodlum" named Lucille Ratliffe, on the grounds that the rest came from "good families." Yet in the court transcripts, few differences can be discerned in the behavior of good girls and bad. The other female defendants may have been less flamboyant, but they were no less sharp-tongued. Was Vivian King a member of the UTW? "Yes, and proud of it." Had she been picketing? "Yes, proud of that." What was a young married woman named Dorothy Oxindine doing on Gap Creek at five o'clock in the morning? "Out airing." Did Lena May Jones "holler out 'scab' "? "No, I think the statement made was 'I wouldn't be a scab' and 'Why don't you come and join our organization.' " Did she laugh at a solider and tell him his gun wouldn't shoot? "I didn't tell him it wouldn't shoot, but I laughed at him . . . and told him he was too much of a man to shoot a lady."[61]

Interviewed over fifty years later, strike participants still refused to make invidious distinctions between themselves and women like Trixie Perry and Texas Bill. Bessie Edens was a settled, self-educated, married woman. But she was also a self-described "daredevil on the picket line," secure in the knowledge that she had a knife hidden in her drawstring underwear. To Edens, who came from a mountain hamlet called Hampton, the chief distinction did not lie between herself and rougher women. It lay between herself and merchants' wives who blamed the trouble on "those hussies from Hampton." When asked what she thought of Trixie Perry and Texas Bill, she answered simply, "There were some girls like that involved. But I didn't care. They did their part."[62]

Nettie Reece, who lived at home with parents who were "pretty particular with [their] daughters," shared Bessie Edens's attitude. After passing along the town gossip about Trixie Perry, she was anxious to make sure her meaning was not misconstrued. "Trixie was not a woman who sold her body," she emphasized. "She just had a big desire for sex. . . . And when she had a cause to fight for, she'd fight." Reece then went on to establish Perry's claim to a certain kind of respectability. After the strike Perry became a hard-working restaurant cook. She was a good neighbor: "If anybody got sick, she was there to wait on them." The six children she bore out of wedlock did well in life, and they "never throwed [their mother] aside."[63]

Family and community solidarity were obvious in the courtroom, implicit in press reports, and confirmed by interviews. By inference, they can also be seen in the living situations of female strikers. Of the 122 activists whose residences could be determined, only six lived or boarded alone. Residing at home, they could hardly have joined in the fray without family toleration or support.[64]

Industrialization, as we know, changed the nature of work, the meaning of time. In Carter County it entailed a shift of economic and political power from the countryside to the town. At issue too were more intimate matters of fantasy, culture, and style.

Implicit in the conflict were two different sexual systems. One, subscribed to by union officials and the local middle class, mandated chastity before marriage, men as breadwinners, and women as housewives in the home. The other, rooted in a rural past and adapted to working-class life, assumed women's productive labor, circumscribed women's roles without investing in abstract standards of femininity, and looked upon sexuality with a more pragmatic eye.

It must be noted at once that this is uncharted territory. There are no studies of gender in preindustrial Appalachia, let alone of sexuality, and discussions of the subject have been limited for the most part to a defense against pernicious stereotypes. The mountain women who people nineteenth-century travel accounts, novels, and social surveys tend to be drudges who married young and aged early, burdened by frequent pregnancies and good-for-nothing men. Alongside that predominant image is another: the promiscuous mountain girl, responsible for the supposed high rate of illegitimacy in the region.[65] We need not dwell on the shortcomings of such stylized accounts, filtered as they are through the lenses of class and cultural "otherness." But it would also be a mistake to discount them altogether, or to oppose them only with examples of mountain folk who conformed quite nicely to outlanders' middle-class norms. The view of married women as drudges is analogous to white observations of Indian life: Women may in fact have taken on agricultural responsibilities seen by observers as inappropriate to their sex, while men engaged in hunting, fishing, and moonshining—and later in logging or coal mining—that seemed unproductive or illegitimate or that took them away from home. Similarly, stripped of moralism, there may be a grain of truth in observations about sexual mores in the backcountry South. The women of Elizabethton came from a society that seems to have recognized liaisons established without the benefit of clergy or license fees and allowed legitimacy to be broadly construed—in short, a society that might produce a Trixie Perry or defend "hussies from Hampton" against the snubs of merchants' wives.[66]

This is not to say that the women of Elizabethton were simply acting on tradition. On the contrary, the strikers dressed the persona of the disorderly woman in unmistakably modern garb. Women's behavior on the witness stand presupposed a certain sophistication: A passing familiarity allowed them to parody ladyhood and to thumb a nose at the genteel standards of the town. Combining garments from the local past with fragments of an expansive consumer culture, the women of Elizabethton assembled their own version of a brash, irreverent Jazz Age style.

By the early 1920s radios and "Ford touring cars" had joined railroads and mail-order catalogs as conduits to the larger world. Record companies had discovered hill-country music, and East Tennessee's first country-music stars were recording hits that transformed ballad singing, fiddle playing, and banjo picking into one of America's great popular-music sounds. The banjo itself was an Afro-American instrument that had come to the mountains with the railroad gangs. Such cultural interchanges multiplied during the 1920s as rural traditions met the upheavals of industrial life. The result was an explosion of musical creativity—in the hills of Tennessee no less than in New York City and other cosmopolitan centers.[67] Arriving for work in the rayon plants, young people brought with them the useable past of the countryside, but they quickly assimilated the speeded-up rhythms, the fashions, the popular culture of their generation's changing times.

Work-related peer groups formed a bridge between traditional loyalties and a novel youth culture. Whether married or single, living with parents or on their own, women participated in the strike in same-sex groups. Sisters boarded, worked, and demonstrated together. Girlfriends teamed up in groups or pairs. Trixie Perry and Texas Bill were a case in point. But there were others as well. Nettie Reece joined the union with her parents' approval but also with her whole "dirty dozen" gang in tow. Ethel and M. C. Ashworth, ages eighteen and seventeen, respectively, came from Virginia to work in the plants. "Hollering and singing [in a] Ford touring car," they were arrested together in a demonstration at Watauga Point. Ida and Evelyn Heaton boarded together on Donna Avenue. Evelyn was hit by a car on the picket line, swore out a warrant, and had the commander of the National Guard placed under arrest. After the strike Evelyn was blacklisted, and Ida attended the Southern Summer School.[68]

The sudden gathering of young people in the town nourished new patterns of heterosociability, and the strike's erotic undercurrent surfaced not only in Trixie Perry's "big desire for sex" but also in the behavior of her more conventional peers. The loyalties of the guardsmen were divided, but their sympathy was obvious, as was their interest in the female strikers. Most of the Elizabethton women were in their teens or early twenties, the usual age of marriage in the region, and the strike provided unaccustomed opportunities for courtship. Rather than choosing a neighbor they had known all their lives, under watchful parental eyes, women flirted on the picket lines or the shop floor. Romance and politics commingled in the excitement of the moment, flowering in a spectrum of behavior—from the outrageousness of Trixie Perry to a spate of marriages among other girls.

What needs emphasis here is the dynamic quality of working-class women's culture—a quality that is sometimes lost in static oppositions between modernism and traditionalism, individualism and family values, consumer and producer mentalities. This is especially important where regional history has been so thoroughly mythologized. Appalachian culture, like all living cultures, embraced continuity and discontinuity, indigenous and borrowed elements.[69] As surely as Anna Weinstock—or Alabama's Zelda Fitzgerald—or any city flapper, the Elizabethton strikers were "new women," making their way in a world their mothers could not have known but carrying with them values handed down through the female line.

Three vignettes may serve to illustrate that process of grounded change.

Flossie Cole's mother, known by everyone on Stoney Creek as "Aunt Tid," was kin to Sheriff Moreland, but that didn't keep her from harboring cardplayers, buck-dancers, and whiskey drinkers in her home. Aunt Tid was also a seamstress who "could look at a picture in a catalog and cut a pattern and make a dress just like it." But like most of her friends, Cole jumped at the chance for store-bought clothes. "That first paycheck, that was it . . . I think I bought me some new clothes with the first check I got. I bought me a new pair of shoes and a dress and a hat. Can you imagine someone going to a plant with a hat on? I had a blue dress and black shoes—patent leather, honey, with real high heels—and a blue hat." Nevertheless before Cole left home in the morning for her job in the rayon plant, Aunt Tid made sure that around her neck—beneath the new blue dress—she wore a bag of asafetida, a strong-smelling resin, a folk remedy to protect her from diseases that might be circulating in the town.[70]

Then there was Myrtle Simmerly, whose father was killed in a logging accident and whose brothers went "out West" to work, faithfully sending money home so that she could finish school. Myrtle was the first secretary hired at the rayon plant, and she used her earnings to buy a Ford roadster with a rumble seat and a wardrobe of up-to-date clothes. For all her modern trappings, Myrtle defended her "hillbilly" heritage and took the workers' side against what she called the "city fathers, the courthouse crew." Asked why she thought women played such active roles in the strike, she spoke from experience: "They grew up on these farms, and they had to be aggressive to live."[71]

Finally, there is visual evidence: a set of sixteen-millimeter films made by the company in order to identify—and to blacklist—workers who participated in the union. In those films groups of smiling women traipse along the picket line dressed in up-to-date clothes.[72] Yet federal conciliator Anna Weinstock, speaking to an interviewer forty years later, pictured them in sunbonnets, and barefooted. "They were," she explained, "what we would normally call hillbillies": women who "never get away from their shacks."[73] This could be seen as the treachery of memory, a problem of retrospection. But it is also an illustration of the power of stereotypes, of how cultural difference is registered as backwardness, of how images of poverty and backwardness hide the realities of working-class women's lives.

The strike, as we know, was defeated, but not without cost to the company and some benefit to the workers. Elizabethton set off a chain reaction across the textile South. "It was supposed to be the leading strike in the South of the textile workers," Bessie Edens explained. "It was the main key to start the labor movement in the South, is what I understood." In Elizabethton itself an autocratic plant manager was recalled to Germany, a personnel officer installed a plant council and an extensive welfare program, wages went up, and hours went down. The new company officials chose symbols of hierarchy and privilege that blended more easily with the American scene. Uniforms were eliminated. At the dedication of a company athletic field in 1930, the "Bemberg Glanzstoff band" marched around the grandstand, followed first by plant officials, then by workingmen carrying banners, and finally by "beautiful women, dressed in rayon suits and costumes of brilliant hues."[74]

To be sure, blacklisted workers suffered for their choices. The depression, followed by the great drought of 1930–1931, devastated the rural economy and put a powerful bludgeon in company hands.[75] Union support inevitably fell away. Rosa Long, for once, was a pragmatist: "I quit the Union because I didn't see anything to them. Wasn't making me a living talking." Yet a committed remnant, supported by the "Citizens Committee," kept the local alive. When the National Labor Relations Act passed in 1935, the Elizabethton plants were among the first to join the Textile Workers Union of America-Congress of Industrial Organizations. Transferring their allegiance to the UTW-AFL in the late 1930s, Elizabethton's workers formed the largest rayon workers' local in the country.[76]

In the community at large, a muted debate over development went on. The local newspaper kept publishing paeons to progress. But the Citizens Committee saw things differently: "Our sons and daughters have been assaulted, arrested and imprisoned because they refuse to bow to the management of the plants. [Concessions to the companies have] defrauded Carter County out of thousands of dollars of taxes rather than bettering the conditions of the county." In some ways at least, the Citizens Committee seems to have taken the more realistic view. The metropolis dreamed of by Elizabethton boosters never materialized. Having bargained away its tax base, the town was forced to default on its bonded debt. Unfinished streets and sidewalks meandered to an end in open fields; houses in subdivisions sat half-finished; chemical wastes from the rayon plants poured into the Watauga River, polluting the clear spring water that had been one of the site's attractions to industry.[77]

The fate of the Elizabethton women is difficult to discern. Interviews traced the road from farm to factory, then focused on the strike itself; they offered only hints of how the experience of the 1920s fit into whole-life trajectories. Still, circumstantial evidence allows at least a few observations. The first is that from the time the rayon plants reopened in the fall of 1929 until World War II, the number of women they employed steadily declined. Perhaps female strikers were more ruthlessly blacklisted, or men preferentially rehired. Perhaps, disillusioned, women simply stayed away. In any case, shrinking opportunities in the rayon mills did not mean that women abandoned wage labor. Although most of the activists whose subsequent histories are known married and had children, they did not permanently leave the work force. Some returned to the old roles of laundress, cook, and housekeeper; others became telephone operators, saleswomen, and secretaries.[78] Still others eventually slipped back into the rayon plants. "They called back who they wanted," said Flossie Cole. "I was out eighteen years. . . . I probably wouldn't ever have gotten back 'cause they blacklisted so many of 'em. But I married and changed my name and World War II came on and I went back to work." Overall, the percentage of Carter County women who were gainfully employed held steady through the 1930s, then leaped upward with the outbreak of war.[79]

But if the habit of female "public work" persisted, its meaning probably did not. Young women had poured eagerly into the rayon mills, drawn at least in part by the promise of

364 / Jacquelyn Dowd Hall

independence, romance, and adventure. As the depression deepened, such motives paled beside stark necessity. One statistic makes the point: The only female occupation that significantly increased during the decade from 1930 to 1940 was domestic service, which rose from 13.4 percent of gainfully employed women to 17.1 percent. When Flossie Cole went "back to the drudge house," she had plenty of company.[80]

Still, despite subsequent hardships, the spirit of the 1920s flickered on. Setting out to explore the strike through oral-history interviews, we expected to find disclaimers or silences. Instead, we heard unfaded memories and no regrets. "I knew I wasn't going to go back, and I didn't care," said Bessie Edens. "I wrote them a letter and told them I didn't care whether they took me back or not. I didn't! If I'd starved I wouldn't of cared, because I knew what I was a'doing when I helped to pull it. And I've never regretted it in any way. . . . And it did help the people, and it's helped the town and the country."[81] For those, like Edens, who went on to the Southern Summer School or who remained active in the union, the strike was a pivot around which the political convictions and personal aspirations of a lifetime turned. For them, there were intangible rewards: a subtle deepening of individual power, a belief that they had made history and that later generations benefitted from what they had done.

The strike, of course, made a fainter impression on other lives. Women's rebelliousness neither redefined gender roles nor overcame economic dependency. Their desire for the trappings of modernity could blur into a self-limiting consumerism. An ideology of romance could end in sexual danger or a married woman's burdensome double day. None of that, however, ought to obscure a generation's legacy. A norm of female public work, a new style of sexual expressiveness, the entry of women into public space and political struggles previously monopolized by men—all these pushed against traditional constraints even as they created new vulnerabilities.[82] The young women who left home for the rayon plants pioneered a new pattern of female experience, and they created for their post-World War II daughters an environment far different from the one they, in their youth, had known. It would be up to later generations to wrestle with the costs of commercialization and to elaborate a vision that embraced economic justice and community solidarity as well as women's liberation.

Notes

This essay is part of a larger study of southern textile workers cowritten by Christopher Daly, Jacquelyn Dowd Hall, Lu Ann Jones, Robert Korstad, James Leloudis, and Mary Murphy. It began as a collaborative endeavor with Sara Evans of the University of Minnesota, who joined me in gathering many of the interviews on which I have relied. Support for this project came from a University Research Council Grant, an Appalachian Studies Fellowship, and a Woodrow Wilson International Center for Scholars Fellowship.

1. Dan Crowe, *Old Town and the Covered Bridge* (Johnson City, Tenn., 1977), 32, 71; Florence (Cole) Grindstaff interview by Jacquelyn Dowd Hall, July 10, 1981 (in Jacquelyn Dowd Hall's possession). The oral-history component of this essay consists of approximately thirty interviews, the most detailed of which were with pro-union activists, a National Guardsman, one of the original German managers of the Bemberg plant, a leader of a company-sponsored organization of "loyal" workers, and members of the sheriff's family. Briefer interviews with workers who remembered the strike but who had not been actively involved are also included.

2. *Elizabethton Star*, March 13, 1929; *Knoxville News Sentinel*, March 13, 1929; Margaret Bowen, "The Story of the Elizabethton Strike," *American Federationist*, 36 (June 1929), 664–68; U.S. Congress, Senate Committee on Manufactures, *Working Conditions of the Textile Industry in North Carolina, South Carolina, and Tennessee*, 71 Cong., 1 sess., May 8, 9, and 20, 1929; *American Bemberg Corp. v. George Miller, et al.*, minute books "Q" and "R," Chancery Court minutes, Carter County, Tenn., July 22, 1929 (Carter County Courthouse, Elizabethton, Tenn.).

3. For the 1929 strike wave, see Tom Tippett, *When Southern Labor Stirs* (New York, 1931); Liston Pope, *Mill-hands and Preachers: A Study of Gastonia* (New York, 1942), 207–330; James A. Hodges, "Challenge to the New South: The Great Textile Strike in Elizabethton, Tennessee, 1929," *Tennessee Historical Quarterly*, 23 (Dec. 1964), 343–57; Irving Bernstein, *The Lean Years: A History of the American Worker*, 1920–1933

(Boston, 1960), 1–43; David S. Painter, "The Southern Labor Revolt of 1929" (seminar paper, University of North Carolina, Chapel Hill, 1974, in David S. Painter's possession); and Jesse Creed Jones, "Revolt in Appalachia: The Elizabethton Rayon Strike, 1929" (honors thesis, University of Tennessee, Knoxville, 1974, in Paul H. Bergeron's possession).

4. On Ella May Wiggins, see Lynn Haessly, " 'Mill Mother's Lament': Ella May, Working Women's Militancy, and the 1929 Gaston County Textile Strikes" (seminar paper, University of North Carolina, Chapel Hill, 1984, in Lynn Haessly's possession); and Lynn Haessley, "Mill Mother's Lament': The Intellectual Left's Reshaping of the 1929 Gaston County Textile Strikes and Songs," *ibid.* Proletarian novels, in contrast to historical accounts, took the perspective and experiences of women as their central concern. See esp. Fielding Burke (Olive Tilford Dargan), *Call Home the Heart* (New York, 1932). See also Sylvia Jenkins Cook, *From Tobacco Road to Route 66: The Southern Poor White in Fiction* (Chapel Hill, 1976), 98–142. For contemporary observations on Elizabethton women, see Matilda Lindsay, "Women Hold Key to Unionization of Dixie," *Machinists' Monthly Journal*, 41 (Sept. 1929), 638–39, 684; Sherwood Anderson, "Elizabethton, Tennessee," *Nation*, May 1, 1929, 526–27; *Knoxville News Sentinel*, May 17, 1929; and Florence Kelley, "Our Newest South," *Survey*, June 15, 1929, 342–44. Sara Evans was the first historian to raise questions about women's roles. See Sara Evans, "Women of the New South: Elizabethton, Tennessee, 1929" (seminar paper, University of North Carolina, Chapel Hill, 1970, in Sara Evans's possession).

5. Anne Firor Scott, "On Seeing and Not Seeing: A Case of Historical Invisibility, *Journal of American History*, 71 (June 1984), 7–8. The new scholarship in Appalachian studies has had little to say about gender. For this point and for a plea for "concrete, empirical, historical research" on class and gender in the region, see Sally Ward Maggard, "Class and Gender: New Theoretical Priorities in Appalachian Studies," paper presented at the Eighth Annual Appalachian Studies Conference, Berea, Ky., 1985, esp. 7 (in Sally Ward Maggard's possession).

6. This scholarship has suggested that the working-class family may serve as a base for resisting exploitation. It has begun to outline the structural factors that include or exclude women from labor movements and to explore the consciousness that informs or inhibits women's collective action. See, for example, Alice Kessler-Harris, " 'Where Are the Organized Women Workers?' " *Feminist Studies*, 3 (Fall 1975), 92–110; June Nash, "Resistance as Protest: Women in the Struggle of Bolivian Tin-Mining Communities," in *Women Cross- Culturally: Change and Challenge*, ed. Ruby Rohrlich-Leavitt (The Hague, 1975), 261–71; Dorothy Thompson, "Women and Nineteenth-Century Radical Politics: A Lost Dimension," in *The Rights and Wrongs of Women*, ed. Juliet Mitchell and Ann Oakley (New York, 1976), 112–38; Jane Humphries, "The Working Class Family, Women's Liberation, and Class Struggle: The Case of Nineteenth Century British History," *Review of Radical Political Economics*, 9 (Fall 1977), 25–41; Carole Turbin, "Reconceptualizing Family, Work and Labor Organizing: Working Women in Troy, 1860–1890," *ibid.*, 16 (Spring 1984), 1–16; Elizabeth Jameson, "Imperfect Unions: Class and Gender in Cripple Creek, 1894–1904," in *Class, Sex, and the Woman Worker*, ed. Milton Cantor and Bruce Laurie (Westport, 1977), 166–202; Thomas Dublin, *Women at Work: The Transformation of Work and Community in Lowell, Massachusetts, 1826–1860* (New York, 1979), esp. 86–131; Ruth Milkman, "Organizing the Sexual Division of Labor: Historical Perspectives on "Women's Work and the American Labor Movement," *Socialist Review*, 10 (Jan.–Feb. 1980), 95–150; Meredith Tax, *The Rising of the Women: Feminist Solidarity and Class Conflict, 1880–1917* (New York, 1980); Temma Kaplan, "Female Consciousness and Collective Action: The Case of Barcelona, 1910–1918," *Signs*, 7 (Spring 1982), 545–66; Susan Levine, "Labor's True Woman: Domesticity and Equal Rights in the Knights of Labor," *Journal of American History*, 70 (Sept. 1983), 323–39; Linda Frankel, "Southern Textile Women: Generations of Survival and Struggle," in *My Troubles Are Going to Have Trouble with Me: Everyday Trials and Triumphs of Women Workers*, ed. Karen Brodkin Sacks and Dorothy Remy (New Brunswick, 1984), 39–60; Louise A. Tilly, "Paths of Proletarianization: Organization of Production, Sexual Division of Labor, and Women's Collective Action," *Signs*, 7 (Winter 1981), 400–17; Sharon Hartman Strom, "Challenging 'Woman's Place': Feminism, the Left, and Industrial Unionism in the 1930s," *Feminist Studies*, 9 (Summer 1983), 359–86; Dolores E. Janiewski, *Sisterhood Denied: Race, Gender, and Class in a New South Community* (Philadelphia, 1985), esp. 152–78; and Ruth Milkman, ed., *Women, Work, and Protest: A Century of U.S. Women's Labor History* (Boston, 1985). In contrast, Leslie Woodcock Tentler has emphasized how family values and the structure of work have encouraged female acquiescence. Leslie Woodcock Tentler, *Wage-Earning Women: Industrial Work and Family Life in the United States, 1900–1930* (New York, 1979), esp. 9–10, 72–80, 180–85.

7. Natalie Zemon Davis, *Society and Culture in Early Modern France* (Stanford, 1975), 124–51. For this phenomenon in the New World, see Laurel Thatcher Ulrich, *Good Wives: Image and Reality in the Lives of Women in Northern New England, 1650–1750* (New York, 1982), 191–97.

8. Michel Foucault, *Power/Knowledge: Selected Interviews and Other Writings, 1972–1977*, trans. and ed. Colin Gordon (New York, 1980), 81.

9. Jesse W. Markham, *Competition in the Rayon Industry* (Cambridge, Mass., 1952), 1–38, 97, 186, 193, 209; Joseph Leeming, *Rayon: The First Man-Made Fiber* (Brooklyn, 1950), 1–82; John F. Holly, "Elizabethton, Tennessee: A Case Study of Southern Industrialization" (Ph.D. diss., Clark University, 1949), 123, 127–28, 133.

10. Bruce Roberts and Nancy Roberts, *Where Time Stood Still: A Portrait of Appalachia* (New York, 1970); William Goodell Frost, "Our Contemporary Ancestors in the Southern Mountains," *Atlantic Monthly*, 83 (March 1899), 311; Arnold J. Toynbee, *A Study of History* (2 vols., New York, 1947), II, 312. For images of Appalachia, see also Henry D. Shapiro, *Appalachia on Our Mind: The Southern Mountains and Mountaineers in the American Consciousness, 1870–1920* (Chapel Hill, 1978). In the 1970s regional scholars posited a neocolonial, or world-systems, model for understanding the "development of underdevelopment" in the Southern Mountains. More recently, they have begun to emphasize the role of indigenous elites, class formation, and the similarities between the Appalachian experience and that of other societies in transition from a semisubsistence to a corporate capitalist economy. See, for example, John Gaventa, *Power and Powerlessness: Quiescence and Rebellion in an Appalachian Valley* (Urbana, 1980); David Alan Corbin, *Life, Work, and Rebellion in the Coal Fields: The Southern West Virginia Miners, 1880–1922* (Urbana, 1981); and Ronald D. Eller, *Miners, Millhands, and Mountaineers: Industrialization of the Appalachian South, 1880–1930* (Knoxville, 1982). For an approach to cultural change, see David E. Whisnant, *All That Is Native & Fine: The Politics of Culture in an American Region* (Chapel Hill, 1983).

11. Eller, *Miners, Millhands, and Mountaineers*, 3–38; Steven Hahn, *The Roots of Southern Populism: Yeoman Farmers and the Transformation of the Georgia Upcountry, 1850–1890* (New York, 1983), 1–169; Holly, "Elizabethton, Tennessee," 1–121; Alfred Hoffmann; "The Mountaineer in Industry," *Mountain Life and Work*, 5 (Jan. 1930, 2–7.

12. J. Fred Holly, "The Co-operative Town Company of Tennessee: A Case Study of Planned Economic Development," *East Tennessee Historical Society's Publications*, 36 (1964), 56–69; Holly, "Elizabethton, Tennessee," 117–20; Eller, *Miners, Millhands, and Mountaineers*, 86–127; Rebecca Cushman, "Seed of Fire: The Human Side of History in Our Nation's Southern Highland Region and Its Changing Years," typescript, n.d., 142–44, North Carolina Collection (Wilson Library, University of North Carolina, Chapel Hill); *Mountaineer*, Dec. 28, Dec. 31, 1887; Nan Elizabeth Woodruff, *As Rare as Rain: Federal Relief in the Great Southern Drought of 1930–31* (Urbana, 1985), 140–57; Ronald D. Eller, "Class, Conflict, and Modernization in the Appalachian South," *Appalachian Journal*, 10 (Winter 1983), 183–86; George F. Dugger, Sr., interview by Hall and Sara Evans, Aug. 8, 1979, transcript, 8–14, Southern Oral History Program Collection, Southern Historical Collection (Wilson Library, University of North Carolina, Chapel Hill). See also David L. Carlton, *Mill and Town in South Carolina, 1880–1920* (Baton Rouge, 1982), 1–39. The problems associated with economic change in Carter County were exacerbated by a high birth rate and by the enclosure of half the county's land area for a national forest reserve. See Si Kahn, "The Government's Private Forests," *Southern Exposure*, 2 (Fall 1974), 132–44; Margaret J. Hagood, "Mothers of the South: A Population Study of Native White Women of Childbearing Age of the Southeast" (Ph.D. diss., University of North Carolina, Chapel Hill, 1938), 260–86; and Woodruff, *As Rare as Rain*, 140–41.

13. U.S. Department of the Interior, Census Office, *Report on the Productions of Agriculture as Returned at the Tenth Census (June 1, 1980)* (Washington, 1883), 84–85, 132, 169; U.S. Department of Commerce, Bureau of the Census, *Fourteenth Census of the United States Taken in the Year 1920: Agriculture*, vol. VI, pt. 2 (Washington, 1922), 446–47.

14. The negotiations that brought the rayon company to Elizabethton can be traced in the John Nolen Papers (Department of Manuscripts of University Archives, Cornell University Libraries, Ithaca, N.Y.). See esp. John Nolen, "Report on Reconnaissance Survey," typescript, box 27, *ibid.*, and John Nolen, "Progress Report and Preliminary Recommendation," typescript, *ibid.* See also Holly, "Elizabethton, Tennessee," 123, 133–38; Hodges, "Challenge to the New South," 343–44; and Dugger interview, 12–14.

15. Hoffmann, "Mountaineer in Industry," 3; *Elizabethton Star*, March 22, 1929; *Knoxville News Sentinel*, March 14, March 22, 1929; Holly, "Elizabethton, Tennessee," 156, 198. For some indirect evidence of discontent with the course of events, however, see *Elizabethton Star*, Jan. 1, Jan. 17, 1929.

16. Accounts of the size and composition of the work force differ widely. I am relying here on Committee on Manufactures, *Working Conditions of the Textile Industry in North Carolina, South Carolina, and Tennessee*, 95; interview with Arthur Mothwurf, *Knoxville News Sentinel*, May 20, 1929; Noel Sargent, "East Tennessee's Rayon Strikes of 1929," *American Industries*, 29 (June 1929), 10–11; and Henry Schuettler interview by Hall, n.d. [1981] (in Hall's possession). The city directory for 1930 showed only 21 married women out of 232 town-dwelling female rayon workers, whereas the figures for men were 375 out of 651. It is likely, however, that the directory underestimated married women's employment by listing only the occupation of the male head-of-household, *Miller's Elizabethton, Tenn., City Directory*, II (Asheville, N.C., 1930). (City directories are extant only for 1926, 1929, and 1930. They were published more regularly after 1936.)

Blacks comprised less than 2 percent of the county's population in 1930, and few were employed in the rayon plants. This is not to say that the county's black population was unaffected by industrialization. The pull of urban growth combined with worsening conditions in the countryside drew blacks to town where they found jobs on the railroads, in construction, and as day laborers. From 1920 to 1930, the black population dropped from 569 to 528 in the county while increasing by 650 percent in Elizabethton. U.S. Department of Commerce, Bureau of the Census, *Fifteenth Census of the United States: 1930. Population*, vol. III, pt. 2 (Washington, 1932). 909.

17. Holly, "Elizabethton, Tennessee," 108–10; *Thirteenth Census of the United States, 1910, Manuscript Population Schedule*, Carter County, Tenn., district 7; *ibid.*, district 15.

18. *Thirteenth Census of the United States, 1910, Manuscript Population Schedule*, Carter County, Tenn., district 10; *ibid.*, district 12. For the prevalence of women's work in preindustrial societies and for the traditional values that permitted families to send their daughters to take advantage of the new opportunities offered by industrialization, see Joan W. Scott and Louise A. Tilly, "Women's Work and the Family in Nineteenth-Century Europe," *Comparative Studies in Society and History*, 17 (Jan. 1975), 36–6). For a somewhat different view, see Dublin, *Women at Work*, 23–57.

19. Grindstaff interview.

20. Bessie Edens interview by Mary Frederickson, Aug. 14, 1975, transcript, 21, Southern Oral History Program Collection; Bessie Edens interview by Hall, Aug. 5, 1979 (in Hall's possession); *Elizabethton Star*, March 8, 1985.

21. Nettie Reece [pseud.] interview by Hall, May 18 and 19, 1983 (in Hall's possession).

22. Grindstaff interview; *Knoxville News Sentinel*, April 10, April 27, May 20, 1929.

23. For men's working conditions, see Hoffmann, "Mountaineer in Industry," 3; Schuettler interview; *Elizabethton Star*, Aug. 15, 1929; *Knoxville News Sentinel*, May 10, 1929; Duane McCracken, *Strike Injunctions in the New South* (Chapel Hill, 1931), 247; Lawrence Range interview by Hall, Aug. 9, 1979 (in Hall's possession); Thomas S. Mancuso, *Help for the Working Wounded* (Washington, 1976), 75–77; Bessie Edens, "My Work in an Artificial Silk Mill," in *Scraps of Work and Play*, Southern Summer School for Women Workers in Industry, Burnsville, N.C., July 11–Aug. 23, 1929, typescript, 21–22, box 111, American Labor Education Service Records, 1927–1962 (Martin P. Catherwood Library, New York State School of Industrial and Labor Relations, Cornell University, Ithaca, N.Y.); Committee on Manufactures, *Working Conditions of the Textile Industry in North Carolina, South Carolina, and Tennessee*, 85. For women's working conditions, see Christine (Hinkle) Galliher, "Where I Work," in *Scraps of Work and Play*, 23; Ida Heaton, "Glanzstoff Silk Mill," in *ibid.*, 24; Edens interview, Aug. 14, 1975, 1–2, 31–32; Edens interview, Aug. 5, 1979; Grindstaff interview; and Dorothy Conkin interview by Hall, June 16, 1982 (in Hall's possession).

24. Committee on Manufactures, *Working Conditions of the Textile Industry in North Carolina, South Carolina, and Tennessee*, 83; Wilma Crowe interview by Hall, July 15, 1981 (in Hall's possession); Hoffmann, "Mountaineer in Industry," 3; Edens interview, Aug. 14, 1975, 32; Grindstaff interview. See also Edens, "My Work in an Artificial Silk Mill."

25. Reece interview. See also Bowen, "Story of the Elizabethton Strike," 666.

26. *Knoxville News Sentinel*, May 13, 1929; *American Bemberg Corp. v. George Miller et al.*, East Tennessee District Supreme Court, Jan. 29, 1930, record of evidence, typescript, box 660, Tennessee Supreme Court Records (Tennessee State Library and Archives, Nashville). See also, *Knoxville News Sentinel*, May 14, 1929; *Elizabethton Star*, Feb. 9, 1929; Holly, "Elizabethton, Tennessee," 217; and "Synopsis of Appeal of Major George L. Berry, President of the International Printing Pressmen and Assistants' Union of North America of Pressmen's Home, Tennessee, with Relation to the Elizabethton Situation," n.d., Records of the Conciliation Service, RG 280 (National Archives). For such uses of Americanism, see Corbin *Life, Work, and Rebellion in the Coal Fields*, 236–52.

27. Ina Nell (Hinkle) Harrison interview by Hall, Aug. 8, 1979, transcript, p. 6, Southern Oral History Program Collection; Albert ("Red") Harrison interview by Evans, Aug. 9, 1979 (in Hall's possession); Evelyn Hardin, written comments in *Scraps of Work and Play*, 25. Most helpful to my thinking about modes of management control were Jeremy Brecher, "Uncovering the Hidden History of the American Workplace," *Review of Radical Political Economics*, 10 (Winter 1978), 1–23; and Richard Edwards, *Contested Terrain: The Transformation of the Workplace in the Twentieth Century* (New York, 1979), esp. 3–34.

28. Scraps of evidence indicate that a number of short-term walkouts occurred before the March strike, but those walkouts were not reported by the newspapers, and accounts of them differ in detail. See Hoffmann, "Mountaineer in Industry," 3–4; E. T. Willson to Secretary of Labor, May 25, June 26, 1929, Records of the Conciliation Service; McCracken, *Strike Injunctions in the New South*, 246; *Knoxville News Sentinel*, March 13, March 15, 1929; Holly, "Elizabethton, Tennessee," 307; and Clarence Raulston interview by Evans and Hall, Aug. 3, 1979 (in Hall's possession).

29. *Knoxville News Sentinel*, March 14, 1929; Christine (Hinkle) Galliher and Dave Galliher interview by Hall,

Aug. 8, 1979, transcript, 5, Southern Oral History Program Collection; Committee on Manufactures, *Working Conditions of the Textile Industry in North Carolina, South Carolina, and Tennessee,* 79. Although interviews provided important information about the motives, actions, and reactions of individuals, they were not a reliable source of constructing a factual chronological overview of the strike. Nor did they yield a detailed account of the inner workings of the local union. The most reliable written sources are the court records; the stories of John Moutoux, a reporter for the *Knoxville News Sentinel;* and a report commissioned by the Bemberg Corporation, Industrial Relations Counsellors, Inc., and Konsul Kummer, comps., "Beright Uber die Striks in Johnson City (Tenn.) ausgebrochen am 12 März und 5. April 1929" (in Hall's possession). Gertraude Wittig supplied me with this document. For the point of view of the local management and other industrialists, see Sargent, "East Tennessee's Rayon Strikes of 1929," 7–32.

30. *Knoxville News Sentinel,* March 14, 1929. For other comments on the religious atmosphere of union meetings, see Galliher interview, 8–9; Tom Tippett, "Southern Situation," speech typescript, Meeting held at the National Board, May 15, 1929, 3, box 25, Young Women's Christian Association Papers, Sophia Smith Collection (Smith College, Northampton, Mass); and Tom Tippett, "Impressions of Situation at Elizabethton, Tenn. May 10, 11, 1929," typescript, 1, *ibid.*

31. *Knoxville News Sentinel,* March 20, March 29, 1929; "Instructions for Adjustment of Wage Scale for Girl Help," March 15, 1929, Records of the Conciliation Service; "Bemberg-Glanzstoff Strike (Counter Proposition from Workers)," March 22, 1929, *ibid.;* "Preliminary Report of Commissioner of Conciliation," March 22, 1929, *ibid.*

32. Grindstaff interview; Committee of Striking Workers[,] Members of United Textile Workers of America to the Honorable Herbert Hoover, April 16, 1929, Records of the Conciliation Service. See also "Preliminary Report of Commissioner of Conciliation," April 16, 1929, *ibid.,* William Kelly to James J. Davis, Secretary, U.S. Department of Labor, April 15, 1929, *ibid.;* "Excerpts," April 16, 1929, *ibid.;* and *Elizabethton Star,* April 15, 1929.

33. Dr. J. A. Hardin to Hon. H. H. Horton, May 16, 1929, box 12, Governor Henry H. Horton Papers (Tennessee State Library and Archives); *Knoxville News Sentinel,* May 6, May 10, May 12, May 14, May 19, May 24, 1929; Bernstein, *Lean Years,* 18.

34. Edens interview, Aug. 14, 1975, 40, 49; Galliher interview, 33; *Knoxville News Sentinel,* March 15, May 14, May 16, May 17, 1929.

35. Mary Frederickson, "Citizens for Democracy: The Industrial Programs of the YWCA," in *Sisterhood and Solidarity: Workers' Education for Women, 1914–1984,* ed. Joyce L. Kornbluh and Mary Frederickson (Philadelphia, 1984), 75–106; Mary Evans Frederickson, "A Place to Speak Our Minds: The Southern School for Women Workers" (Ph.D. diss., University of North Carolina, Chapel Hill, 1981), 92–101; Katharine DuPre Lumpkin interview by Hall, Aug. 4, 1974, transcript, 23–65, Southern Oral History Program Collection; "Marching On," *Life and Labor Bulletin,* 7 (June 1929), 2. See also Marion W. Roydhouse, "The Universal Sisterhood of Women': Women and Labor Reform in North Carolina, 1900–1932" (Ph.D. diss., Duke University, 1980).

36. Alice Henry, "Southern Impressions," Aug. 23, 1927, box 16, National Women's Trade Union League Papers (Schlesinger Library, Radcliffe College, Cambridge, Mass.); Executive Board Meeting, Oct. 30, 1927, box 2, *ibid.; Knoxville News Sentinel,* May 7, March 19, 1929; "Marching On," 1, 3. See also Elizabeth Christman to Mrs. Howorth, June 11, 1929, box 12, Somerville-Howorth Papers (Schlesinger Library).

37. Reece interview; Galliher interview, 26; *Knoxville News Sentinel,* March 14, April 30, May 23, May 25, 1929; Robert (Bob) Cole interview by Hall, July 10, 1981, transcript, 12, Southern Oral History Program Collection; Ina Nell (Hinkle) Harrison interview, 4; Tennessee Federation of Labor, *Proceedings of the Thirty-Third Annual Convention* (Pressmen's Home, Tenn., 1929), 38.

38. *Knoxville News Sentinel,* March 19, April 14, April 27, May 5, May 27, 1929; Cole interview, 6–7; Vesta Finley and Sam Finley interview by Frederickson and Marion Roydhouse, July 22, 1975, transcript, 18–19, Southern Oral History Program Collection; *American Bemberg Corp v. George Miller et al.,* East Tennessee Supreme District Court, Jan. 29, 1930, record of evidence, typescript, box 660, Tennessee Supreme Court Records (Tennessee State Library and Archives); "Hoffman[n] Convicted on Riot Charge: To Appeal Verdict," *Hosiery Worker,* Nov. 30, 1929, 1–2; [company spy] to Horton, April 14, April 15, 1929, box 13, Horton Papers; Mary Heaton Vorse, "Rayon Strikers Reluctantly Accept Settlement," press release, May 27, 1929, box 156, Mary Heaton Vorse Papers, Archives of Labor and Urban Affairs (Walter P. Reuther Library, Wayne State University, Detroit, Mich.); "Norman Thomas Hits at Strike Efficiency," press release, May 27, 1929, *ibid.,* Ina Nell (Hinkle) Harrison interview, 2; *Chattanooga Times,* May 26, 1929.

39. Rays of Sunshine in the Rayon War," *Literary Digest,* June 8, 1929, 12; *Charlotte Observer,* June 2, 1929; *Raleigh News and Observer,* May 24, 1929.

40. *Raleigh News and Observer,* May 24, 1929. See also, *New York Times,* May 26, 1929, sec. 3, 5.

41. Edens interview, Aug. 14, 1975, 43–44; Schuettler interview; Myrtle Simmerly interview by Hall, May 18,

1983 (in Hall's possession); Dugger interview, 22; Ollie Hardin interview by Hall and Evans, Aug. 9, 1979 (in Hall's possession); Effie (Hardin) Carson interview by Hall and Evans, Aug. 6, 1979, transcript, 41, Southern Oral History Program Collection. John Fred Holly, who grew up in Elizabethton and worked at the plant during the 1930s, reported that banker E. Crawford (E. C.) Alexander showed him a copy of an agreement between the company and the Elizabethton Chamber of Commerce assuring the rayon concerns that they would never have to pay weekly wages in excess of ten dollars and that no labor unions would be allowed to operate in the town. Holly, "Elizabethton, Tennessee," 306–07. For earlier manifestations of town-county tensions, see *Mountaineer*, Dec. 28, Dec. 31, 1887, May 2, March 7, 1902. A model for this community-oriented approach to labor conflict is Herbert G. Gutman, *Work, Culture and Society in Industrializing America: Essays in American Working-Class and Social History* (New York, 1976), 234–60.

42. James Myers, "Field Notes: Textile Strikes in the South," box 374, Archive Union Files (Martin P. Catherwood Library); *Raleigh News and Observer*, March 15, 1929. See also Hoffmann, "Mountaineer in Industry," 2–5; and *Knoxville News Sentinel*, March 14, May 20, 1929.

43. Hoffmann, "Mountaineer in Industry," 2–5; Robert (Bob) Moreland and Barbara Moreland interview by Hall, July 11, 1981 (in Hall's possession); Bertha Moteland interview by Hall, July 11, 1981, *ibid.*; *Chattanooga Times*, May 26, 1929; "Resolution Adopted at Citizens Meeting," March 11, 1930, Records of the Conciliation Service; *New York Times*, April 22, 1929, 17; *St. Louis Post Dispatch*, May 26, 1929; *Knoxville News Sentinel*, March 15, March 20, 1929; *Elizabethton Star*, March 15, 1929; Hardin interview; *American Bemberg Corp. v. George Miller, et al.*, East Tennessee Supreme District Court, Jan. 29, 1930, record of evidence, typescript, box 660, Tennessee Supreme Court Records (Tennessee State Library and Archives). For other support from the countryside, see *Knoxville News Sentinel*, March 21, May 10, May 12, May 20, 1929.

44. *Knoxville News Sentinel*, March 19, May 24, 1929; Tippett, "Impressions of Situation at Elizabethton, Tenn.," 1; "Armed Mob in South Kidnaps Organizer Hoffmann," *Hoisery Worker*, March 30, 1929, 2; *American Bermberg Corp. v. George Miller et al.*, Tennessee Court of Appeals, Sept. 5, 1930, records of evidence, typescript, box 660, Tennessee Supreme Court Records (Tennessee State Library and Archives); Honard Ward interview by Hall, n.d. [1981] (in Hall's possession).

45. *Knoxville News Sentinel*, May 15, 1929; Reece interview; McCracken, *Strike Injunctions in the New South*, 246. See also Hardin interview, and Raulston interview.

46. Christine Stansell drew my attention to the importance of generational discontinuity. For the argument that precisely because they are "left behind" by the economic developments that pull men into wage labor, woman-centered families may become repositories of alternative or oppositional values, see Mina Davis Caulfield, "Imperialism, the Family and Cultures of Resistance," *Socialist Revolution*, 4 (Oct. 1974), 67–85; and Helen Matthews Lewis, Sue Easterling Kobak, and Linda Johnson, "Family, Religion and Colonialism in Central Appalachia or Bury My Rifle at Big Stone Gap," in *Colonialism in Modern America: The Appalachian Case*, ed. Helen Matthews Lewis, Linda Johnson, and Don Askins (Boone, N.C., 1978), 113–39. For a review of the literature on women and development, see Ellen Carol DuBois, Gail Paradise Kelly, Elizabeth Lapovsky Kennedy, Carolyn W. Korsmeyer, and Lillian S. Robinson, *Feminist Scholarship: Kindling in the Groves of Academe* (Urbana, 1985), 135–44. For a modern example relevant to the Elizabethton case, see Elizabeth Moen, Elise Boulding, Jane Lillydahl, and Risa Palm, *Women and the Social Costs of Economic Development: Two Colorado Case Studies* (Boulder, 1981), 1–16, 22–23, 171–78.

47. Bessie Edens, "Why a Married Woman Should Work," in *Scraps of Work and Play*, 30–31; Edens interview, Aug. 14, 1975, 14, 21, 34–35; Edens interview, Aug. 5, 1975; Millie Sample, "Impressions," Aug. 1931, box 9, American Labor Education Service Records.

48. Marion Bonner, "Behind the Southern Textile Strikes," *Nation*, Oct. 2, 1929, 351–52; "Scraps From Our Lives," in *Scraps of Work and Play*, 5–11; Raymond Williams, *The Long Revolution* (London, 1961), 48–71.

49. Corbin, *Life, Work, and Rebellion in the Coal Fields*, 92–93; Jameson, "Imperfect Unions"; Nash, "Resistance as Protest"; Tilly, "Paths of Proletarianization"; Bob Korstad, "Those Who Were Not Afraid: Winston-Salem, 1943, "in *Working Lives: The Southern Exposure History of Labor in the South*, ed. Marc S. Miller (New York, 1980), 184–99; Dublin, *Women at Work*; Strom, "Challenging 'Woman's Place.' " For the suggestion that female strikers could fall back on parental resources, see Alice Kessler-Harris, *Out to Work: A History of Wage-Earning Women in the United States* (New York, 1982), 160.

50. For the symbolism of female militancy in other cultures, see Shirley Ardener, "Sexual Insult and Female Militancy," in *Perceiving Women*, ed. Shirley Ardener (New York, 1975), 29–53; Caroline Ifeka-Moller, "Female Militancy and Colonial Revolt: The Women's War of 1929, Eastern Nigeria," in *ibid.*, 127–57; and Judith Van Allen, " 'Sitting on a Man': Colonialism and the Lost Political Institutions of Igbo Women," *Canadian Journal of African Studies*, 6 (no. 2, 1972), 165–81.

51. Thirteenth Census of the United States, 1910, Manuscript Population Schedule, Carter County, Tenn., district 7; *Miller's Elizabethton Tenn., City Directory*, I (Asheville, N.C., April 1929); *Miller's Elizabethton,*

370 / Jacquelyn Dowd Hall

Tenn., City Directory (1930); *Elizabethton Star*, Nov. 14, 1953, Jan. 31, 1986; Reece interview; Carson interview, 25; Nellie Bowers interview by Hall, May 15, 1983 (in Hall's possession); *Knoxville News Sentinel*, May 17, May 18, 1929.

52. *American Bemberg Corp. v. George Miller et al.*, East Tennessee District Supreme Court, Jan. 29, 1930, record of evidence, typescript, box 660, Tennessee Supreme Court Records (Tennessee State Library and Archives).

53. Ibid.

54. *Knoxville News Sentinel*, May 17, 1929.

55. Ibid., *American Bemberg Corp v. George Miller et al.*, East Tennessee District Supreme Court, Jan. 29, 1930, record of evidence, typescript, box 660, Tennessee Supreme Court Records (Tennessee State Library and Archives).

56. *American Bemberg Corp. v. George Miller, et al.*, minute books "Q" and "R," Chancery Court minutes, Carter County, Tenn., July 22, 1929; *American Glanzstoff Corp. v. George Miller et al.*, Court of Appeals, #1, Sept. 5, 1930 (Tennessee Supreme Court and Court of Appeals, Knoxville). On southern women's bawdy humor, see Rayna Green, "Magnolias Grow in Dirt: The Bawdy Lore of Southern Women," *Southern Exposure*, 4 (no. 4, 1977), 29–33.

57. Davis, *Society and Culture in Early Modern France*, 124–51; Ulrich, *Good Wives*, 191–97. For the association of men, rather than women, with individual and collective aggressiveness, see Richard A. Cloward and Frances Fox Pivan, "Hidden Protest: The Channeling of Female Innovation and Resistance," *Signs*, 4 (Summer 1979), 651–69.

58. Elizabethton City Council, minutes, May 23, 1929. Minute Book, vol. 5, 356–57 (City Hall, Elizabethton, Tenn.).

59. *Knoxville News Sentinel*, May 5, 1929; Myers, "Field Notes." For working-class standards of respectability and sexual morality, see Barbara Taylor, *Eve and the New Jerusalem: Socialism and Feminism in the Nineteenth Century* (New York, 1983), 192–205; Ellen Ross, " 'Not the Sort That Would Sit on the Doorstep': Respectability in pre-World War I London Neighborhoods," *International Labor and Working Class History*, 27 (Spring 1985), 39–59; and Kathy Peiss, *Cheap Amusements: Working Women and Leisure in Turn-of-the-Century New York* (Philadelphia, 1986), esp. 88–114.

60. See, for example, Alice Kessler- Harris, "The Autobiography of Ann Washington Craton," *Signs*, 1 (Summer 1976), 1019–37.

61. *Knoxville News Sentinel*, May 18, 1929; *American Bemberg Corp. v. George Miller et al.*, East Tennessee District Supreme Court, Jan. 29, 1930, record of evidence, typescript, box 660, Tennessee Supreme Court Records (Tennessee State Library and Archives).

62. Edens interview, Aug. 5, 1929.

63. Reece interview.

64. I am classifying as "activists" female strikers who appeared as such in newspaper stories, court records, and interviews—and for whom background information could be found.

65. Danny Miller, "The Mountain Woman in Fact and Fiction of the Early Twentieth Century, Part 1," *Appalachian Heritage*, 6 (Summer 1978), 48–56; Danny Miller, "The Mountain Woman in Fact and Fiction of the Early Twentieth Century, Part II," *ibid.*, 6 (Fall 1978), 66–72; Danny Miller, "The Mountain Woman in Fact and Fiction of the Early Twentieth Century, Part III," *ibid.*, 7 (Winter 1979), 16–21; Edward Alsworth Ross, "Pocketed Americans," *New Republic*, Jan. 9, 1924, 170–72.

66. For colonists' views of Indian women, see Mary E. Young, "Women, Civilization, and the Indian Question," in *Clio Was a Woman: Studies in the History of American Women*, ed. Mabel E. Deutrich and Virginia C. Purdy (Washington, 1980), 98–110. For a particularly interesting account of sexual mores, see Olive Dame Campbell Journal, vol. 4, Jan 1900–March 1900, esp. 26–27, 30, 33–34, 42–44, 61, 63–65, 67, 72, 78–80, 82, 92, 97, 102, 107–8, 115, 119–20, box 7, John C. and Olive Dame Campbell Papers, Southern Historical Collection; and Whisnant, *All That Is Native & Fine*, 103–79.

67. Charles K. Wolfe, *Tennessee Strings: The Story of Country Music in Tennessee* (Knoxville, 1977), 22–90; Barry O'Connell, "Dick Boggs, Musician and Coal Miner," *Appalachian Journal*, 11 (Autumn-Winter 1983–84), 48.

68. *Miller's Elizabethton, Tenn., City Directory* (1930); Reece Interview; *American Bemberg Corp. v. George Miller et al.*, East Tennessee District Supreme Court, Jan 29, 1930, record of evidence, typescript, box 660, Tennessee Supreme Court Records (Tennessee State Library and Archives); *Knoxville News Sentinel*, May 16, May 17, 1929; Kelley, "Our Newest South," 343; "Analysis of Union List," Oct. 21, 1929, Records of the Conciliation Service.

69. Whisnant, *All That Is Native & Fine*, 48.

70. Grindstaff interview; Robert and Barbara Moreland interview.

71. Simmerly interview.

72. *Knoxville Journal*, April 22, 1929; sixteen-millimeter film (1 reel), ca. 1929, Helen Raulston Collection

(Archives of Appalachia, East Tennessee State University, Johnson City); sixteen-millimeter film (20 reels), ca. 1927–1928, Bemberg Industry Records (Tennessee State Library and Archives). Mimi Conway drew my attention to these films and, more important, helped prevent their loss or destruction when the Bemberg plant closed.

73. Anna Weinstock Schneider interview by Julia Blodgett Curtis, 1969, transcript, 161, 166, 172–73, 177, box 1, Anna Weinstock Schneider Papers (Martin P. Catherwood Library).

74. Edens interview, Aug. 14, 1975, 4; *Watauga Spinnerette*, 1 (July 1930).

75. Bessie Edens, "All Quiet on the Elizabethton Front," *News of Southern Summer School for Women Workers in Industry*, 1 (Oct. 1930), 2, American Labor Education Service Records; Dugger interview, 18–19; Grindstaff interview; Charles Wolff, Plant Manager, to Employees, Feb. 25, 1930, Records of the Conciliation Service; Wilson to Secretary of Labor, June 26, 1929; "Analysis of Union List."

76. Spencer Miller, Jr., to Davis, March 21, 1930, Records of the Conciliation Service; *American Bemberg Corp. v. George Miller et al.*, East Tennessee District Supreme Court, Jan. 29, 1930, record of evidence, typescript, box 660, Tennessee Supreme Court Records (Tennessee State Library and Archives); Holly, "Elizabethton, Tennessee," 336–68; [U.S. National Labor Relations Board], *Decisions and Orders of the National Labor Relations Board*, vol. 23; April 22–May 28, 1940 (Washington, 1941), 623–29; *ibid.*, vol. 24: May 29–June 30, 1940 (Washington, 1940),727–78.

77. *Elizabethton News*, Aug. 13, 1931; "Resolution Adopted at Citizens Meeting"; Tennessee Taxpayers Association, *A Report with Recommendations Covering a Survey of the Finances and Administrative Methods of the City of Elizabethton, Tennessee*, Research Report no. 46 (Nashville, 1940); Holly, "Elizabethton, Tennessee," 179, 212–16, 279.

78. By the fall of 1929, with the rayon plants in full operation, women made up a smaller percentage of the work force than they had before the strike. Whereas they constituted 44 percent of Glanzstoff workers before the conflict, afterward they made up only 35 percent. Although most of that change can be accounted for by an expansion in the number of male workers, the absolute number of women employed also fell from 850 to 797, while the number of men employed rose from 1099 to 1507. *Knoxville News Sentinel*, May 20, 1929; RR to Willson, Oct. 9, 1929, Records of the Conciliation Service. For Elizabethton activists returning to the work force, see *Miller's Elizabethton, Tenn., City Directory* (1930); Carson interview, 2, 35–38; Edens interview, Aug. 14, 1975, pp. 5–7; Hazel Perry interview by Hall, May 20, 1983 (in Hall's possession); Grindstaff interview; Reece interview; Mamie Horne interview by Hall and Evans, Aug. 6, 1979 (in Hall's possession); and Ina Nell (Hinkle) Harrison interview, 9–10.

79. Bureau of the Census, *Fifteenth Census of the United States: 1930, Population*, vol. III, pt. 2, 909; U.S. Department of Commerce, Bureau of the Census, *Sixteenth Census of the United States: 1940, Population*, vol. II, pt. 6 (Washington, 1943), 616; Grindstaff interview.

80. Ibid.

81. Edens interview, Aug. 14, 1975, 50.

82. For similar conclusions about first-generation immigrant workers, see Peiss, *Cheap Amusements*, 185–88; and Elizabeth Ewen, *Immigrant Women in the Land of Dollars: Life and Culture on the Lower East Side, 1890–1925* (New York, 1985), 264–69. For hints of sexual harassment on the job and for women's vulnerability in a marriage market that was no longer controlled by parents, see Reece interview; and Ina Nell (Hinkle) Harrison interview, 18–22.

24

Making Faces: The Cosmetics Industry and the Cultural Construction of Gender, 1890–1930

Kathy Peiss

In the late nineteenth and early twentieth centuries, American women began to purchase and wear face powder, rouge, lipstick, and other kinds of visible cosmetics. A society that had scorned Victorian women's makeup as a mark of disrepute and illegitimacy had, by the early decades of the twentieth century, embraced powder and paint as essential signs of femininity. Once marking the prostitute and the aristocratic lady as symbols of rampant sexuality and materialistic excess, cosmetics became understood as respectable and indeed necessary for women's success and fulfillment.

Cosmetics, of course, are nothing new. Throughout history and in many cultures, women and men have colored, distorted, and exaggerated their physical features. In the early twentieth century, however, cosmetics took on new meaning in American culture. They became part of an ongoing discourse on femininity that made problematic women's identity in an increasingly commercial, industrial, and urban world. Women linked cosmetics use to an emergent notion of their own modernity, which included wage-work, athleticism, leisure, freer sexual expressiveness, and greater individual consumption. At the same time, new forms of mass culture shaped this discourse, as women began to see their faces differently in a number of novel cultural mirrors: in motion pictures, in mass-market women's magazines and advertising, in shop windows, on fashion runways, and across the counters of department stores.[1]

This essay focuses, however, on the crucial role of the cosmetics and beauty business in popularizing cosmetics and shaping gender definitions. In this century, cosmetics use has been inextricably tied to the emergence of a mass consumer industry. From the 1870s onward, American business has aggressively developed consumer markets, utilizing new techniques of mass production and distribution. In search of expanded and predictable profits, capitalism has promoted the redefinition and commodification of everyday social needs. The cosmetics business, whose financial success lay in defining the outward appearance of femininity, exemplifies this history. In the cosmetics industry, we can see how specific processes of mass production, distribution, marketing, and advertising rendered new social meanings about female identity and made them compelling to women consumers.

Complicating this story, however, is the segmentation of the industry from its inception into three distinct lines of trade. In modern marketing parlance, the industry has long been divided into the "class," "mass," and "ethnic" markets. The class market represents high-priced cosmetic lines, both domestic and imported, whose aura is one of exclusivity and social status. Sold in department stores and exclusive salons, these products are marketed

Reprinted with permission of the author. Originally appeared in *GENDERS* No. 7, Spring 1990.

to wealthy and upwardly mobile middle-class women. "Mass" cosmetic products, the low-priced lines available in drugstores, variety stores, and discount beauty outlets, are marketed to a wide range of consumers, but particularly targeted toward working-class and lower-middle-class women, as well as teenagers. The ethnic market is a contemporary euphemism for the African American beauty industry, although this market includes Hispanic Americans, Asian Americans, and other women of color.

Historically the class, mass, and African American segments of the industry shared certain problems in fostering the popular use of cosmetics, especially in their need to convince women that being "painted" was not only respectable but a requirement of womanhood. In some respects, they came up with similar solutions, which they projected through techniques of mass marketing and advertising. Each appropriated and manipulated a complex set of images about womanhood during a historical period that witnessed major changes in women's experience and status. However, they represented gender in different and contradictory ways that bespeak the divisions of class and race within the industry and, more broadly, within American society. Thus in this essay I first trace the commercialization of cosmetics and their popularization in each segment of the industry. I then turn to the ideological definition of womanhood, focusing on the ways that class and race were inextricably implicated in the cosmetics industry's projections of gendered appearance.

The Commercialization of Cosmetics

Women's cosmetics use in the nineteenth-century United States is difficult to determine with any exactness. Creams, lotions, and tonics—that is, external cosmetic applications involving skin care or therapeutic treatment—were widespread. From the 1840s, family keepsakes and formularies offered recipes to soften and whiten skin, cure freckles, and remove unwanted hair, and were distributed to a wide range of Americans, from middle-class ladies and gentlemen to farmers and mechanics. Many advice books also instructed women in the simple home manufacture of "make-up," that is, cosmetics involving the application of color to the face: pulverized chalk for face powder, beet root for rouge, burnt cloves or green walnut juice for eyebrow and lash coloring. As was the case with medicinal remedies, an oral tradition concerning hair and skin care probably comprised an aspect of women's culture.[2]

Yet the use of makeup was problematic for many nineteenth century women. Among fashionable middle- and upper-class women, the obvious use of powder and paint came into vogue in the 1850s and 1860s, only to decline in the late nineteenth century. For the vast majority of middle-class women, however, enameling the face with a white liquid or visibly tinting it with rouge were objectionable practices. By 1900 the use of face powder seems to have become more common among urban middle-class women, judging from advice books and commentators; even the subtle application of rouge and eyebrow pencil, if concealed, was deemed acceptable.[3]

The use of cosmetics by white working-class and Black women in the latter half of the nineteenth century is even more difficult to determine. Many working-class women refrained from makeup use, given religious beliefs, ethnic cultural traditions, concepts of respectability, and the cost of the products. Probably the most frequent working-class consumers of cosmetics were prostitutes, who signalled their trade to potential customers through the visible use of face powder and rouge. But other working women used these products as well, particularly the subculture of "disorderly" women oriented toward urban nightlife and sexual pleasure. Their use of cosmetics, as well as fancy dress and hair pieces, marked a distinctive and provocative cultural style, if not an oppositional aesthetics. For example, a ruddy complexion, either naturally or artificially induced, seems to have been an ideal among some working women. Reddish cheeks accompanied their boisterous, high-spirited behavior, and offered a sharp contrast to the pale faces of middle-class women. Other working women, who played with the ideal of being "ladies," powdered themselves so much that various employers, from department store managers to household mistresses, barred the use of face powders.[4] While there is even less evidence concerning cosmetics use among Black women, stylishness and adornment were ideals cultivated by postbellum African Americans, signifying freedom and respectability. Although the issue of personal grooming for Black women centered more around hair care, some use of cosmetics, particularly homemade products, is probable.[5]

Whatever the patterns of cosmetic use, consumer resistance to commercially manufactured cosmetics was very high in the nineteenth century. One fear concerned the potential health hazards of so-called patent cosmetics, a term that associated cosmetics with the extravagant claims and often ruinous results of patent medicines. American consumers were increasingly sensitive to the dangers of adulterated products and the substitutions of unscrupulous dealers; in the case of cosmetics, such fears were heightened by the centuries-old tradition of using arsenic, white lead, and other toxic substances in powders and enamels. Advice books often cautioned women, in the words of one, to become their "*own manufacturer*—not only as a matter of *economy*, but of *safety*." Indeed, cosmetics were ideologically linked to a larger critique of commerce and its practice of artifice and deception.[6]

The critique of cosmetics on grounds of health and safety was linked to another powerful, if less specific, set of concerns about what it meant to be "painted." On the one hand, for many Americans, cosmetics were associated with aristocratic excess, undemocratic luxury, and female self-indulgence. Artifice was the mode of parasitical ladies of fashion, who sacrificed health and familial duty in frivolous, self-centered pursuits. On the other hand, the "painted woman" most powerfully signified the prostitute, the immoral, public woman who lived outside the sanction of a middle-class society that valorized women's purity and the home. "Paint" demarcated the boundary between respectability and promiscuity, bourgeois gentility and lower-class vulgarity. If cultural definitions of gender were shaped and bounded by the cultural construction of class and race, then cosmetics contributed significantly to the external marking of those boundaries. Thus, handling social divisions and their cultural markers proved a special problem for the nascent cosmetics industry.[7]

The production of commercial cosmetics remained quite limited in the late nineteenth century. The census of manufactures of 1889 lists only 157 companies whose primary business was perfume and cosmetics. In a period when many consumer goods found a national market, the cosmetics industry was slow to take off. A comparison might be made with patent medicines and soaps, two products that, like cosmetics, were related to physical care and appearance. Sale of these goods gave rise to large corporations that had developed mass production, national distribution, and national advertising by the 1880s. Cosmetics, however, remained a small-scale business, highly entrepreneurial and without a distinctive identity. It was not until the years immediately before and after World War I that the industry experienced substantial growth. In 1914 there were 496 companies manufacturing perfume and cosmetics, and the value of their products was nearly seventeen million dollars; by 1919, although the number of companies had risen only to 569, the value of products climbed dramatically, to almost sixty million dollars.[8]

The Segmentation of the Industry

Commercial manufacture of cosmetics emerged from several distinct lines of trade in the mid-nineteenth century: the manufacture of pharmaceuticals and drugstore supplies, the local business activity of druggists, and commercial beauty culture. Patent medicine makers produced some cosmetic products, particularly those with therapeutic claims. In addition, companies manufacturing perfumery, flavoring extracts, essential oils, and druggists' sundries also included a few cosmetics in their product lines. These were placed before the public through traditional routes of distribution, including drugstores, general stores, and peddlers. Relatively few of them—such as Pond's Extract and Hagan's Magnolia Balm—achieved national distribution or brand name recognition.

More commonplace were the hundreds of local druggists and hairdressers who compounded their own powders and creams, purchasing raw ingredients through wholesalers and jobbers. The catalogs of leading wholesale druggists, for example, contained only a few commercially made preparations but carried a full line of oils, waxes, powders, chemicals, dyes, and perfumes required in cosmetic formulas. In the late nineteenth century, cosmetics manufactured solely for a local or regional market far outnumbered those that achieved national distribution.[9]

Although drugstores were the primary purveyors of commercial cosmetics to the public, it was "beauty culture"—and its commercial exploitation by beauty parlor owners, cosmetic manufacturers, women's magazines, advertisers, and retailers—that fundamentally altered the market for cosmetics. Beauty culture became the crucial intermediary between a women's culture suspicious of powder and paint to one that delighted in them. Beginning in the 1880s, beauty culturists popularized the notion of ritualizing beautification for women. Beauty salons were initially places for the dressing and ornamentation of hair, but by the 1890s had expanded their services to include facial treatments, manicures, and massage. At their most grand, these salons were service stations for elite and middle-class women's enhancement and relaxation.[10] But at a more modest scale, beauty culture was also available to women of lesser means, and was particularly important to African American women; indeed, the latter pioneered in the development of hair and skin treatments and products, creating one of the leading Black-owned businesses in the United States.

The origins of the "class" segment of the cosmetics industry lie in the development of beauty culture for elite and upwardly mobile white women. In salons located on prestigious commercial streets and at expensive resorts, beauty culturists consciously created a paradoxical world of discipline and indulgence, therapy and luxury.[11] For women who had long been enjoined to sacrifice their own desires on behalf of husband and family, the message was irresistible: Women could fulfill the old prescription of "beauty a duty" while at the same time giving in to the siren call of a newer consumerist message. In the words of cosmetologist Susanna Cocroft, "Don't be ashamed of your desire for beauty."[12]

Ironically, beauty culturists generally did not approve of makeup, stressing breathing, exercise, diet, and bathing as the route to natural beauty. Madame Yale, a typical popularizer, warned women to avoid "fashion's glamor and the artificer's whims." For beauty culturists, as for many nineteenth-century Americans, the face was a window into the soul, and complexion problems were indicative of a life that was disordered, out of balance. Thus Susanna Cocroft asked women: "Is your complexion *clear*? Does it express the clearness of your life? Are there discolorations or blemishes in the skin—which symbolize imperfections within?" Beauty culture promised self-transformation that was both internal and external, an idea that resonated powerfully in American middle-class culture (fig. 1).[13]

Beauty culturists initially offered face powder, rouge, and other makeup somewhat apologetically, or even with a tone of exasperation: "Outward applications only have the office of assisting in, and completing, the process which must begin *within*." Madame Yale in the 1890s sold a liquid powder, rouge, and lip tint that she termed "Temporary Beautifiers." She rather grudgingly noted their purchase by "many ladies . . . too indolent to

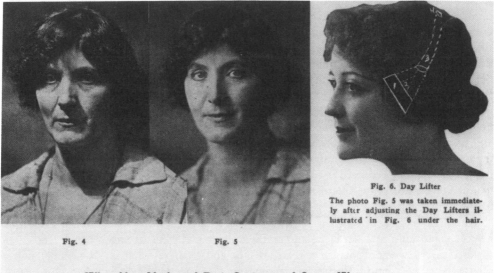

Figure 1. Detail from Susanna Cocroft's "Success Face Lifters" pamphlet. Warshaw Collection of Business Americana, Archives Center, National Museum of American History, Smithsonian Institution. Photo No. 89–14354.

cultivate natural beauty by the Yale System of Beauty Culture" or by "actresses and all whose inclinations or pursuits render 'makeup' necessary."[14]

Nevertheless, the dynamics of beauty culture led to the greater acceptance of cosmetics. By making the complexion, rather than bone structure or physical features, more central to popular definitions of beauty, it popularized the democratic idea that beauty could be achieved by all women if only they used the correct products and treatment. This logic led to the assertion that every woman *should* be beautiful—as a duty to her husband and children, in order to achieve business success, or to find romance—and those who were not beautiful had only themselves to blame.

Beauty culturists also foregrounded the *process* of achieving beauty, not just the end product, and moved that process into popular discourse—in the semipublic environment of beauty salons and in the widely read pages of women's magazines and newspapers. The development of beauty "systems" or "methods" was particularly important. Such "systems" replaced apprenticeship and oral tradition with formal instruction in beauty culture and cosmetology, and proved quite profitable for a number of entrepreneurs who developed beauty schools and correspondence courses. But the notion of a beauty "system" or "method" also changed the consumer's relationship to cosmetics by encouraging the systematic, step-by-step process of beauty application. Beauty culturists, that is, replaced all-purpose creams and lotions with a series of specialized products, each designed to perform a single function. The more entrepreneurial of them not only manufactured these products for the home use of their clients but began to market them to women who did not have direct access to exclusive urban salons, largely through department stores, drugstores, and mail order. By the early twentieth century, beauty culturists' ambivalence toward powder and paint diminished as they saw the possibilities for profit in makeup product lines.[15]

The career of Elizabeth Arden, born Florence Nightingale Graham, illustrates a dominant pattern of entrepreneurship in beauty culture that led to the development of the "class market." She began her career in Eleanor Adair's beauty salon in New York City, first as a receptionist and then as a beauty operator specializing in facials. Soon she became partners with cosmetologist Elizabeth Hubbard, opening a Fifth Avenue salon in 1909 on the strength of Hubbard's products and her own treatment techniques. When their partnership dissolved, Graham took over the salon, lavishly decorated it for an elite clientele, and began to improve on Hubbard's formulas. It was at this time that she transformed herself into Miss Elizabeth Arden, a name she perceived to be romantic and high class. After the first salon was successful, she opened others in a number of cities. Initially the salons offered the usual complexion cures, facials, massage, and hairdressing, but by 1915 Arden had begun to make up her customers, although she did not advertise this service. In 1918, Arden decided to expand sales by going after store orders in fancy retail shops and department stores, often giving them exclusive rights to sell her line in a particular locality. She sent trained representatives or "demonstrators" to teach saleswomen how to sell her products. By 1920, she had developed an extensive product line that included skin care treatments and a full line of face makeup, using Ardena and Venetian as tradenames. According to her biographer, by 1925 Arden's domestic wholesale division was grossing two million dollars each year, from sales to women whose families were in the top three percent income bracket in the United States.[16]

Other beauty culture entrepreneurs, such as Helena Rubinstein and Dorothy Gray, followed the same route to success: first establishing salons for society women, then developing nationally distributed product lines that conveyed a sense of exclusivity and richness to their clientele. At this time, importers also increased the number and variety of products they offered to wholesalers and retailers. Fine-quality imported goods from France and England had long been available to elite women, but by the 1910s firms (such as Coty) from these countries had begun to open branches and offices in the United States to exploit the growing demand for cosmetics. Department store buyers also were increasingly important in providing high-priced goods to the public. Along with beauty culturists, these were critical figures in expanding the class market for cosmetics, countering the image of the painted woman with connotations of gentility, refinement, and social status.

In contrast, the "mass" segment of the cosmetics industry grew out of the pharmaceutical and drugstore trade after 1900, when a few products broke out of their local market and secured national distribution and brand name recognition. Usually these were creams and lotions, often used by both women and men. Hinds' Honey and Almond Cream, for example, was formulated in 1872 by a Portland, Maine drugstore owner who gradually went into manufacturing full time and entered the Boston and New York City markets. In 1905, Aurelius S. Hinds conducted his first nationwide advertising campaign, and five years later added vanishing cream and other products to his line.[17] While Hinds and other skin care products achieved success in the national market, visible makeup such as rouge and lipstick had more limited distribution before World War I.

The outlets for mass market cosmetics were varied. Independent drugstores and general stores remained important, especially in small towns, but sales of cosmetics were boosted by emergent forms of national distribution: chain drugstores and variety stores, department stores, and large mail order outfits, as well as systematized house-to-house selling.[18] The new chain stores aggressively pushed a full range of inexpensive brand name products, as well as private label cosmetics. Both independent and chain merchandisers sought to base drugstore profits not only on the dispensing of medicines and drugs but on the sale of goods consumers needed on an everyday basis, including toiletries. Department store merchandisers similarly found that toiletries and sundries, including soaps, brushes, and rubber goods as well as cosmetics and perfumes, could draw women into the stores; some carried both class and mass products, displaying them in eye-catching cases on the main selling floor.[19]

Mail order houses were initially conservative in the lines they carried, reflecting their small town and rural clientele of housewives and older women. Catalogs of the late nineteenth century tended to group cosmetics inconsequentially with food, patent medicines, and soaps. Yet as early as 1897, Sears offered its own line of toilet preparations, including rouge, eyebrow pencil, and face powder in three colors, as well as such brand names as Ayer's, Pozzoni's, and Tetlow's. The Larkin Company, which began as a soap manufacturer and expanded into general catalog sales, buried cosmetics in the back pages of the 1907 catalog, but by the early 1920s had begun to feature them in the opening pages, accompanied by flowery descriptions and color illustrations.[20]

The advertising of mass-market cosmetics also underwent important changes in this period. Since few companies in the nineteenth century saw cosmetics as their primary product, relatively little money was spent on developing marketing or advertising strategies. Cosmetics were advertised mainly on trade cards, displays, and posters, as well as almanacs, sample envelopes, sheet music, and broadsides. Some firms advertised at expositions and world's fairs; Lundborg's perfume fountain, for example, was a popular attraction at the 1893 Columbian Exposition in Chicago.[21]

Magazine advertising, however, was quite limited before 1900: Only a few firms advertised in women's magazines, and their advertisements (usually for creams and powders, rarely rouge) were set in small type in the back pages—in contrast, for example, to soap advertisements, which often appeared on full pages or magazine covers. In the 1910s, however, large-scale national advertising of cosmetics began in earnest, and by the early 1920s it had become a dominant force in women's magazines.[22]

In the late nineteenth century, manufacturers and advertisers of mass-market cosmetics responded to widespread consumer resistance in several ways. They took pains to stress the safety of their products, seeking to identify them with the widespread cult of health and cleanliness. Some made therapeutic claims for face powders and liquid tints; Stoddart's Peerless Face Powder, for example, was touted as "approved by the medical Profession." The invisibility of the products, moreover, guaranteed that a woman would not be perceived as painted and immoral. Ricksecker's powder, for example, was "*modestly invisible* when used with discrimination." Manufacturers such as Pozzoni's stressed the naturalness and purity of their preparations by using angelic children in their advertising (fig. 2). Even a tag like "Just a Kiss," featured on Tetlow's packaging, played coquetry off against innocence (fig. 3).[23]

While a logical response to consumers' fears, this advertising tactic was ultimately a self-defeating one. The industry's growth depended on its ability to convince women not only to use cosmetics but to buy as many different products as possible. Making appeals to the naturalness and invisibility of cosmetics could not accomplish this; rather, manufacturers needed to convince women of the acceptability of artifice and visible color.

Many companies in the early twentieth century found this a difficult idea to promote; like the beauty culturists, most of them argued that their products merely "improved on nature." Yet the growing importance of color can be seen in the expansion of product lines. Some manufacturers who had succeeded in marketing a cream or lotion began to create coordinated sets of products, somewhat akin to the beauty culturists' notion of "system." Propounding a domino theory of cosmetics use, they argued that once a woman started using face powder, she would inevitably be drawn to complementary, although more daring, products such as rouge and lipstick. Increasingly they appealed to artifice in the pursuit of "natural beauty." Women were urged to buy several face powders and blend

Figure 2. Pozzoni's Face Powder advertising card. Warshaw Collection of Business Americana, Archives Center, National Museum of American History, Smithsonian Institution.

them for a natural look; or buy specialized powders, such as a violet tint to wear under artificial light; or wear matching lip tints and rouge to achieve the "bloom of youth."[24]

At this time, a number of entrepreneurs began to produce and market new cosmetic products that asserted and even celebrated artifice. Lipsticks and eyeshadows in colorful shades, for example, made their appearance on the market after World War I. "Mascaro," which in the nineteenth century had been a general-purpose touch-up for light or greying

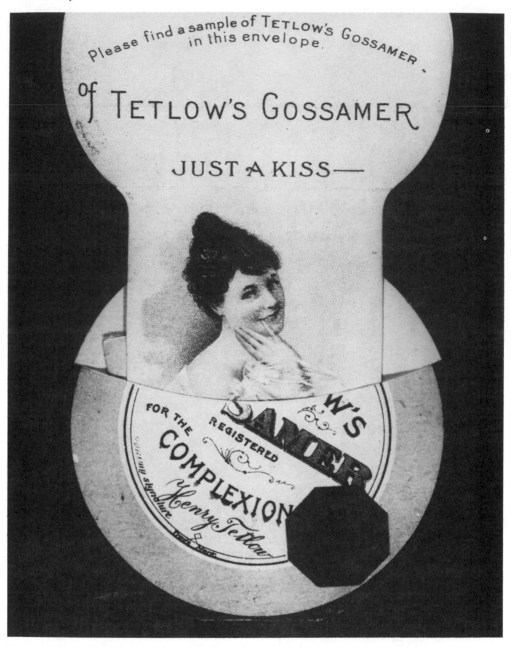

Figure 3. Tetlow's Gossamer "Just a Kiss" powder sample envelope. Warshaw Collection of Business Americana, Archives Center, National Museum of American History, Smithsonian Institution. Photo No. 88–1157.

hair used by both men and women, became specialized as "mascara," a woman's cosmetic for eyelashes. Manufacturers sold cosmetics in luxurious sets to be seen on dressing tables, but even more popular were goods packaged in portable containers. Compacts for face powder and rouge and the lipstick cylinder were marketed in the 1910s, suggesting the increasingly public place of cosmetics.

Manufacturers of mass-market goods often developed a single product, one that was socially unacceptable or controversial, and aggressively promoted it in the trade press and in national advertising. In so doing, they turned to other sources of cultural legitimation than that of middle-class and elite beauty culture.

Social definitions of womanhood were strongly contested from the late nineteenth century onward. The ideal of the "New Woman" represented a departure from concepts of female identity constituted solely in domestic pursuits, sexual purity, and moral motherhood. Yet this new ideal was an unstable one. For some, the New Woman was a mannish, political, and professional woman who had entered the public sphere on its own terms. For others, the New Woman was a sensual, free-spirited girl—in the 1880s a "Daisy," by the 1910s and 1920s a flapper. The latter figure embodied another set of contradictions: She was at once an independent wage-earner, making her own way in the world, and a beautiful, romantic girl, seeking marital fulfillment. This image became increasingly important in the selling of mass-market cosmetics, as manufacturers and advertisers sought to appeal particularly to the rising number of young working women of both middle-class and working-class origins.[25]

An important tactic of the industry was to link cosmetics to emergent forms of popular entertainment and leisure, especially the motion pictures. Mary Pickford's screen image of youthful innocence sold such mass-market creams and lotions as Pompeian in general circulation periodicals and traditional women's magazines (fig. 4). The cosmetics of artifice, in contrast, were heavily advertised in the new confession magazines and "fanzines," such as *True Story* and *Photoplay*, directed at young working-class and middle-class women. Drugstore promotions and display windows also capitalized on the movie craze. Maybelline, for example, marketed its sole product, mascara, by using close-up photographs of movie stars with heavily painted eyes and eyelashes in its magazine advertising and on display cards (fig. 5).[26]

The connection between motion pictures and cosmetics was in some cases quite direct: The movie industry's makeup experts often made technological breakthroughs in products that were then applied to everyday cosmetics. Max Factor, a Russian immigrant, is the most prominent example of a "makeup artist to the stars" who went into cosmetics manufacturing for the mass market. But as important to the cosmetics industry were the "look" and style of female screen stars who promoted the use of color and artifice. Although the theater may have affected everyday makeup practices, the movies were far more influential because of their enormous popularity, and because close-up cinematography could magnify heavily painted lips, eyes, and cheeks. Certainly the cultural style of many working women and early flappers who wore provocative makeup, hair styles, and fashionable clothing was legitimized and reinforced by what they saw on the screen. By the late 1920s, as the Payne Fund studies indicate, young women from a range of socioeconomic backgrounds modelled their cosmetics use, and manners generally, on the movie images they saw. Exploiting the movie industry tie-in, mass-market manufacturers promoted glamor as an integral part of women's identity.[27]

The African American segment of the industry emerged in the late nineteenth century, part of the more general development of an African American consumer market. Constrained even more than white working people by poverty, most Blacks had little spending money for anything beyond the goods essential for survival. Yet a nascent middle class, Black migration, and the growing racial segregation of cities spurred some entrepreneurs to develop businesses serving Black consumers.[28] Some white-owned firms cultivated this market for cosmetics in the Black community as early as the 1890s. The Lyon Manufacturing Company, for example, a Brooklyn-based firm that sold patent medicines, advertised its

Figure 4. Mary Pickford, 1917 Pompeian Beauty Panel. Warshaw Collection of Business Americana, Archives Center, National Museum of American History, Smithsonian Institution.

Figure 5. Maybelline advertisement, *Photoplay* (1920). Courtesy Maybelline, Inc.

Kaitharon hair tonic to Blacks through almanacs and ad cards. The product was touted as a straightener for kinky hair, with testimonials from African American ministers, political leaders, and schoolteachers.[29]

Far more important at this time, however, was the development of African American beauty culture and a hair and skin care industry owned by Blacks. Such figures as Anthony Overton, Annie Turnbo Malone, and Madame C. J. Walker were among the most successful African American entrepreneurs to market face creams, hair oils, and other products. Several Black-owned firms developed out of the drugstore supplies trade or began as small cosmetics companies. Anthony Overton, who by 1916 had built up one of the largest Black-owned businesses in the United States, began his career as a peddler and baking powder manufacturer. He shifted into cosmetics when his daughter's formula for a face powder proved popular in their community. Using networks of distribution he had already established, Overton sold his High Brown Face Powder through an army of door-to-door agents.[30]

Even more significant, however, were the women entrepreneurs who developed African American beauty culture. Beauty culture offered Black women good employment opportunities in the sex- and race-segregated labor market: It required low capitalization, was an easy trade to learn, and was much in demand. Beauty parlors could be operated cheaply in homes, apartments, and small shops, and hair and skin care products could be mixed in one's kitchen to be sold locally. Since drugstores, chain stores, and department stores often refused to locate in the Black community, door-to-door and salon sales were the dominant forms of distribution. Advertising was generally limited to Black-owned newspapers, although large companies like Poro purchased space in many of them throughout the country, achieving a kind of "national" advertising.[31]

Annie Turnbo Malone, founder of Poro, Madame C. J. Walker, and others pioneered in the development of beauty systems that would assure Black women of smooth, manageable hair. White racism had symbolically linked the supposedly "natural" inferiority of Blacks to an appearance marked by unruly, "kinky" hair and slovenliness in dress. As Gwendolyn Robinson has argued in her study of the African American cosmetics industry, the dominant culture's ascription of promiscuity to Black women led them to stress the importance of looking respectable. For Black women, hair care, including straightening, was one external marker of personal success and racial progress, signifying a response to the white denigration of Black womanhood. The beauty culturists asserted and exploited this view in their advertising. Madame Walker, for example, ran a full-page newspaper ad in 1928 whose headline announced: "Amazing Progress of Colored Race—Improved Appearance Responsible."[32]

Like the white beauty culturists, the leading Black entrepreneurs had developed extensive product lines in skin care and cosmetics by World War I, including face creams, bleaches, and powders. Some of these products and beauty systems, especially hair straightening and skin bleaching, were highly controversial in the Black community. They sparked debate over Black emulation of dominant white aesthetics, and over the issue of color differences among African Americans. Cosmetics use not only rendered gender definitions (that is, what constituted female respectability) problematic but tied those definitions to "race consciousness" and Black resistance to white domination as well.

The response of African American beauty culturists was complex, adhering to the dominant aesthetic while asserting the centrality of the industry to collective Black advancement. Unlike the white industry, African American beauty culturists evidenced a genuine commitment to work on behalf of their community. Walker and Malone trained thousands of Black women in their methods to become sales agents, salon owners, and beauty operatives; their promotional literature and handbooks continually emphasized their commitment to Black women's employment and the economic progress of African Americans. In the absence of many commercial outlets, Walker sought a relationship with women's clubs and churches, offering promotions, beauty shows, and product sales to help raise funds for these organizations. Moreover, the sales methods—salon operatives and door-to-door agents selling to friends and neighbors—probably enhanced the web of mutual support and assistance integral to Black women's culture. The integration of this industry with aspects of Black community life and politics sets it apart from the white industry.[33]

Cultural Constructions of Gender, Class, and Race

Despite the difference in their origins, patterns of distribution, and markets, the three segments of the cosmetics industry developed a number of similar products and encountered many of the same issues. The industry converged in certain ways in its handling of gender, responding to social and cultural changes affecting women's attitudes toward appearance, redefining popular notions of female sexual and social respectability to include cosmetics use, and then revising definitions of female beauty into ideals that could only be achieved through cosmetics. Whatever the class and race of cosmetics consumers, all segments of the industry in their advertising and marketing reshaped the relationship between appearance and feminine identity by promoting the externalization of the gendered self, a process much in tune with the tendencies of mass culture.[34]

What to beauty culturists had been a simultaneous process of transforming the interior self and external appearance became in the hands of the twentieth-century cosmetics industry the "makeover." Makeup promised each woman the tools to express her "true" self, indeed, to experiment until she found it. Cosmetics communicated the self to others and infused the self with a sense of esteem and legitimacy. In this new attention to personality and novelty, being able to find yourself and change yourself, cosmetics manufacturers began to reorient their industry away from beauty culture and toward "fashion," allowing for an endless number of "looks" and endless proliferation of products.[35]

But the linkage of female individuality, self expression, and respectability held different meanings in the different contexts under which cosmetics were sold. While a full-scale analysis of the divisions of class and race embedded in the industry's cultural messages cannot be attempted here, I will suggest one route such an analysis might take: the tension between the appearance of Anglo-Saxon gentility and the exploitation of "foreign" exoticism.

While invoking ideas of female self-expression through the use of makeup, the cosmetics industry in the 1910s and 1920s never transcended the problem of class that had been raised in the nineteenth-century identification of "paint" with immorality. The "class" end of the industry had long stressed the gentility and refinement possible through skin care regimens; they now applied this argument to the use of makeup and artifice. The French cachet of imported goods was especially important in conveying status and "chic." Until the 1906 Food and Drug Act prohibited misbranding and false labeling, U.S. companies frequently identified their products as made in Paris.[36] After 1906, they used foreign-sounding, aristocratic tradenames, such as Rubinstein's Valaze line and Arden's Ardena, or they claimed the use of French formulas. Although manufacturing their products in the United States, Arden and Rubinstein commonly made reference to the cosmetic practices of Parisian women as examples American women should emulate. By 1919, national advertisers of cosmetics, particularly of imported brands, had adopted "atmosphere advertisements" depicting the life-styles of the rich and famous. Dorin face powders and compacts, for example, were associated with Saratoga Springs, the Paris Opera, and the races at Ascot: "Not all the users of La Dorine can be members of smart clubs but they are all eager to enjoy as much of the dainty refinement of the fashionable world as they can."[37]

Companies selling cosmetics to Blacks also used images of refinement and social improvement to sell their products, but this strategy must be placed in the overall context of racial stereotyping and Black aspirations. The advertising for the highly successful Overton-Hygienic Manufacturing Company, for example, featured light-skinned, refined-looking, women and appealed more to respectability and gentility than elitism (fig. 6). In contrast, Kashmir Chemical Company, a Black-owned firm with a brief life in the late 1910s and early 1920s, frequently used advertising with very fashionably dressed women sitting at

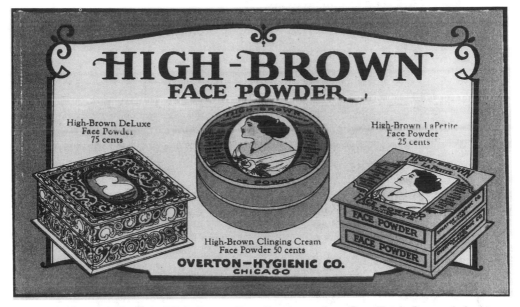

Figure 6. Overton-Hygienic High Brown Face Powder packet. Curt Teich Postcard Archives, Lake County Museum, Wauconda, Illinois.

dressing tables or in automobiles—ads that emulated the elite images common in mainstream magazines.[38]

Mass-market manufacturers stressed the makeover as a route to upward mobility, arguing that a woman's personal success relied on her appearance. As one manufacturer's pamphlet observed, "You can select ten ordinary girls from a factory and by the skillful use of such preparations as Kijja and proper toilet articles . . . you can in a short time make them as attractive and good-looking as most any ten wealthy society girls . . . it is not so much a matter of beauty with different classes of girls as it is how they are fixed up." A similar story is told in a 1924 trade advertisement for Zip depilatory: A dark-skinned woman, her appearance suggesting an eastern or southern European immigrant, is able to achieve social acceptance, implicitly among her Americanized friends, by ridding herself of superfluous hair (fig. 7).[39]

Some manufacturers, particularly at the class end of the industry, sought to dissociate themselves from any cosmetic practices that might be understood as working-class and "vulgar." The trade press, for example, editorialized against putting on makeup in public places, that is, *showing* the artifice; one writer even wanted to start a campaign among sales personnel to advise their customers against the use of too much face powder. Advice books and women's magazines were particularly directive about extreme cosmetic use: Powdering one's nose in restaurants or shops "stamps you as having poor breeding," noted one; another condemned "girls on the streets everyday with their faces daubed like uncivilized Indians." Of vivid red lips, observed yet another, "You cannot afford to make yourself ridiculous if you have started for success, or you want to attract a REAL man."[40] Much of this was a response to young women's cosmetic practices, particularly the "madeup" look of working-class women.

As the reference above to "uncivilized Indians" suggests, manufacturers not only dealt with the cultural identification of "paint" and artifice with class but also with a deeply embedded set of resonances concerning race, ethnicity, and color in American society.

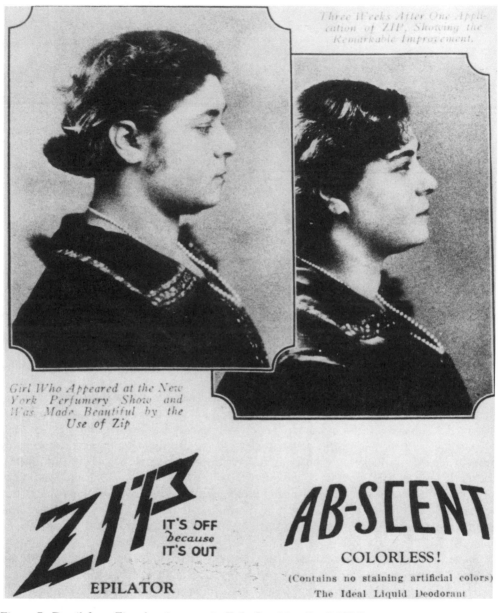

Figure 7. Detail from Zip advertisement, in *Toilet Requisites* (April 1924).

Mass-market manufacturers, for example, often employed exotic images of foreign peoples to advertise products that did not have a distinct place in white bourgeois culture. An instructive comparison might be made with the soap industry, which created advertisements associating cleanliness with colonization and white Anglo-American supremacy (fig. 8). Cosmetics manufacturers, in contrast, used images of American Indian, Egyptian, Turkish, and Japanese women as well as European women to link reluctant Americans to a global cosmetic culture (fig. 9). Versions of "Little Egypt," who caused a furor at the 1893 Columbian Exposition, sold rouge and other cosmetics of artifice. This fascination with

Figure 8. Higgins and Foweler trade card. Warshaw Collection of Business Americana, Archives Center, National Museum of American History, Smithsonian Institution. Photo No. 89–14352.

Figure 9. Murray and Lanham's Florida Water advertising card. Warshaw Collection of Business Americana, Archives Center, National Museum of American History, Smithsonian Institution.

the foreign and exotic, fueled by Western imperialism, can be seen throughout American culture in the late nineteenth century.[41]

In the hands of cosmetics manufacturers, exoticism continued to be powerful long into the twentieth century. Advertisers created narratives about beauty culture through the ages, bypassing the Graeco-Roman tradition in favor of Egypt and Persia. Cleopatra was virtually a cult figure, displayed in advertising to all segments of the market. Kashmir's Nile Queen line, for example, juxtaposed images of genteel black womanhood with frankly sensual representations of naked and semiclothed women (fig. 10). Promotions of lower priced makeup, particularly rouge, eye shadow, and mascara, frequently used exotic "vamp" images.[42]

Advertisers also linked "foreign types" to the realization of women's identity through cosmetics. The Armand complexion powder campaign of 1928 to 1929 instructed women to "find yourself," using a question-and-answer book written by a "famous psychologist and a noted beauty expert"; however, individuality was submerged into a typology that coded appearance and personality together according to ethnic euphemisms—Godiva, Colleen, Mona Lisa, Sheba, Sonya, Cherie, Lorelei, and, of course, Cleopatra (fig. 11).[43]

At the same time, the cosmetics industry at all levels projected contradictory cultural messages linking whiteness with social success and refinement. With the sale of bleach cream and light-colored face powders, this issue became a particularly controversial one within the Black community. Products with names like Black-No-More and Tan Off, many of which were manufactured by white-owned as well as Black-owned companies, baldly appealed to European aesthetic standards and the belief that light-skinned African Americans were more successful and, if women, more desirable as wives. Others struck a more ambivalent tone: Golden Brown Ointment, for example, instructed consumers, "Don't be fooled by so-called 'Skin Whiteners.' " The company admonished that its product "won't whiten your skin—as that can't be done," yet claimed that the ointment produced a "soft, light, bright, smooth complexion" that would "help in business or social life."[44]

It is crucial to note, however, that bleach creams, produced by class and mass manufacturers, were also widely advertised to white women. Until the mid-1920s, when the suntanning craze swept the United States, bleach creams were touted as a means of acquiring a whiteness that connoted gentility, female domesticity, "protection" from labor, the exacting standards of the elite, and Anglo-Saxon superiority. Most of the time advertisers treated such issues obliquely, but they could be quite direct. One series of silhouettes, appearing in a late-nineteenth-century advertisement for Hagan's Magnolia Balm, a skin bleach sold to white women, used physiognomic signifiers to convey that light skin meant Anglo-Saxon gentility. In these images, not only does the woman's skin color lighten upon using the product, but her features undergo a transformation from a stereotyped rural Black woman to a genteel lady (fig. 12). Several decades later, manufacturer Albert F. Wood could declare quite openly: "A white person objects to a swarthy brown-hued or mulatto-like skin, therefore if staying much out of doors use regularly Satin Skin Varnishing Greaseless Cream to keep the skin normally white."[45]

Such explicit and covert attention to race and ethnicity in a business devoted in large part to coloration should not be surprising if we recall the history of this period: the extensive immigration of peoples who looked "different" from earlier western European immigrants and threatened to be unassimilable; intensified consciousness about "race" spurred by legal segregation, heightened violence against Blacks, and northern migration, and the growing acceptance of scientific racism, which ordered human progress, including the attainment of physical beauty, according to racial-ethnic types, with white Anglo-Saxons at the top of that hierarchy. What I would suggest is that the cosmetics industry has

Figure 10. Front cover of Kashmir Chemical Company's Nile Queen pamphlet, 1919. Chicago Historical Society.

Figure 11. "Which of These Alluring Types Are You?" Detail from Armand Complexion Powder ad proof, 1929. N. W. Ayer Collection, Archives Center, National Museum of American History, Smithsonian Institution. Photo No. 89–14353.

BEFORE USING.   USING.   AFTER USING.

Figure 12. Detail from Lyon's Manufacturing Company, "The Secret of Health and Beauty" pamphlet. Warshaw Collection of Business Americana, Archives Center, National Museum of American History, Smithsonian Institution. Photo No. 89–14351.

historically taken discourses of class, ethnicity, race, and gender—discourses that generate deeply held conscious and unconscious feelings of fear, anxiety, and even self-hatred—and displaced them onto safe rhetorical fields, in this case, a language of "color" and "type," a rhetoric of "naturalness," "expressiveness," and "individuality."[46]

The cosmetics industry played a crucial role in defining the appearance of femininity in the early twentieth century, but it was not the only player. How women consumers of different social groups shaped those definitions remains an open question for historical research. The profound changes in women's lives in this period may well have spurred women to indulge new fantasies of beauty and calculate differently its material and psychological benefits. Undoubtedly many women did not receive the intended messages of manufacturers and advertisers passively, but how they used cosmetics and understood their meaning must, at this point, be left to speculation.[47]

Clearly the cosmetics industry responded to a larger cultural field of established and emergent images and definitions of femininity, crosscut by class and race. In various ways, the industry worked with those images, reshaping them in response to its perceptions of women's fears and desires. If, in the early twentieth century, some Americans sought to define female selfhood in meaningful ways (through the act of thinking or through productive labor, for example), the cosmetics industry foregrounded the notion that one's "look" was not only the expression of female identity but its essence as well. In this, the mass, class, and African American ends of the industry converged. Although it may not have controlled the discourse over femininity, the multi-billion-dollar industry that exists today is testimony to its ability to convince women to purchase, as Charles Revson cynically put it, "hope in a jar."

Notes

1. See, e.g., Lary May, *Screening Out the Past: The Birth of Mass Culture and the Motion Picture Industry* (New York: Oxford University Press, 1980); Roland Marchand, *Advertising the American Dream: Making Way for Modernity* (Berkeley: University of California Press, 1985), p. 176–188; Lewis A. Erenberg, *Steppin' Out: New York Nightlife and the Transformation of American Culture, 1890–1930* (Westport, Conn.: Greenwood Press, 1981); Martha Banta, *Imaging American Women: Idea and Ideals in Cultural History* (New York: Columbia

University Press, 1987); William R. Leach, "Transformations in a Culture of Consumption: Women and Department Stores, 1890–1925," *Journal of American History* 71 (September 1984): 319–42.

2. Lois Banner, *American Beauty* (Chicago: University of Chicago Press, 1983). Among the many advice books and formularies, see, e.g., *The American Family Keepsake of People's Practical Cyclopedia* (Boston, 1849); Smith and Swinney, *The House-Keeper's Guide and Everybody's Hand-Book* (Cincinnati, 1868); *The American Ladies' Memorial: An Indispensable Home Book for the Wife, Mother, Daughter* (Boston, 1850); Emily Thornwell, *The Lady's Guide to Perfect Gentility* (New York: Derby and Jackson, 1857). See also Cosmetics files in the Warshaw Collection of Business Americana, Archives Center, National Museum of American History, Smithsonian Institution (hereafter cited as Warshaw), a rich collection of advertising graphics, posters, pamphlets, and ephemera.

3. Banner, *American Beauty*, pp. 42–44, 119; Arnold James Cooley, *Instructions and Cautions Respecting the Selection and Use of Perfumes, Cosmetics and Other Toilet Articles* (Philadelphia: J.B. Lippincott and Company, 1873), p. 428.

4. On working women's subculture, see Christine Stansell, *City of Women: Sex and Class in New York, 1789–1860* (New York: Knopf, 1986); and Kathy Peiss, *Cheap Amusements: Working Women and Leisure in Turn-of-the-Century New York* (Philadelphia: Temple University Press, 1986).

5. Gwendolyn Robinson, "Class, Race and Gender: A Transcultural, Theoretical and Sociohistorical Analysis of Cosmetic Institutions and Practices to 1920" (Ph.D. dissertation, University of Illinois at Chicago, 1984), ch. 2.

6. Lola Montez, *The Art of Beauty: or Secrets of a Lady's Toilet* (New York: Dick and Fitzgerald, 1853), pp. xii–xiii, 47; Cooley, *Instructions and Cautions*; Karen Haltunen, *Confidence Men and Painted Women: A Study of Middle-Class Culture in America, 1830–1870* (New Haven: Yale University Press, 1982).

7. For analyses that speak to the intersection of class and gender in the nineteenth century, see Stansell, *City of Women*, and Nancy Hewitt, "Beyond the Search for Sisterhood: American Women's History in the 1980s," *Social History* 10 (1985), pp. 299–321.

8. For statistics on the cosmetics industry, see U. S. Bureau of the Census, *Census of Manufactures: Patent & Proprietary Medicines and Compounds & Druggists' Preparations* (Washington, D.C.: U.S. Government Printing Office, 1919); and *Toilet Requisites* 6 (June 1921); p. 26. On the patent medicine industry, see James Harvey Young, *The Toadstool Millionaires: A Social History of Patent Medicines in America before Federal Regulation* (Princeton: Princeton University Press, 1961); and Sarah Stage, *Female Complaints: Lydia Pinkham and the Business of Women's Medicine* (New York: Norton, 1979). On soap, see Richard L. Bushman and Claudia L. Bushman, "The Early History of Cleanliness in America," *Journal of American History* 74 (1988); pp. 1213–38.

9. For druggists' formularies, see John H. Nelson, *Druggists' Hand-Book of Private Formulas*, 3rd ed. (Cleveland 1879); Charles E. Hamlin, *Hamlin's Formulae, or Every Druggist His Own Perfumer* (Baltimore: Edward B. Read and Son, 1885). Trade catalogs document wholesale druggists' goods: see, e.g., W. H. Schieffelin and Company, *General Prices Current of Foreign and Domestic Drugs, Medicines, Chemicals . . .* (New York, March 1881); and Bolton Drug Company, *Illustrated Price List* (ca. 1890), both in Archives Center, National Museum of American History; Brown, Durrell and Company, *The Trade Monthly* (Boston, January 1895) and others in *Trade Catalogues at Winterthur, 1750–1980* (Clearwater Publishing Company microfilm collection). For a general history, see Edward Kremers and George Urdang, *Kremer's and Urdang's History of Pharmacy*, 4th ed. (Philadelphia: J. B. Lippincott Company, 1976).

10. Banner, *American Beauty*, pp. 28–44, 202–25. See also Anne Hard, "The Beauty Business," *American Magazine* 69 (November 1909), pp. 79–90.

11. For general background on female cosmetics entrepreneurs, see Margaret Allen, *Selling Dreams: Inside the Beauty Business* (New York: Simon and Schuster, 1981); Maxene Fabe, *Beauty Millionaire: The Life of Helena Rubinstein* (New York: Thomas Y. Crowell, 1972); Patrick O'Higgins, *Madame, an Intimate Biography of Helena Rubinstein* (New York: Viking Press, 1971); Alfred Allan Lewis and Constance Woodworth, *Miss Elizabeth Arden* (New York: Coward, McCann, and Geoghegan, 1972). The latter two biographies, written in breathless prose, include fascinating gossip but are questionable histories.

12. Susanna Cocroft, *How to Secure a Beautiful Complexion and Beautiful Eyes: A Practical Course in Beauty Culture* (Chicago: James J. Clarke and Company, 1911) in Cosmetics, Warshaw. See also her *Beauty a Duty: The Art of Keeping Young* (Chicago: Rand McNally, 1915).

13. Madame Yale, *The Science of Health and Beauty*, (n.p. 1893), p. 6, in Cosmetics, Warshaw; Cocroft, *Beautiful Complexion*.

14. Yale, *Science of Health and Beauty*, p. 26.

15. See n. 11, and also Paulette School, *Beauty Culture at Home* (Washington, D.C.: n.p., 1914); E. Burnham, *The Coiffure*, Catalog No. 37 (Chicago, 1908), in Hair files, Warshaw.

16. Lewis and Woodworth, *Elizabeth Arden*.

17. *Toilet Requisites* 10 (October 1925): 64. *Toilet Requisites*, later *Beauty Fashion*, was the trade journal for buyers and retailers of cosmetics, toiletries, and druggists' sundries; founded in 1916, it is an excellent source for developments in the industry.

18. Alfred D. Chandler, Jr., *The Visible Hand: The Managerial Revolution in American Business* (Cambridge: Harvard University Press, 1977), ch. 7. See also Susan Strasser, " 'Refuse All Substitutes': Branded Products and the Relationships of Distribution, 1885–1920," paper presented at the American Studies Association Annual Meeting, New York, November 1987.

19. See *Fancy Goods Graphics, 1879–1890*; and catalogs from B. Altman and Company, John Wanamaker, Siegel-Cooper, Simpson Crawford Company, R. H. Macy and Company, ranging in date from 1880 to 1920, all in Dry Goods files, Warshaw. *Toilet Requisites* carried extensive coverage of department store counter and window displays. For a general discussion, see William R. Leach, "Transformations in a Culture of Consumption"; and Susan Porter Benson, *Counter Cultures: Saleswomen, Managers and Customers in American Department Stores, 1890–1940* (Urbana: University of Illinois Press, 1986).

20. *Sears General Catalogue*, No. 105 (Fall 1897); Larkin Company Catalogues, No. 55 (1907) and No. 86 (Fall and Winter 1921), in Soap files, Warshaw.

21. For late nineteenth-century advertising, see the material culture sources in Cosmetics, Patent Medicines, and Hair files, in Warshaw. For discussions of the changes in advertising, see Daniel Pope, *The Making of Modern Advertising* (New York: Basic Books, 1983); Robert Jay, *The Trade Card in Nineteenth-Century America* (Columbia, Mo.: University of Missouri Press, 1987); and for a later period, Marchand, *Advertising the American Dream*.

22. See such mass circulation women's magazines as *Ladies Home Journal* and *Delineator*, 1890–1920.

23. Ricksecker's Products brochure; Stoddart's Peerless Liquid and Stoddart's Peerless Face Powder trade cards; Harriet Hubbard Ayer, Recamier Cream, and Recamier Balm advertising cards, all in Cosmetics files, Warshaw.

24. For these trends, and those stated in the following paragraph, see *Toilet Requisites*, 1916–1925.

25. For discussions of this new cultural ideal among middle-class women, see Banta, *Imaging American Women*; Carroll Smith-Rosenberg, "New Woman as Androgyne," in *Disorderly Conduct: Visions of Gender in Victorian America* (New York: Oxford University Press, 1985); Sheila Rothman, *Women's Proper Place: A History of Changing Ideals and Practices* (New York: Basic Books, 1979). On working-class women, see Peiss, *Cheap Amusements*; and Elizabeth Ewen, *Immigrant Women in the Land of Dollars* (New York: Monthly Review Press, 1985).

26. See *Photoplay* and *True Story*, 1920–1925. Also Photoplay Magazine, *The Age Factor in Selling and Advertising: A Study in a New Phase of Advertising* (Chicago and New York: Photoplay, 1922).

27. See, for example, *Toilet Requisites* 9 (March 1925): 46, on using a scene from the film "Male and Female" in a window display. On women's response to the movies, see Herbert Blumer, *Movies and Conduct* (New York: Macmillian, 1933), pp. 30–58; and Peiss, *Cheap Amusements*.

28. Vanessa Broussard, "Afro-American Images in Advertising, 1880–1920" (M.A. thesis, George Washington University, 1987).

29. Lyon Manufacturing Company, *What Colored People Say* (n.p., n.d.) and *Afro-American Almanac 1897* (n.p.), Patent Medicine files, Warshaw.

30. For the most extensive discussion of the Black cosmetics industry, see Robinson, "Class, Race and Gender"; for her treatment of Overton, see pp. 313–39.

31. For insights into cosmetics advertising in Black newspapers, see Claude A. Barnett Papers, Archives and Manuscripts Department, Chicago Historical Society, especially box 262.

32. Robinson, "Class, Race and Gender," pp. 280–282, 347–411, 515. The Walker advertisement appeared in the *Oklahoma Eagle*, 3 March 1928, Rotogravure section, in Barnett Papers, box 262, f4. See also Black Cosmetics Industry File, Division of Community Life, National Museum of American History; "Poro Hair & Beauty Culture" Handbook (St. Louis, 1922), Barnett Papers. There were many other African American beauty culturists: see, e.g., Mrs. Mattie E. Hockenhull, *Imported Method in Beauty Culture. First Lessons* (Pine Bluff, Ark.: Gudger Printing Company, 1917); and W. T. McKissick and Company, *McKissick's Famous Universal Agency or System* (Wilmington, Del.: n.p., n.d.), in Hair files, Warshaw.

33. Robinson, "Class, Race and Gender," pp. 449–551.

34. See Warren I. Susman, *Culture as History: The Transformation of American Society in the Twentieth Century* (New York: Pantheon, 1984), especially " 'Personality' and the Making of Twentieth-Century Culture," pp. 271–85.

35. For an example of this reorientation, see the Armand complexion powder and proofs, 1916–1932, in Armand Co., N. W. Ayer Collection, Archives Center, National Museum of American History, Smithsonian Institution.

36. See *American Perfumer*, 1906–1908, for detailed reporting on the effects of the Food and Drug Act, also

394 / Kathy Peiss

Bureau of Chemistry, General Correspondence, Record Group 97, Entry 8, National Archives. For a general discussion, see James Harvey Young., *The Medical Messiahs: A Social History of Health Quackery in Twentieth-Century America* (Princeton: Princeton University Press, 1967), chs. 1–3.

37. *Toilet Requisites* 4 (August 1919): 10, and 4 (April 1919), p. 3.

38. Overton-Hygienic Manufacturing Company, High Brown Face Powder sample envelope, in Curt Teich Postcard Collection, Lake County Museum, Wauconda, Illinois; Kashmir Chemical Company, Nile Queen Cosmetics advertising, box 4, f1 and f2, in Claude A. Barnett Collection, Prints and Photographs Department, Chicago Historical Society.

39. Countess Ceccaldi (Tokolon Company), *Secrets and Arts of Fascination Employed by Cleopatra, The Greatest Enchantress of All Time* (ca. 1920s), in Cosmetics file, Warshaw; Zip advertisement, *Toilet Requisites* 9. No. 1 (April 1924).

40. *The Secret of Charm and Beauty* (New York: Independent Corporation, 1923), pp. 19, 22–23; Nell Vinick, *Lessons in Loveliness: A Practical Guide to Beauty Secrets* (New York: Longmans, Green and Company, 1930), p. 46; *Toilet Requisites* 5 (April 1920); p.21; and 6 (June 1921), pp. 30–31.

41. Cf. trade cards for Hoyt's German Soap and Murray and Lanham's Florida Water, in Soap and Cosmetics files, respectively. Warshaw, John Kasson in *Amusing the Million: Coney Island at the Turn of the Century* (New York: Hill and Wang, 1978) discusses middle-class interest in exoticism; thanks also to James Gilbert for his helpful insights on this subject.

42. See. e.g., Ceccaldi, *Secrets and Arts of Fascination*; Kashmir Chemical Company, Nile Queen Cosmetics, Barnett Papers. The King Tut craze in 1923 proved profitable to the cosmetics industry: see *Toilet Requisites* 12 (March 1923), p. 25, and unnumbered page following 32.

43. Armand ad proofs, Ayer Book 382, especially Advt. No. 10039, 1929. N.W. Ayer Collection.

44. Golden Brown Ointment advertisement, *New York Age*, 7 February 1920, p. 5. These advertisements abound in the African American press; see e.g., Crane and Company, *New York Age* (5 January 1905), p. 4; M. B. Berger and Company, *New York Age* (14 January 1909), p. 3; Black-No-More, *New York Age* (16 July 1914).

45. Lyon's Manufacturing Company, *The Secret of Health and Beauty* (n.p., n.d.) in Patent Medicines file, Warshaw, Albert F. Wood, *The Way to a Satin Skin* (Detroit, 1923), pp. 8–9, in Archives Center, NMAH.

46. Cf. Frederic Jameson, "Reification and Utopia in Mass Culture," *Social Text 1* (1979), pp. 130–48.

47. Reception analysis is fraught with difficulties for the historian, but for a theoretical model, see Janice A. Radway, *Reading the Romance: Women, Patriarchy and Popular Literature* (Chapel Hill; University of North Carolina Press, 1984); and Michael Denning, *Mechanic Accents: Dime Novels and Working Class Culture in America* (New York: Meuthuen, 1987).

25

Raiz Fuerte: Oral History and Mexicana Farmworkers
Devra Anne Weber

Mexicana field workers, as agricultural laborers, have been remarkable for their absence in written agricultural history. Most studies have focused on the growth of capitalist agriculture and the related decline of the family farm. Concern about the implications of these changes for American culture, political economy, and the agrarian dream has generally shaped the questions asked about capitalist agriculture. If freeholding family farmers were the basis of a democratic society, capitalist and/or slave agriculture were its antitheses. Studies of capitalist agriculture have thus become enclosed within broader questions about American democracy, measuring change against a mythologized past of conflict-free small farming on a classless frontier.

When considered at all, agricultural wageworkers have usually been examined in terms of questions framed by these assumptions. Rather than being seen in their own right, they have usually been depicted as the degraded result of the family farm's demise. The most thoughtful studies have been exposés, written to sway public opinion, which revealed the complex arrangement of social, economic and political power perpetuating the brutal conditions of farmworkers. As was the case with the history of unskilled workers in industry, the written history of farmworkers became molded by the pressing conditions of their lives. The wretchedness of conditions became confused with the social worlds of the workers. Pictured as victims of a brutal system, they emerged as faceless, powerless, passive, and, ultimately, outside the flow of history. Lurking racial, cultural, ethnic, and gender stereotypes reinforced this image. This was especially true for Mexican women.[1]

These considerations make oral sources especially crucial for exploring the history of Mexican women.[2] Oral histories enable us to challenge the common confusion between the dismal conditions of the agricultural labor system and the internal life of workers. They enable us to understand, as Jones and Osterud suggest, the relationship for Mexicanas between the economic system of agriculture and community, politics, familial and cultural life. Oral histories help answer (and reconceptualize) fundamental questions about class, gender, life and work, cultural change, values and perceptions neglected in traditional sources. They also provide an insight into consciousness.

In conducting a series of oral histories with men and women involved in a critical farmworker strike in the 1930s, I began to think about the nature of gender consciousness. How does it intersect with a sense of class? How does it intersect with national and ethnic identity? In the oral histories of Mexican women, their sense of themselves as workers and Mexicans frequently coincided with that of the men, and drew upon similar bonds of

Reprinted with permission from the *Oral History Review*, vol. 17 no. 2, Fall, 1989.

history, community, and commonality. Yet the women's perceptions of what it meant to be a Mexican or a worker were shaped by gender roles and consciousness that frequently differed from that of the men. This seemed to correspond to what Temma Kaplan has defined as "female consciousness." According to Kaplan,

> Female consciousness, recognition of what a particular class, culture and historical period expect from women, creates a sense of rights and obligations that provides motive force for actions different from those Marxist or feminist theory generally try to explain. Female consciousness centers upon the rights of gender, on social concerns, on survival. Those with female consciousness accept the gender system of their society; indeed such consciousness emerges from the division of labor by sex, which assigns women the responsibility of preserving life. But, accepting that task, women with female consciousness demand the rights that their obligations entail. The collective drive to secure those rights that result from the division of labor sometimes has revolutionary consequences insofar as it politicizes the networks of everyday life.[3]

This essay will explore how oral histories can help us understand the consciousness of a group of Mexican women cotton workers (or *companeras* of cotton workers) who participated in the 1933 cotton strike in California's San Joaquin Valley. One was a woman I will call Mrs. Valdez.

Mrs. Valdez and the 1933 Cotton Strike

Mrs. Valdez came from Mexico, where her father had been a *sembrador*, a small farmer or sharecropper, eking out a livable but bleak existence. She had barely reached adolescence when the Mexican revolution broke out in 1910. With the exception of a sister-in-law, neither she nor her immediate family participated in the revolution.[4] As is the case with many noncombatants, her memories of the revolution were not of the opposing ideologies nor issues, but of hunger, fear, and death.[5] Fleeing the revolution, the family crossed the border into the United States. By 1933, she was twenty-four, married with two children, and lived in a small San Joaquin Valley town.

The agricultural industry in which she worked was, by 1933, California's major industry. Cotton, the most rapidly expanding crop, depended on Mexican workers who migrated annually to the valley to work.[6] Large cotton ranches of over three hundred acres dominated the industry. Here workers lived in private labor camps, the largest of which were rural versions of industrial company towns: workers lived in company housing, bought from (and remained in debt to) company stores, and sent their children to company schools. Work and daily lives were supervised by a racially structured hierarchy dominated by Anglo managers and foremen: below them were Mexican contractors who recruited the workers, supervised work, and acted as the intermediary between workers and their English-speaking employers.

With the depression, growers slashed wages. In response, farmworkers went on strike in crop after crop in California. The wave of strikes began in southern California and spread north into the San Joaquin Valley. While conducted under the banner of the Cannery and Agricultural Workers Industrial Union (CAWIU), the strikes were sustained largely by Mexican workers and Mexican organizers. The spread and success of the strikes depended on the familial and social networks of Mexican workers as much as, if not more than, the small but effective and ambitious union. The strike wave crested in the cotton fields of the San Joaquin Valley when eighteen thousand strikers brought picking to a standstill. Growers evicted strikers, who established ad hoc camps on empty land. The largest was near the town of Corcoran, where 3,500 workers congregated. The strikers formed mobile picket lines, to which growers retaliated by organizing armed vigilantes. The strikers held out for over a month before a negotiated settlement was reached with the growers and the California, United States, and Mexican governments.

Mexicanas were a vital part of the strike, and about half of the strikers at Corcoran were women. They ran the camp kitchen, cared for children, and marched on picket lines. They distributed food and clothing. Some attended strike meetings, and a few spoke at the meetings. And it was the women who confronted Mexican strikebreakers. In short, women were essential to this strike, though they have been largely obscured in accounts of its history. Mrs. Valdez went on strike and was on the picket lines. She was not a leader, but one of the many women who made the strike possible.

Voice and Community

Before examining her testimony, a word is in order about voice and tone as a dimension of oral histories. How information is conveyed is as important as what is said and can emphasize or contradict the verbal message. Conversation and social interaction are a major part of women's lives, and gesture and voice are thus particularly crucial to their communications. The verbal message, the "song" of a story, is especially important for people with a strong oral tradition which, as Jan Vansina has pointed out, has meaning as art form, drama, and literature. Oral histories or stories are often dramatic, moving with a grace and continuity that embody analytical reflections and communicate an understanding of social relations and the complexities of human existence.

Mrs. Valdez structured the telling of her oral history in stories or vignettes. Most sections of her oral history had distinct beginnings and endings, interrupted only if I interjected a question. She developed characters, villains and heroes, hardship and tragedy (but little comedy). How this story was constructed and its characters developed embodied her assessment of the conflict.

As she told her story, the characters developed voices of their own, each with separate and distinct tones and cadence, perhaps reflecting their personalities to an extent, but more generally expressing Mrs. Valdez's assessment of them and their role in the drama. Strikebreakers, for example, spoke in high-pitched and pleading voices: the listener understood them immediately as measly cowards. Her rendition of the strikers' voices offered a clear contrast: their words were given in sonorous, deep, and steady tones, in a voice of authority that seemed to represent a communal voice verbalizing what Mrs. Valdez considered to be community values.

Mrs. Valdez's sense of collective values, later embodied in collective action either by strikers as a whole or by women, was expressed in what I would call a collective voice. At times individuals spoke in her stories: the grower, Mr. Peterson; her contractor, "Chicho" Viduarri; and the woman leader "la Lourdes," but more often people spoke in one collective voice which transcended individuality. This sense of community as embodied in a collective voice became a central feature of her narrative, and permeated everything she said about the strike. This manner of telling underscored the sense of unanimity explicit in her analysis of solidarity and clear-cut divisions.[7] How she told the story underlined, accentuated, and modified the meaning of the story itself.

Beyond her use of different voices, Mrs. Valdez's narrative contains substantial nonverbal analysis of the "facts" as she remembered them. Her voice, gestures, and inflections conveyed both implications and meanings. She gestured with her arms and hands—a flat palm hard down on the table to make a point, both hands held up as she began again. Her stories had clear beginnings and often ended with verbal punctuations such as "and that's the way it was." She switched tenses around as, in the heat of the story, the past became the present and then receded again into the past. Vocal inflections jumped, vibrated, climbed, and then descended, playing a tonal counterpoint to her words.

Mrs. Valdez's memories of the 1933 strike focused on two major concerns: providing and caring for her family, and her role as a striker. How she structured these memories says much about her perceptions and her consciousness as a woman, a Mexican, and a worker: it is striking to what extent her memories of the strike focused on the collectivity of Mexicans and, within this, the collectivity of Mexican women.

Mrs. Valdez's sense of national identity, an important underpinning to her narrative, reflects the importance of national cohesion against an historic background of Anglo-Mexican hostility.[8] Mrs. Valdez vividly recounted the United States' appropriation of Mexican land in 1848 and the Treaty of Guadalupe Hidalgo which ceded the area to the United States. She drew from stories of Mexican rebellion against U.S. rule in California and the nineteenth-century California guerrillas, Tiburcio Vasquez and Joaquin Murieta: the knowledge that Mexicans were working on the land which once belonged to Mexico increased her antagonism towards Anglo bosses. Mrs. Valdez may well have felt like another interviewee, Mrs. Martinez, who upon arriving at the valley pointed out to her son and told him "Mira lo que nos arrebataron los bárbaros."[9]

Most of these workers had lived through the Mexican revolution of 1910 to 1920, and they utilized both the experience and legacy within the new context of a strike-torn California. The military experience was crucial in protecting the camp: often led by exmilitary officers, Mexican veterans at the Corcoran camp formed a formidable armed security system. Mrs. Valdez remembers that during the strike stories of the revolution were told, retold, and debated. The extent to which Mexicans employed the images and slogans of the revolution helped solidify a sense of community. Workers named the rough roads in the camp after revolutionary heroes and Mexican towns. Even Mrs. Valdez, whose individual memories of the revolution were primarily of the terror it held for her, shared in a collective memory of a national struggle and its symbols: she disdainfully compared strikebreakers with traitors who had "sold the head of Pancho Villa."[10]

Mrs. Valdez expressed a sense of collectivity among Mexicans. There were, in fact, many divisions—between strikers and strikebreakers, contractors and workers, people from different areas of Mexico, and people who had fought with different factions of the revolution or Cristero movement. Yet conflict with Anglo bosses on what had been Mexican land emphasized an identification as Mexicans (as well as workers) that overshadowed other divisions.

The Community of Mexican Women

Mrs. Valdez remembered a collectivity of Mexican women. By 1933, Mexican women worked alongside men in the fields. Like the men, they were paid piece-rates and picked an average of two hundred pounds per ten-hour day. Picking required strength, skill, and stamina. As one woman recalled:

> But let me describe to you what we had to go through. I'd have a twelve foot sack . . . I'd tie the sack around my waist and the sack would go between my legs and I'd go on the cotton row, picking cotton and just putting it in there. . . . So when we finally got it filled real good then we would pick up the [hundred pound] sack, toss [sic!] it up on our

shoulders, and then I would walk, put it up there on the scale and have it weighed, put it back on my shoulder, climb up on a wagon and empty that sack in.[11]

As Mrs. Valdez recounted, women faced hardships in caring for their families: houses without heat, which contributed to disease, preparing food without stoves, and cooking over fires in oil barrels. Food was central to her memory, reflecting a gender division of labor. Getting enough food, a problem at any time, was exacerbated by the Depression, which forced some women to forage for berries or feed their families flour and water. Food was an issue of survival. As in almost all societies, women were in charge of preparing the food, and Mrs. Valdez's concern about food was repeated in interviews with other women. Men remembered the strike in terms of wages and conditions: women remembered these events in terms of food. Men were not oblivious or unconcerned, but woman's role in preparing food made this a central aspect of their consciousness and shaped the way they perceived, remembered, and articulated the events of the strike.

Mrs. Valdez's memory of leadership reflects this sense of female community. After initially replying that there were no leaders (interesting in itself) she named her labor contractor and then focused on a woman named Lourdes Castillo, an interesting choice for several reasons. Lourdes Castillo was an attractive, single woman who lived in Corcoran. She wore make up, bobbed her hair, and wore stylish dresses. Financially independent, she owned and ran the local bar. Lourdes became involved with the strike when union organizers asked her to store food for strikers in her cantina.

In some respects, Lourdes represented a transition many Mexican women were undergoing in response to capitalist expansion, revolution, and migration. When the revolution convulsively disrupted Mexican families, women left alone took over the work in rural areas, migrated, and sometimes became involved in the revolution. *Soldaderas*, camp followers in the revolution, cooked, nursed, and provided sexual and emotional comfort. Some fought and were even executed in the course of battle. This image of *la soldadera*, the woman fighting on behalf of the Mexican community, was praised as a national symbol of strength and resistance. Yet it was an ambivalent image: praised within the context of an often mythified revolution, the *soldaderas* were criticized for their relative sexual freedom and independence. The term *soldadera* became double-edged. When used to describe an individual woman, it could be synonymous with "whore."

Gender mores in the United States differed from rural Mexico. Some changes were cosmetic manifestations of deeper changes: women bobbed their hair, adopted new dress and make up. But these changes reflected changes in a gender division of labor. Women, usually younger and unmarried, began to work for wages in canneries or garment factories unobserved by watchful male relatives. Some women became financially independent, such as Lourdes, and ran bars and cantinas. Financial independence and a changing gender division of labor outside the house altered expectations of women's responsibilities and obligations. Yet these women still risked the approbation of segments of the community, male and female.

According to Mrs. Valdez, during the strike Lourdes was in charge of keeping the log of who entered and left the camp and spoke at meetings. She was also in charge of distributing food.[12] Lourdes thus reflects women's traditional concern about food, while at the same time she epitomized the cultural transition of Mexican women and the changing gender roles from prerevolutionary Mexico to the more fluid wage society of California. It was precisely her financial independence that enabled her to store and distribute the food. Perhaps Mrs. Valdez's enthusiastic memories of Lourdes suggests Mrs. Valdez's changing values for women, even if not directly expressed in her own life.

While Mrs. Valdez described the abysmal conditions under which women labored, the women were active, not passive, participants in the strike. Women's networks that formed the lattice of mutual assistance in the workers' community were transformed during the strike. The networks helped form daily picket lines in front of the cotton fields. Older women still sporting the long hair and rebozos of rural Mexico, younger women who had adapted the flapper styles of the United States, and young girls barely into their teens rode together in trucks to the picket lines. They set up makeshift child-care centers and established a camp kitchen.

With the spread of the conflict, these networks expanded and the women's involvement escalated from verbal assaults on the strikebreakers to outright physical conflict. When, after three weeks, growers refused to settle, women organized and led confrontations with Mexican strikebreakers. According to Mrs. Valdez, the women decided that they, not the men, would enter the fields to confront the strikebreakers.[13] They reasoned that strikebreakers would be less likely to physically hurt the women.

In organized groups, the women entered the field, appealing to strikebreakers on class and national grounds—as "poor people" and "Mexicanos"—to join the strike. Those from the same regions or villages in Mexico appealed to compatriots on the basis of local loyalties, denouncing as traitors those who refused.

Exhortations turned to threats and conflict. The women threatened to poison one man who had eaten at the camp kitchen—an indication again of the centrality (and their power over) food. But women had come prepared. Those armed with lead pipes and knives went after the strikebreakers. One ripped a cotton sack with a knife. Others hit strikebreakers with pipes, fists, or whatever was handy. Although strikers had felt that the women would not be hurt, the male strikebreakers retaliated, and at least one woman was brutally beaten:

> Las mismas mujeres que iban en los troques . . . que iban en el picoteo. Adentro, les pegaron. Les rompieron su ropa. Les partieron los sombreros y los sacos y se los hicieron asina y todo. Y malos! Ohh! Se mira feo! Feo se miraba. Y nomas miraba y decia "no, no." Yo miraba la sangre que les escurria. [She imitates the strikebreakers in high-pitched, pleading tones:] "No les peguen, déjenlos, no les peguen." [Her voice drops as the voice of the strikers speak:] "Que se los lleve el esto. . . . Si a nosotros nos esta llevando de frio y de hambre pos que a ellos también. No tienen, vendidos, muertos de hambre!" [Her voice rises as the strikebreakers continue their plea:] "Pos nosotros vivemos muy lejos, venimos de Los Angeles . . . tienes que saber de donde, que tenemos que tener dinero pa' irnos." [Her voice lowers and slows as it again becomes the voice of the strikers:] "Si . . . nosotros también tenemos que comer y también tenemos familia. *Pero no somos vendidos!*"[14]

This passage underlines the importance of the female collectivity. The women went in because it was women's business, and they acted on behalf of the community. Mrs. Valdez implied that the men had little to do with the decision or even opposed it. "Porque las mujeres tenemos más chanza. Siempre los hombres se detenian más porque son hombres y todo. Y las mujeres no. Los hombres no nos pueden hacer nada. No nos podian hacer nada pos ahi vamos en zumba."[15]

The issues of confrontation focused around food. This underlines a harsh reality— strikebreakers worked to feed their families; without food strikers would be forced back to work. Her memory reflects the reality of the confrontation but also her understanding of the central issue of the strike. Mrs. Valdez recalls the strikebreakers justifying themselves to the women in terms of the need to feed their families. But the striking women's ultimate rebuke was also expressed in terms of this need: "Si . . . nosotros también tenemos que comer y también tenemos familia. *Pero no somos vendidos!*[16] Food remained central in her memories. Discussions about the strike and strike negotiations were all couched in relation to food. Her interests as a Mexican worker were considered, weighed, and expressed within the context of her interests as a woman, mother, and wife.

As the strike wore on, conditions grew harsher in the Corcoran camp. Growers lobbed incendiaries over the fence at night. Food became hard to get, and at least one child died of malnutrition.[17] In response to public concern following the murder of two strikers, the California Governor overrode federal regulations withholding relief from strikers under arbitration and, over the protestations of local boards of supervisors, sent in trucks of milk and food to the embattled camp. Mrs. Valdez remembers nothing of federal, state, or local government or agencies, but she remembered the food: " . . . rice, beans, milk, everything they sent in."

At a meeting where Lourdes addressed strikers, food, or lack of food, was juxtaposed against their stance in the strike:

> Pa' [Lourdes] decirles que pasaran hambre.
>
> "Mira," dice . . . "aunque alcanzemos poquito pero no nos estamos muriendo de hambre," dice. "Pero no salga. Pero NINGUNO a trabajar . . . aunque venga el ranchero y les diga que, que vamos y que pa' ca. NO vaya ninguno!" dice.
>
> "Miren, aunque sea poquito estamos comiendo . . . pero no nos hemos muerto de hambre. Ta viniendo comida . . . nos estan trayendo comida."
>
> [Mrs. Valdez interjected:] Leche y todo nos daban. . . . Si. Y a todos ahi los que trabajában diciendo que no fueran con ningún ranchero. Que no se creeran de ningún ranchero. Que todos se agarraban de un solo modo que nadien, todos parejos tuvieran su voto, parejos. . . .[18]

Mrs. Valdez was clear about the effects of a united front on both sides, that if one grower broke with the others the rest would follow. [The collective voice speaks:] "No. Y no que no. No. Si nos paga tanto vamos. Y al pagar un ranchero tenían que pagar todos los mismo. Tenían, ves."[19]

Unity and the centrality of women was carried over into her recollection of the final negotiations:

> El portuguese [a growers' representative] . . . le dijera que ahí iban los rancheros . . . a tener un mitin en el campo donde estaban todos ahí campados con la Lourdes Castillo y todo.
>
> "Si," dice. "Ahí vamos a juntarnos todos los rancheros. Y vamos a firmar. Les vamos a pagar tanto. Y vamos a firmar todos para que entonces, sí, ya vayan cada quien a sus campos a trabajar."
>
> "Si," dice [the strikers' representative], "pero no menos de un centavo. No. No salimos hasta que tengan un . . . sueldo fijo. Todos vamos. Pero de ahí en más ni uno vamos. *Ni uno* salimos del camps." Y todo.[20]

The strike was settled, the ranchers had been beaten, and wages went up.

The Structure of Memory

Mrs. Valdez's account of the strike and women—how she structured her memories—tells us more about why Mexicanas supported the strike than interviews with leaders might have. Without the perceptions of women such as Mrs. Valdez it would be more difficult to understand strike dynamics.

Of particular interest is the fact that she remembers (or recounts) a collectivity among Mexican strikers. In her telling, workers speak in a collective voice and act as a united group. She remembers little or no dissent. In her account, *all* the workers on the Peterson ranch walked out together to join the strike, *all* the women were on the picket lines, and *all* the strikers voted unanimously to stay on strike. Growers, also a united group, spoke with one voice as a collective opposition. The lines between worker and grower were clearly drawn. According to Mrs. Valdez it was this unity that accounted for the strikes success.

But within this collectivity of Mexicans was the collectivity of women. Mrs. Valdez focused on female themes and concerns about food, caring for their families and, by extension, the greater community. Women were the actors on the picket line, made decisions about the strike, and acted as a unit. It is perhaps this sense of female collectivity and the concern around the issue of food that accounts for why Lourdes was considered a leader, though she is never mentioned by men in their accounts. Mrs. Valdez stated flatly that the women were braver—men played little part in her narrative. She remembered female leadership, female participation, female concerns, and a largely female victory. While other interviews and sources may disagree (even among women), it does suggest Mrs. Valdez's reality of the strike of 1933.

What Mrs. Valdez did not say suggests the limitations of oral narratives. She either did not know, recall, or choose to recount several crucial aspects of the story: like many other strikers, she remembered nothing of the CAWIU, nor Anglo strike leaders mentioned in other accounts. This was not uncommon, and I discuss elsewhere the implications of this and the nature of Mexican leadership within the strike. The role of the New Deal and the negotiations of the governments—Mexican, United States, and Californian—play no part in her narrative. The visit by the Mexican consul to the camp; visits by government officials; threats to deport strikers—she recounted nothing about the negotiations that led to the settlement of the strike.

Her memory of the strike thus is limited. But the fact that Mrs. Valdez's memories were so similar to those of other women indicates that hers is not an isolated perception. There are also many points at which the memories intersect with the men. We thus may be dealing with a community memory made up of two intersecting collective memories: the collective memory (history) of the group as a whole, and a collective memory of women as a part of this.

Conclusion

Oral narratives reflect peoples' memory of the past: they can be inaccurate, contradictory, altered with the passage of time and the effects of alienation. In terms of historical analysis, Mrs. Valdez's oral history used alone raises questions. Was there really such unity in face of such an intense conflict? There were, obviously, strikebreakers. Were there no doubts, arguments? In part she may have been making a point to me. But it may be also indicative of her consciousness, of the things important to her in the event. Mrs. Valdez also remembers a largely female collectivity. Certainly, from other sources, it is clear men played a crucial role as well. Yet her focus on women provides information unavailable in other sources, and provides a point of view of women. It suggests which issues were important to the female collectivity, how and why women rallied to the strike, and how they used their networks within the strike.

So how may an oral history be used? Seen on its own it remains a fragment of the larger story. Oral narratives must also be read critically as texts in light of the problem of alienation, especially in the United States, where various forms of cultural and historical amnesia seem so advanced. Used uncritically, oral histories are open to misinterpretation and may reinforce rather than reduce the separation from a meaningful past. This is especially true of the narratives of those people usually ignored by written history. Readers may lack an historical framework within which to situate and understand such narratives. The filters of cultural and class differences and chauvinism may also be obstacles. Some may embrace these narratives as colorful and emotional personal statements, while ignoring the subjects as reflective and conscious participants in history.

In the case of the Mexican women farm laborers considered in this essay, oral testimonies are not a complete history, nor can they, by themselves, address the problems of historical amnesia. Used with other material, and read carefully and critically, however, such narratives prove crucial to a reanalysis of the strike. They need to be interpreted and placed within an historical framework encompassing institutional and social relations, struggle, and change. But when this is done, testimonies like that of Mrs. Valdez become a uniquely invaluable source. Used critically, they reveal transformations in consciousness and culture; they suggest the place of self-conscious and reflective Mexican women—and farm laboring women in general—in the broader history of rural women in the United States.

Notes

1. Portions of this essay appear in Devra A. Weber, "Mexican Women on Strike: Memory, History and Oral Narrative," in *Between Borders: Essays on Mexicana/Chicana History* ed. Adelaida Del Castillo (Encino, California: Floricanto Press, 1990), pp. 161–174.
2. I use the term used by the women themselves. They called themselves Mexicans. Although all had lived in the United States over fifty years, all but one identified themselves as Mexicanas by birth, culture, and ethnicity. The one woman born and raised in the United States, and a generation younger, referred to herself interchangeably as Mexicana and Chicana.
3. Temma Kaplan, "Female Consciousness and Collective Action: The Case of Barcelona. 1910–1918," *Signs* (Spring, 1982), p. 545.
4. The sister-in-law is an interesting, if fragmentary, figure in Mrs. Valdez's memory. From Mrs. Valdez's account, the sister-in-law left her husband (Mrs. Valdez's brother) to join a group of revolutionaries, as a *companera* of one of them. When she returned to see her children, she threatened to have the entire family killed by her new lover. It was in the wake of this threat that the family fled to the United States.
5. That these were the main concerns of many Mexicans does not undermine the importance of the revolution in their lives, nor the extent to which the images and symbols of the revolution *later* became symbols of collective resistance, on both a class and national scale.
6. By 1933, the overwhelming majority of Mexican workers did not migrate from Mexico but from settled communities around Los Angeles or the Imperial Valley, adjacent to the Mexican border. Some came from Texas. The point is that they were not the "homing pigeons" described by growers who descended on the fields at harvest and cheerfully departed for Mexico. They were residents, and some of the younger pickers were United States citizens.
7. I want to emphasize that this is *her* analysis. I would disagree with the picture of solidarity: disputes among strikers would, I think, bear this out. Nevertheless, the point is that Mrs. Valdez's historical analysis tells us a great deal about her conception of the strike—and perhaps her conception of what I should be told about it.
8. In Mexico, Mexicans tended to have a greater sense of identity with the town or state they came from than with the country as a whole. These identities were still strong in the 1980s, as were the rivalries which existed between them. It has been argued that the Mexican revolution helped create a sense of national consciousness. One of the primary reasons was its opposition to foreign interests. For those who migrated north, across the Rio Bravo, the sense of opposition to Anglo-Americans was even greater. It was on the border areas, after all, where the corridors of resistance developed, and where many have argued the sense of Mexican nationalism was strongest.
9. "Look at what the barbarians have stolen from us." Interview by author with Guillermo Martinez. Los Angeles, April 1982.

Note: Having encountered strong objections to using the original Spanish in such a text, a word of explanation is in order. Translating another language—especially if the language is colloquial and therefore less directly translatable—robs the subjects of their voices, diminishing the article as a consequence. This is especially true if, as in this case, the language is colloquial and, to those who know Spanish, manifestly rural and working-class. The original text gives such readers an indication of class and meaning unavailable in a translation. It also underscores the value of bridging monolingual parochialism in a multilingual and multicultural society. In any event, full English translations for all quotations will be provided in the Notes.

10. After his death, Villa's corpse was disinterred and decapitated. His head was stolen in the 1920s, and the incident became a legend.

11. Interview by author with Lydia Ramos. All names used here are pseudonyms.

12. It is unclear whether Lourdes did keep the log. In a brief interview, Lourdes confirmed that she spoke at meetings and distributed food.

13. It is unclear exactly who made this decision. Roberto Castro, a member of the central strike committee, said the strike committee decided that women should enter the fields to confront strikebreakers because the women would be less likely to be hurt. The women remembered no such decision, and said that they made the decision themselves. It is hard to fix definitively the origins of the idea, but this may not matter very much: even if the strike committee made the decision, the action was consistent with spontaneous decisions by women that both antedated and followed this strike. Mexican women in Mexico City and other parts of the republic had taken part in bread riots in the colonial period. They had fought in the revolution. And in California, later strikes, in the 1930s but also as recently as the 1980s, were punctuated by groups of Mexican women invading the fields to confront strikebreakers both verbally and physically. In short, it was a female form of protest women had used both before and after the strike.

14. The same women who were in the trucks, who were in the . . . picket line . . . these women went in and beat up all those that were inside [the fields] picking cotton. . . . They tore their clothes. They ripped their hats and the [picking] sacks. . . . And bad. Ohhh! It was ugly! It was an ugly sight. I was just looking and said "No. No." I watched the blood flowing from them.

[She imitates the strikebreakers voice in a high pitched, pleading tone:] "Don't hit us. Leave them [other strikebreakers] alone. Don't hit them."

[Her voice drops as the collective voice of the strikers speaks:] "Let them be set upon. . . . If we are going cold and hungry then they should too. They're cowards . . . sell outs. Scum."

[Her voice rises as the strikebreakers continue their plea:] "Because we live far away, we come from Los Angeles. . . . We need to have money to leave. . . ."

"Yes," she says [her voice lowers and slows as it again becomes the voice of the strikers]. "We also have to eat and we also have family," she says. *But we are not sell outs!*"

15. "Because women take more chances. The men always hold back because they are men and all. But the women, no. The men couldn't make us do anything. They couldn't make us do anything [to prevent us from going] and so we all went off in a flash."

16. "Yes . . . we also have to eat and we also have family. *But we are not sellouts!*"

17. As the local district attorney admitted after the strike, conditions in the strikers' camp were no worse than those of the cotton labor camps. Growers did use the bad conditions, however, to pressure the health department to close the strikers' camp as a menace to public health.

18. She [Lourdes] was telling them that they might have to go hungry for awhile.

"But look," she said . . . "they are bringing us food. We'll each get just a little, but we're not going to starve," she says. "But don't leave. But don't ANYBODY go to work. Even if a rancher comes and tells you 'come on, lets go,' don't anybody go," she says.

"Look, even if its a little bit, we're eating. But we aren't starving. They're bringing us food."

[Mrs. Valdez interjected:]. They brought us milk and everything. Yes, everybody that was working [in the strikers camp] were told not to go with any rancher. They were told not to believe any rancher. But everyone had to stand together as one. Everyone had an equal vote [in what was decided] . . . equal.

19. [The collective voice speaks] "No. And no. [they said] No. No. If you play us this much, then we go. And if one [rancher] pays [the demand] then all the ranchers have to pay the same." They had to, you see.

20. The Portuguese [a growers' representative] told [the strikers representative] that the ranchers . . . were going to have a meeting at [the strikers' camp] with "la Lourdes."

"Yes," he says, . . . "We're going to pay you so much. All of us are going to sign so that then all of you can return to your camps to work."

"Yes," said [the strikers' representative] "But not a cent less. No. We won't go until we have a set wage. Then all of us go. But if there is something more [if there is more trouble] NONE of us go. Not even ONE of us leave the camp."

26

From Servitude to Service Work: Historical Continuities in the Racial Division of Paid Reproductive Labor

Evelyn Nakano Glenn

Recent scholarship on African American, Latina, Asian American, and Native American women reveals the complex interaction of race and gender oppression in their lives. These studies expose the inadequacy of additive models that treat gender and race as separate and discrete systems of hierarchy (Collins 1986; King 1988; Brown 1989). In an additive model, white women are viewed solely in terms of gender, while women of color are thought to be "doubly" subordinated by the cumulative effects of gender plus race. Yet achieving a more adequate framework, one that captures the interlocking, interactive nature of these systems, has been extraordinarily difficult. Historically, race and gender have developed as separate topics of inquiry, each with its own literature and concepts. Thus features of social life considered central in understanding one system have been overlooked in analyses of the other.

One domain that has been explored extensively in analyses of gender but ignored in studies of race is social reproduction. The term *social reproduction* is used by feminist scholars to refer to the array of activities and relationships involved in maintaining people both on a daily basis and intergenerationally. Reproductive labor includes activities such as purchasing household goods, preparing and serving food, laundering and repairing clothing, maintaining furnishings and appliances, socializing children, providing care and emotional support for adults, and maintaining kin and community ties.

Marxist feminists place the gendered construction of reproductive labor at the center of women's oppression. They point out that this labor is performed disproportionately by women, and is essential to the industrial economy. Yet because it takes place mostly outside the market, it is invisible, not recognized as real work. Men benefit directly and indirectly from this arrangement—directly in that they contribute less labor in the home while enjoying the services women provide as wives and mothers, and indirectly in that, freed of domestic labor, they can concentrate their efforts in paid employment and attain primacy in that area. Thus the sexual division of reproductive labor in the home interacts with and reinforces sexual division in the labor market.[1] These analyses draw attention to the dialectics of production and reproduction, and male privilege in both realms. When they represent gender as the sole basis for assigning reproductive labor, however, they imply that all women have the same relationship to it, and that it is therefore a universal female experience.[2]

In the meantime, theories of racial hierarchy do not include any analysis of reproductive labor. Perhaps because, consciously or unconsciously, they are male-centered, they focus

Reprinted by permission of the University of Chicago Press. Originally published in *Signs*, vol. 18, no. 1, 1992.

exclusively on the paid labor market, and especially on male-dominated areas of production.[3] In the 1970s several writers seeking to explain the historic subordination of peoples of color pointed to dualism in the labor market—its division into distinct markets for white workers and for racial-ethnic workers—as a major vehicle for maintaining white domination (Blauner 1972; Barrera 1979).[4] According to these formulations, the labor system has been organized to ensure that racial-ethnic workers are relegated to a lower tier of low-wage, dead-end, marginal jobs; institutional barriers, including restrictions on legal and political rights, prevent their moving out of that tier and competing with Euro-American workers for better jobs. These theories draw attention to the material advantages whites gain from the racial division of labor. However, they either take for granted or ignore women's unpaid household labor and fail to consider whether this work might also be "racially divided."

In short, the racial division of reproductive labor has been a missing piece of the picture in both literatures. This piece, I would contend, is key to the distinct exploitation of women of color, and is a source of both hierarchy and interdependence among white women and women of color. It is thus essential to the development of an integrated model of race and gender, one that treats them as interlocking, rather than additive, systems.

In this article I present a historical analysis of the simultaneous race and gender construction of reproductive labor in the United States, based on comparative study of women's work in the South, the Southwest, and the Far West. I argue that reproductive labor has divided along racial as well as gender lines, and that the specific characteristics of the division have varied regionally and changed over time as capitalism has reorganized reproductive labor, shifting parts of it from the household to the market. In the first half of the century, racial-ethnic women were employed as servants to perform reproductive labor in white households, relieving white middle-class women of onerous aspects of that work; in the second half of the century, with the expansion of commodified services (services turned into commercial products or activities), racial-ethnic women are disproportionately employed as service workers in institutional settings to carry out lower-level "public" reproductive labor, while cleaner, white-collar, supervisory and lower professional positions are filled by white women.

I will examine the ways race and gender were constructed around the division of labor by sketching changes in the organization of reproductive labor since the early nineteenth century, presenting a case study of domestic service among African American women in the South, Mexican American women in the Southwest, and Japanese American women in California and Hawaii, and finally examining the shift to institutional service work, focusing on race and gender stratification in health care and the racial division of labor within the nursing labor force. Race and gender emerge as socially constructed, interlocking systems that shape the material conditions, identities, and consciousnesses of all women.

Historical Changes in the Organization of Reproduction

The concept of reproductive labor originated in Karl Marx's remark that every system of production involves both the production of the necessities of life and the reproduction of the tools and labor-power necessary for production (Marx and Engels 1969, 31). Recent elaborations of the concept grow out of Engels's dictum that the "determining force in history is, in the last resort, the production and reproduction of immediate life." This has, he noted, "a two-fold character, on the one hand the production of subsistence and on the other the production of human beings themselves" (Engels 1972, 71). Although often equated with domestic labor, or defined narrowly as referring to the renewal of labor-power, the term *social reproduction* has come to be more broadly conceived, particularly by social historians, to refer to the creation and recreation of people as cultural and social, as well as physical, beings (Ryan 1981, 15). Thus, it involves mental, emotional, and manual labor (Brenner and Laslett 1986, 117). This labor can be organized in myriad ways—in and out of the household, as paid or unpaid work, creating exchange value or only use value—and these ways are not mutually exclusive. An example is the preparation of food, which can be done by a family member as unwaged work in the household, by a servant as waged work in the household, or by a short-order cook in a fast-food restaurant as waged work that generates profit for the employer. These forms exist contemporaneously.

Prior to industrialization, however, both production and reproduction were organized almost exclusively at the household level. Women were responsible for most of what might be designated as reproduction, but they were simultaneously engaged in the production of foodstuffs, clothing, shoes, candles, soap, and other goods consumed by the household. With industrialization, production of these basic goods was gradually taken over by capitalist industry. Reproduction, however, remained largely the responsibility of individual households. The ideological separation between men's "productive" labor and women's nonmarket-based activity that had evolved at the end of the eighteenth century was elaborated in the early decades of the nineteenth. An idealized division of labor arose, in which men's work was to follow production outside the home, while women's work was to remain centered in the household (Boydstron 1990, esp. 46–48). Household work continued to include the production of many goods consumed by members (Smuts 1959, 11–13; Kessler-Harris 1981), but as an expanding range of outside-manufactured goods became available, household work became increasingly focused on reproduction.[5] This idealized division of labor was largely illusory for working-class households, including immigrant and racial-ethnic families, in which men seldom earned a family wage; in these households women and children were forced into income-earning activities in and out of the home (Kessler-Harris 1982).

In the second half of the twentieth century, with goods production almost completely incorporated into the market, reproduction has become the next major target for commodification. Aside from the tendency of capital to expand into new areas for profit-making, the very conditions of life brought about by large-scale commodity production have increased the need for commercial services. As household members spend more of their waking hours employed outside the home, they have less time and inclination to provide for one another's social and emotional needs. With the growth of a more geographically mobile and urbanized society, individuals and households have become increasingly cut off from larger kinship circles, neighbors, and traditional communities. Thus, as Harry Braverman notes

> The population no longer relies upon social organization in the form of family, friends, neighbors, community, elders, children, but with few exceptions must go to the market and only to the market, not only for food, clothing, and shelter, but also for recreation, amusement, security, for the care of the young, the old, the sick, the handicapped. In time not only the material and service needs but even the emotional patterns of life are channeled through the market (Braverman 1974, 276).

Conditions of capitalist urbanism also have enlarged the population of those requiring daily care and support: elderly and very young people, mentally and physically disabled people, criminals, and other people incapable of fending for themselves. Because the care of such dependents becomes difficult for the "stripped-down" nuclear family or the atomized community to bear, more of it becomes relegated to institutions outside the family.[6]

The final phase in this process is what Braverman calls the "product cycle," which "invents new products and services, some of which become indispensable as the conditions of modern life change and destroy alternatives" (Braverman 1974, 281). In many areas (for example, health care), we no longer have choices outside the market. New services and products also alter the definition of an acceptable standard of living. Dependence on the market is further reinforced by what happened earlier with goods production, namely, an "atrophy of competence," so that individuals no longer know how to do what they formerly did for themselves.

As a result of these tendencies, an increasing range of services has been removed wholly or partially from the household and converted into paid services yielding profits. Today, activities such as preparing and serving food (in restaurants and fast-food establishments), caring for handicapped and elderly people (in nursing homes), caring for children (in child-care centers), and providing emotional support, amusement, and companionship (in counseling offices, recreation centers, and health clubs) have become part of the cash nexus. In addition, whether impelled by a need to maintain social control or in response to pressure exerted by worker and community organizations, the state has stepped in to assume minimal responsibility for some reproductive tasks, such as child protection and welfare programs.[7] Whether supplied by corporations or the state, these services are labor-intensive. Thus, a large army of low-wage workers, mostly women and disproportionately women of color, must be recruited to supply the labor.

Still, despite vastly expanded commodification and institutionalization, much reproduction remains organized at the household level. Sometimes an activity is too labor-intensive to be very profitable. Sometimes households or individuals in them have resisted commodification. The limited commodification of child care, for example, involves both elements. The extent of commercialization in different areas of life is uneven, and the variation in its extent is the outcome of political and economic struggles (Brenner and Laslett 1986, 121; Laslett and Brenner 1989, 384). What is consistent across forms, whether commodified or not, is that reproductive labor is constructed as "female." The gendered organization of reproduction is widely recognized. Less obvious, but equally characteristic, is its racial construction: historically, racial-ethnic women have been assigned a distinct place in the organization of reproductive labor.

Elsewhere I have talked about the reproductive labor racial-ethnic women have carried out for their own families; this labor was intensified as the women struggled to maintain family life and indigenous cultures in the face of cultural assaults, ghettoization, and a labor system that relegated men and women to low-wage, seasonal, and hazardous employment (Glenn 1985; 1986, 86–108; Dill 1988). Here I want to talk about two forms of waged reproductive work that racial-ethnic women have performed disproportionately: domestic service in private households, and institutional service work.

Domestic Service as the Racial Division of Reproductive Labor

Both the demand for household help and the number of women employed as servants expanded rapidly in the latter half of the nineteenth century (Chaplin 1978). This expansion paralleled the rise of industrial capital and the elaboration of middle-class women's reproductive responsibilities. Rising standards of cleanliness, larger and more ornately furnished homes, the sentimentalization of the home as a "haven in a heartless world" (Lasch 1977), and the new emphasis on childhood and the mother's role in nurturing children all served to enlarge middle-class women's responsibilities for reproduction, at a time when technology had done little to reduce the sheer physical drudgery of housework.[8]

By all accounts, middle-class women did not challenge the gender-based division of labor or the enlargement of their reproductive responsibilities. Indeed, middle-class women—as readers and writers of literature; as members and leaders of clubs, charitable organizations, associations, reform movements, and religious revivals; and as supporters of the cause of abolition—helped to elaborate the domestic code (Brenner and Laslett 1986).[9] Feminists seeking an expanded public role for women argued that the same nurturant and moral qualities that made women centers of the home should be brought to bear in public service. In the domestic sphere, instead of questioning the inequitable gender division of labor, they sought to slough off the more burdensome tasks onto more oppressed groups of women.[10]

Phyllis Palmer observes that, at least through the first half of the twentieth century, "most white middle-class women could hire another woman—a recent immigrant, a working class woman, a woman of color, or all three—to perform much of the hard labor of household tasks" (Palmer 1987, 182–83). Domestics were employed to clean house, launder and iron clothes, scrub floors, and care for infants and children. They relieved their mistresses of the heavier and dirtier domestic chores.[11] White middle-class women were thereby freed for supervisory tasks and for cultural, leisure, and volunteer activity or, more rarely during this period, for a career.[12]

Palmer suggests that the use of domestic servants also helped resolve certain contradictions created by the domestic code. She notes that the early twentieth-century housewife confronted inconsistent expectations of middle-class womanhood: domesticity and "feminine virtue." Domesticity—defined as creating a warm, clean, and attractive home for husband and children—required hard physical labor and meant contending with dirt. The virtuous woman, however, was defined in terms of spirituality, refinement, and the denial of the physical body. Additionally, in the 1920s and 1930s there emerged a new ideal of the modern wife as an intelligent and attractive companion. If the heavy parts of household work could be transferred to paid help, the middle-class housewife could fulfill her domestic duties, yet distance herself from the physical labor and dirt, and also have time for personal development (Palmer 1990, 127–51).

Who was to perform the "dirty work" varied by region. In the Northeast, European immigrant women, particularly those who were Irish and German, constituted the majority of domestic servants from the mid-nineteenth century to World War I (Katzman 1978, 65–70). In regions where there was a large concentration of people of color, subordinate-race women formed a more or less permanent servant stratum. Despite differences in the composition of the populations and the mix of industries in the regions, there were important similarities in the situation of Mexicans in the Southwest, African Americans in the South, and Japanese people in northern California and Hawaii. Each of these groups was placed in a separate legal category from whites, excluded from rights and protections accorded full citizens. This severely limited their ability to organize, compete for jobs, and acquire capital (Glenn 1985). The racial division of private reproductive work mirrored this racial dualism in the legal, political, and economic systems.

In the South, African American women constituted the main and almost exclusive servant caste. Except in times of extreme economic crisis, whites and Blacks did not compete for domestic jobs. Until World War I ninety percent of all nonagriculturally employed Black women in the South were employed as domestics. Even at the national level, servants and laundresses accounted for close to half (48.4 percent) of nonagriculturally employed Black women in 1930.[13]

In the Southwest, especially in the states with the highest proportions of Mexicans in the population—Texas, Colorado, and New Mexico—Chicanas were disproportionately concentrated in domestic service.[14] In El Paso nearly half of all Chicanas in the labor market were employed as servants or laundresses in the early decades of the century (Garcia 1981, 76). In Denver, according to Sarah Deutsch, perhaps half of all Chicano/a households had at least one female member employed as a domestic at some time, and if a woman became a widow, she was almost certain to take in laundry (Deutsch 1987a, 147). Nationally, 39.1 percent of nonagriculturally employed Chicanas were servants or laundresses in 1930.[15]

In the Far West—especially in California and Hawaii, with their large populations of Asian immigrants—an unfavorable sex ratio made female labor scarce in the late nineteenth and early twentieth centuries. In contrast to the rest of the nation, the majority of domestic servants in California and Hawaii were men: in California until 1880 (Katzman 1978, 55) and in Hawaii as late as 1920 (Lind 1951, table 1). The men were Asian—Chinese and later Japanese. Chinese houseboys and cooks were familiar figures in late nineteenth-century San Francisco; so too were Japanese male retainers in early twentieth-century Honolulu. After 1907 Japanese women began to immigrate in substantial numbers, and they inherited the mantle of service in both California and Hawaii. In the pre-World War II years, close to half of all immigrant and native-born Japanese American women in the San Francisco Bay area and in Honolulu were employed as servants or laundresses (U.S. Bureau of the Census 1932, table 8; Glenn 1986, 76–79). Nationally, excluding Hawaii, 25.4 percent of nonagricultural Japanese American women workers were listed as servants in 1930.[16]

In areas where racial dualism prevailed, being served by members of the subordinate group was a perquisite of membership in the dominant group. According to Elizabeth Rae Tyson, an Anglo woman who grew up in El Paso in the early years of the century:

> almost every Anglo-American family had at least one, sometimes two or three servants: a maid and laundress, and perhaps a nursemaid or yardman. The maid came in after breakfast and cleaned up the breakfast dishes, and very likely last night's supper dishes as well; did the routine cleaning, washing and ironing, and after the family dinner in the middle of the day, washed dishes again, and then went home to perform similar services in her own home. (Garcia 1980, 327)

In southwest cities, Mexican American girls were trained at an early age to do domestic work and girls as young as nine or ten were hired to clean house.[17]

In Hawaii, where the major social division was between the haole (Caucasian) planter class and the largely Asian plantation worker class, haole residents were required to employ one or more Chinese or Japanese servants to demonstrate their status and their social distance from those less privileged. Andrew Lind notes that "the literature on Hawaii, especially during the second half of the nineteenth century, is full of references to the open-handed hospitality of Island residents, dispensed by the ever-present maids and houseboys" (Lind 1951, 73). A public-schoolteacher who arrived in Honolulu in 1925 was placed in a teacher's cottage with four other mainland teachers. She discovered a maid had already been hired by the principal:

> A maid! None of us had ever had a maid. We were all used to doing our own work. Furthermore, we were all in debt and did not feel that we wanted to spend even four dollars a month on a maid. Our principal was quite insistent. Everyone on the plantation had a maid. It was, therefore, the thing to do. (Lind 1951, 76)

In the South, virtually every middle-class housewife employed at least one African American woman to do cleaning and child care in her home. Southern household workers told one writer that in the old days, "if you worked for a family, your daughter was expected to, too" (Tucker 1988, 98). Daughters of Black domestics were sometimes inducted as children into service to baby-sit, wash diapers, and help clean (Clark-Lewis 1987, 200–201).[18] White-skin privilege transcended class lines, and it was not uncommon for working-class whites to hire Black women for housework (Anderson and Bowman 1953). In the 1930s white women tobacco workers in Durham, North Carolina, could mitigate the effects of the "double day"—household labor on top of paid labor—by employing Black women to work in their homes for about one-third of their own wages (Janiewski 1983, 93). Black women tobacco workers were too poorly paid to have this option, and had to rely on the help of overworked husbands, older children, Black women too old to be employed, neighbors, or kin.

Where more than one group was available for service, a differentiated hierarchy of race, color, and culture emerged. White and racial-ethnic domestics were hired for different tasks. In her study of women workers in Atlanta, New Orleans, and San Antonio during the 1920s and 1930s, Julia Kirk Blackwelder reported that "Anglo women in the employ of private households were nearly always reported as housekeepers, while Blacks and Chicanas were reported as laundresses, cooks or servants" (Blackwelder 1978, 349).[19]

In the Southwest, where Anglos considered Mexican or "Spanish" culture inferior, Anglos displayed considerable ambivalence about employing Mexicans for child care. Although a modern-day example, this statement by an El Paso businessman illustrates the contradictions in Anglo attitudes. The man told an interviewer that he and his wife were putting off parenthood because:

> the major dilemma would be what to do with the child. We don't really like the idea of leaving the baby at home with a maid . . . for the simple reason if the maid is Mexican, the child may assume that the other person is its mother. Nothing wrong with Mexicans, they'd just assume that this other person is its mother. There have been all sorts of cases where the infants learned Spanish before they learned English. There've been incidents of the Mexican maid stealing the child and taking it over to Mexico and selling it. (Ruiz 1987b, 71)

In border towns, the Mexican group was further stratified by English-speaking ability, place of nativity, and immigrant status, with non-English-speaking women residing south of the border occupying the lowest rung. In Laredo and El Paso, Mexican American factory operatives often employed Mexican women who crossed the border daily or weekly to do domestic work for a fraction of a U.S. operative's wages (Hield 1984, 95; Ruiz 1987a, 64).

The Race and Gender Construction of Domestic Service

Despite their preference for European immigrant domestics, employers could not easily retain their services. Most European immigrant women left service upon marriage, and their daughters moved into the expanding manufacturing, clerical, and sales occupations during the 1910s and twenties.[20] With the flow of immigration slowing to a trickle during World War I, there were few new recruits from Europe. In the 1920s, domestic service became increasingly the specialty of minority-race women (Palmer 1990, 12). Women of color were advantageous employees in one respect: they could be compelled more easily to remain in service. There is considerable evidence that middle-class whites acted to ensure the domestic labor supply by tracking racial-ethnic women into domestic service and blocking their entry into other fields. Urban school systems in the Southwest tracked

Chicana students into homemaking courses designed to prepare them for domestic service. The El Paso school board established a segregated school system in the 1880s that remained in place for the next thirty years; education for Mexican children emphasized manual and domestic skills that would prepare them to work at an early age. In 1909 the Women's Civic Improvement League, an Anglo organization, advocated domestic training for older Mexican girls. Their rationale is explained by Mario Garcia:

> According to the league the housegirls for the entire city came from the Mexican settlement and if they could be taught housekeeping, cooking and sewing, every American family would benefit. The Mexican girls would likewise profit since their services would improve and hence be in greater demand. (Garcia 1981, 113)

The education of Chicanas in the Denver school system was similarly directed toward preparing students for domestic service and handicrafts. Sarah Deutsch found that Anglo women there persisted in viewing Chicanas and other "inferior-race" women as dependent, slovenly, and ignorant. Thus, they argued, training Mexican girls for domestic service not only would solve "one phase of women's work we seem to be incapable of handling" but it would simultaneously help raise the (Mexican) community by improving women's standard of living, elevating their morals, and facilitating Americanization (Deutsch 1987b, 736). One Anglo writer, in an article published in 1917 titled "Problems and Progress among Mexicans in Our Own Southwest," claimed, "When trained there is no better servant than the gentle, quiet Mexicana girl" (Romero 1988a, 16).

In Hawaii, with its plantation economy, Japanese and Chinese women were coerced into service for their husbands' or fathers' employers. According to Lind, prior to World War II:

> It has been a usual practice for a department head or a member of the managerial staff of the plantation to indicate to members of his work group that his household is in need of domestic help and to expect them to provide a wife or daughter to fill the need. Under the conditions which have prevailed in the past, the worker has felt obligated to make a member of his own family available for such service, if required, since his own position and advancement depend upon keeping the goodwill of his boss. Not infrequently, girls have been prevented from pursuing a high school or college education because someone on the supervisory staff has needed a servant and it has seemed inadvisable for the family to disregard the claim. (Lind 1951, 77)

Economic coercion also could take bureaucratic forms, especially for women in desperate straits. During the Depression, local officials of the federal Works Project Administration (WPA) and the National Youth Administration (NYA), programs set up by the Roosevelt administration to help the unemployed find work, tried to direct Chicanas and Blacks to domestic service jobs exclusively (Blackwelder 1984, 120–22; Deutsch 1987a, 182–83). In Colorado, local officials of the WPA and NYA advocated household training projects for Chicanas. George Bickel, assistant state director of the WPA for Colorado, wrote: "The average Spanish-American girl on the NYA program looks forward to little save a life devoted to motherhood often under the most miserable circumstances" (Deutsch 1987a, 183). Given such an outlook, it made sense to provide training in domestic skills.

Young Chicanas disliked domestic service so much that slots in the programs went begging. Older women, especially single mothers struggling to support their families, could not afford to refuse what was offered. The cruel dilemma that such women faced was poignantly expressed in one woman's letter to President Roosevelt:

> My name is Lula Gordon. I am a Negro woman. I am on the relief. I have three children. I have no husband and no job. I have worked hard ever since I was old enough. I am willing to do any kind of work because I have to support myself and my children. I was under the impression that the government or the W.P.A. would give the Physical [sic] fit relief clients work. I have been praying for that time to come. A lady, Elizabeth Ramsie, almost in my condition, told me she was going to try to get some work. I went with her. We went to the Court House here in San Antonio, we talked to a Mrs. Beckmon. Mrs. Beckmon told me to phone a Mrs. Coyle because she wanted some one to clean house and cook for ($5) five dollars a week. Mrs. Beckmon said if I did not take the job in the Private home I would be cut off from everything all together. I told her I was afraid to accept the job in the private home because I have registered for a government job and when it opens up I want to take it. She said that she was taking people off of the relief and I have to take the job in the private home or none. . . . I need work and I will do anything the government gives me to do. . . . Will you please give me some work. [Blackwelder 1984, 68–69]

Japanese American women were similarly compelled to accept domestic service jobs when they left the internment camps in which they were imprisoned during World War II. To leave the camps they had to have a job and a residence, and many women were forced to take positions as live-in servants in various parts of the country. When women from the San Francisco Bay area returned there after the camps were closed, agencies set up to assist the returnees directed them to domestic service jobs. Because they had lost their homes and possessions and had no savings, returnees had to take whatever jobs were offered them. Some became live-in servants to secure housing, which was in short supply after the war. In many cases domestic employment became a lifelong career (Glenn 1986).

In Hawaii the Japanese were not interned, but there nonetheless developed a "maid shortage" as war-related employment expanded. Accustomed to cheap and abundant household help, haole employers became increasingly agitated about being deprived of the services of their "mamasans." The suspicion that many able-bodied former maids were staying at home idle because their husbands or fathers had lucrative defense jobs was taken seriously enough to prompt an investigation by a university researcher.[21]

Housewives told their nisei maids it was the maids' patriotic duty to remain on the job. A student working as a live-in domestic during the war was dumbfounded by her mistress's response when she notified her she was leaving to take a room in the dormitory at the university. Her cultured and educated mistress, whom the student had heretofore admired, exclaimed with annoyance: " 'I think especially in war time, the University should close down the dormitory.' Although she didn't say it in words, I sensed the implication that she believed all the (Japanese) girls should be placed in different homes, making it easier for the haole woman."[22] The student noted with some bitterness that although her employer told her that working as a maid was the way for her to do "your bit for the war effort," she and other haole women did not, in turn, consider giving up the "conveniences and luxuries of prewar Hawaii" as their bit for the war.[23]

The dominant group ideology in all these cases was that women of color—African American women, Chicanas, and Japanese American women—were particularly suited for service. These racial justifications ranged from the argument that Black and Mexican women were incapable of governing their own lives and thus were dependent on whites—

making white employment of them an act of benevolence—to the argument that Asian servants were naturally quiet, subordinate, and accustomed to a lower standard of living. Whatever the specific content of the racial characterizations, it defined the proper place of these groups as in service: they belonged there, just as it was the dominant group's place to be served.

David Katzman notes that "ethnic stereotyping was the stock in trade of all employers of servants, and it is difficult at times to figure out whether blacks and immigrants were held in contempt because they were servants or whether urban servants were denigrated because most of the servants were blacks and immigrants" (Katzman 1978, 221). Even though racial stereotypes undoubtedly preceded their entry into domestic work, it is also the case that domestics were forced to enact the role of the inferior. Judith Rollins and Mary Romero describe a variety of rituals that affirmed the subordination and dependence of the domestic; for example, employers addressed household workers by their first names and required them to enter by the back door, eat in the kitchen, and wear uniforms. Domestics understood they were not to initiate conversation but were to remain standing or visibly engaged in work whenever the employer was in the room. They also had to accept with gratitude "gifts" of discarded clothing and leftover food (Rollins 1985, chap. 5; Romero 1987).

For their part, racial-ethnic women were acutely aware that they were trapped in domestic service by racism, and not by lack of skills or intelligence. In their study of Black life in prewar Chicago, St. Clair Drake and Horace Cayton found that education did not provide African Americans with an entree into white-collar work. They noted, "Colored girls are often bitter in their comments about a society which condemns them to the 'white folks' kitchen'" (Drake and Cayton 1962, 246). Thirty-five years later, Anna May Madison minced no words when she declared to anthropologist John Gwaltney:

> Now, I don't do nothing for white women or men that they couldn't do for themselves. They don't do anything I couldn't learn to do every bit as well as they do it. But, you see, that goes right back to the life that you have to live. If that was the life I had been raised up in, I could be President or any other thing I got a chance to be. (Gwaltney 1980, 173)

Chicana domestics interviewed by Mary Romero in Colorado seemed at one level to accept the dominant culture's evaluation of their capabilities. Several said their options were limited by lack of education and training. However, they also realized they were restricted just because they were Mexican. Sixty-eight-year-old Mrs. Portillo told Romero: "There was a lot of discrimination, and Spanish people got just regular housework or laundry work. There was so much discrimination that Spanish people couldn't get jobs outside of washing dishes—things like that" (Romero 1988b, 86).

Similarly, many Japanese domestics reported that their choices were constrained because of language difficulties and lack of education, but they, too, recognized that color was decisive. Some nisei domestics had taken typing and business courses and some had college degrees, yet they had to settle for "schoolgirl" jobs after completing their schooling. Mrs. Morita, who grew up in San Francisco and graduated from high school in the 1930s, bluntly summarized her options: "In those days there was no two ways about it. If you were Japanese, you either worked in an art store ('oriental curios' shop) where they sell those little junks, or you worked as a domestic. . . . There was no Japanese girl working in an American firm" (Glenn 1986, 122).

Hanna Nelson, another of Gwaltney's informants, took the analysis one step further; she recognized the coercion that kept African American women in domestic service. She saw this arrangement as one that allowed white women to exploit Black women economically and emotionally and exposed Black women to sexual assaults by white men, often with white women's complicity. She says:

> I am a woman sixty-one years old and I was born into this world with some talent. But I have done the work that my grandmother's mother did. It is not through any failing of mine that this is so. The whites took my mother's milk by force, and I have lived to hear a human creature of my sex try to force me by threat of hunger to give my milk to an able man. I have grown to womanhood in a world where the saner you are, the madder you are made to appear. (Gwaltney 1980, 7)

Race and Gender Consciousness

Hanna Nelson displayed a consciousness of the politics of race and gender not found among white employers. Employers' and employees' fundamentally different positions within the division of reproductive labor gave them different interests and perspectives. Phyllis Palmer describes the problems of YWCA and other reform groups encountered when they attempted to establish voluntary standards and working hours for live-in domestics in the 1930s. White housewives invariably argued against any "rigid" limitation of hours; they insisted on provisions for emergencies that would override any hour limits. Housewives saw their own responsibilities as limitless, and apparently felt there was no justification for boundaries on domestics' responsibilities. They did not acknowledge the fundamental difference in their positions: they themselves gained status and privileges from their relationships with their husbands—relationships that depended on the performance of wifely duties. They expected domestics to devote long hours and hard work to help them succeed as wives, without, however, commensurate privileges and status. To challenge the inequitable gender division of labor was too difficult and threatening, so white housewives pushed the dilemma onto other women, holding them to the same high standards by which they themselves were imprisoned (Kaplan 1987; Palmer 1990).

Some domestic workers were highly conscious of their mistress' subordination to their husbands, and condemned their unwillingness to challenge their husbands' authority. Mabel Johns, a sixty-four-year-old widow, told Gwaltney:

> I work for a woman who has a good husband; the devil is good to her, anyway. Now that woman could be a good person if she didn't think she could just do everything and have everything. In this world whatsoever you get you will pay for. Now she is a grown woman, but she won't know that simple thing. I don't think there's anything wrong with her mind, but she is greedy and she don't believe in admitting that she is greedy. Now you may say what you willormay [sic] about people being good to you, but there just ain' a living soul in this world that thinks more of you than you do of yourself. . . . She's a grown woman, but she have to keep accounts and her husband tells her whether or not he will let her do thus-and-so or buy this or that. (Gwaltney 1980, 167)

Black domestics are also conscious that a white woman's status comes from her relationship to a white man, that she gains privileges from the relationship that blinds her to her own oppression, and that she therefore willingly participates in and gains advantages from the oppression of racial-ethnic women. Nancy White puts the matter powerfully when she says:

> My mother used to say that the black woman is the white man's mule and the white woman is his dog. Now, she said that to say this: we do the heavy work and get beat whether we do it well or not. But the white woman is closer to the master and he pats them on the head and lets them sleep in the house, but he ain' gon' treat neither one like he was dealing with a person. Now, if I was to tell a white woman that, the first thing she would do is to call you a nigger and then she'd be real nice to her husband so he would come out here and beat you for telling his wife the truth. (Gwaltney 1980, 148)

Rather than challenge the inequity in the relationship with their husbands, white women pushed the burden onto women with even less power. They could justify this only by denying the domestic worker's womanhood, by ignoring the employee's family ties and responsibilities. Susan Tucker found that southern white women talked about their servants with affection, and expressed gratitude that they shared work with the servant that they would otherwise have to do alone. Yet the sense of commonality based on gender that the women expressed turned out to be one-way. Domestic workers knew that employers did not want to know much about their home situations (Kaplan 1987, 96; Tucker 1988). Mostly, the employers did not want domestics' personal needs to interfere with serving them. One domestic wrote that her employer berated her when she asked for a few hours off to pay her bills and take care of pressing business (Palmer 1990, 74). Of relations between white mistresses and Black domestics in the period from 1870 to 1920, Katzman says that in extreme cases "even the shared roles of motherhood could be denied." A Black child nurse reported in 1912 that she worked fourteen to sixteen hours a day caring for her mistress's four children. Describing her existence as a "treadmill life," she reported that she was allowed to go home "only once in every two weeks, every other Sunday afternoon—even then I'm not permitted to stay all night. I see my own children only when they happen to see me on the streets when I am out with the children [of her mistress], or when my children come to the yard to see me, which isn't often, because my white folks don't like to see their servants' children hanging around their premises."[24] While this case may be extreme, Tucker reports, on the basis of extensive interviews with southern African American domestics, that even among live-out workers in the 1960s,

> White women were also not noted for asking about childcare arrangements. All whites, said one black woman, "assume you have a mother, or an older daughter to keep your child, so it's all right to leave your kids." Stories of white employers not believing the children of domestics were sick, but hearing this as an excuse not to work, were also common. Stories, too, of white women who did not inquire of a domestic's family—even when that domestic went on extended trips with the family—were not uncommon. And work on Christmas morning and other holidays for black mothers was not considered by white employers as unfair. Indeed, work on these days was seen as particularly important to the job. (Tucker 1988, 99)

The irony is, of course, that domestics saw their responsibilities as mothers as the central core of their identity. The Japanese American women I interviewed, the Chicana day workers Romero interviewed, and the African American domestics Bonnie Thornton Dill interviewed all emphasized the primacy of their role as mothers (Dill 1980; Glenn 1986; Romero 1988b). As a Japanese immigrant single parent expressed it, "My children come first. I'm working to upgrade my children." Another domestic, Mrs. Hiraoka, confided she hated household work but would keep working until her daughter graduated from optometry school.[25] Romero's day workers arranged their work hours to fit around their children's school hours so that they could be there when needed. For domestics, then, working had meaning precisely because it enabled them to provide for their children.

Perhaps the most universal theme in domestic workers' statements is that they are working so their own daughters will not have to go into domestic service and confront the same dilemmas of leaving their babies to work. A Japanese American domestic noted, "I tell my daughters all the time, 'As long as you get a steady job, stay in school. I want you to get a good job, not like me.' That's what I always tell my daughters: make sure you're not stuck."[26]

In a similar vein, Pearl Runner told Dill, "My main goal was I didn't want them to follow in my footsteps as far as working" (Dill 1980, 109). Domestic workers wanted to protect their daughters from both the hardships and the dangers that working in white homes posed. A Black domestic told Drake and Cayton of her hopes for her daughters: "I hope they may be able to escape a life as a domestic worker, for I know too well the things that make a girl desperate on these jobs" (Drake and Cayton 1962, 246).

When they succeed in helping their children do better than they themselves did, domestics may consider that the hardships were worthwhile. Looking back, Mrs. Runner is able to say,

> I really feel that with all the struggling that I went through, I feel happy and proud that I was able to keep helping my children, that they listened and that they all went to high school. So when I look back, I really feel proud, even though at times the work was very hard and I came home very tired. But now, I feel proud about it. They all got their education. (Dill 1980, 113)

Domestics thus have to grapple with yet another contradiction. They must confront, acknowledge, and convey the undesirable nature of the work they do to their children, as an object lesson and an admonition, and at the same time maintain their children's respect and their own sense of personal worth and dignity (Dill 1980, 110). When they successfully manage that contradiction, they refute their white employers' belief that "you are your work" (Gwaltney 1980, 174).

The Racial Division of Public Reproductive Labor

As noted earlier, the increasing commodification of social reproduction since World War II has led to a dramatic growth in employment by women in such areas as food preparation and service, health care services, child care, and recreational services. The division of labor in public settings mirrors the division of labor in the household. Racial-ethnic women are employed to do the heavy, dirty, "back-room" chores of cooking and serving food in restaurants and cafeterias, cleaning rooms in hotels and office buildings, and caring for the elderly and ill in hospitals and nursing homes, including cleaning rooms, making beds, changing bed pans, and preparing food. In these same settings white women are disproportionately employed as lower-level professionals (for example, nurses and social workers), technicians, and administrative support workers to carry out the more skilled and supervisory tasks.

The U.S. Census category of "service occupations except private household and protective services" roughly approximates what I mean by "institutional service work." It includes food preparation and service, health care service, cleaning and building services, and personal services.[27] In the United States as a whole, Black and Spanish-origin women are overrepresented in this set of occupations; in 1980 they made up 13.7 percent of all workers in the field, nearly double their proportion (seven percent) in the work force. White women (some of whom were of Spanish origin) were also overrepresented, but not to the same extent, making up 50.1 percent of all "service" workers, compared with their thirty six percent share in the overall work force. (Black and Spanish-origin men made up 9.6 percent, and white men, who were fifty percent of the work force, made up the remaining 27.5 percent.)[28]

Because white women constitute the majority, institutional service work may not at first glance appear to be racialized. However, if we look more closely at the composition of specific jobs within the larger category, we find clear patterns of racial specialization. White women are preferred in positions requiring physical and social contact with the public, that is, waiters/waitresses, transportation attendants, hairdressers/cosmetologists, and dental assistants, while racial-ethnic women are preferred in dirty, back-room jobs as maids, janitors/cleaners, kitchen workers, and nurse's aides.[29]

As in the case of domestic service, who does what varies regionally, following racial-ethnic caste lines in local economies. Racialization is clearest in local economies where a subordinate race/ethnic group is sizable enough to fill a substantial portion of jobs. In southern cities, Black women are twice as likely to be employed in service occupations as white women. For example, in Atlanta in 1980, 20.8 percent of African American women were so employed, compared with 10.4 percent of white women. While they were less than one-quarter (23.9 percent) of all women workers, they were nearly two-fifths (38.3 percent) of women service workers. In Memphis, 25.9 percent of African American women, compared with 10.2 percent of white women, were in services; though they made up only a third (34.5 percent) of the female work force, African American women were nearly three-fifths (57.2 percent) of women employed in this field. In southwestern cities Spanish-origin women specialize in service work. In San Antonio, 21.9 percent of Spanish-origin women were so employed, compared with 11.6 percent of non-Spanish-origin white women; in that city half (49.8 percent) of all women service workers were Spanish-origin, while Anglos, who made up two-thirds (64.0 percent) of the female work force, were a little over a third (36.4 percent) of those in the service category. In El Paso, 16.9 percent of Spanish-origin women were service workers compared with 10.8 percent of Anglo women, and they made up two-thirds (66.1 percent) of those in service. Finally, in Honolulu, Asian and Pacific Islanders constituted 68.6 percent of the female work force, but 74.8 percent of those were in service jobs. Overall, these jobs employed 21.6 percent of all Asian and Pacific Islander women, compared with 13.7 percent of white non-Spanish-origin women.[30]

Particularly striking is the case of cleaning and building services. This category—which includes maids, housemen, janitors, and cleaners—is prototypically "dirty work." In Memphis, one out of every twelve Black women (8.2 percent) was in cleaning and building services, and Blacks were 88.1 percent of the women in this occupation. In contrast, only one out of every two hundred white women (0.5 percent) was so employed. In Atlanta, 6.6 percent of Black women were in this field—constituting 74.6 percent of the women in these jobs—compared with only 0.7 percent of white women. Similarly, in El Paso, 4.2 percent of Spanish-origin women (versus 0.6 percent of Anglo women) were in cleaning and building services—making up ninety percent of the women in this field. And in San Antonio the Spanish and Anglo percentages were 5.3 percent versus 1.1 percent, respectively, with Spanish-origin women 73.5 percent of women in these occupations. Finally, in Honolulu, 4.7 percent of Asian and Pacific Islander women were in these occupations, making up 86.6 percent of the total. Only 1.3 percent of white women were so employed.[31]

From Personal to Structural Hierarchy

Does a shift from domestic service to low-level service occupations represent progress for racial-ethnic women? At first glance it appears not to bring much improvement. After domestic service, these are the lowest paid of all occupational groupings. In 1986 service workers were nearly two-thirds (62 percent) of workers in the United States earning at or below minimum wage.[32] As in domestic service, the jobs are often part-time and seasonal, offer few or no medical and other benefits, have low rates of unionization, and subject workers to arbitrary supervision. The service worker also often performs in a public setting the same sorts of tasks that servants did in a private setting. Furthermore, established patterns of race/gender domination-subordination are often incorporated into the authority structure of organizations. Traditional gender-race etiquette shapes face-to-face interaction in the workplace. Duke University Hospital in North Carolina from its founding in 1929 adopted paternalistic policies toward its Black employees. Black workers were highly conscious of this, as evidenced by their references to "the plantation system" at Duke (Sacks 1988, 46).[33]

Still, service workers, especially those who have worked as domestics, are convinced that "public jobs" are preferable to domestic service. They appreciate not being personally subordinate to an individual employer and not having to do "their" dirty work on "their" property. Relations with supervisors and clients are hierarchical, but they are embedded in an impersonal structure governed by more explicit contractual obligations and limits. Also important is the presence of a work group for sociability and support. Workplace culture offers an alternative system of values from that imposed by managers (Benson 1986).[34] Experienced workers socialize newcomers, teaching them how to respond to pressures to speed up work, to negotiate work loads, and to demand respect from superiors. While the isolated domestic finds it difficult to resist demeaning treatment, the peer group in public settings provides backing for individuals to stand up to the boss.

That subordination is usually not as direct and personal in public settings as in the private household does not mean, however, that race and gender hierarchy is diminished in importance. Rather, it changes form, becoming institutionalized within organizational structures. Hierarchy is elaborated through a detailed division of labor that separates conception from execution, and allows those at the top to control the work process. Ranking is based ostensibly on expertise, education, and formal credentials.

The elaboration is especially marked in technologically oriented organizations that employ large numbers of professionals, as is the case with health care institutions. Visual observation of any hospital reveals the hierarchical race and gender division of labor: at the top are the physicians, setting policy and initiating work for others; they are disproportionately white and male. Directly below, performing medical tasks and patient care as delegated by physicians and enforcing hospital rules, are the registered nurses (RNs), who are overwhelmingly female and disproportionately white. Under the registered nurses and often supervised by them are the licensed practical nurses (LPNs), also female but disproportionately women of color. At about the same level are the technologists and technicians who carry out various tests and procedures and the "administrative service" staff in the offices; these categories tend to be female and white. Finally, at the bottom of the pyramid are the nurse's aides, predominantly women of color; housekeepers and kitchen workers, overwhelmingly women of color; and orderlies and cleaners, primarily men of color. They constitute the "hands" that perform routine work directed by others.

The Racial Division of Labor in Nursing

A study of stratification in the nursing labor force illustrates the race and gender construction of public reproductive labor. At the top in terms of status, authority, and pay are the RNs, graduates of two-, three-, or four-year hospital or college-based programs. Unlike the lower ranks, registered nursing offers a career ladder. Starting as a staff nurse, a hospital

RN can rise to head nurse, nursing supervisor, and finally, director of nursing. In 1980 whites were 86.7 percent of RNs, even though they were only 76.7 percent of the population. The LPNs, who make up the second grade of nursing, generally have had twelve months' training in a technical institute or community college. The LPNs are supervised by RNs and may oversee the work of aides. Racial-ethnic workers constituted 23.4 percent of LPNs, with Blacks, who were 11.7 percent of the population, making up fully 17.9 percent. Below the LPNs in the hierarchy are the nurse's aides (NAs), who typically have on-the-job training of four to six weeks. Orderlies, attendants, home health aides, and patient care assistants also fall into this category. These workers perform housekeeping and routine caregiving tasks "delegated by an RN and performed under the direction of an RN or LPN." Among nurse's aides, 34.6 percent were minorities, with Blacks making up 27.0 percent of all aides.[35]

Nationally, Latinas were underrepresented in health care services but were found in nurse's aid positions in proportion to their numbers—making up 5.2 percent of the total. The lower two grades of nursing labor thus appear to be Black specialties. However, in some localities other women of color are concentrated in these jobs. In San Antonio, forty-eight percent of aides were Spanish-origin, while only 15.1 percent of the RNs were. Similarly, in El Paso, 61.5 percent of aides were Spanish-origin, compared with 22.8 percent of RNs. In Honolulu, Asian and Pacific Islanders, who were 68.6 percent of the female labor force, made up 72.3 percent of the NAs but only 45.7 percent of the RNs.[36]

Familial Symbolism and the Race and Gender Construction of Nursing How did the present ranking system and sorting by race/ethnic category in nursing come about? How did the activities of white nurses contribute to the structuring? And how did racial-ethnic women respond to constraints?

The stratification of nursing labor can be traced to the beginnings of organized nursing in the 1870s. However, until the 1930s grading was loose. A broad distinction was made between so-called trained nurses, who were graduates of hospital schools or collegiate programs, and untrained nurses, referred to—often interchangeably—as "practical nurses," "hospital helpers," "nursing assistants," "nursing aides," or simply as "aides" (Cannings and Lazonik 1975; Reverby 1987).

During this period health work in hospitals was divided between male physicians (patient diagnosis and curing) and female nursing staff (patient care) in a fashion analogous to the separate spheres prescribed for middle-class households. Nurses and physicians each had primary responsibility for and authority within their own spheres, but nurses were subject to the ultimate authority of physicians. The separation gave women power in a way that did not challenge male domination. Eva Gamarinikow likens the position of the British nursing matron to that of an upper-class woman in a Victorian household who supervised a large household staff but was subordinate to her husband (Gamarinikow 1978). Taking the analogy a step further, Ann Game and Rosemary Pringle describe the pre-World War II hospital as operating under a system of controls based on familial symbolism. Physicians were the authoritative father figures, while trained nurses were the mothers overseeing the care of patients, who were viewed as dependent children. Student nurses and practical nurses were, in this scheme, in the position of servants, expected to follow orders and subject to strict discipline (Game and Pringle 1983, 99–100).

Like the middle-class white housewives who accepted the domestic ideology, white nursing leaders rarely challenged the familial symbolism supporting the gender division of labor in health care. The boldest advocated, at most, a dual-headed family (Reverby 1987, 71–75). They acceded to the racial implications of the family metaphor as well. If nurses were mothers in a family headed by white men, they had to be white. And, indeed, trained nursing was an almost exclusively white preserve. As Susan Reverby notes, "In 1910 and 1920, for example, less than 3% of the trained nurses in the United States were black, whereas black women made up 17.6% and 24.0% respectively of the female working population" (Reverby 1987, 71–75).

The scarcity of Black women is hardly surprising. Nursing schools in the South excluded Blacks altogether, while northern schools maintained strict quotas. Typical was the policy of the New England Hospital for Women and Children, which by charter could only admit "one Negro and one Jewish student" a year (Hine 1989, 6). Black women who managed to become trained nurses did so through separate Black training schools, and were usually restricted to serving Black patients, whether in "integrated" hospitals in the North or segregated Black hospitals in the South.[37]

White nursing leaders and administrators justified exclusion by appeals to racist ideology. Anne Bess Feeback, the superintendent of nurses for Henry Grady Hospital in Atlanta, declared that Negro women under her supervision had no morals: "They are such liars. . . . They shift responsibility whenever they can. . . . They quarrel constantly among themselves and will cut up each other's clothes for spite. . . . Unless they are constantly watched, they will steal anything in sight" (Hine 1985, 101). Perhaps the most consistent refrain was that Black women were deficient in the qualities needed to be good nurses: they lacked executive skills, intelligence, strength of character, and the ability to withstand pressure. Thus Margaret Butler, chief nurse in the Chicago City Health Department, contended that Black nurses' techniques were "inferior to that of the white nurses, they are not punctual, and are incapable of analyzing a social situation." Apparently Black nurses did not accept white notions of racial inferiority, for Butler also complains about their tendency "to organize against authority" and "to engage in political intrigue" (Hine 1989, 99). Another white nursing educator, Margaret Bruesche, suggested that although Black women lacked the ability to become trained nurses, they "could fill a great need in the South as a trained attendant, who would work for a lower wage than a fully trained woman" (Hine 1989, 101). Even those white nursing leaders sympathetic to Black aspirations agreed that Black nurses should not be put in supervisory positions, because white nurses would never submit to their authority.

Similar ideas about the proper place of "orientals" in nursing were held by haole nursing leaders in pre-World War II Hawaii. White-run hospitals and clinics recruited haoles from the mainland, especially for senior nurse positions, rather than hiring or promoting locally trained Asian American nurses. This pattern was well known enough for a University of Hawaii researcher to ask a haole health administrator whether it was true that "oriental nurses do not reach the higher positions of the profession?" Mr. "C" confirmed this: "Well, there again it is a matter of qualification. There is a limit to the number of nurses we can produce here. For that reason we have to hire from the mainland. Local girls cannot compete with the experience of mainland haole girls. In order to induce haole nurses here we could not possibly put them under an oriental nurse because that would make them race conscious right at the start. And as I said before, Japanese don't make good executives."[38] Because of the racial caste system in Hawaii, Japanese American women who managed to get into nursing were not seen as qualified or competent to do professional work. The chairman of the Territorial Nurses Association noted that:

> before the war (started), our local nurses were looked down (upon) because they were mostly Japanese. . . . The Japanese nurses feel they can get along better with Mainland nurses than local haole nurses. That is true even outside of the profession. I remember

hearing a Hawaiian-born haole dentist say, 'I was never so shocked as when I saw a white man shine shoes when I first went to the Mainland.' Haoles here feel only orientals and other non-haoles should do menial work."[39]

The systematic grading of nursing labor into three ranks was accomplished in the 1930s and forties, as physician-controlled hospital administrations moved to establish "sound business" practices to contain costs and consolidate physician control of health care.[40] High-tech medical and diagnostic procedures provided an impetus for ever-greater specialization. Hospitals adopted Taylorist principles of "scientific management," separating planning and technical tasks from execution and manual labor. They began to hire thousands of subsidiary workers, and created the licensed practical nurse, a position for a graduate of a one-year technical program, to perform routine housekeeping and patient care. With fewer discriminatory barriers and shorter training requirements, LPN positions were accessible to women of color who wanted to become nurses.

The lowest level of nursing workers, nurse's aides, was also defined in the 1930s, when the American Red Cross started offering ten-week courses to train aides for hospitals. This category expanded rapidly in the 1940s, doubling from 102,000 workers in 1940 to 212,000 in 1950 (Cannings and Lazonik 1975, 200–201). This occupation seems to have been designed deliberately to make use of African American labor in the wake of labor shortages during and after World War II. A 1948 report on nursing told the story of how nurse's aides replaced the heretofore volunteer corps of ward attendants: "In response to this request for persons designated as nursing aides, the hospital discovered among the large Negro community a hitherto untapped reservoir of personnel, well above the ward attendant group in intelligence and personality" (Cannings and Lazonik 1975, 201).

One reason for their superiority can be deduced: they often were overqualified. Barred from entry into better occupations, capable, well-educated Black women turned to nurse's aide work as an alternative to domestic service.

In the meantime, RNs continued their struggle to achieve professional status by claiming exclusive rights over "skilled" nursing work. Some nurses, especially rank-and-file general duty nurses, called for an outright ban on employing untrained nurses. Many leaders of nursing organizations, however, favored accepting subsidiary workers to perform housekeeping and other routine chores so that graduate nurses would be free for more professional work. Hospital administrators assured RNs that aides would be paid less and assigned nonnursing functions and that only trained nurses would be allowed supervisory roles. One administrator claimed that aide trainees were told repeatedly that "they are not and will not be nurses" (Reverby 1987, 194).

In the end, the leaders of organized nursing accepted the formal stratification of nursing, and turned their attention to circumscribing the education and duties of the lower grades to ensure their differentiation from "professional" nurses. Indeed, an RN arguing for the need to train and license practical nurses, and laying out a model curriculum for LPNs, warned: "Overtraining can be a serious danger. The practical nurse who has a course of over fifteen months (theory and practice) gets a false impression of her abilities and builds up the unwarranted belief that she can practice as a professional nurse" (Deming 1947, 26). Hospital administrators took advantage of race and class divisions and RNs' anxieties about their status to further their own agenda. Their strategy of co-opting part of the work force (RNs) and restricting the mobility and wages of another part (LPNs and NAs) undermined solidarity among groups that might otherwise have united around common interests.

Nursing Aides: Consciousness of Race and Gender.   The hierarchy in health care has come to be justified less in terms of family symbolism and more in terms of bureaucratic efficiency. Within the new bureaucratic structures, race and gender ordering is inherent in the job definitions. The nurse's aide job is defined as unskilled and menial; hence, the women who do it are, too. Nurse's aides frequently confront a discrepancy, however, between how their jobs are defined (unskilled and subordinate) and what they actually are allowed or expected to do (exercise skill and judgment). Lillian Roberts's experiences illustrate the disjunction. Assigned to the nursery, she was fortunate to work with a white southern RN who was willing to teach her:

> I would ask her about all kinds of deformities that we would see in the nursery, the color of a baby, and why this was happening and why the other was happening. And then I explored with her using my own analysis of things. Sometimes I'd be right just in observing and putting some common sense into it. Before long, when the interns would come in to examine the babies, I could tell them what was wrong with every baby. I'd have them lined up for them. (Reverby 1979, 297–98)

The expertise Roberts developed through observation, questioning, and deduction was not recognized, however. Thirty years later Roberts still smarts from the injustice of not being allowed to sit in on the shift reports: "They never dignify you with that. Even though it would help you give better care. There were limitations on what I could do" (Reverby 1979, 298–99).

She had to assume a deferential manner when dealing with white medical students and personnel, even those who had much less experience than she had. Sometimes she would be left in charge of the nursery and "I'd get a whole mess of new students in there who didn't know what to do. I would very diplomatically have to direct them, although they resented to hell that I was both black and a nurse's aide. But I had to do it in such a way that they didn't feel I was claiming to know more than they did" (Reverby 1979, 298). One of her biggest frustrations was not being allowed to get on-the-job training to advance. Roberts describes the "box" she was in:

> I couldn't have afforded to go to nursing school. I needed the income, and you can't just quit a job and go to school. I was caught in a box, and the salary wasn't big enough to save to go to school. And getting into the nursing schools was a real racist problem as well. So there was a combination of many things. And I used to say, "Why does this country have to go elsewhere and get people when people like myself want to do something?" (Reverby 1979, 299)

When she became a union organizer, her proudest accomplishment was to set up a program in New York that allowed aides to be trained on the job to become LPNs.

While Roberts's experience working in a hospital was typical in the 1940s and 1950s, today the typical aide is employed in a nursing home, in a convalescent home, or in home health care. In these settings, aides are the primary caregivers.[41] The demand for their services continues to grow as treatment increasingly shifts out of hospitals and into such settings. Thus, even though aides have lost ground to RNs in hospitals, which have reorganized nursing services to recreate RNs as generalists, aides are expected to remain among the fastest-growing occupations through the end of the century (Sekcenski 1981, 10–16).[42]

Whatever the setting, aide work continues to be a specialty of racial-ethnic women. The work is seen as unskilled and subordinate, and thus appropriate to their qualifications and status. This point was brought home to Timothy Diamond during the training course he attended as the sole white male in a mostly Black female group of trainees: "We learned elementary biology and how we were never to do health care without first consulting someone in authority; and we learned not to ask questions but to do as we were told. As one of the students, a black woman from Jamaica used to joke, 'I can't figure out whether they're trying to teach us to be nurses' aides or black women' " (Diamond 1988, 40).

What exactly is the nature of the reproductive labor that these largely minority and supposedly unskilled aides and assistants perform? They do most of the day-to-day, face-to-face work of caring for the ill and disabled: helping patients dress or change gowns, taking vital signs (temperature, blood pressure, pulse), assisting patients to shower or giving bed baths, emptying bedpans or assisting patients to toilet, changing sheets and keeping the area tidy, and feeding patients who cannot feed themselves. There is much "dirty" work, such as cleaning up incontinent patients. Yet there is another, unacknowledged, mental and emotional dimension to the work: listening to the reminiscences of elderly patients to help them hold on to their memory, comforting frightened patients about to undergo surgery, and providing the only human contact some patients get. This caring work is largely invisible, and the skills required to do it are not recognized as real skills.[43]

That these nurse's aides are performing reproductive labor on behalf of other women (and ultimately for the benefit of households, industry, and the state) becomes clear when one considers who would do it if paid workers did not. Indeed, we confront that situation frequently today, as hospitals reduce the length of patient stays to cut costs. Patients are released "quicker and sicker" (Sacks 1988, 165). This policy makes sense only if it is assumed that patients have someone to provide interim care, administer medication, prepare meals, and clean for them until they can care for themselves. If such a person exists, most likely it is a woman—a daughter, wife, mother, or sister. She may have to take time off from her job or quit. Her unpaid labor takes the place of the paid work of a nurse's aide or assistant and saves the hospital labor costs. Her labor is thereby appropriated to ensure profit (Glazer 1988). Thus, the situation of women as unpaid reproductive workers at home is inextricably bound to that of women as paid reproductive workers.

Conclusions and Implications

This article began with the observation that the racial division of reproductive labor has been overlooked in the separate literatures on race and gender. The distinct exploitation of women of color and an important source of difference among women have thereby been ignored. How, though, does a historical analysis of the racial division of reproductive labor illuminate the lives of women of color and white women? What are its implications for concerted political action? In order to tackle these questions, we need to address a broader question, namely, how does the analysis advance our understanding of race and gender? Does it take us beyond the additive models I have criticized?

The Social Construction of Race and Gender

Tracing how race and gender have been fashioned in one area of women's work helps us understand them as socially constructed systems of relationships—including symbols, normative beliefs, and practices—organized around perceived differences. This understanding is an important counter to the universalizing tendencies in feminist thought. When feminists perceive reproductive labor only as gendered, they imply that domestic labor is identical for all women and that it therefore can be the basis of a common identity of womanhood. By not recognizing the different relationships women have had to such supposedly universal female experiences as motherhood and domesticity, they risk essentializing gender—treating it as static, fixed, eternal, and natural. They fail to take seriously a basic premise of feminist thought, that gender is a social construct.

If race and gender are socially constructed systems, then they must arise at specific moments in particular circumstances and change as these circumstances change. We can study their appearance, variation, and modification over time. I have suggested that one vantage point for looking at their development in the United States is in the changing division of labor in local economies. A key site for the emergence of concepts of gendered and racialized labor has been in regions characterized by dual labor systems.

As subordinate-race women within dual labor systems, African American, Mexican American, and Japanese American women were drawn into domestic service by a combination of economic need, restricted opportunities, and educational and employment tracking mechanisms. Once they were in service, their association with "degraded" labor affirmed their supposed natural inferiority. Although ideologies of "race" and "racial difference" justifying the dual labor system already were in place, specific ideas about racial-ethnic womanhood were invented and enacted in everyday interactions between mistresses and workers. Thus ideologies of race and gender were created and verified in daily life (Fields 1982).

Two fundamental elements in the construction of racial-ethnic womanhood were the notion of inherent traits that suited the women for service and the denial of the women's identities as wives and mothers in their own right. Employers accepted a cult of domesticity that purported to elevate the status of women as mothers and homemakers, yet they made demands on domestics that hampered them from carrying out these responsibilities in their own households. How could employers maintain such seemingly inconsistent orientations? Racial ideology was critical in resolving the contradiction: it explained why women of color were suited for degrading work. Racial characterizations effectively neutralized the racial-ethnic woman's womanhood, allowing the mistress to be "unaware" of the domestic's relationship to her own children and household. The exploitation of racial-ethnic women's physical, emotional, and mental work for the benefit of white households thus could be rendered invisible in consciousness if not in reality.

With the shift of reproductive labor from household to market, face-to-face hierarchy has been replaced by structural hierarchy. In institutional settings, stratification is built into organizational structures, including lines of authority, job descriptions, rules, and spatial and temporal segregation. Distance between higher and lower orders is ensured by structural segregation. Indeed, much routine service work is organized to be out of sight: it takes place behind institutional walls where outsiders rarely penetrate (for example, nursing homes, chronic care facilities), in back rooms (for example, restaurant kitchens), or at night or other times when occupants are gone (for example, in office buildings and hotels). Workers may appreciate this time and space segregation because it allows them some autonomy and freedom from demeaning interactions. It also makes them and their work invisible, however. In this situation, more privileged women do not have to acknowledge the workers or to confront the contradiction between shared womanhood and inequality by race and class. Racial ideology is not necessary to explain or justify exploitation, not for lack of racism, but because the justification for inequality does not have to be elaborated in specifically racial terms: instead it can be cast in terms of differences in training, skill, or education.[44]

Because they are socially constructed, race and gender systems are subject to contestation and struggle. Racial-ethnic women continually have challenged the devaluation of their womanhood. Domestics often did so covertly. They learned to dissemble, consciously "putting on an act" while inwardly rejecting their employers' premises and maintaining a separate identity rooted in their families and communities. As noted earlier, institutional service workers can resist demeaning treatment more openly because they have the support of peers. Minority-race women hospital workers have been in the forefront of labor militancy, staging walkouts and strikes and organizing workplaces. In both domestic service and institutional service work, women have transcended the limitations of their work by focusing on longer-term goals, such as their children's future.

Beyond Additive Models: Race and Gender as Interlocking Systems

As the foregoing examples show, race and gender constructs are inextricably intertwined. Each develops in the context of the other; they cannot be separated. This is important because when we see reproductive labor only as gendered, we extract gender from its context, which includes other interacting systems of power. If we begin with gender separated out, then we have to put race and class back in when we consider women of color and working-class women. We thus end up with an additive model in which white women have only gender and women of color have gender plus race.

The interlock is evident in the case studies of domestic workers and nurse's aides. In the traditional middle-class household, the availability of cheap female domestic labor buttressed white male privilege by perpetuating the concept of reproductive labor as women's work, sustaining the illusion of a protected private sphere for women, and displacing conflict away from husband and wife to struggles between housewife and domestic.

The racial division of labor also bolstered the gender division of labor indirectly, by offering white women a slightly more privileged position in exchange for accepting domesticity. Expanding on Judith Rollins's notion that white housewives gained an elevated self-identity by casting Black domestics as inferior contrast figures, Phyllis Palmer suggests the dependent position of the middle-class housewife made a contrasting figure necessary. A dualistic conception of women as "good" and "bad," long a part of Western cultural tradition, provided ready-made categories for casting white and racial-ethnic women as oppositional figures (Davidoff 1979; Palmer 1990, 11, 137–39). The racial division of reproductive labor served to channel and recast these dualistic conceptions into racialized gender constructs. By providing them an acceptable self-image, racial constructs gave white housewives a stake in a system that ultimately oppressed them.

The racial division of labor similarly protects white male privilege in institutional settings. White men, after all, still dominate in professional and higher management positions, where they benefit from the paid and unpaid services of women. And as in domestic service, conflict between men and women is redirected into clashes among women. This displacement is evident in health care organizations. Because physicians and administrators control the work of other health workers, we would expect the main conflict to be between doctors and nurses over work load, allocation of tasks, wages, and working conditions. The racial division of nursing labor allows some of the tension to be redirected so that friction arises between registered nurses and aides over work assignments and supervision.

In both household and institutional settings, white professional and managerial men are the group most insulated from dirty work and contact with those who do it. White women are frequently the mediators who have to negotiate between white male superiors and racial-ethnic subordinates. Thus race and gender dynamics are played out in a three-way relationship involving white men, white women, and women of color.

Beyond Difference: Race and Gender as Relational Constructs

Focusing on the racial division of reproductive labor also uncovers the relational nature of race and gender. By "relational" I mean that each is made up of categories (for example, male/female, Anglo/Latino) that are positioned, and therefore gain meaning, in relation to each other (Barrett 1987). Power, status, and privilege are axes along which categories are positioned. Thus, to represent race and gender as relationally constructed is to assert that the experiences of white women and women of color are not just different but connected in systematic ways.

The interdependence is easier to see in the domestic work setting, because the two groups of women confront one another face-to-face. That the higher standard of living of one woman is made possible by, and also helps to perpetuate, the other's lower standard of living is clearly evident. In institutional service work the relationship between those who do the dirty work and those who benefit from it is mediated and buffered by institutional structures, so the dependence of one group on the other for its standard of living is not apparent. Nonetheless, interdependence exists, even if white women do not come into actual contact with women of color.[45]

The notion of relationality also recognizes that white and racial-ethnic women have different standpoints by virtue of their divergent positions. This is an important corrective to feminist theories of gendered thought that posit universal female modes of thinking growing out of common experiences such as domesticity and motherhood. When they portray reproductive labor only as gendered, they assume there is only one standpoint— that of white women. Hence, the activities and experiences of middle-class women become generic "female" experiences and activities, and those of other groups become variant, deviant, or specialized.

In line with recent works on African American, Asian American, and Latina feminist thought, we see that taking the standpoint of women of color gives us a different and more critical perspective on race and gender systems (Garcia 1989; Anzaldúa 1990; Collins 1990.) Domestic workers in particular—because they directly confront the contradictions in their lives and those of their mistresses—develop an acute consciousness of the interlocking nature of race and gender oppression.

Perhaps a less obvious point is that understanding race and gender as relational systems also illuminates the lives of white American women. White womanhood has been constructed not in isolation but in relation to that of women of color. Therefore, race is integral to white women's gender identities. In addition, seeing variation in racial division of labor across time in different regions gives us a more variegated picture of white middle-class womanhood. White women's lives have been lived in many circumstances; their "gender" has been constructed in relation to varying others, not just to Black women. Conceptualizing white womanhood as monolithically defined in opposition to men or to Black women ignores complexity and variation in the experiences of white women.

Implications for Feminist Politics

Understanding race and gender as relational, interlocking, socially constructed systems affects how we strategize for change. If race and gender are socially constructed rather than being "real" referents in the material world, then they can be deconstructed and challenged. Feminists have made considerable strides in deconstructing gender; we now need to focus on deconstructing gender and race simultaneously. An initial step in this process is to expose the structures that support the present division of labor and the constructions of race and gender around it.

Seeing race and gender as interlocking systems, however, alerts us to sources of inertia and resistance to change. The discussion of how the racial division of labor reinforced the gender division of labor makes clear that tackling gender hierarchy requires simultaneously addressing race hierarchy. As long as the gender division of labor remains intact, it will be in the short-term interest of white women to support or at least overlook the racial division of labor, because it ensures that the very worst labor is performed by someone else. Yet, as long as white women support the racial division of labor, they will have less impetus to struggle to change the gender division of labor. This quandary is apparent in cities such as Los Angeles, which have witnessed a large influx of immigrant women fleeing violence and poverty in Latin America, Southeast Asia, and the Caribbean. These women form a large reserve army of low-wage labor for both domestic service and institutional service work. Anglo women who ordinarily would not be able to afford servants are employing illegal immigrants as maids at below minimum wages (McConoway 1987). Not only does this practice diffuse pressure for a more equitable sharing of household work but it also recreates race and gender ideologies that justify the subordination of women of color. Having a Latino or Black maid picking up and cleaning after them teaches Anglo children that some people exist primarily to do work that Anglos do not want to do for themselves.

Acknowledging the relational nature of race and gender and therefore the interdependence between groups means that we recognize conflicting interests among women. Two examples illustrate the divergence. With the move into the labor force of all races and classes of women, it is tempting to think that we can find unity around the common problems of "working women." With that in mind, feminist policy-makers have called for expanding services to assist employed mothers in such areas as child care and elderly care. We need to ask, Who is going to do the work? Who will benefit from increased services? The historical record suggests that it will be women of color, many of them new immigrants, who will do the work and that it will be middle-class women who will receive the services. Not so coincidentally, public officials seeking to reduce welfare costs are promulgating regulations requiring women on public assistance to work. The needs of employed middle-class women and women on welfare might thus be thought to coincide: the needs of the former for services might be met by employing the latter to provide the services. The divergence in interest becomes apparent, however, when we consider that employment in service jobs at current wage levels guarantees that their occupants will remain poor. However, raising their wages so that they can actually support themselves and their children at a decent level would mean many middle-class women could not afford these services.

A second example of an issue that at first blush appears to bridge race and ethnic lines is the continuing earnings disparity between men and women. Because occupational segregation, the concentration of women in low-paying, female-dominated occupations, stands as the major obstacle to wage equity, some feminist policy-makers have embraced the concept of comparable worth (Hartmann 1985; Acker 1989). This strategy calls for equalizing pay for "male" and "female" jobs requiring similar levels of skill and responsibility, even if differing in content. Comparable worth accepts the validity of a job hierarchy and differential pay based on "real" differences in skills and responsibility. Thus, for example, it attacks the differential between nurses and pharmacists but leaves intact the differential between nurses and nurse's aides. Yet the division between "skilled" and "unskilled" jobs is exactly where the racial division typically falls. To address the problems of women of color service workers would require a fundamental attack on the concept of a hierarchy of worth; it would call for flattening the wage differentials between highest-

and lowest-paid ranks. A claim would have to be made for the right of all workers to a living wage, regardless of skill or responsibility.

These examples suggest that forging a political agenda that addresses the universal needs of women is highly problematic, not just because women's priorities differ but because gains for some groups may require a corresponding loss of advantage and privilege for others. As the history of the racial division of reproductive labor reveals, conflict and contestation among women over definitions of womanhood, over work, and over the conditions of family life are part of our legacy as well as the current reality. This does not mean we give up the goal of concerted struggle. It means we give up trying falsely to harmonize women's interests. Appreciating the ways race and gender division of labor creates both hierarchy and interdependence may be a better way to reach an understanding of the interconnectedness of women's lives.

Notes

Work on this project was made possible by a Title F leave from the State University of New York at Binghamton and a visiting scholar appointment at the Murray Research Center at Radcliffe College. Discussions with Elsa Barkley Brown, Gary Glenn, Carole Turbin, and Barrie Thorne contributed immeasurably to the ideas developed here. My thanks to Joyce Chinen for directing me to archival materials in Hawaii. I am also grateful to members of the Women and Work Group and to Norma Alarcon, Gary Dymski, Antonia Glenn, Margaret Guilette, Terence Hopkins, Eileen McDonagh, JoAnne Preston, Mary Ryan, and four anonymous *Signs* reviewers for their suggestions.

1. For various formulations, see Benston (1969), Secombe (1974), Barrett (1980), Fox (1980), and Sokoloff (1980).
2. Recently, white feminists have begun to pay attention to scholarship by and about racial-ethnic women, and to recognize racial stratification in the labor market and other public arenas. My point here is that they still assume that women's relationship to domestic labor is universal; thus they have not been concerned with explicating differences across race, ethnic, and class groups in women's relationship to that labor.
3. See, e.g., Reisler (1976), which, despite its title, is exclusively about male Mexican labor.
4. I use the term *racial-ethnic* to refer collectively to groups that have been socially constructed and constituted as racially as well as culturally distinct from European Americans, and placed in separate legal statuses from "free whites" (c.f. Omi and Winant 1986). Historically, African Americans, Latinos, Asian Americans, and Native Americans were so constructed. Similarly, I have capitalized the word *Black* throughout this article to signify the racial-ethnic construction of that category.
5. Capitalism, however, changed the nature of reproductive labor, which became more and more devoted to consumption activities, i.e., using wages to acquire necessities in the market and then processing these commodities to make them usable (see Weinbaum and Bridges 1976; and Luxton 1980).
6. This is not to deny that family members, especially women, still provide the bulk of care of dependents, but to point out that there has been a marked increase in institutionalized care in the second half of the twentieth century.
7. For a discussion of varying views on the relative importance of control versus agency in shaping state welfare policy, see Gordon (1990). Piven and Cloward note that programs have been created only when poor people have mobilized, and are intended to defuse pressure for more radical change (1971, 66). In their *Poor People's Movements* (Piven and Cloward 1979), they document the role of working-class struggles to win concessions from the state. For a feminist social control perspective, see Abramovitz (1988).
8. These developments are discussed in Degler (1980), Strasser (1982), Cowan (1983), and Dudden (1983, esp. 240–42).
9. See also Blair (1980); Epstein (1981); Ryan (1981); Dudden (1983); and Brenner and Laslett (1986).
10. See, e.g., Kaplan (1987).
11. Phyllis Palmer, in her *Domesticity and Dirt*, found evidence that mistresses and servants agreed on what were the least desirable tasks—washing clothes, washing dishes, and taking care of children on evenings and weekends—and that domestics were more likely to perform the least desirable tasks (1990, 70).
12. It may be worth mentioning the importance of unpaid cultural and charitable activities in perpetuating middle-class privilege and power. Middle-class reformers often aimed to mold the poor in ways that mirrored middle-class values, but without actually altering their subordinate position. See, e.g., Sanchez (1990) for discussion of efforts of Anglo reformers to train Chicanas in domestic skills.

13. U.S. Bureau of the Census 1933, ch. 3, "Color and Nativity of Gainful Workers," tables 2, 4, 6. For discussion of the concentration of African American women in domestic service, see Glenn (1985).

14. I use the terms *Chicano, Chicana,* and *Mexican American* to refer to both native-born and immigrant Mexican people/women in the United States.

15. U.S. Bureau of the Census 1933.

16. *Ibid.*

17. For personal accounts of Chicano children being inducted into domestic service, see Ruíz (1987a) and interview of Josephine Turietta in Elsasser, MacKenzie, and Tixier y Vigil (1980, 28–35).

18. See also life-history accounts of Black domestics, such as that of Bolden (1976) and of Anna Mae Dickson by Wendy Watriss (Watriss 1984).

19. Blackwelder also found that domestics themselves were attuned to the racial-ethnic hierarchy among them. When advertising for jobs, women who did not identify themselves as Black overwhelmingly requested "housekeeping" or "governess" positions, whereas Blacks advertised for "cooking," "laundering," or just plain "domestic work."

20. This is not to say that daughters of European immigrants experienced great social mobility and soon attained affluence. The nondomestic jobs they took were usually low-paying and the conditions of work often deplorable. Nonetheless, white, native-born and immigrant women clearly preferred the relative freedom of industrial, office, or shop employment to the constraints of domestic service (see Katzman 1978, 71–72).

21. Document Ma 24, Romanzo Adams Social Research Laboratory papers. I used these records when they were lodged in the sociology department; they are currently being cataloged by the university archives and a finding aid is in process.

22. *Ibid.*, document Ma 15, 5.

23. *Ibid.*

24. "More Slavery at the South: A Negro Nurse," from the *Independent* (1912), in Katzman and Tuttle (1982, 176–85, 179).

25. From an interview conducted by the author in the San Francisco Bay area in 1977.

26. *Ibid.*

27. The U.S. Labor Department and the U.S. Bureau of the Census divide service occupations into three major categories: "private household," "protective service," and "service occupations except private household and protective services." In this discussion, "service work" refers only to the latter. I omit private household workers, who have been discussed previously, and protective service workers, who include firefighters and police: these jobs, in addition to being male-dominated and relatively well paid, carry some degree of authority, including the right to use force.

28. Computed from U.S. Bureau of the Census (1984), chap. D, "Detailed Population Characteristics," pt. 1; "United States Summary," table 278: "Detailed Occupation of Employed Persons by Sex, Race and Spanish Origin, 1980.28."

29. *Ibid.*

30. Figures computed from table 279 in each of the state chapters of the following: U.S. Bureau of the Census (1984), chap. D, "Detailed Population Characteristics," pt. 6: "California"; pt. 12: "Georgia"; pt. 13: "Hawaii"; pt. 15: "Illinois"; pt. 44: "Tennessee"; and pt. 45: "Texas." The figures for Anglos in the Southwest are estimates, based on the assumption that most "Spanish-origin" people are Mexican, and that Mexicans, when given a racial designation, are counted as whites. Specifically, the excess left after the "total" is subtracted from the "sum" of white, Black, American Indian/Eskimo/Aleut, Asian and Pacific Islander, and "Spanish-origin" is subtracted from the white figure. The remainder is counted as "Anglo." Because of the way "Spanish-origin" crosscuts race (Spanish-origin individuals can be counted as white, Black, or any other race), I did not attempt to compute figures for Latinos or Anglos in cities where Spanish-origin individuals are likely to be more distributed in some unknown proportion between Black and white. This would be the case, e.g., with the large Puerto Rican population in New York City. Thus I have not attempted to compute Latino versus Anglo data for New York and Chicago. Note also that the meaning of *white* differs by locale, and that the local terms *Anglo* and *haole* are not synonymous with *white.* The "white" category in Hawaii includes Portuguese, who, because of their history as plantation labor, are distinguished from haoles in the local ethnic ranking systems. The U.S. Census category system does not capture the local construction of race/ethnicity.

31. Computed from tables specified in *ibid.*

32. The federal minimum wage was $3.35 in 1986. Over a quarter (26.0 percent) of all workers in these service occupations worked at or below this wage. See Mellor (1987, esp. 37).

33. Paternalism is not limited to southern hospitals; similar policies were in place at Montefiore Hospital in New York City. See Fink and Greenberg (1979).

34. See also many examples of workplace cultures supporting resistance in Sacks and Remy (1984) and Lamphere (1987).

35. American Nurses' Association 1965, 6. Reflecting differences in status and authority, RNs earn 20–40 percent more than LPNs and 60–150 percent more than NAs (U.S. Department of Labor 1987a, 1987b).

36. For the national level, see U.S. Bureau of the Census (1984), ch. D, "Detailed Population Characteristics," pt. 1: "United States Summary," table 278. For statistics on RNs and aides in San Antonio, El Paso, and Honolulu, see U.S. Bureau of the Census (1984), ch. D, "Detailed Population Characteristics," pt. 13: "Hawaii"; and pt. 45: "Texas," table 279.

37. For accounts of Black women in nursing, see also Hine (1985) and Carnegie (1986). Hine (1989, ch. 7) makes it clear that Black nurses served Black patients not just because they were restricted but because they wanted to meet Black health care needs. Blacks were excluded from membership in two of the main national organizations for nurses, the National League of Nursing Education and the American Nurses' Association. And although they formed their own organizations, such as the National Association of Colored Graduate Nurses, and enjoyed the respect of the Black community, Black nurses remained subordinated within the white-dominated nursing profession.

38. Document Nu21-I, p. 2, Romanzo Adams Research Laboratory papers, A1989-006, box 17, folder 1.

39. Document Nu10-I, p. 3, Romanzo Adams Research Laboratory papers, A1989-006, box 17, folder 4.

40. This was one outcome of the protracted and eventually successful struggle waged by physicians to gain control over all health care. For an account of how physicians established hospitals as the main site for medical treatment, and gained authority over "subsidiary" health occupations, see Starr (1982). For accounts of nurses' struggle for autonomy and their incorporations into hospitals, see Reverby (1987) and also Wagner (1980).

41. For example, it has been estimated that 80 percent of all patient care in nursing homes is provided by nurse's aides (see Coleman 1989, 5). In 1988, 1,559,000 persons were employed as RNs, 423,000 as LPNs, 1,404,000 as nurse's aides, orderlies, and attendants, and 407,000 as health aides (U.S. Department of Labor 1989, table 22). Nurse's aides and home health care aides are expected to be the fastest-growing occupations through the 1990s, according to Silvestri and Lukasiewicz (1987, 59).

42. For a description of trends and projections to the year 2000, see Silvestri and Lukasiewicz (1987).

43. Feminists have pointed to the undervaluing of female-typed skills, especially those involved in "caring" work (see Rose 1986).

44. That is, the concentration of minority workers in lower-level jobs can be attributed to their lack of "human capital"—qualifications—needed for certain jobs.

45. Elsa Barkley Brown pointed this out to me in a personal communication.

References

Abramovitz, Mimi. 1988. *Regulating the Lives of Women: Social Welfare Policy from Colonial Times to the Present.* Boston: South End Press.

Acker, Joan. 1989. *Doing Comparable Worth: Gender, Class, and Pay Equity.* Philadelphia: Temple University Press.

Adams, Romanzo. Social Research Laboratory papers. University of Hawaii Archives, Manoa.

American Nurses' Association. 1965. *Health Occupations Supportive to Nursing.* New York: American Nurses' Association.

Anderson, C. Arnold, and Mary Jean Bowman. 1953. "The Vanishing Servant and the Contemporary Status System of the American South." *American Journal of Sociology* 59:215–30.

Anzaldúa, Gloria. 1990. *Making Face, Making Soul—Haciendo Caras: Creative Critical Perspectives by Women of Color.* San Francisco: Aunt Lute Foundation.

Barrera, Mario. 1979. *Race and Class in the Southwest: A Theory of Racial Inequality.* Notre Dame, IN, and London: University of Notre Dame Press.

Barrett, Michèle. 1980. *Women's Oppression Today: Problems in Marxist Feminist Analysis.* London: Verso.

———. 1987. "The Concept of 'Difference.'" *Feminist Review* 26(July):29–41.

Benson, Susan Porter. 1986. *Counter Cultures: Saleswomen, Customers, and Managers in American Department Stores, 1890–1940.* Urbana and Chicago: University of Illinois Press.

Benston, Margaret. 1969. "The Political Economy of Women's Liberation." *Monthly Review* 21(September):13–27.

Blackwelder, Julia Kirk. 1978. "Women in the Work Force: Atlanta, New Orleans, and San Antonio, 1930 to 1940." *Journal of Urban History* 4(3):331–58, 349.

———. 1984. *Women of the Depression: Caste and Culture in San Antonio, 1929–1939.* College Station: Texas A&M University Press.

Blair, Karen. 1980. *The Clubwoman as Feminist: True Womanhood Redefined, 1868–1914.* New York: Holmes & Meier.

Blauner, Robert. 1972. *Racial Oppression in America.* Berkeley: University of California Press.

Bolden, Dorothy. 1976. "Forty-two Years a Maid: Starting at Nine in Atlanta." In *Nobody Speaks for Me! Self-Portraits of American Working Class Women,* ed. Nancy Seifer. New York: Simon & Schuster.

Boydston, Jeanne. 1990. *Home and Work: Housework, Wages, and the Ideology of Labor in the Early Republic.* New York: Oxford University Press.

Braverman, Harry. 1974. *Labor and Monopoly Capital: The Degradation of Labor in the Twentieth Century.* New York and London: Monthly Review Press.

Brenner, Johanna, and Barbara Laslett. 1986. "Social Reproduction and the Family." In *Sociology, from Crisis to Science?* Vol. 2, *The Social Reproduction of Organization and Culture,* ed. Ulf Himmelstrand, 116–31. London: Sage.

Brown, Elsa Barkley. 1989. "Womanist Consciousness: Maggie Lena Walker and the Independent Order of Saint Luke." *Signs: Journal of Women in Culture and Society* 14(3):610–33.

Cannings, Kathleen, and William Lazonik. 1975. "The Development of the Nursing Labor Force in the United States: A Basic Analysis." *International Journal of Health Sciences* 5(2):185–216.

Carnegie, Mary Elizabeth. 1986. *The Path We Tread: Blacks in Nursing, 1854–1954.* Philadelphia: Lippincott.

Chaplin, David. 1978. "Domestic Service and Industrialization." *Comparative Studies in Sociology* 1:97–127.

Clark-Lewis, Elizabeth. 1987. "This Work Had an End: African American Domestic Workers in Washington, D.C., 1910–1940." In *"To Toil the Livelong Day": America's Women at Work, 1780–1980,* ed. Carole Groneman and Mary Beth Norton. Ithaca, NY: Cornell University Press.

Coleman, Barbara. 1989. "States Grapple with New Law." *AARP News Bulletin,* 30(2):4–5.

Collins, Patricia Hill. 1986. "Learning from the Outsider Within: The Sociological Significance of Black Feminist Thought." *Social Problems* 33(6):14–32.

———. 1990. *Black Feminist Thought: Knowledge, Consciousness, and the Politics of Empowerment.* New York: Allen & Unwin.

Cowan, Ruth Schwartz. 1983. *More Work for Mother: The Ironies of Household Technology from the Open Hearth to the Microwave.* New York: Basic.

Davidoff, Lenore. 1979. "Class and Gender in Victorian England: The Diaries of Arthur J. Munby and Hannah Cullwick." *Feminist Studies* 5(Spring): 86–114.

Degler, Carl N. 1980. *At Odds: Women and the Family in America from the Revolution to the Present.* New York: Oxford University Press.

Deming, Dorothy. 1947. *The Practical Nurse.* New York: Commonwealth Fund.

Deutsch, Sarah. 1987a. *No Separate Refuge: Culture, Class, and Gender on an Anglo-Hispanic Frontier in the American Southwest, 1880–1940.* New York: Oxford University Press.

———. 1987b. "Women and Intercultural Relations: The Case of Hispanic New Mexico and Colorado." *Signs* 12(4):719–39.

Diamond, Timothy. 1988. "Social Policy and Everyday Life in Nursing Homes: A Critical Ethnography." In *The Worth of Women's Work: A Qualitative Synthesis,* ed. Anne Statham, Eleanor M. Miller, and Hans O. Mauksch. Albany, NY: SUNY Press.

Dill, Bonnie Thornton. 1980. "The Means to Put My Children Through: Childrearing Goals and Strategies among Black Female Domestic Servants." In *The Black Woman,* ed. La Frances Rodgers-Rose. Beverly Hills and London: Sage.

———. 1988. "Our Mothers' Grief: Racial Ethnic Women and the Maintenance of Families." *Journal of Family History* 12(4):415–31.

Drake, St. Clair, and Horace Cayton. (1945) 1962. *Black Metropolis: A Study of Negro Life in a Northern City,* vol. 1. New York: Harper Torchbook.

Dudden, Faye E. 1983. *Serving Women: Household Service in Nineteenth-Century America.* Middletown, CT: Wesleyan University Press.

Elsasser, Nan, Kyle MacKenzie, and Yvonne Tixier y Vigil. 1980. *Las Mujeres: Conversations from a Hispanic Community.* Old Westbury, NY: Feminist Press.

Engels, Friedrich. 1972. *The Origins of the Family, Private Property and the State.* New York: International Publishers.

Epstein, Barbara. 1981. *The Politics of Domesticity: Women, Evangelism, and Temperance in Nineteenth Century America.* Middletown, CT: Wesleyan University Press.

Fields, Barbara. 1982. "Ideology and Race in American History." In *Region, Race, and Reconstruction: Essays in Honor of C. Vann Woodward,* ed. J. Morgan Kousser and James M. McPherson. New York: Oxford University Press.

Fink, Leon, and Brian Greenberg. 1979. "Organizing Montefiore: Labor Militancy Meets a Progressive Health Care Empire." In *Health Care in America: Essays in Social History,* ed. Susan Reverby and David Rosner. Philadelphia: Temple University Press.

Fox, Bonnie, ed. 1980. *Hidden in the Household: Women's Domestic Labour under Capitalism.* Toronto: Women's Press.

Gamarinikow, Eva. 1978. "Sexual Division of Labour: The Case of Nursing." In *Feminism and Materialism: Women and Modes of Production,* ed. Annette Kuhn and Ann-Marie Wolpe, 96–123. London: Routledge & Kegan Paul.

Game, Ann, and Rosemary Pringle. 1983. *Gender at Work.* Sydney: Allen & Unwin.

Garcia, Alma. 1989. "The Development of Chicana Feminist Discourse, 1970–1980." *Gender and Society* 3(2).217–30.

Garcia, Mario T. 1980. "The Chicana in American History: The Mexican Women of El Paso, 1880–1920: A Case Study." *Pacific Historical Review* 49(2):315–39.

———. 1981. *Desert Immigrants: The Mexicans of El Paso, 1880–1920.* New Haven, CT: Yale University Press.

Glazer, Nona. 1988. "Overlooked, Overworked: Women's Unpaid and Paid Work in the Health Services' 'Cost Crisis,'" *International Journal of Health Services* 18(2):119–37.

Glenn, Evelyn Nakano. 1985. "Racial Ethnic Women's Labor: The Intersection of Race, Gender and Class Oppression." *Review of Radical Political Economy* 17(3):86–108.

———. 1986. *Issei, Nisei, Warbride: Three Generations of Japanese American Women in Domestic Service.* Philadelphia: Temple University Press.

Gordon, Linda. 1990. "The New Feminist Scholarship on the Welfare State." In *Women, the State, and Welfare,* ed. Linda Gordon, 9–35. Madison: University of Wisconsin Press.

Gwaltney, John, ed. 1980. *Drylongso: A Self-Portrait of Black America.* New York: Random House.

Hartmann, Heidi I., ed. 1985. *Comparable Worth: New Directions for Research.* Washington, D.C.: National Academy Press.

Hield, Melissa. 1984. "Women in the Texas ILGWU, 1933–50." In *Speaking for Ourselves: Women of the South,* ed. Maxine Alexander, 87–97. New York: Pantheon.

Hine, Darlene Clark, ed. 1985. *Black Women in the Nursing Profession: A Documentary History.* New York: Pathfinder.

———. 1989. *Black Women in White: Racial Conflict and Cooperation in the Nursing Profession, 1890–1950.* Bloomington: Indiana University Press.

Janiewski, Delores. 1983. "Flawed Victories: The Experiences of Black and White Women Workers in Durham during the 1930s." In *Decades of Discontent: The Women's Movement, 1920–1940,* ed. Lois Scharf and Joan M. Jensen, 85–112. Westport, CT, and London: Greenwood.

Kaplan, Elaine Bell. 1987. "'I Don't Do No Windows': Competition between the Domestic Worker and the Housewife." In *Competition: A Feminist Taboo?*" ed. Valerie Miner and Helen E. Longino. New York: Feminist Press at CUNY.

Katzman, David M. 1978. *Seven Days a Week: Women and Domestic Service in Industrializing America.* New York: Oxford University Press.

Katzman, David M., and William M. Tuttle, Jr., eds. 1982. *Plain Folk: The Life Stories of Undistinguished Americans.* Urbana and Chicago: University of Illinois Press.

Kessler-Harris, Alice. 1981. *Women Have Always Worked: A Historical Overview.* Old Westbury, NY: Feminist Press.

———. 1982. *Out to Work: A History of Wage-Earning Women in the United States.* New York: Oxford University Press.

King, Deborah K. 1988. "Multiple Jeopardy, Multiple Consciousness: The Context of a Black Feminist Ideology." *Signs* 14(1):42–72.

Lamphere, Louise. 1987. *From Working Daughters to Working Mothers: Immigrant Women in a New England Industrial Community.* Ithaca, NY: Cornell University Press.

Lasch, Christopher. 1977. *Haven in a Heartless World: The Family Besieged.* New York: Basic.

Laslett, Barbara, and Johanna Brenner. 1989. "Gender and Social Reproduction: Historical Perspectives." *Annual Review of Sociology* 15:381–404.

Lind, Andrew. 1951. "The Changing Position of Domestic Service in Hawaii." *Social Process in Hawaii* 15:71–87.

Luxton, Meg. 1980. *More than a Labour of Love: Three Generations of Women's Work in the Home.* Toronto: Women's Press.

McConoway, Mary Jo. 1987. "The Intimate Experiment." *Los Angeles Times Magazine,* February 19, 18–23, 37–38.

Marx, Karl, and Friedrich Engels. 1969. *Selected Works,* vol. 1. Moscow: Progress.

Mellor, Earl F. 1987. "Workers at the Minimum Wage or Less: Who They Are and the Jobs They Hold." *Monthly Labor Review,* July, 34–38.

Omi, Michael, and Howard Winant. 1986. *Racial Formation in the United States*. New York: Routledge.

Palmer, Phyllis. 1987. "Housewife and Household Worker: Employer-Employee Relations in the Home, 1928–1941." In *"To Toil the Livelong Day": America's Women at Work, 1780–1980*, ed. Carole Groneman and Mary Beth Norton, 179–95. Ithaca, NY: Cornell University Press.

———. 1990. *Domesticity and Dirt: Housewives and Domestic Servants in the United States, 1920–1945*. Philadelphia: Temple University Press.

Piven, Frances Fox, and Richard A. Cloward. 1971. *Regulating the Poor: The Functions of Public Welfare*. New York: Pantheon.

———. 1979. *Poor People's Movements: Why They Succeed, How They Fail*. New York: Pantheon.

Reisler, Mark. 1976. *By the Sweat of Their Brow: Mexican Immigrant Labor in the United States, 1900–1940*. Westport, CT: Greenwood.

Reverby, Susan M. 1979. "From Aide to Organizer: The Oral History of Lillian Roberts." In *Women of America: A History*, ed. Carol Ruth Berkin and Mary Beth Norton. Boston: Houghton Mifflin.

———. 1987. *Ordered to Care: The Dilemma of American Nursing. 1850–1945*. Cambridge: Cambridge University Press.

Rollins, Judith. 1985. *Between Women: Domestics and Their Employers*. Philadelphia: Temple University Press.

Romero, Mary. 1987. "Chicanas Modernize Domestic Service." Unpublished manuscript.

———. 1988a. "Day Work in the Suburbs: The Work Experience of Chicana Private Housekeepers." In *The Worth of Women's Work: A Qualitative Synthesis*, ed. Anne Statham, Eleanor M. Miller, and Hans O. Mauksch, 77–92. Albany: SUNY Press.

———. 1988b. "Renegotiating Race, Class and Gender Hierarchies in the Everyday Interactions between Chicana Private Household Workers and Employers." Paper presented at the 1988 meetings of the Society for the Study of Social Problems, Atlanta.

Rose, Hilary. 1986. "Women's Work: Women's Knowledge." In *What Is Feminism?* ed. Juliet Mitchell and Ann Oakley. 161–83. Oxford: Basil Blackwell.

Ruíz, Vicki L. 1987a. "By the Day or the Week: Mexican Domestic Workers in El Paso." In *Women on the U.S.-Mexico Border: Responses to Change*, ed. Vicki L. Ruíz and Susan Tiano, 61–76. Boston: Allen & Unwin.

———. 1987b. "Oral History and La Mujer: The Rosa Guerrero Story." In *Women on the U.S.-Mexico Border: Responses to Change*, ed. Vicki L. Ruíz and Susan Tiano, 219–32. Boston: Allen & Unwin.

Ryan, Mary P. 1981. *Cradle of the Middle Class: The Family in Oneida County, New York, 1790–1865*. Cambridge: Cambridge University Press.

Sacks, Karen Brodkin. 1988. *Caring by the Hour: Women, Work, and Organizing at Duke Medical Center*. Urbana and Chicago: University of Illinois Press.

Sacks, Karen Brodkin, and Dorothy Remy, eds. 1984. *My Troubles Are Going to Have Trouble with Me: Everyday Trials and Triumphs of Women Workers*. New Brunswick, NJ: Rutgers University Press.

Sanchez, George J. 1990. " 'Go after the Women': Americanization and the Mexican Immigrant Woman, 1915–1929." In *Unequal Sisters: A Multicultural Reader in Women's History*, ed. Ellen Carol DuBois and Vicki L. Ruiz, 250–63. New York: Routledge.

Secombe, Wally. 1974. "The Housewife and Her Labour under Capitalism." *New Left Review* 83(January–February):3–24.

Sekcenski, Edward S. 1981. "The Health Services Industry: A Decade of Expansion." *Monthly Labor Review* (May):10–16.

Silvestri, George T., and John M. Lukasiewicz. 1987. "A Look at Occupational Employment Trends to the Year 2000." *Monthly Labor Review* (September): 46–63.

Smuts, Robert W. 1959. *Women and Work in America*. New York: Schocken.

Sokoloff, Natalie J. 1980. *Between Money and Love: The Dialectics of Women's Home and Market Work*. New York: Praeger.

Starr, Paul. 1982. *The Social Transformation of American Medicine*. New York: Basic.

Strasser, Susan. 1982. *Never Done: A History of American Housework*. New York: Pantheon.

Tucker, Susan. 1988. "The Black Domestic in the South: Her Legacy as Mother and Mother Surrogate." In *Southern Women*, ed. Carolyn Matheny Dillman, 93–102. New York: Hemisphere.

U.S. Bureau of the Census. 1932. *Fifteenth Census of the United States: 1930, Outlying Territories and Possessions*. Washington, D.C.: Government Printing Office.

———. 1933. *Fifteenth Census of the United States: 1930, Population*. Vol. 5, *General Report on Occupations*. Washington, D.C.: Government Printing Office.

———. 1984. *Census of the Population, 1980*. Vol. 1, *Characteristics of the Population*. Washington, D.C.: Government Printing Office.

U.S. Department of Labor. 1987a. *Industry Wage Survey: Hospitals, August 1985*. Bureau of Labor Statistics Bulletin 2273. Washington, D.C.: Government Printing Office.

———. 1987b. *Industry Wage Survey: Nursing and Personal Care Facilities, September 1985.* Bureau of Labor Statistics Bulletin 2275. Washington D.C.: Government Printing Office.

———. 1989. *Employment and Earnings, January 1989.* Bureau of Labor Statistics Bulletin. Washington, D.C.: Government Printing Office.

Wagner, David. 1980. "The Proletarianization of Nursing in the United States, 1932–1945." *International Journal of Health Services* 10(2):271–89.

Watriss, Wendy. 1984. "It's Something Inside You." In *Speaking for Ourselves: Women of the South,* ed. Maxine Alexander. New York: Pantheon.

Weinbaum, Batya, and Amy Bridges. 1976. "The Other Side of the Paycheck." *Monthly Review* 28:88–103.

27

Japanese American Women During World War II

Valerie Matsumoto

> The life here cannot be expressed. Sometimes, we are resigned to it, but when we see the barbed wire fences and the sentry tower with floodlights, it gives us a feeling of being prisoners in a "concentration camp." We try to be happy and yet oftentimes a gloominess does creep in. When I see the "I'm an American" editorial and write-ups, the "equality of race etc."—it seems to be mocking us in our faces. I just wonder if all the sacrifices and hard labor on [the] part of our parents has gone up to leave nothing to show for it?
> —Letter from Shizuko Horiuchi,
> Pomona Assembly Center, May 24,1942

Thirty years after her relocation camp internment, another Nisei woman, the artist Miné Okubo, observed, "The impact of the evacuation is not on the material and the physical. It is something far deeper. It is the effect on the spirit."[1] Describing the lives of Japanese American women during World War II and assessing the effects of the camp experience on the spirit are complex tasks: factors such as age, generation, personality, and family background interweave and preclude simple generalizations. In these relocation camps Japanese American women faced severe racism and traumatic family strain, but the experience also fostered changes in their lives: more leisure for older women, equal pay with men for working women, disintegration of traditional patterns of arranged marriages, and, ultimately, new opportunities for travel, work, and education for the younger women.

I will examine the lives of Japanese American women during the trying war years, focusing on the second generation—the Nisei—whose work and education were most affected. The Nisei women entered college and ventured into new areas of work in unfamiliar regions of the country, sustained by fortitude, family ties, discipline, and humor. My understanding of their history derives from several collections of internees' letters, assembly center and relocation camp newspapers, census records, and taped oral history interviews that I conduced with eighty-four Nisei (second generation) and eleven Issei (first generation). Two- thirds of these interviews were with women.

The personal letters, which comprise a major portion of my research, were written in English by Nisei women in their late teens and twenties. Their writing reflects the experience and concerns of their age group. It is important, however, to remember that they wrote these letters to Caucasian friends and sponsors during a time of great insecurity and psychological and economic hardship. In their struggle to be accepted as American citizens,

Reprinted with permission from the author and *Frontiers*, vol. 8, no. 1, 1984.

the interned Japanese Americans were likely to minimize their suffering in the camps and to try to project a positive image of their adjustment to the traumatic conditions.

Prewar Background

A century ago, male Japanese workers began to arrive on American shores, dreaming of making fortunes that would enable them to return to their homeland in triumph. For many, the fortune did not materialize and the shape of the dream changed: they developed stakes in small farms and businesses and, together with wives brought from Japan, established families and communities.

The majority of Japanese women—over 33,000 immigrants—entered the United States between 1908 and 1924.[2] The "Gentlemen's Agreement" of 1908 restricted the entry of male Japanese laborers into the country but sanctioned the immigration of parents, wives, and children of laborers already residing in the United States. The Immigration Act of 1924 excluded Japanese immigration altogether.

Some Japanese women traveled to reunite with husbands; others journeyed to America as newlyweds with men who had returned to Japan to find wives. Still others came alone as picture brides to join Issei men who sought to avoid army conscription or excessive travel expenses; their family-arranged marriages deviated from social convention only by the absence of the groom from the *miai* (preliminary meeting of prospective spouses) and wedding ceremony.[3] Once settled, these women confronted unfamiliar clothing, food, language, and customs as well as life with husbands who were, in many cases, strangers and often ten to fifteen years their seniors.

Most Issei women migrated to rural areas of the West. Some lived with their husbands in labor camps, which provided workers for the railroad industry, the lumber mills of the Pacific Northwest, and the Alaskan salmon canneries.[4] They also farmed with their husbands as cash or share tenants, particularly in California where Japanese immigrant agriculture began to flourish. In urban areas, women worked as domestics[5] or helped their husbands run small businesses such as laundries, bath houses, restaurants, pool halls, boarding houses, grocery stores, curio shops, bakeries, and plant nurseries. Except for the few who married well-to-do professionals or merchants, the majority of Issei women unceasingly toiled both inside and outside the home. They were always the first to rise in the morning and the last to go to bed at night.

The majority of the Issei's children, the Nisei, were born between 1910 and 1940. Both girls and boys were incorporated into the family economy early, especially those living on farms. They took care of their younger siblings, fed the farm animals, heated water for the *furo* (Japanese bath), and worked in the fields before and after school—hoeing weeds, irrigating, and driving tractors. Daughters helped with cooking and cleaning. In addition, all were expected to devote time to their studies: the Issei instilled in their children a deep respect for education and authority. They repeatedly admonished the Nisei not to bring disgrace upon the family or community and exhorted them to do their best in everything.

The Nisei grew up integrating both the Japanese ways of their parents and the mainstream customs of their non-Japanese friends and classmates—not always an easy process given the deeply rooted prejudice and discrimination they faced as a tiny, easily identified minority. Because of the wide age range among them and the diversity of their early experiences in various urban and rural areas, it is difficult to generalize about the Nisei. Most grew up speaking Japanese with their parents and English with their siblings, friends, and teachers. Regardless of whether they were Buddhist or Christian, they celebrated the New Year with traditional foods and visiting, as well as Christmas and Thanksgiving. Girls learned to knit, sew, and embroider, and some took lessons in *odori* (folk dancing). The Nisei, many of whom were adolescents during the 1940s, also listened to the *Hit Parade,* Jack Benny, and *Gangbusters* on the radio, learned to jitterbug, played kick-the-can and baseball, and read the same popular books and magazines as their non-Japanese peers.

The Issei were strict and not inclined to open displays of affection towards their children, but the Nisei were conscious of their parents' concern for them and for the family. This sense of family strength and responsibility helped to sustain the Issei and Nisei through years of economic hardship and discrimination: the West Coast anti-Japanese movement of the early 1920s, the Depression of the 1930s, and the most drastic ordeal—the chaotic uprooting of the World War II evacuation, internment, and resettlement.

Evacuation and Camp Experience

The bombing of Pearl Harbor on December 7, 1941, unleashed war between the United States and Japan and triggered a wave of hostility against Japanese Americans. On December 8, the financial resources of the Issei were frozen, and the Federal Bureau of Investigation began to seize Issei community leaders thought to be strongly pro-Japanese. Rumors spread that the Japanese in Hawaii had aided the attack on Pearl Harbor, fueling fears of "fifth column" activity on the West Coast. Politicians and the press clamored for restrictions against the Japanese Americans, and their economic competitors saw the chance to gain control of Japanese American farms and businesses.

Despite some official doubts and some differences of opinion among military heads regarding the necessity of removing Japanese Americans from the West Coast, in the end the opinions of civilian leaders and Lieutenant General John L. DeWitt—head of the Western Defense Command—of Assistant Secretary of War John McCloy and Secretary of War Henry Stimson prevailed. On February 19, 1942, President Franklin Delano Roosevelt signed Executive Order 9066, arbitrarily suspending the civil rights of American citizens by authorizing the removal of 110,000 Japanese and their America-born children from the western half of the Pacific Coastal States and the southern third of Arizona.[6]

During the bewildering months before evacuation, the Japanese Americans were subject to curfews and to unannounced searches at all hours for "contraband" weapons, radios, and cameras; in desperation and fear, many people destroyed their belongings from Japan, including treasured heirlooms, books, and photographs. Some families moved voluntarily from the Western Defense zone, but many stayed, believing that all areas would eventually be restricted or fearing hostility in neighboring states.

Involuntary evacuation began in the spring of 1942. Families received a scant week's notice in which to "wind up their affairs, store or sell their possessions, close up their businesses and homes, and show up at an assembly point for transportation to an assembly center."[7] Each person was allowed to bring only as many clothes and personal items as he or she could carry to the temporary assembly centers that had been hastily constructed at fairgrounds, race tracks, and Civilian Conservation Corps camps: twelve in California, one in Oregon, and one in Washington.

The rapidity of evacuation left many Japanese Americans numb; one Nisei noted that "a queer lump came to my throat. Nothing else came to my mind, it was just blank. Everything happened too soon, I guess."[8] As the realization of leaving home, friends, and neighborhood sank in, the numbness gave way to bewilderment. A teenager at the Santa Anita Assembly Center wrote, "I felt lost after I left Mountain View [California]. I thought that we could go back but instead look where we are."[9] Upon arrival at the assembly centers, even the Nisei from large urban communities found themselves surrounded by more

Japanese than they had ever before seen. For Mary Okumura, the whole experience seemed overwhelming at first:

> Just about every night, there is something going on but I rather stay home because I am just new here & don't know very much around. As for the people I met so many all ready, I don't remember any. I am not even going to try to remember names because its just impossible here.[10]

A Nisei from a community where there were few Japanese felt differently about her arrival at the Merced Assembly Center: "I guess at that age it was sort of fun for me really [rather] than tragic, because for the first time I got to see young [Japanese] people. . . . We signed up to work in the mess hall—we got to meet everybody that way."[11]

Overlying the mixed feelings of anxiety, anger, shame, and confusion was resignation. As a relatively small minority caught in a storm of turbulent events that destroyed their individual and community security, there was little the Japanese Americans could do but shrug and say, "*Shikata ga nai*," or, "It can't be helped," the implication being that the situation must be endured. The phrase lingered on many lips when the Issei, Nisei, and the young Sansei (third generation) children prepared for the move—which was completed by November 1942—to the ten permanent relocation camps organized by the War Relocation Authority: Topaz, Utah; Poston and Gila River, Arizona; Amache, Colorado; Manzanar and Tule Lake, California; Heart Mountain, Wyoming; Minidoka, Idaho; Denson and Rohwer, Arkansas.[12] Denson and Rohwer were located in the swampy lowlands of Arkansas; the other camps were in desolate desert or semi-desert areas subject to dust storms and extreme temperatures reflected in the nicknames given to the three sections of the Poston Camp: Toaston, Roaston, and Duston.

The conditions of camp life profoundly altered family relations and affected women of all ages and backgrounds. Family unity deteriorated in the crude communal facilities and cramped barracks. The unceasing battle with the elements, the poor food, the shortages of toilet tissue and milk, coupled with wartime profiteering and mismanagement, and the sense of injustice and frustration took their toll on a people uprooted, far from home.

The standard housing in the camps was a spartan barracks, about twenty feet by one hundred feet, divided into four to six rooms furnished with steel army cots. Initially each single room or "apartment" housed an average of eight persons; individuals without kin nearby were often moved in with smaller families. Because the partitions between apartments did not reach the ceiling, even the smallest noises traveled freely from one end of the building to the other. There were usually fourteen barracks in each block, and each block had its own mess hall, laundry, latrine, shower facilities, and recreation room.

Because of the discomfort, noise, and lack of privacy, which "made a single symphony of yours and your neighbors' loves, hates, and joys,"[13] the barracks often became merely a place to "hang your hat" and sleep. As Jeanne Wakatsuki Houston records in her autobiography, *Farewell to Manzanar,* many family members began to spend less time together in the crowded barracks. The even greater lack of privacy in the latrine and shower facilities necessitated adjustments in former notions of modesty. There were no partitions in the shower room, and the latrine consisted of two rows of partitioned toilets "with nothing in front of you, just on the sides. Lots of people were not used to those kind of facilities, so [they'd] either go early in the morning when people were not around, or go real late at night. . . . It was really something until you got used to it."[14]

The large communal mess halls also encouraged family disunity as family members gradually began to eat separately: mothers with small children, fathers with other men, and older children with their peers. "Table manners were forgotten," observed Miné Okubo. "Guzzle, guzzle, guzzle; hurry, hurry, hurry. Family life was lacking. Everyone ate wherever he or she pleased."[15] Some strategies were developed for preserving family unity. The Amache Camp responded in part by assigning each family a particular table in the mess hall. Some families took the food back to their barracks so that they might eat together. But these measures were not always feasible in the face of varying work schedules; the odd hours of those assigned to shifts in the mess halls and infirmaries often made it impossible for the family to sit down together for meals.

Newspaper reports that Japanese Americans were living in luxurious conditions angered evacuees struggling to adjust to cramped quarters and crude communal facilities. A married woman with a family wrote from Heart Mountain:

> Last weekend, we had an awful cold wave and it was about 20° to 30° below zero. In such a weather, it's terrible to try going even to the bath and latrine house. . . . It really aggravates me to hear some politicians say we Japanese are being coddled, for *it isn't so*!! We're on ration as much as outsiders are. I'd say welcome to anyone to try living behind barbed wire and be cooped in a 20 ft. by 20 ft. room. . . . We do our sleeping, dressing, ironing, hanging up our clothes in this one room.[16]

After the first numbness of disorientation, the evacuees set about making their situation bearable, creating as much order in their lives as possible. With blankets they partitioned their apartments into tiny rooms and created benches, tables, and shelves as piles of scrap lumber left over from barracks construction vanished; victory gardens and flower patches appeared. Evacuees also took advantage of the opportunity to taste freedom when they received temporary permits to go shopping in nearby towns. These were memorable occasions. A Heart Mountain Nisei described what such a trip meant to her in 1944:

> for the first time since being behind the fences, I managed to go out shopping to Billings, Montana—a trip about 4 hours ride on train and bus. . . . It was quite a mental relief to breathe the air on the outside. . . . And was it an undescribable sensation to be able to be dressed up and walk the pavements with my high heel shoes!! You just can't imagine how full we are of pent-up emotions until we leave the camp behind us and see the highway ahead of us. A trip like that will keep us from becoming mentally narrow. And without much privacy, you can imagine how much people will become dull.[17]

Despite the best efforts of the evacuees to restore order to their disputed world, camp conditions prevented replication of their prewar lives. Women's work experiences, for example, changed in complex ways during the years of internment. Each camp offered a wide range of jobs, resulting from the organization of the camps as model cities administered through a series of departments headed by Caucasian administrators. The departments handled everything from accounting, agriculture, education, and medical care to mess hall service and the weekly newspaper. The scramble for jobs began early in the assembly centers and camps, and all able-bodied persons were expected to work.

Even before the war many family members had worked, but now children and parents, men and women all received the same low wages. In the relocation camps, doctors, teachers, and other professionals were at the top of the pay scale, earning $19 per month. The majority of workers received $16, and apprentices earned $12. The new equity in pay and the variety of available jobs gave many women unprecedented opportunities for experimentation, as illustrated by one woman's account of her family's work in Poston:

First I wanted to find art work, but I didn't last too long because it wasn't very interesting . . . so I worked in the mess hall, but that wasn't for me, so I went to the accounting department—time-keeping—and I enjoyed that, so I stayed there. . . . My dad . . . went to a shoe shop . . . and then he was block gardener. . . . He got $16. . . . [My sister] was secretary for the block manager; then she went to the optometry department. She was assistant optometrist; she fixed all the glasses and fitted them. . . . That was $16.[18]

As early as 1942, the War Relocation Authority began to release evacuees temporarily from the centers and camps to do voluntary seasonal farm work in neighboring areas hard hit by the wartime labor shortage. The work was arduous, as one young woman discovered when she left Topaz to take a job plucking turkeys:

The smell is terrific until you get used to it. . . . We all wore gunny sacks around our waist, had a small knife and plucked off the fine feathers.
This is about the hardest work that many of us have done—but without a murmur of complaint we worked 8 hours through the first day without a pause.
We were all so tired that we didn't even feel like eating. . . . Our fingers and wrists were just aching, and I just dreamt of turkeys and more turkeys.[19]

Work conditions varied from situation to situation, and some exploitative farmers refused to pay the Japanese Americans after they had finished beet topping or fruit picking. One worker noted that the degree of friendliness on the employer's part decreased as the harvest neared completion. Nonetheless, many workers, like the turkey plucker, concluded that "even if the work is hard, it is worth the freedom we are allowed."

Camp life increased the leisure of many evacuees. A good number of Issei women, accustomed to long days of work inside and outside the home, found that the communally prepared meals and limited living quarters provided them with spare time. Many availed themselves of the opportunity to attend adult classes taught by both evacuees and non-Japanese. Courses involving handcrafts and traditional Japanese arts such as flower arrangement, sewing, painting, calligraphy, and wood carving became immensely popular as an overwhelming number of people turned to art for recreation and self-expression. Some of these subjects were viewed as hobbies and leisure activities by those who taught them, but to the Issei women they represented access to new skills and a means to contribute to the material comfort of the family.

The evacuees also filled their time with Buddhist and Christian church meetings, theatrical productions, cultural programs, athletic events, and visits with friends. All family members spent more time than ever before in the company of their peers. Nisei from isolated rural areas were exposed to the ideas, styles, and pastimes of the more sophisticated urban youth; in camp they had the time and opportunity to socialize—at work, school, dances, sports events, and parties—in an almost entirely Japanese American environment. Gone were the restrictions of distance, lack of transportation, interracial uneasiness, and the dawn-to-dusk exigencies of field work.

Like their noninterned contemporaries, most young Nisei women envisioned a future of marriage and children. They—and their parents—anticipated that they would marry other Japanese Americans, but these young women also expected to choose their own husbands and to marry "for love." This mainstream American ideal of marriage differed greatly from the Issei's view of love as a bond that might evolve over the course of an arranged marriage that was firmly rooted in less romantic notions of compatibility and responsibility. The discrepancy between Issei and Nisei conceptions of love and marriage had sturdy prewar roots; internment fostered further divergence from the old customs of arranged marriage.

In the artificial hothouse of camp, Nisei romances often bloomed quickly. As Nisei men left to prove their loyalty to the United States in the 442nd Combat Team and the 100th Battalion, young Japanese Americans strove to grasp what happiness and security they could, given the uncertainties of the future. Lily Shoji, in her "Fem-a-lites" newspaper column, commented upon the "changing world" and advised Nisei women:

> This is the day of sudden dates, of blind dates on the up-and-up, so let the flash of a uniform be a signal to you to be ready for any emergency. . . . Romance is blossoming with the emotion and urgency of war.[20]

In keeping with this atmosphere, camp newspaper columns like Shoji's in *The Mercedian*, *The Daily Tulean Dispatch*'s "Strictly Feminine,"and the *Poston Chronicle*'s "Fashionotes" gave their Nisei readers countless suggestions on how to impress boys, care for their complexions, and choose the latest fashions. These evacuee-authored columns thus mirrored the mainstream girls' periodicals of the time. Such fashion news may seem incongruous in the context of an internment camp whose inmates had little choice in clothing beyond what they could find in the Montgomery Ward or Sears and Roebuck mail-order catalogues. These columns, however, reflect women's efforts to remain in touch with the world outside the barbed wire fence; they reflect as well women's attempt to maintain morale in a drab, depressing environment. "There's something about color in clothes," speculated Tule Lake columnist "Yuri"; "Singing colors have a heart-building effect. . . . Color is a stimulant we need—both for its effect on ourselves and on others."[21]

The evacuees' fashion columns addressed practical as well as aesthetic concerns, reflecting the dusty realities of camp life. In this vein, Mitzi Sugita of the Poston Sewing Department praised the "Latest Fashion for Women Today—Slacks," drawing special attention to overalls; she assured her readers that these "digging duds"[22] were not only winsome and workable but also possessed the virtues of being inexpensive and requiring little ironing.

The columnists' concern with the practical aspects of fashion extended beyond the confines of the camps, as women began to leave for life on the outside—an opportunity increasingly available after 1943. Sugita told prospective operatives, "If you are one of the many thousands of women now entering in commercial and industrial work, your required uniform is based on slacks, safe and streamlined. It is very important that they be durable, trim and attractive."[23] Women heading for clerical positions or college were more likely to heed Marii Kyogoku's admonitions to invest in "really nice things," with an eye to "simple lines which are good practically forever."[24]

Resettlement: College and Work

Relocation began slowly in 1942. Among the first to venture out of the camps were college students, assisted by the National Japanese American Student Relocation Council, a nongovernmental agency that provided invaluable placement aid to 4,084 Nisei in the years 1942–46.[25] Founded in 1942 by concerned educators, this organization persuaded institutions outside the restricted Western Defense zone to accept Nisei students and facilitated their admissions and leave clearances. A study of the first 400 students to leave camp showed that a third of them were women.[26] Because of the cumbersome screening process, few other evacuees departed on indefinite leave before 1943. In that year, the

War Relocation Authority tried to expedite the clearance procedure by broadening an army registration program aimed at Nisei males to include all adults. With this policy change, the migration from the camps steadily increased.[27]

Many Nisei, among them a large number of women, were anxious to leave the limbo of camp and return "to normal life again."[28] With all its work, social events, and cultural activities, camp was still an artificial, limited environment. It was stifling "to see nothing but the same barracks, mess halls, and other houses, row after row, day in and day out, it gives us the feeling that we're missing all the freedom and liberty."[29] An aspiring teacher wrote: "Mother and father do not want me to go out. However, I want to go so very much that sometimes I feel that I'd go even if they disowned me. What shall I do? I realize the hard living conditions outside but I think I can take it."[30] Women's developing sense of independence in the camp environment and their growing awareness of their abilities as workers contributed to their self-confidence and hence their desire to leave. Significantly, Issei parents, despite initial reluctance, were gradually beginning to sanction their daughters' departures for education and employment in the Midwest and East. One Nisei noted:

> [Father] became more broad-minded in the relocation center. He was more mellow in his ways. . . . At first he didn't want me to relocate, but he gave in. . . . I said I wanted to go [to Chicago] with my friend, so he helped me pack. He didn't say I could go . . . but he helped me pack, so I thought, "Well, he didn't say no."[31]

The decision to relocate was a difficult one. It was compounded for some women because they felt obligated to stay and care for elderly or infirm parents, like the Heart Mountain Nisei who observed wistfully, "It's getting so more and more of the girls and boys are leaving camp, and I sure wish I could but mother's getting on and I just can't leave her."[32] Many internees worried about their acceptance in the outside world. The Nisei considered themselves American citizens, and they had an allegiance to the land of their birth: "The teaching and love of one's own birth place, one's own country was . . . strongly impressed upon my mind as a child. So even though California may deny our rights of birth, I shall ever love her soil."[33] But evacuation had taught the Japanese Americans that in the eyes of many of their fellow Americans, theirs was the face of the enemy. Many Nisei were torn by mixed feelings of shame, frustration, and bitterness at the denial of their civil rights. These factors created an atmosphere of anxiety that surrounded those who contemplated resettlement: "A feeling of uncertainty hung over the camp; we were worried about the future. Plans were made and remade, as we tried to decide what to do. Some were ready to risk anything to get away. Others feared to leave the protection of the camp."[34]

Thus, those first college students were the scouts whose letters back to camp marked pathways for others to follow. May Yoshino sent a favorable report to her family in Topaz from the nearby University of Utah, indicating that there were "plenty of schoolgirl jobs for those who want to study at the University."[35] Correspondence from other Nisei students shows that although they succeeded at making the dual transition from high school to college and from camp to the outside world, they were not without anxieties as to whether they could handle the study load and the reactions of the Caucasians around them. One student at Drake University in Iowa wrote to her interned sister about a professor's reaction to her autobiographical essay, "Evacuation":

> Today Mr.—, the English teacher that scares me, told me that the theme that I wrote the other day was very interesting. . . . You could just imagine how wonderful and happy *I* was to know that he liked it a little bit. . . . I've been awfully busy trying to catch up on

work and the work is *so* different from high school. I think that little by little I'm beginning to adjust myself to college life.[36]

Several incidents of hostility did occur, but the reception of the Nisei students at colleges and universities was generally warm. Topaz readers of *Trek* magazine could draw encouragement from Lillian Ota's "Campus Report." Ota, a Wellesley student, reassured them: "During the first few days you'll be invited by the college to teas and receptions. Before long you'll lose the awkwardness you might feel at such doings after the months of abnormal life at evacuation centers."[37] Although Ota had not noticed "that my being a 'Jap' has made much difference on the campus itself," she offered cautionary and pragmatic advice to the Nisei, suggesting the burden of responsibility these relocated students felt, as well as the problem of communicating their experiences and emotions to Caucasians.

> It is scarcely necessary to point out that those who have probably never seen a nisei before will get their impression of the nisei as a whole from the relocated students. It won't do you or your family and friends much good to dwell on what you consider injustices when you are questioned about evacuation. Rather, stress the contributions of [our] people to the nation's war effort.[38]

Given the tenor of the times and the situation of their families, the pioneers in resettlement had little choice but to repress their anger and minimize the amount of racist hostility they encountered.

In her article "a la mode," Marii Kyogoku also offered survival tips to the departing Nisei, ever conscious that they were on trial not only as individuals but as representatives of their families and their generation. She suggested criteria for choosing clothes and provided hints on adjustment to food rationing. Kyogoku especially urged the evacuees to improve their table manners, which had been adversely affected by the "unnatural food and atmosphere" of mess hall dining:

> You should start rehearsing for the great outside by bringing your own utensils to the dining hall. Its an aid to normality to be able to eat your jello with a spoon and well worth the dishwashing which it involves. All of us eat much too fast. Eat more slowly. All this practicing should be done so that proper manners will seem natural to you. If you do this, you won't get stagefright and spill your water glass, or make bread pills and hardly dare to eat when you have your first meal away from the centers and in the midst of scrutinizing caucasian eyes.[39]

Armed with advice and drawn by encouraging reports, increasing numbers of women students left camp. A postwar study of a group of 1,000 relocated students showed that 40 percent were women.[40] The field of nursing was particularly attractive to Nisei women; after the first few students disproved the hospital administration's fears of their patients' hostility, acceptance of Nisei into nursing schools grew. By July 1944, there were more than 300 Nisei women in over 100 nursing programs in twenty-four states.[41] One such student wrote from the Asbury Hospital in Minneapolis: "Work here isn't too hard and I enjoy it very much. The patients are very nice people and I haven't had any trouble as yet. They do give us a funny stare at the beginning but after a day or so we receive the best compliments."[42]

The trickle of migration from the camps grew into a steady stream by 1943, as the War Relocation Authority developed its resettlement program to aid evacuees in finding housing and employment in the East and Midwest. A resettlement bulletin published by the Advisory Committee for Evacuees described "who is relocating":

> Mostly younger men and women, in their 20s or 30s; mostly single persons or couples with one or two children, or men with larger families who come out alone first to scout opportunities and to secure a foothold, planning to call wife and children later. Most relocated evacuees have parents or relatives whom they hope and plan to bring out "when we get re-established."[43]

In early 1945, the War Department ended the exclusion of the Japanese Americans from the West Coast, and the War Relocation Authority announced that the camps would be closed within the year. By this time, 37 percent of the evacuees of sixteen years or older had already relocated, including 63 percent of the Nisei women in that age group.[44]

For Nisei women, like their non-Japanese sisters, the wartime labor shortage opened the door into industrial, clerical, and managerial occupations. Prior to the war, racism had excluded the Japanese Americans from most white-collar clerical and sales positions, and, according to sociologist Evelyn Nakano Glenn, "the most common form of nonagricultural employment for the immigrant women (issei) and their American-born daughters (nisei) was domestic service."[45] The highest percentage of job offers for both men and women continued to be requests for domestic workers. In July 1943, the Kansas City branch of the War Relocation Authority noted that 45 percent of requests for workers were for domestics, and the Milwaukee office cited 61 percent.[46] However, Nisei women also found jobs as secretaries, typists, file clerks, beauticians, and factory workers. By 1950, 47 percent of employed Japanese American women were clerical and sales workers and operatives; only 10 percent were in domestic service.[47] The World War II decade, then, marked a turning point for Japanese American women in the labor force.

Whether they were students or workers, and regardless of where they went or how prepared they were to meet the outside world, Nisei women found that leaving camp meant enormous change in their lives. Even someone as confident as Marii Kyogoku, the author of much relocation advice, found that reentry into the Caucasian-dominated world beyond the barbed wire fence was not a simple matter of stepping back into old shoes. Leaving the camps—like entering them—meant major changes in psychological perspective and self-image.

> I had thought that because before evacuation I had adjusted myself rather well in a Caucasian society, I would go right back into my former frame of mind. I have found, however, that though the center became unreal and was as if it had never existed as soon as I got on the train at Delta, I was never so self-conscious in all my life.

Kyogoku was amazed to see so many men and women in uniform and, despite her "proper" dining preparation, felt strange sitting at a table set with clean linen and a full set of silverware.

> I felt a diffidence at facing all these people and things, which was most unusual. Slowly things have come to seem natural, though I am still excited by the sounds of the busy city and thrilled every time I see a street lined with trees, I no longer feel that I am the cynosure of all eyes.[48]

Like Kyogoku, many Nisei women discovered that relocation meant adjustment to "a life different from our former as well as present way of living"[49] and, as such, posed a challenge. Their experiences in meeting this challenge were as diverse as their jobs and living situations.

"I live at the Eleanor Club No. 5 which is located on the west side," wrote Mary Sonoda, working with the American Friends Service Committee in Chicago:

> I pay $1 per day for room and two meals a day. I also have maid service. I do not think that one can manage all this for $1 unless one lives in a place like this which houses thousands of working girls in the city. . . . I am the only Japanese here at present. . . . The residents and the staff are wonderful to me. . . . I am constantly being entertained by one person or another.
>
> The people in Chicago are extremely friendly. Even with the Tribune screaming awful headlines concerning the recent execution of American soldiers in Japan, people kept their heads. On street cars, at stores, everywhere, one finds innumerable evidence of good will.[50]

Chicago, the location of the first War Relocation Authority field office for supervision of resettlement in the Midwest, attracted the largest number of evacuees. Not all found their working environment as congenial as Mary Sonoda did. Smoot Katow, a Nisei man in Chicago, painted "another side of the picture":

> I met one of the Edgewater Beach girls. . . . From what she said it was my impression that the girls are not very happy. The hotel work is too hard, according to this girl. In fact, they are losing weight and one girl became sick with overwork. They have to clean about fifteen suites a day, scrubbing the floors on their hands and knees. . . . It seems the management is out to use labor as labor only. . . . The outside world is just as tough as it ever was.[51]

These variations in living and work conditions and wages encouraged—and sometimes necessitated—a certain amount of job experimentation among the Nisei.

Many relocating Japanese Americans received moral and material assistance from a number of service organizations and religious groups, particularly the Presbyterians, the Methodists, the Society of Friends, and the Young Women's Christian Association. One such Nisei, Dorcas Asano, enthusiastically described to a Quaker sponsor her activities in the big city:

> Since receiving your application for hostel accommodation, I have decided to come to New York and I am really glad for the opportunity to be able to resume the normal civilized life after a year's confinement in camp. New York is really a city of dreams and we are enjoying every minute working in offices, rushing back and forth to work in the ever-speeding sub-way trains, counting our ration points, buying war bonds, going to church, seeing the latest shows, plays, operas, making many new friends and living like our neighbors in the war time. I only wish more of my friends who are behind the fence will take advantage of the many helpful hands offered to them.[52]

The Nisei also derived support and strength from networks—formed before and during internment—of friends and relatives. The homes of those who relocated first became way stations for others as they made the transition into new communities and jobs. In 1944, soon after she obtained a place to stay in New York City, Miné Okubo found that "many of the other evacuees relocating in New York came ringing my doorbell. They were sleeping all over the floor!"[53] Single women often accompanied or joined sisters, brothers, and friends as many interconnecting grapevines carried news of likely jobs, housing, and friendly communities. Ayako Kanemura, for instance, found a job painting Hummel figurines in Chicago; a letter of recommendation from a friend enabled her "to get my foot into the door and then all my friends followed and joined me."[54] Although they were farther from their families than ever before, Nisei women maintained warm ties of affection and concern, and those who had the means to do so continued to play a role in the family economy, remitting a portion of their earnings to their families in or out of camp, and to siblings in school.

Elizabeth Ogata's family exemplifies several patterns of resettlement and the maintenance of family ties within them. In October 1944, her parents were living with her brother Harry who had begun to farm in Springville, Utah; another brother and sister were attending Union College in Lincoln, Nebraska. Elizabeth herself had moved to Minneapolis to join a brother in the army, and she was working as an operative making pajamas. "Minn. is a beautiful place," she wrote, "and the people are so nice. . . . I thought I'd never find anywhere I would feel at home as I did in Mt. View [California], but I have changed my mind."[55] Like Elizabeth, a good number of the 35,000 relocated Japanese Americans were favorably impressed by their new homes and decided to stay.

The war years had complex and profound effects upon Japanese Americans, uprooting their communities and causing severe psychological and emotional damage. The vast majority returned to the West Coast at the end of the war in 1945—a move that, like the initial evacuation, was a grueling test of flexibility and fortitude. Even with the assistance of old friends and service organizations, the transition was taxing and painful; the end of the war meant not only long-awaited freedom but more battles to be fought in social, academic, and economic arenas. The Japanese Americans faced hostility, crude living conditions, and a struggle for jobs. Few evacuees received any compensation for their financial losses, estimated conservatively at $400 million, because Congress decided to appropriate only $38 million for the settlement of claims.[56] It is even harder to place a figure on the toll taken in emotional shock, self-blame, broken dreams, and insecurity. One Japanese American woman still sees in her nightmares the watchtower searchlights that troubled her sleep forty years ago.

The war altered Japanese American women's lives in complicated ways. In general, evacuation and relocation accelerated earlier trends that differentiated the Nisei from their parents. Although most young women, like their mothers and non-Japanese peers, anticipated a future centered on a husband and children, they had already felt the influence of mainstream middle-class values of love and marriage and quickly moved away from the pattern of arranged marriage in the camps. There, increased peer group activities and the relaxation of parental authority gave them more independence. The Nisei women's expectations of marriage became more akin to the companionate ideals of their peers than to those of the Issei.

As before the war, many Nisei women worked in camp, but the new parity in wages they received altered family dynamics. And though they expected to contribute to the family economy, a large number did so in settings far from the family, availing themselves of opportunities provided by the student and worker relocation programs. In meeting the challenges facing them, Nisei women drew not only upon the disciplined strength inculcated by their Issei parents but also upon firmly rooted support networks and the greater measure of self-reliance and independence that they developed during the crucible of the war years.

Notes

For their invaluable assistance with this paper, I would like to thank Estelle Freedman, Mary Rothschild, and members of the women's history dissertation reading group at Stanford University—Sue Cobble, Gary Sue Goodman, Yukiko Hanawa, Gail Hershatter, Emily Honig, Susan Johnson, Sue Lynn, Joanne Meyerowitz, Peggy Pascoe, Linda Schott, Frances Taylor, and Karen Anderson.

1. Miné Okubo, *Miné Okubo: An American Experience*, exhibition catalogue (Oakland: Oakland Museum, 1972), 36.

2. The very first Japanese women to arrive in the United States before the turn of the century were the *ameyuki- san*—prostitutes—of whose lives little is known. For information, see Yuji Ichioka, "Ameyuki-san: Japanese Prostitutes in Nineteenth Century America," *Amerasia Journal*, 4 No. 1 (1977). A few references to the *ameyuki-san* appear in Mildred Crowl Martin's biography, *Chinatown's Angry Angel, The Story of Donaldina Cameron* (Palo Alto: Pacific Books, 1977).

3. In Japan, marriage was legally the transfer of a woman's name from her father's registry to that of the groom's family. Even through the Meiji Era there was enormous diversity in the time period of this formalization; it might occur as early as several days before the wedding ceremony or as late as seven or more years later, by which time the bride should have produced several sons and proven herself to be a good wife and daughter- in-law. For a detailed cross-cultural history of the Issei women, see Yukiko Hanawa, "The Several Worlds of Issei Women," Thesis California State University at Long Beach 1982.

4. Yuji Ichioka. "*Amerika Nadeshiko:* Japanese Immigrant Women in the United States, 1900–1924," *Pacific Historical Review*, 69, No. 2 (May 1980), 343.

5. Evelyn Nakano Glenn has examined the lives of Issei and Nisei domestic workers in the prewar period in her study, "The Dialectics of Wage Work: Japanese American Women and Domestic Servants, 1905–1940," *Feminist Studies*, 6, No. 3 (Fall 1980), 432–71.

6. Sources on evacuation: Robert A. Wilson and Bill Hosokawa, *East to American, A History of the Japanese in the United States* (New York: William Morrow, 1980); Audrie Girdner and Anne Loftis, *The Great Betrayal: The Evacuation of the Japanese-Americans During World War II* (Toronto: Macmillan, 1969); Daisuke Kitagawa, *Issei and Nisei: The Internment Years* (New York: Seabury Press, 1967); Roger Daniels, *The Decision to Relocate the Japanese Americans* (Philadelphia: J. B. Lippincott, 1975).

7. Wilson and Hosokawa, 208.

8. Bettie to Mrs. Jack Shoup, June 3, 1942, Mrs. Jack Shoup Collection, Hoover Institution Archives (hereafter referred to as HIA), Stanford, California.

9. May Nakamoto to Mrs. Jack Shoup, November 30, 1942, Mrs. Jack Shoup Collection, HIA.

10. Mary Okumura to Mrs. Jack Shoup, May 30, 1942, Mrs. Jack Shoup Collection, HIA.

11. Miye Baba, personal interview, February 10, 1982, Turlock, California.

12. Many of the Japanese community leaders arrested by the FBI before the evacuation were interned in special all-male camps in North Dakota, Louisiana, and New Mexico. Some Japanese Americans living outside the perimeter of the Western Defense zone in Arizona, Utah. etc. were not interned.

13. Miné Okubo, *Citizen 13660* (New York: Columbia Univ. Press, 1946), 66.

14. Chieko Kimura, personal interview, April 9, 1978, Glendale, Arizona.

15. Okubo, *Citizen 13660*, 89.

16. Shizuko Horiuchi to Henriette Von Blon, January 24, 1943, Henriette Von Blon Collection, HIA.

17. Shizuko Horiuchi to Henriette Von Blon, January 5, 1944, Henriette Von Blon Collection, HIA.

18. Ayako Kanemura, personal interview, March 10, 1978, Glendale, Arizona.

19. Anonymous, *Topaz Times*, October 24, 1942, 3.

20. Lily Shoji, "Fem-a-lites," *The Mercedian*, August 7, 1942, 4.

21. "Yuri," "Strictly Feminine," September 29, 1942, 2.

22. Mitzi Sugita, "Latest Fashion for Women Today—Slacks," *Poston Chronicle*, June 13, 1943, 1.

23. Sugita.

24. Marii Kyogoku, "a la mode," *Trek* (February 1943), 38.

25. From 1942 to the end of 1945 the Council allocated about $240,000 in scholarships, most of which were provided through the donations of churches and the World Student Service Fund. The average grant per student was $156.73, which in that era was a major contribution toward the cost of higher education. Source: National Japanese American Student Relocation Council, Minutes of the Executive Committee Meeting, Philadelphia, Pennsylvania, December 19, 1945.

26. Robert O'Brien, *The College Nisei* (Palo Alto: Pacific Books, 1949), 73–74.

27. The disastrous consequences of the poorly conceived clearance procedure have been examined by Wilson and Hosokawa, 226–27, and Girdner and Loftis, 342–43.

28. May Nakamoto to Mrs. Jack Shoup, November 20, 1943, Mrs. Jack Shoup Collection, HIA.

29. Shizuko Horiuchi to Henriette Von Blon, December 27, 1942, Henriette Von Blon Collection, HIA.

30. Toshiko Imada to Margaret Cosgrave Sowers, January 16, 1943, Margaret Cosgrave Sowers Collection, HIA.

31. Ayako Kanemura, personal interview, March 24, 1978, Glendale, Arizona.

32. Kathy Ishikawa to Mrs. Jack Shoup, June 14, 1942, Mrs. Jack Shoup Collection, HIA.

33. Anonymous Nisei nurse in Poston Camp to Margaret Finley, May 5, 1943, Margaret Finley Collection, HIA.

34. Okubo, *Citizen 13660*, 139.

35. *Topaz Times*, October 24, 1942, 3.

36. Masako Ono to Atsuko Ono, September 20, 1942, Margaret Cosgrave Sowers Collection, HIA. Prior to the war, few Nisei had college experience: the 1940 census lists 674 second-generation women and 1,507 men who had attended or were attending college.

37. Lillian Ota, "Campus Report," *Trek* (February 1943), 33.

38. Ota, 33–34.

39. Kyogoku, "a la mode," 39.

40. O'Brien, 84.

41. O'Brien, 85–86.

42. Grace Tanabe to Josephine Duveneck, February 16, 1944, Conard-Duveneck Collection, HIA.

43. Advisory Committee for Evacuees, *Resettlement Bulletin* (April 1943), 2.

44. Leonard Broom and Ruth Riemer, *Removal and Return, The Socio-Economic Effects of the War on Japanese Americans* (Berkeley: Univ. of California Press, 1949), 36.

45. Glenn, 412.

46. Advisory Committee for Evacuees, *Resettlement Bulletin* (July 1943), 3.

47. 1950 United States Census, Special Report.

48. Marii Kyogoku, *Resettlement Bulletin* (July 1943), 5.

49. Kyogoku, "a la mode," 39.

50. *Poston Chronicle*, May 23, 1943, 1.

51. *Poston Chronicle*, May 23, 1943.

52. Dorcas Asano to Josephine Duveneck, January 22, 1944, Conard-Duveneck Collection, HIA.

53. Okubo, *An American Experience*, 41.

54. Ayako Kanemura, personal interview, March 24, 1978, Glendale, Arizona.

55. Elizabeth Ogata to Mrs. Jack Shoup, October 1, 1944, Mrs. Jack Shoup Collection, HIA.

56. Susan M. Hartmann, *The Home Front and Beyond, American Women in the 1940s* (Boston: Twayne Publishers, 1982), 126. There is some debate regarding the origins of the assessment of evacuee losses at $400 million. However, a recent study by the Commission on Wartime Relocation and Internment of Civilians has estimated that the Japanese Americans lost between $149 million and $370 million in 1945 dollars, and between $810 million and $2 billion in 1983 dollars. See the *San Francisco Chronicle*, June 16, 1983, 12.

28

Oral History and the Study of
Sexuality in the Lesbian Community:
Buffalo, New York, 1940–1960

Madeline D. Davis and *Elizabeth Lapovsky Kennedy*

We began a study of the history of the Buffalo lesbian community, 1930–1960, to determine that community's contribution to the emergence of the gay liberation movement of the 1960s.[1] Because this community centered around bars and was highly role defined, its members often have been stereotyped as low-life societal discards and pathetic imitators of heterosexuality. We suspected instead that these women were heroines who had shaped the development of gay pride in the twentieth century by forging a culture for survival and resistance under prejudicial conditions and by passing this sense of community on to newcomers; in our minds, these are indications of a movement in its pre-political stages.[2] Our original research plan assumed the conceptual division between the public (social life and politics) and the private (intimate life and sex), which is deeply rooted in modern consciousness and which feminism has only begun to question. Thus we began our study by looking at gay and lesbian bars—the public manifestations of gay life at the time—and relegated sex to a position of less importance, viewing it as only incidentally relevant. As our research progressed we came to question the accuracy of this division. This article records the transformation in our thinking and explores the role of sexuality in the cultural and political development of the Buffalo lesbian community.

At first, our use of the traditional framework that separates the public and private spheres was fruitful.[3] Because the women who patronized the lesbian and gay bars of the past were predominantly working class and left no written records, we chose oral history as our method of study. Through the life stories of over forty narrators, we found that there were more bars in Buffalo during the forties and fifties than there are in that city today. Lesbians living all over the city came to socialize in these bars, which were located primarily in the downtown area. Some of these women were born and raised in Buffalo; others had migrated there in search of their kind. In addition, women from nearby cities, Rochester and Toronto, came to Buffalo bars on weekends. Most of the women who frequented these bars had full-time jobs. Many were factory workers, taxi drivers, bartenders, clerical workers, hospital technicians; a few were teachers or women who owned their own businesses.[4]

Our narrators documented, beyond our greatest expectations, the truth of our original hypothesis that this public bar community was a formative predecessor to the modern gay liberation movement. These bars not only were essential meeting places with distinctive cultures and mores, but they were also the central arena for the lesbian confrontation with

This article is reprinted from *Feminist Studies*, vol. 12, no. 1, (Spring 1986): 7–26, by permission of the publisher, *Feminist Studies, Inc.*, c/o Women's Studies Program, University of Maryland, College Park, MD 20742.

a hostile world. Participants in bar life were engaged in constant, often violent, struggle for public space. Their dress code announced them as lesbians to their neighbors, to strangers on the streets, and of course to all who entered the bars. Although confrontation with the straight world was a constant during this period, its nature changed over time. In the forties, women braved ridicule and verbal abuse, but rarely physical conflict. One narrator of the forties conveys the tone: "There was a great difference in looks between a lesbian and her girl. You had to take a streetcar—very few people had cars. And people would stare and such."[5] In the fifties, with the increased visibility of the established gay community, the concomitant postwar rigidification of sex roles, and the political repression of the McCarthy era, the street dyke emerged. She was a full-time "queer," who frequented the bars even on week nights and was ready at any time to fight for her space and dignity. Many of our fifties' narrators were both aware and proud that their fighting contributed to a safer, more comfortable environment for lesbians today.

> Things back then were horrible, and I think that because I fought like a man to survive I made it somehow easier for the kids coming out today. I did all their fighting for them. I'm not a rich person; I don't even have a lot of money; I don't even have a little money. I would have nothing to leave anybody in this world, but I have that that I can leave to the kids who are coming out now, who will come out into the future, that I left them a better place to come out into. And that's all I have to offer, to leave them. But I wouldn't deny it; even thought I was getting my brains beaten up I would never stand up and say, "No, don't hit me, I'm not gay, I'm not gay." I wouldn't do that.

When we initially gathered this material on the growth and development of community life, we placed little emphasis on sexuality. In part we were swept away by the excitement of the material on bars, dress, and the creation of public space for lesbians. In addition, we were part of a lesbian feminist movement that opposed a definition of lesbianism based primarily on sex. Moreover, we were influenced by the popular assumption that sexuality is natural and unchanging and the related sexist assumption of women's sexual passivity— both of which imply that sexuality is not a valid subject for historical study. Only recently have historians turned their attention to sexuality, a topic that used to be of interest mainly to psychologists and the medical profession. Feminists have added impetus to this study by suggesting that women can desire and shape sexual experience. Finally, we were inhibited by the widespread social reluctance to converse frankly about sexual matters. Thus for various reasons, all stemming, at least indirectly, from modern society's powerful ideological division between the public and the private, we were indisposed to consider how important sexuality might have been to the women we were studying.

The strength of the oral history method is that it enables narrators to shape their history, even when their views contradict the assumptions of historians. As our work progressed, narrators volunteered information about their sexual and emotional lives, and often a shyly asked question would inspire lengthy, absorbing discourse. By proceeding in the direction in which these women steered us, we came to realize that sexuality and sexual identity were not incidental but were central to their lives and their community. Our narrators taught us that although securing public space was indeed important, it was strongly motivated by the need to provide a setting for the formation of intimate relationships. It is the nature of this community that it created public space for lesbians and gay men, while at the same time it organized sexuality and emotional relationships. Appreciation of this dynamic interconnection requires new ways of thinking about lesbian history.

What is an appropriate framework for studying the sexual component of a lesbian community's history and for revealing the role of sexuality in the evolution of twentieth-century lesbian and gay politics? So little research has been done in this area, that our work is still exploratory and tentative. At present, we seek primarily to understand forms of lesbian sexual expression and to identify changes in sexual norms, experiences, and ideas during the 1940s and 1950s. We also look for the forces behind these changes in the evolving culture and politics of the lesbian community. Our goal has been to ascertain what part, if any, sexuality played in the developing politics of gay liberation. As an introduction to this discussion, we shall present our method of research because it has been crucial in our move to study sexuality, and so little has been written on the use of oral history for research on this topic.

Using Oral History to Construct the History of the Buffalo Lesbian Community

The memories of our narrators are colorful, illuminating, and very moving. Our purpose, however, was not only to collect individual life stories, but also to use these as a basis for constructing the history of the community. To create from individual memories a historically valid analysis of this community presented a difficult challenge. The method we developed was slow and painstaking.[6] We treated each oral history as a historical document, taking into account the particular social position of each narrator and how that might affect her memories. We also considered how our own point of view influenced the kind of information we received and the way in which we interpreted a narrator's story. We juxtaposed all interviews with one another to identify patterns and contradictions and checked our developing understanding with other sources, such as newspaper accounts, legal cases, and labor statistics.

As mentioned earlier, we first focused on understanding and documenting lesbian bar life. From the many vibrant and humorous stories about adventures in bars and from the mountains of seemingly unrelated detail about how people spent their time, we began to identify a chronology of bars and to recognize distinctive social mores and forms of lesbian consciousness that were associated with different time periods and even with different bars. We checked and supplemented our analysis by research into newspaper accounts of bar raids and closings and actions of the State Liquor Authority. Contradictions frequently emerged in our material on bars, but, as we pursued them, we found they were rarely due to idiosyncratic or faulty memory on the part of our narrators but to the complexity of bar life. Often the differences could be resolved by taking into account the different social positions of our narrators or the kinds of questions we had asked to elicit the information we received. If conflicting views persisted we tried to return to our narrators for clarification. Usually, we found that we had misunderstood our narrators or that contradictions indeed existed in the community at the time. For instance, narrators consistently told us about the wonderful times in bars as well as how terrible they were. We came to understand that both of these conditions were part of the real experience of bar life.

When we turned our attention to sexuality and romance in this community, we were at first concerned that our method would not be adequate. Using memories to trace the evolution of sexual norms and expression is, at least superficially, more problematic than using them to document social life in bars. There are no concrete public events or institutions to which the memories can be linked. Thus, when a narrator talks about butch-fem sexuality in the forties, we must bear in mind the likelihood that she has modified her view and her practice of butch-fem sexuality in the fifties, sixties, seventies, and eighties. In contrast, when a narrator tells about bars in the forties, even though social life in bars might have changed over the last forty years, she can tie her memories to a concrete place like Ralph Martin's bar, which existed during a specific time period. Although not enough is known about historical memory to fully evaluate data derived from either type of narrative, our guess is, that at least for lesbian communities, they are equally valid.[7] The vividness of our narrators' stories suggests that the potential of oral history to generate full and rich documents about women's sexuality might be especially rich in the lesbian community. Perhaps lesbian memories about sexual ideals and experiences are not separated from the rest of life because the building of public communities is closely connected with the pursuit of intimate relationships. In addition, during this period, when gay oppression marked most lesbians' lives with fear of punishment and lack of acceptance, sexuality was one of the few areas in which many lesbians found satisfaction and pleasure. This was reinforced by the fact that, for lesbians, sexuality was not directly linked with the pain and/or danger of women's responsibility for childbearing and women's economic dependence on men. Therefore, memories of sexual experience might be more positive and more easily shared. But these ideas are tentative. An understanding of the nature of memory about sexuality must await further research.

The difficulty of tying memories about sexual or emotional life to public events does present special problems. We cannot identify specific dates for changes in sexual and emotional life, such as when sex became a public topic of conversation or when role-appropriate sex became a community concern. We can talk only of trends within the framework of decades. In addition, we are unable to find supplementary material to verify and spark our narrators' memories. There are no government documents or newspaper reports on lesbian sexuality. The best one can find are memoirs or fiction written about or by residents in other cities, and even these don't exist for participants in working-class communities of the forties.[8] In general, we have not found these problems to require significant revision of our method.

Our experience indicates that the number of people interviewed is critical to the success of our method, whether we are concerned with analyzing the history of bar life or of emotional and sexual life. We feel that between five and ten narrators' stories need to be juxtaposed in order to develop an analysis that is not changed dramatically by each new story. At the present time, our analysis of the white lesbian community of the fifties is based on oral histories from over fifteen narrators. In contrast, we have only five narrators who participated in the white community of the forties, four for the black community of the fifties, and one from the black community of the forties. Therefore, we emphasize the fifties in this article and have the greatest confidence in our analysis of that decade. Our discussion of the forties must be viewed as only tentative. Our material on the black community is not yet sufficient for separate treatment; so black and white narrators' memories are interspersed throughout the article. Ultimately, we hope to be able to write a history of each community.

Sexuality as Part of the Cultural—Political Development of the Buffalo Lesbian Community

Three features of lesbian sexuality during the forties and fifties suggest its integral connection with the lesbian community's cultural-political development. First, butch-fem roles created an authentic lesbian sexuality appropriate to the flourishing of an independent lesbian culture. Second, lesbians actively pursued rich and fulfilling sexual lives at a time when sexual subjectivity was not the norm for women. This behavior was not only consistent with the creation of a separate lesbian culture, but it also represented the roots of a personal and political feminism that characterized the gay liberation movement of the sixties. Third, although butch-fem roles and the pursuit of sexual autonomy remained constant throughout this period, sexual mores changed in relation to the evolving forms of resistance to oppression.

Most commentators on lesbian bar life in the forties and fifties have noted the prominence of butch-fem roles.[9] Our research corroborates this; we found that roles constituted a powerful code of behavior that shaped the way individuals handled themselves in daily life, including sexual expression. In addition, roles were the primary organizer for the lesbian stance toward the straight world as well as for building love relationships and for making friends.[10] To understand butch-fem roles in their full complexity is a fundamental issue for students of lesbian history; the particular concern of this article is the intricate connection between roles and sexuality. Members of the community, when explaining how one recognized a person's role, regularly referred to two underlying determinants, image, including dress and mannerism, and sexuality.[11] Some people went so far as to say that one never really knew a woman's role identity until one went to bed with her. "You can't tell butch-fem by people's dress. You couldn't even really tell in the fifties. I knew women with long hair, fem clothes, and found out they were butches. Actually I even knew one who wore men's clothes, haircuts and ties, who was a fem."

Today, butch-fem roles elicit deep emotional reactions from many heterosexuals and lesbians. The former are affronted by women assuming male prerogatives; the latter by lesbians adopting male-defined role models. The hostility is exemplified by the prevalent ugly stereotype of the butch-fem sexual dyad: the butch with her dildo or penis substitute, trying to imitate a man, and the simpering passive fem who is kept in her place by ignorance. This representation evokes pity for lesbians because women who so interact must certainly be sexually unfulfilled; one partner cannot achieve satisfaction because she lacks the "true" organ of pleasure, and the other is cheated because she is denied the complete experience of the "real thing." Our research counters the view that butch-fem roles are solely an imitation of sexist heterosexual society.

Inherent to butch-fem relationships was the presumption that the butch is the physically active partner and the leader in lovemaking. As one butch narrator explains, "I treat a woman as a woman, down to the basic fact it'd have to be my side doin' most of the doin'." Insofar as the butch was the doer and the fem was the desired one, butch-fem roles did indeed parallel the male/female roles in heterosexuality. Yet unlike the dynamics of many heterosexual relationships, the butch's foremost objective was to give sexual pleasure to a fem; it was in satisfying her fem that the butch received fulfillment. "If I could give her satisfaction to the highest, that's what gave me satisfaction." As for the fem, she not only knew what would give her physical pleasure, but she also knew that she was neither object of nor receptacle for someone else's gratification. The essence of this emotional/sexual dynamic is captured by the ideal of the "stone butch," or untouchable butch, that prevailed during this period. A "stone butch" does all the "doin' " and does not ever allow her lover to reciprocate in kind. To be untouchable meant to gain pleasure from giving pleasure. Thus, although these women did draw on models in heterosexual society, they transformed those models into an authentically lesbian interaction. Through role-playing they developed distinctive and fulfilling expressions of women's sexual love for women.

The archetypal lesbian couple of the 1940s and 1950s, the "stone butch" and the fem, poses one of the most tantalizing puzzles of lesbian history and possibly of the history of sexuality in general.[12] In a culture that viewed women as sexually passive, butches developed a position as sexual aggressor, a major component of which was untouchability. However, the active or "masculine" partner was associated with the giving of sexual pleasure, a service usually assumed to be "feminine." Conversely, the fem, although the more passive partner, demanded and received sexual pleasure and in this sense might be considered the more self-concerned or even more "selfish" partner. These attributes of butch-fem sexual identity remove sexuality from the realm of the "natural," challenging the notion that sexual perfor-mance is a function of biology and affirming the view that sexual gratification is socially constructed.

Within this framework of butch-fem roles, individual lesbians actively pursued sexual pleasure. On the one hand, butch-fem roles limited sexual expression by imposing a definite structure. On the other hand, this structure ordered and gave a determinant shape to lesbian desire, which allowed individuals to know and find what they wanted. The restrictions of butch-fem sexuality, as well as the pathways it provided for satisfaction, are best captured and explored by examining what it meant for both butch and fem that the butch was the doer; how much leeway was there before the butch became fem, or the fem became butch?

Although there was complete agreement in the community that the butch was the leader in lovemaking, there was a great deal of controversy over the feasibility or necessity of being a "stone butch." In the forties, most butches lived up to the *ideal* of "the untouchable." One fem, who was in a relationship with an untouchable butch at that time, had tried to challenge her partner's behavior but met only with resistance. Her butch's whole group—those who hung out at Ralph Martin's—were the same. "Because I asked her one time, I said, 'Do you think that you might be just the only one?' 'Oh no,' she said. 'I know I'm not, you know, that I've discussed with . . . different people.' [There were] no exceptions, which I thought was ODD, but, I thought, well, you know. This is how it is."

In the fifties, the "stone butch" became a publicly discussed model for appropriate sexual behavior, and it was a standard that young butches felt they had to achieve to be a "real" or "true" butch. In contrast to the forties, a fifties fem, who was out in the community, would not have had to ask her butch friend why she was untouchable, and if there were others like her. She would have known it was the expected behavior for butches. Today our narrators disagree over whether it was, in fact, possible to maintain the ideal and they are unclear about the degree of latitude allowed in the forties or fifties before a butch harmed her reputation. Some butches claim that they were absolutely untouchable; that was how they were, and that's how they enjoyed sex. When we confronted one of our narrators, who referred to herself as an "untouchable," with the opinion of another narrator, who maintained that "stone butches" had never really existed, she replied, "No, that's not true. I'm an 'untouchable,' I've tried to have my lover make love to me, but I just couldn't stand it. . . . I really think there's something physical about that." Like many of our butch narrators, this woman has always been spontaneously orgasmic; that is, her excitement level peaks to orgasm while making love to another woman. Another "stone butch" explains: "I wanted to satisfy them [women], and I wanted to make love—I love to make love. I still think that's the greatest thing in life. But I don't want them to touch me. I feel like that spoils the whole thing—I am the way I am. And I figure if a girl is attracted to me, she's attracted to me because of what I am."

Other butches who consider themselves, and had the reputation of being, untouchable claim that it is, as a general matter, impossible to be completely untouchable. One, when asked if she were really untouchable replied, "Of course not. How would any woman stay with me if I was? It doesn't make any sense. . . . I don't believe there was ever such a class—other than what they told each other." This woman preferred not to be touched, but she did allow mutual lovemaking from time to time during her long-term relationships. A first time in bed, however:

> There's no way in hell that you would touch me . . . if you mean untouchable like that.
> But if I'm living with a woman, I'd have to be a liar if I said that she hadn't touched me.

But I can say that I don't care for it to happen. And the only reason it does happen is because she wants it. It's not like something I desire or want. But there's no such thing as an untouchable butch—and I'm the finest in Buffalo and I'm telling you straight—and don't let them jive you around it—no way.

This narrator's distinction between her behavior on a first night and her behavior in long-term relationships appeared to be accepted practice. The fact that some—albeit little—mutuality was allowed over the period of a long relationship did not affect one's reputation as an untouchable butch, nor did it counter the presumption of the butch as the doer.

This standard of untouchability was so powerful in shaping the behavior of fifties' butches that many never experienced their fems making love to them. By the seventies, however, when we began our interviewing, norms had changed enough so that our butch narrators had had opportunities to experience various forms of sexual expression. Still, many of them—in fact all of those quoted above on "stone butches"—remained untouchable. It was their personal style long after community standards changed. Today these women offer explanations for their preference that provide valuable clues about both the personal importance and the social "rightness" of untouchability as a community norm in the forties and fifties. Some women, as indicated in one of the above quotes, continue to view their discomfort with being touched as physical or biological. Others feel that if a fem were allowed the physical liberties usually associated with the butch role, distinctions would blur and the relationship would become confusing. "I feel that if we're in bed and she does the same thing to me that I do to her, we're the same thing." Another narrator, reflecting on the fact that she always went to bed with her clothes on, suggests that "what it came to was being uncomfortable with the female body. You didn't want people you were with to realize the likeness between the two." Still other butches are hesitant about the vulnerability implicit in mutual lovemaking. "When the first girl wanted to make a mutual exchange sexually, . . . I didn't want to be in the position of being at somebody's disposal, or at their command that much—maybe that's still inside me. Maybe I never let loose enough."

But many untouchables of the fifties did try mutual lovemaking later on, and it came as a pleasant surprise when they found they enjoyed being touched. "For some reason . . . I used to get enough mental satisfaction by satisfying a woman . . . then it got to the point where this one woman said, 'Well, I'm just not gonna accept that,' and she started venturing, and at first I said, 'No, no,' and then I said, 'Well, why not?' and I got to enjoy it." This change was not easy for a woman who had spent many years as an "untouchable." At first she was very nervous and uncomfortable about mutual sex, but "after I started reaching physical climaxes instead of just mental, it went, that little restlessness about it. It just mellowed me right out, y'know." The social pressure of the times prevented some women from experiencing expanded forms of sexual expression they might have enjoyed, and it also put constraints upon some women who had learned mutual sex outside of a structured community. One of our narrators had begun her sex life with mutual relations and enjoyed it immensely, but in order to conform to the community standard for butches, adopted untouchability as her sexual posture. She acceded to this behavioral change willingly and saw it as a logical component of her role during this period.

How was a community able to monitor the sexual activities of its members, and how might people come to know if a butch "rolled over"—the community lingo for a butch who allowed fems to make love to her? The answer was simple; fems talked! A butch's reputation was based on her performance with fems.

Despite the fact that sexual performance could build or destroy a butch's reputation, some butches of the fifties completely ignored the standard of untouchability. Our narrators give two reasons for this. One reason is the opinion that a long-term relationship requires some degree of mutuality to survive. One butch, a respected leader of the community because of her principles, her affability, and her organizational skills, was not only "touchable" but also suspects that most of the butches she knew in the fifties were not "stone butches." "Once you get in bed or in your bedroom and the lights go out, when you get in between those sheets, I don't think there's any male or there's any female or butch or fem, and it's a fifty-fifty thing. And I think that any relationship . . . any true relationship that's gonna survive has got to be that way. You can't be a giver and can't be a taker. You've gotta both be givers and both gotta be takers." The second reason is the pleasure of being touched. Some women experienced this in the fifties and continued to follow the practice.

> When it came to sex [in the fifties] butches were untouchable, so to speak. They did all the lovemaking, but love was not made back to them. And after I found out how different it was, and how great it was, I said, "What was I missing?" I remember a friend of mine, that I had, who dressed like a man all her life . . . and I remember talking to [her] and saying to her, you know you've got to stop being an untouchable butch, and she just couldn't agree. And I remember one time reaching over and pinching her and I said, "Did you feel that?" and she said, "Yes," and I said, "It hurt, didn't it? Well, why aren't you willing to feel something that's good?"

We do not know if in the forties, as in the fifties, butches who preferred a degree of mutuality in lovemaking existed side by side with the ideal of untouchability because we have considerably less information on that decade. Therefore, we cannot judge whether there was in fact a development toward mutual sexuality, the dominant form of lesbian lovemaking of the sixties and seventies, or whether the "stone butch" prescribed ideal and mutual lovemaking couples existed side by side consistently throughout the forties and fifties.

Our information on fem sexuality is not as extensive as that on butch sexuality because we have been able to contact fewer fem narrators. Nevertheless, from the fems we have interviewed and from comments by butches who sought them out and loved them, we do have an indication that fems were not passive receivers of pleasure, but for the most part, knew what they wanted and pursued it.[13] Many butches attributed their knowledge of sex to fems, who educated them by their sexual responsiveness as well as by their explicit directions in lovemaking.

As implied by our discussion of butch sexuality, many fems had difficulty accepting "untouchability." One fem narrator of the forties had a ten-year relationship with an untouchable butch, and the sexual restrictions were a source of discomfort for her. "It was very one-sided, you know, and . . . you never really got a chance to express your love. And I think this kind of suppressed . . . your feelings, your emotions. And I don't know whether that's healthy. I don't think so." But at the same time the majority of these fems appreciated being the center of attention; they derived a strong sense of self-fulfillment from seeking their own satisfaction and giving pleasure—by responding to their butches. "I've had some that I couldn't touch no parts of their bodies. It was all about me. Course I didn't mind! But every once in a while I felt like, well, hey, let me do something to you. I could NEVER understand that. 'Cause I lived with a girl. I couldn't touch any part of her, no part. But boy, did she make me feel good, so I said . . . All right with me . . . I don't mind laying down."

What emerges from our narrators' words is in fact a range of sexual desires that were built into the framework of role-defined sexuality. For butches of the period, we found those who preferred untouchability; those who learned it and liked it; those who learned it and adjusted to it for a time; those who preferred it, but sensed the need for some mutuality; and those who practiced mutuality regularly. For fems, we found those who accepted pleasure, thereby giving pleasure to their lovers; usually such women would aggressively seek what they wanted and instruct their lovers with both verbal and nonverbal cues. Some fems actively sought to make love to their butches and were successful. And finally, we found some women who were not consistent in their roles, changing according to their partners. In the varied sex lives of these role-identified women of the past, we can find the roots of "personal-political" feminism. Women's concern with the ultimate satisfaction of other women is part of a strong sense of female and potentially feminist agency and may be the wellspring for the confidence, the goals, and the needs that shaped the later gay and lesbian feminist movement. Thus, when we develop our understanding of this community as a predecessor to the gay liberation movement, our analysis must include sexuality. For these lesbians actively sought, expanded, and shaped their sexual experience, a radical undertaking for women in the 1940s and 1950s.

Although butch-fem roles were the consistent framework for sexual expression, sexual mores changed and developed throughout this period; two contradictory trends emerged. First, the community became more open to the acceptance of new sexual practices, the discussion of sexual matters, and the learning about sex from friends as well as lovers. Second, the rules of butch-fem sexuality became more rigid, in that community concern for role-appropriate behavior increased.

In the forties there were at least two social groups, focused in two prominent bars, Ralph Martin's and Winters. According to our narrators, the sexual mores of these two groups differed: the former group was somewhat conservative; the latter group was more experimental, presaging what were to become the accepted norms of the fifties. The lesbian patrons of Ralph Martin's did not discuss sex openly, and oral sex was disdained. "People didn't talk about sex. There was no intimate conversation. It was kind of hush, hush . . . I didn't know there were different ways." By way of contrast, this narrator recalls a visit to Winters, where other women were laughing about "sixty-nine." "I didn't get it. I went to [my partner] and said, 'Somebody says "sixty-nine" and everybody gets hysterical.' " Finally her partner learned what the laughter was all about. At that time our narrator would have mentioned such intimacies only with a lover. It wasn't until later that she got into bull sessions about such topics. Not surprisingly, this narrator does not recall having been taught about sex. She remembers being scared during her first lesbian experience, then found that she knew what to do "naturally." She had no early affairs with partners older than herself.

The Winters' patrons had a more open, experimental attitude toward sex; they discussed it unreservedly and accepted the practice of oral sex. These women threw parties in which women tried threesomes and daisy chains. "People would try it and see how it worked out. But nothing really happened. One person would always get angry and leave, and they would end up with two." Even if their sexual adventures did not always turn out as planned, these women were unquestionably innovative for their time. Our narrator from the Winters' crowd reminisced that it was always a contrast to go home to the serene life of her religious family. She also raved about two fems who were her instructors in sexual matters, adding, "I was an apt pupil."

During the fifties the picture changed, and the mores of the Ralph Martin's group virtually disappeared. Sex came to be a conversation topic among all social groups. Oral sex became an accepted form of lovemaking, so that an individual who did not practice it was acting on personal preference rather than on ignorance or social proscription. In addition, most of our fifties' butch narrators recall having been teachers or students of sex.

As in the Winters' group in the forties, an important teacher for the butch was the fem. "I had one girl who had been around who told me. I guess I really frustrated the hell out of her. And she took a piece of paper and drew me a picture and she said, 'Now you get this spot right here.' I felt like a jerk. I was embarrassed that she had to tell me this." According to our narrator, the lesson helped, and she explains that, "I went on to greater and better things."

The fifties also saw the advent of a completely new practice—experienced butches teaching novice butches about sex. One narrator remembers that younger women frequently approached her with questions about sex: "There must be an X on my back. They just pick me out. . . ." She recalls one young butch who "had to know every single detail. She drove me crazy. Jesus Christ, y'know, just get down there and do it— y'get so aggravated." The woman who aggravated her gives the following account of learning about sex:

> And I finally talked to a butch buddy of mine. . . . She was a real tough one. I asked her "What do you do when you make love to a woman?" And we sat up for hours and hours at a time. . . . "I feel sexually aroused by this woman, but if I take her to bed, what am I gonna do?" And she says, "Well, what do you feel like doing?" And I says "Well, the only thing I can think of doing is . . . all I want to do is touch her, but what is the full thing of it . . . you know." So when [she] told me I says, "Really," well there was this one thing in there, uh . . . I don't know if you want me to state it. Maybe I can . . . well, I won't . . . I'll put in terms that you can understand. Amongst other things, the oral gratification. Well, that kind of floored me because I never expected something like that and I thought, well, who knows, I might like it.

She later describes her first sexual experience in which she was so scared that her friend had to shove her into the bedroom where the girl was waiting.

At the same time that attitudes toward discussions of and teachings about sexuality relaxed, the fifties' lesbian community became stricter in enforcing role-appropriate sexuality. Those who deviated from the pattern in the forties might have identified themselves as "lavender butch" and might have been labeled by others as "comme ci, comme ça." Although their divergence from the social norm would have been noticed and discussed, such women were not stigmatized. But the community of the fifties left little room to deviate. Those who did not consistently follow one role in bed were considered "ki-ki" (neither-nor), or more infrequently "AC/DC," both pejorative terms imposed by the community. Such women were viewed as disruptive of the social order and not to be trusted. They not only elicited negative comments, but they also were often ostracized from social groups. From the perspective of the 1980s, in which mutuality in lovemaking is emphasized as a positive quality, it is important to clarify that "ki-ki" did not refer to an abandonment of role-defined sex but rather to a shifting of sexual posture depending upon one's bed partner. Therefore, it was grounded absolutely in role playing. One of our narrators in fact defined "ki-ki" as "double role playing."[14]

These contradictory trends in attitudes and normal of lesbian sexuality parallel changes in the heterosexual world. Movement toward open discussion of sex, the acceptance of oral sex, and the teaching about sex took place in the society at large, as exemplified by the publication of and the material contained in the Kinsey reports.[15] Similarly, the lesbian community's stringent enforcement of role-defined behavior in the fifties occurred in the context of straight society's postwar move toward a stricter sexual division of labor and the ideology that accompanied it.[16] These parallels indicate a close connection between the evolution of heterosexual and homosexual cultures, a topic that requires further research.[17]

At this point, we wish to stress that drawing parallels with heterosexuality can only partially illuminate changes in lesbian sexual mores. As an integral part of lesbian life, lesbian sexuality undergoes transformations that correspond with changing forms of the community's resistance to oppression.

Two developments occurred in this prepolitical period that are fundamental for the later emergence of the lesbian and gay liberation movement of the sixties. The first development was the flourishing of a lesbian culture; the second was the evolving stance of public defiance. The community of the forties was just beginning to support places for public gatherings and socializing, and during this period lesbians were to be found in bars only on weekends. Narrators of the forties do not remember having role models or anyone willing to instruct them in the ways of gay life. The prevalent feeling was that gay life was hard, and if people wanted it, they had to find it for themselves. In the fifties, the number of lesbian bars increased, and lesbians could be found socializing there every night of the week. As bar culture became more elaborate and open, lesbians more freely exchanged information about all aspects of their social lives, including sexuality. Discussion of sex was one of many dimensions of an increasingly complex culture. The strengthening of lesbian culture and the concomitant repression of gays in the fifties led the community to take a more public stance. This shift toward public confrontation subsequently generated enough sense of pride to counter the acknowledged detriments of gay life so that members of the community were willing to instruct newcomers both socially and sexually. Almost all our narrators who came out in the fifties remember a butch who served as a role model or remember acting as a role model themselves. Instruction about sexuality was part of a general education to community life that developed in the context of expanding community pride.

However, the community's growing public defiance was also related to its increased concern for enforcing role-appropriate behavior in the fifties. Butches were key in this process of fighting back. The butches alone, or the butch-fem couple, were always publicly visible as they walked down the street, announcing themselves to the world. To deal effectively with the hostility of the straight world, and to support one another in physical confrontations, the community developed, for butches in particular, rules of appropriate behavior and forms of organization and exerted pressure on butches to live up to these standards. Because roles organized intimate life, as well as the community's resistance to oppression, sexual performance was a vital part of these fifties' standards.

From the vantage point of the 1980s and twenty more years of lesbian and gay history, we know that just as evolving community politics created this tension between open discussion and teaching about sex and strict enforcement of role-appropriate sexual behavior, it also effected the resolution. Our research suggests that in the late sixties in Buffalo, with the development of the political activities of gay liberation, explicitly political organizations and tactics replaced butch-fem roles in leading the resistance to gay oppression. Because butch-fem roles were no longer the primary means for organizing the community's stance toward the straight world, the community no longer needed to enforce role-appropriate behavior.[18] This did not mean that butch-fem roles disappeared. As part of a long tradition of creating an authentic lesbian culture in an oppressive society, butch-fem roles remain, for many lesbians, an important code of personal behavior in matters of either appearance, sexuality, or both.

Notes

This article is a revision of a paper originally presented at the "International Conference on Women's History and Oral History," Columbia University, New York, 18 November 1983. We want to thank Michael

Frisch, Ellen DuBois, and Bobbi Prebis for reading the original version and offering us helpful comments. We also want to thank Rayna Rapp and Ronald Grele for their patience throughout the revision process.

1. This research is part of the work of the Buffalo Women's Oral History Project, which was founded in 1978 with three goals: (1) to produce a comprehensive, written history of the lesbian community in Buffalo, New York, using as the major source, oral histories of lesbians who came out prior to 1970; (2) to create and index an archive of oral history tapes, written interviews, and relevant supplementary materials; and (3) to give this history back to the community from which it derives. Madeline Davis and Elizabeth (Liz) Kennedy are the directors of the project. Avra Michelson was an active member from 1978 to 1981 and had a very important influence on the development of the project. Wanda Edwards has been an active member of the project since 1981, particularly in regard to research on the black lesbian community and on racism in the white lesbian community.

2. This hypothesis was shaped by our personal contact with Buffalo lesbians who came out in the 1940s and 1950s, and by discussion with grass roots gay and lesbian history projects around the country, in particular, the San Francisco Lesbian and Gay History Project, the Boston Area Gay and Lesbian History Project, and the Lesbian Herstory Archives. Our approach is close to and has been influenced by the social constructionist tendency of lesbian and gay history. See in particular, Jonathan Katz, *Gay American History, Lesbians and Gay Men in the U.S.A.* (New York: Thomas Y. Crowell Co., 1976); Gayle Rubin, Introduction to *A Woman Appeared to Me* by Renée Vivien (Nevada: Naiad Press, 1976), iii–xxxvii; Jeffrey Weeks, *Coming Out: Homosexual Politics in Britain from the Nineteenth Century to the Present* (London: Quartet Books, 1977). We want to thank all these sources which have been inspirational to our work.

3. The Buffalo Women's Oral History Project has written two papers on bar life, both by Madeline Davis, Elizabeth (Liz) Kennedy, and Avra Michelson: "Buffalo Lesbian Bars in the Fifties," presented at the National Women's Studies Association, Bloomington, Indiana, May 1980, and "Buffalo Lesbian Bars: 1930–1960," presented at the Fifth Berkshire Conference on the History of Women, Vassar College, Poughkeepsie, N.Y., June 1981. Both papers are on file at the Lesbian Herstory Archives, P.O. Box 1258, New York, New York 10116.

4. We think that this community could accurately be designated as a working-class lesbian community, but this is not a concept many members of this community would use; therefore, we have decided to call it a public bar community.

5. All quotes are taken from the interviews conducted for this project between 1978 and 1984. The use of the phrase "lesbian and her girl" in this quote reflects some of our butch narrators' belief that the butch member of a couple was the lesbian and the fem member's identity was less clear.

6. A variety of sources were helpful for learning about issues and problems of oral history research. They include the Special Issue on Women's Oral History, *Frontiers* 2 (Summer 1977); Willa K. Baum, *Oral History for the Local Historical Society* (Nashville, Tenn.: American Association for State and Local History, 1974); Michael Frisch, "Oral History and *Hard Times:* A Review Essay," *Oral History Review* (1979): 70–80; Ronald Grele, ed., *Envelopes of Sound: Six Practitioners Discuss the Method, Theory, and Practice of Oral History and Oral Tradition* (Chicago: Precedent Publishing, 1975); Ronald Grele, "Can Anyone over Thirty Be Trusted: A Friendly Critique of Oral History," *Oral History Review* (1978): 36–44; "Generations: Women in the South," *Southern Exposure* 4 (Winter 1977); "No More Moanin'," *Southern Exposure* 1 (Winter 1974); Peter Friedlander, *The Emergence of a UAW Local, 1936–1939* (Pittsburgh: University of Pittsburgh Press, 1975); William Lynwood Montell, *The Saga of Coe Ridge: A Study in Oral History* (Knoxville: University of Tennessee Press, 1970); Studs Terkel, *Hard Times: An Oral History of the Great Depression* (New York: Pantheon Books, 1970); Martin B. Duberman, *Black Mountain: An Exploration in Community* (Garden City, N.J.: Doubleday, 1972); Sherna Gluck, ed., *From Parlor to Prison: Five American Suffragists Talk about Their Lives* (New York: Vintage, 1976); and Kathy Kahn, *Hillbilly Women* (New York: Doubleday, 1972).

7. For a helpful discussion of memory, see John A. Neuenschwander, "Rememberance of Things Past: Oral Historians and Long-Term Memory," *Oral History Review* (1978): 46–53; many sources cited in the previous note also have relevant discussions of memory; in particular, see Frisch; Grele, *Envelopes of Sound:* Friedlander; and Montell.

8. See for instance, Joan Nestle, "Esther's Story: 1960," *Common Lives/Lesbian Lives* 1 (Fall 1981): 5–9; Joan Nestle, "Butch-Fem Relationships, Sexual Courage in the 1950s," *Heresies* 12 (1981): 21–24; Audre Lorde, "Tar Beach," *Conditions,* no. 5 (1979): 34–47; and Audre Lorde, "The Beginning," in *Lesbian Fiction,* ed. Elly Bulkin (Watertown, Mass.: Persephone Press, 1981), 255–74. Lesbian pulp fiction can also provide insight into the emotional and sexual life of this period; see for instance, Ann Bannon's *I Am a Woman* (Greenwich, Conn.: Fawcett Publications, 1959) and *Beebo Brinker* (Greenwich, Conn.: Fawcett Publications, 1962).

9. See, for instance, Nestle, "Butch-Fem Relationships"; Lorde, "Tar Beach"; Del Martin and Phyllis Lyon, *Lesbian/Woman* (New York: Bantam Books, 1972); John D'Emilio, *Sexual Politics, Sexual Communities: The*

Making of a Homosexual Minority in the United States, 1940–1970 (Chicago: University of Chicago Press, 1983).

10. For a full discussion of our research on butch-fem roles, see Madeline Davis and Elizabeth (Liz) Kennedy, "Butch-Fem Roles in the Buffalo Lesbian Community, 1940–1960" (paper presented at the Gay Academic Union Conference, Chicago, October 1982). This paper is on file at the Lesbian Herstory Archives.

11. These two main determinants of roles are quite different from what would usually be considered as indicators of sex roles in straight society; they do not include the sexual division of labor.

12. The origins of the "stone butch" and fem couple are beyond the scope of this paper. For an article that begins to approach these issues, see Esther Newton, "The Mythic Mannish Lesbian: Radclyffe Hall and the New Woman," *Signs* 9 (Summer 1984): 557–75.

13. Our understanding of the fem role has been enhanced by the following: Nestle's "Butch-Fem Relationships" and "Esther's Story"; Amber Hollibaugh and Cherrie Moraga, "What We're Rolling Around in Bed With: Sexual Silences in Feminism: A Conversation toward Ending Them," *Heresies* 12 (1981): 58–62.

14. For indications that "ki-ki" was used nationally in the lesbian subculture, see Jonathan Katz, *Gay/Lesbian Almanac, A New Documentary* (New York: Harper & Row, 1983), 15, 626.

15. Alfred C. Kinsey, Wardell B. Pomeroy, and Clyde E. Martin, *Sexual Behavior in the Human Male* (Philadelphia: W.B. Saunders Co., 1948); and Alfred Kinsey et al., *Sexual Behavior in the Human Female* (Philadelphia: W.B. Saunders Co., 1953). Numerous sources document this trend; see, for instance, Ann Snitow, Christine Stansell, and Sharon Thompson, eds, *Powers of Desire: The Politics of Sexuality* (New York: Monthly Review Press, 1983), in particular, Introduction, sec. 2, "Sexual Revolutions," and sec. 3, "The Institution of Heterosexuality," 9–47, 115–71, 173–275; and Katz, *Gay/Lesbian Almanac.*

16. See Mary P. Ryan. *Womanhood in America: From Colonial Times to the Present* (New York: Franklin Watts, 1975).

17. A logical result of the social constructionist school of gay history is to consider that heterosexuality is also a social construction. Katz, in *Gay/Lesbian Almanac,* begins to explore this idea.

18. Although national homophile organizations began in the fifties, no such organizations developed in Buffalo until the formation of the Mattachine Society of the Niagara Frontier in 1969. But we do not think that the lack of early homophile organizations in this city made the bar community's use of roles as an organizer of its stance toward the straight world different from that of cities where homophile organizations existed. In general, these organizations, whether mixed or all women, did not draw from or affect bar communities. Martin and Lyon in chap. 8, "Lesbians United," *Lesbian/Woman* (238–79), present Daughters of Bilitis (DOB) as an alternative for those dissatisfied with bar life, not as an organization to coalesce the forces and strengths of the bar community. Gay liberation combined the political organization of DOB and the defiance and pride of bar life and therefore affected and involved both communities.

29

Race and "Value": Black and White Illegitimate Babies, in the U.S., 1945–1965

Rickie Solinger

There are two histories of single pregnancy in the post-World War II era, one for Black women and one for white. But for girls and women of both races, being single and pregnant revealed that either publicly or privately, their fertility could become a weapon used by others to keep them vulnerable, defenseless, and dependent, in danger without male protection. One aspect of single pregnancy which sharply and powerfully illustrates both the common vulnerability of unwed mothers and the racially distinct treatment they received, is the matter of what an unmarried girl or woman would or could do with her illegitimate child.[1]

Throughout my study of unwed pregnancy in the period before the crucial Supreme Court decision of 1973 (*Roe v. Wade* era),[2] racially distinct ideas about the "value" of the illegitimate baby surface again and again as central to an unmarried mother's fate. In short, after World War II, the white bastard child was no longer the child nobody wanted. The Black illegitimate baby became the child white politicians and taxpayers loved to hate. The central argument of this essay is that the "value" of illegitimate babies has been quite different in different historical eras, and that in the United States during the mid-twentieth century, the emergence of racially specific attitudes toward illegitimate babies, including ideas about what to do with them, fundamentally shaped the experiences of single mothers.

Social, cultural, and economic imperatives converged in the postwar era so as to sanction very narrow and rigid, but different, options for Black and white unwed mothers, no matter what their personal preferences. Black single mothers were expected to keep their babies, as most unwed mothers, Black and white, had done throughout the history of the United States. Unmarried white mothers, for the first time in this country's history, were urged to put their babies up for adoption. These racially specific prescriptions exacerbated racism and racial antagonism in postwar America, and have influenced the politics of female fertility into our own time.

During the Progressive Era of the late nineteenth and early twentieth centuries up through the 1930s, social commentators and social service professionals typically considered an illegitimate baby as a "child of sin," the product of a mentally deficient mother.[3] As such, this child was tainted and undesirable. The girl or woman, Black or white, who gave birth to it was expected by family, by the community, and by the state to bring it up. Commentators assumed that others rarely wanted a child who stood to inherit the sinful character—the mental and moral weaknesses—of its parent. Before World War II, state laws and institutional regulations supported this mandate not so much because there were

---

Reprinted with permission from *Gender & History*, vol. 4, no. 3, Autumn 1992.

others vying for the babies, but to ensure that the mothers would not abandon the infants. State legislators in Minnesota and elsewhere required mothers seeking care in maternity homes to breast-feed their babies for three months or more, long enough to establish unseverable bonds between infant and mother.[4]

Prewar experts stressed that the biology of illegitimacy stamped the baby permanently with marks of mental and moral deficiency, and affirmed that moral conditions were embedded in and revealed by these biological events.[5] Likewise, the unwed mother's pregnancy both revealed her congenital and moral shortcomings and condemned her, through the illicit conception and birth, to carry the permanent stain of biological and moral ruin. The experience of pregnancy she underwent was tied to her moral status in a fixed, direct, and inexorable relationship. Equally important, her motherhood was immutable. While the deficiencies, the stain, and her ruination violated her biological integrity, as well as her social and moral standing in the community, the unwed mother's maternal relation to the child was not compromised. That was also fixed directly and inexorably by the facts of conception and birth.

These attitudes reflected, in part, the importance of bridal virginity and marital conception in mainstream American culture. They also reflected early twentieth-century ideas among moral and medical authorities regarding the strong link between physical, mental, and moral degeneracy and the degeneracy of sex. Until the 1940s, illegitimacy usually carried one meaning; cultural, racial, or psychological determinants which admitted group or individual variability were not sought to explain its occurrence. In this prewar period, social, religious, and educational leaders rarely called for the rehabilitation of unwed mothers, or suggested that there were steps they could take to restore their marriageability and their place in the community. What was lost could not be regained; what was acquired could not be cast off. Consequently, most unwed mothers without family or kinship resources did not have choices to make in that era about the disposition of the bastard child.

After the war, state-imposed breast-feeding regulations and institutional policies asserting the immutability of the white mother's relationship to her illegitimate baby became harder to sustain in the face of a complex and changing set of social conditions. First, the demographic facts of single pregnancy were changing. While birth control and abortion remained illegal and hard to obtain, more girls and women were participating in nonmarital, heterosexual intercourse; thus more of them became pregnant and carried babies to term.[6] As nonmarital sex and pregnancy became more common (and then very common during the later postwar period), it became increasingly difficult to sequester, punish and insist on the permanent ruination of ever-larger numbers of girls and women. This was particularly the case since many of these single pregnant females were members of the growing proportion of the population that considered itself middle class. As a result, it became increasingly difficult for parents and the new service professionals, themselves members of the middle class, to sanction treating "our daughters" as permanently ruined.

In addition, a strain of postwar optimism emerged that rejected the view that the individual white unwed mother was at the mercy of harmful environmental or other "forces" which had the power to determine her fate. The modern expert offered the alternative claim that illegitimacy reflected an emotional, psychological, not environmental or biological disorder and was, in general, a symptom of individual, treatable neuroses. Reliance on the psychological explanation redeemed both American society and the individual female. Moreover, by moving the governing imperative from the body (biology) to the mind (psychology), all of the fixed relationships previously defining white illegitimacy became mutable, indeterminate, even deniable.

Psychological explanations transformed the white unwed mother from a genetically tainted unfortunate into a maladjusted woman who could be cured. While there was no solvent that could remove the biological stain of illegitimacy, the neuroses that fostered illegitimacy could respond to treatment. The white out-of-wedlock child, therefore, was no longer a flawed by-product of innate immortality and low intelligence. The child's innocence was restored and its adoptability established. At the same time, psychologists argued that white unwed mothers, despite their deviate behavior, could be rehabilitated, and that a successful cure rested in large measure on the relinquishment of the child.[7] The white unwed mother no longer had an immutable relationship to her baby.

In postwar America, the social conditions of motherhood, along with notions about the psychological status of the unwed mother, became more important than biology in defining white motherhood. Specifically, for the first time, it took more than a baby to make a white girl or woman into a mother. Without a preceding marriage, a white female could not achieve true motherhood.[8] Accepting these new imperatives, social authorities insisted on the centrality of the male to female adult roles, thereby offsetting postwar concerns that women were aggressively undermining male prerogatives in the United States. Experts explained that the unwed mother who came to terms with the baby's existence, symbolically or concretely, and relinquished the child, enhanced her ability to "function [in the future] as a healthy wife and mother."[9]

Release from the biological imperative represented a major reform in the treatment of the many white unwed mothers who desperately desired a way out of trouble, a way to undo their life-changing mistake. The rising rate and number of white single pregnancies, particularly among unmarried middle-class women, would have created an ever-larger number of ruined girls and women if unwed mothers continued to have no option but to keep their illegitimate children. The opportunity to place an illegitimate child for adoption became, in a sense, an unplanned but fortuitous safety valve for thousands of white girls and women who became unwed mothers but—thanks to the sanctioning of adoption—could go on to become properly married wives and mothers soon thereafter. This arrangement could only work if there was a sizable population of white couples who wanted to adopt infants and who did not mind if the babies had been born to unwed mothers. This condition was met in part because the postwar family imperative put new pressures on and suggested more intense pleasures to infertile couples who in the past would have remained childless. A social scientist in the mid-1950s referred to illegitimate babies as "the silver lining in a dark cloud" and a "blessing" to the many involuntarily childless couples trying to adopt a child.[10] In the early 1950s a leading social-work theorist, using what was becoming a popular metaphor, worried about "the tendency growing out of the demand for babies to regard unmarried mothers as breeding machines ... [by people intent] upon securing babies for quick adoptions."[11]

Through adoption, then, the unwed mother could put the mistake—both the baby *qua* baby, and the proof of nonmarital sexual experience—behind her. Her parents were not stuck with a ruined daughter and a bastard grandchild for life. And the baby could be brought up in a normative family, by a couple prejudged to possess all the attributes and resources necessary for successful parenthood.

Some unmarried pregnant girls considered abortion the best way to efface their mistake, but the possibility in the mid-1950s of getting a safe, legal, hospital abortion was slim, in fact, slimmer than it had been in the prewar decades.[12] But if a girl or woman knew about hospital abortions, she might appeal to a hospital abortion committee, a (male) panel of the director of obstetrics/gynecology, and the chiefs of medicine, surgery, neuropsychiatry, and pediatrics. In hospitals, including Mt. Sinai in New York which set up an abortion committee in 1952, the panel of doctors met once a week and considered cases of women who could bring letters from two specialists diagnosing them as psychologically impaired and unfit to be mothers.[13]

By the early 1950s, doctors claimed that new procedures and medications had eliminated the need for almost all medically indicated abortions.[14] That left only psychiatric grounds, which might have seemed promising for girls and women desperate not to have a child.[15] After all, psychiatric explanations were in vogue, and white unwed mothers were categorically diagnosed as deeply neurotic, or worse. There was, however, a catch. These abortion committees had been set up to begin with because their very existence was meant to reduce requests for "therapeutic" abortions, which they did.[16] It was, in fact, a matter of pride and competition among hospitals to have the highest ratio of births to abortions on record.[17] But even though psychiatric illness was the only remaining acceptable basis for request, many doctors did not believe in these grounds. A professor of obstetrics in a large university hospital said, "We haven't done a therapeutic abortion for psychiatric reasons in ten years. . . . We don't recognize psychiatric indications."[18] So an unwed pregnant girl or woman could be diagnosed and certified as disturbed, probably at considerable cost, but she could not convince the panel that she was sick enough. The committee may have, in fact, agreed with the outside specialists that the abortion petitioner was psychotic, but the panel often claimed the problem was temporary, with sanity recoverable upon delivery.[19]

The doctors were apparently not concerned with questions about when life begins. They were very concerned with what they took to be their responsibility to protect and preserve the links between femininity, maternity, and marriage. One doctor spoke for many of his colleagues when he complained of the "clever, scheming women, simply trying to hoodwink the psychiatrist and obstetrician" in their appeals for permission for abortions.[20] The mere request, in fact, was taken, according to another doctor, "as proof [of the petitioner's] inability and failure to live through the destiny of being a woman."[21] If such permission were granted, one claimed, the woman "will become an unpleasant person to live with and possibly lose her glamour as a wife. She will gradually lose conviction in playing a female role."[22] An angry committee member, refusing to grant permission to one woman, asserted, "Now that she has had her fun, she wants us to launder her dirty underwear. From my standpoint, she can sweat this one out."[23]

For many doctors, however, condemning the petitioner to sweat it out was not sufficient punishment. In the mid-1950s, in Maryland, a doctor would almost never agree to perform a therapeutic abortion unless he sterilized the woman at the same time.[24] The records of a large, midwestern general hospital showed that between 1941 and 1950, seventy-five percent of the abortions performed there were accompanied by sterilization.[25] The bottom line was that if you were single and pregnant (and without rich or influential parents who might, for example, make a significant philanthropic gesture to the hospital) your chances with the abortion committee were pretty bleak. Thousands of unhappily pregnant women each year got illegal abortions, but for thousands of others, financially, morally, or otherwise unable to arrange for the operation, adoption seemed their only choice.

Service agencies, however, found the task of implementing the adoption mandate complicated. Many who worked with white unwed mothers in maternity homes, adoption agencies, or public welfare offices in this period had to braid unmatched strands into a coherent plan. Agency workers were deeply uneasy about separating babies from the one individual who until recently had been historically and culturally designated as best suited, no matter what her marital status, to care for her own baby. In addition, the community response to out-of-wedlock pregnancy and maternity in the United States had historically been punitive.[26] Keeping mother and child together was simultaneously in the child's best interest and the earned wages of sin for the unwed mother. Until the postwar era, most social workers had trained and practiced in this tradition.[27]

After World War II, social workers struggled to discard the two most basic assumptions that had previously guided their work with white unwed mothers. These girls and women were no longer considered the best mothers for their babies. And they would no longer be expected to pay for their illicit sexual experience and illegitimate pregnancy by living as ruined women and outcast mothers of bastard children. Social workers were now to offer them a plan which would protect them from lasting stigma and rehabilitate them for normative female roles. The psychological literature supporting definitions of unwed mothers as not-mothers, the interest of many white couples in obtaining newborn babies, and postwar concepts of family helped social workers accept new ideas about the disposition of illegitimate white babies.

After the war, in all parts of the country, public agencies, national service organizations, and maternity homes allocated resources and developed techniques for separating mother and child. Services became so streamlined that in many maternity homes, such as the Florence Crittenton Home in Houston, "Babies [went] directly from the hospital to children's [adoption] agencies."[28] Indeed, public and private agencies were functioning in an environment in which the separation of single mother and child was becoming the norm. In Minnesota for example, in 1925 there were two hundred such separations; in 1949, one thousand; between 1949 and 1955, approximately seventeen hundred each year. Nationally, by 1955, ninety thousand babies born out of wedlock were being placed for adoption, an eighty percent increase since 1944.[29]

To meet the demand, agencies and individual operators not infrequently resorted to questionable tactics, including selling babies for profit. When the federal government undertook to investigate widespread coercive and profit-oriented adoption practices in the United States in the 1950s, the task was assigned to Senator Estes Kefauver's Subcommittee to Investigate Juvenile Delinquency. This committee was charged with redressing the problem of adoption for profit and assuring the "suitability of the home" for adoptable children, a criterion which could not, by definition, be met in homes headed by unmarried mothers.[30] While illegitimate pregnancy and babies had, in the past, been a private matter handled by family members, perhaps assisted by charity workers, by mid-century, these issues had become public concerns and public business.

The Kefauver committee and the organizations and individuals it investigated defined white unmarried mothers out of their motherhood. If not by law, then *de facto*, they were not parents. This judgment was in line with and supported various forms of state control over single, pregnant girls and women, and those who might become pregnant, including, of course, the state's formal and informal proscriptions against birth control for unmarried girls and women, its denial of access to safe, legal abortion, and its tolerance in many places of unsafe, illegal abortions. The state determined what types of agencies and individuals an unmarried mother could deal with in planning for her child, and either suggested strongly or legislated which ones were "morally wrong." These state prerogatives allowed some agencies and individuals to abuse and exploit childbearing single white women.

A very articulate, eighteen-year-old, unmarried mother from Minnesota wrote to her Governor in August, 1950, illustrating how some public agencies took direct action to separate white babies from their mothers even against the mother's will. She said that a welfare worker in her city told her she could not keep her baby, "that the baby should be brought up by both a mother and a father." Having gotten no satisfaction, she wrote in frustration and anger to President Truman:

> With tears in my eyes and sorrow in my heart I'm trying to defend the rights and privileges which every citizen in the United States is supposed to enjoy under our Constitution [but are] denied me and my baby. . . . The Welfare Department refuses to give me my baby without sufficient cause or explanation. . . . I have never done any wrong and just because I had a baby under such circumstances the welfare agency has no right to condemn me and to demand my child be placed [for adoption].[31]

A year earlier, a young man living in Sterling, Colorado wrote to the Children's Bureau about a similar case. In this situation, a young man and a young deaf woman had conceived a baby out of wedlock, but planned to marry. When the man went to the Denver Welfare Department for assistance a few days before the baby was born, he found that the baby had already been targeted for adoption.[32]

This case, in particular, demonstrates a couple of key assumptions underlying the behavior of some agency workers in matters of out-of-wedlock adoptions. The young mother was deaf. As a handicapped person and an unmarried girl, her maternity, as well as her child, was considered illegitimate and could be rightfully terminated by the authorities. Physically defective women had curtailed rights as mothers, just as physically defective illegitimate babies had diminished opportunities to join the middle class. This case also suggests the very important notion that white babies were so valuable because in postwar America, they were born not only untainted but also *unclassed*. A poor "white trash" teenager could have a white baby in Appalachia; it could be adopted by an upper-middle-class couple in Westport, Connecticut, and the baby would, in that transaction, become upper-middle-class also.

Courts also facilitated adoption abuse. A Chief Probation Officer in the Richmond County, Alabama, Juvenile Court spent a great deal of her time finding and "freeing" white babies for adoption, using her position to legitimize these activities. One unwed mother told of her encounter with the officer, a Miss Hamilton. She said,

> Several hours after delivery [Miss Hamilton] informed me that my baby had been born dead. She told me that if I signed a paper she had, no one, my family or friends would know about the situation, and that everything would be cleared up easily. She described the paper as being a consent authorizing the burial of the child. . . . I signed the paper without really looking at it, as I was in a very distressed and confused condition at the time.[33]

This young woman went on to say that, "Two years later I was shocked to receive in the mail adoption papers from the Welfare Department in California since I was under the impression that the child was deceased."

Illegalities and abuse existed in some mainstream institutions, but a great many of the worst abuses were committed by individual baby brokers—lawyers, doctors, and nonprofessionals cashing in on the misfortune of unwed mothers. In postwar, consumerist America, institutions promoted services and attitudes to protect the out-of-wedlock child from market-driven deals and to see that it was well placed. On the other hand, these same institutions were themselves behaving in market-oriented ways as they promoted a specific, socially beneficial product: the two-parent/two-plus-child family. This double message justified the baby brokers' commoditylike treatment of unwed mothers and their babies. Charlton G. Blair, a lawyer who handled between thirty and sixty adoptions a year in the late 1950s justified his operation by denying he ever "paid one red cent" to a prospective mother of an illegitimate child to persuade her to part with the baby. But in suggesting why the adopting parents were willing to pay up to fifteen hundred dollars for a child, which included the lawyer's $750.00 fee, Blair defined his sense of the transaction very clearly: "If they're willing to pay three thousand dollars for an automobile these days, I don't see why they can't pay this much for a child."[34]

A case which dramatically captures the plight of poor, white, unwed mothers was presented at the Kefauver hearings by Mary Grice, an investigative reporter for the *Wichita Beacon*. Grice testified about a woman, "Mrs. T.," who had been in the adoption business since 1951 or 1952. "Mrs. T." warehoused unwed, pregnant girls in the basement of her home. "She would have them on cots for prospective adoptive parents [who] would come in and she would take them downstairs, and she would point to the girls and say, 'Point out the girl that you want to be the mother of your child.' " Grice's investigation revealed that "Mrs. T." kept on average seven unmarried mothers in her basement at a time and that she would oversee a number of the deliveries herself in the basement. According to Grice, between one hundred and fifty and one hundred and sixty-four adoptions each year of this sort were taking place in Sedgwick County, Kansas. "Mrs. T." often collaborated with Grace Schauner, a Wichita abortionist. Unmarried pregnant girls and women would first see Schauner and if they decided not to have an abortion, they would be referred to "Mrs. T." who would "care for them and sell their infants after birth."[35]

"Mrs. T.'s" girls were poor, so they did not have the information or other resources to resist baby market operators. Because they were female (specifically, white females), their socially mandated shame precluded self-protection and motherhood. Because they were white, their babies had "value." This combination of poverty, race, and gender—in a context which defined white unwed mothers as not-mothers, and defined their babies as valuable—put some white, unwed mothers in a position of extreme vulnerability.

Again, there is no question that for many white unwed mothers, the opportunity to place their babies independently meant that they could get exactly what they needed when they needed it: money to live on, shelter, medical care, and assurances about the placement of the baby, all with no questions asked. "These girls and women were often spared the delays, the layers of authority, the invasions of privacy, the permanent black mark engraved in the files of the welfare department," and they were spared the pressure to reveal the father's name, all of which characterized the bureaucratic agency approach.[36] Their experience demonstrated how difficult it was for institutions to perform simultaneously as agents of social control and as sources of humanitarian assistance for the needy and vulnerable.

An intruder in the courtroom in Miami, Florida, where a section of the Kefauver hearings was held in November 1955, expressed the frustration of some girls and women who felt they had lost control over the disposition of their illegitimate children. This woman stood up, unbidden, and lectured the men before her in a loud voice. She said,

> Excuse me. I am not leaving no court. . . . You have to carry these children nine months and then you have them taken away by the Catholic Charities, and then they throw you out and drag you all over the street. . . . I'm no drunk, I'm no whore. . . . I gave birth to two children and had them taken away from me. I don't sleep nights thinking about my children. What do you people care? Don't take my picture. You people have no feelings at all. That man [a judge testifying that there are plenty of services available for unwed mothers] is sitting there and lying—lying. These people just take other people's children away from them. All that he has said is a lie. My baby was born . . . and I haven't seen it since. . . . How would you like it? Year after year you have to go to the people . . . and ask them why you can't have your children.[37]

Clark Vincent, a sociologist who closely followed the treatment of white unwed mothers in this era, offered the following vision of a world in the near future where the state would have restrained authority to determine who is a mother:

> If the demand for adoptable infants continues to exceed the supply; if more definitive research . . . substantiates that the majority of unwed mothers who keep their children lack the potential for "good motherhood"; and if there continues to be an emphasis through laws and courts on the "rights of the child" superseding the "rights of the parents"; then it is quite probable that in the near future unwed mothers will be "punished" by having their children taken away from them at birth. Such a policy would not be enacted nor labeled overtly as "punishment." Rather it would be implemented under such pressures and labels as "scientific finding," "the best interests of the child," "rehabilitation goals for the unwed mother," and the "stability of family and society."[38]

In postwar America, there was only one public intention for white unwed mothers and their babies: separate them. Toward Black single mothers and their babies, however, there were three broadly different public attitudes.[39] One attitude, often held by middle-of-the-road politicians, social service administrators, and practitioners, maintained that Blacks had babies out of wedlock because they were Negro, because they were ex-Africans and ex-slaves, irresponsible and amoral, but baby-loving. According to this conception, the state and its institutions and agencies could essentially ignore breeding patterns since Blacks would take care of their children themselves. And if Blacks did not, they were responsible for their own mess. Adopting Daniel Moynihan's famous phrase from this period, I call this public attitude toward Black illegitimacy *benign neglect*.

A second response to Black mothers and babies was *punitive*. The conservative, racist politicians who championed this position argued simply that the mothers were bad and should be punished. The babies were expendable because they were expensive and undesirable as citizens. Public policies could and should be used to punish Black unmarried mothers and their children in the form of legislation enabling states to cut them off from welfare benefits, and to sterilize or incarcerate "illegitimate mothers."[40]

I label the third attitude toward Black unwed mothers *benevolent reformist*. Employees at the United States Children's Bureau and many in the social work community who took this position maintained that Blacks who had children out of wedlock were just like whites who did the same. Both groups of females were equally disturbed and equally in need of help, particularly in need of social casework. Regarding the baby, benevolent reformers held that Black unwed mothers should be accorded every opportunity to place the infant for adoption, just like whites.

Despite these different attitudes toward Black women and their babies, proponents of all three shared a great deal. First, they shared the belief that the Black illegitimate baby was the product of pathology. This was the case whether it was a pathology grounded in race, as it was for the benign neglecters and the punishers, or in gender, as it was for the benevolent reformers. Second, all commentators agreed that the baby's existence justified a negative moral judgment about the mother and the mother-and-baby dyad. The Black illegitimate infant was proof of its mother's moral incapacities, its illegitimacy suggested its own probable tendencies toward depravity. Because of the eager market for white babies, this group was cleared of the charge of inherited moral taint, while Black babies were not. Indeed, proponents of each of the three perspectives agreed that the unwed Black mother must, in almost every case, keep her baby. Where they differed was in explaining why this was so. The different answers reflected different strains of racism and carried quite different implications for public policies and practices regarding the Black unmarried mother and her child.

The *benign neglecters* began to articulate their position at about the same time that the psychologists provided new explanations for white single pregnancy. In tandem these developments set Black and white unwed mothers in different universes of cause and effect. According to these "experts," Black and white single mothers were different from each other in several ways. When Black single girls and women had intercourse, it was a sexual, not a psychological act, and Black mothers had "natural affection" for their children, whatever their birth status. The white unwed mother had only neurotic feelings for her out-of-wedlock child. The "unrestrained sexuality" of Black women and their capacity to love the resulting illegitimate children were perceived as inbred traits, and unchangeable, part of Black culture.

Thus, by becoming mothers, even unwed mothers, Black women were simply doing what came naturally. It was also important in this regard that the operative concept of "culture" excised considerations of environment. Environment was not a primary factor in shaping female sexual behavior or the mother's relationship to her illegitimate baby. These were determined by "culture," an essentially biological construct. Therefore, since professionals could only have an impact on the immediate situation—and could not penetrate or rearrange Black "culture," it was futile to consider interfering. The absence of services for these women and their children was justified in this way. Issues regarding Blacks and adoption were quickly dismissed by those who counselled neglect. Agencies claimed that Blacks did not want to part with their babies, and, just as important, Black couples did not want to adopt children.[41]

White policy-makers, and service providers often pointed to the Black grandmothers—willing, able, loving, and present—to justify their contentions that the Black family would take care of its own, and that no additional services were necessary. Yet when grandmothers rendered such service, policy makers labelled them "matriarchs" and blamed them for "faulty personality growth and for maladaptive functioning in children."[42] The mother was similarly placed in a double bind. She was denied services because she was Black—an alleged cultural rather than a racial distinction—and then she was held responsible for the personal and social consequences.[43] The social service system was, in this way, excused from responsibility or obligation to Black unwed mothers.

The *punishers*, both Southern Dixiecrats and Northern racists, drew in part on the "cultural" argument to target both the unwed mother and her baby. They held that Black culture was inherited and that the baby would likely be as great a social liability as its mother. Moreover, they claimed that for a poor Black woman to have a baby was an act of selfishness, as well as pathological, and deserved punishment.[44] Once the public came to believe that Black illegitimacy was not an innocuous social fact but carried a direct and heavy cost to white taxpayers, many whites sanctioned their political representatives to target Black unwed mothers and their babies for attack.[45]

The willingness to attack was expressed, in part, by a special set of tropes which drew on the language and concepts of the marketplace. The "value" assigned to the illegitimate child-as-commodity became useful in classifying the violation of the Black unwed mother in a consumer society. Repeatedly, Black unmarried mothers were construed as "women whose business is having illegitimate children."[46] This illicit "occupation" was portrayed as violating basic consumerist principles including good value in exchange for a good price, for a product which, in general, benefits society. Black unmarried mothers, in contrast, were said to offer bad value (Black babies) at a high price (taxpayer-supported welfare grants) to the detriment of society demographically and economically. The behavior of these women—most of whom did *not* receive Aid to Dependent Children grants for their illegitimate children[47]—was construed as meeting only the consumerist principle that everything can, potentially, be a commodity. These women were accused of treating their reproductive capacities and their children as commodities, with assigned monetary values. From this perspective, Black unmarried mothers were portrayed as "economic women," making calculated decisions for personal, financial gain.[48]

The precise economic principle most grossly violated by these women was, according to many, that they got something (ADC) for nothing (another Black baby); they were cheating the public with a bad sell. The fact that it was, overwhelmingly, a buyer's market for Black babies "proved" the valuelessness of these children, despite their expense to the taxpaying public.[49] White babies entered a healthy seller's market, with up to ten couples competing for every one adoptable infant.[50]

Spokespeople for this point of view believed that Black unmarried mothers should pay dearly for the bad bargain they foisted on society, especially on white taxpayers. But many felt that rather than paying for their sins, Black women were being paid, by ADC grants, an exchange which encouraged additional sexual and fiscal irresponsibility.[51] Thus, society was justified in punishing Black unwed mothers. In addition, the Black unmarried woman, allegedly willing to trade on her reproductive function, willing to use her body and her child so cheaply, earned the state's equal willingness to regard her childbearing capacity cheaply, and take it away, for example, by sterilization legislation.

The ironic truth was that ADC benefits were such inadequate support (and employment and child-care opportunities so meager or nonexistent) that government policies had the effect of causing, not responding to, the economic calculations a woman made that might lead to pregnancy. The average welfare payment per child, per month was $27.29, with monthly averages less than half that amount in most Southern states.[52] The following encounter illustrates the relationship between illegitimacy and economics, from one woman's point of view. "When the case analyst visited the family, the little girl came in with a new dress and shoes. The mother explained that it was the last day of school and the child had begged for new clothes like the other children had. She got them, but the mother's comment was, 'I hope that dress does not cause me another baby.' "[53] This mother's economic and sexual calculations were rooted in poverty and maternal concern, not in some desire to multiply inadequate stipends through additional pregnancies.

The public's interest in casting Black unwed mothers and their babies as consumer violators was reflected in opinion polls which suggested that the American public wanted to withhold federal support, or food money, from illegitimate Black babies.[54] Among dissenters were people who believed it was wrong "to deny food to children because of the sins of the parents."[55] Both groups, however, fell into a trap set by conservative politicians who found it politically profitable to associate Black illegitimacy in their constituents' minds with the rising costs of public welfare grants. The ADC caseload increased in the postwar period for many reasons, including the basic increase in numbers of children and families, and the increase in households headed by women because of divorce, separation, desertion *and* illegitimacy. Between 1953 and 1959, the number of families headed by women rose 12.8 percent while the number of families rose only 8.3 percent.[56] While white sentiment was being whipped up to support punitive measures against Black "subsidized immorality,"[57] only about sixteen percent of nonwhite unwed mothers were receiving ADC grants.[58] Adoption, which was not an option for most Blacks, was the most important factor in removing white children from would-be ADC families. Of unwed white mothers who kept their children, thirty percent, or nearly twice as large a percentage as Blacks, were receiving

Aid to Dependent Children grants in 1959.[59] Yet in the minds of large segments of the white public, Black unwed mothers were being paid, in welfare coin, to have children. The "suitable home" laws which were originally designed, it was claimed, to protect the interests of children, were now instrumental in cutting off ADC payments. These were politicians who had no qualms about using "valueless" Black illegitimate children as pawns in their attempt to squash Black "disobedience" via morals charges.[60]

Led by Annie Lee Davis, a Black social worker at the United States Children's Bureau, many members of the social work community worked unceasingly to convert benign neglecters and punishers into *benevolent reformers*. Davis was a committed integrationist. She was dedicated to convincing the white social service establishment that Black unmarried mothers needed and deserved the same services as their white counterparts. In 1948, Davis addressed this message to her colleagues: "Within minority groups, unmarried mothers suffer guilt and shame as in the majority group." She added, "I know there are those who will challenge this statement," but she insisted, "In the process of adopting the cultural traits of the dominant group in America all groups are striving to be American."[61]

Davis insisted that white public officials and social workers must be brought to believe that Black unwed mothers were psychologically and morally the equals of whites. Only then would Blacks be eligible for the best available services. Ironically, Davis believed that a key element of proof was to establish that Blacks were as interested in adoptive placements for their illegitimate babies as whites were urged to be. Her task was to convince her colleagues that lack of alternate options alone created the custom and the necessity that Blacks kept their illegitimate children.

Benevolent reformers typically took the position that it was unacceptable and potentially racist to assume that Blacks did not want every opportunity that whites had, including adoption. But it was extremely difficult for the reformers to suggest that some Black single mothers wanted their children, and others did not. It was not simply unwed mothers and their babies at issue, it was the Race. For the reformers, constructing an equivalency between Black and white unmarried mothers was the most promising and practical route to social services and social justice.

But even if a Black single mother did consider placing her child for adoption, she knew that the likelihood that the agency would expeditiously approve a couple as adoptive parents was slim.[62] While a white unwed mother could assume a rapid placement, the Black one knew that her child would be forced, in part because of agency practices, to spend months in foster homes or institutions before placement, if that was ever achieved. For example, adoption agencies frequently rejected Blacks who applied for babies, claiming they did not meet the agency's standards for adoptive parents. They also neglected to work with schools and hospitals in contact with Black unwed mothers to improve referral services between these institutions and the agencies, because they feared recruiting Black babies when there might not be homes for them. The reformers had their integrationist vision, but the institutions of society would not cooperate, even when some Black unwed mothers did.

In fact, the evidence from postwar Black communities suggests that the Black unwed mother accepted responsibility for her baby as a matter of course,[63] even when she was sorry to have gotten pregnant.[64] A study in the mid-1960s cautioned the social work profession: "Social work wisdom is that Negroes keep because there is no place to give the baby up, but the study showed . . . that Negroes did not favor adoption, opportunities or their absence notwithstanding." Findings showed that the issue of disposition of the child was the only one that consistently yielded a difference between Black and white respondents, no matter whether they were the unwed mother, her parents, or professional staff. In fact, the Blacks revealed their determination to keep mother and child together and the whites their determination to effect separation, "no matter how [the investigator] varied the content of the questions."[65]

In the same period in Cincinnati, several researchers captured the comments of the mothers themselves. Some girls and women focused on the needs of the baby. One typical respondent claimed, "An innocent child should not be denied his mother's love." Others focused on the strength of their own needs, "I'd grieve myself to death if I let my baby go." A few predicted they would have had nervous breakdowns if they had not been allowed to keep their babies. A representative outlook drew on the sanctified status of motherhood: "The Lord suffered for you to have a baby. He will suffer for you to get food for the baby." Still others expressed themselves in forward-looking, practical terms, "You were less apt to have regrets if you kept the baby than if you let him go."[66]

For many Black unwed mothers the reasons to keep the baby were simply grounded in an immutable moral code of maternal responsibility. A young, Black woman said, "Giving a child away is not the sort of thing a good person would do"; and a teenager asserted, "My parents wouldn't let me give up the baby for adoption."[67] A Black woman in Philadelphia subscribed to this morality. She said, "I sure don't think much of giving babies up for adoption. The mother mightn't be able to give it the finest and best in the world, but she could find a way like I did. My mother had thirteen heads and it was during the Depression. . . . *She* didn't give us away."[68]

The central question for all of these Black, single mothers was how good a mother you were, not whether you were legally married.[69] The overriding stimulus in structuring the personal decisions of these girls and women was a "powerful drive toward family unity, even if the family is not the socially approved one of father, mother and children."[70] In a study of thirty poor, single, Black mothers, only two told the investigators that they would advise another woman in their situation to give the baby up, and both cited difficulties with the welfare office as their reason.[71] The author of the study referred to the "vehemence" of most Black single mothers about their decision to keep the child.[72]

A research team in North Carolina investigating illegitimacy concluded in the early 1960s that one major difference between white and Black unwed mothers was that the white girl generally felt that a "new maturity" had come with the experience of conceiving out of wedlock. The team claimed that this was not true for the Black subjects and explained: "The white subculture demands learning from experience," so the white unwed mother must learn her lesson. The white girl "Has probably been encouraged to look within herself for the reasons for her mistake because the white subculture stresses individual responsibility for error."[73]

These observations capture a great deal of the intentionality underlying the white culture's treatment of unwed mothers under the adoption mandate. For these girls and women, the "lesson" was twofold: no baby without a husband, and no one is to blame but yourself. Learning the lesson meant stepping on the road to real womanhood. The illegitimate child was an encumbrance or an obstacle to following this route. The ability to relinquish was constructed as the first, most crucial, step in the right direction.

Joyce Ladner, in her study of Black women in the 1960s, dealt with the same issue—the relationship between illegitimacy and maturity. She suggested a strikingly different finding: "The adolescent Black girl who becomes pregnant out of wedlock changed her self-concept from one who was approaching maturity to one who had attained the status of womanhood. . . . Mothers were quick to say that their daughters had become grown, that they have 'done as much as I have done.' "[74] The road to maturity for Black unwed mothers was unmediated. Maturity accompanied maternity, the baby's legal status notwithstanding.

Both Black and white women in the postwar era were subject to a definition of maturity that depended on motherhood. The most pervasive, public assumption about Black and white unwed mothers, however, was that their nonmarital childbearing did not constitute maternity in the culturally sanctioned sense. The treatment of these girls and women reinforced the notion that legitimation of sexuality and maternity were the province of the state and the community, and were not the rights of individual girls and women. In the case of white unwed mothers, the community (including the mother, herself, and her family) with government support, was encouraged to efface episodes of illicit sex and maternity. Outside marriage neither the sex nor the resulting child had "reality" in the community or in the mother's life. They became simply momentary mental aberrations. In the case of Black unwed mothers, sexuality was brute biology and childbearing its hideous result. The state, with the support of public institutions, could deface the Black single mother's dignity, diminish her resources, threaten her right to keep her child, and even threaten her reproductive capacity.

In both cases, the policies and practices which structured the meanings of race and gender, sexuality and motherhood, for unwed mothers were tied to social issues—such as the postwar adoption market for white babies, and the white taxpaying public's hostile identification of ADC as a program to support Black unwed mothers and their unwanted babies—which used single pregnant women as resources and as scapegoats.

In the immediate pre-*Roe v. Wade* era, the uses of race combined with the uses of gender, sexuality, and maternity in ways that dealt Black and white unwed mothers quite different hands. According to social and cultural intentions, for the white unwed mother and her baby, relinquishment of the baby was meant to place all scent of taint behind them and thus restore good value to both. The Black unwed mother and her child, triply devalued, had all their troubles before them.

Notes

1. Throughout this essay I have used such expressions as "unwed mother" and "illegitimate baby"—expressions heavily burdened with intended prejudicial meanings—in order to convey the flavor of public discussion of these matters and individuals in the postwar years. I trust it will be obvious that my use of period language does not reflect negative moral judgments on my part. My occasional use of the word "bastard" is a bit more complicated. The word is a technical term, and also, of course, a profound derogation. It is rarely found in the record of public discussion of single pregnancy in these years, although sometimes a politician did not choose to bite his tongue in time. But as I uncovered the public and private fear and rage that structured the treatment of single pregnant women and their babies in this era, I sometimes felt that "bastard" was the only word that expressed the meaning intended by my sources.

2. This essay is taken from a larger study, *Wake Up Little Susie: Single Pregnancy and Race Before Roe v. Wade* (Routledge, New York, 1992).

3. See, for example, Charlotte Lowe, "Intelligence and social background of the unmarried mother," *Mental Hygiene* 4 (1927), pp. 783–94; and Henry C. Schumacher, M.D., "The unmarried mother: a socio-psychiatric viewpoint," *Mental Hygiene* 4 (1927), pp. 775–82.

4. Maryland passed such a law in 1919 and Wisconsin in 1922. It was claimed that these laws would reduce high infant mortality rates, although they were never shown to do so. Maternity home residents were targeted since this group was considered most likely, in its search for secrecy, to abandon its babies. See Elza Virginia Dahlgren, "Attitudes of a Group of Unmarried Mothers toward the Minnesota Three Months Nursing Regulation and its Application," M.A. thesis, University of Minnesota, 1940.

5. See, for example, Percy Kammerer, *The Unmarried Mother* (Little, Brown, Boston, 1918) and Schumacher, "The unmarried mother."

6. Even though many studies published in the postwar era claimed that rates of illicit coition were not rising, the fact that the illegitimacy rates and illegal abortion rates were higher than ever suggests otherwise. See, for example, Alfred C. Kinsey, Wardell B. Pomeroy, Clyde E. Martin, Paul H. Gebhard, *Sexual Behavior in the Human Female* (W.B. Saunders, Philadelphia, 1953), ch. 8. Also see Phillips Cutright, "Illegitimacy

in the United States: 1920–1968," in *Demographic and Social Aspects of Population Growth*, ed. Charles F. Westoff and Robert Parke, Jr. (Commission on Population Growth and the American Future, Washington, D.C., 1969), p. 384.

7. See for example, Mary Lynch Crockett, "An examination of services to the unmarried mother in relation to age at adoption placement of the baby," *Casework Papers, 1960* (Columbia University, New York, 1960), pp. 75–85.

8. See Leontine Young, *Out of Wedlock* (McGraw Hill, New York, 1954), p. 216.

9. Janice P. Montague, "Acceptance or denial—the therapeutic uses of the mother/baby relationship," paper presented at the Florence Crittenton Association of America Northeast Conference, 1964.

10. Winston Ehrmann, "Illegitimacy in Florida II: social and psychological aspects of illegitimacy," *Eugenics Quarterly* 3 (1956), p. 227.

11. Leontine Young, "Is money our trouble?" paper presented at the National Conference on Social Work, 1953.

12. See, for example, Mary Calderone, ed., *Abortion in the United States* (Harper and Brothers, New York, 1958), p. 84, and Edwin M. Gold, Carl L. Erhardt, Harold Jacobziner, and Frieda G. Nelson, "Therapeutic abortions in New York City: a twenty year review," *American Journal of Public Health* 55 (1965), pp. 964–72.

13. Calderone, *Abortion*, pp. 92–3, 139; Alan Guttmacher, "Therapeutic abortion: the doctor's dilemma," *Journal of Mt. Sinai Hospital* 21 (1954), p. 111; Lewis Savel, "Adjudication of Therapeutic Abortion and Sterilization," in *Therapeutic Abortion and Sterilization*, ed. Edmund W. Overstreet (Harper and Row, New York, 1964), pp. 14–21.

14. Calderone, *Abortion*, pp. 86–88.

15. See, for example, J. G. Moore and J. H. Randall, "Trends in therapeutic abortion: a review of 137 cases," *American Journal of Obstetrics and Gynecology* 63 (1952), p. 34.

16. Harry A. Pearce and Harold A. Ott, "Hospital control of sterilization and therapeutic abortion," *American Journal of Obstetrics and Gynecology* 60 (1950), p. 297; James M. Ingram, H. S. B. Treloar, G. Phillips Thomas, and Edward B. Rood, "Interruption of pregnancy for psychiatric indications—a suggested method of control," *Obstetrics and Gynecology* 29 (1967), pp. 251–55.

17. See, for example, Charles C. Dahlberg, "Abortion," in *Sexual Behavior and the Law*, ed. Ralph Slovenko (Charles Thomas, Springfield, IL, 1965), p. 384.

18. Arthur Mandy, "Reflections of a Gynecologist," in *Therapeutic Abortion*, ed. Harold Rosen (The Julian Press, New York, 1954), p. 291.

19. Gregory Zillboorg, "The clinical issues of postpartum psychopathology reactions," *American Journal of Obstetrics and Gynecology* 73 (1957), p. 305; Roy J. Heffernon and William Lynch, "What is the status of therapeutic abortion in modern obstetrics?" *American Journal of Obstetrics and Gynecology* 66 (1953), p. 337.

20. Nicholson J. Eastman, "Obstetric Forward," in Rosen, *Therapeutic Abortion*, p. xx.

21. Theodore Lidz, "Reflections of a Psychiatrist," in Rosen, *Therapeutic Abortion*, p. 279.

22. Flanders Dunbar, "Abortion and the Abortion Habit," in Rosen, *Therapeutic Abortion*, p. 27.

23. Mandy, "Reflections," p. 289.

24. Manfred Guttmacher, "The Legal Status of Therapeutic Abortion," in Rosen, *Therapeutic Abortion*, p. 183. Also see Nanette Davis, *From Crime to Choice: The Transformation of Abortion in America* (Greenwood Press, Westport CT, 1985), p. 73; Johan W. Eliot, Robert E. Hall, J. Robert Willson, and Carolyn Hauser, "The Obstetrician's View," in *Abortion in a Changing World*, Vol. 1, ed. Robert E. Hall (Columbia University, New York, 1970), p. 93; Kenneth R. Niswander, "Medical Abortion Practice in the United States," in *Abortion and the Law*, ed. David T. Smith (Case Western Reserve, Cleveland, 1967), p. 57.

25. David C. Wilson, "The Abortion Problem in the General Hospital," in Rosen, *Therapeutic Abortion*, pp. 190–1. Also see Myra Loth and H. Hesseltine, "Therapeutic abortion at the Chicago Lying-In Hospital," *American Journal of Obstetrics and Gynecology* 72 (1956), pp. 304–311, which reported that 69.4% of their sample were sterilized along with abortion. Also relevant are Keith P. Russell, "Changing indications for therapeutic abortion: twenty years experience at Los Angeles County Hospital," *Journal of the American Medical Association*, 10 January 1953, pp. 108–11, which reported an abortion-sterilization rate of 75.6%; and Lewis E. Savel, "Adjudication of therapeutic abortion and sterilization," *Clinical Obstetrics and Gynecology* 7 (1964), pp. 14–21.

26. See, for example, Michael W. Sedlak, "Young women and the city: adolescent deviance and the transformation of educational policy, 1870–1960," *History of Education Quarterly* 23 (1983), pp. 1–28.

27. See Lillian Ripple, "Social Work Standards of Unmarried Parenthood as Affected by Contemporary Treatment Formulations," Ph.D. dissertation, University of Chicago, 1943.

28. *Directory of Maternity Homes* (National Association on Services to Unmarried Parents, Cleveland, 1960).

29. U.S. Congress, Senate, Judiciary Committee, *Hearings before the Subcommittee to Investigate Juvenile Delin-*

quency, Interstate Adoption Practices, 15–16 July 1955, 84th Congress, 1st sess. (Government Printing Office, Washington, D.C., 1955), p. 200.

30. U.S. Congress, Senate, Judiciary Committee, *Hearings before the Subcommittee to Investigate Juvenile Delinquency, Commercial Child Adoption Practices*, 16 May 1956, 84th Congress, 2nd sess. (Government Printing Office, Washington, D.C., 1956), p. 6.

31. Duluth, Minnesota to Governor Luther Youngdahl, 2 August 1950, and to President Truman, 14 August 1950 Box 457, File 7–4–3–3–4, Record Group 102, National Archives (hereafter cited as N.A.).

32. Sterling, Colorado to Mrs. Lenroot, 21 November 1949, Box 457, File 7–4–3–3–7, Record Group 102, N.A.

33. U.S. Congress, *Hearings, Commercial Child Adoption Practices*, 16 May 1956, p. 120

34. *New York Times* (10 July 1958).

35. U.S. Congress, Senate, Judiciary Committee, *Hearings Before the Subcommittee to Investigate Juvenile Delinquency, Interstate Adoption Practices*, Miami, Florida, 14–15 November 1955, 84th Congress, 1st sess. (Government Printing Office, Washington, D.C., 1956), pp. 54–56. Also see *Wichita Beacon* (31 July and 1–8 August 1955).

36. U.S. Congress, *Hearings, Interstate Adoption Practices*, 15–16 July 1955, p. 206.

37. U.S. Congress, *Hearings, Interstate Adoption Practices*, Miami, Florida, 14–15 November 1955, p. 245.

38. Clark Vincent, "Unwed mothers and the adoption market: psychological and familial factors," *Journal of Marriage and Family Living* 22 (1960), p. 118.

39. See Solinger, *Wake Up Little Susie*, ch. 7, for a fuller discussion of these three public policy perspectives.

40. See Winifred Bell, *Aid to Dependent Children* (Columbia University, New York, 1965) and Julius Paul, "The return of punitive sterilization proposals," *Law and Society Review* 3 (1968), pp. 77–106.

41. See, for example, Andrew Billingsley and Jeanne Giovannoni, *Children of the Storm* (Harcourt, Brace and Javanovich, New York, 1972), p. 142.

42. Patricia Garland, "Illegitimacy—a special minority-group problem in urban areas," *Child Welfare* 45 (1966), p. 84.

43. *Ibid.*

44. See, for example, the editorial, "It Merits Discussion," *Richmond News Leader* (22 March 1957).

45. During the period considered here, Black women in the South were among the first in the United States to receive publicly subsidized birth control, sterilization and abortion services. See Thomas Shapiro, *Population Control Politics: Women, Sterilization and Reproductive Choice* (Temple University, Philadelphia, 1985); Gerald C. Wright, "Racism and the availability of family planning services in the United States," *Social Forces* 56 (1978), pp. 1087–98; and Martha C. Ward, *Poor Women, Powerful Men: America's Great Experiment in Family Planning* (Westview, Boulder, Colorado, 1986).

46. See, for example, *The New York Times* (28 August 1960).

47. See *Illegitimacy and Its Impact on the Aid to Dependent Children Program*, Bureau of Public Assistance, Social Security Administration, U.S. Department of Health, Education and Welfare (Government Printing Office, Washington, D.C. 1960).

48. The *Atlanta Constitution* (25 January, 1951). The *Constitution* reported that the Georgia State Welfare Director, making an argument for denying Aid to Dependent Children grants to mothers with more than one illegitimate child, noted that "Seventy percent of all mothers with more than one illegitimate child are Negro. . . . Some of them, finding themselves tied down to one child are not adverse to adding others as a business proposition."

49. "A study of Negro adoptions," *Child Welfare* 38 (1959), p. 33, quoting David Fanshel, *A Study in Negro Adoptions* (Child Welfare League of America, New York, 1957); "In moving from white to Negro adoptions we are moving from what economists would call a 'seller's market' . . . to a 'buyer's market.'"

50. See, for example, Lydia Hylton, "Trends in adoption," *Child Welfare* 44 (1966), pp. 377–86. In 1960, a government report claimed that in some communities, there were ten suitable applicants for every white infant, *Illegitimacy and Its Impact*, p. 28.

51. One of a number of readers responding irately to a *New York Times* editorial in support of giving welfare grants to unmarried mothers, wrote to the *Times*, "As for your great concern for those careless women who make a career of illicit pregnancy, they should either bear the expense or be put where they can no longer indulge their weaknesses," *New York Times* (7 July, 1961).

52. *New York Times* (9 August, 1959). In late 1958, average monthly family grants in the ADC program were $99.83 nationally, but in the South, ranged between $27.09 in Alabama and $67.73 in Texas. Bell, *Aid to Dependent Children*, p. 224.

53. Hazel McCalley, "The community looks at illegitimacy," Florence Crittenton Association of America Papers, Box 3, Folder: FCAA Annual 11th, 1960–61, Social Welfare History Archives, University of Minnesota (hereafter cited as SWHA); see *Facts, Fallacies and the Future—A Study of the ADC Program of Cook County,*

Illinois (Greenleigh Associates, New York, 1960), p. 29, for a prominent, contemporary discussion concerning how small welfare grants to single mothers were directly responsible for increasing these women's financial and social dependence on men.

54. A Gallup Poll conducted in 1960 found that only "one in ten [respondents] favored giving aid to further children born to unwed parents who have already produced an out of wedlock child." *St. Louis Post Dispatch* (8 August, 1961).

55. *Milwaukee Journal* (9 August, 1961).

56. *Illegitimacy and Its Impact*, p. 30.

57. *Buffalo Currier Express* (5 December, 1957).

58. *Illegitimacy and Its Impact*, p. 36.

59. *Ibid.*

60. See "The current attack on ADC in Louisiana," 16 September 1960, Florence Crittenton Association of American Papers, Box 3, folder: National Urban League, New York City, SWHA.

61. Annie Lee Davis, "Attitudes toward minority groups: their effect on services for unmarried mothers," paper presented at the National Conference on Social Work, 1948.

62. See Seaton W. Manning, "The changing Negro family: implications for the adoption of children," *Child Welfare* 43 (1964), pp. 480–85; Elizabeth Herzog and Rose Bernstein, "Why so few Negro adoptions?" *Children* 12 (1965), pp. 14–15; Billingsley and Giovannoni, *Children of the Storm*; Fanshel, *A Study in Negro Adoption*; Trudy Bradley, "An exploration of caseworkers' perceptions of adoptive applicants," *Child Welfare* 45 (1962), pp. 433–43.

63. Elizabeth Tuttle, "Serving the unmarried mother who keeps her child," *Social Welfare* 43 (1962), p. 418.

64. See *Facts, Fallacies and Future*, pp. 19–20; 552 out of 619 mothers of illegitimate children in this study did not want another child but reported that they had no information about how to prevent conception.

65. Deborah Shapiro, "Attitudes, Values and Unmarried Motherhood," in *Unmarried Parenthood: Clues to Agency and Community Action* (National Council on Illegitimacy, New York, 1967), p. 60.

66. Ellery Reed and Ruth Latimer, *A Study of Unmarried Mothers Who Kept Their Babies* (Social Welfare Research, Inc., Cincinnati, 1963), p. 72.

67. Shapiro, "Attitudes and Values," p. 61.

68. Renee Berg, "Utilizing the strengths of unwed mothers in the AFDC program," *Child Welfare* 43 (1964), p. 337.

69. *Ibid.* Also see Nicholas Lemann, *The Promised Land: The Great Black Migration and How It Changed America* (Knopf, New York, 1991), pp. 59–108.

70. Renee M. Berg, "A Study of a Group of Unmarried Mothers Receiving ADC," Doctor of Social Work dissertation, University of Pennsylvania School of Social Work, 1962, p. 96.

71. Berg, "A Study," p. 93.

72. Berg, "A Study," p. 95.

73. Charles Bowerman, Donald Irish, Hallowell Pope, *Unwed Motherhood: Personal and Social Consequences* (University of North Carolina, Chapel Hill, NC, 1966), p. 261.

74. J. Ladner, *Tomorrow's Tomorrow. The Black Woman* (Doubleday, New York, 1971), pp. 214–5.

30

Ladies' Day at the Capitol:
Women Strike for Peace Versus HUAC

Amy Swerdlow

In mid December of 1962 in the Old House Office Building of the United States Congress, a confrontation took place between a recently formed women's peace movement called Women Strike for Peace (WSP) and the House Committee on Un-American Activities (HUAC). The confrontation took place at a HUAC hearing to determine the extent of Communist party infiltration into "the so-called 'peace movement' in a manner and to a degree affecting the national security."[1] This three-day battle of political and sexual adversaries, which resulted in a rhetorical victory for the women of WSP and a deadly blow to the committee, occurred only twenty years ago.[2] It is a moment in the history of peace movements in the United States in which women led the way by taking a more courageous and principled stand in opposition to cold war ideology and political repression than that of their male counterparts.[3] However, in keeping with the historical amnesia which besets both the history of women and radical movements in America, the WSP-HUAC struggle is largely forgotten.[4]

This article seeks to reconstruct the WSP-HUAC confrontation and the reasons it took the form it did. By analyzing the ideology, consciousness, political style, and public demeanor of the WSP women as they defended their right as mothers "to influence the course of government," we can learn a great deal about the strengths and weaknesses of women's movements for social change that build on traditional sex role ideology and on female culture.[5]

WSP burst upon the American political scene on November 1st, 1961, when an estimated fifty thousand women in over sixty cities across the United States walked out of their kitchens and off their jobs in a one-day women's strike for peace. As a radioactive cloud from a Russian nuclear test hung over the American landscape, these women strikers staged the largest female peace action in the nation's history.[6] In small towns and large cities from New York to California, the women visited government officials demanding that they take immediate steps to "End the Arms Race—Not the Human Race."[7] Coming on the heels of a decade noted for cold war consensus, political conformity, and the celebration of female domesticity, this spontaneous women's initiative baffled both the press and the politicians. The women seemed to have emerged from nowhere. They belonged to no unifying organizations, and their leaders were totally unknown as public figures.

The women strikers were actually responding to a call from a handful of Washington, D.C., women who had become alarmed by the acceleration of the nuclear arms race. So

This article is reprinted from *Feminist Studies*, vol. 8, no. 3 (Fall 1982): 493–520, by permission of the publisher, *Feminist Studies, Inc.*, c/o Women's Studies Program, University of Maryland, College Park, MD 20742.

disheartened were they by the passivity of traditional peace groups, that they had sent a call to women friends and contacts all over the country urging them to suspend their regular routine of home, family, and job to join with friends and neighbors in a one-day strike to end the nuclear arms race.[8]

The call to strike spread rapidly from Washington through typical female networks: word of mouth and chain letter fashion from woman to woman, from coast to coast, through personal telephone calls, and Christmas card lists. Contacts in Parent Teacher Associations (PTAs), the League of Women Voters, church and temple groups, as well as the established peace organizations such as the Women's International League for Peace and Freedom (WILPF) and the Committee for a Sane Nuclear Policy (SANE), also spread the word.

The nature of the strike in each community depended entirely on what the local women were willing, and able, to do. Some marched, others lobbied local officials, a few groups took ads in local newspapers. Thousands sent telegrams to the White House and to the Soviet embassy, calling upon the two first ladies of the nuclear superpowers, Jacqueline Kennedy and Nina Khrushchev, to urge their husbands on behalf of all the world's children to "stop all nuclear tests—east and west." Amazed by the numbers and composition of the turnout on November 1st, *Newsweek* commented:

> They were perfectly ordinary looking women, with their share of good looks; they looked like the women you would see driving ranch wagons, or shopping at the village market, or attending PTA meetings. It was these women by the thousands, who staged demonstrations in a score of cities across the nation last week, protesting atomic testing. A "strike for peace," they called it and—carrying placards, many wheeling baby buggies or strollers— they marched on city halls and Federal buildings to show their concern about nuclear fallout.[9]

The strikers' concern about the nuclear arms race did not end with the November 1st actions. Within only one year, the one-day strike for peace was transformed by its founders and participants into a national women's movement with local groups in sixty communities and offices in ten cities. With no paid staff and no designated leaders, thousands of women in different parts of the country, most of them previously unknown to each other, managed to establish a loosely structured communications network capable of swift and effective direct action on both a national and international scale.

From its inception, the WSP movement was a non-hierarchical participatory network of activists opposed both to rigid ideologies and formal organizational structure. The WSP women called their format simply "our un-organization." It is interesting to note that the young men of Students for a Democratic Society (SDS), a movement founded in the same year as WSP, more aware of their place in the radical political tradition, more aware of the power of naming, and more confident of their power to do so, named their loose structure "participatory democracy." Eleanor Garst, one of the Washington founders, explained the attractions of the un-organizational format:

> No one must wait for orders from headquarters—there aren't any headquarters. No one's idea must wait for clearance through the national board. No one waits for the president or the director to tell her what to do—there is no president or director. Any woman who has an idea can propose it through an informal memo system; if enough women think it's good, it's done. Those who don't like a particular action don't have to drop out of the movement; they just sit out that action and wait for one they like. Sound "crazy"?—it is, but it also brings forth and utilizes the creativity of thousands of women who could never be heard from through ordinary channels.[10]

The choice of a loose structure and local autonomy was a reaction to hierarchical and bureaucratic structures of traditional peace groups like WILPF and SANE to which some of the early leaders belonged. These women perceived the WILPF structure, which required that all programmatic and action proposals be cleared with state and national offices, as a roadblock to spontaneous and direct responses to the urgent international crisis.[11] The willingness of the Washington founders to allow each group to act in the way that suited its particular constituency was WSP's greatest strength and the source of the confidence and admiration that women across the country bestowed on the Washington founders. Washington came to be considered the WSP national office not only because it was located in the nation's capital, but also because the Washington group was trusted by all.

There was also another factor militating against a traditional membership organization. Only the year before the WSP strike, Linus Pauling, the Nobel Laureate in physics and opponent of nuclear testing, had been directed by the Senate Internal Security Subcommittee to turn over the names of those who had helped him gather signatures on a scientists' antinuclear petition. The commandeering of membership lists was not an uncommon tactic of political intimidation in the 1950s. Membership lists of radical organizations could therefore be a burden and responsibility. As they served no purpose in the WSP format, it was a sensible strategy to eliminate them. Another benefit was that WSP never had to assess accurately its numerical strength, thus allowing its legend to grow even when its numbers did not.

From its first day onward, WSP tapped a vast reservoir of moral outrage, energy, organizational talent, and sisterhood—female capacities that had been submerged and silenced for more than a decade by McCarthyism and the "feminine mystique." Using standard pressure group tactics, such as lobbying and petitioning, coupled with direct demonstrative action and civil disobedience, executed with imagination and "feminine flair," the WSP women succeeded in putting women's political demands on the front pages of the nation's newspapers, from which they had largely disappeared since the days of the suffrage campaign. WSP also managed to influence public officials and public policy. At at time when peace marchers were ignored, or viewed as "commies" or "kooks," President John F. Kennedy gave public recognition to the women strikers. Commenting on WSP's first antinuclear march at the White House, on January 15, 1962, the president told the nation that he thought the WSP women were "extremely earnest."

> I saw the ladies myself. I recognized why they were here. There were a great number of them, it was in the rain. I understand what they were attempting to say, therefore, I consider their message was received.[12]

In 1970, *Science* reported that "Wiesner (Jerome Wiesner, Pres. Kennedy's Science Advisor) gave the major credit for moving President Kennedy toward the limited Test Ban Treaty of 1963, not to arms controllers inside the government but to the Women Strike for Peace and to SANE and Linus Pauling."[13]

Although WSP, in its first year, was well received by liberal politicians and journalists, the surveillance establishment and the right-wing press were wary. They recognized early what the Rand Corporation described obliquely as the WSP potential "to impact on military policies."[14] Jack Lotto, a Hearst columnist, charged that although the women described themselves as a "group of unsophisticated wives and mothers who are loosely organized in a spontaneous movement for peace, there is nothing spontaneous about the way the pro-Reds have moved in on our mothers and are using them for their own purposes."[15] On the West Coast, the *San Francisco Examiner* claimed to have proof that "scores of well-intentioned dedicated women ... were being made dupes of by known Communists ... operating openly in the much publicized Women Strike for Peace demonstrations."[16]

That WSP was under Federal Bureau of Investigation (FBI) surveillance from its first public planning meeting in Washington in October 1961, is abundantly evidenced in the forty-three volumes of FBI records on WSP which have been made available to the movement's attorneys under the provisions of the Freedom of Information Act. The records show that FBI offices in major cities, North, East, South, and West—and even in such places as Mobile, Alabama, Phoenix, Arizona, and San Antonio, Texas, not known for WSP activities—were sending and receiving reports on the women, often prepared in cooperation with local "red squads."[17]

Having just lived through the Cuban Missile Crisis of October 1962, WSP celebrated its first anniversary in November with a deep sense of urgency and of heightened political efficacy. But, as the women were making plans to escalate their commitment and their protests, they were stopped in their tracks in the first week of December by HUAC subpoenas to thirteen women peace activists from the New York metropolitan area, as well as Dagmar Wilson of Washington, D.C., the WSP national spokesperson.[18]

It is difficult today to comprehend the emotions and fears such a summons could invoke in individuals and organizations. Lillian Hellman's *Scoundrel Time* gives a picture of the tension, isolation, and near hysteria felt by an articulate and prominent public figure, as she prepared her defense against the committee in 1953.[19] By 1962, cold war hysteria had abated somewhat, as the United States and the USSR were engaged in test ban negotiations, but HUAC represented those forces and those voices in American politics that opposed such negotiations. As a congressional committee, it still possessed the awesome power of an agency of the state to command headlines, cast suspicion, and by labeling individuals as subversives, to destroy careers, lives, and organizations.

The HUAC subpoenas gave no indication of the subject of the hearings, or of their scope. So there was, at first, some confusion about whether it was the WSP connection or other aspects of the subpoenaed women's political lives that were suspect. To add to the confusion, it was soon discovered that three of the women called were not even active in WSP. They were members of the Conference of Greater New York Peace Groups, an organization founded by New Yorkers who had either been expelled from, or who had willingly left, SANE because of its internal red hunt. Of these three women, two had already been named by the committee informers as communists in previous HUAC hearings. One of these women, Elizabeth Moos, had achieved considerable notoriety when she was identified by accused Russian spy William Remington as his mother-in-law and a card-carrying communist. Given these circumstances it was clear that the WSP leadership had some important decisions to make regarding their response to the HUAC hearings. There were two important questions to be faced. First, as WSP had no official membership list, would the movement embrace any woman working for peace even if she were not directly involved in WSP activity? Second, would WSP disavow its members who had past or present communist affiliations, and if WSP did not disavow them, would the movement lose its following and its effectiveness?

The key to WSP unity in the face of the "communist issue" which had divided and disrupted peace, labor, and even civil liberties organizations in the previous decade, was the fact that WSP had previously decided to handle forthrightly and in advance of any attack, the issue of communist inclusion. WSP had, even before the HUAC hearings, decided to reject political screening of its members, deeming it a manifestation of outdated cold war thinking. This decision, the women claimed, was based not on fear or expediency, but on principle. The issue of accepting communists in the movement was brought to the floor of the first national WSP conference in June 1962 by the Los Angeles coordinating council. A prepared statement by the Los Angeles group declared: "Unlike SANE and Turn Toward Peace, WSP must not make the error of initiating its own purges." Treating the issue of communist membership as a question of personal conscience, the Los Angeles group asked, "If there are communists or former communists working in WSP, what difference does that make? We do not question one another about our religious beliefs or other matters of personal conscience. How can we justify political interrogation?" The Los Angeles statement continued, "If fear, mistrust and hatred are ever to be lessened, it will be by courageous individuals who do not hate and fear and can get together to work out tolerable compromises."[20] The argument that "this is a role women would be particularly equipped to play," won over the conference and resulted in the inclusion of a section in the WSP national policy statement which affirmed, "we are women of all races, creeds and political persuasions who are dedicated to the achievement of general and complete disarmament under effective international control."[21]

An emergency meeting of about fifty New York area "key women," along with Dagmar Wilson and other representatives from Washington, was called a few days after the HUAC summonses began to arrive.[22] The first decision made at this meeting was that WSP would live up to the national policy statement that had been arrived at six months earlier and make a reality of the phrase, "We are women of all . . . political persuasions." Following from this decision it was clear that WSP would support and embrace every woman summoned before HUAC, regardless of her past or present affiliations, as long as she supported the movement's campaign against both Russian and American nuclear policies. This meant that in addition to supporting its own women, the three women not active in WSP would also come under the movement's protection if they so desired. They would be given access to the same lawyers as the WSP activists. They would not be isolated or attacked either for their affiliations or for the way they chose to conduct themselves at the hearing. This decision was in sharp contrast to the actions taken by SANE in 1960 when it expelled a leading member of its New York chapter after he invoked the Fifth Amendment at a Senate Internal Security Subcommittee hearing, and then refused to tell Norman Cousins, a cochairman of SANE, whether or not he had ever been a communist.[23]

The decision made by the New York and Washington women not "to cower" before the committee, to conduct no internal purges, to acknowledge each woman's right to act for peace and to conduct herself according to the dictates of her conscience was bold for its day. It was arrived at within the movement, by the women themselves, without consultation with the male leaders of traditional peace and civil liberties groups, many of whom disagreed with this WSP policy.[24] It was based not only on the decision to resist the demonology of the cold war, but also on a sense of sisterhood, on feelings of identification with and empathy for the women singled out for attack. Even the subpoenaed women themselves turned for counsel and support more to each other and the WSP leadership than to their families and lawyers. Working together at a feverish pace, night and day for three weeks, writing, phoning, speaking at rallies, the key women seemed to be acting as if they were a family under attack, for which all personal resources, passions, and energies had to be marshaled. But the family, this time, was "the movement" and it was the sisters, not the fathers, who were in charge.

In response to the subpoenas, a massive campaign was organized for the cancellation of the hearings and for support of WSP from national organizations and public figures. An anti-HUAC statement was composed in New York and Washington which spoke so well to the concerns and the consciousness of "the women" that it succeeded in unifying a movement in shock. The WSP statement on the HUAC inquisition was quoted widely by the press, used by local groups in ads and flyers, in letters to editors, and in speeches. "With the fate of humanity resting on a push button," the statement declared, "the quest for peace has become the highest form of patriotism."[25] In this first sentence, the women set the ground rules for their confrontation with the committee: it was going to be a contest over which group was more patriotic. But the test of "Americanism" according to the WSP rules, was the extent of one's dedication to saving America's children from nuclear extinction. Addressing the issue of communism in the movement, WSP declared: "Differences of politics, economics or social belief disappear when we recognize man's common peril . . . we do not ask an oath of loyalty to any set of beliefs. Instead we ask loyalty to the race of man. The time is long past when a small group of censors can silence the voice of peace." These words would be the WSP *leitmotif* in the Washington hearings. The women were saying, once again, as they had throughout their first year, that for them, the arms race, cold war ideology, and cold war politics, were obsolete in the nuclear age, as was the committee itself. This is the spirit Eric Bentley caught and referred to when he wrote: "In the 1960s a new generation came to life. As far as HUAC is concerned, it began with Women Strike for Peace."[26]

The WSP strategy against HUAC was innovative. An organizing memorandum from the Washington office declared, "The usual response of protest and public statements is too traditional and ineffectual. . . . Let's Turn the Tables! Let's meet the HUAC challenge in the Good New WSP way!"[27] The "new way" suggested by women all over the country was to insist that WSP had nothing to hide. Instead of refusing to testify, as radicals and civil libertarians had done in the 1950s, large numbers of WSP participants volunteered to "talk." Approximately one hundred women sent wires to Representative Francis Walter, chairman of HUAC, offering to come to Washington to tell all about their movement. The offers were refused by HUAC. But, this new WSP tactic pointed up the fact that the committee was less interested in securing information than in exposing and smearing those it chose to investigate. Some WSP groups objected to the free testimony strategy on the grounds that there was a contradiction between denying the right of the committee to exist, and at the same time offering to cooperate with it. But these groups were in a minority. Carol Urner of Portland, Oregon, spoke for all those who volunteered to testify, making it clear that she would not be a "friendly witness." "I could not, of course, divulge the names of others in the movement," she wrote to Representative Walter. "I suppose such a refusal could lead one to 'contempt' and prison and things like that . . . and no mother can accept lightly even the remote possibility of separation from the family which needs her. But mankind needs us too. . . ."[28]

Only three weeks' time elapsed between the arrival of the first subpoenas from HUAC and the date of the Washington hearings. In this short period, the WSP key women managed to develop a legal defense, a national support system for those subpoenaed, and a broad national campaign of public protest against the committee. The women's performance at the hearings was so original, so winning, and so "feminine" in the traditional sense, that it succeeded in capturing the sympathy and the support of large sections of the national media and in strengthening the movement instead of destroying it.

The hearings opened on December 11, 1962, at 10:00 A.M. in the caucus room of the Old House Office Building of the United States Congress in Washington, D.C. Fear, excitement, and exhilaration were in the air as each WSP woman in the audience looked around to see every seat in the room occupied by sisters who had come from eleven states, some from as far as California, in response to a call for their presence from the national leadership. Clyde Doyle, chairman of the subcommittee of HUAC conducting the WSP hearings, opened with a statement of their purpose. Quoting from Lenin, Stalin, Khrushchev, and Gus Hall, he explained:

> Communists believe that there can be no real peace until they have conquered the world. ... The initiated Communist, understanding his Marxist-Leninist doctrine, knows that a Moscow call to intensity the "fight for peace" means that he should intensify his fight to destroy capitalism and its major bastion, the United States of America.[29]

The WSP women in the audience rose as one as the committee called its first witness, Blanche Posner, a retired schoolteacher who was the volunteer office manager for New York WSP. The decision to rise with the first witness, to stand *with* her, was spontaneous. It was proposed only a few minutes before Posner was called, as a note from an unknown source was circulated around the room. Posner refused to answer any questions about the structure or personnel of WSP. She resorted to the Fifth Amendment forty-four times, as the press pointed out in dozens of news stories covering the first day of the hearings. They also reported the way in which Posner took matters into her own hands, lecturing the committee members as though they were recalcitrant boys at DeWitt Clinton High School in the Bronx, where she had taught. Talking right through the interruptions and objections raised by the chairman and by committee counsel, Alfred Nittle, Posner declared:

> I don't know, sir, why I am here, but I do know why you are here, I think ... because you don't quite understand the nature of this movement. This movement was inspired and motivated by mothers' love for children. ... When they were putting their breakfast on the table, they saw not only the wheaties and milk, but they also saw strontium 90 and iodine 131. ... They feared for the health and life of their children. That is the only motivation.[30]

Each time Posner resorted to the Fifth Amendment, she did it with a pointed criticism of the committee or a quip that endeared her to the women in the hearing room who needed to keep their spirits up in the face of charges that Posner had been identified by an FBI informer as a Communist party member while working in New York City as a schoolteacher. One prize exchange between Nittle and Posner led to particularly enthusiastic applause and laughter from WSP women. Nittle asked, "Did you wear a colored paper daisy to identify yourself as a member of the Women Strike for Peace?" Posner answered, "It sounds like such a far cry from communism it is impossible not to be amused. I still invoke the Fifth Amendment."[31]

Most of the witnesses were called because the committee believed it had evidence to link them with the Communist party through identification by FBI informers or the signing of party nominating petitions. But the strategy backfired with Ruth Meyers, of Roslyn, Long Island. She stepped forward, according to Mary McGrory's report in the *Washington Evening Star*, "swathed in red and brown jersey, topped by a steeple crowned red velvet hat," and "she was just as much of a headache to the committee as Posner had been."[32] There was much sparring between Meyers and the committee about the nature and structure of WSP. "Are you presently a member of a group known as Women Strike for Peace?" Nittle asked. "No, sir, Women Strike for Peace has no membership," Meyers answered. Nittle then asked, "You are familiar, I understand, with the structural organization of Women Strike for Peace as evidenced by this plan?" Meyers replied, "I am familiar to the extent of the role that I play in it. I must say that I was not particularly interested in the structure of Women Strike for Peace. I was more involved in my own community activities. . . . I felt that structure, other than the old telephone, has not much of what I was interested in." Nittle then proceeded to deliver what he believed would be the coup de grâce for Meyers. "Mrs. Meyers," he barked, "it appears from the public records that a Ruth Meyers, residing at 1751 East 10th Street, Brooklyn, New York, on July 27, 1948, signed a Communist party nominating petition. . . . Are you the Ruth Meyers who executed that petition?" Meyers shot back, "No, sir." She then examined the petition carefully, and announced, "I never lived in Brooklyn, and this is not my signature."[33] Although the official transcript does not contain this statement, many, including the author, remember that she added, "My husband could never get me to move there." This female remark brought an explosion of laughter and applause. Meyers also invoked the Fifth Amendment. As she left the witness stand, Meyers received a one-minute ovation for humor, grace, and mistaken identity. In the corridor outside the caucus room in front of the TV cameras, she told reporters that she had never been a communist. "But I'll never acknowledge the Committee's right to ask me that question."[34]

Another witness, Lyla Hoffman, chose to tell the committee of her past communist affiliation, asserting that she had left the Communist party, but would not cooperate in naming names or in citing the cause of her resignation. In a statement written after the hearings Hoffman explained, "I felt that it was high time to say, 'What difference does it make what anyone did or believed many years ago? That's not the problem facing humanity today.' But I had to say this in legal terms." She found it very difficult to do so, as the committee was interested only in whether she was a genuine anticommunist or a secret fellow-traveler.[35] Hoffman invoked the Fifth Amendment.

The witnesses that followed Posner, Meyers, and Hoffman, each in her own style, invoked whatever legal and rhetorical strategy her conscience and her situation dictated. They lectured the committee eloquently and courageously on the danger of nuclear holocaust, on women's rights and responsibility to work for peace. In attempting to explain the nonstructured format of WSP, several witnesses suggested that the movement was too fluid and too unpredictable to be comprehended by the masculine mind.

In their most optimistic projections, the WSP women could not have predicted the overwhelmingly favorable press and public response they would receive, and the support and growth for the movement that would result from the HUAC episode. From the outset, the WSP leadership understood that HUAC needed the press to make its tactics of intimidation and punishment work. So, WSP played for the press—as it had done from its founding—and won! The Washington and New York leadership knew that it had two stories; both were developed to the hilt. The first was "motherhood under attack" and the second was the age-old "battle of the sexes." The contest between the sexes, according to the WSP version, involved female common sense, openness, humor, hope, and naiveté versus male rigidity, solemnity, suspicion, and dark theories of conspiracy and subversion. The WSP women, in their middle-class, feminine, political style turned the hearings into an episode of the familiar and funny "I Love Lucy," rather than the tragic and scary inquisition of Alger Hiss.

For the first time, HUAC was belittled with humor and treated to a dose of its own moral superiority. Headlines critical of the committee and supportive of WSP were featured on the front pages of prominent newspapers from coast to coast. The *Chicago Daily News* declared: "It's Ladies Day at Capitol: Hoots, Howls—and Charm; Congressmen Meet Match." Russell Baker's column was headed "Peace March Gals Make Red Hunters Look Silly" and a *Detroit Free Press* story was entitled, "Headhunters Decapitated." A cartoon by Herblock in the *Washington Post* of December 13th showed three aging and baffled committee members. One is seated at the hearing table. One is holding a gavel. Another turns to him and says, "I Came in Late, Which Was It That Was Un-American—Women or Peace?"[36] A story in the *Vancouver* (B.C.) *Sun* of December 14 was typical of many other reports:

> The dreaded House Un-American Activities Committee met its Waterloo this week. It tangled with 500 irate women. They laughed at it. Kleig lights glared, television cameras whirred, and 50 reporters scribbled notes while babies cried and cooed during the fantastic inquisition.

Bill Galt, author of the *Vancouver Sun* story, gave a blow-by-blow description of WSP civil disobedience in the Old House Office Building:

> When the first women headed to the witness table, the crowd rose silently to its feet. The irritated Chairman Clyde Doyle of California outlawed standing. They applauded the next witness and Doyle outlawed clapping. Then they took to running out to kiss the witness. . . . Finally, each woman as she was called was met and handed a huge bouquet. By then Doyle was a beaten man. By the third day the crowd was giving standing ovations to the heroines with impunity.[37]

The hearings were a perfect foil for the humor of Russell Baker, syndicated columnist of the *New York Times*.

> If the House Un-American Activities Committee knew its Greek as well as it knows its Lenin, it would have left the women peace strikers alone. . . . Instead with typical male arrogance it has subpoenaed 15 of the ladies, . . . spent several days trying to show them that women's place is not on the peace march route, and has come out of it covered with foolishness.

Baker, a liberal columnist, understood the committee's purpose and also the "drama of the absurd" that WSP had staged to defeat that purpose. "The Committee's aim was simple enough," Baker pointed out,

> their sleuths studying an organization known as Women Strike for Peace had learned that some of the strikers seemed to have past associations with the Communist Party or its front groups. Presumably if these were exposed, right thinking housewives would give up peace agitation and go back to the kitchen.

The committee had reckoned without female logic, according to Baker:

> How could WSP be infiltrated, witness after witness demanded, when it was not an organization at all? . . . Try as he might, Alfred Nittle, the committee counsel, never managed to break through against this defense.[38]

The *Detroit Free Press* commented: "The House Committee can get away with attacking college students in California, government flunkies who are forced to shrive their souls to save their jobs, and assorted misguided do-gooders. But when it decides to smear an estimated half-million angry women, it's in deep trouble. We wish them nothing but the worst."[39]

Mary McGrory in the *Washington* (D.C.) *Evening Star* played up the difference between the male, HUAC perceptions and those of the female, WSP:

"Why can't a woman be like a man?" sings Henry Higgins in *My Fair Lady*. That is precisely the question the House Committee on Un-American Activities is asking itself today. . . . The committee is trying to find out if the ladies' group is subversive. All it found out was that their conduct in the caucus room certainly was.

"The leader of the group kept protesting that she was not really the leader at all," McGrory observed. Pointing out that few men would deny being leaders, or admit they didn't know what was going on, Mary McGrory reported that:

Dagmar Wilson of Washington, when asked if she exercised control over the New York chapter merely giggled and said, "Nobody controls anybody in the Women Strike for Peace. We're all leaders."

Characterizing Wilson's appearance as the "coup de grâce in the battle of the sexes," McGrory noted that the ladies had been using the Congress as a babysitter, while their young crawled in the aisles and noisily sucked their bottles during the whole proceedings. With a mixture of awe and wonder McGrory described how the ladies themselves, as wayward as their babies, hissed, gasped, clapped entirely at will. When several of their number took the Fifth Amendment, to McGrory's surprise, the women applauded, and

when Mrs. Wilson, trim and beguiling in red wool, stepped up to take the stand, a mother with a baby on one hip worked her way through the crowd and handed her a bouquet of purple and white flowers, exactly as if she were the principal speaker at a ladies' luncheon.

McGrory caught the flavor of Wilson's testimony which was directed not only at the committee, but also at her sisters in the audience. She reported that when Mr. Nittle asked whether the New York chapter had played a dominant role in the group, Wilson replied, "Other cities would be mortified if you said that."

"Was it," Mr. Nittle wanted to know, "Mrs. Wilson's idea to send delegates to a Moscow peace conference?" "No," said Mrs. Wilson regretfully, "I wish I'd thought of that." When Mr. Nittle pursued the question of whose idea it was to send observers to Moscow, Dagmar Wilson replied, "This is something I find very difficult to explain to the masculine mind."

And, in a sense, it was. "Mr. Nittle pressed forward to the clutch question," one, according to McGrory, "that would bring a man to his knees with patriotic protest: 'I would like to ask you whether you would knowingly permit or encourage a Communist Party member to occupy a leadership position in Women Strike for Peace.' " Wilson replied:

Well, my dear sir, I have absolutely no way of controlling, do not desire to control, who wishes to join in the demonstrations and the efforts that women strikers have made for peace. In fact, I would also like to go even further. I would like to say that unless everybody in the whole world joins us in this fight, then God help us.

"Would you knowingly permit or welcome Nazis or Fascists?" asked Mr. Nittle. Mrs. Wilson replied, "if we could only get them on our side."[40] Mr. Doyle then thanked Wilson for appearing and being so helpful. "I want to emphasize," he said,

that the Committee recognizes that there are many, many, many women, in fact a great great majority of women, in this peace movement who are absolutely patriotic and absolutely adverse to everything the Communist Party stands for. We recognize that you are one of them. We compliment you on your leadership and on your helpfulness to us this morning.

Dagmar Wilson tried to get the last word: "I do hope you live to thank us when we have achieved our goal." But Doyle replied, "Well, we will."[41]

The way in which WSP, a movement of middle-class, middle-aged, white women mobilized to meet the attack by a feared congressional committee was energetic and bold, politically nontraditional, pragmatic rather than ideological, moralistic and maternal. It was entirely consistent with the already established program, tactics, rhetoric, and image of this one-year-old movement, labeled by the University of Wisconsin's student newspaper as "the bourgeois mother's underground."[42]

Were these courageous women who bowed to traditional notions of female behavior merely using the politics of motherhood for political advantage? Or had they internalized the feminine mystique? It is useful to examine the backgrounds of the WSP women in seeking to understand their use of their own female culture to legitimate a radical critique of national, foreign, and military policies. The WSP key women were mostly in their late thirties to mid forties at the inception of the movement in 1961. Most of them, then, had come into adulthood in the late 1930s and early 1940s. They were students or workers in the years of political ferment preceding World War II. Many had married just before, during, or right after the war. The majority of these women participated in the postwar baby boom, the rise of middle-class affluence, and the privatism and consumerism connected with suburban life. It was during the 1950s that they made their adjustment to family, parenting, community, and consensus politics.

As a movement born out of, and responding to, the consciousness of the 1950s, WSP projected a middle-class and politically moderate image. In an article celebrating WSP's first anniversary, Eleanor Garst, one of WSP's early image makers, proclaimed:

> Breaking all the rules and behaving with incredible disorder and naivete, "the women" continue to attract recruits until the movement now numbers hundreds of thousands. . . . Furthermore, many of the women behaving in these unaccustomed ways are no odd-ball types, but pillars of the community long courted by civic organizations. Others—perhaps the most numerous—are apolitical housewives who have never before lifted a finger to work for peace or any other social concern.[43]

Although the movement projected an image of political innocence and inexperience, WSP was actually initiated by five women who were already active members of SANE. The women— Dagmar Wilson, Jeanne Bagby, Folly Fodor, Eleanor Garst, and Margaret Russell—had gravitated toward each other because of their mutual distaste for SANE's internal red hunt, which they felt contributed to an escalation, rather than an end to cold war hysteria. Perhaps, more important, they shared a frustration over the slow pace with which the highly structured SANE reacted to international crises. They also resented the reluctance of SANE's male leadership to deal with "mother's issues" such as the contamination of milk by radioactive fallout from nuclear tests.

Dagmar Wilson was forty-five years old, and a political novice when she was moved to call a few friends to her home in the late summer of 1961 to discuss what could be done about the nuclear crisis. At this meeting WSP was born. Wilson was at that time a successful free-lance children's book illustrator, the mother of three daughters and wife of Christopher Wilson, a commercial attaché at the British embassy. Wilson had been born in New York City, had moved to Germany as a very young child, and had spent most of her adult years in England where her father, Cesar Searchinger, was a well-known broadcast correspondent for the Columbia Broadcasting System and the National Broadcasting Company.

Wilson came to the United States prior to World War II, held a variety of professional jobs as an artist and teacher, and finally became a free-lance illustrator. She worked in a studio at home, so as to be available to her children and to insure a smooth-running household. Despite the fact that Wilson was so successful an artist that one of her children's books had become a best-seller, she nevertheless identified herself as a housewife.

> My idea in emphasizing the housewife rather than the professional was that I thought the housewife was a downgraded person, and that we, as housewives had as much right to an opinion and that we deserved as much consideration as anyone else, and I wanted to emphasize . . . this was an important role and that it was time we were heard.[44]

A gifted artist, an intelligent person of good sense, good grace and charm, Wilson possessed the charisma of those who accurately represent the feelings and the perceptions of their constituency, but excel them in passion and the capacity for creative articulation. Having been most of her life a "nonjoiner" Wilson was, as the *New York Times Magazine* reported in a feature story in May 1962, a "political neophyte."[45] Because Wilson had not been involved in U.S. radical politics of the 1940s, she was free from the self-conscious timidity that plagued those who had been involved in leftist organizations and who feared either exposure or a repetition of the persecution and the political isolation they had experienced in the 1950s.

Among the women who met at Wilson's house to plan the emergency peace action was Eleanor Garst, whose direct, friendly, practical, yet passionate political prose played a powerful role in energizing and unifying the WSP women in their first year. It was she who drafted the call for November 1st, and later helped create most of the anti-HUAC rhetoric.

Garst came from a conservative Baptist background. She recalls that everything in her upbringing told her that the only thing a woman should do was to marry, have babies, care for her husband and babies, and "never mind your own needs." Despite this, Garst was the only one of the inner circle of Washington founders, who in 1961 was a completely self-supporting professional woman, living on her own. She was the mother of two grown children. At the time of the founding of WSP, Garst was employed as a community organizer for the Adams Morgan Demonstration project, administered by American University, working to maintain integrated neighborhoods in Washington, D.C. She had become a pacifist in her early childhood after reading about war in novels and poems. Her husband, a merchant seaman, refused to be drafted prior to World War II, a decision that he and Eleanor made together without consulting any other pacifists because they knew none. They spent their honeymoon composing an eighty-page brief against peacetime conscription.

After the war, Garst became a professional political worker, writer, and peace activist on the West Coast before coming to Washington. She had been a founder of the Los Angeles SANE and editor of its newsletter. A forceful and easy writer, Garst had already been published in the *Saturday Evening Post, Reporter, Ladies' Home Journal,* and other national publications when she was asked to draft the letter that initiated the successful November 1st strike.

Folly Fodor, a leading figure in the founding group, had come to Washington in 1960 to follow her husband's job with the U.S. Labor Department. She joined SANE on her arrival in Washington and had been elected to the board. Thirty-seven years old at the time of the founding of WSP, Fodor was the mother of two. Folly Fodor was not new to politics. She was the daughter of parents who had been involved in liberal-to-communist political causes and had herself been a leader in political organizations since her youth. As an undergraduate at Antioch College, in Yellow Springs, Ohio, Folly Fodor had become active in the Young People's Socialist League, eventually becoming "head of it," as she put it. In retrospect she believes she spent too much time fighting the communists on campus, and "never did a goddamn thing." Fodor had been chairperson of the Young Democrats of California and as a Democrat she had clandestinely supported Henry Wallace in 1948. During the mid 1950s, after the birth of her second child, Fodor organized a mothers' group to oppose nuclear testing. So Fodor, like Garst, was not new to radical causes, to peace activity, or to women's groups. She was ready and eager for a separate women's peace action in the fall of 1961.

Two other women who founded WSP, Jeanne Bagby and Margaret Russell, were also already active in the peace cause at the time of the founding of WSP. Bagby was a frequent contributor to *Liberation* magazine. Together the founders possessed research, writing, organizing, and speaking talents that were not unusual for women active in a variety of community, civic, and church groups in the 1950s. All the founders shared a conviction that the men in the peace movement and the government had failed them and that women had to take things into their own hands.

But what of the thousands of women who joined the founders? What was their social and political background and their motivation to take to the streets in peace protest? Elise Boulding, a sociologist and long-time pacifist activist, who became involved in the WSP communications network right after November 1st, decided to try to find out. During the six months in which Boulding edited the *Women's Peace Movement Bulletin*, an information exchange for WSP groups, she kept asking herself whether the WSP women were really political neophytes as they claimed, or "old pros with a well defined idea of some kind of world social order?" Using the resources of the Institute for Conflict Resolution in Ann Arbor, Michigan, where she was working, and with the help of WSP colleagues in Ann Arbor, she composed a questionnaire that was sent to every eighth name on the mailing lists of forty-five local groups. By the fall of 1962, shortly before the summonses from HUAC, 279 questionnaires had been returned from thirty-seven localities in twenty-two states. According to Boulding, the respondents represented a cross section of the movement—not only leaders.[46]

Boulding found that the overwhelming majority of the WSP women were well-educated mothers, and that 61 percent were not employed outside the home. But she concluded that the women who went out on strike for peace on November 1, 1961, and stayed on in the movement in the following months, appeared to be a more complex and sophisticated group than the "buggy-pushing housewife" image the movement conveyed. She characterized the early WSP participants as "largely intellectual and civic-minded people, mostly of the middle class"—very much like the Washington founders themselves.[47]

Most of the women strikers had been liberals, radicals, or pacifists in the 1940s. Although few had been political leaders of any kind, they shared the 1940s belief that society could be restructured on humanistic lines through the direct political action of ordinary people. Dorothy Dinnerstein described the psychological process of depoliticization and privatization that many politically active people experienced in the 1950s. Many radicals, according to Dinnerstein, spent the 1950s in a state of moral shock, induced by the twin catastrophes of Stalinism and McCarthyism. They lost their capacity for social connectedness and, "in this condition they withdrew from history—more or less totally, more or less gradually, more or less blindly into intensely personalistic, inward-turning, magically thing-and-place-oriented life." According to Dinnerstein they withdrew their passion from the larger human scene and sought to invest in something less nightmarish, more coherent and mentally manageable.[48] What the WSP women withdrew into, with society's blessing and encouragement, was the domestic sphere, the management of family, children, home, and local community. Many, when their school-aged children no longer required full-time care, were propelled into the PTAs, League of Women Voters, Democratic party politics, church, synagogue, or cultural activities by their earlier social, political, and humanitarian concerns.

It took the acceleration of nuclear testing by both the capitalist United States and the socialist USSR to convince the WSP women of something they already suspected: that there was no political force in the world acting morally and humanely in the interest of the preservation of life. It took a series of international crises, the example of the civil rights sit-ins, and the Aldermarston antibomb marches in Britain to give the WSP women both the sense of urgency, and of possibility, that are the necessary ingredients for a political movement. Once out in the political arena, the women found that their moral outrage, their real fear for their children's future, and their determination never to be pushed back into the non-political domestic sphere, made them unafraid of a mere congressional committee before which others had quaked.

The women who were drawn to WSP certainly took the job of motherhood seriously. They had willingly chosen to sacrifice careers and personal projects to raise society's children because they had been convinced by the post-Freudians that the making of human beings is a far more important vocation than anything else; and that the making of human beings was a sex-specific vocation requiring the full-time duties of a resident mother.[49] But where the WSP women differed from the majority of their middle-class cohorts was that they saw motherhood not only as a private function, but also as a contribution to society in general and to the future. When they built on their rights and responsibilities to act politically in defense of the world's children, they were invoking not only their maternal consciousness, but their social conscience as well. They were women of heart, emotion, ingenuity, wit, and guile, but they were also serious political thinkers and activists. They chose to rely on their femininity, as most women did in the fifties and early sixties, to create whatever space and power they could carve out for themselves.

The Birmingham (England) Feminist History Group in an article, "Feminism as Femininity in the Nineteen Fifties?" suggests that feminism of the fifties seemed to be more concerned with integrating and foregrounding femininity than in transforming it in a fundamental way.[50] The conduct of WSP before the House Committee on Un-American Activities follows this pattern. The WSP women were not concerned with transforming the ideology of femininity, but rather with using it to enhance women's political power. But in so doing they were transforming that ideology and foreshadowing the feminism that emerged later in the decade.

Very much in the way that the concept of Republican motherhood was used in the late eighteenth century to justify the demand for women's education, and the cult of true womanhood was built upon to project women into the ante-bellum reform movements, WSP used the feminine mystique of the 1950s to legitimize women's right to radical dissent from foreign and military policies. In the repressive political climate of the early 1960s, WSP relied heavily upon sex role stereotypes to legitimize its opposition to cold war policies. But by emphasizing the fact that the men in power could no longer be counted on for protection in the nuclear age, WSP implied that the traditional sex-gender contract no longer worked. And by stressing global issues and international sisterhood, rather than domestic responsibilities, WSP challenged the privatization and isolation of women which was a key element of the feminine mystique. Most important, by performing in relation to HUAC with more courage, candor, and wit than most men had done in a decade of inquisitions, WSP raised women's sense of political power and self-esteem. One of the negative effects for WSP of relying so heavily on the politics of motherhood to project its political message was that it alienated a new generation of younger women who admired the movement's stand for peace, but saw its acquiescence to sex roles stereotypes as regressive. In the late 1960s these younger women insisted upon working for peace not as wives, mothers, and sisters, but as autonomous persons.

Sara Evans in *Personal Politics* points out that those few young women in the civil rights movement who first raised feminist issues within the movement had to step *outside* the sex role assumptions on which they were raised in order to articulate a radical critique of women's position.[51] For WSP it was obviously different. The founders and leaders of WSP certainly did not step outside the traditional sex role assumptions; rather, they stood squarely upon them, with all their contradictions. By using these contradictions to present a radical critique of man's world, WSP began the transformation of woman's consciousness and woman's role.

Notes

I wish to thank my sisters in WSP, particularly Barbara Bick, Eleanor Garst, Ruth Meyers, Ethel Taylor, and Dagmar Wilson for their helpful comments regarding an earlier version of this paper delivered at the "Fifth Berkshire Conference on the History of Women," Vassar College, 16 June 1981. I am indebted also to Alice Kessler-Harris, Joan Kelly, Gerda Lerner, Ruth Milkman, Melanie Gustafson, and Warren Susman for their valuable insights, advice, and criticism. Research for this article was funded in part by a Woodrow Wilson Women's Studies Dissertation Fellowship, 1980.

1. U.S. Congress, House, Committee on Un-American Activities, *Communist Activities in the Peace Movement (Women Strike for Peace and Certain Other Groups), Hearings Before the Committee on Un-American Activities on H.R. 9944.* 87th Cong., 2d. sess., 1962, 2057.

2. Historians and political opponents of HUAC agree that the WSP hearing marked the beginning of the end of the committee's power. Eric Bentley called the WSP-HUAC confrontation, "the fall of HUAC's Bastille." See Eric Bentley, *Thirty Years of Treason* (New York: Viking Press, 1971), 951. Frank Wilkerson of the National Committee to Abolish HUAC wrote to the Washington office after the hearing, "magnificent women . . . You have dealt HUAC its greatest setback." Frank Wilkerson to Eleanor Garst, *et al.*, 14 December 1962. WSP Document Collection in custody of the author. (This collection will go to the Swarthmore College Peace Collection in 1983.) Peace historian Charles De Benedetti said of the HUAC investigation of WSP, "WSP activists challenged for the first time the House Un-American Activities Committee's practice of identifying citizen peace seeking with Communist subversion. . . . The open disdain of the WSP for HUAC did not end the Congress's preference for treating private peace actions as subversive. But it did help break the petrified anti-Communism of Cold War American politics and gave heart to those reformers who conceived peace as more than military preparedness." See Charles De Benedetti, *The Peace Reform in American History* (Bloomington, Ind.: Indiana University Press, 1980), 167–78.

3. In May 1960, Senator Thomas Dodd, vice chairman of the Senate International Security Subcommittee, threatened SANE with congressional investigation if it did not take steps to rid itself of communist infiltrators. SANE responded by voting to exclude all those with communist sympathies. Whole chapters that did not go along with internal red hunts were expelled, as was Henry Abrams, a leading New York activist who refused to tell the Senate committee whether or not he was a communist. Turn Toward Peace also rejected communists or former communists. See Milton S. Katz, "Peace, Politics, and Protest: SANE and the American Peace Movement, 1957–1972" (Ph.D. dissertation, Saint Louis University, 1973) 109–30. Homer Jack, executive director of national SANE, criticized WSP's "welcome everybody" stand. He claimed that it would call into question the political sagacity of groups like his own. See Homer A. Jack, "The Will of the WISP Versus the Humiliation of HUAC," transcript of a talk on Radio Station WBAI, New York, 28 December 1962. (WSP Document Collection). After January 15, 1962, many WSP groups and the Washington office referred to themselves as Women's International Strike for Peace (WISP).

4. The way in which WSP's militant role in the peace movement has been either ignored or trivialized by journalists, peace movement leaders, and historians is illustrated by the following examples. Mary McGrory in her syndicated column described a WSP visit to the White House in the following manner: "This week's Cinderella story has to do with Women Strike for Peace, which after 15 years of drudgery in the skullery

of anti-war activity has been invited to the White House" (*New York Post*, 8 March 1977, 24). Dave Dellinger, one of the most prominent of the male leaders of the 1960s peace movement, devoted about ten lines to WSP in a 317-page book on the history of the civil rights and peace movements from 1965 to 1973. He described WSP as a group fearful of engaging in civil disobedience in the 1967 "Mobilization March on the Pentagon." Nowhere in the book did Dellinger mention that nine months earlier 2,500 WSP women broke through police barricades to bang their shoes on the Pentagon doors which had been shut in their faces. See Dave Dellinger, *More Power Than We Know* (Garden City, N.Y.: Anchor Press, 1975). Lawrence Wittner, in a critical survey of American politics from 1945 to 1974 that focuses on movements of dissent, devoted only four words to WSP. He included the movement in a list of early critics of radioactive fallout. See Lawrence Wittner, *Cold War America from Hiroshima to Watergate* (New York: Praeger Publishers, 1974) 232.

5. For a symposium on the relationship of feminism, women's culture, and women's politics, see Ellen DuBois, Mari Jo Buhle, Temma Kaplan, Gerda Lerner, and Carroll Smith-Rosenberg, "Politics and Culture in Women's History: A Symposium," *Feminist Studies* 6 (Spring 1980): 26–64. Also see Temma Kaplan, "Female Consciousness and Collective Action: The Case of Barcelona, 1910–1918," *Signs* 7 (Spring 1982): 54– 66. Kaplan points out that women's defense of traditional rights, while fundamentally conservative, can have revolutionary consequences.

6. The figure of fifty thousand claimed by the Washington founders after November 1st was accepted in most press accounts and became part of the WSP legend. It was based on reports from women in sixty cities and from newspapers across the country. Often the women's reports and that of the newspapers differed, but even in using the highest figures available I can substantiate only a count of approximately twelve thousand women who struck on November 1st. Nevertheless, this was still the largest women's peace demonstration on record.

7. "End the Arms Race—Not the Human Race" was the central slogan of the November 1st "strike": "Help Wanted" flyer, 25 October 1961, Washington, D.C. See WSP Document Collection. (Mimeographed.)

8. "Dear—, Last night I sat with a few friends in a comfortable living room talking of atomic war." Draft of call to strike by Eleanor Garst, Washington, D.C., 22 September 1961. WSP Document Collection. (Mimeographed.)

9. *Newsweek*, 13 November 1961, 21.

10. Eleanor Garst, "Women: Middle-Class Masses," *Fellowship* 28 (1 November 1962), 10–12.

11. Minutes of the WILPF National Executive Committee stated: "Each branch taking direct action should clear with the National Action Projects Committee. The committee should have, and send out to branches, a list of approved action and a list of the organizations with which we formally cooperate." Women's International League for Peace and Freedom. Minutes of the National Executive Committee, meeting of 28–29 September 1961. Swarthmore College Peace Collection, DG 43, Series A-2, Box 18, 5.

12. "Transcript of the President's News Conference on World and Domestic Affairs," *New York Times*, 16 January 1962, 18.

13. *Science* 167 (13 March 1970), 1476.

14. A. E. Wessel, *The American Peace Movement: A Study of Its Themes and Political Potential* (Santa Monica: The Rand Corporation, 1962), 3.

15. *New York Journal American*, 4 April 1962, 10.

16. *San Francisco Examiner*, 21 May 1962, 10.

17. The FBI files on WSP are located in the offices of the Washington, D.C. law firm of Gaffney, Anspach, Shember, Klimasi, and Marx. These contain hundreds of documents from security officers in major cities to the director of the FBI and from the directors to the security officers. For instance, as early as 23 October 1961, one week before the November 1st strike, the Cleveland office of the FBI already identified one of the WSP planning groups as communist. (FBI Document 100-39566-8). When WSP sent a delegation to lobby the Geneva Disarmament Conference, 2–7 April 1962, the FBI involved Swiss federal police and covert Central Intelligence Agency agents in the American embassy to spy on the women (Legat Bern to Director, FBI 4 April 1962, FBI Document 100-39574-187). An internal security memorandum on 24 July 1962 stated that an informant who had furnished reliable information in the past, made available a list of women "who will be guests of the Soviet Women's Committee in the USSR, 12– 26 July 1962." The list which had been circulated to the press by WSP included the names of twelve women from various parts of the country (FBI Document 100-39566-222).

18. Those subpoenaed were (in order of appearance) Blanche Posner, Ruth Meyers, Lyla Hoffman, Elsie Neidenberg, Sylvia Contente, Rose Clinton, Iris Freed, Anna Mackenzie, Elizabeth Moss, Ceil Gross, Jean Brancato, Miriam Chesman, Norma Spector, and Dagmar Wilson. Spector never testified; she was excused due to illness. *Hearings before Committee on Un-American Activities*, III.

19. Lillian Hellman, *Scoundrel Time* (Boston: Little, Brown & Co., 1976), 99.

20. Los Angeles WISP, Statement I, Ann Arbor Conference, June 9–10, 1962 (WSP Document Collection); *Women Strike for Peace Newsletter*, New York, New Jersey, Connecticut, Summer 1962, 1–2.

21. "WSP National Policy Statement," *Women Strike for Peace Newsletter*, New York, New Jersey, Connecticut, Summer 1962, 1–2.

22. "Key women" was the name used by WSP for those women who were part of the national and local communications network. They were the ones who were called upon to initiate actions or who called upon others to do so.

23. Katz, "Peace, Politics, and Protest," 122–26.

24. Jack, "The Will of the WISP Versus the Humiliation of HUAC."

25. The anti-HUAC statement by WSP was composed by the New York and Washington leadership in their usual collaborative fashion, with no pride or claim of authorship, so it is difficult to know which groups wrote what part. It was distributed through official WSP channels via the national office in Washington.

26. Bentley, *Thirty Years of Treason*, 951.

27. Women Strike for Peace, Washington, D.C., to "Dear WISP's," 6 December 1962 (WSP Document Collection).

28. Carol Urner, to Representative Francis Walter reprinted in *The Women's Peace Movement Bulletin* 1 (20 December 1962): 5.

29. *Hearings before Committee on Un-American Activities*, 2064–65.

30. *Ibid.*, 2074.

31. *Ibid.*, 2085.

32. Mary McGrory, "Prober Finds 'Peacemakers' More Than A Match," *Washington Evening* (D.C.) *Star*, 12 December 1962, A-1.

33. *Hearings before Committee on Un-American Activities*, 2095; 2101.

34. McGrory, "Prober Finds 'Peacemakers' More Than A Match," A-1.

35. Lyla Hoffman, undated typewritten statement (WSP Document Collection).

36. Thirty-seven favorable news stories, columns and editorials were reprinted in a hastily prepared WSP booklet, published less than two weeks after the hearings. Facsimile copies of Russell Baker's column, "Peace March Gals Make Red Hunters Look Silly," appeared on page 2; The *Detroit Free Press* story declaring "Headhunters Decapitated," appeared on page 4; "It's Ladies' Day at Capitol" from the *Chicago Daily News* appeared on page 9; and the Herblock cartoon appeared on page 5. *So Many Great Things Have Been Said*, (Washington, D.C.: Women Strike for Peace, 1963).

37. *Vancouver* (B.C.) *Sun*, 14 December 1962, 2.

38. "The Ladies Turn Peace Quiz into Greek Comedy," *Detroit Free Press*, 16 December 1962, 1.

39. *Detroit Free Press*, 13 December 1962, 8-A.

40. "Nobody Controls Anybody," *Washington* (D.C.) *Evening Star*, 14 December 1962, A-1, A-9.

41. *Hearings before Committee on Un-American Activities*, 2201.

42. *Madison* (Wis.) *Daily Cardinal*, 14 December 1962, 2.

43. Garst, "Women: Middle-Class Masses," 10–11.

44. Interview with Dagmar Wilson, Leesburg, Virginia, September 1977.

45. *New York Times Magazine*, 6 May 1962, 32.

46. On a WSP activity measure, 38 percent rated themselves as "very active," 10 percent as "active," and 42 percent rated themselves as "not active," or only "slightly active." The profile of the majority of the WSP participants that emerged was indeed that of middle-class, well-educated housewives. Sixty-five percent of the women had either a B.A. or a higher degree, at a time when only 6 percent of the female population over age 25 had a B.A. or more. Seventy-one percent of the WSP women were suburb or city dwellers, with the highest concentration in the East Central states, the West Coast, and the Midwest, and with low participation in the Mountain states and the South. The WSPers were concentrated in the twenty-five to forty-four age bracket. Only 5 percent of the group were "never marrieds." Of the married women 43 percent had from one to four children under six; 49 percent had from one to four or more children over eighteen. Sixty-one percent of the women involved in WSP were not, at the time of the questionnaire, employed outside the home. Nearly 70 percent of the husbands of the WSP women who responded to the survey were professionals.

Thirty-eight percent of the women who responded claimed to belong to no other organizations, or at least did not record the names of any organizations in response to questions concerning other community activities. Forty percent of the women were active in a combination of civic, race relations, civil liberties, peace, and electoral political activity. Only 11 percent were members of professional organizations. Boulding concluded that many of the WSP women were nonjoiners. As for their goals in joining WSP activities, the Boulding questionnaire revealed that 55 percent gave abolition of war or multilateral disarmament as their primary goals, and 22 percent gave non-violent solution of all conflict, political and social. The remainder chose as their goals a variety of proposals for world government or limited international controls such as a test ban treaty. As to their reasons for participating in WSP activities: 28 percent of the women said they had joined the movement over concern about fallout, testing, and civil defense, another 4 percent because of the Berlin Wall crisis; but 41 percent listed no specific event, just an increasing sense of urgency about the total world situation and a feeling of the need to make a declaration of personal responsibility. See Elise Boulding, *Who Are These Women?* (Ann Arbor, Mich.: Institute for Conflict Resolution, 1962).

47. *Ibid.*, 15.

48. Dorothy Dinnerstein, *The Mermaid and the Minotaur: Sexual Arrangements and Human Malaise* (New York: Harper Colophon Books, 1976), 259–62.

49. Ashley Montagu, "The Triumph and Tragedy of the American Woman," *Saturday Review* 27 September 1958, 14; Dr. Benjamin Spock, *The Common Sense Book of Baby and Child Care* (New York: Duell, Sloan & Pearce, 1945), 484.

50. "Feminism as Femininity in the Nineteen Fifties?" Birmingham History Group, *Feminist Review* no. 3 (1979), 48–65.

51. Sara Evans, *Personal Politics: The Roots of Women's Liberation in the Civil Rights Movement and the New Left* (New York: Alfred A. Knopf, 1979) 23.

31

To Become an American Woman: Education and Sex Role Socialization of the Vietnamese Immigrant Woman

Gail Paradise Kelly

In late April 1975, 129,000 Vietnamese immigrated to the United States. Before being allowed to settle in this country, they were held in four camps in the U.S., Camp Pendleton in California, Fort Chaffee in Arkansas, Eglin Air Force Base in Florida, and Fort Indian Town Gap in Pennsylvania. At the camps, the immigrants received medical examinations and applied for and awaited entry visas. American authorities, aware that many of the refugees had little exposure to American life, took this waiting time, which for many was about six months, to "introduce" Vietnamese to the country, and teach them behavior deemed minimal for living in an American social setting. Within each refugee camp were scores of programs to do precisely this. They consisted of formal and informal programs, some designed to teach the English language, others offering advice on child raising and medical care, and still others counseling Vietnamese on how to keep houses clean, buy clothes, and so on. These programs are the focus of this paper. I shall analyze how the camps' formal and informal education programs attempted to mold Vietnamese women into roles thought consonant with American culture, but at variance with ones these women had assumed within the Vietnamese family and society.

Women's Roles in Vietnam

Vietnamese women, immigrant and nonimmigrant alike, worked for a living. (Only fourteen percent of women refugees reported their occupations as "housewife.")[1] Vietnamese women, as a whole, worked—they worked out of economic necessity. This was just as true of urban, middle-class women as of peasant women or the urban poor; it has, however, not always been the case in Vietnam. Peasant women worked with the land with their families for survival; they also brought in cash income from petty trading. During the 1920s and 1930s rural markets were filled with women selling prepared food, dogs, handicrafts, and the like—usually to other Vietnamese.[2] In villages depending on fishing, women earned a living either in fishing, marketing fish, producing other foodstuffs on household plots, or in handicrafts. Poverty obliterated sex role divisions that occurred in richer Vietnamese families. Within upper-class families, however, except among urbanized, Westernized groups,

Reprinted by permission of David Kelly.

A slightly different version of this article was published by the author as "The Schooling of Vietnamese Immigrants: Internal Colonialism and its Impact on Women," in *Comparative Perspectives of Third World Women: The Impact of Race, Sex, and Class*, ed. Beverly Lindsay (New York: Praeger Publishers, 1980), pp. 276–296. The editors have added a conclusion to this essay, drawn entirely from that version.

women tended not to be part of economic life. They were sheltered within the household, and their sole function was to produce male heirs for the continuity of the corporate family.

The distinction between women's roles among classes changed drastically over the past twenty years of warfare and inflation in Vietnam.[3] Peasant women continued, as before, to work as farmers, traders, or craftspeople to sustain the family. Petty trade items changed, as many began to sell Coca-Colas and other Western manufactured items siphoned from American stores. The war, especially after 1964, forced urbanization. Strategic hamlets, the establishment of free-fire zones, defoliation programs, search and destroy missions, and programs like Phoenix, which assassinated countless villagers thought to be Vietcong, made the countryside uninhabitable. Cities like Saigon, Hue, and Da Nang swelled. Saigon alone tripled its population between 1962 and 1975. Changes in locale brought changes in peasant women's occupations and intensified the pressures of subsistence. Peasant women became bar girls, prostitutes, laundresses, and maids as well as continued in petty trade in Coca-Cola, cigarettes, liquor and beer, and drugs with urban Vietnamese and the military, both American and Vietnamese. Further, as the toll in death and mutilation of men, mostly of the lower classes who could not afford to buy their way out of military service, increased, women became more often than not the sole support of their families, either as heads of households or as the only persons capable of earning a living. Women emerged from partnership in the struggle for survival of the family to the sole person responsible for that survival.[4]

The war also appreciably altered the roles of the middle-class woman, because the war brought incredible inflation to urban areas, obliterating the buying power of the men supporting the family. The American press has talked much about how this inflation led to widespread corruption that included bribery and theft from American military warehouses. Corruption was one outgrowth of the inflation; another result was extensive moonlighting. Men like Mr. D., whom I interviewed at length, a professor of English at Saigon University, worked three other jobs trying to live in the style to which he and his family was accustomed. Additionally, in his family—and, he claimed, in others of his class in Saigon—five men working full time at several jobs did not produce adequate income. Thus his mother, who, he said, had before 1964 tended solely to the household, began working. She opened a "knitting factory" in the house during the days, employing his sisters, sisters-in-law, and aunts. She had to do this despite the fact that her husband was a highly placed government official, one of her sons was a colonel in the Vietnamese army, another a businessman, and yet another a customs official. Other urban families underwent such experiences. And that experience undermined traditional sex roles of that class within the family and the economy. The war, in short, had changed women's roles in all classes. Women became an integral part of the Vietnamese economy, working often as the sole support of the family.

While women's roles within the family changed dramatically through the war, families themselves survived. Vietnamese immigrated to the U.S. as families. Few refugees came alone, male or female. Of the 5,849 women who were processed at Fort Indian Town Gap, only fifty-three immigrated without relations.[5] Further, those families which came usually spanned three generations, and included brothers and sisters and their children, as well as grandparents. Several of these families had over a hundred members. Motivations for leaving Vietnam also reflected the persistence of the family as the basic unit in Vietnamese life. Many refugees whom I interviewed said they immigrated because they feared the new Vietnamese government would harm them because either a sister, an aunt, a cousin, a second cousin had worked for the Americans.[6]

Vietnamese refugee women, then, were connected to families. Their roles, in reality or by self-definition, were not that of housewife, nor were they those roles arising from

Confucian notions of womanhood which camp officials and, many Americans working with refugees believed. Occupationally, most did not fit into American job categories. For the most part, as I will show in this article, it was assumed that in America they would take on the role of housewife and mother consistant with American conceptions of sex role behavior. This was not only assumed, but enforced; educational efforts in the camps, almost without exception, were directed at resocializing these women to American stereotypic roles in English-language classes, in vocational courses, in cultural orientation meetings, and in printed materials circulated in the camps.[7]

Adult Education: New Language, New Roles

Within the refugee camps there were two types of organized classroom instruction for adults: English classes and vocational training, both run by professional educators under contract from the U.S. Department of Health, Education, and Welfare (HEW). The "school" had but one purpose—to make Vietnamese more "sponsorable." Under the Indochina Refugee Act, Vietnamese could officially enter the United States only if they either had a cash reserve of four thousand dollars per person, or if an American family, group, or organization was willing to assume moral and financial responsibility for the immigrant, either as an individual or as a family, for three years. The responsibilities were such that most Americans were reluctant to assume them unless it was clear that those they sponsored would be self-supporting in a relatively short time. The key to being self-supporting was not only that refugees have skills marketable in the United States, but that the refugees be able to speak English, to enable them to get jobs working with and for Americans. About fifty percent of the refugees could speak some English; of these, only about half could carry on a conversation in English.[8]

Camp authorities therefore placed great emphasis, when the refugee camps opened, on language classes for the refugees. Through HEW funds, they contracted local agencies (in the case of Fort Indian Town Gap, the Pennsylvania State Department of Education; at Fort Chaffee, Fort Smith Community College; at Camp Pendleton, the San Diego County School system) to set up formal instruction, using volunteers wherever possible rather than paid professionals as teachers. Instruction was centered on "survival" English; that is, on teaching only that English considered minimally necessary for functioning in the United States. It was directed only to *heads* of households. The decision to teach only heads of households in practice meant that women and children were excluded from class, for camp authorities, school administrators, and teachers believed that men would support their families and women would care for the family at home. The classes, twenty-six in all, were initially flooded with Vietnamese of both sexes and all ages—and were too large to allow adequate individual work on English pronunciation. Thus, women and children were told to leave.

This led to a large controversy at Indian Town Gap between the Pennsylvania Commission for Women, which assumed the role of immigrant women advocate, and school and camp personnel. The latter justified their policies on several grounds: first, they argued that men, not women, would be breadwinners and therefore had priority; second, that permitting women in class would disrupt the Vietnamese family. Women, they said, might learn the language faster than men, the men would lose "face" because of this, which would, in turn, lead to marital conflicts and divorce. Further, they argued that there were other types of classes for women that would suitably adjust them to American life: classes in birth control, child care, sewing, and cooking, as well as, after September, the Pennsylvania Commission for Women's sessions called "Women in America."[9] In short, American sex role stereotypes were imposed by determining who could go to English class. This broke down several months later as more refugees left the camps and space became available to women.

English classes taught more than language. They were designed to teach immigrants how to live in America and this involved teaching sex role behavior. This was clear in the curricular materials used in class, the conduct of class, and in teacher attitudes. It was explicit in interviews I had with school personnel.

Two types of curricular materials were used in teaching English at Fort Indian Town Gap: The HEW-developed "Survival" English course, and, as a supplement, the MacMillan 900 English language texts. The Survival English course, taught at three levels, had sixteen lessons that covered topics (in the order presented) that included meeting strangers, finding a place to live, occupations, renting apartments, shopping, John's interest, and applying for jobs.[10] The first lesson began with greetings and sex identifications. Students were drilled on phrases such as "Hello," "Good Afternoon," "My name is, . . ." "I'm a man," "I'm a woman." "I'm a boy," "I'm a girl," "Do you speak English?" Subsequently vocabulary taught locations of lavatories, days of the week, numbers, food, time, parts of the body, and job titles. Once vocabulary was introduced as words in isolation, lessons centered on pattern sentences and conversations. In all but two of the sixteen lessons the conversations took place between a "Mr. Brown" and "Mr. Jones" with Mr. Brown responding to Mr. Jones' questions. For example, Mr. Jones (no doubt the refugee) inquired, in the lesson on numbers, how he might go about buying a house. In the lesson on occupations, Mr. Jones asked what kind of job he might get to support his wife and two children. Mr. Jones said he could work as a room clerk, salesman, cashier, laborer, plumber, bricklayer, cook, cleaning person, secretary, typist, seamstress, nurses' aide. Women appeared in the dialogues only in two instances: in a lesson on budgeting and shopping, and in a lesson called "Conversation." Both are explicit in delineating male/female roles. In the conversation Miss Jones becomes part of the drill in two places—with the pattern sentence, "Miss Jones missed the bus to the Miss Universe competition," and "She is an attractive girl."[11] In the shopping sequences, all levels of English classes made it clear that women could shop only for small items. In the basic classes, teaching persons who knew no English, Mrs. Brown shopped for dresses, shoes, food, aspirins, baby needs, and cosmetics; Mr. Brown on the other hand shopped for shirts, houses, cars, and furniture.[12] In the advanced classes this division of labor between the sexes was expanded. "Marie" (no doubt the advanced classes' equivalent of Mrs. Brown) compared prices on food and other commodities, thereby saving her husband *his* hard-earned money. She was wise and would buy nothing but food without consulting her husband, Tim. In the lesson she found out where the cheapest sofa and sewing machine in town could be bought, but took her husband to the stores to decide for them where they should make their purchases.[13]

The MacMillan English Language 900 Series, used as a supplement to Survival English course, was not written specifically for Vietnamese refugees. It is a series of texts designed for non-English speakers, be they Italian, Arab, Chinese, German, or French. These texts, interestingly enough, are quite different from the materials devised specifically for Vietnamese. Women are not absent in the text, nor so inactive. They travel, they work, go to the doctor, shop, ask questions. Despite this, the roles portrayed for women are quite limited. In lesson one, Book Three, for intermediate students, for example, Judy talks with John about buying a new sofa, not because it is needed, but because it's pretty and a bargain.[14] In Unit 2, Barbara and Ella talk about baking a cake for Harry while Frank and Tom discuss hammers and nails; in Unit 4, marriage is discussed, as are bridal dresses; in Unit 5, Mr. James buys a house, and Mabel has coffee klatches with her new neighbors;

in Unit 8, on health and sickness, Dr. Smith and his female nurse give Mrs. Adams advice on her children's health and Mr. Lewis advice on his own health; in Unit 9, mother puts kids to bed and wakes them up while father goes off to work.[15] Designed primarily to teach English, the readers tended to focus less on sex role depictions than on teaching first-and second-person patterns of speech. "I-You" is more apparent in the text than "He-She."

English-language classes, in short, transmitted, as do many American texts used in schools, stereotypical roles—women were noticeably absent in class materials. When they appeared, their qualities were reduced to beauty and interest in it, and their role was that of wife and mother, particularly shopper. It is interesting to note that in the Survival English course, designed specifically for Vietnamese refugees, occupations reserved for American women (typists, seamstresses, nurses' aides) were presented as jobs for Vietnamese men. The programs were not only allocating Vietnamese men into lower-class and female occupations; they also presented immigrant men with roles traditionally reserved for U.S. women. It is Mr. Jones, in the Survival English course, who finds out where stores are, gets a doctor, selects a church, locates the children's school, and so on. In the Survival English materials, women ventured out of the house only to shop.

While the sex bias evident in the MacMillan 900 series may be unconscious—publishers of children's books and school texts in the U.S. have explained their past practices in this way—this was not the case in camp-prepared materials. Many camp officials and school personnel were gravely concerned about the stability of the immigrant family, and the consequences for individuals and the social order should the Vietnamese family disintegrate. (Some veterans of the Agency for International Development working in the camps believed this had already happened under the stress of the war and was the reason the South Vietnamese government fell. They were determined to reconstruct what they thought was the traditional Vietnamese family among the immigrants, believing this to be the only way for them to survive in America.) School teachers, curriculum coordinators, and administrative and resettlement personnel time after time emphasized the role of education in reinforcing the Vietnamese family and the supremacy of the father, which they assumed was characteristic of both Vietnamese and American families. It was through the reinforcement and/or reestablishment of patriarchal relations that immigrants could "adjust" well to America. And, as the curriculum coordinator of the adult school pointed out to me in one of our lengthy interviews, the school's role was not just to teach English; its mission was to help its students "adjust" to America and live happily there.[16]

The teaching materials were not the only elements in formal English instruction that attempted to rob Vietnamese women of their social and economic roles and put Vietnamese men into lower-class and female work-force jobs. In-class instruction also worked in such a manner. An incident in an English class designed for illiterates illustrates this best. This class had more women in it than any other class I observed at Fort Indian Town Gap. (The other classes appeared to be predominantly male; advanced English classes had almost no women in them.) Because the students were illiterate, written materials could not be used. The six-week course had but three units: (1) parts of the body and their names; (2) foods; (3) jobs. All this was constructed by the teachers with the assistance of the curriculum coordinator. Vocabulary was introduced by pointing to an object or a picture of it and learning the English name for it. When pictures or objects were not available, charade was used. In one class the teacher clucked and flapped his arms like a chicken to introduce the term "chicken." He then drilled the class on the phrase, "I want some chicken to eat."[17]

The major emphasis in the classroom was on occupations—teaching Vietnamese refugees how to describe their work skills to prospective employers. In class the teacher began with the phrase, "What kind of work do you do?" He then drew stick figures showing different kinds of work—ditch digging, selling, and so on, naming them all. After introducing phrases like "I am a ditch digger; I am a mechanic," he asked each of his thirty-or-more students, "What kind of work do you do?" The first student to respond was a young man, obviously a former soldier. He responded by imitating a gun with his fingers and replied, "I rat-a-tat-tat." The teacher corrected him with, "I work with my hands." Next to recite was a middle-aged woman, who had lacquered teeth (indicating she came from a rural lower-class family). She made a motion that looked like casting nets (I found out later she came from coastal Vung-Tau and fished for a living). The teacher responded with, "I am a housewife." The woman looked puzzled. The teacher then drew a stick figure on the blackboard representing a woman with a broom in her hand, inside a house. He repeated "I am a housewife," pointing to the woman. She and the women sitting with her began a lively discussion in Vietnamese and started laughing. The teacher then drilled all the women as a group repeatedly with the phrase "I am a housewife."[18]

English classes were the major formal education provided within the refugee camps. The adult school, however, did offer six vocational courses, on electricity, plumbing, carpentry, and home economics. All except the home economics class were simultaneously classes in English terminology appropriate to the skills immigrants already possessed. Perhaps this explains the poor attendance at the classes. Only five or ten students came regularly. The home economics class, conducted in English without a translator, was the only vocational class that taught skills rather than terminology. It was designed primarily for women, to teach them how to use and maintain appliances found in American homes—electric stoves, refrigerators, mixers, and blenders—how to shop in supermarkets; how to tell the difference between nonprepackaged and prepackaged foods and their nutritional values; and how to cook American-style (make chili; pickled beets, gingerbread, jello molds, and so on). Attendance at class averaged seven persons, none of whom spoke English.

Formal education in schools is but one means by which immigrants were prepared for living in America. Within the refugee camps, outside the school, similar efforts occurred. The Pennsylvania Commission for Women, believing that the school and camp authorities were inadequately preparing women for life in America, set up a series of programs called "Women in America" to rectify these "deficiencies," much to the chagrin, I might add, of camp authorities and school personnel.

"Women in America": A Counter to English Classes?

"Women in America" represented to some extent an alternative to the kind of sex role socialization evident in the English language classes. Those who designed it firmly believed in women's rights and fluidity of sex roles, and that Vietnamese women were in a stage of bondage similar to that in nineteenth-century China.[19] The program coordinator, an American woman in her late twenties, had lived several years in Taiwan, Hong Kong, and Japan and saw the Vietnamese family and women's roles within it in light of her limited observations abroad. To her, it was only recently that these women had stopped having their feet bound. According to her, their role was only to produce male heirs for the family and to accede to their mothers-in-law's and husbands' wishes within the household where they were confined. Camp authorities, she told me, through their educational programs and their practices (specifically the practice of not intervening in known cases of wife-beating at Indian Town Gap)[20] reinforced Vietnamese women's traditional roles, which, she believed, were both oppressive and impractical in America. The "Women in America" programs, thus, were set up to explain to immigrant women their roles and rights in the U.S.

"Women in America" was initially designed as a series of meetings dealing topically with life in the American family, women's rights (the right to hold property, abortion, birth control and so on), women at work, and organizations that assist women in whatever they choose to do. What was planned as a series of meetings became six single evening presentations covering basically the same ground each time. This occurred because few of the same people came to more than one session, either because they had found sponsors and left the camps, or through lack of interest or difficulty in finding someone to care for their children.

The content of the classes varied in minor ways at each meeting, depending on responses to them. At several meetings discussion centered on snow or shopping as women, excluded from English-language classes, sought out information about America in general, and took the opportunity to meet Americans to ask questions that intrigued them the most. Generally, the class organizers tried to cover four topics each night before allowing refugees to change the topic: family life, women's rights, jobs for women, and women's organizations. Each of these was presented by the four women from the Pennsylvania Commission for Women, who spoke in English with simultaneous translation into Vietnamese. The first speaker covered the family. Her presentation stressed men's participation in housework and child care and was accompanied by pictures of men bathing children, doing dishes, shopping, and so on. There were almost no pictures of women engaged in these tasks. The second presentation told women they had a right to abortion on demand, could divorce their husbands, could vote, own property, and work if they chose to. It stressed women's right to plan family size, and said that two children was the desirable number for happy families. The third presentation was on jobs. It told Vietnamese women that some American women worked, some chose not to work. With the aid of photographs, the speaker surveyed the world of work for women, showing photos of women as bulldozer operators, nurses, teachers, librarians, salesladies, karate teachers, engineers, corporate presidents, and so on. The person giving the presentation paused when she showed the picture of a nurse at work, and told the class that it was an excellent occupation for women. At this point, a middle-aged immigrant asked if women could be butchers. The response given was that the presenter knew of no woman butchers in America. The final talk was on women's organizations. This was primarily a detailed enumeration of groups like the YWCA, Planned Parenthood, the National Welfare Rights Organization, and the League of Women Voters.[21]

These classes did, indeed, present women's roles and work in quite a different light than did other formal education within the camps. Unlike the English-language classes, women were depicted outside the home, with the possibility of financial independence. The series, however, did not have as much as impact as did the English-language classes, for no more than thirty persons attended the meetings. Several of those who attended were men who, in the discussions following the presentations, made speeches claiming that men in America had no rights at all. The impact of the programs was all the more limited because there was no real incentive for refugees to attend them or take them seriously. Camp authorities and school teachers openly disapproved of the meetings, and ran movies and English classes during the times they were scheduled. Further, camp authorities made it clear to refugees that only by learning English would they adjust well to America. By September, when the Women in America series began, area commanders who were responsible for barrack sections of the camps pressured adults into going to English-language classes; they did not exert any such pressure for persons to attend the series. Most openly, they resented the classes apparently because they believed "Women in America" would disrupt the Vietnamese family, make Vietnamese men anxious about resettling in America and having to cope with aggressive women, and in the long run would make camp authorities' task more difficult.[22]

The Written Word

A discussion of sex role socialization for Vietnamese refugees in the camps would be incomplete without considering other parts of camp life. Refugees learned about American life every day by shopping at the camp (usually done by men); going to the various recreation centers in the camps; watching nightly movies; hanging around resettlement agency offices, chatting with American soldiers and refugee workers about snow, Montana, dating, and hot dogs; and reading materials written in Vietnamese circulated within the camp. The most widely circulated and read material at Fort Indian Town Gap was *Dat Lanh* (Good Land), the daily bilingual camp newspaper published by the U.S. Army Psychological Operations Unit. *Dat Lanh* was not merely a news sheet summarizing national, international, and camp events, it was also a journal intended to supplement the work of schools in preparing Vietnamese to live in America. It was the only bilingual reading material at Indian Town Gap, other than camp notices and government documentary information.

Dat Lanh, which began publication on May 28, 1975, carried three types of articles: camp announcements (meeting and meal times, lists of incoming refugees, notices of sponsorships available to refugees, barrack rules, immigration laws); how-to articles (how to work a telephone, register for a sponsor, buy a car); and informational articles about the United States and its culture. The informational pieces about the U.S. will be the focus of this section, for in them the paper spelled out social behavior expected of persons living in the U.S. The informational articles were broadly of two types: American history and geography, designed to teach the basics of patriotic identification; and information on social behavior. The history and geography articles appeared almost daily. They consisted of atlas-type descriptions of each of the fifty states and the lives of American presidents. On holidays, *Dat Lanh* ran two-to-three-page stories explaining the significance of the day, particularly Memorial Day, Flag Day, the Fourth of July, Labor day, Armed Forces Day, Halloween and Thanksgiving.

The articles on social behavior were in keeping with sex role molding of the English-language classes. Most of these articles, called "The American Way of Life," were addressed to heads of households, presumably male, and explained tipping in restaurants (when the man takes his family out), getting insurance for *his* car and family, buying *his* family clothes, cars, and houses, and so on. Following these articles were short tips on pregnancy, child care, child health, toys, and so on, addressed to mothers. A front page article on July 31, for example, was entitled "Attention Mothers," and described mothers' duties in getting health care for their children. Articles of this nature assumed sex role divisions along stereotypical lines for the Vietnamese family. Other articles openly promoted such sex roles as crucial for Vietnamese to follow if they wished to get along in this country. A *Dat Lanh* front page article on September 7, 1975, for example, entitled "Men and Women" advised men to take their wives on trips, to rise when a woman enters the room, open doors for women, help them push revolving doors since they are not strong enough to push them themselves, pay bills at restaurants, buy tickets, and so on. Further, it told them not to be "frightened" by American women who seem "noisy, aggressive, dominating," and reassured them that most women in America are "quiet, content and gentle" and enjoy being taken care of. The following two issues carried articles on single women's behavior. One of them counseled women on how to find single men. It advised them to join sports clubs, or photography or ballroom dancing classes. Girls should not ask men out, it continued. "In this country the man . . . does the inviting and the planning." The article then pointed out that girls could ask men to their homes for dinner, if they really wanted to impress them.

Education, Role Imposition and Role Reality

This article has described educational efforts directed at Vietnamese immigrants to the U.S. in one resettlement camp, Fort Indian Town Gap, Pennsylvania, particularly the sex role behavior taught through both formal and informal education designed for adults. The roles suggested for women had little correspondence with roles Vietnamese had historically assumed in their own country. Through circumstances of social class, war, and inflation, almost all Vietnamese women had worked to support their families, and through their economic contribution had gained a degree of power within the family, often serving as heads of families. They were not confined to cooking, cleaning, shopping, and child-rearing. The education in the camps proposed to take these women out of the workplace and put them back in the home. Access to English classes, initially restricted to adult males, meant that the women were deprived of an opportunity to enter the American workplace. It was men, not women, who were to be taught the language or how to fill out job applications. Women's education was initially confined to birth control, child care, and maternity classes, conducted in Vietnamese, and home economics classes, none of which involved preparation for life outside the house and the family.

When women entered English-language classes that were key to entering the American economy, they found class materials that relegated them to roles in their homes—for women could only shop and budget and marry. They did not work for a living, even though most Vietnamese women had; nor did they make decisions. "I am a housewife" was the only role model offered, and that role model was presented in such a manner as to imply that assuming such a role was required for living in America. This role socialization was deliberate. Americans, teachers and camp officials alike, believed in the primacy of the family and women's place as housekeeper. Despite their insistence on teaching these roles, they claimed that such relationships were intrinsically Vietnamese, and that retaining such "Vietnamese-ness" would facilitate immigrants' adjustment in the country.

Even the camps' definition of "the family" was somewhat of an anomaly, given the breakup of the Vietnamese family through resettlement. Americans defined the family as nuclear rather than extended, and resettled only nuclear families as units. Thus nuclear families within Vietnamese extended families were settled at different ends of the continent. Solidarity of the Vietnamese family, which depended far more on the trigenerational extended unit than it did upon male supremacy, was therefore not especially preserved.

The Pennsylvania Commission for Women and its representatives, while scarcely able to speak for refugees as a whole, or for Vietnamese women in particular, tried to offer a different view of American life for Vietnamese women and their possible role within it. To some extent, their view was more realistic about changes necessary to survive. Vietnamese were being resettled in an American society in an economic recession, where there were few jobs available to Americans, let alone to immigrants who barely speak English and possess few skills. Jobs for which most refugees were qualified were the lowest-paying in the society. Under American definitions of the nuclear family, the Vietnamese family averaged seven persons. Men working as day laborers, nurses' aides, and so on were not likely to earn enough to sustain an entire family, so that women would be forced to work, either to supplement family income or as the sole source of family income. A year after the camps closed, seventy-three percent of the immigrants who had once been professionals, technicians, managers, and businessmen found themselves blue-collar workers; another seventeen percent became clerical and sales personnel. Only ten percent went into jobs equivalent to those they had held in Vietnam. Most worked in jobs paying minimum wages;

many of these jobs were temporary. Yearly incomes were so low that close to fifty percent of all Vietnamese families in the United States received some form of welfare.

While the camp educational programs were a point of entry of Vietnamese into the society and culture of Americans, they did not serve this purpose equally for men and women. Rather, they prepared only Vietnamese men for integration into the U.S. work force and society; Vietnamese women were not the focus of integrational efforts. "Women in America" alone tried to prepare the women for entry into the U.S. work force. However, like the other educational efforts, this program impinged upon Vietnamese culture and set U.S. terms for Vietnamese adjustment to the society. The educational programs also fostered the lowering of Vietnamese expectations, by preparing men for occupations usually reserved for women in U.S. society. While preparing men for women's roles, they also prepared Vietnamese men to usurp women's roles within the family. The schools taught Vietnamese men to take care of schooling, medical care, shopping, and the like.

English language programs, *Dat Lanh*, and even the "Women in America" programs, regardless of their points of disagreement, were all directed toward getting Vietnamese to enter the society and culture of Americans regardless of their desires. Most Vietnamese were ambivalent about becoming integrated into American society; they opposed the U.S. resettlement policy, openly expressing their desire to remain Vietnamese within the United States. Of this, American were well aware. Article after article in *Dat Lanh* derided Vietnamese unwillingness to leave the "Little Vietnams" of the camps and become Americans. After the camps closed, Vietnamese opposition to U.S. resocialization policies became overt, as they abandoned their original places of resettlement and left the diaspora designed for them, to form their own Vietnamese communities.[23]

Notes

Research for this paper was made possible by grants from the University of Buffalo Foundation; State University of New York at Buffalo Institutional Funds; the SUNY Foundation; and the New York State Council for the Humanities.

1. These statistics are taken from Refugee Demographic Characteristics, Camp Pendleton, September 16, 1975 (mimeo); Refugee Statistical Data, Fort Indian Town Gap, Pennsylvania, November 1975 (mimeo).

2. My discussion of women's roles is based on the following works: Ngo Vinh Long, ed., *Vietnamese Women in Society and Revolution* 1. *The French Colonial Period* (Cambridge: Vietnam Resource Center, 1974); and to a lesser extent on Arlene Eisen Bergman, *Women of Vietnam* (San Francisco: People's Press, 1974); Ngo Tat To, *When the Light is Out*, (Manor: Foreign Languages Publishing House).

3. Changes in women's roles are discussed in Arlene Eisen Bergman, *Women of Vietnam*; Tiziano Terzani, *Giai Phong: The Fall and Liberation of Saigon* (New York: St. Martin's Press, 1976). Several interviews I conducted at Fort Indian Town Gap also detailed these changes, particularly: Interview with Melvin R. Chapman, Area Coordinator, Area 5B, Fort Indian Town Gap, Pennsylvania, November 1975 (Mr. chapman had served with USAID in Vietnam from 1967 to 1975); Interview with Duc-Ting-Nguyen, Teachers' Aide and former University Teacher, Fort Indian Town Gap, Pennsylvania, October 30, 1975; Interview with Dr. Dao, Chief, Family Planning Clinic, Fort Indian Town Gap, Pennsylvania, October 1975.

4. Interview with Duc-Ting-Nguyen, Fort Indian Town Gap, Pennsylvania, October 30, 1975.

5. Refugee Statistical Data, Fort Indian Town Gap, Pennsylvania, November 1975 (mimeo).

6. Interview with Dr. Dao, Fort Indian Town Gap, Pennsylvania, October 1975; Interview with X (a Vietnamese woman of 35), September 26, 1975, Fort Indian Town Gap); Interview with Nguyen-Ngoc-Bich October 15, 1975; Interview with Nguyen Thank Viet, October 15, 1975.

7. My analysis is based on four sources, all obtained in extensive fieldwork at the refugee camps at Fort Indian Town Gap, Pennsylvania, from September to December 1975. These are: (1) curriculum guides, books, and instructional materials used in adult education classes; (2) observations of adult education classes and orientation meetings; (3) interviews with refugee workers, teachers, curriculum specialists and refugees who participated in these programs; and (4) an analysis of the contents of *Dat Lanh*, the bilingual daily newspaper of the camp. I believe that the resocialization efforts that I observed at Fort Indian Town Gap were quite

similar to those at the other refugee centers, since personnel at the camps were remarkably similar and education programs were set up under the supervision of the Department of Health, Education and Welfare and the Indochina Refugee Taskforce in Washington.

8. Refugee Statistical Data, Fort Indian Town Gap, Pennsylvania, November 1975 (mimeo).

9. The school's policy of excluding women from English-language classes initially was discussed in the following interviews: Interview with Phyllis Hesser, Curriculum Coordinator, Adult Education School, Day Program, Fort Indian Town Gap, Pennsylvania, October 29, 1975; November 21, 1975; Interview with Kenneth Adams, Superintendent of Schools, Fort Indian Town Gap, Pennsylvania, September 25, 1975; Interview with Judy Hansen, Director of Information, Pennsylvania Commission for Women, October 29, 1975.

10. This discussion of English-language curriculum is based on an analysis of Survival English Materials collected at Fort Indian Town Gap, Pennsylvania (mimeo).

11. Survival English, Unit I, Lesson I, Basic Course (mimeo).

12. *Ibid.*, Level II, Intermediate, Lesson 4, p. 4.

13. *Ibid.*, Advanced English, Unit 5, "How to Stretch Your Dollar."

14. English Languages Services, Inc. *English 900, Books 1–3*, (New York: Collier Macmillan, Inc., 1975, 16th ed.); Book 3, p. 8.

15. *Ibid.*, Book 3, Unit 2, p. 19; Unit 4, pp. 38–42; Unit 5, p. 49; Unit 8, pp. 77–86; and Unit 9, p. 93.

16. This was explicit in interviews with the following people at Fort Indian Town Gap, Pennsylvania: Melvin Chapman, Area Coordinator, Area 5B, November 1975; Phyllis Hesser, Curriculum Coordinator, Adult Education School, Day Program, October 29, 1975; Jerry Chemiolek, case worker, USCC, October 17, 1975; Peggy Dillon, case worker, USCC, and teacher, Adult Education School, Night Program, November 20, 1975 (she did not agree with this perspective but discussed it at length); Pvt. Richard Lee Blumski, Information Specialist U.S. Army and Teacher, Adult Education School, Night Program, November 20, 1975.

17. Classroom Observation (taped), Adult Education School, Day Program, Fort Indian Town Gap, Pennsylvania, October 30, 1975.

18. *Ibid.*

19. Interview with Judy Hansen, Director of Information, Pennsylvania Commission for Women, Fort Indian Town Gap, Pennsylvania, October 29, 1975.

20. Ms. Hansen is not the only person who spoke about camp authorities ignoring wife-beating. Melvin Chapman, Coordinator, Area 5B, told me in a taped interview that it was camp policy (November 1975.)

21. "Women in America," third session, October 29, 1975, Fort Indian Town Gap, Pennsylvania (taped).

22. This attitude was most clearly expressed by Jerry Chemiolek, USCC case worker, at Indian Town Gap in an interview on October 17, 1975. It was echoed by Phyllis Hessler, Curriculum Coordinator, Adult Education School, Day Program (October 29, 1975.)

23. Gail P. Kelly, *From Vietnam to America: A chronicle of the Vietnamese Immigration to the United States* (Boulder, Col.: Westview Press, 1978), chap. 7.

32

Changing Women: The Crosscurrents of American Indian Feminine Identity

Rebecca Tsosie

> *The Blanket Around Her*
> Maybe it is her birth
> which she holds close to herself
> or her death
> which is just as inseparable
> and the white wind
> that encircles her is a part
> just as
>   the blue sky
> hanging in turquoise from her neck
> oh woman
> remember who you are
> woman
> it is the whole earth
>   —*Joy Harjo*

Laguna novelist Leslie Silko begins *Ceremony* with one word—"Sunrise." The word is simple, yet it encompasses an entire body of culture and thought which revolves around the concepts of birth, regeneration, cyclicity, and the union of masculine and feminine elements. Many American Indian worldviews speak of balanced "opposite" forces which combine as a dynamic whole to form the universe. One may extend the metaphor of "sunrise" further in reference to the contemporary "rebirth" of American Indian cultures, perhaps best illustrated in the growing body of literature by American Indian writers. Kenneth Lincoln makes such an analogy in his comprehensive analysis of American Indian literature, *Native American Renaissance.* Interestingly, Lincoln correlates the dynamics of this movement to gender as he writes, "Native Americans are writing prolifically, particularly the women, who correlate feminist, nativist, and artistic commitments in a compelling rebirth."[1]

The "rebirth" is indeed compelling, though perhaps not unexpected. For too long, Indian women have suffered the burden of Euro-American stereotypes. Following the traditional European perceptions of Indian people as "Noble Savages," or worse, as "Blood-thirsty Savages," Indian women have been cast into a similarly bifurcated role: the "noble" Princess ("Pocahontas") or the more "savage" Squaw, a loathsome, unintelligent "drone."

Reprinted with permission of the author. Originally appeared in the *American Indian Culture and Research Journal*, vol. 12, no. 1 (1988).

Countless Hollywood epics and dime store Westerns have ingrained these stereotypes in American minds, and even today Indian women are frequently approached in terms of these stereotypes.

Importantly, then, contemporary Indian women writers are speaking out against these stereotypes and affirming their own concepts of femininity and "Indianness." Their artistic expressions frequently lean toward traditional beliefs, deeply rooted in the spiritual essence of tribal worldviews; at other times, the same writers speak with an essential understanding of contemporary reality—"Indian" bars, urban ghettos, Ph.D. programs and Oklahoma powwows. In this seemingly contradictory mixture lies the essence of contemporary Indian literature: the active, forceful unity of the dual worlds in which Indian people *must* survive. Paula Allen comments accurately: "From the meeting of the archaic and the contemporary the facts of her life become articulate, and the fact that modern American Indians are both Indian and American becomes very clear."[2]

Perhaps one could say that "American Indian feminine identity" is itself a myth, for the diversity of tribal systems and worldviews is immense, and the thoughts and feelings of Indian women are equally diffuse. However, contemporary Indian women writers have chosen to express both the diversity of Indian people, and the centrality of an Indian "ethos" which emphasizes "life," "motion," and "balance" against the polarized madness of Western technology. They have chosen to stress the critical "female principal" of the universal cycles, and use this natural power to refute the victimization and oppression which characterizes Western patriarchal power structures. By making these choices, these women writers have established a "voice" and an "identity" for the Indian woman which are grounded in the realities of the present, rather than the stereotypes of the past.

By objectively considering the social history of American Indian people and the autobiographical experiences of Indian women in conjunction with the current literature, a dynamic portrait of social change, cultural resilence, and lasting power emerges for the American Indian woman. This portrait counters the American myth of the "Princess and the Squaw" with clarity and dignity, and, one can only hope, with finality.

I

As Patricia Albers notes in the opening chapter of *The Hidden Half,* the male image of the American Indian has always been dominant in the minds of white observers. The "Chief" in feathered regalia, the lithe bison hunter poised above the prey—both images recur in American art and film. The Indian woman, eclipsed by such masculine glory, is either omitted entirely or considered in terms of dichotomous stereotypes—the "noble" Princess or the "savage" Squaw. These images of the Indian woman originated with the bifurcated, ethnocentric observations of early European explorers and traders. Their observations stemmed from the European ideology that Alice Kehoe terms "oppositional dualism," or the stratified, hierarchical Western worldview which perceived the universe as polarized and alienated in a set of opposing categories: "civilized" versus "primitive," "male" versus "female," "Christian" versus "Pagan."[3] This worldview was manifested in European society through social castes, gender inequality, and the rigid dichotomy between the "public" or "market" sphere, versus the "private" or "domestic" sphere. Predictably, the entire system was transposed onto Indian societies by the early European observers, creating gender splits and inequalities which were previously unknown, and tainting Indian women with a version of the "pure" versus the "fallen" woman categorization which had already been applied to European women.

When applied to women of a more "savage" race, as Indian people were considered, this moral categorization assumed significantly more harmful proportions. Rayna Green comments on the long-lasting effects of the "Princess/Squaw" stereotype in her article, "The Pocahontas Perplex: The Image of Indian Women in American Culture." Green traces the "Princess" phenomenon back to traditional European ballads about handsome male adventurers and the beautiful "pagan" (Arabian, Far Eastern) princesses who saved them from the wrath of the "savages" (often at their own personal expense). Green believes that this folktale tradition was transferred to America with the Pocahontas tale, and the subsequent variations of the story, which eventually came to comprise almost a specific genre of American fiction. The Princess was defined by her noble, selfless "love" for a brave white man. But following the European tradition of "oppositional dualism," the Princess received a negative counterpart, the Squaw, who was sullied by actual reference to sexual liaisons with white men.

Naturally, any vestiges of reality inherent in the social history of white/Indian contact became meaningless for the vast majority of Americans for whom the stereotypes became "truth." The "Princess/Squaw" dichotomy does not even approach the historical realities of Indian women, and may be more closely paralleled with what Rayna Green terms the "Virgin/Whore paradox," the categorization of European women as "pure" or "fallen." The primary factor in perceptions of both European women and Indian women became their definition in terms of their relationship with *males*. The Puritan ethic accorded the European woman some status for being a "dutiful" wife and mother: faithful, submissive, pious, and hardworking. "Bad" women blatantly displayed the opposite traits: promiscuity, assertiveness, disregard for Christian precepts, laziness. Importantly, whether "good" or "bad," European women were expected to remain confined to the "private" sphere of love, sex, marriage, and childbirth. Only men could become involved in the "public" sphere of politics, warfare, and Church authority.[4]

Although the same social dichotomy has been applied to Native American groups from first contact to twentieth-century anthropological studies, the distinction between "public" and "private" spheres and gender role differentiation often becomes meaningless in application to traditional Indian systems. As the studies of *The Hidden Half* emphasize, and Paula Allen affirms in *The Sacred Hoop*, gender roles were often flexible and adaptive among the various aspects of society in traditional Indian cultural systems. Perhaps the most dangerous characteristic of European gender categorizations is the tendency to *rank* "duties" into hierarchical layers of "status," thereby ascribing notions of "inferiority" to women's domestic duties, and "superiority" to men's roles in politics and warfare. Such "value judgments" invariably stem from assumptions of the "universal" attributes of the "male/female relationship."[5] Although clearly many Indian societies did ascribe to a degree of task differentiation according to gender, the variable of "importance" attached to these tasks may be a purely European invention. Janet Spector's research on Hidatsa task differentiation reveals the vital role which women played in all phases of the agricultural process.[6] Since the success of the crops often meant the critical difference between survival and starvation, one might perceive the real status which would accrue to competent agriculturalists. In this case, the work of the women complemented the hunting efforts of the men with equal importance.

Patricia Albers also discusses the native integration of "public" and "domestic" spheres in her article on the changing status of Devil's Lake Sioux women.[7] Albers outlines the traditional Sioux ethic which promoted the ideal relationship between male and female as complementary and based on principles of individual autonomy and voluntary sharing. Because of this ethic, Albers claims that the concept of male "dominance" was meaningless for the traditional Sioux. However, Albers agrees with many other authors that U.S.

government policies which, according to patriarchal Euro-American tradition, recognized only male political leaders and only male adults as "head of household," eventually altered the traditional system to a certain extent. Paula Allen supports Albers' view with her discussion of the effects of European colonization on the "gynocratic" social and political systems of the Iroquois tribes and the Cherokee.[8] In such groups, the political and social structures were formerly guided by tribal women; however, with the advent of the Federal "trust" relationship, Indian groups were forced to follow the Anglo model of government, which specified male leadership. However, Albers disputes that the effects of Anglo patriarchy were of final significance. For most Indian groups, the "spheres" remain integrated even today. As Albers comments, despite the preponderance of males on the Devil's Lake Sioux Tribal Council, "To a large extent, tribal politics and domestic politics are the same. . . . The issues that tribal leaders have been faced with in recent years are dominated by domestic concerns that have been critical to both men and women."[9] For many Indian groups, the traditional worldviews which emphasize a holistic, balanced universe continue to counter the Euro-American emphasis on hierarchy and "dominant/subordinate" social roles.

Importantly, a primary distinction between the definition of women by Europeans and that by Indians was the Indian emphasis on individuality. While Europeans defined women in relation to male figures, American Indians generally perceived women and men as individuals with specific talents, abilities, and clan-sanctioned roles. Because Europeans failed to realize this Native emphasis on individuality, they largely ignored the fact that Indian women often played key roles in all of the major political, religious, and economic institutions of the tribe. In Robert Grumet's article on seventeenth- and eighteenth-century coastal Algonkin women, "Sunksquaws, Shamans and Tradeswomen," he maintains that all major tasks were cooperatively performed by men and women on the basis of ability, and that a "corresponding egalitarian sociopolitical organization" characterized most of the mid-Atlantic Algonkin groups during the colonial period.[10] Likewise, in "Farmers, Warriors, Traders: A Fresh Look at Ojibway Women," Priscilla Buffalohead contrasts the popular notion of Ojibway women as "drudges and slaves to men," with the reality of their dynamic roles in the "political, economic and social life of their communities." In addition to the more "expected" roles of food gathering, preparation, and child care, Buffalohead finds evidence of Ojibway women as recognized band leaders, as medicine women, and as warriors. She comments that Anglo officials often chose to ignore these women and deal with male members of the tribe instead. However, in the tribal view, these women were recognized and respected as leaders. Buffalohead concludes that Ojibway society placed a premium value not on gender, but on individuality: "Women as well as men could step outside the boundaries of traditional sex role assignments and, as individuals, make group-respected choices."[11]

The social and political power of Indian women was sanctioned by tribal religious traditions which often emphasized the vital role of female deities. Unlike the European Christian religion, guided by an omnipotent male God, most Indian religions revolved around coequal deities who protected their "creations"—the Earth, sky, animals, crops, and human beings. Because the Earth's natural system depends on cyclical regeneration, the "female" aspects of creation were particularly important. Hence, many of the primary deities were perceived as female. For example, Changing Woman in Navajo belief is a powerful creator-figure who is responsible for the growth of the crops and the birth of all new life. Changing Woman is also perceived as a powerful protectress of what she has created. To this day, the ideal of Navajo womanhood is modeled on the characteristics of Changing Woman. Jennie Joe comments on the strong, protective feelings Navajo women have for their land (which is passed down matrilineally through clan ties). Joe associates these strong traditional ties to the present resistance to federal relocation policies, largely organized by Navajo women: "The defensive actions that these women . . . continue to take fit . . . their perceptions of [the] appropriate role for themselves. This concept includes the role of a warrior. For example, most traditional Navajo women have names that contain the word 'baa', which signifies 'female warrior.' As a female warrior she is expected to fight off . . . whatever poses a threat to the well being of her family and home."[12]

Similarly, the Sioux believe that their Sacred Pipe Religion was given to them by White Buffalo Woman, a female deity who presides over the Four Winds, the primary natural powers of the Great Plains area.[13] To this day, Sioux women are perceived as sacred and powerful. Grace Black Elk, an Oglala Lakota elder and spiritual leader, scoffs at the white feminists who see Indian woman as "slaves to their men." Ward Churchill records her opinions:

> The Lakota have no word for "sexist."
>   The White man does.
> The Lakota does not put his name to his child.
>   White men do.
> For the Lakota, property is the possession of
>   the woman. The generations are the responsibility
>   of the woman. Power is thus in the hands of
>   women. . . .
> Lakota women / are the strength of the people.[14]

Most tribes saw the strongest, most active and articulate tribal women as closely paralleling the traditional female deities. Indian women were accorded great status for their achievements in agriculture, hunting, and hide and meat preparation. Indian people felt that such abilities were divinely sanctioned, hence of the utmost respect; Europeans on the other hand, perceived Indian women as exploited "work drones."[15] Priscilla Buffalohead offers an interesting appraisal of the European attitude toward Indian women: "American Indian women appeared exploited to many nineteenth-century writers if only because their ideal of woman, fostered by the privileged classes of Europe and America, was a frail, dependent person in need of protection."[16] And, indeed, the nineteenth-century Euro-American "ideal" of the passive, self-effacing, delicate, useless woman (personified by Lily Bart in Edith Wharton's novel *The House of Mirth*) was *never* observed by American Indians.

The disparity between European and Native American gender perceptions resulted in a continued Euro-American bias which clouded the realities of American Indian women as dynamic, interactive individuals, in favor of the polarized "Princess/Squaw" stereotype. These stereotypes prevented any conception of the Indian woman as "real," "powerful," or even, at times, "human." Rayna Green notes that, "As some abstract, noble Princess tied to 'America,' and to sacrificial zeal, she [had] power as a symbol. . . . As the Squaw, a depersonalized object of scornful convenience, she [was] powerless. Like her male relatives she [could be] easily destroyed without reference to her humanity."[17] Green associates these dehumanizing stereotypes with the tragic massacre at Sand Creek, and unfortunately history supports her conclusion, with the 1890 massacre at Wounded Knee, and the Baker Massacre of 1870, in which approximately three hundred unarmed Blackfeet women, children and old people were slain by the U.S. Cavalry.[18]

The ethnocentric stereotypes of Euro-American explorers and traders were eventually employed by U.S. policy-makers and military men to sanction policies of removal and genocide. And the stereotypes, which have persisted to the present day, reached mass acceptance among American people as they were popularized and promoted by nineteenth-century writers.

II

Perhaps nineteenth-century fiction concerned with Indian women explains more about nineteenth-century Euro-American women than about Indian women; nonetheless, the stereotypes promoted in these early novels became the basis for many popular twentieth-century "Western" stories and movies, and therefore continue to dominate American perceptions of Indian women.

Karen Elliott discusses the role of Indian women in nineteenth-century popular fiction in her doctoral thesis, "The Portrayal of the American Indian Woman in a Select Group of American Novels."[19] Two of the novels she considers were written in the nineteenth-century Romantic tradition, and these further reinforced the "Noble Princess" stereotype. Ann Stephen's *Malaeska: The Indian Wife of the White Hunter* and Helen Hunt Jackson's *Ramona* were hailed by nineteenth-century do-gooders as charitable contributions to understanding the "Indian Plight." In fact, they probably served more to assuage white guilt for the all-too-recent atrocities committed by the U.S. Cavalry on Indian people.

Initially, *Malaeska* provides no departure from the Pocahontas model. Her father is a "Chief" (hence she is a "Princess"); she marries a brave white man against the wishes of her family, and she has a child. Then—unexpectedly—the white hunter dies, after giving instructions to his wife to take the child to his family in Manhattan. After a successful trip (by canoe, of course), she arrives in the city and the white family "allows" her to remain as a nursemaid to her son. Her true identity as his mother is carefully concealed for the shame it would cause, interesting proof of the nineteenth-century taboos against miscegenation. The end of the story is rather predictable—Malaeska dies of a broken heart after her son commits suicide upon learning of his shameful, mixed-breed ancestry. Throughout the novel, several nineteenth-century stereotypes are reinforced: first, Malaeska is only "noble" by virtue of her marriage to the brave white man; second, Malaeska has no basis in the reality of an American Indian identity—she behaves in the passive, self-effacing, dependent manner of the nineteenth-century Euro-American woman; and finally, the nineteenth-century view of the Indian as the "vanishing American" becomes reinforced, as Malaeska perishes while attempting to become "civilized" and is abandoned by her more "savage" relatives.

The Indian woman receives slightly different treatment in Jackson's *Ramona*, although it is not much better. Ramona is a half-breed, raised by a Spanish woman who keeps Ramona's heritage a secret from her until she falls in love with Alessandro, a young Indian ranch-hand. Ramona elopes with Alessandro, and to his "delight, she began to evidence real signs of her Indianness." In other words, she becomes "attuned to nature," and hears "the trees speak . . . the rocks . . . and the flowers," as all "Noble Savages" do.[20] Ramona and Alessandro live dangerously, preyed upon by evil white men, until Alessandro is murdered. Ramona falls into a deep depression, and from all expectation of nineteenth-century romanticism, we await her death of a broken heart. But Ramona is rescued by her handsome Spanish stepbrother, whom she falls in love with and is duly married to. The "Pocahontas Perplex" is once again resurrected, along with all the other stereotypes: the helpless woman dependent on males for protection (and even for an existence); the pitiful inability of Indians to "make it" in the white world; and the ultimate, inevitable demise of "savagery" (however noble) in the face of "civilization." Interestingly, the *Ramona* story is still enacted yearly at a California pageant, and variations of her story and of poor Malaeska's story are still found in contemporary "pulp" novels and Hollywood productions.

However unfortunate, Ramona and Malaeska remain relatively "good" Indian women. They are not promiscuous; they are not alcoholic and they both care for white men. Slim Girl, in Oliver La Farge's *Laughing Boy,* presents an alternate image.[21] La Farge's novel was written somewhat later than the previous selections, but the "evolution" of the Indian woman has been anything but positive. Slim Girl is the product of the boarding school: she has lost her clan and family ties, she has learned to sell her body to white men for money and trinkets, and to manipulate people for her own gain. Simultaneously aware of her cultural loss, she attempts to reintegrate herself with the Navajo way of life by marrying Laughing Boy—a handsome, naive, and "noble" Indian. Slim Girl finagles a marriage over the protests of Laughing Boy's family, and manages to keep a firm hold on him at her small-town home with the help of small doses of "medicine" (whisky doctored with oranges and sugar). However, Slim Girl continues to prostitute herself to a white man in town— a man who "would have liked to raise her to a position in which he could respect himself if he married her"—because she has learned to depend on the cash income.[22] Although La Farge interjects Slim Girl's attempts to participate as a Navajo woman through the rituals and art of weaving, she never truly succeeds; and just as they are moving back to the reservation for good, she is fatally shot by a misfired bullet meant for Laughing Boy.

However well-intentioned, *Laughing Boy* perpetuates many of the most deleterious stereotypes of Indians, and particularly of Indian women. La Farge appears to support the notion that an Indian cannot successfully bridge two worlds, that the gentle, beautiful Indian woman who nurtures sheep, corn, and babies will be corrupted by a white world she cannot fit into, and become the antithesis of a "good Indian"—a promiscuous, manipulative, materialistic creature with no salvation in either the Indian world or the white world. Hence, *Laughing Boy* both romanticizes the noble "blanket Indian" and denigrates the reality of cultural transition for Indian women. At any rate, the racism and sexism inherent in the Princess/Squaw stereotype lives on in *Laughing Boy,* and Slim Girl ends up the way a lot of "good Indians" did in the Anglo mind—dead.

Interestingly, *Malaeska, Ramona* and *Laughing Boy* have all been hailed as works which are "sympathetic" to Indians, and therefore of some benefit to their "plight." In reality, however, they all acted to misinform the American public on the true problems and possibilities which faced American Indian people. For example, white education was widely perceived by nineteenth-century Indian leaders as necessary, and although the boarding schools were far from ideal, at one time they were the only "option" for Indian people who sought to learn how to manage in the white American world. As many tribes learned, complete ignorance of white ways often had profoundly negative effects, since the "Great White Father" frequently had only his own best interests at heart. Unfortunately, white boarding-schoolteachers often reacted to Indian students in terms of the very stereotypes perpetuated in these novels. This early "conditioning" often influenced the Indian student's self-perception for the rest of his or her life, a fact which must be considered as we examine the changing self-identity of the American Indian woman. Other issues of importance at this time involved the ongoing dilemmas faced by tribes as they experienced increasing miscegenation, controversies over land rights and over their own right to practice Native traditions prohibited by federal "assimilation" policies.

The scanty, romanticized plots of these early novels seem laughable when compared to the realities of the day. However, it is important to consider that policy-makers, influenced by the stereotypical biases of the novels, often applied the same ethnocentric, androcentric attitudes, as they formulated Indian policy. The changing realities faced by Indian women become apparent through analysis of autobiographical and biographical works. The real-life experiences of Indian women mediate between the Euro-American stereotypes and the profusion of issues currently addressed in the contemporary literature of American Indian women.

III

As Gretchen Bataille and Kathleen Sands comment in *American Indian Women, Telling Their Lives,* Indian women's autobiographies are quite different from the male-oriented European autobiographical model, with its emphasis on flamboyant heroism and the dramatic recitation of historical events. The autobiographies of Indian women more closely correlate to the emerging American feminine autobiography, with the same tendency to "sift through their lives for explanation and understanding" in order to "clarify, to affirm and to authenticate" their own roles, as Estelle Jelinek has written.[23] However, the specific tribal orientations of American Indian women clearly receive the primary focus in their autobiographies. Bataille and Sands follow the interpretations of Vine Deloria, Sr., to suggest that, "Indian women have been repositories of tradition and concern for spiritual ideals, upholding the stability of the tribe through both spiritual and generative power."[24] A comparison of autographical experiences from the traditional past with the rapidly modernizing present reveals several important qualities of Indian women's identity which persist in contemporary literature. Among the most important of these themes are the Indian women's unique relationship to the land, her place within the changing social relationships of her tribe, her perceptions of herself as a "traditional" Indian woman or as one influenced by nontraditional concepts and values, and finally, her honest appraisal of her hopes, dreams, and ever-changing, often painful reality.

The following discussion will include excerpts from Nancy Lurie's study of the Winnebago woman, *Mountain Wolf Woman* (born in 1884), the autobiographies of Anna Shaw (Pima, born in 1898) and Helen Sekaquaptewa (Hopi, born in 1898), and the biography of Acoma potter Lucy Lewis (born in 1890), as examples from a primary period of conflict between traditional tribal values and those of white government authorities. Their experiences will be contrasted with those of a more recent generation of Indian women, including Maria Campbell (Metis), the late Micmac activist Anna Mae Aquash, Jeela Alilkatuktuk (Inuit) and Pawnee-Oto writer Anna Lee Walters.

Mountain Wolf Woman's story tells of the tremendous changes and conflicts that faced the traditional Winnebago culture in the early 1900s, when the Anglo culture was imposed upon them. Mountain Wolf Woman's experience reflects the impermanence of Winnebago life during the years following their successive "relocations" by the federal government. As Bataille and Sands note, "She was not tied down to a specific geographical location . . . [but] moved . . . from one location to another" throughout her life.[25] Mountain Wolf Woman exemplifies the transitional phase between traditionalism and adaptive change for Indian people.

The mediational role that Mountain Wolf Woman assumes between "old" and "new" is perhaps best illustrated by her conscious involvement with three religions: the traditional Winnebago religion, Christianity, and the Native American Church. As a child, Mountain Wolf Woman was advised by her father to "Go cry to the thunders." She relates, "We used to sing and scatter tobacco, standing there and watching the stars and the moon. We used to cry because, after all, we were hungry. We used to think we were pitied."[26] Mountain Wolf Woman kept many of the traditional customs, such as the menstrual taboos, and later participated in the traditional Winnebago ceremonies such as the Scalp Dance and the

Medicine Dance. However, her early education at Christian schools had a lasting influence, and when she finally attended the Native American Church, Mountain Wolf Woman found the synthesis of Indian and Christian ritual beliefs which held the greatest meaning for her.

Mountain Wolf Woman's story compares to the experiences of many Indian women who lived during her generation. The pressures to "acculturate" were tremendous, and many Indians responded as Mountain Wolf Woman did: they utilized parts of the white world in conjunction with their own traditional beliefs and value systems. Nancy Lurie comments that Mountain Wolf Woman saw herself in positive terms, as a link between "the historical life of her people and the future generations."[27] Lurie sees this perception as one generated by her traditional responsibilities as wife, mother, and a woman of her lineage. In contrast, Lurie notes, the men of her same generation were affected negatively as their traditional roles in economic provisioning and political decision-making were assumed by paternalistic government agents.

The story of Helen Sekaquaptewa, a Hopi woman born in 1898, illustrates a successful "adaptation" to two worlds which parallels that of Mountain Wolf Woman. Sekaquaptewa was born in the ultratraditional village of Oraibi, and her family was one of those expelled from the original village by the more "progressive" Hopi for their rigid resistance to white schooling, and "Americanization" in general. Sekaquaptewa remembers this violent expulsion and her subsequent (forcible) removal to the Bureau of Indian Affairs (BIA) boarding school. Her childhood was plagued by the factional disputes of her people, which carried over even to the boarding school. Sekaquaptewa remembers that the daughters of the "progressives" teased and tormented the "exiles" mercilessly.[28] And to complicate her "adjustment" to white education, her traditional relatives began to criticize Sekaquaptewa for being too "progressive."

The genuine pain of these conflicting worlds and their attendant value systems permeates the entire autobiography. As a small child, Sekaquaptewa was separated from her family for months at a time in an environment of loneliness, dietary change, and exposure to disease that resulted in the deaths of many Hopi children. Sekaquaptewa learned to speak and read English, and developed the "leadership skills" that the Anglo teachers stressed, but when she was sent back to her family, she faced "a household that looked to the elders, not children, for guidance ... [and] to tradition, not change, for stability."[29] The two environments seemed mutually exclusive, and so, when offered the opportunity to go on to Phoenix Indian School, Sekaquaptewa accepted. She later married a Hopi man from a similar boarding-school background as herself, and details their experiences in the village, where despite their full-blood Hopi ancestry, they were considered "marginal" Hopi. Eventually, Sekaquaptewa emphasizes, she and her husband were accepted into the Hopi village and into the accompanying round of clan duties. However, the effects of their earlier experiences remain pronounced: Sekaquaptewa and some members of her immediate family converted to Mormonism, though it was practiced in conjunction with Hopi ways, and the family established an alternate residence at a cattle ranch below the mesas, a marked departure from Hopi "tradition." Sekaquaptewa sums up the family's attitude: "We chose the good from both ways of living."[30]

Naturally, the reader wonders just how much of Sekaquaptewa's life has been true "choice," and how much a destiny shaped by the conflicting attitudes and policies of Hopi society and U.S. government officials. However, it is important to remember that throughout this critical period, a period characterized by turbulent, accelerated change, Sekaquaptewa retains a sincere appreciation of her Hopi heritage and invariably practices the older system of ethics and values, even as she pioneers different experiences. In this respect she assumes a role similar to that of Mountain Wolf Woman: as a strong mediating force between generations and conflicting value systems. Importantly, Sekaquaptewa retains her love for the Hopi land, and her sense of connection to the matrilineal village of her birth. In that sense, she remains completely "Hopi."

Like Helen Sekaquaptewa, Anna Shaw was born in 1898. However Shaw came from a Christianized Pima family which had, in many respects, already adapted to white ways. Bataille and Sands comment that, in contrast to the forcible removal of Hopi children to the BIA boarding school, "For Pimas, school was an extension of the household—close, filled with friends and kin, approved of by tribal members."[31] Anna Shaw's family supported her progress at school, and applauded her graduation from Phoenix Union High School, the first Indian woman in Arizona to do so. She became the author of two books, *Pima Legends* and her autobiography, *A Pima Past*.

Although Shaw has been criticized for being the "ideal product of the acculturation process advocated in the Indian school system," she stands apart from many other Indian "case histories" of the same generation by her apparent success in *both* worlds.[32] She and her husband emphasized their Pima identity with pride, and did not attempt to "conceal" it as other Indians of the time often did for fear of prejudice. Anna Shaw's autobiography seems to prove what popular opinion seeks always to *disprove*—that an Indian can "make it" in the white world, yet still remain an "Indian." That Shaw achieves this goal seems apparent. After her husband's retirement they moved back to the reservation, where she became involved in reviving traditional Pima arts, edited the tribal newspaper, and helped create a museum of Pima culture. Shaw seems to retain a strong appreciation of the value of the traditional ways and the need to pass them on, thereby refuting arguments of "assimilation," while still exercising her right to join the "modern world" on an equal footing.

It is important to consider Shaw's experiences in a regional and chronological context. The Pima, unlike some other tribes, were located in close proximity to the large urban centers of Phoenix and Tucson. Therefore, they possessed the ability to engage in commerce with the "white world" without necessarily forfeiting their traditional roles. In addition, Shaw completed her education at a time when total "assimilation" was actively encouraged by BIA teachers. Native ways were often denigrated and suppressed. That Shaw continued to nurture tribal traditions and in fact, sought to explain their importance to the American people at large, testifies to her confidence in her Pima identity, rather than her "compromise" to white values.

The story of Acoma potter, Lucy Lewis, contrasts with the experiences of Mountain Wolf Woman, Anna Shaw and Helen Sekaquaptewa. Unlike the other three women, Lewis did not attend white schools, nor did she ever learn English or live in an urban setting. In this sense, Lewis illustrates a far older tradition and lifestyle. Lest one equate "tradition" with a static refusal to permit "change," however, Lucy Lewis's story details both her traditional role as a Pueblo woman—the matriarchal "head" of her family and guarantor of spiritual and traditional continuity—and her radical departure from that role as a widely recognized practitioner of pottery as a fine art form. Lucy Lewis was the first Acoma woman to experiment with different techniques and more detailed designs, and later, the first to "sign" her pottery (against the wishes of tribal leaders) and display it at competitive shows such as the Gallup Ceremonials.[33]

Because of her determination to revive an ancient art in a creative, fulfilling way, Lucy Lewis has inspired many other Pueblo women to learn the art of pottery, develop it through individual styles, and receive acclaim and profit for their artistic achievements. At the same time, Lewis has served her children as a source of spiritual and cultural continuity with

Acoma tradition. Many of her children have lived away from the Pueblo, and all have been educated in white schools; yet they do not feel threatened by their exposure to the white world because of their strong ties to their Acoma heritage.

It is essential to realize that maintaining one's ties to the traditional past, to the ritual and symbolic structures of one's culture, imparts a significant sense of "power." That power includes a sense of identity, connection and self-confidence. The power may vary, according to tribe, gender, or age, but always it is there. In the Acoma tribe, Lewis's daughters explain, the women are inextricably tied to the past through their ritual duties and participation in the ceremonial cycle.

Clearly, each of the women from this generation—Mountain Wolf Woman, Helen Sekaquaptewa, Anna Shaw and Lucy Lewis—has had a strong and vital connection to the traditional past. Though in some cases educated in white schools, "converted" to Christianity, or pioneering a nontraditional role or art form, all of these women have maintained their tribal identities, clan obligations, and traditional value systems. But what about the following generation? What happens when the "power" becomes transmuted through mixed-blood ancestry, birth in urban environments, and displacement from tradition? What happens when the "new ways" seem hopelessly and finally irreconcilable with an "Indian" identity?

Maria Campbell's story centers around conflicts of identity and "place" which are far more severe than those experienced by the women of previous generations. Campbell, a Metis or mixed-blood Cree, was born into Canadian society of the 1940s, arguably even more racist than American society at this time. As a Metis woman, Campbell suffered from both racial and gender-directed oppression. The Metis were victims of discrimination from Canadian whites, as well as from their full-blood Treaty Indian kin, who referred to their mixed-blood relatives as the "Awp-pee-tow-kooson," the "half-people."[34] The Metis held no treaty rights under Canadian law, and were forced to eke out a marginal existence poaching wildlife from government parks, and "squatting" on strips of rocky, muskeg-covered land.

As a child, Maria Campbell was teased by white classmates for eating roasted gophers at lunch, and for dressing in old, mended clothes. For respite, Campbell dreamed of living in a big city like Vancouver, a place of "toothbrushes and pretty dresses, oranges and apples."[35] And eventually she did go to Vancouver, as the wife of a young white man who left her there, battered and penniless and with a baby daughter to support. Too proud to return home to her great-grandmother, Cheechum, and her widowed father, Campbell plunged ahead in her dream of wealth and success; she became a high-priced call girl in a house of prostitution. She had money, satin dresses, and jewels, and rich white men paid to "keep" her, but Campbell admits "Something inside of me died. . . . I had married to escape from what I'd thought was an ugly world, only to find a worse one."[36] Failing to gain an identity which would answer her need for recognition and self-respect, Campbell turned to alcohol and heroin.

Campbell finally realized that by running away from what she was—a half-breed—she was helping to destroy herself. She turned her anger away from herself and toward the society which had labeled Native people in opposing categories, "Metis/Treaty Indian," to further divide and weaken them. Canadian society has done its best to reduce the number of Native "wards" under its care. And too often, the Indian woman has borne the major burden in this process. For example, under the "Indian Act" of Canada, a Treaty Indian woman loses her status if she marries a white, while a white woman gains Indian status and land if she marries an Indian.[37] The patriarchal biases of white bureaucrats together with the androcentric Christianity of the missionaries have dramatically altered traditional

Indian perceptions of women. Campbell summarizes, "The missionaries had impressed upon us the feeling that women were a source of evil. This belief, combined with the ancient Indian recognition of the power of women, is still holding back the progress of our people today."[38]

Although, in a sense, Maria Campbell returns "home" to her ancestral past, embarking on a critical reunion trip to see her Cree great-grandmother, she realizes that for the Metis there *is* no "traditional past" with one set of values, rituals, and attitudes. Years of colonial oppression and miscegenation have fragmented the Metis, and the only unity that remains, aside from certain shared cultural attitudes, is a modern, politically-centered manifestation of Native solidarity. In the larger sense, then, Maria Campbell's "Indian" identity is created largely from the shared bitterness, frustration, and poverty of Canada's diverse Native population. This sense of "Indianness" parallels the "pan-Indianism" that is apparent in large urban centers such as Los Angeles today, characterized by the unified "social consciousness" of Indian people from various tribes and regions, and with varying degrees of "Indian blood." But on a more personal level, Campbell seems to merge her identity with that of her Cree great-grandmother, assuming Cheechum's dreams for the rebirth of the Cree people in her own efforts as a political activist. Although the two women are separated by many years and several "worlds" of experience, they unite in a single spiritual current more ancient than tribal memory or "degree of blood." This spiritual current becomes apparent in the modern literature of authors such as Leslie Silko, Joy Harjo and Louise Erdrich, who are all of mixed Indian/white blood, yet demonstrate a tenacious attachment to their tribal heritage and a lyrical appreciation of the deepest qualities of that heritage.

Like their ancestors, contemporary Indian women display strong ties to the spiritual currents of the past and also to the political realities of the present. The contemporary Indian woman faces a bewildering array of misconceptions, prejudices, and problems. Many Indian women in the last few years have refused to accept the "status quo" of society, and have actively resisted through direct political involvement, as Maria Campbell did, and/or through written works which illuminate their concerns.

In the political arena, Indian women who have been through the white educational system can often appreciate the sophistication of the problems which face their people. The real frustration comes from white bureaucracies and Native political organizations built on the white model, which fail to recognize either the traditional power of Indian women or their modern skills as political facilitators. Jeela Alllkatuktuk, an Inuit woman raised in a traditional family but sent to boarding school as a teenager, explains: "I became involved in community affairs and was elected to the Frobisher Bay Hamlet Council at the age of 19. [While] The Council is supposed . . . to run the community for the people . . . in reality the territorial government controls all the money and all the personnel . . . the councils are [largely] powerless."[39] Alikatuktuk relates this powerlessness to the breakdown of traditional political structures, significantly to the loss of position by women. She claims that in traditional times, the most respected persons were the old women, and many women exerted great influence over camp decisions. Now, Alikatuktuk says, white men have transposed an alien political system onto the Inuit people, along with their own negative attitudes about women. She concludes: "One of our greatest losses is that our young Inuit men are copying the white people in their attitude. Where a white woman can walk without fear an Inuit woman is harassed and propositioned."[40] Alilkatuktuk's statement is corroborated by Indian Health Service worker Phyllis Old Dog Cross for the Navajo. Old Dog Cross documents the dramatic increase of rape on the Navajo reservation (formerly almost unheard of among Navajos, who held women in high esteem, rape is now the number one crime on the reservation) with this explanation: "For the Indian male, the only route to be successful, to be good, to be right, and to have an identity was to be as much like the white man as he could."[41] The modern conflict between genders, for many Indian groups, has largely resulted from patterns learned from white colonial authorities whose policies destroyed traditional egalitarian systems among Indian people.

Because the various government-controlled agencies have failed to provide Indian people with a structure compatible with traditional beliefs, many young Indians have taken a more "militant" stance in all-Indian organizations such as the American Indian Movement. Unfortunately, the effects of patriarchal gender oppression often extend equally to these groups.

In *The Life and Death of Anna Mae Aquash*, Johanna Brand tells the story of a young Micmac woman from Nova Scotia who became involved with AIM during the late sixties and early seventies, and was violently murdered under suspicious circumstances.[42] Anna Mae's story substantiates many of the comments Jeela Alilkatuktuk and Maria Campbell make about the racism and sexism of Canadian officials toward their Indian "wards." Eventually, Anna Mae left her poverty-blighted reserve to go to Boston, where she became involved in various Indian-rights organizations, including AIM. Because of her outspoken endorsement of AIM's most militant activities, many Indian people allege, Anna Mae became a prime target in the FBI campaign against "anti-American agitators." When she was suddenly murdered, and the subsequent investigation conducted hurriedly and incompletely, many Indians became suspicious of political motivations for her death. After Anna Mae's death, many Indian women eulogized her as the "Brave-Hearted Woman," a female warrior in a violent, ongoing war of genocide and oppression. But Brand's biography reveals a far more complex portrait of Anna Mae's struggle.

Brand indicates that Anna Mae was very idealistic about her identity as an Indian woman, and could not reconcile her deeply felt spiritual commitments to the realities of alcoholism, the fast-moving city life, and the mounting political tensions within and around AIM. In part, the tensions were gender-based, because although AIM members claimed to have built their organization on traditional "Indian" precepts and values, it was apparent that some of the male "leaders" adopted a "macho" posturing which more clearly reflected the patriarchal Western mind-set than the traditional egalitarianism which most tribes practiced. One reviewer of Beatrice Medicine's *The Native American Woman: A Perspective* quoted a young AIM woman, Kathleen Smith, on her experience at Wounded Knee:

> The AIM leaders are particularly sexist, never having learned our true Indian history where women voted and participated equally in all matters of tribal life. They have learned the white man's way of talking down to women and regarding their position as inferior. Some . . . actually don't believe women can fight or think, and gave us the impression that we were there for their use and that we should be flattered to have their children. One man said he was helping Indian unity by having a girlfriend from every tribe. They want to keep women divided and fighting for men's friendship and attention.[43]

Aside from gender differences, however, the goals of Indian activism clearly reflected the unified concerns of all Indian people. Shirley Witt, an Akwesasne Mohawk, wrote of Anna Mae's struggle as representative of many Indians who were tired of seeing their people incarcerated, unemployed, alcoholic, and suicidal in racist border towns, who were tired of seeing their children removed to far-off boarding schools and "brainwashed white," and tired of having brothers and sons recruited for a white man's army that didn't care if they came back alive or not.[44] In the "struggle," both genders participated equally. In fact,

Witt claims, after many of the male leaders had been jailed or were trying to escape incarceration in the mid-seventies, it was the women "warriors" who formed the stable core of the Indian movement and kept the concerns alive. And their "concerns" were substantial. Witt offers the statistics of Dr. Connie Uri, Cherokee, who claims that at the Claremore Indian Hospital in July, 1974, sterilization surgery was performed on forty-eight Indian women, most in their twenties. The Indian women activists were the first to bring attention to this forcible sterilization of Indian women in government hospitals. Another area of concern at this time involved adoption procedures regarding Indian children, who were generally placed with higher-income white families, rather than families of their own tribal background. The Indian Child Welfare Act has since been passed, modifying such policies to reflect greater tribal control over the placement of Indian children.[45]

Women of All Red Nations (WARN), an all-women Native activist group, formed as a female counterpart to the American Indian Movement. Currently WARN investigates and calls to attention the various concerns of Indian women. In recent years, these concerns have centered around the massive contamination of Indian water by radioactive waste from uranium mines located on Indian land. Winona La Duke, an Anishinabe and founder of WARN, has assembled statistical evidence of the high birth defect rate on Indian reservations, apparently closely linked to the radioactive contamination of the land and water.[46]

Contemporary Indian women are reasserting the traditional power of their female ancestors in many ways. Many have become strong political leaders for their tribes, such as Ada Deer, Menominee, who was largely responsible for the reinstatement of her tribe to Federal status after its disastrous "termination" by the government in 1961.[47] Other women choose to outline their concerns through written works which illuminate the struggles, failures, and triumphs of their people. Interestingly, many of the "fictional" works written by Indian women are constructed on an autobiographical mode of presentation. Often a central character in the poetry or prose of the Indian woman author will be modeled on the author herself; her experiences become those of the protagonist. Paula Allen describes her novel, *The Woman Who Owned the Shadows*, in this way Allen's novel centers around the quest of Ephanie, a half-breed Laguna woman, as Allen is, for an identity which answers modern realities and traditional needs. Allen observes that the novel "leans on the tradition of autobiography," and that Ephanie was constructed from "qualities and characteristics drawn from her grandmother, mother and herself, as well as fictional elements."[48]

Two concepts are essential in understanding the work of contemporary Indian women writers. The first is to understand the sense of place that permeates the work, as it always has the lives of Indian people. Even among Indian women writers who were born or raised largely in urban environments, there is a strong sense of origin from a specific geographic region, and a concomitant identity which centers around this land. Tribal stories, American Indian autobiographies, and contemporary literature by Indian writers all share this emphasis on "place." However, the Indian women writers perhaps exhibit the most central connections to the land, since, traditionally, the cyclical and regenerative characteristics of the earth were strongly linked to tribal women. To illustrate, Paula Allen refers to the "feminine landscape" of Leslie Silko's novel, *Ceremony*, with this inclusive remark: "We are the land, and the land is mother to us all."[49] Gretchen Bataille and Kathleen Sands comment similarly on the autobiography of Maria Chona, a Papago woman: "Like all works of American Indian literature [her] autobiography is permeated with a sense of place, the inextricable interweaving of language and landscape, the concept that the land is not merely setting for the story, but that the story is formed and shaped by the land, and the land is given significance and vitality in the language."[50] This summary could be applied equally to the work of Leslie Silko, Joy Harjo, Paula Allen, Luci Tapahonso, and countless other Indian women writers. The land unifies tradition and modern experience to reflect the "wholeness" of Indian cultures and nations.

However, along with this sense of "wholeness" and "place," there is a troubling sense of loss, of deprivation and sadness. The idealism which many people ascribe to Indian people via "traditionalism" is countered by the often ugly realities of Indian life on the reservation and in urban areas. Problems such as assault, family violence, alcoholism, incarceration, and murder continually reassert themselves in Indian communities, largely due to widespread socioeconomic deprivation and the significant degree of culture loss (reflected in the loss of tribal languages, rituals, and clan relationships) which now threaten tribal groups. Indian women write consciously of both sides of life—positive and negative— to evoke the power of change and growth for Indian people. The language in the works may be lyrical and delicate, or it may be harsh and tense, as in this paragraph from a forthcoming autobiography by Anna Lee Walters, Pawnee-Oto:

> I have seen handsome people become ugly and disfigured. I have been close when people have been murdered and women raped and given birth. . . . I am familiar with people who have given their children away for a price, cash or a drink. I grew up with children whose parents fought and maimed each other by plan, no accident. I know of men who have given away their daughters.[51]

Walters's work will be an autobiography, but the realism compares to Erdrich's *Love Medicine* and Harjo's poem, "The Black Room."

The idealism of tradition and "place" and the realism of squalid alleys and border town bars may seem paradoxical and incompatible; but then, oftentimes so is the story of Indian survival and the tremendous adaptability of ancient cultures. Students of contemporary Indian literature might take this cue from Joy Harjo in reference to a modern "trickster" story told by a prison inmate:

> Everyone laughed at the impossibility of it,
> but also the truth. Because who would believe
> the fantastic and terrible story of all of our survival
> those who were never meant
>   to survive?[52]

IV

In a metaphorical sense, the diverse works of contemporary Indian women writers combine as a collective whole to generate the rebirth of Native tribal energy and female power. Leslie Silko, Joy Harjo, Paula Allen, and Luci Tapahonso are representative of the many contemporary women writers who have begun to assert this traditional power in written form. Joy Harjo says "we exist / not in words, but in the motion / set off by them," summarizing the power inherent in contemporary literary expression.[53]

These women combine modern experience with an ancient past in a unified continuum, rather than a fragmented assembly of parts. This mode of expression mirrors what Paula Allen calls "the traditional tribal concept of time . . . timelessness," and the complementary understanding of "space" as "multidimensionality."[54] This complex understanding of time and space underlies the ritual construction of many Indian worldviews, as Dr. Alfonso Ortiz affirms in *The Tewa World*.[55]

In conjunction with these concepts, many Indian groups perceive the individual as moving within the constant, natural motion of the universe in "dynamic equilibrium."[56] The relationship of an individual to the universe exists as an ancient, vital bond, as Joy Harjo explains:

> I am memory alive
> not just a name
> but an intricate part
> of this web of motion,
> meaning: earth, sky, stars circling
> my heart
> centrifugal.[57]

Similarly, the relationship of the individual to her ancestors is also continuous and "alive"; Luci Tapahonso writes of a woman who looks into her young daughter's face, "knowing they breathe the same memories, the same blood / dark and wet circulating / forever into time and others."[58]

This sense of connection to the ancient past transcends the modern realities of mixed bloodlines, gender splits, and urban settings, and often appears in modern literature as a surrealist blend of myth and reality. Possibly the best example of this appears in Leslie Silko's novel, *Ceremony*. Significantly, in *Ceremony* a great emphasis rests on the female principles of this universal motion, in accordance with the world view of the matriarchal Laguna people. On a more intricate level, as Paula Allen notes, while *Ceremony* is "ostensibly a tale about a man, Tayo, it is as much and more a tale of two forces: the feminine life force of the universe and the mechanistic death force of the witchery."[59] Allen's comment indicates a major philosophical thread which runs through Pueblo worldviews—the belief that each individual is comprised of both male and female elements, a balanced unity of "life forces" roughly equivalent to the oriental concept of Yin and Yang.

Interestingly, Silko chooses to use a male character to illustrate the competing values of the matriarchal Pueblo culture and the patriarchal Euro-American culture. Louise Erdrich uses a similar approach in *Love Medicine*, with Henry Lamartine, Jr., a Chippewa newly arrived from the horrors of the Vietnam war. Tayo and Henry Jr. are both Indian men who have been mentally "raped" by a Euro-American culture which promotes death and violence and is in direct conflict with the traditional Indian life force. Silko and Erdrich frame the dilemma from a male perspective to reinforce the contemporary realization that the victimization of an individual parallels the victimization of a culture and ethos, and therefore respects no gender boundaries.

Because of this understanding of victimization, which has been an intimate part of American Indian experience (both male and female), contemporary Indian women writers often do not observe the same dichotomy between male "dominance" and female "victimization" that white feminist authors do. Even in Joy Harjo's prose poem, "The Black Room," which concerns the literal rape of a woman, the "rape" is much more complex than a physical act, and can be correlated to "victimization" on a much larger scale:

> Joey had her cornered. Leaned her up against the wall of her room, in black willow shadows his breath was shallow and muscled and she couldn't move and she had no voice no name and she could only wait until it was over—like violent summer storms that she had been terrified of.[60]

When Harjo says "she had no voice / no name" she refers to what many people have called the "mute zone," the chronically passive "victim" mentality of those who have been stripped of identity (a name) and of power (a voice). Tayo and Henry Jr., though male, have succumbed to this victimization through Army indoctrination, much as female rape victims often do through societal judgments ("she asked for it"). For Tayo, the "ceremony" finally allows him to have a "voice." Previously, he has been nearly mute, numbly wading through an existential fog of pain and denial. At the height of his sickness, he perceives the world around him as vague and shadowy; even his own mouth he sees as "an outline . . . like all the other outlines he saw."[61] For Tayo, at this point, the world has no substance, no vitality without the body of tradition and understanding which gives meaning to life.

Tayo learns to transcend the death force of the white witchery by relearning the spiritual power of his Laguna traditions, but Henry Jr. faces a different outcome. Henry Jr. is plagued by memories of the violence and inhumanity of the war he has just experienced. He remembers witnessing the rape of a Vietnamese woman by American soldiers:

> She looked at him. They had used a bayonet. She was out of her mind. You, me, same. Same. She pointed to her eyes and his eyes. The Asian folded eyes of some Chippewas. She was hemorrhaging.[62]

Henry Jr. has witnessed the violent rape of a woman, but he has been similarly victimized by his fellow soldiers, who destroy his own values and perceptions, and leave him "ghost-like," an empty shell of his former self. As his mother realizes: "All his life he did things right, and then the war showed him right was wrong."[63] The Euro-American world which allows the exploitation of women and "Third World" peoples in its quest for power and gain, and then discards the victims without reference to their humanity, conflicts severely with the traditional Indian ethic of balance and mutual respect. Henry Jr., unlike Tayo, has no traditional healer to turn to, and he takes his own life by drowning in the river.

Throughout the works of Indian women writers there is powerful emphasis on transcending victimization to find one's own identity and voice. The initial step in this direction is to define oneself in one's own terms, rather than those of the outer society. For Indian women, this means discarding the Anglo feminine ideal in favor of what Paula Allen appropriately calls "Recovering the feminine in American Indian traditions," in the full title of *The Sacred Hoop*.

Many American women have struggled to counter the nineteenth-century feminine ideal—the beautiful, passive, subordinate woman who received her identity in terms of her affiliation to males. However, even today a "feminine ideal" persists in ad campaigns (the "Virginia Slims Woman") and beauty contests. Modern women are encouraged to adopt the makeup, hairstyle, and clothing that society determines to be "feminine." The "Virginia Slims" woman must always be perfect, always illusive and mysterious. She cannot be "real" (with a "voice," a "name" or an "occupation") or she would destroy her allure and her commercial worth.

For the American Indian woman, the conflict between a traditional identity and the "feminine ideal" promoted by Euro-American society has assumed complex dimensions in relation to the contemporary search for identity. Maria Campbell discusses her aspirations to be a beautiful, revered "lady," which ultimately led her into prostitution and drug addiction, and admits: "Dreams are so important in one's life, yet when followed blindly, they can lead to the disintegration of one's soul."[64] Louise Erdrich illustrates the same conflict through June, in *Love Medicine*. June searches for an identity which will make her feel good about herself, and as society has conditioned women to do, she looks to men for this identity. She maintains a thin veneer of physical attractiveness to cover her inner disintegration, but realizes sadly that she is "truly empty," and eventually walks to her death in a storm.

In *Ceremony*, Tayo's mother shares a fate similar to June's. Like June, Tayo's mother seeks to establish her identity and importance through men; but eventually she faces reality when, "after she had been with them, she could feel the truth in their fists and in their greedy feeble love-making."[65] She grows to feel marginal and inadequate both with the Indian people, who feels shame for her promiscuity and alcoholism, and with the white men who feel contempt for her, and finally dies a lonely, alcoholic death. Both June and Tayo's mother illustrate the consequences of cultural loss and denial. Erdrich and Silko have countered these tragic images with strong Indian women such as Lulu, Marie, and Albertine in *Love Medicine*, and Ts'eh in *Ceremony*, who embody the strength and resilence of their ancestral cultures, even as they adapt and persist in the face of severe opposition.

Defining a contemporary identity becomes critical in achieving such cultural resilience. As Indian women begin to counter the negative effects of the societally-imposed "feminine ideal," they start to assert the older values and perceptions which have always allowed Indian women to maintain a sense of autonomy and self-worth. The process of gaining such an identity entails, first, a realization of one's own oppression; second, the release of one's pain and often self-directed anger; and third, the realization of one's individual self-worth through connections to tradition and kin. This process of "going back home" permeates *Love Medicine* through Lipsha's search for his identity and kin, *Ceremony* through Tayo's ritual connection to his traditional past, and Harjo's collection, *She Had Some Horses*, through Noni Daylight's search for a "voice" and a "self" which can transcend her pain and nihilistic self-denial.

As Noni Daylight realizes, at the root of all pain is fear. For Indian women this may include fear of the cold, anonymous city, fear of going back to the poverty of the reservation, fear of racists and rapists, and of what the schools will "teach" the children, fear of what vision the next drink will bring, and fear of what will happen if there *is* no next drink. Noni Daylight lives with that fear. It grips her heart and dries her mouth and leaves her "a dishrag wrung out over bones":

> Noni Daylight is afraid.
> She waits through traffic lights at intersections
> that at four a.m. are desolate oceans of concrete.
> She toys with the trigger; the heartbeat
> is a constant noise. She talks softly
>
>   softly
> to the voice on the radio. All night she drives.[66]

Noni Daylight is striving for *connection*, as are Maria Campbell, June, Tayo, and Lipsha. Noni Daylight seeks a "voice," and needs to hear the "heartbeat" which tells her she is alive. But she cannot truly find her identity until she realizes, "It is not the moon, or the pistol in her lap / but a fierce anger / that will free her."[67] In these final three lines of "Heartbeat," Harjo discovers an important lesson which might be appropriately used by any person seeking to overcome victimization and assert an individual identity: anger must be used as energy, directed away from the self and worked through, if one is ever to achieve control over one's life. This realization has also received attention in the works of many white feminist writers. Importantly, Paula Allen and Joy Harjo have admitted the bond which all women, regardless of race, have in the struggle to overcome the patriarchal oppression and victimization of Euro-American society. Although both have recognized the significant departures between white feminism and traditional Indian beliefs, they choose to focus on the mutualities of women's experience.

A main tenet of modern feminist thought involves discarding the traditional "passive" role of the female in favor of a more autonomous "active" role. This breaks the "victim mentality," and allows the woman to feel confident about making her own choices and decisions. Adrienne Rich, a white feminist poet, outlines this concept in her acclaimed collection, *Diving Into the Wreck*. As critic Helen Vendler writes, "The forcefulness of *Diving Into the Wreck* comes from the wish not to huddle wounded, but to explore the caverns, scars and depths of the wreckage."[68] By taking this active step, one may discard the internalized anger which, as Rich notes, is often "converted into self-hate and despondency . . . the cause of paralysis."[69] By "paralysis," Rich describes the same numb denial which destroys June and Henry Jr., and threatens to destroy Tayo, and Ephanie in Paula Allen's *The Woman Who Owned the Shadows*.[70]

Joy Harjo correlates this "paralysis" to suicides, which often occur through a "passive" method (drowning, overdose, exposure) because the individual is incapable of making an active decision. In "The Woman Hanging from the Thirteenth Floor Window," Harjo describes a woman who:

> . . . knows she is hanging by her own fingers, her
> own skin, her own thread of indecision . . . .
> She thinks she remembers listening to her own life
> break loose, as she falls from the 13th floor
> window on the east side of Chicago, or as she
> climbs back up to claim herself again.[71]

Harjo intentionally leaves the poem's ending ambiguous to indicate that it is the element of choice, the active power in taking the initiative to save oneself, that is the key to survival. That "choice" is the fundamental theme of the pivotal poem in Harjo's collection, "She Remembers the Future." In this poem, Noni Daylight finally confronts her "other self," the self she has long denied for fear of facing the intense pain and anger that, in fact, *empower* this self. Noni asks the complacent, passive self which contemplates suicide, "Should I dream you afraid / so that you are forced to save / yourself? / Or should you ride colored horses / into the cutting edge of the sky / to know / that we're alive / we are alive."[72]

The act of unifying the two disparate selves, for Noni Daylight, involves the resolution of her seemingly polarized existence into one entity—her "self." Joy Harjo uses Noni Daylight to illustrate her own belief that the contradictions and "polarities" which often fragment Indian people must be reconciled into "an order that is harmonious, balanced and whole."[73] This passage from "She Had Some Horses" illustrate the vital resolution of polarity:

> She had some horses.
> She had horses who got down on their knees for any savior.
> She had horses who thought their high price had saved
>   them.
> She had horses who tried to save her, who climbed in her
>   bed at night and prayed as they raped her.
> She had some horses.
> She had some horses she loved.

> She had some horses she hated.
> These were the same horses.[74]

Harjo has realized that it is this sense of polarity, as she says, of "good/evil, sun/moon, light/dark," which fragments the modern consciousness into near-insanity.[75] The Western world view revolves around polarity—"Christian/pagan," "sacred/secular," "male/female," "technology/nature"—with an attendant imbalance in the judgments of one being superior to its opposite. In the traditional Indian view, as Paula Allen notes, the image of unified balance predominates in the form of the "Sacred Hoop." This view refutes the Western "polarity" which often seems paradoxical, even to Westerners. For example, a white man once asked an old Tuscarora why the polarities of "good and evil," like those of "genius and insanity," often seemed to be "just a hair's breadth apart." The Tuscarora man answered: "There is no such thing as polarity, except in the frail choice of man. If you take the line between your polarities and curve it into a circle, you would have your own answer."[76] It is this understanding of "polarity" which forms the core of American Indian worldviews. Today, the resolution of an artificially imposed polarity restores one to the "primordial center," as Betonie explains to Tayo. For Tayo this means finding the balance between modern life and the older traditions, between the mechanistic forces of technology and the life forces of Laguna tradition.

Contemporary Indian women restore themselves to this balance as they find an identity more appropriate to their unique tribal traditions, and one which emphasizes their own special bond to the female life forces of the universe. Because Indian women have always perceived their regenerative qualities in close concert with the earth's cycles, many contemporary Indian women writers use this theme in their work. Chickasaw poet Linda Hogan writes: "I teach my daughters, / that we are women, / a hundred miles of green / wills itself out of our skin. / The red sky ends at our feet / and the earth begins at our heads."[77] Hogan's image might well coincide with a Navajo sand painting which depicts the circular universe, the unbroken continuum of earth and sky, the female deities arched over the land like rainbows, promising rebirth for a new generation.

In Indian tradition, the births of a woman parallel the other births which belong to the land. Luci Tapahonso explores this connection in relation to sunrise, the ultimate rebirth of the natural world. "The first born of dawn woman / slid out amid crimson fluid streaked with stratus clouds / her body glistening August sunset pink / light steam rising from her like rain on warm rocks."[78] And Joy Harjo relates a human birth to the cycles of the land in much the same way:

> . . . the ground spoke when she was born.
> Her mother heard it. In Navajo she answered
> as she squatted down against the earth
> to give birth. It was now when it happened,
> now giving birth to itself again and again
> between the legs of women.[79]

As Harjo writes, "It was now . . . giving birth to itself again and again," she summarizes the temporal continuity of the Indian universe. This ability to include the traditional past with the changing present characterizes the works of American Indian writers. Linda Hogan offers a concise appraisal of this quality:

> No one is much without the earth
> in their hands

> and I pick up the earth,
> touch the people
> the country
> and the things we try to forget.[80]

Indian women writers, in particular, are all too aware of the modern tendency to "forget" what should not be forgotten: the older traditions, the recent (painful) history, the harsh realism of the modern world. The older Indian people recognized the need to keep memory alive as they perfected the art of oral history. Today, the modern written works of many Indian women fulfill a similar function. Joy Harjo emphasizes the value of "memory":

> Remember that you are this universe and that this
> universe is you.
> Remember that all is in motion, is growing, is you.
> Remember that language comes from this.
> Remember the dance that language is, that life is.
> Remember.[81]

Harjo correlates language and memory to the motion of life. She emphasizes that the past is the current to the future, but only if we allow it to be. In their respective novels, Silko and Erdrich describe what can happen when "memory" is allowed to die, when the natural cycles are broken in the modern "death" of warfare and atomic technology. Just as Lipsha needs to establish his "kinship" to Gerry Nanapush, June, and Lulu in *Love Medicine*, and Tayo must establish his kinship to his Laguna ancestors and traditions in *Ceremony*, so must we all establish our mutual kinship to the land—to the rocks which the Lakota call "Tunkashila" or "grandfather," to the rain-filled clouds which the Hopi call "Kachinas," their spirit ancestors—and to all the living beings which have been born to this land.

This sense of motion, regeneration, and life permeates the work of contemporary Indian women writers. The written expressions of these authors might well be considered a powerful legacy of "survival" for the next generation. In the combined works of these women rests a strong vision for a better future.

In traditional Navajo mythology, a male deity associated with "thought" unites with a female deity associated with "speech" to create the preeminent deity of the Navajo people—Changing Woman.[82] Changing Woman personifies the female life force of the universe, and through her, the ritual structure of the Navajo people was born. Similarly, "thought" and "speech" combine for a dynamic rebirth of the traditional American Indian cultures and belief systems in the contemporary writings of Native American authors. And American Indian women writers have a vital role in this regenerative process. At the conclusion of *Seasonal Woman*, Luci Tapahonso places herself in this continuum of life, art and beauty with a final, gentle prayer:

> bless me hills
> this clear golden morning
> for I am passing through again.
> I can easily sing
> for . . . time is mine
> and these ragged red cliffs
> flowing hills and wind echoes
>   are only extensions
>   of a never-ending prayer.[83]

As Tapahonso realizes, the prayers of generations of people rest in those "ragged red cliffs" and "flowing hills." Their handprints and drawings often remain, etched ghostlike on rock slabs, though their words have long since faded into wind-echoes. However, the "essence" of their prayers remains, giving strength and continuity to a new generation, a generation passing through the "dawn"—once again.

Notes

1. Kenneth Lincoln. *Native American Renaissance* (Berkeley: University of California Press, 1983), preface.
2. Paula Allen. *The Sacred Hoop* (Boston: Beacon Press, 1986), p. 160.
3. Alice Kehoe, "The Shackles of Tradition," in Pat Albers and Beatrice Medicine, eds. *The Hidden Half* (Lanham: University Press of America, 1983), p. 61.
4. Wendy Martin, *An American Triptych* (Chapel Hill: University of North Carolina Press, 1984), pp. 29–30.
5. Albers and Medicine. *The Hidden Half*, p. 13.
6. Janet Spector, "Male Female Task Differentiation Among the Hidatsa," in Albers and Medicine, *The Hidden Half*, p. 95.
7. Patricia Albers, "Sioux Women in Transition," in Albers and Medicine, *The Hidden Half*, p. 175–223.
8. Allen, *The Sacred Hoop*, p. 41.
9. Albers, "Sioux Women in Transition," pp. 216–217.
10. Robert Grumet, "Sunksquaws, Shamans and Tradeswomen," in Etienne and Leacock, eds. *Women and Colonization*, p. 56.
11. Priscilla Buffalohead, "Farmers, Warriors, Traders: A Fresh Look at Ojibway Women," *Minnesota History* 48 (1983), p. 242.
12. Jennie Joe, "Keepers of the Earth Bundle: Navajo Women and Forced Relocation," (manuscript, 1986).
13. Allen, *The Sacred Hoop*, p. 16.
14. Ward Churchill, "Generations of Resistance: American Indian Poetry and the Ghost Dance Spirit," in *Coyote Was Here*, Scholder, ed. (1984), p. 168.
15. Albers and Medicine, *The Hidden Half*, p. 31.
16. Buffalohead, "Farmers, Warriors, Traders," p. 238.
17. Rayna Green, "The Pocahontas Perplex," in *The Massachusetts Review* 16 (1975), p. 713.
18. Vine Deloria, Jr., *Of Utmost Good Faith* (San Francisco: Straight Arrow Books, 1971), p. 156.
19. Karen Sue Elliott, "The Portrayal of the American Indian Woman in a Select Group of American Novels," (University of Minnesota, 1979).
20. *Ibid.*, p. 136.
21. Oliver La Farge, *Laughing Boy* (Massachusetts: The Houghton Mifflin Co., 1929).
22. *Ibid.*, p. 135.
23. Gretchen Bataille and Kathleen Sands, *American Indian Women, Telling Their Lives* (Lincoln: University of Nebraska Press, 1984), p. 8.
24. *Ibid.*, p. 18.
25. *Ibid.*, p. 76.
26. Jane Katz, *I Am the Fire of Time* (New York: E. P. Dutton Publishers, 1977), p. 28.
27. Bataille and Sands, *American Indian Women, Telling Their Lives*, p. 74.
28. *Ibid.*, p. 103.
29. *Ibid.*, p. 104.
30. *Ibid.*, p. 109.
31. *Ibid.*, p. 87.
32. *Ibid.*, p. 95.
33. Susan Peterson, *Lucy Lewis: American Indian Potter* (Tokyo: Kodansha International, 1984), p. 40.
34. Maria Campbell, *Halfbreed* (Toronto: McClellan and Stewart, Ltd., 1973), p. 26.
35. *Ibid.*, p. 114.
36. *Ibid.*, p. 116.
37. John Price, *Native Studies* (McGraw-Hill Ryerson, Ltd., 1978), p. 83.
38. Campbell, *Halfbreed*, p. 144.
39. Jeela Alilkatuktuk, "Canada: Stranger in My Own Land," *Ms.* (February 1974), pp. 8–10.
40. *Ibid.*
41. Allen, *The Sacred Hoop*, p. 192.

42. Johanna Brand, *The Life and Death of Anna Mae Aquash* (Toronto: James Lorimer, 1978).
43. *Off Our Backs* (editorial), vol. 11, no. 2 (February 1981).
44. Shirley Hill Witt, "The Brave-Hearted Woman," *Akwesasne Notes* 8 (Early Summer, 1976); pp. 16–17.
45. Monroe Price and Robert Clinton, *Law and the American Indian* (Charlottesville: The Michie Co., 1983), p. 89.
46. Winona LaDuke, "They Always Come Back," in ed. Brant, *A Gathering of Spirit*, Brant, ed. (Sinister Wisdom Books, 1984), pp. 62–67.
47. Katz, *I Am the Fire of Time*, p. 149.
48. Bataille and Sands, *American Indian Women, Telling Their Lives*, p. 140.
49. Allen, *The Sacred Hoop*, p. 119.
50. Bataille and Sands, *American Indian Women, Telling Their Lives*, p. 49.
51. *Ibid.*, p. 138.
52. Joy Harjo, "Anchorage," in *She Had Some Horses* (New York: Thunder's Mouth Press, 1983), p. 15.
53. *Ibid.*, "Motion," p. 54.
54. Allen, *The Sacred Hoop*, p. 147.
55. Alfonso Ortiz, *The Tewa World* (University of Chicago Press, 1969).
56. Allen, *The Sacred Hoop*, p. 147.
57. Harjo, "Skeleton of Winter," in *She Had Some Horses*, p. 31.
58. Luci Tapahonso, "Her Daughter's Eyes," in *Seasonal Woman* (Tooth of Time Books, 1982), p. 13.
59. Alen, *The Sacred Hoop*, pp. 118–119.
60. Harjo, "The Black Room," in *She Had Some Horses*, p. 25.
61. Silko, *Ceremony*, p. 14.
62. Louise Erdrich, *Love Medicine* (New York: Holt, Rinehart and Winston, 1984), p. 138.
63. *Ibid.*, p. 227.
64. Campbell, *Halfbreed*, p. 116.
65. Silko, *Ceremony*, p. 71.
66. Harjo, "Heartbeat," in *She Had Some Horses*, p. 37.
67. *Ibid.*
68. Martin, *An American Triptych*, p. 191.
69. *Ibid.*, pp. 177–178.
70. Paula Allen, *The Woman Who Owned the Shadows*. (San Francisco: Spinster's Ink Press, 1983).
71. Harjo, "The Woman Hanging from the Thirteenth Floor Window," in *She Had Some Horses*, p. 23.
72. *Ibid.*, "She Remembers the Future," p. 46.
73. Allen, *The Sacred Hoop*, p. 167.
74. Harjo, "She Had Some Horses," p. 64.
75. Allen, *The Sacred Hoop*, p. 166.
76. Ted Williams, *The Reservation* (Syracuse: Syracuse University Press, 1976), p. 254.
77. Linda Hogan, *Seeing through the Sun* (Amherst: University of Massachusetts Press, 1985), p. 44.
78. Luci Tapahonso, "A Breeze Swept Through," in *A Gathering of Spirit*, p. 217.
79. Harjo, "For Alva Benson. And for Those Who I have Learned to Speak," in *She Had Some Horses*, p. 18.
80. Linda Hogan, *Eclipse* (Los Angeles: UCLA America Indian Studies Center, 1983), p. 36.
81. Harjo, "Remember" in *She Had Some Horses*, p. 40.
82. Gary Witherspoon, *Language and Art in the Navajo Universe* (Ann Arbor: University of Michigan Press, 1977), p. 16.
83. Tapahonso, "A Prayer" in *Seasonal Woman*, p. 51.

33

The Development of
Chicana Feminist Discourse, 1970–1980

Alma M. Garcia

Between 1970 and 1980, a Chicana feminist movement developed in the United States that addressed the specific issues that affected Chicanas as women of color. The growth of the Chicana feminist movement can be traced in the speeches, essays, letters, and articles published in Chicano and Chicana newspapers, journals, newsletters, and other printed materials.[1]

During the sixties, American society witnessed the development of the Chicano movement, a social movement characterized by a politics of protest (Barrera 1974; Muñoz 1974; Navarro 1974). The Chicano movement focused on a wide range of issues: social justice, equality, educational reforms, and political and economic self-determination for Chicano communities in the United States. Various struggles evolved within this movement: the United Farmworkers unionization efforts (Dunne 1967; Kushner 1975; Matthiesen 1969; Nelson 1966); the New Mexico Land Grant movement (Nabokov 1969); the Colorado-based Crusade for Justice (Castro 1974; Meier and Rivera 1972); the Chicano student movement (Garcia and de la Garza 1977); and the Raza Unida Party (Shockley 1974).

Chicanas participated actively in each of these struggles. By the end of the sixties, Chicanas began to assess the rewards and limits of their participation. The 1970s witnessed the development of Chicana feminists whose activities, organizations, and writings can be analyzed in terms of a feminist movement by women of color in American society. Chicana feminists outlined a cluster of ideas that crystallized into an emergent Chicana feminist debate. In the same way that Chicano males were reinterpreting the historical and contemporary experience of Chicanos in the United States, Chicanas began to investigate the forces shaping their own experiences as women of color.

The Chicana feminist movement emerged primarily as a result of the dynamics within the Chicano movement. In the 1960s and 1970s, the American political scene witnessed far-reaching social protest movements whose political courses often paralleled and at times exerted influence over each other (Freeman 1983; Piven and Cloward 1979). The development of feminist movements have been explained by the participation of women in larger social movements. Macias (1982), for example, links the early development of the Mexican feminist movement to the participation of women in the Mexican Revolution. Similarly, Freeman's (1984) analysis of the white feminist movement points out that many white feminists who were active in the early years of its development had previously been involved

Reprinted with permission from the author and Sage Publications. Originally published in *Gender and Society*, vol. 3, 1989, copyright held by: Sociologists for Women in Society, c/o Janet Chafetz, University of Houston, Houston, Texas 77004.

in the new left and civil rights movements. It was in these movements that white feminists experienced the constraints of male domination. Black feminists have similarly traced the development of a Black feminist movement during the 1960s and 1970s to their experiences with sexism in the larger Black movement (Davis 1983; Dill 1983; Hooks, 1981, 1984; Joseph and Lewis 1981; White 1984). In this way, then, the origins of Chicana feminism parallel those of other feminist movements.

Origins of Chicana Feminism

Rowbotham (1974) argues that women may develop a feminist consciousness as a result of their experiences with sexism in revolutionary struggles or mass social movements. To the extent that such movements are male dominated, women are likely to develop a feminist consciousness. Chicana feminists began the search for a "room of their own" by assessing their participation within the Chicano movement. Their feminist consciousness emerged from a struggle for equality with Chicano men and from a reassessment of the role of the family as a means of resistance to oppressive societal conditions.

Historically, as well as during the 1960s and 1970s, the Chicano family represented a source of cultural and political resistance to the various types of discrimination experienced in American society (Zinn 1975a). At the cultural level, the Chicano movement emphasized the need to safeguard the value of family loyalty. At the political level, the Chicano movement used the family as a strategic organizational tool for protest activities.

Dramatic changes in the structure of Chicano families occurred as they participated in the Chicano movement. Specifically, women began to question their traditional female roles (Zinn 1975a). Thus, a Chicana feminist movement originated from the nationalist Chicano struggle. Rowbotham (1974, p. 206) refers to such a feminist movement as "a colony within a colony." But as the Chicano movement developed during the 1970s, Chicana feminists began to draw their own political agenda and raised a series of questions to assess their role within the Chicano movement. They entered into a dialogue with each other that explicitly reflected their struggles to secure a room of their own within the Chicano movement.

Defining Feminism for Women of Color

A central question of feminist discourse is the definition of feminism. The lack of consensus reflects different political ideologies and divergent social-class bases. In the United States, Chicana feminists shared the task of defining their ideology and movement with white, Black, and Asian American feminists. Like Black and Asian American feminists, Chicana feminists struggled to gain social equality and end sexist and racist oppression. Like them, Chicana feminists recognized that the nature of social inequality for women of color was multidimensional (Cheng 1984; Chow 1987; Hooks 1981). Like Black and Asian American feminists, Chicana feminists struggled to gain equal status in the male-dominated nationalist movements and also in American society. To them, feminism represented a movement to end sexist oppression within a broader social protest movement. Again, like Black and Asian American feminists, Chicana feminists fought for social equality in the 1970s. They understood that their movement needed to go beyond women's rights and include the men of their group, who also faced racial subordination (Hooks 1981). Chicanas believed that feminism involved more than an analysis of gender because, as women of color, they were affected by both race and class in their everyday lives. Thus, Chicana feminism, as a social movement to improve the position of Chicanas in American society, represented a struggle that was both nationalist and feminist.

Chicana, Black, and Asian American feminists were all confronted with the issue of engaging in a feminist struggle to end sexist oppression within a broader nationalist struggle to end racist oppression. All experienced male domination in their own communities as well as in the large society. Ngan-Ling Chow (1987) identifies gender stereotypes of Asian American women and the patriarchal family structure as major sources of women's oppression. Cultural, political, and economic constraints have, according to Ngan-Ling Chow (1987), limited the full development of a feminist consciousness and movement among Asian American women. The cross-pressures resulting from the demands of a nationalist and a feminist struggle led some Asian American women to organize feminist organizations that, however, continued to address broader issues affecting the Asian American community.

Black women were also faced with addressing feminist issues within a nationalist movement. According to Thornton Dill (1983), Black women played a major historical role in Black resistance movements and, in addition, brought a feminist component to these movements (Davis 1983; Dill 1983). Black women have struggled with Black men in nationalist movements but have also recognized and fought against the sexism in such political movements in the Black community (Hooks 1984). Although they wrote and spoke as Black feminists, they did not organize separately from Black men.

Among the major ideological questions facing all three groups of feminists were the relationship between feminism and the ideology of cultural nationalism or racial pride, feminism and feminist-baiting within the larger movements, and the relationship between their feminist movements and the white feminist movement.

Chicana Feminism and Cultural Nationalism

Throughout the seventies and now, in the eighties, Chicana feminists have been forced to respond to the criticism that cultural nationalism and feminism are irreconcilable. In the first issue of the newspaper, *Hijas de Cuauhtemoc*, Anna Nieto Gomez (1971) stated that a major issue facing Chicanas active in the Chicano movement was the need to organize to improve their status as women within the larger social movement. Francisca Flores (1971b, p. i), another leading Chicana feminist, stated:

> [Chicanas] can no longer remain in a subservient role or as auxiliary forces in the [Chicano] movement. They must be included in the front line of communication, leadership and organizational responsibility. . . . The issue of equality, freedom and self-determination of the Chicana—like the right of self-determination, equality, and liberation of the Mexican [Chicano] community—is not negotiable. Anyone opposing the right of women to organize into their own form of organization has no place in the leadership of the movement.

Supporting this position, Bernice Rincon (1971) argued that a Chicana feminist movement that sought equality and justice for Chicanas would strengthen the Chicano movement. Yet in the process, Chicana feminists challenged traditional gender roles because they limited their participation and acceptance within the Chicano movement.

Throughout the seventies, Chicana feminists viewed the struggle against sexism within the Chicano movement and the struggle against racism in the larger society as integral parts of Chicana feminism. As Nieto Gomez (1976, p. 10) said:

Chicana feminism is in various stages of development. However, in general, Chicana feminism is the recognition that women are oppressed as a group and are exploited as part of *la Raza* people. It is a direction to be responsible to identify and act upon the issues and needs of Chicana women. Chicana feminists are involved in understanding the nature of women's oppression.

Cultural nationalism represented a major ideological component of the Chicano movement. Its emphasis on Chicano cultural pride and cultural survival within an Anglo-dominated society gave significant political direction to the Chicano movement. One source of ideological disagreement between Chicana feminism and this cultural nationalist ideology was cultural survival. Many Chicana feminists believed that a focus on cultural survival did not acknowledge the need to alter male-female relations within Chicano communities. For example, Chicana feminists criticized the notion of the "ideal Chicana" that glorified Chicanas as strong, long-suffering women who had endured and kept Chicano culture and the family intact. To Chicana feminists, this concept represented an obstacle to the redefinition of gender roles. Nieto (1975, p. 4) stated:

> Some Chicanas are praised as they emulate the sanctified example set by [the Virgin] Mary. The woman *par excellence* is mother and wife. She is to love and support her husband and to nurture and teach her children. Thus, may she gain fulfillment as a woman. For a Chicana bent upon fulfillment of her personhood, this restricted perspective of her role as a woman is not only inadequate but crippling.

Chicana feminists were also skeptical about the cultural nationalist interpretation of machismo. Such an interpretation viewed machismo as an ideological tool used by the dominant Anglo society to justify the inequalities experienced by Chicanos. According to this interpretation, the relationship between Chicanos and the larger society was that of an internal colony dominated and exploited by the capitalist economy (Almaguer 1974; Barrera 1979). Machismo, like other cultural traits, was blamed by Anglos for blocking Chicanos from succeeding in American society. In reality, the economic structure and colony-like exploitation were to blame.

Some Chicana feminists agreed with this analysis of machismo, claiming that a mutually reinforcing relationship existed between internal colonialism and the development of the myth of machismo. According to Sosa Riddell (1974, p. 21), machismo was a myth "propagated by subjugators and colonizers, which created damaging stereotypes of Mexican/ Chicano males." As a type of social control imposed by the dominant society on Chicanos, the myth of machismo distorted gender relations within Chicano communities, creating stereotypes of Chicanas as passive and docile women. At this level in the feminist discourse, machismo was seen as an Anglo myth that kept both Chicanos and Chicanas in a subordinate status. As Nieto (1975, p. 4) concluded:

> Although the term "machismo" is correctly denounced by all because it stereotypes the Latin man . . . it does a great disservice to both men and women. Chicano and Chicana alike must be free to seek their own individual fulfillment.

While some Chicana feminists criticized the myth of machismo used by the dominant society to legitimate racial inequality, others moved beyond this level of analysis to distinguish between the machismo that oppressed both men and women and the sexism in Chicano communities in general, and the Chicano movement in particular, that oppressed Chicana women (Chavez 1971; Cotera 1977; Del Castillo 1974; Marquez and Ramirez 1977;

Riddell 1974; Zinn 1975b). According to Vidal (1971, p. 8), the origins of a Chicana feminist consciousness were prompted by the sexist attitudes and behavior of Chicano males, which constituted a "serious obstacle to women anxious to play a role in the struggle for Chicana liberation."

Furthermore, many Chicana feminists disagreed with the cultural nationalist view that machismo could be a positive value within a Chicano cultural value system. They challenged the view that machismo was a source of masculine pride for Chicanos and therefore a defense mechanism against the dominant society's racism. Although Chicana feminists recognized that Chicanos faced discrimination from the dominant society, they adamantly disagreed with those who believed that machismo was a form of cultural resistance to such discrimination. Chicana feminists called for changes in the ideologies responsible for distorting relations between women and men. One such change was to modify the cultural nationalist position that viewed machismo as a source of cultural pride.

Chicana feminists called for a focus on the universal aspects of sexism that shape gender relations in both Anglo and Chicano culture. While they acknowledge the economic exploitation of all Chicanos, Chicana feminists outlined the double exploitation experienced by Chicanas. Sosa Riddell (1974, p. 159) concluded: "It was when Chicanas began to seek work outside of the family groups that sexism became a key factor of oppression along with racism." Francisca Flores (1971a, p. 4) summarized some of the consequences of sexism:

> It is not surprising that more and more Chicanas are forced to go to work in order to supplement the family income. The children are farmed out to a relative to baby-sit with them, and since these women are employed in the lower income jobs, the extra pressure placed on them can become unbearable.

Thus, while the Chicano movement was addressing the issue of racial oppression facing all Chicanos, Chicana feminists argued that it lacked an analysis of sexism. Similarly, Black and Asian American women stressed the interconnectedness of race and gender oppression. Hooks (1984, p. 52) analyzes racism and sexism in terms of their "intersecting, complementary nature." She also emphasizes that one struggle should not take priority over the other. White (1984) criticizes Black men whose nationalism limited discussions of Black women's experiences with sexist oppression. The writings of other Black feminists criticized a Black cultural nationalist ideology that overlooked the consequences of sexist oppression (Beale, 1975; Cade 1970; Davis 1971; Joseph and Lewis 1981). Many Asian American women were also critical of the Asian American movement whose focus on racism ignored the impact of sexism on the daily lives of women. The participation of Asian American women in various community struggles increased their encounters with sexism (Chow 1987). As a result, some Asian American women developed a feminist consciousness and organized as women around feminist issues.

Chicana Feminism and Feminist-Baiting

The systematic analysis by Chicana feminists of the impact of racism and sexism on Chicanas in American society and, above all, within the Chicano movement was often misunderstood as a threat to the political unity of the Chicano movement. As Marta Cotera (1977, p. 9), a leading voice of Chicana feminism pointed out:

> The aggregate cultural values we [Chicanas] share can also work to our benefit if we choose to scrutinize our cultural traditions, isolate the positive attributes and interpret

them for the benefit of women. It's unreal that *Hispañas* have been browbeaten for so long about our so-called conservative (meaning reactionary) culture. It's also unreal that we have let men interpret culture only as those practices and attitudes that determine who does the dishes around the house. We as women also have the right to interpret and define the philosophical and religious traditions beneficial to us within our culture, and which we have inherited as our tradition. To do this, we must become both conversant with our history and philosophical evolution, and analytical about the institutional and behavioral manifestations of the same.

Such Chicana feminists were attacked for developing a "divisive ideology"—a feminist ideology that was frequently viewed as a threat to the Chicano movement as a whole. As Chicana feminists examined their roles as women activists within the Chicano movement, an ideological split developed. One group active in the Chicano movement saw themselves as "loyalists" who believed that the Chicano movement did not have to deal with sexual inequities since Chicano men as well as Chicana women experienced racial oppression. According to Nieto Gomez (1973, p. 35), who was not a loyalist, their view was that if men oppress women, it is not the men's fault but rather that of the system.

Even if such a problem existed, and they did not believe that it did, the loyalists maintained that such a matter would best be resolved internally within the Chicano movement. They denounced the formation of a separate Chicana feminist movement on the grounds that it was a politically dangerous strategy, perhaps Anglo inspired. Such a movement would undermine the unity of the Chicano movement by raising an issue that was not seen as a central one. Loyalists viewed racism as the most important issue within the Chicano movement. Nieto Gomez (1973, p. 35) quotes one such loyalist:

> I am concerned with the direction that the Chicanas are taking in the movement. The words such as liberation, sexism, male chauvinism, etc., were prevalent. The terms mentioned above plus the theme of individualism is a concept of the Anglo society; terms prevalent in the Anglo women's movement. The *familia* has always been our strength in our culture. But it seems evident . . . that you [Chicana feminists] are not concerned with the *familia*, but are influenced by the Anglo woman's movement.

Chicana feminists were also accused of undermining the values associated with Chicano culture. Loyalists saw the Chicana feminist movement as an "anti-family, anti-cultural, anti-man and therefore an anti-Chicano movement" (Gomez 1973, p. 35). Feminism was, above all, believed to be an individualistic search for identity that detracted from the Chicano movement's "real" issues, such as racism. Nieto Gomez (1973, p. 35) quotes a loyalist as stating:

> And since when does a Chicana need identity? If you are a real Chicana then no one regardless of the degrees needs to tell you about it. The only ones who need identity are the *vendidas*, the *falsas*, and the opportunists.

The ideological conflicts between Chicana feminists and loyalists persisted throughout the seventies. Disagreements between these two groups became exacerbated during various Chicana conferences. At times, such confrontations served to increase Chicana feminist activity that challenged the loyalists' attacks, yet these attacks also served to suppress feminist activities.

Chicana feminist lesbians experienced even stronger attacks from those who viewed feminism as a divisive ideology. In a political climate that already viewed feminist ideology with suspicion, lesbianism as a sexual life-style and political ideology came under even more attack. Clearly, a cultural nationalist ideology that perpetuated such stereotypical images of Chicanas as "good wives and good mothers" found it difficult to accept a Chicana feminist lesbian movement.

Cherrie Moraga's writings during the 1970s reflect the struggles of Chicana feminist lesbians who, together with other Chicana feminists, were finding the sexism evident within the Chicano movement intolerable. Just as Chicana feminists analyzed their life circumstances as members of an ethnic minority and as women, Chicana feminist lesbians addressed themselves to the oppression they experienced as lesbians. As Moraga (1981, p. 28) stated:

> My lesbianism is the avenue through which I have learned the most about silence and oppression. . . . In this country, lesbianism is a poverty—as is being brown, as is being a woman, as is being just plain poor. The danger lies in ranking the oppression. The danger lies in failing to acknowledge the specificity of the oppression.

Chicana, Black, and Asian American feminists experienced similar cross-pressures of feminist-baiting and lesbian-baiting attacks. As they organized around feminist struggles, these women of color encountered criticism from both male and female cultural nationalists who often viewed feminism as little more than an "anti-male" ideology. Lesbianism was identified as an extreme derivation of feminism. A direct connection was frequently made that viewed feminism and lesbianism as synonymous. Feminists were labeled lesbians, and lesbians as feminists. Attacks against feminists—Chicanas, Blacks, and Asian Americans— derived from the existence of homophobia within each of these communities. As lesbian women of color published their writings, attacks against them increased (Moraga 1983).

Responses to such attacks varied within and between the feminist movements of women of color. Some groups tried one strategy and later adopted another. Some lesbians pursued a separatist strategy within their own racial and ethnic communities (Moraga and Anzaldua 1981; White 1984). Others attempted to form lesbian coalitions across racial and ethnic lines. Both strategies represented a response to the marginalization of lesbians produced by recurrent waves of homophobic sentiments in Chicano, Black, and Asian American communities (Moraga and Anzaldua 1981). A third response consisted of working within the broader nationalist movements in these communities and the feminist movements within them in order to challenge their heterosexual biases and resultant homophobia. As early as 1974, the "Black Feminist Statement" written by a Boston-based feminist group—the Combahee River Collective—stated (1981, p. 213): "We struggle together with Black men against racism, while we also struggle with Black men against sexism." Similarly, Moraga (1981) challenged the white feminist movement to examine its racist tendencies; the Chicano movement, its sexist tendencies; and both, their homophobic tendencies. In this way, Moraga (1981) argued that such movements to end oppression would begin to respect diversity within their own ranks.

Chicana feminists as well as Chicana feminist lesbians continued to be labeled *vendidas* or "sellouts." Chicana loyalists continued to view Chicana feminism as associated, not only with melting into white society, but more seriously, with dividing the Chicano movement. Similarly, many Chicano males were convinced that Chicana feminism was a divisive ideology incompatible with Chicano cultural nationalism. Nieto Gomez (1976, p. 10) said that "[with] respect to [the] Chicana feminist, their credibility is reduced when they are associated with [feminism] and white women." She added that, as a result, Chicana feminists often faced harrassment and ostracism within the Chicano movement. Similarly, Cotera

(1973, p. 30) stated that Chicanas "are suspected of assimilating into the feminist ideology of an alien [white] culture that actively seeks our cultural domination."

Chicana feminists responded quickly and often vehemently to such charges. Flores (1971a, p. 1) answered these antifeminist attacks in an editorial in which she argued that birth control, abortion, and sex education were not merely "white issues." In response to the accusation that feminists were responsible for the "betrayal of [Chicano] culture and heritage," Flores said, "Our culture hell"—a phrase that became a dramatic slogan of the Chicana feminist movement.

Chicana feminists' defense throughout the 1970s against those claiming that a feminist movement was divisive for the Chicano movement was to reassess their roles within the Chicano movement and to call for an end to male domination. Their challenges of traditional gender roles represented a means to achieve equality (Longeaux y Vasquez 1969a, 1969b). In order to increase the participation of and opportunities for women in the Chicano movement, feminists agreed that both Chicanos and Chicanas had to address the issue of gender inequality (Chapa 1973; Chavez 1971; Del Castillo 1974; Cotera 1977; Moreno 1979). Furthermore, Chicana feminists argued that the resistance that they encountered reflected the existence of sexism on the part of Chicano males and the antifeminist attitudes of the Chicana loyalists. Nieto Gomez (1973, p. 31), reviewing the experiences of Chicana feminists in the Chicano movement, concluded that Chicanas "involved in discussing and applying the women's question have been ostracized, isolated and ignored." She argued that "in organizations where cultural nationalism is extremely strong, Chicana feminists experience intense harassment and ostracism" (1973, p. 38).

Black and Asian American women also faced severe criticism as they pursued feminist issues in their own communities. Indeed, as their participation in collective efforts to end racial oppression increased, so did their confrontations with sexism (Chow 1987; Hooks 1984; White 1984). Ngan-Ling Chow (1987, p. 288) describes the various sources of such criticism directed at Asian American women:

> Asian American women are criticized for the possible consequences of their protests: weakening the male ego, dilution of effort and resources in Asian American communities, destruction of working relationships between Asian men and women, setbacks for the Asian American cause, co-optation into the larger society, and eventual loss of ethnic identity for Asian Americans as a whole. In short, affiliation with the feminist movement is perceived as a threat to solidarity within their own community.

Similar criticism was experienced by Black feminists (Hooks 1984; White 1984).

Chicana Feminists and White Feminists

It is difficult to determine the extent to which Chicana feminists sympathized with the white feminist movement. A 1976 study at the University of San Diego that examined the attitudes of Chicanas regarding the white feminist movement found that the majority of Chicanas surveyed believed that the movement had affected their lives. In addition, they identified with such key issues as the right to legal abortions on demand and access to low-cost birth control. Nevertheless, the survey found that "even though the majority of Chicanas . . . could relate to certain issues of the women's movement, for the most part they saw it as being an elitist movement comprised of white middle-class women who [saw] the oppressor as the males of this country" (Orozco 1976, p. 12).

Nevertheless, some Chicana feminists considered the possibility of forming coalitions with white feminists as their attempts to work within the Chicano movement were suppressed. Since white feminists were themselves struggling against sexism, building coalitions with them was seen as an alternative strategy for Chicana feminists (Rincon 1971). Almost immediately, however, Chicana feminists recognized the problems involved in adopting this political strategy. As Longeaux y Vasquez (1971, p. 11) acknowledged, "Some of our own Chicanas may be attracted to the white woman's liberation movement, but we really don't feel comfortable there. We want to be a Chicana *primero* [first]." For other Chicanas, the demands of white women were "irrelevant to the Chicana movement" (Hernandez 1971, p. 9).

Several issues made such coalition building difficult. First, Chicana feminists criticized what they considered to be a cornerstone of white feminist thought, an emphasis on gender oppression to explain the life circumstances of women. Chicana feminists believed that the white feminist movement overlooked the effects of racial oppression experienced by Chicanas and other women of color. Thus, Del Castillo (1974, p. 8) maintained that the Chicana feminist movement was "different primarily because we are [racially] oppressed people." In addition, Chicana feminists criticized white feminists who believed that a general women's movement would be able to overcome racial differences among women. Chicanas interpreted this as a failure by the white feminist movement to deal with the issue of racism. Without the incorporation of an analysis of racial oppression to explain the experiences of Chicanas as well as of other women of color, Chicana feminists believed that a coalition with white feminists would be highly unlikely (Chapa 1973; Cotera 1977; Gomez 1973; Longeaux y Vasquez 1971). As Longeaux y Vasquez (1971, p. 11) concluded: "We must have a clearer vision of our plight and certainly we cannot blame our men for the oppression of the women."

In the 1970s, Chicana feminists reconciled their demands for an end to sexism within the Chicano movement and their rejection of the saliency of gender oppression by separating the two issues. They clearly identified the struggle against sexism in the Chicano movement as a major issue, arguing that sexism prevented their full participation (Fallis 1974; Gomez 1976). They also argued that sexist behavior and ideology on the part of both Chicano males and Anglos represented the key to understanding women's oppression. However, they remained critical of an analysis of women's experiences that focused exclusively on gender oppression.

Chicana feminists adopted an analysis that began with race as a critical variable in interpreting the experiences of Chicano communities in the United States. They expanded this analysis by identifying gender as a variable interconnected with race in analyzing the specific daily life circumstances of Chicanas as women in Chicano communities. Chicana feminists did not view women's struggles as secondary to the nationalist movement but argued instead for an analysis of race and gender as multiple sources of oppression (Cotera 1977). Thus, Chicana feminism went beyond the limits of an exclusively racial theory of oppression that tended to overlook gender and also went beyond the limits of a theory of oppression based exclusively on gender that tended to overlook race.

A second factor preventing an alliance between Chicana feminists and white feminists was the middle-class orientation of white feminists. While some Chicana feminists recognized the legitimacy of the demands made by white feminists and even admitted sharing some of these demands, they argued that "it is not our business as Chicanas to identify with the white women's liberation movement as a home base for working for our people" (Longeaux y Vasquez 1971, p. 11).

Throughout the 1970s, Chicana feminists viewed the white feminist movement as a middle-class movement (Chapa 1973; Cotera 1980; Longeaux y Vasquez 1970; Martinez

1972; Nieto 1974; Orozco 1976). In contrast, Chicana feminists analyzed the Chicano movement in general as a working-class movement. They repeatedly made reference to such differences, and many Chicana feminists began their writings with a section that disassociated themselves from the "women's liberation movement." Chicana feminists as activists in the broader Chicano movement identified as major struggles the farmworkers movement, welfare rights, undocumented workers, and prison rights. Such issues were seen as far removed from the demands of the white feminist movement, and Chicana feminists could not get white feminist organizations to deal with them (Cotera 1980).

Similar concerns regarding the white feminist movement were raised by Black and Asian American feminists. Black feminists have documented the historical and contemporary schisms between Black feminists and white feminists, emphasizing the socioeconomic and political differences (Davis 1971, 1983; Dill 1983; LaRue 1970). More specifically, Black feminists have been critical of the white feminists who advocate a female solidarity that cuts across racial, ethnic, and social class lines. As Thornton Dill (1893, p. 131) states:

> They cry "Sisterhood is powerful!" has engaged only a few segments of the female population in the United States. Black, Hispanic, Native American, and Asian American women of all classes, as well as many working-class women, have not readily identified themselves as sisters of the white middle-class women who have been in the forefront of the movement.

Like Black feminists, Asian American feminists have also had strong reservations regarding the white feminist movement. For many Asian Americans, white feminism has primarily focused on gender as an analytical category and has thus lacked a systematic analysis of race and class (Chow 1987; Fong 1978; Wong 1980; Woo 1971).

White feminist organizations were also accused of being exclusionary, patronizing, or racist in their dealings with Chicanas and other women of color. Cotera (1980, p. 227) states:

> Minority women could fill volumes with examples of put-down, put-ons, and out-and-out racism shown to them by the leadership in the [white feminist] movement. There are three major problem areas in the minority-majority relationship in the movement: (1) paternalism or maternalism, (2) extremely limited opportunities for minority women . . . , (3) outright discrimination against minority women in the movement.

Although Chicana feminists continued to be critical of building coalitions with white feminists toward the end of the seventies, they acknowledged the diversity of ideologies within the white feminist movement. Chicana feminists sympathetic to radical socialist feminism because of its anticapitalist framework wrote of working-class oppression that cut across racial and ethnic lines. Their later writings discussed the possibility of joining with white working-class women, but strategies for forming such political coalitions were not made explicit (Cotera 1977; Marquez and Ramirez 1977).

Instead, Del Castillo and other Chicana feminists favored coalitions between Chicanas and other women of color while keeping their respective autonomous organizations. Such coalitions would recognize the inherent racial oppression of capitalism rather than universal gender oppression. When Longeaux y Vasquez (1971) stated that she was "Chicana *primero,*" she was stressing the saliency of race over gender in explaining the oppression experienced by Chicanas. The word *Chicana* however, simultaneously expressed a woman's race and gender. Not until later—in the 1980s—would Chicana feminist ideology call for an analysis that stressed the interrelationship of race, class, and gender in explaining the conditions of Chicanas in American society (Cordova et al. 1986; Zinn 1982), just as Black and Asian American feminists have done.

Chicana feminists continued to stress the importance of developing autonomous feminist organizations that would address the struggles of Chicanas as members of an ethnic minority and as women. Rather than attempt to overcome the obstacles to coalition building between Chicana feminists and white feminists, Chicanas called for autonomous feminist organizations for all women of color (Cotera 1977; Gonzalez 1980; Nieto 1975). Chicana feminists believed that sisterhood was indeed powerful but only to the extent that racial and class differences were understood and, above all, respected. As Nieto (1974, p. 4) concludes:

> The Chicana must demand that dignity and respect within the women's rights movement which allows her to practice feminism within the context of her own culture. . . . Her approaches to feminism must be drawn from her own world.

Chicana Feminism: An Evolving Future

Chicana feminists, like Black, Asian American, and Native American feminists, experience specific life conditions that are distinct from those of white feminists. Such socioeconomic and cultural differences in Chicano communities directly shaped the development of Chicana feminism and the relationship between Chicana feminists and feminists of other racial and ethnic groups, including white feminists. Future dialogue among all feminists will require a mutual understanding of the existing differences as well as the similarities. Like other women of color, Chicana feminists must address issues that specifically affect them as women of color. In addition, Chicana feminists must address those issues that have particular impact on Chicano communities, such as poverty, limited opportunities for higher education, high school dropouts, health care, bilingual education, immigration reform, prison reform, welfare, and most recently, United States policies in Central America.

At the academic level, an increasing number of Chicana feminists continue to join in a collective effort to carry on the feminist legacy inherited from the 1970s. In June 1982, a group of Chicana academics organized a national feminist organization called Mujeres Activas en Letras y Cambio Social (MALCS) in order to build a support network for Chicana professors, undergraduates, and graduate students. The organization's major goal is to fight against race, class, and gender oppression facing Chicanas in institutions of higher education. In addition, MALCS aims to bridge the gap between academic work and the Chicano community. MALCS has organized three Chicana/Latina summer research institutes at the University of California at Davis and publishes a working paper series.

During the 1982 conference of the National Association for Chicano Studies, a panel organized by Mujeres en Marcha, a feminist group from the University of California at Berkeley, discussed three major issues facing Chicana feminists in higher education in particular and the Chicano movement in general. Panelists outlined the issues as follows (Mujeres en Marcha 1983, pp. 1–2):

1. For a number of years, Chicanas have heard claims that a concern with issues specifically affecting Chicanas is merely a distraction/diversion from the liberation of Chicano people as a whole. What are the issues that arise when women are asked to separate their exploitation as women from the other forms of oppression that we experience?
2. Chicanas are confronted daily by the limitations of being a woman in this patriarchal society; the attempts to assert these issues around sexism are often met with resistance

and scorn. What are some of the major difficulties in relations amongst ourselves? How are the relationships between women and men affected? How are the relationships of women to women and men to men affected? How do we overcome the constraints of sexism?

3. It is not uncommon that our interests as feminists are challenged on the basis that we are simply falling prey to the interests of white middle-class women. We challenge the notion that there is no room for a Chicana movement within our own community. We, as women of color, have a unique set of concerns that are separate from white women and from men of color.

While these issues could not be resolved at the conference, the panel succeeded in generating an ongoing discussion within the National Association for Chicano Studies (NACS). Two years later, in 1984, the national conference of NACS, held in Austin, Texas, adopted the theme "Voces de la Mujer" in response to demands from the Chicana Caucus. As a result, for the first time since its founding in 1972, the NACS national conference addressed the issue of women. Compared with past conferences, a large number of Chicanas participated by presenting their research and chairing and moderating panels. A plenary session addressed the problems of gender inequality in higher education and within NACS. At the national business meeting, the issue of sexism within NACS was again seriously debated as it continues to be one of the "unsettled issues" of concern to Chicana feminists. A significant outcome of this conference was the publication of the NACS 1984 conference proceedings, which marked the first time that the association's anthology was devoted completely to Chicanas and Mexicanas (Cordova et al. 1986).

The decade of the 1980s has witnessed a rephrasing of the critical question concerning the nature of the oppression experienced by Chicanas and other women of color. Chicana feminists, like Black feminists, are asking what are the consequences of the intersection of race, class, and gender in the daily lives of women in American society, emphasizing the simultaneity of these critical variables for women of color (Garcia 1986; Hooks 1984). In their labor-force participation, wages, education, and poverty levels, Chicanas have made few gains in comparison to white men and women and Chicano men (Segura 1986). To analyze these problems, Chicana feminists have investigated the structures of racism, capitalism, and patriarchy, especially as they are experienced by the majority of Chicanas (Ruiz 1987; Segura 1986; Zavella 1987). Clearly, such issues will need to be explicitly addressed by an evolving Chicana feminist movement, analytically and politically.

Note

AUTHOR'S NOTE: Research for this article was supported by Rev. Thomas Terry, S.J., university research grant awarded by Santa Clara University. Two substantively different versions of this article were presented at the 1985 Annual Conference of the National Association of Chicano Studies, Sacramento, CA, and the 1986 International Congress of the Latin American Studies Association, Boston, MA. I would like to thank Maxine Baca Zinn, Ada Sosa Riddell, Vicki L. Ruiz, Janet Flammang, Judith Lorber, and the referees for their constructive criticism. I am grateful to Francisco Jimenez for his thoughtful editorial suggestions and for his moral support and encouragement during this entire project.

1. For bibliographies on Chicanas see Balderama (1981); Candelaria (1980); Loeb (1980); Portillo, Rios, and Rodriguez (1976); and Baca Zinn (1982, 1984).

References

Almaguer, Tomas. 1974 "Historical Notes on Chicano Oppression." *Aztlan* 5:27–56.

Balderama, Sylvia. 1981. "A Comprehensive Bibliography on La Chicana." Unpublished paper, University of California, Berkeley.

Barrera, Mario. 1974. "The Study of Politics and the Chicano." *Aztlan* 5:9–26.

———.. 1979. *Race and Class in the Southwest.* Notre Dame, IN: University of Notre Dame Press.

Beale, Frances. 1975. "Slave of a Slave No More: Black Women in Struggle." *Black Scholar* 6:2–10.

Cade, Toni. 1970. *The Black Woman.* New York: Signet.

Candelaria, Cordelia. 1980. "Six Reference Works on Mexican American Women: A Review Essay." *Frontiers* 5:75–80.

Castro, Tony. 1974. *Chicano Power.* New York: Saturday Review Press.

Chapa, Evey, 1973. "Report from the National Women's Political Caucus." *Magazin* 1:37–39.

Chavez, Henri. 1971. "The Chicanas." *Regeneracion* 1:14.

Cheng, Lucie. 1984. "Asian American Women and Feminism." *Sojourner* 10:11–12.

Chow, Esther Ngan-Ling. 1987. "The Development of Feminist Consciousness Among Asian American Women." *Gender & Society* 1:284–99.

Combahee River Collection. 1981. "A Black Feminist Statement" 210–18 in *This Bridge Called My Back: Writings by Radical Women of Color,* edited by Cherrie Moraga and Gloria Anzaldua. Watertown, MA: Persephone.

Cordova, Teresa et al. 1986. *Chicana Voices: Intersections of Class, Race, and Gender.* Austin, TX: Center for Mexican American Studies.

Cotera, Marta. 1973. "La Mujer Mexicana: Mexicano Feminism." *Magazin* 1:30–32.

———.. 1977. *The Chicana Feminist.* Austin, TX: Austin Information Systems Development.

———.. 1980. "Feminism: The Chicana and Anglo Versions: An Historical Analysis." 217–34 in *Twice a Minority: Mexican American Women,* edited by Margarita Melville. St. Louis, MO: C. V. Mosby.

Davis, Angela. 1971. "Reflections on Black Women's Role in the Community of Slaves." *Black Scholar* 3:3–13.

———.. 1983. *Women, Race and Class.* New York: Random House.

Del Castillo, Adelaida. 1974. "La Vision Chicana." *La Gente:* 8.

Dill, Bonnie Thornton. 1983. "Race, Class, and Gender: Prospects for an All-Inclusive Sisterhood." *Feminist Studies* 9:131–50.

Dunne, John. 1967. *Delano: The Story of the California Grape Strike.* New York: Strauss.

Fallis, Guadalupe Valdes. 1974. "The Liberated Chicana—A Struggle Against Tradition." *Women: A Journal of Liberation* 3:20.

Flores, Francisca. 1971a. "Conference of Mexican Women: Un Remolino. *Regeneracion* 1(1):1–4.

———.. 1971b. "El Mundo Femenil Mexicana." *Regeneracion* 1(10):i.

Fong, Katheryn M. 1978. "Feminism Is Fine, But What's It Done for Asia America?" *Bridge* 6:21–22.

Freeman, Jo. 1983. "On the Origins of Social Movements." 8–30 in *Social Movements of the Sixties and Seventies,* edited by Jo Freeman. New York: Longman.

———.. 1984. "The Women's Liberation Movement: Its Origins, Structure, Activities, and Ideas." 543–56 in *Women: A Feminist Perspective,* edited by Jo Freeman. Palo Alto, CA: Mayfield.

Garcia, Alma M. 1986 "Studying Chicanas: Bringing Women into the Frame of Chicano Studies." 19–29 in *Chicana Voices: Intersections of Class, Race, and Gender,* edited by Teresa Cordova et al. Austin, TX: Center for Mexican American Studies.

Garcia, F. Chris and Rudolph O. de la Garza. 1977. *The Chicano Political Experience.* North Scituate, MA: Duxbury.

Gomez, Anna Nieto. 1971. "Chicanas Identify." *Hijas de Cuauhtemoc* (April):9.

———.. 1973. "La Femenista." *Encuentro Femenil* 1:34–47.

———. 1976. "Sexism in the Movement." *La Gente* 6(4):10.

Gonzalez, Sylvia. 1980. "Towards a Feminist Pedagogy for Chicana Self-Actualization." *Frontiers* 5:48–51.

Hernandez, Carmen. 1971. "Carmen Speaks Out." *Papel Chicano* (June 12):8–9.

Hooks, Bell. 1981. *Ain't I a Woman: Black Women and Feminism.* Boston: South End Press.

———.. 1984. *Feminist Theory: From Margin to Center.* Boston: South End Press.

Joseph, Gloria and Jill Lewis. 1981. *Common Differences: Conflicts in Black and White Feminist Perspectives.* Garden City, NJ: Doubleday.

Kushner, Sam. 1975. *Long Road to Delano.* New York: International.

LaRue, Linda. 1970. "The Black Movement and Women's Liberation." *Black Scholar* 1:36–42.

Loeb, Catherine. 1980. "La Chicana: A Bibliographic Survey." *Frontiers* 5:59–74.

Longeaux y Vasquez, Enriqueta. 1969a. "The Woman of La Raza." *El Grito del Norte* 2(July):8–9.

———.. 1969b. "La Chicana: Let's Build a New Life." *El Grito del Norte* 2(November):11.

———.. 1970. "The Mexican-American Woman." 379–84 in *Sisterhood Is Powerful,* edited by Robin Morgan. New York: Vintage.

———.. 1971. "Soy Chicana Primero." *El Grito del Norte* 4(April 26):11.

Macias, Anna. 1982. *Against All Odds.* Westport, CT: Greenwood.

Marquez, Evelina and Margarita Ramirez. 1977. "Women's Task Is to Gain Liberation." 188–94 in *Essays on La Mujer,* edited by Rosaura Sanchez and Rosa Martinez Cruz. Los Angeles: UCLA Chicano Studies Center.

Martinez, Elizabeth. 1972. "The Chicana." *Ideal* 44:1–3.

Matthiesen, Peter. 1969. *Sal Si Puedes: Cesar Chavez and the New American Revolution.* New York: Random House.

Meier, Matt and Feliciano Rivera. 1972. *The Chicanos.* New York: Hill & Wang.

Moraga, Cherrie. 1981. "La Guera." 27–34 in *This Bridge Called My Back: Writings by Radical Women of Color,* edited by Cherrie Moraga and Gloria Anzaldua. Watertown, MA: Persephone.

———.. 1983. *Loving in the War Years.* Boston: South End Press.

Moraga, Cherrie and Gloria Anzaldua. 1981. *This Bridge Called My Back: Writings by Radical Women of Color.* Watertown, MA: Persephone.

Moreno, Dorinda. 1979. "The Image of the Chicana and the La Raza Woman." *Caracol* 2:14–15.

Mujeres en Marcha. 1983. *Chicanas in the 80s: Unsettled Issues.* Berkeley, CA: Chicano Studies Publication Unit.

Muñoz, Carlos, Jr., 1974. "The Politics of Protest and Liberation: A Case Study of Repression and Cooptation." *Aztlan* 5:119–41.

Nabokov, Peter. 1969. *Tijerina and the Courthouse Raid.* Aubuquerque, NM: University of New Mexico Press.

Navarro, Armando. 1974. "The Evolution of Chicano Politics." *Aztlan* 5:57–84.

Nelson, Eugene. 1966. *Huelga: The First 100 Days.* Delano, CA: Farm Workers Press.

Nieto, Consuelo, 1974. "The Chicana and the Women's Rights Movement." *La Luz* 3(September):10–11, 32.

———.. 1975. "Consuelo Nieto on the Women's Movement." *Interracial Books for Children Bulletin* 5:4.

Orozco, Yolanda. 1976. "La Chicana and 'Women's Liberation.' " *Voz Fronteriza* (January 5):6, 12.

Piven, Frances Fox and Richard A. Cloward. 1979. *Poor People's Movements: Why They Succeed, How They Fail.* New York: Vintage.

Portillo, Cristina, Graciela Rios, and Martha Rodriquez. 1976. *Bibliography on Writings on La Mujer.* Berkeley, CA: University of California Chicano Studies Library.

Riddell, Adaljiza Sosa. 1974. "Chicanas en el Movimiento." *Aztlan* 5:155–65.

Rincon, Bernice. 1971. "La Chicana: Her Role in the Past and Her Search for a New Role in the Future." *Regeneracion* 1(10):15–17.

Rowbotham, Sheila. 1974. *Women, Resistance and Revolution: A History of Women and Revolution in the Modern World.* New York: Vintage.

Ruiz, Vicki L. 1987. *Cannery Women, Cannery Lives: Mexican Women, Unionization, and the California Food Processing Industry 1930–1950.* Albuquerque: University of New Mexico Press.

Segura, Denise. 1986. "Chicanas and Triple Oppression in the Labor Force." 47–65 in *Chicana Voices: Intersections of Class, Race and Gender,* edited by Teresa Cordova et al. Austin, TX: Center for Mexican American Studies.

Shockley, John. 1974. *Chicano Revolt in a Texas Town.* South Bend, IN: University of Notre Dame Press.

Vidal, Mirta. 1971. "New Voice of La Raza: Chicanas Speak Out." *International Socialist Review* 32:31–33.

White, Frances. 1984. "Listening to the Voices of Black Feminism." *Radical America* 18:7–25.

Wong, Germaine Q. 1980. "Impediments to Asian-Pacific-American Women Organizing." 89–103 in *The Conference on the Educational and Occupational Needs of Asian Pacific Women.* Washington, DC: National Institute of Education.

Woo, Margaret. 1971. "Women + Man = Political Unity." 115–16 in *Asian Women,* edited by Editorial Staff. Berkeley, CA: University of California Press.

Zavella, Patricia. 1987. *Women's Work and Chicano Families: Cannery Workers of the Santa Clara Valley.* Ithaca, NY: Cornell University Press.

Zinn, Maxine Baca. 1975a. "Political Familism: Toward Sex Role Equality in Chicano Families." *Aztlan* 6:13–27.

———.. 1975b. "Chicanas: Power and Control in the Domestic Sphere." *De Colores* 2/3:19–31.

———.. 1982. "Mexican-American Women in the Social Sciences." *Signs: Journal of Women in Culture and Society* 8:259–72.

———.. 1984. "Mexican Heritage Women: A Bibliographic Essay." *Sage Race Relations Abstracts* 9:1–12.

34

Equal Employment Opportunity Commission vs. Sears, Roebuck and Company: A Personal Account

Alice Kessler-Harris

The case exploded into my life in early September of 1984. Had I heard of the suit against Sears, Roebuck, said the lawyer for the Equal Employment Opportunity Commission on the telephone? Did I know that it was the last of the class action cases and that Sears was the largest employer of women outside the Federal government? Discrimination, retail sales, a female work force—would I be willing to testify for the EEOC? But why, I asked, confusedly processing bits of information, do you need a historian to testify? "Well they've got one," came the answer, "and we want you to rebut her testimony. She argues that women were not interested in commission sales, and she cites your work as evidence that Sears was not guilty of discrimination. Do you agree?

No, I thought, I did not agree that women's lack of "interest" could absolve a company of charges of discrimination. Nor could I accept that the complex reality embodied in the notion of "interest" could be so readily simplified. I did think that there was some as yet some undefined difference between men and women. I had argued as much myself. But I had not yet figured out what that meant in terms of historical analysis. And to equate different "interests" with an acceptance of the current distribution of rewards from wage work was, in my judgment, to misunderstand the process by which women struggled for change, as well as to simplify the way difference and inequality have played themselves out historically.

Layers peeled back in the months that followed and the clarity that now seems possible only slowly became visible. A female historian, identified as a feminist, had taken a position in a political trial. She was prepared to testify that other women—working class women, poor women, non-white women—had not wanted well-paying jobs, and would not willingly make the kinds of compromises she herself had made in order to succeed at them. What was to be gained by such testimony? A successful argument would damage women who worked at Sears as well as past and future applicants. Worse, it would set a legal precedent that would inhibit affirmative action cases in the future. For if defendants could justify the absence of women in certain kinds of jobs on the grounds that insufficient numbers of women possessed any interest in them, one could foresee the resulting cycle. Expectations and aspirations conditioned by generations of socialization and labor market experience would now be used to justify continuing discrimination against women. The potential consequences were terrifying. The absence of women from the ranks of plumbers, automobile mechanics or airline pilots could become evidence of their lack of interest in preparing

---

Reprinted with permission from the author and MARHO: The Radical Historians' Organization. Originally appeared in *Radical History Review*, vol. 35, 1986.

for these jobs. Neither employers nor unions could be held responsible for their absence. Women were themselves to blame. And, finally, what would a victory for this kind of argument do to the remnants of the EEOC? Granted that it was now a Reagan appointed and controlled body, still, this case was left over from the Nixon and Carter years. If some of its lawyers were still fighting on behalf of policies this administration had abandoned, and with tactics, it repudiated, should they not be supported?

The elements of the case fell into place slowly. Accused of discriminating against women by failing to hire either new applicants or present employees into commission sales jobs, and by paying managerial women less than men in the same jobs, the company did not dispute the essential fact of the case. Before 1973 (when the EEOC, acting on the complaints of scores of women, and in the wake of the A.T.&T. decision, first brought charges), few women worked in Sears' well-paying commission sales categories.[1] Between 1974 and 1979, under pressure from the EEOC's threatened action, Sears had made some progress in some commission sales categories nationwide. Women had begun to sell such items as sewing machines and draperies, furniture and shoes. In one of the five regional territories into which Sears stores were divided progress had been substantial.[2] But everywhere, the most lucrative jobs in automotive accessories, large appliances, home entertainment, sporting goods and installed home improvements remained stubbornly resistant to female workers. Overall, the EEOC argued, the proportion of women hired or promoted into such jobs was fifty per cent lower than they estimated it should have been.[3] Efforts to reach an agreement with the company on an enforceable affirmative action plan failed, and in 1980 the EEOC determined on court action.

In court, the EEOC relied on statistical methods to prove its case. Producing a few complaintants among the more than one million people who had applied for jobs over the seven-year period in contention would, lawyers feared, create vulnerability if the company could undermine the character of one or two witnesses. Aware that statistical data had been successfully used in the past to demonstrate discrimination in cases involving both women and minorities, EEOC lawyers chose what they thought would be a sure path. They attempted to demonstrate that the absence of women in certain kinds of jobs revealed a pattern of discrimination. Using elaborate statistical techniques that took account of the general and specific work-force experience and educational background of men and women who applied for sales jobs at Sears, the EEOC contended that Sears had fallen far short of good faith efforts at placing women in commission sales jobs. Particularly in contention were the most lucrative jobs selling "big ticket" items such as installed home improvements, carpets, home appliances and auto parts.

Sears' lawyers countered by challenging the notion that a pool of women was available for the jobs it had to offer. The company, they argued, should not be held responsible for the relatively low numbers of women hired in certain categories. Sears had tried, and failed, to find women willing to take those jobs. They were simply not interested in them. A team of lawyers from the Washington based firm of Charles Morgan and Associates[4] presented a series of Sears personnel officials to the court, all of whom testified that even after 1973, when Sears presumably had a goal-oriented affirmative action program, they had had great difficulty in persuading women to take commission sales jobs. As one affirmative action officer testified, "Sears tried very hard to get women into commission selling, despite women's general reluctance to accept these positions."[5] Women, personnel officers agreed, would not willingly undertake the greater competition and financial risk involved in such jobs. And besides, women preferred not to sell items such as men's clothing, fencing equipment, appliances and autoparts because they had no "interest" in them. "Women had to be persuaded to accept commission sales positions . . ." claimed one personnel officer.

"Women were very reluctant to accept positions in the large appliances, installed home improvements, and automotive divisions because they were uncomfortable with selling those product lines or felt they lacked the capacity for the technical aspects of the job."[6]

To prove there was no pool of women available for commission sales jobs, Sears' lawyers drew on the expertise of survey researchers and economists who cited national opinion polls taken in the '50s and '60s that unanimously indicated the prevalence of "traditional" attitudes among women and men regarding the family and women's role within it. And, finally, Sears called on historian Rosalind Rosenberg to provide the broader picture. Women, born and reared before the onset of the contemporary women's movement, she testified, were likely to have internalized traditional values and would thus be less likely than men to accept certain kinds of jobs, even when they carried substantial increases in income.[7]

The EEOC, in rebuttal, contended that Sears had never really tried to find women. The company's affirmative action program was a sham; its personnel people, who kept meticulous records about everything else, could not recall the name of any female job applicant who had actually turned down a job; its interviewing tests for commission sales people were biased.[8] In short, Sears was blind to its own discrimination. "The reasonable inference," argued the EEOC, "to be drawn from the consistent pattern of disparities between the expected and actual female proportion of promotions from full and part time noncommission sales positions to full and part time commission sales positions is that such disparities resulted from discrimination in Sears practices, policies and positions."[9] When only women who had in fact applied for jobs at Sears were counted, EEOC counsel argued, Sears had hired less than fifty per cent of the expected number of women overall. In some departments and regions the figures were much worse, even after the Company was under EEOC investigation.

Sears, drawing once again on Rosalind Rosenberg and others, replied that the EEOC's figures were flawed: the commission incorrectly assumed that men and women were alike and would seek the same kinds of jobs. Sears had tried. Its failure was a result of social circumstances beyond its control. It was, as Rosenberg argued, "naive to believe that the natural effects of these differences was evidence of discrimination by Sears."[10]

How important was the historical evidence in the context of a case that used the expertise of economists, sociologists and survey research experts? To exonerate itself from the charge of discrimination, Sears had to demonstrate that the disproportionately low numbers of women in its most lucrative commission sales jobs could be explained by some factor other than discrimination. A statistical pattern alone would not prove discrimination if Sears could come up with some logical explanation for the absence of women. Sears chose to try to convince the court of three things: that commission sales jobs in fact required competitive, aggressive and risk-oriented personalities; that Sears had made enormous attempts to induce women to take these jobs; and finally, that women's family values and domestic roles had undermined Sears' efforts. It was in this third category that the historical testimony played a role, for an important part of the company's defense rested on whether lawyers could demonstrate that an exceedingly limited pool of women willing to take commission sales jobs had been available in the years before 1973 when charges were first brought, and between 1973 and 1979 when the suit was filed.

Sears apparently counted on finding historical support from the beginning. The case went to trial in Chicago (company headquarters) in early September 1984. It concluded at the end of the following June, the longest case to be tried to date in the seventh circuit. Rosenberg prepared an "offer of proof," a summary of the evidence she was to present in court, sometime before July 1984. On the basis of this, she was deposed (examined by the opposing side as to the content of her testimony) in early July 1984, before the trial began.

I do not know when the EEOC decided it needed a historian to rebut her testimony. I was first contacted in the fall of 1984, and deposed in April 1985, after Rosenberg had testified, and it was clear that my rebuttal would be needed. Because the case was lengthy and drawn out, Judge John Nordberg, a Reagan appointee who was relatively new on the bench, decided about halfway through the trial to ask all witnesses to prepare their direct testimony in writing. This was intended to save time at the trial itself and to facilitate cross-examination. Rosenberg's slightly modified and annotated offer of proof served as her written testimony. Because my offer of proof was prepared under extreme pressure of time, it presented only a two-page outline of my position, on which the written testimony I prepared in May elaborated. After my court appearance in early June, Rosenberg prepared a "sur-rebuttal" on the basis of which she was cross-examined in late June. Neither the EEOC nor I had a chance to respond to this sur-rebuttal, except under the restricted conditions of cross-examination. The unusual circumstance of having two written testimonies (about twenty pages from each of us), as well as Rosenberg's rebuttal, provides a set of documents that lay out the two historical positions in a relatively coherent way, as court proceedings go.[11]

These documents pose a series of challenges to historians of women, the most important of which is why the documents came into existence at all. Historians and other social scientists frequently serve as expert witnesses, and even the unusual circumstance of testifying as to general ideology rather than to particular cases has precedent. According to anthropologist Lawrence Rosen, the 1949–1954 school desegregation cases relied heavily on the expertise of anthropologists who testified that there was no rational basis for keeping schoolchildren of different races apart.[12] But the testimony in the Sears case raises two hotly debated issues. First is the nature of truth and the possibility of claiming it in a case of this kind, and under the conditions that a court of law offers. Given the nature of adversarial proceedings, the historian who does not acknowledge (as C. Vann Woodward did in 1954) that he is "constrained by the limits of his craft" must wonder whether expertise is not merely a cover for more complicated rationalizations of our own values.[13] This raises a second issue: the politics of history. Lawrence Rosen argues that experts must set their own standards for the form of the argument used in a court of law as opposed to those "employed when writing for a scholarly or popular audience," implying what nearly everyone suggests: that witnesses who engage themselves in an adversarial situation necessarily take on the mission of their side. Historian Charles Bolton put this clearly when he described his testimony in a case involving creationism. "Since I was interested in the case and sympathetic to the plaintiff's position, I agreed to investigate the subject and to testify if my findings suited the needs of the attorneys," he said.[14]

Rosenberg studied the data that Sears' lawyers provided and concluded on the basis of it, as well as, presumably, on the basis of her general knowledge of the history of women, that the company was not guilty of discrimination.[15] I looked at the same material (or at any rate at the material that the EEOC provided) and concluded in the light of my work on wage-earning women that an absence of women was more likely to be a consequence of discrimination than of any other cause. There is no point in obscuring these essentially political perceptions or the political decisions that followed from them. Neither of us would have been selected as expert witnesses had we come to the opposite conclusions. Rosenberg later defended her participation in the case on the grounds that discrimination *alone* could not account for the absence of women. Of course not. But this was never the issue. The point is that, in a case that is about discrimination, to argue that discrimination was not the likely explanation is to lend one's expertise to the argument that other explanations are more plausible. What followed was to be expected. Rosenberg marshalled evidence to demonstrate that the absence of women was consistent with a lack of discrimination. I marshalled evidence to demonstrate that the absence of women was probably a result of it.

The capacity to take opposing positions on such a crucial issue deserves scrutiny. How does it happen that two feminist historians faced with the same question could come to such different conclusions? The answer may lie in different understandings of why and how we study the past. For many of us, history is about exploring the nature of social change. We engage in it as professional historians not to explore the past for its own sake but to explain how change happened. Some of us go one step further. In this respect I identify with a comment of Natalie Zemon Davis: "I want to show that even when times were hard, people found ways to cope with what was happening and maybe to resist it. . . . Especially I want to show that it could be different, that it was different, that there are alternatives."[16] As feminist historians, we are particularly concerned to discover what women's lives were like because we know that they simultaneously lived within oppressive systems and found ways to search for the elusive goal of equality. So we are drawn to write the biographies of all kinds of women not because they mirrored the social realities of their worlds, but because they transcended them. We use our knowledge to try to figure out how, despite the overwhelming weight of tradition, change occurs.

The attempt to understand mechanisms of change, then, requires questions about how women have pushed at the boundaries of opportunity. Under what historical circumstances did culture operate to inhibit change and under what circumstances to enhance opportunity? Recent historiography of wage-earning women has involved a search for answers to such questions. We began with the knowledge that most women worked at relatively poor jobs that they sought for a variety of reasons and in a variety of ways. We quickly rejected the biases of an early twentieth-century literature that accepted the values of domesticity, moving beyond its descriptions and illustrations of women's repeated victimization. Instead, we turned to sorting out how particular groups of women were constrained by force (economic and physical) as well as by self-justifying belief systems, and how they took advantage of unique movements to make incremental gains in their positions.

These concerns for the mechanisms of change are negated in the testimony offered by Rosenberg. Sears, seeking to justify the status quo, had set the terms of the discourse. Were there plausible alternative explanations other than discrimination, lawyers asked, for the absence of women in some jobs? Rosenberg had responded with what she later described as a "multicausal" view of history: one in which socialization, family responsibilities, educational practices, government policies, cultural attitudes and employer discrimination all played a part in shaping the contemporary labor force.[17] But, far from explaining the absence of women in certain sectors of the labor market, throwing out a variety of causes merely begs the question of how to order and assess them. As we shall see, Rosenberg had done precisely that. Having accepted the issues as Sears, Roebuck and Co. had chosen to define them, she had responded by presenting a plausible array of alternatives that together added up to a defense of the status quo.

The structure of the argument made to the court followed logically from this essentially political perspective. Rosenberg's position was deceptively simple. Men and women had different interests, goals and aspirations regarding work," she wrote.[18] The EEOC ignored the fact that "many workers, especially women, have goals and values other than realizing maximum economic gain . . ., values shaped in earlier eras."[19] These different goals and values, reinforced by government policies, had led women to emphasize traditional, family-oriented roles, and to make choices about wage work from that perspective. Rosenberg wrote:

Even the semi-subsistence, farming families in seventeenth-century America divided work according to sex. Women cared for the children, prepared the food, nursed the sick, made the clothes, and tended the garden. Men worked the fields, cared for the livestock, and represented the family in the outside world. Many of the jobs that men and women perform in the labor force today are the modern equivalents of traditional male and female tasks. For women these modern equivalents are simply added on to traditional tasks, especially if the woman is a wife and mother. Even as they have entered the labor force in increasing numbers, women have retained their historical commitment to the home. Women's role in American society and in the American family unit has fostered the development of 'feminine' values that have been internalized by women themselves and reinforced by society, through its customs, its culture, and its laws.[20]

For a "multicausal" view of women's condition, these observations reflect a singularly monocausal view of history. They take into account only the suppliers of labor—women—and offer up their domestic roles as the central explanation for the continuation of occupational segregation in the work force. Women had chosen not to look for jobs in nontraditional areas such as commission sales, Rosenberg concluded. Their absence from these jobs was consistent with a finding that there had been no discrimination at Sears.

Given the difficulty of presenting a nuanced historical argument before a court of law (a difficulty I was to experience later), I don't want to debate here the details of the evidence offered. Still, the absence of nuance exposes clearly the structure of the argument on both sides, and it is the outlines of the two positions and their implications that deserve scrutiny. Rosenberg's position lent itself to the uses that Sears' lawyers, Morgan and Associates, made of it.

The case turned on whether Sears employment practices reflected female preferences and values as opposed to those of employers. Lawyers for Sears emphasized women's goals and values, focused on the desire of individuals to fulfill their interests at work, and asserted employers' willingness to hire anyone qualified. Similarly, Rosenberg's testimony assumed the existence of genuine choice for women within an unrestricted labor market. "Because housework and child care continue to affect women's labor force participation even today," she wrote, "many women choose jobs that complement their family obligations over jobs that might increase and inhance [sic] their earning potential."[21] This vision of a labor market operating in response to the needs of women and the family pervades a testimony that lacks any sense that employers, too, make choices in terms of their preconceptions about workers. While no one would want to argue that employers alone discriminate, the decisions made by employers take into account the real costs of equity, and are often buttressed by an ideology that obscures discrimination in which employers and workers alike participate. Rosenberg's position implicitly holds women responsible for the sexual division of labor, offering the reality of a segmented labor market as though it were the product of women's will, but failing to acknowledge that women must confront it whether or not their own inclinations are family oriented.[22]

Such a vision of the labor market suggests that higher wages are incompatible with family responsibilities, an idea affirmed by Rosenberg's statement that "Many workers, especially women, have goals and values other than realizing maximum economic gain."[23] On one level, this statement is of course accurate. Recent research indicates that neither men nor women are interested *solely* in maximizing income. Men tend to choose between work and leisure; women between work, housework and leisure. In the neoclassical paradigm, a rise in wages tips the balance in favor of wage work, so it is hardly radical to view higher wages or available opportunity as responsible for women's willingness to trade housework for a job.[24]

In this context, the notion that some workers have goals and values other than realizing maximum economic gain reveals the essential issue at Sears. According to the EEOC's undisputed calculations, the median salary of full-time commission salespeople in their first year at Sears averaged between three and four dollars an hour more than the average salary of full-time non-commission salespeople.[25] Gaining this wage involved little or no risk. Between 1973 and 1977, Sears paid commission sales people a "draw" against commissions, but the company made up the difference if after one week the employee had not earned the rate of draw. After 1977, Sears guaranteed a minimum salary (estimated on the basis of sales performance) to all commission sales people and salespeople retained their commissions.[26] Personnel officers testified in court that they could recall few people ever fired for failing to make their base salaries. To believe Sears, in short, we would have to believe not only that women were not interested in maximizing income, but that the competition involved in such jobs and their lack of interest in the products sold would deter them from nearly doubling their wages. Since the hours in both non-commission and commission jobs were substantially the same and since earning income is seen by most wage-earning women as a way of meeting family needs, women's objections to commission sales jobs are reduced to the ideological sphere.

Who, then, were the women who preferred to avoid competition and were uninterested in non-traditional jobs? In Rosenberg's testimony, they were women for whom the nineteenth-century prescription of domesticity had become a reality. "Throughout American History," wrote Rosenberg, "there has been a consensus, shared by women, that, for women, working outside the home is subordinate to family." Rosenberg wrote as if all women were middle class. Black, immigrant, and poor women existed only at the periphery of the labor market, instead of at the center of most past and present decisions about wage work. Conceptions such as "traditional" and "non-traditional" work were never defined, and "family life" was reified, wiping out the diverse forms women had adopted to sustain themselves and their dependents.

The result was a conception in which "non-traditional" work and family life appeared as opposites, while "traditional" work was located not in labor market terms but in jobs that sustained notions of the "ideal" family—nursing, part-time, etc.[27] The evident tautology here (if women are doing the job, it must be consistent with family life; if it was consistent with family life, women would do it), was resolved in this schema by the assumption that women, after all, wanted these, and only these jobs. Women's interest in family life led them, with the encouragement of government and educational institutions, to seek out jobs that sustained their family roles and so on in a circular pattern that neatly fit the needs of employers and reaffirmed family life. One can admit the half truth here, namely that many women have accepted prevailing stereotypes about their roles, without negating the ways in which change in women's roles as a whole has resulted from the efforts of a minority of women to break down restrictive barriers. All women have not needed to be construction workers, telephone linemen or tool and dye makers to demonstrate that those options are available to other women.

What is at issue, then, is a conception that is so unalterably middle class and white that the notion of "family needs" is separable from the productive labor of women, inside or outside the home. Historically, women have met the needs of their families where, and as, necessity has required and opportunity has existed. To offer a view of history that suggests that working outside the home is somehow an evasion of family responsibility is to invoke turn-of-the-century middle class condemnation of poor working women.

The unstated assumption of this testimony is that the social root of ideological change lay within the family, as opposed to the sphere of production. Alterations in family demography and inflationary pressures on the family accounted for the surge of interest in jobs in the 1970s. Denying the impact of greater accessibility of jobs through affirmative action plans and legislative intervention, Rosenberg argued that women themselves have been forced, in consequence of demographic and family changes, to seek jobs. Still, they chose to work in areas consistent with her conception of family roles, and thus she could account for the flood of women into the workforce while holding that Sears could not be held responsible for failing to hire women in jobs they and she deemed inconsistent with an unchanging conception of women's roles. In this interpretation, the family was, and remained, the source of women's perceptions of the world around them. Avoiding this pattern was possible, according to the testimony, largely for educated women, who constituted the vanguard of change in the past as in the present.[28] Gone the tradition of radical womanhood embodied in the anarchist experience, or in the lives of black women. Gone too the legion of female trade union activists whose struggles to create opportunity for women highlight the pages of nineteenth- and twentieth-century history. Those were women who often identified with women's "sphere" and nevertheless attempted to fight their disadvantaged status at work. Gone too any conception of consciousness in which the production of household and factory formed a unity in women's minds.

The testimony lacked any conception that the job market and the world of work could and did influence how young girls thought about themselves and how women assessed their possibilities. Failure to understand that aspirations are themselves conditioned by perceptions of available opportunity (that Sears was an important part of this world and complicit in the socialization process) or to put it another way, that ideology and consciousness are both rooted in an everyday experience of which the family is a form as well as a creator, provided the curious gap in perception that allowed Rosenberg to acknowledge on the stand that black women might have had goals and aspirations that varied from those of white women without altering the direction of her testimony a notch.

There was another particularly disturbing problem from the perspective of women's history, however. Rosenberg's testimony offered an interpretation to which many of us had come. Namely, that women's social and cultural differences from men could and should be the subject of historical analysis. And yet, no student of the history of working women that I knew of inferred from that interpretation what was suggested by Rosenberg. What, then, was the level of truth in the argument? That women of all classes and racial groups had had a special relationship to home and family, no one would deny. But the circumstances surrounding that relationship were not merely minor details in an otherwise homogeneous past. An enormous variety of specific experiences divided women and encouraged them to make dramatically different assessments of their work and home options. Granted the differences between men and women, women themselves had understood and used them in varied ways.

Indeed, one of the tensions in women's history that arguably described much of the dynamic of change in women's lives over time was the tension between women's own conception of "difference" and the objective condition of inequality. We had all observed that women, to live, had participated in, even colluded in, their own oppression. But that was not the sum total of their perceptions and understandings of the world around them. Nor did that truth wipe out the ways in which women had continually exerted themselves (in ways consonant with their access to money, resources and education) in a centuries-long struggle for emancipation. If women had sometimes accepted difference as a justification for inequality, they had frequently used it to reach for opportunity when it appeared, and to struggle for political and social change. Changing understandings of cultural difference over time had provided the entering wedges in what could only be interpreted as an effort to achieve greater equality: the domestic feminism of the mid-nineteenth century, the battles for suffrage, and the struggle for protective legislation are cases in point. To use the notion that women had "different" interests to justify their absence from the workplace was to assume that "difference" inevitably affirmed the traditional family.

Historians of working class women have generally not used the idea that way. The notion that women brought with them to the workforce a sense of self and an orientation that was not identical to that of men offered a way of distinguishing their behavior, their values, their commitments and their aspirations from those of men.[29] It helped us to think about workers in gendered terms, as we had earlier learned to think of them in ethnic and racial terms. But gender was one among many patterns that influenced how women worked. To think about women as workers who make choices, conditioned by and responsive to their life experiences, is to say one thing. To think about the generic constraints of a universal female experience defining work orientation is to say something entirely other.

Rosenberg had turned on its head the position to which most students of the subject had come—namely, that women's behavior could be interpreted in light of their own constraints. Instead, she had chosen to universalize her assumptions about what those constraints were likely to be—to saddle all women with a particular interpretation of the domestic code. The result was a series of conclusions that trapped women within a domestic ideology isolated from class, race, ethnicity or region. She had then taken the next step which was to assert that the mechanism of entrapment lay within their own power to remove. Sears was not responsible for women's choices; women were. By implication, corporations that did not hire women were merely responding to women's own needs and interests. This linear and deterministic view of history had inexorably placed responsibility on women's own shoulders—a classic example of blaming the victim.

Reconciling the notion that women could simultaneously operate within and against their society posed little problem for me. Women were part of the society in which they lived, and they continually pushed at the boundaries of opportunity within the contexts of their class and race positions. It was not difficult to explain the existence of simultaneous, seemingly opposite directions in individuals. People could and did have a range of needs and experiences, as well as a range of social understanding within which to place them. Women's behavior was, as much as anything else, a function of their social experience. Change the context, and people would respond in different ways.

A large theoretical literature is consistent with this understanding of the past. Raymond Williams' notion of emergent and residual cultures enable us to understand how some people could hang on to tradition, while their peers moved into the modern world. Charles Sabel's proposition that the multiple world views of workers allowed for a single individual to identify as a member of an ethnic group, as a participant in a family, and as a wage-earner, explained the sometimes conflicting political positions that workers with seemingly identical interests could take. Current empirical literature confirms these speculations. Cynthia Epstein's research on women lawyers points to the importance of opportunity; Brian Greenberg's study of nineteenth-century Albany demonstrates that workers who espouse the idea of free labor also defend their class interests when necessary. Sallie Westwood's explorations of women's factory work reveal the care with which they protect privileges at work while they assign domestic meaning to them.[30]

Rosenberg's testimony lent itself to precisely the purposes for which it was used. That this was no accident is confirmed by the language of the first paragraph of Rosenberg's sur-rebuttal. "It is my professional opinion," she wrote,

> that the overwhelming weight of modern scholarship in women's history and related fields supports the view that other Sears experts and I have put forward—namely, that disparities in the sexual composition of an employer's workforce, as well as disparities in pay between men and women in many circumstances, are consistent with an absence of discrimination on the part of the employer.[31]

Well, yes, but they are also consistent with the presence of discrimination. And if so, why would one want to place one's services at the disposal of, at best, a potentially discriminatory employer?

Rosenberg provided, as her own explanations, two puzzling answers to this question. She had studied Sears' affirmative action program and found it satisfactory; she believed that a successful defense by Sears would encourage other employers to develop good programs. And, she thought, not telling what she had become persuaded was the truth about women would do them "more harm than good."[32] Neither of these is convincing. Whatever we think of the Sears affirmative action program, by its own admission, in a period when goals and targets were widely met by other employers, it failed to meet even its own goals. If her position was based on a study of Sears, why generalize, and why not give women, rather than employers, the benefit of the doubt? Were we to revert to the position that only the slow passage of time would reap change? Rosenberg had never made it clear how women would be harmed by the discussion of a more complex truth.

I preferred to argue that we would never know what women wanted until the doors of opportunity were fully opened. The historical evidence viewed from the perspective of what women had been able to achieve, suggested that given available opportunity, sufficient numbers of women had never been lacking for jobs offered at good pay, even when those jobs were defined as male. An occupationally segregated labor force provided only a description of the labor market constraints, not an explanation of labor market behavior. Labor force needs and the socialization process together explained the structure of the labor force. Neither was independent of the other, I testified, and therefore notions of women's socialization and culture had to be seen in the context of the whole picture. I suggested that women had not "internalized" values and goals. Rather, they had continually modified and altered them as circumstances made it possible to do so.

I acknowledged what all my work had indicated—namely, that women had operated within social constraints that varied for different groups of women as they varied between men and women.[33] But, I argued, those constraints were not unrelated to available opportunities. The existence of something called female culture was not in dispute; its function was. Rosenberg had presented its role as preserving the status quo. I saw it as malleable, as part of the process of change. The key in court would be to demonstrate that sex roles were not rigid as Rosenberg had portrayed them; that women differed widely among themselves; and, crucially, that employers, who used all kinds of differences to discriminate among workers, certainly used gender as well.

These goals were more easily developed than executed. One intuits the difference between working in a library and participating in a court room drama, but until one has experienced it, the disjunction between the two remains abstract. Accustomed to developing the subtle distinctions of an argument, to negotiating about fine points of interpretation, the historian quickly discovers that these skills must be abandoned in testifying. Maintaining a position is as important as the position taken. Consistency is not merely a virtue but evidence of one's expertise. Yet the temptation to overgeneralize or to state a case in its sharpest form must also be resisted. I discovered to my sorrow that either one can be quickly penetrated in a cross-examination.

My written testimony emerged out of an attempt to avoid these two danger points, the product of a two-day ordeal in deposition, and of negotiation with the EEOC lawyer over how much to say and how to say it. Of the two, the deposition was clearly the stronger influence. There, I got my first taste of the clear distinction made by the legal profession between learning the truth and constructing a case; between understanding and persuading. And there, I also learned for the first time, that precisely what I as a historian cared most about would most surely destroy my testimony if I pursued it. My job, I was told, was to answer all questions, but to provide no more information than was demanded. The job of the examining lawyer, Denise Leary, an employee of the firm defending Sears, was to find out as much as she could about what I would testify in writing, and at the trial. Any attempt I made to introduce controversy, disagreement and analysis merely revealed that history was an uncertain tool and invalidated both its findings and my conclusions. She was interested in authority, clarity and weaknesses in my level of knowledge. The basis of both questions and answers was the "offer of proof": in my case a two page statement defining the boundaries within which I was prepared to testify.

I had begun my "offer of proof" with two statements: the first negating the value of prescriptive literature in understanding the behavior of wage-earning women; and the second attacking Rosenberg's testimony for its "numerous omissions and misunderstandings." What, the lawyer wanted to know were these omissions and misunderstandings? What were the areas where I disagreed? Over a two day period, we moved item by item through Rosenberg's testimony as the lawyer asked about, and I responded to, every item. Sometimes the exchanges were funny. More often, they were brutal. Did I not agree that Nancy Cott was a well-respected historian? Well, yes, of course. Then it followed that this point of Rosenberg's for which she had cited Cott as a source must be correct. No, as I understood Cott's position, it did not sustain Rosenberg's argument. Had not Mary Beth Norton argued that women in the revolution knew little about family finances? Yes, but. . . . Did not this support the notion that women's roles were restricted? Not necessarily— after all, Kerber had said X and Berkin said Y, and even Norton in other places modified the argument. Besides, I wanted to scream, this was all irrelevant.

I wanted to explain that history was about change; that to drag the American revolution into today's labor market practices had no meaning at all. That the women those historians had studied, pre-industrial, pre-urban, and white, had little in common with contemporary women workers. But my job was to answer questions. When I tried to introduce diversity, my answers were demeaned. What percentage of married women in 1890 were black or immigrants? What percentage of those worked? Was not the total a relatively small proportion of women as a whole? It depended on how you defined work, I countered: agricultural work, home work, boarders, those added up to significant numbers. And besides, wasn't this case about women *in* the workforce, not about women who could afford to stay out of it? She would ask the questions, thank you. This case was about statistics, she kept reminding me. And when I retreated behind the scattered information that historians possess, she sneered; you just don't know. Oh, for the opportunity to explain what it was that historians did, and how they generalized from limited data!

Rosenberg had cited more than a dozen historians and sociologists in support of points with which I disagreed. Over a weekend break between questions, I looked up as many as I could to see whether and how the citations supported her generalizations. Again and again, I pinpointed misinterpretations, discovered quotes out of context, and arguments made from evidence that pointed in contrary directions.[34] By the second day, I had the hang of it. My answers were more precise, my evidence more targeted, my rebuttals more positive. To refute Rosenberg's argument, I found myself constructing a rebuttal in which subtlety and nuance were omitted, and in which evidence was marshalled to make a point while complexities and exceptions vanished from sight.

In the end, it did not matter. It was not history but its use that went on trial. Just as so much of what we do is not about what is true and what false, what happened and what did not, so the issue here was not about who had correctly interpreted the past, but about how that interpretation was presented in different contexts. Testimony had a double-edged quality. In this case, once given and written, it had a life of its own, at the mercy of cross-examining lawyers, and not subject to qualification. Because it constituted the boundaries within which examination could happen, it had to encompass the totality of my expertise: broad enough to meet the needs of the plaintiff, and yet sufficiently restrained as to offer few loopholes that the defendants could use to undermine it. What sorts of claims to truth could be justified by such expertise? The speculation and tentativeness of an article or a lecture had no place in the courtroom. In a statement of one's own making, one had both leisure and time to play out an argument, to present the negative in order to come to the positive. In a judicial proceeding, not only was there no such time, but doing so jeopardized the case, because it could be and, in my limited experience was, so often cited out of context.

It was no surprise, for example, when the cross examining lawyer challenged not the substance of my testimony, but the language in which it was phrased in a sometimes successful attempt to reduce it to its absurd extremes. So, for example, "women had never failed to take jobs when opportunities presented themselves" (which I had written to mean that sufficient numbers of women were available to fill any job opportunity) got turned into a query about whether it could possibly be true that *all* women availed themselves of opportunity. An argument that the need for income rather than the pursuit of interest drove women into certain kinds of jobs led to a dispute about whether "interest" played any role at all in the kinds of jobs women would take. Though I gathered that such attempts to attack the credibility of witnesses and reduce statements to absurdity were routine parts of every cross-examination, I was nevertheless astonished at how easy it was, within the yes or no format demanded by the court, to agree with statements simply because I could not deny them, not because they represented my understanding of the issues involved.

Deposition, written testimony, cross examination: if I had not fully understood before, they taught me now that with whatever virtue and justice I entered the lists, skill in the fight would tell the tale. What then was a feminist doing in the courtroom at all? I had reacted viscerally to seeing my own work, badly distorted, put to the service of a politically destructive cause. I believed that the success of Sears' lawyers would undermine two decades of affirmative action efforts and exercise a chilling effect on women's history as a whole. To allow the tale told by Sears to pass unchallenged as women's view of their history would encourage others to use it to rationalize an unequal past.

It did not surprise me that history was brought to trial. We have long appealed to the past to justify and rationalize present beliefs and behavior. But I continue to be disturbed that a feminist historian should fail to see the implications of her testimony for working women and for women's history. Rosenberg argued after the trial that she was serving the cause of "careful scholarship." If we insist on pretending that no factors other than employer discrimination play a significant role in shaping women's role in the workforce, we will do women more harm than good," she wrote. But, in fact, she had offered as "careful scholarship" a single-minded interpretation that played down the role of discrimination. She had done this, not in the cause of ordinary women, but in the name of an employer accused of denying women jobs. The past had once again become the creature of conserving ideology—ideology all the more dangerous for remaining unspoken.

The case has been instructive for me. Excited by the possibility of exploring working women's conceptions of gender in order to find a way of probing the pressures to retain and alter tradition, I began, several years ago, to explore the language and symbols with which wage-earning women described their own experiences. I believed—I still believe—that the self-experience of work, as it changes over time, could provide clues about women's relationship to work in the past and in the future. Such symbols were not themselves explanatory, nor could they be interpreted outside the context of material pressures and other social needs. Yet in the search for the dynamism of change, they demanded attention. This would be my way of challenging the particular universalism of labor history. We would, for the first time, have to write books in which "workers" meant women as well as men. One could argue (as I have) that such distinctions, such a breakdown of the universal male would enable women to fight for working conditions that met the legitimate needs of workers who were not male. It could therefore become a political rallying point. But if understanding the way difference can move us toward change offers one way to think about the past, understanding how difference reinforces tradition and legitimizes inequality suggests another. This case reminds us that whether we will or not, writing history is a political act. For my part, then, I am troubled less by the question of how easily careful scholarship is abandoned than by how readily it is distorted and misinterpreted when placed in the service of a political cause.

This case, then, should not serve to stifle our thoughts but to heighten awareness of their political context. Feminist historians have struggled for more than a decade and a half now, not merely to include the experiences of women in history books, but to explore how history itself would be altered by their inclusion. To do that required new frameworks for thought, new ways of thinking. What historical theory, in its vaunted universalism, could not provide we hungrily absorbed from psychology, philosophy, sociology and anthropology. But this case demonstrates that historians have something to return to these disciplines: the empirical evidence that demonstrates that culture is not a static framework, but a moving force. Among the lessons we should learn from this experience is what happens when one historian forgets that history is about change and makes claims to value-free evidence in order to demonstrate that past behavior justifies present injustice. Not the politics but the ethics of history is then called into question.

I don't think that means we should abandon the effort to explore "women's culture" nor should we fail to use the concept to help define the parameters within which a sex-gender system works. Surely there is something useful to the notion that women are somehow "different" from men: such a conception had led us to begin to think of non-universal methodologies in anthropology and psychology; to identify research questions and issues in which distinctions become ways of pursuing knowledge about how and where and when they are created and overcome. The notion has led us to the highest reaches of critical and philosophical speculation.[35] But I think it does mean that we have to remember and articulate, explicitly and consciously, the historical context of the culture about which we speak, for as Ellen Dubois warned us several years ago, what is offered as explanation, can also be used as justification.[36]

The use of historical argument in the Sears case affirms the degree to which historical interpretation is subject to the whims of time. In a period when the politics of the family and efforts to reassert traditional sex roles are in the forefront of a new morality, it illustrates yet again the ease with which political positions are rationalized in the name of scholarship.

Editor's Note: On February 3, 1986, U. S. District Court Judge John A. Nordberg ruled that the EEOC had failed to show that Sears, Roebuck and Company discriminated against women in hiring and promotion for commission sales jobs.

Notes

I very much appreciate the comments and insights of the following friends who willingly helped to sort out the issues involved: Karen Baker, Blanche Wiesen Cook, Eric Foner, Doris Friedensohn, Bert Silverman, Amy Swerdlow, Carole Turbin, and Marilyn Young, as well as RHR's editors. The taped discussion of the faculty seminar in the History and Society program at the University of Minnesota was enormously helpful, as was the commitment of a very special group of graduate students at SUNY Binghamton who, in the Spring of 1985, learned first-hand something of the meaning of Marc Bloch's poignant question, "What is the use of history?"

1. Percentages of women varied by commission sales category. In 1973, 73.5 per cent of Sears 14,794 full time non-commission sales employees were women, but only 15.4 per cent of its 23,867 full time commission sales people were women. Plaintiff's Proposed Finding of Fact and Conclusions of Law—Commission Sales, p. 9; This document like the other court documents cited below was filed in the United States District Court for the Northern District of Illinois, Eastern Division; File no. 79-C-4373, John A. Nordberg, District Judge.

2. Figures for the Midwest were substantially higher than for the four other regions in all commission sales categories. One can speculate that this means that midwestern women were more willing to take such jobs, or that management in this region was more amenable to hiring them.

3. Plaintiff's Pre-trial Brief—Commission Sales Issues (Revised November 19, 1984), p. 50. The EEOC expected that 53.1 per cent of new hires in commission sales would be female; as compared to 27 per cent actually hired.

4. Charles Morgan was a well-known civil rights lawyer in the 1960s. His turn against affirmative action seems to be a consequence of a commitment to fighting for unpopular causes, rather than to the issues involved. See Morgan's piece "Bad for Lawyers, Bad for Lawyering," in the *New York Times* October 11, 1985, A 35.

5. Testimony of Carolyn Rogers, May 7, 1985, 6; cf also, 22, 38, 55, 64, 65.

6. Testimony of J. Richard Howie, May 7, 1985; 4–5.

7. Offer of Proof concerning the Testimony of Dr. Rosalind Rosenberg, items 18, 19, 20. The annotated version, which became Rosalind Rosenberg's written testimony, and which I cite herein, was filed in court on March 11, 1985. The document is not paginated.

8. Plaintiff's Proposed Finding of Fact, 21–22 and 15–18.

9. Plaintiff's Pre-trial Brief, 15.

10. Rosenberg, Offer of Proof, item 24.

11. All of these documents as well as the transcripts of both depositions and the trial testimonies are available from the Clerk of the Court, United States District Court for the Northern District of Illinois, Eastern Division, and will soon be on deposit in the Schlesinger Library in Cambridge, Mass. Rosenberg has claimed that Sears' lawyers wrote the Offer of Proof that was the basis for her deposition and was submitted to the court on March 11, 1985 as her written testimony. Whether or not she actually penned the words, Rosenberg certainly testified to the specific and general contents of the document, as the court transcript makes clear. See 10345–47.

12. Lawrence Rosen, "The Anthropologist as Expert Witness," *American Anthropologist, 79* (September, 1978), 560.

13. Woodward is cited in Paul Soifer, "The Litigation Historian: Objectivity, Responsibility, *The Public Historian,* 5 (Spring, 1983), 51.

14. S. Charles Bolton, "The Historian as Expert Witness: Creationism in Arkansas," *The Public Historian,* 4 (Summer, 1982), 61.

15. On March 11, 1985 toward the end of her first cross examination, Rosenberg admitted that discrimination

was a possible explanation for the data. Asked in re-direct questioning if she thought this was likely, she answered that it was not. Cf. trial transcript 10453, 10459, 10463.

16. Natalie Zemon Davis, "Politics, Progeny, and French History: An Interview with Natalie Zemon Davis," *Radical History Review*, 24 (Fall, 1980), 133.

17. "A Feminist for Sears," *The Nation*, October 26, 1985, 394.

18. Rosenberg, Offer of Proof, item 1.

19. *Ibid.*, item 2.

20. *Ibid.*, items, 5, 10, 16.

21. *Ibid.*, item 11.

22. In the event, this turned out to be one of the most interesting historical issues. Rosenberg characterized my attempt to assert the other side of the dialectical process as "monocausal." I claimed, she held, that employers were solely responsible for discrimination. In charging that my depiction of limited choice for women, within the framework of available opportunity, assumed them to be passive and dependent, she concluded (Written Rebuttal Testimony of Dr. Rosalind Rosenberg, June 25, 1985, 11), that I was guilty of portraying them as victims. I take this attack as demonstration of the validity of my assertion here, and as evidence of the value of a dialectical view of history.

23. Rosenberg, Offer of Proof, item 2.

24. See, for example, Jacob Mincer, "Labor Force Participation of Married women: A Study of Labor Supply," in Gregg Lewis, ed., *Aspects of Labor Economics*, Report of the National Bureau of Economic Research (Princeton: Princeton University Press, 1962), 63–105.

25. According to the EEOC's undisputed figures, the median wage of all full time non-commission salesclerks at Sears in 1979 was $3.50 an hour. In contrast, the average pay of a *first* year commission sales person was $7.50 an hour. Plaintiff's Pre-trial Brief, 27. These figures varied year to year, but the average difference was never less than $2.70 an hour.

26. Plaintiff's Proposed Finding of Fact, 11. Before 1973, commissions were held against a four week draw before the lack of earnings was forgiven.

27. Rosenberg, Offer of Proof, item 4; Deposition of Rosalind Rosenberg, July 2, 1984, 44; and July 3, 1984, 54.

28. Offer of Proof, item 23, Rosenberg Deposition, July 3, 1984, 6.

29. See Carole Turbin, "Reconceptualizing Family, Work and Labor Organizing: Working Women in Troy, 1860–1890," *Review of Radical Political Economics*, 16 (Spring, 1984), 1–16; Ardis Cameron, "Bread and Roses Revisited: Women's Culture and Working-class Activism in the Lawrence Strike of 1912," in Ruth Milkman, ed., *Women, Work and Protest: A Century of Women's Labor History* (Boston: Routledge and Kegan Paul, 1985), 42–61; and Alice Kessler-Harris, "The Debate over Equality for Women in the Workplace: Recognizing Differences," in Laurie Larwood et al., eds., *Women and Work: An Annual Review* vol. 1 (Beverly Hills, CA: Sage Publications, 1985), 141–61.

30. Charles Sabel, *Work and Politics* (Cambridge: Cambridge University Press, 1980); Cynthia Epstein, Brian Greenberg, *Worker and Community* (Albany: SUNY Press, 1985); and Sally Westwood, *All Day, Every Day: Factory and Family in the Making of Women's Lives* (Champagne/Urbana: University of Illinois Press, 1985).

31. Rosenberg, Written Rebuttal Testimony, 1.

32. "A Feminist for Sears," 394.

33. Rosenberg's use of my work to make her case deserves attention. Accusing me of contradicting my own written work in court, she cited twelve pages of examples from my writing that purportedly supported the idea that women operated in obedience to certain kinds of social constraints, never acknowledging that in virtually every instance I had played out both sides of a dialectical process, and repeatedly misquoting, and quoting out of context to make her case.

34. See, for example, the following examples in Alice Kessler-Harris, Deposition, April 15, 1985, 384–85 on the use of Blumstein, Pepper and Schwartz; 473–78 on prescriptive literature; 448 ff. on ideology; 470 ff on male/female differences.

35. See Myra Jehlen, "Archimedes and the Paradox of Feminist Criticism," *Signs* 6 (Summer, 1981), 575–601; and Iris Young, "Socialist Feminism and the Limits of Dual Systems Theory," *Socialist Review*, 50/51 (March/June, 1980), 169–88.

36. Ellen DuBois, "Politics and Culture in Women's History: A Symposium," *Feminist Studies*, 6 (Spring, 1980), 28–36.

35

The Last Taboo

Paula Giddings

The agonizing ordeal of the Clarence Thomas nomination should have taught us a valuable lesson: racial solidarity is not always the same as racial loyalty. This is especially true, it seems to me, in a postsegregation era in which solidarity so often requires suppressing information about any African American of standing regardless of their political views or character flaws. Anita Hill's intervention in the proceedings should have told us that when those views or flaws are also sexist, such solidarity can be especially destructive to the community.

As the messenger for this relatively new idea, Anita Hill earned the antipathy of large segments of the African American community. More at issue than her truthfulness—or Clarence Thomas's character or politics—was whether she *should* have testified against another Black person, especially a Black man, who was just a hairsbreadth away from the Supreme Court. Of course, Anita Hill was not the only Black person who testified against the nomination of Clarence Thomas, nor even the only woman to do so. But the nature of her complaint went further. It forced a mandate on gender: "the cultural definition of behavior defined as appropriate to the sexes in a given society at a given time," to borrow historian Gerda Lerner's definition. For many, what was *inappropriate* was that a Black woman's commitment to a gender issue superseded what was largely perceived as racial solidarity. Still others, I think, reacted to an even greater taboo, perhaps the last and most deeply set one. This was to disclose not only a gender but a sexual discourse, unmediated by the question of racism. What Hill reported to the world was a Black-on-Black sexual crime involving a man of influence in the mainstream community.

The issues of gender and sexuality have been made so painful to us in our history that we have largely hidden them from ourselves, much less the glaring eye of the television camera. Consequently, they remain largely unresolved. I am convinced that Anita Hill, by introducing the issues in a way that could not be ignored, offered the possibility of a modern discourse on these issues that have tremendous, even lifesaving importance for us.

I

It is our historical experience that has shaped or, perhaps more accurately, misshaped the sex/gender issues and discourse in our community. That history was broached by Clarence Thomas himself, when he used the most remembered phrase of the hearings: "high-tech lynching." Thus, he evoked the image of the sexually laden nineteenth-century lynching—

often announced several days in advance to assure a crowd—after which the body was hung, often burned, mutilated, and body parts, including genitals, were fought over for souvenirs. These were low-tech lynchings. Interestingly, it was almost exactly a century ago, in 1892, when the number of African Americans being lynched, 241, reached a peak after steadily escalating since the decade before. Then the epidemic of mob murder against Blacks continued with impunity because of the perception that Black men, no longer constrained by the "civilizing influence" of slavery, had regressed to a primitive state and were routinely raping white women. At that time "rape, and the rumors of rape [were] a kind of acceptable folk pornography in the Bible Belt," observed historian Jacquelyn Dowd Hall.

Although Thomas's application of this phenomenon to his own situation was highly questionable, even ironic, in one way he was substantially correct. Now, as a century ago, white men, regardless of their own moral standing, still exercise the power to judge Blacks on the basis of their perceived sexuality. However, what many failed to take into account with Thomas's evocation was that it was a Black woman, Ida B. Wells, who initiated the nation's first antilynching campaign. For lynching was also a woman's issue: it had as much to do with ideas of gender as it had with race.

Often overlooked is the fact that Black men were thought capable of these sexual crimes *because* of the lascivious character of the women of the race in a time when women were considered the foundation of a group's morality. Black men raped, it was widely believed, because Black men's mothers, wives, sisters, and daughters were seen as "morally obtuse," "openly licentious," and had "no immorality in doing what nature prompts," as Harvard-educated Phillip A. Bruce, brother-in-law of writer Thomas Nelson Page, observed in his influential *Plantation Negro as Freeman* (1889). As one offer of proof, the author noted that Black women never complained about being raped by Black men. Other observers, such as the following southern female writer to the popular periodical *The Independent*, confirmed:

> Degeneracy is apt to show most in the weaker individuals of any race; so negro women evidence more nearly the popular idea of total depravity than the men do. They are so nearly lacking in virtue that the color of a negro woman's skin is generally taken (and quite correctly) as a guarantee of her immorality. . . . And they are evidently the chief instruments of the degradation of the men of their race. . . . I sometimes read of a virtuous negro woman, hear of them, but the idea is absolutely inconceivable to me. . . . I cannot imagine such a creation as a virtuous black woman.

The status of Black women had been dramatically etched into the annals of science earlier in the century. It was in fact personified in the figure of a single South African woman by the name of Sara Bartmann, a.k.a. the "Hottentot Venus." In 1810, when England was in the throes of debate about the slave trade, Ms. Bartmann was first exhibited in London "to the public in a manner offensive to decency," according to observers at the time (Gilman, Sander 1985).

What made Ms. Bartmann such a subject of interest was the extraordinary size and shape of her buttocks, which served as a displacement of the fascination with female genitalia at the time. Sara Bartmann was displayed for five years, until she died, in Paris, at the age of twenty-five. Her degradation by what was defined as science and civilization did not end there. An autopsy was performed, preparing her genitalia "in such a way as to allow one to see the nature of the labia." Her organs were studied and reported upon by Dr. George Cuvier in 1817, coolly comparing Ms. Bartmann's genitalia with that of orangutans. Her sexual organs were then given to the Musée de l'Homme in Paris—where they are still on display.

Sara Bartmann's sexual parts, her genitalia and her buttocks, serve as the central image for the Black female throughout the nineteenth century, concludes Gilman. It was also the image, he notes, that served as an icon for Black sexuality throughout the century.

It is no coincidence that Sara Bartmann became a spectacle in a period when the British were debating the prohibition of slavery. As historian Barbara Fields and others have pointed out, there, as in North America, race took on a new significance when questions arose about the entitlement of nonenslaved Blacks to partake of the fruits of Western liberty and citizenship. In North America, Euro-Americans had to resolve the contradictions between their own struggle for political freedom and that of the Black men and women they still enslaved. This contradiction was resolved (by both pro- and antislavery whites) by racialism: ascribing certain inherited characteristics to Blacks, characteristics that made them unworthy of the benefits of first-class citizenship. At the core of those characteristics was the projection of the dark side of sexuality, now literally embodied by Black females. The use of a broad racial tarbrush, in turn, meant looking at race through the veneer of ideology: an institutionalized set of beliefs through which one interprets social reality. By the nineteenth century, then, race had become an ideology, and a basis of that ideology had become sexual difference. If there was a need for racialism in the late eighteenth century, it became an absolute necessity by the late nineteenth century, when lynching reached its peak. For after the Civil War, the Thirteenth, Fourteenth, and Fifteenth amendments granted freedmen suffrage and Black men and women many of the privileges of citizenship. In a state like Mississippi, which had some of the strongest Black political organizations of any state, this translated into the kind of empowerment that saw, in the 1870s, two Black men serve as U.S. senators, and Blacks as secretaries of state and education, among other high offices. Throughout the South, especially, there was also dramatic evidence of African Americans gaining an economic foothold as the numbers of Black-owned businesses and Black landowners increased.

Additionally, unprecedented numbers of African American men and women were attending both predominantly white and predominantly Black colleges, and aspiring to professional positions deemed out of reach just a generation before. This was even true of Black women. By the 1880s the first Black women were passing state bar exams to become attorneys, and were the first women of any race to practice medicine in the South. By the turn of the century, Booker T. Washington's National Business League reported that there were "160 Black female physicians, seven dentists, ten lawyers, 164 ministers, assorted journalists, writers, artists, 1,185 musicians and teachers of music and 13,525 school instructors." The period saw a virtual renaissance among Black women artists and writers. The Philadelphia-born sculptor Meta Warwick Fuller was under the tutelage of Auguste Rodin; Frances Ellen Harper and Pauline Hopkins published two of the earliest novels by Black women; Oberlin-educated Anna Julia Cooper published *A Voice from the South* (1892), a treatise on race and feminism that anticipated much of the later work of W.E.B. Du Bois; and journalist Ida B. Wells, in 1889, was elected as the first woman secretary of the Afro-American Press Association.

Ironically, such achievements within a generation of slavery did not inspire an ideology of racial equality but one of racial difference, the latter being required to maintain white supremacy. That difference would be largely based on perceptions of sexual difference, and as noted before, the foundation of sexual difference lay in attitudes about Black women.

II

By the late nineteenth century, however, difference would be characterized as its most dualistic: as binary opposition—not just in terms of race and sexuality but of gender and class as well. Such oppositions were effective means of social control at a time when the country was losing its sociosexual mooring in the face of radical and fundamental changes driven (like now) by a technological revolution. For if the late twentieth century was shaped by advances like the computer, the late nineteenth was adjusting itself around innovations such as the typewriter, the gasoline-driven car, the internal-combustion airplane, the sewing machine, the incandescent light, the phonograph, and the radio. Such innovations bring on new systems of marketing and financing them, and thus new possibilities of wealth, as the late nineteenth-century emergence of the Rockefellers, Morgans, Du Ponts, and Carnegies attest. In addition, new corporate cultures increased urbanization, made sex outside of the family more possible, and contributed to the increased commodification of sex in forms of pornography and brothels, as it became more associated with pleasure rather than merely reproduction. At the same time, money and the laborsaving devices allowed middle-class women to spend less time doing domestic housework and more time seeking education and reform outside of the home. Add to this growing numbers of immigrants from eastern and southern Europe, the increasing disparity between the haves and the have-nots (by 1890, the poorest one-half of families received one-fifth of all wages and salaries), labor unrest and unemployment that reached thirty percent in some years during the decade, and the need for control becomes obvious. That control was effectively handled through creating categories of difference through binary opposition. For example, maleness was defined by its opposition to femaleness; whiteness by its opposition to Blackness. The same dualism applied to the concepts of civilization and primitivity, purity and pollutedness, goodness and evil, public and private. The nineteenth-century paradigm regarding sexuality tied all of these oppositions together, which operated to the detriment of Blacks and women in general, and Black women in particular.

For example, in the late nineteenth century, men were believed to have a particularly rapacious sexual drive that had to be controlled. The last thing needed at home was a woman who had the same sexual drive that men had; what was needed was in binary opposition to perceived male sexuality. What was needed was a woman who did not tempt, and was thus synonymous with "good." And so, although in another period women were thought to have strong, even the more ungovernable, sexual drives, by the late nineteenth century, they were thought to have hardly any libido at all. Furthermore, female sexuality was now considered pathological. That meant, of course, that good women did not have erotic feelings, and those who might have had inappropriate urges were recommended to see physicians like J. Marion Sims or Robert Battey, who employed radical gynecological surgery, including clitoridectomies, to "correct" masturbation and other forms of sexual passion (D'Emilio, Freedman, 1988). Such severe methods were necessary to sustain diametrically opposed identities to "bad" women: lower-class women, and especially Black women.

Economically lower-class women fell under the "bad" column by virtue of the fact that they worked outside the home, and thus were uninsulated from the sexual aggression of the society. Certainly, it was the former group of women who made up the growing numbers of prostitutes, a label that could fall even on women more drawn to casual sex than to remuneration, and were of great interest to scientists as well as white, middle-class, female reformers and repressed men. With Sara Bartmann as a model and basis of comparison, their sexual organs were studied, codified, and preserved in jars. Anthropologists such as Cesare Lombrosco, coauthor of the major study of prostitution in the late nineteenth century, *The Prostitute and the Normal Woman* (1893), wrote that the source of their passion and pathology lay in the labia, which reflected a more primitive structure than their upper-class counterparts. One of Lombrosco's students, Abele de Blasio, focused on the buttocks.

His specialty was steatopygia (excessive fat on the buttocks), which was also deemed to be a special characteristic of whores—and, of course, Black women. They would represent the very root of female eroticism, immorality, and disease.

In the medical metaphors of the day, the sexual organs of sexual women were not only hotbeds of moral pathology, but of disease. In the nineteenth century the great fear was of a sexually transmitted disease that was spreading among the population, was incurable, and after invading the body, disfigured and decomposed it in stages. The name of the disease was syphilis, and it was the era's metaphor for the retribution of sexual sin. Despite evidence to the contrary, it was seen as a disease that affected not only persons but groups perceived as both licentious and deviant. Prostitutes of course fell into this category, but it did not seem to affect business. Science even abandoned long-held views to accommodate the paradigm. Formerly, it was believed that Christopher Columbus's sailors had introduced the disease to Europe. Now the new wisdom traced it to a form of leprosy that had long been present in Africa and had spread into Europe during the Middle Ages. At the wellspring of this plague were the genital organs of Black women (Gilman, 1985).

As the epitome of the immorality, pathology, and impurity of the age, Black women were seen in dualistic opposition to their upper-class, pure, and passionless white sisters. It was this binary opposition of women (Black men's sex drives were not seen as inherently different from those of white men, only less controlled) that was the linchpin of race, class, and even gender difference. It was this opposition, furthermore, that also led to lynching. For it was the white women's qualities, so profoundly missing in Black women, that made Black men find white women irresistible, and "strangely alluring and seductive," in the words of Phillip Bruce.

III

Categorizing women through binary opposition had a devastating impact. Even the relatively privileged, middle-class, white women were subjected to the sexual tyrannies of the age. The opposition of public, a male sphere, and private, a female one, led to conclusions that imprisoned women in the home. The eminent Harvard-trained physician Dr. Edward Clarke, for example, wrote in his influential book *Sex in Education* (1873) that education could ruin a woman's sexual organs. Ideas about male sexual irrepressibility in opposition to women's passionlessness were largely responsible for the fact that "rape in marriage was no crime, nor even generally disapproved," "wife-beating was only marginally criminal," and "incest was common enough to require skepticism that it was tabooed," according to historians Linda Gordon and Ellen Carol DuBois (1983). Women would have to untangle and rework paradigms in order to protect themselves and, as DuBois and Gordon note, exercise their right to enjoy the pleasure of sex. Toward this end, white feminists began challenging the oppositional frameworks concerning the sexuality of men and women. For example, Dr. Elizabeth Blackwell, a physician, offered the startling counteropinion that men and women had equal sexual urges, thus providing a rationale for consensual sex in marriage—and for "free lovers" outside of marriage as well. They also regulated the torrent of male sexuality by insisting that women should only be required to have sex when they wanted to get pregnant. Called "voluntary motherhood," it was a "brilliant" tactic, says Gordon, for it "insinuated a rejection of male sexual domination into a politics of defending and improving motherhood." And at a time when they still had little power or even identity outside of the home, women disdained abortion and contraception, insisting—in a world of depersonalized sex—on maintaining the link between sexual intercourse and reproduction. Consequently, say the authors, the principle of marital mutuality and women's right to say no was established among white middle-class couples in the late nineteenth century. This is perhaps evidenced by the fact that although birth control methods were not widely approved, the birthrate among white native-born women declined by 1900 to an average of 3.54–fifty percent below the level of the previous century!

Despite their enlightened views on such issues as a single standard of sexuality for men and women, as well as others, white feminists fell short on issues like nonmarital rape, probably because of its interracial implications. Although they could bring themselves to counter gender oppositions, those which involved race, and to a lesser extent class, seemed to be beyond their reach. This would be left to Black feminists like Ida B. Wells and others who constantly challenged the dualism between good and bad, Black and white, and its implications especially as it affected African American women.

Ida Wells simply turned this paradigm on its head, with her own empirical evidence gathered from her investigation of the circumstances of 728 lynchings that had taken place over the previous decade. Her meticulously documented findings would not only challenge the assumption of rape—which also exonerated Black women to a significant extent—but also included findings about the lynching of Black women, as well as their sexual exploitation at the hands of whites. It was Black women who needed protection, Wells insisted, as "the rape of helpless Negro girls and women, which began in slavery days, still continued without reproof from church, state, or press," thus changing their representation to that of victims. Her most dramatic challenge to the paradigm, of course, was her questioning of the passionless purity of southern white women. There *were* interracial liaisons between Black men and white women, Wells published in her findings, but they were consensual and often initiated by white women. In May of 1892, Wells would publish the editorial that got her exiled from the South: "If Southern white men are not careful . . ." she challenged, "a conclusion will be reached which will be damaging to the moral reputation of their women" (Wells, *On Lynchings* [New York: Arno Press, 1969]). Wells, perhaps the first leader to broach the subject of Black sexual oppression after slavery, had now completely challenged the period's assumptions. Black men were not rapists, white men were; Black women were not doing what "nature prompted," white women were; Wells's framework actually rescued both Black and white women from their dehumanized objectification.

When, in reaction to Wells's ideas, the president of the Missouri Press Association, John Jacks, wrote a letter calling all Black women "prostitutes, thieves and liars," it was the proverbial straw for nascent regional clubs to come together under a national umbrella in 1896. "Read the letter carefully, and use it discriminately" (it was "too indecent for publication"), challenged Boston activist and editor Josephine St. Pierre Ruffin, and "decide if it be not the time to stand before the world and declare ourselves and our principles." Formed as the National Association for Colored Women (NACW), with a membership that would reach fifty thousand by 1916, it would act not only as a means to realize suffrage, education, and community development, but the vessel through which Black women challenged, in public, the beliefs that were getting Black men lynched and Black women raped and exploited. Sexual exploitation was so pervasive that it drove Black women north in search of safer climes. "It is a significant and shameful fact that I am constantly in receipt of letters from still unprotected women in the South," complained the nineteenth-century Chicago activist Fannie Barrier Williams, "begging me to find employment for their daughters . . . to save them from going into the homes of the South as servants as there is nothing to save them from dishonor and degradation." In 1893, before the predominantly white Congress of Representative Women, Williams challenged that Black women should not be disparaged but protected, adding that "I do not want to disturb the serenity of this conference by suggesting why this protection is needed and the kind of man against whom it is needed."

IV

Nevertheless, despite their extraordinary boldness in bringing this issue before the white public, Black women activists were precluded from presenting another kind of critique, one which was also important. The brutal concept of binary opposition prevented them from a frank public discourse concerning intraracial gender relations and sexuality, with which white feminists had been relatively successful. This void was a potentially life-threatening one in a time of adjustment to nonslavery; a time when gender roles, altered first by slavery and then by rapid social and economic changes, were in chaos; a time when the sexuality of both Black men and women had to have been twisted by sexism and racism, and now by numbing poverty. Ghettos were congealing, families were in disarray, domestic violence was on the increase, cocaine and alcohol were being abused, and venereal diseases were increasing at an alarming rate. But in this social-Darwinistic environment, where Blacks were judged harshly, even murderously, by their perceived difference from the white middle-class ideal, where it was believed that the poor deserved to be poor because of moral and character flaws, where a man, as Wells reported, could be lynched under the pretense of beating his wife, how could there be a public discourse about such things? How was one going to explain the higher rates of venereal disease such as syphilis among Blacks? And how was one to explain before a hostile white public that the higher rates of infant mortality were largely due to children inheriting "enfeebled constitutions and congenital diseases, inherited from parents suffering from the effects of sexual immorality and debauchery" (p. 25), as an 1897 report, *Proceedings of the Second Conference for the Study of Problems Concerning Negro City Life,* under the general direction of W. E. B. Du Bois, then at Atlanta University, stated?

Publicly voicing such concerns in a society defined by binary opposition could leave Blacks in general and Black women in particular vulnerable to the violent whims of whites. It is no wonder that the issues of intraracial sexuality and gender has long been tabooed in public discourse. At the same time, not voicing these concerns have left the community, especially women, bereft of the help and protection so needed. As an anonymous Black woman writer, one of the few who dared break the silence of intraracial sexuality, wrote to the *Independent* in 1904, "We poor colored wage-earners of the South are fighting a terrible battle, on the one hand, we are assailed by white men, and on the other hand, we are assailed by Black men who should be our natural protectors." There are sexist backlashes within our community, too.

For Black women, the accumulated effects of assault and the inability to "eradicate negative social and sexual images of their womanhood" had "powerful ideological consequences," concludes historian Darlene Hine. To protect themselves, she observes, Black women created what she calls "a culture of dissemblance." Hine defines this as "the behavior and attitudes of Black women that created the appearance of openness and disclosure but actually shielded the truth of their inner lives and selves from their oppressors"—and I would add, even from ourselves. This is the reason, I think, why we have not forced such sex/gender discourses, seen primarily as disclosures, in our community. It is why feminist issues, though not women's rights issues, are more problematic for us. Not only is feminism specifically associated with our historic binary opposites—middle-class white women—it demands an analysis of sexual issues. This is why to break through the silence and traditional sense of racial solidarity is such a controversial act for us. This, in turn, largely accounts for the vitriol earned by those who indicate a public discourse on sexuality in their work, such as Alice Walker in *The Color Purple* or Ntozake Shange in *For Colored Girls.* ... I think these traditional notions are also the reason why Anita Hill's appearance was so controversial in the Black community. Those who publicly supported her, namely Black scholars and the National Coalition of 100 Black Women—formed in 1970 when the women's movement was making an impact—were those in touch with gender issues and their role in the needed transformation of our institutions and communities. This is the window Black women writers have pointed toward but that Anita Hill, in her first-person, clear, unswervingly direct testimony before the public, has actually opened. It was an act of great inner courage and conviction, to turn back the veil of our Du Boisian double consciousness. It was an act that provided clarity about our new status in the late twentieth century.

V

There would be some that would argue that that status is no more empowered than it was a hundred years ago, thus requiring that we use the same strategies of solidarity. There is no question that, in some ways, the essential aspects of racism and sexism still affect us. This was evident in the statement, "African-American Women in Defense of Ourselves," first appearing in the *New York Times* as a paid ad on November 17, 1991, signed by 1,603 Black women, most of them scholars, in response to the treatment of Anita Hill during the hearings. Insisting that the "malicious defamation of Professor Hill insulted all women of African-American descent," it concluded that "throughout U.S. history, Black women have been stereotyped as immoral, insatiable, perverse; the initiators in all sexual contacts—abusive or otherwise. . . . As Anita Hill's experience demonstrates, Black women who speak of these matters are not likely to be believed. . . ." The words sound very much like those that led women to organize the NACW almost exactly a century ago, and in fact, the similar conditions that previously made us want to wrap ourselves in that protective skin have come back around with a vengeance. Certainly, the late twentieth century, with its dislocating technological revolution, rapacious moneymaking, excesses of sex, guilt and consumption, and incurable diseases viewed as Old Testament warnings should give us pause. For when such a confluence occurs, there are cultural reflexes to create categories of difference, including sexual difference, with all of its murderous Willie Horton, Bensonhurst, David Duke, and Central Park gang-rape implications. And although we may have passed the era that could take a Hottentot Venus seriously, we cannot rest assured that advances in science will save us from such folly. That respectable journals would make connections between green monkeys and African women, for example, or trace the origin of AIDS to African prostitutes—the polluted sexual organs of Black women—reveals our continued vulnerability to racist ideology. It tells us that concepts of racial difference (in this situation, sexual practices) can still be used as weapons of degradation, and that the idea of difference turns on sexuality, and sexuality, in this culture, is loaded with concepts of race, gender, and class. This explains in part why the backlashes against women, Black and non-Black, as well as race, carry a virulence that goes beyond the fear of competition or the sharing of power once so handily monopolized by others.

On the other hand, there have been some fundamental dramatic changes, largely realized by our own struggle for equality and empowerment, that allow us, in fact demand, a new strategy. For although racism still exists, our situation has changed since the sixties in spite of it. It has changed because of two interrelated developments: the sexual revolution and *de jure* desegregation. They are interrelated because sex was the principle around which wholesale segregation and discrimination was organized with the ultimate objective of preventing intermarriage. The sexual revolution, however, separated sexuality from reproduction, and so diluted the ideas about purity—moral, racial, and physical.

Both desegregation and the sexual revolution make dissemblance and suppression in the name of racial solidarity anachronistic, for they were prescribed to divert perceptions of difference, based on sexual difference between Black women and white. Despite the tenacity about ideas of difference, recent sociopolitical developments—further codified by feminist theory as well as Black studies—make binary opposition as a sole indicator of meaning passé.

In the meantime, increasing sexual aggression, including date-rape on college campuses that tends to be underreported by Black women; the number of "children having children," the plague of domestic violence, the breakup of families, and the spread of fatal venereal disease among African Americans at a time when we have more "rights" than ever before, tell us that gender issues are just as important—if not more so—in the Black community as racial issues have always been. More than ever before it is essential that we advance a discourse on sexuality that is liberating for those who engage in it and truncating to the souls of those who do not. As Naima Major, former director of the National Black Women's Health Project—one of the few Black institutions that regularly engages in sexuality issues—said to me, most of the Black women she sees "seem to cut themselves off at the waist," even when they are coming to talk specifically about sexuality.

This is particularly alarming in view of the fact that we are in a sexually aggressive era, one where sex is commodified and often depersonalized, especially for young women. Their worlds were the subject of a study of adolescents aged fifteen to seventeen, conducted by Pat Macpherson and Michelle Fine, and their observations were disturbing. From the stories of these young women, the authors surmised that their generation is more likely to "be aware of, witness to, and victim of" male sexual abuse among both peers and family. Their sexual experiences with peers are not characterized by learning the meaning or enjoyment of sex, or even making choices about engaging in it, but in protecting themselves from what is viewed (as in the past) as the irrepressible sexual drives of the men in their lives. A Black adolescent in this interracial group spoke about not her own sexual preferences but the need to satisfy, indeed mollify, men quickly through cunnilingus so that the evening could end early, and hassle-free. And the authors noted that female adolescents also protect themselves by suppressing signs of their gender: by becoming "one of the boys" through not only dress, but through even misogynist behavior and attitudes. These are issues that were addressed a century ago, under similar sociosexual conditions, but the solutions have not been passed on through families or social institutions. We must begin to do it.

The analysis of how sex/gender systems apply to us in the 1990s becomes urgent when we see that *fifty-eight percent* of Black women beyond the age of eighteen *never* use any form of birth control, according to a 1991 study conducted by the National Council of Negro Women. Yet only one percent of those women said that they wanted to get pregnant, and only two percent said that they did not know how to use birth control. Does this finding indicate ambivalence about separating sexuality from reproduction despite not wanting a child? Does it indicate the desire, however sublimated, to become pregnant? Or, as I suspect, is the finding a reflection of the fact that their male partners look down on birth control?

One thing we know, there seems to be what one might call a cult of motherhood in our community. How else might one interpret the finding of journalist Leon Dash in his book *When Children Want Children* (1988), that nearly a fourth of all unmarried teenage mothers intentionally become pregnant? What does motherhood mean to these youngsters? The ability to exercise maternal authority in lieu of other avenues of self-esteem and empowerment; rebellion against the depersonalization of sex; or perhaps, as a century ago, does this finding represent the effort to control male sexuality? The answers to these questions are important, as the babies of teenagers are more apt to be underweight and thus have learning and other physical disabilities. There is also tragedy in another statistic: forty-eight percent of the teenagers who intentionally got pregnant later regretted their decision.

Even college students, according to a report by the Black Women's Health Project, indicated a conflict about delaying childbearing in the face of "women's traditional and proper role as mother"—"indeed as a respected 'matriarch' in a community beset by failing family structures." Of course, there is also male pressure insinuated in some of these findings. The college students said that they felt intense pressure from male partners who wanted to be fathers—one of the few avenues toward manhood?—as well as from cultural and religious leaders not to have abortions. Although one has to respect religious and/or moral views about this, you have to wonder if young women are making rational, informed decisions about these things—lives depend on it.

Another issue not engaged adequately is one that Leon Dash discovered after hours of interviews with teenagers over the course of an entire year—the time it takes to get beyond their personal dissemblance strategies. Many of the motives behind sexual decisions—for better sometimes, but often for worse—were shaped by the fact that their families had a tremendous amount of sexual abuse within them, sometimes traced through two, three, or more generations. Ironically, Dash's decision to publicly reveal such information caused more consternation among self-conscious middle-class Blacks than the dire implications of the information itself.

If all of this sounds very nineteenth century, there is a reason for it. Black men and women have not had their own sexual revolution—the one we could not have before. We need a discourse that will help us understand modern ideas about gender and sex/gender systems, about male privilege, and about power relations; about the oppressive implications of pornography—something even at least one Harvard professor seems not to understand.

In our considerations of Anita Hill, it is important to understand that she spoke not of a physical transgression on the part of Clarence Thomas, but a verbal one masked in pornographic language. Pornography, "a fantasy salvation that inspires non-fantasy acts of punishment for uppity females," as one historian put it, speaks specifically to power relations between men and women. For African Americans these relations remain unanalyzed in the light of the empowerment of Black male elites like those represented by Thomas, who, since the seventies, have emerged as gatekeepers for the upward mobility of all Blacks in the newly accessible corporate, political, academic, and business spheres of influence. It is men, not women, who control the sociosexual and professional relationships in the Black community. Among other notions that must be dispensed with is the weak male/strong female patriarchal paradigm that clouds so much of our thinking about ourselves.

Implicit in Hill's testimony is the challenge to transcend a past that once protected, but now twists, the deepest sense of ourselves and our identities. The silences and dissemblance in the name of a misguided solidarity must end. A modern and transformative discourse must begin. Anita Hill has broken through. Let us follow.

Notes

In this essay, Gerda Lerner's definition of gender can be found in *The Creation of Patriarchy* (New York: Oxford University Press, 1987). Secondary sources regarding Phillip A. Bruce can be found in *The Black Family in Slavery and Freedom, 1750–1925* by Herbert G. Gutman (New York: Panthcon, 1976); and Jacquelyn Dowd Hall explores lynching and rape in *Revolt Against Chivalry: Jessie Daniel Ames and the*

Women's Campaign Against Lynching (New York: Columbia University Press, 1971). The issue of the *Independent* referred to is dated March 17, 1904; and explications of Sara Bartmann, the Hottentot Venus, can be found in Sander L. Gilman's essay "Black Bodies, White Bodies: Toward an Iconography of Female Sexuality in Late Nineteenth-Century Art, Medicine and Literature," published in Henry Louis Gates, ed., *"Race," Writing and Difference* (Chicago: University of Chicago Press, 1985, 1986). Analysis of sexuality during different periods in American history can be found in John D'Emilio and Estelle Freedman, *Intimate Matters: The History of Sexuality in America* (New York: Harper & Row, 1988). Discussions of the National Association of Colored Women, Black women's status in the nineteenth century and Fannie B. Williams's and Ida B. Wells's antilynching campaign can be found in Paula Giddings, *When and Where I Enter: The Impact of Black Women on Race and Sex in America* (New York: Morrow, 1984). The article by Barbara Fields is entitled "Ideology and Race in American History" and is found in J. Kousser and James M. McPherson, eds., *Race, Region and Reconstruction* (New York: Oxford University Press, 1982). The essay by Ellen DuBois and Linda Gordon is "Seeking Ecstasy on the Battlefield: Danger and Pleasure in Nineteenth Century Feminist Sexual Thought," in *Feminist Studies,* vol. 9., no. 1 (Spring) 1983. The quote by Anna Julia Cooper is in her *Voice from the South* (1893), reprinted by Negro Universities Press (New York) in 1969, pp. 68–69. The report cited under the direction of W. E. B. Du Bois, about Blacks' health and sexuality in the late nineteenth century, is entitled *Proceedings of the Second Conference for the Study of Problems Concerning Negro City Life,* originally published by Atlanta University Publications. See vol. I, reprinted by Octagon Books, 1968. The explanation of the culture of dissemblance is found in Darlene Clark Hine, "Rape and the Inner Lives of Black Women in the Middle West: Preliminary Thoughts on the Culture of Dissemblance," in this volume. The study on contemporary adolescents is "Hungry for an Us: Our Girl Group Talks About Sexual and Racial Identities," by Pat Macpherson and Michelle Fine (unpublished essay). The women-of-color study was underwritten by the National Council of Negro Women with the Communications Consortium Media Center and is entitled "Women of Color Reproductive Health Poll," August 29, 1991. The book in which Leon Dash published his findings on pregnant teenagers is entitled *When Children Want Children: The Urban Crisis of Teenage Childbearing* (New York: Morrow, 1989). The report issued in 1991 by the National Black Women's Health Project is entitled "Report: Reproductive Health Program of the National Black Women's Health Project."

36

Teaching the Differences Among Women from a Historical Perspective: Rethinking Race and Gender as Social Categories

Tessie Liu

During the week-long Southwestern Institute on Research on Women institute in 1989 on teaching women's studies from an international perspective, I experienced several epiphanal moments when a number of my research and teaching preoccupations melded and came into sharper focus. What follows is a progress report on my ruminations on this subject in the year since the institute. In particular, I would like to share the conceptual inversions and reexamination of received categories through which this problem has led me.

What has emerged from this journey is a clearer vision that feminist scholars must not only talk about diversity, but also must better understand how the differences among women are constituted historically in identifiable social processes. In this paper, I explore the importance of race as an analytical tool for investigating and understanding the differences among women. To do so, we must recognize that race is a *gendered* social category. By exploring the connections between race oppression and sex oppression, specifically how the former is predicated on the latter, we will also gain new insights into the relationship between gender and class.

Epiphanal moments, in many ways, occur only when one is primed for them. The lectures and workshops in the week-long seminar addressed questions with which I had been grappling throughout the academic year. My first set of concerns came out of a graduate course in comparative women's history that I taught at the University of Arizona with a colleague who specializes in Latin American history and women's history. Through the semester, students and instructors asked one another what we were trying to achieve by looking at women's experiences comparatively. Beyond our confidence that appreciating diversity would enrich us personally, as well as stimulate in us new questions to pose to our own areas of specialization, we raised many more questions than we found definitive answers. One set of questions, in particular, troubled me. Throughout the semester, I wondered about the relationship between the kinds of comparisons in which we were engaged and feminist theory more generally. Were we looking for some kind of underlying sameness behind all the variations in women's experiences? Was our ultimate goal to build a unified theory of gender that would explain all the differences among women? Much later, I realized that my questions centered on the status of diversity in feminist theory and politics. Especially troubling to me was the lack of discussion on such questions as these: How do feminists explain the differences among women? Are there contradictions between

Reprinted from *Women's Studies International Forum*, Vol. 14, No. 4, pp. 265–276, 1991, with kind permission from Pergamon Press Ltd, Headington Hill Hall, Oxford OX3 OBW, UK.

the focus on differences and the claim to a universal sisterhood among women? How can these tensions be resolved?

The second set of concerns that I brought to this week-long workshop came out of ongoing discussions with my colleagues in the History Department over how to restructure and teach Western civilization if we were to live up to our mandate to incorporate race, class, and gender.[1] Both sets of concerns address the problems of teaching cultural diversity. In this paper, I point out that the intellectual issues raised by adopting a more cross-cultural or international perspective in women's studies parallel the emotional and conceptual hurdles that my colleagues and I encountered in our attempts to integrate race, class, and gender into courses in Western civilization. Further, I suggest that the rethinking required to restructure such courses can be instructive to feminist scholars in offering an opportunity to reassess our own understanding of the relationships among race, class, and gender in feminist analysis.

The mandate to incorporate race, gender, and class into the Western civilization curriculum originated as a political move. But even those of us who pushed for this integration did not have a clear idea of the fundamental intellectual changes entailed. We were initially motivated by the wish to establish diversity. This task is most easily accomplished thematically: that is, every so often, we add a lecture on women, on African Americans, on Native Americans, and so on, aiming for a multicultural representation. Although it marked a good-faith beginning, this approach is particularly problematic in the context of courses like Western civilization. This attempt to introduce diversity merely sprinkles color on a white background, as Abena Busia commented in her lecture to the summer institute. One unintended but very serious effect of merely adding women, other cultures, or even discussions of class conflict and colonialism without challenging the basic structure of the idea of Western civilization is that non-Europeans, all women, the poor, and all intersecting subsets of these identities appear in the story only as victims and losers.

One problem I had not anticipated was the capacity of my students, who are primarily white and middle class, for sympathy and yet distance. To put this more starkly: to many students, they themselves embody the universal norm. In their heart of hearts, they believe that *white* establishes not merely skin color, but the norm from which blacks, browns, yellows, and reds deviate. They condemn racism, which they believe is a problem out there between racists and the people they attack. Analogously, many male students accept the reality of sexism, feel bad about it for women, but think that they are not touched by it. Even though they sympathize, for these students poverty, racism, and even sexism are still other people's problems. Teaching them, I learned an important lesson about the politics of inclusion. For those who have been left out of the story of Western civilization, it is perfectly possible to be integrated and still remain marginal.

Teaching students to appreciate cultural differences with the aim of promoting tolerance may not be a bad goal in itself, but the mode of discourse surrounding tolerance does not challenge the basically Eurocentric worldview enshrined in Western civilization courses. At best, tolerance teaches us to accept differences; at worst, it teaches the necessity of accepting what we fear or dislike. In fact, it often encourages an ethnocentric understanding of differences because this form of comparison does not break down the divisions between *us* and *them*, between *self/subject* and *other*. Most of all, it does encourage us to realize that we are implicated in these differences—that our own identities are constituted relationally within them.

Maintaining the divide between *us* and *them*, I suspect, is one way of distancing the uncomfortable reality of unequal power relations, which come to the fore once we include those previously excluded. Classically, Western civilization courses eschew such discussions of power. The purpose of such courses, structured by very Hegelian notions of the march of progress, is to present world history as the inevitable ascent of Europeans. The noted Islamicist Marshall Hodgson (1963) aptly described this as the "torch theory of civilization": the torch was first lit in Mesopotamia, passed on to Greece and then to Rome, and carried to northern Europe; ultimately, it came to rest on the North American continent during and after World War II. In this story, Europeans and their descendants bear the torch. The privileged subject is white and male, usually a member of the ruling elite, and the multiple social relationships that sustain his privilege are rarely, if ever, examined.

In light of these complexities, the basic problem in reforming Western civilization courses changed. Our new problem was how to de-center the privileged white male (and sometimes female) subject—the *I*—in the story of Western civilization, which, not coincidentally, corresponds closely to the subjectivity students have been socialized to develop in relation to the world. We could not possibly modify or reform this strong underlying message with a sprinkle of diversity. The Euro(andro-)centric viewpoint is embedded in categories of analysis, in notions of historical significance, in beliefs about who the important actors are, and in the causal logic of the story. We cannot integrate race, class, and gender without completely restructuring a course: critiquing foundations, developing new categories, telling a new story. The critical part of the de-centering, however, is the painful process of self-examination. Needless to say, the intellectual and emotional hurdles of such a project must not be underestimated. We are teaching against the grain.

African American feminists in the United States have long argued that the historically privileged white male is paralleled in American feminist discourse by the white female subject. The problem is perhaps most explicitly and succinctly articulated in the title *All the Women are White, All the Blacks are Men, but Some of Us are Brave: Black Women's Studies* (Hull *et al.*, 1982). Introducing and more fully representing women in all their diversity, although a good-faith beginning, is not sufficient in itself to correct the problems. The problem for Black women, as just one example, lies not just in their initial invisibility, but also in the manner in which they enter the mainstream. The real possibility of Black (and other nonwhite) women being brought in as second-class citizens forces us to consider how we as feminists account for and explain the differences among women. What is the status of these differences in feminist theory and politics, especially with respect to the claims of universal sisterhood?

To illustrate the depth of these unresolved problems, let me refer to our discussions on sameness and difference throughout the week-long institute. My personal history is relevant in explaining my reactions. I am an immigrant born in Taiwan to parents who were political refugees from China; my education, however, is completely Western. My feminist consciousness was formed in the context of elite educational institutions, and my specialization is European history. Not surprisingly, I have lived with the contradictions of being simultaneously an insider and an outsider all of my life. The task of explaining why I do not fit anyone's categories is a burden I had long ago accepted. All the same, the week's discussions on sameness and difference stirred within me the undercurrents of unresolved issues and brought into clearer focus how much this problem pervades feminist politics.

The first note of disquiet came on the first day when someone in my discussion group used the term *women of color*. A Palestinian woman, two Chicanas, and I looked at each other and winked knowingly. All of a sudden we were *others*, strangers to each other but placed in the same group. We were all at this conference as feminist scholars, as insiders to the movement, yet suddenly we became outsiders because we had this special affiliation. This concept of diversity (however well meant) begs the question: where is the feminist standpoint in theorizing about the differences among women? Who is the feminist self and, to borrow from Aihwa Ong (1988), "who is the feminist other?" In the previous paragraph, I deliberately used *difference* in the singular rather than *differences* in the plural because I believe that there is an important distinction. *Difference* has become a crucial concept in feminist theory, yet in this context, we are tempted to ask, "different from what or whom?" As *women of color*, we were classed together, in spite of our obvious diversity, simply because we are not white. However well-intentioned such acts of inclusion are, they raise the question: who is doing the comparing? Unless there is an Archimedean point outside social ties from which one could neutrally compare, as feminist scholars we must recognize that all discussions of differences and sameness are themselves inseparable from the power relations in which we live (Jehlen, 1982; Mohanty, 1984). In this sense, I maintain, there is no true international or cross-cultural perspective. We can view the world only from where we stand.

Failure to recognize this fundamental limitation leads to the kind of ethnocentrism hidden in works like Robin Morgan's anthology *Sisterhood Is Global* (1984). Without doubt, Morgan's anthology is an impressive achievement. Covering seventy countries, it provides a wealth of information on women's lives and their legal, economic, and political status. As reviewers Hackstaff and Pierce (1985) point out, however, the implicit argument that women everywhere are fundamentally and similarly oppressed is extremely problematic. In *Sisterhood Is Global*, differences are treated as local variations on a universal theme. As a result, *why* women's experiences differ so radically is never seriously examined. Moreover, the reviewers point out a Western bias implicit in the uncritical and unselfconscious use of crucial terms like *feminism, individual rights,* and *choice,* which retain definitions developed by Western feminists from industrialized countries, however inappropriate such working definitions may be in other cultural and social contexts. The problem is not only that women in other cultures define *feminism* or *self* in distinct ways that Morgan should have acknowledged. More fundamentally, an unproblematic assumption of common sisterhood overlooks the social reality within which texts like *Sisterhood Is Global* are created. Morgan's vision of global feminism does not question the relative power and advantages from which feminists in North America and Western Europe claim the authority to speak in the name of others on the oppression of all women (Mohanty, 1984; Ong, 1988).

This curious result—a catalogue of difference in which the relations among those who are different play no role—is symptomatic of a more general problem with what might be called a *cross-cultural perspective.* The classic anthropological use of *culture* understands the values, beliefs, and politics of various groups and societies as concrete realizations within the compass of human possibility. In an intellectual move with obvious benefits for liberal politics, difference is made a raw fact, irreducible to any hierarchical orderings of evolution or mental progress. A cross-cultural perspective rests on the notion of a transcendental or universal humanness, an essential similarity that makes it possible to understand the beliefs and behavior of others, however strange (Clifford, 1985).

This is a political vision with clear and obvious benefits. In the hands of members of a society that enjoys advantages of wealth and power over those with different cultures, however, it conceals more than it reveals. By not focusing on the unequal distribution of power which permeates relations between groups, the liberal humanist discourse elides the necessary discussion of power. To assert that the differences among women conceal an essential sisterhood is not enough: this quick achievement of solidarity comes at the expense of a real examination of the nature of the connections that actually do exist, by virtue of the fact that we occupy different positions in a world inadequately described as a congeries of reified, discrete *cultures.*[2] Instead, we must understand difference in social structural terms, in terms of interests, of privileges, and of deprivation. Only then can we see the work required to make *sisterhood* more than a rhetorical assertion of common substance. The crucial alternative analytical framework, I argue, entails exploring how diverse women's experiences are constituted reciprocally within relations of power.

On these highly charged issues within feminist politics, Charlotte Bunch (1987), our first speaker in the institute, brought an important perspective on thinking about the differences among women, arguing that we must take differences as the starting point, as the feminist standpoint. In the process of exploring diversity, Bunch assured the audience, the similarities in women's experiences will emerge. For Bunch, however, *difference* is not opposed to *sameness*. Rather, recognizing the differences among women should lead us to ask how our different lives and experiences are connected. In contrast to Morgan, Bunch argues that sisterhood is not a natural category, stemming from an organic community. Rather, an international (or cross-cultural or cross-class) sisterhood is constructed out of common political strategies. In this sense, the possibility of sisterhood begins with the recognition that, despite the vast differences which could divide us, our fates are linked and that very connectedness necessitates common action and common solutions. The fact of difference, however, means that a common cause needs to be constructed; it cannot simply be asserted.

Bunch's perspective is wholly consistent with the general goal of understanding differences across cultures. Yet I think that she asks us to investigate and appreciate diversity not just for its own sake, but also for its strategic importance to feminist politics. The goal of studying women's conditions across regions and cultures is not to demonstrate the sameness of women's oppression, but to understand the connections among the different ways in which women are oppressed (and, perhaps, to understand the connection between some women's privileges and others' deprivations). Because the *connectedness* of experience allows us to formulate strategies for common action, our study of differences must focus on how differences are constituted relationally. As a historian, I interpret these remarks through the possible contributions of my discipline. Methodologically, social history has much to add to the goal of understanding differences relationally. By situating experience as part of specific social processes, social history understands experience as the result of particular actions and actors, actions that establish connections among people and among groups.

In terms of understanding connections, the lessons I have drawn from revising the curriculum for Western civilization are particularly instructive. Moreover, once we change the content of the course from the story of European ascendency to a critical history of European dominance, the global scale and time frame of the modern half of the course (post-1500) offer a framework for thinking through and empirically studying how the differences among women were relationally constituted.[3] This framework is important, I believe, because differences in the world that we have inherited are not neutral facts. The diversity of lived experiences that we encounter today within a single society and among societies around the globe cannot be abstracted from the legacy of colonization, forced contact, expropriation, and continuing inequalities. Of course, the cultures of subjugated peoples cannot be reduced to the fact of their domination alone, any more than the culture of colonizers can be reduced to conquest. Yet no analysis of cultural diversity can be complete without study of the forces that have so fundamentally shaped experience.

In the remainder of this paper, I offer the broad outlines of a conceptual inversion entailed in remaking courses in Western civilization to serve our goal of understanding the differences among women. At present, although within women's studies we speak often of race, class, and gender as aspects of experience, we continue to organize our courses around gender as the important analytical category. This focus is both understandable and logical because, after all, our subject is women. Yet I would like to suggest the usefulness of organizing courses around the concept of race. By understanding how race is a *gendered* social category, we can more systematically address the structural underpinnings of the questions why women's experiences differ so radically and how these differences are relationally constituted.

In order to place race at the center of feminist inquiry, we need first to rethink how we conceptualize race as an analytical category. We tend to think that race is a relevant social category only when we encounter racism as a social phenomenon, in the form of bigotry, for example. Scholars have tried to understand racial hatred by analyzing characteristics like skin color, skull size, and intelligence, which racist ideology deems important, and much of this scholarship has consisted of testing and refuting racial categories. As a result, scholars have let the ideologues of racism set the agenda for discussions of racism within the academy. Although this work is important, I think the scope is too narrow. I would like to suggest that it is fruitful to inquire into the social metaphors that allow racial thinking, that is, the kind of logic or type of reasoning about human relationships that allows racists to believe in the reality of their categories. In other words, we need to move beyond the belief that racial thinking is purely an outgrowth of (irrational) prejudices, because such a belief in fact exoticizes racism, in the sense that it makes racism incomprehensible to those who do not share the hatred. Rather, as I will specify below, the more radical position holds that race is a widespread principle of social organization.

Once we ask what kind of reasoning about the nature of human relationships allows racists to believe in the reality of their categories, we find racial metaphors in benign situations as well as under conditions of discrimination, overt hatred, and even genocide. In other words, even those of us who do not hate on the basis of skin color must realize that racial thinking is disturbingly close to many of the acceptable ways that we conceptualize social relationships. In this sense, placing race at the intellectual center of courses like Western civilization is de-centering, for it attempts to break established habits of categorizing in terms of *self* and *others*. My ideas on this subject, I should add, are still in the formative stages. I have sketched with broad strokes very complex and nuanced social situations in the hope of capturing simple patterns that have been overlooked. In making bold and overly schematic generalizations, I also hope to provoke opposition and controversy as one way to assess the usefulness of these ideas for further inquiry.

Let me begin with several dictionary definitions of race that I found quite surprising and illuminating. Under the first definition in the *Oxford English Dictionary (OED)*, we find *race* as "a group of persons, animals, or plants connected by common descent or origin." As illustrations, the dictionary lists "the offspring or posterity of *a* person; a set of children or descendants; breeding, the production of offspring; (rarely): a generation." In a second set of usages, the *OED* defines *race* as "a limited group descended from a common ancestor; a house, family, kindred." We find as examples "a tribe, nation, or people, regarded as common stock; a group of several tribes or peoples regarded as forming a distinct ethnic stock; one of the great divisions of mankind, having certain peculiarities in common." The last is qualified by this comment: "this term is often used imprecisely; even among anthropologists there is no generally accepted classification or terminology." These definitions are then followed by explanations of the meaning of *race* when applied to animals, plants, and so forth.

It is clear from the first two sets of usage that ideas about descent, blood ties, or common substance are basic to the notion of *race*. What struck me, in particular, was the second set of synonyms for *race:* house, family, kindred. Louis Flandrin (1979) made the reverse discovery when he looked up *family* in a French dictionary, *Petit Robert. Family* refers to "the entirety of persons mutually connected by marriage or filiation" or "the succession of individuals who descend from one another," that is to say, "a line," "a race," "a dynasty." Only secondarily does *Petit Robert* define family in the way we usually mean, as "related persons living under one roof," "more specifically, the father, the mother, the children." These dictionary definitions, taken all together, suggest that race as a social category is intimately linked to one of the basic ways in which human beings have organized society, that is, by kinship. As Flandrin points out, etymologically, at least in England and France, *race* as a kinship term, usually to denote the *patronymic* or *family name*—called literally, the name of the race or *le nom de race*—predated our current usage of the term, which denotes distinct large populations.

Although the specific referent in notions of race is kinship, in order to understand the significance of racial thinking, we need to move beyond these neutral dictionary distinctions. When kinship becomes the key element in a stratified social order, as in dynastic politics or caste systems, the concept of race becomes important. Thus, European society, before actual contact with peoples of different skin tones and different cultures and customs, was organized by racial principles. The operating definition of race was based not on external physical characteristics but on blood ties—or, more precisely, some common substance passed on by fathers. In early modern Europe, when patriarchal rule and patrilineal descent predominated, political power, social station, and economic entitlements were closely bound to blood ties and lineage. Thus, race also encapsulated the notion of class. But class in this society was an accident of birth: either according to birth order (determining which rights and privileges the child inherited) or, more generally, according to the family into which one was born (noble or common, propertied or not). The privileges or stigmas of birth, in this system, were as indelible and as discriminatory as any racial system based on skin color or some other trait. The notion of legitimate and illegitimate birth indicates that blood ties did not extend to all who shared genetic materials, but only those with a culturally defined "common substance" passed on by fathers.

Understanding race as an element of social organization directs our attention to forms of stratification. The centrality of reproduction, especially in the transmission of common substance through heterosexual relations and ultimately through birth as the differentiating mark of social entitlements, for example, allows us to see the gendered dimensions of the concept of race. For societies organized by racial principles, reproductive politics are closely linked to establishing the boundaries of lineages. In a male-dominated system, regulating social relationships through racial metaphors necessitates control over women. The reproduction of the system entails not only regulating the sexuality of women in one's own group, but also differentiating between women according to legitimate access and prohibition. Considered in these terms, race as a social category functions through controlling sexuality and sexual behavior.

To borrow from Benedict Anderson's (1983) insights about the nature of nationalism, racial thinking, as a principle of social organization, is a way to imagine communities. Basic to the notion of race is that an indelible common substance unites the people who possess it in a special community. Importantly, the community described with racial metaphors is always limited; the intent is to exclude in the process of including. Metaphors of common substance simultaneously articulate the quality of relationship among the members of a group, and specify who belongs and who does not, asserting a natural, organic solidarity among people whose relations are described as indelible and nonvoluntary. Thus, it is not accidental that racial thinking borrows its language from biology, particularly from a systemic vision of the natural world wherein hierarchies, differences, and even struggles are described as functional to the survival and health of the whole.

These core concepts in racial thinking are powerful and flexible. Racial metaphors are rife in other forms of community-building. By analogy, kinship terms—*family, brotherhood, sisterhood,* each with its own specific meanings—are often invoked to create a sense of group affiliation: they can be applied to small communities mobilized for political action or to an entire society, in the sense of the body politic. Most notably, such metaphors are central to nationalist movements and nation-building, wherein common language and culture are often linked to blood and soil. The invocation of common substance and frequent use of kinship terms to describe the relationships among members of the political community emphasize the indelible and nonvoluntary quality of the ties and deemphasize conflict and opposing interests. The familiarity of racial metaphors, however, should not lead us to overgeneralize the phenomenon. Racial metaphors are used to build particular kinds of communities, with a special brand of internal politics on which I will later elaborate, but we must remember that forms of community-building exist which do not draw on racial metaphors. For example, there are communities, even families, conceived as voluntary associations built on common values and commitment to common goals, not on indelible ties.

The power and flexibility of racial metaphors lie, I think, in the malleability of notions of common substance. In the colonial societies that Europeans and their descendants created around the world, the older notion of race articulating a lineage-based system of entitlements and privileges was expanded and became the organizing concept through which Europeans attempted to rule subjugated populations. Only in this context of colonization did skin color become the mark of common substance and the differentiating feature between colonizers and the colonized, and, in many cases, between freedom and enslavement. Of course, the qualities designated as superior had power only because of the military force and other forms of coercion which reinforced the political and social privileges accompanying them.

Although colonial societies in the Americas, Africa, and Asia differed greatly in the taxonomy of racial categories and in the degree to which they tolerated sexual unions between colonizers and colonized, and thus had different miscegenation laws and roles for *mestizos,* the underlying problem of creating a hierarchal system of differentiation was similar. As Ann Stoler notes,

> Colonial authority was constructed on two powerful, but false premises. The first was the notion that Europeans in the colonies made up an easily identifiable and discrete biological and social entity; a "natural" community of class interests, racial attributes, political and social affinities and superior culture. The second was the related notion that the boundaries separating colonizer from colonized were thus self-evident and easily drawn (1989, p. 635).

As scholars of colonial societies are quick to point out, neither premise reflected colonial realities. The rulers, divided by conflicting economic and political goals, differed even on which methods would best safeguard European (or white) rule. Yet colonial rule itself was contingent on the colonists' ability to construct and enforce legal and social classifications for who was *white* and who was *native,* who counted as *European* and by what degree, which progeny were legitimate and which were not.

Because racial distinctions claim that common substance is biologically transmitted, race as a social reality focuses particular attention on all women as reproducers of human life (as well as the social life of the group) and at the same time necessarily separates them into distinct groups with special but different burdens. To the degree that colonial authority was based on racial distinctions, then, one could argue that colonial authority itself was fundamentally structured in gendered terms. Although in reality there may have been many types of prohibited unions and contested relationships, "ultimately," as Stoler points out, "inclusion or exclusion required regulating the sexual, conjugal and domestic life of both Europeans in the colonies and their colonized subjects" (1989, p. 635), especially in a racially-based slaveholding society like the American South, where the children of a slave woman were slaves and the children of a free woman were free. Under this juridical system, regulating who had sexual access to which group of women involved economic decisions as well.

In colonial societies as different as Dutch Indonesia (Taylor, 1983), British Nigeria (Callaway, 1987), and the American plantation South (Fox-Genovese, 1988), we find bifurcated visions of womanhood. Women of European descent became the guardians of civilization. Thus, the Victorian cult of domesticity in the colonial world must be seen in the context of demarcations between groups. Because the structure of colonial race privileges focused particularly on limiting access to European status, the elevation of white women as civilization's guardians also confined them within narrow spheres. As the reproducers of the ruling elite, they established through their daily actions the boundaries of their group identity; hence their behavior came under group scrutiny.

By contrast, the images and treatment of colonized women resulted from more complex projections. On the one hand, colonized women were not viewed as women at all in the European sense; they were spared neither harsh labor nor harsh punishment. On the other hand, as the reproducers of the labor force, colonized women were valued as one might value a prize brood mare. Equally, men of European descent eroticized colonized women as exotic, socially prohibited, but available and subjugated sexual objects. In this case, prohibition and availability are intimately connected to desire. Because such unions were socially invisible, the progeny from the union could be denied. Sex, under these conditions, became a personal rather than community or racial matter. In other words, in sexual unions with women from a socially prohibited category, men could step outside the normal restrictions and obligations imposed on sexual activity by shirking responsibility for their progeny.[4]

The same bifurcated images of women appear in European societies as the result of similar processes of creating hierarchy and class distinctions. Students of European history are not used to thinking about race as a relevant category for societies on European soil; these historians, including historians of women, much more readily accept class as the fundamental divide. Yet, despite the presence of more democratically-oriented notions of meritocracy in industrial society, and the dissemination of Enlightenment notions of contractual polity, we should not underestimate the degree to which older (lineage-based) racial thinking rooted in kinship and family alliances remained basic to the accumulation and concentration of capital in propertied families. Racial metaphors (concerns over purity of stock and preservation of social boundaries) pervaded the rationale behind marriage alliances and inheritance. The European upper classes literally thought of themselves as a *race* apart from the common rabble. Belief in the reality of these social distinctions constructed around biological metaphors pervaded bourgeois imagination and social fears. Respectability centered on domestic virtues defended by the upper-class woman, the angel of the hearth. Just as the bourgeoisie championed its own vision of domestic order as a model for civic order, they feared the disorder and contagion of the working class.

This fear is evident in perceptions of nineteenth-century elite social reformers, particularly on such seemingly neutral subjects as social hygiene. In their studies of English and French attempts to control venereal diseases, historians Judith Walkowitz (1980) and Jill Harsin (1985) have shown that regulation focused particularly on policing female prostitutes, and not their male clients. As Walkowitz has demonstrated for the port cities of England, forcing working-class women who occasionally stepped out with sailors to register on police blotters as prostitutes created a distinct outcast group, in a sense professionalizing these women while at the same time isolating them from their working-class neighbors. The ideological assumptions behind such police actions were more explicitly articulated in the French case. As Harsin shows, police regulations explicitly considered street prostitutes, called *les filles publiques* or public women, the source of contagion. Although ostensibly the problem concerned public health and the spread of venereal disease, the solutions reveal that elite social reformers like Parent du Chatalet saw poor working-class women not only as the source of disease, but as infectants of civic order, as sources of social disorder.[5]

The improbability that impoverished street prostitutes could threaten civic order demonstrates the power of the biological metaphors that linked questions of physical health metaphorically to the health of the society (of the body politic). The perception of danger bespeaks how the French upper-class imagination represented working-class women. As the dialectical opposite of the pure and chaste bourgeois angel of the hearth, poor women of the streets symbolized dirt and sexual animality. Whether these perceptions accurately reflected real circumstances is immaterial. It is more important for us to see that elite reformers and the police acted as if their perceptions were true, putting into practice elaborate controls that had material effects on the lives of working-class women and, indirectly, of upper-class women as well. The perception of danger and disorder rests on that prior social reasoning which I have identified as racial metaphors.

The previous analysis of the relationship between prostitution and public health demonstrates both the malleability and the power of racial thinking to structure the terms of political debates and actions. In recent European history, we can find many other examples where racial metaphors provide the basic vocabulary for political discourse. In the latter half of the nineteenth century, the imperatives of competition for empire in a world already carved up by Europeans filtered back into European domestic politics in the form of anxiety over population decline and public health. In the eyes of the state, responsibility for the fitness of the nation rested on women's reproductive capacity, their place in the economy, and their role as mothers in protecting the welfare of children (the future soldiers for the empire) (Davin, 1978). Debates over the "Woman Question," in the form of feminist demands for greater equality within marriage and for political, economic, and reproductive rights, were debated in the context of colonial politics and concerns over the vitality of the master European races. Competition among European nations for colonial empire and their anxieties about themselves as colonizers set the terms for curtailing women's demands for greater freedom of action and autonomy. Antifeminist projects such as economically restrictive protective legislation, bans on birth control, and pronatalist policies went hand in hand with the campaign against women's suffrage.

In the twentieth century, within the European heartland, German National Socialists took these shared assumptions about the relation between national fitness and women's activities to their terrifying extreme. As Gisela Bock's study of women's reproductive rights in Nazi Germany indicates, obsession with race purity and population strength led to a policy of compulsory motherhood with the criminalization of abortion for Aryan women of the superior race and forced sterilization for the inferior races as part of their ultimate extermination (1984). This study of the differential effects of racial policy on women's reproductive rights shocks us into recognizing that the division of women into breeders and nonbreeders is wholly consistent with the logic of racial thinking, whether we encounter such divisions in European dynastic politics or as part of the effort to establish boundaries between colonizers and the colonized. The most disturbing aspect of racial thinking is that it is *not* limited to the terrifying circumstances of genocide for some and compulsory motherhood for others. It is, in many respects, its very banality which should trouble us

This brief survey of the common use and implications of what I have called racial metaphors in colonial contexts as well as in the home countries of colonizers, while hardly satisfactory in terms of detail, has at minimum, I hope, suggested an interesting point of departure for rethinking the connections among gender, race, and class. As Bock's study shows us, racism and sexism are not just analogous forms of oppression; institutionalized racism is a form of sexism. One form of oppression is predicated on the other. Racism is a kind of sexism which does not treat all women as the same, but drives wedges between us on the basis of our daily experiences, our assigned functions within the social order, and our perceived interests and mobilization. Although women everywhere have struggled against prescriptive images and have fought for greater autonomy and control, it should not be surprising that, given their different positions within the system and the vastly different material conditions of their lives, women have fashioned different notions of self, have had different grievances against their circumstances, and have often developed different strategies.

Thinking about differences in the ways that I have suggested in this paper requires overcoming very strong emotional and intellectual barriers. We are all products of societies that have taught us to hate others or, worse, to be indifferent to their suffering and blind to our own privileges and to those who labor to provide them. The historical legacy of these differences makes common bonds difficult to conceive. That which divides us may also connect us, but will not easily unite us. Still, if sisterhood beyond the boundaries of class, race, ethnicity, and nation is a meaningful goal, we must try to develop common strategies for change. As a first step, we can become aware that some of the most fundamental differences arise from our distinct locations within a social system that underprivileges all women, but in different ways. To bridge these differences, we must, as Peggy Pascoe has urged, take a candid look at the shameful side, recognizing that we cannot bury the past or wipe the slate completely clean.[6] We can only strive for empathy and mutual understanding. Some of us face the painful process of reexamining our definitions of *self* and *other*, and of challenging the categories of analysis and conceptions of historical development which support our intimate vision of ourselves in the world. Others face the equally painful task of letting go of anger, not enough to forget it entirely, but enough to admit the possibility of common futures and joint strategies for transformation.

We cannot fully capture and understand the kinds of differences between women based on race and class by such phrases as *diversity of experiences*. By focusing on race as an analytical category in accounting for the differences among women, we are in fact studying race as a principle of social organization and racial metaphors as part of the process of defining hierarchies and constituting boundaries of privilege. The core notion of common substance transmitted through heterosexual intercourse and birth underscores the gendered nature of the concept of race. In a male-dominated society, this concept focuses particular attention on women's activities, on reproductive politics, and more generally, on control over sexuality and sexual behavior. Understanding this process allows us to see how much the identities of different groups of women in the same society are implicated in one another. Although their experiences of oppression differ dramatically, these differences are nonetheless relationally constituted in identifiable social processes.

Notes

This paper has benefited enormously from Ken Dauber's intellectual support and careful readings. I would also like to thank Karen Anderson, Jan Monk, Amy Newhall, and Pat Seavey for their insights and editorial suggestions.

1. Since 1987, all students earning the Bachelor of Arts and Sciences at the University of Arizona have been required to take one course, selected from a designated list, which focuses on gender, class, race, or ethnicity.
2. For a critique of this view of *culture*, see Worsley (1981) and Clifford (1988).
3. Although I am vulnerable, in this move, to the charge that even in the posture of critique, I still privilege a Western perspective, I do so as a politically conscious first step. With regard to my earlier concerns with some of the problems of cross-cultural comparison, a focus on colonialism forces us to keep in the center of our vision the relationship between differences and power.
4. I am indebted to Ken Dauber for this insight. For European parallels in relationships between upper-class men and working-class women, see Davidoff (1983).
5. For interesting parallels see White (1983, 1986) and Guy (1988).
6. Pascoe's talk at Western History Conference in Santa Fe, New Mexico, 1989. See also Pascoe (1990).

References

Anderson, Benedict. 1983. *Imagined Communities: Reflections on the Origins and Spread of Nationalism.* London: Verso.

Bock, Gisela. 1984. "Racism and Sexism in Nazi Germany: Motherhood, Compulsory Sterilization, and the State." In Renate Bridenthal, Atina Grossman, Marion Kaplan, eds., *When Biology Became Destiny: Women in Weimar and Nazi Germany*, pp. 271–296. New York: Monthly Review Press.

Bunch, Charlotte. 1987. "Bringing the Global Home." In Charlotte Bunch, ed., *Passionate Politics*, pp. 328–345. New York: St. Martin's Press.

Callaway, Helen. 1987. *Gender, Culture and Empire: European Women in Colonial Nigeria.* London: Macmillan.

Clifford, James. 1986. "On Ethnographic Allegory." In James Clifford and George Marcus, eds., *Writing Culture: The Poetics and Politics of Ethnography*, pp. 98–121. Berkeley: University of California Press.

——— 1988. *The Predicaments of Culture: Twentieth Century Ethnography, Literature, and Art.* Cambridge, MA: Harvard University Press.

Davin, Anna. 1978. "Imperialism and Motherhood." *History Workshop*, 5, pp. 9–56.

Davidoff, Lenore. 1983. "Class and Gender in Victorian England." In Judith L. Newton, Mary P. Ryan, and Judith R. Walkowitz, eds., *Sex and Class in Women's History*, pp. 16–71. London: Routledge and Kegan Paul.

Flandrin, Jean-Louis. 1979. *Families in Former Times: Kinship, Household, and Sexuality in Early Modern France*, Richard Southern, trans. Cambridge: Cambridge University Press.

Fox-Genovese, Elizabeth. 1988. *Within the Plantation Household: The Black and White Woman of the Old South.* Chapel Hill: University of North Carolina Press.

Guy, Donna J. 1988. "White Slavery, Public Health and the Socialist Position on Legalized Prostitution in Argentina 1913–1936." *Latin American Research Review*, 23(3), pp. 60–80.

Hackstaff, Karla, and Jennifer Pierce. 1985. "Is Sisterhood Global?" *Berkeley Journal of Sociology*, 30, pp. 189–204.

Harsin, Jill. 1985. *Policing Prostitution in Nineteenth Century Paris.* Princeton: Princeton University Press.

Hodgson, Marshall. 1963. "The Interrelations of Societies in History." *Comparative Studies in Society and History*, 5, pp. 227–250.

Hull, Gloria T., Patricia Bell Scott, and Barbara Smith. 1982. *All the Women are White, All the Blacks are Men, but Some of Us are Brave: Black Women's Studies.* Westbury, NY: Feminist Press.

Jehlen, Myra. 1982. "Archimedes and the Paradox of Feminist Criticism." In Nannerl Keohane, Michelle Rosaldo, and Barbara Gelpi, eds., *Feminist Theory: A Critique of Ideology*, pp. 189–215. Chicago: University of Chicago Press.

Mohanty, Chandra Talpade. 1984. "Under Western Eyes: Feminist Scholarship and Colonial Discourses. *Boundaries*, 2(12/13), pp. 333–358.

Morgan, Robin. 1984. *Sisterhood Is Global.* New York: Anchor Press/Doubleday.

Ong, Aihwa. 1988. "Colonialism and Modernity: Feminist Representations of Women in Non-Western Societies." *Inscriptions (Journal of the Group for the Study of Discourse in Colonialism)*, 3/4, pp. 79–93.

Pascoe, Peggy. 1990. "At the Crossroads of Culture." *Women's Review of Books*, 7(5), pp. 22–23.

Stoler, Ann L. 1989. "Making Empire Respectable: The Politics of Race and Sexual Morality in Twentieth Century Colonial Cultures." *American Ethnologist, 16*, pp. 634–660.

Taylor, Jean. 1983. *The World of Batavia.* Madison: University of Wisconsin Press.

Walkowitz, Judith. 1980. *Prostitution and Victorian Society: Women, Class, and the State.* Cambridge: Cambridge University Press.

White, Luise. 1986. "Prostitution, Identity and Class Consciousness in Nairobi During World War II." *Signs,* 11, pp. 255–273.

———— 1983. "A Colonial State and an African Petty Bourgeoisie: Prostitution, Property and Class Struggle in Nairobi, 1936–1940." In Frederick Cooper, ed., *Struggle for the City: Migrant Labor, Capital, and the State in Urban Africa,* pp. 167–193. Beverly Hills, CA: Sage.

Worsley, Peter. 1981. "Marxism and Culture: the Missing Concept." *Dialectical Anthropology,* 6, pp. 103–123.

Selected Bibliographies
African American Women
Compiled by Chana Kai Lee

Anthologies

Bambara, Toni Cade, ed. *The Black Woman: An Anthology*. New York: New American Library, 1970.

Bell, Roseann, Bettye J. Parker and Beverly Guy-Sheftall, eds. *Sturdy Black Bridges: Visions of Black Women in Literature*. Garden City, NY: Anchor Press/Doubleday, 1979.

Crawford, Vicki L., Jacqueline A. Rouse, and Barbara Woods, eds. *Women in the Civil Rights Movement: Trailblazers and Torchbearers*. New York: Carlson, 1990.

Fraser, Walter, Jr., R. Frank Saunders and Jon L. Wakelyn, eds. *The Web of Southern Social Relations: Women, Family, and Education*. Athens, GA: University of Georgia Press, 1985.

Harley, Sharon and Rosalyn Terborg-Penn, eds. *The Afro-American Woman: Struggles and Images*. Port Washington, NY, and London: Kennikat Press, 1978.

Hine Darlene Clark, ed. *Black Women in United States History: From Colonial Times Through the Nineteenth Century*, vols. 1–4. Brooklyn, NY: Carlson Publishing, 1990.

———, ed. *Black Women in United States History: The Twentieth Century*, vols. 5–8. Brooklyn, NY: Carlson Publishing, 1990.

———, ed. *Black Women in American History: Theory and Practice*, vols. 9–10. Brooklyn, NY: Carlson Publishing, 1990.

Hine, Darlene Clark, ed. (with Elsa Barkley Brown and Rosalyn Terborg-Penn, assoc. eds.) *Black Women in America: An Historical Encyclopedia*. Brooklyn, NY: Carlson, 1993.

Hull, Gloria T. *et al.*, eds. *All the Women Are White, All the Blacks Are Men But Some of Us Are Brave: Black Women's Studies*. Old Westbury, NY: Feminist Press, 1982.

Hull, Gloria, ed. *Color, Sex, and Poetry. Three Women Writers of the Harlem Renaissance*. Bloomington: Indiana University Press, 1987.

Lerner, Gerda, ed. *Black Women in White America: A Documentary History*. New York: Vintage Books, 1972.

Lowenberg, Bert and Ruth Bogin, eds. *Black Women in Nineteenth Century Life: Their Thoughts, Their Words, Their Feelings*. University Park: Pennsylvania State University Press, 1976.

Moraga, Cherrie and Gloria Anzaldua, eds. *This Bridge Called My Back: Writings by Radical Women of Color*. Watertown, MA: Persephone Press, 1981.

Morrison, Toni, ed. *Race-ing Justice, En-gendering Power: Essays on Anita Hill, Clarence Thomas and the Construction of Social Reality*. New York: Pantheon Books, 1992.

Pryse, Marjorie and Hortense Spillers, eds. *Conjuring: Black Women, Fiction, and Literary Tradition*. Bloomington: Indiana University Press, 1985.

Shockley, Ann Allen, ed. *Afro-American Women Writers, 1746–1933*. Boston, MA: G.K. Hall, 1988.

Smith, Barbara, ed. *Home Girls: A Black Feminist Anthology*. New York: Kitchen Table Press, 1983.

Smith, Valerie, ed. *African American Writers*. New York: C. Scribner's Sons; Maxwell MacMillan International, 1991.

Wall, Cheryl, ed. *Changing Our Own Words: Essays on Criticism, Theory, and Writing by Black Women*. New Brunswick, NJ: Rutgers University Press, 1989.

White, Evelyn C., ed. *The Black Women's Health Book: Speaking for Ourselves*. Seattle: Seal Press, 1990.

Fiction/Memoir/Poetry

Angelou, Maya. *I Know Why the Caged Bird Sings*. New York: Random House, 1969.

Baker, Nikki. *In the Game*. Jacksonville: Naiad Press, 1990.

Bates, Daisy. *The Long Shadow of Little Rock, A Memoir*. New York: David McKay Co., 1962.

Brown, Elaine. *A Taste of Power: A Black Woman's Story*. New York: Pantheon Books, 1992.

Browne, Martha. *Autobiography of a Female Slave*. Miami, FL: Mnemosyne Publishing Company, 1969.

Butler, Octavia. *Mind of My Mind*. Garden City, NY: Doubleday, 1977.

Clark, Septima. *Echo in My Soul*. New York: E. P. Dutton, 1962.

Davis, Angela. *Angela Davis: An Autobiography*. New York: Random House, 1974.

Dunbar-Nelson, Alice Moore. *The Works of Alice Dunbar-Nelson*, ed. Gloria T. Hull. New York: Oxford University Press, 1988.

Fields, Mamie Garvin with Karen Fields. *Lemon Swamp and Other Places: A Carolina Memoir*. New York: Free Press, 1983.

Forten, Charlotte L. *The Journals of Charlotte Forten Grimke*, ed. Brenda Stevenson. New York: Oxford University Press, 1988.

Grimke, Angelina Weld. *Selected Works of Angelina Weld Grimke*, ed. Carolivia Herron. New York: Oxford University Press, 1991.

Harper, Frances Ellen Watkins. *Iola Leroy, or Shadows Uplifted*. New York: Oxford University Press, 1988.

Hunter-Gault, Charlayne. *In My Place*. New York: Farrar Straus, 1992.

Hurston, Zora Neale. *Dust Tracks on a Road: An Autobiography*. Urbana: University of Illinois Press, 1970.

Jacobs, Harriet (Linda Brent). *Incidents in the Life of A Slave Girl Written by Herself*. Cambridge, MA: Harvard University Press, 1987.

Lorde, Audre. *Zami: A New Spelling of My Name*. Trumansburg, NY: Crossing Press, 1982.

Moody, Anne. *Coming of Age in Mississippi*. New York: Dial Press, 1968.

Morgan, Kathryn L. *Children of Strangers: The Stories of a Black Family*. Philadelphia: Temple University Press, 1980.

Murray, Pauli. *Song in a Weary Throat: An American Pilgrimage*. New York: Harper & Row, 1987.

Morrison, Toni. *Beloved*. New York: Knopf, Random House, 1987.

Naylor, Gloria. *Women of Brewster Place*. New York: Viking Press, 1982.

Shange, Ntozake. *For Colored Girls Who Have Considered Suicide/When the Rainbow is Enuf*. New York: Macmillan, 1977.

Shakur, Assata. *Assata: An Autobiography*. Westport, CT: L. Hill, 1987.

Six Women's Slave Narratives. New York: Oxford University Press, 1988.

Smith, Amanda. *An Autobiography: The Story of Lord's Dealings with Mrs. Amanda Smith, the Colored Evangelist*. New York: Oxford University Press, 1988.

Tarry, Ellen. *The Third Door: The Autobiography of an American Negro Woman*. New York: D. McKay Co., 1955.

Walker, Alice. *The Color Purple*. New York: Harcourt Brace Jovanovich, 1982.

———. *In Search of Our Mothers' Gardens: Womanist Prose*. New York: Harcourt Brace Jovanovich, 1983.

Washington, Mary Helen ed. *Invented Lives: Narratives of Black Women, 1860–1960*. Garden City, NY: Doubleday, 1987.

Wells-Barnett, Ida. *Crusade for Justice: The Autobiography of Ida B. Wells*, ed. Alfreda Duster. Chicago and London: University of Chicago Press, 1970.

Wheatley, Phillips. *The Collected Works of Phillis Wheatley*, ed. John Shields. New York: Oxford University Press, 1988.

Books/Theses/Dissertations

Alexander, Adele Logan. *Ambiguous Lives: Free Women of Color in Rural Georgia, 1789–1879*. Fayetteville: University of Arkansas Press, 1991.

Andrews, Williams, ed. *Sisters of the Spirit*. Bloomington: Indiana University Press, 1986.

Aptheker, Bettina. *Woman's Legacy: Essays on Race, Sex, and Class in American History*. Amherst: University of Massachusetts Press, 1982.

———. *Tapestries of Life: Women's Work, Women's Consciousness, and the Meaning of Daily Experiences*. Amherst: University of Massachusetts Press, 1989.

Braxton, Joanne M. *Black Women Writing Autobiography: A Tradition Within A Tradition*. Philadelphia: Temple University Press, 1989.

Brown, Hallie Q. *Homespun Heroines and Other Women of Distinction.* New York: Oxford University Press, 1988.

Buckley, Gail Lumet. *The Hornes: An American Family.* New York: Knopf, 1986.

Byerly, Victoria. *Hard Times Cotton Mill Girls.* Ithaca, NY: ILR Press, 1986.

Bynum, Victoria E. *Unruly Women: The Politics of Social and Sexual Control in the Old South.* Chapel Hill: University of North Carolina Press, 1992.

Carby, Hazel. *Reconstructing Womanhood: The Emergence of the Afro-American Woman Novelist.* New York: Oxford University Press, 1987.

Carson, Clayborne. *In Struggle: SNCC and the Black Awakening of the 1960s.* Cambridge, MA: Harvard University Press, 1981.

Christian, Barbara. *Black Women Novelists: The Development of a Tradition, 1892–1976.* Westport, CT: Greenwood Press, 1980.

Collins, Patricia Hill. *Black Feminist Thought: Knowledge, Consciousness, and the Politics of Empowerment.* New York: Routledge, 1990.

Cooper, Anna Julia. *A Voice from the South*, ed. Mary Helen Washington. New York: Oxford University Press, 1988.

Davis, Angela. *Women, Race, and Class.* New York: Random House, 1981.

———. *Women, Culture and Politics.* New York: Random House, 1989.

Davis, Marianna. *Contributions of Black Women in America.* Columbia, SC: Kenday Press, 1981.

Devries, James. *Race and Kinship in a Midwestern Town.* Urbana: University of Illinois Press, 1984.

Du Bois, W. E. B. *The Philadelphia Negro: A Social Study.* New York: Schocken Books, 1967.

Frazier, E. Franklin. *The Negro Family in the United States.* Chicago: University of Chicago Press, 1966.

Fox-Genovese, Elizabeth. *Within the Plantation Household: Black and White Women of the Old South.* Chapel Hill: University of North Carolina Press, 1988.

Giddings, Paula. *When and Where I Enter: The Impact of Black Women on Race and Sex in America.* New York: William Morrow and Company, Inc. 1984.

———. *In Search of Sisterhood: Delta Sigma Theta and the Challenge of the Black Sorority Movement.* New York: William Morrow and Company, Inc. 1988.

Gilmore, Glenda. "Gender and Jim Crow: Women and the Politics of White Supremacy in North Carolina, 1896–1920." Ph.D. dissertation, University of North Carolina, Chapel Hill, 1992.

Gottlieb, Peter. *Making Their Own Way: Southern Blacks' Migration to Pittsburgh, 1916–30.* Urbana: University of Illinois Press, 1987.

Gutman, Herbert. *The Black Family in Slavery and Freedom, 1750–1925.* New York: Pantheon Books, 1976.

Guy-Sheftall, Beverly. *Daughters of Sorrow: Attitudes Toward Black Women, 1880–1920.* Brooklyn, NY: Carlson Publishing, 1990.

Hall, Jacquelyn Dowd. *Revolt Against Chivalry: Jessie Daniel Ames and the Women's Campaign Against Lynching.* New York: Columbia University Press, 1979.

Hamilton, Tullia K. Brown. "The National Association of Colored Women, 1896 to 1920." Ph.D. dissertation, Emory University, 1978.

Handy, Antoinette. *Black Women in American Bands and Orchestras.* Metuchen, NJ: Scarecrow Press, 1981.

Harrison, Daphne Duval. *Black Pearls: Blues Queens of the 1920s.* New Brunswick, NJ: Rutgers University Press, 1988.

Hemenway, Robert. *Zora Neale Hurston: A Literary Biography.* Urbana: University of Illinois Press, 1977.

Henri, Forette. *Black Migration: Movement North 1900–1920.* Garden City, NY: Anchor Press, 1975.

Higginbotham, Evelyn Brooks. *Righteous Discontent: The Women's Movement in the Baptist Church, 1880–1920.* Cambridge, MA: Harvard University Press, 1993.

Hine, Darlene Clark. *When the Truth Is Told: A History of Black Women's Culture and Community in Indiana, 1875–1950.* Indianapolis, IN: National Council of Negro Women, 1981.

———. *Black Women in White: Racial Conflict and Cooperation in the Nursing Profession, 1890–1950.* Bloomington: Indiana University Press, 1989.

Holt, Rackham. *Mary McLeod Bethune.* Garden City, NY: Doubleday, 1964.

hooks, bell. *Ain't I Woman: Black Women and Feminism.* Boston: South End Press, 1981.

———. *Feminist Theory: From Margin to Center.* Boston: South End Press, 1984.

———. *Talking Back: Thinking Feminist, Thinking Black.* Boston: South End Press, 1988.

Hunter, Tera W. "Household Workers in the Making: Afro-American Women in Atlanta and the New South, 1861–1920." Ph.D. dissertation, Yale University, 1990.

Jones, Adrienne Lash. *Jane Edna Hunter: A Case Study of Black Leadership, 1910–1950.* Brooklyn, NY: Carlson Publishing, 1990.

Jones, Beverly Washington. *Quest for Equality: The Life and Writings of Mary Eliza Church Terrell, 1863–1954.* Brooklyn, NY: Carlson Publishing, 1990.

Jones, Jacqueline. *Labor of Love, Labor of Sorrow: Black Women, Work and the Family, From Slavery to the Present*. New York: Vintage Books, 1985.

Katzman, David. *Seven Days A Week: Women and Domestic Service in Industrializing America*. New York: Oxford University Press, 1978.

Klotman, Phyllis R. and Wilmer Baatz. *The Black Family and the Black Woman: A Bibliography*. New York: Arno Press, 1978.

Ladner, Joyce. *Tomorrow's Tomorrow: The Black Woman*. Garden City, NY: Doubleday, 1971.

Larison, Cornelius Wilson. *Silvia Dubois: A Biografy of the Slav Who Whipt Her Mistres and Gand Her Fredom*, ed. Jared C. Lobdell, New York: Oxford University, 1988.

Lebsock, Suzanne. *The Free Women of Petersburg: Status and Culture in a Southern Town, 1784–1860*. New York: W.W. Norton, 1984.

Lee, Chana Kai. "A Passionate Pursuit of Justice: The Life and Leadership of Fannie Lou Hamer." Ph.D. dissertation, University of California, Los Angeles, 1993.

Levine, Lawrence. *Black Culture and Black Consciousness*. New York: Oxford University Press, 1977.

Lieb, Sandra. *Mother of the Blues: A Study of Ma Rainey*. Amherst, MA: University of Massachusetts Press, 1981.

Lorde, Audre. *Sister Outsider: Essays and Speeches*. Trumansburg, NY: Crossing Press, 1984.

Mabee, Carleton (with Susan Mabee Newhouse). *Sojourner Truth—Slave, Prophet, Legend*. New York: University Press, 1993.

McAdoo, Harriette. *Black Families*. Beverly Hills: Sage Publications, 1981.

McMillen, Sally G. *Southern Women: Black and White in the Old South*. Arlington Heights, IL: Harlan Davidson, Inc., 1992.

Mills, Kay. *This Little Light of Mine: The Life of Fannie Lou Hamer*. New York: Dutton, 1993.

Mock, Charlotte. *Bridges: New Mexican Black Women, 1900–1950*. Albuquerque, NM: New Mexican Commission on the Study of Women, 1985.

Morton, Patricia. *Disfigured Images: The Historical Assault on Afro-American Women*. Westport, CT: Greenwood Press, 1991.

Noble, Jeanne. *Beautiful Also Are The Souls of My Sisters: A History of the Black Woman in America*. Englewood Cliffs, NJ: Prentice-Hall, Inc., 1978.

Neverdon-Morton, Cynthia. *Afro-American Women of the South and the Advancement of the Race, 1895–1925*. Knoxville: University of Tennessee Press, 1989.

Patterson, Ruth Polk. *The Seed of Sally Good'n: A Black Family in Arkansas, 1833–1953*. Lexington, KY: University of Kentucky Press, 1983.

Perkins, Linda. *Fanny Jackson Coppin and the Institute for Colored Youth, 1837–1902*. New York: Garland, 1987.

Potter, Eliza. *A Hairdresser's Experience in High Life*. New York: Oxford University Press, 1991.

Rhodes, Jane. "Breaking the Editorial Ice: Mary Ann Shadd Cary and the *Provincial Freeman*." Ph.D. dissertation, University of North Carolina, Chapel Hill, 1992.

Richardson, Marilyn, ed. *Maria W. Stewart, America's First Black Woman Political Writer*. Bloomington: Indiana University Press, 1987.

Robinson, Jo Ann Gibson. *The Montgomery Bus Boycott and the Women Who Started It*. Knoxville: University of Tennessee Press, 1987.

Rollins, Judith. *Between Women: Domestics and Their Employers*. Philadelphia: Temple University Press, 1985.

Rouse, Jacqueline. *Lugenia Burns Hope, Black Southern Reformer*. Athens: University of Georgia Press, 1989.

Sacks, Karen. *Caring By the Hour: Women, Work, and Organizing at Duke Medical Center*. Urbana: University of Illinois Press, 1988.

Salem, Dorothy C. *To Better Our World: Black Women in Organized Reform, 1890–1920*. Brooklyn, NY: Carlson Publishing, 1990.

Sims, Janet L. *The Progress of Afro-American Women: A Selected Bibliography and Resource Guide*. Westport, CT: Greenwood Press, 1980.

Smith, Valerie. *Self-Discovery and Authority in Afro-American Narrative*. Cambridge: Harvard University Press, 1987.

Solinger, Rickie. *Wake Up Little Susie: Single Pregnancy and Race Before Roe v. Wade*. New York: Routledge, 1992.

Stack, Carol B. *All Our Kin*. New York: Harper & Row, 1974.

Steady, Filomina Chioma. *The Black Woman Cross-Culturally*. Cambridge, MA: Schenkman Publishing Company, 1981.

Sterling, Dorothy. *Black Foremothers, Three Lives*. Old Westbury, NY: Feminist Press, 1979.

Taylor, Ula Yvette. "The Veiled Garvey: The Life and Times of Amy Jacques Garvey." Ph.D. dissertation, University of California, Santa Barbara, 1992.

Terborg-Penn, Rosalyn. "Afro-Americans in the Struggle for Woman Suffrage." Ph.D. dissertation, Howard University, 1977.

Thompson, Mildred. *Ida B. Wells-Barnett: An Exploratory Study of An American Black Woman, 1893–1930.* Brooklyn, NY: Carlson Publishing, 1990.

Trotter, Joe William. *Black Milwaukee: The Making of an Industrialized Proletariat, 1915–1945.* Urbana: University of Illinois Press, 1985.

Vehanen, Kosti. *Marian Anderson.* Westport, CT: Greenwood Press, 1970.

Wallace, Michele. *Black Macho and the Myth of Superwoman.* New York: Dial Press, 1979.

Wallace, Phyllis. *Black Women in the Labor Force.* Cambridge, MA: MIT Press, 1980.

West, Guida. *The National Welfare Rights Movement: The Social Protest of Poor Women.* New York: Praeger, 1981.

White, Deborah Gray. *Ar'n't I A Woman? Female Slaves in the Plantation South.* New York: Norton, 1985.

Wilson, Emily. *Hope and Dignity: Older Black Women of the South.* Philadelphia: Temple University Press, 1983.

Yee, Shirley. *Black Women Abolitionists: A Study in Activism, 1828–1860.* Knoxville: University of Tennessee Press, 1992.

Yellin, Jean Fagin. *Women & Sisters: The Antislavery Feminists in American Culture.* New Haven: Yale University Press, 1989.

Washington, Margaret, ed. *The Narrative of Sojourner Truth.* New York: Vintage Books, 1993.

Williams, Patricia J. *The Alchemy of Race and Rights.* Cambridge, MA: Harvard University Press, 1991.

Journal/Anthology Articles

Blackett, R.J.M. "The Odyssey of William and Ellen Craft." In *Beating Against the Barriers: Biographical Essays in Nineteenth-Century Afro-American History*, Baton Rouge: Louisiana State University Press, 1986.

Blackwelder, Julia Kirk. "Women in the Work Force: Atlanta, New Orleans, and San Antonio, 1930 to 1940." *Journal of Urban History* 4 (May 1978).

Breen, William J. "Black Women and the Great War: Mobilization and Reform in the South." *Journal of Southern History* 44 (August 1978), pp. 421–40.

Brooks, Evelyn. "Feminist Theology of the Black Baptist Church, 1880–1900." In *Class, Race and Sex: The Dynamics of Control*, eds. Amy Swerdlow and Hanna Lesinger. Boston, MA: G.K. Hall, 1983.

Brown, Elsa Barkley. "Afro-American Women's Quilting: A Framework for Conceptualizing and Teaching African-American Women's History." *Signs* 14 (Summer 1989), pp. 921–929.

———. " 'What Has Happened Here': The Politics of Difference in Women's History and Feminist Politics." *Feminist Studies* 18 (Summer 1992), pp. 295–312.

Collins, Patricia Hill. "The Social Construction of Black Feminist Thought." *Signs* 14 (Summer 1989), pp. 745–73.

Gabin, Nancy. "They Have Placed a Penalty on Womanhood: The Protest Action of Women Auto Workers in Detroit-Area UAW Locals, 1945–1974." *Feminist Studies* 8 (Summer 1982), pp. 373–98.

Geschwender, James A. and Rita Carroll-Seguin. "Exploding the Myth of African-American Progress." *Signs* 15 (Winter 1990), pp. 285–99.

Griffin, Jean T. "West African and Black Working Women: Historical and Contemporary Comparisons." *Journal of Black Psychology* 8 (February 1982), pp. 55–74.

Higginbotham, Evelyn Brooks. "Afro-American Women's History and the Metalanguage of Race." *Signs* 17 (Winter 1992), pp. 251–74.

Omolade, Barbara. "Hearts of Darkness." In *Powers of Desire: The Politics of Sexuality*, eds. Ann Snitow, Christine Stansell, and Sharon Thompson. New York: Monthly Review Press, 1983.

Painter, Nell. "Sojourner Truth in Memory and History: Writing the History of An American Exotic." *Gender and History* 2 (Spring 1990), pp. 3–16.

Simmonds, Felly Nkweto. "She's Gotta Have It: The Representation of Black Female Sexuality on Film." *Feminist Review* 29 (Spring 1988), pp. 10–22.

Simson, Rennie. "The Afro-American Female: The Historical Context of the Construction of Sexual Identity." In *Powers of Desire: The Politics of Sexuality*, eds. Ann Snitow, Christine Stansell, and Sharon Thompson. New York: Monthly Review Press, 1983.

White, E. Frances. "Africa on My Mind: Gender, Counter Discourse and African-American Nationalism." *Journal of Women's History* 2 (Spring 1990), pp. 73–97.

Williams, Patricia. "On Being the Object of Property." *Signs* 14 (Autumn 1988), pp. 5–24.

Asian American Women
Compiled by Brian Niiya

Anthologies

Asian Women United of California, eds. *Making Waves: An Anthology of Writings By and About Asian American Women*. Boston: Beacon Press, 1989.

Berson, Misha, ed. *Between Worlds: Contemporary Asian-American Plays*. New York: Theatre Communications Group, 1990.

Cheng, Lucie, and Edna Bonacich, eds. *Labor Immigration Under Capitalism: Asian Workers in the United States Before World War II*. Berkeley: University of California Press, 1984.

Chock, Eric, and Darrell H. Y. Lum, eds. *The Best of Bamboo Ridge*. Honolulu: Bamboo Ridge Press, 1986.

Hongo, Garrett, ed. and introd. *The Open Boat: Poems from Asian America*. New York: Doubleday, 1993.

Houston, Velina Hasu, ed. *The Politics of Life: Four Plays by Asian American Women*. Philadelphia: Temple University Press, 1993.

Kono, Juliet S., and Cathy Song. *Sister Stew: Fiction and Poetry by Women*. Honolulu: Bamboo Ridge Press, 1991.

Lim, Shirley Geok-lin, and Mayumi Tsutakawa, eds. *The Forbidden Stitch: An Asian American Women's Anthology*. Corvallis, OR: Calyx Books, 1989.

Linking Our Lives: Chinese American Women of Los Angeles. Los Angeles: Chinese Historical Society of Southern California and University of California, Los Angeles. Asian American Studies Center, 1984.

Tsuchida, Nobuya, ed. *Asian and Pacific American Experiences: Women's Perspectives*. Minneapolis: Asian/Pacific American Learning Resource Center and General College, University of Minnesota, 1982.

Watanabe, Sylvia, and Carol Bruchac, eds. *Home to Stay: Asian American Women's Fiction*. New York: Greenfield Review Press, 1990.

Yu, Eui-Young, and Earl H. Phillips, eds. *Korean Women in Transition: At Home and Abroad*. Los Angeles: Center for Korean-American and Korean Studies, California State University, Los Angeles, 1987.

Fiction/Memoir/Poetry

Alexander, Meena. *Fault Lines: A Memoir by Meena Alexander*. New York: The Feminist Press at the City University of New York, 1993.

Brainard, Cecilia Manguerra. *Woman with Horns and Other Stories*. Quezon City, Philippines: New Day Publishers, 1988.

Cha, Theresa Hak Kyung. *Dictee*. New York: Tanam Press, 1982.

Chin, Marilyn. *Dwarf Bamboo*. Greenfield Center, NY: Greenfield Review Press, 1987.

Hagedorn, Jessica. *Dogeaters*. New York: Pantheon Books, 1990.

Hayslip, Le Ly. *When Heaven and Earth Changed Places: A Vietnamese Woman's Journey from War to Peace*. New York: Doubleday, 1989.

Houston, Jeanne Wakatsuki, and James Houston. *Farewell to Manzanar*. Boston: Houghton, 1973.

Jen, Gish. *Typical American*. Boston: Houghton Mifflin, 1991.

Kadohata, Cynthia. *The Floating World*. New York: Viking, 1989.

Kingston, Maxine Hong. *The Woman Warrior: Memoirs of a Girlhood among Ghosts*. New York: Knopf, 1975.

Kogawa, Joy. *Obasan*. Boston: Godine, 1982.

Law-Yone, Wendy. *The Coffin Tree*. New York: Knopf, 1983; Boston: Beacon, 1987.

Lee, Mary Paik. *Quiet Odyssey: A Pioneer Korean Woman in America.* Ed. and introd. Sucheng Chan. Seattle: University of Washington Press, 1990. Excerpt "A Korean/Californian Girlhood" in *California History* 67.1 (March 1988), pp. 42–55.

McCunn, Ruthanne Lum. *Thousand Pieces of Gold.* San Francisco: Design Enterprises of San Francisco, 1981.

Mirikitani, Janice. *Shedding Silence.* Berkeley, CA: Celestial Arts, 1987.

Mukherjee, Bharati. *"The Middleman" and Other Stories.* New York: Grove, 1988.

———. *Jasmine.* New York: Grove, 1989.

Ng, Fae Myenne. *Bone.* New York: Hyperion, 1993.

Ota, Shelley Ayame Nishimura. *Upon Their Shoulders.* New York: Exposition Press, 1951.

Ronyoung, Kim. *Clay Walls.* New York: Permanent Press, 1986.

Sone, Monica, *Nisei Daughter.* Boston: Little, Brown, 1953; Seattle: University of Washington Press, 1979.

Song, Cathy. *Picture Bride.* New Haven: Yale University Press, 1983.

Sui Sin Far. *Mrs. Spring Fragrance.* Chicago: A. C. McClurg, 1912.

Tan, Amy. *The Joy Luck Club.* New York: G. P. Putnam's Sons, 1989.

———. *Kitchen God's Wife.* New York: Putnam, 1991.

Uchida, Yoshiko. *Desert Exile: The Uprooting of a Japanese American Family.* Seattle: University of Washington Press, 1982.

———. *Picture Bride: A Novel.* Flagstaff, AZ: Northland Press, 1987.

Wong, Jade Snow. *Fifth Chinese Daughter.* New York: Harper, 1945.

Yamada, Mitsuye. *Desert Run: Poems and Stories.* Latham, NY: Kitchen Table Women of Color Press, 1988.

Yamamoto, Hisaye. *Seventeen Syllables and Other Stories.* Latham, NY: Kitchen Table Women of Color Press, 1988.

Yamashita, Karen Tei. *Through the Arc of the Rain Forest.* Minneapolis: Coffee House Press, 1990.

Books/Theses/Dissertation

Asis, Maruja M. "Immigrant Women and Occupational Changes: A Comparison of Filipino and Korean Women in Transition." Ph.D. dissertation, Bowling Green State University, 1989.

Brainard, Cecilia Manguerra. *Philippine Women in America: Essays by Cecilia Manguerra Brainard.* Foreword Bienvenido N. Santos. Quezon City, Philippines: New Day Publishers, 1991.

Chan, Sucheng. *Asian Americans: An Interpretive History.* Boston: Twayne Publishers, 1991.

Cheung King-Kok. *Articulate Silences: Hisaye Yamamoto, Maxine Hong Kingston, Joy Kogawa.* Ithaca, NY: Cornell University Press, 1993.

Glenn, Evelyn Nakano. *Issei, Nisei, War Bride: Three Generations of Japanese American Women in Domestic Service.* Philadelphia: Temple University Press, 1986.

Hom, Alice Yee. "Family Matters: A Historical Study of the Asian Pacific Lesbian Network." M.A. thesis, University of California, Los Angeles, 1992.

Ito, Kazuo. *Issei: A History of Japanese Immigrants in North America.* Trans. Shinichiro Nakamura, Jean S. Gerard. Seattle: Executive Committee for the Publication of *Issei*, 1973.

Kikumura, Akemi. *Through Harsh Winters: The Life of a Japanese Immigrant Woman.* Novato, CA: Chandler & Sharp, 1981.

Kim, Elaine H., with Janice Otani. *With Silk Wings: Asian American Women at Work.* San Francisco: Asian Women United of California, 1983.

Ling, Amy. *Between Worlds: Women Writers of Chinese Ancestry.* New York: Pergamon Press, 1990.

Nakano, Mei T. *Japanese American Women: Three Generations, 1890–1990.* Berkeley, CA: Mina Press Publishing, 1990.

Song, Young In. "Battered Korean Women in Urban America: The Relationship of Cultural Conflict to Wife Abuse." Ph.D. dissertation, Ohio State University, 1986.

Takaki, Ronald. *Strangers from a Different Shore: A History of Asian Americans.* Boston: Little, Brown, 1989.

Vallangca, Caridad Concepcion. *The Second Wave: Pinay & Pinoy (1945–1960).* Ed. Jody Bytheway Larson. San Francisco: Strawberry Hill Press, 1987.

Yung, Judy. *Chinese Women of America: A Pictorial History.* Seattle: Chinese Culture Foundation of San Francisco and University of Washington Press, 1986.

Journal/Anthology Articles

Anand, Asha Angela. "Domestic Violence: Cases Reported of its Occurrence in South Asian Immigrant Families." *South Asia Bulletin* 2.1 (March 1982), pp. 84–89.

Chai, Alice Yun. "Korean Women in Hawaii, 1903–1945." In *Women in New Worlds: Historical Perspectives on the Wesleyan Tradition,* ed. Hilah F. Thomas and Rosemary Skinner Keller. Nashville: Abingdon, 1981, pp. 328–44.

————. "Toward a Holistic Paradigm for Asian American Women's Studies: A Synthesis of Feminist Scholarship and Women of Color's Feminist Politics." *Women Studies International Forum* 8.1 (1985), pp. 59–66.

————. "Picture Brides: Feminist Analysis of Life Histories of Hawaii's Early Immigrant Women from Japan, Okinawa, and Korea." In *Seeking Common Ground: Multidisciplinary Studies of Immigrant Women in the United States,* ed. Donna Gabaccia. Westport, CT: Greenwood Press, 1992, pp. 123–38.

Chan, Sucheng. "The Exclusion of Chinese Women, 1870–1943." In *Entry Denied: Exclusion and the Chinese Community in America, 1882–1943.* ed. Sucheng Chan. Philadelphia: Temple University Press, 1991, pp. 94–146.

Cheung King-Kok. "The Woman Warrior versus the Chinaman Pacific: Must a Chinese American Critic Choose Between Feminism and Heroism?" In *Conflicts in Feminism,* eds. Marianne Hirsch and Evelyn Fox Keller. New York: Routledge, 1990, pp. 234–51.

Chu, Judy. "Asian American Women's Studies Courses: A Look Back at Our Beginnings." *Frontiers* 8.3 (1986), pp. 96–101.

Chung, Sue Fawn. "Gue Gim Wah: Pioneering Chinese American Woman of Nevada." In *History and Humanities: Essays in Honor of Wilbur S. Shepperson,* ed. Francis X. Hartigan. Reno: University of Nevada Press, 1989, pp. 45–80.

Davidson, Lani. "Women Refugees: Special Needs and Programs." *Journal of Refugee Resettlement* 1.3 (May 1981), pp. 16–26.

Gee, Emma. "Issei Women." In *Counterpoint: Perspectives on Asian America,* ed. Emma Gee. Los Angeles: Asian American Studies Center, University of California, 1976, pp. 359–64. Originally published in *Asian Women.* Berkeley: Asian American Studies, University of California, 1971, pp. 8–15.

Glenn, Evelyn Nakano. "The Dialectics of Wage Work: Japanese-American Women and Domestic Service, 1905–1940." *Feminist Studies* 6.3 (September 1980), pp. 432–71.

————. "Occupational Ghettoization: Japanese American Women and Domestic Service, 1905–1970." *Ethnicity* 8.4 (December 1981); pp. 352–86.

————. "Racial Ethnic Women's Labor: The Intersection of Race, Gender and Class Oppression." *Review of Radical Political Economics* 17.3 (1986), pp. 86–108.

Goodman, Catherine Chase. "The Caregiving Roles of Asian American Women." *Journal of Women and Aging* 2.1 (1990), pp. 109–20.

H., Pamela. "Asian American Lesbians: An Emerging Voice in the Asian American Community." In *Making Waves: An Anthology of Writings By and About Asian American Women,* ed. Asian Women United of California. Boston: Beacon Press, 1989, pp. 282–90.

Hirata, Lucie Cheng. "Chinese Immigrant Women in Nineteenth-Century America." In *Women of America: A History,* eds. Carol Ruth Berkin and Mary Beth Norton. Boston: Houghton, 1979, pp. 223–44.

————. "Free, Indentured, Enslaved; Chinese Prostitutes in Nineteenth Century America." *Signs: Journal of Women in Culture and Society* 5.1 (1979), pp. 3–29.

Hirayama, Kasumi K. "Evaluating Effects of the Employment of Vietnamese Refugee Wives on their Family Roles and Mental Health." *California Sociologist* 5.1 (December 1982), pp. 96–110.

Hori, Joan. "Japanese Prostitution in Hawaii during the Immigration Period." *Hawaiian Journal of History* 15 (1981), pp. 113–23.

Ichioka, Yuji. "*Ameyuki-san.* Japanese Prostitutes in Nineteenth Century America." *Amerasia Journal* 4.1 (1977), pp. 1–22.

————. "*Amerika Nadeshiko:* Japanese Immigrant Women in the United States, 1900–1924." *Pacific Historical Review* 49.2 (May 1980), pp. 339–57.

Kaw, Eugenia. "Medicalization of Racial Features: Asian American Women and Cosmetic Surgery." *Medical Anthropology Quarterly* 7.1 (March 1993), pp. 74–89.

Kibria, Nazli. "Power, Patriarchy and Gender Conflict in the Vietnamese Immigrant Community." *Gender & Society* 4 (1990), pp. 9–24.

Kim, Bok-Lim C. "Asian Wives of U.S. Servicemen: Women in Shadows." *Amerasia Journal* 4.1 (March 1977), pp. 91–115.

Kim, Elaine H. " 'Such Opposite Creatures': Men and Women in Asian American Literature." *Michigan Quarterly Review* 29 (December 1990), pp. 68–93.

Lee, Patricia. "Asian Immigrant Women & HERE Local 2." *Labor Research Review* 11 (1988), pp. 29–38.

Ling, Amy. "Creating One's Self: The Eaton Sisters." In *Reading the Literatures of Asian America,* ed. Shirley Geok-lin Lim and Amy Ling. Philadelphia: Temple University Press, 1992, pp. 305–18.

Ling, Susie H. "The Mountain Movers: Asian American Women's Movement in Los Angeles." *Amerasia Journal* 15.1 (1989), pp. 51–67.

Loo, Chalsa, and Paul Ong. "Slaying Dragons with a Sewing Needle: Feminist Issues for Chinatown's Women." *Berkeley Journal of Sociology* 27 (1982), pp. 77–88.

Mar, Don. "Chinese Immigrant Women and the Ethnic Labor Market." *Critical Perspectives of Third World America* 2.1 (September 1984), pp. 62–71.

Matsumoto, Valerie. "Desperately Seeking 'Deirdre': Gender Roles, Multicultural Relations, and Nisei Women Writers of the 1930s." *Frontiers. Journal of Women's Studies* 12.1 (1991), pp. 19–32.

Mau, Rosalind Y. "Barriers to Higher Education for Asian/Pacific-American Females." *The Urban Review* 22.3 (1990), pp. 183–97.

Mazumdar, Sucheta. "A Woman-Centered Perspective on Asian American History." In *Making Waves: An Anthology of Writings By and About Asian American Women*, ed. Asian Women United of California. Boston: Beacon Press, 1989, pp. 1–22.

Nomura, Gail M. "*Tsugiki*, A Grafting: A History of a Japanese Pioneer Woman in Washington State." *Women's Studies* 14.1 (1987), pp. 15–37.

Peffer, George Anthony. "From Under the Sojourner's Shadow: A Historiographical Study of Chinese Female Immigration to America, 1852–1882." *Journal of American Ethnic History* 11.3 (Spring 1992), pp. 41–67.

Peterson, Sally. "Translating Experience and the Reading of a Story Cloth." *Journal of American Folklore* 101.399 (1988), pp. 6–22.

Scott, George M., Jr. "To Catch or Not to Catch a Thief: A Case of Bride Theft Among the Lao Hmong Refugees in Southern California." *Ethnic Groups* 7 (1988), pp. 137–51.

Song, Young I. "Single Asian American Women as a Result of Divorce: Depressive Affect and Changes in Social Support." *Journal of Divorce and Remarriage* 14.3–4 (1991), pp. 219–30.

Southard, Naomi, and Rita Nakashima Brock. "The Other Half of the Basket: Asian American Women and the Search for a Theological Home." *Journal of Feminist Studies in Religion* 3 (Fall 1987), pp. 135–50.

Sunoo, Sonia S. "Korean Women Pioneers of the Pacific Northwest." *Oregon Historical Quarterly* 79.1 (March 1978), pp. 50–63.

Tajima, Renee E. "Lotus Blossoms Don't Bleed: Images of Asian Women." In *Making Waves: An Anthology of Writings By and About Asian American Women*, ed. Asian Women United of California;. Boston: Beacon Press, 1989, pp. 308–17.

Takaki, Ronald. "They Also Came. The Migration of Chinese and Japanese Women to Hawaii and the Continental United States." *Chinese America: History and Perspectives* (1991), pp. 3–19.

Thaker, Suvarna. "The Quality of Life of Asian Indian Women in the Motel Industry." *South Asia Bulletin* 2.1 (March 1982), pp. 68–73.

Thompson, Janice L. "Exploring Gender and Culture with Khmer Refugee Women: Reflections on Participatory Feminist Research." *Advances in Nursing Science* 13.3 (March 1991), pp. 30–48.

Wong, Linda. "The Esther Lau Trial: A Case Study of Oppression and Sexism." *Amerasia Journal* 3 (1975), pp. 16–26.

Wong, Morrison G., and Charles Hirschman. "Labor Force Participation and Socioeconomic Attainment of Asian American Women." *Sociological Perspectives* 26.4 (October 1983), pp. 423–46.

Wong, Sau-ling Cynthia. "Ethnicizing Gender: An Exploration of Sexuality as Sign in Chinese Immigrant Literature." In *Reading the Literatures of Asian America*, eds. Shirley Geok-lin Lim and Amy Ling. Philadelphia: Temple University Press, 1992, pp. 111–29.

Woo, Deborah. "The Socioeconomic Status of Asian American Women in the Labor Force: An Alternative View." *Sociological Perspectives* 28.3 (July 1985), pp. 307–38.

Yang, Eun Sik. "Korean Women of America: From Subordination to Partnership, 1903–1930." *Amerasia Journal* 11.2 (1984), pp. 1–28.

Latinas

Compiled by Vicki L. Ruiz

Anthologies

Acosta-Belen, Edna, ed. *The Puerto Rican Woman.* 2nd ed. New York: Praeger, 1986.

Alarcón, Norma, Ana Castillo, and Cherríe Moraga, eds. "The Sexuality of Latinas" Special issue of *Third Woman* 4 (1989).

Armitage, Sue and Elizabeth Jameson, eds. *The Women's West.* Norman: University of Oklahoma Press, 1987.

Cortés, Carlos, ed. *Cuban Exiles in the United States.* New York: Arno Press, 1980.

———, ed. *Regional perspectives of the Puerto Rican Experience.* New York: Arno Press, 1980.

de la Torre, Adela and Beatríz Pesquera. *Building With Our Hands:* New Directions in Chicana Studies. Berkeley: University of California Press, 1993.

Del Castillo, Adelaida. *Between Borders.* Los Angeles: Floricanto Press, 1989.

Jensen, Joan and Darlis Miller. *New Mexico Women: Intercultural Perspectives.* Albuquerque: University of New Mexico Press, 1986.

López, Adalberto, ed. *The Puerto Ricans, Their History, Culture and Society.* Cambridge; MAL Schenkman Publishing Co., 1980.

Melville, Margarita B., ed. *Mexicanas at Work in the United States.* Houston: Mexican American Studies Center, University of Houston, 1988.

Melville, Margarita B., ed. *Twice a Minority: Mexican-American Women.* St. Louis: C. V. Mosby Co., 1980.

Mohanty, Chandra Talpade, Ann Russo, and Lourdes Torres, eds. *Third World Women and the Politics of Feminism.* Bloomington: Indiana University Press, 1991.

Mora, Magdelena and Adelaida Del Castillo, eds. *Mexican Women in the United States: Struggles Past and Present.* Los Angeles: University of California, Chicano Studies Publications, 1980.

National Association for Chicano Studies, *Voces de la Mujer.* Austin: University of Texas Mexican American Studies Center, 1986.

"Oral History and Puerto Rican Women." Special issue of *Oral History Review,* 16:2 (Fall 1988).

Rodríguez, Clara, Virginia Sánchez Korrol, and José Albers, eds. *The Puerto Rican Struggle: Essays on Survival in the United States.* Maplewood, NH: Waterfront Press, 1984.

Ruiz, Vicki L., ed. "Las Obreras: The Politics of Work and Family." Special double issue of *Aztlán* 20:1–2 (1993).

———. and Susan Tiano, eds. *Women on the United States-Mexico Border: Responses to Change.* Westminster, MA: Allen and Unwin, 1987; reprint ed. Westview Press, 1991.

Sánchez, Rosaura and Rosa Martínez Cruz, eds. *Essays on La Mujer.* Los Angeles: University of California Chicano Studies Publications, 1977.

Schlissel, Lillian, Vicki L. Ruiz, and Janice Monk, eds. *Western Women: Their Land, Their Lives.* Albuquerque: University of New Mexico Press, 1988.

Sutton, Constance R. and Elsa M. Chaney, eds. *Caribbean Life in New York City: Sociocultural Dimensions.* New York: Center for Migration Studies of New York, 1987.

Fiction/Memoir/Poetry

Alvarez, Julia. *How the Garcia Girls Lost Their Accents.* Chapel Hill: Algonquin Books of Chapel Hill, 1991.

Anzaldúa, Gloria. *Borderlands/La Frontera.* San Francisco: Spinsters/Aunt Lute Book Company, 1987.

————. *Making Face, Making Soul/Haciendo Caras*. San Francisco: An Aunt Lute Foundation Book, 1990.

Augenbraum, Harold and Illan Stevens. *Growing Up Latino: Memoirs and Stories*. Boston: Houghton Mifflin, 1993.

Castañeda, Antonia, Tomás Ybarra-Frausto, and Joseph Somers. *Literature Chicana*. Englewood Cliffs: Prentice-Hall, 1972.

Castillo, Ana. *So Far From God*. New York: W. W. Norton, 1993.

Chávez, Denise. *The Last of the Menu Girls*. Houston: Arte Público Press, 1986.

Cisneros, Sandra. *House on Mango Street*. Houston: Arte Público Press, 1985.

————. *Woman Hollering Creek*. New York: Random House, 1991.

Corpi, Lucha. *Delta's Song*. Houston: Arte Público Press, 1989.

————. *Eulogy for a Brown Angel*. Houston: Arte Público Press, 1992.

Curiel, Barbara Brinson. *Speak To Me From Dreams*. Berkeley: Third Woman Press, 1989.

de Hoyos, Angela. *Selected Poems/selecciones*. San Antonio: Dezkalazo Press, 1979.

García, Cristina. *Dreaming in Cuban*. New York: Knopf, 1992.

Gaspar de Alba, Alicia. "Excerpts from the Sapphic Diary of Sor Juana Inés de la Cruz." *Frontiers*. 12:3, pp. 171–179.

Gómez, Alma, Cherríe Moraga, and Mariana Romo Carmona, eds. *Cuentos: Stories by Latinas*. New York: Kitchen Table Women of Color Press, 1983.

Gutiérrez, Ramón and Genaro Padilla. *Recovering the U.S. Hispanic Literary Heritage*. Houston: Arte Público Press, 1993.

López-Medina, Sylvia. *Cantora*. Albuquerque: University of New Mexico Press, 1992.

Mohr, Nicholasa. *Rituals of Survival: A Woman's Portfolio*. Houston: Arte Púlico Press, 1985.

Mora, Pat. *Borders*. Houston: Arte Público Press, 1986.

————. *Chants*. Houston: Arte Público Press, 1984.

————. *Nepantla: Essays from the Land in the Middle*. Albuquerque: University of New Mexico Press, 1993.

Moraga, Cherríe. *Giving up the Ghost*. Los Angeles: West End Press, 1987.

————. *Loving in the War Years*. Boston: South End Press, 1983.

————. and Anzaldúa, Gloria, eds. *This Bridge Called My Back: Writings by Radical Women of Color*. Watertown, MA: Persephone Press, 1981.

Morales, Aurora Levins. *Getting Home Alive*. Ithaca: Firebrand Books, 1986.

Ponce, Mary Helen. *Hoyt Street*. Albuquerque: University of New Mexico Press, 1993.

Ortiz, Judith Cofer. *The Line of the Sun: A Novel*. Athens, GA: University of Georgia Press, 1989.

Quiñonez, Naomi. *Sueño de Colibri/Hummingbird Dream*. Los Angeles: West End Press, 1985.

Rebolledo, Tey Diana, Erlinda Gonzáles-Berry, and Teresa Márquez. *Las Mujeres Hablan: An Anthology of Nuevo Mexicana Writers*. Albuquerque: El Norte Publications, 1988.

Rebolledo, Tey Diana and Eliana S. Rivera. *Infinite Divisions: Anthology of Chicana Literature*. Tucson: University of Arizona Press, 1993.

Trujillo, Carla, ed. *Chicana Lesbians: The Girls Our Mothers Warned Us About*. Berkeley: Third Woman Press, 1991.

Villanueva, Alma Luz. *The Ultraviolet Sky*. Tempe: Bilingual Press, 1988.

Zamora, Bernice. Restless Serpents. Menlo Park: Diseños Literarios, 1974.

Books/Theses/Dissertations

Allen, Ruth. *The Labor of Women in the Production of Cotton*. Reprint edition. New York: Arno Press, 1975.

Alvarez, Robert, Jr. *Familia: Migration and Adaptation in Baja and Alta California, 1880–1975*. Berkeley: University of California Press, 1987.

Año Nuevo Kerr, Louise. "The Chicano Experience in Chicago: 1920–1970." Ph.D. dissertation, University of Illinois, Chicago Circle, 1976.

Blackwelder, Julia Kirk. *Women of the Depression: Caste and Culture in San Antonio, 1929–1939*, College Station: Texas A&M Press, 1984.

Blea, Irene Isabel. "Bessemer: A Sociological Perspective of a Chicano Barrio." Ph.D. dissertation, University of Colorado, Boulder, 1980.

Boone, Margaret S. *Capital Cubans: Refugee Adaptations in Washington, D.C.* New York: AMS Press, 1989.

Buss, Fran Leeper. *Forged under the Sun/Forjada bajo el sol*. Ann Arbor: University of Michigan Press, 1993.

Cabeza de Baca, Fabiola. *We Fed Them Cactus*. Albuquerque: University of New Mexico Press, 1954.

Camarillo, Albert. *Chicanos in California*. San Francisco: Boyd and Fraser, 1984.

Castañeda, Antonia I. "Presidarias y Pobladoras: Spanish-Mexican Women in Frontier Monterey, Alta California, 1770–1821." Ph.D. dissertation, Stanford University, 1990.

Cortera, Marta. *The Chicana Feminist*. Austin: Information Systems Development, 1977.

———. *Diosa y Hembra: The History and Heritage of Chicanas in the U.S.* Austin: Information Systems Development, 1976.

Craver, Rebecca McDowell. *The Impact of Intimacy: Mexican-Anglo Intermarriage in New Mexico, 1821–1846*. El Paso: Texas Western Press, 1982.

Davis, Marilyn. *Mexican Voices/American Dreams: An Oral History of Mexican Immigration to the United States*. New York: Henry Holt and Company, 1990.

Deutsch, Sarah. *No Separate Refuge. Culture, Class and Gender on an Anglo-Hispanic Frontier in the American Southwest, 1880–1940*. New York: Oxford University Press, 1987.

Doran, Terry, Janet Satterfield, and Chris State. *A Road Well-Traveled: Three Generations of Cuban American Women*. Fort Wayne, ID: Latin American Educational Center, 1988.

Elasasser, Nan, Kyle MacKenzie, and Yvonne Tixier y Vigil. *Las Mujeres: Conversations with the Hispanic Community*. Old Westbury: Feminist Press, 1980.

Gamio, Manuel. *The Life Story of the Mexican Immigrant*. Chicago: University of Chicago Press, 1931; reprint New York: Dover Publications, 1971.

Gil, Vincent Edward. "The Personal Adjustment and Acculturation of Cuban Immigrants in Los Angeles." Ph.D. dissertation, University of California, Los Angeles, 1976.

González, Deena J. *Refusing the Favor: Spanish-Mexican Women of Santa Fé, 1820–1880."* New York: Oxford University Press, forthcoming.

Griffith, Beatrice. *American Me*. Boston: 1948; reprint Westport: Greenwood Press.

Griswold del Castillo, Richard. *La Familia: The Mexican-American Family In The Urban Southwest*. Notre Dame: University of Notre Dame Press, 1984.

Guerin-Gonzáles, Camille. *Mexican Workers and American Dreams: Immigration, Repatriation, and California Farm Labor, 1900–1939*. New Brunswick: Rutgers University Press, forthcoming.

Gutiérrez, Ramón A. *When Jesus Came, the Corn Mothers Went Away: Power and Sexuality in New Mexico, 1500–1846*. Stanford: Stanford University Press, 1990.

Infante, Isa María. "Politicization of Immigrant Women from Puerto Rico and the Dominican Republic." Ph.D. dissertation, University of California, Riverside, 1977.

Kingsolver, Barbara. *Holding The Line: Women in the Great Arizona Mine Strike of 1983*. Ithaca: ILR Press, 1989.

Lamphere, Louise, Patricia Zavella, Felipe Gonzales, with Peter Evans. *Sunbelt Working Mothers: Reconciling Family and Factory*. Ithaca: Cornell University Press, 1993.

MacCorkle, Lyn. *Cubans in the U.S.: A Bibliography for Research, 1960–1983*. Westport, CN: Greenwood Press, 1984.

Martin, Patricia Preciado. *Songs My Mother Sang To Me: An Oral History of Mexican American Women*. Tucson: University of Arizona Press, 1992.

Martin, Patricia Preciado and Louis Bernal. *Images and Conversations: Mexican-Americans Recall A Southwestern Past*. Tucson: University of Arizona Press, 1983.

Martínez, Elizabeth. *500 Years of Chicano History in Pictures*. Albuquerque: Southwest Organizing Project, 1991.

Mirandé, Alfredo and Evangelina Enríquez. *La Chicana: The Mexican-American Woman*. Chicago: University of Chicago Press, 1979.

Monroy, Douglas Guy. "Mexicanos in Los Angeles, 1930–1941: An Ethnic Group In Relation To Class Forces." Ph.D. dissertation, University of California, Los Angeles, 1978.

Orozco, Cynthia E. "The Origins of the League of United Latin American Citizens (LULAC) and the Mexican American Civil Rights Movement in Texas with an Analysis of Women's Political Participation in a Gendered Context, 1910–1929." Ph.D. dissertation, University of California, Los Angeles, 1992.

Pedraza-Bailey, Sylvia. *Political and Economic Migrants in America: Cubans and Mexicans*. Austin: University of Texas Press, 1985.

Pesquera, Beatríz. "Work and Family: A Comparative Analysis of Professional, Clerical and Blue Collar Chicana Workers." Ph.D. dissertation, University of California, Berkeley, 1985.

Rodríguez, Clara. *The Ethnic Queue in the United States: The Case of Puerto Ricans*. San Francisco: R and E Research Associates, 1974.

———. *Puerto Ricans: Born in the U.S.A.* Westminster, MA: Unwin and Human, 1989.

Rodríguez, Gregorita. *Singing For My Echo: Memories of a Native Healer of Santa Fe*. Santa Fe: Ocean Tree Books, 1988.

Rose, Margaret. "Women in the United Farm Workers: A Study of Chicana and Mexicana Participation in a Labor Union, 1950–1980." Ph.D. dissertation, University of California, Los Angeles, 1988.

Ruiz, Vicki L. *Cannery Women, Cannery Lives: Mexican Women, Unionization, and the California Food Processing Industry, 1939–1950*. Albuquerque: University of New Mexico Press, 1987.

Sánchez, George J. *Becoming Mexican American: Ethnicity, Culture, and Identity in Chicano Los Angeles, 1900–1945*. New York: Oxford University Press, 1993.

Sánchez-Walker, Marjorie. "Woven Within My Grandmother's Braid: The Biography of a Mexican Immigrant Woman, 1898–1982." M.A. thesis, Washington State University, 1993.

Strachwitz, Chris with James Nicolopulos, eds. *Lydia Mendoza: A Family Autobiography*. Houston: Arte Público Press, 1993.

Segura, Denise. "Chicana and Mexican Immigrant Women in the Labor Market: A Study of Occupational Mobility and Stratification." Ph.D. dissertation, University of California, Berkeley, 1986.

Sheridan, Thomas. *Los Tucsonenses*. Tucson: University of Arizona Press, 1986.

Taylor, Paul S. *Mexican Labor in the United States*. 2 vols. Berkeley: University of California Press, 1930.

Trotter, Robert T. and Juan Antonio Chavira. *Curandersimo*. Athens, GA: University of Georgia Press, 1981.

Tuck, Ruth. *Not With The Fist*. New York: Harcourt, Brace and Co., 1946; reprint New York: Arno Press, 1974.

Williams, Norma. *The Mexican American Family: Tradition and Change*. Boston: G.K. Hall, 1990.

Zavella, Patricia. *Women's Work and Chicano Families: Cannery Workers of the Santa Clara Valley*. Ithaca: Cornell University Press, 1987.

Journal/Anthology Articles

Arguelles, Lourdes. "Undocumented Female Labor in the United States Southwest: An Essay on Migration, Consciousness, Oppression and Struggle." In *Between Borders*, ed. Adelaida Del Castillo. Los Angeles: Floricanto Press, 1989, pp. 299–312.

Baca Zinn, Maxine. "Mexican-American Women in the Social Sciences." *Signs* 8:2 (1982), pp. 259–72.

———. "Political Familialism: Toward Sex Role Equality in Chicano Families." *Aztlán* 8:8 (1975), pp. 13–26.

Baer, Barbara and Glenna Matthews. "The Women of the Boycott." In *America's Working Women: A Documentary History—1600 to the Present*, ed. Rosalyn Baxandall, Linda Gordon, and Susan Reverby. New York: Vintage Books, 1976, pp. 363–372.

Benmayor, Rina. "Testimony, Action Research, and Empowerment: Puerto Rican Women and Popular Education." In *Women's Words: The Feminist Practice of Oral History*, eds. Sherna Berger Gluck and Daphne Patai. New York: Routledge, 1991, pp. 159–174.

Boone, Margaret S. "The Use of Traditional Concepts in the Development of New Urban Roles: Cuban Women in the United States." In *A World of Women*, ed. Erika Bourguignon. New York: Praeger, 1980, pp. 236–267.

Cantarow, Ellen, "Jessie López de la Cruz." In *Moving the Mountain: Women Working for Social Change*, ed. Ellen Cantarow. Old Westbury: Feminist Press, 1980, pp. 94–151.

Casal, Lourdes and Andrés R. Hernández. "Cubans in the United States: A Survey of the Literature." *Cuban Studies/Estudios Cubanos*, 5:2 (July 1975), pp. 25–51.

Castañeda, Antonia I. "The Political Economy of Nineteenth Century Stereotypes of Californianas." In *Between The Conquests*, ed. Michael R. Ornelas. Iowa: Kendall Hunt Publishing, 1991, pp. 87–105.

Castañeda, Antonia I. "Spanish and English Speaking Women on Worldwide Frontiers: A Discussion of the Migration of Women to Alta California and New Zealand." In *Western Women: Their Land, Their Lives*, eds. Lillian Schlissel, Vicki L. Ruiz, and Janice Monk. Albuquerque: University of New Mexico Press, 1988, pp. 283–300.

Chabram-Dernersesian, Angie. "I Throw Punches for My Race, but I Don't Want to Be a Man: Writing Us—Chica-nos (Girl, US)/Chicanas—into the Movement Script." In *Cultural Studies, 81–95*, eds. Lawrence Grossberg, Cary Nelson, and Paula Treichler. New York: Routledge, 1992, pp. 81–95.

Durón, Clementina. "Mexican Women and Labor Conflict in Los Angeles: the ILGWU Dressmakers; Strike of 1933." *Aztlan* 15 (Spring 1989), pp. 145–162.

Franzen, Trisha. "Differences and Identities: Feminism and the Albuquerque Lesbian Community." *Signs* 18:4 (Summer 1993), pp. 891–906.

García, Mario T. "The Chicana in American History: The Mexican Women of El Paso, 1880–1920: A Case Study." *Pacific Historical Review* 49:2 (May, 1980), pp. 315–37.

Gaspar de Alba, Alicia. "Tortillerismo: Work by Chicana Lesbians." *Signs* 18:4 (Summer 1993), pp. 956–63.

González, Rosalinda M. "Chicanas and Mexican Immigrant Families 1920–1940: Women's Subordination and Family Exploitation." In *Decades of Discontents: The Women's Movement, 1920–1940*, eds. Lois Scharf and Joan Jensen. Westport: Greenwood Press, 1983, pp. 59–83.

González, Yolanda Broyles. "Toward a Re-Vision of Chicano Theatre History: The Women of El Teatro Campesino." In *Making a Spectacle: Feminist Essays on Contemporary Women's Theatre*, ed. Lynda Hart. Ann Arbor: University of Michigan Press, 1989, pp. 209–238.

Gutiérrez, Ramón A. "Community, Patriarchy, and Individualism: The Politics of Chicano History and the Dream of Equality." *American Quarterly* 45:1 (March 1993), pp. 44–72.

———. "Honor, Ideology, Marriage Negotiation and Class-Gender Domination in New Mexico, 1690–1846." *Latin American Perspectives* 12:1 (Winter 1985), pp. 81–104.

Hernández, Inés. "Sara Estela Ramírez." *Legacies* (1989), pp. 13–26.

King, Lourdes Miranda. "Puertorriqueñas in the U.S.: The Impact of Double Discrimination." *Civil Rights Digest* 6:3 (Spring 1974), pp. 20–27.

Korrol, Virginia Sánchez. "On the Other Side of the Ocean: The Work Experiences of Early Puerto Rican Migrant Women." *Caribbean Review* 8:1 (January–March 1979), pp. 22–28.

Miranda, Gloria E. "Hispano-Mexican Childrearing Practices in Pre-American Santa Barbara," *Southern California Historical Quarterly*, 65:4 (Winter 1983), pp. 307–20.

Ortiz, Vilma. "Migration and Employment among Puerto Rican Women." *Latino Studies Journal*, forthcoming.

Prieto, Yolanda. "Cuban Women in New Jersey: Gender Relations and Change." In *Seeking Common Ground: Multidisciplinary Studies of Immigrant Women in the United States*, ed. Donna Gabaccia. Westport: Greenwood Press, 1992, pp. 185–202.

Rich, B. Ruby and Lourdes Arguelles. "Homosexuality, Homophobia, and Revolution: Notes Toward and Understanding of the Cuban Lesbian and Gay Male Experience." *Signs* 9:4, (Summer 1984, Autumn 1985), pp. 683–699, 120–36.

Ruiz, Vicki L. "The Flapper and the Chaperone: Historical Memory Among Mexican American Women." In *Seeking Common Ground: Multidisciplinary Studies of Immigrant Women in the United States*, ed. Donna Gabaccia. Westport: Greenwood Press, 1992, pp. 141–158.

Segura, Denise. "Chicana and Mexican Immigrant Women At Work," *Gender and Society*, 3:1 (March 1989), pp. 37–52.

——— and Pesquera, Beatríz. "Beyond Indifference and Apathy: The Chicana Movement and Chicana Feminist Discourse." *Aztlán* 19:2 (Fall 1988–1990), pp. 69–92.

Sosa, Riddell, Adaljiza. "Chicanas and El Movimiento." *Aztlán*, 5:2 (Spring and Fall 1974), pp. 155–65.

Ybarra, Lea. "When Wives Work: The Impact on the Chicano Family." *Journal of Marriage and the Family* 44:1 (February 1982), pp. 169–78.

Zavella, Patricia. " 'Abnormal Intimacy': The Varying Work Networks of Chicana Cannery Workers." *Feminist Studies*, 11:3 (Fall 1985), pp. 541–57.

———. "Reflections on Diversity among Chicanas." *Frontiers*, 12:2 (1991), pp. 763–85.

Native American Women
Compiled by Annette Reed Crum

Anthologies

Ahenakew, Freda and H.C. Wolfart, eds. *Kohkominawak Otacimowini wawa: Our Grandmothers' Lives As told In Their Own Words*. Saskatoon, Saskatchewan: Fifth House Publishers, 1992.

Albers, Patricia and Beatrice Medicine, eds. *The Hidden Half: Studies of Plains Indian Women*. Washington D.C.: University Press of America, 1983.

Allen, Paula Gunn, ed. *Spider Woman's Granddaughters: Traditional Tales and Contemporary Writing by Native Women*. New York: Ballantine Books, 1989.

Armitage, Susan and Elizabeth Jameson, eds. *The Women's West*. Norman: University of Oklahoma Press, 1987.

Brant, Beth [Degonwadonti] ed. *A Gathering of Spirit, A Collection by North American Indian Women*. Ithaca, NY: Firebrand Books, 1984.

Bruchac, Joseph, ed. *Songs From This Earth On Turtle's Back: Contemporary American Indian Poetry*. New York: The Greenfield Review Press, 1983.

Clifton, James A., ed. *Being and Becoming Indian: Biographical Studies of North American Frontiers*. Chicago: Dorsey Press, 1989.

Etienne, Mona and Eleanor Leacock, eds. *Women and Colonization: Anthropological Perspectives*. New York: Praeger Publishers, 1980.

Green, Rayna, ed. *That's What She Said: Contemporary Poetry and Fiction by Native American Women*. Bloomington: Indiana University Press, 1984.

Lerner, Andrea, ed. *Dancing on the Rim of the World: An Anthology of Contemporary Northwest Native American Writing*. Tucson: University of Arizona Press, 1990.

Lesley, Craig, ed. *Talking Leaves, Contemporary Native American Short Stories: An Anthology*. New York: Bantam Doubleday Dell, 1991.

Niatum, Duane, ed. *Harper's Anthology of Twentieth Century Native American Poetry*. New York: Harper, 1988.

Perreault, Jeanne and Sylvia Vance, eds. *Writing the Circle: Native Women of Western Canada*. Edmonton, Alberta: New West Publishers Limited, 1990.

Roscoe, Will, ed. *Living the Spirit: A Gay American Indian Anthology*. New York: St. Martin's Press, 1988.

Schlissel, Lillian, Vicki L. Ruiz and Janice Monk, eds. *Western Women: Their Land, Their Lives*. Albuquerque: University of New Mexico Press, 1988.

Silman, Janet. *Enough Is Enough: Aboriginal Women Speak Out*. Toronto, Ontario: The Women's Press, 1987.

Spittal, W.G., ed. *Iroquois Women: An Anthology*. Ohsweken, Ont.: Iroqrafts, 1990.

Trafzer, Clifford, ed. *Earth Song, Sky Spirit*. New York: Doubleday, 1993.

Fiction/Memoir/Poetry

Allen, Paula Gunn. *The Woman Who Owned The Shadows*. San Francisco: Spinsters Ink, 1983.

———. *Skins and Bones: Poems 1979–87*. Albuquerque: West End Press, 1988.

Bruchac, Joseph, ed. *Survival This Way: Interview with Native American Poets*. Tucson: University of Arizona Press, 1987.

Burns, Diane. *Riding the One-Eyed Ford*. New York: Contact II, 1981.

Cook-Lynn, Elizabeth. *Then Badger Said This*. Fairfield, WA: Ye Galleon Press, 1983.

————. *The Power of Horses and Other Stories*. New York: Arcade Publishing, 1990.

————, *From the River's Edge, A Novel*. New York: Arcade Publishing, 1991.

Cruickshank, Julie. *Life Lived Like a Story: Life Stories of Three Yukon Native Elders*. Lincoln: University of Nebraska Press, 1990.

Deloria, Ella Cara. *Waterlily*. Lincoln: University of Nebraska Press, 1988.

Erdrich, Louise. *Love Medicine*. New York: Holt and Company, 1984.

————. *Jacklight: Poems*. New York: Holt and Company, 1984.

————. *The Beet Queen*. New York: Holt and Company, 1986.

————. *Tracks*. New York: Holt and Company, 1988.

Glaney, Diane. *Offering: Poetry and Prose*. Duluth MN: Holy Cow!, 1988.

Hale, Janet Cambell. *The Jailing of Cecilia Capture*. New York: Random House, 1985.

————. *Bloodlines, Odyssey of a Native Daughter*. New York: Random House, 1993.

Harjo, Joy. *What Moon Drove Me to This*. Berkeley: Reed and Cannon, 1979.

————. *She Had Some Horses*. New York: Thunder's Mouth Press, 1982.

————. *In Mad Love and War*. Middletown, CT: Wesleyan University Press, 1990.

Hogan, Linda. *Seeing Through the Sun*. Amherst: University of Massachusetts Press, 1985.

————. *Mean Spirit*. New York: Athenaeum, 1990.

Johnson, Emily Pauline. *Flint and Feather: The Complete Poems of Pauline Johnson*. Ontario: Mills, 1972.

Mourning Dove (Hum-ishu-ma). *Cogewea: The Half-Blood*. Lincoln: University of Nebraska Press, 1981 (1927).

Rose, Wendy. *The Halfbreed Chronicles and Other Poems*. Los Angeles: West End Press, 1985.

Silko, Leslie Marmon. *Ceremony*. New York: Viking Press, 1977.

————. *Storyteller*. New York: Richard Seaver, Random House and Grove Books, 1981.

————. *Almanac of the Dead*. New York: Simon and Schuster, 1991.

Swann, Brian and Arnold Krupat, eds. *I Tell You Now: Autobiographical Essays by Native American Writers*. Lincoln: University of Nebraska Press, 1987.

Walters, Anna Lee. *The Sun Is Not Merciful*. Ithaca, NY: Firebrand, 1985.

Whiteman, Roberta Hill. *Star Quilt*. Minneapolis: Holy Cow! Press, 1984.

Zitkala-Sa (Gertrude Bonnin). *Old Indian Legends*. Lincoln: University of Nebraska Press, 1985 (1901).

————. *American Indian Stories*. Lincoln: University of Nebraska Press, 1985 (1921).

Books/Theses/Dissertations

Allen, Elsie. *Pomo Basketmaking: A Supreme Art for the Weaver*, ed. Vinson Brown. Happy Camp, CA: Naturegraph Publishers, Inc., 1972.

Allen, Paula Gunn. *The Sacred Hoop: Recovering the Feminine in American Indian Traditions*. Boston: Beacon Press, 1986.

Bahr, Diana Meyers. *From Mission to Metropolis: Cupeno Indian Women in Los Angeles*. Norman: University of Oklahoma Press, 1993.

Bataille, Gretchen, M. *Native American Women: A Biographical Dictionary*. New York: Garland Publishing, Inc., 1991.

————. and Kathleen Mullen Sands, eds. *American Indian Women: Telling Their Lives*. Lincoln: University of Nebraska Press, 1984.

————. *American Indian Women: A Guide to Research*. New York: Garland Publishing, Inc., 1991.

Barbour, Philip L. *Pocahontas and Her World*. New York: Houghton Mifflin, 1970.

Beck, Peggy V. and Anna L. Walters. *The Sacred Ways of Knowledge, Sources of Life*. Tsaile, AZ: Navajo Community College Press, 1992, (1977).

Bennett, Kay. *Kaibah: Recollections of a Navajo Girlhood*. Los Angeles: Western Lore, 1964.

Boyer, Ruth McDonald and Narcissus Duffy Gayton. *Apache Mothers and Daughters*. Norman: University of Oklahoma Press, 1992.

Brave Bird, Mary (formerly Mary Crow Dog). *Ohitika Woman*. New York: Grove Press Inc., 1993.

Brown, Jennifer S. H. *Strangers In Blood: Fur Trade Families In Indian Country*. Vancouver: University of British Columbia, 1981.

Buchanan, Kimberly Moore. *Apache Women Warriors*. El Paso: Texas Western Press, 1986.

Campbell, Maria. *Halfbreed*. Lincoln: University of Nebraska Press, 1973.

Canfield, Gae Whitney. *Sarah Winnemucca of the Northern Paiutes*. Norman: University of Oklahoma Press, 1983.

Chona, Maria. *Papago Woman*, ed. Ruth Underhill. Prospect Heights, IL: Waveland Press, 1985 (1935).

Clark, Ella Elizabeth and Margot Edmonds. *Sacajawea of the Lewis and Clark Expedition*. Berkeley: University of California Press, 1979.

Colson, Elizabeth, ed. *Autobiographies of Three Pomo Women*. Berkeley: Archelogical Research Facility, Dept. of Archeology, University of California, 1974.

Coltelli, Laura. *Winged Words, American Indian Writers Speak*. Lincoln: University of Nebraska Press, 1990.

Cox, Bruce Alden. *Native People Native Lands: Canadian Indians, Inuit and Metis*. Ottawa: Carleton University Press, 1987.

Crary, Margaret. *Susette La Flesche: Voice of the Omaha Indians*. New York: Hawthorne Press, 1973.

Crow Dog, Mary with Richard Erdoes. *Lakota Woman*. New York: Harper Perennial, 1990.

Cuera, Delphina. *The Autobiography of Delphina Cuero*, ed. Florence Shipek. Menlo Park, CA: Ballena Press, 1991 (1970).

Deer, Ada and R. E. Simon, Jr. *Speaking Out*. Chicago: Children's Press, 1970.

Devens, Carol. *Countering Colonization: Native American Women and Great Lakes Missions, 1630–1900*. Berkeley: University of California Press, 1992.

Foreman, Carolyn Thomas. *Indian Women Chiefs*. Washington, D.C.: Zenger Publishing, 1954.

Green, Norma Kidd. *Iron Eyes' Family: The Children of Joseph La Flesche*. Lincoln: Johnson Publishing Co., 1969.

Green, Rayna. *Native American Women: A Contextual Bibliography*. Bloomington: Indiana University Press, 1983.

Hopkins, Sarah Winnemucca. *Life Among the Piutes: Their Wrongs and Claims*, ed. Mrs. Horace Mann. Bishop, CA: Sierra Media Inc. 1969 (1883).

Howard, Harold P. *Sacajewea*. Norman: University of Oklahoma, 1971.

Hungry Wolf, Beverly. *The Ways of My Grandmothers*. New York: Morrow, 1980.

Hurtado, Albert L. *Indian Survival on the California Frontier*. New Haven: Yale University Press, 1988.

Jones, David. *Sanapia: Commanche Medicine Woman*. New York: Holt, Rinehart and Winston, 1972.

Katz, Jane B. *I Am the Fire of Time: The Voices of Native American Women*. New York: E.P. Dutton, 1977.

———. *The Song Remembers: Self-Portraits of Native Americans in the Arts*. Boston: Houghton Mifflin, 1980.

Kelly, Jane Holden. *Yaqui Women: Contemporary Life Histories*. Lincoln: University of Nebraska Press, 1978.

Leacock, Eleanor Burke. *Myths of Male Dominance: Collected Articles on Women Cross-Culturally*. New York. Monthly Review Press, 1981.

Linderman, Frank B. *Pretty-Shield: Medicine Woman of the Crows*. New York: John Day Co., 1972, originally published as *Red Mother*, 1932.

Lurie, Nancy. *Mountain Wolf Woman, Sister of Crashing Thunder*. Ann Arbor: University of Michigan Press, 1961.

Mankiller, Wilma and Michael Wallis. *Mankiller: A Chief and Her People, An Autobiography by the Principal Chief of the Cherokee Nation*. New York: St. Martin's Press, 1993.

Menchu, Rigoberta. *I, Rigoberta Menchu: An Indian Woman in Guatemala*, ed. Elisabeth Burgos-Debray. New York: Verso, 1984.

Mihesuah, Devon A. *Cultivating the Rosebuds: The Education of Women at the Cherokee Female Seminary, 1851–1909*. Urbana: University of Illinois Press, 1993.

Modesto, Ruby and Guy Mount. *Not For Innocent Ears, Spiritual Traditions of a Desert Cahuilla Medicine Woman*. Arcata, CA: Sweetlight Books, 1980.

Niethammer, Carolyn. *Daughters of the Earth: The Lives and Legends of American Indian Women*. New York: Collier Books, 1977.

Ohoyo Resource Center. *Words of Today's American Indian Women: Ohoyo Makachi*. Wichita Falls, TX: Ohoyo Resource Center, 1981.

Pascoe, Peggy. *Relations of Rescue*. New York: Oxford University Press, 1990.

Peterson, Jacqueline L. "The People In Between. Indian-White Marriage and the Generation of a Metis Society and Culture in the Great Lakes Region, 1680–1830." Ph.D. dissertation, University of Illinois, 1981.

Peterson, Susan. *The Living Tradition of Maria Martinez*. Tokyo: Kodanska International, 1977.

Pitseolak, P. *Pictures Out of My Life*. New York: Oxford University Press, 1971.

Potts, Marie. *The Northern Maidu*. Happy Camp, CA: Naturegraph, 1977.

Powers, Marla N. Oglala. *Women, Myth, Ritual, and Reality*. Chicago: University of Chicago Press, 1986.

Red Horse, John, August Shattuck, and Fred Hoffman. *The American Indian Family: Strengths and Stresses*. Isleta, NM: American: American Indian Social Research and Development Associates, 1981.

Reyer, Carolyn. *Cante ohitika Win (Brave-hearted Women): Images of Lakota Women from the Pine Ridge Reservation, South Dakota*. Vermillion: University of South Dakota Press, 1991.

Rubinstein, Charlotte Streifer. *American Women Artists: From Early Indian Time to the Present*. Boston: G.K. Hall and Company, 1982.

Spicer, Edward H. *People of Pascua*, eds. Kathleen M. Sands and Rosamond B. Spicer. Tucson: University of Arizona Press, 1988.

Stedman, Raymond William. *Shadows of the Indian, Stereotypes in American Culture*. Norman: University of Oklahoma Press, 1984.

Stewart, Irene. *A Voice In Her Tribe: A Navajo Woman's Own Story*. Socorro, NM: Ballena Press, 1980.

Stockel, H. Henrietta. *Women of the Apache Nation*. Reno: University of Nevada Press, 1991.

St. Pierre, Mark. *Madonna Swan, A Lakota Woman's Story*. Norman: University of Oklahoma Press, 1991.

Thompson, Lucy (Che-na wah Weitch-ah-wah). *To The American Indian: Reminiscences of a Yurok Woman*. Berkeley: Heyday Books, 1991 (1916).

Udell, Louise, ed. *Me and Mine: The Life Story of Helen Sekaquaptewa*. Tucson: University of Arizona Press, 1969.

Van Kirk, Sylvia. *Many Tender Ties: Women in Fur-Trade Society, 1670–1870*. Norman: University of Oklahoma Press, 1980.

Welch, Deborah. "An American Indian Leader: The Story of Gertrude Bonnin, 1876–1939." Ph.D. dissertation, University of Wyoming, 1985.

Qoyawayma, Polingaysi (Elizabeth White). *No Turning Back, A Hopi Indian Woman's Struggle to Live in Two Worlds*, ed. Vada F. Carlson. Albuquerque: University of New Mexico Press, 1964.

Journal/Anthology Articles

Albers, Patricia and William James. "Illusion and Illumination: Visual Images of American Indian Women in the West." In *The Women's West*, eds. Sue Armitage and Elizabeth Jameson. Norman: University of Oklahoma Press, 1987, pp. 35–50.

Allen, Paula Gunn, ed. "Special Issue: Native Women of New Mexico." *A Journal of Contemporary Literature* 3.2 (Fall 1978).

———. "Beloved Women: Lesbians in American Indian Culture." *Conditions* 7 (1981), pp. 67–87.

Anderson, Karen. "Commodity Exchange and Subordination: Montagnais-Naskapi and Huron Women, 1600–1650." *Signs: Journal of Women in Culture and Society* 11.1 (Fall 1985), pp. 48–62.

Anderson, Robert. "The Northern Cheyenne War Mothers." *Anthropological Quarterly* 29.3 (1956), pp. 82–90.

Bates, Craig D. "Dorothy Stanley, 1924–1990." *News From Native California* 5.1 (November/January 1990–91), pp. 6–8.

Blackwood, Evelyn. "Sexuality and Gender in Certain Native American Tribes: The Case of Cross-Gender Females." *Signs: Journal of Women in Culture and Society* 10 (1984), pp. 27–42.

Brady, Victoria, Sarah Crome and Lyn Reese. "Resist! Survival Tactics of Indian Women." *California History* 63 (Spring 1984), pp. 140–151.

Brown, Judith K. "Iroquois Women: An Ethnohistorical Note." In *Toward An Anthropology of Women*, ed. Rayna R. Reiter. New York: Monthly Review Press, 1975, pp. 235–251.

Buckley, Thomas. "Menstruation and the Power of Yurok Women: Methodology in Cultural Reconstruction." *American Ethnologist* 9.1 (1982), pp. 47–60.

Buffalohead, Priscilla A. "Farmers, Warriors, Traders: A Fresh Look at Ojibway Women." *Minnesota History* 48.6 (1983), pp. 236–244.

Cameron, Barbara. "Gee You Don't Seem Like An Indian From The Reservation." In *This Bridge Called My Back: Writings of Radical Women of Color*, eds. Cherríe Moraga and Gloria Anzaldúa. Watertown, Mass: Persephone Press, 1981, pp. 46–52.

Canadian Woman Studies/Les Cahiers de la Femme. Special Issue: Native Women. Downview, Ontario: York University Publication. 10.2 & 3 (Summer/Fall 1989).

Chato, Genevieve and Christine Conte, "The Legal Rights of American Indian Women." In *Western Women: Their Land, Their Lives*, eds. Lillian Schlissel, Vicki L. Ruiz and Janice Monk. Albuquerque: University of New Mexico Press, 1988, pp. 227–258.

Christensen, Rosemary A. "Indian Women: An Historical and Personal Perspective." *Pupil Personnel Services* 4 (July 1975), pp. 12–22.

Clark, Jerry E. and Martha Ellen Webb. "Susette and Susan LaFlesch: Reformer and Missionary." In *Being and Becoming Indian: Biographical Studies of North American Frontiers*, ed. James A. Clifton, Chicago: Dorsey Press, 1989, pp. 136–159.

Cook, Katsi. "Seeking the Balance: A Native Women's Dialogue, Panel Presentation at the State of Indian American Conference Cornell University October 10, 1992." *Akwe:kon, A Journal of Indigenous Issues* 10:2 (Summer 1993), pp. 16–29.

DuBois, Cora. "Tolowa Notes." *American Anthropologist* 34.2 (1932), pp. 248–262.

Frederickson, Vera Mae, ed. "School Days in Northern California: The Accounts of Six Pomo Women." *News From Native California* 4.1 (Fall 1989), pp. 40–45.

Frisbie, Charlotte J. "Traditional Navajo Women: Ethnographic and Life History Portrayals." *American Indian Quarterly* 6 (1982), pp. 11–33.

Green, Rayna. "The Pocahontas Perplex: The Image of Indian Women In Popular Culture." *Massachusetts Review* 16 (Autumn 1975), pp. 678–714.

———. "Native American Women: Review Essay." *Signs: Journal of Women in Culture and Society* 6 (Winter 1980), pp. 248–267.

———. "Women in American Indian Society." In *Indians of North America*, ed. Frank W. Porter III. New York: Chelsea House Publishers, 1992.

Hailstone, Vivien. "The Past is but the Beginning of the Beginning." *News from Native California* 7 (Winter 1992–1993), pp. 4–5.

Hauptman, Laurence M. "Alice Jemison: Seneca Political Activist." *The Indian Historian* 12.2 (1974), pp. 15–40.

———. "Designing Woman: Minnie Kellogg, Iroquois Leader." In *Indian Lives: Essays on Nineteenth- and Twentieth-Century Native American Leaders*, eds. L.G. Moses and Raymond Wilson. Albuquerque: University of New Mexico Press, 1985, pp. 159–188.

Heizer, Robert F., ed. "Disease, Liquor and Sexual Exploitation of Indian Women." In *The Destruction of California Indians*. Lincoln: University of Nebraska Press, 1993 (1974), pp. 271–286.

Higham, John. "Indian Princess and Roman Goddess: The First Female Symbols of America." *Proceedings of the American Antiquarian Society* 100.1 (1990), pp. 45–79.

Hogan, Linda ed. *Frontiers: Special Issue on Native American Women* 6:3 (1981).

Holland-Braund, Kathryn E. "Guardians of Tradition and Handmaidens to Change: Women's Roles in Creek Economic and Social Life During the Eighteenth Century." *American Indian Quarterly* 14.3 (1990), pp. 239–258.

Indigenous Woman. A Publication of the Indigenous Women's Network. Lake Elmo, MN.

Jaimes, M. Annette. "American Indian Women: At the Center of Indigenous Resistance in North America." In *The State of Native America: Genocide, Colonization, and Resistance*, ed. M. Annette Jaimes. Boston: South End Press, 1992, pp. 311–344.

Jamieson, Kathleen. "Multiple Jeopardy: The Evolution of A Native Women's Movement." *Canadian Ethnic Studies* 13.1 (1981), pp. 130–143.

———. "Sisters under the Skin: An Exploration of the Implication of Feminist Materialist Perspective Research." *Canadian Ethnic Studies* 13.1 (1981), pp. 130–43.

———. "Sex Discrimination and the Indian Act." In *Arduous Journey: Canadian Indians and Decolonization*, ed. J. Rick Ponting. Toronto: Mc Clelland and Stewart, 1986, pp. 112–136.

Johnson, David L. and Raymond Wilson. "Gertrude Simmons Bonnin, 1876–1938: 'Americanize the First Americans.'" *American Indian Quarterly* 12.1 (Winter 1988), pp. 27–40.

Johnson, Rhonda and Winona Stevenson and Donna Greschner. "Peekiskwetan." *Canadian Journal of Women and the Law*. 6.1 (1993), pp. 153–171.

Johnson, Tomas H. "Maud Clairmont: Artist, Entrepreneur, Cultural Mediator." In *Being and Becoming Indian: Biographical Studies of North American Frontiers*, ed. James A. Clifton, Chicago: Dorsey Press, 1989, pp. 249–275.

Kidwell, Clara Sue. "Indian Women as Cultural Mediators." *Ethnohistory* 39.2 (1992), pp. 97–107.

Klein, Alan M. "The Plains Truth: The Impact of Colonialism On Indian Women." *Dislectical Anthropology* 7.4 (1983), pp. 299–313.

Klein, Laura F. "Contending with Colonization: Tlingit Men and Women in Change." In *Women and Colonization: Anthropological Perspectives*, eds. Mona Etienne and Eleanor Leacock. New York: Praeger Publishers, 1980, pp. 88–108.

Knack, Martha E. "Contemporary Southern Paiute Women and the Measurement of Women's Economic and Political Status." *Ethnology* 28 (1989), pp. 233–248.

La Duke, Winona. "In Honor of Women Warriors." *American Heritage* 16 (1981), pp. 10–13.

La Pointe, Charlene. "Boarding Schools Teach Violence." *Plainswomen* 10.4, pp. 3–4.

Leacock, Eleanor. "Montagnais Women and the Jesuit Program for Colonization." In *Women and Colonization: Anthropological Perspectives*, eds. Mona Etienne and Eleanor Leacock. New York: Praeger Publishers, 1980, pp. 25–42.

Lynch, Robert N. "Women in Northern Paiute Politics." *Signs: Journal of Women in Culture and Society* 11.2 (1986), pp. 352–366.

Mathes, Valerie Sherer. "American Indian Women and the Catholic Church." *North Dakota History* 47 (Fall 1980), pp. 20–25.

———. "Native American Women in Medicine and the Military." *Journal of the West* 21.2 (April 1982), pp. 41–48.

————. "Dr. Susan La Flesche Picotte." In *Indian Lives: Essays on Nineteenth- and Twentieth-Century Native American Leaders,* eds. L.G. Moses and Raymond Wilson. Albuquerque: University of New Mexico Press, 1985, pp. 61–90.

————. "Susan La Fresche Picotte, M.D.: Nineteenth-Century Physician and Reformer." *Great Plains Quarterly* 13.3 (Summer 1993), pp. 172–186.

McDonald, Michael. "Indian Status: Colonialism or Sexism?" *Canadian Community Law Journal* 9 (1986), pp. 23–48.

McGill, Marsha Ann and Emma Mitchell. "California Women's Clubs Past and Present." *News From Native California* 4.3 (Spring 1990), pp. 22.

Medicine, Beatrice. "Indian Women Tribal Identity as Status Quo." In *Woman's Nature: Rationalizations of Inequality,* eds. Marion Lowe and Ruth Hubbard. New York: Pergamon, 1983, pp. 63–73.

————. "Native American (Indian) Women: A Call for Research." *Anthropology and Education Quarterly* 19.2 (1988), pp. 86–92.

Metcalf, Ann. "From Schoolgirl to Mother: The Effects of Education of Navajo Women." *Social Problems* 23.4 (June 1976), pp. 535–544.

————. "Navajo Women in the City: Lessons From a Quarter Century of Relocation." *American Indian Quarterly* 6.1 & 2 (Spring-Summer 1982), pp. 71–89.

Mihesuah, Devon A. "Too Dark to Be Angels: The Class System among the Cherokees at the Female Seminary." *American Indian Culture and Research Journal* 15.1 (1991), pp. 29–52.

Miller, Jay. "Mourning Dove: The Author as Cultural Mediator." In *Being and Becoming Indian: Biographical Studies in North American Frontiers,* ed. James A. Clifton. Chicago: Dorsey Press, 1989, pp. 160–182.

Moore, Kimberly Beth. " 'Braver Than Most and Cunning in Strategy': Historical Perspectives on Apache and Other Native American Women Warriors." Ph.D. dissertation, Texas Tech University, 1984.

Nash, June. "Aztec Women: The Transition from Status to Class in Empire and Colony." In *Women and Colonization: Anthropological Perspectives,* eds. Mona Etienne and Eleanor Leacock. New York: Praeger Publishers, 1980, pp. 134–148.

Navajo Women: American Indian Quarterly: Special Issue. (1982).

Ortiz, Bev. "Beyond the Stereotypes." *News From Native California* 5.1 (November/January 1990–1991), pp. 32–33.

Patterson, Victoria D. "Indian Life in the City: A Glimpse of the Urban Experience of Pomo Women in 1930s." *California History* 71 (Fall 1992), pp. 402–431.

Peterson, Jacqueline. "Women Dreaming: The Religiopsychology of Indian-White Marriage and the Rise of Metis Culture." In *Western Women: Their Land, Their Lives,* eds. Lillian Schlissel, Vicki L. Ruiz and Janice Monk. Albuquerque: University of New Mexico Press, 1988, pp. 47–76.

Riley, Glenda. "Some European (Mis) Perceptions of American Indian Women." *New Mexico Historical Review* 59 (July 1984), pp. 237–266.

Ross, Luana. "Major Concerns of Imprisoned American Indian and White Mothers." In *Gender: Multi-Cultural Perspectives,* ed. Judy T. Gonzalez-Calvo. Dubuque, IA: Kendall-Hunt Publishing Co., 1993.

Rothenberg, Diane. "The Mothers of the Nation: Seneca Resistance to Quaker Intervention." In *Women and Colonization: Anthropological Perspectives,* eds. Mona Etienne and Eleanor Leacock. New York: Praeger Publishers, 1980, 63–87.

Schlegel, Alice. "Male and Female in Hopi Thought and Action." In *Sexual Stratification: A Cross-Cultural View,* ed. Alice Schlegel. New York: Columbia University, 1977, pp. 245–269.

Shepardson, Mary. "The Status of Navajo Women." *American Indian Quarterly* 6 (1982), pp. 149–169.

Smith, Sherry L. "Beyond Princess and Squaw: Army Officers' Perceptions of Indian Women." In *The Women's West,* eds. Sue Armitage and Elizabeth Jameson. Norman: University of Oklahoma Press, 1987, pp. 63–76.

Smits, David D. "The Squaw Drudge: A Prime Index of Savagism." *Ethnohistory* 29.4 (1982), pp. 281–306.

Sugar, Fran. "Entrenched Social Catastrophe: Native Women in Prison." *Canadian Woman Studies* 10.2&3 (Summer/Fall 1989), pp. 87–89.

Szasz, Margaret Connell. " 'Poor Richard' Meets the Native American: Schooling for Young Indian Women in Eighteenth Century Connecticut." *Pacific Historical Review* 49 (May 1980), pp. 215–235.

Trennert, Robert A. "Educating Indian Girls at Nonreservation Boarding Schools, 1878–1920." *Western Historical Quarterly* 13.3 (July 1982), pp. 271–290.

Wagner, Sally Roesch. "The Iroquois Influence on Women's Rights." *Akwe:kon Journal* 9.1 (Spring 1992), pp. 4–15.

Wallace, Michele. "Wilma Mankiller." *Ms.* 16.7 (January 1988), pp. 68–69.

Waterman, T. T. and A. L. Kroeber. "Yurok Marriages." *University of California Publications in American Archaeology and Ethnology* 335 (1943), pp. 1–14.

Welch, Deborah. "American Indian Women: Reaching Beyond the Myth." In *New Directions in American Indian History*, ed. Colin G. Calloway. Norman: University of Oklahoma Press, 1988, pp. 31–48.

Willard, William. "Zitkala-Sa: A Woman Who Would Be Heard." *Wicazo Sa Review* 1 (Spring 1985), pp. 11–16.

Wilson, Terry P. "Osage Indian Women During a Century of Change, 1870–1980." *Prologue: The Journal of the National Archives* 14 (Winter 1982), pp. 185–201.

Witt, Shirley Hill. "Brave Hearted Women." *Akwesasne Notes* 8.2 (1976), pp. 16–17.

———. "Native Women Today: Sexism and the Native American Woman." *Civil Rights Digest*. 6.3 (1974), pp. 29–35.

Zastro, Leona M. "American Indian Women as Art Educators." *Journal of American Indian Education* 18 (October 1978), pp. 6–10.

Index

Notes on Contributors

Yamila Azize-Vargas was born in Puerto Rico. She did her BA at the University of Puerto Rico and her Ph.D. at the University of Pennsylvania. She is the author and editor of several books about women in Puerto Rico: *Luchas de la mujer en Puerto Rico* (a history of feminism in Puerto Rico 1898–1930), *La mujer en Puerto Rico: ensayos de investigación* (editor, research essays), *Hacia un currículo no sexista* (editor, resource book on curricular change), *La realidad del aborto en Puerto Rico* (Abortion in Puerto Rico, Spanish and English editions), *Mujer y Ciencia: investigación y currículo* (editor, science research esays). Since 1987, she has been director of the Women's Studies Program at the University of Puerto Rico, Cayey Campus.

Paula Baker is Associate Professor of History at the University of Pittsburgh, where she teaches nineteenth- and twentieth-century U.S. history. She is also author of *Moral Frameworks of Public Life: Gender, Politics, and the State in Rural New York, 1870–1930* (Oxford University Press, 1991).

Jeanne Boydston is Associate Professor of History at the University of Wisconsin-Madison. She is the author of *Home and Work: Housework, Wages and the Ideology of Labor in the Early Republic* and is coauthor of *The Limits of Sisterhood: The Beecher Sisters on Women's Rights and Woman's Sphere*. She is currently working on a study of wage-earning women and the development of political culture in early national Philadelphia.

Elsa Barkley Brown teaches in the Department of History and Center for Afro-American Studies at the University of Michigan. Her articles have appeared in *Signs, Sage, History Workshop Journal,* and *Feminist Studies.*

Hazel V. Carby is Professor of English, African and African-American Studies, and American Studies at Yale University and author of *Reconstructing Womanhood: The Emergence of the Afro-American Woman Novelist.*

Annette Reed Crum (Tolowa) is a Ph.D. candidate in Ethnic Studies at the University of California at Berkeley. She earned her M.A. in History at U.C., Davis under the expert mentorship of Vicki L. Ruiz. Annette teaches a summer course entitled *Native American Women* in the Department of Native American Studies at U.C., Davis. Her dissertation will be a tribal history of the Tolowa in northwestern California. Her research interests include Native American History, Native American Women, California Indians, and History of the American West.

Madeline D. Davis is the Chief Conservator for the Buffalo and Erie County Public Library System. A gay and lesbian rights activist since 1970, she is also co-director of the Buffalo and Erie County Public Library System. She has been a gay and lesbian rights activist since 1970 and is co-director of the Buffalo Women's Oral History Project. She is the coauthor of *Boots of Leather, Slippers of Gold: The History of a Lesbian Community.* As a singer, songwriter, poet and actress she has sought to forward lesbian and gay culture as the cutting edge of revolution. She has recently performed in Jane Chambers' "Last Summer at Bluefish Cove", and Sarah Dreher's "This Brooding Sky", as well as numerous concerts for gay causes. She is currently doing research on lesbian sexuality and friendships.

Ellen Carol DuBois is Professor of History at UCLA. She is the author of *Feminism and Suffrage: The Emergence of an Independent Women's Movement in America, 1848–1969*, and the editor of *The Elizabeth Cady Stanton-Susan B. Anthony Reader.* Her forthcoming book is a biography of Harriot Stanton Blatch and a revisionist history of the women's suffrage movement in the twentieth century.

Alma M. Garcia is Associate Professor of Sociology and Ethnic Studies at Santa Clara University. She is also the Director of the Women's Studies Program. Her past publications include articles on Chicana Studies and curriculum reforms, twentieth century agrarian movements in Mexico, and Chicana feminist theory. Present research includes a study of entrepreneurship among Mexican American women and a regional study of Mexican agrarian movements during the 1930s. Garcia has served as president of the National Association for Chicano Studies (NACS) and of Mujeres Activas en Letras y Cambios Sociales (MALCS).

Paula Giddings, a journalist, is the author of *When and Where I Enter: The Impact of Black Women on Race and Sex in America*, and *In Search of Sisterhood: Delta Sigma Theta and the Challenge of the Black Sorority Movement*. In 1993, she was named a fellow of the National Humanities Center and the Guggenheim Foundation.

Evelyn Nakano Glenn is Professor of Women's Studies and Ethnic Studies at the University of California, Berkeley. She has written extensively on women, work and technology issues. She is the author of *Issei, Nisei, Warbride* and senior editor of *Mothering: Ideology, Experience and Agency*. Her current research centers on the race and gender construction of women's work, which is based on a comparative historical study of African American, Latina and Asian American women's labor.

Deena J. González is Associate Professor of History at Pomona College and Chair of Chicano Studies at Claremont. She is currently editing *The Dictionary of Latinas in the United States* for Garland Press and working on a third book on Chicana feminism. Her first book, *Refusing the Favor: The Spanish-Mexican Women of Sante Fe, 1820–1880* is forthcoming from Oxford University Press. She has also published articles in *California Sociologist, Outlook*, and in the first edition of *Unequal Sisters*.

Linda Gordon is the Florence Kelley Professor of History at the University of Wisconsin-Madison. Her books include *Woman's Body, Woman's Right: The History of Birth Control in America* (orig. 1976, 2nd ed., Penguin 1990); *Heroes of Their Own Lives: The Politics and History of Family Violence* (Viking/Penguin, 1988); *Women, the State and Welfare* (University of Wisconsin Press, 1990). The material in this article appears in her most recent book, *Pitied But Not Entitled: Single Mothers and the History of Welfare* (Free Press, 1994).

Jacquelyn Dowd Hall is Julia Cherry Spruill Professor of History and director of the Southern Oral History Program at the University of North Carolina at Chapel Hill. She is the coauthor of *Like a Family: The Making of a Southern Cotton Mill World* (1987). In 1993 Columbia University Press issued a new edition of her first book, *Revolt Against Chivalry: Jessie Daniel Ames and the Women's Campaign Against Lynching*, with a new introductory chapter and an epilogue. Her articles have appeared in the *American Historical Review*, the *Journal of American History, Feminist Studies, Signs*, the *Women's Review of Books, Radical History Review*, and *Southern Exposure*. Her most recent publication is "O. Delight Smith's Progressive Era: Labor, Feminism and Reform in the Urban South" in *Visible Women*, ed. Nancy A. Hewitt and Suzanne Lebsock.

Nancy A. Hewitt, Professor of History at Duke University, is the author of *Women's Activism and Social Change: Rochester, New York, 1822–1872* (Cornell, 1984) and editor of *Women, Families and Communities: Readings in American History* (HarperCollins, 1990) and *Visible Women: New Essays on American Activism* (Illinois, 1993). She is currently completing a study of Anglo, African American, and Latin women in Tampa, Florida, 1885–1945, and beginning a multicultural synthesis of antebellum women's history.

Darlene Clark Hine is John A. Hannah Professor of American History at Michigan State University. She is editor of Carlson's Publishing's sixteen-volume series, *Black Women in United States History: From Colonial Times to the Present* (1990). Her books include *Black Women in White: Racial Conflict and Cooperation in the Nursing Profession, 1890–1950* (1989); *Women's Culture and Community in Indiana, 1875–1959* (1981); and *Black Victory: The Rise and Fall of the White Primary in Texas* (1979). She has also published over fifty research articles on black history and is currently the editor of a two volume set, *Black Women in America: An Historical Encyclopedia* (Brooklyn: Carlson Publishing, 1993). Hine has also edited *The State of Afro-American History, Past, Present, and Future* (1986).

Joan M. Jensen is Professor Emerita in the History Department at New Mexico State University where she taught Women's History and also directed the Women's Studies Program. Her most recent publications are *Promise to the Land: Essays on Rural Women* (1991) and *One Foot on the Rockies: Women and Creativity in the Modern American West* (forthcoming from University of New Mexico Press).

Gail Paradise Kelly was Professor of Education and Chairperson of the Department of Educational Organization, Administration of Policy at SUNY/Buffalo. She wrote *From Vietnam to America*, coauthored *Feminism in the Disciplines* and most recently was a coeditor and contributor to *Emergent Issues in Education: Comparative Perspectives*. She also served a term as president of the Comparative Education Society.

Elizabeth Lapovsky Kennedy is a founding member of Women's Studies at the State University of New York at Buffalo and Professor in the Department of American Studies. She was trained as a social anthropologist at the University of Cambridge, Cambridge England and did two years of field work with the Waunan in Colombia South America. Over the past twenty years she has worked to build the field of women's studies and pioneered studies of lesbian community. She is coauthor of *Feminist Scholarship: Kindling in the Groves of Academe* with Ellen DuBois et al. (University of Illinois Press, 1985) and *Boots of Leather, Slippers of Gold: The History of a Lesbian Community* (Routledge, 1993), with Madeline D. Davis.

Alice Kessler-Harris, Professor of History and Director of the Women's Studies Program at Rutgers University, is author, most recently, of *A Woman's Wage: Historical Meanings and Social Consequences*. She is currently exploring the usages of gender in creating social policy in the twentieth century United States.

Chana Kai Lee is Assistant Professor of History at Indiana University, Bloomington, where she teaches twentieth century U.S. history and recent Afro-American history. For her doctoral thesis, she completed a biography of Fannie Lou Hamer titled "A Passionate Pursuit of Justice: The Life and Leadership of Fannie Lou Hamer, 1917–1967."

Tessie Liu is Assistant Professor of History at Northwestern University and a member of the editorial collective of *Gender and History*. She is currently researching a new book tentatively entitled *Genealogies of Race: Citizenship and Difference in Modern France*. Her monograph, *The Weaver's Knot: Contradictions of Class Struggle and Family Solidarity in Western France, 1750–1914* (Cornell University Press, 1994) studies the role of gender inequality in the successful resistance of male artisans to capitalist relations of production.

Valerie Matsumoto is Associate Professor of History and Asian American Studies at the University of California, Los Angeles. She is the author of *Farming the Home Place: A Japanese American Community in California, 1919–1982* and is currently working on a book about Nisei women writers in the 1930s.

Joanne Meyerowitz is Associate Professor of History at the University of Cincinnati. She is the author of *Women Adrift: Independent Wage Earners in Chicago, 1880–1930* (University of Chicago Press, 1988) and the editor of *Not June Cleaver: Women and Gender in Postwar America, 1945–1960* (Temple University Press, 1994).

Brian Niiya is the assistant coordinator of the UCLA Asian American Studies Center Reading Room/Library.

Peggy Pascoe is Associate Professor of History at the University of Utah. The author of *Relations of Rescue: The Search for Female Moral Authority in the American West, 1874–1939* (1990), she is at work on a history of laws against interracial marriage tentatively titled *What Comes Naturally: Race, Sex, and Marriage Law, 1870–1993*.

Kathy Peiss teaches history and women's studies at the University of Massachusetts at Amherst. She is author of *Cheap Amusements: Working Women and Leisure in Turn-of-the-Century New York* (Temple University Press, 1986) and coeditor of *Passion and Power: Sexuality in History* (Temple, 1989). She is currently completing a study of cosmetics in American culture entitled *Making Faces* (Basic Books).

Theda Perdue, Professor of History at the University of Kentucky, is author of *Slavery and the Evolution of Cherokee Society, 1540–1866* (1979), *Native Carolinians* (1985), and *The Cherokee* (1988), and she is editor of *Cherokee Editor* (1983) and *Nations Remembered* (1980). A fellow of the D'Arcy McNickle Center for the History of the American Indian at the Newberry Library, she currently is working on books on Cherokee women in the eighteenth and early nineteenth centuries and on Cherokee removal.

Barbara M. Posadas is Associate Professor of History and Director of the M.A. Option in Historical Administration at Northern Illinois University. Born in Chicago to a Filipino father and a Polish-American mother, she earned a Ph.D. in United States history at Northwestern University. Her articles on the Filipino old-timers' community in Chicago have appeared in *Labor History*, *Amerasia Journal*, the *Journal of American Ethnic History*, and the *Illinois Historical Journal*.

Vicki L. Ruiz chairs the Department of History at The Claremont Graduate School. She teaches courses in Chicano history, U.S. women's history, the West, and immigration studies. She is currently completing a manuscript on the history of Mexican women in the United States from 1900 to the present.

George J. Sánchez is Associate Professor of History and American Culture at the University of Michigan. He teaches courses in Latino history and ethnicity in the United States, and is presently the director of the Program in American Culture. He is the author of *Becoming Mexican American: Ethnicity, Culture and Identity in Chicano Los Angeles, 1900–1945* (1993) and is currently writing a book on racial attacks against recent Latino and Asian immigrants to the United States.

Rickie Solinger is the author of *Wake Up Little Susie: Single Pregnancy and Race Before Roe V. Wade* (Routledge, 1992) and *The Abortionist: A Woman Against the Law* (The Free Press, 1994). She lives in Boulder, Colorado.

Christine Stansell is a longtime feminist who teaches American history and women's studies at Princeton University. She is the author of *City of Women: Sex and Class in New York, 1789–1860* and coeditor (with Ann Snitow and Sharon Thompson) of *Powers of Desire: the Politics of Sexuality.* Her essays and reviews have appeared in scholarly journals and journals of opinion, including *Feminist Studies, The Nation,* and *The New Republic.* She is writing a book about American radical intellectuals and artists in the early twentieth century.

Amy Swerdlow is Professor of History and Director of the Graduate Program in Women's History *Emerita,* Sarah Lawrence College. She writes on women's movements for peace and social justice in the nineteenth and twentieth centuries. Her most recent publications are: *Women Strike for Peace: Traditional Motherhood and Radical Politics in the 1960s* (University of Chicago Press, 1993) and "Abolition's Conservative Sisters: The New York City Anti-Slavery Societies, 1834–1840" in *An Untrodden Path: Anti-Slavery and Women's Political Culture,* John C. Van Horne and Jean Fagan Yellin, eds. (Cornell University Press, 1994).

Meredith Tax is the author of a history book, *The Rising of the Women* (1980), a children's book, *Families* (1981), and two historical novels, *Rivington Street* (1982) and *Union Square* (1988). She has just completed a memoir, *Ritual.* She has been active in the women's movement since 1968, in Boston, Chicago, and New York. With Grace Paley, she founded the Women's Comittee of PEN American Center in 1986. In 1991, she became the founding Chair of the Women Writers' Committee of International PEN.

Rebecca Tsosie is Visiting Professor of Law at Arizona State University College of Law, where she teaches Federal Indian Law and Property. She is on leave from the law firm of Brown & Bain, where she practices in the areas of litigation, Indian law and environmental law. Ms. Tsosie received her Bachelor's degree in American Indian Studies from UCLA in 1987, and received her J.D. from the UCLA School of Law in 1990. Ms. Tsosie is of Pascua Yaqui descent and is married to Richard Tsosie, a Navajo silversmith and sculptor. They have two children, Daniel and Lisa.

Sylvia Van Kirk grew up in Edmonton, Alberta and received her B.A. and M.A. degrees at the University of Alberta. She received her Ph.D. at the University of London, England and is now Associate Professor of Canadian History and Women's Studies at the University of Toronto. Her research focuses on the role of women in the early frontier societies of Western Canada. She is the author of *"Many Tender Ties": Women in Fur Trade Society in Western Canada, 1670–1870* (University of Oklahoma Press, 1982) and numerous related articles. Her most recent work focuses on the role of women in the Cariboo gold rush in mid-nineteenth century British Columbia.

Devra Anne Weber is the author of *Dark Sweat, White Gold: California Farm Workers, Cotton and the New Deal* (University of California Press, 1994) and articles on Mexican labor in the United States. She is Assistant Professor in the Department of History at the University of California, Riverside.

Deborah Gray White is Professor of History at Rutgers University. She is the author of *Ar'n't I A Woman? Female Slaves in the Plantation South,* a book which explores the lives of black women on southern plantations during slavery. Her forthcoming work, to be published by W. W. Norton Inc., is titled *Too Heavy A Load. Ideas of Race, Class, and Gender in Black Women's Organizational Life, 1896–1980.* This work looks at classism and sexism within black America, and explores the definitions of black sisterhood and feminism over time.

Judy Yung is Assistant Professor in American Studies at the University of California, Santa Cruz. She is the author of *Chinese Women of America: A Pictorial History* (1986) and co-author of *Island: Poetry and History of Chinese Immigrants on Angel Island, 1910–1940* (1980). Her forthcoming book will be *Unbound Feet: Social Change for Chinese Women in San Francisco* (1995).